Mary &
the Art of
Prayer

Mary &
the Art of
Prayer

The Hours of the
Virgin in Medieval
Christian Life and
Thought

Rachel Fulton Brown

Columbia University Press
New York

Columbia University Press
Publishers Since 1893
New York   Chichester, West Sussex
cup.columbia.edu

Support for this book was generously provided through fellowships from the John Simon Guggenheim Memorial Foundation and the American Council of Learned Societies.

Library of Congress Cataloging-in-Publication Data
Names: Fulton Brown, Rachel, author.
Title: Mary and the art of prayer : the hours of the Virgin in medieval Christian life
    and thought / Rachel Fulton Brown.
Description: New York : Columbia University Press, 2017. | Includes bibliographical
    references and index.
Identifiers: LCCN 2017009362 (print) | LCCN 2017034281 (ebook) |
    ISBN 9780231181686 (cloth) | ISBN 9780231181693 (pbk.) |
    ISBN 9780231543712 (ebook)
Subjects: LCSH: Catholic Church. Little office of the Blessed Virgin Mary. |
    Mary, Blessed Virgin, Saint—Prayers and devotions. | Mary, Blessed Virgin,
    Saint—Devotion to. | Spiritual life—Christianity—History.
Classification: LCC BX2025 (ebook) | LCC BX2025 .F85 2017 (print) |
    DDC 264/.020150902—dc23
LC record available at https://lccn.loc.gov/2017009362

Cover design: Lisa Hamm
Cover image: © Mondadori Portfolio/Electa/
Paolo e Federico Manusardi/Bridgeman Images

For my mother, the strongest woman in my life,
and in memory of my father, who sent me on the quest.

Contents

List of illustrations   xi

List of tables   xii

Acknowledgments   xiii

Notes to the Reader   xv

    On the Name of the Lord   xv

    On the Citation of Scripture   xv

    Approach to the Work   xvii

Invitatory   xxiii

    How to Read This Book   xxvi

    The Virgin Clothed with the Sun   xxxi

1 The Hours of the Virgin   1

    A Little History of the Office   7

    "Seven times a day I have praised you" (Psalm 118:164)   26

2 Ave Maria   47

    Saluting Mary: Ave   56

        Saying the Ave   59

        Learning the Ave   65

    Naming Mary: MARIA   72

        Container of the Uncontainable   76

Full of Grace   81

Aves in the Psalms   85

"And the virgin's name was Mary" (Luke 1:27)   93

3 Antiphon and Psalm   103

Mary in the Temple   111

The Lord and the Lady of the Temple   120

Miriam, the Mother of the Son of the Most High   133

Mary, the *Theotokos*, the Living Temple of God   146

Mary in the Psalms   161

The Night Office, or Matins   169

First nocturn, on Sunday, Monday, and Thursday   170

Second nocturn, on Tuesday and Friday   175

Third nocturn, on Wednesday and Saturday   184

The Seven Hours of the Day   194

Lauds, sung at sunrise   197

Prime, sung at the first hour of the day (about 6 a.m.)   209

Terce, Sext, and None, sung at the third, sixth,
and ninth hours (about 9 a.m., 12 p.m., and 3 p.m.)   211

Vespers, sung at sunset   221

Compline, sung at bedtime   230

4 Lesson and Response   237

Lectio prima. Ars grammatica. Richard of Saint-Laurent
and the Names of Mary in Scripture   251

Lectio ii. Ars rhetorica. Conrad of Saxony on
What the Angel Said to Mary   309

Lectio iii. Ars dialectica. Pseudo-Albert's Questions About
What Mary Knew   324

5 Prayer 345

How to serve Mary 368

Reasons to serve Mary 389

Mary as intercessor 395

The miracle of Theophilus 400

Mary as bride 414

Beautiful from head to toe 423

Mary as temple 433

The Lord enters into his Creation 439

Compline: Sor María de Jesús de Ágreda and the Mystical City of God 459

. . . .

Appendix: Handlist of Manuscripts and Printed Editions of Richard of Saint-Laurent's *De laudibus beatae Mariae virginis libri XII* 481

Notes 485

Bibliography 563

Abbreviations 563

Hours of the Virgin: Printed Editions 564

Printed Sources and Translations 564

Scholarly Studies 576

Index of Scriptural Citations 605

Index of Manuscripts Cited 617

General Index 619

List of Illustrations

Figure 1. Diagram of the structure of the book. Drawing by Thomas Rush Brown. xxxvii

Plate 1. Shrine of the Virgin, Rhine valley, ca. 1300. Closed. xxxiv

Plate 2. Shrine of the Virgin, Rhine valley, ca. 1300. Open. xxxv

Plate 3. Tree of Jesse, Annunciation. Book of Hours, France, ca. 1500–1510. xlii

Plate 4. Virgin and Child enthroned, with kneeling devotee. Book of Hours, England, ca. 1260. 46

Plate 5. Virgin and Child in majesty, Auvergne, France, ca. 1175–1200. 50

Plate 6. Calendar, Annunciation. Book of Hours, France, ca. 1400–1414. 55

Plate 7. Annunciation, "Incipit horae beatae marie virginis." Book of Hours, Belgium, ca. 1475. 71

Plate 8. Mary of Burgundy praying with her book, the Virgin and Child in church. Book of Hours, Flanders, ca. 1477. 102

Plate 9. Virgin and Child enthroned. Psalter ("The Melisende Psalter"), Jerusalem, 1131–1143. 110

Plate 10. Virgin and Child enthroned, with kneeling nun. Psalter ("The Shaftesbury Psalter"), Dorset, England, second quarter of the twelfth century. 160

Plate 11. "Tota pulcra es, amica mea, et macula non est in te." *Hore intemerate virginis Marie secundum usum Romanum: totaliter ad longum sine require, cum pluribus orationibus in gallico et latino.* Thielman Kerver, Paris, 1502. 236

Plate 12. Mary appears to the author, who is dressed as a Dominican friar. Richard of Saint-Laurent, *De laudibus beatae Mariae virginis,* lib. 1. Copied in Paris or French Flanders, between 1250 and 1299. 250

Plate 13. Mary as Mother nursing the Child. Richard of Saint-Laurent, *De laudibus beatae Mariae virginis,* lib. 6. Copied in Paris or French Flanders, between 1250 and 1299. 262

Plate 14. Mary as sun, moon, and stars. Richard of Saint-Laurent, *De laudibus beatae Mariae virginis*, lib. 7 Copied in Paris or French Flanders, between 1250 and 1299.   269

Plate 15. Mary as Earth, with contemplative Dominican. Richard of Saint-Laurent, *De laudibus beatae Mariae virginis*, lib. 8. Copied in Paris or French Flanders, between 1250 and 1299.   276

Plate 16. Mary as ark and throne, with contemplative Dominican. Richard of Saint-Laurent, *De laudibus beatae Mariae virginis*, lib. 10. Copied in Paris or French Flanders, between 1250 and 1299.   281

Plate 17. Mary as city of God. Richard of Saint-Laurent, *De laudibus beatae Mariae virginis*, lib. 11. Copied in Paris or French Flanders, between 1250 and 1299.   292

Plate 18. Abbot Robert of Clairmarais presents Richard's book to the Virgin and Child. Richard of Saint-Laurent, *De virtutibus*. Copy dedicated by Robert of Clairmarais (abbot, 1257–1264) to Robertus de Bethunia.   308

Plate 19. Annunciation, "Hier beghint dei metten von onser soeter vrouwen gehtide." Book of Hours, The Netherlands, ca. 1475.   323

Plate 20. How to serve Mary: Mary shows the Child to a kneeling crowd. Richard of Saint-Laurent, *De laudibus beatae Mariae virginis*, lib. 2. Copied in Paris or French Flanders, between 1250 and 1299.   344

Plate 21. Mary punches the devil and retrieves the charter for Theophilus. Book of Hours ("The De Brailes Hours"), Oxford, England, ca. 1240.   401

Plate 22. The woman clothed with the sun, holding the child. Book of Hours, The Netherlands, ca. 1475.   414

Plate 23. Opening Madonna triptych, France, possibly Sens, ca. 1180–1220. Closed.   434

Plate 24. Opening Madonna triptych, France, possibly Sens, ca. 1180–1220. Open, showing scenes of the Passion.   440

Plate 25. Triptych with Madonna and Child with Crucifixion, Annunciation, Coronation of the Virgin, and Presentation in the temple. Catalonia, Spain, ca. 1340–1348.   457

LIST OF TABLES

Table 1. Psalm Numbering   xvi

Table 2. The Hours of the Virgin (for the most part)   3

Table 3. Psalms and Lessons of the Marian Office (Use of Rome)   168

Acknowledgments

Rhetorically, prayer may take many forms. In acknowledgments, it takes the form of thanksgiving.

I am grateful to Mary, for choosing me to write this book on her behalf and trusting me, a cradle Presbyterian, with the recovery of the devotion with which medieval Christians prayed to her.

I am grateful to the Andrew W. Mellon Foundation for giving me a year (2004) as a New Directions Fellow to study cognitive and biological psychology, that I might develop the tools that I needed to "get inside" the medieval practice of prayer.

I am grateful to the John Simon Guggenheim Memorial Foundation and the American Council of Learned Societies for fellowships to spend two years (2008–2009, 2012–2013) to concentrate on writing this book. Thanks to their generosity, funds were likewise available to bring this book to press. Thanks also to the University of Chicago where I teach for leave during this time.

I am grateful to Christopher Fletcher for serving as my research assistant for two years, for photocopies and rich conversation whenever he brought materials to me.

I am grateful to Google Books, Hathi Trust, and the staff of the Joseph Regenstein Library for making it possible to do much of the work for the latter part of this book from my couch. I am particularly grateful to David K. Larsen for setting up the Scan & Deliver service at the library so as to make its collection more accessible to those of us working from home.

I am grateful to the British Library and the Regenstein Library Department of Special Collections for access to the Books of Hours in their care, and to Wellesley College Library, Special Collections, for access to their beautiful manuscript of Richard of Saint-Laurent's *De laudibus beatae Mariae virginis*.

I am grateful to the late Erik Drigsdahl for maintaining his magnificent site on Books of Hours and for advice on the books that he knew.

I am grateful to the students in my courses on Mary and Mariology (spring 2012, autumn 2015), The Psalms in Medieval Christianity (autumn–winter 2014–2015), Medieval Biblical Exegesis (autumn–winter 2011–2012), Praying by the Book (spring 2007), and Spiritual Exercises: History and Practice (spring 2006) for helping me read the texts on which much of this book is based, and to my students in Tolkien: Medieval and Modern (spring 2005, 2008, 2011, 2014) for being willing to subcreate with me.

I am grateful for the opportunities I had to present portions of this work in progress to the Medieval Studies Workshop at the University of Chicago, Brent House Episcopal Campus Ministry, the Medieval Intellectual History Seminar, St. Louis University, the University of California at Los Angeles, the University of California at Berkeley, the University of Mississippi, Marquette University, the University of Minnesota, DePaul University, Northwestern University, the University of Virginia, Villanova University, Yale University, the University of Wisconsin–Madison, the Medieval Academy of America, and the American Society of Church History.

I am grateful to Lynn Botelho, Caroline Walker Bynum, Steve Heyman, Nathaniel Goggin, Susan Melsky, Barbara Newman, Victor Pisman, and Jeffrey Stackert for conversation, scholarly advice, and constant encouragement, and to Barbara Friend Ish for helping me rewrite the opening meditation.

I am grateful to my three readers for the Press, particularly my devil's advocate who made the argument against why my book should be published, and to my two angels for encouraging me to revise. I am more grateful than words can express to my editor Wendy Lochner for not giving up on my book throughout its lengthy review.

I am grateful to my mother for her generosity in helping me finish this book.

I am grateful to my husband Jonathan Brown for insisting even in my darkest moments that Mary wanted me to write this book, and to our son Rush for letting me drag him around all those churches in Belgium, for drawing the schema for the book, and for always being there when I needed a hug.

And I am grateful to my dog, for being my Joy. Every scholar needs a dog to get her outside for walks and to look at the trees.

Feast of St. Margaret of Scotland, A.D. 2016
Chicago, Illinois

⋈otes to the Reader

ON THE NAME OF THE LORD

In the ancient Hebrew tradition, the Divine Name or "Tetragrammaton" (יהוה) was believed to be too sacred to speak out loud; accordingly, when reading from the scriptures, cantors would substitute the word Adonai, meaning "Lord." When the scriptures were translated into ancient Greek, this spoken word was rendered Κύριος (Lord). Translated into Latin, the Name as spoken became Dominus (Lord). In the King James Version of the scriptures published in 1611, the translators rendered the Name in capitals: Lord. According to medieval as well as ancient Christians, Jesus was not just a lord in the sense of a master or ruler; his proper name was (and is) Lord.

ON THE CITATION OF SCRIPTURE

One of the great challenges in describing a devotion that crosses so many periods in history is choosing which version of the scriptures to use as a standard reference. Given that our focus is the devotion to the Virgin Mary in the Middle Ages of the Latin West, all scriptural citations unless otherwise marked refer to the Vulgate, in particular using the Septuagint/Vulgate numbering for the Psalms, except when otherwise indicated. For translation of the Psalms, Job, Proverbs, Ecclesiastes, the Song of Songs, Wisdom, and Ecclesiasticus, I have consulted *The Vulgate Bible, Volume 3: The Poetical Books. Douay-Rheims Translation*, edited by Swift Edgar with Angela M. Kinney (Dumbarton Oaks Medieval Library; Cambridge: Harvard University Press, 2011). For the Bible as a whole, I have consulted *The Holy Bible: Douay-Rheims Version. Translated from the Latin Vulgate,*

Diligently Compared with the Hebrew, Greek, and Other Editions in Diverse Languages. The Old Testament: First Published by the English College at Douay, A.D. 1609; The New Testament: First Published by the English College at Rheims A.D. 1582 (Charlotte, N.C.: Saint Benedict Press, 2009). Medieval Christian commentators on the scriptures often refer to other translations, typically not in order to critique the version of the text with which they were most familiar but to expand the possibilities of interpretation, believing as they did that every translation was always only an approximation of God's speaking to the world, including the original Hebrew or Greek. For references to the scriptures more closely approximating the Masoretic Hebrew of the Old Testament, particularly in chapter 3, I have consulted *The Holy Bible: Revised Standard Version. Translated from the Original Languages Being the Version Set Forth A.D. 1611, Revised A.D. 1881–1885 and A.D. 1901, Compared with the Most Ancient Authorities and Revised A.D. 1946–1952, Second Edition of the New Testament A.D. 1971* (Nashville, Tenn.: Nelson, 1952, 1971). For references to the Septuagint Greek translation of the Old Testament cited by the Orthodox homilists, I have consulted

TABLE I Psalm Numbering

Septuagint/Vulgate	Hebrew/Revised Standard Version
1–8	1–8
9	9–10
10–112	11–113
113	114–115
114	116:1–9
115	116:10–19
116–145	117–146
146	147:1–11
147	147:12–29
148–150	148–150
151	

The Septuagint with Apocrypha: Greek and English, edited by Sir Lancelot C. L. Brenton (London: Samuel Bagster and Sons, 1851; reprint Hendrickson, 1986); and *A New English Translation of the Septuagint and the Other Greek Translations Traditionally Included Under that Title*, edited by Albert Pietersma and Benjamin G. Wright (New York: Oxford University Press, 2007). In giving these citations, my goal throughout has been to keep as close as possible to the sense of the texts as read and cited by the ancient and medieval exegetes, so as to enable the modern reader to get inside the scriptures as Mary's medieval devotees read them while praying her Hours. For the Hours of the Virgin according to the Use of Rome, I have followed *The Little Office of the Blessed Virgin Mary in Latin and English. In Conformity with the 1961* Editio Typica *of the Roman Breviary Being That Permitted by* Summorum Pontificum (London: Baronius, 2007).

APPROACH TO THE WORK

In approaching a work of literature or history, including the scriptures, medieval readers trained in the arts of grammar and rhetoric were accustomed to inquire into six things: the title of the work (*titulus*), its subject matter (*materia*), its purpose (*intentio*), its usefulness (*utilitas*), the part of philosophy to which it belongs (*pars philosophiae*), and its manner or method of treating its subject (*modus tractandi*).[1]

The title of the present work is *Mary and the Art of Prayer: The Hours of the Virgin in Medieval Christian Life and Thought*.

Its subject matter is the complex of psalms, chants, and other prayers known as the Hours of the Virgin with which Christians in medieval Europe served Mary, the Mother of the one whom they recognized as the Lord worshiped in the psalms of the Old Testament.

Its purpose is to provide a history of this service, while at the same time suggesting what it would have been like for medieval Christians to imagine Mary in this way.

It is intended to be useful to students of history, devotion, prayer, theology, liturgy, and exegesis who are interested in not only the structures of medieval religious thought but also its experience as an exercise of affect, intellect, and imagination.

Its author writes as an historian and believing Christian, but she is not a theologian, although she would argue that in writing about the history of devotion to Mary it is impossible not to make certain theological claims, as even the claim that the scriptures "say very little about Mary" with which most modern histories of devotion to Mary typically begin is itself grounded in particular confessional convictions.

The book's manner or method of treating its subject is expected to be somewhat challenging, crossing as it does the boundaries that modern scholars typically place between observation and experience, between the primary world of provable "facts" and the secondary world of imagination or "faërie." Accordingly, following an introduction to the history of the devotion of saying the Hours or "Little Office" of the Virgin in chapter 1, it then invites its readers in subsequent chapters to imagine themselves as medieval Christians saying this Office, including its invitatory (chapter 2), its antiphons and psalms (chapter 3), its lessons (chapter 4), and prayers (chapter 5).

It is the author's hope that this exercise will prove intellectually stimulating as well as enjoyable, even if, as with all real adventures, it may feel dangerous at times.

As the storytellers say, "Once upon a time . . ."

"I wonder what sort of tale we've fallen into?" [said Sam].

"I wonder," said Frodo. "But I don't know. And that's the way of a real tale. Take any one that you're fond of. You may know, or guess, what kind of a tale it is, happy-ending or sad-ending, but the people in it don't know. And you don't want them to."

"No, sir, of course not. Beren now, he never thought he was going to get that Silmaril from the Iron Crown in Thangorodrim, and yet he did, and that was a worse place and a blacker danger than ours. But that's a long tale, of course, and goes on past the happiness and into grief and beyond it—and the Silmaril went on and came to Eärendil. And why, sir, I never thought of that before! We've got—you've got some of the light of it in that star-glass that the Lady gave you! Why, to think of it, we're in the same tale still! It's going on. Don't the great tales never end?"

—J. R. R. Tolkien, *The Lord of the Rings* (1955), bk. 4, chap. 8

The Gospels contain a fairy-story, or a story of a larger kind which embraces all the essence of fairy-stories. They contain many marvels—peculiarly artistic, beautiful, and moving: "mythical" in their perfect, self-contained significance; and among the marvels is the greatest and most complete conceivable eucatastrophe. But this story has entered History and the primary world; the desire and aspiration of sub-creation has been raised to the fulfillment of Creation. The Birth of Christ is the eucatastrophe of Man's history. The Resurrection is the eucatastrophe of the story of the Incarnation . . . There is no tale ever told that men would rather find was true, and none which so many sceptical men have accepted as true on its own merits. For the Art of it has the supremely convincing tone of Primary Art, that is, of Creation . . . [This] story is supreme; and it is true. Art has been verified. God is the Lord, of angels, and of men—and of elves. Legend and History have met and fused.

—J. R. R. Tolkien, "On Fairy-Stories" (1947)

And in the sixth month, the angel Gabriel was sent from God into a city of Galilee, called Nazareth, to a virgin espoused to a man whose name was Joseph, of the house of David: and the virgin's name was Mary. And the angel being come in, said unto her: "Hail, full of grace, the Lord is with thee: blessed art thou among women." Who having heard, was troubled at his saying and thought with herself what manner of salutation this should be.

—Luke 1:26–29

The swelling of the stream maketh glad the city of God: the Most High hath sanctified his tabernacle. God is in the midst of her, she shall not be moved.

—Psalm 45:5–6

In all these I sought rest, and I shall abide in the inheritance of the Lord. Then the Creator of all things commanded, and said to me: and he that made me rested in my tabernacle, and he said to me: "Let thy dwelling be in Jacob, and thy inheritance in Israel, and take root in mine elect." And so was I established in Sion, and in the holy city likewise I rested; and my power was in Jerusalem, and I took root in an honourable people, and in the portion of my God his inheritance, and my abode is in the full assembly of Saints.

—Ecclesiasticus 24:14–16

Invitatory

Come, let us praise the Lord with joy!
Let us joyfully sing to God, our savior.

—Psalm 94:1

Devotion requires an object. Like the imagination, devotion takes its shape and purpose from its object. Without an object, there can be no devotion. Just as, in philosopher and literary critic Elaine Scarry's words, "it is impossible to imagine without imagining something," so it is impossible to be devout (or to love) without having devotion for or to something. To paraphrase Scarry, as in imagination, so in devotion there is "no activity, no 'state,' no experienceable condition or felt-occurrence separate from its object." Likewise, as in imagination, the attributes that devotion is understood to have "tend to be derived from whatever 'imagined object' happens to have been taken as a representable instance of imagining."[1] As with the imagination, so with devotion; it is the characteristics of the object that define it as an activity or experiential state. It is the object that defines the experience of devotion. Love of the object shapes the one loving, even as the one loving, through the imagination, gives shape to the object. The lover requires a beloved to love, even as the beloved creates the lover through love.

For nearly two thousand years, Christians have defined themselves through their love of God, identifying God as love and themselves as lovers of God (1 John 4:7–12). For much of that time, they have also identified themselves as lovers of God's mother, the Virgin Mary who gave birth to the child Jesus of Nazareth, whom the angel Gabriel promised her would be called the Son of the Most High (Luke 1:32). But just as it took many centuries for Christians to explain for themselves what it meant to say that the child born of Mary was the Son of God (Luke 1:35), so it took many centuries for them to explain what it meant to say that a human woman had given birth to the Maker of heaven and earth. Nevertheless, throughout much of that time, Christians were convinced that the mystery had been foreshadowed in the scriptures—particularly the psalms—that they read and sang out of devotion to Mary and her Son.

This is a book about devotion, about the way it works as an exercise of the imagination and as an expression of love for a particular object, the Virgin Mother of God. It is not, however, a book about devotion in the abstract, nor, the author would argue, could such a book be written and still be about devotion. Rather, this book is intended as a kind of handbook, itself an exercise in describing the object of devotion so as to get inside the experience of loving that object, to see the beloved as her lovers have seen her, and perhaps thereby to understand something of their love. As such, it is likewise an invitation to participate in that love, if only for the sake of experiment. More academic readers may prefer to think of themselves as participating in an exercise of empathy or, if you will, make-believe.

This book invites the reader: Imagine! Imagine that you are a devotee of Mary and her Son; a medieval devotee of the Virgin, skilled in the recitation of her Office, that cycle of psalms, chants, lessons, and prayers said daily throughout the High Middle Ages and later by every man, woman, or child who could read and, as we shall see, even by many who knew the texts only by heart or in part. As you sing to her the chants and psalms of her Office, imagine that you know yourself joined by all the creatures in heaven and on earth in worship of their Creator, made visible to his creatures through the Incarnation of the Son, and that the Lady to whom you sing is the one who made him visible by giving birth to him.

Allow yourself to be absorbed in the sound and the meaning of the words you are singing about Mary and her Son. Know that for you there is no greater joy to be had than in singing her praises and giving thanks for her Son, because the words that you sing are the very ones sung by the angels and saints before the throne of the Lord whose mother she is. As you imagine yourself in the presence of the Virgin when the angel Gabriel came to her and said, "Hail, full of grace, the Lord is with you" (Luke 1:28), you feel your mouth filled with the sweetness of the angel's greeting, just as Mary herself rejoiced to feel the baby conceived in her womb. As her devotee you want nothing more than to spend your days—and nights, for much of the Office was said at night—naming her so as to savor the mystery of how the Lord showed himself to the world. You could never weary of describing her, because she herself is the most perfect image and likeness of the Lord whom she bore in her womb, the unspotted mirror of his majesty and the very image of his goodness (Wisdom 7:26).

Notice the effect that this exercise of singing and imagination has on you and on the way in which you understand the meaning of the psalms. Like all her most ardent devotees, you realize you know how to praise her because she is described everywhere in the scriptures, because she is Wisdom who was with God from the beginning and who danced and played before him as he created heaven and earth (Proverbs 8:22–31). You also know that he created her to be the ark, temple, throne, and glorious city by which he entered into his creation, to whom he espoused himself and who now, as Tree of Life and Queen, stands by his throne interceding on behalf of all those who pray to her. Your greatest hope is to become like her by serving her, the servant of the Lord, the very reflection of the Creator in whose image you have been made. Even more, by loving her, you hope yourself to be transformed by love and thus discover the true meaning of devotion in love. And that transformation and understanding of love is the greatest reward any human being could ever seek.

"Prayer," as the liberal French theologian Auguste Sabatier (d. 1901) once famously put it, as cited by the American philosopher and psychologist William James (d. 1910), "is religion in act; that is, prayer is real religion."[2] For medieval Christians, prayer was above all an exercise in lifting the mind and soul to God.[3] One might lift the mind and soul to God for many different reasons, in thanksgiving, supplication, intercession, confession, petition, or promise (1 Timothy 2:1), but at root prayer was understood as an exercise in attention, that is, an exercise in focusing one's intellect and affect (*intellectus et affectus*) utterly upon God. As the twentieth-century mystic Simone Weil (d. 1943) averred, clearly echoing this tradition:

> The key to a Christian conception of studies is the realization that prayer consists of attention. It is the orientation of all the attention of which the soul is capable toward God. The quality of the attention counts for much in the quality of the prayer. Warmth of heart cannot make up for it. The highest part of the attention only makes contact with God, when prayer is intense and pure enough for such a contact to be established; but the whole attention is turned toward God.[4]

"I will pray," the apostle Paul told the Corinthians, "with the spirit, I will pray also with the understanding, I will sing with the spirit, I will sing also with the understanding" (1 Corinthians 14:15). "Let us stand to sing the psalms," Benedict of Nursia (d. ca. 547) cautioned his monastic brothers, "in such a way that our minds are in harmony with our voices."[5] Over the centuries, ancient and medieval Christians developed various practices to help train their attention on God, some as simple as reciting a single verse of a psalm, some involving far more complicated practices of reading and meditation, always, however, with the conviction that it was not the practice as such that mattered, but rather the object. More to the point, for medieval Christians, prayer was not, as it has become in much of modern American culture, primarily a technology of "self-discovery" or "self-realization," nor was it intended to be. Neither was it an exercise in achieving "flow" or a certain "altered state" of consciousness, whether mystical, affective, imagistic, or absorbed, although, as with all such exercises of concentrated attention, such states could—and did—result.[6] It was God, not the psychological state of the one praying, that was the focus, and it was above all the Virgin Mary to whom medieval Christians turned in order to focus their attention on God.

Medieval Christians prayed to Mary because they believed that it was she who, by her consent to the Incarnation of the Son of God in her womb, made the God-man visible to the world and so, as the Lord Christ, the principal focus of prayer. It was likewise, as medieval Christians understood it, at the moment of her overshadowing by the Holy Spirit (Luke 1:35) that God revealed himself to humanity as triune, one God in three persons. As the great twelfth-century visionary abbess Hildegard of Bingen (d. 1179) explained the mystery: "The Father is declared through the Son, the Son through creation, and the Holy Spirit through the Son incarnate."[7] Just as it was Mary who carried the Son of God in her womb, so for her medieval devotees it was the work of the Office of the Virgin, with its Marian antiphons framing psalms of praise to the Creator of heaven and earth, to make this relationship clear.

HOW TO READ THIS BOOK

Standing one day in a dark toolshed, medievalist, novelist, and Christian apologist C. S. Lewis (d. 1963) had an enlightening experience.[8] As he tells it:

> The sun was shining outside and through the crack at the top of the door there came a sunbeam. From where I stood that beam of light, with the specks of dust

floating in it, was the most striking thing in the place. Everything else was almost pitch-black. I was seeing the beam, not seeing things by it.

Then I moved, so that the beam fell on my eyes. Instantly the whole previous picture vanished. I saw no toolshed, and (above all) no beam. Instead I saw, framed in the irregular cranny at the top of the door, green leaves moving on the branches of a tree outside and beyond that, 90 odd million miles away, the sun.

At which, Lewis came to a sudden realization:

Looking along the beam [he opined], and looking at the beam are very different experiences.

"Which"—Lewis asked readers of the *Coventry Evening Telegraph*, where he first published this "Meditation in a Toolshed"—"is the 'true' or 'valid' experience" if "you get one experience of a thing when you look along it and another when you look at it"? Which experience (he asked them to consider) tells you most about, say, love or religion or chivalry: looking *at* the beam and describing what you see from the outside, or looking *along* it to see what the lover or devotee or knight offering his lady his service sees? And why should what those who look only *at* the beam see (the beam itself, the dust motes floating in it) be taken as more real or objective than what those who look *along* it are enabled to see (the leaves of the trees, the sun)? Surely, both the lover (whose whole world changes when he gazes upon his beloved) and the biologist (who sees a man driven by his hormones and genes); the mathematician (whose mind is filled with contemplations of "timeless and spaceless truths about quantity") and the cerebral physiologist (who, looking inside the mathematician's head, sees only "tiny movements in the grey matter"); the savage (who believes his dancing brings babies and rain) and the anthropologist (who identifies the dance as a particular type of fertility ritual); the little girl (who cries when her doll breaks as if she has lost a real friend) and the psychologist (who explains that the girl's "nascent maternal instinct has been temporarily lavished on a bit of shaped and coloured wax") all consider their experiences "valid" and "true," whether they are looking along the beam (the lover, the mathematician, the savage, the little girl) or looking at it (the biologist, the cerebral physiologist, the anthropologist, the psychologist). How do you decide whose experience is the real one? Can you?

Once this distinction between looking *at* and looking *along* is grasped, common sense, not to mention common experience, would seem to suggest caution. And yet, Lewis observed, "you can hardly ask [this] question without noticing that for the last fifty years or so [Lewis was writing in 1945] everyone has been taking the answer for granted." In his words:

> It has been assumed without discussion that if you want the true account of religion you must go, not to religious people, but to anthropologists; that if you want the true account of sexual love you must go, not to lovers, but to psychologists; that if you want to understand some "ideology" (such as medieval chivalry or the nineteenth-century idea of a "gentleman"), you must listen not to those who lived inside it, but to sociologists.

Not, Lewis would insist, that there are not important insights to be gained from looking *at* rather than *along* religion or sexual love or chivalry, quite the reverse. Rather, he averred, the real problem is that in recent years, "the people who look *at* things [taking, as scholars would now say, an etic approach] have had it all their own way," while "the people who look *along* things [as it were, emically] have simply been brow-beaten." Worse,

> [it] has even come to be taken for granted that the external account of a thing somehow refutes or "debunks" the account given from inside. "All these moral ideals which look so transcendental and beautiful from inside," says the wiseacre, "are really only a mass of biological instincts and inherited taboos."[9] And no one plays the game the other way round by replying, "If you will only step inside, the things that look to you like instincts and taboos will suddenly reveal their real and transcendental nature."

Simply put, Lewis contended, it is time for the browbeating to end, for the practical reason that we cannot know from the outset which account is true: "We do not know in advance whether the lover or the psychologist is giving the more correct account of love, or whether both accounts are equally correct in different ways, or whether both are equally wrong." Ideally, according to Lewis, "[one] must look both *along* and *at* everything," otherwise we condemn ourselves before we have even started to the idiocy that there is no such thing as thought, only movements of the gray matter in our brains, for "if the outside vision were the correct one all thought (including this thought itself) would be valueless." But this is self-contradictory: "You cannot," Lewis insists, "have a proof that no proofs matter." Nor if the exterior account is the only valid one would there be such a thing as pain, since (as Scarry herself would put it), pain, having no object, can only be experienced by its sufferer. Even the words that we use to describe pain have no referent other than the pain itself, which only the sufferer can know. To study pain, as Lewis puts it, one must have looked *along* pain, not only *at* it as a kind of neural event. The very subject of study exists only if one has "been inside" pain by actually suffering.

So, likewise, this book argues, with devotion and prayer, particularly devotions like that of medieval Christians to the Virgin and her Son.

For too long, our scholarship has privileged those would who look *at* devotion as something to be explained from the outside, rather than allowing ourselves to look *along* devotion to see what the devout might see. We have looked *at* prayer as a practice rather than *along* prayer to its object, seeing only the beam ("religious experience") rather than the sun ("God"). So convinced, indeed, have we become that what those who are looking along the beam see cannot be valid or true that we—as, for example, Scarry or Ludwig Feuerbach (d. 1872) before her—have persuaded ourselves that what they see can only be a figment of their imagination, something made up rather than something held in the mind with attention; an artifact of their own making rather than, as they experience it, the light by which they see. (The entailments of the metaphor of the beam are clearly derived from Lewis's own understanding of God.) Even those who consider themselves Christians often spend more time looking *at* the beam than *along* it, worrying more about "experiencing" Christ than about Christ, as if their experience of itself could prove the truth of their faith when, in fact, what they are doing is standing outside of the very beam into which Christ invites them to step so that they might see him as the truth and the light by which they live.[10]

The effects of this focus on experience rather than Christ are clear to see in the loss of faith many have experienced since the nineteenth century, particularly those most influenced by critical theologians like Feuerbach.[11] Seen from the outside, those attending to something others cannot see can only appear ridiculous. All of the gestures, actions, and words people use when focused on an object make no sense to those focused only on the one having the experience, unless they themselves are focused on the same object and are therefore, likewise, looking along the beam. The devotee does not kneel or sing or light candles or burn incense before an image of the Virgin because she wishes to have the experience of kneeling or singing or looking at candles or smelling incense, any more than the fan leaps and yells because he wishes to have the experience of leaping and yelling. She kneels and sings and lights candles and burns incense because these are the responses she has to seeing the Virgin, just as the fan leaps and yells because these are the responses he has to seeing his favorite athlete perform.

Nor will the experience of kneeling or singing as such make the devotee see the Virgin any more than leaping and yelling will make the fan see the athlete. It is not, in other words, the practices that call forth the experience, but the attention to the object that calls forth the practices.

Nor is this insight at all new. Prayer, as every medieval Christian knew, was not something you did so as to have a certain kind of feeling that would thereby prove that God existed. (As Anselm, abbot of Bec and archbishop of Canterbury [d. 1109], and his many followers understood it, God was "that-than-which-nothing-greater-can-be-conceived," that is, by the mind, not just by the heart.) Rather, prayer was what you did because you were paying attention to God. As Anselm prayed in his *Proslogion*: "O Lord . . . I long to understand a little of your truth, which my heart already believes and loves. For I do not seek to understand so that I may believe, but I believe so that I may understand."[12] Looked *at* from the outside, such practices as reciting the Office or saying the Ave Maria cannot help but to appear "mechanical," a "vain exercise of words" or "mere repetition of sacred formulae" (as Sabatier would put it[13]), effective only insofar as they induce certain physiological or neurological states such as might be detected through functional magnetic resonance imaging. Rather, as Lewis would contend and Anselm most likely agree, it is only when we look *along* such practices to the object on which they were focused that they appear as the machines (*machinae*) that they were intended to be—engines, as Mary's medieval devotees would put it, for lifting the mind to God.[14]

From this perspective, theory, at least in the modern sense of the word, can take us only so far. We need some way of stepping into the beam so as to gaze at the object rather than the experience. If we want to understand the experience, we need some way of partaking in it, not just looking at it from the outside. We need to become spectators, not in the modern sense of those looking at something from the outside, but rather in the ancient sense of *theoria*, attending to something so perfectly as to forget one's own purposes and to become totally involved in what one sees.[15] This is not as alien an experience as it might at first seem, even for those who prefer looking at the beam; even in looking at the beam, they are still having the experience of attending to the beam. In Lewis's words, "you can step outside one experience only by stepping inside another." We are all looking along one beam or another, even as we look at others standing within the beam we have not entered. If, Lewis cautions, we insist that their inside experience is misleading—that what they see cannot be as true or valid as what we see—then we, too, are forced to confess that we may have been misled by the object that we have taken for our sun.

THE VIRGIN CLOTHED WITH THE SUN

Stepping from the darkness into the light can be disorienting. It takes some time for one's eyes to adjust to the brightness. At first, one may be dazzled   or blinded. Many may prefer to close their eyes and retreat. But those with the willingness to allow themselves to look along the beam may see something that they did not expect to see. Such new insights may be unsettling and difficult to understand. In the present instance, the greatest stumbling block many readers of this book will most likely encounter (other than faith that what they are seeing can be trusted) is the degree to which medieval Marian devotion depended on the scriptures, and not just those passages in the Gospels (Matthew 1:18–2:23, 12:46–50; Mark 3:31–35, 6:3; Luke 1:26–2:52; John 2:1–12, 19:17–30) with which most modern histories of Mary more or less apologetically begin. The scriptures, we are told, say relatively little about Mary.[16] How then, it is asked, could medieval Christians say so much about her? At least since the sixteenth century, the almost invariable answer to this question has been: they must have made it up or have drawn from that magical reservoir—"paganism."[17] And yet, as we shall see, this was hardly the way in which Mary's medieval devotees understood their sacred texts.[18]

The Office of the Virgin Mary, like the Divine Office on which it was modeled, was above all an exercise in reciting the psalms. Almost invariably, studies of the Marian Office, particularly studies of any lavishly illuminated Book of Hours with which wealthier late medieval Christians said their prayers, take the presence of the psalms for granted, some even arguing on the basis of the images contained in many of these books that medieval Christians barely read the texts, so focused would they have been on the illuminations in the margins.[19] Other studies assume, on the basis of the images, that the psalms they introduce and frame were read as replicating the narrative of the earthly life of the Virgin represented in the pictures, when, as our reading of the texts will hopefully show, the relationship between text and image was somewhat more complicated. A very few studies suggest that the psalms should be read as saying something about the relationship between Mary and God or between Mary and her devotees, but even these typically default into more general arguments about how Mary represents a type of the Church (which she may, if not quite for the reasons usually invoked) or imply that the Marian frame in which the psalms appear in her Office had little to do with the meaning of the texts.

But what if, *Mary and the Art of Prayer* invites its readers to imagine, contrary to more recent traditions of reading the psalms, there was a tradition of reading according to which the psalms make mention of the Virgin Mary *all the time*?

What if, according to this tradition of interpretation, just as the Lord of the psalms might be identified as Jesus Christ, so the Virgin Mary might be identified, not as a "type" of the Church, but as herself the Lady who gave birth to the Lord and stood beside his throne in gold-woven robes as his queen (Psalm 44:10)? What if, in this tradition, not only the psalms, but indeed the whole of scripture made mention of the Virgin Mary over and over and over again as the one through whom the Lord entered into his creation and made his face shine upon the world? To attempt to read the psalms and the other texts of the Marian Office in this way is to step into a beam that will require us to see not only the Virgin but indeed the whole of Christianity in a light most modern Christians, not to mention most modern scholars, have never seen, so convinced have we become that those who saw by it could only be deluded—or mad.[20]

As every good modern exegete knows, medieval exegetes read into the scriptures all sorts of things that were never there.[21] How else to explain their elaborate figures, tropes, and typologies, for example, of Mary as the burning bush, Gideon's fleece, the tower of David, or the temple of Solomon? Even modern Catholics seem to be embarrassed by this tradition, despite Henri de Lubac's magisterial four-volume effort to revive the "four senses of Scripture" for contemporary exegetical practice.[22] More recently, the medieval monastic practice of *lectio divina* has become popular among both scholars and religious readers alike, but more as a meditative technique than as an exercise grounded in a particular tradition of interpretation.[23] Even medievalists who study this interpretive tradition typically prefer to bracket it as "the way medieval Christians read the Bible," without asking whether perhaps there might have been some grounds for it other than allegory (whatever that means)—or wishful thinking.[24]

Drawing on the work of Old Testament scholar Margaret Barker, *Mary and the Art of Prayer* proposes an alternative. When medieval Christians like the canon, archdeacon, and penitentiary Richard of Saint-Laurent (d. ca. 1250), the Franciscan preacher Conrad of Saxony (d. 1279), or the anonymous author of the thirteenth-century *Mariale* long attributed to the Dominican Albert the Great insisted that the scriptures throughout showed forth Mary, they did so on the basis of an interpretive tradition they saw going back to the very origins of Christianity. From this perspective, medieval Christians sang the psalms of the Old Testament in praise of the Virgin Mother of God not because they were desperate for ways in which to invent her cult, but because they believed that the scriptures they sang were quite literally about her and her Son—and, indeed, always had been. Mary was the lens through which they read scripture, because in their understanding Mary was the one who had made God visible to the world. She was the Mother of the Word who spoke through the scriptures.

Herself Wisdom, she was the Mother of Wisdom by which the deaf hear and the blind see. Accordingly, as Richard of Saint-Laurent explained, everything that was said in scriptures about Wisdom could likewise be expounded of her as the Mother of Wisdom, so perfectly was she filled with wisdom when Wisdom rested in her womb.[25]

While the primary purpose in invoking Barker's reconstruction of this interpretative tradition is to help us see the medieval devotion to the Virgin in a new light, there is potentially a further benefit to this approach in the way it helps us to reimagine the origins of Mary's cult. If we accept, as Barker herself argues, that this understanding of the Lady as Wisdom went back well before the earliest Christians claimed to have beheld the glory of the Lord in the person of Jesus of Nazareth (John 1:14), then the medieval tradition appears not as the product of fancy or excess devotion, but rather, as the medieval liturgists and commentators themselves insisted, as a continuation of the very tradition out of which Christianity arose. From this perspective, Mary appears not (as the sixteenth-century reformers feared) as the mother goddess manqué invented (as some modern scholars have provocatively suggested) by the early Christians so as to relieve the otherwise overwhelming masculinity of their monotheism (it was always more complicated than this criticism suggests), but rather even more provocatively if in proper orthodox fashion, as the reason that Christians describe God as Trinity. More particularly, Mary, or rather, the Lady who was present in the ancient temple before the seventh-century B.C.E. reforms of King Josiah cast her out (2 Kings 23 RSV), appears as the reason that Christians looked to the birth of a Son who would show forth his glory and thereby make the Father known (John 1:18), suggesting possibly—just possibly—that what her medieval devotees believed about her was not just devotionally, but historically true, with profound implications for the way in which we understand the subsequent history of the relationship between those who called themselves "Christians" and their rivals and fellow heirs of the temple tradition, the Jews.[26] Medieval Christian artists attempted to represent this mystery visually in the form of statues of the Virgin and Child that opened to reveal the Trinity within.[27] Our argument will be that the Office of the Virgin attempted to represent this mystery verbally through its choice of antiphons and psalms.

Barker's reconstruction of the ancient and medieval interpretive tradition is presented more fully in chapter 3, but first we need to set the scene. Chapter 1 gives a history of the adoption of the Marian Office from its first appearance

PLATE 1 Closed, the statue represents the Virgin holding the Child. Shrine of the Virgin, Rhine valley, ca. 1300. Metropolitan Museum of Art, Gift of J. Pierpont Morgan, 1917, Accession number 17.190.185.

PLATE 2   Opened, the statue reveals the mystery: the Trinity (the dove at God's breast and the body of Christ on the cross are missing), God whom the heavens could not contain, contained within the womb of the Virgin. The painted images on the wings tell the story of the Incarnation, reading left to right, top to bottom: Annunciation, Visitation, Nativity, Presentation in the temple, visit of the Magi, annunciation to the shepherds. Shrine of the Virgin, Rhine valley, ca. 1300. Metropolitan Museum of Art, Gift of J. Pierpont Morgan, 1917, Accession number 17.190.185.

in the sources at the turn of the eleventh century to its formal promulgation after the Council of Trent, as well as an introduction to the symbolism of the liturgical hours and the overall structure of the Office. Chapter 2 invites the reader to imagine saying the invitatory antiphon of the Office (Ave Maria) as a salutation to the Virgin and explores the various meanings of Mary's name attributed to her in the Middle Ages, including those titles taken from the scriptures that have struck many modern exegetes as particularly absurd. Why did medieval Christians name Mary in the way that they did, as ark, tabernacle, temple, throne, and city of God? It is a mystery, it would seem, to which we have lost the key. Invoking Mary herself as our interpretive guide, chapter 3 takes us into the heart of the Office, with its complex interweaving of antiphons (or framing chants) and psalms. Here is where our argument of necessity becomes most speculative, suggesting as it does a reading of the psalms of the Marian Office on the basis of the imagery Barker has shown to have been integral to the ancient temple tradition as she reconstructs it, as well as to the Orthodox devotion to Mary as Theotokos.

Chapter 4 is intended as a balance to this more speculative reading. If, as chapter 3 has argued, the psalms and antiphons of the Marian Office reveal Mary as the Lady of the temple, did medieval Christians read the texts in this way? In answer, this chapter offers a close reading of three of the most important thirteenth-century *summae* written in praise of Mary, themselves in effect commentaries on the imagery of the Marian Office although they have rarely if ever been read in this way. For our purposes, the *De laudibus beatae Mariae virginis* of Richard of Saint-Laurent is particularly valuable as the single most comprehensive contemporary effort to demonstrate the way in which the scriptures speak of Mary, while Conrad of Saxony's popular *Speculum beatae Mariae* (itself long believed to have been the work of the great Franciscan theologian Bonaventure) and Pseudo-Albert's *Mariale, sive CCXXX Quaestiones super Evangelium Super missus est* illustrate further how this imagery was used in describing Mary as Wisdom and Queen. Chapter 5 turns to the many miracle stories written about the effects of prayer to Mary to show the way in which this imagery informed even the most humble devotions to the Lady, as sinners from the poorest almsman to the king of Spain sought to serve her as the Mother of the Lord. This understanding of their service is contrasted with the way in which the medieval devotion to the Virgin has typically been read in the nineteenth and twentieth centuries, suggesting a critique not only of the modern reading of her medieval cult, but also of our understanding of medieval theology, liturgy, and devotion more generally. The epilogue suggests, by way of Sor María de Jesús de Ágreda's seventeenth-century masterpiece *Mystica Ciudad de Dios*, how this tradition

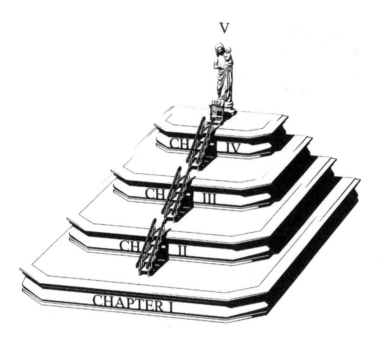

FIGURE I   Diagram of the structure of the book.

Drawing by Thomas Rush Brown.

continued to inform Marian devotion well into the early modern period, while at the same time, by way of the reception of Sor María's book, how—and at what cost—it was lost.

As the journey before us is a long one, a diagram may be helpful here to conceptualize the relationship of the various parts of the argument (see figure 1). Just as Mary as the Mother of God was believed by her medieval devotees to have provided the support or "frame" for God's entry into history, so the history of the Office as told in chapter 1 provides the supporting frame for the practice of saying the Ave Maria, itself the antiphon for the invitatory psalm, Psalm 94. This invitatory frame is described in chapter 2. In chapter 3, the antiphons for the Office provide the supporting frame for the recitation of the psalms, giving a Marian frame to the reading of the scriptures, while, in chapter 4, the recitation of the psalms in the Marian Office provides the frame for the commentaries that Richard, Conrad, and Pseudo-Albert wrote on the angel Gabriel's greeting. Ascending the steps, we move up and into the mystery, until in chapter 5 we arrive at the practice itself, expressed through the miracle stories that have hitherto been the most important and oft-cited witnesses to this devotion.

The figure of the Virgin crowns the ascent, as if arising from it, so that the practice of serving Mary is seen to arise from the singing of the antiphons and psalms of her Office. The purpose of chapter 5 is to tie together all of the threads drawn out in the first four chapters while at the same time providing a correction to the way in which medieval Marian devotion has been read for the better part of two centuries in the English-speaking tradition. Within this tradition, it has been typically assumed that devotion to the Virgin Mary was above all "popular" rather than learned, while at the same time it was thought that if there were a learned tradition of devotion to Mary, it must have been at odds with what the "common people" believed. As chapter 1 shows, however, of all of the devotions associated with Mary, the recitation of her Hours was arguably the single most popular devotion among both clergy and laity, women and men, to judge at the very least from the production of Books of Hours, not to mention, as chapter 2 shows, the practice of saying the Ave Maria as an abbreviated Office and later the rosary as an abbreviated psalter. Other than occasional rubrics in the Books of Hours (a subject still awaiting a comprehensive study), the most abundant evidence we have for what medieval people thought about performing the Office, including the Ave Maria, comes in the form of the miracle stories, themselves, as is shown in the first part of chapter 5, hitherto read almost invariably as witnesses to the way in which devotion to the Virgin challenged, rather than participated in, the rich complex of imagery that we can see in the commentaries, even as, as we shall see in chapter 4, the commentaries have themselves been rejected by certain scholars in the twentieth century as evidence of the contaminating "decadence" of "proper" Marian devotion.

The purpose of chapter 5 is to show, on the basis of the miracle stories, first, how medieval Christians understood their devotions in the Office as "service," and second, how our understanding of the image of Mary in the miracle stories changes when read through the frame of the imagery found in her Office described in chapter 3 and explicated in the commentaries described in chapter 4. More particularly, the second part of chapter 5 explicitly challenges three of the most frequent criticisms levied by modern scholars and Christians alike against the orthodoxy of medieval Marian devotion: first, that she subverts God's justice through her intercession; second, that descriptions of her beauty were at base profane; and third, that devotion to Mary distracts from contemplation of God. In each instance, the chapter shows how these modern critiques of the Virgin as she appears in the miracle stories are challenged by the imagery of Mary visible in the antiphons and psalms of the Office and developed through the commentaries of Richard, Conrad, and Pseudo-Albert. One story in particular, that of Theophilus, is critical here for a number of reasons: (1) Richard alludes to it constantly throughout his work as the principal example of Mary's power as intercessor; (2) illuminations illustrating it appear in the oldest extant English Book of Hours (London, British Library, Add. 49999, the De Brailes Hours), thus associating the story closely with the significance of the devotional practice; and (3) as one of the oldest extant stories of Mary's intercessory role, not to mention the best known of all her miracles, it is an important witness to the antiquity of the temple imagery in Marian devotion as well as a significant link between the devotion as it developed in the East and its transmission to the Latin West. Long as this chapter is, indeed, long as this book is, the author's main concern is that she will have only just scratched the surface of what it meant for medieval Christians to pray to Mary. It is her hope, nevertheless, that what little she has been able to show helps make clear why so many medieval women and men were said to experience such joy in reciting the angel's greeting in Mary's name, and why, as they strove to praise her, they did so in the language of the Psalms.

Mary &
the Art of
Prayer

PLATE 3 Left: The tree of Jesse, showing the ancestors of Mary and Jesus as flowers coming forth from Jesse's root (Isaiah 11:1). Right: the Annunciation, with God sending the dove of the Holy Spirit from heaven to overshadow Mary. Note the creatures in the margins. Book of Hours, France, ca. 1500–1510. Tree of Jesse, Annunciation. Book of Hours, France, ca. 1500–1510. Use of Nevers. Chicago, The University of Chicago Library, Special Collections 348, fols. 6v–7r.

1

The Hours of the Virgin

I f you have ever seen a medieval manuscript or a picture from a medieval manuscript on a Christmas card, you most likely have seen a Book of Hours. You would not be alone. Oft-remarked then as now for the beauty of their illuminations, Books of Hours were literally the best sellers of their day. Thousands, perhaps even tens of thousands of manuscript Books of Hours survive, particularly from the fifteenth and early sixteenth centuries.[1] With the advent of printing, Books of Hours became available in hundreds of editions, some as luxurious as the manuscripts on which they were modeled, others affordable even to the average artisan.[2] As various as their makers and patrons, Books of Hours typically contain a wide variety of scriptural, liturgical, and devotional texts, including calendars, excerpts from the Gospels, prayers to the Virgin Mary and other saints, various cycles of psalms (Penitential and Gradual), litanies, and the Office of the Dead.[3] It is fair to say that, even in their printed editions, no two Books of Hours are necessarily alike, their contents typically personalized and annotated by their owners for private devotional use.[4] But the reason that they are called Books of Hours and not books of prayer is that every Book of Hours contained some version of the *Horae beatae Mariae virginis* or "Hours of the Blessed Virgin Mary," now better known as the *Officium parvum beatae Mariae virginis* or "Little Office of the Virgin Mary."[5] So popular would this daily liturgical cursus of hymns, chants, psalms, lessons, and prayers become (thus the great popularity of the books, which English readers would come to call "prymers"), that by the later Middle Ages, every European Christian—man, woman, or child; monk, nun, cleric, or layperson—who could read would have been able to recite at least some of these hours by heart, and even those who could not would have been able to say the invitatory antiphon (Ave Maria) in lieu of the full Office.[6] In the mid-fifteenth century, the scholars at the newly founded Eton College said their Matins of the Virgin while making their beds.[7]

And yet, even in its popularity, there was a paradox: prior to the promulgation in 1571 of the *Officium beatae Mariae Virginis* as revised in accordance with the recommendations of the Council of Trent, strictly speaking there was no such thing as *the* Office of the Virgin Mary.[8] To be sure, some Uses[9] were more widespread than others—those of Sarum (Salisbury) and York in England; that of Rome in Italy, Flanders, and in the later fifteenth century, France; that of Geert Grote's Dutch translation in the Low Countries—but for centuries, variety remained the norm. Hundreds of different Uses have thus far been identified, and there is little to suggest that even current lists are exhaustive.[10] To a certain extent, this variation should come as no surprise to those familiar with the complexities of the medieval liturgy. Even for the principal feasts of the Virgin, the texts of the liturgy varied from monastery to monastery, cathedral to cathedral.[11] At least with respect to their lessons and chants, however, the latter tended to draw from a recognizable repertoire, itself heavily dependent upon the Franko-Gregorian appropriation of the Song of Songs for the Marian feasts.[12] With the Office of the Virgin, the only real core was the choice of hymns and psalms and even here, particularly for Prime, the Little Hours, Vespers, and Compline there was significant variation. Only at Matins, where the psalms were the same as those for the Feasts of the Purification, Assumption, and Nativity of the Virgin, and at Lauds, where the psalms were taken from the regular secular cursus for Sunday, was there anything like a standard observance (see Table 2).[13]

Post-Tridentine expectations of liturgical conformity might lead us to suspect that contemporaries found this diversity somewhat troubling, but such does not seem to have been the case. Every devout Christian man or woman—from the queen and her ladies to the abbess of the local convent, the bourgeois wife anxious to impress her neighbors, and the child just learning her ABCs; from the master general of the Dominicans to the duke and duchess of Burgundy, the brothers and sisters of the Common Life, and the married daughters of the knight Geoffrey de la Tour-Landry—might be saying the Matins of the Blessed Virgin first thing in the morning, "reverently," as one spiritual director advised a certain English gentleman, "and not too fast," but there is nothing to suggest that anything other than custom, local observance, and/or personal preference dictated which version of the Marian Office he or she might use.[14] Skeptics might wonder whether for the majority of Mary's devotees it made any difference. Surely, or so it has often been suggested, medieval Christians who owned such beautifully illuminated prayer books were only looking at the pictures (or showing them off to their friends), not reading the texts. And, to be sure, it is the pictures that have tended to attract most recent collectors and scholars, particularly those less versed (or less interested) in the intricacies of the medieval liturgy.[15] Nevertheless,

TABLE 2 The Hours of the Virgin (for the most part)

MATINS (night Office)

- Invitatory (Ave Maria), with Psalm 94
- Hymn ("Quem terra pontus sidera")
- One of three nocturns according to the day of the week. Each nocturn consists of three psalms, each having its own antiphon.
  - I: Psalms 8, 18, and 23 (Sunday, Monday, and Thursday)
  - II: Psalms 44, 45, and 86 (Tuesday and Friday)
  - III: Psalms 95, 96, and 97 (Wednesday and Saturday)
- Versicle and response
- Three lessons, each preceded by a blessing and followed by a responsory, with versicle and response. The Te Deum follows the third lesson.

LAUDS (daybreak)

- Five psalms, each with its own antiphon
  - Psalms 92, 99, 62, and 66
  - Canticle of the Three Children ("Benedicite opera omnia," Daniel 3:57–88, 56)
  - Psalms 148–150
- Capitulum or "little chapter" with or without responsory
- Hymn ("O gloriosa Domina"), with versicle and response
- Canticle of Zacharias (Benedictus, Luke 1:68–79), with antiphon
- Prayer, followed by Suffrages of the Saints, with versicle and response

THE LITTLE HOURS (Prime: 6 a.m.; Terce: 9 a.m.; Sext: 12 p.m.; and None: 3 p.m.)

- Hymn
- Three psalms, with one antiphon
  - Prime: highly variable
  - Typical cycles starting with Terce:
    - a) Psalms 119, 120, 121; 122, 123, 124; 125, 126, 127
    - b) Psalms 122, 123, 124; 125, 126, 127; 128, 129, 130
    - c) Psalm 118 divided into parts vv. 33–80; 81–128; 129–176
- Capitulum with responsory
- Prayer, with versicle and response

(continued)

TABLE 2 *(Continued)*

VESPERS (sunset)

- Five psalms, each with its own antiphon
  - ○ Typical cycles:
    - ▪ a) Psalms 109, 112, 121, 126, and 147
    - ▪ b) Psalms 121, 122, 123, 124, and 125
    - ▪ c) Psalms 128, 129, 130, 131, and 132
- Capitulum, with or without responsory
- Hymn ("Ave maris stella"), with versicle and response
- Canticle of Mary (Magnificat, Luke 1:46–55), with antiphon
- Prayer, with versicle and response

COMPLINE (bedtime)

- Three (monastic cursus) or four (secular cursus) psalms, with or without antiphons
  - ○ Typical cycles:
    - ▪ a) Psalms 12, 42, 128, and 130
    - ▪ b) Psalms 128, 129, and 130
    - ▪ c) Psalms 131, 132, and 133
    - ▪ d) Psalms 30, 86, and 116
- Hymn
- Capitulum, with versicle and response
- Canticle of Simeon (Nunc Dimittis, Luke 2:29–32), with antiphon
- Prayer, with versicle and response

for all their beauty, images in fact make up only a small part of the contents of most Books of Hours. Unless you were saying, for example, Matins from memory (which is possible, given its repetition, day after day for most of one's life), you would very rapidly finish reading the opening versicle ("Domine, labia mea aperies"—*Lord, open my lips*) accompanying the image of the Annunciation and need to turn the page. What you would then find would be not more images (except perhaps marginally, and these often far from devotional), but page after page of text, most—albeit not all—of it taken from the Psalms.[16]

Various and however much supplemented by additional devotions as they might be, the texts of the Hours of the Virgin mattered. Indeed, it is arguably their very variety that is the most telling witness to the significance of the Hours in high and late medieval Christian devotion. This was not an Office enjoined upon the laity by an authoritarian clergy; nor, despite the fact that it had come, by the later fourteenth century, to be considered obligatory upon all cathedral and collegiate clergy "by virtue of the general custom of all nations," was it in its origins anything other than voluntary.[17] Rather, just as the laity seems to have requested resources for participating in the liturgical observances of the regular clergy and the friars, so the friars and secular clergy themselves looked to the innovations of the monasteries.[18] Neither, although the ever-vigilant Peter Damian (d. 1072/1073) did his utmost to promote it, can the composition of the Marian Office be accredited to any one community, never mind any one author.[19] To date (to the best of my knowledge), some ten different Offices copied in the eleventh and twelfth centuries have been published; another seven have been identified in manuscript.[20] The two oldest of these, although both from mid–eleventh century England and from communities as closely associated as Canterbury and Winchester, differ in almost every particular, other than their selection of psalms.[21]

How did this optional Office, so obscure in its origins, come to be on the lips of so many in Christendom? One is almost tempted to say, with the Bostonian historian and belle-lettrist Henry Adams (d. 1918), because the Virgin herself wished it so. But this is to anticipate.[22] What we can see as historians is a growth of interest in keeping this Office or something like it beginning from the later tenth century among certain monastic individuals and spreading rapidly over the course of the eleventh and twelfth centuries to monastic and cathedral communities from as far south as Monte Cassino to as far north as the diocese of York. From the second quarter of the thirteenth century, we have evidence for its observance among certain ladies of the English West Midlands who had removed themselves from secular society to live as recluses or "ancresses."[23] At about the same time, laypeople, especially women, seem to have begun to make special requests of professional (that is, nonmonastic) bookmakers for books containing the Hours of the Virgin as observed by their clerical, particularly mendicant, spiritual advisers. This, at least, seems to have been the case with the oldest known extant Book of Hours to be produced in England (London, British Library, Add. 49999), itself the work from around the year 1240 of the Oxford-based illuminator and scribe William de Brailes.[24] We have already noted the general self-imposition of the observance on cathedral colleges and the monastic orders by the fourteenth century. Whether copied into psalters, as remained the custom particularly in

England well into the fifteenth century, or as the centerpiece of the increasingly popular Books of Hours, the Hours of the Virgin underpinned the prayer life of communities (convents, cathedral colleges, hospitals, houses of the Common Life, confraternities) and individuals (Peter Damian, Matilda of Tuscany, Gundulf of Bec, Manegold of Lautenbach, Humbert of Romans, Louis IX of France, Gertrude of Helfta, Geert Grote, Margery Kempe, Thomas More) for some five hundred or more years.

A full history of the development of the Hours of the Virgin is beyond the scope of our present exercise, involved as such a history would be with not only the monastic reforms of the eleventh and twelfth centuries and the new emphasis on lay education stimulated by the Fourth Lateran Council and the rise of the friars in the thirteenth, but also the great burgeoning of devotion to the Virgin that these centuries witnessed more generally.[25] There is likewise much work still to be done with the manuscripts and with tracing the distribution of textual variants and Uses. Our concern being with the role of the Marian Office in the practice and experience of prayer to the Virgin, it is not so much the details as the fact of this development that requires our attention here.

To this end, the first part of this chapter offers a review of the evidence that we have to date for the origins and adoption of the Marian Office. Although much of this story has been available, at least in parts, for the better part of a century, there remains a tendency in much recent scholarship on Books of Hours to imply, if unintentionally, that the Marian Office, while clearly monastic in its origins, was somehow specifically designed with the laity in mind, as an "abbreviated breviary" or substitute for the full monastic cursus of prayer.[26] As we shall see, as much in the thirteenth, fourteenth, and fifteenth centuries as in the eleventh and twelfth, the Marian Office was an observance kept by clergy and regular religious who, it should be noted, could both read and understand its texts and who still found it added something significant to their day, above and beyond the Hours of the Divine Office they were canonically obliged to observe. Nor were the laity (anchoresses, beguines, hospital workers, brothers and sisters of the Common Life, householders) who adopted the Office for their own devotions necessarily any less likely to be able to understand and appreciate the complexity of its texts; quite the reverse.

The second part of this chapter offers a description of the Marian Office itself, its overall structure, and the significance of praying the various Hours, as well as some indication of the differences between the earlier versions of the Office and its later, more widespread and local Uses. Again, it is not the purpose here to provide a full account of the development of the Marian Office in all of its temporal and regional complexities, but rather to suggest, by way of comparison, how differences in Use can help us to think about the meaning of the Virgin's Office for its practitioners. The Marian Office, like the Divine Office on which it was modeled, offered a way of structuring not only time—punctuating the night and day with moments of prayer—but also understanding. It was not just that the Marian Office provided medieval European Christians with an opportunity to pray to the Virgin Mother of God. Rather, its appeal lay specifically in the way in which it structured this prayer, imaginatively as well as theologically.

Laypeople today may find it difficult to discern the meaning and purpose of praying the monastic Hours—although with the work of Kathleen Norris and Phyllis Tickle this is beginning to change—but for the laity of the Middle Ages, as for the monks, nuns, and clergy, ordered, regular prayer was invariably the ideal.[27] To understand the place that the Virgin held in the hearts, minds, and imaginations of medieval European Christians, we must first appreciate why they strove to structure their prayers in the way that they did, whether, as with the Marian Office, according to the Hours of the monastic day; or, as with the rosary, according to the number of the psalms. As we shall see, far from constraining prayer, structure inspired it. Keeping the Hours, including attending Mass, enabled medieval Christians not only to think about the Virgin, but through Mary, to think about God. In return, God and his Mother came to them through the prayers of the liturgy and rewarded them with their presence, sometimes in visions; sometimes, more modestly, with sensations of lingering sweetness. Spontaneous as such experiences might seem to be, they were in fact predicated on hours—and Hours—of practice. If medieval Christians experienced the Virgin as real, it was not just because they longed for a mother to comfort them or a patron to intercede for them, but because they were practiced at imagining her, hour after hour, day after day. In order to appreciate the precise contours and theological implications of this imagining that will be our focus in subsequent chapters, it is first necessary to establish the practice by which it was sustained.

A LITTLE HISTORY OF THE OFFICE

By the early decades of the twelfth century, when monasteries and cathedral chapters across Europe had begun to observe a votive Office of the Virgin, there were almost predictable efforts to insist that its introduction went back to before Charlemagne's day.[28] According to Peter the Deacon, librarian of the great Benedictine abbey of Monte Cassino, it was Pope Zachary (d. 752) himself who had imposed the obligation upon his own community, "at all times in both summer and winter, before the night as well as the day office, as soon as the brothers will have assembled in choir, [to begin] the office of St. Benedict; afterwards, they should begin the office that the Rule enjoins; to which should be added also the office of the holy Mother of God and Virgin Mary (*sanctae Dei Genitricis et Virginis Mariae officio*)."[29] Peter noted that both additional observances were "canonical offices of seven hours," presumably so as to distinguish them from other, less comprehensive devotions, such as the Saturday votive Mass of the Virgin and its accompanying commemorative Office, the former of which really did go back (almost) to Charlemagne or, rather, his adviser Alcuin of York (d. 804).[30]

Peter's promotional efforts notwithstanding, others would date the observance of the Marian *Horae* to the mid-tenth century at the earliest, although even here there are questions about what, exactly, Mary's devotees were saying. Writing like Peter the Deacon in the first half of the twelfth century, the Benedictine chronicler Hugh of Flavigny recalled how Berengerius, bishop of Verdun (940–962), once literally stumbled upon Bernerius, the provost of his cathedral, whom he had found lying prostrate in the dark chanting Matins of the blessed Virgin (*matutinarium beatae Virginis cursum*). That same night the Virgin herself appeared to the bishop and berated him for treating her devoted cleric with such disrespect, upon which she ordered Saint Thecla, who had accompanied her along with Saint Agnes, to strike the bishop on the foot with which he had kicked the provost. Berengerius limped, or so Hugh told it, for the rest of his days.[31] Somewhat less colorfully if rather more proximate to his subject, Gerhard of Augsburg (writing between 982 and 993) described how his bishop Ulric of Augsburg (d. 973), latterly proclaimed a saint by Pope John XV (d. 996), kept the hours of the Divine Office (*cursus quotidianus*) in choir with the chapter of his cathedral whenever he was at home. In addition, Gerhard noted, Ulric was accustomed to recite "one *cursus* in honor of St. Mary, Mother of God; another in honor of the holy Cross; a third in honor of all saints, as well as many other psalms and the whole psalter daily."[32]

An appendix to Wulfstan of Winchester's biography of Saint Aethelwold of Winchester (d. 984), preserved in a twelfth-century manuscript copied by the monastic historian Ordericus Vitalis, attributes a similar triple cursus of psalmody to the saintly Anglo-Saxon bishop: the first, "to the praise of the blessed Mother of God and ever-virgin Mary"; the second, "to the honor of the blessed apostles Peter and Paul and to all those serving the humanity of our Savior in person"; the third, "asking for the support of all the saints that, protected by their pious intercession, we may deserve to overcome the manifold deceptions of the crafty Antichrist and his members and to receive, by the reward of Christ, the palm of celestial prizes."[33] The question here, as with

Ulric's devotions, is whether any of these three cursus constituted a complete cycle of *Horae* to be said throughout the day or whether—like the Office preserved in the so-called Prayerbook of Aelfwine (London, British Library, Cotton Titus D.xxvi+xxvii), copied sometime between 1012 and 1035 at Winchester—they were each rather a single Office to be said but once a day.[34] Although the note to Saint Aethelwold's vita claims that the bishop had these *horas regulares* "written down in very many places," none of the books (if the *Horae* were written in books and not just in unbound pamphlets or on single leaves) would seem to have survived.

In Aelfwine's prayer book, the Office *in honore sancte Mariae* is accompanied not as in Aethelwold's devotional cursus by Offices of Saints Peter and Paul, and All Saints, but rather by Offices of the Trinity and the Holy Cross.[35] Each calls for the recitation of three psalms; in fact, the same psalms in all three cases (53, 117, and 118 *usque in finem*) followed by the Athanasian creed *Quicumque vult*, with antiphons, chapters, responsories, versicles, hymns, and collects as appropriate to their intention. The structure of the offices with its three psalms is closest to that of monastic Vespers, including the Magnificat, but the psalms themselves are more commonly associated with the secular cursus for Sundays at Prime.[36] It is perhaps noteworthy that, some fifty or sixty years before Aelfwine compiled his devotions at Winchester, the authors of the "Monastic agreement of the monks and nuns of the English nation" or *Regularis concordia*, led by Aethelwold, had recommended the recitation of three additional antiphons at both Vespers and Lauds, to follow the psalms for the king, queen, and *familiares* of the monastic community. These antiphons, most likely suffrages or memorials including an antiphon, versicle, response, and collect, were to be sung in honor of the Holy Cross, Saint Mary, and the saint to whom the community's church was dedicated.[37] Significantly, Winchester, where Aethelwold was bishop and the *Regularis concordia* compiled, was refounded as a monastery in 964 and rededicated to the Trinity, the Virgin Mary, Saint Peter, and (possibly) All Saints.[38] While neither Aethelwold's *Horae regulares* nor Aelfwine's Offices seem to have been intended for corporate recitation, it would seem more than likely that both represent expansions on the somewhat shorter devotional suffrages appended as per the *Regularis concordia*'s recommendation to the morning and evening offices kept in choir. Neither was, however, properly speaking a canonical—that is, full daily—office.

Other than Peter the Deacon's rather fanciful backdating of the Office as performed at Monte Cassino, there would accordingly appear to be little evidence to suggest that anything like an "office of seven hours" was kept in honor of the Virgin prior to the first half of the eleventh century. As Hugh of Flavigny told the story, the provost Bernerius was disturbed by his bishop while chanting Matins of the blessed Virgin. Another somewhat older source says that Bernerius was celebrating her *memoria* or suffrage.[39] Saints Ulric and Aethelwold seem to have celebrated offices similar to those copied by Aelfwine into his prayer book. But, again, none of these offices can be said to have been properly speaking an "Office of the Virgin," nor were they, apparently, understood as specifically Marian devotions, in the sense that they might be somehow separable from the other devotions—to the Trinity, to the holy cross, to the saints—with which they were typically said. By the twelfth century, in contrast, Mary herself had taken to appearing in person in defense of those, like Bernerius, who kept her Office faithfully, "extending [themselves] in praise of the mother of the Lord," or so Hugh of Flavigny put it.[40] Clearly, something had changed.

I have shown elsewhere how changes in the image of Christ and the Virgin Mary coincided with—and, I would argue, seem to have been directly occasioned by—anxieties surrounding the coming of the year 1033 and its possible apocalyptic implications, particularly the expectation that Christ himself might return in the flesh.[41] Intriguingly, it is within a generation of this date that the Office of the Virgin seems to have been given its earliest form and, even more suggestively, to have been taken up in some of the very regions (southern England, northern Italy) and by some of the very people (Peter Damian) most closely associated with the development of the newly articulated devotion to Christ in his incarnate humanity and to the Virgin in her compassion for her Son's suffering. Miracle stories like Hugh's circulating in the early twelfth century would attribute the liturgical innovation to the Virgin herself, whether by direct instruction of her devotees or in response to her intercession on their behalf. Nor are we, at this point, in a position to gainsay such accounts. Contemporaries in the mid-eleventh century seem to have recognized the Marian Office as a novelty, but neither could (or would) they say whose idea it had originally been. The best we can say is that it seems to have come into existence in multiple forms at about the same time within a decade or so of the millennium of Christ's Passion and to have spread quickly over the course of the next fifty or so years such that by the early decades of the twelfth century, for all anyone knew, it really had been instituted, or so Prior Dominic of Evesham told it, by the pope in gratitude to the Virgin for intervening with Saint Peter when the pope put the saint's lamp out. That is, as other stories would have it, if it had not been instituted by Mary herself.[42]

As already noted, arguably the two earliest extant manuscript witnesses to the full devotional Office of the Virgin come from mid–eleventh century England.[43] The one (London, British Library, Cotton Tiberius A.iii) is a miscellany containing one of the two extant copies of the *Regularis concordia*, alongside some for-ty-odd additional texts ranging from prognostics on dreams and the phases of the moon to homilies on the Passion, lists of the precious stones mentioned in the book of Revelation, a dialogue between boys wanting to speak Latin, and the rule of Benedict. Many of the texts are in Old English or Latin with an Anglo-Saxon gloss.[44] The Marian Office or *Votiva laus in veneratione sancte marie virginis* appears on folios 107v–115v, immediately following (on the same folio) an Anglo-Saxon treatise on the ceremonies of Holy Week and preceding (not on the same folio) the Benedictine rule, but as the manuscript was dam-aged by fire in 1731 and all of the folios trimmed and inlayed into separate pieces of paper, it is impossible to determine whether this ordering represents the orig-inal arrangement of items. The *Votiva laus* itself concludes with a litany of saints that points with a fair degree of certainty to a community at Canterbury, more particularly the Benedictine community at Christ Church.[45] As Archbishop Lanfranc's *Consuetudines* compiled for Christ Church around 1080 make no mention of such a devotional office, it would seem to be clear that this obser-vance predated his reform and was not in fact introduced into England by the Norman monks who accompanied him.[46]

The other manuscript (London, British Library, Royal 2 B. V) has proven somewhat more controversial to locate definitively. Although the manuscript— a Latin psalter with canticles and interlinear Anglo-Saxon gloss copied in a tenth-century hand—was rebound in 1757, it would appear to have survived in more or less its original form, with the notable exception of the first seven folios con-taining the Marian Office.[47] A prayer appended to the head of the Office makes special appeal to Saints Mary, Machutus (Malo), and Eadberga on behalf of a community that had been robbed by an enemy of a certain possession, suggesting that perhaps the Office was initially adopted as an emergency measure after the community had suffered this loss.[48] Paleographically, it would seem to be fairly clear that the psalter itself was copied at Winchester, most likely for the Nun-naminster, but opinions diverge on whether the Office was appended there or at Canterbury.[49] The prefatory prayer, however, would seem to point most clearly to Saint Mary's at Winchester, where Edberga (d. 960), daughter of Edward the Elder, had been a nun and possibly abbess.[50] At the Conquest, the convent had been deprived of the manor of Icene (Itchen Abbas), which King William granted to Hugh Fitz Baldric. The abbess contested this alienation in 1086, and the manor was restored to the nuns.[51] Did the nuns maintain the recitation of the Marian Office following the successful conclusion of their suit? It is impossible to be sure.[52] The idiosyncrasy of its choice of lessons and hymns—unique, so far as I have been able to determine—would tend to suggest at the very least that the nuns did not share their devotion with others, and yet the manuscript containing their extraordinary Office has survived.[53]

Other communities found that it was rather more perilous to abandon their newly adopted devotions to the Virgin Mother of God. At least, this is what Mary's great champion, the monk, cardinal, and ardent reformer Peter Damian contended in relating the calamities that befell the monks of the Benedictine community of Saint Vincent's on Mount Petra Pertusa (at the Furlo Pass). As Peter told it in a letter written to a community of hermits in May 1066, the monks at Saint Vincent's had already had the custom for some three years of saying the Office of the Blessed Virgin along with the canonical hours each day, when one of their number, a certain Gozo, "an unworthy character, but a man of keen and brilliant talent," began to argue that such an observance was not only unprofitable (*supervacua*), but indeed superstitious (*superstitiosa*). The regular observance commanded by Benedict was, he insisted, "more than enough, nor should the burden of a new invention (*novae adinventionis pondus*) be imposed upon the brethren." Gozo prevailed. "Immediately," Peter observed,

> such a hail of adversity, such a storm of wars and afflictions struck their monastery that menacing swords daily threatened the monks with death and destruction. On all sides there were raids and devastation; rural holdings with buildings and cottages went up in flames; dependents and serfs of that holy place were brutally killed. Not only the phantom of death, but death itself stalked its prey, so that the monks were overcome by the nausea of living, since in the crash of war they found it impossible to maintain the monastic office, so profitable to their peace.

The monks appealed to the emperor in Germany (at this time, most likely, Henry III) who issued pragmatic sanctions bearing the imperial seal against their enemy (most likely, Duke Godfrey of Lorraine), but to no avail. Enjoined as a mediator, Peter rebuked his fellow Benedictines. Because the monks had "cast from their monastery the Mother of Peace itself, they deserved to be engulfed by the winds and the waves of tribulation and disaster." And, indeed, only when they received a penance and "promised henceforth never to neglect the customary praises of the Mother of God" did their tribulations cease. "Therefore," Peter admonished his readers, "they who lightly tear up the statutes of their elders should bear these events in mind, and should fear with good reason lest the sword of God's anger come upon them."[54]

Monks and hermits were not the only ones whom Peter Damian encouraged in the recitation of Mary's Office. According to his biographer John of Lodi,

Peter preached tirelessly to the secular clergy throughout the Roman province in support of the "office of all the hours" (*omnium horarum officia*) in honor of the Mother of God that he and the members of his community were accustomed to recite.[55] Peter likewise recommended the Office to laypeople. Writing to a certain nobleman of Ravenna around the year 1045/1046, Peter recalled a conversation they had had the previous year at the episcopal residence in Ravenna, during the course of which Peter had argued that "the canonical office, consisting of seven hours, should be performed by all Christian faithful as a daily task of service to God." Everyone sins, Peter asserted; therefore, everyone has need of the remedy for sin. Accordingly, just as the principal vices to which humanity is prone number seven, so also the hours from Lauds to Compline. Nor should the laity excuse themselves from this service, as if it were something prescribed only for monks or only for those at leisure to attend the Office when chanted by a priest in church. Whether riding on horseback or working in the fields, Peter insisted, "if there are psalms to say, say them." For those without skill in letters, there was always the Lord's Prayer. For those whose spirit burned "a little more fervently with the love of God," however, there were the Hours of the Virgin Mother of God.[56]

Just as the monks of Saint Vincent's found that—novelty though her Office might be—it was imprudent to neglect the Virgin's due, so Peter averred, "of this I am certain, that whoever strives to recite these hours daily in her honor will have the mother of the Judge as his helper and advocate in his day of need." This, at least, is what one cleric found when, near death and reflecting on the sins with which he had defiled his flesh, he called on the Virgin, saying, "O gate of heaven, window of paradise, and true Mother of God and man, you are my witness that 'seven times a day I praised you' [Psalm 118:164], and although I am a sinner, although I am unworthy, I did not cheat you of any of the canonical hours in your honor." Upon which—or so Peter had heard the story told, although, he cautioned, he could not be certain from his source that it had really happened—the Mother of God appeared to the dying man, "and gently comforting him, declared that through the generosity of God's mercy his sins had been forgiven."[57] A cleric of the church of Nevers, likewise accustomed to pay the Virgin's debt of praise daily *per singulas horas*, was even more highly favored. As the cleric lay dying—or so Peter had heard from his nephew who was studying in Gaul where the rumor was current—the Mother of God appeared to him visibly (*visibiliter*) and, pressing her breast, caused several drops of her milk to fall onto his lips. Soon the cleric had recovered his strength and was back singing psalms in choir with his brothers; it was even said that a few drops of milk could still be seen on his lips. Again, Peter was cautious about how much could be known for certain from this story, but hopeful of its implications:

But what words the Blessed Virgin spoke to him, even though in passing they were told to me, because I am not certain, I will not report them, since I am afraid to deviate, even slightly, from the truth. Nevertheless, one can conjecture from this that the glorious Virgin instilled the healing milk onto the very lips with which he had praised and honored her, so that by this member of the body by which the venerable cleric had exalted and glorified her, in a fitting exchange he should receive the medicine that restored his health.[58]

Whether thanks directly to Peter Damian or, as Peter might insist, Mary, every devout Christian who was anyone—especially, but not exclusively among those of a monastic bent—was saying the Hours of the Virgin by the turn of the century.[59] The saintly queen Margaret of Scotland (d. 1093) went to church every morning to say Matins (*Matutinas*) of the Holy Trinity, the Holy Cross, and Saint Mary, while Countess Matilda of Tuscany (d. 1115) "never stopped listening to [Mary's] office day or night."[60] Queen Margaret's daughter, Queen Matilda of England (d. 1118), was close friends with Archbishop Anselm of Canterbury (d. 1109) and through him, or so I have argued elsewhere, with the well-traveled *presbyter et scholasticus* Honorius Augustodunensis.[61] In his *Gemma animae*, Honorius was careful to note that "we sing the Office of Saint Mary (*cursum de sancta Maria*) not because we are bound by any law, but for the sake of devotion."[62] Yet another friend of Anselm's, Gundulf (d. 1108), fellow monk at Bec and latterly bishop of Rochester, heard all the Hours of the Virgin (*omnibus Horis de S. Maria*) on his deathbed, just as his spirit was about to leave his body.[63] And Anselm's nephew and namesake, the abbot of Bury St. Edmund's, was accustomed to say every day both a Mass and, following the canonical hours, additional hours in honor of Mary.[64] This younger Anselm (d. 1148) is perhaps best known for his promotion of the controversial feast of Mary's Conception. As R. W. Southern has shown, Abbot Anselm was also responsible for some of the earliest collections of miracle stories celebrating the Virgin, a number of which he seems to have heard during his youth in Rome, including quite possibly Peter Damian's account of the Virgin's healing milk [65]

For her part, Countess Matilda, likewise a friend of the elder Anselm, may have acquired the custom of saying the Marian Office from her spiritual father and Peter Damian's friend, Pope Gregory VII (d. 1085), who encouraged the countess to throw herself at the feet of the Mother of the Lord and pour out her tears "from an humble and contrite heart."[66] A generation or so later, Gregory himself was remembered as having been pope at the time when monasteries throughout Christendom began "to sing a new song, celebrating in great numbers the *cursus beatae Mariae*."[67] Gregory's great supporter, William of Hirsau (d. 1091), noted in the customary for the reform of his community that "the daily office in honor of St. Mary" (*cursus quotidianus de S. Maria*) should be recited by the *capellanus S. Mariae* at Christmas, its octave, and All Saints, presumably in addition to the festal offices for those days.[68] Here William may have been influenced by the account Ulrich of Zell (d. 1093) compiled for him of the observances kept at Ulrich's monastery of Cluny under his abbot Hugh (d. 1109). According to Ulrich, the monks at Cluny were accustomed to sing the Hours of the Virgin (*horas de S. Maria*) while baking the hosts for the Eucharist, all the while taking care not to let their spit fall on the breads.[69] Ulrich's contemporary, Bernard of Cluny, noted somewhat less colorfully that the abbot had ordered the sick monks in the infirmary to observe "all the hours of St. Mary" (*omnes horas de sancta Maria*), albeit "all" at this time does not seem to have included Compline.[70] Somewhat more impressively, if, that is, later reports are to be trusted, yet another monk of Cluny, Odo, alias Pope Urban II (d. 1099), ordered all of the clergy and laity to recite the Hours of the Blessed Virgin daily in order to obtain Mary's support for the great expedition he preached in November 1095 at Clermont.[71]

The Virgin, aided by Peter the Venerable of Cluny (d. 1156), soon remedied the absence of Compline from her Hours, as over the course of the twelfth century, more and more communities adopted her Office.[72] The Grandmontines remembered their founder Stephen of Muret (d. 1124) as having been especially vigilant in saying the divine offices, including those of the blessed Virgin.[73] In the constitutions that he drew up for the canons regular of Saint Mary in Porte near Ravenna, Peter de Honestis (d. 1119), himself a relation of Peter Damian's exemplar Romuald, included the Hours of the Virgin among the various devotions that the brothers might choose to observe.[74] Likewise, Manegold of Lautenbach (d. after 1103) specified in the rule that he composed for the community of Marbach in Upper Alsace that while the fifteen Gradual Psalms were to be said before Matins and the seven Penitential Psalms and the litany after Prime, the Hours of the Virgin were to be said after each of the hours of the ordinary Office.[75] Both Peter's and Manegold's compilations were widely adopted by communities of Augustinian canons, Peter's throughout Italy and Germany, Manegold's in the south of Germany and in Switzerland.[76]

Meanwhile, the White (as opposed to the Augustinian Black) Canons of the reforming Premonstratensian order were busy sweeping away all such accretions to the traditional Divine Office. Unlike the White Monks of the order of Cîteaux upon whose reforms Norbert of Xanten (d. 1134) modeled his own, however, the White Canons of Prémontré maintained the recitation of the Marian Office.[77] Somewhat ironically, given their later fame as Mary's promoters, the Cistercians initially eschewed the Hours of the Virgin as superfluous to their corporate observance. It would, in fact, be more than a century after the founding of their motherhouse before they would officially adopt this form of service to their patronal Lady.[78] Individual monks might, however, say the Hours of Saint Mary and the Office of the Dead while traveling.[79]

Cathedrals dedicated to the Virgin were rather more open than the early generations of Cistercians to the choral adoption of Mary's Hours. The ordinal for the cathedral of Laon, composed by its deacon Lisiard between 1155 and 1168, includes detailed rubrics for the celebration of the Marian Office, incidentally providing one of our earliest glimpses into how the Office was performed. The rubrics make clear that the Marian Office, like the Divine Office, was sung in choir every day throughout the year, including Sundays, the only exceptions being the days from Christmas through the octave of Saint Stephen, Epiphany, Maundy Thursday through the Saturday after the octave of Easter, Ascension, and Pentecost and its octave. The various solo parts would be taken by a priest (opening versicles, benedictions), a *clericulus* (invitatory antiphon and psalm, antiphons, lessons), and subdeacon (responsories). Less clear, however, is whether the service required the participation of other members of the community or just these three.[80] Detailed evidence from other cathedral communities is typically available only from the thirteenth century; however, as at Laon, so also at Cambrai, Chartres, Paris, and Reims the Marian Office would seem to have become a central feature of the daily liturgy by the second half of the twelfth century.[81] At Paris, as elsewhere, where the main altar was dedicated to the Virgin, "there was [in Rebecca Baltzer's words] nowhere else in the cathedral more appropriate for her daily Office than in the choir, with the altar of the Virgin ever before the performers."[82] Every church dedicated to Notre Dame was, in a very real sense, Mary's, as were the clergy who served her by singing her praises at its very heart.

Newly rebuilt and rededicated in 1218 to Saints Mary, Peter, Oswald, and Wulfstan, the cathedral church of Worcester adopted an unusually elaborate sequence of Marian Offices, adapting the observance season by season with alternative antiphons, responsories, and hymns.[83] It was the Office as celebrated at the new cathedral at Salisbury (New Sarum) that was, however, to become standard in Books of Hours circulating in England, the earliest known extant of which (the De Brailes Hours) postdates the earliest evidence for the observance at Salisbury (1230s) by only some ten or so years.[84] At about the same time, the Franciscans were busy popularizing what was in later centuries to become the official Use of the post-Tridentine Catholic Church. True to the mandate of their founder to be obedient to the pope, the Franciscans did not compose their own Office of the Virgin but rather adopted that used by Innocent III (d. 1216) in his chapel at the Lateran Palace. What relationship this curial Office of the Virgin bore to the Marian Office originally celebrated in the days of Gregory VII is unclear.[85] For their part, the Dominicans, insistent that their order was under the special protection of the Mother of Truth, developed their own version of the Marian Hours.[86] As the fifth master general of the order Humbert of Romans (d. 1277) observed in his model sermon for the Marian feasts,

> among all the men and women saints, there is none who is remembered as much as the blessed Virgin. She has the most images in our churches, she has her own day in every week, she has a special Office which is said every day, and many churches hold a procession in her honour every day and make a remembrance of her; and throughout the world she has more feast days than any other saint.[87]

According to the Dominican constitutions of 1228, the brethren were to say the Matins of the blessed Virgin "according to the time of the year" as soon as they heard the first signal to get up. They would then make their way to the choir only after they had finished this initial devotion.[88]

As with their devotion to Christ and his Mother more generally, so with the Office of the Virgin, the friars were eager to communicate this observance to those not already bound by the customs of a religious order, that is, the laity. In his model sermon for "girls living in the world," Humbert explicitly recommended that "they know how to recite at the appropriate time the Psalter, or the Hours of the Blessed Virgin, or the Office for the Dead, or other prayers to be recited to God." Thus educated, such girls would be ready, if they so chose, to enter the religious life, but even if they chose rather to live a virgin life at home, or so Humbert contended, their exercises might still lead them, like Paula and Eustochium, "to a deep understanding of holy Scripture."[89] How these "girls" were to learn their Psalter and Hours was another question altogether. Prior to the early thirteenth century, as we have already noted, the Hours of the Virgin, although widespread in monastic and cathedral practice, rarely took written form, at least insofar as we can tell from the manuscript record. Of the fifteen or so examples that survive from before the year 1200 (this is only a ballpark figure), about half are appended to psalters or breviaries, but the others appear in a wide variety of contexts (homiliaries, collectars, devotional and liturgical miscellanies), almost as if it was unclear where best to record this new devotional ordo despite its dependence on the canonical Office.[90] With the coming of the friars, particularly the Dominicans, the status of the Marian Office seems to have changed, such that where previously it had existed, in textual form at least, as at best a kind of appendix to the Psalter, from the second quarter of the thirteenth century it was to become the centerpiece of a new codicological format, the Book of Hours.

As with the Marian Office, so with the Book of Hours, we do not know who was the first to suggest the idea of a book specially dedicated to just those observances (the Hours of the Virgin, the Penitential and Gradual Psalms, the Litany and Collects, as well as, latterly, the Office of the Dead) kept by those who were not necessarily members of a religious order or of the clergy.[91] It is perhaps significant that one early exemplar, that made by William de Brailes in Oxford, includes on its closing folios (102v–105v) a number of prayers copied in French, apparently as part of the original commission, indicating three local Dominicans by name (Richard of Newark, Richard of Westey, and Bartholomew of Grimston) for whom the book's user was to pray a Pater Noster and an Ave Maria "out of love" (*par charite*).[92] There is also evidence that the book was altered—somewhat clumsily and in a different, Italianate hand, but before it was bound—so that its original owner could say Vespers according to the Dominican Use, presumably along with those same friars for whom she (or he) was accustomed to pray.[93]

Even more suggestive, or so Bella Millett has argued, are the instructions given in the Middle English *Ancrene Wisse* composed a decade or two earlier on how the anchoresses (*ancresses*) for whom it was written were to spend their day. Unlike the recluse whom Aelred of Rievaulx (d. 1166) advised in his *De institutione inclusarum*, the anchoresses being laywomen were not expected to say the whole of the Divine Office as prescribed by Benedict, but rather only the Hours of the Virgin "as [they themselves had] written them out."[94] Millett does not go so far as to insist that it was, in fact, the anchoresses who invented the Book of Hours, but, she contends, it is intriguing that the devotions prescribed for the women by their (most likely) Dominican adviser conform so closely to the devotions typically included in such books: the Hours of the Virgin, said separately, each "at its own time"; the Hours of the Holy Spirit, optionally, before the Hours of the Virgin; the *Pretiosa* or monastic "Capitular Office" recited after Prime; the *Placebo* (Vespers) and the *Dirige* (Matins and Lauds) from the Office of the Dead; the Commendation of the Dead; the Litany; the Seven Penitential Psalms (6, 31, 37, 50, 101, 129, and 142); and the Fifteen Gradual Psalms (119 through 133, corresponding to the fifteen steps of the temple that Mary was believed to have ascended when only three years old); along with prayers and meditations on the Five Wounds of Christ, the Five Joys of the Virgin in English, and multiple Aves and Paters, all carefully calculated to recall the Six Works of Mercy, the Seven Gifts of the Spirit, the Nine Orders of Angels, the Ten Commandments, and the Twelve Apostles.[95]

All of the above, with the exception of the Joys, was to be said in Latin, in all a schedule that would most likely fill some four hours of every day.[96] Millett has shown how the instructions accompanying this schedule, particularly for saying Matins, have close parallels with those that appear in the earliest Dominican Constitutions, down to the details of when to make the sign of the cross, when to bow, and when to kneel. For example, on kneeling or bowing "according to the time": "in Chapter at the prayer *Sancta Maria*, and in every prayer, when the name of the Blessed Virgin is mentioned" (Dominican Constitutions); "at the *Ave Maria* and wherever you hear Mary's name uttered" (*Ancrene Wisse*).[97] That the anchoresses' schedule was modeled on that of the Dominican brethren is likewise clear from references to the time at which "we say the *Placebo* and *Dirige*" (that is, "after the food graces"), as well as, in at least one early manuscript (London, British Library, Cotton Nero A.xiv), the modifications that those anchoresses who did not know or could not say Matins might make to their observances as compared with "how our lay-brothers say their Hours."[98]

But the Office of the Virgin was hardly a service just for anchoresses, any more than the Book of Hours or something like it was exclusively their book. At about the same time as the Dominicans in England were advising pious recluses on how to say the Hours of the Virgin, their brethren across the Channel were actively organizing the beguines of the southern Low Countries into enclosed communities or courts.[99] Prior to this intervention, devout virgins like Marie d'Oignies (d. 1213), Margaret of Ypres (d. 1234), and Beatrice of Nazareth (d. 1268) had already been accustomed to honor the Virgin with genuflections and multiple repetitions of the angelic salutation, whether in place of (as with Beatrice) or prefacing (as with Marie) the 150 Psalms.[100] As Judith Oliver has shown, the mid–thirteenth century coming of the friars brought with it not only a dramatic increase in the production of Psalters and Psalter-Hours, but also the expectation that beguines would say the Office of the Virgin every day.[101] Whether this observance was intended as a mitigation of the intense use such celebrated beguines as Marie and her contemporary Odilia of Liège (d. 1220) made of their psalters is unclear. What is certain is that these were women for whom such books were not simply fashionable props but essential equipment for their lives of service and prayer.[102]

Two hundred years earlier, Peter Damian had insisted that every Christian, cleric, monastic, or layperson, skilled or unskilled in letters, should consider the canonical Office of seven hours "a daily task of service to God," because, as Peter put it, all have sinned and all therefore have need of the remedy for sin. In the first half of the thirteenth century, many—particularly in the south of Europe—began to take Peter's advice to heart, establishing confraternities of penitents for the purpose of living ascetically while still in the world. Typically, the *clerici*[103] who enrolled in these confraternities were expected to say the full Divine Office, while those who did not know the Office would say multiple Paters and Aves.[104] For those like the anchoresses and beguines, who knew their Psalter but were not trained in the monastic Hours, some thirteenth-century statutes, as, for example, those of the new *Militia Beatae Virginis* drawn up by the Franciscan Rufo de Gurgone in 1261, would seem to suggest that it was permissible to substitute the Hours of the Virgin specifically in place of the Divine Office.[105]

Even more pointedly, according to the statutes for many hospitals and leprosaria, as with the clergy who were required to recite the canonical Divine Office, so those hospital workers—some semireligious under vows, others still lay, including husbands and wives who served together—who knew the Hours of the Virgin were expected to say them every day.[106] The gradations specified in the widely adopted statutes for the hospital of Montdidier as copied for use at Amiens in 1233 are particularly instructive in this respect. Everyone who knew the canonical hours (*horas canonicas noverit*), whether *clericus* or *laicus*, but especially priests (*sacerdotes*), was to observe them at the appropriate times (*eas horis statutis persolvat*), while those who knew the Hours of the Blessed Virgin Mary (*horas Beate Virginis Marie*) were to sing them (*eas decantet*). Those who knew the seven Penitential Psalms but neither the canonical nor the Marian Hours were to sing the psalms *pro matutinis*, prefaced by a Pater Noster, *Deus in adiutorium meum intende*, and Gloria Patri, and followed by a Kyrie Eleison, another Pater Noster and a prayer. Those who did not know even the Penitential Psalms were to sing *Miserere mei Deus* (Psalm 50) seven times at Matins and once at each of the following six hours, according to the same ordo. Nor were those exempt who knew only the three basic texts that all Christians should know (Pater Noster, Ave Maria, Credo in Deum). If they did not know them on entry into the community, they were to be so instructed while probationers. Their Matins were to consist of twenty-five Pater Nosters and the same number of Aves, with a Credo in Deum at Matins, Prime, and Compline, recited, again, according to the ordo for the Penitential Psalms.[107]

Recent scholarship has tended to concentrate on the lower end of these requirements, noting that for the majority of late medieval Christians, it would have been unusual to know anything more than those texts that the probationers at Montdidier would have learned.[108] And yet, surely the most intriguing aspect of these statutory provisions is how it is assumed that there will be lay brothers and sisters who already know the Hours of the Virgin and who, as the statutes for the leprosarium at Lille (1239) put it, might prefer to say them in lieu of the recitations of Paters and Aves.[109] How had these lay brothers and sisters learned the Marian Hours? Paradoxically, given what was said earlier about the importance of the development of this new codicological form, the answer cannot be "from their Books of Hours" or even "from their Psalter-Hours," at least, that is, if the numbers of extant manuscript copies are anything to go by. Books of Hours may have been the best sellers of the fifteenth century (as already noted, they survive in the thousands), but they are, in fact, relatively rare for the some one hundred fifty years prior to that. Exact numbers are curiously difficult to come by, but of the nearly eight hundred surviving manuscript Books of Hours or Psalter-Hours known to have been used in England, fewer than three dozen can be dated before the end of the thirteenth century, while only some hundred or so are extant from the following century.[110] Similarly, of the 337 Hours and Psalter-Hours noted by Victor Leroquais in his survey of the holdings in the Bibliothèque nationale in Paris, only eighteen date to before 1400 and only nine of these to before 1300.[111] Such books as the De Brailes Hours were luxuries that not everybody could afford. Nevertheless, somehow laypeople were learning their Hours of the Virgin. The question is whether it was necessarily *from books*, that is, from books in the way that early extant manuscripts—for the most part, exceptional even in their own day—have led us to expect.

The German Empire offers an interesting counterexample to the regions where the illuminated Books of Hours would eventually become most popular. Of the Books of Hours known to have been produced in German-speaking regions prior to 1400, only one ('s-Heerenberg, Huis Bergh, 52, inv.-no. 239) has anything like the number of illustrations typical of the more famous English, French, Flemish, and Italian exemplars of the same period.[112] Unillustrated prayer books are rather more numerous, but these do not always contain the elements that readers elsewhere would have associated with Books of Hours. Moreover, as much as prior to printing no two Books of Hours were ever identical, whether in decoration or in selection and arrangement of pieces, extant books of prayer made in Germany are even more idiosyncratic. One such prayer book, now in the collection at the Pierpont Morgan Library (M. 739), was copied in the early decades of the thirteenth century, most likely for Hedwig of Silesia (d. 1243), although somewhat confusingly the calendar follows the Premonstratensian Use, while Hedwig was more closely associated with the Cistercian convent of Trebnitz (Trzebnica), cofounded with her husband Duke Henry I the Bearded in 1202/1203.[113] The manuscript is particularly remarkable for an extensive picture cycle with vernacular inscriptions (fols. 9–24v) telling the whole of salvation history from the fall of the angels to the Last Judgment. The *cursus sancte marie* follows in Latin on folios 25-[101v], the Hours of the Virgin being interspersed with the Hours of the Trinity, the Holy Spirit, the Holy Cross, and All Saints, but with only occasional decorations. The manuscript concludes with Vespers for the Dead and the Litany, followed by prayers to God, the Virgin, and the saints, Vespers for the Burial of the Virgin, prayers against evildoers and for rain, a short Psalter, and yet more prayers for self and friends, again with minimal illustration. Whatever the function of the pictures in the first part of the book, it cannot have been as a support for learning the Office and other prayers, except as a relatively sophisticated reminder of the historical and typological context in which they were to be said.

Like the Hours and Psalter-Hours of the Low Countries, England, and France, many of these German prayer books were closely associated with women, whether as donors or readers. Even more frequently, however, like Hedwig's book, German Books of Hours include not only rubrics but also whole texts in the vernacular.[114] The majority of these early vernacular Books of Hours come from the same general region as Hedwig's family (Bavaria, Bohemia, Austria), although at least one mid–fourteenth century exemplar is known to have belonged to a house of Dominican nuns in the diocese of Constance.[115] Again, far from being simply a beautiful prop for devotions said indifferently or with lit-tle attention to their textual meaning, such Books of Hours strongly suggest that the particulars of the Office mattered even to those who could not follow them in the original Latin. While some might lament the apparent decline in stan-dards of Latin education the existence of such books implies (many of them were made for nuns), the fact that most of these books were not illustrated should give us pause. The use of images may have been closely associated with the pasto-ral care of nuns, but—it would seem—knowing the Hours of the Virgin meant knowing the words.

This liturgical hunger is nowhere more vividly instanced than in the some two thousand extant manuscript copies of the Hours of the Virgin as rendered into Dutch by educational critic and reformer Geert Grote (d. 1384).[116] With the exception of Grote's translation of the Dominican Henry Suso's (d. 1366) *Cursus de Aeterna Sapientia* or *Hours of Eternal Wisdom*, the contents of Grote's vernacular compilation were somewhat more typical of Latin Books of Hours than those in the German vernacular tradition: the calendar, the Hours of the Virgin, the Holy Spirit, and the Holy Cross, a second longer Hours of the Holy Cross, the Seven Penitential Psalms, the Litany, and the Vigils or Office of the Dead.[117] Nevertheless, the spirit of Grote's *Getijdenboek* is far from that too often indiscriminately attributed to ecclesiastics in the later Middle Ages, of fear that the laity might somehow gain access to the texts of scripture, ironically, given that it was, after all, the Psalms above all on which the Hours of the Virgin depended.[118] Grote's Hours were popular particularly among those women and men known as the "Modern Devout" or "sisters and brothers of the Common Life," who gathered in houses throughout the Oversticht, Guelders, Utrecht, Holland, Flanders, and Brabant, and in cities as far-flung as Cambrai, Liège, Cologne, Wesel, and Münster, to live a life of work and prayer.[119] Like the beguines before them, the Devout supported themselves through their own labor, copying books—especially Books of Hours—and setting up schools.[120] For Gerhart Zerbolt of Zutphen (d. 1398), librarian of Master Geert's house at Deventer and one of the Devout's great apologists, it went without saying that the laity, like the clergy, should pray with understanding and, if necessary, in their own language if they did not understand the words in Latin.[121] Nor were laypeople always satisfied with "simple prayers written in ordinary words." Rather, Zerbolt contended, the "more devout" explicitly preferred the psalms as they encountered them in their little prayer books (*libellos oracionum*) finding them "more enkindling" and "more affective" than other prayers.[122]

By the turn of the fifteenth century, saying the Hours of the Virgin had been an established practice in monasteries and cathedrals throughout Christian Europe for some three hundred years and among educated laypeople in their own devotions for at least two hundred, even longer for those of the nobility with close ties to the monks and nuns of their day. Simply to list those known to have kept this observance would involve compiling a who's who of late medieval society, necessarily suggesting that even those for whom we have no definite evidence that they knew the Office must—in fact—have.[123] Even extant Books of Hours can give us only a partial appreciation of the degree to which the Hours of the Virgin had become a feature of daily life. Louis IX (d. 1270) may have learned his psalms from the beautifully illuminated Psalter that his mother owned (Leiden, Universiteitsbibliotheek, BPL 76 A).[124] Likewise, he may have ensured that his own children learned their Hours of the Virgin from equally beautiful tomes, but as we have already noted, pictures were not essential for learning one's *Horae* nor, arguably, were one's ABC's.[125] Beatrice of Nazareth had learned to recite the entire Psalter by the age of five "without flaw and in the right order" (*absque quolibet offendiculo ex ordine*), before being sent to study with the beguines at Zoutleeuw after her mother's death. Her father was described by her biographer as being of only middling class and was himself to become a lay brother of the Cistercian convent of Florival or Bloemendaal where he had previously served as general manager (*generalis dispensator*) of the community's temporal goods. As a sister at Bloemendaal, Beatrice was to become a skilled copyist herself, but her biographer gives no indication of what books her parents owned or how, exactly, she was able to memorize the psalms.[126] Perhaps, after all, some laypeople learned their Hours by heart such that Eustache Deschamps (d. ca. 1406) was correct to ridicule the ladies of the bourgeoisie for their penchant for luxurious Books of Hours "of gold and azure, rich and smart / Arranged and painted with great art / Covered with fine brocade of gold."[127] Certainly, it was possible to say one's Hours without so much visual and tactile finery.

Nevertheless, laypeople were eager for books and by the early decades of the fifteenth century, the booksellers of Paris and—especially following the Treaty of Arras in 1435—Flanders were willing and able to supply them.[128] The workshops of Ghent and Bruges in particular specialized in crafting Books of Hours for export in addition to the thousands of books that they must have made for use at home. To date, some two hundred fifty Books of Hours produced in the Low Countries between the 1390s and 1520s for use in England have been identified (typically, Use of Sarum); one can only speculate on how many were lost during the Reformation.[129] As Nicholas Rogers has put it, such books "looked more expensive than [they] really [were]," while still being well within the purchasing power of "middling merchants and local gentry."[130] In the 1460s, the merchant John Browne of Stamford ordered his Book of Hours from Bruges and had it customized with silver-gilt clasps ornamented with miniatures of the Virgin and Child and Saint Veronica set in crystal.[131] It may well have been one such book (*boke*) that Margery Kempe (d. after 1438), wife, mother of fourteen, and inveterate weeper, was praying from (*hir boke in hir hand*) when a stone fell from the roof of her parish church, striking her on her head and her back and, we may presume, knocking her book from her hands.[132] As the daughter of the town's mayor and herself a brewer (albeit not a very successful one), Margery was moderately well-to-do, but it is unclear whether she herself could read (most scholars assume she could not). She had the book of her own experiences copied out for her by two different scribes, while her own "reading" consisted of listening to books read to her by a sympathetic priest.[133] And yet, she still considered it necessary to own a book from which to pray.

By the end of the century, movable type printing had made book ownership possible for those even further down the social scale than a merchant of Stamford or the mayor's daughter of King's Lynn. Whereas in the early fourteenth century, a Book of Hours might cost anywhere between eight *livres* and six *sous*—at its most expensive, more than a years' worth of daily labor for a female agricultural worker in southern France; at its cheapest, as much as fourteen days' labor for a woman, if only half that for a man—by the later fifteenth century, even shopkeepers and artisans could afford to own books.[134] But printing did more than bring books down in price. It also made it possible for readers to do something that anyone reading a modern printed book will more or less take for granted but that had been quite literally impossible hitherto: it allowed two or more people to read exactly the same text in the same layout at exactly the same time without having to look at the same physical book.[135] Whereas, as we have noted, no two manuscript Books of Hours were ever exactly alike, printed editions might run to more than a thousand copies apiece, all with identical pages, tables of contents, indices, images, and texts.[136] To be sure, there were still often significant differences from edition to edition, never mind from Use to Use, but if, for example, a family wanted to pray its Hours of the Virgin together, every family member could now potentially read from his or her own personal copy of a book, all the while—as we now say—staying on the same page.

Around 1478, the English publisher William Caxton (d. ca. 1492) brought out in octavo format the earliest known edition for English (presumably Sarum) Use. A quarto edition of (again, presumably) the same Use came out almost the very next year (ca. 1480).[137] Other publishers soon followed suit, the French *libraire* Antoine Vérard (d. 1512) initiating in September 1485 a run of some eighty editions of *Horae* with a small Book of Hours for the Use of Rome, printed in Paris in both Latin and French.[138] By 1500, some twenty or more editions of the Sarum Use had been printed at Westminster, London, or Paris, along with one printed by Gerard Leeu at Antwerp.[139] In the first decade of the sixteenth century, Parisian printers and/or publishers, including Antoine Vérard, Gilles and Germain Hardouyn, Thielman Kerver, Philippe Pigouchet, and Simon Vostre, together issued on average some twenty-nine editions of Books of Hours per year, ranging from as few as nineteen to as many as fifty-two before 1510.[140] By 1530 there were possibly as many as 760 different editions of Books of Hours in print, some hundred or more produced for the English market alone.[141] It is in this context that we must imagine Hans Holbein (d. 1543) drafting his famous study of Thomas More and his family at prayer in the late 1520s. Not only is almost everyone holding a book, but—as Eamon Duffy has pointed out—"everyone is holding the *same* book. . . . Through Holbein's eyes, we are privileged flies on the wall at a London bourgeois household's family prayers, and the More family are about to start a *communal* recitation of Our Lady's Matins."[142]

At long last, it would seem, the laity had realized what had in fact been its desire all along: to share in the life of prayer enjoyed by the religious and clergy, reciting the Hours in common.[143] This is the report that one Italian traveler famously gave of the English in the reign of Henry VII (d. 1509): "The common people [that is, those involved in trade, fishing, or navigation] . . . all attend Mass every day, and say many Paternosters in public, the women carrying long rosaries in their hands, and any who can read taking the office of our Lady with them, and with some companion reciting it in the church verse by verse, in a low voice, after the manner of churchmen."[144] It is surely therefore all the more ironic, not to say poignant, that within a lifetime of this traveler's report, the clergy themselves would cease to observe the Marian Office as a communal obligation—an obligation that, as we have seen, had been voluntarily and, indeed, eagerly assumed over the previous six centuries by secular and religious alike. Even more ironic, given its history, were the reasons Pope Pius V (d. 1572) gave in his bull *Quod a nobis* (1568) for removing this prescription from the rubrics, namely, "on account of the many labors of this life," such that those who were occupied with much business might not risk further danger of sin. (Recall how Peter Damian championed the Hours as a defense against sin.) It was better, Pope Pius argued, for the Office of the Blessed Virgin, the Office of the Dead, the Seven Penitential Psalms, and the Gradual Psalms to be said or sung out of devotion than as a duty. "Therefore," the Pope declared, "so that the will and desire of the faithful might be all the more aroused to this salutary custom . . . we loosen the penance upon them enjoined in the prescribed rubrics."[145]

"SEVEN TIMES A DAY I HAVE PRAISED YOU" (PSALM 118:164)

There is yet a further irony in the pope's concern about whether Christians should feel obliged to say the Office of the Virgin. Even as it removed the obligation (if there ever really was one) to say the Marian Hours, Pius's bull touched upon a tension going back to the origins of Christianity itself and, arguably, still very much alive in contemporary discussions of Christian practice. How, exactly, should Christians pray? Voluntarily or prescriptively? Spontaneously, as the Holy Spirit moves them (Romans 8:26), or regularly, as a service to God (Psalm 118:62, 164)? Paul enjoined the Thessalonians to "pray without ceasing" (1 Thessalonians 5:17).[146] But Jesus himself had insisted that prayer should be brief (Matthew 6:7). Nor was it at all immediately clear even for the early Christians when and where Christians should pray, whether in secret, alone (Matthew 6:5–6), or in community, together (Acts 1:14). Early Christians seem to have recognized certain regular hours for prayer—Clement of Alexandria (d. ca. 215), Tertullian (d. ca. 225), Hippolytus (d. ca. 235), Origen of Alexandria (d. 254), and Cyprian of Carthage (d. 258) all refer to prayers said at the third, sixth, and ninth hours of the day (counting from dawn), as well as to those said at morning, evening, and night—but the day hours seem to have been kept only privately, as a personal rather than communal devotion.[147] By the fourth century, it was customary for the people to gather in the churches for prayer twice daily, in the morning and the evening. As Eusebius of Caesarea (d. ca. 340) exulted, commenting on Psalm 64:9 ("exitus matutini et vespere delectabis"): "For surely it is no small sign of God's power that throughout the whole world in the churches of God at the morning rising of the sun and at the evening hours, hymns, praises, and truly divine delights are offered to God."[148] Nevertheless, it was, in fact, only later in the fourth century with the spread of monasticism from the desert to the cities and the consequent merger of the morning and evening prayers with those said during the night and day that something like the full cycle of canonical hours subsequently popularized by Benedict of Nursia would come to be observed.[149]

Explanations for the schedule were nearly as old—and as varied—as the schedule itself. According to Tertullian, the day hours had been hallowed above all by the tradition of the Church. The apostles had first received the outpouring of the Holy Spirit at the third hour of the day (Acts 2:1–4, 14–15). Peter had gone up to the roof to pray at the sixth hour when he received his vision of the creatures in the sheet (Acts 10:9–16). Peter and John were going to the temple to pray at the ninth hour when John restored a paralytic to health (Acts 3:1–10).[150] For his part, Hippolytus (or, more precisely, the *Traditio apostolica* ascribed to him) related these customary hours for prayer to the remembrance of the events of Christ's Passion. At the third hour, Christ was nailed to the cross (Mark 15:25). At the sixth hour, darkness fell (Matthew 27:45; Mark 15:33; Luke 23:44). At the ninth hour, Christ cried out and breathed his last and his side, "pierced with the spear, poured forth water and blood, and lighted the rest of the day's span and brought it to evening" (Matthew 27:46–50; Mark 15:34–37; Luke 23:44–46; cf. John 19:34).[151] As for the prayers at midnight: "the elders who gave us the tradition taught us that at that hour all creation is still for a moment, to praise the Lord; stars, trees, waters stop for an instant, and all the host of angels (which) ministers to him praises God with the souls of the righteous at this hour. That is why believers should take good care to pray at this hour." And at cockcrow or dawn: "at that hour, as the cock crew, the children of Israel denied Christ, whom we know by faith, our eyes looking towards that day in the hope of eternal light at the resurrection of the dead."[152]

The monastic fathers Basil of Caesarea (d. 379) and John Cassian (d. 435) likewise invoked the coming of the Spirit at the third hour and Peter and John's going up to the temple at the ninth in justification for praying at these times, but whereas Cassian would argue that the sixth hour recalled both Christ's sacrifice and Peter's vision, Basil alluded rather to the hope expressed in Psalm 90:6, that those praying should elude "the arrow flying in the day" and "the attack of the noon-day demon."[153] According to Basil, Christians should pray in the morning so as to consecrate the first movements of the mind and the soul to God, and when the day is finished, to give thanks "for what has been given us during the day or for what we have done rightly," or else to confess "what we have failed to do." Prayer is also appropriate upon going to bed, to "ask that our rest may be without offence and free from phantasies," while Paul and Silas showed that it was necessary to rise again at midnight so as to praise God (Acts 16:25). Likewise, or so Basil explained, the psalmist says: "I rose at midnight to praise you for the judgments of your righteousness" (Psalm 118:62). "None of these times," Basil cautioned, "should be neglected by those who have chosen a life dedicated to the glory of God and his Christ."[154]

Attentive readers will note that here Basil discriminates seven occasions for prayer: at midnight, at dawn, at the third, sixth, and ninth hours of the day, at evening, and at bedtime. Missing only is the Office for the first hour of the day (Prime) so as to round out what would be become, thanks above all to the rule of Benedict, the standard cycle of Christian prayer for the better part of a thousand years. Given the significance that later authors, not to mention illuminators of Books of Hours, gave to the sequence of *Horae*, it is perhaps surprising that prior to Benedict we have no clear explanation for why, in fact, Christians should rise not only at midnight, but also "seven [rather than six or five or three] times a day" to pray. The closest scholars have been able to come is a reference that Cassian makes in his *De institutis coenobiorum* to a morning Office (*Matutina*) of three psalms and prayers said "according to the fashion fixed of old in the observance of terce and sext," which additional office, he says, had been instituted "in our own time" to prevent the monks from spending too much time in bed between the night Office, celebrated with the daily vigils, and the third hour or Terce.[155] Traditionally, it was contended that Cassian was here speaking of Prime, but more recently it has been argued that he was rather describing a sort of "second matins" or Lauds.[156] In either case, what is significant for our purposes is the justification that Cassian gives for the innovation: "Although this scheme seems to have been devised in response to a particular circumstance and appears to be quite recent . . . nonetheless it corresponds very clearly in a literal way to that number of which blessed David speaks (although it also has a spiritual meaning): 'Seven times a day I have praised you for the judgments of your righteousness' " [Psalm 118:164].[157] Accident of the monks' sluggishness though it may have been, it was a scheme that was to have a profound effect on the conceptualization of and significance attributed to the medieval observance of a regular cycle of prayer, including, above all, the Hours of the Virgin.

Why, indeed, pray "seven times a day"? For Benedict, the number itself would seem to have been of spiritual significance (*septenarius sacratus numerus*), although in his *Rule* he gives no explanation other than its grounding in the text of the psalm as to why, noting simply: "We will fulfill this sacred number of seven if we satisfy our obligations of service at Lauds (*matutinum*), Prime, Terce, Sext, None, Vespers and Compline, for it was of these hours during the day that he said: 'Seven times a day have I praised you.' "[158] Later commentators on the Divine Office would be somewhat more expansive, not to say inspired. For Smaragdus of Saint-Mihiel-sur-Meuse (d. after 826), abbot of the monastery of Castellio and author of the earliest known complete commentary on Benedict's *Rule*, the seven times a day that the monks gave praise to their Creator recalled the seven days of creation and the seven gifts of the Holy Spirit. Citing Cassian—or, rather, more accurately, the seventh-century Spanish *Regula Cassiani* compiled from the *De institutis coenobiorum*—Smaragdus likewise invoked the early Christian interpretation of the Hours, including the more recent additions of Prime and "Twelfth" (presumably Vespers): Prime, "for the start of the day"; Terce, "because the Holy Spirit is acknowledged to have come down upon the apostles at the same hour"; Sext, "because the spotless victim, our Lord Jesus Christ, while hanging on the cross at the same hour, freed those liable to punishment from the eternal bonds of their sin"; None, "because at that same hour our Lord went down to hell and set free from there the souls of the saints which were being held there shut up in darkness, and took them with him to heaven"; and Twelfth, "for the ending of the day." Three of these times, Smaragdus (or rather his source) noted, were celebrated "even by the apostles" (cf. Acts 2:1–4; 10:9–12; 3:1), whereas Prime and Twelfth "were later additions of the Fathers." And yet, even in the Psalms, there is evidence that morning and evening prayers were "always offered in the Lord's temple. And so David says of evening prayers: 'Let my prayer be directed like incense in your sight; the raising of my hands like an evening sacrifice' (Psalm 140:2). While of morning prayers he says: 'O God, my God, unto you do I keep watch at break of day' (Psalm 62:2); and: 'I will meditate on you in the morning hours, for you have been my help' (Psalm 62:7–8)."[159]

Smaragdus's younger contemporary Hrabanus Maurus (d. 856), latterly abbot of Fulda and archbishop of Mainz, was, if anything, even more elaborate in his interpretation of the canonical hours. According to Hrabanus, Lauds (which he, like Benedict and Smaragdus, calls *Matutina*) celebrates the Resurrection of Christ who, rising from the dead at dawn, saved his people and condemned the devil and all his minions to eternal captivity. Prime, the first hour of the day when the sun appears in the east, is the most appropriate time to pray for the coming of the sun of justice, that those walking in his light may evade the shadows of sin and the snares of death. Terce is the hour at which Christ's Passion began, when the Jews called for the Lord to be crucified; likewise, it is the hour at which the Spirit descended upon the apostles. Sext is the hour at which Christ ascended the cross, offering himself to the eternal Father so as to liberate humanity from the power of the enemy and from perpetual death; it is, therefore, the hour at which it is most suitable to pray through his Passion to be restored to eternal life. None is the hour at which Christ commended his spirit into the hands of the Father; therefore, it is appropriate for the faithful at this hour to commend themselves to God with devout prayer, much as Peter and John ascended to the temple at this hour to pray. In the Old Testament, Vespers marks the hour at which it was the custom to offer sacrifices of spices and incense (Psalm 140:2), while in the New Testament, it is the hour at which the Savior instituted the mystery of his body and blood, that is, the sacrifice of the Mass. Concerning Compline, David prophesied: "I will not lie on the couch where I sleep, nor give my eyes to sleep or my eyelids to rest until I have found a place for the Lord, a dwelling for the God of Jacob" (Psalm 131:3–5); so, likewise, at this hour the devout prepare a place in their hearts for the Lord, much as it was at the eleventh hour, that is, the end of the day that the body of the Savior was laid in the tomb. As for nocturns or vigils (what later liturgists would call Matins), both Isaiah (cf. Isaiah 26:9) and David (Psalm 118:62) marked the middle of the night with prayer. It was likewise at this time that the angel struck down the firstborn sons of the Egyptians, indicating for Christians that it is important to keep watch lest they find themselves in danger, too. Christ more than once warned the apostles always to keep watch and himself spent the night in prayer, while Paul and Silas rose during the middle of the night to pray and sing hymns to God (Acts 16:25).[160]

With Smaragdus and Hrabanus, both of whose commentaries were well known in the eleventh and twelfth centuries when the Office of the Virgin was first being designed, we may perhaps begin to understand why Peter Damian should insist that every Christian pray not only daily, but also according to the seven hours of the canonical day; likewise, why it was essential for Peter and his contemporaries that the Office of the Virgin should be an office "of all the hours." It was not just—as many modern Christians experience the Hours—so as to break up the workday into regular intervals and thus remind Christians of their debt to God. Nor was it, as Phyllis Tickle has suggested, simply an artifact of the ancient Roman forum day, marked by bells at the first, third, sixth, ninth, and twelfth hours of the day.[161] Prayer, to be sure, was "work"—indeed, *the* work—of God (*opus Dei*), but its structuring according to the hours at which the apostles had been accustomed to pray was understood not simply as a service, but also as at once a reenactment and a remembrance of the history of salvation, from the creation and the prophecies of the Old Testament, through the events of the Passion and the coming of the Holy Spirit at Pentecost. The hours were more than just a schedule disciplining the monks, nuns, and clergy to an awareness of God. They were themselves a story to be recapitulated and relived day after day.

Nor was the story they enacted ever monovalent. We have noted above how Peter Damian championed the seven hours of the day as an antidote against "the seven principal vices from which all other infectious forms of vice derive."[162] For Honorius Augustodunensis, as for later liturgical commentators ultimately dependent on him, including Johannes Beleth (writing 1160–1164), Sicardus of Cremona (d. 1215), and William Durandus (d. 1296), the seven hours of the day recalled the seven ages in the life of a man which (as Beleth, Sicardus, and Durandus put it) humanity would have enjoyed if not for sin: infancy (Lauds or *Matutina*), childhood (Prime), adolescence (Terce), youth (Sext), old age (None), senility (Vespers), and the end of life (Compline).[163] Again, for Honorius, as for Sicardus, the seven hours of the day referred to the seven ages of history, here the microcosm of the day mirroring the macrocosm of all secular time: Lauds (*Matutina*), the time that Adam and Eve spent in Paradise praising God; Prime, the time during which Abel, Enoch, and other just people praised God; Terce, the time that Noah, having emerged from the ark, blessed God; Sext, the time that Abraham and the other patriarchs glorified God; None, the time when the prophets magnified God under the law; Vespers, the time when the apostles and their followers sang hymns to God; and Compline, the time when the just will give thanks to God under the Antichrist.[164] And, again, as Beleth put it, the seven hours of the day recalled the seven gifts of the Holy Spirit, the night Office representing the time of misery during which the human race was held captive by the devil, with the Offices of the day representing the time of redemption and liberation under Christ, the sun of justice.[165]

By far the most prominent—not to mention devotionally resonant—schema associated with the Hours, however, was that identifying the Offices of the day with the stations of the Passion. Already in the late eleventh century, the Flemish monk Goscelin of Saint-Bertin (d. after 1099) had advised the English recluse Eva: "Consecrate all the hours to the sufferings of Christ. In the middle of the night adore his capture and incarceration, in the morning his flagellation, at the third hour his being delivered up to be crucified . . . at the sixth hour his hanging from the cross, at the ninth hour his death, at vespers his burial."[166] Likewise, in his reading of the canonical hours, Peter Damian recalled the Gospels' witness to the hours of the Passion: "at [Terce], as we read in Mark, our Redeemer was crucified. . . . At [Sext], as the other evangelists testify, our Savior hung on the cross for the salvation of all men. . . . The ninth hour, moreover, is distinguished in its own right in that at that hour the Lord is described as having completed the mystery of his passion, and died."[167] With the commentaries of the twelfth and later centuries, every hour of the liturgical day, not just the evangelically attested three, was to be caught up in the drama and given a christological significance. For Rupert of Deutz (d. 1129), the drama began during the night Office with the birth of Christ. At Lauds (*Matutina*), Peter denied Christ three times, while confusingly enough, again at dawn, the angels announced the Resurrection of the Lord to the women. At Prime, the Lord was spat upon, mocked, slapped, bound, and brought before Pilate. At Terce, he was crowned with thorns and crucified "by the tongues of the Jews." At Sext, he was raised upon the cross and physical darkness fell upon the earth as the true light passed to the illumination of the Gentiles. At None, Jesus cried out with a loud voice and sent forth his spirit, while his side was pierced with a lance and the elements of the Church—blood by which humanity was redeemed and water by which it was washed clean—poured forth. At Vespers, the Lord was buried, just as he took bread and wine in his hands to show forth in truth his body and blood. Finally, according to Rupert, the hour of Compline commemorates at once the Passion of the Lord and the future suffering of the martyrs as well as the peace between God and men accomplished by his Resurrection.[168]

Thus far, everything that has been said about the significance of the canonical hours could apply as much to the Divine Office in its entirety as to any individual Office for the day. It must also be admitted that at first glance the majority of these schema do not seem to have much to do with the development of the Hours of the Virgin in particular. And yet, with the commemorative focus on Christ, that on his Mother could never be far behind.[169] Indeed, if we accept a remarkable prayer that Anselm of Lucca (d. 1086) composed for Countess Matilda of Tuscany as a reflection of the meditations that she was to make while reciting her daily Office of the Virgin, it is possible that, devotionally at least, the Hours of the Virgin were acknowledged as a vehicle for this type of imaginative engagement long before its more famous articulation in the fourteenth-century Franciscan *Meditationes vitae Christi*. In the course of her prayer as guided by Anselm, Matilda was to focus in turn on certain events in the life of the Virgin: the Annunciation, the finding of the twelve-year-old Jesus in the temple, the Crucifixion, the Virgin's death, and her Assumption, each recalled as if Matilda herself were present "at that hour" when the event itself was taking place. For example, at the first of these "hours" Matilda was to pray: "My sins outnumber the sands of the sea and I am not worthy to be counted among your handmaidens nor to be introduced into your chamber. . . . [cf. Song of Songs 1:3]. And yet, I look to the time when Gabriel enters to greet you, that after him I may enter boldly into the secret chamber of your prayers." And at the hour of the Crucifixion: "And yet again . . . I look to that time when you will come to the cross of your Son, that when you and the holy women are given over to John's custody, suffering with you I may console you in your immense grief until you forgive me and pardon my iniquities."[170]

Similarly, in the *Meditationes vitae Christi*, once thought to be the work of Bonaventure, but more recently attributed to the Tuscan John of Caulibus and likewise apparently written for a female recipient, the reader is to imagine herself (or himself) present at each of the canonical hours, beginning with Christ's prayer and arrest in the garden of Gethsemane at Matins and proceeding through his flagellation and mocking at Prime, his carrying the cross at Terce, his Crucifixion at Sext and his death at None, his deposition from the cross at Vespers, his burial at Compline, and his Resurrection during the night Office.[171] Over and over again, the author of the *Meditationes* exhorts the reader, "carefully look at each and every event"; "notice every detail as if you were present"; "contemplate and watch carefully all the actions and each and every affliction of your Lord. As closely as you can, suffer together with him."[172] Significantly, each hour is accompanied by a corresponding meditation on the experience of the Virgin so that, for example, at Matins, after Christ has been taken from the garden, the reader is to imagine Mary's prayer: "I beg you, most holy Father, if it pleases You, do not let my son die," and to respond in kind: "Pity her now that you see her so afflicted."[173] Likewise, at None, when Christ gave forth his final cry as he was dying, the author reflects: "O what kind of mother's grief was there then, when, so devastated, she witnessed him weaken, fail, weep and die!"[174] And at Vespers, as John, Mary Magdalene, and Mary's sisters sat with her by the cross, he asks the reader: "Do you see how many times she died this day? Certainly as many times as she witnessed some new atrocity against her son. In fact, Simeon's prophesy was truly fulfilled: 'A sword,' he said to her, 'shall pierce your own soul' (Luke 2:35), for this happened to her many times this day."[175]

We may catch a glimpse of the way in which at least one of Mary's devotees experienced this interpretive resonance in the account of a spiritual conversation that the Benedictine nun Gertrude of Helfta (d. 1301/2) had one night while keeping vigil before Matins. Wearied by her contemplation of his Passion and most likely unwell, otherwise she would have been in choir for the Divine Office, Gertrude begged the Lord to teach her "what honor or service I could now show your most blessed Mother, since I cannot perform the Hours due to her." Christ responded by offering Gertrude a series of meditations praising him for the virtues of the Virgin Mother according to which she imitated him at every stage of his suffering.

"*Lauda me*," the Lord enjoined Gertrude. "Praise me": At Matins, for the Virgin's integrity in conceiving and giving birth to him, thus imitating his innocence in being taken captive, insulted, and mocked for redemption of humanity. At Prime, for the Virgin's readiness to receive him more and more, thus imitating his humility in condescending to be judged by an infidel (*Sarraceno homine*). At Terce, for the ardent desire with which she drew him from the bosom of the Father into her virgin womb, thus imitating that desire with which he desired human salvation when he was scourged, crowned with thorns, and bore on his shoulders the shameful and infamous cross. At Sext, for that hope with which she aspired always to seek his glory, thus imitating that longing with which he, hanging on the cross, thirsted for the salvation of human souls. At None, for that most ardent love between his divine heart and the immaculate Virgin that joined his divine nature to human nature in her womb, thus imitating the immensity of his love as he died on the cross for the redemption of humankind. At Vespers, for the constancy of her faith even after his death, when all but she despaired, thus imitating the faithfulness with which he, now dead and taken down from the cross, followed humankind even to depths of hell so as to transport them to the joys of paradise. And at Compline, for her most praiseworthy perseverance in goodness and virtue even unto the end, thus imitating him in handing over his incorruptible body for burial "in human fashion, to show that I would refuse nothing, however vile, for human salvation."[176]

Perhaps the most fully developed account of the way in which the hours of the liturgical day might sustain a meditation on Mary's role in the work of salvation comes, however, in the so-called *Myroure of oure Ladye*, an early fifteenth-century commentary on the Divine Office composed in Middle English for the sisters of the Monastery of Saint Savior and Saint Bridget of Syon of the Order of Augustine (or Syon Abbey).[177] The Bridgettine or Birgittine nuns observed not a daily, but rather a weekly Office of the Virgin, with a full complement of psalms, chants, and readings designated for each day of the week. Here, as in the regular Benedictine Office, the seven-hour cycle of the day was overlaid upon the seven-day cycle of the week, each day for the Birgittines recalling an age in the history of the world as it pertained to the Virgin Mother, with the hours of the day carrying the recollection of, among other things, the seven deadly sins, the seven sacraments, the seven gifts of the Holy Spirit, the creation of the world in six days with God's rest on the seventh, the seven ages of man, and the seven ages of the world.[178]

According to the *Myroure*, on Sundays, the nuns were to meditate on the glory of the blessed Trinity and the love that God had for the Virgin "endelesly as presente in the syghte of hys Godly forknowynge." On Mondays, they were to "beholde and se wyth [their] gostly eyen" the angels as they rejoiced in the Virgin as yet unborn but already loved more even than themselves. On Tuesdays, the nuns were to reflect on the creation and fall of Adam and on how he and all the patriarchs and prophets had foreknowledge of the Virgin. On Wednesdays, they were to contemplate the conception and birth of the Virgin, God's love for humankind's salvation, and the Virgin's love on earth. On Thursdays, they were to think on the excellence of the Virgin's virtues, her beauty in body and soul, and the wonder of the Incarnation of Our Lord Jesus Christ in her, while on Fridays, their meditation was to turn to Our Lady's sorrows at his Passion. On Saturdays, they were to recall the life of the Virgin from the time of the Passion to her Assumption in body and soul into heaven, considering thereby how the joy that the Trinity had of her on Sundays before she was made was fulfilled on Saturdays "effectually in dede" after her death.[179]

The nuns' hourly meditations were likewise to focus on the Virgin, nor should they be concerned that in so concentrating their attention their service might in some way be opposed to that said in honor of the Lord, "for [Our Lady's] wyl was neuer contrary to his blessyd wyll." Accordingly, just as at *Matyns* the Lord rose again from death into life, so "som say," there is a star that appears at this time that guides sailors to their right port. This star is "our mercyfull lady . . . that socoureth mankynde in the troubelous se of this worlde, & bringeth her louers to the hauen of helth: therefore yt is worthy that she be serued, & praysed at matyns time." Again, at Prime, Our Lord Christ was led before Pilate; in the same hour after his Resurrection he appeared to Mary Magdalene (Mark 16:9; John 20:1–18) and to his disciples as they were fishing (John 21:4–14). Likewise, at Prime, there is a star that appears in the heavens before the sun, "as yf yt were the leder or brynger forth of the sonn." So Mary came before and brought forth that "sonn of rightwysnes," Our Lord Jesus Christ. At Terce, Christ was scourged, crowned with thorns, and scorned; at the same hour he appeared after his Resurrection to the women as they were coming from the tomb (Matthew 28:9–10). And, again, as Terce is the hour at which laborers are accustomed to have their dinner, so Our Lady brought forth for us at this time him who is the bread of life.

At Sext, the Lord was crucified and given vinegar and gall. At the same hour after his Resurrection he appeared to Saint James and, on the day of his Ascension, ate with his apostles (Mark 16:14–20). This is likewise the hour at which the sun "waxeth more hotte"; thus, through Our Lady, "the euerlastyng sonn hath shewed the hete of his charite more largely to mankynde." At None, Our Lord cried out and gave up his soul and his side was opened, pouring forth blood and water for our redemption. At the same hour on Easter day he appeared to Saint Peter. None is also the hour at which the sun is at its highest (confusingly, since this should be around mid-afternoon): "& the hyest grace & mercy that euer was done to man in erth, was broughte in by mene of our lady." At Vespers (or "euensonge") on Maundy Thursday, Our Lord ate with the apostles and ordained the sacrament of his body and blood. At the same hour on Good Friday, his body was taken down from the cross, and on Easter Sunday he met with two of his disciples on the way to Emmaus, to whom he made himself known in the breaking of the bread (Luke 24:13–35). And, again, at Evensong, the day "fayleth moche"; nevertheless, "our ladys grace help-eth" when all other help fails. At Compline on Maundy Thursday, Our Lord sweated blood as he prayed, while at the same hour on Good Friday he was buried, and on Easter Sunday he appeared to the apostles in the house where they had locked themselves away for fear of the Jews and said, "Peace be with you" (John 20:19). Compline is the Office at the end of the day, so, likewise, at the end of our life "we haue moste need of our ladys helpe, and therfore in all these houres we ought to do her worship & praysyng." Moreover, so con-sonant was the life of the Virgin with that of her Son that all the pains that he is said to have suffered "in all these .vii. houres . . . our lady his moder sufferyd the same paynes in her harte by compassion, & therfore," the author of the *Myroure* concluded, "yt is conuenient to prayse her & do her seruice in all the same houres."[180]

"Seven times a day have I praised you." Taken as a template for how and when exactly Christians should pray, the psalmist's exclamation was frustratingly brief, nor, as we have seen, does it seem directly to have influenced the times at which early Christians were accustomed to pray. As an explanation after the fact for the development of the canonical hours, it was, however, seemingly prophetic. At the very least, later commentators on the liturgy were to take it as such. Under these circumstances, it was perhaps inevitable that the Office of the Virgin should take the form that it did, modeled as it was on the canonical

Office dedicated to the service of God. And yet, one might still ask why it was an Office in honor of Mary rather than, for example, the Trinity, the Holy Spirit, or the Holy Cross that was to become the centerpiece of late medieval monastic, clerical, and lay devotion. Our survey of the meanings attributed over the centuries to the liturgical hours would seem to suggest one compelling—perhaps even the most compelling—reason. For medieval Christians, praise of and prayer to their Lady was in and of itself always and at the same time praise of and prayer to the Trinity and to the Lord Jesus Christ. It was, therefore, not only appropriate ("conuenient") but indeed obligatory ("we ought") to praise and pray to the Virgin at those same times at which Christians offered prayer and praise to God. The events in her life were so intimately bound up with those of her Son that, in fact, to praise him as the author of human redemption was at the same time to praise her as the Mother who gave birth to God in the flesh. Her virtues were his virtues, her joys and sufferings were his—and vice versa. As Christ told Gertrude when she asked what service she might offer in honor of his Mother, "Praise me."

Over and over again, commentators on the liturgy appealed to the events in Christ's Passion as a justification for Christians to pray at particular hours during the day. As we have seen, this same justification could also apply to the praise and prayers that they offered to the Virgin Mary at those same hours through her particular Office. Spiritually if not historically speaking, there was, in fact, nothing accidental in the schedule that Benedict prescribed in his *Rule*. As medieval Christians saw it, God himself had indicated through his own sufferings the times at which it was most appropriate to pray. From this perspective, time was not simply a limited resource to be divided between sleep, work, and prayer, but itself full of meaning, an experience as well as a sign of God's engagement with his creation. It was something sacred to be lived, every hour an act of remembrance situated at once within the history of salvation and the particular experience of God and his Mother.[181] Moreover, it would have been unthinkable (at least, theoretically) to find this schedule in any way burdensome. Had not God himself suffered throughout the whole of the day so as to redeem humanity from its sins? The least that Christians could do was to observe the hours of their Lord's Passion as particularly solemn, compassionating the Virgin Mother as she herself suffered with her Son.

Nor was the Marian Office a product—as later reformers would have it—of a somehow excessive desire to honor the Mother of God over her Creator and Son.[182] As we shall see, the particular texts of her Office, while drawing in part on antiphons, responsories, lessons, prayers, and hymns originally composed for use on Mary's various feasts (her Purification, the Annunciation, her Assumption, and her Nativity) were themselves always of necessity subordinated to the texts of the Psalms it was the core of her—indeed, any—Office to recite. Much as the Virgin Mother carried the Son of God in her womb, so the texts of her Office carried the praise of God at their heart. Again, we can see this dependence not only in the overall structure of her Hours, but also in the way in which the commentators, including Gertrude, explained its significance. Mary's Hours did not, at least, not in any straightforward narrative or literal way, "recall significant episodes in Mary's life," any more than they told the history of salvation from Adam to Antichrist or rehearsed the life of the individual human being from infancy to old age.[183] (As we shall see, things were rather more complicated than that.) And yet, at a typological or experiential level, they did, just as they recalled the insults and agonies Christ suffered over the course of the day of his death or the joys of the women and the apostles to whom he appeared on the day of his rising to life from death.

The illuminations in some of the earliest English Books of Hours attest as much. In the early thirteenth-century De Brailes Hours (London, British Library, Add. 49999, ca. 1240), the Hours of the Virgin are prefaced not, as would be the case in most later manuscript and printed Books of Hours, with images from the narrative of Christ's infancy (the Annunciation, Visitation, Nativity, annunciation to the shepherds, adoration of the Magi, presentation in the temple, massacre of the innocents, and the flight into Egypt), but rather with complex four-part images from the narrative of his Passion: at Matins, the betrayal of, scourging of, mocking of, and spitting at Christ, accompanied by Peter's denial (fol. 1); at Prime, Christ's judgment before Annas, Caiaphas, Pilate, and Herod (fol. 32); at Terce, Christ again before Pilate, and Pilate's washing his hands while Christ is turned over to the Jews (fol. 39); at Sext, Christ accosted by the Wandering Jew, Christ carrying the cross, Christ being disrobed, and Christ standing before the cross, awaiting his Crucifixion (fol. 43v); and, at None, Christ on the cross between the two thieves, Mary and John at the foot of the cross, and Christ's side pierced by Longinus's spear (fol. 47v).[184] (The illuminations for Vespers and Complins have been excised, while that for Lauds—the Visitation—belongs to a subordinate cycle of smaller images illustrating the individual texts of Matins and Lauds.) Clearly, William de Brailes had been reading his Honorius, Beleth, and Sicardus, or at the very least listening to sermons based on their texts.

In contrast, the Hours of the Virgin in the slightly later Egerton Hours (London, British Library, Egerton 1151, ca. 1260) are illustrated with a cycle of images depicting the activities of a typical day (again, some images are missing). At Matins, the owner of the book kneels at prayer before the Virgin and Child (fol. 7); at Prime, a man watches the sunrise (fol. 38); at None, two musicians play while a man and two women dance (fol. 47); at Vespers, a woman kneels while two monks sing the evening prayers (fol. 50); and at Compline, two men get ready for bed (fol. 57v), suggesting a meditation on time much as that later invoked in the Birgittines' *Myroure*.[185] The images for the Hours of the Virgin in the somewhat more luxurious Salvin Hours (London, British Library, Add. 48985, ca. 1270) return to the narrative of the Passion, albeit without keeping as strictly to the traditional interpretation of the Hours as did William de Brailes in his images. The opening for Matins, for example, includes a full-page miniature of the Tree of Jesse, with scenes from the infancy of Christ in accompanying roundels, while the text of the Office itself ("Deus in adiutorium meum intende") begins with an image of Judas's kiss (fols. 1v–2). At Lauds, Christ appears before Annas (fol. 7), and at Prime, before Caiaphas (fol. 29), while at Terce, he appears before Pilate, after which (in the margin) Pilate washes his hands (fol. 32v). At Sext, Christ is mocked and denied by Peter (fol. 35). At None, he is scourged (fol. 37v). At Vespers, he is crucified between Longinus with his spear and Stephaton with his bucket and sponge (fol. 40). At Compline, however, he rises again from the tomb (fol. 43v).[186] Again, this christological reading of the Marian Hours would have made perfect sense to those for whom the hours of prayer were by definition an occasion to think at once about God's suffering in time and about his Mother's participation with him in that suffering and its subsequent joys.

In what sense then, if any, was this Marian Office "little," if in fact it contained devotions for the full complement of canonical hours according to the monastic as well as cathedral tradition (see Table 2)? As we have seen, however popular it would eventually become among the laity, the Office of the Virgin was monastic and clerical in its origins. There was no need from this perspective to make it somehow less complicated or easier to learn. Nor, in fact, was the Marian Office in its earliest form strictly speaking "abbreviated" so as to make it less intrusive on the monastic or secular day.[187] The whole point of the Office, as Peter Damian would insist, was that it honored the Virgin at all seven (with the night Office, eight) canonical hours of the liturgical day, and to do so required a full complement of hymns, psalms, lessons, and prayers. Typically, and even in monasteries, the Marian Office for the night Office or Matins followed the secular (that is, cathedral) use of three nocturns of three psalms and three lessons or readings each, although some communities, like Worcester, kept the full monastic use of twelve psalms with, however, still only three lessons.[188] However—and in this respect at least Matins of the Virgin as recited each day would have been shorter than the same Hour for either the Marian feasts (Purification, Annunciation, Assumption, Nativity and, where it was celebrated, Conception) or the commemorative Saturday Office of the Virgin—it was the custom in some (perhaps, to judge from the Books of Hours, most) communities to recite the three nocturns in rotation over the course of the week, the first on Sundays, Mondays, and Thursdays; the second on Tuesdays and Fridays; and the third on Wednesdays and Saturdays.[189] It was this shortened observance of Matins that would eventually earn the Marian Office its epithet "Little" (*Parvum*), not necessarily a reduction in either the complexity or number of any of its texts.[190]

Accompanying the psalms and lessons of each nocturn would be certain chants: short sentences (*antiphona*) for the psalms, somewhat more complicated responsories for the lessons. While, as we shall see in chapter 3, the psalms for the Marian Office drew from a relatively but never wholly consistent repertoire, the antiphons, responsories, and lessons could vary widely from Use to Use, thus inflecting the meaning of the psalms at the Office's core. So, for example, while the first psalm at Matins was more or less invariably *Domine Dominus noster* (Psalm 8), its antiphon might be anything from "The Holy Spirit descended in you, Mary, lest you fear to bear the Son of God in your womb" (Canterbury, Christ Church, eleventh century)[191] to "You are exalted, holy Mother of God, above the choirs of angels to the heavenly kingdom" (Winchester, Nunnaminster, eleventh century)[192] to "Blessed are you among women and blessed is the fruit of your womb" (Fonte Avellana, eleventh century, Peter Damian's community).[193] The third of these antiphons would become standard for the Uses of Sarum, York, Rome, and Geert Grote among others, but the Use of Paris would take up the second, while no community other than Canterbury seems ever to have used the first for this location in the Marian Office, although it was regularly used in a slightly different form on the first Sunday of Advent and for the Feast of the Annunciation. At Mouzon in the eleventh century, the antiphon for the same psalm was: "Almighty Lord, have mercy on us and save us through the prayers and merits of the most blessed Mother of God and all the saints,"[194] while at in least one community in the diocese of York in the twelfth century, it was: "Our dwelling in you is as of all those that rejoice, holy Mother of God."[195] And at Westminster toward the end of the same century, it was: "We confess you, Mary, by right queen of heaven, from whose bridal chamber the sun of justice came forth."[196] Similar variations attended the selection of antiphons for the remaining psalms. Conversely, while the choice of responsories was relatively somewhat more consistent (perhaps owing to the responsories' own greater musical as well as textual complexity), the choice of lessons was even more eclectic than that of the antiphons for the psalms.

The remaining hours, while structurally simpler, shared the same tendency to local variation within a context of occasional consistency, the latter most particularly in the selection of hymns. The hymn for Matins was usually—albeit not always—the magnificent "Quem terra, pontus, aethera" traditionally ascribed to Venantius Fortunatus (d. 600/609).[197] At Paris, however, it was "O quam glorifica luce coruscas."[198] Lauds as recited in honor of the Virgin, with its five psalms (Psalms 148–150 being recited under one Gloria Patri and, therefore, counting only as one), chapter (*capitulum*) with short responsory, hymn, versicle and response, antiphon and canticle (Luke 1:68–79, the song of Zacharias or the Benedictus), and collect or prayer, was structurally more or less identical with the Office for that Hour as recited for any other festal or ferial observance; likewise the Little Hours of Prime, Terce, Sext, and None. Prime of the Virgin, like ferial (as opposed to Sunday) Prime of both secular and monastic use, typically consisted of a hymn, three psalms with one antiphon (although here there were significant variants in number as well as choice of psalms, some Marian Uses having as many as five), a chapter with short responsory, a versicle and response, and various concluding collects and/or prayers; while Terce, Sext, and None each consisted of a hymn, an antiphon with three psalms, a chapter with short responsory, a versicle and response, and a collect or prayer.

Again, as with Matins, the choice of antiphons for each of these Marian Hours might vary greatly even when the psalms did not, which, nevertheless, the psalms did, if according to a somewhat recognizable pattern (see Table 2). This was particularly the case with Prime and None, so much so that in his groundbreaking tests for the localization of manuscripts, first proposed in 1920, Falconer Madan was confident that it was possible to determine the Use of any given manuscript version of the Marian Hours simply by checking the antiphons and chapters for these two Hours.[199] Erik Drigsdahl's important online database of variants has now demonstrated that this is not in fact the case—one needs to check rather more texts to determine whether one is working with any given Use—but it is telling that simply on the basis of his limited test Madan was able to discern some ninety or more different Uses. Drigsdahl, in comparison, identified more than six hundred variants in Use.[200] By far the majority of these disparate Uses seems to have been developed in the fourteenth or fifteenth centuries, but again, it is telling that of the handful of Marian Offices that survives from before 1200, no two share more than the occasional text. So, for example, in the eleventh-century Office from Canterbury (London, British Library, Cotton Tiberius A.iii), the fourth antiphon for Lauds is the same as that found in the eleventh-century Office from Winchester (London, British Library, Royal 2 B.V), as are the chapter and collect at None, the third antiphon at Vespers, and the first responsory at Matins, but otherwise, the two Offices share only their arrangement of psalms, not necessarily the degree of similarity one would expect from two communities so closely associated as Christ Church and the Nunnaminster.[201]

If Lauds with its five psalms was the single most regular Hour of the Marian Office and Prime its most variable, at least in the choice of psalms, Vespers and Compline fell somewhere in between, depending on whether they followed monastic or secular use. Monastic Vespers and, therefore, Vespers of the Virgin as observed in most eleventh- and twelfth-century monastic communities, had four psalms, whereas secular Vespers and, therefore, Vespers of the Virgin according to most cathedral Uses, had five. In both secular and monastic uses, so also in the Office of the Virgin; however, the psalms would be followed by a chapter with short responsory, a hymn (in the Office of the Virgin almost invariably "Ave maris stella"), antiphon and canticle (Luke 1:46–55, the song of Mary or the Magnificat), and a collect or prayer. Although according to legend Compline was not originally included in the Hours of the Virgin, at least as kept at Cluny, elsewhere, including Canterbury and Winchester, it was already part of the Office in the mid-eleventh century. Once again, however, there was a choice to be made between the secular and monastic structures for this Hour, whether four psalms followed by a chapter with short responsory, a hymn, an antiphon with canticle (Luke 2:29–32, the song of Simeon or Nunc Dimittis), and concluding prayers as per the secular use; or three psalms followed by a hymn, chapter but no responsory, and prayers, omitting the Nunc Dimittis as per the monastic use. Nor, as at Matins, do the authors of the Marian Office seem to have felt constrained to adhere strictly to one or the other use. At Paris in the thirteenth century, for example, the Compline of the Virgin included four psalms and the Nunc Dimittis, but the hymn preceded the chapter rather than, as in the usual secular Office, the reverse.[202]

There were also, at least in some communities, variations in the Marian Office from season to season of the liturgical year. The thirteenth-century antiphoner for the Benedictine community serving the cathedral of Worcester contains no fewer than four distinct seasonal alternatives for the daily Office of the Virgin: for Advent, from the Octave of the Epiphany to the Purification, from the Purification to Easter, and in Eastertide, with additional antiphons for the Magnificat to be used after Pentecost through the Nativity of the Virgin.[203] Likewise, the late thirteenth- or early fourteenth-century breviary for the Benedictine community near Winchester (Hyde Abbey) distinguishes the

Hours of the Virgin as sung during Advent, from Christmas to the Purification of the Virgin, during Eastertide, and throughout the rest of the year.[204] Most laypeople, to be sure, would not have been familiar with such internal variants, although some books of Hours do include additional texts (antiphons, lessons, responsories, hymns, chapters, and collects) for Advent.[205] Nevertheless, by the later fourteenth century, there were always the Offices of the Holy Spirit and of the Holy Cross, not to mention the many suffrages and other prayers typically appended to the Marian Office ("Obsecro te," "O intemerata," the Fifteen Joys of the Virgin, the Seven Requests to Our Lord, the "Salva sancta facies," the "Stabat mater," the Seven Prayers of Saint Gregory, the Seven Verses of Saint Bernard, "Adoro te, Domine Jesu Christe, in cruce pendentem," the Fifteen Oes of Saint Bridget) with which the laity and clergy alike could supplement their devotions.[206] (Note, as with the Hours, the emphasis on the number seven.) The Hours of the Virgin in most Books of Hours may have been unvarying from season to season, but we have no reason to suppose that their observance was.

It is, of course, another question altogether whether and to what extent most laypeople or, indeed, even most monastics and clerics would have been aware of the way in which the Hours of the Virgin differed from Use to Use. The care with which the original owner of the De Brailes Hours made sure to have Vespers copied out according to the Dominican Use suggests that at least some were mindful of these variants. Certainly all those artists and scribes who peopled the workshops of Ghent and Bruges making books of Hours for export would have known the difference between the Uses of Sarum and York; likewise those working in Rouen making books for the Uses of Coutances, Lisieux, Evreux, and elsewhere.[207] Similarly, there seems little reason for there to have been distinct Uses for towns as proximate as Amiens, Arras, Beauvais, Chartres, Lille, Laon, Paris, Reims, and Rouen unless their composers and presumably users had some sense of wanting to honor the Virgin in their own, particular, local way. Intriguingly, however, the only controversy specifically over Use of which I am aware—prior, that is, to 1571—had more to do with the language in which the texts were said than with the texts themselves.

As we have seen, Gerhart Zerbolt defended the use of Geert Grote's Dutch version of the Hours on the basis that the laity should understand the texts they were praying, particularly the psalms. He said nothing, however, about their choice of psalms or their arrangement according to Use.[208] As Paul Saenger has shown, there was much concern in the later Middle Ages over whether one should pray silently or aloud, with or without full comprehension of the words that one was saying.[209] And yet, there would seem to have been curiously little attention given to the sheer diversity of Uses with which Christians were accustomed to pray, other than through the efforts of the scribes and printers to make them available for purchase. It was good business after all. Between 1485 and 1512, Antoine Vérard alone published Books of Hours for as many as seven different identifiable Uses, including Rome, Paris, Poitiers, Rouen, Bourges, Quercy, and (in two editions) Sarum.[210] While more than half of Vérard's some eighty different editions were Use of Rome, including a number in both Latin and French, his contemporary and presumably competitor Simon Vostre seems to have specialized in Hours customized for local Use, averaging some ten or eleven editions per year in the first decade of the sixteenth century.[211] A half-century or so later, the great Antwerp printer Christopher Plantin (d. 1589) did his best to make the newly authorized *Officium beatae Mariae Virginis* (as of 1571, its official title) available to as many Roman Catholic Christians as possible (thirty-seven editions in all by 1589, thirty-three in duodecimo or smaller); nevertheless, Pope Pius's insistence that there should be only one version of the Marian Office publishable only under license and only in Latin was a watershed in more ways than one.[212]

This, then, was the structure according to which Mary's medieval devotees kept her Hours. Seven times each day, every third hour from morning till evening (approximately 6:00 a.m. [Prime], 9:00 a.m. [Terce], noon [Sext], 3:00 p.m. [None], sunset [Vespers] and bedtime [Compline]), and once in the night (around 2 a.m. by our clocks, although the laity seem to have said their Matins along with Lauds at dawn), they turned their attention to God and his Mother. While there is still much to learn from the many thousands of Books of Hours that survive from the later Middle Ages about the context in which medieval Christians kept their devotions to the Mother of God, about this much we can be sure: every devout European Christian who was anyone (or, as Deschamps would have it, aspired to be), and even many whose names we will never know, was saying the Hours of the Virgin, voluntarily and, for those who could afford it, with the aid of personalized books.[213] But why, after all, did they say *this* Office? Why were they so drawn to *this* devotion, rather than, say, one to a local saint (although Books of Hours, of course, included suffrages to the saints) or, more explicitly, to the Three Persons of God? This is a question that few scholars have even thought to ask, more often than not taking for granted that medieval Christians were drawn to the devotion out of a general desire to honor the Virgin.[214] Perhaps C. S. Lewis was right after all. We need to do more than stand outside the light, looking at the beam, in order to understand this devotion. More particularly, looking *at*—as opposed to looking *along*—the Books of Hours, not to mention the Hours of the Virgin at their heart, cannot tell us why medieval Christians were so committed to this practice rather than any other that might similarly engage their attention and thus, if we go by more recent standards of valuation, result in absorptive "flow." It is time for us to step into the beam to see what Mary's medieval devotees said they saw, as hour after hour, day after day, they lifted their voices in praise of the Lady and her Lord.

PLATE 4 Virgin and Child enthroned between angels with thuribles; a woman kneels in prayer before them with her open book. Monkey and rabbit musicians accompany her. Opening of the Office of the Virgin: "Domine labia mea aperies . . ." Book of Hours ("Egerton Hours"), England (Oxford or West Midlands), ca. 1260. Not Use of Sarum, variants Use of Arras. London, British Library, Egerton 1151, fol. 7r.

2

Ave Maria

Imagine the scene, if you will.[1] It is dark, except for the light of a few candles, and silent, except for the breathing of those around you. Someone coughs. You are, perhaps, tired, because you have already been singing and listening for some time, praising God through the watches of the night. Still in your stall, you turn with your brothers (or sisters) toward the altar and repeat, once again, the opening dialogue of Matins, led by your priest:

Domine, labia mea aperies.

Lord, open my lips.

To which you as part of the choir reply:

Et os meum annuntiabit laudem tuam.

And my mouth shall show forth your praise.

Again, the priest lifts up his voice:

Deus, in adjutorium meum intende.

God, come to my assistance.

To which the choir responds:

Domine, ad adjuvandum me festina.

Lord, make haste to help me.

The latter is spoken rather than sung, followed by a Gloria Patri.[2] And then, as if with the voice of an angel, the *versicularius* intones the familiar chant:

> Ave Maria, gratia plena.
>
> *Hail Mary, full of grace.*

You with the rest of the choir respond in full (CAO #1041, 1539):

> Ave Maria, gratia plena, dominus tecum. Ave Maria, gratia plena, dominus tecum.
>
> *Hail Mary, full of grace, the Lord is with you. Hail Mary, full of grace, the Lord is with you.*

At once, the *versicularius* continues, intoning the psalm (Psalm 94):

> Venite exultemus Domino, iubilemus Deo salutari nostro: preoccupemus faciem eius in confessione: et in psalmis iubilemus ei.

You respond, yet again:

> Ave Maria, gratia plena, dominus tecum.

The one text is as habitual as the other; you have sung both every morning for the better part of your life. You have no need to look at the words or to think about the reciting tone; this exchange comes to you as easily as breathing. "Venite," the psalm invites you.

> *Come, let us sing unto the Lord. Let us rejoice before God, our Savior. Let us come into his presence with thanksgiving, and rejoice before him with psalms (vv. 1–2).*

"Hail Mary," you respond, "full of grace, the Lord is with you," weaving the words that the angel Gabriel spoke to the Mother of God at the Annunciation (Luke 1:28) in among the verses of the psalm.

Perhaps, as you sing, a glint of light catches your eye, and you turn to see a pair of amber beads swaying gently in front of the image of the Blessed Virgin. Almost idly, you recall how Isabella, the wife of William Belgrafe, had bequeathed them to Our Lady along with her gold and silver ring only last year.[3] You begin to think on the joy with which Mary herself must have exulted when she understood that she was to become Bride of God and Mother of Our Lord. Suddenly, it is as if you were present yourself at the very moment when Gabriel came to her in that "pryue chaumbure" where she was accustomed to say her prayers and meditate, with Isaiah, on the manner of the Incarnation.[4] You hear her speak:

> Quoniam Deus magnus Dominus et rex magnus super omnes deos: quoniam non repellet Dominus plebem suam: quia in manu eius sunt omnes fines terre: et altitudines montium ipse conspicit.

> *For the Lord is a great God, and a great King above all gods. For the Lord will not cast off his people. For in his hand are all the ends of the earth: and the heights of the mountains he beholds* (vv. 3–4).

And you realize that she is waiting for you to speak in return: "The Lord is with you." To which she responds with even greater joy:

> Quoniam ipsius est mare et ipse fecit illud; et aridam fundauerunt manus eius: venite adoremus et procidamus ante Deum, ploremus coram Domino qui fecit nos: quia ipse est Dominus Deus noster: nos autem populus eius et oues pascue eius.

> *For the sea is his, and he made it: and his hands formed the dry land. Come, let us worship and fall down before God, let us weep before the Lord who made us: for he is the Lord our God, and we are his people and the sheep of his pasture* (vv. 5–7).

You are amazed to find your mouth filled with an extraordinary sweetness, like honey, as once again you repeat the angel's greeting: "Hail Mary, full of grace, the Lord is with you."[5] And in little more than a whisper, so that you are not sure whether you are hearing it or not, a voice admonishes you: "Slow down! I want to savor the joy that I have when you say those words, most especially *Dominus tecum*, for then it seems to me that my Son is in me, just as he was when, God and man, he deigned to be born from me for the sake of sinners."[6]

Abashed, you find yourself wanting to fall to your knees and bow down with every repetition of the angel's words and wonder what it would be like to say the salutation fifty, a hundred, or even a hundred and fifty times, when once again the Virgin's voice breaks in:

> Hodie si vocem eius audieritis nolite obdurare corda vestra: sicut in exacerbatione secundum diem tentationis in deserto vbi tentauerunt me patres vestri: probauerunt et viderunt opera mea.

PLATE 5 Altar statue, the Virgin and Child in majesty, Auvergne, France, ca. 1175–1200. Metropolitan Museum of Art, Gift of J. Pierpont Morgan, 1916, Accession number 16.32.194.

If you hear his voice today, harden not your hearts: as in the provocation according to the day of temptation in the wilderness where your fathers tempted me: they proved me and saw my works (vv. 8–9).

As you answer: "The Lord is with you," you think miserably on your sins and your hardness of heart, especially your failure to honor God and his Mother as you should, for did she not suffer even as her Son as he died on the cross for our sins?⁷ Almost as if he could read your thoughts, her Son replies:

Quadraginta annis proximus fui generationi huic et dixi semper hi errant corde ipsi vero non cognouerunt vias meas quibus iuraui in ira mea si introibunt in requiem meam.

For forty years I was nigh to this generation, and I said: always they err in heart, for truly they have not known my ways: I swore to them in my wrath they shall never enter into my rest (vv. 10–11).

Trembling, indeed, pleading, you turn to the Virgin Mother once again: "Hail Mary, full of grace, the Lord is with you," hoping against hope that she might be able to assuage the wrath of the Judge, her Son. "Glory be to the Father, and to the Son, and to the Holy Spirit," you sing. "As it was in the beginning, is now and ever shall be: world without end. Amen." Thankfully, you hear the *versicularius* intone once again: "Hail Mary, full of grace," and you answer: "The Lord is with you," knowing that he "whom earth and sea and sky adore" vouchsafed in truth to be enclosed within her womb.⁸

"Today," the great Cistercian abbot Bernard of Clairvaux (d. 1153) advised his brothers as he turned their attention to the opening verse of the Song of Songs, "we read in the book of experience (*Hodie legimus in libro experientiae*): 'Let him kiss me with the kiss of his mouth.' But," he cautioned them,

it is not given to just anyone to say these words from within (*ex affectu*). . . . I think that no one is able to understand what [this kiss] is except the one who receives it; for it is a "hidden manna" [Revelation 2:17], and only he who eats it still hungers for more. It is a "sealed fountain" [Song of Songs 4:12], to which no stranger has access; only he who drinks still thirsts for more.⁹

What was it like for medieval Christians to pray, hour after hour, day after day, to the Virgin Mother of God? Much like Bernard when confronted with the mystical kiss of the Song, this is not a question that most recent scholars, including historians, have found themselves readily equipped to answer. The odd (if often repeated) miracle story, the chipped and faded (if still much-loved) image before which her devotees were accustomed to kneel, the evocative (if historically and scripturally problematic) advice on how to imagine oneself in her earthly presence, the repetitive (if poetic) chants and psalms of her liturgy: these are the fragmentary objects and texts upon which we depend to imagine their devotional world. As the fin de siècle American tourist Henry Adams—marveling at the forces brought to bear on the medieval construction of the Virgin's cult—once put it: "All the steam in the world could not, like the Virgin, build Chartres."[10] And yet, like Adams, historians have been hard pressed to explain her appeal in other than the most psychologically reductive (or etic) terms, for example, because medieval monks and other clerics were simultaneously fascinated and repelled by the female body or because, as oblates, they had never known their mothers.[11] Did medieval Christians pray to her as if to a goddess, as the sixteenth-century reformers who rejected her cult feared they had and many twentieth-century feminist scholars have hoped modern Christians might?[12] Or was she rather for them a model or type of the Church, as Catholic theologians following Vatican II have tended to argue?[13]

To be clear, no, not at least as we see her in the sources associated with her medieval cult.[14] Even at the height of her popularity in the Middle Ages, Mary was not revered as a goddess in the pagan sense of the term, that is, as if she were not a creature but herself somehow divine—although, as well shall see, this did not mean that she was not revered as other than a humble woman, as the sixteenth-century reformers seem to have preferred. Nor was she subsumed into the Church such that every image of her was always already understood as a type of the communal Body of Christ, as certain twentieth-century Catholic studies have tended to imply.[15] As the one who remained steadfast in faith during the days of her Son's entombment, she was the first member of the Church that had been born in the water and blood that flowed from Christ's side, but for all their love of personification allegories, her medieval devotees would never have insisted that she or Christ was thereby identical with, never mind subordinate to Ecclesia. Nor would Mary's medieval devotees have accepted the preeminently Protestant claim that the scriptures say "so little" about her, any more than they would have accepted the more recent historical-critical insistence that, of the scriptures, only the texts of the New Testament contain any reliable information about the life, death, and Resurrection of the Lord Jesus Christ. If, as they believed, Christ spoke to them through the Psalms, so Mary spoke to them through Proverbs, the Song of Songs, Ecclesiasticus (Sirach), and the Wisdom of Solomon. Indeed, as we shall see, some like Richard of Saint-Laurent, a canon of the metropolitan chapter of Rouen, would insist that nearly all of the scriptures showed forth her praise insofar as they contain images of her spiritual and physical beauty and of the mystery of her relationship with God. Mary as her medieval devotees described her may not have been a goddess in her own right (that is, uncreated, herself the Creator)—much of the wonder of the Incarnation depended on the fact that she was not—but she had borne God in her womb, and for this reason she was not only blessed among women as her cousin Elizabeth exclaimed (Luke 1:42), but indeed exalted above all the choirs of the angels, as the first antiphon for the first nocturn for the feast of her Assumption proclaimed.[16]

Nor was devoting oneself to the Virgin Mary somehow necessarily easier or less terrifying than praying directly to God. Mary, like the elephant, might be "lacking in bile" as the great Dominican preacher Jacobus de Voragine (d. 1298) put it and, therefore, only accidentally "severe," but even her sweetness had its limits. Like the elephant in battle, when provoked, she too could be "terrible as the ordered ranks of the army" (Song of Songs 6:3, 9), battling on humanity's behalf against the demons but also against sinners at the judgment, for whom "at the end she would no longer pray."[17] Indeed, as our imaginative exercise has already shown, prayer to Mary might be just as much an occasion for abjection over one's sins as prayer to Christ. Certainly, this is what Anselm of Canterbury found when he attempted to write a prayer worthy of her attention. "Good Lady," he prayed, "a huge dullness is between you and me, so that I am scarcely aware of the extent of my sickness. I am so filthy and stinking that I am afraid you will turn your merciful face from me."[18] The point for medieval Christians like Anselm was not that praying to Mary made prayer easy, but rather, as we shall see, that Mary, by giving her consent to bear the Creator of all things in her body and so make the God-man visible to the world, made prayer possible in a way that it had not hitherto been before. It was for this reason that Mary's medieval devotees delighted to recite the words with which the angel Gabriel had greeted her at the moment of the Incarnation: every repetition recalled for her—and them—the joy that she had felt when divinity joined itself with humanity in her womb. It was, they insisted, not possible to praise her enough, whom God had loved so much as to take his very flesh from her.

"Prayer," as Dionysius the Carthusian (d. 1471) put it, following a tradition going back through Thomas Aquinas (d. 1274) to John of Damascus (d. 749), "is defined as 'a lifting up (*ascensus*) of the mind and soul to God.' "[19] One of the most effective ways to assist this mental and spiritual *ascensus*, or so medieval Christians believed, was to address themselves to the woman through whom God had descended to the world in flesh. Indeed, in their experience, the more often they repeated the angel's salutation to her ("Ave Maria, gratia plena"), the deeper their appreciation of the mystery of God's Incarnation became ("Dominus tecum"). While later critics following the sixteenth-century reformers have tended to see in this practice either a superstitious dependence on the efficacy of sheer repetition or, more sympathetically, a powerful if nevertheless somewhat mindless or mechanical form of self-hypnosis, medieval commentaries on the text—not to mention the Virgin's own plea that her devotees not say her salutation too fast—make it clear that, like the Virgin herself, Gabriel's greeting was pregnant with God. It was for this reason—not the Virgin's purported capriciousness in honoring her devotees—that repeating it mindfully, with devotion, could have such profound spiritual benefits. Certainly, it might seem a little thing to say "Ave Maria, gratia plena, Dominus tecum" fifty or a hundred or even a hundred and fifty times a day, but only if one had no sense of the mystery contained therein.

To judge from the sermons that they preached both within their own monastic or collegiate communities and, in the vernacular, to the laity at large, as well as the hymns, litanies, and psalters they composed in her praise, likewise the popularity of such works as Conrad of Saxony's (d. 1279) *Speculum beatae Mariae virginis*, itself an extended commentary on the angelic salutation, medieval monks, nuns, canons, and friars relished the opportunity to savor this mystery and encouraged their audiences to do likewise. As we shall see, one of the things that they enjoyed most was meditation on Mary's name, including all of the titles and typologies discovered of her in creation and in the scriptures. Mary, as they saw her, was God's handmaid, to be sure (Luke 1:38), but she was also Ark of the Covenant, Seat of Wisdom, Tower of Ivory, Litter of Solomon, Cedar of Lebanon, Garden of Delights, and Star of the Sea, not to mention Virgin of Virgins, Mother of Mercy, Queen of Heaven, and Bride of God. More to the point, Mary, as the Mother of God, the Creator of all things, was in Anselm's words the "mother of all re-created things."[20] The most perfect of all God's creatures, Mary herself was the most perfect mirror of God, the one—as the great Italian poet Dante Alighieri (d. 1321) put it in his *Paradiso*—whose "face is most like / the face of Christ" and by whose radiance humanity is prepared for the vision of God.[21] This is the way that the Benedictine abbess Hildegard of Bingen hailed her:

O how great
in its strength is the side of man,
from which God produced the form of woman.
He made her the mirror
of all his beauty
and the embrace
of his whole creation.[22]

Earth, sea, and sky; sun, moon, and stars; flowers, trees, spices, fruits; birds and beasts; precious metals and gemstones; the products of the mechanical, architectural, and liberal arts: all were invoked as symbols for or attributes of her virtues and beauty.[23] A creature herself, Mary reflected the virtues and beauty of all God's creatures; and yet, she had carried within her womb "he whom the whole world could not contain."[24] This was the mystery evoked at every recitation of the angel's words: "Dominus tecum." Little wonder if, as the Benedictine poet Gautier de Coincy (d. 1236) put it, Mary "is the sea that no one exhausts" (*mers que nus n'espuise*).[25] She it was whom God filled with himself.

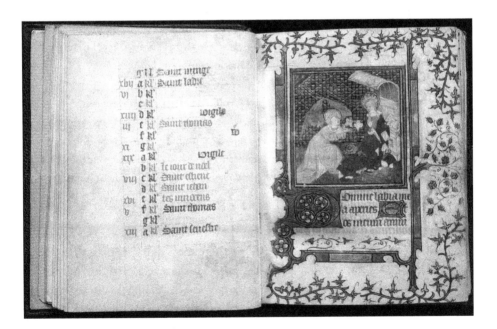

PLATE 6   Calendar, Annunciation. Book of Hours, France, ca. 1400–1414. Use of Châlons-sur-Marne. Chicago, The University of Chicago Library, Special Collections 26, fols. 12v–13r.

Photo courtesy of Special Collections Research Center, The University of Chicago Library.

Of all of the practices associated by the later Middle Ages with devotion to the Virgin—veneration of her milk, clothing, and house(s); pilgrimage to the shrines of her wonder-working statues; imaginative meditation on the events of her life leading to the conviction that she might appear to the meditants in visions—none so exercised the concern, if not the ridicule, of the sixteenth-century reformers as the recitation of the greeting of the angel Gabriel as, in effect, a prayer. In part one might argue that their concern was justified. By the later fifteenth century, the angel's salutation as recorded by Luke had been supplemented not only with Mary's proper name (Gabriel had said only, "Chaire, kecharitomene [Χαῖρε, κεχαριτωμένη]," in Jerome's translation, "Ave, gratia plena"), as well as with Elizabeth's greeting ("et benedictus fructus ventris tui," itself supplemented with Jesus' name), but also with a concluding nonscriptural plea: "Sancta Maria, Mater Dei, ora pro nobis peccatoribus nunc et in ora mortis. Amen."[26] Regardless of the fact that this second part of the Ave Maria was not to become standardized until the latter part of the sixteenth century (a standardization owing, not incidentally, to Protestant attacks on the recitation of the Ave Maria as such), the reformers, beginning with Martin Luther (d. 1546), were adamant that what the angel and Elizabeth had said to Mary was not a prayer but simply a greeting intended to honor and praise her.[27] As the English martyr Hugh Latimer (d. 1555) defended his rejection of the hitherto customary devotional use of the Ave:

> As for the *Ave Maria*, who can think that I would deny it? I said it was a heavenly greeting or saluting of our blessed lady, wherein the angel Gabriel, sent from the Father of heaven, did annunciate and shew unto her the good-will of God towards her, what he would with her, and to what he had chosen her. But I said, it was not properly a prayer, as the *Pater noster*, which our Saviour Christ himself made for a proper prayer.[28]

Arguably even more problematic than the form of the words was the way in which Christians had been accustomed to salute the Virgin. Again, in Latimer's words: "I did not speak against well saying of [the Ave Maria], but against superstitious saying of it, and of the *Pater noster* too."[29] Paramount among such superstitions according to the reformers was the repeated recitation of the Ave Maria—as, for example, in the devotions of the rosary—in the hope of acquiring spiritual merit and, thereby, indulgences. Such practices were not only vain, but impious, their observance the very definition of "popery." Accordingly, Archbishop of Canterbury Edmund Grindal's Visitation Articles of 1576 specifically inquired whether any of the clergy encouraged their parishioners "to pray in an unknown tongue, [rather] than in English, or to put their trust in a certain number of prayers, as in saying over a certain number of beads, Lady-Psalters, or other like."[30] This distrust of the mere numbering of prayers would later translate itself among the reformers' modernist descendants into a distrust of the very use of such scripted, "artificial" prayers, for how, they argued, could any "vain exercise of words" or "mere repetition of sacred formulae" have anything to do with "the very movement itself of the soul" that is the essence of "religion in act," that is, prayer?[31] More recent phenomenological investigations have tended to be somewhat more sympathetic to such regular practices as chanting the psalms or, as with the rosary, keying meditations to the repeated recitation of short phrases or mantras.[32] Contrary to the sixteenth-century reformers' conviction that such practices were at best vain, at worst the work of the devil, the tendency now is to assume that chanting Mary's name over and over again could indeed induce visions and sensations of sweetness. From this perspective, chanting almost any sacred or even not so sacred text with the proper breath control and attention would have much the same spiritual effect.[33]

Medieval Christians who devoted themselves to the recitation of the Ave Maria would have been as befuddled by the sixteenth-century reformers' insistence that it was "only" a salutation (that, after all, was its point) as they would by the more recent conviction that the specific words one uses in such exercises do not really matter. To their understanding, saluting the Virgin in Gabriel's and Elizabeth's words was not so much a prayer in the sense of a petition for something, as a service, much as chanting the Psalter as a whole in the course of the Divine Office was a service to God. The point was not, by way of such exercises, to change one's own intellectual, spiritual, or emotional state, but to please God and his Mother. To be sure, singing the Divine Office or saying the Ave Maria might have powerful—and, indeed, manifold—spiritual, emotional, and even corporeal effects: stirring the soul to contrition for sins, melting the heart to greater devotion, ravishing devout souls and causing them to receive spiritual gifts, making the heart joyous and sweet, driving away evil spirits, and overcoming the bodily and spiritual enemies of the church. But, above all, as the Birgittine *Myroure of oure Ladye* put it, "holy chyrche songe . . . pleasyth so moche god, that he desyreth and ioyeth to here yt."[34] It was for this reason that the monks and nuns of the medieval church spent their lives singing the psalms: not because they thought thereby to achieve ecstasy (although some most certainly did), but because the Psalms were the words with which God had praised himself and therefore the words he most desired to hear.[35] As Augustine of Hippo explained in his commentary on Psalm 144 (*Exaltabo te Deus*):

"So that God might be well praised by man, God praised himself [in the scriptures]; and because he has deigned to praise himself, therefore man knows how to praise him."[36]

Likewise the words with which the angel Gabriel greeted the Mother of God. As Jacobus de Voragine put it, citing "Bernard," "This salutation was composed in the council chamber (*in secretario*) of the Trinity and written by the finger of God" (cf. Exodus 31:18).[37] To recite Gabriel's salutation was neither to ask something of Mary nor to attribute it to her divinity. Rather, it was to rejoice with her and to congratulate her, as if to say, or so Richard of Saint-Laurent put it: "O blessed Virgin, I rejoice with you and give you joy in your salvation and glory."[38] If God saw fit to address her in this way through his angel, how much more ought human beings to congratulate her, being as they are in her debt for so many blessings? John the Baptist leapt in his mother's womb as Mary approached (Luke 1:41), while her Son himself rose to meet and adore her—"that is, salute her"—in heaven (3 Kings 2:19). "We ought, therefore," Jacobus chided his audience, "to blush not to salute her after such as these have saluted her."[39] Richard of Saint-Laurent was, if anything, even more forceful in his recommendations for saluting the Virgin. "When, therefore, we say *Ave, Maria*," he insisted, "we ought to humble ourselves before her like servants (*servi*) before their Lady."[40] Nor was this humiliation to be strictly spiritual:

> For [Richard argued] if we salute so affectionately and diligently, if we bare our heads, if we bow and rise to our feet and bend our knees and repeat our salutation again and again to the intimate friends and relatives and companions of the great whose counsel or support we need at court, and we seek to obtain their benevolence with gifts and services, and we prevail in this way, what should we do for the mother at the court of her only Son, whom not only can she supplicate effectively, but also command with her maternal authority?[41]

Just as Mary herself served humanity in her body by giving flesh to her Son, so (Richard averred) Christians ought to serve her not only in their hearts, but also with all of their bodily members and all of their senses: bowing their heads before her images whenever they passed them; averting their eyes from all vanities and praying with groans and tears; closing their ears to all obnoxious sounds and their noses to all meretricious scents; restraining their appetites so as not to give in to drunkenness or gluttony; doing good works with their hands; embracing their enemies with their arms; bending their knees before her altars and images and whenever they recited her name, "because she says with the Son: 'To me every knee shall bow' (Isaiah 45:24)."[42]

Saying the Ave

Stories told of the lives of the holy—and the not-so-holy—bear ample witness to these practices, particularly the reverence given to Mary's images and the genuflections with which she was regularly greeted. Moreover, as Herbert Thurston argued more than a century ago following the great Benedictine historians Luc d'Achery (d. 1685) and Jean Mabillon (d. 1707), such stories likewise prove that the recitation of the Ave Maria as such had its origins not as a freestanding devotion, but rather in the genuflections or bows offered with the invitatory antiphon at the outset of the Office of the Virgin, as, for example, in both London, British Library, Cotton Tiberius A.iii and Royal 2 B.V.[43] Once again, as with the Hours of the Virgin, Peter Damian is one of our earliest witnesses to this development. As Peter or, rather his friend Stephen, cardinal priest of the Apostolic see, told it:

> I remember hearing of a certain cleric, who was simple, good for nothing, flighty and tactless. In addition, he seemed to have no talent for the religious life, no quality that reflected the gravity and decorum pertaining to canonical discipline. But among these dead ashes of a useless life, one tiny flame continued to burn. Daily he would go to the holy altar of the blessed Mother of God, and there reverently bowing his head would recite this angelic and Gospel verse (*angelicum atque evangelicum versiculum*): "Hail Mary, full of grace, the Lord is with you: blessed are you among women."

Eventually, the cleric's bishop caught wind of his uselessness and deprived of him the benefice upon which he depended to live, at which the Virgin was not pleased. Appearing to the bishop in his sleep along with a man carrying a torch in one hand and a rod in the other, she ordered him to be whipped and chastised him for depriving "my chaplain who daily prayed to me" of his stipend. "Therefore," Peter concluded, "if this cleric was rewarded with food for his body just for having sung one prayerful verse, with what confidence can those who daily recite all the hours of the office to the blessed queen of the world look forward to eternal refreshment?"[44]

As with the full Office of the Virgin, this "abbreviated Office" was to become popular among monastics, clergy, and laity alike over the course of the next century or so, such that even those who could say only the invitatory antiphon were able to participate in Mary's service.[45] As early as 1125, Franco, abbot of the Brabantine house of Afflighem, insisted: "Of good right does every condition, every age, every degree honour Mary with the angelical salutation; of good right does every voice, every tongue, every conscious being cry aloud to Mary with

the angel: 'Ave Maria, gratia plena, Dominus tecum; benedicta tu in mulieribus.' "[46] As Baldwin of Ford (d. 1190, Acre), bishop of Worcester and archbishop
of Canterbury, put it in one of the earliest extended commentaries on the Ave
Maria: "The matter of our salvation begins with a salutation, and the commencement of our reconciliation is consecrated by a proclamation of peace. . . . O saving
greeting, spoken by the angel, instructing us in how we should greet the Virgin!
O joy of the heart, sweetness to the mouth, seasoning of love!"[47] The Benedictine
nun and visionary Elisabeth of Schönau (d. 1165), who was accustomed to salute
the Virgin in this way, enjoyed a vision of Mary standing at an altar and arrayed
in a vestment "like a priestly chasuble," while on her head she wore a "glorious
crown decorated with four precious gems, and the angelic salutation, 'Hail Mary,
full of grace, the Lord is with you,' was inscribed around it."[48]

Much as Richard of Saint-Laurent had insisted they should be, these recitations
of the Ave Maria were typically accompanied by genuflections, usually before her
images, sometimes multiplied tens or even hundreds of times. As the biographer
of the Premonstratensian canon Hermann Joseph (d. 1241) explained:

> It is the common custom in our order, and I think that the same is true of
> other orders also, that as often as the venerable name of the Most Holy Virgin
> is mentioned in the Collect, in the Creed, in the Preface, and in the Angelic
> Salutation which is said for the Invitatory (*in Salutatione Angelica, quæ dicitur pro
> Invitatorio*), the community makes a momentary reverence (*veniam*) in peniten-
> tial or ferial seasons by falling upon their knees, and on festivals with the hand.

Hermann himself was accustomed to make a full prostration at every mention of
Mary's name, at which he experienced a scent of extraordinary sweetness, more
pleasing than that of any flower or other perfume.[49] According to her biographer Jacques de Vitry, the beguine Marie d'Oignies was sometimes so overcome
with devotion that she would salute the blessed Virgin eleven hundred times a
day, keeping this observance for forty days in a row. First, she would genuflect
six hundred times without pause; second, she would recite the whole Psalter,
standing, genuflecting, and offering the angelic salutation at the conclusion of
each psalm; third, moved even more strongly by the spirit of devotion, she would
genuflect three hundred times while striking herself with the rod of discipline,
going so far as to draw blood with the last three blows "to give flavor to the others"; finally, she would consummate the sacrifice (*sacrificium consummabat*) with
fifty more simple genuflections.[50] Less spectacularly if no less devoutly, the teen-
aged beguine Margaret of Ypres said every day four hundred Pater Nosters and
four hundred Ave Marias "with the same number of genuflections, as well as fifty

psalms," most likely short verses accompanied by salutations to the Virgin. Worn out by these devotions, Margaret sometimes found it difficult to stand. "At such times," according to her biographer Thomas of Cantimpré, "she could palpably feel the touch of two angels, one on her right side and one on her left, lifting her by the elbows," who would sustain her until she could recite ten more salutations to Mary, at which she would revive and be able to finish her prayers.[51] The Cistercian nun Beatrice of Nazareth maintained a similar observance, reciting every day, "with genuflections, the psalter of the Blessed Virgin (*psalterium beate virginis*) which," her biographer explained, "consists of as many repetitions of the angelic salutation as there are psalms in David's psalter."[52]

Strange as these devotional exercises may seem today, it would seem that in the Middle Ages the Virgin Mother was greatly pleased by such attentions, as those who related the stories of her miracles were eager to attest.[53] The Cistercian Caesarius of Heisterbach (d. ca. 1240) told the story of a certain recluse who lived next to the church of Saint Severinus in Cologne "during the time of the schism between Alexander and Paschal," whom the matrons of the city would often visit. One of these women confessed to the recluse "she could not say the name of Our Lady without tasting a wonderful sweetness." Upon being asked the cause of such a great favor, she responded: "Every day in her honor I have been accustomed to say Ave Maria fifty times with the same number of genuflections (*veniis*), through which I have earned such sweetness that all the spittle of my mouth seems to be turned to honey during the time of prayer." Encouraged by the matron's example, the recluse took up the exercise himself. After six weeks, he, too, began to sense in his mouth and throat a sweetness "far surpassing the sweetness of honey" every time he greeted the Virgin.[54]

Other effects of saluting the Virgin were even more tangible, if not always enjoyed by their recipients while they were alive. A certain monk who always devoutly said her Hours was healed of a tumor in his throat by a drop of her milk.[55] A monk who fell into a river and drowned on his way to see his mistress was rescued from the demons who came to demand his soul because, as the Virgin said, "I know that he never left the monastery without saluting me."[56] A certain cleric who drowned while drunk was buried in unconsecrated ground until, that is, his body was exhumed and a tag was found hanging from his mouth inscribed with the words with which he had been accustomed to salute the Virgin: "Ave Maria, gratia plena, Dominus tecum."[57] An unlettered knight who had entered the Cistercian order but could learn only the two words "Ave Maria" was found after his burial to have a lily growing from his mouth on one leaf of which were inscribed in letters of gold the same two words with which he had so devoutly honored the Virgin.[58]

Sometimes the circumstances were even more complicated, often leading more recent readers to insist that Mary rewarded her devotees without regard for their overall spiritual or moral status.[59] And yet, as Anne Clark has elegantly shown, such stories of Mary's favor "often suggest a more subtle message in which devotion to Mary is part of a complex religiosity."[60] One such story, first recounted by the Benedictine Guibert of Nogent (d. 1124) and retold numerous times thereafter, including in the vernacular, concerned an adulteress, the wife of whose lover prayed to the Virgin to punish her, only to be told that the Virgin couldn't:

> Why [the Virgin reproved the wife in a vision] do you ask me for revenge over that woman? Clearly I can do nothing against her because daily she announces to me my joy, than which nothing is more pleasing for me to hear from any creature. Do you think that against her on your behalf I ought to be provoked, who, as if to remind me, cries out so sedulously concerning my ineffable glory?[61]

Other versions of the story recounted how the adulteress made her devotions before the image of the Virgin "every day on bare knees" (Jean Gobi), "[bowing] a hundred times, with her forehead touching the ground" (Alfonso X). All, however, emphasized how her devotions rendered her apparently immune against the Virgin's anger.[62] Understandably incensed at the Virgin's reply and vowing to withdraw her own devotional attentions since the Virgin would not (again, apparently) help her, the wife railed against her rival when she met her entering the church: "O most foul one, how many torments will you inflict on my soul?"

> I had only one hope, that the Virgin Mother of God might cast sentence of revenge against you, but already I have failed utterly in this hope, for she told me that that *Ave*, with which you capture her attention every day, has softened her to such a degree that it is unbefitting for her to do anything against you.[63]

At which—perhaps contrary to expectations if not to the logic of the story—the adulteress immediately repented and, in one version at least, knelt before the Virgin's image and vowed to become a nun.[64] As the *cantigas* of King Alfonso X el Sabio (d. 1284) told it: "Thus the Virgin caused these two women to mend their quarrel, whereas formerly they had snarled at each other with hatred as bitter as green grape juice."[65] As Clark has observed, the point of the story is not that saluting the Virgin allows the adulteress somehow to "get away" with her sin, but rather that her devotions accomplish not only her conversion but also her reconciliation with the woman whom she had wronged. Like the knight who converted from a life of robbery upon learning that the only thing protecting him from a demon sent to capture his soul was his daily recitation of the Ave Maria, so with the adulteress: there was nothing that pleased the Virgin and dismayed the demons so much as reminding the Mother of God of her greatest joy.[66]

Nor was it enough to say the angelic salutation a certain number of times without proper attention or in a rush. Again, King Alfonso's *cantigas* related a story that was widely known of a nun (in other versions, named Eulalia, sometimes of Saxony, at others of Saint Edward's at Shaftesbury) who was accustomed to say every day a thousand Ave Marias with much "weeping and moaning and a great deal of sighing." One night, however, the Virgin herself appeared to the nun (some said while she was asleep; others, including Alfonso's *cantiga*, that she was not) and reproved her:

> If you wish me to be pleased by your prayer, when you say the salutation which the holy angel gave me, say it calmly and do not hurry, for we assure you that when I hear how God visited me, I derive so much pleasure therefrom . . . that I tell you it seems to me then that I have God the Father [*sic*], Beloved and Son, within my body again. Therefore, we beseech you that you adopt a way of praying very slowly. . . . Leave out two parts of what you formerly said and say well the third, and we shall love you more for this.[67]

As other versions made clear, the delight that the Virgin experienced on hearing the words *Dominus tecum* "uttered lingeringly" (*prolixius*) was itself impossible to express in words, so great a thrill of joy (*magnum gaudium*) had she experienced on feeling her Son within her when he deigned to be born from her for the salvation of humankind.[68] Think of the butterflies that you feel in your gut on catching sight of your beloved or, if you have been pregnant, the feeling of your child moving in your womb for the first time multiplied beyond reckoning, as if somehow you could contain the whole of creation in your very body. This—her medieval devotees were convinced—was what the Virgin felt every time they saluted her with these words. As the Carthusian Ludolph of Saxony (d. 1377) put it in his popular *Vita Christi*, citing "Bernard": "For you, Virgin Mary, to hear this angelic verse, the *Ave*, was like a kiss. Indeed, most blessed one, you are kissed as often as you are devoutly greeted by the *Ave*. Therefore," he urged his readers, "go to her image, bend your knees, and press kisses upon it, and say the *Ave*."[69]

Significantly, it was not only the Virgin who benefited from such recitations, as the nun Gertrude of Helfta learned one year as she and her sisters celebrated the Feast of the Annunciation. On the vigil of the feast, when the martyrology was read, Gertrude saw Christ turn to his Mother and "[salute] her with a most pleasing inclination of his head, as if to renew in her that sweet and inestimable joy which she had felt when His incomprehensible Divinity took flesh in her womb, and united itself to our nature."[70] Even more striking, or so one of her sisters recorded, was the vision that Gertrude experienced as the nuns intoned the invitatory for the Office of the feast itself:[71]

> While the *Ave Maria* was chanted at Matins, Gertrude beheld three most effica-
> cious streams, which flowed with a sweet impetuosity from the Father, the Son,
> and the Holy Spirit into the heart of the Blessed Virgin, and flowed back again
> from her heart with the same efficacious impetuosity to their original source. By
> this inflowing of the Holy Trinity, it was given to the Blessed Virgin to be the
> most powerful after the Father, most wise after the Son, and most benign after
> the Holy Spirit. Gertrude understood also that every time the angelic salutation,
> that is, the *Ave Maria*, is recited with devotion by the faithful on earth, that
> these aforesaid streams overflowing with an even more efficacious force, flowed
> over the Blessed Virgin and into her most holy heart, and thus with a wonder-
> ful sweetness returned to their source. From that overflowing, little streams of
> joy, of delight, and of eternal salvation are splashed over on the persons of all
> the saints and angels, and especially on those on earth who are mindful of the
> angelic salutation, through which in every one is renewed every good which they
> have obtained through the Incarnation of the Son of God.[72]

At Gertrude's wondering what form of devotion would be most acceptable to the Virgin at this time, the Mother of God instructed her to say forty-five Ave Marias each day during the octave of the feast, that is, forty-five times six or 270 repetitions of the salutation, the same as the number of days that her Son spent in her womb.[73]

Once again, such service was so pleasing to the Virgin as to render her inca-pable of refusing anything that her devotees might ask, for indeed, the Virgin explained, "they would [thereby have rendered] her the same service as if they had attended her with the greatest care from the moment of conception to the time of the birth." Accordingly, the Virgin went on, this was the way in which Gertrude should say the salutation. At the word "Ave" she should desire "the alle-viation of those weighed down with heaviness." At the word "Maria" she should look for "the penitent to continue in good works." At the words *gratia plena* she should long for "the taste of grace for those who had it not." At the words *Domi-nus tecum* she should ask "indulgence for all sinners," while at *benedicta tu in mulieribus* she should desire "grace for those who had begun to live well." At *ben-edictus fructus ventris tui* she should long for "the perfection of the elect." Finally, she should conclude each Ave with the words *Jesus, splendor paternae charitatis*

[Jesus, splendor of fatherly love] "for true knowledge," and *figura substantiae ejus* [figure of his substance] "for Divine love."[74] Another time, when Gertrude had offered the Virgin a hundred and fifty Aves, "praying that she might be present in her maternal piety at the hour of [Gertrude's] death," every word that she repeated appeared "like a piece of gold offered before the tribunal of the Judge, and commended by him to his Mother," who, like a good steward, kept them until that time as she should need them for Gertrude's consolation and aid at her death.[75] In return Gertrude offered similar sets of Aves along with the one hundred fifty psalms to assist her sisters at their death.[76]

Learning the Ave

Under such circumstances it was therefore hardly a small thing—as it were, merely an educational minimum—to insist, as did diocese after diocese over the course of the thirteenth century, that every Christian man and woman know how to recite the angelic salutation and do so as the council held at Coventry in 1237 mandated, "seven times a day," as per the injunction of "the Prophet, who said, 'I have praised you seven times a day.' "[77] Such legislation makes clear once again that saying the Ave Maria was understood as itself an abbreviated form of the full canonical office of seven hours offered in praise of the Virgin. So, for example, according to the *Ancrene Wisse*, while the recluses themselves were expected to say the Hours of the Virgin kneeling or bowing every time they said Mary's name, as we have seen, those who did not know the full Office or for some reason or other could not say it were to recite thirty Pater Nosters, with an Ave Maria after each Pater, and a Gloria Patri after each Ave for Matins; likewise, they were to say twenty Paters, Aves, and Glorias for Vespers and fifteen each at every other hour. Presumably these recitations did not include the five Aves that every anchoress was expected to say each morning kneeling before Mary's statue and the Pater and Ave that she was to say before and after each of the seven daily hours, nor the multiple repetitions of Paters and Aves throughout the day accompanying her other devotions to God and the Virgin, but this is not clear. The sisters were, however, allowed to cut ten repetitions along with their genuflections from Matins and five each from the other hours if they were ill.[78]

Likewise, as we have seen, there were the statutes promulgated at more or less the same time throughout Europe allowing all those serving in hospitals to substitute recitations of the Pater Noster and Ave Maria for the offices they might otherwise not be able to say.[79] As the statutes for the hospital of Notre-Dame founded in 1237 by the countess Jeanne of Lille explained, the sisters and lay brother who knew them were to say the Hours of the Virgin, while those who did not were to observe the following ordo: twenty-five Pater Nosters and as many Ave Marias or seven psalms or seven repetitions of *Miserere mei Deus* (Psalm 50) at Matins; seven Pater Nosters and as many Ave Marias or two repetitions of *Miserere mei Deus* at each of the hours of Prime, Terce, Sext, None, and Compline; ten Pater Nosters and as many Ave Marias or three repetitions of *Miserere mei Deus* at Vespers, thus fulfilling the service of the canonical hours despite the fact that they did not (yet?) know the full text of the Marian Office.[80]

Similar concerns would appear to be behind the rules of life for the various confraternities of the Virgin established over the course of the thirteenth and fourteenth centuries.[81] The instructions for the observance kept by the Dominican confraternities of Pisa according to the rule established in 1312 are particularly telling. While the clergy were to recite the full Divine Office and those who were not clergy but were able to read were to say the Hours of the Virgin, the other members of the confraternity were to say every day twenty-five Pater Nosters and twenty-five Ave Marias with a Gloria Patri followed by a brief *lauda*: "Benedetto sia lo nome del nostro segnore Ihesus Christo e della sua dolce madre Vergine Maria." The Pater Nosters and Ave Marias were to be distributed over the course of the day, with five each to be said at Matins and Vespers, and three for each of the four Little Hours plus Compline.[82] Similar provisions were made by Munio de Zamora in 1285 in his rule for the order of the brothers and sisters of the Penitents of Saint Dominic. The brothers and sisters were required to say the canonical hours (*horas canonicas*) daily, consisting of twenty-eight Pater Nosters and Ave Marias for Matins, fourteen Pater Nosters and Ave Marias for Vespers, and seven Pater Nosters and Ave Marias for each of the other hours.[83]

Notably, both of these confraternity rules also include instructions for saying additional Pater Nosters and Ave Marias. At Pisa, while the clergy and laity who knew them were to say the Seven Penitential Psalms every day "for the living and the dead of our company," everyone else was to substitute seven Pater Nosters and seven Ave Marias following the *Requiem aeternam*.[84] Likewise at Pisa, everyone was to say a Pater Noster, an Ave Maria and the Gloria Patri both before and after eating, along with the *lauda*: "Benedecto sia quel segnore, che ci à creato, recomperato e pasciuto, e ongne fedele anima defunta per la misericordia di Dio riposi in sancta pace. Amen."[85] Among the order of the Penitents of Saint Dominic, those who knew them would say either *Miserere mei Deus* (Psalm 50) or *Laudate* (Psalm 148 or 150?) before and after meals, while the others would say a Pater Noster.[86] As with the provisions made for the hours at Lille, so with the rules of the confraternities and order of Penitents, structurally the Pater Nosters and Ave Marias were clearly standing in for the psalms that the brothers and sisters would otherwise say, pointing at once to the importance attached to praying according to the canonical horarium and to the way in which saying the Ave Maria, like the Divine Office itself, was understood as a service to God.

Instruction in saying the Pater Noster and Ave Maria was accordingly widespread, including in some regions efforts to make the texts available in the vernacular, whether as a part of the Office of the Virgin or incorporated into more extended, often poetic meditations on the Ave Maria itself.[87] Arguably even more significant was the provision made by the friars, particularly in the context of the Marian confraternities, for preaching every Wednesday (Dominicans) or Friday (Franciscans) of the week, in addition to the sermons that were preached every day throughout Lent and on feast days.[88] Such sermons might range over the whole content of the liturgical year, necessarily including each of the four major feasts of the Virgin (Purification, Annunciation, Assumption, and Nativity). At least once a year, on the Annunciation (March 25), congregations would hear a sermon on the significance of the angel's greeting. Some of these sermons were preached extempore, but some were collected and published as models for subsequent delivery, thus providing an important glimpse into the way in which late medieval audiences were taught to think about the Ave Maria and the Virgin Mother to whom it was addressed.[89]

But this was not all. For those friars and other clergy interested in exploring the mystery of the angelic salutation in more depth, perhaps simply for themselves, perhaps in preparation for their own sermons, in addition to these model sermons, a number of thirteenth-century commentators penned whole treatises explicating Gabriel's and Elizabeth's words, one of the most prominent of which was the commentary on the Ave Maria or *Speculum seu salutatio beatae Mariae virginis* written by the Franciscan Conrad of Saxony.[90] In similar fashion, the Rouen canon Richard of Saint-Laurent framed his *De laudibus beatae Mariae virginis* as an exposition of the angelic salutation, while an anonymous Austrian or Bavarian monastic contemporary compiled some two hundred thirty *quaestiones* on the particulars of the evangelical event.[91] Friars like Conrad seem to have particularly enjoyed meditations on Mary's name. The Franciscan preacher Servasanctus of Faenza (d. ca. 1300) compiled a whole psalter of titles based on a declension of the grammatical elements (letters, syllables, words, phrases) in the salvific exordium (Luke 1:28), while late in life, the Dominican Jacobus de Voragine added to the Marian sermons that he had preached during the liturgical year a compilation of one hundred sixty meditations on her various titles, symbols, and attributes, arranged according to the letters of the alphabet.[92] For Servasanctus, as, indeed, for Richard, unlocking the mystery of the angel's Ave involved understanding the whole of creation, while for Jacobus, every recitation of the angelic salutation invoked a veritable encyclopedia of names for the Virgin Mother of God.

Almost unknown today, all five of these works enjoyed a marked popularity throughout the later Middle Ages and well into the seventeenth century. Long believed to be the work of the Franciscan Saint Bonaventure, Conrad's *Speculum* survives in some 247 known manuscripts, the vast majority from the fourteenth and fifteenth centuries, with provenances from across both eastern and western Europe.[93] Running to some 840 double-columned pages in the 1898 edition, Richard's *De laudibus beatae Mariae virginis* was nevertheless copied into manuscript upward of thirty times, while the *Mariale, sive CCXXX quaestiones super Evangelium "Missus est Angelus Gabriel,"* running to more than three hundred double-columned pages in the same 1898 edition, is known in as many as thirty-two extant copies, including copies made before 1300 in both Cologne and Paris.[94] Servasanctus's one hundred-fifty-chapter *Mariale* is extant in some fifteen known manuscripts with provenances ranging from the Franciscan convent of Santa Croce in Florence to the cathedral library in Valencia, the Augustinian house at Glatz (Bohemia), the Benedictine community of Bury St. Edmunds, the Carmelite house in Paris, the Augustinian house at Bordeaux, and the monastery of Saint Cyprian in Murano (this last copy also includes an incomplete version of Richard's *De laudibus*).[95] Albeit hardly as well known as his *Legenda aurea*, Jacobus's alphabetic *Mariale* also enjoyed a wide circulation, surviving in as many as sixty fourteenth- and fifteenth-century manuscripts, as well as at least three early printed editions.[96] Conrad's *Speculum* was printed four times by 1521 as the work of Bonaventure,[97] while Richard's *De laudibus beatae Mariae virginis* passed into print as early as 1473 along with the *Mariale, sive CCXXX quaestiones super Evangelium* as the work of the Dominican Albert the Great.[98] Although Richard's *De laudibus beatae Mariae virginis* was published under his own name by Jean Bogard in 1625 (as well as among the works of Albert in 1651),[99] the *Mariale, sive CCXXX quaestiones super Evangelium* was accepted as the work of Albert until 1952.[100] Meanwhile, the copy of Servasanctus's *Mariale*, which had made its way from Bologna to Glatz as a gift of Archbishop Ernestus of Prague (d. 1364), was printed in 1651 as the work of the archbishop himself.[101]

It would be easy to go on. Almost every aspect of late medieval European Christian religious life was marked—and enhanced—by salutation of the Virgin. From the invitatory sung at Matins to the threefold Ave Marias recited with the Franciscans' encouragement at the ringing of the bells at the end of the day (the "Angelus"), from the multiple genuflections made before the images of Mary to the ubiquitous altarpieces and Books of Hours depicting the angel kneeling before the Virgin in imitation of her earthly devotees, from the Mary-psalters of the twelfth, thirteenth, and fourteenth centuries to the fully developed rosary of the fifteenth said while fingering one's beads, the mystery of the words spoken by the angel was invoked aurally, visually, corporeally, and haptically day after day.[102] So familiar, indeed, was the practice of saying the Ave Maria that it might even be used, as one late fourteenth-century handbook for household management famously put it, to time how long one should allow eggs to cook or sugar to melt for a glaze.[103] And yet, for all its familiarity, the Ave Maria never ceased to enchant. Just as the Virgin herself never wearied of being reminded of her joy, so her devotees—monks, nuns, friars, canons, clerics, beguines, anchoresses, lay brothers and sisters, kings, ladies, knights, matrons, and members of her confraternities—seem never to have wearied of saluting her, for, as their poetic reiterations of the angel's greeting, likewise their commentaries, sermons, and treatises made clear, these were words that contained a mystery in which they themselves longed to participate and yet which mere words could hardly contain.

"Let him kiss me with the kiss of his mouth" (Song of Songs 1:1). This—or so her medieval devotees averred—is what Mary exclaimed when she understood herself about to bear in her womb "him whom kings and prophets had not deserved to hear or see."[104] "What is this exclamation so great, so unlooked for?," wondered the Benedictine abbot Rupert of Deutz at the beginning of his commentary on the Song of Songs *de Incarnatione Domini*:

> O blessed Mary, the inundation of joy, the force of love, the torrent of delight covered you entirely, possessed you totally, intoxicated you inwardly, and you sensed what eye has not seen and ear has not heard and what has not entered into the heart of man, and you said: "Let him kiss me with the kiss of his mouth."[105]

This was the mystery of Mary's overshadowing, the mystery of the kiss with which the Trinity espoused her at the moment of the Incarnation. As the great teacher (*Doctor Universalis*) Alan of Lille (d. 1203) explained in his commentary on the Song of Songs, the kiss of verse 1:1 was a triple kiss, the first kiss being that of the Incarnation by which the divine is joined to human nature; the second, that of the Holy Spirit, by which the Son kisses the Father and the Father loves the Son; the third, that of the presence of the doctrine of Christ. "These are the kisses," Alan elaborated, "by which the Father kisses the Son, the bridegroom the bride, the Lord the handmaiden, the son the mother, the nursling the nurse." Accordingly, these were the kisses that Mary invited on hearing the angel's "Ave."[106]

The Premonstratensian prior Philip of Harvengt (d. 1183) was, if anything, even more explicit, particularly about the identity of Mary's divine lover.

According to Philip, "hearing that she had been betrothed to the Son of God and was to give birth to God and man," the Virgin burned with the Spirit or rather with love, for that which the angel had promised was to be accomplished in her. As the Virgin herself remembered the moment: "The voice of the angel that had told me of such great blessings fell silent, and the Son of God who betrothed himself to me a virgin approached," at which she cried out:

> Let him kiss me with the kiss of his mouth. . . . Let him touch me with his mouth; let his touch fill me with great grace; let him deem me worthy of his kiss; let him make me fertile with his spirit. For indeed there is in a kiss of the mouth not only the exterior joining of the lips, but also a certain internal exhalation, which if it is pure will be filled with a sweet taste, as if the one kissing pours a sweet spirit into the one kissed.[107]

Who could not—Philip's contemporary Amadeus, the Cistercian bishop of Lausanne (d. 1159), enthused—want to know what Mary's experience at this moment had been like? As Amadeus apostrophized the Virgin ("the most precious impress of the divine seal [*agalma*], the most holy vessel in which the Word of God was conceived") in the third of eight homilies that he composed in her praise:

> We pray you, Lady, most worthy Mother of God, not to scorn those who seek in fearfulness, ask in piety, knock in love; we ask, by what feeling were you moved, by what love were you held, by what incitement were you stirred when these things took place in you and the Word took flesh from you? Where was your soul, where your heart, where your mind, where your sense, where your reason?[108]

Amadeus was not the first nor the last to be seized by this pious curiosity.[109] Some two hundred years later, Mary's devotees were still wondering, in response to which the Carthusian Ludolph of Saxony suggested a remedy, purportedly citing Amadeus's own teacher, Bernard:

> O, if you were strong enough to sense of what sort and how great was that fire sent from heaven, that consolation conferred, that solace infused! how great the lifting up of the Virgin Mother, how great the ennoblement of the human race, how great the condescension of majesty! If you are able to hear the Virgin singing with joy, I think that you should begin to rejoice with her equally for so great a blessing and never cease to sing thanks to God. So that therefore you may be able to renew such a great joy for the Virgin and recall it to mind, do not neglect to salute her repeatedly with the sweet verse of the Angel and to imprint kisses of devout salutation on her feet, saying: *Ave, Maria.*[110]

Two hundred years earlier, Amadeus' contemporary and fellow Cistercian Aelred of Rievaulx (cited by Ludolph as "Anselm") had been equally insistent in advising his sister in her life as a recluse on how she was to imagine the arrival of the angel in the Virgin's chamber:

> Hear him as he utters his greeting, and so, filled with amazement and rapt out of yourself, greet your most sweet Lady together with the angel. Cry out with a loud voice: "Hail, full of grace, the Lord is with you, blessed are you among women." Repeat this several times and consider what this fullness of grace is in which the whole world shared when the Word was made flesh and dwelt among us, full of grace and truth. Wonder at the Lord who fills earth and heaven being enclosed within the womb of a maiden, whom the Father sanctified, the Son made fertile, and the Holy Spirit overshadowed.[111]

It would be surprising indeed if such regular practice did not leave a sweet taste in the mouth.

PLATE 7 Annunciation, "Incipit horae beatae marie virginis." Book of Hours, Belgium, ca. 1475. Use of Ghent. Chicago, The University of Chicago Library, Special Collections 184, fols. 61v–62r.

NAMING MARY: MARIA

Sweet it may have been to repeat the angel's salutation in this way, but who, after all, was this maiden to whom Gabriel had been sent? Even with the angel's example it was—or so her medieval devotees soon realized—another thing altogether to adequately describe, not to mention praise, the one saluted daily in their recitation of her Hours in whose womb "the Lord who fills earth and heaven" had been enclosed. For many, like the Franciscan Walter of Wimborne (fl. 1260s), it was difficult to even know where to begin. As Walter confessed at the outset of his *Marie Carmina*, a poetic retelling of the life of Mary and Christ:

Once I wrote a song of Mary
Six in feet, its truth contrary.
Now verse I draw from quiver rude;
O grace, let me a poet prove.
In praise I sharpen blunted pen
To cry the Virgin's praise again.
But, oh, that words would harmonize
In style with that which I do prize.
Vile, brief, and rude though writing be,
In praise of you, it's oratory.
And all the writer bums become
Like tongues of angels, cherubim.
If all the world turned into quills
And atoms scribes, for all their skills
This host could not her praise reveal
Nor even match the Virgin's heel.
As many scribes as there are leaves,
Rocks, pebbles, groves, or dripping seas
Could not the Virgin worthily
Describe in all eternity.
If scribes were numbered with the stars
That twinkle in the face of Mars
Or drops of rain that on earth fall,
The matter's weight would crush them all.
To praise, therefore, love urges me
The Virgin in her majesty;
And mildly she calls me to stand,

The offered reed to take in hand.
But I that pen accept with fear;
To her dictation I adhere,
Incapable of finding sense,
With her support my sole defense.
My reed is blunt and rather slow;
My love lukewarm, my thinking low.
A student rude, I take my seat
To write that which she says is meet.[112]

But why was it so difficult to write about Mary? Surely, as the sixteenth-century reformers would insist, everything that one needed to know about her had been encompassed in her response to the angel's greeting (Luke 1:38: "Behold, the handmaid of the Lord"): namely, that she was humble and obedient, a true handmaiden (*ancilla*) of God, most likely engaged in housework when the angel arrived.[113] What more needed to be said? In a word: everything. Praising Mary, or so her medieval devotees contended, was more than simply a matter of showing the proper respect to the woman in whom God had taken up his dwelling on earth. It was in a very real sense an exercise in praising God, for it was after all he to whom she had given birth.

What did it mean to say with the prophet Jeremiah, "the Lord has created a new thing on the earth: a woman shall compass a man" (31:22), when that "man" was himself the Creator of heaven and earth? Or with Ecclesiasticus, "he that made me rested in my tabernacle" (24:12), when that "tabernacle" was the space of the Virgin's womb? Visually, the magnitude of the mystery is perhaps best expressed through contemporary iconography of the *mappa mundi*. For example, in the monumental map made in the late thirteenth century for the Benedictine convent at Ebstorf in Lower Saxony, the world itself is shown as the body of Christ with his head, hands, and feet peeking just over the oceanic frame, and in the late thirteenth-century map now in the cathedral at Hereford, as it was originally framed, Gabriel and Mary stood on either side of the world, enclosing the creation in the moment of the angel's greeting.[114] Representations of Christ as Creator such as those that appear as frontispieces for a number of the more lavishly illustrated thirteenth-century *Bibles moralisée* make a similar point: Christ enthroned holds the cosmos in his bosom with his left hand while he measures its dimensions with an architect's compass in his right.[115] And yet, it was in just this way, or so her devotees marveled, that Mary had carried Christ in her womb and supported him as a baby on her lap, just as they beheld her doing every day in the sculpted and painted images before which they knelt in prayer.[116]

The miracle was not just that a virgin had become pregnant and given birth, but rather that he who was the Creator of all things had entered into his own creation—the Artist into his Work—by way of one of his own creatures and, further, had lived for nine months in her womb. What kind of artist (*artifex*) not only could, but would be willing to become subject in this way to the material limitations of his own art? It would be as if the Oxford philologist J. R. R. Tolkien (d. 1973) were somehow not simply the author of *The Lord of the Rings*, but there in the story with Frodo, Sam, and Gollum, struggling their way into Mordor; or with Eowyn and Merry, fighting the Witch King to the death; or with Pippin trying to persuade Gandalf to come to Faramir's aid. But, again, this is what medieval Christians believed: that the Maker had somehow entered "into the thing that He [had] made . . . than which He is beyond measure greater," like the "singer into his tale or the designer into his picture. How"—or so the devout Catholic Tolkien imagined his artistic subcreation the woman Andreth wondering as she whispered of this hope to the Elf Finrod—"could He the greater do this? Would it not shatter Arda [the world], or indeed all of Eä [creation]?"[117]

Medieval Christians wondered much the same thing. How could the Maker of heaven and earth enter into his creation—physically, materially, corporeally, historically—without shattering the very thing he had made? Their answer: through Mary. "O Lady," Anselm of Canterbury marveled in the third of the three great prayers that he wrote in her praise, "you showed to the sight of all the world its Creator whom it had not seen. . . . [By] you the elements are renewed, hell is redeemed, demons are trampled down and men are saved. . . . O woman full and overflowing with grace, plenty flows from you to make all creatures green again." Over and over again in his prayer, Anselm emphasizes that it was Mary through whom the Creator of all things came into the world. She it was who was the "gateway of life, door of salvation, way of reconciliation, approach to recovery" and "the palace of universal propitiation, cause of general reconciliation, vase and temple of life and universal salvation." For Anselm, the metaphors invoked through Mary's many titles were hardly as passive as some more recent critics of this traditional imagery have argued, but paradoxically—awe-inspiringly—active.[118] Mary was no mere passage to be taken and then forgotten, no mere vessel to be filled and then discarded by God. Rather, as both container (*aula, vas, templum*) and way (*porta, ianua, via, aditus*) she was herself an agent in making God visible to his creatures: "You showed to the world its Lord and its God whom it had not known." Without Mary, God would have remained invisible, "Father of all created things," yet still "only ruling invisibly over them all." Through Mary, God revealed himself to the world as at once its Creator and Redeemer: "God who made all things made himself of Mary and

thus he refashioned everything he had made. . . . So God is the Father of all created things, and Mary is the mother of all re-created things. . . . For God gave
birth to him by whom all things were made and Mary brought forth him by
whom all are saved." According to Anselm, it was for this reason that "nothing
equals Mary, nothing but God is greater than Mary": Mary, as vessel, as way, was
the human, creaturely agent of the Creator's entry into his creation.[119]

Hildegard of Bingen—or, rather, her heavenly voice—explained the mystery
perhaps most succinctly: "The blessed and ineffable Trinity showed itself to
the world (*se mundo manifestauit*) when the Father sent into the world his
Only-Begotten, conceived by the Holy Spirit and born of the Virgin, so that
humans, born so diversely and bound by so many sins, should be brought
back through Him to the way of truth."[120] More lyrically, again in Hildegard's
words—or rather those of the chorus of Heaven praising the Virgin through
whom the Trinity was made visible to the world:

> O splendid jewel, serenely infused with the Sun!
> The Sun is in you as a fount from the heart of the Father;
> It is His sole Word, by Whom He created the world,
> The primary matter, which Eve threw into disorder.
> He formed the Word in you as a human being,
> And therefore you are the jewel that shines most brightly,
> Through whom the Word breathed out the whole of the virtues,
> As once from primary matter He made all creatures.[121]

What Hildegard sought to capture in her music, medieval sculptors attempted
to convey visually in statues in which Mary's abdomen or chest is inset with a
polished crystal, the Christ-child within shining forth from her body like the
very sun.[122] In Hildegard's imagery, Mary is at once material and transparent,
the luminous matter (*lucida materia*) in which the Word took human form and
through which he breathed forth his virtue into the world. She is the creature
through whom God entered into his creation, the "prime matter of the world"
(*prima materia mundi*), which Eve had perturbed. Like a jewel sparkling in the
sun, Mary was infused with light, filled with God. And yet, as a sequence by the
Augustinian canon Adam of Saint Victor (d. 1146) for the Feast of the Nativity
(Christmas) put it, the Son came forth from her without shattering her, that is,
without breaking the seal of her chastity, just as a crystal "moistened and placed
in the sunlight emits a little spark of fire" without breaking.[123] Here Mary's unbroken seal of virginity stands in for the whole of creation, which God, its Maker,
miraculously entered without destroying it, like light shining through a jewel.

Container of the Uncontainable

Mary was a mystery which, it would seem, only metaphor could adequately contain, if, that is, the metaphor were expanded to include the whole of heaven and earth and everything—animal, vegetable, and mineral, natural and artificial—therein. "Not only heaven and earth," or so the anonymous early thirteenth-century author of a series of sermons on the antiphon Salve Regina put it,

> but also other names (*aliis nominibus*) and words of things (*rerum vocabulis*) fittingly designate the Lady. She is the tabernacle of God, the temple, the house, the entry-hall, the bedchamber, the bridal-bed, the bride, the daughter, the ark of the flood, the ark of the covenant, the golden urn, the manna, the rod of Aaron, the fleece of Gideon, the gate of Ezekiel, the city of God, the heaven, the earth, the sun, the moon, the morning star, the dawn, the lamp, the trumpet, the mountain, the fountain of the garden and the lily of the valley, the desert, the land of promise flowing with milk and honey, the star of the sea, the ship, the way in the sea, the fishing net, the vine, the field, the ark, the granary, the stable, the manger of the beast of burden, the store-room, the court, the tower, the castle, the battle-line, the people, the kingdom, the priesthood.

Nor was this all:

> She is the sheep, the pasture, the paradise, the palm, the rose, the river, the draught, the dove, the column, the clothing, the pearl, the candelabra, the table, the crown, the scepter, the bread, the oil, the wine, the tree, the rod, the cedar, the cypress, the plane-tree, the cinnamon, the balsam, the myrrh, the frankincense, the olive, the nard, the crocus, the reed, the pipe, the pen, the gum, the sister and mother.

"Indeed," the already long-winded preacher apologized, "that I might briefly conclude, all Scripture was written concerning her and about her and because of her, and for her the whole world was made, she who is full of the grace of God and through whom man has been redeemed, the Word of God made flesh, God humbled and man sublimed."[124]

As Richard of Saint-Laurent and his contemporaries read the scriptures, it would take a book—indeed, many books—just to begin to elucidate all of the figures of Mary contained therein. It took Richard twelve: one to establish the angelic salutation as the model for all addresses to the Virgin Mary; one to explain why and how Mary ought to be praised by her servants; four to list the privileges, virtues, beauties, and names of Mary; and six to enumerate all of her figures in heaven and on earth mentioned in the Bible. According to her medieval devotees, not just scripture, but all of creation was reflected in Mary, "the mirror of great purity," as the German minnesinger Heinrich von Meissen or Frauenlob (d. 1318) put it, "in which God saw himself from the beginning." "I was with him," Frauenlob has Mary declare, echoing Wisdom 7:26, "when he formed the whole creation; he gazed at me with desire unceasing."

> I carried him who carries earth and sky
> and yet am still a maid.
> He lay in me and left me without labor.
> Most certainly
> I slept with Three—
> till I grew pregnant with God's goodness.

And what goodness!

> I am the field that bore in season
> wheat for the sacred mysteries. . . .
> I am the throne the Godhead
> never fled—since God slipped inside. . . .
> All that the prophets prophesied—
> of me alone their words were said.[125]

Whether clerical hyperbole expressing an underlying ambivalence about elevating a mere woman to such heights of cosmic and theological significance (as at least one recent scholar has put it), or blasphemy, making Mary (as the sixteenth-century reformers would have it) equal to God, the one thing such metaphorical and titular exuberance, once tapped, could hardly be was restrained.[126]

For Richard of Saint-Laurent, there was seemingly nothing to which Mary, "the tabernacle and the triclinium of the whole Trinity," could not be compared.[127] She was the heaven (including the Zodiac), the firmament, the sun, the moon, the horizon, the morning star, the dawn, the daybreak, the morning, the light, the day, the cloud. She was the earth, the threshing-floor, the plain, the field, the mountain, the hill, the desert, the rock. She was the fountain, the well, the stream, the river, the torrent, the water, the pond, the riverbed, the bucket, the lake, the jug, the shell, the canal, the pipe, the aqueduct, the bath, the fishpond, the pool, the vein, the spring water, the cistern. Nor were her figures limited to things in the natural world. She was the ark, the throne, the chair, the litter (*ferculum*), the settle, the tribunal, the seat, the teacher's chair (*cathedra*), the footstool, the couch, the rest, the dwelling, the storeroom, the nest, the cell, the medicine chest, the treasure chest, the library, the temple treasury, the women's quarters, the place, the granary, the mill, the oven, the kiln, the forge, the palace of the highest emperor, the court, the tabernacle, the bridal bed, the house, the temple, the city, the camp, the castle, the village, the tower, the rampart, the wall, the ship, and the ark of Noah. And (in one of the most elaborate images of all) she was the garden enclosed praised by the Beloved in the Song of Songs, along with all of its delights, fragrances, flowers, herbs, trees, and birds. Mother, beloved, sister, dearest one, daughter, bride, wife, widow, good woman, virgin, virago, prince, queen: Mary bore all of these titles in her relationship with God, along with those of the celestial, terrestrial, built, and cultivated world.[128]

Hard as it may be to believe, there were those who might argue that even Richard had not been encyclopedic enough in his scope. For Frauenlob, the Virgin was also the weasel who "bore the ermine who bit the snake," the lion's roar "that roused its cub from death's first flood," the fire "in which the phoenix renewed its youth," and the Grail "that healed the noble King's great woe."[129] For Jacobus de Voragine, she was likewise the bee, the dove, the ivory, the elephant, the chicken, the lily, the pearl, the sheep, the mirror, and the fleece, not to mention (as Richard had) the almond, the cedar, the cypress, the galbanum, the olive, the palm tree, and the rose. As Jacobus explained: "For just as according to the philosophers, those things which are scattered among the animals by nature are gathered together in human beings through reason, like simplicity in the dove, kindness in the lamb, liberality in the lion; so all the graces which are given to others are gathered together in Mary at the same time."[130] Accordingly, for the fourteenth-century Dominican compiler of the French *Rosarius*, Mary was the panther (or leopard) in her temperance, the swallow in her desire for contemplation, the stork in her loftiness of life, the ewe in her suitability for sacrifice to God, the whale in her protection of others, the lark in that she was full of grace, the salamander in her adaptability, the bee in her sweetness, the swan in her song at death, the nightingale in her nobility, the pigeon in her removal from the world, the tortoise in the hardness of her shell, the dromedary to the camel that is Christ, and the falcon in the gentility of her heart and body.[131] Not to be outdone, the English Franciscan Walter of Wimborne likewise composed, in addition to his lengthy *Marie Carmina*, a 164-stanza poem in Latin inspired in part by the images compiled by Richard in his *De laudibus beatae Mariae virginis*, hailing the Virgin as (among other things) phoenix of virgins, key of heaven, maidenly gem, room (*zeta*) of the Word, abyss of honey, saw of death, incense of heaven, shield of sinners, and wagon of God.[132]

To be sure, such efforts to describe Mary in all her referential glory could, if the Spirit so willed, lend themselves to what some might call a certain elitist (a.k.a. educated) obscurantism, but their point was not mere—or not merely—showing off.[133] Rather, and rather more modestly, they were an attempt to capture in nouns or names (*nomina*) that which all the words in the world could not hope to describe. There are four reasons, Jacobus contended, that God's human creatures are not able to praise Mary sufficiently. First, on account of their weakness; second, on account of their unworthiness; third, on account of her dignity; fourth—and, arguably, most important—on account of the insufficiency and poverty of words, "because suitable words do not exist for us (*verba idonea nobis deficiunt*)."[134] As Dante, arguably the greatest poet of the Middle Ages, perhaps in all of Christendom, excused himself for not describing the Virgin more fully in his *Paradiso*,

> And even if my speech were rich as my
> imagination is, I should not try
> to tell the very least of her delights.[135]

Indeed, or so one anonymous fourteenth-century Flemish poet somewhat mischievously suggested, arguably the greatest praise one might give to Mary would be to admit that he could never praise her enough. As the poet set the scene, "once there were three masters, proficient in learning and chosen in wisdom," who met one day to discuss how best they might praise the Virgin. The first, Albert of Cologne (that is, Doctor Albertus Magnus [d. 1280]), argued that if all the flowers, grass, herbs, beasts, and even the stars of heaven were to have tongues and could speak as wisely as the masters from Paris to the Danube, they could not thank her or praise her virtues and nobility enough. The second, Henry Formater (that is, the Doctor Solemnis Henry of Ghent [d. 1293]), argued that if every drop of water in the seas and rivers, every grain of sand, all the rain, hail, and snow which has fallen since the beginning of the world had tongues and could speak as wisely as the masters from Paris and Montpellier, they could not thank her or praise her chastity and virtue enough. The third, Jacob van Maerlant (d. ca. 1300), the hero of the piece despite the fact that he wrote not in Latin but in Dutch and was no philosopher but merely a poet, argued that if all the fish in the sea, the worms in the ground, the beasts in the forest, the birds in the air, and the crops in the field had tongues and, moreover, even if they were joined by all the saints, angels, apostles, confessors, martyrs, and virgins, who then did nothing but speak her praises with a hundred thousand tongues, every one the wisest in the world, still they could not thank and praise the Virgin enough.

At which—somewhat predictably, given the circumstances—the great scholastic philosophers Albert and Henry declared Jacob their master "because you have spoken the praise of Mary better than we did. This we admit."[136]

Under such circumstances, even the language of scripture might come to seem inadequate. The great Franciscan Doctor Seraphicus Bonaventure of Bagnoreggio (d. 1274) put the mystery this way in the first of the sermons that he preached for the Feast of the Annunciation:

> Because the mystery of the incarnation of the Lord is so secret and deep that no understanding is able to seize it, no tongue able to unfold it, the Holy Spirit, condescending to human weakness, wished that it be described by many metaphors (*metaphoris*), by which as if led by the hand, we might come to some knowledge of it. For, according to the Apostle [Romans 1:20], "the invisible things of God are made comprehensible through those visible things that have been made."[137]

"A rod shall come forth out of the root of Jesse, and a flower shall rise up out of his root, and the Spirit of the Lord shall rest upon him" (Isaiah 11:1); "The Lord will give goodness, and our earth shall yield her fruit" (Psalm 84:13); "He who created me rested in my tabernacle" (Ecclesiasticus 24:12). According to Bonaventure, all of these visible things (root, rod, and flower; the earth and her fruit; the tabernacle in which the Creator rested) were ways of attempting to express the same incomprehensible mystery: how the immensity of the eternal majesty confined itself in Mary's womb. As the Mother of God Mary was the temple in which "the whole Divinity dwelt corporeally" (cf. Malachi 3:1).[138] She was the house of David in which "the true David, Christ, dwelt and dedicated to himself and blessed for all eternity" (cf. 2 Kings [Samuel] 7:29).[139] And she was the ark of the covenant in which "all the treasures of wisdom and knowledge are hidden because in her she contained the flesh of Christ" (cf. 2 Chronicles 5:8).[140] Indeed, as Bonaventure understood it, without Mary, that "wonderful vessel, the work of the Most High" (Ecclesiasticus 43:2), the whole universe would be deformed: "For if you take the Mother of God from the world, in consequence you take the incarnate Word, without which the deformity of sinning and the error of sinners would remain."[141]

Nor was it only Mary whom Divinity had infused. Isaiah heard the seraphs surrounding the throne of the Lord calling, "The whole earth is filled with his glory" (Isaiah 6:3), which is to say, the humanity of the Son of God "filled the most sacred womb of the Virgin and in consequence the whole universe. . . . [and] that plenitude which was in the Virgin Mary overflowed into the whole Church."[142] Filling the Virgin's womb, God the Creator overflowed in his goodness to suffuse the whole of creation, now transformed in both grace and meaning. "He who created me rested in my tabernacle" (Ecclesiasticus 24:12), that is, Bonaventure explained, he who was Creator was also the inhabitant of that which he had created because he was both God and man, Alpha and Omega. Inhabiting the Virgin corporeally, he likewise rested sacramentally in the tabernacle of the militant Church (that is, the Church on earth), while at the same time resting spiritually in the tabernacle of the faithful soul as well as sempiternally in the tabernacle of the celestial court. "Thus," Bonaventure argued, "what is said [in this text] is true in every mode, namely literally, allegorically, morally, and anagogically."[143]

Full of Grace

It would be hard to imagine—would it not?—how such an indwelling could not have had some effect on the Virgin, other than her giving birth, although many since the sixteenth century have insisted that it did not, that Mary was "just a housewife" who was obedient to God. Perhaps the most contested effect of this indwelling since the mid-nineteenth century, and thus in the modern historiography of her cult, has been her preservation whether before or after her conception from sin.[144] For Mary's medieval devotees, however, the effects included not only her spiritual, but also her intellectual state, often to what some would later ridicule as a preposterous extent. Never mind (although the debate was a fierce one) whether she was conceived without original sin or only sanctified in her mother's womb, what did the Virgin in whom the Creator of all things had made his dwelling *know*? According to the thirteenth-century *Mariale, sive CCXXX quaestiones super Evangelium* of Pseudo-Albert the Great, everything: Mary had knowledge of all of the mechanical arts, especially those having to do with weaving, and all of the liberal arts, including those of the trivium (grammar, rhetoric, dialectic) along with civil and canon law, physics and medicine, and those of the quadrivium (music, astronomy, arithmetic, and geometry), not to mention theology and all the matter of Peter Lombard's *Sentences*, the textbook of the Scholastics.[145] As Hilda Graef writing in the mid-twentieth century somewhat dismissively commented, "had the author lived in our own time he no doubt would have added aeronautics and nuclear physics"—and why not?[146] Moreover, Pseudo-Albert would insist, Mary had not only perfect knowledge of the Incarnation "through grace and singular experience," but also perfect knowledge of the Trinity "without mediation," as well as knowledge of her own predestination; of souls and spirits, angels, and demons; of the scriptures, what ought to be done and what ought to be contemplated; of all creatures "through nature, grace, and contemplation"; and of "evening and morning," that is, first and last things. Indeed, Pseudo-Albert concluded, "there was nothing of which she was ignorant," whether of action or contemplation, by nature or grace; rather, her knowledge of all things was perfectly complete.[147]

The German poet Heinrich von Mügeln (d. 1369) would concur. In his *Der meide kranz* (The Virgin's garland), the seven liberal arts plus Philosophy, Medicine, Alchemy, Metaphysics, and Theology meet at the court of Emperor Charles IV (d. 1378) in Prague to debate which among them is to hold the place of honor as a jewel in Mary's crown. As Charles judges the case, Theology is necessarily the victor, for her truth surpasses that of all of the other arts. Philosophy "speaks of corruption and generation and the rightful operations of Nature," but Theology speaks of the one who rules over and nourishes Nature. Grammar "uses words and teaches the parts of speech," but she forgets that Word "which became flesh in the maiden and which never separates itself from the divine essence." Arithmetic counts and measures everything from the sands of the sea to the stars of heaven, but Theology describes "how the king allowed himself to receive numberless wounds for our sake." Music "lured God into the depths of the heart" so that he "took on humanity from the maiden," but she did not master that tune that was "composed on the cross by the child of the maiden and the Word of God." Astronomy teaches the movement of the stars and what events will happen in the future: "For that reason," she argues, "I may stand in the crown of the Virgin who spun three persons out of one Word, painlessly; the rays of the sun did not break her glass." But Theology teaches about him "who has embedded the stars into the grail of heaven and who may pull them down again."[148] And so forth. All twelve arts in the end are nevertheless admitted to adorn the Virgin's garland, for each, while itself inadequate to the task of describing her in full, contributes to the understanding and praise of the Virgin, she who gave birth to the Truth surpassing all human arts.

While full of the knowledge of the Creator and his creation, Mary was likewise, as the angel had put it, "full of grace," a fullness only intensified by the fact that "the Lord [was with her]." All virtues, Pseudo-Albert would contend, were embodied in her—faith, hope, charity, justice, obedience, worship, penitence, prudence, fortitude, perseverance, temperance, chastity, sobriety, modesty— along with the gifts of the Holy Spirit (Isaiah 11:2–3), the Beatitudes (Matthew 5:3–11), and the fruits of the Spirit (Galatians 5:22–23).[149] She had the graces of healing, working miracles, prophecy, discernment of spirits, tongues, and the interpretation of scriptures (1 Corinthians 12:9–10). And she was an apostle, a prophetess, an evangelist, and a pastor (Ephesians 4:11).[150] She also, of course, had a perfect body, perfect complexion (warm and dry), and perfect health, and, therefore—Pseudo-Albert reasoned according to contemporary physiological theory—black eyes and black hair.[151] At her death, she was (as the Church sings) "exalted above all the choirs of the angels," because she possessed all the properties of all the hierarchies of the angels. Likewise, she was "blessed among women" because she possessed "in the highest degree all singular blessings singularly, and all universal blessings universally," including the blessings of Adam and Eve, of Abraham on Isaac, of Jacob's blessings on his sons, and Balaam's blessings on Israel.[152] In short, as Albert the Great's fellow Dominican Thomas Aquinas would put it in his commentary on the angelic salutation, the Virgin "surpasses the angels in her fullness of grace, which is greater in her than in any angel. . . . Grace filled her soul . . . Grace overflowed into her body [fitting it for the conception of God's Son]. . . . [And] grace overflows from her onto all mankind."[153]

Leaving to one side later anxieties about how far one could or should go in praising the Virgin, perhaps we may now begin to appreciate how, from the perspective of her high and late medieval devotees, even hyperbole might come to seem inadequate. As the thirteenth-century Franciscan Conrad of Saxony put it in his popular meditation on the angel's greeting:

The grace of which [Mary] was full was certainly immense. An immense vessel (*vas*) cannot be full, unless that is also immense wherewith it is filled. Mary was a vessel beyond measure (*vas immensissimum*), since she could contain Him who is greater than the Heavens. Who is greater than the Heavens? Without doubt He of whom Solomon says: "If heaven and the heaven of heavens cannot contain thee, how much less this house which I have built?" (3 Kings 8:27). It was not indeed the house which Solomon built, but she who is signified by that house, which could contain God (*sed domus per illam significata Deum capere potuit*). You, therefore, O most immeasurable Mary (*immensissima Maria*), are more capacious than the Heavens, because "he whom the Heavens cannot contain was carried in your womb."[154] You are more capacious than the world, because He whom the whole world cannot contain, "being made man, was enclosed in you."[155] If Mary's womb then had such immensity, how much more had her mind? And if so immense a capacity was full of grace, it was fitting that that grace which could fill so great a capacity, should also be immense. Who can measure the immensity of Mary?. . . . Mary is a heaven, as much because she abounded in heavenly purity, heavenly light, and other heavenly virtues, as because she was the most high throne of God. . . . Mary was also the earth which brought forth for us that fruit of which the same Prophet says: "The earth has given its fruits" (Psalm 66:7). Mary is also an abyss in goodness and deepest mercy; whence she obtains for us the mercy of her Son, as it were "an abyss calling upon an abyss" (Psalm 41:8).[156]

For Conrad and, indeed, the majority of his contemporaries, it was inconceivable that one might praise Mary "too much," as if it were even possible to praise her, like God to whom she had given birth, enough. Never mind how (although, of course, they were certain that she had been a virgin), Mary had carried in her body the Author of the World. To minimize Mary would be to suggest that one might minimize God.

Of course Mary was "full of grace"; *of course* she enjoyed all of the gifts of the Holy Spirit; *of course* she was filled with nine plenitudes—the overflowing of grace, the illumination of wisdom, the fruits and riches of a good life, the anointing of mercy, the fecundity of the divine offspring, the perfection of the universal Church, the fragrant sprinkling of sweetly scented fame, the reflection of the divine glory, and the joy of eternal happiness—surpassing even the plenitudes of the nine orders of angels.[157] "She alone," as Conrad put it, "above all creatures was in the body most familiar with God. For, what was never granted to any other creature, nor will ever be granted again in eternity, she bore God for nine months in her womb, she nourished God 'from her breasts full of heaven,' for many years she sweetly brought up our Lord."[158] "She, who is our moon and our lamp, was illuminated by the Lord," her mind filled with the light of wisdom before she conceived him, her body with Wisdom after her consent.[159] Her body was the house filled with the majesty of the Incarnate Word on the throne of whose mind the Lord sits (cf. Isaiah 6:1); therefore, Conrad explained, "it is said in the third book of Kings (8:11): 'The glory of the Lord had filled the house of the Lord.' "[160]

And who is this Lord who is "with [her]"? Generally speaking (*generaliter*), he is the "Lord of all creatures," "of all things visible and invisible," who has made Mary "the universal Lady of all things—the Lady, I say, of heaven and the Lady of the world."[161] More specifically (*specialiter*), he is a "most loving, most just, most sure, and most renowned Lord" of his rational creatures, loving in his infinite mercy, just in his judgments and equity, sure in his fidelity, renowned over all the earth.[162] Most particularly (*singulariter*), however, he is the Lord who inhabits the singular court of Mary's body and soul, in relation to whom Mary is at once Daughter of the Lord Father, Mother of the Lord Son, Bride of the Lord Holy Spirit, and Handmaid of the Lord Three-and-One.[163] As such, she is accordingly the dawn (*aurora*) irradiated by the Eternal Sun and preparing for his rising (Song of Songs 6:9); the rod (*virga*) smoking with incense (Song of Songs 3:6), flowering with virtues (Numbers 17:8), golden to the perfect and contemplative (Esther 15:15), and iron to demons and sinners (Psalm 2:9), from which the flower foreseen by Isaiah (11:1) sprouted; and the Queen (*regina*) of the Eternal King, entering into his glory (3 Kings 10:1–2). "Behold, therefore," Conrad concluded, "O most sweet Virgin Mary; behold, truly 'the Lord is with you,' as the sun is with the dawn going before it, as the flower is with the flowering rod, as the king is with the queen entering in."[164] Mary, in other words, defines (encompasses, makes visible) God because it is she—as Daughter, Mother, Bride, Handmaid, Dawn, Rod, and Queen—whom he is with.

Aves in the Psalms

But *how* does one praise the human woman in whom Divinity dwelt? (It is impossible to overstress how mind-boggling this question is, banal as the idea of the Incarnation has become some two thousand years after the conception and birth of the one whom Christians call Lord.) According to Mary's medieval devotees, faute de mieux with a list, ideally one prefacing every attribute or title—just as the angel had—with "Hail!" Such lists are perhaps most familiar to more recent Christians in the form of devotions like the Litany of Loreto, formally approved by Pope Sixtus V in 1587 but well attested in older versions from the twelfth century at the latest, when the recitation of the Ave Maria was already gaining in popularity, as liturgical historian G. G. Meersseman has shown.[165] Even by the twelfth century, however, this practice of hailing Mary in all her attributes and titles was centuries old, going back to the very origins of the formal cult of the Virgin in the East following Mary's official recognition at the council of Ephesus in 431 as Theotokos or "Mother of God."[166] Perhaps the most telling—certainly the most liturgically resonant—product of this recognition was the magnificent twenty-four-strophe hymn in Greek famously sung standing ("Akathistos") over the course of single night in thanksgiving for the deliverance of the city of Constantinople from its Avar and Persian besiegers in August 626.[167] By the ninth century, as Meersseman has shown, the "Akathistos" hymn with its twelve groups of twelve greetings to the Virgin, each punctuated by the paradoxical refrain "Ave, sponsa insponsata" (Hail, bride unwedded), had been translated into Latin, most likely by the Greek Christophorus I, bishop of Venice under the Franks (803–807).[168] At about the same time, similar greeting hymns began to be composed in the West, including the much-loved "Ave maris stella" (Hail, star of the sea), subsequently adopted as the hymn for Vespers in the Office of the Virgin.[169] In the tenth century, such compositions often took the form of meditations on the various titles of the Virgin arranged according to the letters of the alphabet: "Auroram.... Beatam domum.... Columbam.... David praecelso parientem filium.... Egressa virga Jesse de radice est...."[170] From the twelfth century, however, it became the custom to compose whole "psalters" of Aves, each verse recalling a corresponding verse or image from the Psalms.[171] While such "Mary-psalters" have been often invoked as precursors to the later fourteenth- and fifteenth-century recitation of the rosary, particularly its numbering of Aves in imitation of the Psalms, what is surely these psalters' most striking characteristic is their painstaking effort—psalm by psalm—to salute the Virgin in all her titular abundance.[172]

To take but one example: the earliest as well as one of the most popular of these psalters would appear to come from the Cistercian monastery of Pontigny, although at least one early thirteenth-century manuscript (London, British Library, Arundel 157, fols. 146–159) attributes it to Anselm of Canterbury.[173] The Arundel version includes, among others, the following preparatory prayer suggesting the psalter's purpose:

Suscipe, regina celi, que mente deuota
Cantica de psalmis offero sumpta sacris.
Cumque salutaris in eis et magnificaris
Pauperis atque mei sis memor et miseri.

Queen of heaven, accept these songs
that devoted I offer from the sacred psalms.
And when in them you are saluted and magnified,
be mindful of me, miserable and poor.[174]

The psalter itself consists of 150 salutations, from "Ave, porta paradysi" (Hail, gate of paradise) (Psalm 1) to "Ave, fili; salve, mater" (Hail, son; greetings, mother) (Psalm 150), including "Ave, templum sanctum dei" (Hail, holy temple of God) (Psalm 5), "Ave, lucerna seculi" (Hail, lamp of the age) (Psalm 10), "Ave, virgo pulchra tota" (Hail, all beautiful virgin) (Psalm 25), "Ave, domus ubertatis" (Hail, house of plenty) (Psalm 35), "Ave, simplex ut columba" (Hail, simple as a dove) (Psalm 54), "Ave, terra ferens fructum" (Hail, earth bearing fruit) (Psalm 66), "Ave, prima columpnarum" (Hail, first of columns) (Psalm 74), "Ave pulchra sicut luna" (Hail, beautiful as the moon) (Psalm 80), "Ave, ancilla domini" (Hail, handmaid of the Lord) (Psalm 85), "Ave, virgo, celi porta" (Hail, virgin, gate of heaven) (Psalm 96), "Ave, ovis centesima" (Hail, one hundredth sheep) (Psalm 99), "Ave, virga iustitie" (Hail, rod of justice) (Psalm 109)—and so on, from psalm to psalm, with no apparent logic other than that of pairing each salutation with a verse from the Psalms. The point is not, however, as in the meditations that would later come to be associated with the various decades of the rosary, to recall particular events in Mary's or her Son's life, but rather, as the prefatory prayer suggests, to salute and magnify the Virgin through the Psalms. If there is a fullness here (which there most definitely is), it is not that of narrative, but rather that of praise, the Psalms that God so loved to hear provid-ing the structure for praising his Mother, and vice versa, the Aves giving occa-sion for praising God. The first few verses may give us a taste of the way in which this interwoven praise works.[175]

The psalter begins:

Et erit tanquam lingnum (*sic*) quod plantatum est, secus decursus aquarum quod fructum suum dabit in tempore suo. (Psalm 1:3)

And he [or she] *will be like a tree* (lignum) *that is planted by running waters which will give its fruit* (fructum) *in its time.*

The accompanying Ave provides, as it were, the gloss:

Aue porta paradysi lignum uite quod amisi.
Per te michi iam dulcessit, et salutis fructus crescit.

Gate of paradise, tree (lignum) *of life that I have lost.*
Through you for me already the fruit (fructus) *of salvation becomes sweet*
and grows.

While the rhyme scheme of the Ave emphasizes the loss of paradise (*paradysi/amisi*) as against the increase of sweetness (*dulcescit/crescit*), the pairing with the psalm verse focuses the attention on the tree and its fruit: Christ is, of course, the fruit that Mary bore. Accordingly, it is she who is the Tree of Life on which the fruit ripened, an image recalling at once the Tree of Life in the garden of paradise (Genesis 2:9) and the Cross-Tree from which Christ, the fruit of salvation, hung. As Conrad of Saxony put it, citing Revelation 22:2: "The tree of life (*lignum vitae*) is Mary, the mother of life; or the tree of life is the tree of the Cross; or else the tree is Jesus Christ, the author of life, who is also the fruit of life."[176] According to Richard of Saint-Laurent, the running waters by which the tree is planted may be read as, among other things, streams of scripture, wisdom, and grace that help ripen the fruit, that is, make it available to humankind.[177]

The psalm admonishes:

Apprehendite disciplinam nequando irascatur dominus et pereatis de uia iusta. (Psalm 2:12)

Embrace discipline (disciplinam) *lest the Lord be angry* (irascatur) *and you perish from the just way* (uia).

And the Ave reassures:

> Aue morum disciplina, uita uia, lux diuina.
> Iram dei mitigasti quando Christum generasti.

> *Hail, discipline* (disciplina) *of customs, way* (uia) *of life, light divine.*
> *You softened the anger* (iram) *of God when you gave birth to Christ.*

Here the parallels are between Mary's discipline in its divine inspiration (*disciplina/divina*) and between her act of generation and the softening of God's anger (*mitigasti/generasti*). Somewhat surprisingly, Mary, rather than Christ, is here "the way" because it is she who mitigated God's anger against sinners through her teaching and habits; likewise, she shows sinners the way to the path of justice by giving birth to God's Son.

The one praying cries out:

> Voce mea ad dominum clamaui et exaudiuit me de monte sancto suo. (Psalm 3:5)

> *I have cried* (clamaui) *to the Lord with my voice and he heard* (exaudiuit) *me from his holy mountain* (de monte).

And the Virgin hears:

> Aue uirgo cuius clamor nostri fuit pius amor.
> Qui de monte exauditur uerbum carni cum unitur.

> *Hail, virgin, whose shout* (clamor) *was pious love for us,*
> *Which was heard* (exauditur) *from the mountain* (de monte) *when the*
>   *Word was joined to flesh.*

According to Conrad, Mary is the "holy mountain" because it is she from whom the stone, Christ, was cut without hands (cf. Daniel 2:45), and because she is lofty in her life and manners and excellent in her merits.[178] Her shout (*clamor*) of love (*amor*) which the Lord heard (*exauditur*) from his mountain was the consent that she gave to the angel's words: "Let it be to me according to your word" (Luke 1:38), at which the Word became flesh (*unitur*) in her womb. Likewise, the Ave suggests, she is a mountain for others from which they may lift their voices to God.

The psalmist prays:

Signatum est super nos lumen uultus tui domine; dedisti leticiam in corde meo.
(Psalm 4:7)

Lord, let the light of your face (uultus tui) *set its mark* (signatum est) *upon us; you gave me gladness in my heart.*

On which the Ave reflects:

Aue cuius refulgentem splendor patris fecit mentem.
De splendore reuultus tui fac signentur serui tui.

Hail, the one whose mind the splendor of the Father made to reflect
[a shining light].
Let your servants be marked (signentur) *with the splendor of your countenance* (vultus tui).

Mary's mind (*mentem*) shone with a great splendor (*refulgentem*) because it
was there that the Lord rested on his throne.[179] Indeed, as Conrad explained,
citing Bernard of Clairvaux: "Heavenly Wisdom built for himself a house in
Mary: for he so filled her mind that from the very fullness of her mind her
flesh became fecund, and the Virgin by a singular grace brought forth that
same Wisdom, covered with a garb of flesh, whom she had first conceived in
her mind."[180] Because, moreover, her mind was so marked by her contemplation of God, her face shone in likeness to her Son's, whose mirror she was
both in spirit and in flesh.[181] After the Son, indeed, she was the true light (as
Richard put it) "illuminating all those who come into the world."[182] Likewise,
her servants are marked by her and filled with joy when "irradiated by her life
and example" and "illuminated by her patronage and mercy," they are incited
to good.[183]

The psalmist rejoices:

Introibo in domum tuam domine; adorabo ad templum sanctum tuum et con-
fitebor nomini tuo. (Psalm 5:8, with changes)

I will enter into your house, O Lord; I will worship in your holy temple (templum
sanctum) *and I will confess your name.*

And the Ave concurs:

> Aue templum sanctum dei ad quod currunt omnes rei.
> Vt ab hoste liberentur a quo capti detinentur.
>
> *Hail, holy temple* (templum sanctum) *of God, to which sinners run,*
> *That they may be liberated from the enemy by whom, taken captive, they*
> *have been detained.*

As Bonaventure put it, Mary's womb was the temple "made by the power of the Father, adorned by the wisdom of the Son, dedicated by the grace of the Holy Spirit, and filled with the presence of the Incarnate Word."[184] Jacobus would agree: the Father founded the temple, the Holy Spirit consecrated it, and the Son inhabited it. Accordingly, it—that is, Mary—is full in four ways: her womb for receiving God in the flesh; her intellect for receiving the understanding of the divine light directly, not just through God's works; her affect for having compassion on sinners "for whom she obtains God's mercy," the tempted "whom she protects from the Devil," and those leaving this world "whom she leads with her hands into heaven"; and her merit for assisting all those in the world and at judgment.[185] Likewise, for Richard of Saint-Laurent: "Mary is the temple because it is through her that we offer prayers to Christ."[186] The Ave verse likewise recalls the medieval legal tradition of sanctuary, whereby those who took refuge in a church would be safe from arrest, as well as the Virgin's fabled intervention on behalf of those who sought her protection from their captivity to the devil and sin, most notably, Theophilus.[187] As the temple of God, that is, his habitation, Mary is also the house built by Wisdom (Proverbs 9:1), founded, constructed, and stabilized by the three Persons of the Trinity.[188] It is there that "I will confess your name," because it was through Mary that God as Trinity revealed himself to the world. Accordingly, as Richard put it, "the heart of the Virgin may be rightly called the tabernacle and *triclinium* of the whole Trinity," because the whole Trinity rested in her soul while he who was wandering as a soldier in the world rested in her flesh: "For Christ about to come forth to fight against the world and the Devil armed himself in the womb of the Virgin, putting on poverty against pride and virgin flesh like a shield against luxury and excess."[189]

And so forth, as the titles of the individual psalms put it, *in finem*, "to the end." Even though we are only to stanza five, the reader is doubtless already wondering how much longer such an exhaustive itemization could possibly go on. And yet, even if we were to follow the psalter through its remaining 145 stanzas all the way to the end, this is not to say that the itemizing of Mary's attributes would be in any way complete. Indeed, other psalters would emphasize wholly other verses of the Psalms and consequently different images and words. While certain themes would recur (for example, Mary as Tree of Life, temple, and house of God), no two psalters invoke exactly the same set of attributes or give each the same meaning. For the author of the psalter from Pontigny, for example, Psalm 2 was an occasion for meditating on the Virgin's discipline as the way of life (Psalm 2:12), but for archbishop of Canterbury Stephen Langton (d. 1228), it recalled rather the grumbling of the nations (*gentes fremuerunt*) against the one to whom her body had given birth (Psalm 2:1).[190] Like the author from Pontigny, Stephen's later successor as archbishop Saint Edmund of Abingdon (d. 1242) would invoke the Virgin as "salvific discipline" (*disciplina salutaris*) in his verse for Psalm 2, but for Psalm 3, he would focus on her as the "healing of our disease" (*nostri salus morbi*) and on the blessing (*benedictio*) poured out through her over the people (cf. Psalm 3:3, 9) rather than on her shout.[191] As her medieval devotees read them, the Psalms, like the Virgin herself, were inexhaustible, every word a hint as to her praise.

And yet, remarkably, for some it would seem that even the Psalms were not enough. Whether out of frustration or simply in an attempt to expand even further the scope of their salutations, other poets, for example, the Benedictine abbot Engelbert of Admont (d. 1331) and the Franciscan poet and former schoolmaster Walter of Wimborne, would dispense with the formal psalm structure altogether, retaining only (if that) the number of the psalms. For Engelbert, Mary was preeminently the rose, every stanza of his psalter beginning with the same salutation: "Ave, rosa." But how many different roses he invokes!

> Ave, rosa, flos aestive, O Maria, lucis vivae suave habitaculum . . .
> *Hail, rose, flower of summer, O Mary, sweet habitation of the living light!*
> Ave, rosa non vulgaris, disciplinae puellaris exemplum et regula . . .
> *Hail, rose uncommon, example and rule of maidenly discipline!*
> Ave, rosa verni roris, te divini ros amoris totam sic roraverat . . .
> *Hail, rose of vernal dew, the dew of divine love wholly you bedewed!*
> Ave, rosa paradisi, per quam morbi sunt elisi. . . .
> *Hail, rose of paradise, through whom all disease is crushed!*
> Ave, rosa sola potis, ferre vim rhinocerotis et invictum capere . . .
> *Hail, rose alone able to bear the strength of the unicorn and to capture the*
>   *unconquered one!*[192]

For Walter, in contrast, like Richard of Saint-Laurent on whom he seems to have depended for many of his images, it is difficult to say what the Virgin was not:

> Hail, virgin, mother of Christ,
> you who by your modesty merited
> to be called phoenix of virgins;
> hail, virgin, whose fruit
> gave to us the end of sorrow and
> the limit of lamentation.
> Hail, beautiful virgin,
> for whose praise neither prose
> nor meter suffices;
> hail, virgin, turning-post (*meta*) of evil,
> vein of life, through whom the death (*theta*)
> of foul death is accomplished.
> Hail, glorious virgin,
> you who are the comment and gloss
> of prophetic scripture,
> whose gloss lays bare
> that which is veiled
> by the hard shell of the letter.
> Hail, virgin, key of heaven,
> hail, new ship weighed down
> with novel wares,
> through whom on full sails
> is brought the full light from heaven
> to the blind and wandering.
> Hail, maidenly gem,
> hail, bright star of the sea,
> hail, treasure-chest of the divinity,
> hail, torch and lantern
> whom the supernal light sets light,
> firebrand of eternal light.
> Hail, virgin, whose womb,
> diligently sealed (*sigillatus*),
> swelled with a new growth;
> without pain or torment,
> the splendor and figure of the Father

wished to be born from you.
Hail, virgin, room (*zeta*) of the Word,
chastely pregnant by chaste breath,
not impure seed;
to you worthily we offer odes,
you who knot God with mud,
and mother with virgin.
Hail, virgin, cell of the Word,
concealing the light-beam of divinity
under a cloud of flesh;
hail, virgin, medicine-chest of God,
through whom the clouded, bleary, blind
mind receives its salve.
Hail, virgin, abyss of honey,
you who drive far away the ancient gall
of death and sorrow,
you who with the needle of providence
joined God with mud
and the lowest with the highest.
Hail, virgin, saw of death,
whose womb is a casket
of celestial incense;
hail, virgin, whom the power
of the bountiful spirit made sacred,
fortunate, and fertile.[193]

"Hail, gracious virgin. . . . Hail, sweetness of the mind. . . . Hail, incense of heaven . . . Hail, shield of sinners . . . Hail, cloud shot through with the flames of Phoebus and adorned with the rainbow of divinity. . . . Hail!" And so on for 164 Victorine stanzas, through metaphors even Richard had not explored.[194]

"And the virgin's name was Mary" (Luke 1:27)

How, in the end, does one describe the indescribable? Perhaps, as Walter himself suggested at the outset of the second of his great efforts to describe the Virgin (*Marie Carmina*), one cannot: even if the whole of creation were transformed into pens, parchment, and ink and all its creatures into scribes, one could not hope to praise adequately even the least of the virtues of the one who contained the uncontainable in her womb.[195] Her very existence was (and, for the faithful, still is) a paradox, exceeding the capacity of human reason to comprehend. For all the metaphors that one might invoke to describe her (and they were, as we have seen, legion), nothing in truth, or so her medieval devotees insisted, was remotely like her, not the heavens or the earth, not the sun or the moon, not the garden enclosed or the litter of Solomon, not the temple or the ark, not the jewel, gate, ship, house, city, elephant, or dove—for, after all, she alone of all his creatures had given birth to God. No list of attributes, unless itself infinite, could encompass divinity—and yet, mind-bogglingly, Mary had. As Anselm had put it: "Nothing equals Mary, nothing but God is greater than Mary." What mere words could one use to describe the one in whom the Word had dwelled? All of them? None of them? Or perhaps, paradoxically—as Walter himself eventually realized—there was only one: "Mary." In Walter's words: "All other praise is exiguous."[196]

Maria: this—according to the Vulgate tradition on which medieval European Christians depended—was the name of the virgin to whom the angel was sent (Luke 1:27), the name given to her by God as recorded by the evangelist.[197] "Ave Maria": what more needed to be said? "Your name," argued Richard of Saint-Laurent, citing the Song of Songs (1:2),

"is as oil poured out; therefore, the young maidens loved you" exceedingly. Rightly is this name "Maria" compared to oil: because above all the names of the saints this name, after the name of the Son, refreshes the tired, strengthens the weak, gives light to the blind, penetrates the hard [of heart], restores the weary, anoints the struggling, rots the yoke of the Devil, and floats above all names just as oil above all other liquids. For the whole Trinity gave to her this name that is above all other names after the name of her Son, that in her name every knee should bend . . . in heaven, earth, and hell; and that every tongue should confess the grace, glory, and virtue of this most holy name (cf. Philippians 2:10–11). For there is no more powerful aid in any other name after the name of the Son, nor is there any name under heaven given to human beings after the sweet name of Jesus from which so great a salvation is poured out to humankind (cf. Acts 4:12).[198]

Never mind the Virgin's various titles, everything that one needed to know in order to praise her could be learned simply from her name—or so the Franciscan Bernardino de Busti (d. 1513) would argue in his vast but oft-printed *Mariale* of sixty-three sermons in twelve parts, six of which sermons he dedicated to elucidating the mysteries of "M.A.R.I.A."[199] In Bernardino's reading, although the immensity of Mary's glory exceeds the capacity of all human words to express,[200] so filled with meaning is her name that even the very shapes of the individual letters are signs pointing Christians to her virtues: "M" with its three "I's" joined into one is for her faith in the Trinity. "A" with its top open and curved to the left is for her hope in adversity. "R" with its two turnings is for her love of God and her neighbor. "I" in its simplicity is for her humility. And "A," again with its open curve to the left, is for her largess.[201]

Nor, as Bernardino would have it, was it only Mary's virtues that the letters of her name could reveal, in so many ways and through so many figures did they speak of her glories. Simply to give the outlines of this literal multiplicity took Bernardino nearly fifty double-columned pages in the 1511 black-letter edition of his work, over sixty in the 1588 edition printed in Roman type. Like Richard of Saint-Laurent, Bernardino read Mary's name as a veritable treasury of significations, she herself having been filled with him in whom were hidden all the treasures of wisdom and knowledge (Colossians 2:3).[202] And why not? After all, as "Jerome, Ambrose, Bernard, Anselm, and Bartholomeus of Pisa" all attest (or so Bernardino argued), this was the name her Son gave to her, the name by which the angel greeted her at the Incarnation of the Word, about which the psalmist rightly cries: "How admirable is your name in the whole earth!" (Psalm 8:2), and Mary herself may be heard to say in the words of the prophet Malachi (1:11): "From the rising of the sun even to its going down, my name is great among the peoples and in every place."[203] Thus buttressed by scripture on the one hand and learned authorities on the other, who would not be emboldened (or, at the very least, curious) to open her name and discover the many treasures contained therein?

Appropriatively (*quae dicitur appropriationis*), or so Bernardino explained, "M" is for pearl (*margarita*) because pearls staunch the flow of blood and strengthen the heart; likewise, Mary through the grace which she pours out on her lovers has the virtue of staunching the flow of sin. "A" is for diamond (*adamas*) because it is the gemstone of reconciliation and love, and Mary reconciles the human race with God and establishes them in love. "R" is for ruby (*rubinus*) because it has the virtue of making its wearers glad; the gracious Virgin makes those devoted to her happy. "I" is for jasper (*iaspis*) because it protects against harm; likewise, the Virgin protects those who pray to her against all evils and dangers. "A" is for *allectorius*, a gem found in the maw of a cock, because it brings honors and fortune; Mary brings her devotees great good fortune, for as "Bernard" (actually the Carolingian monk Paschasius Radbertus) put it, "there is nothing of virtue, nothing of splendor, nothing of glory with which she does not shine."[204]

In similar fashion, according to Bernardino, but on a different level, figuratively (*quae dicitur figurationis*), the letters of Mary's name point to the various women mentioned in the scriptures whose lives prefigured hers. "M" is for Michal, the wife of David, king and prophet, between whom and Abner there could be no friendship unless Abner sent her to the king (2 Kings [Samuel] 3); likewise, there could be no friendship between her Son and humankind until the Virgin was born into the world. "A" signifies Abigail, also the wife of David, who pleaded on behalf of her husband Nabal that David not wreak his vengeance upon him (1 Kings [Samuel] 25); in the same way, Mary goes out to meet God adorned with all her virtues so as to turn his wrath away from humankind. "R" denotes Rachel, the wife of Jacob, who bore Joseph, whose name mean "savior" (Genesis 30); Mary bore Christ, the Savior of the world. "I" indicates Judith, who killed Holofernes (Judith 13); likewise, Mary through the merit of her humble virginity killed Lucifer, prince of demons, by crushing his power. "A" is for Abishag, the Sunamite chosen over all the daughters of Israel to attend King David in his old age (3 Kings 1:1–4); in the same way, Mary was chosen over all other women to minister to the heavenly king (Ecclesiasticus 24:14).[205]

Again, as Bernardino would have it, on yet another level, significantly (*quae dicitur significationis*), the letters of Mary's name point to her various roles in relation to humanity and God. Mary is a mediator (*mediatrix*) because she mediates between God and humankind, Christ and the Church, the three Persons of the Trinity and the three states of humanity (virgins, continent, and married), reconciling sinners to God, interceding for them daily and communicating between those who are still in the world and the saints who are already on the way to heaven. Likewise, she is her devotees' helper (*auxiliatrix*); their renewer, restorer, and reconciler (*restauratrix, reparatrix, reconciliatrix*); their illuminator (*illuminatrix*), and their advocate (*advocata*).[206] Yet again, she is the Mother of all things (*mater universorum*), the of the treasury of God (*arca thesaurorum Dei*), the Queen of heaven and earth (*regina celorum et totius orbis*), the Empress of heaven and earth (*imperatrix celi et terra*), and the Augusta of the whole world (*augusta totius orbis*).[207] In her prerogatives, she is the hand of God (*manus Dei*), five-fingered, rounded, golden, and hyacinth; the bee of God (*apis Dei*) feeding on the dew of heaven and giving birth to the sweetness of paradise; the rule of life for everyone living (*regula omnium viventium*); the urn of God (*ydria Dei*); the almond and celestial tree (*amygdala, arbor celestis*).[208] And she is the mother of mercy (*mater misericordiae*), the aqueduct (*aqueductus*) flowing out of paradise (Ecclesiasticus 24:41), the earth besprinkled with celestial dew (*rore perfusa*) giving forth plants (Deuteronomy

32:2), the door (*ianua*) and gate of paradise, and the forecourt (*atrium*) and habitation of God.[209]

Above all, however, Bernardino concluded, Mary is the star: of the heavens, of the pole, of the morning, of the king, and of the sea.[210] As Jerome had explained in his commentary on the Hebrew names, "Maria" means "stella maris" or "star of the sea"; therefore, Bernardino noted, "the Church sings, 'Ave maris stella.' "[211] Some two hundred years earlier Conrad of Saxony had likewise elaborated on this traditional etymology: "Mary is spiritually a 'bitter sea' to the demons, officially 'star of the sea' to men, eternally 'illuminatrix' to the angelic spirits, and universally 'lady' to all creatures."[212] As star of the sea, she guides all those "who sail through the sea of the world in the ship of innocence or penance to the shore of the heavenly country," because she is pure by living purely, radiant by bringing forth eternal light, and useful by directing humanity to the shores of its home country.[213] Jacobus de Voragine would concur: Mary's name is pleasing and sweet, like honey in the mouth, a song in the ear, and joy in the heart. She is illuminated like the woman clothed with the sun and the moon at her feet and on her head a crown of twelve stars (Revelation 12:1); she illuminates the dark places of the earth and warms the cold; and she is bitter on account of the blindness of her people, the sufferings of her Son, and the separations from her Son that she had to endure. She is the lady to whom angels, human beings, and demons all kneel. And she is the star of the sea on whom the whole court of heaven attends.[214]

Why was the virgin's name "Maria"? Again in Richard of Saint-Laurent's words: because she is illuminated by the light of the Father, the grace of the Holy Spirit, and the Son of God who is the true sun of justice. She is the *illuminatrix* of the world because she bore the True Light. She is a bitter sea by reason of her compassion at her Son's suffering. She is the Lady offering her Son to the world, as in her images. And she is the star of the sea exalted over all the orders of the angels: because she is fixed in the firmament of heaven, that is, the scriptures; because she illuminates the world by light of her virtues; because she is on fire with love, especially by him whom she conceived; because she appears little in her humility before God; because she attracts others to her, drawing them through the curtains of the tabernacle, that is, the Church of God; because she shines brilliantly in times of cold, as when at her Son's Passion the love of all others chilled; because she stands in her obedience; because she is scintillating in the excellence of her conversation; because she is continually moving from virtue to virtue and from activity to contemplation; because she illuminates those whom she guards and fights against the devil for her servants; because she was and is always at the right hand of God; because she serves him through all eternity;

because she joyfully gives her light; because she is beautiful in the honesty of her life; because in her and through her the Father laughs with his creatures; because she adorns the Church and illumines the night; because she foretells future events and shows the astrologers, that is, the prophets, to have been telling the truth; because she excites the lazy to work and guides those sailing through the sea of the world to the port of salvation.[215]

Why was the Virgin's name "Maria"? Mary's "faithful Bernard" (*fedel Bernardo*)—for Dante, he needed no other introduction—put it perhaps most famously in the second of his four homilies *super "Missus est,"* cited by all of the authors whom we have considered above, in full by Richard in his commentary on the Ave:

> Surely [the Virgin Mother] is very fittingly likened to a star. The star sends forth its ray without harm to itself. In the same way the Virgin brought forth her son with no injury to herself. The ray no more diminishes the star's brightness than does the Son his mother's integrity. She is indeed that noble star risen out of Jacob (Numbers 24:17) whose beam enlightens this earthly globe. She it is whose brightness both twinkles in the highest heaven and pierces the pit of hell, and is shed upon earth, warming our hearts far more than our bodies, fostering virtue and cauterizing vice. She, I tell you, is that splendid and wondrous star suspended as by necessity over this great wide sea, radiant with merit and brilliant in example.

Accordingly, Bernard "aflame with love" (*ond'io ardo tutto d'amor,* as Dante put it) encouraged his fellow lovers of Mary:

> O you, whoever you are, who feel that in the tidal wave of this world you are nearer to being tossed about among the squalls and gales than treading on dry land, if you do not want to founder in the tempest, do not avert your eyes from the brightness of this star. When the wind of temptation blows up within you, when you strike upon the rock of tribulation, gaze up at this star, call out to Mary. Whether you are being tossed about by the waves of pride or ambition or slander or jealousy, gaze up at this star, call out to Mary. When rage or greed or fleshly desires are battering the skiff of your soul, gaze up at Mary. When the immensity of your sins weighs you down and you are bewildered by the loathsomeness of your conscience, when the terrifying thought of judgment appalls you and you begin to founder in the gulf of sadness and despair, think of Mary. In dangers, in hardships, in every doubt, think of Mary, call out to Mary. Keep her in your mouth, keep her in your heart. Follow the example of her life and you will obtain the favor of her prayer. Following her, you will never go astray.

Asking her help, you will never despair. Keeping her in your thoughts, you will never wander away. With your hand in hers, you will never stumble. With her protecting you, you will not be afraid. With her leading you, you will never tire. Her kindness will see you through to the end. Then you will know by your own experience how true it is that "the Virgin's name was Mary."[216]

All this and more, medieval European Christians hoped and claimed to experience by saluting Mary in the words with which the angel sent from God had greeted her. And yet, much like the angel in many medieval images of the Annunciation, having noted as much, we are arguably only at the threshold of understanding what Mary's devotees said they saw in her.[217] We have, after all, said only the invitatory antiphon and psalm for her Office and are in the process of singing its first hymn. So what if medieval Christians believed their oft-repeated salutations of the Virgin brought her great joy and them a sweet taste to the mouth? So what if they insisted that all their attempts at naming her as the "mother of all re-created things" taxed the very limits of human language and understanding? Where—other than in their desire to exercise their onomastic skills—did they get the idea to read the scriptures in the way that they did, as filled with names for her, almost none of which (other than her actual name) were invoked by the evangelists Matthew, Mark, or Luke? (John, as we shall see, was another matter, particularly as the author of the book of Revelation.) More particularly, why did they invoke *these* metaphors—ark, tabernacle, temple, house, throne, city, mountain, river, tree, mirror, virgin, bride, queen—as a way of describing her relationship with God? And where did they get the idea that it was appropriate to talk about her in the language of the Psalms, as following the invitatory Ave they did hour after hour, day after day in the recitation of her Office?

The thirteenth-century Franciscan preacher Servasanctus of Faenza thought he knew.

"Dearest brothers," Servasanctus invited his readers in the preface to his *Mariale*, paraphrasing the Venerable Bede's opening to his homily on Luke 1:26–38, "let us listen with intent ear to the exordium of our salvation that we might merit to attain the promised gift of salvation."[218] After all, the friar reasoned, if there is not a jot or tittle of the law empty of mystery (cf. Matthew 5:18), how much the more must that brief and blessed word of the evangelist (Luke 1:28) be full of significance. Accordingly, he proposed, "let us see (*videamus*) what and how many are the elements (*quae et quot sunt elementa*) of this exordium!"

There are, the learned friar calculated, eighty-three elements or letters, most perfectly summed up (because eight is the number of completion) in the three theological virtues that the Apostle Paul enumerated (1 Corinthians 13:13); thirty-seven syllables, signifying Mary, her faith in the Trinity and the divine law, and the plenitude of sevenfold grace with which she was filled; and fifteen words, signifying the fifteen steps of virtue that she ascended, plus five distinctions or phrases. The angelic salutation itself contains nine words ("Ave, gratia plena, Dominus tecum: benedicta tu in mulieribus"), signifying that Mary was full of the graces of all the saints and angels.[219] And what do we get once we have counted all the elements? Servasanctus does the arithmetic for us: "Collect, if you will, all these into one, and add that which is customarily added at the end of this salutation, and you will have one hundred and fifty, the same as the number of the psalms of David."

"But surely," we may imagine Servasanctus's late thirteenth-century readers to have protested, for this is the era of the scholastic disputation, in which friars like Servasanctus's brothers at the *studium generale* in Florence were trained, "you are not saying that this means the Psalms of David contain the praises of the Virgin Mary?" (Or perhaps if they protested it was only gently; to judge from the widespread distribution of his work, Servasanctus clearly found a sympathetic audience.)

Not exactly: we have not yet finished our calculations. "Seek," Servasanctus would have his readers, "in heaven, on earth, in the sea, in every abyss, in the Scriptures, in its figures and in its creatures, until you find the same number as it were of harpists playing their harps in praise of Mary (*quendam chorum cytharoedorum cytharizantium cytharis suis laudes Mariae*), so as to make up a pleasing psalter with harp (*ut sit Psalterium jucundum cum cythara*), so that just as the praises of Christ are sung with the psalter of David, so on this harp the praises of the Virgin might be sung." And how many such harpists do we find when we search the heavens, the earth, the seas, the abyss, the scriptures, its figures and creatures? Exactly as many as we found elements in the exordium of salvation, subdivided according to their natures. In natural things (*in rebus naturalibus*), we find eighty-three; in made things (*in rebus artificialibus*), we find thirty-seven; in moral dispositions (*in moralibus*), we find fifteen; in orders of the saints, five; in orders of the angels, nine; and one that sums up all the others (*Magnificata*). If, as we have seen, for Bernardino it was possible to discover Mary's virtues in the very shapes of the letters that went together to make her name, so it would seem, according to Servasanctus, all the creatures of creation—or, at the very least, 150 of them—sang out in her praise from the letters, syllables, words, and phrases of the angelic salutation.

And yet, we are still not finished, so intricate a mystery does the exordium contain. To unlock it, or so Servasanctus would have it, we must do more than calculate the number of these creaturely "harpists." Rather, Servasanctus insisted, in all of these, if we look carefully, we find (and this is very significant for Servasanctus's purposes), the elements (*elementa*) of Mary's praise, for they show her in their forms (*quasi quaedam facies ipsam Virginem utcumque*), represent her in figure (*quasi in aenigmate repraesentantes*), name her (*quasi quaedam vocabula nomen Virginis interpretantia*), and wrap the plenitude of her graces in parables (*quasi quaedam parabola gratiarum eius plenitudinem involutam*) through the particulars they contain (*pro particulis continentes*). For, argued Servasanctus, just as in the words of the Philosopher (that is, Aristotle) "those things which are dispersed in animals by nature are gathered together in man by reason"[220]—simplicity in the dove, kindness in the lamb, liberality in the lion—so all the graces and blessings that are bestowed upon others in part are gathered together in Mary in full, as indeed, we read about her in Proverbs 31:29: "Many daughters have gathered together riches: you have surpassed them all."

And yet—Servasanctus continued—for all her riches as a creature, in Mary herself there is an even greater mystery. "In me," Wisdom says in Ecclesiasticus 24:25, "is all grace of the way (*gratia omnis viae*), that is [according to Servasanctus], of every creature, which is a way to the Creator (*id est omnis creaturae, quae est via ad Creatorem*), for Mary, the book of life and the mirror and the exemplar either is or contains all these things (*haec enim omnia est aut continet liber vitae et speculum et exemplar MARIA*)." As Servasanctus would have it, Mary, the "mother of fair love, and of fear, and of knowledge, and of holy hope" (Ecclesiasticus 24:24), is *the* way to the Creator because she is the book of life containing all the creatures of creation, who herself promises, speaking as Wisdom: "They that explain me shall have life everlasting" (Ecclesiasticus 24:31). "And I wept," says John in Revelation 5:4, cited by Servasanctus, "because no man was found worthy to open the book, nor to see it."

The elements of the evangelical exordium precisely calculated to the number of the Psalms, the same number of harpists discovered in the natural and artificial creatures of creation singing the praises of the Virgin, just as King David sang the praises of Christ, the creature Mary as the book of life, mirror, and exemplar of the Creator containing all the creatures of creation, Wisdom promising in Ecclesiasticus that they who explain her shall have eternal life: these are mysteries indeed. We have heard the angel greet her. Clearly, to understand and experience the Virgin's psalter as Servasanctus hoped his fellow Christians might, somehow we need to learn to read this book.

PLATE 8 Mary of Burgundy is shown praying with her Book of Hours, while through the
window she can be seen kneeling before the Virgin and Child for whom she has sung the psalms.
Her prayer has made them visible to her and brought her into their presence. Book of Hours,
Flanders, ca. 1477. Use of Rome. Made for Mary of Burgundy (1457–1482), the daughter of
Charles the Bold. Vienna, Österreichische Nationalbibliothek, Cod. 1857, fol. 14v.

3

Antiphon and Psalm

The Office of Matins continues.[1] Having saluted the Virgin and hymned her praise as the one in whose womb the Maker of all things enclosed himself—

Quem terra, pontus, aethera
colunt, adorant, praedicant,
trinam regentem machinam
claustrum Mariae baiulat.

He whom earth, and sea, and sky,
worship, adore, proclaim,
who rules their triple fabric
Mary's cloistered womb contains.

Cui luna, sol et omnia,
deserviunt per tempora,
perfusa caeli gratia
gestant puellae viscera.

He whom the moon, sun, and everything
serve throughout all time,
bedewed with heavenly grace
the maiden's vitals bore.

Beata mater, munere
cuius supernus artifex,

mundum pugillo continens,
ventris sub arca clausus est.

Blessed mother, by whose
gift the celestial maker,
containing the world in his fist,
is enclosed in the ark of the womb.

Benedicta caeli nuntio,
fecunda sancto Spiritu,
desideratus gentibus,
cuius per alvum fusus est.

Blessed by the messenger of heaven,
made fruitful by the Holy Spirit,
through whose womb was he brought forth,
the one longed for by the peoples.

Gloria tibi, Domine,
qui natus es de virgine,
cum Patre et sancto Spiritu,
in sempiterna saecula. Amen.

Glory to you, Lord,
born from the virgin,
with the Father and the Holy Spirit,
now and forever. Amen.[2]

—you turn your attention once again to the *versicularius*, now intoning the pregnant antiphonal phrase: "Benedicta tu." As the choir answers with the first of the three psalms of the nocturn, you begin to reflect on how appropriate it is that the antiphon itself should reiterate Elizabeth's greeting to Mary (Luke 1:42: "Blessed are you among women and blessed is the fruit of your womb") when the psalm for which the Marian antiphon provides the frame is a celebration of the greatness of the Lord as Creator and of the place of man (*homo*) in his creation:

Benedicta tu.

Blessed are you.[3]

Domine, Dominus noster, quam admirabile est nomen tuum in universa terra! Quoniam elevata est magnificentia tua super caelos.

O Lord, our Lord, how admirable is your name in all the earth, for your magnificence is exalted above the heavens.

Ex ore infantium et lactantium perfecisti laudem propter inimicos tuos ut destruas inimicum et ultorem.

Out of the mouths of babes and sucklings you have perfected praise because of your enemies, that you might destroy the enemy and the avenger.

Quoniam videbo caelos tuos, opera digitorum tuorum, lunam et stellas quae tu fundasti.

For I will behold your heavens, the works of your fingers: the moon and the stars, which you have founded.

Quid est homo, quod memor es eius, aut filius hominis, quoniam visitas eum?

What is man that you are mindful of him? or the son of man that you visit him?

Minuisti eum paulominus ab angelis; gloria et honore coronasti eum et constituisti eum super opera manuum tuarum.

You have made him a little lower than the angels, with glory and honor you have crowned him: and you have set him over the works of your hand.

Omnia subiecisti sub pedibus eius, oves et boves universas, insuper et pecora campi, volucres caeli et pisces maris qui perambulant semitas maris.

You have put all things in subjection under his feet, sheep and all oxen, and the beasts of the field. The birds of the air and the fishes of the sea that walk through the paths of the seas.

Domine, Dominus noster, quam admirabile est nomen tuum in universa terra!

O Lord, our Lord, how admirable is your name in all the earth![4]

Gloria Patri et Filio et Spiritui Sancto. Sicut erat in principio et nunc et semper et in saecula saeculorum. Amen.

Glory be to the Father, and to the Son, and to the Holy Spirit. As it was in the beginning, is now, and ever shall be: world without end. Amen.[5]

Ruminating further, you recall reading just the other day how Psalm 8 (*Domine, Dominus noster*) is one of a number of psalms that speak directly about the two natures of Christ, its first part praising the majesty of his divinity, its second hymning the humility and glory of his humanity.[6] Accordingly, as you recite the psalm, you find yourself wanting to linger over every syllable of every word, the better to squeeze the honey of its spiritual meaning from the comb of its letters.[7] You are struck in particular by the second part (or colon) of the first verse: "Quoniam elevata est magnificentia tua super caelos." What was it that Cassiodorus said about this verse? Oh, yes: "the *magnificence* is the secret of the Lord's incarnation, and amongst its various wonders we acknowledge above all as a gift bestowed on us the fact that God deigned to become man, and endured the cross for the salvation of all." A blessed fruit, indeed, especially now that the Lord Christ has been elevated above the heavens and all creatures to sit at the right hand of the Father![8] And how appropriate that newborn babes should have perfected his praise, whose magnificence exceeds even that of the scriptures, not to mention the understanding of all rational creatures![9]

Augustine had something rather pointed to say in this respect, did he not? About the heretics and those who pass for philosophers among the superstitious Gentiles and how they are wrong to think that faith may be bypassed on the way to knowledge? Now you remember: it is for this reason that they are in fact the enemies of the truth, because they try to persuade people to worship and venerate the elements of the world, when it is the Son of God who is the power and wisdom of God "by which everyone who is made wise by the truth is enlightened."[10] And what (you ask yourself, still following Augustine) are "the works of your fingers" if not the scriptures by which God has brought knowledge of his magnificence down within the range of nurslings and infants, that through these books, written by the saints through the operation of the Holy Spirit, they might be "nurtured and strengthened to scale the heights and understand things eternal, through the humility of faith rooted in a history which has been worked out within time"?[11] Again, you muse, how appropriate that this same psalm should point both to the wonders of creation, "all of which the Lord has ordered by that power of His wisdom which is beyond understanding," and to the fleshly weakness that "the Lord-Man himself, born of the virgin Mary . . . condescended to bear"![12] How was it that Cassiodorus put it? "The Creator of angels was made less than the angels," but only "*a little less*, because though He took on a mortal body He had no sin." Now, resurrected, he has been "crowned with glory and honor," and every creature is subjected "under his feet," worshipping and adoring the Creator. Aptly, therefore, "*crown* . . . is applied to the circle of the world, because the entire circumference of the universe was fashioned in its image."[13] Likewise fittingly, you now realize, the psalm ends as it began, the Church having sung of the Incarnation and Resurrection now returning to her praise of he who is "alpha and omega, beginning and end" (cf. Revelation 1:8).[14]

Blessed indeed, you reflect, coming back to yourself at the familiar Gloria Patri, was she who bore such fruit in her womb, even as the antiphon bears (introduces and concludes) the recitation of the psalm celebrating his divine and human magnificence and glory. Suddenly, it occurs to you that perhaps this is the key to understanding the book of Mary's Hours, every psalm framed, indeed embraced, by its corresponding antiphon, like the Son of God seated in his Mother's lap. Your eye falls once again on the image of the Blessed Virgin, and just for a moment it is as if the Child enthroned in her arms smiles at you.[15] So that's it, is it? This is the way to crack open the hard shell of the letter to reveal the sweet nut of the spirit within; this is the way to lift the veil of the text's literal meaning from the spiritual sense it conceals.[16] Mary is the comb containing the honey, the shell protecting the nut, the veil concealing the Holy of Holies, the antiphon framing the psalm. She is the one both who contains and who shows us the way to Christ. That would explain why the Office, ostensibly offered in praise of Mary, still depends so heavily on the psalms: it is not only about her, it is also about her Son whom she makes visible to the world. But surely, you pause to consider, this is the case with the Divine Office as a whole, including the offices offered in praise of the saints on their feast days? Perhaps every performance of the Divine Office should be experienced as a sort of dialogue, a conversation between the scriptural texts and their antiphonal and (for the lessons) responsorial frames. And yet, is it not striking that it is the Marian Office that your community appends to every recitation of the Divine Hours, almost as if to remind you that it was Mary through whom the Word came bodily—historically, literally—into the world so that the spiritual sense of the prophecies King David made in his psalms might be fulfilled?

Not everyone, you remind yourself, is able to extract all these various levels of meanings from the psalms. Some, even in your own community, have access only to the literal meaning of the texts, such that, while you are filling the pauses between the verses of the psalms with meditations on their allegorical, tropological, and anagogical mysteries (as the traditional division of the spiritual senses would put it), they are occupying themselves with greetings to Mary or short ejaculations like "Christ Jesus, son of the living God, have mercy on us." Moreover, you consider, other even simpler souls understand not even the literal sense of the texts and find themselves rather in darkness, at least with respect to the words. During the psalmody, they occupy themselves with making imaginary pictures: Gabriel greeting the Virgin, Mary conceiving the Word, Mary greeting Elizabeth, and so forth. For them, it is only the number of the psalms that has any significance. Thus, for example, the five psalms at Lauds they refer to the five wounds of Christ, all the while drawing imaginary pictures of Christ "crucified on the floorboards (*super formas*)." Alternately, they refer the first three verses of each psalm to the Holy Trinity, the next five to the wounds of Christ on the cross, and the next five to the joys of the Virgin, while they may refer "nine verses to the nine orders of angels, twelve to the twelve apostles, and other verses to the martyrs, confessors, virgins and all the saints familiar to them."[17] And yet, who is to say that they, like you, do not make good use of their time? After all, as the psalm you have just been singing itself says, "out of the mouths of babes and sucklings, you have perfected praise," so efficacious is the recitation of the psalms even when those saying them do not have access to their full sense.

"But Mary kept all these words, pondering them in her heart" (Luke 2:19).[18] It is a curious feature of the medieval European Christian tradition that while there are more books than anybody could ever hope to read of commentary on the Psalms, many of them still extant only in manuscript, and more manuscript copies of the Psalms, including Books of Hours, than any other book of the Bible, we know comparatively little about the way in which they were experienced and understood as they were prayed.[19] This is particularly the case with the Hours of the Virgin, but it is likewise true for the psalms as they were recited in the Divine Office more generally. Indeed, the Cistercian Stephen of Sawley (d. 1252), on whose *De informatione mentis circa psalmodiam diei et noctis* the above meditation largely depends, is one of the few to have written explicitly about this experience, and even he does so largely to apologize for not being able to say more.[20] Moreover, even such prolific monastic commentators on scripture and the liturgy as Honorius Augustodunensis (fl. early twelfth century) and

Rupert of Deutz make only scattered, typically indirect references to the experience—as opposed to the symbolism—of performing the texts of the Office.[21] As the twentieth-century Benedictine Dom Jean Leclercq (d. 1993) once famously observed, monks like Stephen, Honorius, and Rupert "wrote little about their attitude toward the liturgy: its importance was quite taken for granted; for men [and women] who were living constantly under its influence, it hardly needed any commentary."[22]

And yet, in other ways, arguably above all with respect to the Marian Office, medieval Christians wrote about it all the time. Perhaps not in the form that we might like—full commentaries on the significance of each of the texts as they appear in the Office, as, for example, Ethelred Taunton offered in his *The Little Office of Our Lady: A Treatise Theoretical, Practical, and Exegetical* published in 1903—but indirectly in their commentaries and sermons on the Ave Maria and the meaning of Mary's name as well as directly in the texts of the Office itself. If their understanding of the meaning and importance of the Marian Office is nowhere (or only rarely) explicitly stated, it is everywhere assumed in the texts, chants, and images with which they prayed. Arguably, from this perspective, to understand the experience of saying the Office, particularly something so embedded in the daily life of even the most ordinary medieval Christians as the Hours of the Virgin, all that we would need to do is to say it ourselves, paying proper attention to the choice of texts and their juxtapositions, much as the preachers and commentators did when they wrote about the meaning of particular antiphons and psalms. But would we? As everyone who has ever attempted to read a medieval commentary on scripture and found it boring or nonsensical or to make sense of the intricacies of the medieval liturgy and found them abstruse and overly elaborate knows, the real problem is that we (modern scholars, modern Christians, devotees and skeptics alike) do not know how to read these sources anymore.

It is not just that so many centuries intervene. The world has changed, and with it the way in which we think about almost everything in it: tradition, the scriptures, the role of God in creation. If, as we shall see in the concluding chapter on Sor María de Jesús de Ágreda, even as late as the seventeenth century, it was still possible to see the Virgin in the figures of the Old Testament so beloved of her medieval devotees, by the eighteenth century this tradition had become even in Catholic countries the object of Enlightened ridicule. By the nineteenth century, particularly for Protestant Anglophone audiences, it had been almost entirely forgotten, so much so that Henry Adams looking on the magnificence of Chartres could explain it only as the response to a woman's fancy, the latter albeit a "force . . . as potent as X-rays."[23] More recently, as we have noted, it has been

PLATE 9 Virgin and Child enthroned. "*Oratio ad sanctam Mariam*: Sancta Maria, succurre miseris, iuva pusillanimes, refove flebiles, ora pro populo, interveni pro clero, intercede pro devoto femineo sexu. Sentiant omnes tuum levamen quicumque celebrunt tuum nomen. Sancta Maria virgo regis semper invicti mater castissima, ora et intercede pro cunctis fidentibus tuis patrociniis . . ." Psalter ("The Melisende Psalter"), Jerusalem, 1131–1143. Probably made for Melisende (1105–1161), queen of Jerusalem, by Basilius in the monastery of the Holy Sepulcher. London, British Library, Egerton 1139, fol. 202v.

difficult for scholars to read the exuberant efforts of Mary's medieval devotees to catalogue her many titles as anything other than clerical wordplay intended more to dazzle its hapless audiences than to enlighten them.[24] How, following the Reformation's revaluation of the tradition of scriptural exegesis on which the medieval image of the Virgin depended, the Enlightenment's revaluation of the idea of the Creator God, and the Romantics' revaluation of the role of emotion (as opposed to intellect) in faith, not to mention the construction of the whole modern edifice of scientific scholarship and history according to which medieval views of the world appear more often than not as grotesque, superstitious, or simply wrong—how under such circumstances is it possible to catch even a glimpse of what medieval Christians saw or heard when they read or sang the psalms and other chants in the Office of the Virgin?

The Cistercian Stephen of Sawley would have it that Mary herself is somehow the key: "when you arise in the middle of the night to praise the Lord, recite first Matins of the Blessed Virgin with such devotion as if you were there at the birth of Jesus Christ which is believed to have happened at that hour. Addressing the Blessed Virgin as if she were present (*praesentialiter*), direct your intention either to her or to her son by means of the hymns and psalms, lessons and responsories."[25] With the unspoken corollary: "And she will help you to understand their *materia* or themes." After all, as the Dominican Pseudo-Albert would insist, she knows everything there is to know about the scriptures and the mysteries contained within them. Indeed, as the Franciscan Servasanctus would have it, she herself is the book containing all the creatures of creation which shows the way to the Creator, to explain which is to have everlasting life.

More prosaically, with or without the Virgin's guidance, there are two things that we need to discover to read Mary's book and hear the psalter of creation singing her praises in the way that Servasanctus, Pseudo-Albert, Stephen, and their medieval contemporaries did: (1) where the image of Mary at the core of her Office came from, and (2) how to read the psalms as Marian.

MARY IN THE TEMPLE

Sing with me, can you hear the creatures? Let us name them, if we can. Light, heaven of heavens, crystalline heaven, firmament, sun, moon, morning star, star of the sea, star, constellation, day, noon, dawn, rainbow, cloud, mist, snow, dew, air, flood, sea, port, river, Ganges, Nile, Tigris, Euphrates, Doryx, Jordan, aqueduct, fountain, well, earth, paradise, field, desert, valley, mountain, rock, mineral, gold, gemstone, tree, root, shoot, cedar, cypress, palm tree, rosebush, olive tree, plane tree, fig tree, vine, terebinth, silver fir, tree of Sethim, pomegranate, almond tree, bush, mulberry tree, chaste-tree, grove, spice bed, cinnamon, balsam, myrrh, storax, galbanum, onyx, fragrant resin, frankincense, opobalsam, nard, flower, lily, bee, turtledove, dove, hind, sheep, fleece, neck, heart, exemplar, book, mirror, new vessel, vessel of gold, city, castle, wall, tower, gate, window, house of God, court, bridal chamber, throne, litter, couch, granary, dining room, cellar, oven, treasure chest, ship, ladder, fishnet, ark of Noah, cloister, tabernacle, temple of God, Holy of Holies, ark of the Covenant, mercy seat, golden altar, veil, candelabra, column, courtyard, virago, mother, one, perfect, chosen, queen, lady, daughter, sister, friend, bride, handmaiden, nurse, advocate, cymbal-player, virgin of virgins, queen of confessors, queen of martyrs, queen of apostles, queen of patriarchs and prophets, queen of angels, of archangels, of virtues, of powers, of principalities, of dominions, of thrones, of cherubim, of seraphim, *Magnificata*.[26]

Count with me, how many do we find? One hundred fifty harpists singing the praises of the Mother of God, showing forth the Virgin and naming her as the one in whom the Creator took his rest (cf. Ecclesiasticus 24:12). Where did all these names come from? According to Servasanctus: scripture, at least most of them. A few—crystalline heaven, star of the sea, constellation, chaste-tree, opobalsam, cloister, lady, advocate, virgin of virgins, and Mary's thirteen titles as queen—do not appear in scripture, but all of the other one hundred twenty-eight do, as Servasanctus makes clear with great chains of citations, the vast majority taken from Ecclesiasticus, the Song of Songs, or the Psalms, with a handful (about six) taken from the New Testament and the remainder from other books in the Old Testament.[27]

As we have seen, Servasanctus was hardly alone in scouring the scriptures for mentions of Mary. Richard of Saint-Laurent, Conrad of Saxony, Jacobus de Voragine, Bonaventure of Bagnoreggio, Pseudo-Albert, Frauenlob, Walter of Wimborne, Engelbert of Admont, not to mention countless anonymous preachers and poets, all were convinced that the scriptures spoke all the time about Mary, not just those passages in Matthew, Mark, Luke, and John on which most modern descriptions of Jesus's mother depend. Even Anselm of Canterbury, who tended to bury his citations of scripture in allusion and liturgical echoes, found it impossible to speak about Mary without referring to her Old Testament names: "palace of universal propitiation . . . vase and temple of life"; while Hildegard of Bingen, even more allusively, still talked about her as "mirror" (cf. Wisdom 7:26), "fountain" (cf. Song of Songs 4:12), "closed portal" (cf. Ezekiel 44:1), and "sun" (cf. Psalm 88:38).[28]

The twelfth-century *Speculum virginum*, written in dialogue form for a community of German canonesses, contains a veritable cascade of such references, without apology and without full citations, suggesting at the very least that the author did not expect them to be unfamiliar to the women for whom he was writing. As the master Peregrinus explains to his disciple Theodora,

> If I tried to say anything about the Lord's Mother it would be an act of reckless presumption rather than learning. For the magnitude of grace divinely granted to Mary exceeds my faculty of speech, since she was chosen before she was born to conceive the eternal Word, and crowned once born with the perfection of all blessings.

Nevertheless, he tries:

> She then is the bride of the eternal king; she is daughter, mother, and virgin; dove, sister, and beloved; unique mother of the unique Son of God, foreordained in heaven before she was born to be the Mother of God's Son. . . . She is the dawn, the sun, the moon, and the star: the dawn preceding the Sun of justice in its rising; the sun in whom the Creator himself set the tabernacle of his body, and came forth like a bridegroom from his chamber; the moon radiant from its Creator's splendor . . .; and the star of the sea, because she is the path, the harbor, and the life of sailors in this worldly darkness. In paradise she is the flower and fruit of trees that exude the finest balsam, and the green shoot of all spices. . . . Since she is mother and virgin, she is revealed by a mystic figure in the bush that burned and was not consumed. In the tabernacle of Moses, fashioned with such variety of materials and such marvelous art, she is supremely figured in the branch of Aaron and the golden urn. She is the dry branch that flowered among the other dry branches, bearing flower and fruit before the whole mass of humankind which had withered in sin. . . . The golden urn which preserved the manna symbolizes the purity of her mind and body in its gold, displaying the manna—that is, the Word of God, "the food of angels" [Wisdom 16:20]—to all the faithful. Do you see that all the labor of the wondrous tabernacle and its most precious hangings—"in gold and silver, purple and linen, twice-dyed scarlet" and every precious stone [Exodus 25:3–4]—pertained to those four things [the tabernacle, the ark, the golden urn, and the branch of Aaron] in which the future mysteries of the Mother and Son were chiefly hidden for our

future age?. . . . Indeed, you will find many things proclaiming and bearing witness to the Lord's Mother in the prophets' writings and miracles, and if we were to scrutinize and discuss every one of them, our dialogue would exceed all bounds. For what speech can contain her whom the Son of God chose before the commencement of time to be his temple . . . who alone was preserved to redeem humankind?[29]

The question before us now is not whether medieval Christians knew these titles for the Virgin (to judge from our surviving sources, all those who wrote about Mary did), but whether there was a method in this exegetical madness other than, for example, looking for feminine nouns (particularly when not all of them are feminine, for example, *templum*, n.).[30]

Where did this practice of reading the scriptures as filled with references to Mary come from? There are, roughly speaking, two options: one, it was invented by the medieval devotees of the Virgin as a way of expressing their desire to honor her. Two, it was part of the tradition out of which Christianity developed in the first place. (A third possibility, that it was learned by medieval Latin Christians from their Orthodox brethren in the East—which, as we shall see, it was—is simply a variant on the first, with the early Christians of the Greek, Syrian, Coptic, Armenian, Georgian, and Ethiopic traditions being the primary inventors.) The former is the argument made almost invariably by most modern scholars, who would date the emergence of devotion to Mary only some time after the composition of the Gospels and other texts of the New Testament.[31] The latter is the argument made by Mary's medieval devotees, that the scriptures, most especially those of the Old Testament, spoke about Mary all the time because they were originally about her, just as they were about her Son. As Peregrinus put it in his dialogue with Theodora:

All these things, wrapped and veiled in symbolic foreshadowings, have been revealed to our age more clearly than light by the gracious gifts of heaven . . . If then you seek Mary with a subtle understanding, you will find her in heaven before all creation; you will see her in paradise and in Noah's ark in the flood; you will see her among the patriarchs and wandering with the people of God in the desert; you will find her among the judges and kings, coming forth from the royal stock and blooming among the Jews like a rose among thorns.[32]

You will find her, Peregrinus insists, because she was always there.

More than just the devotion to the Virgin depends on this claim; it is fundamental to the history of Christianity itself. "What do you think of the

Christ?," Jesus asked the Pharisees. "Whose son is he?" According to Matthew, they responded: "The son of David." At which Jesus asked them: "How is it then that David, inspired by the Spirit, calls him Lord?" In proof of which, Jesus quoted a psalm:

> The Lord said to my Lord,
> Sit at my right hand,
> till I put thy enemies under thy feet.

And then he asked the Pharisees to interpret it: "If David thus calls him Lord, how is [the Christ] his son?" "And no one," the evangelist noted, "was able to answer him a word, nor from that day did any one dare to ask him any more questions" (Matthew 22:41–46 RSV).[33] Everything, it would seem, hinged upon the interpretation of this psalm (Psalm 109 Vulgate, 110 RSV): the identity of the Christ, his relationship to King David, Jesus's authority to teach (cf. Mark 12:35–37; Luke 20:41–44; Acts 2:34–35; Hebrews 5:5–6). Nor to this day has the question been resolved, at least for those who do not accept the Christian answer. To rehearse the claims made repeatedly in the New Testament about the identity of Jesus, not to mention his mother Mary, whom the angel Gabriel claimed would bear a child who would be called "holy, the Son of God" and "Son of the Most High" (Luke 1:32, 35 RSV), is to ask *the* question on which the whole Christian tradition depends: Why did Jesus's followers identify him as they did, not just as their friend and rabbi, but, in the Apostle Peter's words as recorded by the evangelist, as "the Christ, the Son of the Living God" (Matthew 16:16 RSV)? Why? According to the evangelists: because in Jesus, as they read them, the scriptures were fulfilled. To put it mildly, many of Jesus's contemporaries, particularly among his own people, disagreed.[34]

No matter how many ways you slice it, there is no way that both of these readings of the scriptures can be true, the one insisting that Jesus fulfilled the prophecies, the other that he did not, both, however, claiming the same scriptures as the key to the recognition and understanding of God's presence among his people. Nor from within either tradition of interpretation, the one claimed by the followers of Jesus, the other by those who did not recognize him as the Christ, is it possible to discern which, in fact, is the correct one. (Whether the tradition on which the scriptures were dependent gives an accurate representation of reality is another question altogether, but that is not a question that we, as historians, are equipped to answer.) As Old Testament scholar Margaret Barker has put it in reflecting on the problem of discerning the origins of Christian practices such as the Eucharist, which practice she argues is better read in the context of the ancient temple liturgy for the Day of Atonement than in first-century C.E. synagogue observances of Passover:

> *There can be no certainty that what the Eucharist became was different from Jesus' original intention.* . . . Data becomes significant only in context, and if a synagogue context is assumed because Christians called their assemblies "synagogues" (Jas 2.2), or a Passover context is assumed, because Jesus was crucified at Passover, data can be put into those frameworks, and a picture constructed which may be inaccurate because it is based on false assumptions. If other contexts are considered, then the same data can convey something very different, because a different set of associations is implicit in the proposed contexts.[35]

How we read the origins of Christianity depends on what frame we choose; likewise, the meaning of the texts to which Christians have for centuries appealed as proofs for who they thought Jesus was. So, for example, the great sixteenth-century reformer John Calvin (d. 1564) insisted against both the Jews and his fellow reformer Michael Servetus (d. 1553, in Calvin's Geneva, burned at the stake) that the Word of God manifested himself to Abraham and the patriarchs in the form of an angel: "For though he were not clothed with flesh, yet he descended as in an intermediate form, that he might have more familiar access to the faithful." This is the angel whom Jacob wrestled, after which he declared: "I have seen God face to face" (Genesis 32:30); this, likewise, is the angel whom Paul said led the people in the wilderness (1 Corinthians 10:4). "Still clearer and stronger," Calvin insisted, "is the passage of Malachi, in which a promise is made that the messenger who was then expected would come to his own temple [Malachi 3:1]. The temple certainly was dedicated to Almighty God only, and yet the prophet claims it for Christ. Hence it follows," Calvin concluded, "that he is the God who was always worshipped by the Jews."[36] It was likewise, those following the tradition of reading the scriptures on which the medieval devotion to the Virgin depended would insist, with Mary. As Theodora put it, in answer to Peregrinus's expositions of the scriptures in which Mary shone forth: "It is a most fitting and spiritual affair that all the most profound and noble sacraments granted to the ancient people should pertain to the beauty and glory of Mary, who visibly bore 'the beauty of justice' [Jeremiah 31:23] 'in whom all the fullness of deity dwells bodily' [Colossians 2:9]."[37] And yet, it would be the followers of the reformers like Calvin who would come to insist that the scriptures say "so little" about her.

As with the disjuncture between the Jewish and Christian traditions of reading the scriptures about Jesus, so with the disjuncture between the Orthodox,

Catholic, and Protestant traditions of reading the scriptures about Mary: we are at an impasse. However much Catholic scholars following the medieval tradition insist she is there, particularly in the Old Testament, Protestant scholars say she is not, including in those passages of the New Testament that the Catholic tradition has read consistently about her, particularly the description in Revelation 12:1 of the woman clothed with the sun, the moon at her feet, and her head encircled with stars.[38] It is yet another instance of the Rubin face-vase ambiguity with which all converts are familiar: both traditions of interpretation cannot be true (or even seen) at the same time and yet somehow must be, else one or the other tradition must be accepted as false.[39] Arguably more so than almost any other aspect of the larger Christian tradition, Mary is on the cusp of the disruption in the way of reading the Old Testament that occurred in the sixteenth century, making it more or less impossible for modern interpreters to read the scriptures like a medieval Christian.[40] Our problem as historians is to try to see this older tradition from within: to read the scriptures as once medieval Christians did, taking the psalms as historically or literally about Jesus as the Lord made present in his temple by (or with) his Lady Mother. Rather than starting from the assumption that the medieval tradition was wrong, what if we imagined for the sake of experiment that it was right?

Although she herself has not described it in this way, this, in effect, is the tradition that the maverick (as she is often called) Methodist lay theologian Margaret Barker has been attempting to recover in her studies of the Old Testament, its apocrypha, and pseudepigrapha, as preserved and developed by the earliest Christians.[41] In Barker's reading of the scriptures (both those included in present-day Christian and rabbinic Bibles and those accepted by the early Christians but subsequently forgotten or suppressed[42]), the earliest Christians were Jews steeped in the traditions of the worship of the temple as it was before King Josiah's (reigned 641–609 B.C.E.) famous Deuteronomic reform (2 Kings 23 RSV).[43] From this perspective, Christianity emerges not as a radical break from the ancient Hebrew tradition, but rather as the fulfillment of a tradition going back to the temple of Solomon, including the claim that the Virgin would give birth to the Son of the Most High.

While at odds with most standard modern interpretations of the relationship between the Old and New Testaments, this reading, in broad strokes as well as in particulars, bears a surprising and provocative resemblance to the way in which medieval exegetes read the scriptures, above all in their emphasis on both the temple as the place where God becomes present and the Virgin as the Mother, Bride, and Daughter of Wisdom. Intriguingly, it has received its most sympathetic reception from pastoral theologians like the former Archbishop of

Canterbury, Rowan Williams, who awarded Barker a Lambeth Degree in 2008 "in recognition of her work on the Jerusalem temple and the origins of Christian liturgy which has made a significant new contribution to our understanding of the New Testament and opened up important fields for research," and Orthodox scholars like the Byzantinist, Father Andrew Louth, who commented to one of the readers for the press for *Mary and the Art of Prayer* "that [while] Barker's work isn't entirely convincing as a history of Israelite religion . . . it does present a very good picture of how that religion was probably seen by early Christian writers." Whether or not this reconstruction is correct in all its particulars,[44] like Sigmund Mowinckel's groundbreaking work on the cultic origins of the psalms in the worship of the pre-exilic temple, it is, I would venture, worth our attention here insofar as it challenges us to rethink the frames with which we have viewed both the older Christian tradition and the texts to which it appealed.[45] If problematic (much like the medieval exegetical tradition) as history, nevertheless, I would contend that Barker's attempt at reconstructing this older tradition offers a powerful and much needed heuristic for rethinking why medieval Christians read the psalms and other Old Testament texts in the way that they did, as speaking everywhere about Mary as the Lady in whom the Lord became present to the world. As I read her work, Barker encourages us, if you will, to step into the light and look along the beam by which early and medieval Christians claimed to see the Lady and her Lord and thereby to consider, if only for a moment, that what they saw might have been not just historically or theologically, but possibly even substantively real. (As my readers for the press would have me caution you, "*Caveat lector! Hic sunt dracones!*" But we knew that, we're medievalists; dragons come with the territory, it says so in the psalms.[46])

As Barker reconstructs it, the core of the tradition to which the earliest Christians appealed was the temple seen as representing creation, itself divided by a veil into the visible (created, material, earthly) and invisible (uncreated, heavenly) worlds. "The Holy of Holies, with the golden chariot throne, was the invisible world of God and the angels," while "the great hall of the temple represented the material world . . . with Adam, the human being, as the high priest." The veil dividing the great hall from the Holy of Holies was woven from four colors—purple, blue, scarlet, and white—to represent the four elements that "screened the glory of God from the material world." The Holy of Holies thus screened by the veil was, therefore, "a hidden place," beyond matter and time. "Rituals in the Holy of Holies were rituals in eternity, and those who entered the Holy of Holies passed between heaven and earth." The Holy of Holies itself was a great golden cube housing the ark on which the glory of God rested, enthroned above the cherubim (Psalm 99:1 RSV; 2 Chronicles 3–5).

The temple was served by priests "after the order of Melchizedek" (Psalm 110:4 RSV; cf. Hebrews 5:6), clothed in white linen when they entered the Holy of Holies, while the Davidic kings themselves, once anointed, were seen as "transformed by their anointing and enthronement into sons of God, into the human presence of Yahweh"—that is, the Lord.[47]

Nor in this tradition, as Barker reads it, was the Lord, the Son of the Most High, alone in his temple: his Mother was with him. The earliest Christians described her as a woman clothed with the sun, crowned with stars, with the moon under her feet, who gave birth to a male child who was to rule all the nations (Revelation 12:1–2); as a bride, clothed in fine linen (the garment worn by the priests as they stood before the Lord in the Holy of Holies) (Revelation 19:8); and as a bejeweled city (Revelation 21:9–21). This bride, mother of her son, was the queen of heaven for whom the women of Jerusalem once burned incense, poured out libations, and baked cakes "bearing her image" (Jeremiah 44:15–19). She was Miriam, ancestress of the royal house, the mother of the kings of Jerusalem.[48] She was Wisdom, the Tree of Life (Proverbs 3:18), whom Solomon sought as his bride (Wisdom 8:2), who was with the Lord as he brought all things into creation (Proverbs 8:22). And she was (in Barker's words) "the lady [who] was the genius of Jerusalem."[49] She was also expelled from the temple, along with the anointed kings, her cakes, and her candelabra-trees, in the course of King Josiah's reforms (cf. 2 Kings 23:6–7 RSV, on the destruction of the Asherah). And yet, she, like her Son, was destined to return—or so at least those who came to call themselves Christians (that is, "little anointed ones") believed.

We have encountered many of these images already in the medieval efforts to discover Mary's name: Mary as the tabernacle of God, the temple, the house, the bedchamber, the bride, the daughter, the ark of the covenant, the golden urn, the manna, the rod of Aaron, the gate of Ezekiel, the city of God. For Richard of Saint-Laurent, Mary was "the tabernacle and the *triclinium* of the whole Trinity." For Bonaventure, she was the temple in which "the whole Divinity dwelt corporeally," the house of David in which "the true David, Christ, dwelt," and the tabernacle in which her Creator rested (Ecclesiasticus 24:12). For Conrad of Saxony, she was the container signified by the house which Solomon built (3 Kings 8:27), a vessel more capacious than heaven and earth, because he whom the whole world could not contain was enclosed in her womb. This is the Virgin celebrated in the hymns, chants, psalms, lessons, and prayers of the Marian Office: the Mother of the Lord who bore the Son of God in her womb just as the ark of the covenant held the flowering rod of Aaron and the golden urn of manna, the bodily temple through whose material veil the Son of God passed from heaven (the Holy of Holies) to earth (the visible world). The imagery is clear in the magnificent ancient hymn long attributed to Venantius Fortunatus (d. ca. 609) which was sung every morning in her Office by her medieval European devotees (and which we have just sung earlier in this chapter): Mary's womb enclosed the Creator who rules earth, sea, and sky; filled with the grace of heaven, a maiden gave birth from her body the one whom the sun, moon, and all other creatures serve. Over and over again, the hymn emphasizes that it is the Maker of all things (*supernus artifex*) whom the ark of Virgin's womb contained (*ventris sub arca clausus est*), and that it is through her womb that he who contains everything in his hand (*mundum pugillo continens*) came forth into the world (*cujus per alvum fusus est*). But who, after all, was this Maker of all things, and why did he need a Mother? In a word, according to Barker, he was the Lord, whose mother was the holy place, the living temple, where he became present to the world.

The Lord and the Lady of the Temple

In the beginning (as Barker tells it), there was El, the Most High, the deity served by the high priest Melchizedek (Genesis 14:18–20). There was also El Shaddai, "the God with Breasts [alt. of the mountains]" who appeared to the patriarchs (Exodus 6:3). And there was Yahweh, the Lord, the Great Angel of Israel, who appeared in human form to close the door of the ark (Genesis 7:16).[50] As Barker reads it, according to the ancient mythology as well as it can be recovered from the pre-Masoretic versions of the Song of Moses preserved in the Septuagint and in the Dead Sea Scrolls found at Qumran, Yahweh [יהוה], the Lord [*Adonai*, Greek κύριος], was the Son of the Most High given Israel as "his allotted heritage [portion LXX]," while other angels were allotted other nations "according to the number of the sons [angels LXX] of God," which they ruled as guardians or shepherds (Deuteronomy 32:8–9).[51] Although it is at times unclear in Barker's exposition exactly how, there were yet other angels who were themselves aspects of Yahweh, the Lord, the Great Angel of Israel. Thus the great declaration of Deuteronomy 6:4 RSV: "The Lord our God (*'elohim*, a plural noun) is One Lord." In Barker's words: "The plurality of Yahweh was a Unity, but the plurality could be perceived and described as his angels."[52]

But Yahweh, the Lord, the Son of the Most High, was present to his people in other ways as well, above all through the worship offered in the temple. Like the angels who bore Yahweh in their names, so the high priest bore the Name on his forehead when he entered the Holy of Holies to offer the annual sacrifices of atonement (Exodus 28:36–38; Leviticus 16:1–34).[53] In an important sense, when he emerged carrying the sacrifices, the high priest *was* Yahweh made manifest to his people; likewise, when the anointed king sat upon the throne, so, too, he bore the presence of the Lord before all Israel (1 Chronicles 29:20–23).[54] It was in this sense (or so Barker has argued) that the early Christians, most notably the author of the letter to the Hebrews, recognized Jesus as Lord: "Although he was a Son, he learned obedience through what he suffered; and being made perfect he became the source of eternal salvation to all who obey him, being designated by God a high priest after the order of Melchizedek" (Hebrews 5:8–10 RSV). Nevertheless, whereas earthly priests like Aaron served merely as "a copy and shadow of the heavenly sanctuary" designed according to the pattern shown to Moses on the mountain (Hebrews 8:5 RSV; citing Exodus 25:40), "[Jesus] Christ has entered, not into a sanctuary made with hands, a copy of the true one, but into heaven itself, now to appear in the presence of God on our behalf" (Hebrews 9:24 RSV). "Therefore," as the Apostle Paul exclaimed in his letter to the Philippians, quoting one of the most ancient Christian hymns, "God has highly exalted him and bestowed on him the name which is above every name, that at the name of Jesus every knee should bow, in heaven and on earth and under the earth, and every tongue confess that Jesus Christ is Lord, to the glory of God the Father" (Philippians 2:9–11 RSV). This, as Barker puts it, is "why Christians worshipped Jesus": "The name above every name is Yahweh, and the allusion is to Isaiah 45:23: 'To me every knee shall bow, every tongue shall swear,' originally said of Yahweh, but here of Jesus. The hymn proclaims that Jesus has been given the Name, and so all creation acknowledges that Jesus Christ is Yahweh," that is, the Lord.[55]

According to Barker, it is highly significant that Paul makes this declaration by quoting a hymn. For, as she has shown, music, arguably even more so than sacrifice, was at the heart of temple worship as the early Christians understood it.[56] Even before the first temple was built, King David appointed "certain of the Levites as ministers before the ark of the Lord, to invoke, to thank, and to praise the Lord, the God of Israel" with harps, lyres, cymbals, and trumpets (1 Chronicles 16:4–6 RSV; cf. 1 Chronicles 15:16). He likewise gave them a song to sing on the day in which they brought the ark into Jerusalem (1 Chronicles 16:7–11 RSV):

> O give thanks to the Lord, call on his name,
> make known his deeds among the peoples!
> Sing to him, sing praises to him, tell of all his wonderful works!
> Glory in his holy name;
> let the hearts of those who seek the Lord rejoice!
> Seek the Lord and his strength,
> seek his presence continually!

As they processed into the city, David, Chenaniah, the leader of the singers, and all of the singers themselves, along with those carrying the ark, were clothed in fine linen, the same fabric worn by the high priests in the Holy of Holies. Thus arrayed, "all Israel brought up the ark of the Lord with shouting, to the sound of the horn, trumpets, and cymbals, and made loud music on harps and lyres" (1 Chronicles 15:28 RSV). Under the order of the king, the singers serving before the Lord were to "prophesy with lyres, with harps, and with cymbals" (1 Chronicles 25:1 RSV). And "the number of them along with their brethren, who were trained in singing to the Lord, all who were skillful, was two hundred and eighty-eight" (1 Chronicles 25:7 RSV). At the consecration of the temple built by David's son Solomon, "the Levitical singers, Asaph, Heman, and Jeduthun, their sons and kinsmen, arrayed in fine linen, with cymbals, harps, and lyres, stood east of the altar with a hundred and twenty priests who were trumpeters; and it was the duty of the trumpeters and singers to make themselves heard in unison in praise and thanksgiving to the Lord" (2 Chronicles 5:12–13 RSV). As the singers and priests praised the Lord with one voice, "the house, the house of the Lord, was filled with a cloud, so that the priests could not stand to minister because of the cloud; for the glory of the Lord filled the house of God" (2 Chronicles 5:13–14 RSV). Likewise, when King Hezekiah restored the temple, he stationed the Levites with their cymbals, harps, and lyres, and the priests with their trumpets alongside the altar so that "when the burnt offering began, the song to the Lord began also, and the trumpets, accompanied by the instruments of David king of Israel. The whole assembly worshiped, and the singers sang, and the trumpeters sounded; all this continued until the burnt offering was finished" (2 Chronicles 29:25–28 RSV).

Notably, in Barker's account, the Deuteronomists following King Josiah would have none of this.[57] Their version of the story, recorded in the books of Samuel and Kings, makes no mention of the Levitical musicians (2 Samuel 6:16–19 RSV) or of the music at the dedication of the temple (1 Kings 8:1–11 RSV) or of the music at King Hezekiah's restoration of the temple (2 Kings 18:1–8 RSV). Barker suggests why. For the Deuteronomists, it was axiomatic that the Lord could only be heard, never seen. As "Moses" (or, rather, the Deuteronomists) reminded the people of Israel, when they stood at the foot of Mount Sinai "[burning] with fire to the heart of heaven, wrapped in darkness, cloud, and gloom," "the Lord spoke to you out of the midst of the fire; you heard the sound of words, but saw no form; there was only a voice" (Deuteronomy 4:11–12 RSV). In contrast, the early Christians who looked to the temple tradition were emphatic that the Lord could be seen. In the words of the evangelist: "We have beheld his glory, glory as of the only Son from the Father" (John 1:14 RSV). Likewise: "Isaiah . . . saw his glory and spoke of him" (John 12:41 RSV; cf. Isaiah 6:1–3). But how, in the temple tradition, was this seeing understood? In the person of the high priest, anointed and vested in the colors of the temple veil? In the clouds of incense billowing forth from the Holy of Holies? With masked priests taking the part of the four living creatures—the lion, the ox, the eagle, and the man—whom the prophet Ezekiel saw surrounding the sapphire throne upon which he beheld "a likeness as it were of a human form," possibly the king (Ezekiel 1:4–28)? As Barker acknowledges, given the state of the evidence, it is impossible to be sure. What is clear is that it had something to do with music—and singing. It was music that made the glory of the Lord visible in the temple, however that glory was "seen." As Barker puts it: *"Music invoked the presence."*[58]

The Psalms—traditionally attributed to the same King David who instituted the temple musicians—are replete with this imagery of the presence. "The Lord is in his holy temple, the Lord's throne is in heaven" (Psalm 11:4 RSV)—that is, in the Holy of Holies that represented heaven with the cherubim surrounding the throne (2 Chronicles 3–5). Accordingly, the psalmist cries out: "Give ear, O Shepherd of Israel, thou who leadest Joseph like a flock! Thou who art enthroned upon the cherubim, shine forth!" (Psalm 80:1 RSV). "The Lord reigns; let the peoples tremble! He sits enthroned upon the cherubim: let the earth quake!" (Psalm 99:1 RSV). This is the way in which Isaiah saw the Lord, "sitting upon a throne, high and lifted up," surrounded by seraphim crying out: "Holy, holy, holy is the Lord of hosts; the whole earth is full of his glory" (Isaiah 6:1–3 RSV). "And the foundations of the thresholds shook at the voice of him who called, and the house was filled with smoke" (Isaiah 6:4 RSV)—arguably the same smoke with which the temple was filled as the musicians sang (2 Chronicles 5:13–14). Again and again, the psalmist sings of longing to behold the glory or face of the Lord: "Let thy face shine on thy servant" (Psalm 31:16 RSV); "Hide not thy face from thy servant; for I am in distress, make haste to answer me" (Psalm 69:17 RSV); "Hear, O Lord, when I cry aloud, be gracious to me and answer me! Thou hast said, 'Seek ye my face.' My heart says to thee, 'Thy face, Lord, do I seek.' Hide not thy face from me" (Psalm 27:7–9 RSV). And indeed, as the people sang, or so the psalmist asserted, the Lord appeared in his glory, "enthroned upon the praises of Israel" (Psalm 22:3 RSV).[59]

Who was this King of glory (cf. Psalm 24:7–10 RSV) who shone forth from his temple as the people played music and sang? Medieval Christians believed they knew. As the great twelfth-century theologian Peter Lombard (d. 1160) put it in his commentary on the Psalter: "The title [of this book] is as follows: HERE BEGINS THE BOOK OF HYMNS OR SOLILOQUIES OF THE PROPHET [DAVID] CONCERNING CHRIST ... The subject-matter of this book is the whole Christ (*totus Christus*), that is, the betrothed and His spouse (*scilicet sponsus et sponsa*)."[60]

In Barker's words: "To say that the Psalms were re-read, that is, *re-interpreted*, by the Church, is to make a distorting assumption. If the Christians declared 'Jesus is Yahweh' [יהוה], then they would have read the Psalms in their original sense, as praise to Yahweh, the God of Israel."[61] In harmony with this reading, "the revelation of Jesus Christ which God gave him to show to his servants what must soon take place" (Revelation 1:1) provides an image of how the earliest Christians envisaged the ancient temple worship, including the place of music and song.[62]

As the seer (whom Barker identifies as Jesus himself) looked, he saw a door opening in heaven: "At once I was in the Spirit, and lo, a throne stood in heaven, with one seated on the throne!" (Revelation 4:2 RSV). Surrounding the throne were twenty-four thrones upon which were seated twenty-four elders in white garments and golden crowns, while "from the throne [issued] flashes of lightning, and voices and peals of thunder" (Revelation 4:5 RSV). Along with the twenty-four elders, there were also four living creatures surrounding the throne, the first like a lion, the second like an ox, the third with the face of a man, and the fourth like an eagle (cf. Ezekiel 1:4–14). "And," the seer recorded, "the four living creatures, each of them with six wings, are full of eyes all round and within, and day and night they never cease to sing: 'Holy, holy, holy, is the Lord God Almighty, who was and is and is to come!' " (Revelation 4:8 RSV). To which song the twenty-four elders, throwing down their crowns, replied, singing: "Worthy art thou, our Lord and God, to receive glory and honor and power, for thou didst create all things, and by thy will they existed and were created" (Revelation 4:11 RSV). When the creatures and elders beheld the Lamb standing in their midst, they likewise cried out in song:

> "Worthy art thou to take the scroll and to open its seals,
> for thou wast slain and by thy blood didst ransom men for God
> from every tribe and tongue and people and nation,
> and hast made them a kingdom and priests to our God,
> and they shall reign on earth." (Revelation 5:9 RSV)

Heaven, by the seer's account, was filled with music and song. "Then I looked," he continues,

> and lo, on Mount Zion stood the Lamb, and with him a hundred and forty-four thousand who had his name and his Father's name written on their foreheads. And I heard a voice from heaven like the sound of many waters and like the sound of loud thunder; the voice I heard was like the sound of harpers playing on their harps, and they sing a new song before the throne and before the

four living creature and before the elders. No one could learn that song except the hundred and forty-four thousand who had been redeemed from the earth. (Revelation 14:1–3 RSV)

Here we may note that the singers are those who bear the Name on their foreheads—just as the high priest did as he ministered in the Holy of Holies. It is surely likewise significant that the seer heard the 144,000 singing as if with one voice, just as the temple musicians were commanded to sing and play (2 Chronicles 5:12–13). The voice from heaven sounds like water and thunder, arguably the same voice that Isaiah heard coming forth from the angelic throne and shaking the thresholds of the temple (Isaiah 6:1–4). Ezekiel heard a similar sound "of many waters, like the thunder of the Almighty," made by the wings of the four living creatures surrounding the chariot throne (Ezekiel 1:24 RSV). The new song, however, had not been heard before: it was the song of the Christians bearing the Great Angel's new name (Revelation 3:12).

According to the seer, there was yet a third choir in heaven, this one comprising those who had conquered the beast:

And I saw what appeared to be a sea of glass mingled with fire, and those who had conquered the beast and its image and the number of its name, standing beside the sea of glass with harps of God in their hands. And they sing the song of Moses, the servant of God, and the song of the Lamb, saying,

> "Great and wonderful are thy deeds,
> O Lord God the Almighty!
> Just and true are thy ways,
> O King of the ages!
> Who shall not fear and glorify thy name, O Lord?
> For thou alone art holy.
> All nations shall come and worship thee,
> for thy judgments have been revealed." (Revelation 15:2–4 RSV)

Once again, we see the emphasis on the singers bearing the holy Name and the unison of their song, this time in contrast with those who bore the name of the beast. The sea of glass mingled with fire appears likewise in the visions of 1 Enoch, one of the most important witnesses to the temple tradition. We may likewise recall that Solomon's temple had a floor of gold (1 Kings 6:30 RSV); according to Josephus, the interior of the temple was so completely covered with gold that "the whole temple shined and dazzled the eyes of such as entered, by the splendour of the gold that was on every side of them."[63] Throughout Jesus's revelation, the seer's imagery depends on that of the temple tradition: the throne, the four living creatures, the Name borne upon the forehead, the white garments, the voice like thunder coming forth from the lightning, the musical instruments, the worship of the Lord in song. As the seer beheld it, the only thing missing from the heavenly city (itself, like the Holy of Holies, a great golden cube [Revelation 21:16]) was, of course, the temple: "for its temple is the Lord God the Almighty and the Lamb. And the city has no need of sun or moon to shine upon it, for the glory of God is its light and its lamp is the Lamb" (Revelation 21:22 RSV).

And what did the angel show the seer standing alongside this shining temple-Lamb? A tree—but not just any tree. Rather,

> he showed me the river of the water of life, bright as crystal, flowing from the throne of God and of the Lamb through the middle of the street of the city; also, on either side of the river, the tree of life with its twelve kinds of fruit, yielding its fruit each month; and the leaves of the tree were for the healing of the nations. (Revelation 22:1–2 RSV)

But why a tree? Because—as Barker explains and, as we have already seen, medieval Christian liturgists, hymnographers, homilists, and exegetes believed—the Lady of the temple, the Mother of the Lord, was there in the heavenly city with her Son, the Lamb, for it was the Lady who was the river of Wisdom flowing out of paradise and the Tree of Life from which the faithful could eat for healing and redemption.[64]

"I was exalted," Wisdom praises herself,

> like a cedar in Lebanon and as a cypress tree on Mount Zion.
> I was exalted like a palm tree in Kadesh and as a rose plant in Jericho;
> as a fair olive tree in the plains and as a plane tree by the water in the
>   streets was I exalted . . .
>
> I have stretched out my branches as the turpentine tree [terebinth],
> and my branches are of honour and grace.
> As the vine I have brought forth a pleasant odour: and my flowers are the
>   fruit of honour and riches. . . .
>
> I, Wisdom, have poured out rivers.
> I, like a brook out of a river of a mighty water; I, like a channel of a river,
>   and like an aqueduct, came out of paradise. (Ecclesiasticus 24:17–19,
>   22–23, 40–41)

"Happy is the man who finds wisdom," Solomon, the son of David, told his son, "and the man who gets understanding . . . She is more precious than jewels, and nothing you desire can compare with her . . . She is a tree of life to those who lay hold of her; those who hold her fast are called happy" (Proverbs 3:13, 15, 18 RSV). Moses encountered her (or so Barker has argued) in the burning bush (Exodus 3); the patriarchs set up altars to her under her trees (Genesis 12:4–7); lamps and incense were burned in the temple in her honor; the menorah, it may be recalled, was a stylized almond tree (Exodus 25:31–37). And King Josiah expelled her when "he brought out the Asherah [like the menorah, most likely a stylized tree] from the house of the Lord," carried it to the brook Kidron, "and burned it . . . and beat it to dust and cast the dust of it upon the graves of the common people" (2 Kings 23:6 RSV).[65] Here, we should note, Barker is far from alone in seeing the Asherah as a significant element in the pre-Deuteronomic temple cult.[66] She is, however, somewhat less usual in her insistence that the early Christians had access to this cult through their readings of the scriptures. As Barker observes: "Later Jewish tradition hoped that five items from the first temple would be restored in the temple of the Messiah: the fire, the ark, the menorah, the Spirit and the cherubim."[67] In Barker's reading, according to the earliest Christian tradition, all five items have been restored, at least insofar as they have been realized in the worship of the Church (cf. Hebrews 9): the ark appears in Revelation 11:19; the menorah in the Tree of Life in Revelation 22:1–2; the cherubim with the heavenly throne in Revelation 4; the fire and the Spirit, arguably, at Pentecost.

In support of her reading of the Asherah as Lady Wisdom, Barker points to what she identifies as traces of the Lady's cult throughout the most ancient versions of the Hebrew scriptures, traces that may at times be verified through the archeological record. Most striking is the evidence of the hundreds of small, female "pillar" figurines discovered in excavations throughout the southern Levant. Often described as possible representations of Astarte, the Canaanite fertility goddess, most of these figurines have, however, been found in Jerusalem—the center of the temple cult. Significantly, Barker observes, "none can be dated after the time of Josiah."[68] Barker sees the figurines as evidence of devotion to El Shaddai, "the God with breasts," whom she also associates with the great Ugaritic goddess Athirat or Asheratah, the Virgin Mother of the seventy sons of the high god El (cf. Deuteronomy 32:8–9). Athirat was the Great Lady, the Bright One, the goddess of the sun, the "nursing mother" of the earthly king, himself known as the Morning and Evening Star, over whom she hovers in the surviving iconography as a sun with wings (cf. Malachi 4:2, where the "sun of righteousness" is promised to rise "with healing in its [her] wings"). Athirat was also typically portrayed carrying a spindle. Her full name in Ugaritic "is disputed: in the form *athirat yam* it may have been 'the lady who treads the sea/sea dragon.' "[69] Can it therefore (Barker asks) really be a coincidence that the Christian seer beheld this "great portent . . . in heaven," "a woman clothed with the sun, with the moon under her feet, and on her head a crown of twelve stars," threatened by a dragon while giving birth to a child who was "to rule all the nations with a rod of iron" (Revelation 12:1–6 RSV)? He names himself, after all: "I Jesus . . . am the root and the offspring of David, the bright morning star" (Revelation 22:16 RSV).

How Athirat or, as she was known in Jerusalem, Asherah came to be identified with Wisdom, Barker never fully explains, but if the pillar figurines with their prominent breasts represent Asherah as nursing mother, their wide-open eyes could support the association with Wisdom and the vision that she imparted to her devotees. Likewise, the white linen dresses and fiery red faces on those on which traces of paint survive, as well as the disks which some of them hold: all, according to Barker, are possible attributes of the Lady as Wisdom, above all the disks, which Barker identifies as loaves of bread. We may recall that the exiles in Egypt complained to Jeremiah that their present calamities had come upon them because the women were no longer making their customary offerings of libations and cakes to the Queen of Heaven (Jeremiah 44:15–19). Barker goes so far as to suggest that the Queen of Heaven or Wisdom was likewise associated with the showbread or bread of the Presence the priests consumed on the sabbath (Exodus 25:23–30; Leviticus 24:5–9). Both the Queen's cakes and the showbread were shaped; the cakes were made "bearing her image," and the showbread was baked in a special, albeit secret mold.[70] The showbread itself was considered "a most holy portion" of the offerings made to the Lord, the only cereal offering that was taken into the temple itself. Having thus been made holy, it could only be served on dishes of pure gold. These plates themselves had to be set on a table covered in gold, while Aaron and his sons were to consume their portion of the holy bread "in a most holy place." Wisdom, Barker argues, fed her devotees with this very same bread. "Come," Wisdom invited them, "eat of my bread and drink of the wine I have mixed. Leave simpleness, and live, and walk in the way of insight" (Proverbs 9:5–6 RSV). According to Barker, later rabbinic tradition likewise associated the bread of the Presence with Wisdom: "The House of Wisdom is the tabernacle, and Wisdom's table is Bread of Presence and wine."[71]

In Barker's telling, Wisdom or Asherah or the Lady had yet other attributes in the ancient temple tradition, all of which were to become, along with the river of paradise, the Tree of Life, and the bread of the Presence, significant symbols of Mary as the Virgin Mother of God. Christians were (and are) so-called because they, like Christ, have been anointed with the chrism of baptism. Likewise, in the temple tradition, the anointing oil was a sacrament of Wisdom. The priests of the temple were anointed with a special oil compounded of the finest spices—liquid myrrh, sweet-smelling cinnamon, aromatic cane, cassia, and olive oil—which was so holy that whoever presumed to copy it or use it on "an outsider" should be "cut off from his people." The same perfumed oil was used to anoint the tent of meeting, the ark of the testimony, the golden table and its utensils, the golden lampstand and its utensils, the golden altar of incense, the bronze altar for the burnt offerings and its utensils, and the bronze laver and its base. Everything thus anointed became "most holy," as well as anything that touched that which had been anointed (Exodus 30:22–33). The kings of the temple tradition were similarly holy—and, therefore, wise. At David's anointing by Samuel, "the Spirit of the Lord came mightily upon [him]" (1 Samuel 16:13 RSV), while Isaiah prophesied of a branch that should grow out of the root of Jesse: "And the Spirit of the Lord shall rest upon him, the spirit of wisdom and understanding, the spirit of counsel and might, the spirit of knowledge and the fear of the Lord. And his delight [lit. perfume] shall be in the fear of the Lord" (Isaiah 11:1–3 RSV).[72]

Elsewhere, as Barker shows, the Spirit of the Lord is even more explicitly identified with Wisdom: "Who shall know thy thought, except thou give them wisdom, and send thy Holy Spirit from above?" (Wisdom 9:17). By her own description, Wisdom flowed with the perfumes of the anointing oil:

> I gave a sweet smell like cinnamon and aromatical balm. I yielded a sweet odour like the best myrrh, and I perfumed my dwelling as storax and galbanum and onyx and aloes and as the frankincense not cut, and my odour is as the purest balm. (Ecclesiasticus 24:20–21)

"Behold," she cries out in the street, "I will pour out my spirit on you; I will make my words known to you" (Proverbs 1:23 RSV)—just as the oil of the anointing was poured out over the priests and Davidic kings. Significantly, as Barker points out, according to the Babylonian Talmudic tradition, at the time of Josiah, the anointing oil was taken out of the temple and hidden, along with the ark, Aaron's flowering almond rod, and the jar of manna[73]—all of which, as we have already seen, were to be explicitly identified with the Virgin Mary.

Like Athirat, Wisdom was also understood as the mother of the earthly, anointed king. "Ask a sign of the Lord your God," the prophet Isaiah commanded King Ahaz (Isaiah 7:10–11 RSV). Or, rather, according to Barker, as the pre-Masoretic Qumran Isaiah scroll puts it: "Ask a sign of the Mother of the Lord your God," the pre-Christian Isaiah scroll differing from the later rabbinic reading of the text by one highly suggestive letter.[74] And what sign would the Lord give? Again, the details are significant. In the Hebrew, the sign reads (Isaiah 7:14):

"Behold, the virgin [:'almah, including the definite article] shall conceive and bear a son, and shall call his name Immanuel ['God is with us']." Likewise, the Septuagint translates 'almah as παρθένος, "virgin." Barker argues that this virgin was, in fact, the Virgin, like the Great Lady Athirat, who was also known as the Virgin and who gave birth to the Morning Star, the child upon whose shoulders the government would rest (cf. Isaiah 9:6 RSV): "And his name will be called 'Wonderful Counselor, Mighty God, Everlasting Father, Prince of Peace.' " Or, as the Septuagint translation of the four-part title put it: Μεγάλης βουλῆς ἄγγελος, "Angel of Great Counsel," that is, Barker contends, the Angel of Wisdom.

As Barker reads it, some of the most important evidence for the relationship between Lady Wisdom and her royal Son can be recovered only by careful attention to the revisions that the post-Deuteronomic editors made to the Psalms, above all Psalms 45 and 110 RSV, both having to do with the enthronement and anointing of the king. Psalm 45:9 RSV is usually read, "at your right hand stands the queen in gold of Ophir," but the word for "queen" is an unusual one (segal), suggesting a woman who has been disgraced rather than honored. As the king's bride is described separately as "daughter" (Psalm 45:10 RSV), Barker suggests that the queen thus subsequently slurred must have been the king's mother, standing at his right hand to crown him on his wedding day, just as she is described in the Song of Songs: "Go forth, O daughters of Zion, and behold King Solomon, with the crown with which his mother crowned him on the day of his wedding, on the day of the gladness of his heart" (3:11 RSV).[75]

Psalm 110 RSV—one of the single most critical psalms for the identification of Jesus as the Son of God and high priest in the order of Melchizedek, as we have already seen—is even more complicated. As Barker reconstructs it, this psalm was originally intended to describe how a human being (the king) became the divine son (an angel) through his anointing by Wisdom. The critical passage is now translated from the Hebrew: "upon the holy mountains [alt. in holy array]. From the womb of the morning like dew your youth [alt. the dew of your youth] will come to you" (110:2–3 RSV), but Barker, drawing on the Septuagint Greek, suggests a rather different reading: "In the glory of the holy one, with dew from the womb I have begotten you as the Morning Star."[76] In comparison, the Vulgate reads:

Tecum principium in die virtutis tuae in splendoribus sanctorum: ex utero, ante Luciferum, genui te.

With thee is the principality in the day of thy strength, in the brightness of the saints; from the womb before the Day Star I begot thee. (Psalm 109:3)

Like the child born of the woman clothed in the sun (Revelation 12:1–6), the king came forth from the Holy of Holies, anointed by his mother Wisdom and resurrected (or reborn) as an angel, bearing the presence of the Lord. These were the "sons" whom Isaiah promised would marry Jerusalem (Isaiah 62:5), the anointed ones to whom Wisdom gave birth.[77]

In the ancient tradition, Wisdom had likewise been present at the dawn of creation, before there was heaven and earth, before the bounds of the earth, seas, and skies were drawn. As she cried out at the gates of the town from the path where she took her stand:

> The Lord created me at the beginning of his work,
> the first of his acts of old.
> Ages ago I was set up,
> at the first, before the beginning of the earth.
> When there were no depths I was brought forth,
> when there were no springs abounding with water.
> Before the mountains had been shaped,
> before the hills, I was brought forth;
> before he had made the earth with its fields,
> or the first of the dust of the world.
> When he established the heavens, I was there,
> when he drew the circle on the face of the deep,
> when he made firm the skies above,
> when he established the fountains of the deep,
> when he assigned to the sea its limit,
> so that the waters might not transgress his command,
> when he marked out the foundations of the earth,
> then I was beside him, like a master workman;
> and I was daily his delight,
> rejoicing before him always,
> rejoicing in his inhabited world
> and delighting in the sons of men. (Proverbs 8:22–31 RSV)

As Barker notes, there are a number of words in this passage for which the meaning of the Hebrew is uncertain, most notably 'amon (verse 30), here rendered "master workman," but in the Septuagint translated ἁρμόζουσα, "harmonizer."[78] As the Creator set the bounds of his creation or, rather, more literally, *engraved* them (that is, their structures or patterns), Wisdom was there with him on Day One, holding all things in harmony as the angels (likewise, according to the temple tradition, creatures of Day One) sang. Medieval Christians would later appeal to this same passage as a proof text for the doctrine of the Immaculate Conception. As a witness to the older temple tradition, it is most important for what it suggests about the way in which Wisdom was seen as the partner or consort of the Creator, standing beside him in heaven, the Holy of Holies, just as the Queen stood beside her Son. "Let us," God (plural in the Hebrew) said, "make man in our image, after our likeness." And, accordingly, "God created man in his own image . . . male and female he created them" (Genesis 1:26–27 RSV). Writing at a time when memories of his service as a priest in the original temple cult were still fresh, Ezekiel described the Lady as she had formerly appeared in the Holy of Holies, as the Spirit of the Living One (feminine singular) impelling the wheels of the chariot throne upon which the likeness of the glory of the Lord appeared in human form (Ezekiel 1:20–21, 26–28). After the capture of Jerusalem by the Babylonians, he saw this same living chariot throne with its four wheels and fourfold living creature(s) going out from the house with the glory of the Lord (Ezekiel 10), the implication being, it would seem, that if Wisdom were no longer in temple, neither was the Lord.[79]

In Barker's reconstruction, contrary to the Deuteronomic tradition upon which later rabbinic and Protestant readings of the Old Testament ultimately depend, the worship of Yahweh and his Asherah, the Lord and his Lady, the Son of the Most High and his Mother Wisdom was neither a corruption of the original temple cult nor an alien or syncretistic import. It *was* the original temple tradition. Worshipping the Queen of Heaven did not bring about the fall of the temple to the Babylonians; rather, rejecting her worship did—at least, that is what the exiles in Pathros in the land of Egypt told Jeremiah (Jeremiah 44:15–19). Why King Josiah and his ministers cast her out of the temple is something of a mystery, even if the results—a focus on the Law given to Moses on Mount Sinai as the basis for the covenant between God (now conceived monotheistically) and his people Israel—are clear (cf. 1 Kings 15:1–13 RSV).[80] For the Israelites taken captive and deported to Babylon, it was this covenant that was to become the focus of their tradition; these were the people who, according to the first-century C.E. historian Josephus, came to be called *Ioudaioi*, "Jews."[81]

But not all of the inhabitants of Jerusalem were taken to Babylon and not all of them had accepted the Deuteronomist reforms. Some of these, as Jeremiah tells us, fled to Egypt; others to Arabia and Ethiopia; others as far as the border area between China and Tibet. Among these communities, Barker has argued, memories of the Lady remained strong, particularly as she was associated with Wisdom.[82] The book of Ecclesiasticus or the Wisdom of Jesus Ben Sirach was translated into Greek by his grandson while he was living in Egypt in the second century B.C.E. The Wisdom of Solomon, like Ecclesiasticus one of the most important sources of Wisdom imagery, was likewise written in Alexandria most likely some thirty years either side of the birth of Jesus.[83] Even what were to become the canonical scriptures retained traces of the rejection of Wisdom: "How long," Wisdom cries aloud in the book of Proverbs, "O simple ones, will you love being simple? How long will scoffers delight in their scoffing and fools hate knowledge?" (Proverbs 1:22 RSV). The book of 1 Enoch, known to the early Christians and quoted in the New Testament letter of Jude (1:14–15, citing 1 Enoch 1:9), is even more explicit about Wisdom's exile:

> Wisdom found no place where she might dwell;
> Then a dwelling-place was assigned her in the heavens.
> Wisdom went forth to make her dwelling among the children of men,
> And found no dwelling-place:
> Wisdom returned to her place,
> And took her seat among the angels.
> And unrighteousness went forth from her chambers;
> Whom she sought not she found,
> And dwelt with them,
> As rain in a desert
> And dew on a thirsty land.[84]

And yet, for many of those who longed for the ancient traditions of the temple as they had been before the reform, there was still hope that the Lady would one day return to earth from her seat among the angels—and along with her, her Son.[85]

Miriam, the Mother of the Son of the Most High

When in the eighteenth year of his reign King Josiah cast the Asherah out of the temple, he also expelled the women who customarily wove for her. There are difficulties with the translation of the relevant passage (2 Kings 23:7 RSV; 4 Kings 23:7 LXX), but as Barker reconstructs it, it would seem to suggest that the women were weaving "linens" (reading the Hebrew *battim* as *baddim*; LXX χεττιν) that is, white garments, in the house of the "holy ones" (*qedôsîm*; LXX καδησιμ, "angels" rather than "male prostitutes," as it is usually translated).[86] According to the *Protevangelium* or *Infancy Gospel of James*, our earliest witness (other than the canonical Gospels) to an interest in Mary's biography, typically dated to the mid- or late second-century C.E., Mary, too, had been a weaver for the temple, although, when the angel Gabriel appeared to her bearing his great tidings, she was spinning not linen, but purple to be used in weaving a new veil. We may recall that one of the Lady Athirat's attributes was likewise a spindle.[87]

This is the story as "James" (traditionally believed to have been James, the brother of Jesus) told it.[88] When Mary was three years old, her parents Anna and Joachim took her to the temple as an offering to the Lord, where she lived until she was twelve, "brought up like a dove and fed by an angel." At her reception, the priest "kissed her and blessed her" and sat her on the third step of the altar, "and the Lord put grace on her and she danced with her feet and all the house of Israel loved her." Beloved as she was, she could not be allowed to remain in the temple once she started to menstruate, lest she defile it (cf. Leviticus 15:19), so the high priest put on the vestment with the twelve bells (cf. Exodus 28:33–34) and went into the Holy of Holies to pray about what should be done with her. An angel appeared and told him to assemble the widowers of the people and the Lord would give a sign as to who should take her as wife. Joseph "threw down his adze" and gathered together with the other widowers before the high priest. Each of the men brought with him a rod, which the high priest took into the temple, where he prayed. When the high priest came back out of the temple, he distributed the rods, giving the last to Joseph. "And behold, a dove came out of the rod and flew onto Joseph's head" (cf. Numbers 17:1–11, where Aaron is chosen as high priest when his rod sprouts and produces blossoms and ripe almonds).

Soon thereafter the priests decided to make a new veil for the temple and chose Mary as one of seven virgins from the tribe of David to help with the work. They brought the virgins into the temple and cast lots to see who would weave which part of the fabric: the gold, the amiantus ["undefiled"], the linen, the silk, the hyacinth-blue, the scarlet, and the true purple (cf. Exodus 26:1). "The pure purple and scarlet fell by lot to Mary," who took them home and started to spin. As the *Protevangelium* tells it, the angel first spoke to Mary when she had gone out to the well to draw water, at which she heard only a voice saying, "Hail, highly favored one, the Lord is with you, blessed are you among women" (cf. Luke 1:28, 42). Trembling, she went back to her house, "took the purple and sat down on her seat (*thronos*) and drew out the thread." At which moment, the angel of the Lord stood before her and said, "Do not fear, Mary; for you have found grace before the Lord of all things and shall conceive by his Word." Hearing which, she considered and asked, "Shall I conceive by the Lord, the living God, and bear as every woman bears?" "Not so, Mary," the angel replied, "for the power of the Lord shall overshadow you; wherefore that holy one who is born of you shall be called the Son of the Most High. And you shall call his name Jesus; for he shall save his people from their sins." And Mary answered: "Behold, the handmaid of the Lord [is] before him: be it to me according to your word." After which, she "made ready the purple and scarlet and brought them to the priest, [who] blessed her and said, 'Mary, the Lord God has magnified your name, and you shall be blessed among all generations of the earth' " (cf. Luke 1:42, 48).

There are a number of ways to read what "James" is doing here with the more familiar version of the Annunciation from Luke, the more usual being to assume that the author was making things up for the sake of readers for whom the story as it appears in Luke was somehow inadequate. As J. K. Elliott puts it in his introduction to the text: "In accord with the demands of popular piety responsible for the growth of much apocryphal material, [the *Protevangelium of James*] sets out to satisfy curiosity about Jesus' antecedents by filling in the gaps left in the canonical material." But this is to beg the question why the author gives the details that he does; for example, that Mary was spinning when the angel arrived. Elliott suggests an economic motive: "Our author is concerned to tell us that Jesus' parents were not poor: Joseph is a building contractor; Mary spins, but not for payment."[89] But why should Mary be spinning *the veil for the temple* if the author's only purpose in giving us this detail was to prove that she worked?

As Barker would have it: because Mary was Wisdom restored to her temple, dancing with her feet to the delight of the Lord in the Holy of Holies (Proverbs 8:30).[90] Like the woman clothed with the sun, Mary came forth from heaven (that is, the Holy of Holies) to give birth to her child, who passed through the veil of her womb without tearing it. (Appropriately, another theme of the *Protevangelium* is the defense of Mary's virginity *in partu*.) She was at work weaving a new veil for the temple at the moment of the Incarnation not in order to demonstrate her industry, but because the veil, like the garment of the high priest, was symbolically the flesh that her Son put on both to conceal his glory and to become visible to the world. She was spinning the purple and scarlet rather than the linen because it was linen that the priests (and angels) wore in the Holy of Holies (or heaven) (Leviticus 16:4; cf. Revelation 1:13), but scarlet (fire), blue (air), purple (water), and white (earth) that they wore when outside the veil on earth.[91] This same veil was torn in two, from top to bottom, at her Son's death (Matthew 27:51; Mark 15:38; Luke 23:45), as he opened the "new and living way" into the sanctuary "through the curtain, that is, through his flesh" (Hebrews 10:19–20 RSV). In icons of the Annunciation, Mary is often shown holding a spindle, as Barker observes, "the ancient symbol of the Great Lady." Barker concludes: "The Queen of Heaven and her Son were Mary and her Son, and just as Jesus was proclaimed the Lord, the God of Israel, so Mary was depicted as the Great Lady, his Mother."[92]

Hitherto, the tendency in Marian scholarship has been to read such imagery retrospectively, assuming that because "so little" was said about Mary in the Gospels, early Christian and medieval authors were forced to hunt through the scriptures to find things to say about her (a.k.a. read into the scriptures the things they wanted to find). But this, to judge from the sources that we have, is not what the early Christian and medieval authors thought they were doing in reading the scriptures for traces (or "types") of Mary, any more than they thought they were making things up when they insisted that Jesus was Lord. If Jesus was the Messiah, the anointed one who bore the presence of Yahweh before his people, the Angel of Great Counsel prophesied by Isaiah, the Son born of the Virgin who would bear the Name "God is with us," the great High Priest who at his death passed through the veil of his flesh into the heavens so as to sit at the right hand of the Most High, then, as Barker has argued, for the early Christians as for their medieval heirs, she who gave birth to the Son of the Most High (cf. Luke 1:32) *was* Wisdom, the Mother, Bride, and Daughter of the Lord, the queen who stood beside him in gold of Ophir as he received his crown (cf. John 19:2, 25). Even her name, Miriam, was suggestive of the older tradition. As Barker notes, according to this tradition, Miriam, the sister of Moses and Aaron, had been stricken with leprosy (the punishment for blasphemy) for speaking out against Moses when he married a Cushite (that is, foreign) woman (Numbers 12). Aaron spoke up for her, and she was healed, but otherwise she "had no further place in the story. This was the ruling family: Moses the lawgiver, Aaron the high priest, and Miriam, the *older* sister who disappeared from the scene." And yet Miriam was honored as "the ancestress of the royal house, the mother of the kings of Jerusalem."[93] Miriam, like Wisdom, was associated with water (cf. Ecclesiasticus 24:40–43). Significantly, it was also recorded that, after Miriam died and was buried at Kadesh (the "holy place"), "there was no water for the congregation; and they assembled themselves together against Moses and against Aaron" (Numbers 20:1–2 RSV). Perhaps this is why, Barker suggests, as the *Protevangelium of James* tells it, the angel Gabriel first came to Mary with his good news when she had gone out to draw water from the well."[94]

What was the appropriate way in which to honor the Lady who had given birth to the Lord? As with the hotly contested efforts that early Christians made to identify her Son, so—as best as we can determine from the (admittedly scanty) evidence—there were likewise heated debates among the early Christians about how, or even whether, to worship her.[95] Famously, writing in the 370s, Epiphanius of Salamis (d. 403) included in his *Panarion* or "medicine chest" of heresies a condemnation of certain women in Arabia who were accustomed to "prepare a certain carriage with a square seat and spread out fine linens over it on a special day of the year." They would then "put forth bread and offer it in the name of Mary," after which "they [would] all partake of the bread."⁹⁶ For Epiphanius, at the time serving as bishop of Salamis, the women's practice was "ridiculous," clearly "the malady of the deluded Eve all over again," for "never at any time has a woman been a priest."⁹⁷ Even worse, according to Epiphanius, was the suggestion that the women were offering the bread in Mary's name, that is, as if she were God. Tellingly, he likens their error to that which Jeremiah condemned when he ordered the women in Pathros not to burn incense and offer cakes to the "queen of heaven" (Jeremiah 44:15–23).⁹⁸ Elsewhere, Epiphanius even goes so far as to accuse the women of worshipping Mary as a pagan goddess like Persephone or Thermutis, thus persuading many modern readers that the Kollyridians (as he called the women) "were some sort of Christian goddess worshippers who elevated Mary to be a part of the Godhead."⁹⁹

Who was this Virgin whom Isaiah had prophesied would give birth to the Lord (Isaiah 7:14)? Epiphanius was categorical: "Yes, of course Mary's body was holy, but she was not God. Yes, the Virgin was indeed a virgin and honored as such, but she was not given us to worship; she worships Him who, though born of her flesh, has come from heaven, from the bosom of his Father."¹⁰⁰ If she is to be praised, it should be like Elijah, "who was virgin from his mother's womb, always remained so, and was taken up but has not seen death," or John, "who leaned on the Lord's breast," or St. Thecla; but she is not to be worshiped, "nor any of the saints."¹⁰¹ And yet, Epiphanius nevertheless concurred that Mary was deserving of honor, for "her womb became a temple, and by God's kindness and an awesome mystery was prepared to be the dwelling place of the Lord's human nature."¹⁰² Significantly, Epiphanius also knew that Mary's parents were named Anna and Joachim and that an angel had appeared to her father to announce her conception, just as the *Protevangelium of James* had said.¹⁰³

There is one other source from antiquity, the so-called *Six Books Dormition Apocryphon*, originally written in the fourth century in Greek but for which the earliest manuscripts extant are from the fifth century in Syriac, which likewise includes an account of bread offered liturgically in honor of Mary, here in the context of the commemoration of Mary's dormition or "falling asleep."¹⁰⁴ The apocryphon lists three feasts to be kept in honor of Mary: one to be kept two days after the Nativity (December 24 or January 6, depending on local tradition), one on May 15 "on account of the seeds," and the third on August 13 "on account of the vines." Bread was to be offered at each of these feasts. According to the apostles' instructions, this bread was to be kneaded and baked on the night immediately preceding the feast. In the morning, the priest was to offer it up with incense and lights while the people stood before the altar "with psalms of

David." The Old and New Testaments and the account of Mary's death were read, and "the whole service [was to be] concerning these offerings." Three times the priest was instructed to say: "In the name of the Father, and of the Son, and of the Holy Spirit, we celebrate the commemoration of my Lady Mary." "And (simultaneously) with the word of the priest who speaks, the Holy Spirit shall come and bless these offerings; and when everyone takes away his offering, and goes to his house, great help and the blessing of the blessed one shall enter his dwelling and establish it for ever."[105] The Virgin to whom the people made their offerings may not have been the Most High (the Father) or the Lord (her Son), but she was clearly more than just another saint, as Epiphanius would insist—or was she? Prior to the great council held at Ephesus in 431, it was, it seems, still difficult to be sure.[106]

The parable coined in the twelfth century by Alan of Lille would have it that "a thousand roads lead men forever to Rome,"[107] but by the fourth and fifth centuries C.E. all roads having to do with the person and natures of Christ led inevitably to Constantinople, likewise those having to do with the person and nature of his Mother. Thanks to the councils held under the emperors' auspices at Nicaea in 325 and at Constantinople in 381, orthodox Christians of the early fifth century knew not only that Jesus was Lord, but also, in the words of the Nicene-Constantinopolitan Creed, that he was "the only-begotten Son of God, begotten of the Father before all worlds, [God of God], Light of Light, very God of very God, begotten, not made, being of one substance [essence] with the Father, by whom all things were made."[108] Who, however, his Mother was had not yet been clarified, despite the fact that there is evidence that there were already (or still) those who were accustomed to pray to her as Θεοτόκος, "God-bearer" or "Mother of God," by the end of the third century in Egypt, saying: "We take refuge beneath the protection of your compassion, Theotokos. Do not disregard our prayers in troubling times, but deliver us from danger, O only pure and blessed one."[109] By the early fifth century, feasts were observed in her honor in both Jerusalem and Constantinople, the former on August 15, the latter on the day following the Nativity of Christ. In Jerusalem, the feast was known as the Memory of Mary and celebrated at the church of the Kathisma (or "seat") on the road to Bethlehem where, according to the *Protevangelium*, Christ had been born. In Constantinople, "the Virgin's festival" was likewise associated with the celebration of Mary's giving birth to her Son, with an additional emphasis on her virginity.[110] According to the homily that Proclus (d. 446), future patriarch of the city but at the time titular bishop of Cyzicus, preached on the feast on December 26, 430, the Virgin's festival attracted travelers from far and wide.[111]

"Lovely is the gathering!" Proclus exclaimed to the multitude assembled in the Great Church of Constantinople dedicated to the Holy Wisdom of God, where the festival was being kept.[112] "See how both the earth and sea serve as the Virgin's escorts: the one spreading forth her waves calmly beneath the ships, the other conducting the steps of travelers on their way unhindered."[113] Fatefully, among those in the audience that day was the patriarch of Constantinople, Nestorius of Antioch (d. ca. 451), who (according to the historian Socrates), on his elevation in 428, had promised the Emperor Theodosius II (d. 450): "Give me, my prince, the earth purged of heretics, and I will give you heaven as a recompense. Assist me in destroying heretics, and I will assist you in vanquishing the Persians."[114] For Nestorius, those in need of purging included not only Arians, Apollinarians, Eunomians, Macedonians, Novatians, Messalians, Quartodecimans, Gnostics, and Manicheaens, but also the populace of the city (with its fondness for animal bouts, athletic games, and mimes), the local monks (who resisted his efforts at regulating them), the bishops of Rome and Alexandria (to whom Nestorius omitted to send the customary gifts and greetings upon his election), and, above all, the sister of the emperor and avowed virgin Pulcheria (d. 453), whom he accused of promiscuity with at least seven different lovers.

The insults to the imperial princess did not end there.[115] Nestorius refused to recognize Pulcheria as "bride of Christ" in his public prayers (as she claimed was her prerogative thanks to her vow of virginity), "effaced a special portrait of her that had been placed in the sanctuary, and removed her robe from an altar table where it had served as a covering."[116] He also refused to let her take communion at the altar on Easter Sunday because, he said, no woman could enter there. And he began to preach against the title Theotokos, "for," as one of his presbyters Anastasius put it, "Mary was but a human being, and it is impossible that God could be born from a human being."[117] As Nestorius saw it, "the story of Christ is not the passion of God made flesh, but the exculpation and victory of a representative human being before God." As Nicholas Constas observes in his detailed account of the controversy: "At times, Nestorius' rhetoric on this question reached such a pitch that he seemed to be postulating two completely different subjects within the one Christ: the transcendent Word of God, and the mortal man Jesus in whom the Word was pleased to dwell."[118] Thus, Nestorius insisted, Mary could not be "birth-giver of God," only "birth-giver of Christ" (*Christotokos*). Significantly, in Antiochene theology, women were not considered to participate in the "image of God" either.[119] Unsurprisingly, Pulcheria was not pleased, having purposefully modeled herself on the Virgin Mary; she is often assumed to have been behind the sermon that Proclus, one of her closest advisors, preached at the festival on December 26.

Ironically, Nestorius likewise encouraged Proclus to preach that day, urging him to address the crowds, many of whom, as Proclus suggests, had traveled to the city specifically for the feast.

Nor were they to be disappointed, at least those for whom the title Theotokos had a special place in their devotion to the Mother of the Lord. As one eleventh-century scribe noted in the margin to his manuscript: "This sermon demonstrates that the Holy Virgin Mary is the 'Theotokos', and that the one born from her is neither 'solely God' nor 'merely man,' but 'Emmanuel' [cf. Isaiah 7:14; Matthew 1:23], who is both God and man without confusion or alteration.' "[120] And, indeed, this is the claim with which Proclus concluded, citing the prophet Ezekiel's vision of the temple's closed gate, through which none should pass but the Lord, the God of Israel (Ezekiel 44:1–2): "There you have a clear testimony to the Holy and 'God-bearing' (*Theotokou*) Mary. Let all contradictions now cease."[121]

Important as it was to be in the history of Christian doctrine and devotion, not to mention Marian piety, arguably even more riveting for our purposes are the images with which Proclus set out to support this claim:

> She who called us here today [Proclus reminded his listeners] is the Holy Mary; the untarnished vessel of virginity; the spiritual paradise of the second Adam; the workshop for the union of natures; the market-place of the contract of salvation; the bridal chamber in which the Word took the flesh in marriage; the living bush of human nature, which the fire of a divine birth-pang did not consume; the veritable swift cloud who carried in her body the one who rides upon the cherubim; the purest fleece drenched with the rain which came down from heaven, whereby the shepherd clothed himself with the sheep; handmaid and mother, virgin and heaven, the only bridge for God to mankind; the awesome loom of the divine economy upon which the robe of union was ineffably woven.[122]

As Jesus would put it, echoing the prophets who lamented the people's rejection of Wisdom, "He who has ears to hear, let him hear" (Matthew 11:15; cf. Isaiah 6:10; Jeremiah 5:21).[123] The burning bush ablaze but not consumed by the presence of divinity (Exodus 3:2), the cloud carrying within her the glory of the One enthroned upon the cherubim (Isaiah 19:1; Ezekiel 1:26), the fleece drenched (or anointed) with the dew of heaven (Judges 6:36–38), the Virgin-heaven giving birth to her Son: these, as we have seen, were images not just of Mary, but of Wisdom, the Lady of the temple and Mother of the Lord; likewise, the image of the loom on which the "robe of union was ineffably woven." Proclus elaborated:

The loom-worker was the Holy Spirit; the wool-worker the overshadowing power from on high. The wool was the ancient fleece of Adam; the interlocking thread the spotless flesh of the Virgin. The weaver's shuttle was propelled by the immeasurable grace of him who wore the robe; the artisan was the Word who entered in through her sense of hearing.[124]

Industrious as they may have wanted to prove themselves as aristocratic ladies, it can hardly be a coincidence that the virgin princess Pulcheria and her women spent their days weaving, nor that Pulcheria had donated one of her robes to be used as a covering for the altar upon which the priest was accustomed to lay the Eucharistic bread.[125]

As Pulcheria and her women seem to have seen her, Mary, the Virgin Theotokos, was the Lady with her spindle, the Mother who gave birth to the Morning Star, the Living One whom Ezekiel saw in the chariot throne. If the scriptures were filled with her images—as Proclus would insist in homily after homily—this was why.[126] Mary was the "living temple" built by the Word, the dwelling of the One whom heaven itself could not contain.[127] She was the "bridal chamber [in which] the Word of God pitched the tent of the mystery of the incarnation," and the "ark, containing not the Law, but bearing in her womb the Giver of the Law."[128] And she was a lampstand (in the prophet Zechariah's words) "all of gold, with a lamp on the top of it, and seven conduits for the oil" from whose belly "beams of light flashed forth," on that day "when the Virgin imitated heaven . . . when a sun made flesh emerged from her womb; when she shaped the light into human form."[129] "O womb," Proclus exclaimed as he stood before the people of Constantinople on that fateful December day,

> in which was drawn up the bond that gave us all liberty! O belly, in which was forged the sword that defeated death! O field, in which Christ, nature's farmer, himself sprouted forth unsown as an ear of corn! O temple, in which God became a priest, not by changing his nature, but by his mercy clothing himself with him who was "according to the order of Melchizedek"! [Hebrews 5:10] "The Word became flesh" [John 1:14], even if the Jews disbelieve the Lord who said so. God has put on the form of a human being, even if the Greeks ridicule the wonder.[130]

As Proclus put it in yet another homily that he would later preach as patriarch on the Feast of the Nativity:

> [The Lord's] richly appointed throne is the Virgin Theotokos. His consular toga is his seedless flesh . . . Strange is his apparel, and his tunic is exceedingly unique.

Its fabrication is wondrous, for it has no share in any human craftsmanship. O Virgin, maiden who knew not man, and mother who knew not pain! Where did you find the flax to weave the robe with which the Lord of creation has clothed himself today? What sort of loom was your womb, upon which you wove the tunic without seam? [cf. John 19:23] But [Proclus apostrophized] I seem to hear Nature responding instead of the Virgin, for I take care to assess the rationale of a virgin birth. "I am unable," Nature says, "to make garments of flesh without the mingling of a man. Besides my loom produces only soiled garments. I clothed Adam, but he was stripped naked, and he covered himself with fig-leaves and shame." In order, then, to mend the ruined robe, Wisdom (σοφία) became a weaver in the virginal workshop, and by means of a shuttle propelled by divine artifice, she clothed herself in the robe of the body.[131]

Strikingly, here Wisdom herself takes the part of the Lord, weaving for herself the robe with which she will enter through the veil of the womb into creation. And yet, it is Mary who is the one who supplies the thread with which Wisdom weaves in the "virginal workshop" of her womb. It is Mary who weaves the tunic without seam, the fleshly, material robe with which the high priest, her Son, clothed himself as he entered into his creation. So is Wisdom (Sophia) weaver or wearer, creator or creature, Mary or God?

This, in a nutshell, is the great mystery with which Proclus and his contemporaries were grappling in arguing over whether to call Mary "God-bearer," Theotokos, Mother of God. Wisdom, they knew from the scriptures, was with God at the creation, standing beside him in heaven, the Holy of Holies, as he engraved the patterns of the world. Just as it was she who carried him like a cloud as he rode upon the chariot of the cherubim, so it was she in whose image and likeness he crafted Adam and Eve, male and female. She was beside him "like a master workman" (Proverbs 8:30; 'amon in the Hebrew, ἁρμόζουσα in the Greek), joining together the bonds of the everlasting covenant between heaven and earth, human and divine.[132] Like Eve (Hebrew hawwah), she was mother of all living, the Living One (Hebrew hayyah) whom Ezekiel saw in the temple in the midst of the glory of the throne.[133] As Wisdom exulted in the book of Ecclesiasticus, from which the scriptural readings were to be taken for Mary's feasts:

> I came out of the mouth of the most High, the firstborn before all
>   creatures:
> I made that in the heavens there should rise light that never faileth, and
>   as a cloud I covered all the earth:
> I dwelt in the highest places, and my throne is in a pillar of a cloud.

I alone have compassed the circuit of heaven, and have penetrated into
the bottom of the deep, and have walked in the waves of the sea,
And have stood in all the earth: and in every people,
And in every nation I have had the chief rule:
And by my power I have trodden under my feet the hearts of all the high
and low: and in all these I sought rest, and I shall abide in the inheri-
tance of the Lord.
Then the creator of all things commanded, and said to me: and he that
made me, rested in my tabernacle,
And he said to me: Let thy dwelling be in Jacob, and thy inheritance in
Israel, and take root in my elect.
From the beginning, and before the world, was I created, and unto the
world to come I shall not cease to be, and in the holy dwelling place I
have ministered before him. (Ecclesiasticus 24:5–14)

And yet, the Lady's Son, too, was somehow Wisdom, one with God at the
creation. "I and the Father are one," Jesus told the Jews who had asked him
whether he was the Christ (John 10:30). As the evangelist put it, echoing
Ecclesiasticus (and Genesis):

In the beginning was the Word (λόγος), and the Word was with God, and
the Word was God. He was in the beginning with God; all things were made
through him, and without him was not anything made that was made. In him
was life, and the life was the light of men. The light shines in the darkness, and
the darkness has not overcome it. (John 1:1–5 RSV)

So the Word, too, was with God from before creation, like Wisdom, "the image
of the invisible God, the first-born of all creation, for in him all things were
created, in heaven and on earth, visible and invisible . . . He is before all things,
and in him all things hold together" (Colossians 1:15–17 RSV). Appointed by
the Father "the heir of all things," it was he "through whom [God] also created
the world. He reflects the glory of God and bears the very stamp of his nature,
upholding the universe by his word of power" (Hebrews 1:2–3 RSV).

So was (or is) Wisdom female (Sophia) or male (Logos), mother or son? How
could this mystery be explained?[134] As the Apostle Paul cautioned the Corinthians
seeking certainty, "Jews demand signs and Greeks seek wisdom, but we preach
Christ crucified, a stumbling block to Jews and a folly to Gentiles, but to those
who are called, both Jews and Greeks, Christ the power of God and the wisdom
of God" (1 Corinthians 1:24 RSV). But who, then, or what was Wisdom? Was

she the Lady or the Lord? Was she (or he) the Word or the Mother of the Word? Could the creation exist without him (or her)? Was she creator or creature, the dwelling place or the one who dwells (cf. Psalm 90:1 LXX)? Somehow, it seems, much as the Christ her Son was both God and man, the image and reflection of God, Wisdom was both creature and creator, the temple and presence of God. "[Wisdom]," explained "Solomon," writing sometime in the second or first century B.C.E. in Alexandria, "is a vapour [alt. breath] of the power of God, and a certain pure emanation of the glory of Almighty God. . . . For she is the brightness of eternal light, and the unspotted mirror of God's majesty, and the image of his goodness" (Wisdom 7:25–26). "For we say," argued the great Jewish exegete Philo of Alexandria (d. 50 C.E.),

> that the high priest is not a man, but is the word (*logos*) of God . . . For Moses says that he cannot be defiled neither in respect of his father, that is, the mind, nor of his mother, that is, the external sense; because, I imagine, he has received imperishable and wholly pure parents, God being his father, who is also the father of all things, and Wisdom being his mother, by means of whom the universe arrived at creation. [Moreover, he] is anointed with oil, by which I mean that the principal part of him is illuminated with a light like the beams of the sun, so as to be thought worthy to be clothed with garments. And the most ancient word of the living God is clothed with the word as with a garment, for it has put on earth, and water, and air, and fire [that is, as Philo explains elsewhere, the four-colored fabric of the temple veil], and the things which proceed from those elements.[135]

Likewise, Proclus suggested through the complexly woven imagery of his homilies, the Virgin Theotokos, Lady Wisdom, clothed the high priest, the Word of God, in the elements of creation when she wove the fabric of his fleshly garment in the loom of her virginal womb. His Mother, she had been with him at the creation of the world, just as he was with the Father. The mirror of his majesty, she was herself the brightness of the eternal light that shone forth from the temple as he came forth like a bridegroom from his bridal chamber (cf. Psalm 18:6), like the Lord passing through the closed gate of his sanctuary (cf. Ezekiel 44:1–2). Becoming incarnate, the Word put on the stuff of Wisdom, the elements (or threads) that she helped him create (or spin). To disassociate the Lord from his Mother would be as difficult as unpicking the seams of his tunic, which had none. Just as the Lord Jesus Christ was God incarnate, neither merely man nor solely God, so (as Proclus famously put it as he preached in Constantinople on the day of her feast) "the same one was both with the Virgin and of the Virgin; by his 'overshadowing,' he was with her; by becoming incarnate, he was of her. . . . As man, Emmanuel opened the gates of human nature; as God, he left the bars of virginity unbroken . . . [just] as the prophet Ezekiel said."[136]

Unlike Pulcheria and the rest of the (possibly) largely female crowd, who enthusiastically applauded Proclus's rhetorical tour de force, Patriarch Nestorius was not at all pleased, and he rose immediately to make his protest. "It is not surprising," he conceded, "that you who love Christ should applaud those who preach in honor of the blessed Mary, for the fact that she became the temple of our Lord's flesh (*templum Dominicae carnis*) exceeds everything else worthy of praise."[137] (Note that even Nestorius used the imagery of the temple in talking about Mary's womb.) "But," he cautioned, putting forth an argument that would be used to this day in countering efforts to afford Mary the devotion many believe she deserves, "we should not honor or praise her more than is fitting, lest we seem to confound the dignity of the Word of God."[138] Aside from the philosophical objections that he insisted the Greek (*paganus*) would raise against the idea of a God who was born, died, and buried, manifestly most troubling of all for Nestorius was the image of Jesus the Word as priest, not to mention his mother's womb as temple: "I cannot admit that God 'became a priest,' for if God is both creator and priest, to whom is the sacrifice of priests offered?" Moreover, for Nestorius, it was not Mary's womb that was the temple, but Jesus's body, which died: "The Word who dwelt in the temple formed by the Holy Spirit is one (*alius*), and the temple itself is another (*aliud templum*), different from God who dwells within it."[139] Elsewhere, to drive the point further home, Nestorius would insist: "A creature did not produce the Creator, rather she gave birth to the human being, the instrument of the Godhead. The Holy Spirit did not create God the Logos . . . Rather, he formed out of the Virgin a temple for God the Logos, a temple in which he dwelt."[140]

Addressing the council convened the next summer to examine Nestorius's theology, Cyril (d. ca. 444), the patriarch of Alexandria, would beg to differ. "Hail, Mary the Theotokos, the revered treasure of the whole world, the inextinguishable lamp, the crown of virginity, the scepter of orthodoxy, the indissoluble temple, the container of the uncontainable, mother and virgin," he would exclaim to the bishops, clergy, and people gathered in the Church of Mary at Ephesus.[141] The bishops agreed. "If anyone does not confess the Emmanuel to be truly God, and the holy virgin to be Mother of God (for she gave birth in the flesh to the Word of God made flesh), let him be anathema," the council pronounced at the conclusion of their review of Nestorius's errors.[142] Mary, as Cyril would insist in homily after homily, was more than just a womb for Christ's human nature. She was the temple in which God put on flesh, her body the sacred enclosure (χώρα) containing the uncontainable God.[143] If Nestorius could not see her as Mother of God, then, Cyril argued, he could not see Jesus Christ as truly God as well as truly man. "We do not say," Cyril argued in a letter to Nestorius that was read out at the council and recorded in its proceedings,

> that [the only-begotten Word of God] cast aside what he was, but ... he remained what he was, God in nature and truth. We do not say that his flesh was turned into the nature of the godhead or that the unspeakable Word of God was changed into the nature of the flesh ... For although visible as a child and in swaddling cloths, even while he was in the bosom of the virgin that bore him, as God he filled the whole of creation and was fellow ruler with him who begot him. ... But we do not say that the Word of God dwelt as in an ordinary man born of the holy virgin, in order that Christ may not be thought of as a God-bearing man. For even though "the Word dwelt among us," and it is also said that in Christ dwelt "all the fulllness of the godhead bodily," we understand that, having become flesh the manner of his indwelling is not defined in the same way as he is said to dwell among the saints. ... There is therefore one Christ and Son and Lord.[144]

Not, as Nestorius would have it, two Christs: one, human, of the flesh, the other divine. As much as, more famously, Nestorius's position was a rejection of the hypostatic union of the two natures in Christ, so, arguably, if Barker's reconstruction as presented here is correct, it was a rejection of the temple tradition upon which the identification of Jesus as Lord and his Mother as Lady Wisdom historically as well as theologically depended.[145] As the people of Constantinople celebrating Nestorius's condemnation would exult,

> Mary, the Holy Virgin, who gave birth to God in the flesh, has overthrown Nestorius! ... O Christ, our God, it is you who have conquered; o cross, it is you who have won! ... There is only one faith, there is only one council ... Thousands of years to Pulcheria, she is the one who strengthened the faith![146]

The Lady and her Son had returned.[147]

Mary, the Theotokos, the Living Temple of God

It was night, and the people of Constantinople were singing:

> Hail, through whom joy shall shine forth;
> Hail, through whom the curse shall cease;
> Hail, recalling of fallen Adam;
> Hail, deliverance of the tears of Eve;

Hail, height hard for human thoughts to scale;
Hail, depth hard even for the eyes of angels to pierce;
Hail, since you are the chair (καθέδρα) of the king;
Hail, since you bear him who bears all;
Hail, star causing the sun to shine;
Hail, womb of the divine Incarnation;
Hail, through whom the creation is made new;
Hail, through whom the Creator is worshipped;
Hail, bride unwedded. (strophe 1)[148]

The year, or so tradition tells it, was 626, and the city had been under siege for over a month. Heraclius (d. 641) was emperor and Sergius I (d. 638) was patriarch, and the people were gathered outside the walls of the city in the church of Holy Mary at Blachernai; the church, or so tradition tells it, had been founded almost two hundred years earlier by the Empress Pulcheria and housed a great relic of the Virgin, her *maphorion* or veil.[149] The people were standing—thus, the hymn that they sang came to be known as the Ἀκάθιστος, "not sitting"—in thanksgiving for the Virgin's protection against their enemies, the Avars and the Sassanid Persians, whom, they believed, she had miraculously driven away.[150] Like the church where they were gathered, the hymn was already centuries old, most likely, as Leena Mari Peltomaa has argued, going back to the decades immediately following the council of Ephesus during the lifetime of the Empress Pulcheria.[151] But, as we have seen, the imagery by which they invoked their Virgin defender was even centuries older.[152]

Hail, tabernacle of God and the Word;
Hail, greater than the Holy of Holies;
Hail, ark gilded by the Spirit;
Hail, inexhaustible treasury of life;
Hail, precious diadem of pious kings;
Hail, holy exaltation of devout priests;
Hail, immovable tower of the Church;
Hail, impregnable wall of the kingdom;
Hail, through whom trophies are raised up;
Hail, through whom enemies fall;
Hail, healing of my body;
Hail, protection of my soul;
Hail, bride unwedded. (strophe 23)

We know these titles, we have heard them before.[153] Again and again, the hymn invokes the imagery of the temple and its Lady, Wisdom, as the one who harmonizes heaven and earth (Proverbs 8:30), the Tree of Life bearing fruit and fragrant oils (Ecclesiasticus 24:23), the chariot throne in the Holy of Holies bearing the Lord among the seraphim (Ezekiel 1:4–28; Isaiah 6:1–2), the gate of the sanctuary through which only the Lord might pass (Ezekiel 44:1–2), the golden lampstand (Zechariah 4:2), the table on which the showbread was offered (Exodus 25:23–30), and the mother of the Morning Star who gives light to the world (Psalm 109:3). In the words of the "Akathistos," Mary, "yearning to grasp a knowledge unknowable," is herself "initiate of sacred counsel," "celestial ladder by which God descended," "bridge leading those from earth to heaven" (strophe 3). "Hail," the hymn salutes her in the voice of Gabriel, "you who surpass the knowledge of the wise . . . you who illuminate the minds of the faithful" (strophe 3). "Hail," it cries in the voice of the unborn child of Elizabeth, "vine-twig of unfading bud . . . treasure of undying fruit" (strophe 5). "Hail," it rejoices with the shepherds, "since heavenly things rejoice with the earth . . . since earthly things chant with the faithful" (strophe 7). "Hail," it acknowledges her in the voices of the Magi, "mother of the star that never sets . . . bright dawn of the mystical day . . . you who protect the initiates of the Trinity . . . you who showed forth the Lord Christ, who loves humankind" (strophe 9).

"A new creation has the Creator revealed, / manifesting himself to us, his creatures" (strophe 13). She is "the tree of glorious fruit on which the faithful feed . . . the wood of fair shading leaves where many shelter" (strophe 13). The Word, "present wholly among those below, / yet in no way absent from those above," condescended to be born, and the Virgin, seized by God, hears herself praised:

> Hail, container of the uncontainable God;
> Hail, gate of hallowed mystery;
> Hail, tidings doubted by unbelievers;
> Hail, undoubted boast of believers;
> Hail, all-holy chariot of him who is above the Cherubim;
> Hail, excellent dwelling-place for him who is above the Seraphim;
> Hail, you who bring opposites together;
> Hail, you who unite virginity and childbirth;
> Hail, through whom sin is remitted;
> Hail, through whom Paradise is opened;
> Hail, key to the kingdom of Christ;
> Hail, hope of eternal blessings;
> Hail, bride unwedded. (strophe 15)

"Wordy orators" who attempt to describe her fall "dumb as the fishes," at a loss to explain how she "remained virgin / and yet had the power to bear a child," but the faithful cry aloud:

> Hail, vessel of the wisdom of God;
> Hail, treasure of his providence;
> Hail, you who reveal lovers of wisdom as unwise;
> Hail, you who refute practitioners of wisdom as unreasonable;
> Hail, since the cunning disputants are shown to be fools;
> Hail, since the myth-makers have withered in silence;
> Hail, you who have torn asunder the tangled webs of the Athenians;
> Hail, you who have filled the nets of the fishermen;
> Hail, you who draw us forth from the depths of ignorance;
> Hail, you who illuminate many with knowledge;
> Hail, ship for those who wish to be saved;
> Hail, haven for the seafarers of life;
> Hail, bride unwedded. (strophe 17)

As the hymn would have it, unlike those who would follow the falsely reasoned arguments of the Jews and the Greeks (cf. 1 Corinthians 1:24), those who follow the Theotokos have access to true wisdom. She is the source of enlightenment, the one who enables those whom she anoints to see the Lord in his glory. She, not the "cunning disputants" and "myth-makers" of the Athenians, is the source of truth, because it is she who makes the Lord visible on his throne. Thus, the hymn exults, "we see the holy Virgin as a torch full of light, / shining upon those in darkness," just as the lampstand burned before the Holy of Holies in the temple. "For by kindling the immaterial light / she guides all to divine knowledge, / illuminating the mind with brilliance." Like the Lady who gave birth to the Morning Star, she is the "beam of the spiritual sun" and the "lampstand of the light that never wanes." She is the "soul-illuminating lightning" and the "thunder [striking] down [her] enemies" that came forth from the chariot throne. She kindles "the many-beamed lantern" (that is, the lampstands in the temple) and makes "the many-streamed river gush forth" (that is, the four-streamed river of Paradise, Genesis 2:10–14). In bestowing the Holy Spirit on her anointed ones (cf. Wisdom 9:17), she "[prefigures] the baptismal font" and "[takes away] the filth of sin." Like the great bronze sea that stood in the forecourt of the temple (2 Chronicles 4:2), she is the "basin that washes clean the conscience." And she is the "bowl wherein is mixed the wine of mighty joy" offered for the atonement of sins. Above all, she is the "scent of Christ's fragrance" and the "life of mystical feasting," the perfumed oil with which Wisdom anoints her children and the fruit-bearing Tree of Life with which she feeds them (strophe 21).[154] "We all praise you," the hymn concludes, "as a living temple, O Theotokos (ὡς ἔμψυχον ναόν Θεοτόκε). / For the Lord who holds all in his hands dwelt in your womb" (strophe 23).

There are many ways we might explain the presence of this imagery in this, arguably the Virgin's most famous hymn, sung in full in the Orthodox Church every year since the tenth century on Friday evening in the fifth week in Lent, in parts over the course of the whole season of Lent such that, as Peltomaa puts it, "the Akathistos characterizes the whole Orthodox world's preparation for Easter."[155] Byzantinists Vasiliki Limberis and Bissera Pentcheva would point to the resonances in its repeated salutations with the titles accorded the ancient pagan goddesses of Byzantium, latterly Constantinople: Isis as the goddess of rivers and weaving, Athena as the goddess of seafarers, Rhea as the mother of the gods, Tyche and Victoria as the goddesses of civic prosperity and victory.[156] In the great outpouring of homilies that they wrote in observance of her principal feasts founded over the course of the sixth century, Mary's seventh- and eighth-century Orthodox devotees would insist rather that all of her titles, now more usually designated as "types" or "allegories," could be found in the scriptures (for the Old Testament texts, the Septuagint; the New Testament was, of course, originally written in Greek). As the great hymnographer Andrew of Crete (d. 740?) put it in the fourth of four homilies that he preached on the Nativity of the Virgin (celebrated on September 8): "For there is not, indeed there is not, any place in the whole of the God-inspired Scripture where, on going about, one would not see signs of [the Virgin Mary] scattered about in diverse ways." "See," Andrew exclaimed,

> how she is adorned with names of many meanings and revealed very clearly in many places in Scripture, as, for example, whenever [scripture] calls her a virgin, a young maiden, a prophetess, then bridal chamber, house of God, holy temple, second tabernacle, holy table, sanctuary, mercy-seat, golden censer, holy of holies, cherubim of glory, golden jar, tablets of the covenant, priestly staff, scep-tre of the kingdom, diadem of beauty, horn in which [is contained] the myrrh of unction, alabaster jar [of perfumes; cf. Exodus 30:34–38], candlestick, breath [cf. Wisdom 7:25], lampstand, wick, chariot, shrub, rock, land, garden, country, field, spring, ewe-lamb, drop, and as many other [types] as the renowned inter-preters of the Spirit foreseeingly call her in accordance with the mystical insight that [reveals itself] in symbols (συμβόλοις).[157]

If, by the eighth century, for Andrew and his contemporaries the wonder lay in how many ways the Spirit revealed the Virgin to them in the scriptures, for us it should surely be in how uncannily their lists of symbols recalled the Lady who had once been present in the temple along with her attributes: the Tree of Life and the river of paradise; the cherub throne and the golden lampstand; the table of the showbread and the perfumed oils; the clouds of incense and the crown with which she crowned the king, her Son; the ark of the covenant, the jar of manna, and Aaron's flowering rod—not to mention the Holy of Holies and Wisdom herself.[158] The "Akathistos" set the pattern, if not always the rhetorical boundaries, for the most exuberant such lists. (References to the Old Testament throughout this subsection are to the Septuagint version.)

"Hail," Modestus, archbishop of Jerusalem (d. ca. 634), the author of one of the most elaborate seventh-century homilies for the feast of Mary's Dormition (or "falling asleep," celebrated on August 15) cried out:

Hail, woman so desired by God, living temple of the Most High, whom no place can contain! In you the personified, uncreated Wisdom of God the Father dwelt, and built the Temple of his body. . . .

Hail, holy Mother of God! The king of glory, the Lord Jesus, chose you to be his spiritual kingdom on earth. . . .

Hail, daughter of Joachim and mother of the God who created all things! You are summoned by him to share in blessedness beyond all joy of the holy ranks who are called blessed on earth and in heaven.

Hail, spring of healing! You have poured forth Christ, who cures every illness. . . .

Hail, glorious Mother of everlasting light, which is by nature and substance the true God! He has shone forth from you in our substance on earth, and has "let the light of his face shine upon us" [cf. Psalm 4:6]. . . .

Hail, divine altar erected on God's foundation! Through you the atoning and saving sacrifice for the whole world came forth, Christ our God. For from you, holy Mother of God, he put on that vestment of flesh prepared for him by the Holy Spirit, and came forth as "a priest forever, according to the order of Melchizedek" [Psalm 109:4; cf. Hebrews 5:6], as scripture says.[159]

"Hail," the great theologian John of Damascus invited his audience to exclaim with the angel Gabriel in the third of three homilies that he preached for the same feast in the church at Gethsemane at the site of Mary's tomb:

Hail, you who were destined to be Mother of God! Hail, you who were chosen before all ages by God's will, most holy shoot of the earth, vessel of the divine fire, sacred image of the Holy Spirit, spring of the water of life, paradise for the tree of life, living branch of the holy vine that flows with nectar and ambrosia, river filled with the perfumes of the Spirit, field of divine wheat, rose glowing with virginity and breathing the fragrance of grace, lily robed like a queen, ewe who gave birth to the Lamb of God who takes away the sin of the world, workshop of our salvation, higher than the angelic powers, servant and mother![160]

"Hail," Germanus I (d. ca. 742), patriarch of Constantinople from 715 to his forced resignation in 730 for his defense of the icons, exulted in the first of two homilies that he preached for the entry of the Virgin into the temple at age three (feast celebrated on November 21):

Hail, the shining cloud that lets fall drops of spiritual, divine dew on us, having today, at your inconspicuous entrance into the holy of holies, caused a radiant sun to shine on those held in the shadow of death!. . . .

Hail, the most delightful and rational paradise of God . . . in which the life-giving wood flowers into a knowledge of truth, and which bestows immortality on those who taste of it.

Hail, the palace of the All-Ruler, God, who was sacredly built, undefiled, and most pure, [and] who has encompassed his greatness while guiding all your people in mystically directed enjoyment!. . . .

Hail, the new Zion and divine Jerusalem, holy "city of the great Ruler God, in whose citadels God himself is known" [cf. Psalm 47:3–4]. . . .

[Hail,] the truly golden and shining . . . lampstand with seven lights that is lit by inaccessible light and enriched by the oil of purity, guaranteeing a rising of brightness to those who are blinded by mist in the gloom of transgression. . . .

Hail, the holy throne of God, the divine offering, the house of glory, the most beautiful ornament and chosen vessel and universal place of propitiation, and heaven declaring the glory of God! [cf. Psalm 18:2].[161]

"Hail," Germanus (unable to contain himself) continued in the oration that he delivered for the Feast of the Annunciation of "the Supremely Holy Theotokos" (celebrated on March 25):

Hail, favored one, the royal robe, purple in appearance, that clothed the King of Heaven and of earth who was made flesh!

Hail, favored one, the spice-bearing earth and life-bearing container and new vase of unguent for the Spirit, that filled the whole universe with a perfumed scent!

Hail, favored one, truly the golden censer and the pure and all-holy and spotless treasury of purity!

Hail, favored one, all-golden and wholly unblemished beauty, and transcendent and truly most marvellous dwelling-place of the Word!

Hail, favored one, who caused the Sun that is eternal to arise for the world in flesh, [a Sun] who dazzled the whole of creation with his goodness!

Hail, favored one, the all-bright cloud of the life-giving Spirit, which carries the rain of compassion and sprinkles all creation!

Hail, favored one, salvation of those born on earth, who transformed grief into joy, and joined the things on earth with those in heaven, and who loosed the dividing wall of enmity!

Hail, favored one the divinely sealed and divinely entered gate of our life, through whom the Co-eternal Word of the God and Father passed! [cf. Ezekiel 44:1–2]

Hail, favored one, untouchable plant of purity and shady tree of compassion and gold-purple lily of true virginity!

Hail, favored one, the heifer unused to the yoke, who fed the fatted calf and carried in her womb that heavenly greatness![162]

Hail, favored one, the spotless ewe-lamb, who cherished in her undefiled hands that purple-dyed sheep which was willingly sacrificed on behalf of everyone! [cf. Numbers 6:14]

Hail, favored one, blameless and unwedded maiden who showed her relatives a strange conception and inexplicable birth-giving that was without travail!

Hail, favored one, ark of the sanctuary and divinely-planted rod of righteousness, which flowered with the genuine flower!

Hail, favored one, the golden lampstand bearing a bowl, and shining tabernacle, and table which contained in itself the life-giving bread!

Hail, favored one, the cherubic and most strange seat for the King of Glory, and truly an imperial palace for the flesh of the Word!

Hail, favored one, in whom the living and honored and divinely ruled city, being fortified, is always honored!

Hail, favored one, the all-gold jar of manna and the tabernacle truly made of purple, which the new Bezaleel adorned in golden style!

Hail, favored one, forever purple, God-bearing cloud and spring eternally pouring out grace for everyone!

Hail, favored one, the high and exalted throne of the Creator and Redeemer of all things, who holds all things in his hand whether in heaven or on earth!

Hail, favored one, the living temple of magnificent glory, for the One who became human on our behalf and took on flesh for the sake of our salvation!

Hail, favored one, who brings Life and nourishes the Nourisher; who provides milk for the One who formerly caused honey to spring forth from a rock!

Hail, favored one, mountain of God, rich mountain, shaded mountain, uncut mountain, visible mountain of God! [cf. Psalm 67:16; Habakkuk 3:3; Daniel 2:45][163]

Hail, favored one, exultation of the soul, universal object of worship for the whole world, and truly good mediator for all sinners!

Hail, favored one, joy of the afflicted and formidable protectress of those who with sincere hearts confess you as Theotokos!

Hail, favored one, who carried in your womb the benevolent Master for the general salvation of the human race!

Hail, favored one, marvellous and compassionate refuge for all Christians and spectacle loftier than all magnificent beauty![164]

"Hail, favored one!" Germanus ventriloquized the angel saluting her. "For you are about to become heaven, a temple containing God, and a living tabernacle of God, wider, higher and more marvellous than the seven firmaments."[165]

And what a heaven she was! There was almost nothing that such a living tabernacle could not contain and, therefore, nothing that did not signify her, or so Andrew of Crete seemed determine to prove as he scoured the scriptures for signs of her. She was the bramble bush that burned but was not consumed (Exodus 3:3); the rod that came forth from the root of Jesse (Isaiah 11:1); the root of Jesse that arose to rule over the Gentiles (Isaiah 11:10); the holy ground on which Moses stood (Exodus 3:5); the desirable land (Psalm 105:24); the land from which truth arose (Psalm 84:12); the land of Thaeman and the mountain from which God will come (Habakkuk 3:3); the rock cut without hands (Daniel 2:45); the mountain in which God was pleased to dwell (Psalm 67:17); the fruitful olive tree in the house of the Lord (Psalm 51:10); the ark of holiness (Psalm 131:8); the throne of the Lord (Isaiah 6:1); the closed gate (Ezekiel 44:2); Zion (Isaiah 59:20), which the Lord chose as a habitation for himself (Psalm 131:13); mother, because a man will say, "Zion is my mother" (Psalm 86:5); the litter of Solomon (Song of Songs 3:9) and his couch (Song of Songs 3:7); a scroll (Ezekiel 2:9–3:1); a book (Isaiah 29:11); the volume [or scroll] on which the prophet was commanded to write (Isaiah 8:1); the altar tongs bearing the coals that purified the prophet's lips (Isaiah 6:6–7); the virgin who would conceive and bear Immanuel (Isaiah 7:14); the prophetess who bore a son (Isaiah 8:3–4); the queen standing beside the Lord's right hand in gold-woven robes (Psalm 44:10); the beloved who is all fair (Song of Songs 4:7), whom the bridegroom invites to come from Lebanon (Song of Songs 4:8), whose lips drip honey and whose garments are like the fragrance of Lebanon (Song of Songs 4:11); the sister-bride with beautiful eyes (Song of Songs 4:10); the enclosed garden and sealed fountain (Song of Songs 4:12); the daughter whose beauty the king desired (Psalm 44:11–12) and who exceeds all others in wealth and power (Proverbs 31:29); the betrothed of Joseph (Luke 1:26–27); the cloud on which the Lord sits (Isaiah 19:1); the appearance of the likeness of the glory of the Lord that appeared like a rainbow in a cloud on a rainy day around the cherub throne (Ezekiel 1:28); the appearance of amber (Ezekiel 1:27); the day pouring forth speech and the night proclaiming knowledge (Psalm 18:3); heaven from which the Lord looked out (Psalm 32:13); the heaven of heavens that belongs to the Lord (Psalm 113:24); the East (Psalm 67:33–34); the West (Psalm 67:5); the sun in which the bridegroom set his tabernacle (Psalm 18:5–6); the city of God (Psalm 86:3), gladdened by the streams of the river (Psalm 45:5), who will not be moved (Psalm 45:6); the brick inscribed with the city, Jerusalem (Ezekiel 4:1–2); a fearful place, the house of God and the gate of heaven (Genesis 28:17), blessed by the glory of the Lord (Ezekiel 3:12), a tabernacle for the God of Jacob (Psalm 131:4–5); the fleece on which the Lord comes as rain (Psalm 71:6); blessed among women (Luke 1:42), from whom the Son of God was born under the law (Galatians 4:4); blessed in her belief that the Lord would fulfill what was spoken to her (Luke 1:45) and in her womb and her breasts (Luke 11:27); Mary (Luke 1:30), who would conceive a bear a Son (Luke 1:31) who would save his people from their sins (Matthew 1:21) and be called Son of the Highest and Son of God (Luke 1:32–35); Mary, who magnifies the Lord (Luke 1:46–47).[166]

Just as the scriptures bore witness to the Lord, the Son of the Most High, who rode upon the clouds and sat enthroned upon the cherubim and came forth from the Holy of Holies like a bridegroom coming forth from his bedchamber, so, Andrew and his contemporaries believed, they bore witness to the heaven who bore him.[167] In this respect, perhaps the greatest mystery was, in fact, how she could be both a person (Mary, the mother, daughter, sister, beloved, virgin, prophetess, and bride of God) and a place (heaven, the temple, the tabernacle, the house, the ark, the throne, the litter, the mountain, the cloud, the city, the sun, the tree) in which God, himself the one "who has no place, because he *is* the place of all other beings," dwelled.[168] Who other than Wisdom could encompass this mystery? Who other than the Lady could encompass the Lord (cf. Jeremiah 31:22)? "My soul," Mary exclaimed, "magnifies the Lord" (Luke 1:46), as, her devotees would insist, how could it not? She was the one who made the Lord visible to the world, clothing him with flesh as he passed through the veil, magnifying his glory as he came forth from her womb. Mary was the one who, harmonizing heaven and earth, scripture and human understanding, made it possible to discern God. "Hail," Andrew greeted her yet again, the intellectual mirror of discerning foreknowledge, through which the renowned interpreters of the Spirit mystically contemplated the infinitely powerful condescension of God on our behalf. Hail, foreseeing optical instrument, by means of which those who were overshadowed by the gloomy shadow of sin were mightily illumined and received the Sun of righteousness, rising with glory from on high![169]

"Be glad in her, heaven!" Andrew exclaimed. "For she imitated you, who could not contain the Lord, in yourself, when she contained him without constriction."[170] "She is the great world in miniature, the world containing him who brought the world from nothingness into being, that it might be the messenger of his own greatness."[171] "Hail, mediator of law and grace, seal of old and new covenants, manifest fulfillment of all prophecy, acrostic of the God-inspired truth of the Scriptures, the living and also most pure volume of God and the Word in which, wordlessly and without writing, the Writer himself, God and the Word, is read each day!"[172]

Mirror, magnifier, acrostic: Mary was the one and only lens through which to read the truth about God and his creation. She was "the new refuge of all Christians . . . the vision which was mystically foreshadowed of old in Moses' bush . . . David's divinely embroidered purple robe . . . [the] cherubic throne, supremely great, fiery and lofty, holding in its womb the Lord King Sabaoth . . . where the seraphim stand by covered by their wings . . . and cry out loudly that fearful hymn since they cannot support the sight of his unbearable glory."[173] "Behold," Andrew invited his listeners as they celebrated the Feast of the Dormition,

the new ark of God's glory, containing "the golden vase, Aaron's rod that blossomed, and the tablets of the covenant" [Hebrews 9:4]. Behold, the summation of all the things which the oracles of the prophets foretold . . . Behold the altar of expiation in the Holy of Holies, set up in the sanctuary of the tent of God's presence. At some times, she is covered over with the Seraphs' wings; at others, she is the place where our sins are expiated through the mystery of Jesus' own initiation. The yoke of slavery to the Law no longer rests on the true Israel, since Christ has written for us a bill of liberation, of free and spiritual worship, using as his parchment the body he took from the Virgin. The priests' yearly procession into the holy place is no longer practiced, for "the great high priest, Christ Jesus, has passed through the heavens" [Hebrews 4:14], with the flesh he took on and with its rational, intellectual soul, in order to offer his mystical sacrifice in the virgin's sanctuary as in a temple, always interceding for us. He offers sacrifice and is himself offered; bringing his holocaust forward, he becomes the sacrifice; sanctifying himself for our sakes, he sanctifies those who have sacrificed him.[174]

Mary herself was the Holy of Holies that contained God; her body was the sanctuary in which her Son, the great high priest, offered himself as a sacrifice. She was the new ark, bearing the tablets of the covenant written not on stone, but on the flesh and in the blood of her child. His sacrifice supplanted the sacrifices of atonement offered annually by the priests (Leviticus 16:1–34), and she was the place in which this expiation occurred.

As Germanus apostrophized preaching on the same feast, "No one is filled with the knowledge of God except through you, all-holy One; no one is saved but through you, Mother of God."[175] It is, therefore, he reasoned, appropriate that Christians should adorn the temples that they have built in her honor with images of her:

> For if the temple of Solomon once represented heaven in an earthly image, will not the temples built in honor of you, who became the living temple of Christ, all the more justly be celebrated as heavens on earth? The stars speak out with tongues of flame in the heavenly firmament; and the material colors of your icons, O Mother of God, dazzle us with the representation of your gifts.[176]

Likewise, Germanus argued, it was appropriate that Mary's body, "the living temple of the all-holy godhead of the Only-begotten," not be ultimately confined by a tomb.[177] John of Damascus concurred. As the "living and rational tabernacle of God," Mary was "the receptacle not just of the activity of God [as were the tablets upon which the Spirit wrote on Mount Sinai], but essentially of the hypostasis of the Son of God [made flesh in her by the Holy Spirit and her blood]."[178] Accordingly, just as King Solomon called together the elders of Israel and the priests to carry the ark of the covenant into the temple at Jerusalem (3 Kings 8:1–6), so when Mary, "the tabernacle of the Lord's glory," died, the apostles gathered together in Jerusalem to convey her body, "the spiritual ark, not of the Lord's covenant but of the very person of God the Word, the new Solomon himself, the King of Peace and master-builder of the universe," to its tomb as to a bridal chamber, from which, on the third day it was lifted up, "so that she, his first love, should be taken up to that 'greater and more perfect tabernacle . . . to heaven itself' " (cf. Hebrews 9:11, 24).[179] It is for this reason, John cautioned his listeners, that "we do not call her a goddess—we will have none of such pedantic classical fabling—for we proclaim her death. But we recognize her as Mother of the God who became flesh," and so we praise her with sacred songs and dance in her honor with Miriam the prophetess to the sound of tambourines (Exodus 15:20) and "shout in our hearts the cry of victory for the ark of the Lord God."[180]

Not everyone, to be sure, was equally impressed with such arguments, most particularly (or so the preachers felt obliged to remind their listeners as they retold the story of Mary's death or "falling asleep") the Jews. As Stephen Shoemaker has shown, the oldest traditions in these stories date back to as early as the third or fourth century, possibly even the second century, at all events well before the council of Ephesus.[181] By the eighth century, although there were still Christians, particularly in the West, who had doubts about what had happened to Mary's body after it had reached its not necessarily final resting place, all were agreed that on the way to its tomb, the "spiritual ark of the very person of God the Word" (as John of Damascus had put it) had been attacked. According to John of Thessalonica (r. 610–649), in what would become the most widely cited version of the story in both East and West, as the apostles processed through the streets of Jerusalem with Mary's bier, singing hymns and blessing God, Satan entered into the priests of the city, who, filled with anger at the sound of the singing, said to each other, "Come, let us go out and kill the Apostles, and let us burn the body that bore that sorcerer!"[182] So they rose up with swords and shields and went out to put the apostles to death. But the angels who were accompanying the apostles in the procession struck the priests blind so that they found themselves blundering against the city walls. One of their number, however, managed to retain his ability to see and catch up with the bier, at the sight of which he raged: "Here is the dwelling of the one who despoiled our people; what tremendous glory she has!" (Or, as the Latin version of the story put it: "Behold the tabernacle of the man who troubled us and all our nation, what glory it has received.") Laying hold of the bier, he attempted to upset it so as to pull the body to the ground, but "immediately his hands adhered to the bier and were severed from his elbows, and remained hanging from the bier."

In great pain, the priest cried out to the apostles for help, at which Peter turned and said to him: "If you believe that Jesus is the Son of God, whom you rose up against, imprisoned and put to death, surely you will be released from this predicament." To which the priest replied: "Did we not realize that he is the Son of God? But what shall we do, when avarice darkens our eyes?" But Peter said to him: "If now you believe with your whole heart, go and kiss the body of Mary, and say, 'I believe in you and in the God who was born of you.' " Then the chief priest began to bless holy Mary, "in the Hebrew language, for three hours, and did not allow anyone to touch her, offering witness-texts from the holy books of Moses and the other prophets that it is written about her that she would be the temple of the God of glory." (In the Latin, my translation: "And he began to praise God greatly and to draw witness from the books of the Old Testament to Mary, that she was the temple of God.") And those who heard him describe these traditions "were struck with wonder," because they had not heard them before. Then Peter commanded the priest to pray to Mary that he be made whole, and, immediately, he was. Once the priest regained the use of his hands, Peter gave him a strand from the branch of the palm that the Great Angel had brought to Mary from paradise for the apostles to carry before her bier, "for by it," the angel had explained, "many shall be healed."[183] Taking the strand, the priest went back to the city, where he found all those whom the angels had struck with blindness weeping and bemoaning their state: "Woe to us, for what happened to the Sodomites has also happened to us! For in ancient times God struck them with blindness, and afterwards he sent fire from heaven and burnt them up." But when the priest spoke to the people about the faith, telling them what had happened to him and laying the strand of palm upon their eyes, "those who believed began to see, while those who did not believe did not see, but remained blind."

Thanks to the great tragedies suffered by the Jews at the hands of Christians in the intervening centuries, it is understandably difficult for most modern readers to see in this episode anything other than a mean-spirited if not intentionally hostile attack by Christian storytellers on their long-standing rivals in the interpretation of the scriptures.[184] Read as an account not of an actual event (however vividly described) but of the argument of a tradition, it perhaps makes rather more sense. That the hands of the priest stuck to the bier when he tried to overturn it recalls the far more extreme punishment inflicted upon Uzzah, the son of Abinadab, who put out his hand to steady the ark of God as it was being brought to Jerusalem from the house of his father "with songs and lyres and harps and tambourines and castanets and cymbals": "And the anger of the Lord was kindled against Uzzah; and God smote him there because he put forth his hand to the ark, and he died there beside the ark of God" (2 Kings [Samuel] 6:1–7). In contrast, the priest who attempted to overthrow the new ark, the body of Mary, did not die, but was healed and made whole. Likewise, the people who had been struck blind by their rejection of Wisdom were given sight again when their eyes were touched with a branch from the tree of paradise, after which they were able, like the priest, to recognize the signs of her scattered throughout scripture. Vision, not vengeance, is the moral of the story as it was typically told, although, to be sure, those who rejected the Virgin were said to have remained blind, just as Wisdom herself had said they would (cf. Proverbs 1:20–33).

"Behold," John, monk and priest of Euboea (fl. eighth century), intoned as he preached on the Conception of the holy God-bearer and Virgin (kept on December 9 in the East), "a new ark is being constructed by the Creator,

PLATE 10 Virgin and Child enthroned, with kneeling nun. Psalter ("The Shaftesbury Psalter"),
Dorset, England, second quarter of the twelfth century, from the Benedictine nunnery of Saint
Edward, Shaftesbury. London, British Library, Lansdowne 383, fol. 165v.

Photo courtesy of The British Library, London.

which is countless thousand times stronger than the one in the time of Noah and in that of Moses! . . . This is the beginning of the new covenant, of the new and God-receiving ark that was formed in Anna's womb, out of the root of Judah, Jesse, and David."[185] "O what a marvel," he wondered as he told the story of her presentation by her parents in the temple. "The living temple and cherubic throne is brought into a temple constructed from stones. . . . For she is a throne and a place and a dwelling-place of the Emmanuel and All-Ruler, Christ."[186] She is the daughter of God about whom King David sang in the psalm: "Hear, O daughter of God, and see, and incline your ear, and forget your people and your father's house. And the King will desire your beauty" (Psalm 44:11–12).[187] And she is the queen who was brought into the temple accompanied by her fellow virgins (Psalm 44:15): "For she is the temple of the great King since, as Queen, she was about to lead the virgins as undefiled ones into a King's temple, for her honor and glory." "See," John urged his listeners, "see, descendants of Reuben and his sons . . . the Sun of Righteousness . . . is great and terrible before all those who encircle him. He is the Lord, mighty and powerful. . . . He is the Creator who fashioned a new heaven and throne that was unconsumed with fire out of the earth which had grown old." Accordingly, John invited them in the words of the psalms that, as we shall see, would be sung daily in the Virgin's honor as well as on her feasts:

> "Sing to the Lord a new song; sing to the Lord, all the earth. Sing to the Lord, bless his name" [Psalm 95:1–2], that a virgin girl is offered in a temple, that he who sanctifies the temple may dwell in her; and having dwelt in her womb, may not consume [it] . . . "Sing and exult and sing psalms" [Psalm 97:4]. . . . [For] behold, a throne more wonderful than the cherubic one is made ready on earth, about which it has been written: "God is in the midst of her, and she shall not be moved!" [Psalm 45:6].[188]

MARY IN THE PSALMS

Mary, or so her medieval Christian devotees insisted, was everywhere in scripture, particularly, to judge from the sermons that they preached and the hymns that they sang in her Office as well as on her feast days, the books of Wisdom and the Psalms. And not just the scriptures: books upon books could be written—and, as we shall see in more detail in chapter 4, were—on the ways in which the Virgin's images filled heaven and earth. For her medieval devotees, however, the greatest repository of such images was always the liturgy of the Divine Office, drawing as heavily as it did for both its texts and images on the references to the Virgin that could be found, when properly read, in scripture. By the end of the sixth century, the church in Constantinople kept four major feasts in honor of the Theotokos: the *Hypapante* or Presentation in the Temple (February 2), the Annunciation by the angel Gabriel (March 25), the Dormition ("Falling Asleep") of the Virgin (August 15), and the Nativity of the Virgin (September 8). By the eighth century, when the oldest extant liturgical sources become available in Latin and Greek,[189] liturgical calendars in the East also included the Entry of the Mother of God into the Temple (November 21), and the Conception of Saint Anne of the Virgin Mary (December 9).[190] The four oldest feasts (Presentation or Purification, Annuncia-tion, Dormition or Assumption, and Nativity of the Virgin) had been introduced to the Roman liturgy by the time of Pope Sergius I (r. 687–701), while certain communities, particularly in England, also adopted the Feast of the Virgin's Con-ception (December 8) before the Norman Conquest of 1066.[191]

Like the feasts of the liturgical year commemorating the events of salvation history, these Marian feasts commemorated specific events in the life of the Virgin: her conception, her birth, her entry into the temple at age three, the conception of her Son, his birth, his presentation in the temple, and her death and Assumption into heaven. Nevertheless, as we have seen, to judge from the sermons preached on her feast days and the choice of liturgical texts, all of them as they were established in the East also celebrated to one extent or another Mary's role as Wisdom, the living temple of God. In the East, this imagery was encapsulated in the magnificent hymn sung standing ("akathistos") every year during the Fridays of Lent. In the West, perhaps not coincidentally following the translation of the "Akathistos" into Latin, it was to receive its fullest expression in the daily Office kept in honor of the Virgin.[192] We have already noted the way in which Mary's later medieval devotees expanded upon the angel's greeting in their meditations, sermons, treatises, psalters, and poetry; thanks to Barker (or, as her medieval devotees would likely have put it, Wisdom herself), we may now appreciate better the ultimate source of much of their more recherché imagery. Likewise, thanks to what we have learned about the history of this imagery, we are now in a position to attempt what hitherto seemed inaccessible to us: a read-ing of the Marian Office in full, particularly the imagery of the psalms. We have discovered where the imagery at the core of Mary's Office came from. Now it is time to learn how to read her psalms.

A word or two of caution before we continue. As noted in chapter 1, other than its ubiquity in the devotional life of the medieval West, the only thing consistent about the Office of the Virgin as it was observed prior to 1571 was its variety. To suggest that there was ever a single understanding of what the Office meant would be as misleading as to suggest that there was ever a single selection of chants, psalms, lessons, and prayers through which medieval Christians expressed their devotion to the Mother of God. What we will be looking for in our reading are patterns and themes, not an overarching authoritative text. There were, however, certain things that the Office most definitely was not, one of which we have already noted in our discussion of the symbolism associated with the hours of the day at which it was said. Unlike the historiated initials or full-page images that typically accompanied it in the more sumptuous Books of Hours, the Office did not rehearse particular events in Mary's earthly life. Rather, as we shall see, the Office itself is above all a celebration of Mary as the Mother of the Lord, the Lady of the temple as the container of God. Insofar as it has a narrative, it is that of Mary's cosmic biography as the Queen of Heaven, not her earthly biography as the humble maiden of Nazareth, at least, not in the way in which those looking for a "realistic" account might prefer.

Moreover, just as the Office as such did not invite its practitioners to meditate on Mary's more earthly activities, neither did it invite them to empathize with her as if she were just another human being. Unlike the meditations on the life of Christ and the Virgin so popular among medieval Franciscans and modern scholars alike, the purpose of the Office was not to imitate Mary, but to praise her. It was to gather with the angels before the throne of God and sing the new song that only those bearing the Name could sing (Revelation 14:1–3). In this respect, its purpose was more mythological than historical, more to do with heaven than earth. Its main themes were not earthly suffering and human experience, but the presence of the Lord in his temple and in angelic song. Praising the Virgin through the texts of her Office, medieval Christians were, as it were, lifted out of time into eternity. Like the Virgin herself, they were assumed, if not bodily, then vocally into the presence of God, their music, like that of the temple musicians, invoking the presence of the Lady and her Lord. Accordingly, saying the Office was not so much an experience (in the sense of something shared with Mary or Christ) as an exercise in attention; its goal not the transformation of self into Other, but its emptying so as to become an instrument for making a great noise before the Lord. We have already noted how repeating the angel's salutation was believed to bring Mary herself great joy (chapter 2). How much the more, or so medieval Christians believed, must she have delighted in hearing the praises offered through her to God, amplified as they were by praises of the temple in which God once dwelled!

What, exactly, did medieval European Christians see as they attended to the Lady through the antiphons and psalms of her Office? If, as devotees, we now have perhaps more than enough evidence to go on, as historians, we are inevitably still somewhat at a loss. If Mary's feasts date back to as early as the fifth century in Constantinople and Jerusalem and sermons on their themes to about the same time, detailed commentaries on these themes appear only in the twelfth and thirteenth centuries in the West, some five hundred or more years after the adoption of the Marian feasts in Rome, some three hundred or so years after the translation of the "Akathistos" into Latin, some hundred years or thereabouts after the adoption of the practice of saying her daily Hours, by which time, as we have already seen, medieval Christians simply knew that these texts were about her, although they did not necessarily know why.[193] *Lex orandi, lex credendi*, as the theologians say. Prayer precedes the formal articulation of the faith; devotion more often than not predates explanation, often by hundreds of years.[194] Practically speaking, given that no medieval commentator ever attempted what we are about to do now—offer a reading of the psalms as they appear in the Office of the Virgin framed by their antiphons, not to mention give a full historical explanation of where the texts of the Marian liturgy came from—we do not have the sources to explain why medieval Christians said the psalms and other scriptural texts that they did in honor of the Virgin, except indirectly through their sermons on her feasts and commentaries on her names, unless, of course, we take seriously what they insisted all the time, that they used these texts because they were about her as the Mother of the Lord.[195]

This is not, of course, the way that the psalms of the Marian Office tend to be read today. In his explanation of the Marian Hours, Roger Wieck notes simply: "The Psalms of the Old Testament do not, of course, make mention of the Virgin Mary."[196] Rebecca Baltzer, commenting on the Parisian Office of the Virgin, suggests an ecclesial reading for texts that otherwise do not seem to pertain to Mary as a woman: "The texts of the Little Office of the Virgin, which echoed so frequently in the choir of the cathedral, reminded the clergy again and again of the equation between Mary and the Church."[197] Even Ethelred Taunton, despite writing an entire book on the Marian Office, seems to have had difficulty reading the psalms in a Marian sense. For the most part, he relies not on the Marian antiphons, but rather on the exegesis of the Fathers for his interpretation of the psalms—not, in itself, a bad method (we will make use of it ourselves, particularly the readings of Augustine and Cassiodorus that would have been most familiar to the authors of the liturgy in the West), but not one that goes very far to explain the centrality of Mary in Christian devotion other than as "the example of what a creature can become by grace." If, in Taunton's reading, the point of saying the psalms is to become more like Christ, every psalm being, as he puts it, "a picture of the Soul of Jesus in Himself," then the question must become how it is that honoring Mary aids the soul in this process.[198] Likewise, if, as Baltzer and others have argued, Mary was seen in the High Middle Ages through her Office above all as a type of the Church, what was it about her that suggested to her medieval devotees that she might be compared to the Church—or, perhaps more accurately, that the Church might be compared to her? The answer, as we hope to show, lies in the way in which medieval Christians prayed the psalms of the Marian Office: as texts that, in fact, pertained directly to her as the Mother of the Lord, not just allegorically or figuratively, but in their most literal, historical sense.

With which caution(s), a word on the methodology that we will use for our Marian reading of the psalms. Given the complexities of the tradition with which we are concerned, it is difficult to chose a single perspective from which to construct our reading. Somehow, we need to explain at once how the psalms may have had a potentially Marian significance for the earliest Christians who sang them for her feasts, while at the same time accounting for the difficulties that later readers have had in understanding why these texts were used in her service. If, on the one hand, as suggested earlier following Barker, the origins of devotion to the Virgin go back to the way in which the earliest Christians read the scriptures for signs of the temple worship that they believed had been restored through Mary and her Son, then we would want to look for ways in which the psalms might have originally been read (possibly even written) in this way, as speaking about the Lady and the Lord. On the other hand, we likewise need to acknowledge the fact that this is not the way the commentaries that the authors of the Marian liturgies themselves would have been reading—most particularly, those of Augustine of Hippo (d. 430) and Cassiodorus (d. 585), who relied closely on Augustine—suggested they read the psalms, which commentaries, if the monks and nuns who seem to have been responsible for first developing the Marian Office had taken as authoritative, would seemingly have precluded seeing Mary in the psalms at all.[199] If, as a practice, the Marian Office was wholly a product of the West, as an exercise in exegesis it seems to have depended rather on imagery for the Virgin imported from the East, making it, much like Mary herself, an ineffable hybrid, simultaneously virgin and mother, the scepter of orthodoxy whom only the people—or, in this case, the authors and interpreters of her liturgies—could see.

Nor, arguably, can we rely at this point on what would otherwise—and will, in chapter 4—be our best witnesses to the way in which later medieval Christians read the psalms and other Wisdom texts as Marian, namely, the extended commentaries on her titles written in the thirteenth century by Richard of Saint-Laurent, Conrad of Saxony, and Pseudo-Albert (Servasanctus's commentary

166 ANTIPHON AND PSALM

came to my attention too late to include in full; Jacobus de Voragine's depends less closely on titles found in scripture), for the simple reason that they are too late. By the time that Richard, Conrad, Pseudo-Albert, Jacobus, and Servasanctus were writing, Mary's most devoted Western servants had already been singing her Office for nearly two hundred years, in the case of the psalms taken from the liturgies for her feasts, for at the very least nearly five hundred (we cannot know for sure; again, our sources are too late, the earliest antiphoners for the Divine Office that we have postdate the introduction of Mary's feasts to Rome by more than two hundred years). While invaluable as witnesses to the continuity of the tradition, Richard, Conrad, Pseudo-Albert, Jacobus, and Servasanctus are nevertheless somewhat less useful—or, at the very least, less immediately convincing—as witnesses to its origins.

Like the Marian Office itself, our method must therefore be composite, fourfold, if you will, for those familiar with the fourfold method typically invoked in studies of medieval exegesis.[200] If, in John Cassian's famous formulation, historically, Jerusalem meant the city of the Jews, for us, historically, the question is how the psalms were understood in the temple tradition as speaking about the Lady and her Lord, while allegorically, much as Cassian would recommend, we will be concerned with the way in which the psalms were read by the Latin Fathers Augustine and Cassiodorus following the New Testament tradition as speaking about Christ. Anagogically, as Cassian put it, Jerusalem is the heavenly city, "the mother of us all"; likewise, the antiphons of her Office will help us see Mary, the temple of God, as the frame for the psalms containing her Son. Tropologically, Jerusalem points, as Cassian would put it, to that "which has to do with improvement of life and practical teaching, as if we were to understand by these two covenants practical and theoretical instruction, or at any rate as if we were to want to take Jerusalem or Sion [Zion] as the soul of man, according to this: 'Praise the Lord, O Jerusalem: praise thy God, O Sion' (Psalm 147:1)."[201] Our fourth level of interpretation will be the Orthodox homilies preached in celebration of Mary's feasts, the oldest direct witnesses that we have to the way in which the psalms were read in a Marian sense for her liturgies. Taunton, the only modern scholar known to me to have attempted anything like a comprehensive exegesis of the Marian Office, is invoked for the sake of comparison, so as to help us appreciate the difficulties in reading the Office as its original compilers intended, now that the lens through which they viewed the Virgin has been largely obscured. Again, our goal is not to provide a definitive exegesis, but rather to attempt to see the psalms as they may have been read by the compilers of the Marian liturgies upon which her Office was based, as speaking about Mary just as they spoke about Christ, her Son.[202]

While it is at this point still to be established how the specifics of the Eastern devotion were transmitted to the West—Mary Clayton would point us to close ties between England and Rome in the seventh century when the Marian feasts were introduced there by Greek and Syrian popes, as well as to England's early adoption of the Feast of Mary's Conception, possibly owing to the presence of Anglo-Saxons in Constantinople in the eleventh century and, conversely, of a Greek monk named Constantine at Malmesbury around 1030[203]—most scholars agree the West inherited them directly over the course of the seventh and eighth centuries.[204] To judge from both the choice of psalms for the Marian feasts in the Western liturgies and, as we shall see in chapter 4, the resonances with the Eastern use of the scriptures in later Latin exegesis, the connections must have been significant.[205] In his history of Rome under the Greek popes, Andrew Ekonomou notes that, as archbishop of Gortyna, Andrew of Crete was a suffragan of the Roman pontiff and therefore most likely "had contact if not in person or by emissaries then certainly through correspondence with all the popes from Sergius I [d. 701] through Gregory III [d. 741]." Might this correspondence have included his homilies for the Marian feasts? Ekonomou says, to judge from the correspondences in the Roman observances with Andrew's themes, most likely, yes.[206] We may likewise note, once again, that the "Akathistos" hymn was translated into Latin by the early ninth century, according to Meersseman, by a Greek bishop of Venice, and that along with the "Akathistos" came the whole cascade of titles with which Mary's Orthodox devotees had been accustomed to greet her.[207] It is also important to emphasize that our earliest evidence for the antiphons associated with the psalms of the Marian Office comes from about this same time, from the oldest extant Office book for the Gregorian chant, now known as the antiphoner of Compiègne (Paris, Bibliothèque nationale, lat. 17436), but which most likely was written at the royal abbey of Saint-Médard of Soissons, possibly in May 877 for the dedication of the chapel of Sainte-Marie-de-Compiègne.[208] Soissons, we may note, was known for its merchants in the ninth century, and in 889 its bishop required all its churches to have chasubles of silk, a fabric which at that time came only from the East.[209]

For reasons that will be explained more fully below, our reading of the Marian Office will follow the Use of Rome. Following the use of the Latin West, citations from the scriptures are taken from the Vulgate, unless otherwise indicated. *Psalms are indicated by italics*; **antiphons are in bold**; ***antiphons taken from the psalms they frame are in bold italics***. For the way in which the antiphons and psalms would have been performed in the Office, see the exercise at the beginning of this chapter.

TABLE 3 Psalms and Lessons of the Marian Office (Use of Rome)

Matins

- Psalm 8 *Domine, Dominus noster*
- Psalm 18 *Caeli enarrant*
- Psalm 23 *Domini est terra*
- Psalm 44 *Eructavit cor meum*
- Psalm 45 *Deus noster refugium*
- Psalm 86 *Fundamenta eius*
- Psalm 95 *Cantate Domino*
- Psalm 96 *Dominus regnavit*
- Psalm 97 *Cantate Domino*
- Ecclesiasticus 24:11–13, 15–16; 24:17–20

Lauds

- Psalm 92 *Dominus regnavit*
- Psalm 99 *Jubilate Deo*
- Psalm 62 *Deus, Deus meus*, and Psalm 66 *Deus misereatur nostri*
- Daniel 3:57–88, 56 *Benedicite*
- Psalm 148 *Laudate Dominum*, Psalm 149 *Cantate Domino*, and Psalm 150 *Laudate Dominum in sanctis*
- Song of Songs 6:8

Prime

- Psalm 53 *Deus, in nomine tuo*
- Psalm 84 *Benedixisti, Domine*
- Psalm 116 *Laudate Dominum*
- Song of Songs 6:9

Terce, Sext, and None

- Psalms 119–127 The Gradual Psalms
- Ecclesiasticus 24:15, 16, 19–20

TABLE 3 (*Continued*)

Vespers

- Psalm 109 *Dixit Dominus*
- Psalm 112 *Laudate, pueri*
- Psalm 121 *Laetatus sum in his*
- Psalm 126 *Nisi Dominus*
- Psalm 147 *Lauda Jerusalem*
- Ecclesiasticus 24:14

Compline

- Psalm 128 *Saepe expugnaverunt*
- Psalm 129 *De profundis*
- Psalm 130 *Domine, non est*
- Ecclesiasticus 24:24

The Night Office, or Matins

If the core of the Divine Office was the recitation of the psalms, the core of the psalmody was the night Office or Hour of Matins. Typically, even in monasteries, the psalmody for Matins in the Marian Office followed that of the secular or Roman cursus of three nocturns of three psalms each, each psalm introduced by its own antiphon, as established by the ninth century for her major feasts: I: 8, 18, 23; II: 44, 45, 86; and III: 95, 96, and 97. These are the psalms that appear in the earliest extant antiphoners or chant books for the Offices of the Feasts of the Purification (February 2), Annunciation (March 25), Assumption (August 15), and Nativity of the Virgin (September 8).[210] It is likely that their use in the Marian liturgy in the West goes back even farther. Certainly, the oldest extant selections of texts used for the masses celebrated in her honor suggest a strong association with Psalm 44 *Eructavit cor meum*.[211] More so than for any of the other hours, these were the psalms that defined the daily Marian Office as Marian.[212] Likewise, for these psalms, the antiphons in the Use of Rome for the Marian Office are, with only two exceptions (Psalm 95 and 96), those associated with them in the ninth-century antiphoner of Compiègne for the Feast of the Purification; the exceptions appear in the same antiphoner as antiphons for the same psalms for the Feast of the Assumption. Accordingly, these antiphons are among the oldest Latin witnesses we have to the way in which these psalms were read as Marian, quite possibly going back to the original chants that were used from the seventh century in Rome when the feasts were adopted by the popes from the East.[213]

FIRST NOCTURN, ON SUNDAY, MONDAY, AND THURSDAY

Psalm 8 *Domine, Dominus noster*

Above, in the opening meditation for this chapter, we have already suggested a reading of this first psalm as a celebration of Mary as the one who held the Creator in her womb. According to the antiphon, Mary was **blessed among women, and blessed [was] the fruit of [her] womb.**[214] As Taunton reads it, the antiphon "directs our mind to Our Lady as the choicest and most perfect creature of God,"[215] but the psalm the antiphon frames suggests rather more than just that she is to be crowned with glory and honor, like the *man* of whom the Lord is *mindful* and whom he has made *a little less than the angels* (vv. 5–6). Barker translates verse 5 slightly differently from most, suggesting a reference not just to "man," but to "the son of Adam," that is, "man" in his role as high priest sharing in the knowledge of the Most High and the wisdom of the sons of heaven, that is, the angels. In Barker's reading, the psalm encapsulates, as does Adam, the work of creation, over which he rules as priest and king, maintaining the correspondence between heaven and earth according to the patterns or form (*demût*) with which the creation was engraved. Here, she suggests, there is likewise an association with the ruler to whom Micah prophesied Bethlehem, that is, the Lady would give birth, who would feed his flock "in the majesty of the name of the Lord his God" (Micah 5:2–4 RSV): "His role was to uphold the comparison, the pattern of heaven on earth."[216] As Wisdom, the Lady herself participated in the design of this pattern. The Lord created her first, "at the beginning of his work . . . before the beginning of the earth," and she was with him when he established the heavens, that is, the engravings of creation; she was beside him "like a master workman," harmonizing heaven and earth (Proverbs 8:22–31 RSV). "Hence," in Barker's words, "[the psalm describes] the original Adam: a glorious male-female image of the Creator, destined to be great and to uphold the creation in peace."[217] Blessed indeed, as the choirs sang in the antiphon, was the woman who gave birth to the Creator of the world, the Lady who stood beside the Creator as he brought the world into being!

Psalm 18 *Caeli enarrant*

According to Augustine, "this psalm is sung about Christ, as is abundantly clear from a line in it: *He is like a bridegroom coming forth from his tent*."[218] The bridegroom is Christ "who proceeded from the virginal womb where God was joined with human nature as a bridegroom is united with his bride."[219] Cassiodorus would concur: "With this great simile [the psalmist] unfolded the mystery of His Incarnation. By this miraculous dispensation, He came forth from a virgin womb to reconcile the world to the Godhead, and with a Bridegroom's love to join himself to the Church."[220] Both Augustine and Cassiodorus suggest that this psalm has to do with the preaching of the coming of Christ, whether (as for Augustine) by the evangelists or (as for Cassiodorus) by the apostles and prophets. These preachers are the *heavens* that have proclaimed the glory of God (v. 2). Both commentators likewise point to the importance the psalm places on the apostles' preaching in all the languages of the world (v. 4), Augustine taking the opportunity to remind his listeners that they are called upon to sing with understanding, "to know and perceive with clear hearts what [they] have sung together with harmonious voices."[221] And both commentators see in the reference to the bridegroom's *going out . . . from the end of heaven* (v. 7) a revelation of the Trinity, of the Son's eternal procession from the Father and of the *heat* of the Holy Spirit from which no one can hide. Accordingly, both read the second part of the psalm (vv. 8–12) as the law revealed by the Father and the Son through the Spirit, first through Moses and then in the Gospels. In the third part of the psalm (vv. 13–15), as Cassiodorus puts it, "[the psalmist] begs the Lord to be cleansed of secret vices, asking that He make the psalmist worthy in His eyes."[222]

Other than the reference to the *sun* in which the bridegroom *set his tabernacle* (v. 6), there is (apparently) very little in this psalm to suggest a Marian reading. And yet, the antiphon proclaims: **Like choice myrrh you have given forth the odor of sweetness, holy Mother of God.**[223] Taunton infers a reference here to the gifts of the Magi, the myrrh denoting mortification and the penance "by [which] alone . . . we can repair the destruction sin has brought upon God's creation,"[224] but the antiphon speaks rather of sweetness, alluding to the fragrance given forth by Wisdom from her tree (Ecclesiasticus 24:20–21). Appropriately, the second part of the psalm would seem to recall some of Wisdom's gifts: the conversion of souls and the reception of wisdom (v. 8), the *rejoicing* of hearts and the *enlightening* of the eyes (v. 9), chaste *fear of the Lord . . . enduring forever* (v. 10). The psalm itself attributes these gifts to the law of the Lord, his testimony, justice, commandments, and judgment, all of which are *more to be desired* *than gold and many precious stones, and sweeter than honey and the honeycomb* (v. 11). But, as we have seen, in the temple tradition, it was not the law given to Moses, but rather Wisdom herself through whom the king anointed by her perfumed oil received the spirit of the Lord by which he was illumined and thus enabled to see (v. 12). Significantly, as Nicolas Wyatt has argued, this may in fact have been the original context in which this psalm was composed.[225]

As Wyatt reads it, the psalm in its original sense alludes not to the law as it was imparted to Moses, but rather to the ritual anointing of the king following his "birth" as the Morning Star, the offspring of El, the moon, and his bride, the sun. Drawing on the liturgy for such rituals, the first part of the psalm describes the sun and the moon and their meeting in the heavens, as the heavens sing out the glory of El and the firmament proclaims the work of his hands (v. 2). There is no speech to describe what day utters to day and night to night because human eyes and ears cannot perceive this heavenly exchange (vv. 3–4), and yet it fills the whole earth (v. 5). The bridegroom, the moon, sets his tabernacle in his bride, the sun, and comes forth again like a hero as he completes his circuit of the heavens (vv. 6–7). Following this sacred marriage, the second part of the psalm describes the blessings received by the king on his anointing as the Morning Star, the son of El and the Lady (cf. Psalm 109: 2–3). Wyatt imagines the priest touching the king in turn on different parts of his body, symbolizing each of the divine powers that the king was to receive: his breast (the teaching of Yahweh), his head (the testimony of Yahweh), his heart (the precepts of Yahweh), his eyes (the commandments of Yahweh), and his throat (the speech of Yahweh). That these were gifts of Wisdom rather than the Mosaic law is clear from how precious they were. As Solomon put it, "Happy is the man who finds wisdom, and the man who gets understanding, for the gain from it is better than gain from silver and its profit better than gold . . . She is more precious than jewels, and nothing you desire can compare with her" (Proverbs 3:13–14 RSV; cf. Job 28:12–19). As Wisdom herself put it, "For my spirit [LXX: memorial] is sweet above honey, and my inheritance above honey and the honeycomb" (Ecclesiasticus 24:27). We may likewise recall that it was in Wisdom's tabernacle that the Creator of all things took his rest (Ecclesiasticus 24:12).

Psalm 23 *Domini est terra*

Once again, the psalm opens by recalling the Lord's work as the Creator of *the earth . . . and the fullness thereof . . . [which] he hath founded . . . upon the seas and hath prepared . . . upon the rivers* (vv. 1–2). The title of the psalm sets the scene: "On the first day of the week, a psalm of David." Cassiodorus explains: "*The first day of the week* indicates the Lord's day, the first after the sabbath, the day on which the Lord rose from the dead." This day is called the Lord's day "because on that day He stabilised the world, for by rising again on it He is seen to lend succour to the world and is declared also its Maker."[226] For Cassiodorus, as for Augustine, the earth thus stabilized is more specifically the Church, filled with a holy multitude and anchored by faith against the stormy waves of vice. In their reading, according to the second section of the psalm, only those established in the Church are able to *ascend into the mountain of the Lord* [and] *stand in his holy place* (vv. 3–4), that is, only the "innocent in action and pure in thought" (Augustine), "whose activities hurt no-one, and who [strive] to lend succour to the best of [their] power" (Cassiodorus).[227] Such persons set their hearts not on transient or passing things, but only on eternity; thus they receive a *blessing from the Lord* and pardon for their sins (v. 5). *This is the generation* (v.6) "reborn from the spring of holy baptism, and which recommends its faith through devoted works."[228] The third section of the psalm then turns to those who have previously closed their hearts against the Lord and invites them to open themselves to *the King of Glory* that he might enter through the eternal gates of baptism, anointing, and preaching (v. 7). *Who is this King of Glory?* The psalmist replies: *The Lord who is strong and mighty, the Lord mighty in battle* (v. 8). Cassiodorus explains: "If you examine this statement, it will shown to be appropriate to Christ alone. . . . and here the wicked presumption of the Jewish people is well proved by each word."[229] As Augustine put it: "Handle his scars and you will find them healed, see his human weakness restored to immortal strength. This glorification of the Lord was owed to the earth, where he did battle with death, and it has been paid in full."[230] Thus, in Cassiodorus's words: "The whole of this psalm is concerned with the teaching of manners, for it warns us to abandon superstitions and faithfully to serve the true and holy God."[231]

But what, if anything, does the psalm teach us about Mary? The antiphon encourages its singers: **Before the couch of this Virgin repeat to us the sweet songs of the drama.**[232] What drama would that be? Taunton suggests an allusion to the drama or play of the Song of Songs, in which Solomon "sings of the spiritual espousals between Jesus Christ and the soul, between the Head and the Members of the Mystical Body."[233] As I have shown elsewhere, however, in a Marian context the drama of the Song of Songs refers not to Christ and the Church or Christ and the soul, but rather to the relationship between Mary and her Son, more specifically in the context of this antiphon, to the liturgical *historia* of her death and Assumption into heaven. The antiphon itself is alluded to in a sermon on the *thalamos Mariae* (bridal chamber of Mary) attributed to Augustine, and it appears in the ninth-century antiphoner of Compiègne in a long series of antiphons to be sung *in evangelio* at Lauds for the Feast of the Assumption.[234] These antiphons, I have argued, were intended to recount the narrative of the Virgin's death, which, for the Carolingians at least, was problematic because it was nowhere recounted in scripture. In lieu of the apocryphal stories so beloved in the East, the Carolingians turned instead to the Song of Songs, wherein they found (or so they believed) a more reliable account of what happened when Mary died as prophesied by the Holy Spirit in the songs sung by the Church—songs themselves taken largely from the Song of Songs, as the monk Paschasius Radbertus (d. 865) made clear in the sermon that he wrote for his friends the nuns at Soissons so that they would have something to read in church on the day of the feast.[235]

These were the "sweet songs of the drama," according to Paschasius, which the antiphon invited the nuns to sing, the songs taken from the Song of Songs (3:6; 6:9): "Who is this who ascends through the desert like a column of smoke from the spices? Who is this who ascends like the rising dawn, beautiful as the moon, chosen as the sun, terrible as a battle line drawn up from the camps?" "*Quae est ista?*" the choirs sang, marveling at the ascent of the Virgin. "*Quis est iste?*" the psalm replied, wondering at the entry of the king of glory into his temple (v. 8). Who was this, indeed? In his commentary, Ugaritic scholar Mitchell Dahood notes that this psalm, like Psalm 18 [19 RSV], was most likely intended for use in the temple liturgy, in this case, for the procession of the ark of the covenant, perhaps even (as Taunton notes) for the original procession of the ark led by David from the house of Obededom to Mount Zion.[236] Dahood also notes that the psalm's "dialogue structure . . . suggests that it was sung by alternating choirs," perhaps the very same choirs that David appointed to serve before the Lord with horns, trumpets, lyres, harps, and cymbals as the ark was brought into Jerusalem (1 Chronicles 15:25–28; cf. 2 Samuel 6:12–15 RSV). Barker suggests further that the *mountain of the Lord* to which the pilgrims with clean hands and pure hearts ascend (vv. 3–4) should be identified with the tower of David to which the bride is compared in Song of Songs 4:4, the tower being the Holy of Holies built out upon the wall of the city and rising some one hundred fifty meters from the valley floor.[237]

We have already noted how Mary herself was identified with the ark, particularly as her body was carried from her deathbed to its tomb. She was likewise the temple into which the King of Glory, the Lord strong and mighty in battle, entered at his Incarnation. And, as Andrew of Crete noted, she was the holy mountain in which the Lord was pleased to dwell. Like the ark, she bore the presence and glory of the Lord, and she was the gate through which only the Lord might enter. As Barker reads the psalm:

The Psalmist had seen the Glory of the Lord entering the temple in human form. He sang of the King of Glory entering the ancient doors.... What had he seen? Elsewhere in his world he might have seen a statue dressed in golden robes being taking into a temple, but Jerusalem had no statues. The King, the royal high priest, was God with his people, Immanuel, and so the King of Glory entering the temple was probably the human king in his role as the visible presence of the Lord.[238]

It was for this reason, Barker argues, that the early Christians looked for the Lord to come in human form as the royal high priest who would sacrifice for them in the temple (Hebrews 8): this is the way he was described in the psalms. As translated by Jerome (v. 2), Psalm 23 even suggested the name of his mother, for as Creator, the Lord had founded the very earth upon her, that is, upon the seas (*maria*). We may recall that according to the "Akathistos" (strophe 21), another of the Lady's attributes was the sacred river, upon which, or so the psalmist would have it, the Lord prepared the earth.

SECOND NOCTURN, ON TUESDAY AND FRIDAY

Psalm 44 *Eructavit cor meum*

Of all the psalms, this is the one most often associated with the Virgin Mary. Here, the antiphon itself is taken from the psalm (v. 5): ***In your comeliness and your beauty go forth, proceed prosperously, and reign.***[239] Like the Song of Songs, the psalm has long been identified as an *epithalamium* or (in Cassiodorus's words) "*laus thalami*," a song sung in praise of a bridegroom and a bride at their wedding. And, indeed, in his exegesis Cassiodorus explicitly compares the psalm's descriptions of the bridegroom and bride with those given by "the most wise Solomon" in the Song of Songs: "So we append exemplary passages from the Book [called the Song of Songs] in this psalm as the occasion demands; thus those who praise, though separated by their eras, may appear to have spoken the one message with the harmony of prophecy."[240] As Cassiodorus reads it, first (vv. 3–10) the psalm praises the bridegroom in four modes (*a forma, a potestate, a causa iudicii*, and in the person of His bride); then (vv. 11–18) it praises the bride, likewise in four modes (*a specie*, with respect to the bridegroom's honor, in her members, and in her progeny). In his reading, as in Augustine's (not to mention that of every other medieval Christian commentator on the psalm), the bridegroom is, of course, Christ (cf. Matthew 9:15; Mark 2:19; Luke 5:34–35). Traditionally, however, determining the identity of the bride has proven somewhat more complicated. Liturgically, the psalm, like the antiphon, is also associated with the Common of Virgins, as well as with other virgin saints (Agnes, Agatha, Cecelia, and Mary Magdalene); the same verse also appears as a responsory for the Common of Virgins in the monastic cursus of chants and as an alleluia in the masses for both the Nativity and Assumption of the Virgin and in the masses for Lucia, Agnes, Pudentiana, and Euphemia.[241] Accordingly, Taunton suggests: "This Antiphon fixes for us the idea of the glory and majesty of the Heavenly Bridegroom . . . and the reflected glory which the Spouse hath, even as the moon reflects the splendours of the sun. Our ever dear and blessed Lady is the type and model of all spouses to God; she alone is all fair, and without the slightest stain [cf. Song of Songs 4:7]."[242] For Augustine, as for Cassiodorus, however, the marriage celebrated in the psalm is not that of an individual bride, but rather that of a king and his people, "the Savior and those who are to be saved," that is, the Church.[243]

Virgin or Church? An individual bridegroom and bride, or a people and their king? There are further complications. What kind of marriage was this psalm celebrating? A royal one, to be sure, but in what context? Who was the bridegroom, and who was the bride? Although, as we have said, Cassiodorus concentrates throughout his reading of the psalm on Christ's relationship to the Church, he reads v. 5 (that is, the text for the antiphon) through Psalm 18:6, as a reference to the Incarnation: "*Come forth*, as the Bridegroom from the maiden's womb; in the words of Scripture: *And he as a bridegroom coming out of his bridechamber*."[244] This is likewise the way that Augustine reads the principal imagery of the psalm: "Perhaps you are wondering whether there is any bridal chamber (*thalamus*) at this wedding to which we have been invited? Yes, there is; why else would another psalm say, *He has pitched his tent in the sun, and he is like a bridegroom coming forth from his tent*? The nuptial union is effected between the Word and human flesh, and the place where the nuptial union is consummated is the Virgin's womb."[245] Again, we find the emphasis on Mary as the dwelling or chamber (*thalamus*) of the Lord whom God has anointed (v. 8): "*Therefore God, thy God, hath anointed thee*. The anointed Christ signifies both king and priest, for these offices were assumed by most sacred anointings; the very name of Christ comes from the holy chrism."[246] As Augustine put it: "Nowhere else were kings and priests anointed; it was done only in that kingdom where Christ's coming was prophesied, where he was anointed, and from where the name of Christ was to come."[247] We may recall that in the temple tradition, as in our reading of Psalm 18 above, it was Wisdom who provided the anointing oil that brought forth the king as a son of God. This psalm, like Psalm 18, is a temple song, not just an epithalamium. The marriage celebrated has to do with the presence of the Lord.[248]

Who, then, is it whom the antiphon invites to *go forth, proceed prosperously, and reign*? In the psalm, it is the king as mighty warrior (that is, the Lord; cf. Psalm 23:8) with his sword girded upon his thigh, beautiful, blessed by God, anointed, and seated upon his throne, his scepter in his hand and his garments perfumed with myrrh, stacte (aloes), and cassia (vv. 3–9). The daughters of kings delight in his glory, and *the queen [stands] at [his] right hand in gold of Ophir* [LXX: clothed in vestiture wrought with gold, and arrayed in diverse colors] (v. 10), just as Solomon suggested she would on the day of his wedding (cf. Song of Songs 3:11). Both Augustine and Cassiodorus tend to conflate the queen and the bride; Cassiodorus even explicitly identifies the queen with the one who says in the Song of Songs (1:1), "Let him kiss me with the kiss of his mouth."[249] But in the psalm itself the queen is distinct from the daughter who is called to forget her people and the house of her father (v. 11) so that sons might be born from her (v. 17). As Barker describes it, the scene is one with which the worshippers in the temple tradition would have been familiar, the queen mother standing beside the king in his glory as the daughter of the king was brought into the temple of the king followed by her fellow virgins (vv. 15–16). As Barker notes, it was the mother of the king who was said to have had a special devotion to Asherah, just as it was the king who was said to have borne the presence of the Lord before his people. This is the reason, or so Nicolas Wyatt suggests, that David married Bathsheba: she was the Great Lady of Jerusalem; therefore, it was her son, Solomon, who had the strongest claim of all David's sons to succeed his father as king (1 Kings 1 RSV). Solomon, in his turn, married his son Rehoboam to Ma'acah, a devotee of Asherah (1 Kings 15:2, 9–13 RSV; 2 Chronicles 15:16 RSV).[250] Indeed, the chroniclers were careful to record the names of all of the mothers of the kings (1 Kings 15:2, 10; 22:42; 2 Kings 8:26; 12:1; 14:2; 15:2, 33; 18:2; 21:1, 21:19; 22:1; 23:31, 36; 24:8, 18 RSV), suggesting (as Barker notes) "that she was an important figure," perhaps even Asherah herself.[251] In the psalm, as Barker reads it, it was Wisdom, his mother, who stood beside the king in gold-woven robes as he received his bride.[252]

Whether the earliest Christians saw the queen mothers in precisely this way, if not Augustine and Cassiodorus, nevertheless those in the East were certain that King David was referring to Mary, the Mother of the Lord, in this psalm.[253] For Chrysippus of Jerusalem (d. 479) preaching for the August Feast of the Virgin at the Church of the Kathisma on the chants for the day, it was Mary herself who was the daughter whom the psalm invited to incline her ear as well as the queen standing beside her Son. "Concern yourself," Chrysippus imagined King David singing to her, "no longer with your earthly relations, for you will be transposed into a heavenly kingdom, and hear, he says, how the creator and ruler of all will be your lover. 'For the king,' he says, 'desires your beauty' [v. 12], the Father himself will take you for his bride, the Spirit will assist in the bridal arrangements, and the Son will partake of the very comeliness of your temple."[254] In what may very likely be the earliest complete account of the life of the Virgin Mary, attributed in the manuscript tradition to Maximus the Confessor (d. 662) and, as Stephen Shoemaker has argued, an important source for the later devotional emphasis on Mary's compassionate suffering at the Crucifixion, the identification of the psalm's bride with Mary is complete.[255] The author of the *Life* reads the psalm more or less verbatim as a description of the Virgin as "blessed queen and daughter and the mother of God," arguing that "even if some have interpreted these words as being about the Church, there is nevertheless nothing at all that impedes understanding them as being about the holy Theotokos." Accordingly: "*The queen stood at your right* (v. 10) . . . foretells her Presentation in the Temple [at age three] and her location to the right of the altar in the Holy of Holies, which is truly regarded as being to the right of God." Her *gold-woven robes* (v. 10) indicate her many-hued virtues adorned with good works and godly thoughts; these virtues increased as she grew in age, "and that is why *the king desired her beauty* (v. 12), and he dwelt within her."[256] At the end of her life, her Son likewise desired "that he could place her at his right hand beautifully adorned with golden tassels in many colors and proclaim her queen of all creatures, and . . . that she would pass behind the veil and dwell in the Holy of Holies," and so he sent the angel Gabriel to her to announce her death.[257]

"But come to me, David," Germanus of Constantinople imagined Mary's mother Anna inviting the psalmist as she led her daughter to the temple,

> our forefather and divine father, plucking your lyre, make an even more harmonious sound on the strings of the Spirit with your divinely inspired mouth, signifying distinctly the procession of your women [in the words], "Virgins shall be brought to the King behind her; her companions shall be brought [to you]" (Psalm 44:15 LXX). Behold, the multitude of young people is forming a chorus in the streets, while [the daughter] of the King, my child, whom you yourself called daughter, is led through the sanctified dwelling places into the holy temple, in a happy and joyful state, so that she may fulfill your prediction. "For all the glory of the King's daughter," you said, is robed from within "in golden fringed garments" (cf. Psalm 44:14 LXX), [that is] in her undefiled and spotless virginity, and adorned with incomparable comeliness . . .[258]

Andrew of Crete saw Mary in the same psalm as he imagined the hymn sung by those gathered round her body on her deathbed. Note especially the parallels Andrew draws with the Song of Songs, as well as the references to the queen mother, the crown with which she crowned her Son, and her anointing perfumes.

This (according to Andrew) is what the apostles, angels, and holy souls of the saints sang (citations, LXX):

> God's ancestor David prayed to Christ on your behalf, saying, "Arise, Lord, you and the ark of your holiness" (Psalm 131:8). He also referred by anticipation to your death when he sang prophetically, "The rich among the people will make supplication before your face" (Psalm 44:13). "Behold all the glory of the king's daughter within; she is robed and ornamented in cloth fringed with gold" (Psalm 44:14). The holy book of Canticles described you in advance, when it made this hidden allusion: "Who is this who comes up from the desert like a column of smoke, breathing myrrh and incense made from all the merchant's powders?" (Song 3:6). The same holy book also foretold you when its author wrote, "Here is Solomon's resting-place; he has made its posts of silver, its base of gold, its steps of porphyry. Within it is paved with stone, [a gift of] love from the daughters of Jerusalem" (Song 3:7,10). And further: "Come out, daughters of Zion, [and gaze] on King Solomon. He is wearing the crown with which his mother crowned him on his wedding day, on the day of his heart's delight" (Song 3:11). See her, daughters of Zion, and call her blessed; queens and concubines, praise her, for the fragrance of her garments is beyond all perfume (cf. Song 6:8, 4:10). . . . Let holy Solomon sing to you yet another verse: "You are as lovely as Jerusalem, and the fragrance of your garments is as the fragrance of Lebanon" (Song 6:3, 4:11). You are the new flask of inexhaustible myrrh; you are the gladness of the oil that anoints us (cf. Psalm 44:8). . . . You are the crown of kingly power, woven by the high priest; you are the "throne on high" (cf. Isaiah 6:1), the gate that stands high above the heaven of heavens; you are the queen of all humanity. . . . Aside from God alone, you are higher than all beings.[259]

Psalm 45 *Deus noster refugium*

At first glance, the contrast with the previous psalm could hardly be more marked. Gone are the bridegroom and bride, gone are the perfumed vestments and anointing oil, gone are the daughters and virgins and queen. God may be *our refuge and strength* (v. 2), but nowhere is there any suggestion that this strength might include his mother. Or is there? Like Psalm 44, the psalm is entitled *Unto the end . . . for the sons of Core* [Korah], which Cassiodorus explains means that the psalm refers to the Lord Christ and that it is sung by Christians because *Core* in Hebrew means Calvary, and Christians are those who have embraced the sign of the cross.[260] For Cassiodorus, accordingly, the psalm may be divided into three parts: in the first part, the sons of Core declare "that they do not fear the troubles of life, because God is known as their refuge and strength"; in the second part, "they state that Christ appears in the midst of the Church and has deigned to build it on Himself as on the firmest of rocks"; in the third part, "the mass of believers is invited to gaze on the great things of God" as he "shatters the arms of wickedness, banishes wars, and transforms the sadness of the faithful into eternal joys."[261] Augustine's reading is similar. According to its title, the psalm is "about the hidden things" because "he who was crucified on Calvary [that is, "the bald place," reading "Korah" as "baldness"] rent the veil asunder so that the secret places of the temple were exposed to view." Likewise, *unto the end* is a reference to Christ, who brought the law to perfection and is the end of Christians' journey because "in him we possess the Father, because he is in the Father, and the Father in him. He and the Father are one." Christ is thus the only refuge for Christians: "He is God, and when we flee to him, we are strong. No Christian will be strong in himself or herself; but God, who has become our refuge, will supply the strength."[262]

The antiphon, like the second part of the psalm, suggests, however, yet another relationship: ***God will help her with his countenance; God is in the midst of her, she shall not be moved.***[263] As with the antiphon for Psalm 44, so this antiphon is taken from the psalm (cf. Psalm 45:5 LXX); it likewise was used for the Common of Virgins and other virgin saints. Who then is *she* whom God will help? The preceding verse gives the answer (v. 4): *The stream of the river maketh the city of God joyful; the Most High hath sanctified his own tabernacle.* How is it, Augustine asks, that the psalm says, " 'God is in the center of it'?. . . . Does this mean that God is confined in a place, in such a way that, while the things around him have ample room, he who is encircled is cramped for space? Heaven forbid! You must not think of God like that." Rather, Augustine insists, it is that God "whose throne is in the souls of the devout is not hemmed in by any place," nor does he waver if human hearts change. Accordingly, "if the word 'sanctified' is used, it is obvious that we should understand these powerful impulses [of the river] to be those of the Holy Spirit, by whom every godly soul that believes in Christ is sanctified, to make it a citizen of the city of God."[264] Cassiodorus, more prosaically, suggests simply that the "tabernacle of the most High is either the Church or His glorious assumption of a human body," and his justice is in the midst "because he always has regard for the faithful." Further, "the Church cannot be moved as it is seen to be founded on the most solid rock which is the Lord Christ."[265] For Taunton, in comparison, it was Mary's "ceaseless union with God, ever keeping the *Word of God in her heart*, that is, fashioning herself upon the model of her divine Son, and making Him live in her, [that] kept her immovable."[266]

From a Marian perspective, or so her Orthodox devotees would most likely argue, such readings are curiously opaque. After all, what could be more obvious than that Mary herself was the tabernacle whom the Most High sanctified or that Mary was the city of God made joyful by the flowing stream? Certainly, this is the way the Orthodox homilists read it. "Hail," Modestus of Jerusalem saluted her in his encomium on her Dormition, "refuge of mortals with God! He made us his own through you, and became 'our refuge and strength' (Psalm 45:1 LXX), working through us great healing and giving strength to the whole world."[267] "Her whole being," reflected John of Damascus on the feast of her Nativity, "is the bridal chamber of the Spirit; her whole being is a city of the living God which 'the flowings of the river gladden' (Psalm 45:4 LXX); [that is] floods of the gifts of the Holy Spirit."[268] Thus, John imagined, the apostles sang at her burial, "crying out divine hymns to the music of the harp of the Spirit": " 'We shall be filled with the riches of your house; holy is your temple, wonderful because of [God's] salvation' (Psalm 64:4–5 LXX); and again, 'The Most High has made his tabernacle holy' (Psalm 45:5 LXX)."[269] "Behold," we may recall John of Euboea greeted her, "a throne more wonderful than the cherubic one is made ready on earth, about which it has been written: 'God is in the midst of her, and she shall not be moved' (Psalm 45:5 LXX)."[270]

Psalm 86 *Fundamenta eius*

The theme of the city continues. As John of Damascus put it, asking who would not praise the Mother of God, not so much as to glorify her as to win eternal glory for oneself: "The tabernacle of the Lord's glory, after all, is in no need of glory from us; [she is] the city of God, of whom 'glorious things are spoken,' as holy David says to her: 'Glorious things are spoken of you, City of God!' (v. 3 LXX)"[271] As we should by now expect, this is not quite the way that Augustine and Cassiodorus would explain this imagery.[272] Once again, the psalm is addressed *to the sons of Core*, that is, as Cassiodorus puts it, "faithful Christians to whom the prophet proclaims the city of God, so that their longing for this great glory may be enhanced." The psalm is *of a canticle* because it is intended "to raise us from the tents of this world to an understanding of the heavenly city."[273] Augustine would concur: "In this psalm a city is sung about and celebrated, a city of which we are citizens by virtue of being Christians, a city from which we are absent abroad as long as we are mortal, and towards which we are traveling."[274] Both focus on the earthly city of Zion as a foreshadowing or representation of the heavenly Jerusalem "which, as the apostle says, *is the mother of us all* (Galatians 4:26)."[275] In the first part of the psalm (as Cassiodorus would have it), the prophet proclaims the heavenly city; in the second, he rebukes the synagogue for not knowing God when the Gentiles believed in Him; in the third, in a single verse (v. 7), he touches on "the blessedness of the age to come."[276] This is likewise the way that Taunton explains the Marian sense of the psalm, as revealed through the use of this last verse as its antiphon: "She is called in the Litany 'The Cause of our joy;' and the spiritual Zion, the Church, rejoices, for her Founder comes from her, and by her."[277]

John or Germanus would read the city (or the psalm) rather differently in reference to Mary. Likewise the antiphon: *Just as of all those who rejoice*, **our** *habitation is in you*, **holy Mother of God.**[278] What does it mean to say that Christians dwell not in God, as we might expect, but rather in the Mother of God? Arguably, the answer goes back to the way in which the earliest Christians, including the author of Revelation, understood the city of Jerusalem, not just as a place where the Lord became visible, but as itself (or, rather, herself) the bride of the Lamb (Revelation 21:2). Jerusalem, the mother of kings, was herself the Lady of the Lord. Barker explains how this could be.[279] On the one hand, there is the witness of Isaiah, promising Jerusalem that she would one day be restored:

> You shall be a crown of beauty in the hand of the Lord,
> and a royal diadem in the hand of your God.
> You shall no more be termed Forsaken,
> and your land shall no more be termed Desolate,
> but you shall be called My Delight Is In Her,
> and your land Married;
> for the Lord delights in you,
> and your land shall be married.
> For as a young man marries a virgin,
> so shall your sons marry you,
> and as the bridegroom rejoices over the bride,
> so shall your God rejoice over you. (Isaiah 62:3–5 RSV)

On the other hand, there are the parallels between Wisdom as described in the Wisdom of Solomon and the bride as she appears in Revelation. "Her have I loved," King Solomon asserts, "and have sought her out from my youth, and have desired to take for my spouse, and I became a lover of her beauty" (Wisdom 8:2). Like the bride of the Lamb who is the true Solomon, Wisdom whom Solomon sought as his bride is filled with the glory of God (Wisdom 7:25; cf. Revelation 21:22); like the Lady clothed with the sun who gave birth to the Morning Star,

she is "more beautiful than the sun, and above all the order of the stars" (Wisdom
7:29; cf. Revelation 12:1–2, 22:16). Thus, like the city-bride, she needs no other
light. She is more precious than gold or silver or precious gems (Wisdom 7:9; cf.
Psalm 18:11), the very materials with which the heavenly city is built (Revelation
21:10–21), decked as a bride with jewels for her husband (Isaiah 61:10) just as the
prophet had promised (Isaiah 54:11–12). She is vast, reaching mightily "from end
to end" (Wisdom 8:1), but "no defiled thing enters into her" (Wisdom 7:25), just
as the city extends 12,000 stadia (some 1,500 miles) in each direction and yet is
closed to all who are unclean (Revelation 21:16, 27). She preserved the one first
formed by God "when he was created alone, and she brought him out of his sin,
and gave him power to govern all things" (Wisdom 10:1–2). God loves none but
he who dwells with her (Wisdom 7:28).

 *A man shall say, "Zion is my mother," and such a man was born in her; and the
Highest himself has founded her* (v. 5 LXX). "But who is this man?" Augustine asks.

> The psalm tells us, if we listen and have the wit to hear. . . . What could be plainer,
> my brothers and sisters? True it is that *glorious things are spoken of you, city of
> God*. Think about it: *"Zion, my mother," a man will say*. What man? He who *was
> made man in her*. . . . He founded the city in which he was to be born, just as he
> created the mother from whom he was to be born. . . . On our account he who as
> the Most High founded the city calls the city "Mother."[280]

It is almost as if Augustine has anticipated the very objections most modern
readers would bring to the Marian use of this psalm: How is it that a man would
call Zion the city "mother," not to mention Wisdom or bride? *I will make mention of Raab and Babylon to them that know me: behold also the Philistines, and
Tyre, and the people of the Ethiopians: these were born there*, the psalmist replies
(v. 4 LXX). These were the peoples, Barker suggests, who looked to the Lady
as she had once been before King Josiah's reforms, who knew the Lord and the
city founded upon the holy mountain (another aspect of the Lady) in which
he once dwelled.[281] But, as Isaiah promised, one day a shoot would come forth
from the rod of Jesse, and the Spirit of the Lord would rest upon him, and
Wisdom would return: "The wolf shall dwell with the lamb, and the leopard
shall lie down with the kid, and the calf and the lion and the fatling together,
and a little child shall lead them. . . . They shall not hurt or destroy in all my holy
mountain; for the earth shall be full of the knowledge of the Lord as the waters
cover the sea" (Isaiah 11:6, 9 RSV). This, argues Barker, was the mother in whom
the God-man was born. As Germanus put it, preaching on the consecration of
the ναός (lit. temple) of the Mother of God:

"Glorious things have been spoken of you, O city of God," sang the divine David to us in spirit. Again it is indeed most evident concerning whom such "glorious things" have been spoken . . .: Mary, the supremely chaste and surpassingly unblemished Theotokos. He who is truly King of Kings and Lord of those who rule took up his abode in her; or in other words, the whole fullness of divinity dwelt bodily in her.

"She indeed is a glorified city," he continued, "she is a Zion that is apprehended by the mind."[282] Mary's medieval devotees would concur; of course *the Lord loves the gates of Zion, more than all the tabernacles of Jacob* (v. 2 LXX): she was his mother, his bride, his Lady, his delight, his Miriam, his Wisdom, his queen, dancing beside him as he made the world.

THIRD NOCTURN, ON WEDNESDAY AND SATURDAY

Psalm 95 *Cantate Domino*

"So far as the literal sense is concerned," Cassiodorus comments, "the heading [of this psalm: *A canticle of David, when the house was built after the captivity*] points to the time when the temple at Jerusalem is known to have been refurbished by Torobabel son of Salathiel, after it had been levelled to the ground by a hostile band of Chaldeans."[283] Oddly, however, or so both Cassiodorus and Augustine remark, the psalm says nothing of building a building, nothing of hewing stones or laying foundations or erecting pillars. It must, therefore, they reason, have to do with building the house of living stones in which Christ dwells, that is, with "proclaiming the first and second coming of the Lord."[284] Accordingly, as Cassiodorus reads it, in the first part of the psalm (vv. 1–6), the psalmist exhorts the peoples of the earth "to sing to the Lord and to announce through the whole world the coming of the Lord's incarnation, for He is the true Lord over all gods." In the second part of the psalm (vv. 7–13), the psalmist "advises the different races first to offer themselves and then to perform the tasks of proclamation by recounting both comings of the Lord, the first when he was judged by man and the second when He will come to judge the world."[285] For Cassiodorus as well as Augustine, the psalm is at once a call to praise and a confession of faith. *Sing ye to the Lord*, the psalm cries out, *and bless his name: shew forth his salvation from day to day* (v. 2), that is, Cassiodorus suggests, in both the Old and New Testaments, "for both shine with the brightness of the eternal sun." *Declare his glory among the Gentiles: his wonders among all people* (v. 3), that is, to all nations wholly the mystery of his Incarnation, but, Cassiodorus cautions, "the Jew must listen, and realise that he was spurned through his wicked stubbornness; for [the psalmist] says, 'Declare it not to the Jews, but to the Gentiles.' "[286] *For the Lord is great, and exceedingly to be praised: he is to be feared above all gods* (v. 4), that is, Augustine insists, more than the demons to which the nations paid cult.[287] *For all the gods of the Gentiles are devils* (v. 5) or demons (*daemones*), that is, Cassiodorus explains, substances "created by God which like that of the good angels [are] superior to men, but which because of the effect of [their] pride [have] reached the stage of abandoning [their] natural dignity, and [are] always engaged in evil activities ... These are precisely the gods of the gentiles."[288] *But*, the psalm proclaims, *the Lord made the heavens. Praise and beauty are before him: holiness and majesty [are] in his sanctuary* (vv. 5–6).

To whom, then, is this psalm most appropriately addressed if the Gentiles worship demons and the Jews fail to recognize the Lord? Provocatively, the antiphon exclaims: **Rejoice, Virgin Mary, you alone have destroyed all heresies in the world.**[289] Taunton comments, aptly:

> If the Sacred Humanity no longer needs a Mother's loving care, Jesus wills that His mystical Body, the Church, should look to her in all needs and troubles, certain that it will never ask amiss. So, in a special way, is she the guardian of her Son, the Divine Truth, and thus the great destroyer of false doctrine, [as, for example, at the Council of Ephesus when Nestorius] began to attack the Divinity of our Lord [and] denied Mary's title of Mother of God; ...it was the glorious vindication of this name [Theotokos] that secured the truth, that Jesus, her Son, is very God and very Man. The Antiphon sounds like a cry of triumph after the Council of Ephesus, which condemned the Nestorian heresy.[290]

But why, we might still ask, is this antiphon associated with this particular psalm, and why should this psalm be sung in honor of Mary? Once again, Barker suggests, if indirectly, what may be perhaps the most compelling reason.

Say among the nations, "The Lord reigns!" (Psalm 96:10): this is the way the verse reads in the Revised Standard Version as well as in the Hebrew. It is not, however, the way that Augustine and Cassiodorus knew the psalm.[291] Rather, as they quoted it, the psalm exhorted: *Say among the nations, "The Lord hath reigned from the wood"* (*Dominus regnavit a ligno*). Why *from the wood*? For Augustine, as for Cassiodorus, *a ligno* is clearly a reference to the cross and to Christ's identity as Lord: "The Lord," Augustine echoes the psalm, "has established his sovereignty from a tree. Who is it who fights with wood? Christ. From his cross he has conquered kings, brought them into subjection and affixed his cross to their foreheads, so that now they glory in it, knowing that in it lies their salvation."[292] Cassiodorus is slightly more cautious, noting that "other translators do not render *from the wood*, but it is enough for us that it is maintained by the authority of the seventy interpreters [that is, the Septuagint]. The Lord's cross," he contends, "corrected the debased and twisted world when it converted the hearts of pagans by the rule of faith."[293] What happened to *from the wood* in those other translations? Justin Martyr, writing in the second century C.E., thought he knew. The Jews (that is, the correcting scribes of the Second Temple) took the words away from their copies of the scriptures.[294] As Barker remarks: "If the Lord reigning from the tree was such a sensitive text, it must have been very important to the early Church."[295]

Whose tree was it from which the Lord reigned? If we accept Barker's reconstruction of the temple tradition, the Lady's, of course. Accordingly, from within this tradition, as the Lady, Mary is the one who destroys all heresies because she is the one who reveals the Lord as he really is: the Maker of the world and the one who suffered on the cross. She is the one who anointed and enthroned him as the divine Son and the one in whom he took his rest (Ecclesiasticus 24:12). Thus, as the scriptural lessons for Matins of her Office would put it, she was "established in Zion" and her "power was in Jerusalem," where she "took root in an honourable people," and her abode was in the "full assembly of saints" (Ecclesiasticus 24:15–16). And thus she was "exalted like a cedar in Lebanon, and as a cypress tree on Mount Zion ... like a palm-tree in Kadesh, and as a rose plant in Jericho, as a fair olive tree in the plains, and as a plane tree by the water in the streets" (Ecclesiasticus 24:17–19). To reject the Mother, as the earliest Christians repeatedly insisted, was to reject her Son, as indeed those who came to identify themselves as "Jews" (as opposed to "Christians") did. In the temple tradition, the Lord was the Great Angel, more to be feared than all of the other angels or sons of the Most High because it was he whom the Most High had established to reign over Israel (cf. Deuteronomy 32:8–9).[296] It was he who had established the world, setting it firm above the waters, so that the heavens might rejoice and the earth be glad, the sea be moved, and the field joyful, and *all the trees of the wood rejoice before the face of the Lord, because he cometh* (vv. 11–13). This is why the earth was invited to sing a *new song* (v. 1): it was through the Lord that the earth had been made, and it was through the Lord that it was (to be) renewed, thus the "new song" that those who bore the Name on their foreheads sang before the throne in heaven (Revelation 14:1–3).[297] Mary, as the Mother of the Lord, was, as it were, the author of this song, the first to bear the Name, not only on her forehead, but also in her womb.

There is another reason that this psalm was most likely associated with the Virgin Mary. According to 1 Chronicles 16:23–34, it was originally composed, like Psalm 23, to be sung before the ark of the covenant once it had been brought to dwell in Jerusalem. The ark, we may recall, like the Asherah King Josiah burned, was made out of wood (Exodus 25:10).

Psalm 96 *Dominus regnavit*

A psalm, the title declares, *for the same David when his land was restored again to him. David*, of course, or so Augustine and Cassiodorus explain, means "Christ," "for Christ was born of Mary, who was of David's line; therefore Christ could aptly be spoken of in prophecy as 'David,' since he was to be David's descendant."[298] His land was restored to him after his Resurrection, when those who had called for him to be crucified believed in him and were forgiven. Once again, as in Psalm 95, the psalm proclaims the Lord as the one who is exalted above all other gods (v. 9); further, it explicitly condemns those who worship *graven things and that glory in their idols* (v. 7), calling upon the heavens and the earth to rejoice because it is he who reigns (v. 1). *The Lord hath reigned.* "This," Augustine observes, "is sung of him who stood before a judge, was slapped, scourged, spat upon, crowned with thorns, punched, hung on a tree, and insulted as he hung there. It is sung of him who died on the cross, was pierced with a lance, was buried, and rose again."[299] Might this have been the same Lord described in Psalm 95:10 as reigning *from the wood*? Augustine does not specify, but what he says about the following verse is arguably even more intriguing: *Clouds and darkness are round about him; justice and judgment are the establishment of his throne* (v. 2). Why should his throne be surrounded with *clouds and darkness*? According to Cassiodorus, it is the wicked who see him this way, "just as the sun appears shadowy to the bleary-eyed," while the clean and pure of heart see rather his justice.[300] Augustine is even more particular: "People who have believed in him form his throne. He has made them his seat because Wisdom is enthroned in them, that Wisdom who is the Son of God. We may hear in another passage of scripture an important teaching that supports this interpretation: *the soul of a just person is the throne of Wisdom* (Proverbs 12:23 LXX)."[301]

    Grant that I may praise you, sacred Virgin: give me strength against your enemies, the antiphon pleads.[302] Taunton remarks: "The reason why we seek to praise our ever dear and blessed Lady is on account of the strength we receive through her to combat not only our enemies, but her foes also."[303] Who might those foes be? At a guess, those who would deny that her son was, in fact, the Lord, but what about those who would deny her? More to the point, why sing *this* psalm in her honor? Arguably, because, as we have seen, in the temple tradition, just as the Lady was the bride, the city, and the tree, so, as Wisdom, she was both the cloud and the throne, as well as the fire that went before the Lord (v. 3), the lightning (v. 4), and the glory (v. 6). We have encountered these images more than once. In the "Akathistos" she is hailed as the "chair of the king" (strophe 1), the one "shining upon Egypt the light of truth" as its idols "fell down unable to endure [her] power" (strophe 11), "the pillar of fire, guiding those in darkness," and "the protection of the world, wider than the cloud" (strophe 11). Likewise, she was the "all-holy chariot of him who is above the cherubim" (strophe 15) and the one who "like thunder [strikes] down the enemies" (strophe 21).[304] As Proclus saw her, she was "the veritable swift cloud who carried in her body the one who rides upon the cherubim,"[305] while for Andrew of Crete, she was the "high and exalted throne" upon which Isaiah saw the Lord sitting in a house "full of his glory" (Isaiah 6:1 LXX) as well as the "swift cloud" upon which the Lord would be sitting when he would come to Egypt "and the idols [lit. handmade things] of Egypt [would] be moved at his presence, and their heart [be] faint within them" (Isaiah 19:1 LXX). She was likewise, for Andrew, the "appearance of fire, and its brightness round about. As the appearance of the [rain]bow when it is in the cloud in days of rain, so," as the prophet Ezekiel described the figure on the sapphire throne (1:27–28 LXX), "was the form of the brightness round about: this was the appearance of the likeness of the glory of the Lord."[306]

As Barker has shown, all of the above—the cloud, the throne, the fire, the lightning, the glory—were images or aspects of Wisdom.[307] They were, likewise, the images of Wisdom that the Deuteronomists were most determined to appropriate for their depiction of the Law, including her role in casting down the idols worshipped in Egypt, where, we may recall, Jeremiah found the women making offerings to the Queen of Heaven soon after the destruction of the temple (Jeremiah 44:15–19), and where, centuries later, the books of Ecclesiasticus and Wisdom were written. "As a cloud," Wisdom exulted, "I covered all the earth: I dwelt in the highest places, and my throne is in a pillar of cloud" (Ecclesiasticus 24:6–7). It was as this same pillar of fire and cloud, or so Barker has argued, that Wisdom led the people of Israel out of Egypt and from which the Lord looked down on the host of the Egyptians as they attempted to cross the Red Sea (Exodus 13:21–22, 14:24). As the author of the Wisdom of Solomon writing in Alexandria put it: "[Wisdom] delivered the righteous people and blameless seed from the nation that oppressed them . . . [and] guided them in a marvellous way, and was unto them a cover by day, and a light of stars in the night; [she] brought them through the Red Sea, and led them through much water: but she drowned their enemies, and cast them up out of the bottom of the deep" (Wisdom 10:15–19 LXX). Wisdom, the Lady, was there in the pillar of cloud, bearing the Lord, her Son, and protecting her people against their enemies.[308]

This same pillar of cloud would "descend and stand at the door of the tent" whenever the Lord came to speak to Moses (Exodus 33:9). Along with the glory and the fire, the cloud was likewise there when Moses ascended the mountain on which he received his vision of the tabernacle (Exodus 24:15–18)—the same tabernacle which, as we have seen, was, like the temple, itself patterned on the whole of creation.[309] King Solomon described the Lord as dwelling in "thick darkness" (1 Kings 8:12 RSV); when the temple was finished and the ark of the covenant installed in the Holy of Holies underneath the cherubim, "a cloud filled the house of the Lord, so that the priests could not stand to minister because of the cloud; for the glory of the Lord filled the house of the Lord" (1 Kings 8:10–11 RSV). In Barker's words: "The story of Moses on Sinai was modelled on the king entering the holy of holies, where he was enthroned as the divine Son and given the Lord's decree. . . . It was not until the story of the Exodus was joined with the stories of the patriarchs that Sinai [the holy mountain] was attributed to Moses and incorporated into the Exodus saga."[310] In the Deuteronomist tradition, Moses, as the bearer of the Law, took over the role of Wisdom. The Law usurped the Lady as the source of wisdom and understanding (Deuteronomy 4:6), her pillar was cast out of the temple, and Moses became the one who witnessed the days of creation.[311]

Psalm 97 *Cantate Domino*

Sing ye to the Lord a new canticle, the psalmist exults, *because he hath done wonderful things!* What wonderful things?, Augustine and Cassiodorus ask. Clearly, Cassiodorus notes, once again the Lord here is Christ, for the psalm is *for David himself*, and, as we have seen, "David" means "Christ," while the psalm itself "[tells] of the glory of His incarnation and second coming." The song is *new* because it is to be sung by the new man, "not the old man who has not yet relinquished Adam's sins." The new man sings a new song because he has been saved by the *right hand* and *holy arm* of the Lord (v. 1), that is the Word and the deeds of the Son.[312] According to the psalmist, the Lord has revealed his justice to the Gentiles (v. 2) and his truth to the house of Israel (v. 3); indeed, *all the ends of the earth have seen the salvation of our God* (v. 3). As Augustine puts it: "God's right hand, God's arm, God's salvation, and . . . God's justice: our Lord and Savior Jesus Christ is all these." Further, Augustine explains " 'Israel' means 'One who sees God.' If we see him now by faith, we shall see him in vision later . . . We are 'Israel' by faith now, but later we shall be 'Israel' in face-to-face vision."[313] In Cassiodorus's words: "By *Israel* is denoted every faithful person who beheld God with a pure heart."[314] Accordingly, the psalmist exclaims (vv. 4–9):

> Sing joyfully to God, all the earth: sing, rejoice, and hymn.
>
> Hymn the Lord on the harp: on the harp with the words of a psalm.
>
> With hammered trumpets and sound of horn
>
> make a joyful noise in the sight of the Lord our king.
>
> Let the sea be stirred up, and the fullness thereof:
>
> the world and all who dwell therein.
>
> The rivers shall clap their hands to that same purpose:
>
> the mountains shall exult before the face of the Lord
>
> because he cometh to judge the earth.
>
> He shall judge the world with justice, and the people with equity.[315]

Where is the Lady in this psalm? At first glance, the antiphon would appear to be less than helpful: **After giving birth, you remained inviolate, Virgin; Mother of God, intercede for us.**[316] What does the Virgin's giving birth have to do with praising the Lord in song? Or the Mother of God with his coming in judgment? Not to put too fine a point on it: everything. As we have seen, in the temple tradition to which the early Christians saw themselves as heirs, singing and making music were not simply the ornaments of worship; they were the very essence of worship. David appointed musicians "to invoke, to thank, and to praise the Lord, the God of Israel" (1 Chronicles 16:4 RSV), not just to accompany the priests in making their offerings, but because music itself invoked the presence of the Lord.[317] It was as the musicians played and the singers sang that the house of the Lord was filled with his glory, a cloud so thick that the priests could not stand to serve (2 Chronicles 5:13–14). Moreover, as Barker has shown, it was singing through which the Lord had accomplished creation, or so the pseudepigraphal second-century B.C.E. *Book of Jubilees* suggested.[318] On Day One, the Lord created

> the heavens which are above and the earth and the waters
>
> and all the spirits which serve before him—
>
> the angels of the presence,
>
> and the angels of sanctification,
>
> and the angels [of the spirit of fire]
>
> [and the angels] of the spirit of the winds,
>
> and the angels of the spirit of the clouds,

and of darkness, and of snow and of hail and of hoar frost,
and the angels of the voices and of the thunder and of the lightning,
and the angels of the spirits of cold and of heat,
and of winter and of spring and of autumn and of summer
and of all the spirits of his creatures which are in the heavens and on
    the earth,
the abysses and the darkness, eventide [and night],
and the light, dawn and day, which He hath prepared in the knowledge
    of his heart.

"And thereupon," the angel of the presence told Moses on the mountain, "we [that is, the angels] saw His works, and praised Him, and lauded before Him on account of all His works."[319] As Barker reads it: "The praise of the angels in Day One was at the heart of the creation, and their song was part of the process of creation."[320]

"Holy, holy, holy is the Lord of hosts," sang the seraphim whom Isaiah saw surrounding the throne, "the whole earth is full of his glory" (Isaiah 6:3 RSV). Enoch heard the same song as he stood in the Holy of Holies. "Holy, holy, holy, is the Lord of Spirits," the hosts of heaven sang, "he filleth the earth with spirits."[321] The seer of the revelation of Jesus Christ heard it, too: "Holy, holy, holy, is the Lord God Almighty, who was and is and is to come!" (Revelation 4:8 RSV). In other words, as Barker explains, Yahweh, the Lord of Hosts or, rather, "He who causes the Hosts to be," is "the One who enables the many to exist . . . prompted, it would seem, by the praises of the angels."[322] In Barker's words:

> The process of creation was the great mystery of the holy of holies—how the One became the many, the invisible hosts and then the visible creation—and so John heard the heavenly song continue: "[Worthy art thou, our Lord and God, to receive glory and honor and power,] for thou didst create all things and by thy will they existed and were created" (Revelation 4:11).[323]

As the Lord demanded of Job: "Where were you when I laid the foundations of the earth . . . when the morning stars sang together, and all the sons of God [LXX: angels] shouted for joy?" (Job 38:4,7 RSV).

Accordingly, within this tradition, singing was likewise seen as a part of the process of atonement and, therefore, of re-creation. As Barker notes, the only time that the priests like Isaiah would have "heard" the Sanctus was when they had entered the Holy of Holies to offer the sacrifices of atonement.[324] "Woe is me!" Isaiah cried when he saw the throne and heard the song, "for I am lost;

for I am a man of unclean lips, and I dwell in the midst of a people of unclean lips; for my eyes have seen the King, the Lord of hosts!" But far from being lost, Isaiah was saved, as one of the seraphim took a burning coal from the altar and touched it to his lips, saying, "Behold, this has touched your lips; your guilt is taken away, and your sin forgiven" (Isaiah 6:5–7 RSV). Likewise, the seer of the New Testament beheld, before the throne, the Lamb who was slain and who, as the "new song" of the living creatures and elders put it, "by [his] blood didst ransom men for God" (Revelation 5:9 RSV). And how did the living creatures and elders know who this Lamb was? Because, as Isaiah had prophesied, he was born of the Virgin (Isaiah 7:14), that is, of the Lady with the moon at her feet and clothed with the sun (Revelation 12:1–6), just as the antiphon proclaimed. Just as the Lady had been present with the Lord at creation (Proverbs 8:22–31), so she was there with him as he brought about its renewal. Thus, at his birth, the angels, surrounded by the glory of God, sang: "Glory to God in the highest, and on earth peace among men with whom he is pleased!" (Luke 2:14 RSV). The Lord, the high priest, had come forth at Bethlehem from the Holy of Holies, the Virgin's womb, "to be ruler in Israel" and bring peace to the earth (Micah 5:2–4) by wedding himself once again to the Lady, his bride.[325] "And in that day," the Lord promised Israel, "you will call me, 'My husband,' . . . and I will make for you a covenant on that day with the beasts of the field, the birds of the air, and the creeping things of the ground; and I will abolish the bow, the sword, and war from the land. . . . I will betroth you to me in faithfulness; and you shall know the Lord" (Hosea 2:16, 18, 20 RSV).[326] At which betrothal, once again, all creation would sing (cf. Revelation 21). "Sing, O heavens," Isaiah invited the cosmos, "for the Lord has done it; shout, O depths of the earth; break forth into singing, O mountains, O forest, and every tree in it! For the Lord has redeemed Jacob, and will be glorified in Israel" (Isaiah 44:23 RSV; cf. 49:13–18).

But, of course, the one upon whom the spirit of Wisdom rested would bring not only redemption and peace, but also judgment. In the words of Isaiah: "He shall not judge by what his eyes see, or decide by what his ears hear; but with righteousness he shall judge the poor, and decide with equity for the meek of the earth; and he shall smite the earth with the rod of his mouth, and with the breath of his lips he shall slay the wicked" (Isaiah 11:3–4 RSV). The earliest Christians knew to expect the Lord to come in this way. After all, Jesus had told them as much. In his words, as recorded by the evangelist Matthew, at the end of the age, "then will appear the sign of the Son of man in heaven, and then all the tribes of the earth will mourn, and they will see the Son of man coming on the clouds of heaven with power and great glory" (Matthew 24:30 RSV). And, Jesus continued: "When the Son of man comes in his glory, and all the angels with him, then he will sit on his glorious throne. Before him will be gathered all the nations, and he will separate them one from another as a shepherd separates the sheep from the goats, and he will place the sheep at his right hand, but the goats at the left" (Matthew 25:31–33 RSV). As Barker explains, in the temple tradition in which Jesus was speaking, animals like sheep and goats indicate human beings, while "man," as in "the man Gabriel" (Daniel 9:21) was used to indicate an angel.[327] The sign of the "Son of man" may, therefore, be read as the sign of the Angel of Great Counsel prophesied by Isaiah (9:6 LXX), the "Wonderful Counselor, Mighty God, Everlasting Father, Prince of Peace" who would rule with righteousness and of whose peace there would be no end. It can hardly been coincidental, Barker insists, that this angel-child upon whose shoulders the government was to rest would come in glory riding on a cloud surrounded by angels. Here, once again, the Lord was not without his Lady, nor the king without his bride.

What hope did the sheep and the goats have at the great judgment? As we have noted, the seer in Revelation saw the Tree of Life, that is, the Lady, standing beside the throne of the Lamb, thus suggesting that the Mother of the Lord was, once again, there with him in the Holy of Holies, "and the leaves of the tree were for the healing of the nations" (Revelation 22:2). As Barker reads the tradition, Adam, in his sin, had rejected the Tree of Life (that is, the tree of Wisdom) in favor of the tree of the knowledge of good and evil (Genesis 3). With Wisdom's return, Adam, that is, man would be able to eat of her fruits and thus share once again in the wisdom of the angels. This new Adam, born from the root of the tree of Jesse, would be beautiful and great and fill the earth with the knowledge of the Lord and reign over it in peace.[328] The covenant between heaven and earth would be restored; the son of Adam, made "little less than the angels," would once again be crowned "with glory and splendor" and rule over creation (cf. Psalm 8:5–9). Significantly, like Ezekiel in his vision of the chariot, Enoch standing in the Holy of Holies saw four presences surrounding the throne and "[uttering] praises before the Lord of glory." The first, Michael, "the merciful and long-suffering," was "[blessing] the Lord of Spirits for ever and ever." The second, Raphael, "who is set over all the diseases and wounds of the children of men," was "blessing the Elect One and the elect ones who hang upon the Lord of Spirits." The third, Gabriel, "who is set over all the powers," was "[praying and interceding] for those who dwell on the earth and [supplicating] in the name of the Lord of Spirit," while the fourth, Phanuel, "who is set over the repentance unto hope of those who inherit eternal life," was "fending off the Satans and forbidding them to come before the Lord of Spirits to accuse them who dwell on the earth."[329] We may recall that it was the angel Gabriel, that is, the intercessor, who was sent to announce to Mary that she was to become the Mother of the new Adam, the Lord, who was to rule over the house of

Jacob for ever, and of whose kingdom there would be no end (Luke 1:26–33, 3:38). As Taunton points out, commenting on the antiphon, "Jesus came to us through [Mary]. She has given Him to the world. . . . This Antiphon, then, teaches us her office of Intercessor between us and Jesus."[330]

"Today," John of Damascus rejoiced on the Feast of the Nativity of the Virgin, "is the beginning of salvation for the world. 'Cry aloud to the Lord, all the earth, praise and exult and sing psalms' (Psalm 97:4 LXX). Lift up your voice, 'Lift it up, fear not!' (Isaiah 40:9). For a Mother of God, from whom the Lamb of God who takes away the sin of the world has been pleased to be born, has been born for us in a holy sheepfold."[331] "Your light outshines the sun," Germanus told her, "your honor is above that of all creation, your excellence before that of the angels. . . . For when he who was born of you shall come 'to judge the world in justice' (Psalm 97:9 LXX), 'they will see and will beat their breasts' (Zechariah 12:10 LXX) who have not already wished to confess you, in good faith, as Mother of God."[332] As John of Euboea explained at the feast of her Conception: "This is the praise and the songs of the exulting daughters of Judea, 'Sing and exult and sing psalms!' (Psalm 97:4 LXX). For behold, the devil who usurped our nature has been conquered! Behold, a throne more wonderful than the cherubic one is made ready on earth. . . . For she is a throne and a place and a dwelling-place of the Emmanuel and All-Ruler, Christ."[333]

The Seven Hours of the Day

Unlike the psalms for Matins, those for the remaining hours of the Marian Office (Lauds, Prime, Terce, Sext, None, Vespers, and Compline) were not necessarily specific to the Marian feasts as such, nor, with the exception of Lauds, were they consistent from Use to Use.[334] As for the Marian feasts, those for Lauds followed the cursus for Sundays used in secular churches, with seven psalms and one canticle sung under five antiphons: Psalms 92 (with antiphon), 99 (with antiphon), 62 and 66 (under one antiphon), the *Benedicite* or Canticle of the Three Children (Daniel 3:57–88, 56) (with antiphon), and Psalms 148–150 (under one antiphon).

For the Little Hours (Prime, Terce, Sext, and None), each hour including three psalms sung under one antiphon, there were a variety of uses, with the greatest variation at Prime. At Fonte Avellana in the eleventh century and at Paris by the thirteenth, the psalms for Prime were 1, 2, and 5, while at Monte Cassino in the eleventh century and in England in the twelfth, they followed the weekday secular cursus of 53, 118:1–16, 17–32, and *Quicumque vult* (the Athanasian creed).

By the thirteenth century at Oxford as well as Sarum by the fourteenth, the psalms for Prime were 53, 116, and 117, while at Rome by the fifteenth century they were 53, 84, and 116. Following the Dominicans, Geert Grote used the first three Gradual Psalms, Psalms 119, 120, and 121, at Prime. For Terce, Sext, and None, the usage was somewhat simpler, focusing either, as in the daily secular cursus, on Psalm 118, divided into three sections for each hour, or on the first nine (out of fifteen) Gradual Psalms, as in the regular monastic cursus for Tuesday through Saturday. The former usage, kept at Monte Cassino as well as in eleventh-century England, seems to have been the older, but the latter appears at Fonte Avellana by the beginning of the twelfth century and was to become standard, except with the Dominicans and Grote, who continued at Terce with Psalm 122, having sung the first three Gradual Psalms at Prime.

For Vespers, the earliest English monastic uses and at Monte Cassino included four psalms (109, 121, 126, and 131) under four antiphons, while, following the secular cursus for Tuesdays, Vespers at Oxford, Paris, Sarum, and York had five of the Gradual Psalms (121, 122, 123, 124, and 125). The Dominicans as well as the Use of Rome likewise had five psalms (109, 112, 121, 126, and 147), all of which were associated with Vespers throughout the week; these psalms, however, were likewise those used for the Marian feasts, suggesting a possibly more particular focus. At Hyde Abbey at the turn of the fourteenth century, Vespers for the Office of the Virgin included the five Gradual Psalms, but the same hour for the Marian feasts followed the monastic usage of four. At Compline, both the Roman and the Dominican uses continued with the Gradual Psalms, starting respectively with Psalm 128 and Psalm 131 and including three psalms under one antiphon. At Monte Cassino as in the earlier English monastic uses, the psalms for Compline followed the daily secular cursus of four psalms (4, 30, 90, and 133) under one antiphon, while at Oxford, Paris, Sarum, and York the psalms were 12, 42, 128, and 130.

In what sense, if at all, were these psalms considered particularly Marian, if, with the possible exception of Vespers, they were simply those used anyway during the Divine Office in the regular course of the week? Much depended on the choice of the antiphons, which, as we shall see, gave each of the hours a specifically Marian inflection, even if the psalms were not chosen specially for her. And yet, perhaps, after all, they did not need to be, any more than they needed to be chosen especially for her Son, the Lord Jesus Christ, about whom and for whom and through whom, as all ancient and medieval Christian commentators knew, all of the psalms had been written in the first place. We have already noted how Psalm 109, the first psalm at Vespers, was originally associated with the anointing and rebirth of the king as the son of Wisdom and high priest in the order of Melchizedek. *From the womb before the day star I begot thee*, the psalm (v. 3 Vulgate) proclaims. **While the king was at his rest, my nard gave forth the odor of sweetness**, the antiphon (Use of Rome) exults, recalling the "sweetness" with which Wisdom anointed her Son as he came forth from her "chamber."[335] To paraphrase the evangelist (cf. John 12:26), where the Lord is, there shall be his Mother also. But it is not just that, according to the Orthodox homilists, the psalms as such speak of Mary as the Mother of the Lord, which, as we have seen in our reading of the psalms for Matins, they would arguably seem to do, as least according to the authors of the liturgy for her feasts. A true daughter of David, she likewise spent her life singing them, or so her medieval devotees would insist. Once again, much depends on the temple tradition to which the earliest Christians believed themselves to be heirs, here inflected through the monastic tradition upon which the Office depended.

As we have seen, according to the *Protevangelium of James*, Mary's mother Anna, much as Samuel's mother Hannah, promised her daughter while an infant as an offering to the Lord (cf. 1 Samuel 1:22–28 RSV).[336] Mary, therefore, like Samuel, grew up with the priests who were serving the Lord, but as a girl she was not, of course, able to assist in the sacrifices. How, then, did she spend her days? The author of the so-called *Gospel of Pseudo-Matthew*, a Latin version of the *Protevangelium* extant in some eight known manuscripts from as early as the ninth century and translated into Old English before the twelfth century, thought he (or she) knew: Mary prayed. More particularly, she alternately worked and prayed according to a rule (L: *regulam*; OE: *haligne regol*). From dawn to the third hour, she prayed (L: *a mane usque ad horam tertiam orationibus insisteret*); from the third to the ninth hour, she worked at her weaving; she prayed again from the ninth hour until the angel brought her (as the Old English version of the story put it) "heavenly sweet food" (OE: *heofonlice swetnysse*), which she ate from his hand. She kept to her prayers and praises of God even after the more senior virgins had ceased for the day, so that there was no one more learned in the wisdom of the law of God, more humble in humility, more eloquent in singing the psalms (L: *in carminibus Davidicis eloquentior*), or more perfect in virtue. More specifically, as the Anglo-Saxon translator put it: "She was humbler and more joyous in praise of God and purer in her thoughts and more excellent in the songs of David (*dauidiscum sangum wraetlicre*) than any of the [other virgins] had been before."[337]

In her account of Mary's childhood, the tenth-century Saxon canoness Hrotsvitha of Gandersheim (d. ca. 1002) was likewise careful to specify that, while living in the temple, Mary was "ever zealous in chanting the psalms of David" (*carminibus semper studiosa Davidis*). "[Mary's] one ambition," or so Hrotsvitha explained, "was to persevere in prayer and to be constant in singing the divine praises" from darkest night up to the third hour of the day and then again from the ninth hour until evening.[338] As Otfrid von Weissenburg (d. after 871) told it in his *Evangelienbuch*, a versified version of the Gospels in Old High German, the angel Gabriel found Mary similarly employed when he came to her with his good news: "He went into the palace, he found her praising God, / With her psalter in her hands, singing it through until the end (*mit salteru in henti, then sang si unz in enti*), / She was making fine cloths / Out of costly threads—she always did that gladly."[339] As well she might! After all, as we have seen, according to the temple tradition, it was by singing the psalms that the ancient Israelites invoked the presence of the Lord, just as it was by weaving that the Mother of the Lord made for him the garment which he wore when he came into the world as high priest. Accordingly, as her medieval devotees told it, Mary, like her devotees, spent her days (and nights) singing the psalms. But how, once again, did they—and she—understand what they sang? As with the third nocturn for Matins, the antiphons and psalmody for Lauds for the Use of Rome follow that for the same hour for the Feast of the Assumption in the ninth-century antiphoner of Compiègne.[340]

LAUDS, SUNG AT SUNRISE

Psalm 92 *Dominus regnavit*

The Lord hath reigned, he is clothed with beauty: the Lord is clothed with strength, and hath girded himself. For he hath established the world which shall not be moved (v. 1) The themes of the first psalm for the day are ones with which we are already familiar: the Lord reigns (from the tree?), he is clothed (with the scarlet and purple which his mother wove for him?), he has girded himself (as a mighty warrior, with his sword upon his thigh?), he is beautiful and strong (like the royal bridegroom awaiting his bride?), he has established the world which shall not be moved (like the holy city in its midst?). Following its inscription (*Praise in the way of a canticle for David himself on the day before the sabbath, when the earth was founded*), Augustine explains that this psalm is to be read with reference to the sixth day of creation, on which God made all the animals and, finally, human beings "in his own image and likeness." Likewise, the Lord Jesus Christ came in the sixth age, "so that human beings might be reshaped in God's image."[341] Accordingly, in Augustine's reading, the psalm celebrates the Lord as both creator and re-creator, the one who laid the foundations of the earth and of the Christian faith (cf. 1 Corinthians 3:11). *Thy throne is prepared from of old;*

thou art from everlasting (v. 2). And who, we might ask, was that throne (*sedes*) prepared from of old? Who else but the Mother of the Lord, the Seat of Wisdom (*sedes Sapientiae*) "set up, from eternity and of old, before the earth was made" (Proverbs 8:23), who brought forth the Lord "in the splendor of the saints from the womb before the day star" as sacrifice and high priest? The parallel with Psalm 109:3 suggested here is Augustine's, albeit without the explicit Marian reference.[342]

The floods have lifted up, O Lord: the floods have lifted up their voice. The floods have lifted up their waves with the noise of many waters (vv. 3–4). Once again, Augustine's parallel is suggestive: "The Spirit himself is the mighty river whence many other rivers derive. Concerning that river another psalm says: 'The vehement impulses of a river give joy to God's city'" (Psalm 45:5).[343] And who was that city made joyful by the voices of the river? The psalmist recalls: "The Most High hath sanctified his own tabernacle" (Psalm 45:5), that is, as we have seen, his Mother. Or, following Barker's reconstruction of the temple tradition, we might read the psalm this way: the psalm depicts the Lord as king enthroned above the waters, that is, the waters of heaven and earth separated by the firmament just as the Holy of Holies was separated from the great hall of the temple by the veil.[344] These were the waters (the "sea of glass") that the seer saw spreading out before the throne "like crystal" (Revelation 4:6, 15:2), in fulfillment of the prophet's promise that "the Lord in majesty will be for us a place of broad rivers and streams, where no galley with oars can go, nor stately ship can pass" (Isaiah 33:21 RSV). *Wonderful are the surges of the sea: wonderful is the Lord on high!* (v. 4). Could (we may imagine the authors of Mary's liturgy asking) the imagery here be any clearer? Who, after all, lifted up her voice to the Lord more wonderfully than Mary, the star of the sea, as she rejoiced in God her savior and cried out: "Holy is his name"? (cf. Luke 1:46–55) *Thy testimonies are become exceedingly credible: holiness becometh thy house, O Lord, unto length of days* (v. 5). It is easy to imagine how the identification of Mary with the house of the Lord becoming in its holiness would most likely have become by this point irresistible to the medieval readers of her psalms.

If the above interpretation from a Marian perspective does not satisfy, the antiphon suggests yet another reading: **Mary has been assumed into heaven: the angels rejoice and, praising, they bless the Lord.**[345] What (again, we may imagine the authors of Mary's liturgy asking) could be more appropriate than that the angels, like the rivers, should lift up their voices at this hour to wonder at the Assumption of the woman who, clothed with the sun, gave birth to the Morning Star who brought salvation to the world? "Today," or so John of Damascus apostrophized her on the feast of her Dormition,

the angels minister to you as you go home to your Son. . . . In their godly enthu-
siasm, they sing holy hymns to you, the source of the Lord's body that is for us
a stream of life. . . . Heaven received your soul with joy. The powers [of heaven]
met you with holy hymns and splendid ceremony, crying out words such as
these: " 'Who is this who ascends, robed all in white' [Song 8:5], 'spreading over
us like the dawn, beautiful as the moon, singular as the sun?' " [Song 6:9]. . . . You
have gone on to the very royal throne of your Son, where you see him with your
own eyes and rejoice; you stand beside him in great, indescribable freedom.[346]

In the imagery of the Office, it is dawn, and the queen has taken her place
beside the king, now sitting on his throne from which the waters of life flow out
through the heavenly city, "and night shall be no more" (cf. Revelation 22:1–2, 5).
As Taunton comments: "The Assumption of Our Lady is the image of ours; even
as hers was modelled on that of the Resurrection and Ascension of her Divine
Son."[347]

Psalm 99 *Jubilate Deo*

"*Psalmus in confessione*," the Vulgate inscription reads. "*A psalm for thanksgiving*,"
the Septuagint avers. "'Confession,'" Augustine explains, "is understood by
scripture in two senses: there is the confession of one who praises, and the
confession of one who groans. . . . Men and women confess when they praise
God, and they confess when they accuse themselves; and the tongue has no
nobler function."[348] This, then, according to Augustine, is a psalm of praise; there
is no nobler work in which human beings could be engaged. *Sing joyfully to God,
all the earth! Serve ye the Lord with gladness* (v. 1). We have already remarked
more than once the importance of singing both for the work of creation and for
those in the temple tradition who would invoke the presence of the Lord. As
Augustine and Cassiodorus would have it, psalmody itself is a kind of spiritual
work to be offered to God with great joy. In Cassiodorus's words: "Singing means
uttering praises with the voice alone, whereas reciting a psalm means proclaiming
the Lord's glory by good works. Singing and reciting a psalm are themselves *the
victim of jubilation*."[349] It is, therefore, a work for which one should prepare with
great care. You would not, Augustine argues, attempt to sing before some musical
expert without having proper musical training lest your singing grate on his ears.
How much the more, he would insist, should Christians prepare themselves to
sing to God, "who so shrewdly judges the singer, who so closely scrutinizes every
detail, who listens with such discrimination?"[350] Even more important, however,
is that they sing with joy. "Playing psalms is a cheerful activity," Augustine

insists.[351] Nor is it something about which they should be anxious: "Anyone who praises God can be wholly free from anxiety, because there is no possibility that we shall ever be ashamed of the one we have praised."[352] Even less should they worry that it should become boring: "Praising God, loving God, will never not satisfy us. If you weary of love, you will weary of praise; but if love is everlasting, because that beauty can never cloy, have no fear that you will find yourself unable to praise for ever him whom you will have strength to love for ever."[353] Therefore, *come*, the psalmist urges, *come in before his presence with exceeding great joy* (v. 2).

"When," Augustine wonders, "should we shout for joy? When," he answers, "we praise what is beyond utterance, that is, the whole of creation, the earth, the sea, the sky, and all the creatures in them, including us."[354] *Know ye*, the psalmist cautions, *that the Lord, he is God: he made us, and not we ourselves. We are his people and the sheep of his pasture* (v. 3). Here, Cassiodorus argues, the psalmist teaches what it means to be Christian: *know* that the Lord is "the very God who made heaven and earth, who fashioned us as well to His image and likeness," and that *we are his people* whom he feeds with the "abundant and sweet feast provided by the holy Scriptures."[355] *Go ye into his gates with praise, into his courts with hymns, and give glory to him* (v. 4), that is, praise him with songs of praise. As Augustine put it: "Confess that you did not make yourselves, and praise him by whom you were made." *Praise ye his name, for the Lord is sweet; his mercy endureth for ever and his truth to generation and generation* (v. 5). "Never think that you will weary of praising him," Augustine assured his listeners. "Your songs of praise are like eating: the more you praise, the more strength you acquire, and the more delightful does he become whom you are praising."[356]

How, according to her medieval devotees, might the Mother of the Lord have sung this psalm? The antiphon sets the scene: **The Virgin Mary has been assumed to the heavenly chamber, where the King of kings sits upon his starry throne.**[357] "My soul," Mary cried out at her cousin Elizabeth's blessing, "doth magnify the Lord, and my spirit hath rejoiced in God my Saviour" (Luke 1:46–47). How much the more, we may imagine, must she have rejoiced to enter through the gates of the heavenly city and come into his presence as the angels sang their hymns of praise! "Because," she once sang to her cousin, "he that is mighty hath done great things to me; and holy is his name. And his mercy is from generation unto generations, to them that fear him" (Luke 1:49–50). Now, or so the antiphon invites Mary's devotees to imagine, she stands beside his starry throne, singing joyfully unto God and serving him with gladness just as she once served him with humility, praising her Son as Creator and Lord, and pleading for his mercy on behalf of his people, his sheep. Nor, having been assumed into his presence, could she ever weary in praising his name or confessing him as her Son, the King of kings who "hath put down the mighty from their seat, and hath exalted the humble" (Luke 1:52). Thus Hannah rejoiced as she offered her son Samuel to the Lord (1 Samuel 2:1–10 RSV); thus, or so the antiphon suggests, Mary, the Mother of the Lord, must now rejoice standing beside the throne of her Son.

Psalms 62 *Deus, Deus meus* and 66 *Deus misereatur nostri*

The first two psalms with their antiphons having set the heavenly scene, the next two psalms, sung under one antiphon, turn inward to the voice of the soul, first in the singular ("I"), then in the plural ("we"). Again, the theme is the joyful confession and praise of the Lord for his mercy as Creator and judge, with the soul, as it were, answering the invitation of the previous psalms to rejoice and sing. According to Augustine, Psalm 62 is spoken in the person of Christ, who suffered for humanity and who still suffers in the world as the Church, while for Cassiodorus, the speaker is "that spiritual bride, who embodies the limbs of the Lord Savior."[358] The antiphon suggests yet a third bride: **We run to the odor of your ointments: the young maidens have loved you exceedingly.**[359] The text of the antiphon is adapted from the Song of Songs (1:2–3), which, as we have already seen, was understood liturgically with reference to Mary.[360] In the Song of Songs, depending on how one reads the dialogue, it is ambiguous whom the young maidens love, but in the antiphon they take the part of the virgins of Psalm 44:15–16 following the bride into the palace of the king. These, if we follow the *Protevangelium* and the *Gospel of Pseudo-Matthew*, would seem to be the Virgin's companions who lived with her in the temple. If, however, we follow the stories of her Dormition, they might rather be the holy souls who are led with her to heaven.[361] In either case, it is the Virgin whom they love and to whose fragrance they are drawn. Under this antiphon, it is she, therefore, who would seem to cry out in the words of the psalm: *O God, my God, to thee do I watch at break of day. For thee my soul hath thirsted, for thee my flesh—O how many ways!* (Psalm 62:2). As Augustine explains, the flesh thirsts just as much as the soul, "because even for our flesh there is the promise of resurrection"[362]—just as, with her Assumption, the Virgin herself was promised by her Son.

These, or so John of Damascus imagined, were the words which the Lord spoke to her just before she died: "Come, my blessed Mother, 'into the place of my rest' [Psalm 131:8 LXX]. 'Arise, come, my dear one,' beautiful among all women; 'for behold, winter has passed, and the time of pruning has come' [Song 2:10–12]. 'My dear one is beautiful, and there is no blemish in you'

[Song 4:7]. 'The odor of your ointments surpasses all fragrance' [Song 1:3]."³⁶³ Hearing which, Mary "committed her soul to the hands of her Son" and was carried up into heaven, rising (as Song of Songs 3:6 put it) "from the desert like a column of smoke," fragrant with all the powders of the merchant. "How beautiful you are, how sweet!" John imagined the company of heaven rejoicing at her ascent. " 'You are the flower of the plain, like a lily among thorns (Song 2:1–2). 'Therefore the young maidens love you—we rush towards the fragrance of your myrrh' (Song 1:2–3)." On her arrival, John assured her, " 'The king [bore] you into his chamber' (Song 1:4)," as all the ranks of angels accompanied her to his throne, praising her as "the mother of their Lord."³⁶⁴ Accordingly, or so it seems the psalmist foretold, she cried out: *In a desert land and where there is no way and no water* [I thirsted]: *so in the sanctuary have I come before thee to see thy power and thy glory* (Psalm 62:3). There, she blesses his name and lifts up her hands, and praises her Son with joyful lips, and her soul is filled with *marrow and fatness* (Psalm 62:4–6). But, O how she longed for him before she died! "Upon my bed by night, I sought him whom my soul loves: I sought him, and found him not" (Song 3:1). Flooding her bed every night with prayerful tears, she thirsted for him "like a deer that yearns for running streams" (Psalm 41:1), running across the mountains "like a gazelle or a young hart" (Song 2:17).³⁶⁵ *If*, the psalmist spoke for her, *I have remembered thee upon my bed, I will meditate on thee in the morning, because thou hast been my helper. And I will rejoice under the covert of thy wings: my soul hath stuck close to thee: thy right hand hath received me* (Psalm 62:7–9). "I will rise now," the bride exclaims in the Song of Songs, "and go about the city. . . . I will seek him whom my soul loves. . . . When I found him, I held him, and would not let him go. . . . O that his left hand were under my head, and that his right hand embraced me!" (Song of Songs 3:2, 4; 2:6). *But they*, the psalmist continued, *have sought my soul in vain, they shall go into the lower parts of the earth; they shall be delivered into the hands of the sword, they shall be the portions of foxes* (Psalm 62:10–11). "The watchmen found me," the bride recalls, "as they went about in the city; they beat me, they wounded me, they took away my mantle" (Song 5:7; cf. 3:3). "Catch us," she begs her beloved, "the foxes, the little foxes, that spoil the vineyards"—that is, the powers of hell whom Mary begged not to have to see at the hour when her soul went out of her body³⁶⁶—"for our vineyards are in blossom" (Song 2:15). *But the king shall rejoice in God*, the psalmist promises, *all they shall be praised that swear by him* (Psalm 62:12). "Go forth, daughters of Zion," the bride invites her followers, "and behold King Solomon, with the crown with which his mother"—that is, Mary would insist, myself—"crowned him on the day of his wedding," and praise him "on the day of the gladness of his heart" (Song 3:11).

In the second of the two psalms, accordingly, or so the antiphon suggests, we hear the voice of the daughters who have run in the fragrance of the bride: *May God have mercy on us, and bless us: may he cause the light of his countenance to shine upon us* (Psalm 66:2). We have already noted how, in the temple tradition, the worshippers sang to invoke the presence of the Lord and cause his face to shine.[367] Here it is the virgins who, accompanying Mary, surround the throne of the Lamb and sing: *Let people confess to thee, O God: let all people give praise to thee . . . for thou judgest the people with justice and directest the nations upon earth* (Psalm 66:4–5). This is the Lord as he appeared in his sanctuary in his power and glory (cf. Psalm 62:3), coming to judge the earth with his Mother at his side. Thus the psalmist exclaims: *The earth hath yielded her fruit* (Psalm 66:7). That is, as the bride heard her beloved say: "Arise, make haste, my love, my dove, my beautiful one, and come. For now the winter is past, the rain is over and gone. The flowers have appeared in our land, the time of pruning is come: the voice of the turtledove is heard in our land. The fig tree has put forth her green figs: the vines in flower yield their sweet smell. Arise, my love, my beautiful one, and come" (Song of Songs 2:10–13). And so, according to the ancient tradition, Mary did.

Daniel 3:57–88, 56 Benedicite

Properly speaking, the fourth text of Lauds is not a psalm, but a canticle. It is an excerpt from the so-called *Canticle of the Three Children*, that is, of Shadrach, Meshach, and Abednego, "servants of the Most High God," whom Nebuchadnezzar, king of the Chaldeans, had ordered cast into a fiery furnace for refusing to worship the golden idol he had made (Daniel 3). The song, which calls upon *all ye works of the Lord* to praise and exalt him, appears in both the Septuagint and the Vulgate, but not, significantly, in the Hebrew version of the book of Daniel, for reasons which should by now not be difficult to understand, dependent as the song is on the angel mythology of the temple tradition.[368] Augustine himself cited it as proof that the angels were creatures of God, noting that, as God put it in the book of Job, "when the stars were made, all my angels praised me with a great voice" (Job 38:7); thus, Augustine reasoned, the angels had to have been made before the fourth day.[369] As we have already noted, according to the *Book of Jubilees*, the angels were, in fact, creatures of Day One (that is, *dies unus*, as Augustine put it), along with the spirits of the winds, clouds, darkness, snow, hail, hoarfrost, thunder, lightning, cold, heat, seasons, darkness, light, dawn and day, and "all the spirits of his creatures which are in the heavens and on the earth."[370] As Barker notes, the list of the Lord's works that appears in the *Benedicite* sung by the three men as they walked among the flames in the furnace follows a similar pattern: first the angels, then the heavens, the waters and powers, sun, moon and stars, showers, dew and spirits, fire, heat, winter and summer, dews, hoarfrost, frost and cold, ice, snow, nights and days, light, darkness, lightnings and clouds, the earth, mountains and hills, fountains, seas and floods, the whales and other creatures that move in the waters, the fowls of the air, the beasts, cattle, and sons of men, Israel, the priests and servants of the Lord, the spirits and souls of the just, the holy and humble at heart, and the three singers themselves.[371] *Blessed art thou in the firmament of heaven*, they sang as the flames of King Nebuchadnezzar's furnace flickered about them, *and worthy of praise, and glorious for ever* (Daniel 3:56).

Blessed are you of the Lord, daughter; because through you we have been made partakers of the fruit of life, the daughters of men answered them, or, perhaps more accurately, the daughters of Zion praising the queen in the antiphon.[372] Like the early Christians (or so the antiphon invites us to imagine), they had entered with her into the Holy of Holies to stand before the throne of the Lamb (cf. Revelation 14:4) and sing with the angels the wonders of the Lord's works, praising him for his creation (cf. Revelation 4:11). In Augustine's words: "The substances that praise him were made through him. The three young men in the fiery furnace sang of the entire creation as praising God; the hymn of all the beings that praise him resounds from earthly things to things of heaven, and back again from heavenly beings to those of earth."[373] For Augustine, however, it was not the creatures themselves, other than the angels and human beings, who praise God, but rather the creatures as contemplated by the angels and human beings: "All these thing are good because God who made them is good, and all of them praise him when studied in the right spirit, the spirit of piety and wisdom."[374] And indeed, as the "Akathistos" put it, what better guide might the daughters have in their contemplation than that "tree of glorious fruit upon which the faithful feed," herself the one upon whom the spirit of Wisdom rested? As those "children of the Chaldeans," the Magi exclaimed when they "saw in the Virgin's hands / him who with his hand fashioned humankind":

> Hail, you who closed the furnace of deception;
> Hail you who protect the initiates of the Trinity;
> Hail, you who have cast the inhuman tyrant from his dominion;
> Hail, you who showed forth the Lord Christ, who loves humankind![375]

This is the way that John of Damascus hymned her in his canon for the Feast of the Dormition:

> When commanded not to adore him who created them,
> Three sons of Israel
> Chose, in their courage, to defy even furnaces,
> Braving the fire, as they sang exultantly,
> "Praised be the God of Abraham; may the Lord be blessed forever!"
>
> Come, young men and gentle maidens, join the festival;
> Honor that maiden, the
> Mother of God today; come, elders and emperors,
> Masters and magistrates, join our canticle:
> "Praised be the God of Abraham; may the Lord be blessed forever!"
>
> . . .
>
> The lads who were cast into the furnace
> Were rescued by Mary's Son, who guides the universe—
> Then by a prefiguring, now becoming flesh in her,
> Waking the world to victory, inspiring anthems of praise;
> O come, acclaim the works of the Savior,
> And call him blessed forever and forever!
>
> Your name, too, O spotless, holy Virgin,
> The powers and principalities now celebrate,
> Angels with the archangels, thrones and dominions all,
> Cherubim, too, and seraphim, aglow with awe-struck, burning acclaim;
> So we, mere men and women, dare praise you
> And call you blessed forever and forever![376]

Psalms 148 *Laudate Dominum*, 149 *Cantate Domino*, and 150 *Laudate Dominum*

The psalmody for Lauds rises to its crescendo, calling once again on all the creatures of the Lord in heaven and on earth: *Praise the name of the Lord, for he spoke, and they were made; he commanded, and they were created. He hath established them for ever and for ages and ages; he hath made a decree, and it shall not pass away ... The praise of him is above heaven and earth, and he hath exalted the horn of his people* (Psalm 148:5–6, 14). All the familiar voices are invoked, along with the voices of the people: the angels and all the hosts, the sun and moon, stars and light, the heavens of heavens and the waters above the heavens (that is, the waters above which the Lord is enthroned), the earth, dragons, and deeps, fire, hail, snow, ice, stormy winds, mountains and hills, fruitful trees and cedars, beasts and cattle, serpents and feathered fowls, kings, princes, and judges, young men and maidens, old and young (Psalm 148:2–4, 7–12). Israel and the saints are invited to sing a new song and the children of Zion to be joyful *in their king*—that is, Augustine explains, in Christ, who is "our king and our priest," who "took flesh from us . . . from the womb of his virgin mother, so that he might offer it clean for us who were unclean"[377]—praising him in chorus and singing to him *with the timbrel and the psaltery: For the Lord is well pleased with his people and he will exalt the meek unto salvation* (Psalm 149:1–4). The saints (or "holy ones") will rejoice in glory and come with two-edged swords in their hands to execute his judgment (Psalm 149:5–9), as all the instruments of the temple (trumpet, psaltery, harp, timbrel, choir, strings, organs, and cymbals) sound with praise for his mighty acts (*virtutibus*) and the multitude of his greatness (Psalm 150:2–5). *Praise ye the Lord*, the psalmist cries out, *in his holy places: praise ye him in the firmament of his power!* (Psalm 150:1). The temple setting is unmistakable, translated, by way of the antiphon, to the court over which the Lady and Lord of heaven preside.[378]

"Hallelu-jah!" (*Alleluia*) each of the three psalms begins, that is, Barker translates, "Make the Lord shine forth [from his Holy of Holies]!"[379] **You are beautiful and comely, daughter of Jerusalem: terrible as an army set in array**, the antiphon exclaims, here borrowing from Song of Songs 6:3.[380] Who better to make the Lord shine forth from his holy places than the mother who gave birth to him from the sanctuary of her womb? But if she was beautiful and comely, why was she so terrifying? Because, of course, as Barker notes, in the temple tradition, the Lady was not only mother of the king, but guardian of the city.[381] As Shaddai, the mighty mountain "in which God is well pleased to dwell," she scattered kings in battle, and snow fell on her peaks (Psalm 67:14–18). The prophet Isaiah described her as bringing destruction on the day of the Lord as he mustered his hosts for battle (Isaiah 13:2–6), and the prophet Micah entreated her: "Arise and thresh, O daughter of Zion, for I will make your horn iron and your hoofs bronze; you shall beat in pieces many people, and shall devote their gain to the Lord" (Micah 4:13 RSV). No wonder the saints were expected to come forth with *two-edged swords in their hands* (Psalm 149:6): she was leading them. As the prooemium appended to the "Akathistos" after her victory over the Avars saluted her: "To you, our leader in battle and defender, O Theotokos, I, your city, delivered from sufferings, ascribe hymns of victory and thanksgiving."[382] Accordingly, Andrew of Crete called upon all the people of the city—the fathers and patriarchs, prophets, priests, and apostles, martyrs, doctors, and souls of the just, saints, kings, rulers and ruled, *young men and virgins, old men and youths* (Psalm 148:12)—to run together and praise her as she, the camp of God, "left the tents of Kedar [cf. Psalm 119:5 LXX] for the incorporeal tents of a new life." "All nations, bless her," he exhorted his fellow citizens on the feast of her Dormition, "all tongues, call her blessed; sing to the Mother of God, all tribes of the earth—sing! Begin to sing and sound the cymbals, raise a joyful cry, magnify her, sing her praises!"[383] As well they should, given that she was their protectress and queen.[384]

At this point in the Marian Office, as we have already noted, there were certain choices to be made in the selection of psalms, never mind the antiphons, which were always more various than the above exposition has been able to indicate, concentrating as it has on explicating the psalms through the antiphons with which they appear in the oldest extant antiphoner for the Marian feasts as well as in the latterly standard Use of Rome. Should one follow the Use of Fonte Avellana or Oxford, Paris or Sarum, Monte Cassino or Rome?[385] That of Fonte Avellana would seem to recommend itself as the inspiration for Paris, but that of Monte Cassino and the English monasteries of Winchester and Muchelney would seem to be the older, following as it does the standard secular cursus for weekdays (suggesting less innovation on the part of its authors). The Uses of Oxford and Sarum share two out of three psalms at Prime with that of Rome, and like Rome as well as Paris, they use the Gradual Psalms for the Little Hours of Terce, Sext, and None, but the Roman Use followed the proper psalms for the Marian feasts for Vespers, while Paris, Oxford, and Sarum repeated five of the Gradual Psalms. Rome differed from Paris, Oxford, and Sarum at Compline as well, this time the Roman Use continuing with the Gradual Psalms, while the northern uses followed a selection first witnessed at Saint Alban's, and, possibly, Fonte Avellana. And, as we have noted, the Dominicans and Geert Grote's popular Dutch translation of the Marian Office followed yet another pattern of psalms, so as to include all fifteen Gradual Psalms (119 through 133) over the course of the day.

Here, unlike with the antiphons and psalms for Matins and Lauds, the dominant patterns of usage are not necessarily the earliest, while the earliest and/or dominant are not necessarily the most Marian, as, arguably, the Dominican concentration on the Gradual Psalms in fact was. One might simply comment on all of the psalms used for a particular hour, but not only would this be unwieldy, not to mention taxing even further the patience of the reader; it would also, in effect, be unrepresentative of the Office as it was practiced, elongating the day at the expense of the night. And yet, choosing only one cursus of psalms would be likewise unrepresentative of the complexity with which Mary's medieval devotees thought about her, able as they were to see her in more psalms than the structure of the Office allowed for any one day. For consistency's sake, it seems best that we go, as the Church did after Trent, with Rome, given that the antiphons we have been using for our exegesis thus far were adopted there, too. But again, unlike with the antiphons and psalms for Matins and Lauds, we have no earlier witnesses to the association of these texts liturgically; the earliest antiphoners from the ninth and tenth centuries give only the texts for Matins, Lauds, and, occasionally, Vespers, not those for the other hours of the day. To make things even more complicated, if they weren't sufficiently so already, there were also seasonal variations within particular uses, such that even at Rome, there might be different antiphons associated with particular hours of the Marian Office in Advent and at Christmastide than during the rest of the year. On the one hand, we risk saying too much (as if one could ever say enough about Mary); on the other, we risk saying too little (which, truth be told, she might in her humility prefer). Perhaps, in our dilemma, we may appreciate why there were so many variations on Mary's Office, intended as it was to praise the queen standing beside the king in her multicolored robes (Psalm 44:10). One might as easily attempt to describe the rainbow surrounding the king's sapphire throne—according to Barker, yet another image of the Lady, as well as the sign of the everlasting covenant that El Shaddai set in the cloud.[386] We must choose but a single hue to follow here, so as to be able to trace the arc of the bow, all the while remembering that the Lady's glory came in many colors, all of them brilliant, all revealing her mystery in magnificent and often startling ways.

We continue, therefore, following the Use of Rome in our choice of antiphons and psalms. Although not associated with these particular psalms—because the manuscript does not give psalms for the day hours after Lauds—all but one of the nine antiphons for the Little Hours and Vespers (there is no antiphon in the Roman Use for Compline) appear in the antiphoner for Compiègne among the antiphons used for the Feast of the Assumption, the four for the Little Hours at

Lauds, four of the five for Vespers in a series of antiphons to be used *in evange-lio*. Seven of these nine, including the odd one out, are taken from the Song of Songs; the other two refer explicitly to Mary's Assumption. Although not in the antiphoner of Compiègne, the ninth antiphon, **Dum esset rex** (CAO #2450), appears as a chant for the votive Office of the Virgin and for the Common of Virgins in the antiphoner of Albi (Albi, Bibliothèque municipale Rochegude, 44, ca. 890), according to CANTUS, the only other known relatively complete ninth-century source for the chants of the Divine Office.[387] All of the antiphons, in other words, are once again among our most ancient sources for the way in which her Western devotees honored the Virgin in their liturgy.

PRIME, SUNG AT THE FIRST HOUR OF THE DAY (ABOUT 6 A.M.)

Psalms 53 *Deus in nomine tuo*, 84 *Benedixisti Domine*,
and 116 *Laudate Dominum*

The antiphon under which these three psalms were sung, the same with which the hour of Lauds began, reminds us once again of our heavenly setting: **Mary has been assumed into heaven: the angels rejoice and, praising, they bless the Lord.**[388] The queen has been received into the court of the king, the Lady has returned to the temple where the Lamb who was slain now reigns from the tree. Like Queen Esther, she now sets herself to pray for her people, that they might be spared the anger of the king (Esther 5, 7, 15). According to its inscription, David composed Psalm 53 when the Ziphites came to Saul and told him, "Do you not realize that David is hiding among us?" (cf. 1 Samuel 23:19 RSV). Who, Augustine asks, are these Ziphites, the enemies of David? Their name means "those who flourish" or "flower," thus, "the flourishing children of this world," who trust in their own riches, rather than in the ways of God. Esther, however, trusted not in her riches, but in her humility, "and in her prayer [to the king] she confessed that all her royal insignia were of no more value to her than a dirty rag."[389] As the antiphon suggests, Mary, now assumed to stand beside the Lord in heaven, comes before her spouse and king with similar humility to petition for her people, praying to him, in David's words: *O God, hear my prayer; give ear to the words of my mouth* (Psalm 53:4). "Behold," Maximus the Confessor wondered in the conclusion to his *Life* of the Virgin,

> what mind will fathom, or what tongue will express, or what master scribe's hand will write the innumerable multitude of the graces and benevolences of the holy and ever-virgin Theotokos, which she manifested and manifests from day

to day among the human race? She is the ardent intercessor with her son, Christ God, for all those who entreat her ... the calm harbor of all those buffeted by waves ... the guide on the way of life for all who have gone astray ... the one who seeks and converts those who are lost ... the help and support of those who are afflicted ... the intercessor and mediator of those who are penitent.[390]

More exalted than the thrones, cherubim, and seraphim, she is now a second mediator for humanity, "a second offering of our nature to the Father after the first one who was himself sacrificed one time on behalf of all, and she is ever living to intercede on behalf of those who approach God through her."[391] As the psalmist prayed: *I will freely sacrifice to thee and will give praise, Lord, to thy name because it is good* (Psalm 53:8), that is, Augustine explains, "I will sacrifice to you" not because "you have given me productive estates ... gold and silver ... a huge fortune, lots of money and a position of honor," but because "I can find nothing better than your name."[392]

Lord, thou hast blessed thy land, the psalmist continues. *Thou hast turned away the captivity of Jacob ... Convert us, O God, our saviour, and turn off thy anger from us. Wilt thou be angry with us for ever, or wilt thou extend thy wrath from generation to generation?* (Psalm 84:2, 5–6). No, Maximus would insist; not if the Virgin Mary can help. She is "our advocate and intercessor" with the Lord, who "[turns] away his wrath and anger, which comes justly on account of our sins and transgressions, but [she spreads] forth his mercy and sweetness upon us. How great," Maximus exclaims, thinking on her intercession for her people with her Son, "are your supernatural benefactions and mercies, O holy Virgin!"[393] As Maximus would have it, Mary is the one through whom God turns again and brings his people to life, the one through whom he grants them salvation and speaks *peace unto his people* (Psalm 84:7–9). *Surely*, the psalmist reassures the people of the Lord, *his salvation is near to them that fear him, that glory may dwell in our land* (Psalm 84:10). As Barker reads it: "The voice in the psalm gives a glimpse of the land revived and the eternal covenant restored for the people who do not return to their ways of rejecting Wisdom. The glory returns."[394] Just as, in Barker's words, "Wisdom and the throne of glory had originally been together in Day One, the holy of holies," so now Mary, the mother of Wisdom, is together with her Son in heaven where, as the seventh-century homilist Theoteknos of Livias put it, "she has free access to God" and "is available to us all as our intercessor." It is she, Theoteknos would insist, to whom the prophet David refers in the psalm as *peace*, when he says, *Righteousness and peace have kissed. Truth has sprung up from the earth* (Psalm 84:11–12 LXX). "Mary is peace," Theoteknos explains. "Christ is righteousness and Christ is truth. The Mother of God is the earth [yielding *its fruit*] (Psalm 84:13 LXX), [that is] the bread that will never fail us, Christ."395 Andrew of Crete would concur: Mary was the "land causing the truth to arise" when the mercy of the Son met with the true assumption of humanity in the Virgin's womb, thus joining heavenly things to those on earth so as to "bring about in us the salvation which the Father was well pleased [to effect] through him."396 Augustine suggests a similar reading: "*Truth has sprung up from the earth*, because Christ was born from a woman . . . because the Son of God has come forth from the flesh. . . . Truth was born from the virgin Mary, that he might be in a position to offer sacrifice for those who needed justification, the sacrifice of his passion, the sacrifice of the cross."397 For Cassiodorus, the meeting of mercy and truth, justice and peace also signifies the meeting of the Old and New Testaments, united by the incarnation "in an interlinked chain . . . [and] a reciprocal harmony," while "Truth springs from the earth when the confession of a sinner is offered, and Justice looks down from heaven when there is forgiveness of sins."398

Accordingly, the third psalm of the hour exults: *Alleluia! O Praise the Lord, all ye nations! Praise him, all ye people! For his mercy is confirmed upon us, and the truth of the Lord remaineth for ever* (Psalm 116:1–2). With the Virgin in heaven, or so her medieval devotees insisted, Wisdom has been restored to the earth. She was also, thereby, or so the psalms for the following hours suggest, restored to the temple, where she was daily the Lord's delight (cf. Proverbs 8:30).

TERCE, SEXT, AND NONE, SUNG AT THE THIRD, SIXTH, AND NINTH HOURS OF THE DAY (ABOUT 9 A.M., 12 P.M., AND 3 P.M.)

How did she come there? As with Prime, the antiphons for the other Little Hours of the day in the Roman Use reiterate those used at Lauds. At Terce, Mary is **assumed to the heavenly chamber, where the King of kings sits upon his starry throne.**399 At Sext, **we run to the odor of [her] ointments**, while **the young maidens [love her] exceedingly.**400 At None, she is **beautiful and comely . . . terrible as an army set in array.**401 With the psalms for these hours, however, the setting is arguably somewhat different. With the antiphons, we are still, as it were, in heaven, the queen standing beside the throne, but the psalms focus rather on the location of the throne in the temple at the top of its fifteen steps. This, at least, is the way in which the psalms sung at these hours had been read since antiquity, both in the rabbinic and in the Christian tradition.

The psalms for the hours of Terce, Sext, and None in the Use of Rome as in the Rule of Saint Benedict belong to a group of fifteen psalms, each of which bears the same title: *sir hammaalot*, translated in the Septuagint as Ὠιδὴ τῶν ἀναβαθμῶν ("Song of degrees") and in the Vulgate as *Canticum graduum* ("Song of steps" or "Song of ascents"). The title, a technical one, has been variously explained: as a "pilgrim song" sung by the people as they "went up" to Jerusalem for the three great annual festivals of Passover, Weeks, and Tabernacles (cf. Exodus 23:14–17; Deuteronomy 16:16; 1 Kings 12:28 RSV; Matthew 20:17; Luke 2:41); as a song sung by the exiles returning from Babylon as they "went up" to the holy city; or as a song sung by the Levitical priests as they ascended the fifteen steps from the court of the women to the hall of the Israelites in the temple, the latter being a tradition from the Mishnah attributed to Rabbi Eliezer ben Jacob and dating to about 200 C.E. that was known to Jerome.[402] Poetically, the psalms also share an "ascending" structure, as Dahood explains, "in which each verse takes up and repeats a word or clause from the preceding verse," prompting some scholars to suggest that this is the "ascent" to which the title refers.[403] For Augustine, in contrast, the ascent is one to be made primarily in the heart. There are fifteen psalms just as there were fifteen steps in the temple, but the steps of the psalms are those that have been placed in the heart, "set up by God through his grace."[404] These steps the soul climbs from "the valley of weeping," not with bodily feet, but "by loving. While you are climbing," Augustine avers, "the song of ascents rings out." And what does the soul climb? The mountain, that is, the Lord Jesus Christ, who made himself into a valley of weeping in his Passion that fallen human beings might ascend to eternal life.[405] For Cassiodorus, the fifteen psalms signify the mystery of the Old and New Testaments, the number seven denoting "the week occasioned by the sabbath of the Old Testament," while the number eight signifies the Lord's day on which he rose again. As the psalmist mounts the fifteen steps, he begins with the renunciation of the world and ascends by way of the merits of the saints to "the perfect and eternal love of the Lord, which as we know is set at the very summit of the virtues."[406] As with Augustine, although Cassiodorus notes that the number of psalms alludes to the physical steps in Solomon's temple, the psalmist's ascent is to be read as that of the soul. Further, both Augustine and Cassiodorus note that while in Latin it is impossible to tell which way the steps (*gradus*) are leading, in Greek the direction is clear: the steps lead up (ἀνα).[407]

By the later Middle Ages, as is well-known, it was simply assumed that Mary herself must have sung these same psalms as, like the Levitical priests, she ascended the steps of the temple, albeit at the age of three. As Jacobus de Voragine told it in his *Legenda aurea*: "Around the Temple there were fifteen steps, corresponding to the fifteen Gradual Psalms, and because the Temple was built on a hill, there was no way to go to the altar of holocaust . . . except by climbing the steps. The virgin child was set down at the lowest step and mounted to the top without help from anyone, as if she were already fully grown up."[408] By the fifteenth century, or so the N-Town *Mary Play* would have it, the three-year-old Mary not only mounted the fifteen steps on her own, but cited the first verse of each psalm in both Latin and the vernacular as she climbed.[409] In the play, the bishop marvels at such learning in a child so young. We may wonder rather at how Mary came to be so closely associated with the Gradual Psalms, particularly given, as we have noted, that the earliest versions of her Office as attested in the manuscripts used Psalm 118.[410]

A partial answer to this development may appear in the late eleventh-century *Liber confortatorius*, written by the monk Goscelin of Saint-Bertin for his friend, Eva, who had recently left her nunnery at Wilton to become a recluse. In advising Eva on how to structure her daily prayer, Goscelin told her the following vividly imagined story, which, he said, he had heard from a certain learned monk (*a quodam monacho non indocto*):

> The Virgin [Mary], unique among all others, who would give birth to God, once rose in the middle of the night, as was her sacred custom, to sing divine hymns. As she rose [she] intoned the gradual psalm; and when she arrived at the verse where it says, "May the Lord watch over your comings in and goings out" [Psalm 120:8]—at that very moment the Archangel Gabriel entered with heavenly splendor, so that the Virgin appeared to be receiving him with this greeting. More importantly, she received the one who the messenger said would be born of her, and the Lord would be watching over his "going in," in his conception, and over his "going out," in his birth. Thus, her spirit rejoicing from this angelic message in God her savior, she entered the Synagogue chanting the following psalm: "I was glad when they said to me, let us go into the house of the Lord" [Psalm 121:1].[411]

In her recent exegesis of this passage, one of the very few from this period that we have giving us such imaginative detail of the Virgin's devotional life, Monika Otter concentrates on the way in which Goscelin suggests that he, as a monk, understood the performance of the Gradual Psalms, sung since the ninth century as the monks, like Mary in the story, made their way from their dormitory to the choir for Matins. As Goscelin tells it, the monk, again like Mary, experiences the Gradual Psalms as the moment of the Annunciation, anticipating, as it were, the Ave Maria with which the Marian Office at Matins began (the suggestion, according to Otter, is intentionally erotic).[412] For our purposes, however, it is the more striking not that Goscelin imagines himself as a monk participating in the moment of Mary's impregnation with God, but that he imagines her as a nun, experiencing the coming of the Lord as she was singing "divine hymns." Such, as we have seen, was the expectation in the temple, that is, that singing would invoke the presence of the Lord; such, Goscelin would seem to suggest, was Mary's experience as she mounted the steps of the temple in song.

In the N-Town play, Mary reflects step by step on all fifteen of the Gradual Psalms, suggesting that here, at least, she was following the Dominican Use or, possibly, Geert Grote's practice of reciting all fifteen psalms over the course of Prime, Terce, Sext, None, and Compline. But, as we have noted, in the Roman Use, which we are following, as well as those of Paris, Sarum, and Oxford, she would have said only the first nine of the psalms during Terce, Sext, and None, concluding with Psalms 128, 129, and 130 at Compline. What was Mary thinking as she climbed the steps of the temple or, as Goscelin imagined it, made her way to the choir, singing the Gradual Psalms?

Psalms 119 *Ad Dominum*, 120 *Levavi oculos*, and 121 *Laetatus sum in his*

It is the third hour of the day. According to the *Mary Play*, with her first step the three-year-old Mary commented on the first verse of Psalm 119: "The fyrst degre gostly applyed, / It is holy desyre with God to be."[413] At the very least, this suggests that she—or, more prosaically, the author of the play—may have been reading Augustine, who likewise suggests that with this psalm the Christian begins to think about addressing himself to the ascent in the heart by scorning "earthly, perishable, temporal things" and resolving to follow Christ.[414] In Cassiodorus's words, here "the first step of the virtues is taken, in which the prophet abandons earthly vices, and with tearful confession begs to be freed from the affliction of this world." Almost immediately, however, the climber encounters *wicked lips* and *a deceitful tongue* (v. 2) who attempt to dissuade her from making the ascent. "Why," Cassiodorus imagines them asking, "do you torture yourself, fleeing from worldly honours and abandoning human attractions, with the result that you both lose the world and fail ever to attain what you long for?"[415] But Mary, the antiphon assures us, **has been assumed to the heavenly chamber, where the King of kings sits upon his starry throne.**[416] She has, as Andrew of Crete put it, "left the tents of Kedar for the incorporeal tents of a new life."[417] It is easy to imagine how she suffered as a sojourner in this life [dwelling] *with the inhabitants of Kedar* (v. 5), above all how much she longed to be once again with her Son.[418] Now, however, or so the antiphon invites us to imagine, she has begun her ascent to be with him in heaven, that is, in the Holy of Holies in the temple, as once she was in life when he dwelled within her as in the Holy of Holies.

I have lifted up my eyes to the mountains from whence help shall come to me, the psalmist prays. *My help is from the Lord, who made heaven and earth* (Psalm 120:1–2). "The secunde [degre]," the child Mary explained as she ascended the temple steps, "is stody with meke inquysissyon, veryly, / How I xal have knowynge of Godys wylle." Barker notes that this psalm is one of only five in which Yahweh is named as the one "who made heaven and earth" (cf. Psalms 113:23; 123:8; 133:3; 145:5–6), suggesting the equation between Yahweh and El and the exclusion of the Lady and her Son characteristic of the Deuteronomists' reforms.[419] Oddly, Augustine makes relatively little of the phrase at this point. Cassiodorus, however, reads in these two verses a categorical syllogism: "*My help is from the Lord, who made heaven and earth*. Every person whose help is from the Lord who made heaven and earth gets his help from the true God. So my help is help from the true God"[420]—with which syllogism, presumably, the Deuteronomists could not help but be pleased, proving as it does the identity of the Lord with the Most High, except that this would seem to prove the Christians' point that Jesus was true God as well. Clearly, this is a matter for "meke inquysissyon, veryly." But for Mary, this inquiry has an ethical aspect as well as a theological one: to know God's will. As Modestus of Jerusalem explained, she herself is the one through whom Christians learn to ascend: "So it is written, 'My help comes from the Lord, who made heaven and earth': through her, he has made known to us the way to ascend to him by right faith, and by the good life that leads to heaven."[421] She is likewise, as Germanus of Constantinople suggested, the one who watches over the faithful and "neither sleeps nor slumbers" (cf. Psalm 120:4). "So," he averred, "we confess, in our faith, that we have [her] with us as a companion on our journey," for although her body may have fallen asleep according to her human nature, her heart keeps watch over Christians even now (cf. Song of Songs 5:2).[422]

And how does she help Christians ascend? *I rejoiced*, Goscelin imagined that she answered Gabriel, *at the things that were said to me, "We shall go into the house of the Lord"* (Psalm 121:1). As if to say: "The thrydde [degre] is gladnes in mende in hope to be, / That we xall be savyd all thus." Mary, as her medieval devotees would have it, is the one through whom humanity has been saved because it is she who gave birth to the Savior. She has gone into the house of the Lord and has been welcomed into his court where he sits over the house of David on his seat of judgment (Psalm 121:2, 5). The Lord watched over her as he went into her at his conception and came out at his birth (cf. Psalm 120:8); likewise, he preserved her at her death, so that now, as the antiphon puts it, she stands beside his starry throne in heaven, praying *for the peace of Jerusalem and abundance for them that love* [him] (Psalm 121:6).

Psalms 122 *Ad te levavi*, 123 *Nisi quia Dominus*, and 124 *Qui confidunt*

It is noon. Mary continues her ascent up the temple steps, as, according to the antiphon, **the young maidens** follow her, rejoicing in **the odor of her ointments.**[423] "The fourte [degre]," she tells her companions, "is meke obedyence as is dette / To Hym that is above the planetys sefne." Thus, the psalmist says: *To thee have I lifted up my eyes who dwellest in heaven* (Hebrew: who are enthroned in heaven).[424] In Psalm 120, the psalmist lifted up his eyes to the mountains; now, as Cassiodorus puts it, he lifts up "the eyes of his heart to the Lord Himself."[425] But how, Augustine wonders, can human beings hope to ascend to heaven when there is such an enormous distance between heaven and earth and yet, "there are no ladders to be seen. Are we not," he asks his listeners, "indulging in wishful thinking when we sing a *Song of Steps*, a song of ascending? No," he assures them. "We ascend to heaven if we think of God, who arranges ascents in our hearts. But," he anticipates their objection, "what does it mean, to ascend in the heart?" He answers: "To draw closer to God" And how does one do that? By lifting up the eyes "to him who dwells in heaven" rather than focusing on oneself.[426] As the psalmist puts it, the eyes of the faithful should be on the Lord God *as the eyes of servants are on the hands of their masters, as the eyes of the handmaid are on the hands of her mistress* (Psalm 122:2). (Cassiodorus notes how the psalmist takes care to mention both sexes.) Thus, the antiphon suggests, the eyes of the young maidens are on the hands of their mistress, Mary, as she lifts up her eyes to her Son, enthroned above the cherubim in heaven, and prays: *Have mercy on us, O Lord, have mercy on us* (v. 3). Or perhaps it is the maidens themselves who pray: *For we are greatly filled with contempt. For our soul is greatly filled: we are a reproach to the rich, and contempt to the proud* (vv. 3–4).

"The fyfte [degre]," Mary cautions the maidens, "is propyr confessyon, / That we be nought withowth God thus." As the psalmist put it: *"If it had not been that the Lord was with us,"* let Israel now say, *"if it had not been that the Lord was with us when men rose up against us, perhaps they had swallowed us up alive"* (Psalm 123:1–3). Who is singing in this psalm, Augustine wonders, given that sometimes the psalms seem to speak in the singular and at others in the plural? Cassiodorus answers: "the holy confessors," who are "aware of the great dangers from which, as from the onrush of a torrent, they have escaped through God's mercy," who, in the first part of the psalm, "confess that they have been freed from so many raging hardships solely through His pity," and in the second, "give thanks that they have not been deceived by their persecutors."[427] Augustine suggests, rather, that it is all the members of the body of Christ, the body "toiling on earth" while the "head looks down from heaven and cares for the body." The body, that is, the members of Christ are singing because "they are in love. . . . Sometimes they sing in their troubles and at other times, when they are singing in hope, they sing exultantly." And what do they hope? "We believe now, and hereafter we shall see. When we believe, we live in this present world in hope; when we see, we shall enjoy the reality in the world to come. Then we shall see God face to face. But face-to-face vision depends on our having cleansed our hearts." This is the confession that the singers invite their listeners to make through the psalm. "Listen to it," Augustine exhorts his listeners,

> as though you were hearing yourselves. Listen as though you were looking at your own reflection in the mirror of the scriptures. When you gaze into the scriptural mirror your own cheerful face looks back at you. When in your exultant hope you observe the likeness between yourself and other members of Christ, the members who first sang these verses, you will be certain that you are among his members, and you too will sing them.[428]

The singers are happy, Augustine explains, "because they have escaped." From what? According to the psalm: *Our soul hath passed through a torrent . . . Our soul hath been delivered as a sparrow out of the snare of the fowlers. The snare is broken, and we are delivered* (Psalm 123:5, 7). In other words, from sin and death, just as the Virgin Mary, the Mother of *the Lord, who made heaven and earth* (Psalm 123:8) was preserved from corruption in her falling asleep.

On the sixth step, the psalmist recalls the location of the temple on the mountain of Zion and the city in which those who trust in the Lord dwell: *They that trust in the Lord shall be as Mount Zion; he shall not be moved for ever that dwelleth in Jerusalem* (Psalm 124:1–2). Mary comments: "The sexte [degre] is confidens in Goddys strenght alon; / For of all grace from Hym comyth the strem." Perhaps the maidens following in her fragrance recall at this point how Mary herself was the mountain "which surpasses and transcends every hill and every mountain, [that is to say], the height of men and of angels. . . . Mountain of God," John of Damascus eulogized her, "rich mountain, curdled mountain, rich mountain, the mountain which God has been pleased to dwell in [cf. Psalm 67:16–18]. . . . Summit more holy than Sinai, which is covered not only by smoke, nor shadow, nor tempest, nor fearful fire, but by the shining illumination of the all-holy Spirit."[429] "Truly," John of Euboea remarked on the feast of her Conception, "the mountain of Zion rejoiced and the daughters of Judea exulted (cf. Psalm 47:12) . . . when the temple of God was now brought to God in a temple, when an undefiled girl paradoxically walking into the holy of holies on the fleetest of feet [went] to dwell there."[430] Mounting the steps, Mary progresses ever further in contemplation, ascending in virtue as she ascends in mind, longing for the heights but wary of losing her footing. As Augustine comments: "As we make our ascent and lift our souls to the Lord our God with love and devotion, [the current] psalm teaches us to pay no attention to the prosperous folk of this world."[431] Just so, as Germanus told it, Mary kept herself focused on God as she went up to the "threshold of the holy dwelling-place, for whose splendor of beauty the happy daughters of Jerusalem weave praise as they rejoice."[432]

Psalms 125 *In convertendo*, 126 *Nisi Dominus*, and 127 *Beati omnes*

It is the middle of the afternoon, about the ninth hour. **You are beautiful and comely, daughter of Jerusalem**, the daughters of Jerusalem praise her, terrible as an army set in array.[433] To which the psalmist replies: *When the Lord brought back the captivity of Zion we became like men comforted* (Psalm 125:1). Mary explains to the daughters who are accompanying her on her way up the steps: "The sefte [degre] is undowteful hope of immortalyte / In oure Lordeis grace and mercy." In this, as in the next two steps, Mary's reading of the psalm in the *Mary Play* coheres almost word for word with Augustine's, albeit Augustine's exegesis is of course much more extended. Once again, Augustine reminds his listeners that Psalm 125 is a "Song of Steps . . . sung by people who are ascending. And to what other place," he asks, "can they be ascending but to the Jerusalem on high that is mother of us all, the city in heaven?" Why do they sing as they ascend? Because, Augustine explains, even as they sigh with longing to return to the heavenly city from which they have been exiled, they do so in hope of redemption. "What kind of redemption are they awaiting? That perfect redemption of their humanity of which we have seen an exemplar in the Lord, who rose from the dead and ascended into heaven." Although they still "groan at the prospect of death," the singers become *like people comforted* "because he [who] was the first to rise from the dead . . . gave us hope; distressed though we are at present, this hope has brought us comfort."[434]

Likewise, or so Andrew of Crete would insist, Mary's falling asleep should give the singers hope, for by her example, they learn how they will be transformed: "[Death] touched her enough to let her experience that sleep that is [to be] for us . . . a kind of ecstatic movement towards the things we only hope for during this life, a passage that leads us on towards transformation into a state like that of God."[435] Thus, Andrew imagined, the apostles sang as they gathered around her deathbed: "This is the final goal of the covenants God has made with us. . . . This is the first step to all ascent, to all contemplation; the holy tabernacle of him who made the world; the vessel that received the inexhaustible wisdom of God; the inviolate treasury of life. . . . Through this woman, the pledge of our salvation has been made and kept, in that this marvelous creature has both reached the limits of our lot and has paid the common debt proper to our nature."[436] Now, however, she has ascended into heaven where, living "by the torrents of eternal delight, in the meadows of incorruptibility, near the spring of life that is always new," she enjoys "the beauty of [her] Son" and delights "in his inexhaustible joy and in the beatitude that never grows old." "There," the apostles concluded their hymn, "is the goal of all our past and present hopes, the sum of all good things, the revelation of all that is hidden and will only be seen in days to come. . . . There the Father is worshipped, the Son is glorified, the Holy Spirit is praised in song."[437] Or, as the psalmist might put it: *Then was our mouth filled with gladness and our tongue with joy. Then shall they say among the Gentiles, "The Lord hath done great things for them"* (Psalm 125:2).

Having given the daughters hope of heaven, with her next step, however, Mary cautions them: "The eyted [degre] is contempt of veynglory in us. For Hym that al mankende hath multyplyed." In the words of the psalmist: *Unless the Lord build the house they labour in vain that build it. Unless the Lord keep the city he watcheth in vain that keepeth it* (Psalm 126:1). As Augustine explains, noting that the title of this psalm includes Solomon's name: "This man Solomon had built a temple to the Lord, which was a type and figure of the Church and of the body of the Lord. . . . [This] house is also a city, for God's house is nothing else but God's people. . . . And this city is Jerusalem." Jerusalem has its guardians, as well as its builders and watchmen, but their labor is futile unless the one who sees their thoughts guards them himself. But there is a condition: "If we want to be kept safe under the wings of God, guarded by him who was humbled for our sake and exalted for our protection, let us be humble."[438] It is vain for human beings, as the psalmist says (v. 2), *to rise before the light*, that is, before Christ; only *after [they] have sitten*, that is, humbled themselves, should they attempt to rise. And "when," Augustine imagines his listeners might ask, "do we rise up?" "Think now," he answers them,

> when was Christ exalted? After his death. That means that you too must hope for your rising up after death. . . . That is the kind of rising you must hope for.

Be a Christian with that in view, not with an eye to happiness in this world. If you try to be a Christian for the sake of this world's happiness, you are trying to rise before the light, and you will inevitably remain in darkness, for he who is your light sought no worldly happiness. Let yourself be changed, then, and follow your light. Rise as he rose. Sit down first, and rise up only after that, *after I have given sleep to his beloved.*[439]

And the reward for this humility? According to the psalmist, children, *the fruit of the womb* (v. 3), which Augustine reads as the children of the Church, those children, as Cassiodorus puts it, "born of water and the holy Spirit" from the Virgin's womb.[440] Mary, while the humble handmaid of the Lord is also, or so the antiphon reminds its singers, the guardian and mother of the anointed ones, that is, the baptized, who will rise with her after their deaths and ascend with her to heaven; it is she who, **terrible as an army set in array**, leads the daughters into the city of God.

But they are not there yet. Before they ascend, the psalmist suggests, they must learn to fear the Lord. *Blessed,* he says, *are all they that fear the Lord, that walk in his ways* (Psalm 127:1). According to the *Mary Play*, Mary would agree. In her words: "The nynte [degre] is a childely fer indede, / With a longyng love in our Lorde that ay is." Augustine explains: "Let us listen to this psalm in the certainty that it is speaking about Christ. We are grafted into Christ's body; we have been made Christ's members. So let us walk in the Lord's ways and fear him with a chaste fear that abides for ever, in eternity." But what does it mean, Augustine asks, to fear the Lord with a "chaste fear (*timor castus*) enduring for ever" (cf. Psalm 18:10)? (We may recall from our discussion of Psalm 18 that such holy fear was one of the gifts of Wisdom.) Imagine, Augustine suggests, two women, one chaste, who fears her husband, the other an adulteress, who also fears her husband. "The chaste woman fears that her husband may go away; the adulteress fears that hers may return." Now, Augustine encourages his listeners, imagine that Christ, the bridegroom to whom humanity has been wedded, is absent, "in a sense. He gave us his Holy Spirit as his pledge (*arrha*), but he is absent himself; he redeemed us with his blood, but now he has gone away. . . . Question your conscience," Augustine challenges his audience. "Do you want him to come back, or would you prefer him to delay his return?" Chaste fear is like the fear of the chaste woman, who longs for her husband's return and "dreads any delay in his coming, so, when he has come, will it dread his going away." In contrast, "a fear not yet chaste . . . stands in dread of the Lord's presence and is frightened of being punished." So how do Christians know if their fear is chaste? Augustine offers another test:

Suppose God came and spoke to us here in his own voice (he never ceases to speak through his scriptures [*per litteras suas*], of course). But now, imagine that he is here and saying to one of you, "Do you want to sin? All right, go ahead, then: sin. Do anything that gives you pleasure. Anything that you love on earth shall be yours. You are angry with someone? Fine: let him die. You want to lay violent hands on someone? He is yours to seize. If you want to hit someone, you can hit him. If you want someone condemned, condemned he shall be. Whatever you want for yourself, you shall possess it. No one is to oppose you, no one is to say to you, 'What are you doing?' No one will say to you, 'Don't do that.' No one will say, 'Why did you do it?' All the earthly things you crave shall be yours in abundance. You shall live to enjoy them not just for a time but always. But there is just one reservation: you will never see my face."

"You groaned when I said that, my brothers and sisters," Augustine, ever the consummate catechist, remarks. "Why did you groan? Only because chaste fear has been born in you, the fear that *endures for ever and ever*." Chaste fear, as Augustine puts it, weeps and groans at the prospect of never being able to see the Lord's face, just as the psalmist so often prayed (cf. Psalm 79:2–8).[441] Much as it had been the goal of the temple tradition, so we may imagine it was the Virgin's goal as she ascended the steps of the temple at age three as well as her most fervent prayer as she lay on her deathbed: to gaze upon the face of the Lord, the bridegroom whom she loved.[442] As Augustine would have it, it was likewise the goal—or, at the very least, should be—of the daughters of Jerusalem who followed her in her ascent.

VESPERS, SUNG AT SUNSET

Psalm 109 *Dixit Dominus*

The Lord said to my Lord: "Sit thou at my right hand until I make thy enemies thy footstool" (v. 1). It is difficult to imagine a more appropriate psalm with which Vespers in honor of the Virgin might begin (although, of course, in some Uses it was Psalm 121). As Barker has shown, no other psalm was as critical for the identification of Jesus as Lord or his mother as the Lady who anointed him at his birth. As we have seen, Jesus himself quoted it when he challenged the Pharisees to explain how it was that they could say that the Christ was the son of David when David himself, "inspired by the Spirit, calls him Lord" (Matthew 22:41–46; cf. Mark 12:35–37; Luke 20:41–44). The Letter to the Hebrews cites the same psalm as proof that Christ "did not exalt himself to be made a high priest, but was appointed by him who said to him, 'Thou art my Son, today I have begotten thee' [Psalm 2:7]; as he says also in another place, 'Thou art a priest for ever, after the order of Melchizedek' [Psalm 109:4]" (Hebrews 5:5–6 RSV). For Cassiodorus, Psalm 109 is "the sun of our faith, the mirror of the heavenly secret, the chest of the holy Scriptures, in which all that is told in the proclamation of both testaments is spoken in summary."[443] For Augustine, the psalm "speaks prophetically of our Lord and Savior Jesus Christ with such certainty and clarity that we cannot doubt that it is he who is proclaimed here."[444] Dahood, like Barker, notes its resemblance to Psalm 2, where the Lord acknowledges the king as his son.[445] For Barker, both psalms point to the ritual in which the king entered into the Holy of Holies where, anointed (or "bedewed"), he was "begotten" (or resurrected) as the Melchizedek priest, that is, "the presence or face of the Lord, Immanuel." It was in this sense, she contends, that Jesus of Nazareth claimed to have been the Son of God, the human presence of Yahweh, by way of his anointing by John at his baptism, when the heavens opened and the Spirit of God came down on him like a dove and a voice from heaven declared: "Thou art my beloved Son; with thee I am well pleased" (Mark 1:10–11; cf. Matthew 3:16–17; Luke 3:21–22 RSV).[446]

But whose voice did Jesus hear coming down like a dove? The Synoptic Gospels do not say, but according to the *Gospel of the Hebrews* (or Nazarenes) as cited by Jerome in his commentary on Isaiah 11:2, it was "the whole fount of the Holy Spirit [who] descended and rested upon him, and said to him, 'My Son, in all the prophets I was waiting for you, that you might come, and that I might rest in you. For you are my rest; and you are my firstborn son, who reigns forever.' "[447] And who was this "Spirit"? According to the same gospel as cited by both Origen and Jerome: his mother. As Origen has it in his commentary on John 2:12: "If any accept the Gospel of the Hebrews, here the Savior says: 'Even so did my mother, the Holy Spirit, take me by one of my hairs, and carry me to the great Mount Tabor.' "[448] "Spirit," Jerome explains, just in case anybody was worried, "is of feminine gender in Hebrew."[449] As, we may note, so is Wisdom in Hebrew (*chokhmah*), as well as in Latin (*sapientia*) and Greek (σοφία, *sophia*).[450] "In all these [creatures]," Wisdom declares in the first lesson for Matins of the Marian Office in the Roman Use, "I sought rest (*requiem quaesivi*). . . . Then the creator of all things commanded, and said to me: and he that made me rested in my tabernacle (*requievit in tabernaculo meo*)" (Ecclesiasticus 24:11–12). "And so," she declares in the second lesson for Matins, as well as in the little chapter at Terce, "was I established in Zion, and in the holy city likewise I rested (*requievi*), and my power was in Jerusalem" (Ecclesiasticus 24:15). Continuing the second lesson at Sext, she elaborates:

"I took root in an honorable people, and in the portion of my God his inheritance: and my abode is in the full assembly of saints" (Ecclesiasticus 24:16). While in the third lesson and at None, she asserts: "In the streets, like cinnamon and aromatic balm, I gave forth a sweet fragrance: like the choicest myrrh, I yielded a sweetness of odor" (Ecclesiasticus 24:19–20). Now, at Vespers, in the first antiphon, she rejoices in the words of the bride (Song of Songs 1:11): **While the king was at his rest, my nard gave forth the odor of sweetness.**[451] And, in the words of the psalm, she confirms: *In the brightness of the saints, from the womb, before the day-star, I have begot thee . . . "Thou art a priest for ever according to the order of Melchizedek"* (Psalm 109:3–4).[452]

As Mary's ancient and medieval devotees read these texts, Wisdom sought her rest in the city on the mountain, and the Creator of all things came to rest in her; the Spirit sought her rest in her firstborn son, and the Lord, the maker of heaven and earth, came to rest in the tabernacle of his Mother's womb. The human being is anointed in the assembly of the holy ones and comes forth from the Holy of Holies bearing the presence of the Lord; the King of kings rests in the chamber of his bride, and she gives forth the sweet fragrance of the oil with which she anointed him as priest. The woman clothed with the sun gives birth to the Morning and Evening Star; she rises like the dawn, "beautiful as the moon, chosen as the sun, terrible as an army set in array" (Song of Songs 6:9, the little chapter at Prime), and the daughters of Zion declare her most blessed (cf. Song of Songs 6:8, the little chapter at Lauds). Even Augustine, not otherwise famous for his devotion to the Virgin Mary, seems to have known something of this mystery. "As we learn from the book of Revelation," he avers,

> the human Jesus was born of a virgin in a solitary place. . . . The woman bore him to rule his people with an iron rod. But this woman is the ancient city of God, of which a psalm sings, *Glorious things are spoken of you, city of God* (Psalm 86:3). . . . As a man he was made lowly, yet all the while he was the Most High who established the city in which he was himself made man. This is why the woman who bore him is said to have been clothed with the sun, the very sun of righteousness, unknown to the godless. . . . This woman who was clothed with the sun was pregnant with a male child and about to give birth. Her child was he who had founded Zion, and the woman was the city of God, protected by the radiant light of him whom she was bearing in the flesh. With good reason, too, was she depicted with the moon under her feet, because in her strength and holiness she trampled on the mortality of flesh which, moon-like, waxes and wanes.[453]

Here, the virgin who gives birth to the human mediator between God and humanity in the flesh is at once the woman whom the seer beheld in the heavens clothed with the sun and the glorious city of Zion. The child born of her is also the one who founded the city and who will therefore say of her, "Zion, my mother" (cf. Psalm 86:5). *Out of Zion*, the psalmist assures "my Lord," *will the Lord send forth the scepter of thy power* (Psalm 109:2), "and thou shalt rule them with a rod of iron" (Psalm 2:9)—just as the male child born of the virgin and caught up to God and his throne was to rule all the nations "with an iron rod" (Revelation 12:5).[454]

"Hail, divine altar erected on God's foundation!" Modestus of Jerusalem greeted Mary in his homily for her Dormition:

> Through you the atoning and saving sacrifice for the whole world came forth, Christ our God. For from you, holy Mother of God, he put on that vestment of flesh prepared for him by the Holy Spirit, and came forth as "a priest forever, according to the order of Melchizedek," as Scripture says; and he has decreed that he will take you as his partner, in order to provide forever a propitiary sacrifice for all humanity, as you intercede for them.[455]

Germanus of Constantinople likewise insisted that it was the Spirit who begot the Son *from the womb before the morning star*, although by this point, of course, the Conciliar Fathers had agreed that "Spirit" must share the same substance with the Father such that "the Father makes the activity of the all-holy Spirit his own" in begetting the Son.[456] But what if, instead, they had followed the *Gospel of the Hebrews* in acknowledging the Spirit as Jesus's *mother*? As Augustine observed: "By his birth from the Father, as God-with-God, co-eternal with his Begetter, [the Lord] is not a priest. He is a priest only because of the flesh he assumed, the body he received from us to offer as a sacrificial victim for us."[457] In other words, what if he is *a priest for ever according to the order of Melchizedek*, that is, a priest of the Most High, only through his birth from the Virgin? After all, as the antiphon declares, it is the Lady who anointed him priest with her nard.

Psalm 112 *Laudate pueri*

Alleluia, the title of this psalm declares. That is, as we have seen: "Make the Lord shine forth [from the Holy of Holies]."[458] Like Psalms 148–150 at Lauds, this is a psalm of praise, a psalm invoking the presence of the Lord. It invites the children of the Lord to praise his Name *from the rising of the sun unto the going down of the same*, proclaiming him exalted *above all the nations and his glory above the heavens* (vv. 1–4). *Who is as the Lord our God?* the psalmist asks. He is the one *who dwelleth on high and looketh down on the low things in heaven and in earth, raising up the needy from the earth and lifting up the poor out of the dunghill that he may place them with princes, with the princes of his people* (vv. 5–8). As if to say with Hannah, the mother of Samuel, as she offered her son in the temple: "He raiseth up the needy from the dust, and lifteth up the poor from the dunghill: that he may sit with princes, and hold the throne of glory" (1 Kings [Samuel] 2:8). Or with the Virgin herself: "He hath put down the mighty from their seat, and hath exalted the humble. He hath filled the hungry with good things; and the rich he hath sent empty away" (Luke 1:52–53). This is why, Augustine explains, the psalmist calls the singers "children" (*pueri*): it is to remind them of the humility with which the Lord says that they are to approach the kingdom of God. "People who think themselves important do not sing these words," he told his brethren, "nor did those who, though knowing God, did not glorify him as God or give him thanks."[459] Thus, Mary would sing, "he hath received Israel his servant (L: *puerum suum*), being mindful of his mercy" (Luke 1:54).

His left hand under my head, and his right hand shall embrace me, the antiphon asserts in the words of the bride (Song of Songs 2:6, 8:3).[460] He *maketh a barren woman to dwell in a house the joyful mother of children* (v. 9), the psalmist concurs. Or, as Mary put it: "As he spoke to our fathers: to Abraham and to his seed for ever" (Luke 1:55). Augustine explains: "He who dwells in the heights . . . multiplies Abraham's seed like the stars of heaven . . . [and] like the sand on the seashore by separating that merciful, uncountable multitude from the waves on the left [hand] and from the bitter, salty sea of unbelief."[461] Read from within the temple tradition on which we have argued the devotion to the Virgin was founded, the imagery here is dense and complex. Mary is the bride embraced by the divine bridegroom who, although a virgin, brings forth many children of Abraham. Her Son lifts the children up from the earth to the heavens, where he has established heavenly thrones for them. He sets the lowly whom he has raised up from the dunghill on his right hand with the princes of his people, separating them from those on the left who do not praise his Name (cf. Revelation 4–5, 12). Proverbs suggests yet another reading of the scene. "Blessed is the man that findeth Wisdom," the king declares. "Length of days is in her right hand, and in her left hand riches and glory" (Proverbs 3:13, 16). The setting is the mountaintop, where the Lord dwells on high and the Tree of Life stands to one side (cf. Proverbs 3:18). By Wisdom, "the Lord . . . hath founded the earth, hath established the heavens by prudence. By his wisdom the depths have broken out and the clouds grow thick with dew" (Proverbs 3:19–20).

Alternatively yet again, this is the scene as one second-century B.C.E. Greek writer put it, as cited in the fourth century C.E. by Eusebius of Caesarea in his *Preparatio evangelica*. The speaker is Moses, describing his vision on Mount Sinai:

> Methought upon Mount Sinai's brow I saw
> A mighty throne that reached to heaven's high vault,
> Whereon there sat a man of noblest mien
> Wearing a royal crown; whose left hand held
> A mighty sceptre; and his right to me
> Made sign, and I stood forth before the throne.
> He gave me then the sceptre and the crown,
> And bade me sit upon the royal throne,
> From which himself removed. Thence I looked forth
> Upon the earth's wide circle, and beneath
> The earth itself, and high above the heaven.
> Then at my feet, behold! a thousand stars
> Began to fall, and I their number told,
> As they passed by me like an armed host:
> And I in terror started up from sleep![462]

Here, as Barker reads it, Moses "(or someone) ascending Sinai [has] been fused with the person who entered the holy of holies to be made king."[463] There, as in the temple tradition, he is shown the archetypes of all things, whence seated on the throne he looks out on the whole of creation, just as Wisdom once did as she stood beside (or supported) the throne. As we have seen, in this reading of the tradition, Moses (that is, the Law) has supplanted Wisdom as the one on whom the Lord bases his covenant, but in Revelation it is the Lamb who is seated upon the throne and to whom all the creatures on heaven and earth sing: "To him who sits upon the throne and to the Lamb be blessing and honor and glory and might for ever and ever!" (Revelation 5:13 RSV). In the psalm as sung at Vespers in the Virgin's Office, the poor and needy one lifted up from the earth and set with the princes is at once the human king seated upon his throne in the Holy of Holies, and, by virtue of the antiphon, Wisdom or the Virgin herself, lifted up in her humility to sit beside the Lamb in heaven.[464]

Psalm 121 *Laetatus sum in his*

With this psalm, at Terce, Mary was assumed to the heavenly chamber, where the King of kings sits upon his starry throne.[465] Now, according to the antiphon for Vespers, she rejoices: **I am black but beautiful, daughters of Jerusalem: therefore the king has loved me, and brought me into his chamber** (cf. Song of Songs 1:4, 3).[466] *I rejoiced,* she reiterates in the psalm, *at the things that were said to me, "We shall go into the house of the Lord"* (v. 1). But why does she say, I am black? In the Song of Songs, she elaborates: "I am black but beautiful . . . as the tents (*tabernacula*) of Kedar, as the curtains of Solomon. Do not consider me that I am brown, because the sun hath altered my colour" (1:4–5). Taunton suggests that here we see Mary at the foot of the cross, "smitten with grief and plunged in a sea of woe,"[467] but the psalm as well as the other antiphons for the hour arguably tell against this reading. She is black, but also beautiful, [rejoicing] *at the things that were said to* [her]. The setting is still her Assumption and her welcome into the court of heaven, as the use of this antiphon for the Feast of the Assumption likewise suggests.

But there is still something of a mystery why she should be "black." The same verse of the Song of Songs is often cited in explanation of the numerous "Black Madonnas" venerated throughout the later Middle Ages, but as with so many mysteries associated with devotion to the Virgin, the difficulty remains why the Song of Songs should describe the bride in this way, never mind why this verse should be applied to the Virgin long before any of her dark-faced statues are known to have been made.[468] One popular explanation is that here we have a reference to the queen of Sheba, black because she came from the south (1 Kings 10:1–13 RSV), but in the Song of Songs, the bride compares herself rather to the "tents of Kedar" and "the curtains of Solomon," that is, to the hangings of the tabernacle or temple where the ark was kept. Peter J. Leithart notes that "the word for curtains is used almost exclusively with reference to the curtains that made up the tabernacle (Exodus 26:1–13; 36:8–17; Numbers 4:25) or the curtains of David's ark-tabernacle (2 Samuel 7:2; 1 Chronicles 17:1)." While it does not appear in the temple descriptions, "the word is used once, tantalizingly, in connection with Nebuchadnezzar's defeat of the nomads of Kedar (Jeremiah 49:28–29); the king of Babylon carries away Kedar's tents, flocks, and tent curtains."[469]

Kedar was a son of Ishmael, the son of Abraham driven out into the desert when Isaac was born (Genesis 16:15; 21:8–21; 25:13). In the psalms, as we have seen, the tents of Kedar are associated with exile, sojourning in the midst of lying lips and treacherous tongues (Psalm 119:2–5); in Isaiah, "the villages that Kedar inhabits" are set in the desert (Isaiah 42:11 RSV), while Ezekiel associates "all the princes of Kedar" with Arabia (Ezekiel 27:21 RSV). According to Isaiah, however, there would come a time when "all the flocks of Kedar . . . [and] the rams of Nebaioth" would serve before the altar of the Lord, "bring gold and frankincense, and proclaim the praise of the Lord . . . and I [the Lord] will glorify my glorious house" (Isaiah 60:6–7 RSV). "For behold," the prophet promised Zion, "darkness shall cover the earth, and thick darkness the peoples; but the Lord will arise upon you, and his glory will be seen upon you. And nations shall come to your light, and kings to the brightness of your rising" (Isaiah 60:2–3 RSV)—just as the Magi came (from Arabia?) with their gifts of gold, frankincense, and myrrh to worship the child in his mother's arms under the star (Matthew 2:9–11).[470]

The end of exile and the flocks ministering at the altar, the bride beautiful as the curtains of the temple and the Lord beheld in his house surrounded by his glory: all of the signs point to the Lady, exiled from the temple, but at long last restored. "Arise, shine," the prophet invited her city, "for your light has come, and the glory of the Lord has risen upon you" (Isaiah 60:1 RSV). *For thither*, the psalmist responded, *did the tribes go up, the tribes of the Lord*, including all those, like Kedar and Nebaioth (the firstborn of Ishmael, the patriarch of the Gentiles), who had been exiled from the temple but whom Isaiah prophesied would return *to praise the name of the Lord* (Psalm 121:4).

Psalm 126 *Nisi Dominus*

But now the exile is over, and the Lord calls out to his Lady in the words of the antiphon: **Now winter is past, the rain is over and gone: arise, my beloved, and come** (cf. Song of Songs 2:11, 13).[471] As with the previous psalm, we have sung this psalm already at None, where the antiphon praised the Lady **as beautiful and comely . . . terrible as an army set in array.**[472] Now the bridegroom invites his beloved daughter of Jerusalem to arise and come into the house that he built and the city which he keeps (Psalm 126:1). But the Virgin herself is also the house built by the Lord and the city over which he watches. Now, as we have seen, he calls to her, or so John of Damascus imagined, saying: "Come, my blessed Mother, 'into the place of my rest' [Psalm 131:8 LXX]. Arise, come, my dear one, beautiful among all women; 'for behold, winter has passed, and the time of pruning has come' [Song 2:10–12]."[473] "Arise, O Lord," the psalmist urged, "into your resting place: thou and the ark, which thou hast sanctified" (Psalm 131:8). "Today," John preached yet again on the feast of her Dormition,

the living city of God is transported from the earthly Jerusalem to "the Jerusalem which is on high" (Hebrews 12:22), she who has brought forth, as her own first-born, "the first-born of all creation" (Colossians 1:15), the only-begotten of the Father (cf. John 1:14), now dwells in the "assembly of the first-born" (Hebrews 12:23). The living, spiritual ark of the Lord has "gone up to the resting-place" of her Son (Psalm 131:8 LXX).[474]

At Monte Cassino as well as in the earliest English monastic uses, Psalm 131 appears as the fourth of four psalms at Vespers, following Psalms 109, 121, and 126, for reasons which are hopefully now clear. While Psalm 126 speaks of the house and city of God, Psalm 131, like Psalms 23 and 95, was originally composed to be sung for the Feast of the Ark when it was carried in procession up to Jerusalem.[475] As her medieval devotees would have it, Mary, the mother of Wisdom, the first-born of all creation, was herself lifted up to dwell in the assembly of the firstborn; herself the city in which God chose to dwell, she now dwells with the angels in the city of the living God; herself the ark in which the Lord took his rest, she now takes hers in him. As she (that is, Wisdom) says in the little chapter for this same hour: "From the beginning and before the world, was I created, and unto the world to come I shall not cease to be, and in the holy dwelling I have ministered before him" (Ecclesiasticus 24:14).

Psalm 147 *Lauda Jerusalem*

Thus the Virgin, the city and ark of the Lord, the Tree of Life and the bride of the king stands beside the throne of her Son in heaven. **You have become beautiful and sweet in your delights, holy Mother of God**, the antiphon assures her, paraphrasing yet again the words of the bridegroom in the Song of Songs (7:6 Vetus Latina).[476] *Praise the Lord, O Jerusalem! Praise thy God, O Zion!* the psalm invites her. *Because he hath strengthened the bolts of thy gates, he hath blessed thy children within thee* (vv. 1–2). "Blessed," the seer said, "are those who wash their robes [alt. do his commandments], that they may have the right to the tree of life and that they may enter the city by the gates" (Revelation 22:14 RSV). At this point in her Office, the Virgin Mother of God appears in all her magnificence and beauty, as the living city of God set upon the holy mountain, her gates open to receive the children of the Lord whom she has anointed with her sweetness and feeds with the bread of heaven. There in that city reigns the Angel of Great Counsel, the Prince of Peace (Isaiah 9:6; cf. Romans 5:1). As the psalmist tells it: [He] *hath placed peace in thy borders and filleth thee with the fat of corn* (Psalm 147:3).

"There," in heaven, Taunton suggests (if not quite with the meaning we would give it here), "the saints shall know the sweetness of the Eternal Word with no type nor veil between them; there they shall put their lips to the very

Source of wisdom, and no longer drink of the mere rills of droppings which come down to water the earth."[477] In the ancient tradition, as we have seen, it was the Lady who was the "very Source of wisdom." It was she who surrounded the Lord with glory as he sat upon his throne; it was she who was the source of the anointing oil by which he was made present in human form in the body of the king; it was her tree from which he reigned. It was she who "came out of the mouth of the most High, the firstborn before all creatures" (Ecclesiasticus 24:5); she herself was the first fruit of his word that *runneth swiftly* as he *sendeth forth his speech to the earth* (Psalm 147:4). She was there with him at the creation of the spirits of snow and hail and hoarfrost, the snow which, according to the psalmist, *he giveth like wool*, the hoarfrost (or mist) which he *scattereth like ashes*, and the crystal ice which *he sendeth like morsels* (vv. 5–6). She was there as he sent out his Word to make his wind (or spirit) blow and his waters run (v. 7), for, as the Wisdom of Solomon put it, "she is the breath of the power of God . . . She reacheth therefore from end to end mightily, and ordereth all things sweetly" (7:25, 8:1). Through her, the Lord *declareth his word to Jacob* (Psalm 147:8) and "shewed him the kingdom of God and gave him the knowledge of the holy things" (Wisdom 10:10). Through her, he chose kings for his people and commanded them "to build a temple on [his] holy mount and an altar in the city of [his] dwelling place, a resemblance of [the] holy tabernacle, which [he] prepared from the beginning" (Wisdom 9:7–8). Through her, "who was present when [he made] the world" (Wisdom 9:9), he made known *his justices and his judgments to Israel* (Psalm 147:8), "what was agreeable to [his] eyes and what was right in [his] commandments" (Wisdom 9:9). *He hath not done in like manner to every nation, and his judgments he hath not made manifest to them* (Psalm 147:9), only to those who live in Jerusalem where his throne is. As Solomon prayed: "Give me Wisdom that sitteth by thy throne, and cast me not off from among thy children" (Wisdom 9:4), those blessed children who dwell within Jerusalem, the "vision of peace," the heavenly city of God.[478]

COMPLINE, SUNG AT BEDTIME

Psalms 128 *Saepe expugnaverunt*, 129 *De profundis*, and 130 *Domine non est*

There are but three steps left to climb, three of the Gradual Psalms left to sing. In the Roman Use, there is no antiphon at this point, simply the psalms and a little chapter taken, like the lessons for Matins as well as the little chapters for Terce, Sext, None, and Vespers, from Ecclesiasticus 24. Here, at bedtime, Wisdom proclaims: "I am the mother of fair love and of fear and of knowledge and of holy hope" (Ecclesiasticus 24:24). As a toddler—or so her medieval devotees imagined—Mary climbed the steps of the temple, singing the song of ascents; now, as queen, she has once again taken her place in the Holy of Holies, there to intercede before the throne. This is the way Germanus of Constantinople envisioned her reception by the high priest Zacharias as she crossed the threshold into the temple when she was three:

> Come then to me, little child, who is more exalted than the heavens! Come, infant that is seen and understood as the divine workshop! . . . Come, peep into an inaccessible and awesome inner chamber, you, who will become an immense and unsearchable vessel! Enter the front doors of the chancel, you who are breaking up the front doors of death! Look upon the curtain [that is, veil]. . . . Draw near that you may venerate the table. . . . Pass through the building of the whole sanctuary, as if breathing out a fragrance of incense. . . . Go up, go up onto the threshold of the holy dwelling-place, for whose splendor of beauty the happy daughters of Jerusalem weave praise as they rejoice, and earthly kings give blessings. . . . Be seated, O Lady. It is fitting for you, the Queen, who have been glorified above all earthly queens, to sit upon such a threshold. It is fitting that the hallowed place should become a dwelling-place for you, the most cherubic throne. Behold, I have worthily vouchsafed to you, as Queen of all, the preeminent throne; raise up, then, those who have fallen![479]

It is arguably appropriate, therefore, that the last three psalms of the Office should be psalms not only of the temple steps, but also of supplication for help against enemies, sin, pride, and despair. As the Virgin herself explained in the N-Town *Mary Play*: "The tende [degre] is myghty soferauns of carnal temptacyon; / For the fleschly syghtys ben fers and fel," while "the elefnte is accusatyff confessyon of iniquite, / Of which ful noyous is the noyis," and "the twelfte is mekenes that is fayr and softe / In mannys sowle withinne and withowte."

"*Often have they fought against me from my youth*," the psalmist laments in the voice of Israel. "*The wicked have wrought upon my back; they have lengthened their iniquity*" (Psalm 128:1, 3). In the first section of this psalm, or so Cassiodorus reads it, "the prophet . . . urges Israel [that is, God's Church] to tell of the great struggles and the nature of the guile which they have endured from their enemies, so that none of the faithful may seem to despair because of their afflictions."[480] These afflictions went back all the way to Abel, through the sufferings of Lot, Job, and those of the people of Israel under Pharaoh, up to those of the Church when the

Lord suffered on the cross "when the foolish thought that she had lost the Lord whom she proclaimed as the Begetter of her life." "Many most holy persons were attacked by afflictions and hazards," Cassiodorus observes, but nevertheless the Church "grows under the persecution of the wicked, and expands through her grief." The Lord, however, "is patient and great-souled and bears with sinners," subjecting them rather to "his sweet yoke with the humility which brings salvation."[481] In the second section of the psalm, the prophet turns to the foes of the Church and prophesies what will "befall them at the future judgment."[482] As the psalmist puts it: *Let them all be confounded and turned back that hate Zion*, that is, according to both Augustine and Cassiodorus, those that hate the Church. *Let them be as grass upon the tops of houses which withereth before it be plucked up* (Psalm 128:5–6). Passersby will not bless them, nor will they be gathered in at the harvest, but rather they will be accursed by their own stubbornness in hating the city of the Lord.

In the next psalm, accordingly, the sinner cries out to the Lord: *Out of the depths I have cried to thee, O Lord. Lord, hear my voice. Let thy ears be attentive to the voice of my supplication* (Psalm 129:1–2). How is it, Cassiodorus wonders, that the prophet, who has by now ascended to the eleventh step, should thus prostrate himself and cry out from the depths? Because, Cassiodorus explains, he knows that it is always possible to fall into sin, "for at what moment do we not sin in thought, or err through excess of words, or slip through thoughtless action? So," Cassiodorus insists the psalmist is telling his audience, "there is this one safe course for the person living in this world: continually to bend low with devoted prayers, so that despite our inability to be free from guilt, we may deserve to be pardoned through the kind offices of devotion."[483] Nevertheless, as a song of the steps, this is a psalm about contemplation, that is ascent, not falling. The psalmist bends low in humility even as his spirit mounts to the heights. It is, likewise, a psalm of hope, as the psalmist cries out for forgiveness from the Lord. *My soul hath relied on his word*, the psalmist says. *My soul hath hoped in the Lord . . . because with the Lord there is mercy and with him plentiful redemption* (Psalm 129:4–5, 7). This psalm, according to the medieval tradition, as well as being the twelfth Gradual Psalm, is the sixth of the so-called Penitential Psalms (6, 31, 37, 50, 101, 129, and 142).[484] Here, in the final hour of the day, the Virgin's ascent up the steps of the temple intersects with the sinner's plea for her protection, as the soul keeps watch from morning until night (Psalm 129:6).

Almost ready for sleep, the soul makes its concluding petition: *Lord, my heart is not exalted, nor are my eyes lofty. Neither have I walked in great matters nor in wonderful things above me* (Psalm 130:1). "This psalm," according to Augustine, "brings to our attention the humility of a servant of God . . . who stands for the entire body of Christ." Although the psalmist speaks in the singular, Augustine argues, the psalm is in fact "the prayer of all who are within Christ's body," that is, his temple:

> All who believe in Christ form the temple—at least, all who believe in him in such a way to love him. . . . All who believe in this way are like the living stones from which God's temple is built. . . . Believers form the temple in which prayer is offered to God and heard by him. If a person prays anywhere else than in this temple, he is not heard in a way that would bring him to the heavenly peace of Jerusalem, even if he is heard when he prays for various temporal good, which God has given even to pagans. . . . To be heard in a way conducive to eternal life is something quite different, and it is granted only to one who prays in the temple of God.[485]

Augustine goes on to contrast this living temple with that ancient temple "which was no more than a type . . . [of] the real temple which it signified," but even he seems to distinguish between the temple as the assembly of the faithful and the Holy of Holies where the Lord, "who was both priest and victim, offered himself and entered once for all into the holy of holies."[486] What he does not do, as we should by now expect, is identify the temple with Mary in the way that his contemporaries in Constantinople would. Augustine died in August the year before the council at Ephesus, only a few months before Proclus gave his great homily on the Feast of the Virgin.

We may wonder for the moment why the devotion to the Virgin did not develop in North Africa in the same way that it did in the East, but even in the fifth century, the stories of her childhood in the temple and posthumous Assumption into heaven were making their way west, even if initially to be met with some skepticism, and a great church (Santa Maria Maggiore) was built in her honor around 440 in Rome.[487] By the sixth century, when Cassiodorus was writing, Emperor Justinian (d. 565) was busy consecrating a new church in Jerusalem dedicated to the Holy Mother of God, the Ever-Virgin Mary, which dedication, according to Barker, was purposefully associated with the Feast of the Entry of the Theotokos into the Temple on which Germanus would later preach.[488] By the end of the seventh century, as we have noted, the Annunciation, Assumption, and Nativity of Mary, "Mother of God and ever virgin," along with the Feast of "St. Simeon which the Greeks call *Hypapante*," were being observed in Rome with a litany sung in procession from the church of Sant' Adriano in the Roman Forum to the basilica of Santa Maria Maggiore.[489] Although the feasts themselves may have been adopted in the West as much as a century before Pope Sergius I issued his decree standardizing the processions, as we have shown direct evidence for the antiphons and psalms chanted on these days comes only from the ninth century, by which time the feasts had also been adopted north of the Alps. How much the specific choice of antiphons and psalms for these feasts—and, thus, by extension, for the Marian Office—depended on Eastern practice is a question, to the best of my knowledge, impossible to answer with the evidence we have in hand. Although often alluding to the chants of the people, the homilists do not tell us everything that they sang, only how they read the scriptures in search of the Lady Mother of God. Like the devotion to the Virgin itself, however, what is now hopefully clear from our reading of the antiphons and psalms is the extent to which even in the Marian Office as it developed in the West, its choice of texts spoke to the traditions of the East. In the next chapter, we will see some of the ways Mary's devotees in the West grappled with how to understand (and worship) the Virgin whom they encountered in the Office. Now, however, it is time for bed.

In the words of the canticle Nunc Dimittis, sung at the close of the day: "Now," the aged Simeon exulted as, inspired by the Spirit to come into the temple, he took the baby Jesus in his arms,

> thou dost dismiss thy servant, O Lord, according to thy word in peace.
> Because my eyes have seen thy salvation,
> Which thou hast prepared before the face of all peoples:
> A light to the revelation of the Gentiles, and the glory of thy people
>   Israel. (Luke 2:29–32)

"The glory of the Lord shall be revealed," Isaiah had prophesied, "and all flesh together shall see, that the mouth of the Lord hath spoken" (Isaiah 40:5); "the Lord hath prepared his holy arm [alt. Holy One] in the sight of all the Gentiles, and all the ends of the earth shall see the salvation of our God" (Isaiah 52:10). Just as Simeon had hoped they would, the mother and her child had returned to the temple, the glory once more surrounding the Lord as she held him in her arms. Israel, the "one who sees God," could once again see the Lord, the Great Angel, the Prince of Peace, the Son of the Most High, because the Lady had made him visible to them.[490] *As a child that is weaned is towards his mother*, the psalmist prayed, prophetically suggesting the image of the Son enthroned in his mother's lap, *so reward in my soul. Let Israel hope in the Lord from henceforth, now and for ever* (Psalm 130:2–3). **We fly to your patronage, O holy Mother of God**, Christians as early as the third century had prayed, their prayer here sung as an antiphon for the canticle, **despise not our petitions in our necessities; but deliver us always from all dangers, O glorious and blessed Virgin.**[491] Now that the Lady was there in the temple with her Son, or so those who honored the Virgin through the psalms of her Office would argue, they could at long last be assured that she would.

PLATE 11 "Tota pulcra es, amica mea, et macula non est in te." Mary with some of her many names, reading left to right, top to bottom: "Electa ut sol, pulcra ut luna, porta celi, stella maris, sicut lilium inter spinas, exaltata cedrus, plantacio rosae, turris David cum propugnaculis, oliva speciosa, puteus aquarum viventium, virga Iesse floruit, speculum sine macula, fons ortorum, ortus conclusus, civitas Dei." *Hore intemerate virginis Marie secundum usum Romanum: totaliter ad longum sine require, cum pluribus orationibus in gallico et latino.* Paris: Thielman Kerver, 1502. Use of Rome. New York, The Morgan Library and Museum, Accession PML 126023.

4
Lesson and Response

All the while that you have been singing antiphons and psalms in her praise, your eyes have returned again and again to the image of the Blessed Virgin that first caught your eye at the invitatory Ave Maria for Matins.[1] Now, however, as you greet her, you can no longer look upon her simply as a maid of Nazareth praying and meditating in her chamber on the prophecies of Isaiah.[2] Rather, she has been transfigured before your eyes into the great Lady of the temple and Queen of heaven, even as the song of the angels fills your heart, mind, and ears:

> Quae est ista quae progreditur quasi aurora consurgens, pulchra ut luna, electa ut sol, terribilis ut castrorum acies ordinata?
>
> *Who is she who comes forth like the rising dawn, beautiful as the moon, chosen as the sun, terrible as an army set in array?* (Song of Songs 6:9, little chapter for Prime, my translation)[3]

At once, if only for a moment, it is as if a veil has been pulled aside and you can see the woman enthroned for who she really is: the bright sapphire throne upon which the One in the likeness of a man appeared (cf. Ezekiel 1:26). Wisdom herself, she is likewise the throne of Wisdom, the one created *from the beginning and before the world* who ministered before the Creator of all things *in the holy dwelling place* (Ecclesiasticus 24:14, little chapter for Vespers). You realize now why the daughters of Zion *declared her most blessed* and why the queens *praised her* (Song of Songs 6:8, little chapter for Lauds) as she stood beside the throne (Psalm 44:10). She, as much as her Son, was the one whom they had been waiting for, the Lady restored to her place in the worship of the Lord.

At which realization, you hear her speak:

In omnibus requiem quaesivi, et in haereditate Domini morabor. Tunc praecepit, et dixit mihi Creator omnium, et qui creavit me, requievit in tabernaculo meo, et dixit mihi: In Iacob inhabita, et in Israhel hereditare, et in electis meis ede radices.

In all these I sought rest, and I shall abide in the inheritance of the Lord. Then the creator of all things commanded and said to me, and he that made me rested in my tabernacle, and he said to me: "Let thy dwelling be in Jacob, and thy inheritance in Israel, and take root in my elect." (Ecclesiasticus 24:11–13, first lesson for Matins)

As with the elders who threw down their crowns before the One seated upon the throne (Revelation 4:10), your desire for understanding moves you to cry out to her:

R. Sancta et immaculata virginitas, quibus te laudibus efferam nescio. * Quia quem caeli capere non poterant, tuo gremio contulisti.

*R. O holy and immaculate virginity, I know not with what praises I shall extol you. * For he whom the heavens could not contain, you bore in your womb.* (first responsory for Matins)[4]

You beg to know more about her so that you might praise her as she deserves. She answers:

Et sic in Zion firmata sum, et in civitate sanctificata similiter requievi: et in Hierusalem potestas mea. Et radicavi in populo honorificato, et in parte Dei mei haereditas illius, et in plenitudine sanctorum detentio mea.

And so was I established in Zion, and in the holy city likewise I rested, and my power was in Jerusalem. And I took root in an honourable people, and in the portion of my God his inheritance, and my abode is in the full assembly of saints. (Ecclesiasticus 24:15–16, second lesson for Matins)

The veil flutters again, and you catch a glimpse of the Holy of Holies concealed within, the Lady surrounded by the hosts of the Lord. You venture to salute her:

R. Beata es, Virgo Maria, quae Dominum portasti Creatorem mundi. * Genuisti qui te fecit, et in aeternum permanes virgo.

*R. Blessed are you, Mary, who bore the Lord, the Creator of the world. * You gave birth to him who made you, and you remain a virgin for ever.* (second responsory for Matins)[5]

You hear a sound as of many waters and of thunder as the living creatures who surround the throne spread out their wings and sing: "Glory be to the Father, and to the Son, and to the Holy Ghost," even as the Virgin turns her shining face toward you.

> Quasi cedrus exaltata sum in Libano, et quasi cypressus in Monte Zion. Quasi palma exaltata sum in Cades, et quasi plantatio rosae in Hiericho. Quasi oliva speciosa in campis, et quasi platanus exaltata sum iuxta aquam in plateis. Sicut cinnamomum et balsamum aromatizans odorem dedi. Quasi myrrha electa dedi suavitatem odoris.

> *I was exalted like a cedar in Lebanon, and as a cypress tree on Mount Zion. I was exalted like a palm tree in Kadesh and as a rose plant in Jericho. As a fair olive tree in the plains, and as a plane tree by the water in the streets was I exalted. I gave a sweet smell like cinnamon and aromatic balm. I yielded a sweet odor like the best myrrh.* (Ecclesiasticus 24:17–20, third lesson at Matins)

You notice a sweet smell coming from the altar on which her image stands (could it be only the incense with which the thurifer has censed the altar and whose smoke now fills the church?), and you feel your lips burn as if touched by a hot coal (cf. Isaiah 6:7). Perhaps it is only that you have been singing for so long that now your throat feels parched and your lips are on fire. Or perhaps it is the love with which your heart has started to burn that you find yourself bursting with desire to sing:

> Felix namque es, sacra Virgo Maria, et omni laude dignissima. * Quia ex te ortus est sol justitiae, * Christus Deus noster.

> *R. Surely happy are you, holy Virgin Mary, and most worthy of all praise. *For out of you arose the Sun of justice, * Christ our God.* (third responsory for Matins)[6]

Happy, indeed, is the Virgin who gave birth to the Son of the Most High! In the words of Wisdom, echoing the words heard by Moses from the burning bush (Exodus 3:14) and the apostles from the mouth of the Word (John 6:35; 8:12; 11:25; 14:6; 15:5), the Lady of the Office declares:

> Ego mater pulchrae dilectionis et timoris et agnitionis et sanctae spei.

> *I am the mother of fair love and of fear and of knowledge and of holy hope.* (Ecclesiasticus 24:24, little chapter for Compline)

As you recall from your reading (*lectio divina*) just the other day, the passage continues:

> *In me is all grace of the way and of the truth. In me is all hope of life and of virtue. Come over to me, all ye that desire me, and be filled with my fruits, for my spirit is sweet above honey, and my inheritance above honey and the honeycomb. My memory is unto everlasting generations. They that eat of me shall yet hunger, and they that drink of me shall yet thirst. He that hearkeneth to me shall not be confounded, and they that work by me shall not sin. They that explain me shall have life everlasting.* (Ecclesiasticus 24:25–31)

Like Moses, wary of stepping on holy ground (Exodus 3:5), you pause, troubled by what you have just heard. This is not the way, you realize, that the masters in the schools with whom you are familiar have tended to speak of the Virgin Mary, when they speak of her at all. The Lombard (d. 1160), whose great compendium of sentences culled from the Fathers, particularly Augustine, has become the basis for the study of what the masters call "theology (*theologia*)," barely mentions her even in the context of the Incarnation, except to ask whether the flesh taken from her by the Word was free from sin.[7] Far from identifying her with Wisdom, as in the lessons and little chapters of her Office, Peter ignores her. For him, as for the Latin Fathers upon whom he largely depends, it is Christ who is *the power of God, and the wisdom of God* (1 Corinthians 1:24) and *in whom are hid all the treasures of wisdom and knowledge* (Colossians 2:3). Accordingly, for Peter, it is the Lord, not the Lady, who speaks in the books of Proverbs, Ecclesiasticus, and Wisdom, who *came out of the mouth of the Most High, the firstborn before all creatures* (Ecclesiasticus 24:5).[8] Have you, you begin to wonder, perhaps carried your reading of the antiphons and psalms of her Office *too far* such that you are now misunderstanding the lessons that you have just heard?[9]

If, for our purposes in trying to understand the way in which medieval Christians prayed the Marian Office, it is curious that as scholars we as yet know so little about the way in which they understood and experienced the recitation of the psalms, it is surely even more curious how contentious over the centuries the place of the Virgin in the Christian tradition has proven to be. The debate, as we have seen, was at the center of the argument in the fifth century between Nestorius of Antioch and Cyril of Alexandria over how to describe Christ as the incarnate Word. It was revived with perhaps even more vigor in the sixteenth century, when Hugh Latimer, bishop of Worcester, exulted in a letter to the then Chancellor of the Exchequer and ardent Anglican reformer Thomas Cromwell (d. 1540), that he hoped "our great Sibyll" (he means the statue of Our Lady of Worcester) would, along with "her older sister of Walsingham, her young sister of Ipswich, with their two other sisters of Doncaster and Penrice . . . make a jolly muster in Smithfield; [even if] they would not be all day in burning."[10] (It may or may not be significant that the statues depicting Mary as the throne of Wisdom that Cromwell ordered collected and burned were, like the Asherah over two thousand years before, made of wood; certainly the reformers knew their Old Testament.) It continued well into the eighteenth century, as we shall see in the concluding chapter on Sor María de Jesús de Ágreda. Indeed, if now relatively somewhat muted, it remains with us to this day, both in the ecumenical conversations between Catholics and Protestants about how to include Mary in their theologies and in the debates within Catholicism that have followed Vatican II about the way in which to talk about her, as co-Redemptrix or type of the Church.[11] Fraught as these discussions have been (and continue to be), as a witness to the difficulties that American Protestants in particular have had with making sense of the medieval devotion to Mary, there is arguably no better guide than the Bostonian belle-lettrist Henry Adams, who, on his *fin de siècle* tour of the Virgin's cathedrals in northern France, found himself drawn to her for reasons that even he could not fully explain.[12]

Albeit, according to his own account in his autobiographical *The Education of Henry Adams* published in 1918, "Adams never tired of quoting the supreme phrase of his idol Gibbon [as he stood] before the Gothic cathedrals"—"I darted a contemptuous look on the stately monuments of superstition"—he was nevertheless obliged to admit that over the course of his tour he had begun "to feel the Virgin or Venus as a force," even though his friend and fellow traveler Augustus St. Gaudens could not. After all, Adams opined: "The idea [of the goddess as the force of female energy] died out long ago in the German and English stock." But at what cost? "Symbol or energy the Virgin had acted as the greatest force the Western world ever felt, and had drawn man's activities to herself more strongly than any other power, natural or supernatural, had ever done before." Even now, he could still feel her power, of this much Adams "the historian" (the epithet is his) was sure.[13]

But could he explain her? He would try. She was Woman, he told his nieces (or "those who are willing . . . to be nieces in wish") in the imaginative travelogue *Mont Saint Michel and Chartres* that he privately published for them in 1904.[14] Her people built churches for her just like little girls make houses for their dolls, because they understood that she was capricious and childlike in her love of beauty, color, and light: "Her taste was infallible; her sentence utterly final." Her people loved her because she cared little for theology and even less for divine or human law. Keeping court over the people who came to worship in her palaces, she reigned as Queen of Heaven in spite of every earthly pope or king. "Had the Church controlled her, the Virgin would perhaps have remained prostrate at the foot of the Cross." But the Church could not. The bourgeois of medieval France invested "an enormous share of his capital" in building her cathedrals (eighty) and churches (more than five hundred)—"five thousand million francs . . . a thousand million dollars" over the course of the century between 1170 and 1270, and that in dollars of 1840 (Americans, according to Adams, always understand something if you put it in terms of money)—simply in order to please her: "For three hundred years [the investment in the Virgin] prostrated France."[15] Nevertheless, while the popes and philosophers failed to constrain her, her troubadours delighted to sing her praises in "the childish jingle" of their "mediaeval Latin." As one such "nursery rhyme" believed to have been composed for her by "the lyrical poet" Adam of Saint Victor put it:

> Salve, Mater pietatis,
> Et totius Trinitatis
>   Nobile Triclinium!
> Verbi tamen incarnati
> Speciale majestati
>   Praeparans hospitium!

> *Hail, Mother of Divinity!*
> *Hail, Temple of the Trinity!*
>   *Home of the Triune God!*
> *In whom the incarnate word had birth,*
> *The King! to whom you gave on earth*
>   *Imperial abode.*[16]

It was with this image of her in mind, Adams explained (his primary purpose being, in fact, to introduce his nieces not so much to the Virgin as to her art), that her medieval artists depicted her in stone and even more effectively in glass. At Chartres, in Adams's view, they captured her perhaps most effectively in the window now in the choir next to the south transept but originally most likely positioned in the center of the apse and known as Notre Dame de la Belle Verrière (Our Lady of the Beautiful Stained Glass Window). As Adams read this window over a century ago:

> The Empress Mother sits full-face, on a rich throne and dais, with the child in her lap. . . . She wears her crown; her feet rest on a stool, and both stool, rug, robe and throne are as rich as color and decoration can make them . . . she holds no sceptre; the Holy Ghost seems to give her support which she did not need before. . . . Exquisite as the angels are who surround and bear up her throne, they assert no authority. . . . The effect of the whole, in this angle which is almost always dark or filled with shadow, is deep and sad, as though the Empress felt her authority fail, and had come down from the western Portal to reproach us for neglect. The face is haunting.

Perhaps, Adams hazarded, it is because the window is "very old" (albeit it has been often restored) that it has so much "personality, and there it stands alone." "For seven hundred years" (at Adams's writing), pilgrims had been coming to Chartres, hoping to see the Virgin, and so, Adams imagined, in this window as elsewhere in her church, they did:

> Yet wherever we find her at Chartres, and of whatever period, she is always queen. Her expression and attitude are always calm and commanding. She never calls for sympathy by hysterical appeals to our feelings; she does not even altogether command, but rather accepts the voluntary, unquestioning, unhesitating, instinctive faith, love and devotion of mankind. She will accept ours, and we have not the heart to refuse it; we have not even the right, for we are her guests.[17]

Who was this Queen for whom the people of Chartres built such a beautiful palace of stone and glass, color and light? For Adams, writing at the turn of the twentieth century, the great difficulty in answering this question seemed to be one of feeling: if Chartres made no economic sense, perhaps the tourist could recapture something of what her medieval worshippers felt, although, he cautioned his American readers, there was nothing to be found here of mysticism for those who knew their "Lohengrin, Siegfried and Parsifal." In all its elaborate imagery, "[even] what seems a grotesque or an abstract idea is no more than the simplest child's personification," nor should one look for anything approaching "[t]heology in the metaphysical sense" in the great church's architectural symbolism: "Chartres represents not the Trinity, but the identity of the Mother and Son. The Son represents the Trinity, which is thus absorbed in the Mother. The idea is not orthodox," Adams concedes. "But this is no affair of ours. The Church watches over its own."[18]

In her recent study of the music, art, and architecture through which the people of Chartres imagined the Virgin, medieval musicologist Margot Fassler offers a rather different reading of the mysterious window which Adams found so haunting and yet lacking in orthodox authority. "The first thing to notice about the window," she comments, "is the emphasis on the Virgin's robe. As the light comes through the window, the blue robe enshrines the Virgin's body with a gleaming cloud"—just as, we may recall, in the temple tradition Wisdom enveloped the Lord like a cloud as he rode upon the cherubim (Isaiah 19:1; Ezekiel 1:4–28). "The Christ Child's body, clothed in the purple appropriate to his royal stature, is framed by that of his mother, whose shimmering garment completely surrounds him like a cloth halo made splendid by light"—just as, according to the early Christians the purple of the temple veil framed the Lord as he entered into the world from the Holy of Holies (Hebrews 8–9). "Radiant too is her restored head, surrounded as it is by a beaded orb of light that is the same radiant blue as her robe"—for so, as her Orthodox devotees depicted her in their icons, the face of the Virgin must have shone when she gazed upon her Son, the Lord (cf. Exodus 34:29–35). "Around the Virgin and Child is rich ruby-red glass, the bejeweled counterpart to the luminous blue robe, which shines all the more brightly because of the contrast. The tent of the tabernacle was red (see Exodus 26:14), and the use of the color here may be symbolic." At this point, the identification of the Virgin as the tabernacle is Fassler's. She continues:

The Child holds a book that deliberately resembles a tablet, and on it is written in uncial letters, "Omnis Vallis Implebitur" ("Every valley shall be filled": Luke 3:5). These are the opening words of the antiphon sung for the canticle at Lauds on Ember Saturday in Advent. . . . Many who saw this window could supply the rest of the text on the book Christ holds because it was sung in the liturgy and hence was well known. . . . "Every valley shall be filled" continues by proclaiming, "all flesh shall see the salvation of God." The mystery was *seen*: the very act of seeing means that history has changed, and a new Holy of Holies has been built within the Temple. . . . Notre Dame de la Belle Verrière offers another way of saying the same thing, in accordance with the prophecy of Hebrews 9. "To see the salvation of God" within the Tabernacle meant that a new order had come to it, and what had been a closed and invisible mystery had been offered to human senses.[19]

There is yet more in the composition of Notre Dame de la Belle Verrière to identify Adams's mysterious Queen with the Lady of the temple whom we have discovered in her antiphons and psalms. To either side of the Virgin in the twelfth-century window as it was enhanced in the thirteenth century stand eight angels, two holding thuribles that intrude into the original twelfth-century core. In Fassler's reading: "The likely original angels faced each other, as the angels in the Holy of Holies are said to have done. They provide the appropriate cloud of incense," with which, as we have seen, the Lord was believed to have become present in his temple (2 Chronicles 5:13–14). Along with the lower four angels, who also hold thuribles, these same angels also hold pots of manna in their hands, recalling the manna kept in a golden pot in the ark according to Hebrews 9. Again, in Fassler's reading: "This is a visual sign that the viewer has entered the holiest place of a New Testament configuration of the Temple." The other two angels hold candles, recalling the candelabra of the temple, while four angels (for a total of twelve, plus two to either side of the dove of the Holy Spirit at the top) stand directly beneath the Virgin's throne, each holding a golden pillar with which, in Fassler's reading, to support the Virgin's veil, alluding at once to the physical relic kept at Chartres, "which was a veil for the tabernacle of her body," but also to the veil of the tabernacle itself, which surrounded the Holy of Holies (Exodus 26:31–33). Fassler translates the same twelfth-century sequence that Adams cited as an example of the jingle-like quality of medieval Latin hymns:

> Hail, mother of piety
> and noble resting place
> of the entire Trinity,
> yet with special majesty
> preparing a welcome
> for the incarnate Word.

In Fassler's reading, as celebrated at Chartres, "Mary, when overshadowed by the Holy Spirit, becomes the new tabernacle filled with the eternally begotten Godhead. Her body contains the flesh of Christ but also, as he is one with the rest of the Trinity, encompasses the Trinity itself."[20] A great mystery, indeed, possibly even orthodox (*pace* Adams), arguably worthy of the attention of the most sophisticated theologians (*pace* Lombard), if only they knew how to see and read the Word![21]

Mary, as all those who rose early in the morning throughout the Middle Ages to sing her antiphons and psalms knew, was not only the Virgin whom

Isaiah had prophesied would give birth to a son whom she would call Immanuel (Isaiah 7:14). She was also Wisdom, whom *the Lord created . . . at the beginning of his work* to play beside him as he established the heavens and marked out the foundations of the earth (Proverbs 8:22–31; cf. Psalm 8). It was she who anointed the king at his birth as the Morning Star, the mother of the bridegroom who set his tabernacle in the sun (Psalm 18). She was the ark bearing the presence of the Lord in the Holy of Holies (Psalm 23), the queen standing beside the throne of the king on his wedding day (Psalm 44), the tabernacle sanctified by the Most High as his dwelling place (Psalm 45). She was the city of God of whom glorious things were said, the dwelling of all those who rejoice (Psalm 86), the heavenly Jerusalem arrayed like a bride for her bridegroom, the Lady clothed with the sun (Revelation 21:2, 12:1). She was the Tree of Life standing beside the throne of the Lamb (Revelation 22:2), the wood from which the Lord reigned (Psalm 95), the cloud, the throne, the lightning, and the glory upon which the Lord rode (Psalm 96). Great were the mysteries sung in her praise as the people anticipated the Lord's coming in judgment, filling heaven and earth with the glory of his presence (Psalm 97). Her Son may have come into the world as but a little child, but he was expected to return as the Great Angel of the Most High, the Son of Man riding on a cloud, seated at the right hand of Power and surrounded by all the hosts of heaven in his glory (cf. Matthew 24:30; 25:31; 26:64). *Make thy face to shine upon thy servant!*, the psalmist prayed (Psalm 30:17). Mary was the Lady who made the Lord visible to the world, the cloud filling the Holy of Holies, the glory surrounding the throne, the chariot throne bearing the presence of the Lord before his people so that his face might shine upon them. Like the ark or the temple, she was the place where God became manifest in his creation; a creature herself, she was filled with divinity when the Son of God took on flesh in her womb. Like the ark or the temple, therefore, she contained great mysteries worthy of attentive contemplation, even as she herself had pondered these great mysteries in her heart. As the Franciscan lector and provincial general Conrad of Saxony wondered in his *Speculum* or *Mirror of the Blessed Virgin Mary*, "Oh, who shall relate, or who can even imagine, in what contemplations daily that holy Zion, that holy mind of Mary, was employed, while she fervently revolved in her mind all those mysteries known to herself above all mortals?"[22]

What contemplations, indeed? If the authors of the liturgy themselves did not give us commentary on the antiphons and psalms that they designated for Mary, their successors in serving—most notably for our purposes, Conrad, Richard of Saint-Laurent, Pseudo-Albert, and Servasanctus—did, at great length and in consummate scriptural detail. It should by now come as no surprise that, as with the texts of her liturgy, rich as they are as sources for understanding the way in which her medieval devotees saw the Virgin Mother of God, these commentaries have not been easy for modern readers to make sense of, even those who are interested in the history of devotion to Mary. When they have not ignored them—as, for example, in Luigi Gambero's recent survey of Mary among the medieval Latin theologians, which includes an entry on Conrad,[23] but none on Richard or Pseudo-Albert (he may be forgiven Servasanctus, about whom almost all of us have until recently been ignorant)—they have tended to dismiss them, chiding them at once for their devotional exuberance and for failing to advance sober doctrine as sober theologians should. Hilda Graef's important survey *Mary: A History of Doctrine and Devotion*, published in two volumes in 1963 and 1965 in the midst of the discussions being held at Vatican II, has been extremely influential in this respect. On the one hand, Graef, a laywoman, was deeply devoted to Mary; on the other, as the cautionary epigraph to her book suggests, she was likewise anxious not to put the Madonna "above her Son" by attributing more to her than proper Church doctrine allowed. Accordingly, while feeling it her responsibility as an historian to leave in much "questionable material" that her readers might find disconcerting, Graef nevertheless took it upon herself to criticize "where I felt criticism was necessary, even in the case of canonized saints." In this respect, she hoped to be objective, not "glossing over the deviations" in the development of Marian doctrine which modern readers might find embarrassing or off-putting, particularly those among "our separated brethren" (that is, Protestants). "It has seemed to me," she averred, "that there would be a much better chance of making them understand our devotion to [the Mother of our Lord Jesus Christ] if we [that is, Catholics] frankly admitted that it has at times outrun discretion."[24]

High on Graef's list of such "questionable material" were the vast exegetical *summae* of Richard of Saint-Laurent and Pseudo-Albert. Both, in her view, were more or less equally dangerous, since they both circulated throughout Europe in both manuscript and print well into the seventeenth century as the work of Albert the Great, the attribution of the *Mariale, sive CCXXX quaestiones* not being challenged until as recently as 1952.[25] (She gives Conrad about a page, under the rubric "Some Lesser Figures"; Servasanctus she did not know.) We have already noted how ridiculous Graef found Pseudo-Albert's insistence on Mary's knowledge of theology and the arts.[26] She was even more critical of Richard, particularly his tendency to attribute to Mary scriptural texts more usually read (at least, in recent centuries) as pertaining solely to her Son. In Graef's estimation:

> It should quite frankly be admitted that this work, the first fairly system-atic treatise [on medieval Marian devotion], combines a number of traits that could only have an unfortunate influence. The opposition of Mary, the Queen of mercy, to Christ as the King of justice and vengeance, the constant and undiscriminating application to her of New-Testament sayings referring to her divine Son [including, we may note, the Lord's Prayer], her share in the eucharistic elements, and other features, did considerable injury to sane Marian doctrine and devotion, all the more as the work went very soon under the name of St. Albert and so was regarded with the veneration due to that great theologian. Compared with it the other work mistakenly attributed to him, the *Mariale Super Missus Est* [our Pseudo-Albert], is more sober, despite its exaggerations.[27]

The adjectives Graef applies throughout her description of Richard's work are perhaps the most telling. In her account, Richard's *De laudibus beatae Mariae virginis*, like Pseudo-Albert's *Mariale, sive CCXXX quaestiones super Evangelium "Missus est Angelus Gabriel,"* contains "a good deal of questionable material besides much that remains valuable." Richard's description of Mary's flesh as being one with that of her Son's and so consumed, like his, in the sacrament is "a view that is quite inadmissable." "Indeed, there is at times an unhealthy strain in Richard's spirituality, as when he devotes a whole book to the beauty of Mary, of which six pages describe her spiritual and no less than forty her physical beauty, though it must be admitted," Graef concedes, "that much of this space is taken up by allegorical explanations, especially in his detailed exposition of Mary as the neck." "And how [according to Richard] is [Mary] to be honoured?" Not with any practices that Graef herself could recommend: "Richard of St.-Laurent chiefly recommends external practices, and those not always in the best of taste. The various members of her body are to be adored (in the sense of venerated) and blessed through genuflexions and the recitations of *Hail Marys*, and all holy desires, meditations and good works should be addressed to her."[28]

We will have occasion to consider Richard's devotional recommendations in more detail in chapter 5. Here we are concerned with learning how to read his commentary on Mary's name, to which, Richard argues–much to Graef's chagrin–"every knee on heaven, on earth, and under the earth should bow except that of her Son" (cf. Philippians 2:9–10).[29] Our challenge, as with our reading of the antiphons and psalms of the Marian Office, is to learn to read like a medieval devotee of Mary, with all the images of her in scripture at our fingertips, looking not for formal theological doctrine, but for those things that, as the Benedictine Arnold of Bonneval (d. ca. 1157) put it, the scriptures contain "in very truth."[30] If, in chapter 3, our project was to suggest the way in which the authors of the Marian liturgy explored this devotional mystery, the Marian antiphons containing and framing the psalms that Augustine and Cassiodorus read as speaking always already of Christ, our project in this chapter is to practice this interpretation by reading the commentaries that Richard, Conrad, and Pseudo-Albert wrote in order to explain the Virgin whom they encountered in the liturgy, above all in the scriptures that they read and sang as referring to her. Whereas in the previous chapter our method was one of compiling references from disparate sources, whether Barker's reconstruction of the temple tradition, Augustine and Cassiodorus's christological reading of the psalms, the Marian antiphons composed for her feasts, or the Orthodox homilists' citations of the psalms and other scriptural texts assigned to the liturgies for the same, in this chapter, we shall stand back and allow the commentators themselves to suggest the references. Accordingly, while our method in the previous chapter was to compose a reading on several different levels, here, in contrast, it is largely to paraphrase, our goal being to provide not a commentary on our commentators, but a close reading of their texts so that their reading of the scriptures and other texts of Mary's Office may offer, as it were, a commentary on ours. Despite their popularity in their own day, these three works are for most modern readers (including modern Mariologists) unfamiliar and for the most part unread. If our primary purpose is to use these texts as a way of testing our own exegesis of Mary's Office, it is also hoped that our paraphrase translation may make them more accessible to those who would like to study the medieval devotion to the Virgin in more depth but who otherwise might find the original works too daunting. We have met these authors already in our survey of the way in which they and their contemporaries saluted Mary in chapter 2, and we have practiced our interpretation of the texts of her liturgy in chapter 3. Now it is time to test what we have learned by reading Richard's, Conrad's, and Pseudo-Albert's explanations of what their devotion meant.

As we shall see, to praise Mary—and, therefore, her Son—properly, or so Richard of Saint-Laurent, Conrad of Saxony, and Pseudo-Albert insisted, it was necessary to understand her, and by understanding her thereby be moved to love. Unlike many of Mary's more modern devotees, for whom the focus has been largely on the little that can be known (or imagined) of her earthly life, Mary's medieval servants—for so, Richard avers, they should be called—were far more focused on her heavenly presence as the queen to whom they offered their praises and prayers. (Here, Adams was on the right track, even if he did not have access

PLATE 12 Mary appears to the author, who is dressed as a Dominican friar. Richard of Saint-Laurent, *De laudibus beatae Mariae virginis*, lib. 1. Copied in Paris or French Flanders, between 1250 and 1299. Wellesley, Wellesley College 19, fol. 1.

Reproduction courtesy of Wellesley College Library, Special Collections. Photo by James Marrow.

to the deeper scriptural reasoning behind the emphasis on Mary as Queen.) Even as they meditated on her childhood in the temple, her conversation with the angel Gabriel, her meeting with her cousin Elizabeth, her giving birth to her Son at Bethlehem, her presentation of her Son in the temple, her attendance at the marriage of Cana, or her standing beside her Son's cross as he died, they were mindful of her cosmic stature as the Lady (*Domina*) of their Lord (*Dominus*). Moreover, if, as they believed, her Son was, in fact, *the image of the invisible God, the firstborn of every creature* in whom *it hath well pleased the Father that all fulness should dwell* (Colossians 1:15, 19), she was the one in whom that image made his habitation and through whom he manifested his presence to the world, *the unspotted mirror of God's majesty and the image of his goodness* (Wisdom 7:26). To love her, they contended, it was necessary to see her. And to see her, one needed to know how to read, above all how to read the scriptures through which she and her Son spoke to the world, above all the books of Wisdom and the Psalms.

A reading from the book of Wisdom, as the liturgists say.[31] All scriptural citations and allusions unless otherwise indicated are those given by Richard, Conrad, and Pseudo-Albert, although not all are marked by their modern editors as such, so thoroughly had the medieval authors absorbed the language of Wisdom and made it their own. (Pro tip: It helps to have a Vulgate to hand; quotations from the scriptures are indicated by italics.) It is perhaps not insignificant, albeit originally accidental to our purposes, that each of these three works represents in its method one of the three great arts associated with language, Mary being, after all, the Mother of the Word.

LECTIO PRIMA. ARS GRAMMATICA. RICHARD OF SAINT-LAURENT AND THE NAMES OF MARY IN SCRIPTURE

Writing, as he explained in the prologue to his massive work (over 840 double-columned pages in the 1898 edition), at the behest of his friends, both monks and nuns in the Cistercian order (although he himself was not a Cistercian), Richard begged his readers not to judge his work too harshly. He was, he insisted, simply trying to offer them a taste of the sweetness that poured forth from the holy womb of the Virgin Mary for the sake of the famished earth. Nevertheless, just as the sweet harmony of resounding cymbals might be shattered by the ringing of a little broken bell, so he worried that his efforts to add something so unpolished to the praises of Mary "whom the morning stars praise together, and for whom all the sons of God make a joyful melody" (cf. Job 38:7) might seem rather to diminish than to augment them. "For I know," he averred, "that her praise is so ineffable, that no living man, even if he were to speak with the tongues of angels and of men (cf. 1 Corinthians 13:1), or knew perfectly the language of heaven, could speak it, because she is greater than any praise. For," Richard acknowledged, "this glory the heavenly creator (*artifex*) has reserved for himself, whose special work (*opus speciale*) is the Virgin mother, and he will not give her over to another." Indeed, so great is her beauty that no creature but only the bridegroom who created her knows all of her secrets (cf. Song of Songs 4:1). And yet, burning with love for her and urged on by her promise that *they that explain me shall have life everlasting* (Ecclesiasticus 24:31), Richard nevertheless hoped to say a little something in her praise.[32]

Richard's method in praising the Virgin is highly instructive, if easy to take for granted.[33] He had been frustrated, Richard explained, that none of the Fathers had hitherto gone through the scriptures gathering together all of the testimonies to Mary and bundled them together into chapters (or sheaves). Not wishing to seem like a eunuch trying to deflower a virgin, that is, like someone trying to expound the scriptures without proper understanding, Richard proposed rather to imitate the prudence of bees, who collect nectar for making honey and wax from wherever they can. Taking his subject matter from modern doctors and ancient theologians alike, he proposed (mixing metaphors yet again) to raise up new little plants with water from their well, feed famished hearts with strengthening bread made from their comparisons, and fill the chalice of contemplation with wonderful sweetness pressed from their grapes. His work, Richard hoped, would have two principal fruits for the devout reader: a more enlightened understanding and a more ardent disposition, the better both to know and to love the Virgin (*ut ad intellectum cognitio, ad affectum dilectio referatur*). Those with less capacity for understanding might benefit if they ruminated over his work like animals that divide the hoof; those with greater subtlety in study—if, that is, they could put aside their pride—might find in it the opportunity to move on to greater things.

> If, however [Richard demurred], anyone should judge me rash in assembling
> such concordances, he ought to know, that truly whatever the ancients said
> concerning divine Wisdom (*de Sapientia divina*), the moderns expound
> concerning the mother of Wisdom (*de matre sapientiae*) for whom with Wisdom

so intricate is the union (*tam multiplex est unio*), that while her generation may
be univocal (*quod cum univoca sit generatio*) [that is, of a single species or name],
she is called Wisdom by equivocation (*quasi emphabolice* Sapientia *nominatur*)
[that is, ambiguously, with names referring both to divine Wisdom and to Mary].

(Here Richard the cathedral canon was showing off his grammatical chops
for those educated in the schools.) Nor, Richard continued, having given all
the explanation he deemed necessary to defend his exegetical mode, would he
apologize for his garrulity: "If I speak at length about sweet Mary it is because
the subject matter is exceedingly sweet; and because I have the leisure and it was
good to be here, it was pleasing to ruminate on such sweetness for a long time."
Better, he reasoned, to go on at length than that his brevity become an obstacle
for the simple for whose sake he began to write, lest he lose the reward promised
by the Mother of God to those who explained her (cf. Ecclesiasticus 24:32).[34]

True to his inner bee, Richard gathered together abundant citations from
authors both ancient and modern so as, as he put it in his second prologue,
to make his offering of goat's hair in lieu of the scarlet, blue, linen, and purple
which he lacked (cf. Exodus 25:4), lest he go against the precept of the law in
the sight of God and the blessed Virgin and give nothing.[35] Judging from his
bee-gleanings as identified in his text, Richard's favorite author was, without a
doubt, the Cistercian Bernard of Clairvaux (more than two hundred citations),
but he also cites frequently from other eleventh- and twelfth-century writers,
including Fulbert of Chartres (d. 1028), Peter Damian, Anselm of Canterbury
(thirty citations), Hugh (d. 1141) and Richard of Saint Victor (d. 1173), Ekbert
of Schönau, Peter Comestor (as Petrus Manducator) (d. 1178), "Magister
Adam," Innocent III, and Alan of Lille. Thirteenth-century authorities appear
more often anonymously, but include Thomas Gallus (d. 1246), John Halgren
of Abbeville (d. 1237), and William of Auvergne (d. 1249). Richard's references
to the Fathers and early medieval *auctoritates* are likewise copious, adverting to
Ignatius, Origen, Cyprian, Athanasius, Basil, Hilary, John Chrysostom, Augustine (some one hundred citations), Ambrose (thirty), Jerome (seventy), Cyril
of Alexandria, Sedulius, Fulgentius, Boethius, Cassiodorus, Gregory the Great
(sixty), Ildefonsus, Maximus, John of Damascus (eight), Bede (ninetten), Alcuin,
Hrabanus Maurus, and Remigius of Auxerre, as well as schoolroom texts like the
Eclogue of Theodulus, albeit not all of these references are to works now recognized as belonging to the authorities to whom Richard and his contemporaries
attributed them. Most notable among these misattributions are the treatises
or sermons ascribed to Augustine and Jerome on the Virgin's Assumption.
The latter, famously, is now recognized as the work of Paschasius Radbertus

(*Cogitis me*), but under the authority of Jerome, it provided the lessons for Mary's feast throughout the later Middle Ages.[36]

Richard likewise makes regular use, particularly in the latter part of his exposition on Mary's names, of descriptions taken from Isidore of Seville's *Etymologiarum*. He is also fond of providing etymologies for Mary's various titles in Greek, while every so often he provides translations of particular terms in French (*Gallice*) and explanations of certain letters in Hebrew. Even more frequently, Richard refers to the ordinary and interlinear glosses (*Glossa, Glossa interlinearis*) on the scriptures as well as to various unnamed contemporaries (*quidam*), one of the most important of which A. Fries identified as the Dominican Hugh of Saint Cher (d. 1263), to whom Richard sent a personalized copy of his work.[37] Significantly for our purposes, Richard even refers on several occasions to alternative readings of the scriptures according to the Septuagint.[38] Nor, as someone highly educated in the liberal arts (as one might expect of one of Wisdom's devotees), was Richard's reading confined to Christian authors. Aristotle (as "the Philosopher"), Cicero (as Tullius), Seneca, Lucan, Cato (of the *Disticha*), Ovid, Horace, and Virgil (the latter four typically identified simply as "the Poet") all make an appearance on his pages. To the witness of these learned authorities, Richard added not only the chants and hymns sung of the Virgin by the Church, but also the stories told of her miracles, above all that of Theophilus, as well as the apocryphal accounts of her childhood (*De infantia Salvatoris*) and death (*Transitus*), albeit the latter only once, Richard apparently preferring the account provided by "Jerome" in *Cogitis me*.[39] At one point, despite his professed desire in his prologue to remain anonymous, Richard betrays a certain local pride, citing as witness to the beauty of Mary's hair a relic of the same which "we see at Rouen" (it was, apparently, golden).[40] At another point, perhaps significantly, Richard cites at length, albeit anonymously, a conductus also found in the *Hortus deliciarum* of Abbess Herrad of Hohenbourg (d. 1195).[41] Like Herrad, Richard described himself as a bee collecting nectar from wherever he could; also like Herrad, Richard was particularly fond of the imagery of gardens and trees.[42]

By far the majority of Richard's bee-gleanings come, however, from scripture, particularly those books most closely associated with Wisdom: Ecclesiasticus, Proverbs, Wisdom, and Job. No bee, of course, could resist the many flowers and trees of the Song of Songs, but Richard's ability to discover testimonies to the Virgin in scripture did not end there. Most striking for our purposes are the many references Richard makes to the psalms, particularly those sung in Mary's honor on her feast days and in her daily Office, likewise to the visions and prophecies of Isaiah, Ezekiel, and Revelation, which, thanks to Barker, we may now recognize as having been integral to the temple tradition to which the early Christians appealed and upon which the Orthodox homilists built their understanding of Mary.

But this was not all. Richard had one even more important source upon which all his others depended. As we have already noted in chapter 2, one of Richard's favorite titles for Mary was *triclinium totius Trinitatis*, the same phrase that Henry Adams found so theologically obscure.[43] Perhaps even more provocatively, if very much to our purposes in learning to read the scriptures like one of Mary's medieval devotees, Richard insisted that Mary herself was a book—and not just any book, but *the* book in which it was possible to read the mysteries of God. As he explained, commenting on Matthew 1:1 which was read as the lesson for the Nativity of the Virgin, Mary herself might be read as the *book of the generation of Jesus Christ*, the great book upon which the Lord commanded Isaiah to write (Isaiah 8:1), great in its dignity, in the depth of its learning (*scientiae*), in the inscrutability of its sayings (*sententiae*), in its difficulty and utility; great because written by the action of the Holy Spirit (cf. Psalm 44:2); great because written in large and legible letters (that is, her virtues; cf. Habakkuk 2:2–3). As Richard reads her, Mary is the sealed book (Isaiah 29:11) kept by the side of the ark (Deuteronomy 31:26) as a testimony against the Jews, and she is the book that John saw, sealed with the seven seals (Revelation 5:1) and containing all knowledge (*scientia*) necessary to salvation. She is sealed because "no one knows the mother except the Son and anyone to whom the Son chooses to reveal her, just as Christ says of the Father" (cf. Matthew 11:27; Luke 10:22). She is the book given to the seer to eat (Revelation 10:8–11), sweet to the taste, that is, in her memory and examples, but bitter in the stomach, because she makes temporal and carnal delights seem bitter to those who imitate her.[44]

What, according to Richard, should one do with such a book? Just what the voice from heaven ordered. *Take this book*, the angel commanded John, *and eat it* (Revelation 10:9). That is, Richard explained, "Take it with understanding (*per intellectum*) and eat it with affection (*per affectum*) . . . keeping it always in your heart."[45] The intention of this Mary-book—or so Richard elaborated following the *accessus* used in the schools—is to make peace between heaven and earth, reconcile sinners with the Son, and to make known to sinners the will of God; thus she is called *nostra mediatrix* and *advocata*. The subject matter of this book is the wisdom of God (*sapientia Dei*) hidden from the ages. The lesson of this book is the way to true knowledge (*via ad veram scientiam*). As this book says of it/herself (Ecclesiasticus 24:30–31):

> *He that hearkeneth to me shall not be confounded*, behold the education and reward of its hearers; *and they that work by me*, that is, according to what I teach, *shall not sin*, behold the profit of following the precepts of this book; *and they that explain me shall have everlasting life*, behold the reward of teachers.[46]

Thus the utility of this book. Accordingly, just as Mary kept in her heart all the things that she had heard, so, Richard suggested in his second prologue, he had done what he could to collect what he had *seen* (cf. Revelation 1:11), that is, *understood* about her in the scriptures, so that his listeners might hear, recall, and profit from what they had heard, becoming, like her, an archive or library of scripture (*armarium Scripturarum*).[47]

But with this difference: unlike ordinary libraries, Mary was hardly a passive repository for books. Rather, Mary herself was an avid reader of scripture (cf. Ecclesiasticus 39:1–3):

> She sought out the wisdom of the ancients, that is, sought in her heart, and occupied herself in the prophets. She kept the sayings of renowned men and entered into the subtleties of parables. She searched out the hidden meanings of proverbs and was conversant in the secrets of parables.[48]

Herself wise, she diligently studied to pierce the surface of the letter or of figures found therein and to seek the mystical and moral sense with all her heart. Moreover, not only was she wise, but through her words, prayers, and deeds she was also a teacher of wisdom (*sapientiae Dei magistra*) (cf. Wisdom 8:4).[49] After all, she was the Mother of Wisdom (*mater sapientiae*), that is, of Christ, filled up like the Phison and Euphrates by the king born from David (cf. Ecclesiasticus 24:35–36) with all the knowledge of the scriptures: "For he who opened the minds of the Apostles so that they might understand the scriptures (cf. Luke 24:45) filled his mother all the more powerfully with the spirit of wisdom and understanding," and not only for the nine months in which he dwelt in her womb, but all the years of his childhood as he was living with her. As "blessed Anselm" put it: "What of God did she not know, in whom the wisdom of God lay hidden, and from whose womb he made for himself a body?"[50] Instructed by her Son in "the hidden and uncertain aspects of his wisdom," that is, "the secrets of the sacred Scriptures" up to "the marrow of the spiritual sense," after his Ascension, she became the teacher of the evangelists and the apostles, thus fulfilling the prophecy, *For the law shall go forth out of Zion, and the word of the Lord out of Jerusalem* (Micah 4:2), that is, Richard explains, from the Virgin who is represented by Zion and Jerusalem.[51]

It was for this reason that Richard, in Graef's words, "placed [Mary] in constant parallel to Christ and even to God the Father."[52] Not, as Graef worried, because Richard wanted to put the Madonna "above her Son," but because divine Wisdom had taken his rest in her, and so assimilated her to himself. As the Lord says of her in the psalms (Psalm 131:14): *This is my rest for ever and ever; here will I dwell, for I have chosen it.* "*In all these*," Wisdom himself says (Ecclesiasticus 24:11), "*I sought rest, and I shall abide in the inheritance of the Lord*, that is, in the blessed Virgin Mary, in her body for nine months, but never to leave her soul." "But note," Richard goes on, "that Mary was not only made the hostess or guest-house of the Son of God, but rather of the whole Trinity, whose *triclinium* she is." Thus, Richard says Job says speaking in the persona of Mary (Job 29:4–6): "*When God was secretly in my tabernacle,* that is, the Son in my womb. *When the Almighty was with me,* that is, God the Father through indwelling grace. *And the rock poured me out rivers of oil,* that is, the Holy Spirit poured into me the gifts and favors of every grace."[53] In Richard's words: Mary was "the habitation not only of the Son, but indeed of the whole Trinity, and a joyous habitation at that. Thus it seems possible to read that verse of Psalm 86:7 in this way: *As of all who rejoice,* namely of the three persons, *the habitation is in you.*"[54] Mary is the place (*locus*) chosen and sanctified by God *that* [his] *name be there* (2 Chronicles 7:16); *a high and glorious throne, the place of our sanctification* (Jeremiah 17:12) because "she is the temple of God in which the divine mysteries are celebrated." For this reason, she is likewise a place terrible to demons and the powers of the air (cf. Genesis 28:17), a place of peace (Psalm 75:3), and a place of prayer (*locus orationis*).[55]

Moreover, Richard explains, God made her precisely in order that she might be such a place and that he might dwell in her. She is his greatest work, finely and artistically crafted "because she is the work of the wisdom of God or the Holy Spirit, who is the maker (*artifex*) of all things."[56] She is the special work of God (*speciale opus Dei*) and his principal one (*opus speciale et principale*),[57] first in dignity and prefiguration (*primarium opus Dei dignitate et praefiguratione*). *In the beginning,* as the scriptures say, *God created heaven and earth* (Genesis 1:1). *In the beginning,* Richard pulls back the scriptural veil, God created his dwelling Mary. As she says in Proverbs 8:22 "secundum aliam litteram" (which "other letter" Richard does not say; he is here most likely quoting the liturgy): *The Lord created me in the beginning of his ways* (the Vulgate reads "possessed"). Again, she says: *The firstborn before all creatures . . . From the beginning and before the world was I created* (Ecclesiasticus 24:5, 14). Accordingly, Richard contends, she contains in herself all the secrets of God (*arcana Dei*), that is, the virtues known only to God, or rather her Son, unknown to the world, hidden in her through the Incarnation.[58] In this respect, she is also the temple and the house that Wisdom built for herself (Psalm 64:5; Proverbs 9:1), through which "we offer prayers to Christ."[59] And she is the throne upon which Wisdom sits in his Incarnation; sitting in this chair (*cathedra*) Christ is most wise because he is the wisdom of the Father (cf. 2 Kings [Samuel] 23:8; John 13:13; 1 Corinthians 1:30).[60]

But, we might pause for a moment to ask, if Mary is the house that Wisdom built for him/herself as well as the throne upon which Wisdom sits, who, according to Richard, is Wisdom, and who is Mary? Moreover, what does it mean to say that Wisdom dwelled in her if she was the creature of Wisdom?

Was she, then, somehow greater than her own Maker that she could thus contain her (or is it him)? Arguably, here, in a nutshell, we encounter once again the principal mystery upon which the medieval devotion to the Virgin depended: Mary was the one who contained in her womb him whom heaven and earth could not contain. No human being before or since has experienced the indwelling of God in this way. Not even the kings of the temple tradition were said to have given birth to God; rather, they themselves were anointed as sons of God, becoming angels, but not God-bearers. Mary, in contrast, and as Richard took some pains to point out, was not God but the Mother of God; God dwelled in her, the city that he made for himself, even as he held her in his hand.[61] If at this point, again in Graef's words, "the difference between the divine-human Christ and his human mother tends to be more and more obliterated"[62]; this arguably is why: like heaven, like the temple, like the Holy of Holies, like the ark, there was no part of Mary, body, mind, or soul, that was not filled utterly with the grace of God. Accordingly, she was, in Richard's word, "deified" (*deificata*), that is, made like God. Not made God, nor made a god(dess), but made *like God*, and, therefore, able as Wisdom to teach others about God.

It is instructive to note how, according to Richard, Mary does this. Mary, Richard explains, could not have been more full of grace than if she herself were "joined to the divinity, that is, unless she herself were God."[63] Nevertheless, when the Son of God dwelled in her, in her were hidden *all the treasures of wisdom and knowledge* of God (Colossians 2:3), so that she was "in some sense deified" (*quoddammodo deificata*).[64] It is for this reason that the bridegroom says of her in the Song of Songs (4:7):

> *Thou art all beautiful, my beloved....* For just as iron taken from the fire is not only fiery, but rather wholly fire; and just as the air illuminated by the sun ... takes on its color and is made wholly sun; and just as a drop of water poured into a jar of the best wine changes wholly to the taste, odor, and color of wine; and just as clear and pure glass illuminated by the sun changes to the brightness and color of the sun; and just as pure white wool dyed with the blood of the murex or shellfish is colored through and through with the dye, so when Mary's soul was filled with the Holy Spirit, and especially when that heavenly light, that is, the Son of God descended into her, she was now made not only full of light, but was wholly deified (*deificata*).[65]

Nor was she the only one affected by this descent. The Son of God, too, was changed—insofar as the unchangeable God can change—when he took on flesh from her (*carnem assumens, in ea informatus est*); so, likewise, the blessed Virgin "announced to us ineffably out of the omnipotence of God a certain divinity" (*quoddam divinum nobis ineffabile ex Dei omnipotentia nuntiavit*).[66]

After all, Richard asks, how could she not have been in some sense deified, having been made wholly fiery by the Son who is fire?[67] The real question is what effect this deification had on her. Here, as indeed throughout Richard's exegesis of those things that figure her in scripture, the Virgin's divinity, to coin a phrase, is in the details. *King Solomon*, we are told, *made a great throne of ivory, and overlaid it with the finest gold. It had six steps, and the top of the throne was round behind* (3 Kings 10:18–19). As Richard explains, King Solomon is, of course, Christ, that is, Eternal Wisdom, and the throne, that is, the Virgin, is his special work, because in this work above all the Maker of the dawn and the sun showed his wisdom.[68] She is made of the most precious materials, gold and ivory, because nothing like her was made in all his kingdoms, heavenly, earthly, or infernal.[69] She has six steps to signify the six workings of the Holy Spirit in her body and soul or the six virtues by which Christ ascended into her.[70] Even more to the point, *the top of the throne*—that is, Mary's intellect—*was round behind*: *round* to signify eternity, *behind* "because it is not yet clear what we will be." What does this mean? As Richard would have it: Mary was round, that is, without corners or beginning or end; thus she was wholly illuminated by divinity, whose dwelling she was:

And in God, so to speak, she was deified (*deificata*), made a participant in divine eternity, without corners or turnings. *From behind* means the end of the body: because in life there is no perfect happiness, but only in the life to come. Then the likeness of the divine image (*divinae imaginis similitudo*) will shine forth in our mind or understanding through our memory, reason, and will.[71]

In other words, special as she was, Mary, having been filled with God, was no more or less than the image of what a human being is—or, rather, what all human beings will be, when filled with God in the life to come.

This is why it is so important, Richard would insist, for Christians to serve her: "Because she drank first from the fount of eternal wisdom, she is able to reveal the secrets of God to whom she wills." In her words (Ecclesiasticus 24:46): *I will pour out doctrine as prophecy and will leave it to them that seek wisdom.*[72] Wisdom, it is said, is *the brightness of eternal light and the unspotted mirror of God's majesty and the image of his goodness* (Wisdom 7:26). According to Richard, there are three such mirrors, the most perfect of which is the Son, who is the image of the Father: "For just as the image of a thing is seen in a mirror and through the image the thing, so in the Son and through the Son, the Father is seen: in the Son, because he is a mirror; through the Son, because he is the image." The second is "the human mind made to the image and likeness of God," but this mirror, of course, is not without spot. The third is "every creature in which traces of the whole Trinity shine forth, as Augustine says, in being, power, manner, and wisdom."[73] It is this mirror, as the Apostle Paul says (1 Corinthians 13:12), through which human beings now see in figures (*in aenigmate*), particularly, or so Richard would argue, figures of the Virgin Mary. For she, too, is a mirror, but of a very special sort. As a fountain, she is the source of a pool of great clarity, which shows an image to those who gaze into it.

As Richard would insist:

> Mary is an *unspotted mirror* for the souls of the faithful, in which they ought to gaze continuously. For so great is her purity that anything greater [than she] under God cannot be thought, just as blessed Anselm says; for she was worthy to conceive him, as Jerome says, who reformed in us the image deformed by the old Adam, when through her love and obedience the wax of human nature was made warm and pliable and was impressed once again with the seal, that is, the Son of God, in her virginal womb.[74]

This is the image that fountain shows, the Son of God who is the face of the Father (cf. Psalm 12:1), but only to those who are close to her in love, purity, and humility and who look with both eyes of the soul, namely the intellect and affect or faith and love.[75] Mary is the *brightness of eternal light* because through her the eternal light, that is the Father and the Son, is seen. Thus the psalmist says of her (Psalm 35:10): *For with thee is the fountain of life, and in thy light we shall see light*. Mary, in other words, is the Lady who answers the psalmist's prayer that the Lord make his face shine upon his servants. Filled with the light of her Son, she gave birth to the true light that he might become visible to the world.[76] Herself filled with divine light, she illuminates the eyes, that is, the intellect and affect of her servants, "the intellect with knowledge of herself and God, the affect with love of God and neighbor."[77] To say, therefore, as Richard emphatically and insistently does, that that which is said in scripture of divine Wisdom may also be read of Mary is something of a tautology, for to speak of Mary is to speak of God.[78] This is why, to his mind, it is worth their while for Mary's servants to spend so much time poring over every image of her that they can find in the scriptures, which, because she herself is the book in which they read about God, are more or less by definition chock-full of her. More specifically, the scriptures are full of her names: Mary, mother, good woman, queen, heaven, sun, moon, dawn, cloud, earth, mountain, fountain, river, ark, throne, tabernacle, bedchamber, house, temple, city of God, tower, ship, garden, flower, tree—every property of which tells Mary's fellow creatures something about her and, therefore, about God.

As Richard would have it, to praise Mary (and therefore God) properly, it was important to understand her, but to understand her, it was necessary to be able to name her—and not just name her, but inquire into every aspect of her name. The technique that Richard uses to inquire into the scriptures is that which is typically described as "allegorical," that is, looking for the symbolism in words and things so as to discern their spiritual significance, but it might more properly be termed "grammatical," that is, inquiring into the properties of nouns or names. This was a technique that Richard would have learned in the schools along with his approach to the authors.[79] It, like Mary, is at the heart of much of what has made the medieval understanding of scripture so difficult to appreciate for modern readers no longer trained to read for signs of Wisdom as opposed to historical "facts." Confusingly enough, Richard would most likely insist (although he does not say so in quite so many words) that he was reading scripture not allegorically but literally (*ad litteram*) in his insistence that "the words of Wisdom are the words of Mary."[80] Allegorically speaking, what he was attempting to do (as Barker might put it) was to pull away the veil of the temple so as to behold the mysteries within—in the temple tradition, "allegories," "proverbs," or "parables" all being, like the heavenly visions of the prophets, moments at which the parallels between heaven and earth were made visible. Like Mary, the temple was a place at which the two creations, earthly and heavenly, intersected, and heaven and earth were revealed as "counterparts of each other in one reality [in which] time and eternity show the same patterns." Within this tradition, this is the reason that earthly things (like temples and arks and rivers and mountains) might be used to talk about heavenly things (like God and his glory): they were not opposites, but aspects of the same reality differently perceived, the earthly by way of the corporeal senses, the heavenly by way of the eyes of the soul.[81]

As we have seen, in the temple tradition, it was Wisdom, or rather the Lady, who gave light to the eyes; likewise, in the Gospels, giving sight to the blind is taken as one of the signs that Jesus was (and is) the Lord, her Son. As Richard would have it, Wisdom, or rather Mary (*sapientia vel Maria*), was the one who made the shadows of ignorance flee and gave birth to the true light, Christ.[82] In his reading, she is also the one by whose light the scriptures are to be read, the one illuminating their every mystery and opening the intellect and affect to the knowledge and love of God. *Who is she*, the angels wondered, *who comes forth like the rising dawn, beautiful as the moon, chosen as the sun, terrible as an army set in array?* (Song of Songs 6:9). To answer the angels' question: here, according to Richard, are but a few of her names. Again, all references or allusions to scripture are Richard's.

PLATE 13 Mary as Mother nursing the Child. Richard of Saint-Laurent, *De laudibus beatae Mariae virginis*, lib. 6. Copied in Paris or French Flanders, between 1250 and 1299. Wellesley, Wellesley College 19, fol. 192.

Mary

At the Incarnation, when the angel Gabriel came to her, then, in Richard's words, "the Angel of Great Counsel entered into her heart."[83] "Note," Richard comments almost casually, "that just as the name of the Son is poured out in seven [sic] names, where it says (Isaiah 9:6): *Admirabilis, Consiliarius*, etc., thus Mary's name can be fittingly poured out through its interpretations." These, according to Richard, are the four most common meanings of Mary's name: light-giver (*illuminatrix*), Lady (*Domina*), bitter sea (*mare amarum*), and star of the sea (*stella maris*). Properly speaking, Mary was the light-giver and star of the sea at her Son's Nativity, "when she sent forth the ray illuminating the whole world and made manifest to the world the true light, namely when the true sun of justice arose from her"; the Lady in the offering of her Son, when she presented him in the temple; and the bitter sea at his Passion, when the sword passed through her soul also. She is the light-giver because she makes light the darkness; the Lady because she protects Christians like a strong tower and conquers their enemies; the star of the sea because she guides their journey through the sea of this world; and a bitter sea because she makes bitter the harmful delights of the world. She was illuminated by the Father of lights, from whom descends every perfect gift from above (cf. James 1:17); by the grace of the Holy Spirit, when he sanctified her womb and came upon her (cf. Luke 1:35); and by the Son of God, the true sun of justice, at his conception, "whom she received and carried wholly in her heart and wholly in her womb."[84] Thus she gives light to the whole Church both on earth, like the window in Noah's ark, and in heaven, as she says in Ecclesiasticus 24:6: "*I made that in the heavens there should rise light that never faileth*, that is, I gave birth to Christ who is the unfailing light in the heavens." After the Son, she is *the true light, which enlighteneth every man that cometh into this world* (John 1:9), just as her Son, the Wisdom of God, gave light to the one born blind when he spat on the ground and made clay of his spittle and spread the clay on his eyes (John 9:6).[85]

Mother

I am the Mother of fair love and of fear and of knowledge and of holy hope, Wisdom, that is, Mary, declares in Ecclesiasticus 24:24. Love, explains Richard, is beautiful when it is natural, that is, directed toward the one who deserves love, namely God; singular, when the faithful soul admits no other lover except God; and whole, when the soul loves with the whole heart, that is, the whole intellect without error, the whole soul, that is, the whole will without opposition, and the whole mind, that is, the whole memory without forgetfulness. Fear is beautiful when it is the fear of God and neglects nothing, doing nothing which ought not to be done, omitting nothing which ought to be done. Knowledge (*agnitio*) is beautiful when it come from faith and the knowledge (*scientia*) of the sacred scriptures; it is even more beautiful when it comes through revelation and the understanding of prophecy; it is most beautiful when it enjoys the presence and experience of that which is believed by faith. Hope is holy and beautiful that comes from faith and merits; it is holier and more beautiful when it comes by revelation and the witness of conscience; it is holiest and most beautiful when it is secure (cf. Romans 8:38–39). *Come over to me*, the glorious Virgin promises her servants, *all ye that desire me, and be filled with my fruits* (Ecclesiasticus 24:26), with the love that is its own reward, the fear that is the religiousness of knowledge that keeps and justifies the heart (Ecclesiasticus 1:17–18), the knowledge that inflames desire that they should desire what they know all the more, and the hope that does not disappoint (Romans 5:4).[86]

These are the fruits that Mary as mother pours out from herself like a stream from a fountain on those who desire her, teaching them what they should seek (God), what they should flee (sin), what they should fear (hell), and what they should hope for (the heavenly homeland). Love moves them to seek, fear to flee, knowledge to believe, and hope to hope. Mary is mother because, receiving these four things from God, she sent them out into the light. Her love was pure because she despised all temporal things and vowed herself to virginity. As the mother of fear, she fled not only sin, but the actions of sinners, humbling herself before Elizabeth even as she was magnified through the conception of her Son. She gave an example of believing what ought to be believed and of hoping what ought to be hoped, for she knew that *one thing is necessary* (Luke 10:42), to *seek first the kingdom of God* (Matthew 6:33). Therefore, she says: *In me is all hope of life and of virtue* (Ecclesiasticus 24:25). She is "the hope of life, because through her we hope to have life, and of virtue, that is, of constancy." Before her birth, death reigned in the world, but through Mary who gave birth to Christ, death has been overcome. In her is all hope of life and virtue because in her are all the cardinal and theological virtues, which she bestows through her prayers and examples upon those who hope in her. As it says in Proverbs 29:25: "*He that trusteth in the Lord* [*Dominus*], that is, in Mary, which in Syriac means 'Lady' (*Domina*), *shall be set on high*."[87]

Again, Mary is the Mother of beautiful love because she is the Mother of Christ, who is beautiful. As it says in Hebrews 1:3: *Who being the brightness of his glory*, and in Psalm 44:3: *Thou art beautiful above the sons of men*. Through the love which he had for the human race, Christ bound himself to human nature.

Through the love which he has for his creatures, he binds them to himself: "because he who is joined to God is one spirit with him, namely by the unity of love and grace" (cf. 1 Corinthians 6:17). Therefore, Mary is called the Mother of beautiful love "because she makes her lovers and friends to resemble Christ her Son, who is most beautiful, reshaping (*refigurans*) the likeness of the Son in them through grace, which they lost through sin. This happened with Theophilus: for after he was reconciled to the Son through the mother's mediation and had taken holy communion, his face shone like the sun."[88] *In me*, the Mother of beautiful love says, *is all grace of the way and of the truth* (Ecclesiasticus 24:25), because Christ, the way and the truth, upon whom the spirit of the Lord, the spirit of wisdom and understanding rested (Isaiah 11:2), rested in her (Psalm 131:14).[89]

Good Woman

This is the name that Mary's Son used in speaking to her: *Woman, what is that to me and to thee?* (John 2:4); and: *Woman, behold thy son* (John 19:26). She is woman by reason of her sex, but not, Richard hastens to add, owing to any corruption of her virginal integrity. Or she is called woman through antonomasia (that is, as an epithet) because when Christ put on flesh in her womb, he took on all the weaknesses of the flesh except four. As the Son says to the mother (Job 10:11): *Thou hast clothed me with skin and flesh*. Mary softens the Son in another way as well, reconciling him to the human race so that he forgets the punishment that he would have inflicted upon humanity for its sins. Thanks to her prayers and merits, he now tolerates even major sins, when once he punished even minor sins severely. "For it is a fact," noted Richard, who likewise served as penitentiary at Rouen and so presumably had some knowledge about the kinds of sins to which his fellow Christians were prone, "that modern Sodomites or lechers sin much more gravely than did those ancient ones who were punished so harshly." Moreover, "it is usual for a mother to be more merciful to her children than a father. Accordingly, while God the Father gave us his Son as a father and king of justice, to moderate his justice he gave us a mother of piety and queen of mercy. . . . For this reason she is described as our advocate (*advocata*) standing at the right hand of the Son . . . because it is extremely proper for there to be a queen of mercy accompanying the king of justice."[90]

Mary is also the woman who was to tread on the head of the serpent (Genesis 3:15), as well as the woman sought by Solomon, who said: *Who shall find a strong woman?* (Proverbs 31:10). Until he came to Mary, she could not be found. But who found her? No one except Christ, who by the grace of her strength in vowing herself to virginity and the humility that he beheld in her, gave himself to her in payment for her double virtue, for, as Solomon put it, *far, and from the uttermost coasts is the price of her* (Proverbs 31:10). Here, according to the gloss, the strong woman may be understood not only as Mary, but also as the Church and the faithful soul, for all were bought with a great price (1 Corinthians 6:20). Mary's price, that is Christ, came from afar, when he descended from heaven into her womb: "because *his going out is from the highest heaven* [Psalm 18:7], and from her he assumed flesh and blood or, rather, a body, which for her as for us he offered on the cross." His going out was *from the highest heaven*, that is, from the Father's majesty to the hidden depths of the womb, "which neither Angel nor any other creature penetrated or was able to find." Concerning which womb the Father says to the Son: *From the womb before the daystar I begot thee* (Psalm 109:3). Likewise, Mary is the pearl of great price, so pure in body and soul that to purchase her the celestial merchant gave all that he had without exception. Whence it is sung in her antiphon: "O marvelous exchange! The creator of the human race, taking a body with a living soul, deigned to be born of a virgin, and becoming man without man's seed, bestowed upon us his divinity." Mary, in return, gave herself wholly to God, and with this exchange claimed for herself everything divine. For God chose her and bestowed upon her everything of his own (*omnia sua propria, id est, divina*). As her Son says in John 16:15: *All things whatsoever that the Father hath, are mine.* "The Father has immortality, eternity, and light: the Son and the Holy Spirit have these, too. And the Virgin Mary has these, too, albeit in a different way (*sed aliter et aliter*)."[91]

Queen

If on earth Mary was woman, in heaven she is queen. As the psalmist says of her: *The queen stood on thy right hand in gilded clothing, surrounded with variety* (Psalm 44:10). And what a queen she is! Prompt to serve or to minister, standing always before her king; prompt to offer aid, always ready to help; prompt to contradict her servants' adversaries accusing them in the court of her only-begotten Son, acting as their advocate by speaking on their behalf before God; ceaselessly and steadfastly giving aid to her servants, never forsaking them unless they forsake her; royal in dignity, authority, power, and majesty; granted to sit at the right hand of her Son, just as Solomon had a seat brought for his mother Bathsheba that she might sit beside him (3 Kings 2:19); clothed in beautiful and precious clothing, that is, a glorified body, and in a multitude of virtues, merits, dignities, and honors; an example to others, that those who see her might understand, be edified, and invited to imitate her.[92] Thus she stands, ministering before the Trinity *in the holy dwelling place* (Ecclesiasticus 24:14), to Elizabeth when she was pregnant (Luke 1:56), and to the Son of God born from her, who himself *came not to be served, but to serve* (Matthew 20:28). And she stands as a most faithful helper to the embattled and especially to her servants, against whom the world, the flesh, and diverse demons make war.[93]

She may be recognized as a queen in a variety of ways: through her royal lineage and noble birth from the tribe of Judah and the stock of David; through her anointing by the Holy Spirit with the *oil of gladness* (Psalm 44:8) from her mother's womb; through her betrothal *in faithfulness* (Hosea 2:20) to her heavenly bridegroom; through the gifts of grace, glory, and the heavenly kingdom with which she was betrothed; through the dignity by which she was exalted to share with her Son in the heavenly kingdom; through the power by which she assists sinners like Theophilus who invoke her faithfully as she sits on the throne of judgment (cf. Proverbs 20:8, said of the king); through the generosity with which she bestows the gifts of grace, the clothing of virtue, and the treasures of merit on her servants; by her guardians, the angel Gabriel, the virgin John the Baptist [*sic*], and the multitude of angels given charge over her (Psalm 90:11); through her coronation at her Assumption, just as her Son promised her (Song of Songs 4:8); and through the size of her kingdom *from sea to sea and from the river unto the ends of the earth* (Psalm 71:8) with its three provinces, celestial, terrestrial, and infernal. In her reign, she is figured by two queens: the Queen of Sheba and Esther. Just as King Ahasuerus offered Queen Esther up to half his kingdom (Esther 7:2), so Christ has shared out his kingdom with Mary, giving her the share of mercy while retaining justice for himself.[94]

As it is written (3 Kings 10:2–3, 13):

> *The queen of Sheba entered into Jerusalem with a great train, and riches, and camels that carried spices, and an immense quantity of gold, and precious stones. She came to king Solomon and spoke to him all that she had in her heart. And Solomon informed her of all the things she proposed to him . . . And King Solomon gave the queen of Sheba all that she desired, and asked of him: besides what he offered her of himself of his royal bounty.*

Likewise Mary entered into the heavenly Jerusalem at her Assumption. "Jerusalem," Richard explains, "may be interpreted as 'vision of peace' (*visio pacis*) and signifies eternal life, in which he who is our peace, Christ, is seen face to face, who in the pouring out of his blood on the cross made peace for us with God the Father, whom now we see veiled on the altar in the appearance of bread and wine.

For faith goes before knowledge (*cognitionem*), and merit [before] its reward, which will be to see him in the future just as he is."[95] Mary, however, has entered into this vision now *with a great train*, that is, all of the angels and saints who came out to greet her as she was "assumed to the heavenly chamber, where the King of kings sits upon his starry throne."[96] As Jerome says: "Today the blessed Virgin entered joyfully into the joys of eternal life as the choirs of Angels sang alternating hymns." Just so David brought the ark into the city with joy: *And there were with David seven choirs* (2 Kings [Samuel] 6:12), that is, the choirs of the angels, patriarchs, prophets, apostles, martyrs, confessors, and virgins, all singing her praise.[97] She entered with riches, that is, her twelve privileges (which Richard describes at length in book 3); camels carrying spices, that is, sinners bearing the fasts, vigils, prayers, tears, pilgrimages, and suchlike of true penance that make a good odor before the Lord; and gold and precious stones, that is, the virtues with which through grace she bedecks her lovers and imitators. She spoke what was in her heart, that is, on behalf of her lovers and imitators, and Solomon, that is, her Son, who is neither willing nor able to refuse her anything, gave her whatever she asked.[98]

Heaven

Do not I, the Lord asked, speaking through the prophet Jeremiah (23:24), *fill heaven and earth?*—that is, the mind and body of Mary. And note, Richard observes, that the Lord says first *heaven* then *earth*: "because the Virgin first conceived him in her mind through faith and love, then in her womb through the union of natures." Mary is called heaven (*coelum*) from *celando* "because she conceals for us the secrets of God," prudently veiling the divine mysteries from the wicked, but revealing them clearly to the evangelists. She is most high (Psalm 90:9), elevated above all earthly things in her contemplation of eternal things; most beautiful, shining with the glory of the stars (Ecclesiasticus 43:10), that is, the splendor of her virtues; most subtle in her understanding of divine things, of the Incarnation of the Lord, and in her mercy; most hot, wholly on fire with love, having enclosed in her womb he who is a consuming fire (Deuteronomy 4:24; Hebrews 12:29); most orderly (Job 38:33), in thought, sight, hearing, smell, taste, touch, gait, movement, and gesture, ever obedient to the divine will; always turning, never tired, according to the example of her Son (Psalm 18:6); illuminated by her Son, the sun of justice; and quickly moving, to see Elizabeth when she had conceived the Savior, to Nazareth when she was about to give birth, to Egypt when Herod threatened to kill her Son, back

PLATE 14 Mary as sun, moon, and stars. Richard of Saint-Laurent, *De laudibus beatae Mariae virginis*, lib. 7. Copied in Paris or French Flanders, between 1250 and 1299. Wellesley, Wellesley College 19, fol. 236.

to Nazareth when Herod died, following her Son as he went about through villages and towns and standing beside his cross.[99]

She is spherical and moving in a perfect circle, as heavenly bodies do, lacking beginning and end, wholly pure, without angles in her simplicity, of all figures having the greatest capacity, for in her womb the One made man enclosed himself, whom the whole world could not contain. She is extended and stretched out (Isaiah 40:22), covering her lovers like a tent (Psalm 103:2); her name stretches out to the ends of the earth, likewise her mercy and love for her enemies and friends. She is most strong (Job 37:18), in the constancy of her mind and the firmness of her faith. She is shining and most splendid in her examples, "for her beautiful life illuminates the whole Church." She is most peaceful, a place of peace (Psalm 75:3), where no evil comes (Psalm 90:10). God dwells in her (Psalm 103:19; Isaiah 66:1; Acts 7:49); likewise, she is the habitation of the angels, that is, all the virtues (Galatians 5:22–23). Nothing wicked and no vices dwell within her (Psalm 5:6); from her descend the dew and rain upon the earth (Isaiah 45:8). The waters are above her (Psalm 28:3), that is, the abundance of graces which she had from above or the tears which she shed at the Passion of her Son and after his Ascension as she longed to be with him. Her proper color is sapphire or hyacinth or a mixture of white and sapphire, and she contains within herself the twelve signs of the Zodiac, each, of course, with its own symbolism.[100]

Sun

First God created heaven and earth; then he created the firmament in the midst of the waters (Genesis 1:6; Psalm 18:2); then he created the lights in the firmament, that is, the sun and the moon (Genesis 1:14). Mary is the sun. As it says of her in the Song of Songs (6:9): *beautiful as the moon, chosen as the sun.* Likewise, in Ecclesiasticus 26:21: *As the sun when it riseth to the world in the high places of God, so is the beauty of a good woman for the ornament of her house.* And, again, in Psalm 88:38: "*His throne,* that is, the blessed Virgin, [will be] *as the sun in my sight.*" Like the sun, Mary has no equal, shining in celestial glory before all other saints.[101]

The whole world is filled with the splendor of her miracles and will be until the day of judgment. Thus it is sung in her sequence:

> As the sun outshines the moon,
> and the moon outshines the stars,
> so Mary is worthier
> than all other creatures.[102]

Mary is the firstborn before all other creatures, that is, worthier than all pure creatures; just as there is only one sun, so Mary is alone Mother and Virgin. In this sense, she may be compared to the phoenix, which is a singular bird having no father. Likewise, she is called *chosen as the sun*, because just as the sun was made to give light to the whole earth (Genesis 1:16), so Mary was made by God the Trinity "that she might beseech mercy, pardon, grace, and glory for the whole world from God." Just as Christ was chosen out of thousands of men (Song of Songs 5:10), so Mary was chosen out of thousands of women, whence it says in the Song of Songs (6:8): *She is the only one of her mother, the chosen of her that bore her.* Like a good woman who beautifies her house or the sun that illuminates the moon, so Mary gives light to the whole Church, as it is sung at her Nativity. She is chosen as the sun because she illuminates the intellect with true knowledge and inflames the affect with true love.[103]

She is called sun because she gives whatever she has to both the good and the bad. For the bad, she asks pardon and grace, as with Theophilus; for the just, she beseeches, increases, and preserves grace. She attracts the waters of the sea, that is, the people of the world, to the worship of her Son through the heat of her piety, love, prayers, merits, and examples, and she draws them off from the saltiness of vice, making sinners sweet. Just as the sun is the eye of the material world, so she is "the light of creatures and the mirror of the creator, than which no earthly creature is more beautiful, more useful, more bright, by whose shining all other lights are as not" (cf. Job 25:5). Her principal privileges are five: her size, that is, her humility, the virtue by which all souls are measured by God (Matthew 18:4); her power, that is, her faith, because faith is the power of the soul (Mark 9:22); her utility, that is, her mercy, because after the mercy of God nothing is more useful to the human creature; her brightness, that is, her purity, which Richard explains elsewhere under a separate title; and her heat, that is, her love, because love is the heat of the soul, which, again, Richard explains elsewhere under a separate title on the properties of the servants of Mary (the cross-references are his).[104]

The sun begins the day with its rising, ends it with its setting, and divides it into parts with its movement; likewise, Mary gives order to the life of the Christian through the example of her life, so that what is said of her Son may also be said of her: *By thy ordinance the day goes on* (Psalm 118:91). The sun makes darkness flee and gives light to the world of shades; Mary drives out heresies, just as the Church sings: "Gaude, Maria, virgo." Nevertheless, she never turns her face from even the vilest sinner who invokes her faithfully, unlike those who are "great in letters, riches, or honors" who neglect to invoke her.[105]

Moon

According to Tullius, moon (*luna*) is derived by syncope from *Lucina* (the goddess of childbirth, "she who brings to light") or *lucens nocte* (shining at night). Whence Virgil says: "Chaste Lucina, favor me" (*Eclogue IV*, with changes). According to Isidore, *luna* is derived from *luminum una* (one of the lights) because, as it says in Genesis 1:16, God made two lights, one, the sun, that is, Christ, the sun of justice, to rule the day, and the other, the moon, that is, Mary, to rule the night, that is, to illuminate sinners, and the stars, that is, the just. Mary is the Mother of grace, filled with mercy toward sinners just as a mother is merciful to her children. While the sun is both hot with justice and bright with mercy, the moon is merciful without the severity of the sun's heat and is therefore easier for those with weak eyes to gaze upon. Unlike the sun, the moon waxes and wanes, but no other light is as like the sun. There is nothing (that is, no other planet) between the sun and the moon,[106] whence the moon says: *Let him kiss me with the kiss of his mouth* (Song of Songs 1:1). Sometimes the moon has the color of iron, when she mortified the members of her body in penance or at the Passion of her Son, when he had *no beauty or comeliness* (Isaiah 53:2) and she was darkened through her compassion. The bone marrow of animals increases and decreases with changes in the moon; so, too, the virtues of grace that moisten the bones of her servants' natural virtues increase or decrease through Mary's grace and prayers (Proverbs 3:8).[107]

Like the moon when it is dark, Mary was conceived in original sin, but at her sanctification she began to increase in light. Then she appeared with her two horns, humility of mind and virginity of flesh. She was like a half-moon before the conception of her Son, when she was living in the temple. At the Annunciation, the angel called her *full of grace*, for then she was fully illuminated by the sun of justice. She was eclipsed at the Passion of her Son, when she was turned to blood (Joel 2:31), but full once again at her Assumption, perfect for all eternity (Isaiah 30:26). She is *beautiful as the moon* (Song of Songs 6:9) because illuminated by the true sun of justice she sheds the light of heavenly knowledge and the conversation of the Gospel on the night of this age. The moon grows for fourteen days and then it appears full; likewise, Mary is believed to have been aged fourteen when she conceived the Son of God. While she was full, she was without the stain of sin, but she did not lack the stain of human misery; just so, she suffered with her Son through her compassion as she stood beside his cross. When the sun of justice had ascended into heaven and she was left behind in the world for a time, she instructed the primitive Church, that is, the apostles and other disciples along with the holy women, through her example, joining with them in prayer (Acts 1:14). Her Nativity begins all the Church's solemnities, whence it says in Ecclesiasticus 43: *From the moon is the sign of the festival day* (v. 7); and *the moon in all her season is for a declaration of times and a sign of the world* (v. 6). For she was the sign of the fullness of time, and from her arose Christians' every festivity, namely Christ the Lord, who is all their joy. Whence she is called *the city of our solemnity* (Isaiah 33:20).[108]

Dawn

In French (*Gallice*), dawn is *alba* or *aube*, from *albedine* (whiteness), while in Latin, according to Isidore, *aurora* comes from *auro* (gold) on account of its splendor. The Virgin was white inside and out in holiness of body and spirit; she was resplendent inside and out like gold, pure in her virginity (Revelation 21:18), fiery in her love (Revelation 3:18), and best in wisdom because she tasted and saw (Genesis 2:12). Dawn is a golden hour (*aurea hora*) because it brought the golden age, as it is said of Saturn: "Ordering the golden age throughout the earth." The dawn is breezy (*aura*) with the grace and breath of the Holy Spirit (Song of Songs 5:16), dripping (*auro rorans*) with the dew of prayers and merits (Job 4:16), the hour of dew (*hora roris*) because at his conception the Son of God descended in her like dew (Hosea 14:6), whom she conceived through her ear (*per aurem*) (Song of Songs 5:4), whence the Church sings: "You conceived our Lord through your ear, that you might be called blessed among women."[109]

Likewise, dawn is the hour of birds (*avium hora*), who at that time begin to raise their voices in praise of the Mother and the Son. The birds of the world are spiritual men, while the birds of heaven are the angels, who praise her harmoniously. Whence she is able to say with her Son (Job 38:7): *when the morning stars praised me together and all the sons of God made a joyful melody*. Birds are those faithful souls who fly with wings of virtue and whose thoughts are on the heavens, who open their mouths in praise of Mary and her Son and to give thanks to the Lord for the blessings of his Incarnation and Passion (2 Corinthians 9:15). These souls kept vigil through all the watches of the night, from the time of Noah and Abraham when the signs of Mary were hidden, through the time of Moses and those who were taught by the law, through the time of the prophets and their certain predictions, to the time of the saints desiring that the promises of the Lord be fulfilled. Mary is the dawn who brought an end to the night of the law with the light of the New Testament, gave birth to him who revealed the truth against the night of ignorance, and brought the light of grace against the night of sin. With the birth of Christ from the Virgin, the shadows of scripture recede, *all their treasures are opened and the clouds fly out like birds* (Ecclesiasticus 43:15).[110]

Dawn comes forth from the shadows, and afterward gives birth to the sun. Likewise, the Virgin came forth from the ancient fathers, who lived in the shadows of sin, in the darkness of ignorance, under the shadow of the law. Like the dawn, she gave birth to the true sun.

> *In the beginning, God created heaven and earth,* that is, the soul and body of Mary, but *the earth was void and empty* before the grace of sanctification, *and darkness was upon the face of the deep,* because she was conceived in original sin. And God said as if by predestination: *Be light made, and light was made,* when he sanctified her (Genesis 1:1–3). And from that light according to the opinion of some was made the body of the sun. But most of all there was light at [her] conception over the whole world.

God separated the light, that is, the predestined, from the darkness, that is, vices, through their prayers and examples, and Mary from the shadows of the synagogue, for she was a rose among thorns, born from the Jews. Her Nativity came before the human nativity of Christ, but she received all her splendor from his divinity, whence it says (2 Kings [Samuel] 23:4): *As the light of the dawn, when the sun riseth, shineth in the morning without clouds.*[111] Just as the dawn comes before the sun, so Mary in her virtues shows the image of the Son about to be born from her. She is the mediator between the day, Christ, and the night, the sinner: "Just as it is impossible to come from the shadows of the night into the light without the mediation of the dawn, so it is impossible to come from the shadows of vices to the light of grace and virtue without the mediating intercession of Mary." She is the image and model (*forma et modulus*) of all goodness, giving the form of penitence standing beside the cross, of the active life ministering to Elizabeth, and of the contemplative life speaking with Gabriel and persevering in prayer with the holy women and the apostles: "For she gave birth to Christ, who came into the world that he might repair his image in our souls deformed by the old Adam."[112]

Who is she, the angels wondered, *who comes forth like the rising dawn, beautiful as the moon, chosen as the sun, terrible as an army set in array?* (Song of Songs 6:9). Mary was the dawn at her Nativity, beautiful as the moon in the conception of her Son, chosen as the sun at her Assumption, and most powerful in her assistance, like an army set in array. She advances into heaven over all the orders of the angels and the saints, whence it is sung of her: "I saw the beautiful one ascending like a dove over the rivers of water."[113]

Cloud

Mary is the cloud of which the prophet spoke: *The Lord will ascend upon a swift cloud, and will enter into Egypt* (Isaiah 19:1). She is swift (*levis*) because the Holy Spirit lifted the weight of original sin from her at her sanctification and purified her from all trace of sin at the conception of her Son. Descending into her at the Incarnation, the Lord assumed the flesh from her in which he appeared visible to the world. As the prophet put it (Baruch 3:38): *Afterwards he was seen upon the earth* who previously had been invisible in his divinity. Thus while previously he had been a hidden God (Isaiah 45:15), riding on Mary he ascended in the knowledge (*cognitionem*) of men who previously had known little or nothing about him. As a cloud, Mary is white in her virginity and purity, whence it says: *And I saw: and behold a white cloud and upon the cloud one sitting like to the Son of man, having on his head a crown of gold and in his hand a sharp sickle* (Revelation 14:14). This was the Lord sitting on the cloud, his divinity crowned with eternal wisdom and holding in his hand the power of judgment. The cloud was suspended between heaven and earth because Mary is the mediatrix between God and sinners; it was watery with an abundance of graces and charisms, and with all the words of wisdom that Mary conserved in her heart. As a cloud, Mary was given these two offices (Psalm 104:39): to protect her servants from the heat of the sun of justice and to illumine them with her prayers and examples like fire, "because she is the light showing the light of virtue, and she protects us against the devil like a fiery wall, and against vices and sin."[114]

Earth

Mary is the earth from which the new Adam was formed, the earth of which it is said no man had tilled and from which a spring rose to water the face of the earth (Genesis 2:5–6). She is the land of Havilah where is found the best gold, that is, the flesh of Christ, as well as bdellium, that is, the soul of Christ, filling the whole world with the fragrance of its virtues and examples, and onyx with its bands of white, that is, the divinity of Christ, shining with the brightness of eternal light and the figure of the Father (Genesis 2:11–12; Wisdom 7:26). She is the land of Gerar where Isaac sowed (Genesis 26:12); the land flowing with the honey of virginity and the milk of fertility (Numbers 14:8; Ezekiel 20:15); the land promised to the Jews and restored to Christians; a good land of brooks, waters, fountains, plains, and hills where deep rivers arise, of wheat, barley, vineyards, fig trees, and pomegranates, a land of oil and honey (Deuteronomy 8:7–9),

PLATE 15 Mary as Earth, with contemplative Dominican. Richard of Saint-Laurent, *De laudibus beatae Mariae virginis*, lib. 8. Copied in Paris or French Flanders, between 1250 and 1299. Wellesley, Wellesley College 19, fol. 239.

flowing with charisms, graces, and virtues. She is a land of wheat who bore Christ, the grain of wheat, and she is the granary of scripture, where holy souls are fed. She is a land of hills and plains, expecting rains from heaven, whom the Lord visits (Deuteronomy 11:11–12), the earth hung upon nothing (Job 26:7), that is, humility which relies only on God.[115]

She is the land blessed by the Lord (Psalm 84:2), who sanctified her in her mother's womb (Psalm 45:5), extinguished all trace of sin in her (Luke 1:35), and granted her the power of giving birth (Jeremiah 31:22): "This land God alone inhabited, God alone cultivated, and he alone this land bore." This is the land where humanity was liberated from its captivity to the devil (Psalm 84:2), where through the prayers of Mary its sins are forgiven and covered with the mantle of flesh with which Mary clothed God (Psalm 84:3; Ezekiel 16:8). She is the earth visited, watered, and enriched by God (Psalm 64:10), the land that gives forth fruit (Psalm 84:13), as can been seen in her images, where she holds her fruit in her hands, offering him to all. She is the center of the earth, where God has wrought salvation (Psalm 73:12), the land of the Lord (Psalm 23:1). She is the earth that stands forever while the generations pass away (Ecclesiastes 1:4); alone among the elements she is immovable and firm. She is the earth poised with three fingers (Isaiah 40:12), the work of the Trinity; the thirsty earth from which the root grew (Isaiah 53:2), and the land upon which no man walked (Jeremiah 2:6).[116]

She is called earth (*terra*) from *terion* (Greek: place), that is, *statio* (Latin: standing place), because *the earth standeth forever* (Ecclesiastes 1:4), while fire, air, and water move; ground (*solum*) because of her constancy in preserving her vow of virginity and in the stability of her faith when the Lord was in the tomb; earth (*tellus*) because she carries her servants (*nos tollit*) and they carry her fruits (*tollimus fructus suos*); soil (*humus*) because she is moist with charisms and graces; dry (*arida*) because in her the waters of earthly concupiscence have no place (Genesis 1:9); mud (*limus*) because she was watered by the Holy Spirit that from her Christ might be formed; and clay (*argilla*) because on her works of stone might be securely founded and in her were cast all the vessels of the temple of Solomon (3 Kings 7:46–50). As the earth, she is decorated with diverse flowers, that is, virtues, clothed with many kinds of medicinal herbs, walked upon in her humility and by the enemies of her Son (Psalm 55:3), thirsty in her desire for grace, flat in places in her gentleness, but mountainous in others in her excellence. Every building, that is, every good work, is founded upon her through faith in the Incarnation; she takes up the falling and helps them to rise (Revelation 12:16). She is the only thing standing between her servants and the abyss; without her help, they would fall at once into sin and thence into hell, just like Korah, Dathan, and Abiram (Numbers 16:31–32).[117]

Mountain

Mary is a mountain in her eminence, immobile in her humility, a fat mountain (Psalm 67:16–17) curdled like cheese in her virginal integrity, fat with the fat of love, the lard of devotion, the richness of fertility, the oil of mercy and piety, the butter of gentleness, the honey of contemplation, and the thickness of singular grace. She is the mountain upon which the true Jews were accustomed to worship (John 4:20–21), the mountain in Armenia where the ark rests (Genesis 8:4), the mountain of vision where Abraham intended to sacrifice his son (Genesis 22:14), and the mountain of Gilead (Genesis 31:21), which means "heap of witnesses," "because in her come together all the testimonies of the scriptures of the Old and New Testaments, and all the oracles of the Prophets as well as the deeds of the Patriarchs bear witness to her." She is the mountain of Horeb, the mountain of Tabor, and the mountain of Olives. She is the mountain in which God was pleased to dwell corporeally for nine months and spiritually without end (Psalm 67:17). She is the mountain that Daniel saw (Daniel 2:34), the height of human nature before it fell into sin, cut without hands "because the flesh of Christ, the temple of God, is figured by the temple of Solomon, in whose construction there was heard neither hammer nor ax nor any tool of iron (3 Kings 6:7), but its maker and builder was God (Hebrews 11:10)." She is that shadowy mountain from which God comes to humanity (Habakkuk 3:3, according to an alternate reading). And she is the mountain of the house of the Lord exalted above all other hills (Isaiah 2:2), that is, all other saints; higher than the adjacent land, that is, every pure creature, and inferior only to Christ. She may be seen from afar: "for the sound of her piety and mercy resounds through every corner of the earth." And she is suitable for fortifications and mirrors: "for in her examples we are able to see as if in a mirror what ought to be avoided and what ought to be embraced."[118]

Fountain

Mary is the fountain of gardens (Song of Songs 4:15), that is, of the Church and the consciences of the just. The river of this fountain is Christ the Lord, whom

Wisdom pours out to water her garden (Ecclesiasticus 24:42). She is a sealed fountain, rising up out of the earth to water the face of the earth (Genesis 2:6), sealed with the seal of her Son and of the Trinity (Song of Songs 8:6), that is, with the beauty of the divine likeness more distinctly than any other creature. She is the fountain coming forth from the house of the Lord (Joel 3:18), that is, blessed Anna, "in whom the blessed Trinity dwelled by grace," or the family of the Lord, namely the ancient fathers Abraham, Isaac, and Jacob, or the double house of the Lord, both royal and priestly, who waters the torrent of thorns, that is, of sinners. She is the fountain of Shiloah (Isaiah 8:6) next to the mountain of Zion (John 9:7), the fountain of which Zechariah says (Zechariah 13:1): *In that day there shall be a fountain open to the house of David, and to the inhabitants of Jerusalem: for the washing of the sinner, and of the unclean woman.* She is open to her friends, but closed to her enemies; open to the clean, but closed to the unclean; open to the penitent, but closed to the impenitent; open by mercy, but closed by justice. As a fountain, she both descends lower than all other creatures through her humility in conceiving God and ascends above all other pure creatures at her Assumption. She reveals the waters lying hidden in the earth: "for through her the goodness and humanity of the Savior appeared to us, who before had been a hidden God in the land of the living."[119]

River

The river of God is filled with water (Psalm 64:10), that is, Mary is filled with the charisms of grace, whence she is *gratia plena.* She is the river that *maketh the city of God joyful* (Psalm 45:5), that is, both the Church and the faithful soul. She takes her waters from the fountain, that is, from the Lord, who is a fountain of living water (Jeremiah 2:13), or, rather, from the divine plenitude, that she might pour it out for her servants. She makes fertile her surroundings, that is, the consciences of those joined to her in love, watering the hearts of her lovers with her prayers and examples. In this river was born "that singular and eternal fish, Christ the Lord, who like a fish was caught in the waters of the human race by the hook of our mortality, that he might give to us eternal life, and in whose mouth was found the coin of our redemption" (cf. Matthew 17:26). She is signified by the four rivers that flow out of the earthly paradise (Genesis 2:10–14), as described in Ecclesiasticus 24:35–37: the Phison or Ganges, in whose sands are found precious stones, that is, the gifts of grace with which the wise Virgin is filled; the Tigris, filled with grace in the days of new fruits, flowing swiftly against the Assyrians, that is, the proud, with the example of her humility; the Euphrates, filled with senses, that is, the spiritual senses, the red color of love, the white of chastity, the green of holiness, the odor of spiritual discretion, and the taste of spiritual wisdom; and the Gihon or Nile *in the time of the vintage*, that is, standing beside her Son when like a grape he was pressed on the winepress of the cross. Likewise, she will stand by him on the day of judgment, pouring out the waters of her graces onto the dry hearts of sinners. *I, Wisdom*, Mary says, *have poured out rivers* (Ecclesiasticus 24:40): "Just as when one river rises out of another, I was filled with wisdom from that king born of David. Thus I ought to be called Wisdom, because I am the mother of the eternal wisdom of God, and so ought to be called by the same name (*et univoca debet esse generatio*)."[120]

Ark

And Beseleel made also the ark of setim wood: it was two cubits and a half in length, and a cubit and a half in breadth, and the height was of one cubit and a half: and he overlaid it with the purest gold within and without. And he made to it a crown of gold round about. (Exodus 37:1–2)

Mary is the ark because in her God hid himself (Isaiah 45:15). The material ark was built to preserve memorials of the divine activity: the rod (*virga*) in memory of the liberation from Egypt, the manna in memory of the feeding in the desert, the tablets of the giving of the Law (Hebrews 9:4). Mary, the spiritual ark, was made "that in her might be placed the price of our liberation." The rod signifies his divine nature, for the Son of God is the power (*virtus*) of God (Psalm 109:2); the two tablets signify his created nature, namely his soul, with its intellect and affect; the manna signifies his corporeal nature, pure of all stain of original sin except its penalties. This manna is the bread that Wisdom prepared (Wisdom 16:20), and the bread for which Christians pray, saying: "Give us today our daily bread."[121]

The ark, that is, Mary, was made of two materials: setim wood and purest gold, namely flesh and spirit, flesh that never experienced the corruption of lust or decay, and a spirit shining with perfect wisdom, the habitation of divinity. But the urn of manna which she contained, that is, the body of Christ filled with the manna of divinity, was wholly gold, wholly without the stain of sin. Alternately, the manna signifies the sweetness of divinity and of eternal bliss, while the rod signifies the right of rule that he has as heir and the tablets his knowledge of both laws which he had as priest (Malachi 2:7). Or, again, the

PLATE 16   Mary as ark and throne, with contemplative Dominican. Richard of Saint-Laurent, *De laudibus beatae Mariae virginis*, lib. 10. Copied in Paris or French Flanders, between 1250 and 1299. Wellesley, Wellesley College 19, fol. 264.

ark signifies the body of Christ, the golden urn his soul, and the manna the sweetness of his divinity:

> For Christ is manna, that is, the celestial bread filled with every delight and every sweet taste, the bread of Angels, that man ate. He is the bread whom the little ones asked for, but before the coming and birth of Mary, there was no one to break it for them (cf. Lamentations 4:4). But Mary made this bread that was broken on the cross. . . . Thus we ought to cry out to her assiduously: "Our mother who is in heaven, give us today our daily bread from your ark, that is, from the ark, which you are" (cf. Matthew 6:11). For since she is a mother, she most freely gives this bread to her children, that is, to her imitators. Whence it is said of her: *All expect of thee that thou give them food in season* (Psalm 103:27).[122]

Mary is the ark because she contains the tablets of the Ten Commandments, the tablets of the knowledge of the divine law written on her heart (Jeremiah 31:33). She had perfect knowledge of the law "because the author of the Scriptures dwelt in her," whence she taught the apostles and was the teacher (*magistra*) of the New Testament. For in the ark were contained both Deuteronomy and the tablets of the covenant, that is, both the old and the new law: "Thus her whole life and her every action are a lesson (*lectio*) and instruction for Christians, just as Augustine said of Christ." Again and more subtly, Mary as the ark contains both the manna of the sweetness of divine contemplation and the rod of the rectitude of perfect action as well as the tablets of the understanding of the spiritual meaning of the law. In her was placed the testament, that is, the law of the covenant of the Lord:

> because she binds us in covenant to the whole Trinity . . . and through her God's covenant with us is confirmed. . . . But through the Virgin the Son of God came to us, and was made Emmanuel, that is, God with us, that both the Son and the mother might lead us back to the Father. . . . Whence in the hours of the blessed Virgin Mary we say to Christ: "Remember, author of salvation . . ."[123]

Mary is the ark of propitiation because she is the mother and queen of mercy, propitiating the Lord through her merits and intercession for her servants' sins (cf. 1 John 2:2). She is the ark of sanctification (Psalm 131:8) because she was sanctified in the womb, because Christ descended into her and there sanctified himself as man through himself as Word, and because her servants are sanctified through her in the present and will be glorified in future. She is the ark of the covenant seen in the temple (Revelation 11:19) because she is the secret of God (Isaiah 24:16), which he has closed and no one opens (Revelation 3:7). In her are hidden all the treasures of wisdom and knowledge (Colossians 2:3), whence someone has said of her:

> Hail, rich ark of Christ,
> who poured out treasure,
> by which all are enriched.[124]

And she is the ark in which folded clothing is kept: "for Christ, whom the whole world could not contain, as it were folded and humbled himself, and enclosed himself in the ark of her womb." Her dimensions are the three theological virtues: her length faith, her height hope, and her width love. She is covered over with gold inside and out in both her virginity and her fertility; her crown is gold because she is the Mother of the highest king, and her power is in the heavenly Jerusalem (Ecclesiasticus 24:15).[125]

Throne

> *King Solomon also made a great throne of ivory, and overlaid it with the finest gold. It had six steps, and the top of the throne was round behind, and there were two hands on either side holding the seat, and two lions stood, one at each hand. And twelve little lions stood upon the six steps on the one side and on the other; there was no such work made in any kingdom.* (3 Kings 10:18–20)

Mary is called throne because the king humbled himself and sat down in her and took on the form of a servant so as to exercise his power as judge. Christ is called Solomon ("peaceful") because he thinks thoughts of peace (Jeremiah 29:11); the throne is described as Solomon's work because it is the work of eternal wisdom (Proverbs 9:1), who in this work especially showed his wisdom, for she is *an admirable vessel, the work of the Most High* (Ecclesiasticus 43:2) that he made for himself to sit in and no other (Ezekiel 44:3), not the flesh, not the world, not the devil, not Bacchus, not Venus, not Mercury, not Mars, but himself—albeit also for humanity and the angels, but in a different way.[126]

He made the throne out of ivory, that is, Mary, the first to vow herself to virginity, whom he magnified above all others in her fertility. Ivory comes from the bones of elephants. In Greek *elephas* means "mountain," while the Indians call the elephant *barro*, for its trumpeting (*barritus*); likewise, Mary is compared to a mountain on account of her excellence (see above, "Mountain"). Elephants are by nature cold, so that by their blood they extinguish the burning of the serpent's venom; they are enemies of the dragon, just as the blessed Virgin is the enemy of the ancient serpent who seduced Eve. They have small tongues but great wisdom, just like the Virgin, who spoke few words. If they find someone who is lost, they guide him back to the way, just as the Virgin guides those wandering in the byways of vice back to the way of life with her prayers, merits, and examples. Elephants are chaste when married and widowed, preserving their virginity in the whiteness of their bones. They carry towers on their backs (1 Maccabees 6:37), just as the edifice of the Catholic Church is supported by the prayers, patronage, and example of Mary. They are not frightened by the sight of blood, but rather incited to battle, just as the Virgin did not fear to die at the sight of her Son's blood pouring out on the cross but rather wanted, if not to offer her soul for his, then whatever she could.[127]

Ivory is fleshless, hairless, dry, hard, cold, solid, white, shining, red when it ages, strong, durable, and suitable for making vessels for use in the sanctuary, like the pyx in which the body of Christ is kept along with the hosts from which it is made. The blessed Virgin is the throne of Solomon, "for in her the true peacemaker rested and sat corporeally for nine months." Other sons may be crowned kings after they are born from their mother, but Christ was crowned by his mother on the day of his conception (Song of Songs 3:11); thus the wise men from the East sought him, asking, *Where is he that is born king?* (Matthew 2:2). Mary was a great throne, constructed from the most precious materials, exquisitely crafted, durable for all eternity (Hebrews 1:8), enclosing the one who could not be enclosed (Ecclesiasticus 24:8), large enough to hold a giant, like the sun in her brilliance (Psalm 88:38), bearing the authority of the most just judge (Psalm 9:5, 8–9). She was overlaid with the finest gold, that is, Christ, the highest wisdom, by whom she was clothed (Revelation 12:1). She was bright with celestial wisdom, enlightening with her example both angels and men, pure in her immunity from sin, red in her virginal modesty, natural beauty, singular patience, and burning love, weighty in her humility, solid in the constancy of her mind, malleable in her obedience, without price whose price was Christ (Proverbs 31:10; see "Good Woman").[128]

We have already noted the six steps by which the Son ascended to his seat, making her a participant in his divine eternity when he sat upon his throne. There divine Wisdom took his rest because *there his place was in peace, and his abode in Zion* (Psalm 75:3). There the new Adam was placed in the paradise of the blessed Virgin, when a woman encompassed a man (Jeremiah 31:22), that he might till her and keep her (Genesis 2:15). The two lions to either side of her were John the Baptist and John the Evangelist (because they both lived in the desert, the Baptist literally, the Evangelist spiritually as seer) or John the Evangelist and Gabriel (who had Mary's body and soul in their care), while the twelve steps were the ancient fathers from whom she was born or the twelve apostles standing before her and serving her. Such a work was never made in any kingdom, in heaven, on earth, or in hell, nor will there be her like again. On this throne Christ sits as judge, *just, strong, and patient* (Psalm 7:12), judging with the power given to him by the Father *because he is the Son of Man* (John 5:27). It is a throne of grace, not a tribunal of judgment, because Mary, full of grace, is a fountain of grace, pouring out grace for the remission of sins and helping sinners not to fall back into their sins. There, like the sun in his sight *and a faithful witness in heaven* (Psalm 88:38), she prays for sinners and bears witness that the Son of God was made man for them, even as she shows him her breasts and calls upon him to remember his throne (Jeremiah 14:21). Whence, in the general confession, it is said: "I confess to God and blessed Mary . . ."[129]

Tabernacle

"*Lord*, the psalmist asked, *who shall dwell in thy tabernacle* (Psalm 14:1) that is, in the blessed Virgin? As if to say: 'No one, but you alone.' " Christ has multiple tabernacles: first and most worthy, the body that he took from the Virgin. Second, the body of the Virgin herself. Third, the Church militant. Fourth, the Church triumphant. Fifth, the body of the just man. Sixth, any ordered religion. Let us, Richard says, take each in order. Of the first, the psalmist says: *He hath set his tabernacle in the sun* (Psalm 18:6), that is, in the Virgin when he assumed human nature from her, when he who is eternal entered into time and took on that which he had not had, hunger, thirst, fatigue, sleep, and the like. Of the second, she herself says: *He who created me rested in my tabernacle* (Ecclesiasticus 24:12). Note, Richard observes, that a tabernacle or tent is proper to knights and pilgrims: "For just as a knight about to fight arms himself in his tent, that he might go out armed to battle, thus Christ about to fight the devil for his disinherited bride, namely the Church, put on the armor of human flesh in the womb of the blessed Virgin as in a tent." Likewise, when the Son of God became a pilgrim, that is, a stranger and a sojourner from heaven on earth at the Incarnation, Mary received him in her tent. She is the tabernacle placed in the midst of the camp (Leviticus 26:11); the tabernacle of the true Moses, adorned and constructed and covered with skins dyed red and blue and with goat's hair, that is, virtues of every kind; and the tabernacle of the covenant from which the cloud was taken up (Numbers 10:11–12; see "Cloud") at the Assumption of her body "because in her was made the covenant between God and man through the marriage with the flesh assumed [from her]." The third tabernacle, the Church militant, is figured through that tabernacle and its vessels, which Moses made in the desert. The fourth, the Church triumphant, is that which the seer beheld in heaven (Revelation 21:3) and which cannot be moved (Isaiah 33:20). The fifth tabernacle is the body of the just man, to which Peter refers (1 Peter 1:13), while the sixth is any ordered religion where spiritual knights dwell in their cloisters and fight against the devil (Numbers 24:5–6).[130]

Bedchamber

Mary is called bedchamber because in her womb the Son of God married himself to human nature like a bridegroom to his bride; thus, as Cyril of Alexandria put it, he came forth from her womb *like a bridegroom coming out of his bridechamber*, as it says in the psalm (Psalm 18:6). And note, Richard observes, that when kings and great men build houses for themselves "they build their own bedchambers with greater care and to a more elegant design, where there is better and purer air and gardens nearby where birds sing, spices and flowers give forth their fragrances, grasses grow, trees give fruit, the south wind blows, and the sun appears first before other parts of the house." Like-wise, when Wisdom, the Maker of all things (*omnium artifex*), built his house (Proverbs 9:1), the work of the Holy Spirit, he designed it with the utmost care. His interior chamber was the mind of the Virgin, which the whole Trinity inhabited; his exterior chamber, from which he went out into his house, was the Virgin's womb, through which God came into the world. His upper chamber was the blessed life of the Virgin, in which Mary is already embraced by her bridegroom, as she says in the Song of Songs (2:6): "*His left hand is under my head, and his right hand shall embrace me*. And thus at her assumption the bedchamber ascended to the bedchamber, namely the interior and exterior to the superior: for all believe that she was assumed at the same time with her body, although this may not be asserted [as certain]."[131]

The walls of this bedchamber were *carved with divers figures and carvings ... cherubims and palm trees, and divers representations, as it were standing out, and coming forth from the wall* (3 Kings 6:29), all painted by the Holy Spirit, *who by his continual diligence varieth the figure, and shall give his heart to the resemblance of the picture, and by his watching shall finish the work* (Ecclesiasticus 38:28). The figures and carvings were picked out in a multitude of colors—the white of virginity, the green of perpetual sanctity, the gold of love, the azure of voluntary poverty, the sapphire of celestial conversation, the hyacinth of contemplation, the lilac of most innocent purity, the rose of virginal modesty, the livid blue of compassion, the vermilion of spiritual martyrdom, the red ocher of singular patience, the saffron of angelic likeness, the black of humility, the pallor of mortification, the crystal of celestial wisdom, the purple of royal dignity, the marble of every virtue and grace—in a variety of images and forms, with likenesses of the angels in harmony, of the patriarchs in faith and hope, of the prophets in knowledge of future things, of the apostles in zeal, of the martyrs in patience, of the confessors in temperance, of the virgins in humility and innocence, and of all the saints in justice and virtues of every kind. The bedchamber itself was large enough to hold the one who fills heaven and earth (Jeremiah 23:24), but closed against sleepless dragons and roaring lions, sealed with the seal of virginity, and furnished with arms (see "House"). Nothing unclean might enter into her in thought, word, or deed (Revelation 21:27). She was bright, peaceful, fragrant, flowing with delights, noble, wonderful, and rich, filled with all the treasures of wisdom and knowledge, and suitable for the celestial bridegroom. She also contained a dressing-room, in French *la garderobe*, that is, her virginal womb, "in which the high priest put on his vestments of most pure flesh."[132]

House

Wisdom hath built herself a house; she hath hewn her out seven pillars (Proverbs 9:1). Wisdom, that is, the Maker of all things (Wisdom 7:21), has built, that is, constructed, a place in which to live in that form of building called a house ("*a forma, vel specie, vel architectura, ubi dicitur, domum*"), and hewn out with great diligence or care seven columns to strengthen and distinguish it. Mary is this special work, filled with the glory of the Lord (Ecclesiasticus 42:16), which God made that the angelic nature might be repaired after its fall (Psalm 109:6), human nature renewed (Revelation 21:5), and corporeal nature *delivered from the servitude of corruption into the liberty of the glory of the children of God* (Romans 8:21). He built this house for himself, who built heaven for the angels, hell for the demons and the damned, the world for fallen man, the land for the beasts, the waters for the fish, the air for the birds, and the firmament for the stars. But although only he lived in this house, he gave it to the angels for their restoration, to man and human nature for our reparation, and to the lower creatures for their liberation, that innocence and the angelic life might be restored, peace made between God and man, and the devil conquered and trod upon (Genesis 3:15).[133]

He hewed out seven columns to support it: columns of iron for strength (Jeremiah 1:18), of marble for chastity (Song of Songs 5:15), of brass for humility (3 Kings 7:15), of silver for faith (Song of Songs 3:10), of gold for wisdom (Ecclesiasticus 26:23), of cloud for poverty (Exodus 13:21; Ecclesiasticus 24:7), and of fire for love (Exodus 13:21). Its walls are foursquare with fear and desire, grief and joy; its beams are cedar and its rafters of cypress trees (Song of Songs 1:16), that is, the bodies of Christ and of Mary are free of corruption, never eaten by worms. Its pavement was made of precious marble (2 Chronicles 3:6), sculpted with pictures showing the virtues of the patriarchs and prophets, and its gate was always closed to the devil and to the habit of sin, but open to lead humanity into its sabbatical rest (Ezekiel 46:1). Alternately, the seven columns may be read as the seven gifts of the Holy Spirit "which rested in Christ resting in Mary," or the three theological and four cardinal virtues, or the seven virtues that may be elicited from the seven words that Mary spoke as recorded in the Gospels, or the seven virtues that James attributes to Wisdom "which support the house of wisdom [that is, Mary or the perfect soul] against the seven deadly sins" (James 3:17). Wisdom built this house not only for herself, but also for her servants, that it might pour forth for them the gifts of grace, the ointments of virtue, medicines against sickness, and the like. As the psalmist said of Christ in the person of all the faithful: *We shall be filled with the good things of thy house* (Psalm 64:5). This house fills Mary's servants with all the good things that they lack as many times as they come to it, because she asks pardon for their sins lest they be as nothing, gains grace for them lest they be empty, and repairs their nature lest they remain like mud: "And she does this not only once, but as many times as truly penitent we flee to her."[134]

Mary is the treasury of the Lord filled with virtues and graces, the place of his heart (3 Kings 9:3), and the House of the Forest of Lebanon (3 Kings 7:2), which, according to the Master in his *Historia*, was divided into two parts: the lower part was called *netota*, that is, perfumery (*pigmentaria*), where Solomon kept perfumes and incense for use in the temple and the house of the king, that is, the virginal odor of Mary so pleasing to God, while the upper part was called the armory (*armaria*), where he kept the arms for the protection of the king and for the beauty of the house, that is, the virtues with which Mary protects the Church and those ruling themselves well.[135]

Temple

The psalmist continues: *We shall be filled with the good things of thy house; holy is thy temple, wonderful in justice* (Psalm 64:5–6). A house is the proper dwelling of a man, while the temple is the dwelling of God. Mary is called both house and temple because she was the dwelling of God and man. She is called temple because her servants offer through her their prayers to Christ. In this temple, offerings are made to the Lord, even as the Son offers his humility to the Father in the womb of the blessed Virgin. Here the Lord is worshipped, and here the mother worships the Son. Here prayers are spoken, as when Mary's servants say, "Remember, author of salvation . . ."[136] Here sacrifices are made to the Lord, as when the mother is martyred through the Son or as many times as the Lord is beseeched in a spirit of humility and with contrite heart (Daniel 3:39; Psalm 50:19). This temple is signed inwardly and outwardly with the cross, inwardly in memory of the Passion, outwardly in imitation of her Son (Song of Songs 8:6). Relics are kept in this temple, that is, the examples of the saints for imitation, as well as that most precious relic, the Son of God enclosed in the virginal womb, along with the charisms of all graces, just as the priests carried the names of the twelve sons of Israel on their breast as a memorial and a remembrance (Exodus 28:9–12). It is aspersed with holy water, full of grace, and filled with the waters of the wisdom of salvation and with holy tears, especially at the time of the Lord's Passion. In it are placed the table of propitiation (that the soul might be fed on the scriptures), the altar of incense (made of setim wood because the articles of faith are incorruptible), and the candelabrum with its seven lights (namely, the heart, which is like the sun in the microcosm of the body, illuminating the temple with its seven gifts), and here there is singing and psalmody, for *in his temple all shall speak his glory* (Psalm 28:9), to the honor of the Son by glorifying Mary: "For she is the queen and the leader of the choirs of virgins, who sing to the Lord a new song without ceasing, of which it is said (Revelation 14:3): *No one could say the song.*" And the priest of this temple is the Lord Christ (Psalm 10:5).[137]

Everything about this temple is significant of Mary. It is a *basilica* because there worship and sacrifices are offered to the king (*basileus*), and there the king of heaven took his rest. It is called the Holy of Holies (*sancta sanctorum*) because no one except the priest enters into it. It has a sacristy (*sacrarium*) where the sacred books of both Testaments are kept, that is, Mary's knowledge of the scriptures, along with the sacred vestments (her virtues), reliquaries (blessed members of Christ), and sacred vessels. It has a mercy seat (*propitiatorium*) or oracle of purest gold (Exodus 37:6), where the angel of the Lord appeared to Moses. Mary is the mercy seat whom the whole Trinity gave to be humanity's *propitiatrix* before the Son, "by praying on our behalf for our sins and by showing him the womb in which she carried him and the breasts which he sucked." The temple has a porch or vestibule (3 Kings 6:3), where Mary brings penitent sinners like Theophilus back to her Son, and it has a gate (Ezekiel 44:1–3) through which God has access to his creatures and they have access to God. This gate looks to the east because through it Christ, the true East, entered into the world. It is also the gate of heaven (Genesis 28:17) and the gate of light "because through her the true sun of justice enlightened and enlightens the Church and the faithful soul with rays of grace." Whence it is sung:

> Hail, gate of light,
> most excellent of gates,
> revealing the king of glory.[138]

Along with its gate, this temple also has a window to let in light and to allow those inside to see out. Mary is a window, opening her mouth to pray for her servants and illuminating their consciousness (*conscientia*) with the light of the Savior. She is likewise figured by that crystal window, which, according to Hebrew tradition, Noah made in the ark, "which signifies the Church." Just as crystal "moistened by the dew of heaven and set in the sun produces a little spark of fire without breaking," so moistened by celestial dew Mary bore Christ, the light of the Church, without losing the seal of her virginity, as the poet so elegantly says:

> If a crystal is made moist
> And placed in sunlight
> It sends out a little spark of fire.
> The crystal is not broken,
> The seal of chastity
> Is not broken in childbirth.[139]

She is also the ladder of Jacob (Genesis 28:12–13) seen only in dreams, that is, when the soul is asleep and free of worldly occupations, for her excellence is not visible except to those, like Jacob, who have struggled against vices and sins. To climb this ladder requires feet, that is, loving her and giving thanks to her continuously; hands, that is, at every instant doing whatever pleases her; and knees, that is, kneeling before her images and altars and at every recitation of her name. And she is a winding staircase leading up to the middle room and from the middle to the third (3 Kings 6:8), like a round tower at the corner of the Church, guiding those up from virtue to virtue by her example.[140]

Above all, however, she is the *vas admirabile, opus Excelsi* (Ecclesiasticus 43:2), the vessel who contained him whom the whole world could not contain, who was herself contained by him. Thus every vessel used in the temple may be read of her, of which it is said: *And the multitude of vessels was innumerable* (2 Chronicles 4:18; cf. 3 Kings 7:47). She is the new vessel filled with salt (4 Kings 2:20); the golden urn filled with manna (Exodus 16:33); the *massy vessel of gold adorned with every precious stone* (Ecclesiasticus 50:10); the vessel of crystal, of sapphire, of emerald, of ivory, of gold, and of silver where the sacramental body of the Lord is kept. She is a round drinking bowl (*crater*) adorned with gems (Song of Songs 7:2; Ecclesiasticus 32:7), a cup with two handles (*cratera*), a phial of oil (*lechytus*), a casket for ointments and perfumes (*pyxis*), a vessel for oil made out of bronze or silver (*lenticula*), a drinking cup like a ship (*cyathus* or *cymbia*), a siphon for putting out fires (*syphon*), an alabaster box (*alabastrum*), a wine-jar (*oenoforum*), a plate for holding food (*discus*), a salver (*scutella*), a saltcellar (*salmum*), an urn (*urna*), a chalice (*calix*), a phial of glass or silver or gold (*phiala*), a milk pail (*mulchrum*), a vessel for washing the hands (*scyphus*), an ewer for blessed water (*urceus*), a leather bottle (*uter*), a basin for washing the feet (*pelvis*), and a bottle for holy oil (*ampulla*) "because Christ the priest placed in the blessed Virgin the oil of the future good of the sick, that is, the mercy which signs sinners, and the sacred chrism, that is, the spiritual ointment of spiritual kings, priests, and champions, without which no one is sanctified or able to be made truly Christian in name."[141]

City of God

According to Isidore, "A city (*civitas*) is a multitude of people (*concors hominum*) united by a bond of community, named for its citizens (*a civibus*), that is, from the residents of the city (*urbis*) because it has jurisdiction over and contains the lives of many. Now *urbs* is the name for the actual buildings, while *civitas* is not the stones, but the inhabitants." All of these things may be applied to the blessed Virgin, because she is that city of which it is said in the psalm: *Glorious things are said of thee, O city of God* (Psalm 86:3). Mary is a city (*civitas*) because in her dwell a unity of citizens (*civium unitas*), that is, a complete harmony of sensitivity and reason (*sensualitas et rationis plena concordia*). The citizens of this city are holy thoughts, devout affections, fervent desires, and the like, all of which live together in necessary unity. These citizens are governed by the counsel of the Holy Spirit,

PLATE 17 Mary as city of God. Richard of Saint-Laurent, *De laudibus beatae Mariae virginis*, lib. 11. Copied in Paris or French Flanders, between 1250 and 1299. Wellesley, Wellesley College 19, fol. 319.

Reproduction courtesy of Wellesley College Library, Special Collections. Photo by James Marrow.

so that the flesh never desires anything against the spirit nor the spirit against the flesh, but all live together in this place of peace (Psalm 75:3). She is called the city of God to differentiate her from the city of Babylon, where the devil lives and the Lord will not enter (Hosea 11:9). But no one lives in her except God.[142]

There are many things to commend about this city, beginning with its foundations. As the psalmist puts it: *The foundations thereof are in the holy mountains* (Psalm 86:1), that is, in the patriarchs, kings, and prophets from whose lineage she was born, but above all, in Christ, who supports the whole Church (Matthew 16:18), especially the Virgin. Mary is also the foundation of the temple that Solomon built with great and costly stones (3 Kings 5:17–18), that is, her virtues. She is also to be commended for her gates, as the psalmist says: *The Lord loveth the gates of Zion above all the tabernacles of Jacob* (Psalm 86:2). Mary is called Zion because it was the most prominent place in Jerusalem, just as Mary is most prominent in both Churches (that is, militant and triumphant). Her gates are her five senses, which are always closed against anything harmful or indecent but open to everything good as well as to every sinner calling upon her for mercy. She is to be commended for her reputation, again in the words of the psalm: *Glorious things are said of thee, O city of God* (Psalm 86:3), through the patriarchs under the obscurities of figures and through the prophets under the enigmas of words, as in Isaiah 7:14: *Behold, a virgin shall conceive*; Isaiah 11:1: *A rod shall come forth*; Jeremiah 31:38: *A city shall be built to the Lord from the tower of Hanameel*; Numbers 24:17: *A star shall rise out of Jacob*; and Song of Songs 6:8: *The daughters* [of Zion] *saw her and declared her most blessed, the queens and concubines, and they praised her*.[143]

Still in the words of the psalm, the city of God is to be commended for her helpfulness in the conversion of sinners and in recalling them from evil, that is, the city of Babylon: *I will be mindful*, she says, *of Rahab*, that is, of sinners, *and of Babylon knowing me* (Psalm 86:4). Many now dwell in her who before were citizens of Babylon, as she says: *Behold, the foreigners and Tyre and the people of the Ethiopians, these were there* (Psalm 86:4), having fled to her through penitence. *Shall not Zion say, "This man and that man is born in her?" And the Highest himself hath founded her* (Psalm 86:5), that is, having founded her he was born man in her, something that never before had been heard, that an architect should first build a house and then be born in it. Accordingly, *the Lord shall tell in his writings of peoples and of princes of them that have been in her* (Psalm 86:6), that is, in the writings of both people (that is, the poor prophets like Amon, the Gentiles like the Sybil and Job, the commentators on scripture, and the saints other than the apostles) and princes (that is, the kings and nobles like David and Isaiah, the Jews, the editors of scripture, and the apostles), the dignity of blessed Mary and of both Churches shall be told, not by Plato, Aristotle, and Socrates, but by those who were in the city, that is, the Church. Moreover, everyone who lives in her will rejoice (Psalm 86:7). Thus it is sung of her in the antiphon: "Just as of all those who rejoice, our habitation is in you, holy Mother of God." Mary, indeed, is "the refuge and hope of all the faithful, because she is impregnable and most strong, and terrible as an army set in array. She is also rich with an abundance of graces and virtues because she is full of grace and glory. And she is great in the breadth of her love, by which all are embraced. Thus the Church sings: 'We fly to your protection, holy Mother of God.' "[144]

This city is likewise commended many other places in scripture: for its builder and maker (Hebrews 11:10); for its ruler and king of justice, Melchizedek (Psalm 22:1; Genesis 14:18); for its foundation on Christ and humility (1 Corinthians 10:4; Psalm 103:5; Revelation 21:10–11); for its brightness (Isaiah 60:19; Tobit 13:13; Revelation 21:11, 23–24), soundness (see the title on her sanctification), and purity (Revelation 21:18, 27); for its materials (Revelation 21:18); for its extent (Zechariah 14:10; Jeremiah 31:38); for the length of its walls, even to the region of death (Jeremiah 31:39–40); for its defense of the fatherland (Isaiah 26:1); for its foursquare shape (Revelation 21:16); for the height of its towers (Judith 1:1–3); for the strength of its walls (Revelation 21:12, 18; Isaiah 26:1; Song of Songs 8:9); for the guardians of its walls, that is, the angels (Isaiah 62:6); and for the dignity of its names—Salem, the city of Melchizedek; Jerusalem, the vision of peace and the seat of the king (2 Kings [Samuel] 5:9) in the middle of the world (Ezekiel 5:5); Zion, where salvation is given (Isaiah 46:13); Nazareth, the city of Galilee where she conceived and raised her Son; Bethlehem, the house of bread, where she gave birth to the living bread descended from heaven; Jericho, the moon; Capernaum, the field of fatness or village of consolation; Bethulia, the virgin of the Lord (Judith 6:7); Tanis, where the Lord wrought wonders (Psalm 77:43); and Laish, where the people dwelt without fear (Judges 18:7). It is commended for the novelty of its name (Isaiah 60:14, 62:2); for the width of its streets paved with transparent gold (Revelation 21:21; Song of Songs 3:2); for its security and peace (Psalm 147:3; Revelation 21:25); for the passage that it provides to those who want to reach the Son (Isaiah 48:2; 54:15; 55:5; 56:6–7); because whoever wants to be saved needs to seek her as a helper (Isaiah 62:12); because through her is rebuilt that which was broken down by Eve (Isaiah 58:12); for her immunity from sin (Isaiah 60:18); because in her and through her the Lord is magnified and praised (Psalm 47:2); because the whole world rejoices in her (Isaiah 65:18); and because the rectors of souls attribute to her and her grace the conversion of their souls and the glory of their own conscience (Revelation 21:24).[145]

Many excellent things are found in this city: hostels and hospitals, temples, churches, and oratories, convents and monasteries. There lives Melchizedek, the king of justice who is also its bishop and priest. There many people dwell, "foreigners and Tyre and the people of the Ethiopians" (Psalm 86:4), "for the people of this city are all the true faithful, whence it is said: *And thy people shall be all the just, they shall inherit the land for ever (Isaiah 60:21)." Its temple is Christ (Revelation 21:22), who dwells in the palace of the king of glory (Proverbs 9:1), and its law is clemency and kindness (Proverbs 31:26), written on the heart (Psalm 36:31): "Do not do to another what you do not want done to yourself" (cf. Tobit 4:16). There are found the fountain of mercy, the well of the one who lives and sees (Genesis 16:14), many cisterns and channels and pipes, rivers of gifts and of graces "just as may be seen in certain most noble cities, like Paris, Rome, and Rouen," fishponds (Song of Songs 7:4), and the bubbling springs of many rivers and streams (Song of Songs 4:15). The city has a harbor, the anchorage of hope, where the ship of the mind may find refuge against the perils of the sea. There ships dock, bringing "*thy sons from afar, their silver, and their gold*, that is, eloquence and wisdom, *with them, to the name of the Lord thy God* (Isaiah 60:9)." In this city are meadows, grasses, pastures, and fruit-bearing trees (olives, vines, palms, figs, and pomegranates), fertile fields (Deuteronomy 8:7–10), watered gardens (Numbers 24:5–6; Jeremiah 31:12), shady groves (Genesis 21:33), wooded mountains (Isaiah 35:2), forests for hunting (Psalm 49:10) and for honey-making bees (1 Kings [Samuel] 14:26), every kind of bird (Psalm 49:11), ponds filled with fish (Ezekiel 47:10), fat animals of every kind (3 Kings 4:22–28), and precious metals of every kind (Deuteronomy 8:9; Isaiah 60:17; 2 Chronicles 1:15). There money is minted, coins (*drachma*) having the image and superscription of the king "because 'Christian' comes from 'Christ.' " The citizens of this city are precious stones (1 Peter 2:5), farmers, vintners, herdsmen, architects, merchants, and traders, selling the best corn (Ezekiel 27:17), spices of every kind (Ecclesiasticus 24:21), perfumes (Ecclesiasticus 24:20), medicines (Ecclesiasticus 38:4), resin ("the Son of God, whom she offers to all, just as she figures his image"), all kinds of clothing (Isaiah 52:1) and textiles (Isaiah 19:9; 1 Chronicles 4:21; Exodus 35:25–26).[146]

Tower

As the bridegroom says to the Church in the Song of Songs (4:4): *Thy neck is as the tower of David, which is built with bulwarks. A thousand bucklers hang upon it, all the armour of valiant men.* Mary is the neck of the Church, that is, the peak of its excellence, because she is the tower of the true David, that is, of Christ, standing as a refuge for sinners in the midst of the Church. She is the highest tower of the Church because she has the deepest foundations, that is, her humility, and on account of the loftiness of her contemplation and her knowledge of eternal things. She is upright before God, never turning to the left in adversity or to the right in prosperity, but always directing herself toward God (Psalm 24:5). She is strong, squared by the four cardinal virtues, protecting and guarding those who live in the camp or the city of the Church. Like the lighthouse that Ptolemy built at Alexandria, she gives forth a great light, guiding those who walk through the sea of the world to the right way and the port of salvation. She is built with bulwarks, that is, walled with virtues and graces, and hung with bucklers, that is, with the examples of her given throughout scripture, with the help that she offers to those venerating her and fleeing to her, as with Theophilus, and with the testimonies (*documenta*) of her words, inciting her servants and instructing them how to fight. Therefore, like Theophilus, they ought continually to cry out to her: "Be to me, O Lady, *a tower of strength against the face of the enemy* (Psalm 60:4). *Overthrow them that fight against me. Take hold of arms and shield, and rise up to help me* (Psalm 34:1–2)."[147]

Ship

Some say that a ship (*navis*) is so-called because it needs a skilled captain (*gnavum rectorem*), that is, one who is experienced, wise, and vigorous, and who knows how to guide it through the dangers of the sea. Therefore, it is said (Proverbs 1:5): *He that understandeth shall have the helm* (*gubernacula*). Mary is rightly called ship because her helmsman (*gubernator*) and captain is Christ, the wisdom of the Father, who governs her (Psalm 22:1). Thus, it says of her in Proverbs 31:14: *She is like the merchant's ship; she bringeth her bread from afar.* This verse, Richard notes, comes under the letter ה, "which may be interpreted 'to be' (*esse*) or 'to live' (*vivere*) or 'taking' (*suscipiens*) or 'undertaking' (*susceptio*), all of which are appropriate to this ship. For indeed, through the bread of life which she received from heaven and carried in her womb, she had truth as he is in the present life, has everlasting life now, and will receive glory in eternity from him whom she received (*suscepit*) when he came down from heaven into her glorious guestroom," as, indeed, will Christians who receive this bread through her. She was the first to receive from heaven that bread who is being (*esse*) and life (*vivere*), by whom Christians are received and whom they receive through her, the merchant's ship. Whence it is said (Wisdom 14:5): "*Those passing over the sea*, that is, the world, *by ship*, that is, by Mary, *are saved.*"[148]

As ship, Mary is to be commended above all for seven things. First, for her builder and Maker, God the Trinity (Hebrews 11:10; Ecclesiasticus 43:2;

Psalm 117:23), or rather, the Wisdom of God, namely the Son (Proverbs 9:1), or rather the Holy Spirit, the Maker of all things (Wisdom 7:21), or rather Beseleel and Ooliab, as with the ark (see "Ark"). Second, for her framework of virtue, strong and incorruptible like setim wood (Isaiah 40:20). Third, for her cargo of graces and good works. Fourth, for her utility, carrying bread from heaven, which was fulfilled to the letter (*ad litteram*) when she carried Christ, the living bread, in her womb. Fifth, for her material, again like the ark of the covenant as well as the ark of Noah (Genesis 6:14), of setim wood, dried of all harmful moisture by the heat of the Holy Spirit. Sixth, for her end (as the Philosopher would put it) that through this ship the bread of angels might be brought to men "that by tasting it they might become angels." Seventh, for her form or shape, of which there are four parts: her prow, or prudence; her hull, or strength; her keel, or temperance; and her poop, or justice. She is high stem and stern (*alta in capitibus*), that is, in her genealogy, in her sanctification in her mother's womb, and in her Assumption; open to the rains of grace and the charisms of gifts; wide in the middle, namely in the desires of her heart, that she might be filled with the merchandise of good works; of great size, like Noah's ark, so as to hold all the elect and carry them to the harbor of life; hollow with humility so as to have room for the true bread; covered against the powers of the air; pitched within and without with chastity; divided into cabins, like paradise with its many mansions; a vessel beyond price (*vas sumptuosissimum*).[149]

Her mast is of applewood, with its beam making the shape of the cross, her sail the holy desire with which the Holy Spirit inspired her (Song of Songs 4:16). Her anchor is the fear of the Lord, her castle the four cardinal virtues, her arms the virtues described by the Apostle Paul (Ephesians 6:11), her oars good works, her rudder prudence, her helmsman the providence of God the Father, her sailors and oarsmen the holy angels ministering to their captain, Christ (Hebrews 1:14), and her cargo the riches of human salvation. She is moved in part by the breezes, in part by her oars, that is, by grace from above and by activity from below, and does battle for the safety of her servants against pirates and thieves, that is, the powers of the air. When the Lord slept in the boat of the cross, a great storm arose threatening to overwhelm the Church with its waves (Matthew 8:24), but Mary was the strong woman who alone held the rudder with constant faith: "because the whole ship of the Church was then supported by her faith, namely from Friday evening through Holy Saturday, for which reason the universal Church venerates her especially every Saturday and sings her canticle at Mass on that day." The merchant for which she was made is, however, Christ, "who by her came from heaven into the world to do business, sell, and buy. For a merchant travels from his homeland into another country in hope of profit and with the desire to make purchases: thus Christ came at his incarnation from heaven to earth to buy and redeem our souls."[150] He is the bread that she bought from the Father with the price of her virginity and humility and that was baked in the oven of her womb by the fire of the Holy Spirit and baked again on the altar of the cross and for which Christians pray to God the Father, saying: "Our mother who is in heaven, give us today our supersubstantial or daily bread."[151]

Garden

Mary is the earthly paradise planted by God, where the Tree of Life and the tree of the knowledge of good and evil grew (Genesis 2:8–9), that is, Christ, who is the Tree of Life and the tree of knowledge in whom all the treasures of wisdom and knowledge are hidden (Colossians 2:3). The waters of the flood did not cover her, and the waters of the four rivers flowed out from her over the whole earth (Genesis 2:10), that is, the four rivers of the Gospels. Enoch and Elijah walked in her, and Christ was placed in her (Genesis 2:15) not by carnal generation but solely by the working of the Trinity. She is guarded by angels (Genesis 3:24; Song of Songs 3:7; Psalm 90:11), always verdant, planted with all kinds of plants, grasses, and trees, that is, virtues. She is a paradise of pleasure (*paradisus voluptatis*) or, as another translation has it, *a paradise in Eden toward the East* (LXX), where "Eden" in Hebrew means "delights (*deliciae*)" in Latin. Her womb is the paradise where the whole Trinity took its rest (Ecclesiasticus 24:11), filling it with creatures, and from which the Son of God came forth like the river Dioryx (Ecclesiasticus 24:41–42) in four streams (tears, sweat, blood, and water). As Abbot Ekbert said to her:

> Truly you are the paradise of God, who gave to the world the tree of life, from which whoever eats shall have eternal life. The fountain of life which came forth from the mouth of the Most High leapt from your womb, and dividing into four heads went out to water the face of the dry earth, making joyful the city of God. For everyone who drinks from it will never thirst. And you are more than a paradise: for he who drinks water from it will thirst again. O how much you gave to the world, who merited to be the aqueduct of such healing water![152]

As garden her properties are fifty (the number is clearly significant, although Richard does not elaborate why, plus he identifies only forty-nine), which may be divided under twelve heads.

1. She is *enclosed* (Song of Songs 4:12) spiritually and corporeally in her virginity, to the exterior through her five senses, in her interior through voluntary poverty, by a wall of divine protection and a moat of the plenitude of grace, and by her silence. She is *fortified* by the key of David (Isaiah 22:22; Revelation 3:7), that is, the grace of spiritual wisdom, or the power of closing and opening the scriptures. This key opens hearts to the understanding of the faith, mouths to the preaching of the Word, the understanding of the scriptures, and the natures of things; the senses to knowledge, the affect to devotion, the tongues of the doctors to teaching, and the hearts of the people to believing. She is *bolted* with the bolt of virginity, which was never pulled back by God or man, whence it says of her in the psalm: *He hath strengthened the bolts of thy gates* (Psalm 147:2).[153]

2. She is *guarded* by God the Father (Isaiah 41:13), by the Father, Son, and Holy Spirit as one (Isaiah 42:6), by Christ at his Incarnation, placed in her as the new Adam (Genesis 2:15), by the angels (Psalm 90:11; Song of Songs 3:11), by Gabriel, that is, the strength of God, and by John, the grace of God. She is *sealed* with the seal of virginity because she is the secret of God (Isaiah 24:16) and placed by Christ as a sign against Jews, pagans, and heretics. She is *uncovered* so that she might receive the dew, sun, rain, air, and the like that come down from above (James 1:17) (as Richard shows at length in a later section; see below, chapter 5, "The Lord enters into his Creation").[154]

3. She was *implanted* at the Incarnation when that noble shoot, the Word made flesh, was grafted onto the trunk of humanity in the garden of her womb (James 1:21). She was *cultivated* by the whole Trinity, whose works are inseparable, but especially by divine inspiration, the Wisdom of the Son, and the discipline of the Holy Spirit, as well as by the teaching of her mother and father, angelic advice (that is, when she was in the temple growing up), and the like (Ezekiel 36:35). She was *planted* by the Father with the Tree of Life, that is, Christ (Genesis 2:8), and she was *husbanded* by God, as are all the just (1 Corinthians 3:9; John 15:1).[155]

4. She is *enriched* with grace, love, devotion, and every charism and anointed with the oil of mercy (Mark 12:1; Psalm 22:5), *ditched* with chaste fear and compassion for her Son suffering on the cross, *sown* not with the seed of a man, but by a mystical breath, that is, the Word of God (Luke 8:11), and *bedded* with fragrant spices, that is, virtues, graces, and gifts, and with flowers, that is, holy thoughts (Song of Songs 6:1).[156]

5. She is *leveled* so as to be watered with virtues and graces more easily, *extended* through piety and love, *secret*, like the earthly paradise, removed from all other habitations, so that when the angel Gabriel came to her, he had to go into her secret chamber where she offered her prayers (Luke 1:28), *pleasant* or

delightful (which delights, again, Richard treats at length in a later section of the book), and *high* above all other earthly things (Isaiah 58:11, 14), inferior only to Christ, as Anselm says: "Nothing equals Mary, nothing but God is greater than Mary."[157]

6. She is *healing*, filled with medicinal herbs, perfumes, spices and trees, each having its own virtue, with Christ, who is the physician and medicine against every disease (Ecclesiasticus 38:4), and with the antidote of salvation (Ezekiel 47:12). She is *fragrant*, flowing with aromatical spices (Song of Songs 4:16), *restorative* because there the air is purer, the breeze calmer, the light more temperate, the rest sweeter, the song more pleasing, the tree leafier, the fruit riper than in any other saint, all of whom still speak as if they were in the village, but Mary's conversation is wholly in the city of paradise, *saturated* with blessings (Hebrews 6:7), yet *thirsty* in her desire for glory and grace (Psalm 41:3).[158]

7. She is *moist* with the waters of grace (Jeremiah 17:8), *watered* by the fountain of Christ (Isaiah 58:11; Ecclesiasticus 24:42; Genesis 2:6), *drenched* with rain because Christ descended upon her like rain on the fleece (again, Richard treats this descent more fully elsewhere), and *bedewed* (ditto).[159]

8. She is *dripping* with Christ-rain (Psalm 64:11), *flowing* with grace-dew, *cloudy* so as to cover the sun of justice dwelling in her (3 Kings 8:12), and *steamy* (see "Tree").[160]

9. She is *dense* with herbs, plants, spices, and trees (Song of Songs 4:13–14; Ezekiel 47:7, 12; Revelation 22:2; Ecclesiasticus 24:17–23), and *shady*, shading sinners with her prayers, merits, and examples from the fervor of divine anger and the heat of their own crooked desires. She is *concealing*, for in her Christ hid for nine months (Isaiah 45:15), there assuming the cloud of human flesh so as to conceal himself from the devil and the princes of this world (1 Corinthians 2:8), and she is *full of hiding-places* "in a good sense, that is, convenient for finding shelter," whether for Christ or for those fleeing from the world, flesh, and the devil (Psalm 103:18).[161]

10. She is *clean* because nothing unclean enters into her (Revelation 21:27), *purifying* with her dew those who walk in her in meditation and imitate her through their works, *wonderful* in three things—in herself because as a virgin she bore God, in her flower which she never lost, and in her fruit, Christ, or more particularly, the flesh of Christ—and *inviolate* because nothing unclean or uncircumcised passes through her (Isaiah 52:1).[162]

11. She is *secure* because she is not open to evildoers, that is, demons or vices, so that they cannot take away those who have fled to her for safety, *steadfast* in the plenitude of her virtues and delights, which never wither, grow old, or decay (Ezekiel 47:12), *lush* with grasses, leaves, fruits, fragrances, fronds, birds,

fountains, and the like (Song of Songs 4:13–14), with which she takes away the yoke of her servants' ancient captivity, pacifies the anger of divine indignation, and blots out the mark of human iniquity, and *flowing with delights* (Song of Songs 8:5).[163]

12. She is *generous*, inviting all to share in her delights (Matthew 11:28; Ecclesiasticus 24:26), and *inexhaustible*. As Master Hugh of Saint Victor put it, "Rightly is she called *full of grace*, because from her rose the fountain of grace"; therefore, she says (Ecclesiasticus 24:14): *Unto the world to come I shall not cease*, namely to show mercy to the wretched of the world. She is *fulfilling*, whence she says (Ecclesiasticus 24:26): *Be filled with my fruits*, and invites Christ and his friends into her garden (Song of Songs 5:1): *Let my beloved come into his garden, and eat the fruit of his apple trees*. Which he does, saying (Song of Songs 5:1): *I am come into my garden, my sister, my spouse . . . I have eaten the honeycomb with my honey*, that is, taken delight in her life of both action and contemplation, *I have drunk my wine with my milk. Drinking* at his invitation, she, too, is inebriated with her own fruit as if with a threefold wine: first, with the wine of compassion through her suffering with sinners; second, with the wine of devout prayer as she prays for them; third, with the wine of happiness and rejoicing, as she rejoices with those making progress in virtue and grace. Having himself drunk from her garden, God wants his servants and friends of his mother to be filled as well (Song of Songs 5:1): *Eat, friends, and drink*, he calls to them, *and be inebriated, my dearly beloved!* Mary feeds her guests first and most worthily with that glorious fruit, Christ, "which we receive in the sacrament"; second, with her virginal flesh, which her servants also receive in the sacrament, "because the flesh of Christ is the flesh of Mary, just as the flesh of mother and son are one flesh"; third, with the words of the Gospel, which are the words of God, and which the Spirit of truth taught her; fourth, with her example; fifth, with herself, "for to eat herself with love and devotion is to restore herself spiritually"; and sixth, with everything tender and tasty, the bread of life, the flesh of the immaculate lamb (Exodus 12:5), the best grain, the fish of faith, the egg of hope, the bread of love, the fruits of holy belief, the grape of the memory of the Passion, and the pomegranate in which many seeds are kept under one rind, so as to make her servants preserve and love their fraternal unity. She is like a butler, dispensing graces from the wine cellar of the king (Song of Songs 2:4). And she is *playful*, for she is the ark before which David danced *with all his strength* (2 Kings [Samuel] 6:14), just as John the Baptist leaped before her in his mother's womb (Luke 1:44). Just so her servants ought to leap or kneel as many times as they greet her or come before her altars or images.[164]

Flower

The flower of the garden is Christ, who blossomed at his Nativity (Isaiah 11:1), withered at his Passion (Nahum 1:4), and bloomed again in his humanity at his Resurrection (Psalm 27:7). As flower he is pure, fragrant, slight, tender, beautiful, concave, multicolored, vernal (Song of Songs 2:10–14), pleasant to the touch, abounding in water, fruit-bearing, inclined, light, common, medicinal, delicate, has a mother (the earth, a tree, or a grass) but no father, feeds the bees and provides them with honey and wax, receives the Holy Spirit (Isaiah 11:1–2), spreads his odor without being seen, does not harm his mother but distinguishes and beautifies her, adorns the head, and beautifies the temple—all of which properties the Virgin as flower shares.[165]

I am the flower of the field and the lily of the valleys, the bridegroom, Christ, says to his bride in the Song of Songs (2:1). "I who am by nature God, I am the flower of the field, that is, the Son of the Virgin." Christ is the flower of the field, not the garden, because he is the beauty and glory of the world where he fights to win the prize (Isaiah 28:5) and the lily of the valleys because he is the beauty and glory of the humble to whom he reveals the splendor of his divinity rather than to the proud. *As the lily among the thorns*, the bridegroom continues, *so is my love among the daughters* (Song of Songs 2:2). Mary is a lily among the thorns because she was born among the Jews, but was herself without thorns. She gave forth her fragrance when she was pierced by the thorns but never returned evil for evil or a curse for a curse. Just as a lily relieves pain and dampens fevers, so with her prayers and examples Mary protects her servants from harm, easing the pains of their souls and extinguishing their lustful desires.[166]

Christ and Mary are also signified by the rose, of which it is said: *Like a rose plant in Jericho* (Ecclesiasticus 24:18). Jericho may be interpreted "moon" or, as someone else says, "its odor": "because the mouth of every Christian ought to be fragrant, resounding with the praises of Mary, just as the mouth is fragrant when chewing aromatic spices." Mary is red like the rose with the blood of her Son because she suffered with him in her heart as he suffered in his body.[167] Likewise, she is white like the lily in her virginity, innocence, and immunity from sin; red like the rose in her natural beauty, virginal modesty, exceptional love, singular patience, and compassionate martyrdom; purple like the violet because she is appropriate to the King of kings and again in her martyrdom because purple is the color of blood; blue like the hyacinth in her heavenly conversation; golden yellow like the crocus in her wisdom and love; azure blue in her voluntary poverty; livid in her compassion for her Son; and green with the vigor of her faith.[168] Like the myrtle, which the herbalists say is good for "many necessities of women," Mary is good for all the necessities of the faithful soul, while like the pomegranate she helps those sleep who before could not *except they have done evil, and ... made some to fall* (Proverbs 4:16).[169]

Tree

I made me great works, Solomon says in Ecclesiastes (2:4–5). *I built me houses and planted vineyards. I made gardens and orchards and set them with trees of all kinds.* Mary is the garden or orchard planted by the hand of Wisdom with every kind of tree, that is, every virtue. She is the *vine* (Ecclesiasticus 24:23) bringing forth the pleasant odor of doctrine and turning the law and the prophets into the fruit of the Gospels through her reading.[170] She is the *olive tree* (Ecclesiasticus 24:19), exalted in the plains, beautiful in her bud and oil, that is, her Son, in the flowers of her holy desires, in the leaves of her words, and in the fronds and branches of her active and contemplative works.[171] She is the *bush* (Exodus 3:2–3) in which the Lord appeared to Moses as a flame of fire, because *our God is a consuming fire* (Hebrews 12:29) who came forth from the midst of the bush, that is, the virginal womb.[172] She is the *cedar* exalted in Lebanon (Ecclesiasticus 24:17), that is, in Christ, in the world, in heaven, and in the Cistercian order "because all of the churches of that order are dedicated to her." As cedar, she provided the material for the building of the temple, that is, the body of the Lord. Serpents, that is, demons, flee from her fragrance, and her sap protects books against bookworms, that is, heretics, and old age "because grace is especially given to those loving her to understand the holy Scriptures better from day to day . . . for she reveals deep things out of darkness [to the friends of God and prophets whom she teaches] . . . and thus she does not allow the holy Scriptures to grow old."[173]

She is the *palm tree* exalted in Kadesh (Ecclesiasticus 24:18), that is, "translated" from original sin at her sanctification, from virginity to fertility at the Incarnation, and from a humble maiden to the highest queen at her Assumption. Her fronds are used for the aspersion of holy water, that is, the grace of the Holy Spirit, by Jesus, the great high priest according to the order of Melchizedek, "because in her he *took hold of the seed of Abraham* (Hebrews 2:16)," and as a sign of victory "because she fights for us against invisible enemies."[174] She is the *cypress tree* exalted on Mount Zion (Ecclesiasticus 24:17), that is, in the militant Church "in which God is seen through a mirror in figures" and on the mountain of the triumphant Church, for Zion means "mirror" or "mirrors" and Mary is blessed among both angels and men. Alternately, Zion means the mirror in which man sees his own image. Mary is exalted as a cypress because through her the image of God is reformed in the soul and the body restored to health through the Resurrection because cypresses are healing, too.[175] She is *frankincense* uncut, growing on the mountain of Lebanon (Ecclesiasticus 24:21), which when burned emits a fragrant smoke, that is, love, perfuming its dwelling, that is, showing through her works that her conversation is in heaven.[176] She is the *plane tree* exalted by the water in the streets (Ecclesiasticus 24:19), her broad leaves shielding her lovers against the heat of exterior tribulation and interior temptation as well as against the heat of her Son, the sun of justice: "Therefore," Richard advises his readers, "love her and serve her, that the sun not burn you by day nor the moon by night."[177]

She is the *cinnamon* (Ecclesiasticus 24:20) that grows far away, in Arabia, India, and Ethiopia, because even in these remote regions, there is veneration for Mary.[178] Her bark, that is, her patience, is hard and the color of death because Mary is dead to the world and knows only the sweet odors of paradise. Chewing her makes the mouth fragrant, as for example with Jostius, a monk at the monastery of Saint Bertin in Saint-Omer, whose mouth, eyes, and ears were found filled at his death with five roses of exceptional color and scent because every day he had sung five prayers to the blessed Virgin with the utmost devotion.[179] Mary is the *myrrh* (Ecclesiasticus 24:20) that comes from Arabia and preserves dead bodies from decay. It is bitter on account of the bitterness that Mary suffered at the Passion of her Son. Like myrrh, Mary preserves her servants from corruption through the grace of her prayers, merits, and examples, and her thoughts and affections drip with the purest myrrh, that is, the odor of her virginity.[180] She is *storax* in her strength, *galbanum* in her temperance, *onyx* in her prudence, *aloes* in her justice, and *balsam* in her love (Ecclesiasticus 24:21).[181] And she is the *terebinth* (Ecclesiasticus 24:22), stretching out her branches of honor and grace from the middle of paradise so as to shade sinners with the example of her works. Her sap is the best medicine for sick souls and her branches bear the fruit of redemption and salvation. As the terebinth, moreover, she gives her servants a model for how to pray: just as the terebinth is short yet fruitful, so likewise prayer is often more profitable if it is brief.[182]

She is the *tree* (*arbor*) in the midst of the earth (Daniel 4:7–9), that is, in the midst of the Church, common to all without exception, just as her image stands to the right of the crucifix in the middle of the church. Her leaves, that is, her words, were most beautiful, full of mystery and healing to all, and her sight, that is, her eyes, looked out to the ends of the earth with mercy for all sinners, including Theophilus. Her fruit was beyond measure "because he whom the whole world could not contain, enclosed himself made man in her womb," and "*in it was food for all*, that is, angels and men, because through her man ate the bread of angels, and through her angels and men eat the sacrament of her Son at the table of the altar, as if in one refectory."[183] Again, she is the *tree (lignum)* of life in the midst of paradise (Genesis 2:9), that is, in the midst of the church, where her image is to be found next to the crucifix holding her Son as if offering him to all.[184] She is planted by the waters (Jeremiah 17:8), because she sends out her roots, that is, her intellect and affect, to the waters of grace: "and therefore she does not fear the heat of lust or the drought of eternal fire, nor does she ever cease to offer the fruit of piety and mercy, daily giving us on the way as well as the angels and blessed in the fatherland the fruit of her womb. Whence we should continually pray: 'Our mother, who is in heaven, give us today our daily bread, who is your fruit.' "[185]

And she is the *rod, wand, scepter,* or *shoot (virga)* coming forth out of the root of Jesse (Isaiah 11:1), springing up from Israel (Numbers 24:17), sent forth out of Zion by the Lord (Psalm 109:2). She has fewer leaves than most trees because she spoke fewer words in her humility; she is smooth, without knots or bark, that is, without sin; she is flexible and light, favorable to her servants' petitions if they are just and made in the name of her Son. She acts as a mediator between her root, the human race, and her fruit, her Son, for she is the golden scepter of Ahasuerus, mediating access to the king (Esther 4:11). "And note," Richard reflects,

> that there is only a small difference between these two names, *virga* and *virgo*, and that the near identity of these two names on account of their identity of meaning [is shown] through those [letters] in which they differ, namely *o* [and] *a*. Whence Revelation 1:8: *I am α and ω the beginning and the end.* And just as these two letters are the perfectives of these two names, thus the Son of God who is α and ω, through his incarnation perfected Mary, who is *virga* and *virgo*.

(Richard observes further that these two letters are not Hebrew, but Greek, "because in the letter [*ad litteram*] wisdom began with the Greeks," and further, that they teach that "not only theological, but also philosophical wisdom is from the Lord God.") But how can readers be sure that when the prophet Isaiah said, *There shall come forth a rod (virga)* without any qualifier that he meant them to understand that the Virgin (*Virgo*) was a perfect rod? Because, Richard explains for the one and only time in his entire work, "it is the custom of sacred Scripture that whenever it makes a metaphor for something perfect out of something irrational or something inanimate, if that thing is mentioned by its general name, the most perfect thing of its kind is to be understood." Thus, he argues, readers of scripture should understand only the best properties of a thing as applying to Mary.[186]

Accordingly, the Virgin Mary is the rod that Jeremiah saw keeping watch (Jeremiah 1:11) because she wakes her servants from the sleep of sin with her prayers, merits, and examples. She is the rod that Jonathan dipped in honey and carried to his mouth, at the taste of which his eyes were enlightened (1 Kings [Samuel] 14:27); just so will her servants' interior eyes, that is, their intellect and affect be opened to knowledge and love of her and her Son if they keep her in their mouths by praying, praising, blessing, confessing, preaching her great works, and crying out to her: "O clement, O loving, O sweet Virgin Mary." She is the rod with which Moses struck the rock twice and brought forth water (Exodus 17:6; Numbers 20:11) because she strikes Christ, the rock, with her virginal purity and maternal dignity through her prayers, that he might pour forth for sinners the waters of grace. She is the golden rod or scepter of Ahasuerus (Esther 4:11) made by the hand of celestial Wisdom from the gold of Ophir (virginity flourishing in feeble flesh), of Arabia (humility at sunset, that is, in thinking on her setting), and of Hevilah (love). She is the rod of Aaron that settled the argument against Moses and Aaron when it budded, flowered, and gave forth almonds (Numbers 17:8), that is, budded with good habits, flowered with virtue, and gave forth the fruit of good works. She is the rod of the high priest that came forth from the root of Jesse (Isaiah 11:1) because she gave birth to him who is both king and priest. And she is the rod called Beauty and the rod called Cord which the Lord placed before his flock (Zechariah 11:7), that is, the rod of discipline or internal virtues and beauty and the rod of measuring by which her servants restrain their flesh with poverty, affliction, and penance. These are the seven rods that Jacob, that is, God the Father, placed in the water troughs (Genesis 30:37–39), that is, "in the mirror of the Scriptures, that gazing upon them we might conceive various offspring, that is, various dispositions of virtue."[187]

Nor does this exhaust the ways in which Mary is tree. In addition to all of the trees and rods mentioned above, Mary is also the *pomegranate, fig, almond, mulberry, sycamore* (which Christ climbed in order to become visible to humanity), *fir, willow, oleaster, pine, chestnut, laurel* (because Mary crowned him champion), *box tree,* and *elm.*[188]

"*Thou art all beautiful, my beloved*" (Song of Songs 4:7). Mary, mother, good woman, queen, heaven, sun, moon, dawn, cloud, earth, mountain, fountain, river, ark, throne, tabernacle, bedchamber, house, temple, city of God, tower, ship, garden, flower, tree: the list could go on and on. And, indeed, for Richard, it did. Everything in scripture pointed to Mary because everything in scripture pointed to God and his creation, and Mary was the special work of God, the mirror of her Creator, reflecting his image for all who gazed upon her. All of creation was suffused with significance when read through her because she was the one through whom God had entered into his creation, filling her and, through her, everything in it with his glory and grace. Far from opposing Mary to God or absorbing God into Mary, Richard saw Mary as a way of making God visible, just as in the temple tradition her servants had prayed that the Lady (the cloud, the throne, the temple, the city, the tree) might do for the Lord. Her names were legion (she was, after all, terrible as an army set in array) because she contained in her womb the Maker of all things, the divine Wisdom who made all things through her. By giving birth to God, Mary made God known to the world, just as the scriptures made God known through his Word. For Richard, reading the scriptures through Mary *was* reading the scriptures about God: Mary was the key that made the scriptures understandable and without which they remained shrouded in mystery.

Mary was the one—as the Cistercian Amadeus of Lausanne put it in his sermons, printed with Richard's in Antwerp in 1625—standing between the Old and New Testaments, mediating between the prophecies and signs and their fulfillment at the Incarnation. (Recall that Richard said he was writing at the behest of his Cistercian friends; perhaps they had been reading Amadeus, who was, like Arnold of Bonneval, a friend of Bernard of Clairvaux.) In Amadeus's telling: "[Like] the tree planted in the midst of paradise, [Mary] raises her head to the height of heaven and, conceiving by the heavenly dew, brings forth the fruit of salvation, the fruit of glory, the fruit of life." With Mary, that which had hitherto been "cloaked in mysteries and metaphors" was "now celebrated in festal rite."

As Amadeus invited his readers:

> Let us, therefore, enter the Holy of Holies and gaze upon the mercy seat, which has above it two cherubim gazing upon it and overshadowing it as they face each other with wings outstretched. There among other things shines the golden urn enclosing hidden manna. There is Aaron's rod which budded. . . . The golden urn is blessed Mary . . . who in her sacred womb bore the bread of angels which comes down from heaven and gives life to the world. The priestly rod signifies that same glorious one who, descended from a priestly and royal stock, gave birth to the King of saints, who is a priest for ever after the order of Melchizedek.

And the cherubim? "The two cherubim mean the two Testaments, for 'cherubim' means the fulness of knowledge, and the fulness of knowledge is in the Testaments. Rightly do the cherubim cover the mercy seat which they gaze upon as they face each other, for they conceal under figures and riddles the Christ whom the Testaments agree in proclaiming."[189] As Richard explained the mystery, Mary was Wisdom who taught her medieval devotees how to read the scriptures about Wisdom, the one through whom they came to the fullness of knowledge about the One whom she bore in her womb. In Richard's telling, having been filled with Wisdom, Mary not only knew God, but became like God, "deified" in her assimilation to the image in which she, like all other human beings, had been made. To name her, to understand her, to love her was to name, understand, and love God. What more pleasing occupation could there be than, as Richard put it, "to ruminate on such sweetness for a long time"? As Wisdom herself had promised: *They that explain me shall have life everlasting* (Ecclesiasticus 24:31) because in explaining her, they explained God, his work, and his Wisdom made visible through her to the world.

PLATE 18 Abbot Robert of Clairmarais presents Richard's book to the Virgin and Child. Richard of Saint-Laurent, *De virtutibus*. Copy dedicated by Robert of Clairmarais (abbot, 1257–1264) to Robertus de Bethunia. Saint Omer, Bibliothèque municipale 174, fols. 2v–3r.

LECTIO II. ARS RHETORICA. CONRAD OF SAXONY ON WHAT THE ANGEL SAID TO MARY

What it was like being filled with such Wisdom? For Richard, as we have seen, for all her names, Mary was above all a book or, rather, *the* book in which Wisdom had inscribed her/himself for his/her creatures to read. For Conrad of Saxony, in contrast, she was above all a place or, rather, *the* place (*locus*) where God might be found, as the angel Gabriel had said to her when he came to her with the good news that she was to become the Mother of God: "The Lord is with you." As Conrad explained in the prologue to his commentary on the angelic salutation, it was for this reason that he chose the text that he did, that by praising Mary he might find a way to worthily praise God:

> Since as blessed Jerome says, "there is no doubt that whatever is worthily said of his mother belongs wholly to the glory of the praise of God," therefore desiring to say something to the praise and glory of Our Lord Jesus Christ concerning the praise and glory of his most glorious mother, I have judged it fitting to take for my subject matter the most sweet salutation of his mother.

It is a difficult subject, Conrad averred in proper five-part friarly fashion,

> because of the great incomprehensibility of the matter,
> because of the slenderness of my knowledge,
> because of the aridity of my speech,
> because of the unworthiness of my life, and
> because of the supreme glory and praiseworthiness of the person who is
> to be praised.

(Appropriately for a Franciscan trained in the art of preaching, everything that Conrad says breaks down into such orderly, typically numbered parts.) Nevertheless, buttressing his exposition with copious quotations from Augustine (more often than not, pseudo; most often Ambrosius Autpertus's sermon on the Assumption), Jerome (most often, as with Richard, Paschasius Radbertus's *Cogitis me*), Anselm (particularly his third prayer to Mary), and Bernard (usually himself, but frequently Ekbert of Schönau's *Sermo panegyricus*), Conrad ventured to offer "this little gift written in honor of so a great queen that in it, as in a dark mirror, the simpler lovers of this queen should at least faintly see (*speculentur*) what and how great she is." Thus, he explained, the title of his work: *Speculum Mariae*, "Mirror of Mary," because in it might be glimpsed something of "Mary's life, grace, and glory." "Therefore," Conrad prayed before embarking on his exposition, "my most kind lady, Mary, graciously accept this little service that your poor lover offers you. For with this little gift, with this little work on your salutation I salute you; with bended knee, with head bowed, with heart and mouth, I salute you, and saluting you I say, 'Hail, Mary.' "[190]

Like Richard, Conrad makes frequent appeals to the many different names of Mary to be found in the scriptures.[191] Unlike Richard, Conrad does not structure his work around Mary's names, in part because his work is much shorter (only a tenth of the length of Richard's; arguably the reason it was copied so much more frequently than Richard's), but also because names as such are less his concern than is showing the way in which whatever is said of Mary "belongs wholly to the glory of the praise of God." While for Richard, if we may make such distinctions between two such thematically similar works, Mary is the one who is most *like* God, for Conrad, Mary is the one who is most *with* God, as the angel acknowledged in his salutation: "The Lord is with you." This emphasis on Mary's relationship with the Lord is perhaps most visible in the way in which Conrad describes Mary's relationship to the Trinity. As Conrad explains, Mary is singularly (*singulariter*) in body as well as in soul the court of the Lord (*aula Domini*), of whom it is said in the psalm (92:5): *Holiness becometh thy house, O Lord.*

> This singular Lord of Mary was with Mary so singularly that he made her singularly Lady, so that "never before was one seen like her, nor shall she have one after her," for she was made singularly the daughter of the Lord, the mother of the Lord, the bride of the Lord, and the handmaid of the Lord.... If we wish to assign her to each of the three divine Persons, we can say that the Lord who is singularly with Mary is the Lord Father, the Lord Son, the Lord Holy Spirit, the Lord Three and One. He is the Lord Father, of whom Mary is the most noble daughter; he is the Lord Son, of whom Mary is the most worthy mother; he is the Lord Holy Spirit, of whom Mary is the most beautiful bride; he is the Lord Three and One, of whom Mary is the most obedient handmaid. Assuredly, Mary is the daughter of the most high eternity, the mother of the most high truth, the bride of the most high goodness, the handmaid of the most high Trinity.[192]

Whereas Richard emphasized the unity of the Trinity's working in Mary, Conrad saw Mary as distinguishing the three persons, defining God as Trinity by her relationship to God Three in One. She was with the Father as daughter (Ruth 3:10; Psalm 44:14), with the Son as mother (Luke 1:43; Ecclesiasticus 24:24), with the Holy Spirit as bride (Hosea 2:19–20), with the Lord Three in One as handmaid (Luke 1:38; 1 Kings [Samuel] 25:41).[193] "The Lord is therefore with you," Conrad concludes, "the Lord whose daughter you are, than whom none is more noble; the Lord whose mother you are, than whom none is more wonderful; the Lord whose bride you are, than whom none is more lovable; the Lord whose handmaid you are, than whom none is more humble, nor ever was, nor ever will be in eternity. Therefore, Lady," he prayed, "because so great a Lord is with you in such a manner and is so much with you, grant that by grace he may also be with us."[194]

What did it mean for the Lord to be *with* Mary in this way? This is the mystery to which the angel invited her with his salutation: "Hail, Mary, full of grace, the Lord is with you; blessed are you among women, and blessed is the fruit of your womb." Accordingly, Conrad invited her,

> "Listen, most sweet virgin Mary, hear things new and wonderful, *listen, daughter, and see and incline thy ear* [Psalm 44:11]. *Listen* to Gabriel, that glorious messenger, *see* the wonderful manner of your fecundity, *incline thy ear* to a fruitful consent. *Listen* to what is announced to you by God the Father; *see* how the Son of God is to become incarnate from you; *incline thy ear* to the Holy Spirit, who is about to work wonderful things within you."[195]

As Conrad would have it, every phrase of the angel's greeting was pregnant with meaning, even as it bore to Mary the Annunciation of the Word. Appropriately, Conrad's exposition of the salutation is addressed not only to readers, but also to listeners[196], who, like Mary, are invited, because they have ears, to *listen*: "Because *you have ears to hear, hear*! (Matthew 11:15)."[197] While written as a continuous commentary, Conrad's exposition is structured like a series of sermons, each theme and subtheme divided conveniently into definitional lists the better to impress themselves on the memories of his audience.[198] At the same time, Conrad invites the Virgin—and, therefore, his audience—to *see*, recalling both her role as mother in making her Son visible to the world and Wisdom's invitation to her devotees to come to her that they might see the Lord in his glory, shining *in his days as the morning star in the midst of a cloud and as the moon at the full* (Ecclesiasticus 50:6).[199] As with our reading of Richard, all citations from and references to scripture are Conrad's.

Ave Maria

As Conrad explains, following Richard, Mary's name means at once "bitter sea" (*amarum mare*), "star of the sea" (*stella maris*), "light-giver" (*illuminatrix*), and Lady (*Domina*), referring in turn to her relationship to the demons, men, angels, and the whole of creation. She is a bitter sea to the devil and his angels because,

as a sea, she is filled with all the graces of the Holy Spirit, which flow into her like
the rivers into the sea (cf. Ecclesiastes 1:7), and she was filled with bitterness at the
Passion of her Son (cf. Luke 2:35; Ruth 1:20).[200] She is the star of the sea for men
sailing through the sea of the world in the ship of innocence or penance, most pure,
as Wisdom (7:29) says of her: *For she is more beautiful than the sun and above all the
order of the stars*; most radiant, by emitting eternal light and giving birth to the Son
of God, as it is said of her in Numbers (24:17): *A star shall rise out of Jacob and a rod
shall spring up from Israel*; and most useful because she guides men to the heavenly
country just like the star that led the three Magi to her Son.[201] She is the light-giver
wonderfully illuminated by the presence of the Lord, as it says in Revelation (18:1):
*I saw another angel come down from heaven, having great power: and the earth was
illuminated with his glory*. The Son of God is the Angel of Great Counsel, while
the earth illuminated by his glory is Mary, "who, just as she was illuminated by his
grace in the world, is now illuminated by his glory in heaven, that being thus illuminated, she may become a light-giver in the world and in heaven."[202] Like Wisdom,
Mary gives light to the world: by the example of her most luminous life, by the
benefits of her gracious mercy, and by her most resplendent glory,

which illuminates the whole of heaven, just as the sun illuminates the world, as it
says in Ecclesiasticus 42:16: *The sun giving light hath looked upon all things, and full
of the glory of the Lord is his work*. *The sun giving light* is Mary, who is *beautiful as the
moon, chosen as the sun* (Song of Songs 6:9): *beautiful as the moon* through grace,
chosen as the sun through glory. *Full of the glory of the Lord is his work*. The most
excellent work of the Lord is Mary.... Therefore the sun giving light, Mary, shining
in her glory, has looked upon all things, because through all the angels and through
all the saints she spreads out the illumination of her glory.[203]

She is also Lady of all creatures in heaven, on earth, and in hell, as Augustine
(actually, Ambrosius Autpertus) says: "If I call you heaven, you are higher; if I call
you the mother of nations, you are greater; if I name you lady of the angels, you
are proved to be so by everything; if I call you the form of God (*formam Dei*),
you are worthy of this name."[204]

Gratia Plena

Bitter sea, star of the sea, light-giver, and Lady, Mary was likewise full of a
fourfold grace: the grace of gifts, the grace of speech, the grace of privileges, and
the grace of rewards. She was full of the grace of the gifts of the Holy Spirit, for

which her servants may hear her giving thanks in Ecclesiasticus 24:25: *In me is all grace of life and of the truth.*[205] She is the rod from which the flower on which the Holy Spirit rested with all his gifts came forth (Isaiah 11:1–3). What wonder is it, therefore, Conrad asks, that she, too, should be filled with such gifts? The grace of truth set her in order "above herself through the gift of wisdom, below herself through the gift of counsel, within herself through the gift of understanding, without herself through the gift of knowledge." Likewise, the grace of life set her in order "towards the devil through the gift of fortitude, towards her neighbor through the gift of piety, and towards God through the gift of fear." These are the seven pillars of the house that Wisdom built for herself (Proverbs 9:1), whoever desiring which should look for the flower of the Holy Spirit in the rod: "For through the rod we come to the flower, and through the flower to the Spirit resting on him, while through Mary we come to Christ, and through Christ we find the grace of the Holy Spirit."[206] Mary was full of the grace of speech, that is, of the lips, as the psalmist says (Psalm 44:3): *Grace is poured abroad in thy lips*, so much so that she might be prefigured by Judith, of whom it is said (Judith 11:19): *There is not such another woman upon earth in look, in beauty, and in sense of words.* Like the bride in the Song of Songs (4:11), her lips were as a *dropping honeycomb*, whether she was speaking to angels (Luke 1:34, 38), to men (Luke 1:40; John 2:5), or to God (Luke 1:46, 2:48; John 2:3).[207]

Like the seven gifts of the Holy Spirit and the seven words she spoke in the Gospels, the grace of her privileges was sevenfold: first, that she was above all men free from sin and most pure, having been sanctified in her mother's womb; second, that she was above all men full of grace; third, that she alone was a mother and an inviolate virgin; fourth, that she alone was the ineffable Mother of the Son of God; fifth, that she was above all creatures in the body most familiar with God, whom she bore for nine months in her womb, nursed with her breasts "full of heaven," and kissed and embraced for many years most familiarly; sixth, that she alone is above all creatures most powerful with God; and seventh, that she is most excellent in glory above all the blessed, so that "whatever after God is more beautiful, whatever sweeter, whatever pleasanter in glory, that is Mary, that is in Mary, that is by Mary."[208] And she is full of the grace of rewards, as it says of her in Ecclesiasticus 26:19: *A holy and chaste woman is grace upon grace.* Again, her rewards are seven, four of the body—clarity, subtlety, agility, and impassibility—and three of the soul: knowledge, love, and enjoyment, or, "as the moderns put it," vision, enjoyment, and possession.[209]

And why, Conrad asks, should she not be endowed with these gifts more so than all the other blessed souls who also enjoy them in heaven? What wonder is it if the soul of Mary is already illuminated by knowledge and immersed in eternal light? As Bernard says: "She penetrated the most profound abyss of divine wisdom beyond what could be believed, so that as far as the condition of a creature is capable without personal union, she was seen to be immersed in that inaccessible light." What wonder is it if her soul is already most fruitful in love when she is herself most beloved? As Augustine (again, Ambrosius Autpertus) says: "The King of kings, loving you before all as true mother and beautiful bride, has joined himself to you in a loving embrace." What wonder is it if her soul should already be immersed in the most delightful enjoyment (*fruitio*) when she was fed most sweetly by the blessed fruit of her womb? As Augustine (here, in the anonymous *De assumptione* upon which much of the discussion of Mary's bodily assumption depended in the later Middle Ages) says: "Mary's soul enjoys Christ in brightness, and always present, always beholding [him], always thirsting to see [him], she is fed beyond all accounting by his glorious sight."[210]

So great, indeed, is Mary's plenitude of grace that she surpasses not only all earthly, but all heavenly creatures, that is, all the orders of the angels in her fullness (a theme that, as we shall see, Pseudo-Albert would explore at even greater length).

First, she is full of the illumination of wisdom in her understanding because she is the moon (Song of Songs 6:9) and the lamp (Psalm 27:29), fully illuminated with the light of wisdom and truth by the eternal sun. "Behold," Conrad exclaims, "if Mary was full of the light of wisdom which she received from the eternal sun before she conceived him, how much more full was she when she so wonderfully conceived this sun and so entirely received him within herself!"[211]

Second, she is full of the overflowing of grace in her affections because she is the sea into which all the rivers of the gifts of grace gather together (Genesis 1:10; Ecclesiastes 1:7; Ecclesiasticus 24:25). "Of the fullness of this sea," Conrad observes, "it is likewise said in the psalm [95:11]: *Let the sea be moved and the fulness thereof.* Let the sea be moved," Conrad prays, "let Mary be moved, let her be moved by our sighs and mortifications, let her be moved by our tears and prayers, let her be moved by our alms and other venerations. Let her be moved, I say, fully, that she may pour out on us from her fullness."[212]

Third, she is full of the riches of the good life in her actions because she is the earth, as it says in the psalm [23:1]: *The earth is the Lord's and the fulness thereof,* and in Isaiah 45:8: *Let the earth be opened, and bud forth a savior!* Conrad explains: "The fruits and riches of this most full earth, Mary, are the works, manners, examples, and diverse merits of the most holy life of Mary. The Lord looked upon her with such riches and filled her with such goods, as it says in Ecclesiasticus 16:30: *God looked upon the earth and filled it with his goods.*"[213]

Fourth, she is full of the anointing of mercy and the oil of piety because she is the woman who, having closed the door of her house and gathered together all of her vessels, found them miraculously full of oil, as the prophet Elisha had promised, saying, *When they are full, take them away* (4 Kings 4:4). Her house was closed up because she is also the gate, as Ezekiel says: *This gate shall be shut, it shall not be opened, and no man shall pass through it: because the Lord God Israel hath entered in by it* (Ezekiel 44:2). Her vessels are her affections and actions, desires and benefits, which are full of the oil of mercy that she pours out on all, as Bernard says: "Mary has opened the bosom of her mercy to all, that all may receive of her fullness: the captive, redemption; the sick, healing; the sad, consolation; the sinner, pardon; the just, grace; the angel, joy; and finally the whole Trinity, glory; the person of the Son, the substance of human flesh."[214]

Fifth, she is full of the fecundity of divine offspring because she is the house on whose throne the Lord sits, on the throne of whose mind the Lord rested (cf. Isaiah 6:1). "O truly blessed, O truly stable throne," Conrad exclaims,

> just as it is said in 3 Kings 8:13: *Thy most firm throne for ever.* This most high throne is in the intellect, raised up on the affections; it is most high over men, raised up over angels.... On this throne, Mary, on this throne, I say, of her mind, the Lord was seated, and the house of her body was full of the majesty of the Incarnate Word.... Therefore, it is said in 3 Kings 8:11–12: *The glory of the Lord had filled the house of the Lord. Then Solomon said: "The Lord said that he would dwell in a cloud."* Therefore, the house of the Lord, Mary, was filled with the glory of the divine majesty by the cloud of the humanity assumed by God; that cloud, I say, of which it is said in Ecclesiasticus 43:24: *The medicine of all is in the speedy coming of a cloud.* And again in Ecclesiasticus 50:6: [He shone in his days] *as the morning star in the midst of a cloud.* For like the star in a cloud is the Word in the flesh assumed by him.[215]

Sixth, she was full of the perfection of the universal Church because, as she herself might put it in the words of Ecclesiasticus 24:16: *My abode is in the full assembly of saints*, that is, in all their perfections and graces.[216]

Seventh, she is full of the besprinkling of fragrant fame because she is the field full of flowers in whom the treasure of the angels, rather, the treasure of God the Father, is hidden, as it says in Genesis 27:27: *Behold, the smell of my son is as the smell of a full field, which the Lord has blessed.* Of this fragrance, she herself could say, with Wisdom: *I gave a sweet smell like cinnamon and aromatical balm. I yielded a sweet odor like the best myrrh* (Ecclesiasticus 24:20). This good odor was like cinnamon in the shell of her conversation, like balm in the anointing of her devotion, and like myrrh in the bitterness of her Purification; or, again, like cinnamon in her deeds, like balm in her contemplation, and like myrrh in her passion, so full was she of that odoriferous balm of the Holy Spirit who overshadowed her.[217]

Eighth, she is full of the reflection or representation or expression of the divine glory because antonomastically (*antonomastice*) she is the work of the Lord, as it says in Ecclesiasticus 42:16: *Full of the glory of the Lord is his work*; and in Ecclesiasticus 43:2: *An admirable vessel, the work of the Most High*. She is truly wonderful, for a similar work cannot be found, whence it says in 3 Kings 10:20: *There was no such work made in any kingdom*. Not in heaven or on earth or in limbo, "for this work is full of the glory of the Lord, which shines above all pure creatures most fully in Mary . . . Therefore, full of the glory of the Lord is his work, Mary, because, as it is said in Isaiah 6:3: *The earth is full of his glory*."[218]

Ninth, she is full of the enjoyment of eternal happiness, as Jerome (that is, Paschasius Radbertus) says: "Full indeed of grace, full of God, full of virtues, she could not but possess fully the glory of eternal splendor." Whence Anselm salutes her: "O woman full and overfull with grace, from the overflowing of whose plenitude every creature gains life anew!"[219]

Dominus Tecum

There is a reason, of course, that Mary is so full of all of these things: wisdom, grace, the riches of a fruitful life, mercy, fecundity, perfection, fame, glory, and joy. As the angel told her: *The Lord is with you*, that is, "the Lord of all creatures in general (*generaliter*), the Lord specially (*specialiter*) of rational creatures, the Lord singularly (*singulariter*) of your virginal court, O Mary!" She is the one, as it says in Wisdom (8:3), whom *the Lord of all things loved*.[220] As Lord of all things universally, of all things visible and invisible, he is a Lord most power-ful in will (Psalm 134:6), most wise in truth (Psalm 146:5), most wealthy in his possessions, in heaven and on earth (Psalms 23:1; 88:12), reigning in eternity (Exodus 15:18; Psalm 101:13). Accordingly, she whom he is with is powerful (Ecclesiasticus 24:15), wise (1 Kings [Samuel] 25:3), rich (Proverbs 31:29), and enduring forever as his throne (Psalm 88:38).[221] As the Lord specially of rational creatures, lawgiver, judge, and king (Isaiah 33:22), he is a Lord most loving in his infinite mercy (Psalm 85:5), most just in his equity (Psalms 10:8; 118:137; 144:17), most sure in his fidelity and most faithful in his surety (Psalm 144:13), and most renowned for fame (Jeremiah 10:6; Psalms 148:11–12; 112:2–3). Likewise, she whom he is with is the merciful throne upon which he sits in truth (Isaiah 16:5), the rod of Aaron, "straight and erect by justice and equity, flowering in virginity, fruitful in fecundity" (cf. Numbers 17:8), the most faithful dove of Noah "who stood forth as most faithful *mediatrix* between the Most High of Noah and the world submerged in a spiritual flood" (cf. Genesis 8:6–11), and Ruth, whose name was celebrated in Bethlehem (Ruth 4:11), as well as Judith, who was greatly renowned (Judith 8:8), as, for example, when Mary intervened on behalf of Theophilus.[222] And, as we have already seen, as the Lord singularly of her virginal court, Father, Son, and Holy Spirit, God Three in One, he is the Lord of whom she is the most noble daughter, the most worthy mother, the most beautiful bride, and the most devout handmaid.[223]

"Truly," Anselm praised her, "*the Lord is with you*, to whom the Lord gave himself, that all nature in you might be in him." "*The Lord is with you*, with you, most certainly, with you," Conrad exulted, repeating himself even more than usual in thinking on Mary's relationship with the Lord. "He was with you, he is with you, he will be with you." Above all, the Lord was, is, and will be with Mary in three ways: like the sun with the dawn, like the flower with its stem, and like the king with his queen.[224] Mary is the dawn of the world "prepared in a most singular manner by the eternal sun, [who] marvelously irradiated, herself prepares for the rising of this sun." She was born like the dawn out of the night of sin through her sanctification in her mother's womb and progressed throughout her life in the light of grace and virtue (Song of Songs 6:9), so that her Son's rising was unaccompanied by any cloud of sin, as it says 2 Kings [Samuel] 23:4: *As the light of the dawn, when the sun riseth, shineth in the morning without clouds.* Christ is the sun conceived without the clouds of original sin, the fire conceived in the bush without the burning of carnal desire, the stone conceived without the hands of a marital embrace. As sun, he enlightens the intellect; as fire, he enkindles the affections; as rock, he strengthens against fault. Now, therefore, Mary, the dawn, holds the place nearest to him, the eternal sun, in heaven, because she received him in three ways: spiritually, in her mind; corporeally, in her body; and eternally, in glory.[225]

The first place that Mary received the Lord was in her mind, peaceful and quiet, as the psalmist says (Psalm 75:3): *His place is in peace, and his abode in Zion. Zion*, Conrad explains, may be interpreted "mirror" (*speculum*) or "contemplation" (*speculatio*), for "whoever desires God to dwell in his mind, or to contemplate God in his mind, must make a place for him in the peace of his mind, for without peace of mind no one comes to speculative contemplation (*speculationem contemplationis*)." Mary's mind was such a place, a holy Zion, in which, filled with the Holy Spirit, she revolved (as Jerome, a.k.a. Paschasius put it) "all that she had heard, all that she had seen, all that she had heard" of the divine mysteries that had been made known to her before all other mortals.[226]

The second place that Mary received the Lord was in her womb, from which the river, her Son, came out of the paradise of pleasure to water the garden of the universal Church (cf. Genesis 2:10). The third place that Mary received the Lord is the place of glory, of which the Lord said to Job (38:12): *Didst thou shew the dawn its place?*, as if to say, "Not you, but I." It is her place because it is distinct from all other places of the saints; hence it is said (3 Kings 8:6): *The priests brought the ark of the covenant of the Lord into its place.* This place, Mary's place, is above all the choirs of the angels, as Bernard attests: "Neither was there in the world a more worthy place than the temple of the virginal womb, in which Mary received the Son of God, nor in the heavens a more worthy place than the royal throne to which the Son of Mary raised Mary."[227]

Again, the Lord is with Mary as the flower is with its budding stem (*virga*), as it is said in Isaiah (11:1): *And there shall come forth a rod (virga) out of the root of Jesse, and a flower shall rise up out of his root.* Mary is a rod smoking with incense for beginners and penitents, rising up from the desert, that is, the heart of the sinner, by her prayers (Song of Songs 3:6); a rod of wood for those who are advancing in virtue, bearing flowers and fruits (Numbers 17:8); a rod of gold for those entering into the king in contemplation with her two handmaids or powers of the soul, the intellect, which proceeds through knowledge (*per cognitionem*), and the affections, which proceed through love (*per dilectionem*), strengthening the soul against fear of the divine justice and the splendor of divine glory (Esther 4:11); and a rod of iron to demons and incorrigible sinners, as it says in the psalm (2:9): *Thou shalt rule them with a rod of iron.* This is the Lady to whom Christians pray with "Innocent," saying: "Hail, nourishing mother of God, who owing to the dignity by which you are the mother of God are able to command angels and demons, restrain the demons lest they harm us; charge the angels to protect us!"[228] The flower which came forth from her is likewise fourfold: of precious virginity, which flowered in the desert (Isaiah 35:1); of virtuous reputation of manners and life (Ecclesiasticus 24:23), flowering in the earth of her active life (Song of Songs 2:12) and in the bed of her contemplative mind (Song of Songs 1:15); of miraculous fecundity, coming forth without sin from the root of Jesse (Isaiah 11:1) only to be crushed by dying like a sinner (Job 14:2); and of glorious immortality, flowering in the beauty of her glorified body and fruiting in the beatitude of her soul, as the psalmist says (27:7): *My flesh hath flowered again.* (Here Conrad affirms his belief in the bodily assumption, "[which] the holy doctors seem to think as probable and strive to prove with reason, and the faithful embrace with pious opinion."[229])

Last, but hardly least, the Lord is with Mary as the eternal king is with his queen, as the psalmist says (44:10): *The queen stood on thy right hand.*[230] Here

Conrad refers his readers to his own sermons on the Assumption, where he treats her attributes as queen more fully: As queen, she enters into Jerusalem with a great company of angels and with great riches (3 Kings 10:1–2), more than any other soul (Proverbs 31:29). Her camels, that is, the senses and powers of her soul, carry the spices of her good example and reputation, the gold of wisdom and contemplation, and the precious stones of her virtues and good works. She stands at the right hand of the king in gilded clothing, surrounded with variety (Psalm 44:10), that is, in the bright gown of her body, shining like the sun (Revelation 12:1), white with virginity, red with charity, and splendid with truth. The king sets a throne for his mother, and she sits at his right hand (3 Kings 2:19). The king is Christ: *He is the king of glory* (Psalm 23:10), while the Mother of the king is Mary: *I am the mother of fair love and of fear and of knowledge and of holy hope* (Ecclesiasticus 24:24). Her throne is set above all the orders of the angels to the right of the king, where she sits to reign and stands to help those who are still in the world. The king loved her *more than all other women and placed a crown on her head* (Esther 2:17). She is the ark for which Beseleel, that is, Christ, made a golden crown (Exodus 37:1–2), and she is the woman seen in the heavens with a crown of twelve stars, that is, twelve prerogatives on her head (Revelation 12:1).[231] She is also the throne upon which the Lord sits, as the psalmist says (88:38): *His throne is as the sun in my sight*, whose throne was the body and soul of his mother Mary, "who today is believed to be one with the Son in body (*una cum Filio corporaliter*) in the sight of God the Father." As his throne, she is ivory in her virginity, gilded with love (3 Kings 10:18), like the ark, containing the manna of his divinity in the golden urn of his humanity (Exodus 37:1; Hebrews 9:4). She is also sapphire and lifted up above the firmament, that is, the angels, in her conversation (Ezekiel 1:26), and a pillar of cloud in her piety, protecting sinners like Theophilus from the heat of the sun (Ecclesiasticus 24:7; Psalm 104:39); and she is like the sun in her glory in heaven, while like the moon in the world (Psalm 88:38; Song of Songs 6:9).[232] In all these ways, the Lord is with her, and she with him, reflecting his glory like the moon, shining in her contemplation of him like the sun, as is shown in her *Speculum*.

Benedicta tu in mulieribus

Mary, according to Conrad, is therefore blessed indeed: blessed on account of the plenitude of her graces, in her heart by the grace of gifts (Ecclesiasticus 40:17), in her mouth by the grace of her lips (Psalm 44:3), in her works by the grace of manners (Jeremiah 31:23); blessed on account of the majesty of the person who took flesh from her, the fruit born from her womb, sprung up from the earth (Psalm 84:2, 12); blessed on account of the multitude of her mercy, because through her God is made favorable to man (1 Kings [Samuel] 25:32–33), man is made acceptable to God (Isaiah 19:24–25), and the devil is made superable by man (Judith 13:22); blessed on account of the magnitude of her glory, as Ezekiel says (3:12): *Blessed is the glory of the Lord from its place.*[233] As Conrad explains: "The glory of the Lord is the glorious mother of the Lord, who is truly blessed because of the glory which she has from her twofold place: she is blessed, I say, from the place where her Son rested with her in her womb; she is also blessed from the place where she rests with her Son in heaven."[234] She is also blessed in the excellence of her virtues, with which she counters the seven capital sins: by her humility against pride, her love against envy, her mildness against anger, her diligence against sloth, her generosity against avarice, her temperance against gluttony, and her chastity against lust.[235] She is blessed because she was a wife, more blessed because she was a widow, most blessed above all who loved virginal chastity. Therefore, (Pseudo-)Augustine exclaims: "O woman blessed above women, who knew no man, yet encompassed a man in her womb!"[236]

Et benedictus est fructus ventris tui

Likewise blessed, or so her cousin Elizabeth prophetically exclaimed, is the fruit of Mary's womb, whom she brought forth, as Bede puts it, from "the temple of her virginal womb ... *And our earth will give its fruit* [Psalm 84:13], because the same virgin, who had her body from the earth, brought forth a Son co-equal indeed in divinity with God the Father, but in the reality of his flesh consubstantial with her."[237] This fruit is wellborn because he is born from her royal and virginal womb as well as from the womb of the eternal Father (Psalms 131:11; 109:3; Wisdom 18:15; Hosea 14:9; Isaiah 4:2). He is delightful in his fragrance (Ecclesiasticus 24:23) and beauty (Leviticus 23:40); white in his divinity, but ruddy in his humanity (Song of Songs 5:10), he is the brightness of eternal light (Wisdom 7:26). He has great strength to save the lost (Ecclesiasticus 1:22), multiply the number of those who are to be saved (Psalm 4:8), and preserve all those he has saved (Proverbs 11:30). And he is abundant enough to satiate the rational soul, which the whole world and every creature cannot satisfy (Psalm 103:13), to feed all of those who are to be saved

(Daniel 4:9), and never to fail in satisfying souls and angels (Ezekiel 47:12).[238] Moreover, he is the fruit not of Mary's womb alone, but of the mind of every faithful and virtuous soul: the fruit of the humble against pride, of the loving against envy, of the meek against anger, of the diligent against sloth, of the generous against greed, of the abstinent against gluttony, and of the chaste against lust.[239] Mary herself, above all human beings, "was most worthy of this fruit, because," Conrad explains, "above all she was most disciplined in good, as Bede well shows, when, commenting on her *Magnificat*, he puts these words into her mouth: 'I offer the whole affection of my soul in the praises of thanksgiving; all my life, all that I feel, all that I discern in contemplating his magnitude, all this I employ in observing his commands.' "[240] She was most fittingly said to be like a beautiful fruit-bearing olive tree (Ecclesiasticus 24:19) because, as John of Damascus says: "Mary, planted in the house of the Lord and fattened by the Spirit, became the dwelling place of every virtue like a fruit-bearing olive tree."[241]

This is the fruit promised by Wisdom, the blessed fruit of those who exercise themselves in good and flee from sloth and all other vices (cf. Wisdom 3:11).[242] Its benefits to those who eat of it are twelve, six as a remedy against evil, and six for the attainment of good, on account of which all men rightly praise its effects, as it is written: *Let the people praise you, O God; let all the people give praise to thee. The earth hath yielded her fruit* (Psalm 66:6–7). Its first effect is the expiation of mortal sin, as Isaiah says (27:9): *This is all the fruit, that the sin thereof should be taken away.* Its second effect is to create peace between God and man and between angels and men, again, as Isaiah says (57:19): *I created the fruit of the lips, peace, peace to him that is far off and to him that is near.* Its third effect is to heal the wound of original sin, "whence we read in Revelation 22:2 that the angel showed John *the tree of life, bearing twelve fruits, yielding its fruits every month, and the leaves of the tree were for the healing of nations.*" Its fourth effect is to relieve the hunger or famine of the soul, so that the animals of God should not perish, as it is promised in the book of Joel (2:22): *Fear not, ye beasts of the field, for the beautiful places of the desert have blossomed, for the tree hath brought forth its fruit.* Its fifth effect is to avoid the anger of the judge, for, as it says in the psalm (57:12): *If indeed there be fruit to the just, there is indeed a God that judgeth them on the earth.* Its sixth effect is to deliver all those who will be converted to her, that is, the earth, from the pains of hell or eternal death, as is promised in 4 Kings 18:32: *I will take you away to a fruitful land, and plentiful in wine, a land of bread and oil and honey, and you shall live, and not die.*[243]

Its seventh effect is the renunciation of or contempt for temporal goods, whence it says in the Song of Songs (8:11): *A man shall offer for this fruit a thousand pieces of silver*, that is, as it says in the interlinear gloss, "by leaving all temporal things." For, indeed, as Wisdom says in Proverbs (8:19): *My fruit is better than gold and the precious stone, and my blossoms than choice silver*. Its eighth effect is to enrich or fill the rational soul, as it says in Proverbs (12:14): *By the fruit of his mouth each one shall be filled with good things*, that is, through preaching, praise, and prayer, as well as through the sacrament. Its ninth effect is the perfection or consummation of the spiritual life, for, as it says in the psalm (1:3–4): [The blessed man] *shall be like a tree which is planted near the running waters, which shall bring forth its fruit in due season. And his leaf shall not fall off, and all whatsoever he shall do shall prosper*. Its tenth effect is to multiply the universal Church; therefore, it is said in Proverbs 31:16: *With the fruit of her hands she hath planted a vineyard*. Its eleventh effect is to restore the ruin of the empyreal realm, concerning which the Lord says (Ezekiel 17:23): *On the high mountain of Israel I shall plant it, and it shall shoot forth into branches and bear fruit*. The twelfth effect of Mary's blessed fruit is to perpetuate the eternal glory, which would not be perpetual unless he preserved it, as it says in Proverbs (11:30): *The fruit of the just is a tree of life*. These, concludes Conrad, are the twelve fruits we read of in Revelation that the angel showed to John and that came into the world through the blessed fruit of Mary's womb.[244]

"There is no doubt," as Jerome (a.k.a. Paschasius) put it, "that whatever is worthily said of his mother belongs wholly to the glory of the praise of God."[245] This, for Conrad, was the principal mystery: how to praise Mary worthily so as to praise God, the Lord who was with her and the fruit of her womb. Conrad found, as he believed, the key in the words with which the angel greeted her, its five sweet phrases (including the blessing uttered by Elizabeth) encapsulating wonderfully the mystery of God's presence with her, as the sun with the dawn, the flower with its stem, and the king with his queen, dwelling with her and in her in body and mind, even as she took her place beside him in heaven in body and mind. While for Richard the grammarian, as we have seen, Mary was above all the book of the generation of the Word, for Conrad the preacher, as for the authors of the Orthodox homilies upon which, as we have argued, the liturgy of her Office depended, Mary, above all, was the *locus* or place where God was: the throne, the temple, the city of Zion in which the incarnate Word took his rest.[246] She was the burning bush, the pillar of cloud, and the ark because, as his mother, she was the glory of the Lord, just as she had been in the temple. When the angel said to her, therefore, "The Lord is with you," he indeed spoke a great mystery: the Lord of Israel, the Angel of Great Counsel, had made her his holy habitation and therefore exalted her not only above all other women, but also above all other creatures in heaven as well as on earth. He sat in her mind as on a throne and filled the house of her body with his glory, just as, in the ancient temple tradition, the Lord was enthroned upon the cherubim and filled the temple with his glory. *For*, as the book of Wisdom put it, *she is the brightness of eternal light and the unspotted mirror of God's majesty and the image of his goodness* (Wisdom 7:26). According to Conrad, Mary's mind was such a mirror, her body such a temple, and therefore the Lord was with her in his majesty, filling her body and soul with the grace of his presence.

PLATE 19 Annunciation, "Hier beghint dei metten von onser soeter vrouwen gehtide." Book of Hours, The Netherlands, ca. 1475. Use of Geert Grote. Chicago, The University of Chicago Library, Special Collections 347, fols. 16v–17r.

Photo courtesy of Special Collections Research Center, The University of Chicago Library.

LECTIO III. ARS DIALECTICA. PSEUDO-ALBERT'S QUESTIONS ABOUT WHAT MARY KNEW

This being the thirteenth century and the height not only of Marian devotion, but also of Scholasticism, there could not help but be *quaestiones*.[247] If Mary was full of grace, did this mean that she was full of as much grace as possible or full of the highest grace or full of all graces? If she was full of the knowledge and love of God, did she have faith? Did her knowledge include the mechanical and liberal arts? In what way was she exalted above the angels? Sometime in the latter half of the century, one of Mary's servants as yet known only as Pseudo-Albert set out to answer as many of these questions as he could, taking as his starting point the moment when the angel arrived to give the Virgin the good news that she was to become the Mother of God. In the end, following strict Scholastic methods of disputation, Pseudo-Albert discovered as many as 230 such questions about the sacred event, up to and including, as Hilda Graef put it, "such irrelevancies, absurd to the modern reader, as the sex, age and clothes in which the angel appeared to Mary, the colour of her complexion and hair, and other questions hardly of interest to the serious theologian."[248] Even more absurd to Graef than Pseudo-Albert's attention to these physical and sartorial irrelevancies, however, was the fact that he insisted Mary was "full" not just of the grace of becoming the Mother of God, but of "every grace in which a pure creature could share." According to Graef, this emphasis on Mary's plenitude of grace constituted "a considerable departure from the traditional view which places her divine motherhood at the centre," particularly since, as Graef took care to point out, the angel never said that Mary was "full of grace" [*gratia plena*] only "highly favored" [*kecharitomene*].[249] Despite Pseudo-Albert's otherwise commendable emphasis on Mary's compassion for her Son at his Crucifixion, therefore, Graef felt herself obliged to agree with René Laurentin's assessment of the work, as manifesting "the first symptoms of decadence" to which, in her view, the late medieval devotion to Mary was so regrettably prone, even if, in comparison with Richard of Saint-Laurent's *De laudibus*, Pseudo-Albert's *Mariale* was "more sober, despite its exaggerations."[250] But how, after all, we might still ask, could one exaggerate, never mind say enough, about the woman who gave birth to God?

Like Conrad, Pseudo-Albert—who seems to have been working in Austria or southern Germany, possibly in a Benedictine or Cistercian convent, albeit one with close Dominican ties[251]—may have used Richard's work,[252] although the correspondences could as well be evidence of the degree to which the Marian tradition of the High Middle Ages was itself "decadent," if by "decadent" we mean ultimately dependent upon the temple tradition and reading Mary as (the Mother of) Wisdom. That said, Pseudo-Albert does add one element to the praises of Mary that does not feature in the other two works and may rightly be called "decadent," if by "decadent" we mean departing from the temple tradition in which Adam and Eve, the Lord and his Lady together were understood as bearing the "image and likeness" of God (Genesis 1:26–27).[253] For Pseudo-Albert, it seems, it was not enough to praise Mary as exalted among women; it was also necessary to imply that she was exalted in spite of her sex, the female sex being (as he put it) later by nature yet prior in sin.[254] Even he, however, was quick to point out that, although women are excluded from holy orders on account of the "unworthiness of their sex and their greater tendency to sin," both the Old and the New Testaments told stories of prophetesses who were capable of explaining the scriptures, of whom Mary was undoubtedly one. Moreover, he averred, if John the Baptist was a prophet and more than a prophet because he pointed to God with his finger (Matthew 11:9; Luke 7:26), Mary herself could not help but be more than a prophetess, capable of explaining the whole of the law (*totius legis explanatrix*), for she, after all, pointed to the Son with her whole body when as a virgin she gave birth to him whom the prophets and scriptures had foretold.[255]

Mary, being a woman, might not have received the sacrament of holy orders; nevertheless, or so Pseudo-Albert reasoned, being "full of grace," she possessed all the grace, dignity, and power of the priesthood above even that of the pope, for while the pope is the servant of the servants of God, Mary is the Queen and Lady of the Angels and Empress of the whole world. (So much for the inferiority of her sex!) By Pseudo-Albert's reckoning, while the ministers of the Church have spiritual and temporal power as vicars or delegates of God, Mary has a perpetual plenitude of heavenly power by canonical authority (*ex auctoritate ordinaria*); and while the ministers of the Church have the power of binding and loosing through the use of the keys, she has the lawful power of binding and loosing by command (*per imperium*). She likewise possesses equally and excellently the special dignities and graces of each of the individual orders: with the exorcists, she has the power to cast out demons (Genesis 3:15); with the doorkeepers, she admits the clean and keeps out the unclean (Ezekiel 44:2–3); with the acolytes, she bears light (Song of Songs 3:6; Numbers 24:17). With the lectors, she interprets the scriptures according to the letter about herself (*ad litteram in seipsa*) (Isaiah 7:14; Luke 1:31). With the subdeacons, she makes known the apostolic teachings, "whence she is signified by the ark, in which were the manna and rod of Aaron [Numbers 17:10; Hebrews 9:4], that is, divine wisdom."

With the deacons, she treasures the Word of the Lord, both to tell others the story and to fulfill the counsels of God (Luke 2:19). With the priests, she fashions the body of the Lord by herself (*per seipsam*) and communicates it to the faithful. With the bishops, she ordains priests through the obligation of continence (Isaiah 52:11), consecrates spiritual temples by inspiring them to chastity, and consecrates virgins by adorning them with virtues and espousing them to her Son (Wisdom 6:20). With the pope, she has care for all the churches, a plenitude of spiritual power, and a universality of privileged actions, because if he is the father of fathers, she is the mother of all Christians or, rather, of all the good (Wisdom 7:11–12), and while the pope has a plenitude of power only in this life, she has power in heaven, purgatory, and hell.[256]

So, likewise, Pseudo-Albert reasoned, Mary, being full of grace, received the fullness of all the other sacraments, of baptism, confirmation, communion, confession and penance, marriage, and extreme unction. She was also full of virtue, of faith, hope, love, justice, fortitude, perseverance, temperance, chastity, sobriety, and modesty. Again, she was full of the blessings promised in the Beatitudes, of poverty, meekness, mourning, hungering and thirsting for justice, mercy, purity of heart, peace, and the crowns of the martyrs, confessors, and virgins (Matthew 5:3–12). She was likewise full of the gifts of grace (1 Corinthians 12:8–10) as well as of all the properties of the nine orders of the angels, not to mention blessed with all the blessings of the patriarchs. And she was full of the gifts of the Holy Spirit, of understanding, counsel, fortitude, knowledge, piety, and fear of the Lord (Isaiah 11:2–3). Above all, however, according to Pseudo-Albert, she was full of Wisdom:

> That the most blessed Virgin was wiser than any other creature, is indicated by the fact that the book which is entitled *Wisdom*, is especially interpreted concerning her: the Church interprets what is said of the Lord's wisdom as if it is said of her, as is evident in the epistles [that is, the lessons for the Office and Mass] which are read of her. In wisdom, however, there is nothing of stupidity or ignorance: therefore the most blessed Virgin was full of wisdom. But in faith, wisdom is not full, but only in part, as it is said: *For we know in part, and we prophesy in part* (1 Corinthians 13:9). Therefore, the most blessed Virgin did not have faith, but full knowledge.[257]

And what knowledge she had! As blessed Bernard put it, as cited by Pseudo-Albert:

> Who indeed can, except perhaps she who alone deserved to have this most blessed experience, who can grasp by his intelligence and discern with his reason not only the way in which the inaccessible splendor could pour itself out into the

virginal womb but also how, in order that she might support the approach of the inaccessible, it became a shade for the rest of this body, a small portion of which he had vivified and appropriated? And perhaps it was for this reason the angel used the words *he will overshadow you*, because the event was so great a mystery that the Trinity wished to accomplish it in the Virgin alone and with her alone, and she alone was allowed to understand it because she alone was allowed to experience it.[258]

Which, arguably, leaves us at an impasse before we have even started. What point could there be in asking questions about Mary's experience at the Annunciation, if she alone was allowed to understand what the Trinity wished to accomplish in her?

As Pseudo-Albert would put it, all the point in the world! Mary alone may have been allowed to experience the mystery of her overshadowing, but, as Pseudo-Albert noted in the epigraph to his work as a whole, as Wisdom, she had made a great promise to those who sought her:

Wisdom, as it is written (Wisdom 6:13–17), *is glorious and never fadeth away and is easily seen by them that love her and is found by them that seek her. She preventeth them that covet her so that she first sheweth herself unto them. He that awaketh early to seek her shall not labour, for he shall find her sitting at his door. To think therefore upon her is perfect understanding, and he that watcheth for her shall quickly be secure. For she goeth about seeking such as are worthy of her, and she sheweth herself to them cheerfully in the ways and meeteth them with all providence.* It is also written (Ecclesiasticus 24:29–31): *They that eat me shall yet hunger, and they that drink me shall yet thirst. He that hearkeneth to me shall not be confounded, and they that work by me shall not sin. They that explain me shall have life everlasting.*

Accordingly, Pseudo-Albert took heart: "Supported by trust in this lavish promise, I put my hand to this work, even though there are others who surpass me greatly in understanding and knowledge." Like Richard, Pseudo-Albert implored his readers not to ascribe anything in his work that might strike their ears as somehow novel or dubious to rashness on his part, but only to simple devotion. His purpose, Pseudo-Albert contended, was not to praise the glorious Virgin with falsehoods or to try to impress others with a lofty style of speech, but only "to offer through simple words a gift of devotion to those like me who are unlearned and simple." To help the reader, he had divided the work into titles the better to shed light on what follows. "Know," he advised, "that anything in it that strikes you as reasonable, comes from God as the maker of all good things," for, as Augustine himself put it,

> For my part I declare resolutely and with all my heart that if I were called upon to write a book which was to be vested with the highest authority, I should prefer to write it in such a way that a reader could find re-echoed in my words whatever truths he was able to apprehend. I would rather write in this way than impose a single true meaning so explicitly that it would exclude all others, even though they contained no falsehood that could give me offence.

As for what it is possible to say about the Virgin, Augustine says in his book on Genesis that (in Pseudo-Albert's paraphrase) "neither in spiritual nor in corporeal things is there anything empty [of meaning]." Moreover—here Pseudo-Albert paraphrased John of Damascus without attribution: "The most blessed Virgin is not surpassed by any of the famous in anything," whether in her purity from sin or in the blessings that descended upon her. Indeed, Pseudo-Albert contended, "there was no good lacking in her of which a pure creature was capable in the present life."[259] Accordingly, while it is true, as Graef points out, that Pseudo-Albert concerned himself with such apparent irrelevancies "as the sex [male], age [youth], and clothes [white] in which the angel appeared to Mary, the colour of her complexion [white and ruddy] and her hair [black, like her eyes],"[260] by far the majority of his questions (well over half of the total) have to do with demonstrating how Mary, the Mother of Wisdom, was full of the gifts of wisdom, knowledge, and grace. Once again, as in our readings of Richard and Conrad, the citations from scripture are Pseudo-Albert's.

The first thirty or so questions set the scene. For example: *Q. 12 What was Mary doing when the angel came to her with his good news?* She was engaged in contemplation, in silence and hope, as befits the most prudent Virgin about to become the Mother of Wisdom and to be elevated in substance to the highest proximity to God.[261] *Q. 29 Why was it fitting for the Mother of God to be called Mary?* Because this name means Lady (*Domina*), star of the sea (*stella maris*), illuminated one (*illuminata*), light-giver (*illuminatrix*), and bitter sea (*amarum mare*).[262] *Q. 30 Why does the Evangelist say: "He went in," and was the door open or closed when the angel entered?* Clearly, the door was closed because Mary was praying. As Bernard says: "Angels are accustomed to taking their stand beside those who pray, and they delight in those whom they see lifting pure hands in prayer." Moreover, "angelic spirits are not hindered by walls." When the angel went in to her, he found Mary with her knees bent, her pure hands lifted up, and her eyes fixed on heaven as with tears and great devotion she poured out prayers to the Father for the Incarnation of the Son.[263] *Q. 31 Whether it was fitting for the angel's greeting to begin with "Ave"?* While the angel might have said rather "*Salve*" or "*Gaude*" or "*Pax vobis*," he said "*Ave*" because the Virgin was "*a vae*," without woe, whether of error in her reason, of pain in her desires, or of shame in her motivations.[264] *Q. 32 Why does the Church customarily add "Mary" to the salutation, by saying: "Hail Mary"?* It would seem to be a problem that the Church adds something to what the Gospel says when it is expressly forbidden in Revelation 22:18–19 to add anything to scripture, but then we should have to ask why the angel seems to omit Mary's name from his greeting. Instead of her proper name, however, speaking as the mouth of the Lord (Isaiah 62:2), he gives her a new name, *gratia plena*, proper only to her: "For no other creature is full of grace susceptively (*susceptive*) except the blessed Virgin, who alone received so much, that a pure creature could receive no more." The Church adds Mary's proper name to the salutation that through it she might be inclined to her servants in their necessity, while the angel's name for her recalls her dignity.[265]

Q. 35 What is meant by the plenitude of grace in Mary?

Now that was the question! Or, rather, that was questions 35 through 164, some of which were easier to answer than others, albeit all ultimately in the affirmative. After all, as it says of her in Ecclesiasticus 24:25: *In me is all grace of the way and of the truth.* "Therefore," Pseudo-Albert argues, "she was full of all grace. Moreover," he avers, "in the art of logic (*in arte logica*), that which is undefined is understood universally; likewise, the benefits of princes are interpreted in the broadest sense. Therefore, since the Lord in his privilege named her through the angel *gratia plena*, because it does not specify a particular grace, [this name] should be understood universally for all."[266] *Q. 36 Were the sacraments contained in this plenitude?* Yes, as we have already seen, including the grace and dignity of holy orders, for seven reasons: her own humility, in order to avoid scandal, in order to fulfill the commandments, on account of her supererogation of merits, in order to confound the heretics, especially those who would assert that she was not a human being but an angel, in order to instruct the perfect, and in order to make sinners culpable.[267]

Q. 44 Did the blessed Virgin have faith?

It would seem at first not, for, as Pseudo-Albert reasoned, just as her love in this life exceeded that of any other creature, so her knowledge exceeded that of any other creature, including those, like Paul, who had been rapt up to the third heaven. Likewise, she was purer in heart than any other creature, joined more closely to God through knowledge and love than any other creature, lifted higher to the knowledge of God than any other creature. Moreover, as we have already seen, she was full of wisdom, suggesting that she had no need of faith.[268] It would likewise seem, Pseudo-Albert averred, that the Virgin did not have hope, for just as her knowledge transcended faith, so in its certainty it transcended hope.[269] She had love, of course, greater and more excellent than any other pure creature; likewise, she had justice, obedience, devotion, penitence, prudence, perseverance, temperance, chastity, sobriety, and modesty in behavior and dress.[270] She was also most excellent in her disposition and acts of worship, for as Mother of God, her worship of God was greater beyond comparison than that of any of the other servants of God, in the acts of her heart (knowledge and love), of her mouth (praise and prayer), and of works (genuflections, adorations, sacrifices, and the like):

> [For] she made of her heart and body a temple of the Holy Spirit, in which the Son of God dwelled bodily, in which she offered to God in herself and in the supreme chastity of her heart and body that sacrifice more acceptable than any other sacrifice, rather her son himself and the Son of God, not as bread and wine translated into his body and sacrificed under other species, but in the flesh and blood according to which his body was made, in the proper species in which she bore him and offered him for us all willingly at his passion.[271]

But did the Virgin have faith? Clearly struggling, Pseudo-Albert returned to this question in his summary *responsio* on the theological and cardinal virtues, which he prefaced with a lengthy prolegomenon on the ways in which creatures ascend to the vision or knowledge of God.[272]

As Stephen Mossman notes, Pseudo-Albert's conclusion at this point—that of course Mary had the habit of faith—is somewhat unconvincing, insisting rather disingenuously that both the habit of faith and the habit of rapture were able to coexist, albeit only the more perfect (rapture) within the less perfect (faith), not vice versa, for "as long as there is the habit of faith in the [mental] power, so there is something obscure . . . but when the [mental] power has been wholly deified (*deiformis*), there is something most similar to that purification which is in the heavenly kingdom."[273] In contrast, Pseudo-Albert was much more convinced of the plenitude of Mary's knowledge, which she experienced not, like Adam, in ecstatic sleep, nor, like Paul and John, in rapture, but in a way surpassing all other creatures in this life, the closest ever achieved to that vision of the heavenly kingdom, so pure in mind, full of grace, and exalted by the love of God was she even before she was lifted up into heaven after her death. Now, of course, having been assumed into heaven she enjoys a vision of God above even that of the angels, who are able to see God without any bodily form. Above all these visions is that of the Lord Jesus Christ, who sees God most perfectly in himself and his blessedness through the grace of understanding, his soul joined to the divine nature by the grace of union, and beyond the ability of all creatures by reason of his divinity, for only the Trinity enjoys perfect vision of itself. Nevertheless, Mary excelled all other creatures in the perfection, persistence, and manner of her knowing from the time when she became Mother of God to her Assumption into heaven, for "her life was always hidden with Christ in God and present to the angelic court, and she dwelled within the sanctuary of God." Indeed, so great a light filled her intellect that it was like the body of the Lord at the transfiguration, when he appeared to the apostles in the brightness of his glory (Matthew 17:1–8; Mark 9:1–7; Luke 9:28–36). While Peter and those who were with him were thrown into a stupor, likewise Paul when he was lifted up *whether in body, I do not know, or out of body, I know not, God knoweth* (2 Corinthians 12:3), Mary was not, because her intellect was more deified (*deiformior*) because proportionally more filled with light.[274]

Q. 62 How was the sevenfold plenitude of grace apportioned between the sevenfold gifts contained in that plenitude?

Just as the most blessed Virgin was filled with the virtues, so she was filled with the gifts of the Holy Spirit (Isaiah 11:2–3) in a way above that of any other creature in this state of life.[275] As it says in Proverbs (11:2): *Where humility is, there also is wisdom.* Mary had humility beyond comparison; therefore, her wisdom, too, was beyond comparison. Wisdom, according to Pseudo-Albert, "is a certain spiritual taste of prime truth by way of the highest good," and taste, as the Philosopher says, is a certain kind of touch in which there is a discernment of the thing tasted and a delight in the conjunction of the taster with the thing tasted. Mary excelled all others in her taste and, therefore, in her wisdom because she was so close to God in love, never failing to discern good from evil, delighting beyond comparison in her hope and certainty, and full of spiritual sweetness, tasting nothing but God for the sake of God.[276] Mary likewise excelled all other creatures in this life in her understanding, for while earthly wayfarers (*viatores*) know God only "through images without light with the obscurity of faith" and those in heaven (*comprehensores*) know "the uncreated light by the uncreated light without images," she alone knew God "in created light, but without images":

> In this way she knows the uncreated through the created, and that light was neither a medium like a mirror, a trace, or an image, nor as a sign is a medium between the perception and the signified, but as the light of the sun is a medium binding the visible object to sight.[277]

Mary excelled all other creatures in her counsel, having been anointed (1 John 2:20) and overshadowed by the Spirit of truth (John 16:13), for to her alone was revealed in its fullness the greatest secret of all, the mystery of the Incarnation; therefore, she was not ignorant of any lesser secret. Moreover, the blessed Virgin is most familiar with and most beloved of the Son of God, as well as most wise, the one "of whom the book of love, that is the Song of Songs, and the book of Wisdom are expounded, so that those things which are said of Wisdom are understood of her." Just as perfect Wisdom knows all secrets, so the blessed Virgin had perfect knowledge universally of all secrets, as befits her as universal counselor (*consiliatrix*).[278] She had greater fortitude than all other wayfarers because she overcame God, death, and the devil, greater knowledge, greater piety, and greater fear.[279] She likewise had the actions of all of these gifts in knowledge and affection (*in cognitione et affectione*) "in a middle way between the state of life and the state of the heavenly kingdom," for she knew herself to have been sanctified in the womb, to be the Mother of God, and not to be able to sin, and thus she knew that she could not be separated from God (cf. Romans 8:38–39).[280]

Q. 95 How were the gratuitous gifts of grace present in the blessed Virgin?

As the Apostle Paul promised (1 Corinthians 12:8–10):

> *To one indeed, by the Spirit, is given the word of wisdom* (sapientia), *and to another, the word of knowledge* (scientiae), *according to the same Spirit; to another faith in the same Spirit, to another the grace of healing in one Spirit, to another the working of miracles, to another prophecy, to another the discerning of spirits, to another diverse kinds of tongues, to another interpretation of speeches.*

Of course Mary had faith, as has already been established (albeit Pseudo-Albert seems somewhat more confident in his own proofs this second time around). Likewise, she had the grace of healing because from her came forth the flesh of Christ (Ecclesiasticus 38:4; 43:24; 24:41); the working of miracles because she accomplished a miracle above nature by encompassing God (Isaiah 66:8; Jeremiah 31:22); prophecy because she had divine inspiration through the presence, grace, and indwelling of the Holy Spirit (Luke 1:35); discernment of spirits because she was more spiritual than others, therefore more judicious than others (1 Corinthians 2:15) and never deceived; diverse kinds of tongues because she is the advocate for everyone and talked with many kinds of people; and the interpretation of speeches because she understood everything said in the scriptures.[281] Her wisdom and knowledge, however, were even more incomparable, for, as Pseudo-Albert would contend, Mary knew everything.

She knew and was able to see the angels and spiritual beings as they really were (*per speciem propriam*). (Here Pseudo-Albert adduces a variety of proofs, philosophical, natural, and theological on whether her soul had such an ability, concluding, of course, that she did because, after all, Paul says that he saw the celestial hierarchies, as did the blessed Dionysius; therefore, Mary must have been able to as well.[282]) She also had knowledge of all of the mechanical arts, particularly those subtler and nobler arts associated with women, including embroidery and silk-working and sewing and weaving and the like.[283] And she had knowledge of all of the liberal arts in full, for, as it says in Proverbs (9:1): *Wisdom hath built herself a house; she hath hewn her out seven pillars*, that is, the seven liberal arts. Likewise, it says in the Song of Songs (4:4): *A thousand shields hang upon* [the tower of David], *all the armour of valiant men*. The tower of David is the holy scriptures, while the shields are the physical sciences; therefore, the liberal sciences pertain to the fortification of the holy scriptures; therefore, the saints know them; therefore, the blessed Virgin knew them. She knew grammar because, as the Damascene says, she was brought up in the temple, where the virgins were instructed; likewise, it says in Luke (2:51): *Mary kept all these words*, on which the gloss notes: "In diverse prophets"; therefore, she knew how to read. She knew rhetoric because she understood the scriptures perfectly, and, as Augustine says, the scriptures contain many colors of rhetoric. She knew civil and canon law because she is her servants' advocate before God against the cunning of the devil, and because she is the empress, she is able to establish and interpret the law. She knew logic in order to understand the scriptures, confound heretics, and strengthen the faith, and in all of its parts: *tentativa*, because she never succumbed to temptation; *sophistica*, because she knew all the devices of the devil; *dialectica*, because she knew how to solve problems; and *demonstrativa*, because she derived the most noble passion (mercy) from the most noble subject (the highest good) when through her God showed the greatest mercy in the work of redemption.[284]

She knew physics and medicine because, as the Philosopher says, the knowledge of the soul pertains to everything, and Mary had perfect knowledge of her soul. Likewise, many mysteries are figured in the sacred scriptures through the properties of precious stones, the species of animals and trees, and of other natural things; since the Virgin had perfect knowledge of the scriptures, she knew the natures of things as well, including how to heal the body and soul. She knew the arts of the quadrivium because she was perfect in affect and intellect; therefore, she loved all things lovable and knew all things knowable. Likewise, it is said that Abraham knew these sciences and was enriched by them; therefore, the Virgin ought to have known them. She knew music, since in both the old and new law song was used in the worship of God; moreover, her harmonious voice was the most delightful thing that the Son of God ever heard. She knew astronomy, for astronomy is necessary to theology and understanding the work of creation. She knew arithmetic in order to understand the mystical meanings of the numbers in scripture, as well as how to compute the numbers of years and the dates of various feasts. And she knew geometry, because there are in scripture many measures and measurements, for example, of the tabernacle and the temple, all of which she understood. Above all, she knew theology, for she fulfilled the commandments by which she had understanding (Psalm 118:104), her path lighted by the lamp of the Word (Psalm 118:105); she bore the golden crown of the preachers and was anointed with those things pertaining to salvation, as it says in the gloss (1 John 2:27), and she was figured by the ark that contained the law of Deuteronomy; therefore, she knew the whole law. She likewise knew everything included in the *Sentences* (that is, the textbook of theology used in the schools): everything pertaining to the Trinity, the predestination, power, and will of God; to angels, the works of the six days, and the status of man; to the Incarnation of the Word and his virtues, which she knew through her experience and in herself; and to the sacraments of grace and the Resurrection, her body even in this life being after the body of God most similar to the glorified body of the Resurrection.[285]

In fine, Mary knew everything, for did not the Lord promise as much, saying (John 16:13): *When the Spirit of truth comes, he will teach you all truth*? To know everything is a good thing; therefore, either the soul of the blessed Virgin was capable of this good or not. If so, then she would have been given this good, but if not, then we have to ask why. The Virgin, Pseudo-Albert concludes, knew everything not as Christ knows everything perfectly *per modum patriae*, nor as the apostles knew everything imperfectly *per modum viae*, but rather in a middle way, her soul knowing what Christ's soul knew, but less perfectly. Thus, by a most special grace, she had perfect knowledge of the Trinity "without mediation," of the mystery of the Incarnation "through grace and singular experience," of her own predestination "through revelation and reason," of her soul and spirits "as they really are (*per proprias species*) dispositively by nature, fully by grace," so that she was able to see angels, souls, and demons. She had perfect knowledge of everything pertaining to the state of this life "through the inpouring and inspiration of grace," and she had perfect knowledge of the scriptures, of what to do and what to contemplate. She had knowledge of her own future "through revelation and in the mirror of her reading," and she knew everything pertaining to the heavenly kingdom "through the revelation of contemplation." She had knowledge of all creatures "through nature, grace, and contemplation," of the evening (that is, last things) "through nature and through grace" and of the morning (that is, creation) "through grace." Through nature and grace, she was perfect in all her works and, therefore, in her knowledge, by which she ordered all her actions. She had perfect knowledge of everything pertaining to her blessedness in this life, while in her soul there was nevertheless nothing useless or irrelevant, but throughout she was full of grace.[286]

Q. 152 Whether if, as Dionysius says, the higher orders of angels have the properties of the lesser orders more excellently and the blessed Virgin is above all the orders of the angels, then she possesses the properties of all the angels?

It would seem so, for while angels as messengers and ministering spirits bear news through created words, she bears news through the uncreated word. Moreover, as (Pseudo-) Dionysius says in his book *de coelesti hierarchia* (here Pseudo-Albert is showing off his scholastic chops with his knowledge of the angelic hierarchies, a topic of much interest among the theologians of his day):

> According to the correct account which we have already frequently given, the superior Orders [of the celestial hierarchy] possess abundantly the sacred properties of the inferior ones, but the lowest do not possess the superposed universality of the highest, although the first-manifested illuminations are partially conveyed to them through the first Order, in proportion to their capacity.[287]

The Virgin is superior to all the celestial ranks; therefore, she abundantly possesses all of their properties, most particularly purgation, illumination, and perfection, for she "was shining in her purity, than which under God no greater is known." Just as the angels minister to the Lord (Daniel 7:10; Hebrews 1:14), so, like the sisters Mary and Martha (Luke 10:38–42), Mary ministered to him through her actions and in her contemplation. As Augustine (rather, Ralph of Escures) asked: "What of wisdom did she not know, in whom the wisdom of God lay hidden and in whose womb Christ made for himself a body? In Mary, therefore, were hidden all the treasures of the wisdom and knowledge of God."[288] Again, as (Pseudo-)Dionysius explains: "Hierarchy is, as I see it, a divine order and knowledge and activity." That the blessed Virgin has all three of these things is clear because she had imperial power, that is, order, with respect to all the angels; therefore, because her power was greater than that of all the angels, so likewise was her knowledge and activity. Last but not least, "there is one property that is common to all angels: angels always see the face of the Father. And this vision is their whole reward." But Mary's reward was incomparably superior to that of the angels; therefore, her vision is superior to that of all the angels.[289]

Mary likewise possesses all the properties of each of the nine orders of the angels. While the angels are known to God's other creatures through understanding, the most blessed Virgin is known to them through experience; so while they are of higher rank than humanity and not brothers or sons, she is her servants' superior, mother, sister, and daughter, who guards all universally, just as the Angels guard each individually. Like the Archangels, she receives illuminations from above, excels the Angels and all other saints in grace, justice, and nature, and as *mediatrix* and *adjutrix* leads those inferior to her to join the order of the angels so that its number might be restored. Like the Principalities, she imitates the Prince of Princes in immunity from evil (Wisdom 6:20) and in communicating all good things (Wisdom 7:11), fully formed through her virtues in the likeness of God in whom she dwells (*qui habuit deiformissimas virtutes*) as she says in Ecclesiasticus (24:7): *I dwelt in the highest places*, and leading all creatures back to him from whom they came by joining with him in person. Like the Powers, she was well-ordered in her dignity, the founder (*inventrix*) and mistress (*ordinatrix*) of the order of virgins as well as the repairer (*reparatrix*) and restorer (*restauratrix*) of the order of angels, and leading all toward the divine by the example of her virtues. Like the Virtues, she was strong in the face of opposition, constant in the face of difficulty, and enduring in the face of evil, particularly at the Passion of her Son; she was never slowed down by weakness even though she, unlike the angels, bore the burden of the flesh, and she was generous toward those below her, giving God to the world and the world to God and to men the kingdom of heaven. Like the Dominions, she is free from all servitude, invincible against enemies, neither prodigal nor miserly but generously strict, serving no creature but God alone, having no need of subjects, being most like God in both his humanity and his divinity, *the mirror of his majesty and the image of his goodness* (Wisdom 7:25–26), her will ordered for ruling, conforming herself and her servants to God while pursuing nothing vain, conformed wholly to the divine lordship by sharing in the Passion of her Son.[290]

Like the Thrones, she dwells in the high places and her throne is a pillar of cloud (Ecclesiasticus 24:7), for she is that sapphire throne Ezekiel saw over the firmament (Ezekiel 1:26), that is, above all the choirs of angels. She is the light surrounding the king, for she enclosed in her womb him whom the heavens could not contain, and the place in which the king took his rest, making for himself from her a body that he joined in the unity of his person and never put off. She is the true litter that the true Solomon made for himself (Song of Songs 3:9), which carried him into the world and around the world, when he ascended on a swift cloud and entered into Egypt (Isaiah 19:1). Like the Cherubim, she wholly encompasses him because she entered into the innermost part of the Father's mercy and drew forth the only-begotten Son from her heart; she led back to God everything that came from God; her actions were wholly assimilated to God (*deiformissimos actus habuit*) when she gave birth to him as God and man whom God begot before God; and she was an example and mirror and star of the sea for all re-created things, the teacher (*doctrix*) of the discipline of God illuminating all. Like the Seraphim, she moves, that is, lives in love, because she was the beginning of uncreated life and for her servants the cause of eternal life. She is unceasing, that is, perpetual in her love, because she was never able to sin, and she is fiery with a love that is nevertheless calm in the midst of temptation and strife. She is even sharper in her wisdom than the angels, for while the Seraphim participate accidentally (*accidentaliter*) in created wisdom, she was in essence (*essentialiter*) the Mother of uncreated wisdom. She is above even the Seraphim in the vehemence of her love, like a dove ascending through contemplation above the rivers of waters, that is, above all the choirs of the angels (here Pseudo-Albert is quoting a responsory for the feast of the Assumption), for she had before all the greatest treasure above, where, therefore, her heart was (Matthew 6:21), herself wholly given to God, filled body and soul with God. She is more intent, that is, she enters more into herself than the angels, because she penetrated to the innermost parts of her heart so as to bring forth from the innermost bowels of her mercy the Son from the innermost heart of the Father, thus pouring out all the riches of his mercy while, dwelling in the sanctuary of God, she made visible the Wisdom hidden from the ages, now clothed in flesh. She not only does not descend, but rises up, drawing others with her, never allowing anything to divert her from her Son.[291]

Q. 162 Whether the name Queen of Mercy is properly suited to the blessed Virgin?

It would seem not, for there are other names by which she could be known, better suited to her dignity, the most worthy being Mother of God. Likewise, she has been exalted to the highest position of glory; therefore, she should be called Queen of glory, because just as her Son is called King of glory, so she should be called Queen. Moreover, where she is queen, there is, as the gloss says, no mercy (*misericordia*) because there is no misery (*miseria*) in heaven; therefore, she should be called Queen of heaven because she reigns there above all the orders of the angels. Again, while glory is proper to heaven, mercy is proper to earth, but grace is common to both heaven and earth; therefore, she should be called Queen of grace. Again, as her Son is the emperor over kings, so she is empress over queens; therefore, she should be called Empress of mercy. Again, the higher orders of angels are named according to their gifts; the highest gift is love; therefore, she should be called Queen of love. Again, her Son is called God of peace and love; therefore, she should be called Queen of peace and love. Again, she is higher than the Seraphim, therefore higher than love, but nothing is higher than love but God; therefore, she ought to be named after God; therefore, she ought to be called Goddess of mercy (*dea misericordiae*). Again, her Son is called King of kings and Lord of lords (1 Timothy 6:15; Revelation 19:16); therefore, she ought to be called Queen of queens and Lady of ladies. Again, her Son is called God of gods (*Deus deorum*); therefore, she ought to be called Goddess of goddesses (*dea dearum*). Again, (Pseudo-)Dionysius says: "You will find, however, that the divine Word [*eloquia*] calls not only these supercelestial essences gods, but also the holy men and most beloved of God among us." Since, therefore, the blessed Virgin was most beloved of God and lifted above all other creatures to the illumination of the divine, she most of all is to be called Goddess of gods (*dea deorum*).[292]

But, in fact, it is more suitable that she be called Queen of mercy because the kingdom of mercy is greater in power and dignity than the kingdom of glory, grace, or justice, for while there is glory in heaven, there is mercy also on earth and in purgatory and in hell. Likewise, the Mother shares the patrimony and property of the Son, which is mercy. Only mercy encompasses the whole kingdom of God; therefore, as she is queen where he is king, she is Queen of mercy. Again, just as she is called queen of France who is lady over everything in France, so the most blessed Virgin is properly, truly, and legally lady over everything in the mercy of God, whether mercy is construed transitively, because she is the cause of all mercy, or intransitively, because she is mercy, the place prepared by the Holy Spirit for the throne (Isaiah 16:5). Moreover, the dominion of mercy makes exiles kings, sinners godlike (*deiformissimos*) and more beautiful angels, and rules with love over heaven and earth. For all these reasons, it seems that the most proper name for the most blessed Virgin should be Queen rather than Empress, for while Empress is a name of severity and fear, Queen is a name of providence and equity. "It is for this reason," Pseudo-Albert observes, "I believe that God is never called Emperor in the Bible, but King, for this is the name of majesty." Likewise, if she were called Goddess of goddesses, she might not seem to be the goddess or queen of sinners or demons. Nor does it seem proper that she should be called Queen of power or wisdom, for just as wisdom includes power, but not vice versa, so mercy includes both power and wisdom, but not vice versa, whence the Queen of mercy is also Queen of power and wisdom, but not vice versa. A similar argument applies to justice, grace, and glory, all of which are likewise contained in mercy.[293]

Q. 164 *What comes to us [that is, her servants] out of Mary's plenitude of graces?*

As Wisdom says in Ecclesiasticus (24:41): "*I, like an aqueduct, came out of the paradise of God*, that is, out of the delights of the mercies of God." Thus, her servant says in Wisdom (7:11): *All good things came to me together with her, and innumerable riches through her hands.* Likewise, her plenitude was that of a vessel not only filled to the brim with created graces, but also filled at the same time with uncreated grace, whom she received and enclosed for nine months. For she was not only a vessel, but *an admirable vessel, the work of the Most High* (Ecclesiasticus 43:2), as the Church sings: "Virgin Mother of God, he whom the whole world could not contain, enclosed himself made man in your womb." She was that admirable vessel, containing at the same time both the water of humanity and the wine of divinity without confusion of nature or properties, who as Virgin conceived, bore, and remained virgin after giving birth, for she was *the enclosed garden, the sealed fountain* (Song of Songs 4:12), and *the closed gate* (Ezekiel 44:2) through whom only the king entered and went out. Like a fountain, she flowed continually with grace, for she was that *little fountain, which grew into a river, and abounded into many waters* (Esther 10:6), from which a plenitude of graces flows out onto the human race.[294]

According to Pseudo-Albert, six things in particular flow to her servants out of Mary's plenitude of grace.

One, the price of redemption (*pretium redemptionis*), for she is that *bag of money* (Proverbs 7:20) in which were hidden *all the treasures of the wisdom and knowledge of God* (Colossians 2:3), whom *the blessed man who hath not walked in the counsel of the ungodly* (Psalm 1:1) took up, that is, at her Assumption, when he *returned on the day of the full moon* (Proverbs 7:20). She is that *strong woman, whose price is beyond reckoning* (Proverbs 31:10), who *reacheth therefore from end to end mightily and ordereth all things sweetly* (Wisdom 8:1). That price was received at the Annunciation and paid out on the day of the Passion, but although the Jews believed that it was copper, when tested in the fire (Psalm 16:3), numbered (Psalm 21:18), and weighed on the cross, it was found to be of the purest gold, that is, God.

Two, the water of washing (*aqua ablutionis*), for she is that fountain of which Zechariah (13:1) says: *In that day there shall be a fountain open to the house of David, and to the inhabitants of Jerusalem, for the washing of the sinner, and of the menstruating woman.* Likewise, she is that fountain prefigured in 2 Kings (Samuel) 23:15, when David said: *O, that some man would get me a drink of the water out of the cistern that is in Bethlehem by the gate!* The most blessed Virgin is a fountain pouring out blessings for all, but a well for those who are especially devoted to her, and a cistern for the refreshment of sinners, whence she cries out to them (Ecclesiasticus 24:26): *Come over to me, all ye that desire me, and be filled with my fruits.* The water of this cistern is Christ, who is a fountain of life springing up into life everlasting (John 4:14), for which the Jewish people thirsted (Isaiah 41:17; Job 30:30; Psalm 142:6). Whence the Lord said to Moses (Numbers 20:8): "*Speak to the rock,* that is, to the blessed Virgin, who is hard against tribulation, heavy against instability, cold against lust: *and she will give you waters.*" Accordingly, when the angel spoke to her, Mary opened her treasury, that is, her fountain, and the waters of life poured forth from the cistern in Bethlehem.

Three, the bread of refreshment (*panis refectionis*), for she is *like the merchant's ship, bringing her bread from afar* (Proverbs 31:14), that is, from heaven (John 6:51), which she invites her servants to eat (Proverbs 9:5): *Eat my bread, and drink the wine which I have mixed for you.* God the Trinity mixed the wine of divinity with the water of humanity when he joined human nature with the divine; the blessed Virgin mixed this wine when she believed and consented. She likewise made her bread, when, like the woman in the Gospel (Matthew

13:33; Luke 13:20), she took and hid three measures of flour, that is, the body, soul, and divinity of Christ, until it was leavened by her faith. This is the bread for which the little ones hungered, but there was no one to break it for them (Lamentations 4:4), which was milled at the Incarnation and broken at the Passion so as to feed the hungry, as Isaiah (58:7) sought.

Four, the medicine of healing (*medicina curationis*), for *the Most High hath created medicines out of the earth* (Ecclesiasticus 38:4), and *a medicine for all is in the speedy coming of a cloud* (Ecclesiasticus 43:24), that is, in the most pure flesh of Christ formed into a body, which comes to her servants out of her plenitude. Whence she says (Ecclesiasticus 24:41): *I like the river Dioryx came out of paradise*, that is, out of God. "Dioryx" may be interpreted as "the medicine of generation," for Christ heals every infirmity.

Five, the weapons of attack (*arma expugnationis*), for, as the Master says in his *Historia*, the House of the Forest of Lebanon (3 Kings 7:2) was divided into two parts, the upper part for the storage of spices and perfumes for the use of the temple, the lower part for the armory for the protection of the king and the beauty of the house. (Here Pseudo-Albert gets what the Master says backward: Peter says the lower part of the house was for the spices, the upper for the armory.)[295] The most blessed Virgin was this house which Solomon built for himself (Proverbs 9:1), in which were kept medicines against the wounds of sins, and arms against the world and the devil. More particularly, Solomon made golden shields that he kept in this house. "I will go in," he says to her, "to this admirable tabernacle, because he whom the heavens could not contain, you enclosed in your womb." He entered into his tent and armed himself and there put on the shield of goodwill and became the light-bearer (*lucifer*). The psalmist says (Psalm 5:13): *Thou hast crowned us as with the shield of thy goodwill*, because what here is called a shield (*scutum*), in the Song of Songs (3:11) is called the crown (*diadema*) with which his Mother, that is, the Virgin Mary, crowned him on the day of his espousals, that is, at the Annunciation. It is with such a crown or shield that the king crowns the saints when he wants to honor them and share with them his divine properties (Esther 6:7–8), whence the woman clothed with the sun had on her head a crown of twelve stars (Revelation 12:1), because the most blessed Virgin crowned all the saints.

Six, the reward of recompense (*praemium remunerationis*), as it says in the psalm (126:3): *Behold the inheritance of the Lord, children, the reward of the fruit of the womb.* And in Genesis (15:1): *I will be thy reward exceedingly great.* "Thus," Pseudo-Albert concludes, "we see how the plenitude of the Virgin poured forth perfect blessings of all kinds on the human race," for she is that glorious city of God, in whose dwelling all rejoice (Psalm 86:3, 7), the field filled with flowers and fruits whom the Lord has blessed (Genesis 27:27), in whom the plenitude of divinity, the Father, Son, and Holy Spirit dwelt corporeally, full of love because she was full of God and God is love (1 John 4:8). "For all these reasons, therefore, it is clear how the most blessed Virgin was full of all grace, all plenitude, all reason of plenitude, and grace in every way."[296] As the logicians say, Q.E.D.

Here ends the lesson. *R. Thanks be to God.* Perhaps now, thanks to Richard, Conrad, and Pseudo-Albert, we can understand what or who it was medieval Christians saw when they read the scriptures, particularly the psalms, looking for the Lady and her Lord. "Quae est ista quae ascendit quasi aurora consurgens?," the angels sang.[297] Who was this Lady rising like the dawn for whom her medieval servants built such beautiful palaces at Chartres, Rouen, Paris, Amiens, Reims, Laon, Noyon, Coutances, and Bayeux[298] so that from morning to night they might sing for her their angelic antiphons, psalms, responsories, and hymns? If, for Henry Adams, she was Woman delighting in color and light but not much concerned with theology, and for Graef she was the Madonna who was "not pleased when she is put above her Son," for Richard, Conrad, and Pseudo-Albert, as we have seen, she was the book of the generation of Jesus Christ, the mirror of Wisdom, and Queen of mercy, made like God in her contemplation of God, filled with the plenitude of the divine in both heart and mind, her soul overflowing with the love of God just as her body contained him whom the heavens could not contain. As Richard, Conrad, Pseudo-Albert, and their fellow servants of Mary believed, to serve her was to serve God whose most perfect mirror she was; to look upon her was to look upon her Son in whose image and likeness she had been made. This was the reason, according to Richard, that everything said in the scriptures of Wisdom might also be said of her (*Maria*); it was likewise the reason that Conrad insisted the Lord was so fully with her (*Dominus tecum*) and that Pseudo-Albert insisted she was full of grace (*gratia plena*). Exalted above the angels in her maternity, she was the one through whom God became visible to the world, the creature through whom the Creator entered into his creation that he might be seen. Just as the sun shone through the colored glass of her beautiful window at Chartres, so the light of God shone through her into the world, taking on flesh without breaking the seal of her virginity, taking his rest in the noble *triclinium* of her womb. Far from absorbing the Trinity (in Adams's words), she was the one through whom the Trinity made itself known to the world as Father, Son, and Holy Spirit, the Lady through whom the Lord showed his face to his people. To describe her in all her names was to describe God, in whose name all the creatures of the world had been created. This was the reason, or so her medieval devotees like Richard, Conrad, and Pseudo-Albert believed, that the scriptures spoke about her all the time: because to speak about her was to speak about God, her Creator, Beloved, and Son. This was the reason they sang to her, as in the hymn for her Office that Richard sang at Rouen:

> Remember, author of salvation,
> that once you took the form
> of our body by being born
> from the virgin undefiled . . .
> Glory be to you, Lord,
> born from the virgin,
> with the Father and the Holy Spirit
> for ever and ever. Amen.[299]

As her medieval servants would have it, to praise Mary was to praise him who was with her, as the angel had said, because to praise Mary, the most perfect creature of God, was to praise God to whom she had given birth. In a word, her servants like Richard, Conrad, and Pseudo-Albert praised her as the Holy of Holies and heaven of heavens because they believed Mary was the temple, the mirror, the book in which Christians might learn about God.

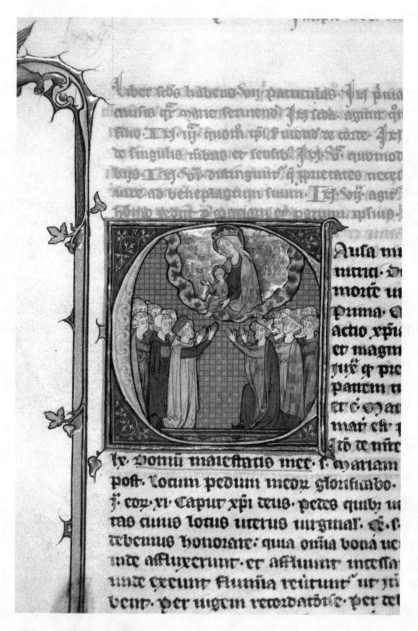

PLATE 20 How to serve Mary: Mary shows the Child to a kneeling crowd. Richard of Saint-Laurent, *De laudibus beatae Mariae virginis*, lib. 2. Copied in Paris or French Flanders, between 1250 and 1299. Wellesley, Wellesley College 19, fol. 36v.

5
Prayer

illed with knowledge of the Lady and her Lord and burning with love for them both, you fall to your knees, prayers pouring from your lips.[1]

Deus, qui de beatae Mariae Virginis utero Verbum tuum, angelo nuntiante, carnem suscipere voluisti; praesta supplicibus tuis, ut qui vere eam genitricem Dei credimus, ejus apud te intercessionibus adjuvemur.[2]

God, who willed that, at the angel's annunciation, your Word should take flesh from the womb of the blessed Virgin Mary, grant us, your humble supplicants, as we believe her to be truly the Mother of God, that we may be assisted by her intercessions with you. (Matins, Lauds)

As you pray—

Deus, qui virginalem aulam beatae Mariae Virginis in qua habitares, eligere dignatus es; da, quaesumus, ut sua nos defensione munitos, jucundos facias suae interesse commemorationi.[3]

God, who deigned to choose the virginal court of the blessed Virgin Mary in which to dwell, grant, we beseech, that guarded by her defense, we may joyfully take part in her commemoration. (Prime)

—you remind yourself that you are in the presence of a king and queen more powerful than any mere earthly rulers and to whom you are obliged for both your life and your salvation.[4] Chastening yourself for your previous lapses in attention, you beg for her help in praying to her Son.

Deus, qui salutis aeternae, beatae Mariae virginitate foecunda, humano generi praemia praestiti; tribue, quaesumus, ut ipsam pro nobis intercedere sentiamus, per quam meruimus auctorem vitae suscipere, Dominum nostrum Jesum Christum.[5]

God, who by the fruitful virginity of blessed Mary has bestowed rewards upon the human race, grant, we beseech, that we may experience her intercession, through whom we merited to receive the author of life, our Lord Jesus Christ. (Terce)

You remind yourself not to speak too quickly, lest you drop syllables[6] from your praise of the one who contained in her womb he who cannot be contained.

Concede, misericors Deus, fragilitati nostrae praesidium, ut qui sanctae Dei genitricis memoriam agimus, intercessionis ejus auxilio, a nostris iniquitatibus resurgamus.[7]

Grant, merciful God, support for our weakness, that we who remember the holy Mother of God may, by the help of her intercession, rise up from our sins. (Sext)

Focusing your understanding (*intellectus*) as well as you can on the meaning of the words, you find your affection (*affectus*) stirred more and more to devotion as your mind lifts ever upward to God in faith, hope, and love.

Famulorum tuorum, quaesumus Domine delictis ignosce; ut qui tibi placere de actibus nostris non valemus, genitricis Filii tui Domini nostri Jesu Christi intercessione salvemur.[8]

Lord, we beseech, forgive the offenses of your servants, that we who are unable to please you by our actions, may be saved by the intercession of the Mother of your Son, our Lord Jesus Christ. (None)

For a moment, you find yourself reflecting on the different rhetorical modes in which you might pray—giving thanks, making petitions, confessing your sins, asking for intercession:

Concede nos famulos tuos, quaesumus, Domine Deus, perpetua mentis et corporis sanitate gaudere; et gloriosa beatae Mariae semper Virginis intercessione, a praesenti liberari tristitia, et aeterna perfrui laetitia.[9]

Grant us, we beseech, Lord God, your servants to rejoice in perpetual health of body and mind, and by the glorious intercession of blessed Mary ever Virgin, to be delivered from present sorrow and to enjoy eternal happiness. (Vespers)

But then your devotion stirs again, and you forget everything but the love of God and his Mother, as you pray:

> Beatae et gloriosae semperque Virginis Mariae, quaesumus, Domine, intercessio gloriosa nos protegat, et ad vitam perducat aeternum.[10]
>
> *We beseech, Lord, let the glorious intercession of the blessed and glorious ever Virgin Mary protect us and guide us to eternal life.* (Compline)

You begin to sing the concluding antiphon:

> Salve, regina, mater misericordiae, vita, dulcedo, et spes nostra, salve! Ad te clamamus, exules filii Hevae; ad te suspiramus, gementes et flentes in hac lacrymarum valle. Eia ergo, advocata nostra, illos tuos misericordes oculos ad nos converte; et Jesum benedictum fructum ventris tui, nobis post hoc exilium ostende. O clemens, o pia, o dulcis Virgo Maria![11]
>
> *Hail, queen, mother of mercy, our life, our sweetness, and our hope! To you we cry, exiled children of Eve, to you we sigh, weeping and mourning in this vale of tears. Come, then, our advocate, turn your merciful eyes on us, and our long exile past show us Jesus, the blessed fruit of your womb. O merciful, o pious, o sweet Virgin Mary!*

But even as you intone the opening phrase, you find yourself rising like incense from the holocaust of your prayer, drawn by the marvelous power of God out of your body and led by an angel to a glorious city built out of gold and precious stones. There, surrounded by all the orders of the heavenly city—saints, patriarchs, prophets, apostles, martyrs, confessors, virgins, widows, and all the rest of the faithful—you behold a glorious lady, exceeding bright and fair, more beautiful than any other creature you have ever imagined or seen. On her head she wears a crown of dazzling stars, and her clothing is wrought with gold and precious stones. She is seated on a throne likewise wrought with precious stuffs and surrounded by angels singing praises to God.[12] Her face shines with divine light as she turns toward you and smiles.[13] You feel your heart swell with love for her as your tongue is moved by the spirit of wisdom and understanding to cry out: "Teach me," you beg of her, "how to serve you!"[14] She gestures toward the angels, who, you now realize, are intoning the psalms for her Hours, their melodies so sweet and the harmony of their voices so marvelous that no words could possibly describe their song. You falter, knowing that you could never sing as beautifully as they, even if you were able to remember all of the words without having to read them in a book (as spiritual intelligences, angels do not need physical books), never mind understand them without having to ask one of your fellow choristers.[15]

But then you recall a story that you once heard a minstrel sing about a tumbler who, because he had no learning when he became a monk other than to leap and to jump, made an office of his tumbling before the image of Mary by turning somersaults in her praise. "Clearly," you think to yourself, "there is more to serving Mary than simply singing skillfully, for how otherwise could the tumbler's tumbling have been acceptable to her?" You then think on the other stories you have heard about the ways in which Mary rewarded her servants for reciting the angel's greeting or the Salve Regina (which you are singing now) and how, when all seemed lost, she was there to intercede for them, even Theophilus, who had contracted himself in writing to serve the devil rather than God and his Mother. "So is it easy or hard to serve Mary?" you wonder. "Does it really not matter what I do in this life so long as I serve her?" You have heard some say how her Son cannot refuse her if she pleads on your behalf and how she restrained him when he would have destroyed the world in his judgment.[16] But you have also heard about how she punished those who made vows to her and did not keep them. Sometimes, Mary seems to side with sinners, like the thief Ebbo whom she saved from hanging because he saluted her so devoutly when he prayed, or the abbess whose pregnancy she helped to conceal because the sinner chanted her Hours so sweetly, but at other times, the Virgin seems to demand rather more, as when she chastised the cleric who had once said her Hours at a time when they were still said by only a few, but who had become sluggish in her service and had taken another bride. "O impious and most stupid man!" she is said to have chided him. "Why have you, trapped in another love, abandoned me when I had been your friend? Surely you have not found another one better? I warn you neither to fail me nor take another wife, with me scorned!"[17] And what about those stories where she defends Christians in battle, only to turn around and pray for Christians, Jews, and Saracens alike, albeit, as Richard of Saint-Laurent put it, "in different ways" (*aliter tamen et aliter*)?[18] How and why can or should you serve such an awesome and beautiful Lady?

"What is man," the psalmist asked,

> *that thou art mindful of him: or the son of man that thou visitest him? Thou hast made him a little lower than the angels; thou hast crowned him with glory and honour and hast set him over the works of thy hands.* (Psalm 8:5–6)

Holy, holy, holy, the Lord God of hosts, all the earth is full of his glory, sang the seraphim whom Isaiah saw above the throne (Isaiah 6:1). *Come*, the psalmist sang,

> *let us praise the Lord with joy! Let us joyfully sing to God, our saviour. Let us come before his presence with thanksgiving and make a joyful noise to him with psalms, for the Lord is a great God and a great king above all gods, for in his hand are all the ends of the earth, and the heights of the mountains are his, for the sea is his, and he made it, and his hands formed the dry land.* (Psalm 94:1–5)

Praise ye the Lord, and call upon his name, King David commanded the priests to sing as they carried the ark into Jerusalem, *make known his doings among the nations! Sing to him, yea, sing praises to him: and relate all his wondrous works!* (1 Chronicles 16:7–11).

To sing with the angels the praises of the Lord the Maker of heaven and earth: this, according to the temple tradition upon which, as Margaret Barker has taught us, early and medieval Christianity depended, was the reason that God had crowned human beings with his glory and set them over the works of his hands.[19] Like the angels, human beings were called to serve the Lord, as it says in the Septuagint translation of Deuteronomy 32:43 that was known to the early Christians:

> *Rejoice, ye heavens, with* [the Lord], *and let all the angels of God worship him; rejoice ye Gentiles, with his people, and let all the sons of God strengthen themselves in him.*

As the author of the letter to the Hebrews confirmed, citing the verse from Deuteronomy as it appears in the Septuagint but no longer in the modern Hebrew:[20]

> *And again when [God] bringeth in the first begotten into the world, he saith: "And let all the angels of God adore him."* (Hebrews 1:6)

What is man?, the psalmist asked. As the Apostle Paul told his fellow Christians:

> *The first man* [that is, Adam] *was of the earth, earthly; the second man* [that is, Jesus Christ] *from heaven, heavenly . . . Just as we have borne the image of the earthly, let us bear also the image of the heavenly.* (1 Corinthians 15:47, 49)

The man from heaven is the man serving as high priest in the order of Melchizedek, the Son begotten on the day of his anointing, as the Lord says in the psalms (cf. Hebrews 5:5–6): *"Thou art my Son. This day I have begotten thee"* (Psalm 2:7); and *"Thou art a priest for ever according to the order of Melchizedek"* (Psalm 109:4). According to the ancient tradition, Christians, having been anointed at their baptism, were likewise priests, robed, like the angels, in white (Revelation 7:13–14), and restored to the glory of Adam before the fall. And again, like the angels, they were one in the Lord, as Paul said:

> *For as many of you as have been baptized in Christ, have put on Christ. There is neither Jew nor Greek: there is neither bond nor free: there is neither male nor female. For you are all one in Christ Jesus.* (Galatians 3:27–28)

Accordingly, Paul insisted, Christians should regard their bodies as [temples] *of the Holy Spirit* (1 Corinthians 6:19) and prepare themselves *as a living sacrifice, holy, pleasing unto God . . . reformed in the newness of* [their] *mind* (Romans 12:1–2), that is, by their anointing into Wisdom (1 John 2:20, 27). For, as John foretold, by thus serving the Lord, they would one day see him: *And his servants shall serve him: and they shall see his face: and his name shall be on their foreheads* (Revelation 22:3–4). As the Apostle Peter told the baptized who, like the high priests before them, bore the Name:

> *But you are a chosen generation, a kingly priesthood, a holy nation, a purchased people: that you may declare his virtues, who hath called you out of darkness into his marvellous light.* (1 Peter 2:9)

Holy, holy, holy, Lord God Almighty, who was, and who is, and who is to come! sang the living creatures around the throne (Revelation 4:8). *Thou are worthy, O lord our God, to receive glory, and honour, and power: because thou hast created all things; and for thy will they were, and have been created,* sang the twenty-four elders in return (Revelation 4:11).

This was the service that monks and nuns, canons, canonesses, and friars offered throughout the Middle Ages in their singing of the Divine Office. Likewise, this was the service to which medieval Christians believed they had been called as they sang the Hours of the Virgin, the Office of prayer they offered to the Mother of the Lord. As the psalmist prayed: *Let my prayer be directed as incense in thy sight, the lifting up of my hands as evening sacrifice* (Psalm 140:2). This, as ancient and medieval Christians understood it, was their "real religion," their "religion in act" (as Auguste Sabatier would put it): to sing to the Lord whom the Most High had crowned with glory, bestowing on him the *name which is above all names: that in the name of Jesus every knee should bow, of those that are in heaven, on earth, and under the earth: and that every tongue should confess that the Lord Jesus Christ is in the glory of God the Father* (Philippians 2:9–11), because Jesus the Anointed One was

> *the image of the invisible God, the firstborn of every creature: for in him were all things created in heaven and on earth, visible and invisible, whether thrones, or dominations, or principalities, or powers: . . . Because in him, it hath well pleased the Father, that all fulness should dwell: and through him to reconcile all things unto himself, making peace through the blood of his cross.* (Colossians 1:15–16, 19–20)

As Jordan of Saxony (d. 1237) warned his Dominican brothers: "When the brothers stand in choir for the Divine Office each one should be on his guard against being lazy and disinterested. Rather he should compel his spirit to stand in reverence and eagerly to sing to God before the angels who are present there, saying with the psalmist: *In the sight of the angels I shall sing to you* (Psalm 137:1)."[21] Likewise, as Dionysius the Carthusian put it in his great summary of the tradition: "To praise God is a most noble, heavenly and angelic act. It is worthier than the prayer of supplication."[22] This was the reason medieval Christians sang at the preparatory prayer of every Mass as they offered the host to be consecrated that it might become the "bread of angels" (Psalm 77:25):

> *Holy, holy, holy, Lord God of hosts!*
> *Heaven and earth are full of your glory.*
> *Hosanna in the highest.*
> *Blessed is he that comes in the name of the Lord.*
> *Hosanna in the highest.*[23]

As the Mass preface put it, in singing the Sanctus that Isaiah heard, medieval Christians were singing "with the angels and archangels, with thrones and dominations, and with all the hosts of the heavenly army." In this way, they believed, they were serving before the Lord just as the seer of Revelation had seen their counterparts serving in heaven.[24] Likewise, this was the service that they offered in their singing of the psalms, lifting their voices to heaven in praise of the one who made heaven and earth:

> *The heavens shew forth the glory of God, and the firmament declareth the work of his hands. Day to day uttereth speech, and night to night sheweth knowledge. There are no speeches nor languages where their voices are not heard. Their sound hath gone forth into all the earth, and their words unto to ends of the world.* (Psalm 18:1–5)

Sing ye to the Lord a new canticle! Sing to the Lord, all the earth! Sing ye to the Lord, and bless his name. Shew forth his salvation from day to day! (Psalm 95:1–2)

The Lord hath reigned; let the earth rejoice; let many islands be glad! Clouds and darkness are round about him; justice and judgment are the establishment of his throne. (Psalm 96:1–2)

Alleluia. Praise ye the Lord from the heavens! Praise ye him in the high places! Praise ye him, all his angels! Praise ye him, all his hosts! Praise ye him, O sun and moon! Praise him, all ye stars and light! Praise him, ye heavens of heavens, and let all the waters that are above the heavens praise the name of the Lord, for he spoke, and they were made; he commanded and they were created. He hath established them for ever and for ages of ages; he hath made a decree, and it shall not pass away. Praise the Lord from the earth, ye dragons and all ye deeps, fire, hail, snow, ice, stormy winds, which fulfil his word, mountains and all hills, fruitful trees and all cedars, beasts and all cattle, serpents and feathered fowls, kings of the earth and all people, princes and all judges of the earth, young men and maidens! Let the old with the younger praise the name of the Lord, for his name alone is exalted. The praise of him is above heaven and earth, and he hath exalted the horn of his people, a hymn to all his saints, to the children of Israel, a people approaching to him. Alleluia. (Psalm 148)

As we have seen, medieval Christians likewise sang these same psalms day after day, night after night in service of Mary, the Mother of the One who made the dragons and all deeps.

Modern Christians have a tendency to worry about what liturgy and prayer will do for them—whether it "works," as the headlines say.[25] Medieval Christians, to judge from the treatises that they wrote and the stories that they told about their experience of prayer, worried rather whether they had prepared themselves properly to sing and to pray with understanding and devotion, their minds, as the monastic father Benedict of Nursia would put it, in harmony with their voices. This, arguably, is why they worried about whether they felt anything—above all, love—as they sang or prayed: not, at least not purposefully, so as to experience feelings of bliss or ecstasy (although, of course, some, perhaps even many, did, much to their joy and delight), but because they believed that that was their obligation as creatures, as the Lord Jesus Christ had said:

> *And thou shalt love the Lord thy God, with thy whole heart, and with thy whole soul, and with thy whole mind, and with thy whole strength.* (Mark 12:30)

That is, you shall love the Lord with your heart *and* soul *and* mind *and* strength: not just with your affections, but with your intellect and reason and will as well. To be sure, or so her medieval servants would insist, there were benefits to be had from singing the psalms with proper attention and love, not the least of which being the Mother of the Lord's willingness to intercede on one's behalf with her Son, the judge. But arguably even more bracing were the promised effects of neglecting such service to the Lady and Lord:

> *Wisdom preacheth abroad; she uttereth her voice in the streets . . .*
>   *"O children, how long will you love childishness and fools covet those things which are hurtful to themselves and the unwise hate knowledge? Turn ye at my reproof. Behold: I will utter my spirit to you and will shew you my words. Because I called and you refused, I stretched out my hand, and there was none that regarded. You have despised all my counsel and have neglected my reprehensions. I also will laugh in your destruction and will mock when that shall come to you which you feared."* (Proverbs 1:20, 22–26)

As her ancient and medieval devotees imagined her, the Lady might be merciful and kind, but being Wisdom, she did not suffer gladly those foolish enough to reject her, any more than her Son suffered those who dishonored her who had borne him in her womb. The anointing of Wisdom opened the eyes to see God, but rejecting her brought only calamity, destruction, tribulation, and distress. *Come,* Wisdom invited her little ones, *eat my bread and drink the wine which I have mingled for you. Forsake childishness, and live, and walk by the ways of prudence* (Proverbs 9:4–5). And yet, as the Apostle Paul warned, citing Isaiah 29:14, those who followed Wisdom might themselves look foolish to the world: *For the word of the cross, to them indeed that perish, is foolishness; but to them that are saved, that is, to us, it is the power of God. For it is written: "I will destroy the wisdom of the wise, and the prudence of the prudent I will reject."* (1 Corinthians 1:18–19)

    "Serve me," Lady Wisdom commanded her devotees, "and I will reward you. Ignore me, and I will laugh at your destruction." We have already noted the difficulties that Mary's modern followers like Henry Adams and Hilda Graef have had with the way in which the Lady's medieval devotees imagined her through their reading of the scriptures, particularly the way in which her devotees like Richard of Saint-Laurent, Conrad of Saxony, and Pseudo-Albert read her as Wisdom in relation to God. Arguably, however, an even greater stumbling block for many modern readers has been the effects that Mary's medieval devotees expected their imaginings to have; or, perhaps more accurately, the effects that modern readers have assumed Mary's medieval devotees expected their imaginings to have, most notably her more or less guaranteed intercession on her servants' behalf with her Son. For Adams, Mary's propensity—as he imagined her medieval devotees imagined her—to intercede on behalf of even the most recalcitrant sinners was yet further proof of the fact that, if the medieval Virgin cared little for theology, she cared even less for justice.

"She alone," as Adams put it to his nieces, "represented Love. The Trinity were, or was, One, and could by the nature of its essence, administer justice alone." Not so Mary. As witnessed in the stories that poets like Gautier de Coincy told about the miracles that she worked on her servants' behalf, Mary was, as Adams read it, "by essence illogical, unreasonable and feminine," so much so that devotion to her was "in substance a separate religion" from that worship more properly offered to her Son. If the Church had had its way, "the Trinity would never have raised her from the foot of the Cross, had not the Virgin of Majesty been imposed by necessity and public unanimity, on a creed which was meant to be complete without her." But "the people loved Mary because she trampled on conventions; not merely because she could do it, but because she liked to do what shocked every well-regulated authority. Her pity [unlike, Adams implies, God's] had no limit."[26]

"True it was," Adams opined,

> that the Virgin embarrassed the Trinity; and perhaps this was the reason, behind all the other excellent reasons, why men loved and adored her with a passion such as no other deity has ever inspired: and why we, although utter strangers to her, are not far from getting down on our knees and praying to her still. Mary concentrated in herself the whole rebellion of man against fate; the whole protest against divine law; the whole contempt for human law as its outcome; the whole unutterable fury of human nature beating itself against the walls of its prisonhouse, and suddenly seized by a hope that in the Virgin man had found a door of escape. She was above law; she took feminine pleasure in turning Hell into an ornament; she delighted in trampling on every social distinction in this world and the next. She knew that the universe was as

unintelligible to her, on any theory of morals, as it was to her worshippers, and she felt, like them, no sure conviction that it was any more intelligible to the Creator of it. To her, every suppliant was a universe in itself, to be judged apart, on his own merits, by his love for her,—by no means on his orthodoxy, or his conventional standing in the Church, or according to his correctness in defining the nature of the Trinity.[27]

Graef would concur in broad strokes with this assessment, if with somewhat less glee. In Graef's view, Mary, as her medieval devotees like Richard of Saint-Laurent imagined her, grievously overreached her proper function as God's Mother. According to Graef, in Richard's account,

> Mary, the Mother, is more merciful than Christ, the Father: "Now God the Father gave us his Son as our Father and King of Justice, and to moderate his justice he gave us the Mother of Pity and the Queen of Mercy. For often the mercy of this mother graciously liberates what the justice of this Father would rightly condemn." The mercy of Christ disappears completely in this division of labour between him and his Mother; further, Mary actually changes the "temper" of the Godhead, if we may so express it, for Richard writes ingenuously: "Mary has so softened the Lord, and still continues to do so by her merits and prayers, that he now patiently tolerates even great sins, whereas before he mercilessly avenged even quite small ones."[28]

(Richard, as we have noted, was the penitentiary at Rouen, which means he was empowered to hear confessions of both clergy and laity and enjoin appropriate penances; in addition to his *De laudibus beatae Mariae virginis*, he was also the author of a treatise, still unpublished, *De charitate et aliis virtutibus*, on how to prepare for confession and penance, suggesting, at the very least, that he was thinking here of particular "great" sins that Mary might encourage her Son to tolerate.[29]) For Graef, it was one thing "to surround Mary with such tokens of love and respect" as, for example, the endearments with which her medieval devotees hailed her in the Salve Regina ("queen, mother of mercy, our life, our sweetness, and our hope!"). It was quite another "to say that God obeys her, that we can appeal from God's tribunal to hers, that she rules over the kingdom of mercy while leaving to her Son only that of justice, and similar things which, as [Cardinal John Henry] Newman says, 'can only be explained by being explained away.' "[30]

Aside from the tendency to read Mary into scriptures that "do not, of course, make mention of her," three things in particular have tended to exercise (or excite) modern scholars and Christians like Adams and Graef about the service medieval Christians offered Mary and the stories that they told about the miraculous benefits they hoped to receive in return: one, the apparent expectation that serving her was somehow easier or less demanding of virtue than serving God, particularly given her willingness to intercede for sinners based on their devotion to her; two, the emphasis that their descriptions of her placed on her physical beauty; and three, the conviction that in focusing on Mary medieval Christians were not worshipping God. In the words of the psalmist: *Praise the Lord from the earth, ye dragons and all ye deeps!* There are magical creatures here! More prosaically: As with the medieval exegetes' reading of scripture that we explored in chapters 3 and 4, so with the stories that Mary's medieval devotees told about the blessings they enjoyed in her service that we will be reading here— many centuries intervene, during which (to put it mildly) there have been many changes in the way in which Christians, not to mention scholars, think about the purpose and benefits of religious worship, particularly the kind of praises and prayer offered to Mary and God in her Office. If, for the former Augustinian friar Martin Luther, "the kind of babbling and bellowing that used to pass for prayers in the church was not really prayer" but only "singing or reading exercise," for many more recent critics it was hardly even that.[31]

As the Unitarian chemist and political theorist Joseph Priestley put it, writing in 1790:

> Christians deeply tinctured with these notions [of ascetic retreat for the sake of the soul], thought that *prayer* would greatly assist in this grand operation [of achieving union with God] and do more for them than mere *meditation* could for the heathen philosophers. Hence, to the most mortified state that the body could bear, they added the mental exercises of incessant meditation and prayer; and this indolent contemplative mode of life they imagined to be the most perfect that human nature was capable of in this world.[32]

A hundred or so years later, the Protestant theologian Auguste Sabatier, while more sympathetic than Enlightened *philosophes* like Priestley to the practice of prayer as such, was no more convinced that the medieval monks and nuns, not to mention those who would imitate them by saying Mary's Office, necessarily knew how to pray. As he put it writing in 1897, as cited by the Harvard psychologist William James in 1902:

> Religion is nothing if it be not the vital act by which the entire mind seeks to save itself by clinging to the principle from which it draws its life. This act is

prayer, by which term I understand no vain exercise of words, no mere repetition of sacred formulae, but the very movement itself of the soul, putting itself in a personal relation of contact with the mysterious power of which it feels the presence—it may be even before it has a name by which to call it. Wherever this interior prayer is lacking, there is no religion; wherever, on the other hand, this prayer rises and stirs the soul, even in the absence of forms or of doctrine, we have living religion.[33]

So much, many would have it, for the wordy exercises and repetitious formulae of the medieval Office; much better the spontaneous prayer of the heart! As Friedrich Heiler, himself a Lutheran convert from Roman Catholicism, argued in 1932:

> Prayer is the free, spontaneous expression of experiences which emerge on the heights of the devotional life and which deeply stir the soul. It is not subject to any religious or philosophical criticism, is burdened with no intellectual problems and is not bound up with traditional rules and formulas. Its deepest motive is the burning desire of the heart which finds its rest in blissful union with God or in assured trust in Him. It is fundamentally the same motive infinitely purified, refined and enlightened, which gives birth to all the manifestations of primitive religion, the desire for power, peace, and blessedness.[34]

Even more to the point for those wishing to understand the traditional rules and formulae of the medieval Office, Heiler notes: "Whenever a suppliant writes down in words his most fervent prayer, he feels only too deeply that the written words are but a faint reflection of the burning prayer of his heart."[35]

Nor has it helped that for many modern scholars, including Adams, the thing that arguably made the medieval devotion to the Virgin Mary most distinctive from this perspective was its appeal to the people, who, by definition in most late nineteenth- and twentieth-century narratives, had little interest in theology and even less in scripted, regular prayer. As Evelyn Underhill put it in the preface to her translation of twenty-five of the most popular miracles of the Virgin, published in 1906:

> Though now almost entirely forgotten, for over four centuries the Miracles of Our Lady occupied a very prominent place in popular literature. They are the fairy-tales of mediaeval Catholicism; the result of the reaction of religion on that spirit which produced the romances of chivalry. These tales bring us to the Courts of Paradise, but the atmosphere is still that of the Courts of Love.

By turns homely and heroic, visionary and realistic, they do in literature that which the Gothic sculptors do in art; make a link between heaven and earth, give actual and familiar significance to the most awful mysteries of the faith, and set the Queen of Angels in the midst of her faithful friends. As other fairy tales, behind their apparent if adorable absurdities, carry a secret message for those who can pierce the veil, so in these legends great mysteries are often concealed. It was in this form that those mysteries were able to come out from the cloister[36] and spread themselves in the world; for it was amongst the people that the Mary-legends prospered, and to the people that they were primarily addressed. They adorned sermons, they provided subjects for poetry, painting and sculpture, they were a part of the texture of common life.[37]

If for Underhill, the miracle stories were "fairy-tales" concealing great mysteries (here, to be fair, I think she is on the right track), for Eileen Power writing some twenty years later, the mystery that they concealed was clear (in the course of her fuller description, Power cites both Underhill and Henry Adams):

> It is true that kings gave the lead [to Mary's cult] (it probably began at the Byzantine court) and that learned doctors organised the cult and worked out its doctrinal justification; but beyond all this it was essentially popular. In this matter the people ran away from the church, which followed panting in their rear; and the medieval Virgin is essentially their creation, a figure of popular folklore even more than a figure of doctrinal devotion, and much more than a figure of cold history. "The middle ages," says Dr. Coulton, "thus made for themselves a new Redeemer, endowed with all the qualities that they needed most and fashioned with every poetic liberty which the reticence of the four evangelists permitted. If the early Christians had known more about the Mother of the Lord the medieval mind would have known far less. There grew up practically a Gospel of Mary, with all those details that are lacking in the four Gospels, and Acts of Mary, to supply all that is not said about her in the Acts." Above all there grew up those hundreds of stories, passed from mouth to mouth and in version after version, which we know as the Miracles of Our Lady. . . . There are many collections of these miracles, but the people did not depend upon the written word for their diffusion. The very absence of popular education tightened the Virgin's hold on her worshippers.[38]

In his groundbreaking 1953 account of the earliest collections of these miracles, made, as he showed, in the monasteries of early twelfth-century England, R. W. Southern challenged the argument that the collections were "popular" (that is, lay or illiterate) in origin, without, however, challenging the essential "popular-ity" of the stories themselves. As Southern read it:

> The world in which we move [in the miracle stories of the Virgin] is one of unbounded, unbridled imagination. Time and place lose all significance, and we come under the sway of a universal power, uncramped by local ties, and exer-cised with an appearance of caprice for the protection of all who love the person from whom these benefits flow. Like the rain, this protective power of the Virgin falls on the just and the unjust alike—provided only that they have entered the circle of her allegiance. . . . In a word, [the stories] are popular, and speak to the common man wherever he might be. The circle of those devoted to the Virgin appears almost as a wonderful club, a supernatural order of chivalry, confined to no single class or country.[39]

Similarly, in a more recent study published in 2000, David Flory argues that the devotion to the Virgin as evidenced in the miracle stories of thirteenth-century poets like the jongleur Rutebeuf (d. ca. 1277) operated outside the normal strictures of Trinitarian orthodoxy, not to mention scripture. In Flory's reading, as Rutebeuf himself sensed:

> Marianism short of soaring lyricism and a profoundly direct emotional appeal does not work, at least at the popular level. When drawn too tightly and too quickly into orthodox devotion, it disappears, both because no place has been prepared for it next to Trinitarianism (an intellectual task that was to require nearly two millennia) and because there is so little scriptural support for it. The Mary Mediatrix of Marian literature is, in the final analysis, a popular construc-tion that the Church has only slowly, over a very long period of time, incorpo-rated into orthodoxy. Where Jacques de Vitry has seen the problems of Marian devotion—sentimentality and doctrinal inexactness—Rutebeuf has sensed its power, and he as an artist offers, in beautifully elaborated form, the Mary in which most believe and that will eventually become incorporated—largely intact—into Church dogma [in the nineteenth and twentieth centuries with the papal con-stitutions on the Immaculate Conception (1854) and the Assumption (1950)].[40]

They that explain me, Wisdom promised, *shall have life everlasting* (Ecclesias-ticus 24:31). How is it, we might ask yet again, that the key to this mystery has been so repeatedly lost such that even now, centuries after the Lord showed him-self to the world in his glory (John 1:14), his Mother remains so difficult to see, even to those who have been anointed in the name of the Three in One? Perhaps, after all, we might counter: Wisdom has only herself to blame, speaking as she has over the millennia always in riddles so as to confound the wise.

As William of Malmesbury (d. ca. 1143) famously explained in the preface to his collection of miracle stories—one of the earliest, as Southern showed, inspired by the collections of William's fellow monastics Anselm of Bury St. Edmunds (d. 1148) and Dominic of Evesham (d. after 1145)—he had compiled the collection because he believed that stories would be an "apter means of kindling love for this Lady in the souls of the simple (*simplitium*)" than the learned writings of the great (*a maioribus dicta*). In William's words:

> Reasonings (*ratiocinationes*) may awaken the faith of the perfected, but it is the narration of miracles (*miraculorum narratio*) that awakens the hope and charity of the simple (*simplitium*), just as a sluggish fire when oil is thrown on it. Reasonings teach that she *can* pity the pitiable, but it is examples of miracles (*exempla miraculorum*) that teach that she *wishes* to do what she is able to do.[41]

Likewise, Dominic insisted in the preface to his collection that he was writing for the "simple" (*simplices*) rather than "learned ears" (*doctas aures*).[42] It is possible that both William and Dominic meant these assertions literally, that they were writing, as Benedicta Ward argued, for "the edification of the unlearned," even if those "unlearned" included the nobility, the "knights and ladies as appeared in their pages."[43] William claimed that the stories were so popular that, in his day, the story of Julian the Apostate was "sung in the streets" (*cantitatur in triviis*) and that of Ebbo the Thief was "told and retold among the laity with zest" (*studio apud saeculares maxime frequentatur*).[44] Certainly, this is the way, as Adrienne Williams Boyarin points out, the stories have more often than not been read in the scholarship: "as 'popular rather than learned', as 'the stuff of popular homiletics', or as a kind of 'vulgarization' of hagiographical literature only representative of the 'universal' medieval notion of Mary's power and mercy," hardly the stuff of serious literary analysis, never mind sophisticated reasonings about theology.[45] And yet, Richard of Saint-Laurent, Conrad of Saxony, and Pseudo-Albert said they were writing for the *simplices*, too, and it is highly unlikely that they expected readers who did not know their scriptures well.[46]

As Underhill herself sensed in her description of the miracle stories as "fairy-tales," something else is going on here. Such stories, in her words, "carry a secret message for those who can pierce the veil." What veil would that be? That of the temple, of course. Such stories are parables; it is the way Wisdom speaks. As Barker observes:

[In Hebrew as in Greek] a proverb or parable was the same word [H: *mašal*; Gr: *parabole*], and it imparted wisdom . . . Wisdom was at the Lord's side before there was a material creation. . . . Since she was with the Lord before the material world was made, she belonged, in temple terms, in the holy of holies. Wisdom was described as the breath of the power of God, and it was the breath of God that transformed Adam from a creature of clay into a living being (Wisdom 7:25; Genesis 2:7). . . . The breath of God gave Adam the power of speech, and words themselves were a form of Wisdom. Since she joined all things together in harmony, the literary forms for expressing Wisdom were parables and proverbs—noting similarities, comparing opposites, the basis for natural science. Since she was also a mighty angel, one of the assembly of God Most High (Ecclesiasticus 24:2), she revealed herself as did the angels. To know Wisdom was to know her role in the creation.[47]

God gave Solomon wisdom, and the king spoke in parables about trees, beasts, fowls, creeping things, and fishes (3 Kings 4:32), while Jesus, most famously, spoke in parables about the kingdom of heaven (Mark 4:11), but both, according to Barker, were talking about the same thing, the insight that they had received into the secrets of creation.[48] In the temple tradition, such secrets were preserved for the high priests, the only ones permitted to enter the Holy of Holies, but in Christianity, all of the faithful were baptized into the mysteries and, thus, into the wisdom of the Lord. As Barker has shown, Miriam, the sister of Aaron the high priest, was said to have been the mother of Beseleel, the builder of the tabernacle who was "filled with the Spirit of the *ʾelohim*, with wisdom, intelligence, knowledge, and all craftsmanship" (Exodus 35:31 RSV); Miriam was likewise remembered as the ancestress of King David, to whom the plan of the temple was revealed (1 Chronicles 28:18–19).[49] God, as Job put it, might be the one *who doth things great and incomprehensible and wonderful of which there is no number* (Job 9:10), but he did these wonderful things (*mirabilia*) through Wisdom, his daughter, mother, and bride. Thus the psalmist sang: *O Lord how manifold are thy works! With Wisdom thou hast made them all* (Psalm 103:24).[50]

"The eternal wisdom of God," Dominic of Evesham explained at the outset of his collection of *mirabilia*,

> "reaching from end to end mightily, and ordering all things sweetly," since it ordered all things in measure, number, and weight [cf. Wisdom 11:21] in an ineffable way before time, among other things which it established for the benefit of the human race, chose the most blessed and glorious Virgin Mary for its mother,

who, just as the splendor of the sun is brighter than all the faithful, so with the help of divine grace she shines forth to all the world more advantageously than all the saints in this age.[51]

In her miracles, Dominic argued, Mary excelled "the shining faith of the patriarchs, the wonderful prophesies of the prophets, the clear preaching of the apostles, the strong examples of the martyrs, the firm doctrine of the confessors, and the remarkable modesty of the virgins," for, in her, virginity was fertile and maternity augmented true virginity; in her singularly were examples of all the virtues and a fullness of all grace because through her was the beginning of redemption and the reconciliation with God the Father of the whole human race. How then, Dominic asked his readers and listeners, was it possible to keep silent and not say something about her virtues? Accordingly, he had scoured sources both old and new at the behest of his brothers and friends so as to provide food for the soul, that they might "learn to trust more in the wisdom of God than in some spark of worldly knowledge":

> For since it is true that we are endowed neither with the eloquence of Cicero nor the knowledge of Homer or Virgil to approach so great a matter, unwilling lest we fail by writing anything unfitting for it, we pray the wisdom of almighty God, that he who gave knowledge to all the wise and made the tongues of infants also eloquent [cf. Wisdom 10:21], grant us worthy skill to tell the praises of his incomparable mother Mary.[52]

Significantly, Dominic arranged the first four of his stories, his so-called "Elements Series," to illustrate Mary's power over the elements of creation: fire, when she rescued the Jewish boy from the oven into which his father had cast him for taking communion; air, when she rescued Theophilus from the power of the devil, a spirit of the air; water, when she rescued a pregnant woman caught by the tide on the causeway to the church of Mont Saint Michel; and earth, when she brought back to life the warrior Mercurius so that he might kill Julian the Apostate, man being made of earth.[53] In Dominic's telling, Mary, like Wisdom, knew the secrets of creation as evidenced by her control over their creaturely stuff.

Arguably even more telling of his purpose in revealing Mary as Wisdom, however, is the contrast that Dominic draws in his preface between his ability as an author and that of the ancients. Rather than attempt to describe Mary's miracles and virtues in the high style of a Cicero, he proposed to adopt a humble style (*humili stilo*), for which he begged his readers' indulgence. "If," he urged them, "you should find here any fault of barbarism or solecism, let us be pardoned, because we are compelled by that love of Mary, the holy mother of God, which to all true Christians is common and exceedingly sweet, to attempt such an excellent work with little learning."[54] His obligatory protestations of modesty aside, Dominic surely knew that his Latin is not easy or simple (unlike, for example, Richard of Saint-Laurent's), so what is he claiming here? Not, in fact, that his brothers and friends for whom he was writing were "unlearned," but rather that they were highly learned indeed: they knew their Cicero and Homer and Virgil, otherwise how would they be able to spot barbarisms and solecisms in Dominic's prose?[55] They also, being well-versed in the Fathers as well as the pagan classics—as Dominic's allusion to the style (*humilis*) in which he was writing shows—knew their Augustine, arguably the most rhetorically skilled commentator on scripture the Christian tradition has ever known. They would also, accordingly, know that, committed as he was to the art of speaking well, Augustine was particularly concerned with the role of style, including the lowliest, in expressing Christian truth, not to mention in unlocking the obscurities of scripture in which that truth had been veiled.

This is the way Augustine understood his role as a Christian teacher, that is, a teacher of Wisdom. Sometime around 399–405, Deogratias, a deacon of the church in Carthage, wrote to bishop Augustine asking for help in catechizing, that is, instructing the pagans who were coming to him wanting to become Christians. Too often, Deogratias complained, he did not know what to say; worse, when he did, he worried that what he said was profitless and distasteful to his listeners, so much so that sometimes he even bored himself. Augustine reassured his friend, he had felt the same way, too. And yet, Augustine asked Deogratias to consider, how much the more frustrated must God have felt in his efforts to communicate with his human children? As Augustine put it, starting from the heights of rhetoric himself:

> Now if the cause of our sadness lies in the circumstance that our hearer does not apprehend what we mean, so that we have to come down in a certain fashion from the elevation of our own conceptions, and are under the necessity of dwelling long in the tedious processes of syllables which come far beneath the standard of our ideas, and have anxiously to consider how that which we ourselves take in with a most rapid draught of mental apprehension is to be given forth by the mouth of flesh in the long and perplexed intricacies of its method of enunciation; and if the great dissimilarity thus felt (between our utterance and our thought) makes it distasteful to us to speak, and a pleasure to us to keep silence, then let us ponder what has been set before us by Him who has *showed us an example that we should follow His steps* [1 Peter 2:21]. For however much our

articulate speech may differ from the vivacity of our intelligence, much greater is the difference of the flesh of mortality from the equality of God. And, nevertheless, *although He was in the same form, He emptied Himself, taking the form of a servant,*—and so on down to the words *the death of the cross* [Philippians 2:7–8]. What is the explanation of this but that He made Himself *weak to the weak, in order that He might gain the weak* [1 Corinthians 9:22]? Listen to His follower as he expresses himself also in another place to this effect: *For whether we be beside ourselves, it is to God; or whether we be sober, it is for your cause. For the love of Christ constrains us, because we thus judge that He died for all* [2 Corinthians 5:13–14]. And how, indeed, should one be ready to be spent for their souls, if he should find it irksome to him to bend himself to their ears? For this reason, therefore, He became a little child in the midst of us, (and) like a nurse cherishing her children. For is it a pleasure to lisp shortened and broken words, unless love invites us? And yet men desire to have infants to whom they have to do that kind of service; and it is a sweeter thing to a mother to put small morsels of masticated food into her little son's mouth, than to eat up and devour larger pieces herself. In like manner, accordingly, let not the thought of the hen recede from your heart, who covers her tender brood with her drooping feathers, and with broken voice calls her chirping young ones to her, while they that turn away from her fostering wings in their pride become a prey to birds [cf. Matthew 23:37].[56]

Surely, Augustine averred, if God, like a mother hen, so humbled himself to the capacity of human understanding that he took on flesh in the Virgin's womb so as to make himself heard by his children, Deogratias must not despair at having to adapt his language to the capacity of his listeners, however rude and unlearned they might be and however far his own speaking might feel from the understanding of his heart.

Augustine made a similar argument in favor of what Ciceronian rhetoricians called the low or humble style (*sermo humilis*) in the fourth book of his *De doctrina christiana*, or *On Christian Teaching*, written some years after his letter to Deogratias.[57] While at all times, Augustine acknowledged, the Christian teacher ought to prefer speaking with wisdom to speaking with eloquence, this did not mean that he might never choose to speak according to the high or sublime style (*sermo sublimis*) appropriate to the lofty matters of theology and praise of God. Nevertheless, Augustine went on, while Cicero argued for matching the style of one's oration to the matter addressed, low for pecuniary transactions, high for matters of life or liberty, for Christian orators there could be no such necessary correspondence between style and matter, since everything that they were talking about as Christians was great (*magna*), concerned as they were with the eternal salvation of the soul. Accordingly, Augustine advised, given their threefold aims of teaching for the sake of instruction, delighting so as to keep their listeners' attention, and moving so as to stir them to love of God, Christian orators must take care to adapt their speaking to the capacities of their audience, just as the Word of God adapted himself through the Incarnation to the capacities of his. Himself the Word, God spoke with a similar attention to human capacity in the scriptures, the model, as Augustine set out to demonstrate throughout his *De doctrina christiana*, for all Christian teaching in words. And yet, as Augustine conceded, how defective the scriptures sometimes seem, with their lack of harmonious endings and other rhetorical ornaments! (It could be, he acknowledged, the translators' fault, but he didn't think that was the entire reason; in his view, the original authors purposefully avoided such ornaments.) If, for those like Augustine who had been educated in the classical arts of grammar and rhetoric (the same in which Dominic and his monastic brothers would have been educated), the scriptures seemed crude and barbarous, therein, or so Augustine argued, lay their greatest mystery: "We were snared by the wisdom of the serpent: we are set free by the foolishness of God."[58] The role of the Christian teacher, like the storyteller, was to unlock this wisdom for the simple souls God became incarnate to save.

As Augustine, his fellow classically educated Fathers, and their liberally educated medieval followers saw it, all Christian teaching by definition was intended for the *simplices* insofar as it was steeped in the language of the scriptures through which Wisdom humbled him/her/itself so as to be comprehensible in human terms. The scriptures spoke purposefully in a humble style (*sermo humilis*) while concealing great mysteries within. Again, as Barker notes: this is the way Wisdom speaks, in parables and proverbs, veiling mysteries behind simple words. (Mary's Son made a particular point of speaking in this way.) In Erich Auerbach's magisterial description of this understanding of scripture's "simple" style, according to the Fathers:

> The purpose of this humility or lowliness of style is to make the Scriptures available to all; the humblest of men should be drawn to them, moved by them, at home in them. Yet Scripture is not always simple; it contains mysteries and hidden meaning; much of it seems obscure. But even the difficult ideas are not presented in a learned, "haughty" style that would intimidate and repel the simple man. On the contrary, anyone who is not light-minded (hence, superficial and lacking in humility) can find his way to the deeper meaning; Scripture "grows with the children," that is to say, children grow into an understanding of it. Nevertheless, few get to the core of it; the essential

is not learning but true humility in keeping with the humility of the style: there is no fundamental difference between the profound, obscure passages and those that are clear and simple; the former merely open up deeper levels of understanding.[59]

As Augustine, Dominic, and all those educated in this tradition of grammar, rhetoric, and scriptural interpretation saw it, compared to God, all human beings are like children. How else, Mary's medieval devotees would insist, than through stories told in the simple style of scripture would Wisdom speak to her children so as to delight, instruct, and move them to love and serve her as they had been created to do?

Here, then, is the answer to the principal conundrum that modern readers of the medieval Mary miracle stories have found so difficult to resolve: whether, in their "fairy-tale" quality and appeal to the "simple," the stories were ultimately orthodox or popular, as if the two (theology and love for Mary) were necessarily opposed. In a word, like the devotion to the Lady as Wisdom, they were both—orthodox and popular, arguably the most orthodox literature of their day. When medieval Christian authors like Dominic, William, Richard, Conrad, and Pseudo-Albert insisted they were writing for the *simplices*, they meant they were writing for Christians, those who had made themselves fools for Christ by rejecting the wisdom and eloquence of the philosophers in favor of the wisdom contained in the Word. Likewise, when they told stories about Mary for the *simplices*, they were seeking not merely to delight and move their audiences to love and serve her, but also to instruct them in her mysteries, just as Wisdom him/her/itself had taught his/her/its children through parables and proverbs. As Claire Waters notes in her recent discussion of these stories:

> If [Mary's] miracles can be seen as one of the most accessible and broadly disseminated modes of [Marian] devotion (along with prayers and rituals that the miracles themselves often promote), it does not necessarily follow that they fail to do justice to the fundamental theological teachings concerning God's mother. The miracles provide an intensely vivid account of Mary's relation to Christ and, by extension, the theology of the Incarnation, and do so while insisting that the heights of theological complexity are, in fact, immediately adjacent to, if not overlapping with, the most quotidian and homely of practices.[60]

Of course, her medieval devotees would insist, Mary confounds the wisdom of the wise, not to mention those who would refuse to temper justice with mercy. What else would she do, being the Mother of the Son who said, "Suffer the little children to come unto me, and forbid them not; for of such is the kingdom of God" (Mark 10:14; cf. Matthew 19:14; Luke 18:16)?

In the medieval miracle stories, as in the commentaries on the scriptures in which her medieval devotees like Richard, Conrad, and Pseudo-Albert attempted to explain her, Mary, that is, Wisdom, the mother, daughter, and bride of Wisdom, is the one who gives sight to the blind and who makes the deaf hear.[61] She is the one who feeds her servants with the bread of life and gladdens them with wine (Proverbs 9:5; Ecclesiasticus 24:29). She is the one who gives them the skill to make things like arks and veils and tabernacles and temples and psalms (Exodus 35:31; 1 Chronicles 28:11–19; 4 Kings 23:7; Proverbs 7:21–22). She is the one who dances before the Lord as he separates the waters from the land and subdues the waves (Proverbs 8:22–31). She is the one who protects the walls of the city, the tower looking out over the land (Psalm 60:4), guarding her people against their enemies (Wisdom 10:1–21). She is the one who chastises and heals, inspires and rebukes.[62] She is the one who stands beside the throne, the Tree of Life bearing healing fruits (Proverbs 3:18; Revelation 22:2). And because she is also the temple, she is the place where her servants pray (2 Chronicles 7:15–16). She is beautiful and terrible like the ordered ranks of an army (Song of Songs 6:9), a bride arrayed for her bridegroom, bedecked with gold and precious stones (Revelation 21). She is also a mother grieving for her children on whom the devil makes war (Revelation 12:17). She is the Queen of heaven (Jeremiah 44:18) and the Mother of the Lord (Isaiah 7:14, 9:6), the one who gives birth to the Morning Star (Revelation 22:16) and anoints him as king with her dew (Psalm 109:3). Her name is above all names other than her Son's (Philippians 2:9–10), himself the great high priest bearing the Name as he enters the Holy of Holies to make sacrifice for the atonement of sins (Hebrews 4:14–5:10). Now that she has been assumed, like him, into heaven, she sits at the right hand of God, where she pleads with the Lord on behalf of her servants, the Living One whom Ezekiel saw, now returned to her temple (Ezekiel 10:15). She is the mother and wife of the king to whom the people pray (3 Kings 1:17–21; Esther 15:3). Like her Son, she rewards her servants and casts down all those who reject her (1 Kings [Samuel] 2:30; Proverbs 1:20–33). Above all, however, she is the one who makes God visible, the bush burning with the presence of the Lord (Exodus 3:2), the throne on which the Lord appears in human form (Ezekiel 1:26). She wove the veil through which he passed when he came into the world (Hebrews 10:19–20). She was there at his side when he worked his first miracle (John 2:1–11), and she was there under the cross as he offered himself up for the salvation of humankind (John 19:25–27). The first-born of all creation (Ecclesiasticus 24:5), she was the one who magnified the

Lord (Luke 1:46–55), making him visible to all the world, even as she humbled herself before him as his creature. And she is the one who speaks in parables, so that her children might understand her, pulling back the veil of the Holy of Holies that she helped weave so as to reveal the mysteries of the kingdom hidden within.

Christians, that is, the "little anointed ones," would be fools indeed not to serve her with all their hearts, souls, minds, and strength, however "simple" they might seem in the eyes of the world.

HOW TO SERVE MARY

This is the way one thirteenth-century poet, as yet unknown, told the story of one such simple soul.[63] Once upon a time, there was a minstrel who, having grown weary of his wanderings in the world, entered the Holy Order at Clairvaux. But while he was handsome in body and skilled at leaping, tumbling, and dancing, he had no other learning, no Pater Noster or chant or *Credo* or Ave Maria (*le salu*) that might avail for his salvation. Noticing that the monks conversed with each other only in signs, he decided that he, too, should keep silence, but otherwise he did not know what to say or to do. On the one hand, the monks and converts whom he observed seemed to him overly gloomy, what with all their lamenting, weeping, groaning, and sighing; but, on the other, they all had some service that they performed, while he had none. He saw the priests serving at the altar, the deacons at the gospels, the subdeacons at the vigils, and the acolytes standing ready to read the epistles. One recited the responsory (*vers*), another the lesson, while the choristers said their psalters, the converts their *Miserere mei* (Psalm 50), and the simplest (*li plus nice*) their *patrenostres*.[64]

"O wretched me! What am I doing?," the minstrel exclaimed. "For there is none here so caitiff but who vies with all the rest in serving God after his trade (*ne serve Deu de son mestier*); but I have no business (*mestier*) here, for I know not what to do or say." Anxious lest he be found out for his lack of service and thrown to the dogs for doing nothing but eating and amusing himself, he prayed:

Holy Mary, mother! Pray your sovereign Father that he hold me in his pleasure, and send me his good counsel, that I may have power to serve him and you (*que lui et vos puisse servir*), and may earn the victuals that I take: for I know well that I misreceive them.

One day, maddened with grief, he searched the monastery until he came upon a crypt, where he discovered an altar with an image of Mary, as indeed God, "who well knows how to call his own to him," had intended him to. Hearing the signal for Mass, he leapt up, dismayed. "Ah!," he cried,

> how am I ashamed! Now each one will say his stave, but I am like an ox at tether, doing naught but browse and spoiling victuals for no good. Shall I say it? Shall I do it? By the mother of God, I will! I shall ne'er be blamed for it, if I do what I have learned, and serve the mother of God in her monastery according to my trade (*Si servirai de men mestier / La mere deu en son mostier*). The rest serve in chanting, and I will serve in tumbling (*Li autre servent de canter / Et jo servirai de tumer*).

Accordingly, he stripped himself of his robe and, wearing only his undershirt, turned to the image and addressed himself to the Virgin:

> Lady, to your protection I commend my body and my soul. Sweet queen, sweet lady, despise not what I know: for I would fain essay to serve you in good faith, if God aid me, without guile. I can nor chant, nor read to you; but, certes, I would pick for you a choice of all my finest feats. Now, may I be like the bull-calf that leaps and bounds before his mother. Lady, who are no whit bitter to such as serve you truly, whatsoever I am, may it be for you.

At which, the minstrel began to leap and spring before her, high and low, under and over, pausing only to throw himself once again on his knees before her image and salute her before returning to his somersaults—the somersault of Metz and that of Champaign, the French somersault, the Spanish somersault, the somersault of Brittany and that of Lorraine—exerting himself to do the best that he could. As he tumbled, he said to her:

> Lady, this is a choice performance. I do it for no other but for you; so aid me God, I do not—for you and for your son! And this I dare avouch and boast, that for me it is no playwork. But I am serving you, and that pays me (*Mais jo vos serf et si m'aquit*). The others serve, and so do I (*Li altre servent et jo serf*). Lady, despise not your servant (*vo serf*), for I serve you for your joy. Lady, you are the *mon-joie* that kindles all the world.

All through the Mass, he continued his tumbling, walking on his hands and weeping with his eyes, adoring the Lady "with heart and body, feet and hands," and promising always to be her minstrel, "for he knew not how else to pray," until he was dripping with sweat and could no longer stand.

Putting his clothes back on, the minstrel saluted the image: "Adieu, sweetest friend. For God's sake be not cast down, for if I can I will come again. At every hour I would serve you the very best that may be, if it please you, and if I can." And then, again, still looking at the image, he sighed: "Lady, what a pity that I know not all those psalters! Right gladly would I say them for love of you, most sweet Lady. To you I commend my body and my soul." Thereafter, the minstrel returned to the crypt at every hour of the liturgical day to render his service and homage (*son servise et son homage*), none of the other monks—only God—knowing what he did while he was there. "Now, do you suppose," the poet asks his audience, "that God would have prized his service had he not loved? Not a whit, however much he tumbled! But it was his love that he prized." Do everything that you may—weep, sigh, groan, pray, fast, take the discipline, go to Mass and Matins—but, the poet admonished his readers,

> if you love not God with all your heart, all these good things are thrown away—be well assured—and avail you naught at all for your salvation. . . . God asks not gold nor silver, but only true love in folks' hearts. And this man loved God unfeigningly, and that was why God prized his service.

The minstrel loved, in other words, as the Lord had said he should, with all his heart and soul and mind and strength, and thus his service was as acceptable as that of any of the priests with their Masses, the deacons with their gospels, the subdeacons with their vigils, the acolytes with their epistles, the choristers with their psalters, or the other laybrothers with their Pater Nosters and *Miserere meis*—as, indeed, the Lady herself would prove.

The minstrel continued this service at all the liturgical hours of the day for many years, until at long last one of the other monks began to wonder what he was doing while the others were in the church. When, however, the monk discovered his secret, he rejoiced, for although he laughed at the minstrel's tumbling, he could see that it was offered without guile. "May God count it for penance!" he avowed. "And, for my part, in sooth, I think no ill of it; for I take it he does according to his lights and in good faith, because he would not fain be idle." The monk went to the abbot, who cautioned him to say nothing until the abbot himself had had a chance to observe the tumbler's office. Hiding themselves by the altar in the crypt, they saw the minstrel perform all his somersaults, "leaping and dancing and saluting the image, and tripping and bounding, until he came to faint," his body dripping with sweat. At which point, the abbot looked and saw a Lady (*Dame*) "so glorious descend from the vault that none e'er saw one so precious and so richly arrayed." With her were many angels and archangels, who ranged round the minstrel to sustain and comfort him. "Then [the angels] pressed to serve (*servir*) him, because they longed to repay the service (*deservir / Le servise*) that he did their Lady." The Queen herself fanned the minstrel with a white napkin to cool his body, neck, and face. While the abbot and monk kept watch, the scene repeated itself a good four times, "for at every hour it came to pass that the Mother of God came to aid and succor her man, for she well knows how to rescue her own." The minstrel himself, however, had no inkling that he was in such fair company, but rendered his service solely out of love.

The lesson that the minstrel's tumbling taught the abbot and monk of Clairvaux recurs in story after story that her medieval devotees told of their service to the Lady: "God rejects no one who comes to him in love, of whatsoever trade (*mestier*) he be, if only he love God and do right." Whether her servants were rich or poor, skilled or unskilled, learned or unlearned, secular, cloistered, or clerics, it was their love for the Virgin and her Son that counted, not this or that form that their service took, as her poets and jongleurs took pains to make clear.

Peter Ivern of Sieglar, a minstrel, was playing his lute before the image of the Virgin at Rocamadour, and prayed: "Lady, if my playing and singing please you or your Son, my Lord, then grant me a piece from the countless measures of wax which are hanging here." At once, a little piece of wax fell down onto his instrument—and did so a second and third time when the guardian of the shrine snatched it away accusing Peter of being a "magician and caster of spells." Seeing which, all the people at the shrine began praising God as one, lifting their voices to the heavens. Meanwhile, Peter "began to weep with joy and returned the piece of wax which he had been given to God the giver, praising him *with timbrel and dance, with strings and pipe* [cf. Psalm 150:4]."[65]

A rich merchant from Portugal took care "whenever he went to buy and sell his goods, if he found a beautiful and tasteful gift which seemed to him suitable for the altar, he always tried to take it to [Mary]." One day, while sailing near the coast of Spain on his way to Flanders, his ship was struck with a storm. "Oh, Mother of God," he prayed when he fell into the sea, "may your goodness come to my aid, you who are Holy and Mighty Lady. . . . My Lady, in your mercy, do not abandon me because I cause you trouble for a little while, and if you will bring me now out of these waves, I will serve you forever and obey your command." At once, "like a good Mistress who cares for her own," Mary drew him out of the waves and the sea became calm.[66]

A knight of Provence vowed that he would make for Mary's statue every day a chaplet of roses and, when he could not find roses, he would say an Ave Maria in place of every rose. One day as he was riding, he dismounted and knelt facing east to say his Aves, when a group of his enemies came along. When, however, "they were about to kill him in their rage, they saw him all surrounded with celestial light." They also saw "a Maiden weaving a chaplet of roses, and he was there with Her, tying roses on the other end of the chaplet." Nor did they have the power to approach him. "Let us turn from here at once," they said to each other, "for it does not please God that we kill this man, for he is a servant of His." As one of them put it to the others: "It is a very serious thing to wage war with the Mother of Our Lord, whom we see beside him, more beautiful than any flower, helping him to make the chaplet, for She would destroy us as water destroys salt." And so they went away, while the knight, like the tumbler, had not been aware of anything, but only loved the Mighty and Worthy Lady all the more when he heard of what she had done for him.[67]

Adam, a priest and monk of Locheim, had been accustomed when he was but a boy to say the angel's salutation. While a scholar at Münster in Westphalia, he was accustomed to stop on his way to school or to Matins before a certain chapel of the Mother of God, where he would make three genuflections and say three Aves. One night, thinking that he had heard the bell for Matins, he rushed to the church but found it still closed, upon which he saluted the Virgin in his usual way. On rising, he found the doors of the church opened, "and so great a light in the church, that it was like the blaze of the noon-day sun." Entering the church in wonder, he "saw seven most beautiful matrons sitting before the high altar, one in the midst who was more dazzling than the others." The Lady in the middle called to him and asked him about the sickness (*scabies*) he had on his head and why care had not been taken to heal him. When he said that his friends had done everything they could to no avail, she responded: "I am the Mother of Christ and the patroness of this church. Because you have been zealous to keep me in mind, I will cure you. Take the fruit of the spindle wood and have your head washed with it three times before mass in the name of the Father, Son, and Holy Spirit, and immediately you will be cured."[68]

A lay brother (conversus) of the Cistercian order in Spain "was so fervent and devout in his worship of the blessed Virgin, so absorbed and intent in chanting her Hours, that not only did he carry in his memory every verse but even every word, and thus with great labors almost continuously said his Hours" (*sicque horam horae cum maximis laboribus pene continuaret*). After seventeen years of such service, it happened that he fell grievously ill and a companion of his was sent to attend upon him. "Yesterday," the dying brother told his friend, "Our Lady visited me and foretold that in seven days I should go to be with the Lord. And she added: 'Because you have served me more earnestly than all other mortals, I will do for you what I have never yet done for anyone.' And throwing her arms around my neck, she gave me a kiss."[69]

A poor man who lived on alms "honored the holy Mother of God, Mary—as much as he could and understood how to—with his whole heart, so that for her love he would also give generously, even from the alms that were given to him, to other paupers." As he lay dying, he prayed to her to have mercy on him and give him the happiness of paradise. And, indeed, those who were attending him heard her say to him: "Come, beloved, and as you have asked, you will enjoy fully the rest of Paradise." "Then at once his soul left his body and was conducted by angels into the joy of Paradise, where, just as the holy Mother of God had promised, he rejoiced with the company of saints."[70]

Nor was it only men whom Mary favored. As the Cistercian Caesarius of Heisterbach put it: "There is neither male nor female in her eyes. She was born woman and she herself gave birth to the chief of men, Christ. Both sexes she visits and consoles, to both she reveals her secrets," as the examples of her miracles show.[71]

A woman who never did anything good except salute the Virgin every day and hear Mass in her honor on Saturdays was near death, and she prayed: "Lady Queen and Mother, although I have never done anything good, yet I trust in your mercy and commend my soul to you." When the devils came for her soul, they said, "She is ours," but the Mother of Mercy prevented them, saying: "You know not that she has saluted me daily with the angel's salutation and has said a mass in honor of me and in her death agony commended her soul to me." Said the devils: "She has committed very many crimes." To whom Mary replied: "That soul may never be damned that has served me and has committed her soul to me." At which the devils fled and Mary took the woman's soul with her.[72]

A nun in Spain "loved Holy Mary above all else and therefore constantly said the hours from beginning to end, never failing to repeat prime, tierce, sext, vespers, none, complins, and matins before Her statue." But the devil tempted her to run away with a certain abbot, who kept her as his paramour in Lisbon. When she became pregnant, however, he abandoned her, at which (or so the Cistercian Caesarius of Heisterbach told the story) she became a prostitute and lived like this for fifteen years. In King Alfonso's telling, she returned to the convent, where to her surprise she had not been missed (Caesarius explained that Mary had taken her place), until it came time for her to have her baby. "My Lady," she prayed before the Virgin's statue, "I come to you as a woman who acknowledges the great error she has committed. But, dear Lady, remember that I have performed some service for you, so save my person from falling into disgrace and my soul from being taken by the devil to burn in Hell. I ask you this with fear, for I am ashamed to beg you for anything, but I ask it of you as a favor." When the baby was born, the Holy Queen arrived and instructed an angel to take the child and care for him. Many years later, much to his mother's delight, a handsome youth arrived at the convent and, joining the choir at vespers, began to sing the Salve Regina "as he had been commanded to do by the Holy Virgin Mary who had cared for him for a long time, for She does not abandon those She loves, even though they err against Her."[73]

A woman named Jutta who lived at the castle of Veldenz venerated the image of the Virgin in its chapel "with the highest honor, making before it salutations, prayers, and many petitions for pardon." One day, her daughter, whom she had sent to a nearby village to be brought up, was playing outdoors when a wolf seized her by the throat, threw her over its back, and set off for the woods nearby. Going to the chapel "in great bitterness of heart," Jutta seized the image of the Savior from his mother's bosom and declared: "Lady, never shall you have you Son back again unless you restore to me my child unhurt." "Wonderful humility of the Queen of heaven!" Caesarius exclaimed. Following the wolf's tracks, the people of the village found the little girl, who told them: "Mummart has bitten me," as indeed the marks on her neck proved. Her daughter now safe, Jutta rushed to give thanks before the sacred image and put back the Child, saying: "Because you have given me back my daughter, behold, I restore to you your Son."[74]

Nor, according to her troubadours, did the Virgin accept only the service of Christians, however much at other times, like Wisdom, she might call down destruction upon those who refused to acknowledge her or her Son.

A Jewish woman was suffering in childbirth. For all their skill, there was nothing that the midwives could do but wait for death to end her pains. Suddenly, as she gasped for breath, tortured in body and soul, "a light from heaven shone forth above her, and with the light a voice was heard saying: 'Call on the Mother of Jesus, and you shall be delivered; invoke the name of Mary, and you shall be saved.' " The light from heaven withdrew, "but within by the virtue of those healing words the woman was illuminated right through her heart, and, putting her faith and trust in the Lord, she called on the name of Mary in a loud voice, and at once by a happy delivery brought forth her son without any pain." As King Alfonso told the story, when the Jewish women who were attending her heard her call to Mary, they "fled from the house and denounced her, calling her 'heretic,' 'apostate,' and 'Christian convert.' " She, however, went straight to the church after her days of purification were over. "She waited no longer for the Messiah but was baptized [along with her daughter and son] as soon as she entered."[75]

A Moorish woman from Borja had a beautiful son who died of disease. Seeing how the Christians went to Holy Mary of Salas and hearing of the miracles that the Virgin performed for them, the grieving mother ventured to put her trust in her. When the other Moorish women protested to her about this, she said to them: "Friends, if God protects me from harm, I believe that my hope will overcome your objections, for I shall take my son to Holy Mary of Salas right away, with this waxen image which I have bought for her. I shall keep watch in the church of the most blessed Holy Mary, and I believe that She will sympathize with my woe." Accordingly, the woman carried her dead son to Salas, where she said to the Virgin: "If your law does not lie, give me my son, and I will make my peace with you." The Mooress kept watch but a single night and the Virgin revived her son, for, as the refrain to King Alfonso's *cantiga* put it, "*The Virgin will aid whoever trusts in Her and prays faithfully to Her, although he be a follower of another law.*" Like the Jewess, the Mooress at once became a Christian, holding Mary in great reverence for restoring to life her son who had been dead for three days.[76]

It would be easy to go on—the stories, told in both Latin and the vernacular, prose and verse, at length and in précis, number in the thousands—but their scope and tenor are hopefully by now clear.[77] Monks, nuns, priests, bishops, knights, merchants, minstrels, peasants, kings, queens, widows, mothers, children, and old people, even Muslims and Jews: all appear as servants acknowledged by Mary. This diversity in the status of her servants is a feature in both those collections made at particular shrines like Rocamadour and by monks, preachers, and poets who composed more "universal" collections. William of Malmesbury used it explicitly as the organizing principle for his.[78] While authors like the notary-priest Gonzalo de Berceo (d. before 1264), the monk-minstrel Gautier de Coincy, the preacher-reformer Jacques de Vitry (d. 1240), the troubadour Rutebeuf, and the poet-king Alfonso X el Sabio expressed different concerns in their retellings of these stories, the theme of service owed to Mary as Mother of the Lord runs like a scarlet thread throughout, much like the thread Mary herself spun for the temple veil.

In Gonzalo de Berceo's telling, Saint Ildefonsus of Toledo (d. 667), whom Mary gifted with a chasuble ("angelic work, not woven by human kind") for his devoted service,

> . . .was always partial to the Glorious One,
> Never did man have more love for lady,
> he sought to serve Her with all his might,
> and did so sensibly and most prudently.[79]

Indeed, as Gonzalo put it in his story of the foulmouthed prior who nevertheless always stood for the Hours of the Virgin and who said her Office *de suo corde toto*:

> [It] is *summum bonum* to serve such a Lady,
> Who knows how to aid Her servants in such an hour;
> this Lady is a good shelter; She is a good shepherdess;
> She helps everyone who prays to Her with a good heart.[80]

Likewise, as Gonzalo observed in his conclusion to the story of the Jewish boy who converted after the "Lady Who was in the golden chair, with Her Son in her arms, sitting on the altar" saved him from the furnace into which his father had thrown him (much as, as Barker has argued, the Great Angel protected the three boys whom King Nebuchadnezzar threw into the furnace, where they sang the *Benedicite*):

> Such is Holy Mary who is full of grace,
> for service She gives Glory, for disservice punishment;
> to the good she gives wheat, to the evil oats,
> the good go to Glory, the others go in chains.
> Whoever renders Her service is fortunate,
> whoever rendered disservice was born in a harsh hour,

the ones gain grace, and the others rancor;
the good and the evil are revealed by their deeds.
Those who offend Her or disserve Her
won mercy if indeed they asked Her for it;
never did she refuse those who loved Her,
nor did She throw in their faces the evil they had done.[81]

In Gautier de Coincy's telling, the young cleric who betrothed himself to her statue saying, "My Lady, I will serve you all my life, from now on (*Dame . . . tout mon aage / D'or en avant te servirai*)," learned a similar lesson on the night of his wedding to another woman: "It is not right," Mary rebuked her forgetful servant, "nor loyal what you do to me. . . . You leave the rose for the nettle, and the wild rose for the elder tree. Wretch!"[82]

And yet, according to her minstrels, the Lady would reward even the (apparently) slightest service with favor, as Jacques de Vitry recounted of a certain gambler who, having lost all his money at dice, was offered a loan by a certain powerful Jew if only he would deny Christ, his Mother, and the saints, but the gambler refused. One day, as the luckless dicer was passing by a statue of the Virgin Mary, it bowed to him, as though expressing thanks. A certain rich man saw the statue bow and, wondering, asked the man: "How can this be? Did you perform some service for the Blessed Virgin?" The gambler replied: "I served neither God nor her." Then remembering, he said: "A certain Jew wanted to make me rich if I were to deny Blessed Mary, but I preferred to remain poor rather than deny her." The rich man was so impressed that he bestowed not only wealth, but also the hand of his daughter on the gambler so that he became much wealthier than even the Jew would have made him. "Behold," Jacques concluded his *exemplum*, "how good it is to serve and honor Blessed Mary!"[83] "*Cursed be he who will not praise Her who contains all goodness*," sang King Alfonso the Wise of Castille, Toledo, León, Galicia, Seville, Córdoba, Murcia, Jaén, and the Algarbe. "Cursed be the one who will not praise Her who has no equal in goodness nor will ever have while the world shall last, for God made no other like Her, nor ever will again."[84]

Perilous as it was to neglect praising Mary, serving her, as the stories showed, might take many forms. Calling on her name, bowing before her images, making pilgrimage to her shrines, sending her gifts, giving alms, saluting her with the angel's greeting, and saying her Hours were all acceptable forms of service, all meriting her blessing. While potentially simple in form, what these services were not was necessarily easy. The Jewess who cried out to Mary in labor risked being done to death by the Jewish midwives who were in attendance upon her, or so

Johannes Herolt told the story. The Mooress who made a pilgrimage to her shrine risked similar rejection, although King Alfonso does not say that the other Moorish women wished to kill her. The gambler who refused to deny her was reduced to poverty; when the statue bowed to him, he was nearly naked (*nudus*) and looked like a vagrant (*ribaldus*). The cleric whom the Virgin rebuked for forgetting his promise to serve her gave up his earthly bride on their wedding night and entered a monastery. The pauper who lived on alms gave up the very alms which he had begged for his survival. Even the sinful woman who did nothing but salute Mary every day and hear her Mass on Saturdays did something, or so the story implies, that not everyone was able or willing to do, at least not without a certain discipline. Arguably, the point in all of these stories is not, as many modern readers like Henry Adams have tended to assume, the capriciousness of Mary's favor or, as others have argued, her purported dislike of the Jews (she could be equally harsh to Christians who neglected her, as Wisdom warned), but rather the great importance of the service to which all of humanity is called in praise of the Lord and his Mother.

Nor was such service strictly speaking "popular," if by "popular" we mean having little basis in orthodox, scriptural tradition. Mary, as we have seen, was the one through whom the Lord became visible to the world; she was his image and mirror, even as he was *the image of the invisible God* (Colossians 1:15). Accordingly, Richard of Saint-Laurent observed, "Before [Mary's] altars and images, and at the recitation of her name, the knee should bow, because she says with the Son (Isaiah 45:23): *To me every knee shall bow*," for the Trinity has bestowed upon her a name "which is above all names after the name of her Son," and she is the queen of all three kingdoms, in heaven, on earth, and in hell.[85] In the miracle stories, the images of the Virgin are typically described as sitting on the altar, while in the illuminations accompanying King Alfonso's *Cantigas*, they are clearly shown as images of Mary as the throne of Wisdom.[86] As we have seen, in the temple tradition, the prophet Ezekiel beheld *the likeness of a throne . . . and seated above the likeness of a throne . . . a likeness as it were of a human form* (Ezekiel 1:26–27), while the prophet Daniel beheld *the ancient of days* seated upon a throne of fiery flames, and *a thousand thousands served him* (Daniel 7:9–10). Likewise, the twenty-four elders of John's vision fell down before the throne and the One who sat upon it while the four living creatures sang: *Holy, holy, holy is the Lord God Almighty, who was and is and is to come!* (Revelation 4:2–11).[87] As the Lady standing beside the throne while the living creatures sang, Mary herself took especial delight in the hymns and other chants composed in her honor, as miracle story after miracle story sought to make clear.[88] Sometimes, as King Alfonso told it, she even went so far as to help in their composition so that through her, the Mother of the Lord, the thrice-holy Trinity might be praised, as the priest of the church of Saint Victor in Paris put it: "*Nobile triclinium . . .* noble dwelling, there are three chambers in you: God the Father and His Son and the Holy Spirit came to dwell therein to show us love."[89]

From this perspective, even the tumbler's tumbling may be seen to have a basis in the temple tradition, that is, the scriptures read as fulfilled through Jesus, the son of Miriam. Just as Wisdom danced and played before the Lord (*ludens coram eo omni tempore, ludens in orbe terrarum*) (Proverbs 8:30–31), so King David "danced with all his might before the Lord" (*saltabat totis viribus ante Dominum*) as the priests bore the ark of the covenant into the city and Michal, the daughter of Saul, *looking out through a window, saw King David leaping and dancing before the Lord: and she despised him in her heart* (2 Kings [Samuel] 6:14–16). As Jan Ziolkowski comments in noting the parallels between the story of the tumbler and that of David's dancing, the verses of the scriptural passage "capture the energy of David's dance, his near-nakedness when he engages in it, its athleticism, and the scorn with which it is greeted."[90] And yet, like King David's dancing before the ark, the tumbler's tumbling may be seen as yet another form of temple service, as Richard of Saint-Laurent made clear: Mary herself is represented by the ark of the covenant before which David danced bound with a linen ephod or, as it says in 1 Chronicles 15:27, a robe of fine linen. "Likewise," Richard exhorted, "we ought to leap and dance before the blessed Virgin in truth," bound with purity of flesh and spirit and making music with the instruments of good works. Accordingly, he observed, "in this garden [that is, Mary] or, rather, before this ark we leap so many times as we salute her with bended knees or ask her pardon before her altars or her images."[91] Even more to the point for our purposes in understanding of the importance of his service, the tumbler did not simply tumble in service to Mary; he tumbled according to the schedule of the liturgical hours. Like the Ave Marias recited by so many of Mary's servants, the minstrel offered his tumbling not to spite the regular service of his fellow monks, but to participate in it as best he could. As the minstrel put it: "The rest serve in chanting, and I will serve in tumbling." And yet, still he sighed: "Lady, what a pity that I know not all those psalters!"[92]

The point of the stories like that of the tumbler was not whether this or that form of service (verbal or nonverbal, simple or complex) was more acceptable to Mary—all forms were acceptable insofar as they were offered with love—but that service should be offered by everyone (kings and people, princes and judges, young men and maidens, the old and the young, as the psalmist put it) to the best of one's ability and, like David dancing before the ark, with all one's might. So important, indeed, did medieval Christians believe that it was to serve Mary that even those who knew "all those psalters" worried whether they knew how to serve Mary as they ought, for, after all, as Richard of Saint-Laurent put it, she was the special work of God (*speciale opus Dei*), born wholly holy (*nata tota sancta*), like the star that rose out of Jacob (Numbers 24:17). The monk of Canterbury who, already saying his prayers "many times a day with great reverence," still felt called upon to ask Mary "with all his heart to give him much needed wisdom so that he might know how to serve Her well" cannot have been alone.[93] After all, compared to Mary, herself Wisdom and the Mother of Wisdom, all other human creatures are, as Augustine told Deogratias, like little children, dependent on her and her Son to teach them the ways of God. As she says in Ecclesiasticus (24:24–25): *I am the mother of fair love and of fear and of knowledge and of holy hope* [in whom] *is all grace of the way and of the truth.* No wonder the tumbling minstrel of Clairvaux was so anxious to offer her at least some form of service, however humble, for how, even knowing the psalters, could one ever hope adequately to praise or serve the one who had contained in her womb him whom the whole world could not contain? Gracious Lady that she was, Mary was more than willing to make allowances for the limitations of her servants, but she had little patience with those who neglected her entirely, for in neglecting her, they neglected God. As King Alfonso put it:

> *He who says that it is naught for a man to serve the Virgin is impudent and a man of bad faith.* For if there is gain in doing service for a good man, how much more is there in serving the Holy Virgin whence we receive all blessings. He who does not believe in this, his belief is worth nothing, for he disbelieves in God, His Son, and Her who is His Mother.[94]

As the stories that they told by the thousands show, all Mary's medieval servants from the king on his throne to the minstrel leaping and bowing before her altar would concur: it was important to prepare oneself properly for serving Mary, whatever form one's service took. But how? Here, curiously, at least to judge from our extant sources, they were comparatively reluctant to say, perhaps because it would be so hard to describe a service by definition so open to variation, limited only by her servants' desire to please. Or perhaps they said little because it seemed obvious, given how carefully they prepared themselves to speak when seeking mere earthly blessings. As Richard of Saint-Laurent himself observed (always eager to elaborate), even those who present themselves at the court of earthly ladies and lords bare their heads, bow and kneel, and repeat their greetings over and over again as they seek to capture their lordships' benevolence with gifts and services. How much the more, therefore, ought those who appear before the most powerful Mother at the court of her only begotten Son offer her reverence and praise! As Richard enjoined his fellow servants, perhaps thinking of the very story we have just read, set as it was in the Cistercian monastery of Clairvaux, like the minstrel or jongleur who exerts himself leaping and singing before the table groaning with temporal food, so ought Christians to prepare themselves heart and mind, body and soul to feast at the table of the Mother of the Lord.[95] They should not, however, expect such preparation to be easy. Indeed, as Richard set out to show in book 2 of his *De laudibus beatae Mariae* (the fullest such discussion of which I am aware prior to the seventeenth century, thus arguably its subsequent popularity in both manuscript and print[96]), to serve Mary properly would require the whole not only of their hearts, minds, and souls, but also of their bodily strength, all their senses and all their members, but most particularly their mouths, with which they spoke and sang. (These are the external practices that were so troubling for Graef.) Only thus, Richard would insist, could they hope to serve the Lord their God and the Lady his Mother as they should, rising like incense in their praises and prayers to that heavenly vision for which they longed. This, Richard would argue, if he had been able to answer his future countryman Sabatier, was their "real religion," their "religion in act," that is, their prayer. As in our reading of Richard in chapter 4, all citations from scripture are his.

To begin with, Richard told his fellow servants, they ought to serve Mary with both their hearts and minds. Indeed, Richard reminded them, it is impossible to know everything about Mary because "infinite are those things about the Virgin that exceed the human intellect."[97] What they could not know, however, Richard assured them, they should nevertheless piously believe, trusting in her goodness, hoping in her, and loving her as the wise man loves Wisdom (Wisdom 7:10–11). Just as the wise man loved Wisdom from his youth and sought to espouse himself to her (Wisdom 8:2), so she, like her Son, loves those who love her (Proverbs 8:17). She is that precious pearl (Matthew 13:46) to be preferred before kingdoms and thrones, powers and dignities, more precious than silver or gold or any precious stone (Wisdom 7:8–9).[98] Accordingly, Richard averred, her servants owe her not only their faith, hope, and love, but also their obedience, reverence, humility, and fear. They ought to attend to her counsels so as not to be confounded (Ecclesiasticus 24:30); comport themselves decently before her eyes in thought, desire, and deed (Habakkuk 1:13); and revere her as the spiritual sanctuary of the Lord (Leviticus 26:2). They ought to adore her with bended knees and hands outstretched, their knees bent in humility and their hands open to receive her blessings. "*Ad litteram*," as Richard put it: "As many times as we salute her or pass her temples, images, or altars, we ought to bend the knee, bare our heads, and humble ourselves like servants before their lady or ladies-in-waiting before their queen," for just as the Jews did before the Lord (Nehemiah 8:6), so ought her servants to do also before the Lady.[99]

Moreover, Richard continued, Mary's servants ought to think and meditate upon her continually, for so she thinks about their peace and salvation (Jeremiah 29:11). As it says in Ecclesiasticus (24:39): *Her thoughts are more vast than the sea and her counsels more deep than the great ocean*. Indeed, just as it is impossible for human understanding to count the drops of the sea, so it is impossible for the human intellect to comprehend her thoughts, her love, piety, humility, goodness, and everything else that pertains to her. And yet, Richard assured his fellow servants, they should think upon her as well as their human fragility allowed, holding in their thoughts all those things that pertain to her honor and glory. As it says in Wisdom (6:16): *To think upon her is perfect understanding, and he that watches for her shall quickly be secure*. Likewise, Richard advised his readers, they ought continually to direct the gaze of their mind and lift their spiritual eyes to her, as it says in Ecclesiasticus (4:16): "*He who looks upon her*, that is, Wisdom, whether Christ on the cross or Mary herself, he looks, I say, with the eye of faith and true love, so that the eyes of her servant drip continually for her."[100]

Again, Richard contended, Mary's servants should rejoice with her for the grace she found before God and compassionate her for the suffering she shared with her Son. They ought never to forget her (Psalm 136:6) because she never forgets them (Isaiah 49:15). Rather, they ought with tears and groans to sigh for her as the faithful souls wept for Zion (Psalm 136:1), singing with the Church: "To you we sigh, weeping and mourning [in this vale of tears]" (here Richard is quoting the Salve Regina). They ought to yearn for her, saying, "Lady, all my desire is before you" (cf. Psalm 37:10), and bind themselves to her service with all their heart, never ceasing to praise her. Whence it says in Proverbs (4:8–9): "*Take hold on her*, that is, Wisdom or, rather, Mary so as to serve her, *and she shall lift you up*, from earthly things to heavenly." Likewise, as it says in Ecclesiastes (8:3): "*Be not hasty to depart from her face*, [for] all those who serve and minister stand before the face of Christ and Mary, as the [angel] Raphael said (Tobit 12:15)." How dangerous it is to neglect her service is shown by the calamities that, according to Peter Damian, befell one community when, at the suggestion of a certain "sarcastic and eloquent brother," they suspended the recitation of her Hours. Rather, Richard admonished, her servants ought to sing wisely (Psalm 46:8), thinking carefully on the words of their mouths (Psalm 5:3), and turning over in their hearts what they say in prayer, as Augustine puts it, lest the Mother say with the Son: *This people honors me with their lips, but their heart is far from me* (Matthew 15:8).[101]

Having thus prepared their hearts and minds to serve her, Richard advised his fellow servants, they ought also to prepare their bodies. They ought to serve her with their faces and heads, worshipping before her face (Isaiah 66:23) as before her Son's holy temple (Psalm 137:2) and bowing at the sound of her name and before her images, particularly those in which they see her seated on a throne to the right of her Son, for, as it says in the book of Barlaam and Josaphat, "the reverence given to an image passes to the exemplar of the image." They ought to serve her with their eyes, averting them from all vanities and looking upon her images with reverence so as to impress them fully on the memory of their hearts. They ought to serve her with their ears, listening gratefully to honorable things said about her but eschewing anything dishonorable they hear. They ought to serve her with their noses, abhorring the perfumes of harlots (Proverbs 7:17) and following instead after the odor of her good example and teaching, drawn like a curtain by a curtain (Exodus 26:3; 36:10) to *Come* (Revelation 22:17). They ought to serve her with their sense of taste, refraining from intemperance in food and drink and observing the vigils of her feast days and Saturdays with fasting so as to rejoice more fully the next day in that sacrament which is their refreshment and will in future be their joy.[102]

As they serve her with their senses, Richard averred, so Mary's servants ought to serve her with their bodily members. They ought to serve her with their shoulders, mercifully carrying the burdens of their brother's infirmity and patiently bearing the weight of present tribulations for the sake of her honor and love. They ought to serve her with their hands, keeping them clean from all impurity and all illicit work so that they might lift only pure hands to her in prayer (1 Timothy 2:8). They ought likewise to adorn and provide for her oratories, altars, and images, prepare lights for her feasts and on Saturdays, and prepare clean and honorable vestments for ministering before her, even as they read in her miracles she provided vestments from heaven for blessed Bonus of Clermont and blessed Ildefonsus of Toledo. They ought to serve her with their arms, embracing her with their love and service, reconciling themselves with their enemies, and purifying themselves by giving alms (Ecclesiasticus 7:33–36). They ought to serve her with their breasts, feeding the simple with the milk of simple teaching and explaining her to them (Ecclesiasticus 24:31). They ought to serve her with their loins, girding them by her example with continence and strengthening their arms with good works (Proverbs 31:17). They ought to serve her with their knees, kneeling before her altars and images and at the recitation of her name (Isaiah 45:23). And, above all, they ought to serve her with their feet by avoiding the ways of evil and remembering her constantly with devotion, so that they might say with the psalmist (Psalm 121:2): "*Our feet were standing in your courts, O Jerusalem*, that is, you, O Mary." Whence, Richard comments, it is said among other things in the story of Theophilus that she greatly loves the Christian people (*genus Christianorum*), "especially those who with right faith and pure conscience run to her temple."[103]

But what—as so many of Mary's servants were clearly anxious to know, given their newly invented Books of Hours—should they say once they got to her temple? That is, how ought they to serve her with their mouths? According to Richard: with praise, exaltation, prayer, confession, blessing, study, teaching, preaching, magnification, singing, thanksgiving, and solemnizing her Saturdays, vigils, and feasts. They ought to praise her, Richard insisted, just as they praised the Lord her Son (Psalm 144:21), for she says with him in Psalm 49:23: *The sacrifice of praise shall glorify me*. They ought to exalt and praise her above all the saints after her Son (Daniel 3:57), blessing her as they blessed the Lord as much as they could (Ecclesiasticus 43:33), searching out her glorious acts, showing forth the power of her majesty, and declaring her mercy (Ecclesiasticus 18:3–4). They ought to pray to her without ceasing (1 Thessalonians 5:17), which, as Bede explains, means keeping her daily Hours according to the rite of the Church, for so she prays for all her servants, like Bathsheba before her son King Solomon (3 Kings 1:17–21), continually pleading for them with her Son, as she did for the first time when she said: *Son, they have no wine* (John 2:3). This is the reason her servants invoke her under three names in the litanies, saying: "Holy Mary, pray for us. Holy Mother of God, pray for us. Holy Virgin of virgins, pray for us." She is the temple of Solomon of which the Lord says (2 Chronicles 7:15–16): *My eyes shall be open, and my ears attentive to the prayer of him that shall pray in this place. For I have chosen, and have sanctified this place.* Thus her servants ought to pray continually with blessed Anselm, saying:

> Mary, I beseech you, by that grace through which the Lord willed to be with you and you willed to be with him, that on account of that same grace, your mercy and grace be with me . . . For, O most blessed one, everyone who turns away from you and whom you oppose, must needs be lost, just as whoever turns to you and whom you regard with favor, shall not perish.

For, indeed, Mary easily gains whatever she asks of her Son, whence she is figured by Judith, to whom it was said (Judith 8:29): *Pray for us, for you are a holy woman, and one fearing God*; and by Esther, to whom it was said (Esther 15:3): *Call upon the Lord, and speak to the king for us, and deliver us from death.*[104]

Likewise, Richard advised, her servants ought to confess her, believing in her in their hearts and confessing her with their mouths, praising her as they praised the Son *with the voice of* [their] *lips and with the canticles of* [their] *mouths and with harps* (Ecclesiasticus 39:20) and confessing their sins to God and to her so that, like the moon, she might be for them *a faithful witness in heaven* before her Son (Psalm 88:38). They ought to bless her unceasingly with heart and voice, for through her virginal childbearing the curse of Eve (*Hevae*) has been converted into blessing, whence the angel said to her: *Ave, gratia plena.* Accordingly, they ought to bless and salute every member of her body with the angel's greeting: her feet by which she carried the Lord (two Aves), her womb in which she carried him (one Ave), her heart in which she believed firmly in him and fervently loved him (one Ave), the breasts with which she nursed him (two Aves), the hands with which she cared for him (two Aves), the mouth, tongue, and lips with which she gave him the happy kisses of human redemption (two Aves plus two Aves), the nostrils with which she smelled the sweet fragrance of his humanity (two Aves), the ears with which she delighted to hear his sweet speech (two Aves), the eyes with which she looked upon him with devotion (two Aves), the body and soul which Christ consecrated with every blessing (two Aves). They ought to say these twenty Aves before her image or altar daily with as many genuflections, just as the psalmist said (Psalm 144:2): *Every day will I bless you, and I will praise your name for ever and ever.* In particular, with the woman in the crowd (Luke 11:27), they ought to bless Mary's womb because it was there that God was made man (John 1:14), the Word a child, the immortal mortal, the great small, the Creator a creature. Moreover, it was for this purpose that the Father and the Son created her *in the Holy Spirit and saw her and numbered her and measured her* (Ecclesiasticus 1:9), so that he who was invisible might be made visible, he who was innumerable might be made numerable, and he who was immeasurable might be measured, constrained within her virginal womb.[105]

There were yet more ways that Mary's servants might serve her with their mouths. They ought—Richard continued, warming to his task—to study all Mary's works, examples, and words, everything that the evangelists say about the time and place of the Lord's conception, his Incarnation, and Passion, and how Mary ministered to him during them. They ought to explain her (Ecclesiasticus 24:31), that is, her life, words, examples, and preaching, by imitating her ("because life teaches more efficaciously than the letter") so as to attain eternal life, that is, the life of contemplation illuminated by wisdom, that is, Christ and Mary. They ought to preach, first about God, then about Mary, first however rising out of sin through penance "because *praise is not seemly in the mouth of a sinner*" (Ecclesiasticus 15:9). They ought to magnify her as much as they were able in heart, word, and deed whenever they were called to serve, love, and praise her, saying with the psalmist (cf. Psalm 33:4): "Magnify the Lady with me, and let us extol her name together!"[106]

And her servants ought to sing to her, again as the psalmist says (cf. Psalm 104:2): "Sing to her, sing praises to her, tell all her wondrous works!" But note again, Richard warned, that whoever wishes to sing before Christ or Mary ought first to make ready his heart and soul (Psalm 56:8), cleansing them of all hypocrisy and other impurities and adorning them with virtues like a temple with colorful curtains. Moreover, even as the just man says to Christ or Mary (Psalm 70:6): *Of thee shall I continually sing*, so it seems that all the just ought to be like minstrels (*joculatores*) singing before Christ, Mary, and the saints. Likewise, even as those minstrels who compose songs (*cantilenas*) to perform at court hope to receive gifts from those for whom they sing, so her servants hope to receive many benefits from Christ and Mary. Accordingly, they ought to sing before them and about them with great devotion and not just anywhere, but in church, even as King Hezekiah prayed: *O Lord, save me, and we will sing our psalms all the days of our life in the house of the Lord* (Isaiah 38:20). "This," Richard comments, "is clearly against those who rarely or never say her Hours in Church." Again, the psalmist asks: "*How shall we sing the song of the Lord* or the Lady, that is, Mary, *in a strange land*, that is, outside the Church [cf. Psalm 136:4]. And note," Richard observes, "that it is said *of you I shall sing* (*in te cantatio*), not only tell (*narratio*), against those who never sing her office (*contra eos qui numquam dicunt suum officium ad notam*)," particularly those clerics, White Monks, and White Canons who refuse to sing so as to spare their voices (by the by suggesting that it was more common in his day to speak rather than sing Mary's Hours, at least among the Cistercians and Augustinian canons for whom Richard was originally writing). The blessed Virgin herself sings in mind and spirit just as Miriam the sister of Moses sang when the army of Pharaoh was cast into the sea (Exodus 15:20–21). Thus, the bridegroom says to her in the Song of Songs (2:14): *Let your voice sound in my ears, for your voice is sweet*. So, likewise, ought her servants to sing and pray with their spirit and understanding (1 Corinthians 14:15), singing the seven vocal hours (*horae vocales*) with the psalmist (Psalm 118:164), performing the seven bodily hours (*horae reales*) through the works of mercy, and observing the seven spiritual hours (*horae spirituales*) in the three theological and four cardinal virtues as well as those listed in Galatians (5:22–23), for thus they more fully imitate her.[107]

According to Richard, thus admonished, Mary's servants—which means, as we have seen, ideally everyone—were still not yet ready to serve Mary as they ought. Having prepared their hearts, bodies, and words (including thanking God the Trinity for all the blessings that they receive through Mary and observing Saturdays in her honor and all her vigils and feasts), they must also, or so Richard would caution, prepare their souls. Whereas under the old law, sacrifice was made literally with animals (Leviticus 1), under the new law Christians make sacrifice to the Lord spiritually with humble spirit and contrite heart (Psalm 50:19). They should therefore prepare their souls with as much care as the animals were prepared, washing their minds with contrition and confession so that they are free of all impurity or stain (Isaiah 1:16), clearing the house of their conscience of the dinner of lust, the dust of greed, and the cobwebs of pride so that nothing filthy remains within. They ought to trim their beard and tonsure (here Richard betrays his own personal grooming habits), cutting off their virility and their presumption of strength and casting out all superfluous and harmful thoughts from their minds. They ought to trim their nails and adorn the house of their conscience with virtues just as they adorn the house of the Lord with tapestries or curtains and the leafy boughs of trees. Separating out the sacrificial animals, that is, their bodies from all animality, they ought to bind their hearts with the twin cords of love and fear, offer them at the door of the tabernacle, that is, to the mercy of God, and as penitents hand them over to the priest. There, at the door of the tabernacle, they ought to let their hearts be slaughtered by the grief of contrition and the work of satisfaction, skinned so that their interior may be wholly revealed, cut into parts through contrition for their individual sins, their parts washed with alms and tears and then bound together and placed on the fire of good works. Having been wholly burned up on the altar by love, they would then make a pleasing odor of compunction and devout prayer before the Lord, the odor of their good example inviting others to do the same.[108]

What will such humble and contrite souls, once sacrificed, be like? As Jerome (that is, Paschasius Radbertus) told Paula and Eustochium (that is, the nuns of Soissons) in the sermon that he wrote for them on the Feast of the Assumption: "Most beloved, love the one you worship and worship the one you love: you will truly worship and love her if you strive to imitate with your whole heart the one whom you praise." That is, Richard explained, the more her servants love and worship Mary, the more they ought to become like her: *pure*, ministering before the Lord and the Lady in the holy place (Ecclesiasticus 24:14) as reverently as they minister before their earthly lords, serving the mother and her Son in holiness and justice (Luke 1:74–75), abstaining from all lusts (Ecclesiasticus 18:30) and from all perverse thoughts which separate them from God (Wisdom 1:3);

perfumed by the example of her chastity, piety, and humility (Ecclesiasticus 39:17–20) and fragrant in thought, word, and deed; *upright* because through her the Lord has broken the chains of their necks (Leviticus 26:13) that they might rightly love the Mother and her Son (Song of Songs 1:3), their love directed to God for the sake of God rather than bent toward earthly things, their voices joined in harmony unanimously praising Mary and Christ (Psalm 33:4); *devout*, loving God and the blessed Virgin with the pious and humble affection generated by contrition and in the tenderness of heart and mind easily released in tears; *Hebrew*, that is, in transit from one state to another, from vice to virtue, from good to better, from better to best, from merit to reward, from doubt to surety, from time to eternity, from faith to hope, from hope to the thing hoped for, from the spark of love to the furnace (Isaiah 31:9), "for the glorious Virgin calls to her service especially those who are in transit" (Ecclesiasticus 24:26), that is, everyone; *compassionate* and *congratulatory*, sharing with Mary in her grief and joy (Romans 12:15); *truthful* in heart without duplicity, in action without falsity, and in deed without vanity; *taciturn*, like Mary, of whose words are read only seven in the Gospel, lest in much speaking they have occasion for sin (Psalm 140:3–4); *fervent* against slothfulness, idleness, tepidity, and negligence; *discreet* in their fervor, their service reasonable, not excessive (Romans 12:1); *humble*, doing everything in her honor according to the example of the Lord, who, although he was rich, became poor (2 Corinthians 8:9), sharing in the weakness of human nature, thus becoming like a servant lesser in status to the one he serves; *pious* and *merciful* because she is the mother of pity and mercy; *modest* before all (Philippians 4:5) in speech, clothing, and diet; *just*, for *he that possesses justice shall lay hold on her*, that is, justice, wisdom, or Mary, *and she will meet him as an honorable mother and will receive him as a woman married as a virgin* (Ecclesiasticus 15:1); *peace-making*, because he who wishes to serve at Mary's pleasure must first make peace with her Son through penance; *simple*, that is, without the folds (*sine plica*) of duplicity and simulation, unlike (Richard takes care to note) many of those clerics or religious who sing before Christ and Mary more like monkeys than men; *patient* with the murmurings of the impious, the loss of temporal goods, injury to their members, the difficulty of their work, the tribulations of the flesh, the contempt of the world, and the illnesses of the body; *honest*, that is, well-composed; *modest*, blushing to do or say or think anything shameful, harmful, or wicked; *happy*, serving neither out of sorrow nor necessity, but out of joy (Ecclesiasticus 35:11); *zealous*, serving not out of fear, but out of love; and *studious*, always diligently inquiring about how to please the one whom they serve.[109]

Such, as Richard would have it, were the "simple" souls, like the tumbler, who had perfected themselves in the service of Mary, for *they that serve her shall be servants to the holy one, and God loves them that love her* (Ecclesiasticus 4:15).[110]

REASONS TO SERVE MARY

"He who would seek perfect love and understanding," King Alfonso the Wise sang,

> *let him woo Holy Mary.* For She makes all things clearly understood and through understanding makes us know Our Lord and enjoy His blessing and lose our fear of the devil. . . . This Lady gives us wisdom and befriends us and saves us from going astray.[111]

"No man should doubt in any way," the king sang, in yet another song,

> *that God took on human flesh in the Virgin* . . . for were it not so, we should not see the King Who would judge our bodies and souls. . . . Nor should we see God in any other way, nor have the compassionate love shown by his works, if He were not visible to our eyes, my friends.

Thus, the king argued,

> we owe our love to Him [who assumed flesh from the Virgin and allowed Himself to be killed for us] . . . and to the Holy Virgin . . . for through Her He performed all these miracles which I have related to you [in my songs].[112]

Indeed, as Richard of Saint-Laurent would have it, Wisdom, that is, Mary, is omnipotent,

> for, as we read in her miracles, she has saved many already certain of their damnation, many drowning in water, many victims of sudden death, who while they were living commended themselves to her patronage; and many who without penance would have died in mortal sin, she powerfully wrested from the jaws of the devil and returned to life so that they might be able to do penance. For she is as clever and subtle for the salvation of sinners as the devil is clever and subtle for their damnation.[113]

For Henry Adams, as indeed for many scholars since, the reason that Mary's medieval servants served her was simple: because she protected them from the wrath of her Son, however sinful they might be, with the added benefit of embarrassing the Trinity whose law she ignored. In G. G. Coulton's words, as cited by Power: "The middle ages thus made for themselves [in Mary] a new Redeemer, endowed with all the qualities that they needed most and fashioned with every poetic liberty which the reticence of the four evangelists permitted." As Power herself put it: "[The Virgin] stood for faith and not for good works, for love and not for justice. The medieval man felt that with her he always had a chance; he had only to believe in her and she would not desert him."[114] In Benedicta Ward's reading, Mary as she appeared in the miracle stories was "a figure of mercy without bounds . . . Anyone might take liturgical actions, and the stories stress the extent of the power of the Virgin and the lightness of the required devotions for the most heavy sins to be removed."[115] Likewise, for David Flory, stories of Mary's miracles above all "[exalt] the Virgin in her role as Mediatrix, offering to the poor and often wretched sinner an extreme and readily accessible intercessional grace. This grace, however, especially as it functions in a typical miracle plot, often subtly contravenes rigid theological principles (which many, even in the Church, considered oppressive) and effectively subverts the very authoritarian structures within which it seemed to be working"—just as Adams said.[116]

Richard of Saint-Laurent, cathedral canon and penitentiary of Rouen—whom, we may recall, Hilda Graef chided as being too "decadent" in his devotions, particularly his insistence on Mary's role as Mother of pity and Queen of mercy, not to mention his attention to her physical beauty—would insist that things were rather more complicated. By Richard's count (because, of course, he counted) there were no fewer than forty reasons "to serve the Mother of God [which] you ought to do while you live, if you wish to live after death," only some of them having to do with the miracles that she worked on her servants' behalf in pleading for them before the judge (see nos. 10, 17–19, 21, 24, 25, and 39):

1. Because the Son of God, whose every action is a lesson for Christians, honors and magnifies his Mother, according to the commandment (Exodus 20:12): *Honor thy father and thy mother.*

2. Because the Holy Spirit commands that Mary be honored (Psalm 98:5): *Adore the footstool of his feet, because it is holy.*

3. Because whatever reverence and honor is shown to the Mother redounds wholly unto the Son, and vice versa. Whence it says in Ecclesiasticus 4:15: "*Those who serve her serve the holy one,* that is, Christ, who is the Holy of Holies, *and those who love her, God loves.*"

4. Because through her and in her and out of her, the glory of the Father and of the Son and of the Holy Spirit is increased. Whence it says in Psalm 47:2: *Great is the Lord and exceedingly to be praised in the city of our God, in his holy mountain*; and in Psalm 86:3: *Glorious things are said of you, city of God.*

5. Because through her and in her and with her and by her the world has, had, and will have every good, that is, Christ, who is every good and the highest good and the one without whom there is no good, who alone is good, whence he says (Luke 18:19): *No one is good except God alone.*

6. Because with Mary is found every good. Whence she says (Proverbs 8:35): *He who finds me, finds life and will receive salvation from the Lord.*

7. Because she loves those who love her, nay, rather, she serves those who serve her. Whence she says (Proverbs 8:17): *I love those who love me.* But whomever is loved by the Mother is also loved by the Son and by the whole celestial court; therefore, she says with the Son (John 14:21): "*He who loves me, shall be loved by my Father,* and by my Son, *and I will love him.*"

8. Because it is the highest honor, the greatest glory and the greatest utility to serve Mary and to be one of her household (*familia*). For to serve her is to reign, just as Boethius says of the Lord.

9. Because drawing water with the bucket of humble and devout prayer from the fountain of life, that is, God, she sprinkles her servants with great drops, especially if they have suitable vessels [to catch the water in].

10. Because she reconciles her servants and lovers most effectively with her angry Son: for she speaks peace unto his people and unto his saints (Psalm 84:9); thus, they invoke her above all other saints, as with Theophilus.

11. Because it is her kindness that no one should be frightened to come to her.

12. Because so great is her mercy that she drives no one away from her.

13. Because she builds up her servants with gifts and charisms that they might become a worthy habitation for her Son and the Holy Spirit, as it says in Proverbs 14:1: *The wise woman builds her house,* that is, her household (*familiam*).

14. Because through her prayers and examples she adorns her servants with manifold virtues (Proverbs 31:21–22), with the white linen of chastity, the twice-dyed scarlet of love, the hyacinth blue of celestial desire, and the purple of royal dignity [that is, with the fabrics and colors of the temple veil; cf. Exodus 26:1]

15. Because she offers up the prayers and sacrifices of her servants, and especially those that are dedicated to her, in the sight of the divine majesty.

16. Because just as the Son is the mediator between God and man, so she is her servants' mediator with the Son, that is, through her mediation the Son comes to them and by way of her they come to the Son.

17. Because she is her servants' advocate with the Son, just as the Son is their advocate with the Father; rather, she brings their troubles and petitions to the Father and the Son.

18. Because she represents those invoking her humbly with sweet words before her angry Son, at which the Son is easily pacified.

19. Because for the salvation of her servants, she is able not only to supplicate her Son like the other saints, but also to command him with her maternal authority.

20. Because she is the tree of life for all those who lay hold of her (Proverbs 3:18) with particular love and service.

21. Because often those whom the justice of the Son condemns, the mercy of the Mother sets free, for even as the justice of the Son says: *I will kill, and I will strike*, so the mercy of the mother responds: *I will make to live, and I will heal* (Deuteronomy 32:39), and so they flee to her like Theophilus and have nothing to fear, for she promises (Ecclesiasticus 24:6): "*As a cloud I covered all the earth*, from the anger of God, as if from the heat of the sun."

22. Because given that she is the treasury of the Lord and the treasurer of his graces, she enriches abundantly those serving her with spiritual gifts (Proverbs 8:20–21; Wisdom 7:14).

23. Because confessing the virgin birth leads to salvation, from which the blessing of God the Father follows.

24. Because she protects her servants most effectively from the threefold adversary, namely the world, the flesh, and the devil, for whom she is terrible as the ordered ranks of the army (Song of Songs 6:3) and a tower against the face of the enemy (Psalm 60:4), as is read in her miracles.

25. Because in Mary all those find refuge who, fearing the justice of God, are afraid to come to him.

26. Because she gives food to the hungry and drink to those who thirst. Whence it may be said of her just as of the Son: "Cast your thoughts on the Lady (*Domina*), and she will sustain you" (cf. Psalm 54:23). Moreover, because the flesh of Christ and the flesh of Mary are one flesh, it is her flesh that Christians receive in the sacrament. Thus she says (Ecclesiasticus 24:29): "*They that eat me shall yet hunger* because those who taste her sweetness shall long to know more about her."

27. Because given that she is the Mother of Wisdom who is the Son of God, she mercifully instructs her servants in the law of the Son. Whence it is said concerning her (Wisdom 7:27): *She makes the friends of God and prophets*, that is, the wise. For indeed, because she drank first from the font of eternal wisdom, she is able to reveal the mysteries of the secrets of God to whomever she wants.

28. Because if her favor has been withdrawn from her servants on account of their sins, as swiftly as they repent, it will be returned to them. Whence she says with the Son (Zechariah 1:3): *Return to me, and I shall return to you.*

29. Because salvation is in her hand, such that Christians ought to say to her more truly than the Egyptians said to Joseph (Genesis 47:25): *Our salvation is in your hand.*

30. Because by serving her are attained days of grace and glory. Whence she says to her servant (Proverbs 9:11): *For by me your days will be multiplied, and years will be added to your life.*

31. Because after the Son, she is Lady (*Domina*) of all creatures: whence she is called Lady, and for that reason ought to be served like a Lady.

32. Because he who loves and honors the Mother of the Lord, freely is able to ask mercy from the Father and the Son, because she is his house and the habitation of his glory (Psalm 25:8).

33. Because through the incarnation of the Word that was accomplished in her, the sinful soul is returned to the unity of the Church (Jeremiah 31:21–22).

34. Because through Mary and, therefore, through Christ whom Christians have through Mary, whatever was lost through Adam and Eve is restored to them.

35. Because through her conception and giving birth the wonderful dignity and prerogative of human nature is increased, namely, because the Son of God about to redeem the world assumed not angelic nature (Hebrews 2:16), but rather human nature in her and through her.

36. Because wishing her servants to attain victory that they might win the crown, and knowing that only he who competes lawfully will be crowned (2 Timothy 2:5), she arranges wars and temptations for her lovers, and permits them to be afflicted from time to time. But with temptation she gives increase so that they are able to bear up, and she aids them with virtue that they might achieve the crown, for she is the one who gives strength to the weary with her prayers, merits, and examples (Wisdom 10:12).

37. Because those who serve her in the present will see her most glorious face in the future (Job 33:26; Revelation 22:3–4; Wisdom 6:17).

38. Because she rewards her servants with the glorious fruit of her womb (Proverbs 8:19), just as she is depicted in her images holding her Son, as if giving him to her servants.

39. Because she protects the souls of her servants going out of their bodies from the attack of the powers of the air, to whom she is terrible as the ordered ranks of an army, as is often read in her miracles.

40. Because she will glorify in the future those serving and honoring her in the present. Whence she says with the Son (1 Kings [Samuel] 2:30): *Whoever will have honored me, I will glorify him: who however contemns me will be cast down.*[117]

All of which is to say: because she is Wisdom, who invites her servants to offer prayers through her to the Lord who became present in her as in his temple. This is not an image of the Virgin with which most modern scholars or, indeed, modern Christians are familiar, certainly not its deep foundations in scripture. As we saw in chapter 4, it took Richard seven of the twelve books that he wrote on her praises to elucidate the ways in which her servants might invoke her through her many names. His contemporaries, including Conrad of Saxony, Pseudo-Albert, Servasanctus of Faenza, Jacobus of Voragine, and many others, found even more ways to celebrate her through the prophecies, proverbs, and psalms of scripture written, as they believed, about her and her Son. How we evaluate this tradition of reading her, as present like her Son everywhere in scripture, inevitably depends, as we have seen, as much on our own confessional convictions as it does on the evidence of the texts—evidence that, as we have likewise noted, has itself been the subject of continuing confessional debate. Arguably, our evaluation of the purposes and appeal of her late medieval cult as evidenced in the miracle stories so beloved of Richard and his contemporaries is similarly constrained by our own confessional frames: Did her intercession on her servants' behalf, as they imagined it, confound or realize God's justice? (Adams would say the former.) Were her servants, like Richard, inappropriately attentive to her physical beauty as a woman? (Graef would say yes.) Did Mary distract from their contemplation of God? (Define "God.")

These are not easy questions to answer. As Adams himself rightly sensed, and I would now argue based on what I have learned in learning how medieval Christians prayed Mary's Hours, devotion to Mary fueled the construction of more than just the cathedrals at Chartres, Paris, or Rouen; it was "the greatest force the Western world had ever felt, and [drew] man's activities to herself more strongly than any other power, natural or supernatural, had ever done."[118] Devotion to the Virgin touched on almost every aspect of late medieval Christian life, as hopefully our reading of her miracles has begun to suggest: from ideas about serfdom and vassalage in the service offered to Mary, to the conventions of courtly love in the descriptions of her as bride, to the longing for the beatific vision at the heart of Christian worship, realized, or so her servants would insist, through Mary as the Mother of God. Just as, Servasanctus would insist, all the creatures of creation sang out in praise of the one who contained him whom the heavens could not contain, so, as we have seen in the catalogues that Servasanctus and his contemporaries made of her titles and attributes, particularly her knowledge, thinking about Mary encompassed and framed the whole of medieval spiritual and intellectual life, from meditations on the creatures created by her Son, all his works from the angels of Day One to the animals and human beings of day six, to the inner workings of the soul in its virtues and relationship with God which, they believed, Mary perfected. As I hope to show in a subsequent study, thinking about Mary as the city of God was arguably at the center of the development of both the science of the natural world (a.k.a. creation) and the making of human artifacts (including cities as well as other goods) in the later Middle Ages, as well as the construction of the reflective, penitential, virtuous self imagined through the psalms and other chants by which late medieval Christians prayed her Hours. Indeed, I would now argue, through Mary, as her medieval devotees insisted, a new world came into being, a world that some would argue we are in the process of losing for neglect of her.[119] More modestly here, by way of conclusion, I have time and space to suggest but a few of the ways in which our reading of the Virgin as found in the texts of her Office changes the way in which we read her as a figure of devotion, as seen in three of her most popular guises: as intercessor in her relationship with her servants, as bride in her beauty as a creature, and as temple in her relationship with God. Arguably, how we read her in these roles changes everything that modern scholars have hitherto believed about the significance of her medieval cult, just as how we read her Son changes everything about the way in which we see God and his relationship to the world, not to mention the purposes of prayer. *Hic sunt dracones!* As with our reading of Mary's names, Richard of Saint-Laurent is our most eloquent, not to mention exhaustive, witness to this tradition, along with the stories told of her miracles.

Mary as Intercessor

A certain man "who was religious in name only, but, wherever true religion was concerned, hard-hearted and careless" nevertheless "was in the habit of praying to the Blessed Virgin and saying once every day a hundred 'Hail, Mary's.' " One day, near death, he was caught up in an ecstasy, where the devils "charged him before the Great Judge seeking a sentence that would adjudge him to be theirs. God, therefore, knowing his manifold sins, said that he must be condemned." God's Mother, meanwhile, "came offering schedules in which were contained all the 'Hail Mary's,' and begging her Son to allow [the man] to receive a milder sentence." The devils countered with many books full of the man's sins, which, when the books on both sides were put into the scales, far outweighed the schedules of salutations. At which, Mary pleaded with her Son: "Remember, Beloved, that Thou didst receive of my substance, visible, tangible and sensible substance; give to me one drop of Thy blood shed for sinners in Thy passion." To which request her Son replied: "It is impossible to deny thee anything. Yet know that one drop of my blood weighs heavier than all the sins of the whole world. Receive therefore thy request." And, indeed, when she placed the drop of blood in the scales "all those sins of the religious [man] weighed against it as light as ashes." The devils departed in confusion, crying: "The lady is too merciful to Christians; we fail as often as she comes to contend with us." The man, however, recovered, "related the whole tale, and became a monk."[120] That is, thanks to the Virgin's intervention, he changed his ways and, we may infer, became religious in heart, word, and deed as well as in name.

Who, in the scale of things, should we assume is at fault here, other than the sinner: Mary, for asking her Son for a drop of his blood, or the devils, for presuming that the soul was already theirs? It is, after all, theologically orthodox to insist that Christ sacrificed himself for the redemption of sins, opening by his blood *a new and living way* into the sanctuary *through the veil, that is to say, his flesh* (Hebrews 10:19–20). Here, Mary simply reminds him of the blood he shed in the flesh ("visible, tangible and sensible substance") that he took from her. Or is the fault that Christ says he can deny his mother nothing, when, in fact, she is asking for something he has already done, his blood having been *offered once* [at his Passion] *to exhaust the sins of many* (Hebrews 9:28)? Or is it simply that she asks? To some, including Graef, it would seem the latter: that Mary asks or has to ask or in asking somehow changes the Godhead, as, for example, in Richard of Saint-Laurent's description of Mary as "[softening] the Lord with her merits and prayers, so that he now patiently tolerates even great sins, whereas before he mercilessly [*durissime*] avenged even quite small ones."[121] In Graef's view, as we have seen: "The mercy of Christ disappears completely in this division of labour between him and his Mother."[122] And yet, elsewhere, Richard makes it clear that the mercy of Mary (that is, the Lady) and the justice of Christ (that is, the Lord) are, in fact, one because both are of God. As it says in Deuteronomy 32:39 (as commented by Richard): "*See that I alone am, and there is no other God besides me: I will kill,* says the justice of the Son; *and I will make to live,* responds the mercy of the Mother: *I will strike,* says the justice of the Son; *and I will heal,* responds the mercy of the Mother, *and there is none that can deliver out of my hand.*"[123] Moreover, Richard avers: "It is just and right that [such a sweet, renowned, festive, devout, powerful, and sweet salutation as the Ave Maria] should be recited famously and devoutly by Christians on earth, when, as is truly believed, the inhabitants of heaven recite it regularly to the honor and glory of the glorious Virgin" because it was with these words that Christ "determined to save the world through her as *mediatrix*."[124] Mary, according to Richard, has the power that she does because she "is the queen of that city whose king is her Son, and according to the laws the king and queen enjoy the same privileges. Therefore the same power is common to the mother as to the Son, and her omnipotence is an effect of his, because *there is no power except from God* (Romans 13:1)."[125] Her power, in other words, *is* God's; she is his instrument, his angel, if you will, not his superior.

The question, as always with the medieval devotion to the Virgin, is not whether Mary as Mother of Jesus was trying to play God in place of her Son, but whether and how Mary as the Mother of the Lord belongs in Christian tradition. It all depends on how we read the scriptures. Once upon a time, there was a certain man who begged Abbot Odo of Cluny (d. 942) for admission to the monastery so that he might do penance for his youth spent as a thief. Imitating the Israelites as they rebuilt Jerusalem, the novice monk put one hand to the sword of obedience while laboring to learn the Psalter with the other, and in such labor soon came to the end of his life. As he lay dying, or so he told Abbot Odo, a woman "of most glorious person and most excellent power" appeared to him and asked: "Do you know me?" He replied: "No, lady." "I," she said, "am the mother of mercy (*mater misericordiae*)," and revealed to him that he would die in three days, which he did. Thereafter, or so Odo's biographer John of Italy explained, it was Odo's custom to invoke Mary under this name.[126] "That truly," one twelfth-century version of this story explained, "holy Mary, the mother of Christ, is truthfully the mother of mercy, is also attested by the psalmist when he writes about the Lord Jesus Christ, her Son, saying: *My God, my mercy* (*Deus meus, misericordia mea*) [Psalm 58:18]. Since therefore Christ is our mercy, and holy Mary is the mother of that same mercy, we ought not to despair that she who gave birth to our mercy will help us in our necessities."[127] As Pseudo-Albert put it in his *Mariale*: "[Mary] is the queen of that which is mercy, whence Esther, who is a figure of the blessed Virgin, is called by the name Edissa, which is interpreted *mercy* (Esther 2:7)."[128]

As Richard of Saint-Laurent explained it, Mary is but one of humanity's advocates in the court of God (*curia Dei*). The first is the Holy Spirit, who *asks (postulat) for us with unspeakable groans* (Romans 8:26; RSV: *intercedes for us with sighs too deep for words*) and appeases the Father's anger against sinners. The second is the Son of God *always living to make intercession for us* (Hebrews 7:25), who like a good champion shows the Father the signs (*stigmata*) of his Passion and advocates for sinners with the Father for the remission of sins and the grace of the Holy Spirit, whence he says (John 14:16): "*I will ask the Father, and he shall give you another Paraclete*, that is, comforter." The third advocate is the blessed Virgin, especially with her Son, who beseeches for her servants every good, for indeed there was no advocate for them with the Son before Mary was born, but the Father said (Genesis 2:18): "*It is not good for man to be alone*, that is, it is not enough for there to be only one advocate or mediator or intercessor for the human race in heaven, when it has so many and such dangerous cases before me. *Let us make him a helper*, that is, the blessed Virgin, who may make the case for the human race before the Son, just as the Son before me." (This is why, Richard explains, she is called "our advocate" in the Salve Regina.) The fourth advocate in the court of God is each soul's guardian angel, whence it says in Daniel 12:1 that Michael stands for the children of his people. The fifth advocate is alms, as it says in Ecclesiasticus (29:15): *Shut up alms in the heart of the poor, and it shall obtain help for you against all evil.* The sixth advocate is prayer, whence it says in Psalm 87:3: "*Let my prayer come in before you*, as the gloss explains: Here is shown the great power of pure prayer, which like a certain person enters in before God, and there accomplishes what the flesh cannot."[129]

Accordingly, Richard continued, the scriptures contain many figures of Mary acting as mediator or intercessor with her Son. Just as she told him at the marriage at Cana: *They have no wine* (John 2:3), so Bathsheba, sitting on a throne set for her at his right hand, asked her son King Solomon that Abishag the Shunammite be given to his brother Adonijah as his wife (3 Kings 2:19–20). Again, as Richard puts it, we see Mary in the figure of Esther, to whom her husband King Ahasuerus said: *What is your petition, Esther, that it may be granted to you? And what will you have done? Although you ask the half of my kingdom, you shall have it.* And she responded: *If I have found favor in your sight, O king, give to my people what I request* (Esther 7:2–3). Mary's hands, Richard explains, are *full of hyacinths* (Song of Songs 5:14), that is, blue stones like the color of the sky, "because whatever good she does shines with celestial intention and comes forth from the font of eternal wisdom. Further, hyacinths have the grace of obtaining: for whatever it pleases her to give, she obtains easily by praying to her only-begotten Son, who not only gives her what she asks, but also urges her to ask for it."[130] Like Abigail, she is most prudent and beautiful, placating King David's anger against the foolishness of her husband Nabal (that is, the human race) with the wisdom of her words (1 Kings [Samuel] 25). Like the wise woman of Thecua, she reconciles Absalon with his father David for the killing of his brother Ammon (2 Kings [Samuel] 14). Like the wise woman of Abela, she asks Joab, the commander of David's army: *Do you not seek to destroy a city and to overthrow a mother in Israel?* Then she cuts off the head of Seba who had stirred up sedition against David and throws it over the wall to Joab and the city is saved (2 Kings [Samuel] 20:14–22). "Thus," explains Richard, "Mary treads under foot Barabbas, that is, she casts down the devil, who on account of the sedition that he stirred up in heaven, the kingdom of the true David, and of the murder that he did when he killed himself and his accomplices in that sedition ... is called a murderer from the beginning (John 8:44), into the prison of hell (Luke 23:25)."[131]

Mary, Richard insisted, is merciful, as how could she not be, for God, who is love, rested corporeally in her womb for nine months. Are Christians then to believe, Richard asks, that the Son of God should not honor his Mother or to doubt that this love did not pass into her through her womb? This, he says, is why her servants sing to her: "*Salve, regina, mater misericordiae*," remembering that as queen she is able, and being merciful she is willing to help them. She is called the Mother of mercy, that is, of Christ, "who antonomastically is called mercy," whence the psalmist says (Psalm 143:2): *My mercy and my refuge*. Indeed, her first petition of her Son was for mercy, when she said to him: *Son, they have no wine* (John 2:3), as if to say: "Son, men are hungry and thirsty and in need of the mercy of your pity and love that the wine of divine grace might hereafter make them glad, whom hitherto the savorless taste of the observance of the law have made sad." Accordingly, "with the prayers and merits of his mother, Christ changes the waters of sin into the wine of grace and the waters of misery into the wine of consolation."[132] Moreover, like her Son, who promised the thief crucified on his right hand not just that he would remember him, but that the thief would be with him that day in paradise (Luke 23:43), Mary gives more than she is asked, even as Rebecca, when Eliezar, the servant of Abraham, asked her for water, offered to draw water not only for him, but also for all of his camels (Genesis 24:18–19).[133]

Again, Richard reminded her servants, Mary is that city of God of whom glorious things are said (Psalm 86:3). She is glorious in her priestly and royal lineage (Psalm 44:14), in her sanctification in her mother's womb (Ezekiel 3:12), in her most singular humility, which God had regard for and strengthened and on the strength of which he filled her with every virtue and grace (Ecclesiasticus 43:10), in her primitive and fertile virginity (Isaiah 35:2), in the flower of her fertility (Luke 1:35), in her most excellent maternity (Isaiah 42:8), in giving birth to the redemption of her people (John 8:36), in the singular honor given to her that at her death her body should not decay but be assumed with her soul into heaven (Psalm 72:24), in the glorification of her body before the day of judgment (Esther 15:4), in the exaltation of humanity in her as in the Son above the nature of the angels (Ezekiel 10:4), in the plenitude of power that she exercises over the whole celestial court (Ecclesiasticus 24:15) such that at her name every knee in heaven, on earth, and in hell should bow (Philippians 2:10), and in the commanding power of her prayers. She shows her Son her womb and her breasts so that she cannot be refused, just as blessed Bernard (more likely, Arnold of Bonneval) says. Praying for those who run to her, she obtains from her Son the grace of compunction, as when she obtained wine for those at the wedding

(John 2:3); the grace of reconciliation, as when the woman of Thecua reconciled Absalon with David (2 Kings [Samuel] 14); and the washing away of sins, as when Abigail asked to wash the feet of the servants of David (1 Kings [Samuel] 25:41). And she obtains the blotting out of the chirograph of the devil, as when Esther annulled and reversed the letters of Aman ordering the destruction of the Jews (Esther 8:5). Concerning which chirograph it is said (Colossians 2:14): "*Blotting out the chirograph of the decree that was against us, which was contrary to us*, which Mary did through the mediation of her Son." Indeed, Richard notes, invoking yet again his favorite miracle story of the Virgin: "Her kindness was never denied anyone however much a sinner, if only he converted to her with his whole heart, as is clear in [the story of] Theophilus, who denied her with her Son."[134]

THE MIRACLE OF THEOPHILUS

But what exactly—or so, at this point, we might finally ask Richard—is it that the story of Theophilus makes clear? Significantly, although he alludes to it more than two dozen times throughout the course of his *De laudibus beatae Mariae virginis*, Richard never felt it necessary to retell the story in any detail, in part because it was not his purpose to write a narrative of Mary's life and miracles, but arguably even more so because he deemed that there was little need to tell it. All of his readers, he assumed, would already know how the story goes, as, indeed, by the middle of the thirteenth century when he was writing, it was a reasonable assumption that they would.

To the best of our knowledge, the story made its first appearance in the West in the late ninth century in what later tradition would claim to be a translation from the sixth-century original Greek of one Eutychian, purportedly an eyewitness to the events recounted in the tale. While given the state of the manuscripts (there are three in Greek, the two earliest dating to the eleventh century, the third to the fifteenth) the actual dating and authorship of the story are subject to some doubt, the tale's first Latin author is known to have been a certain Paul the Deacon of Naples, who, as Adrienne Williams Boyarin has noted in her recent study of the story in England, "was an important member of a small school of translators whose project included making Byzantine hagiography accessible to the West."[135] The story was versified in Latin in the tenth century by the canoness Hrotsvitha of Gandersheim and paraphrased in Old English in his sermon for the Feast of the Assumption by Aelfric of Eynsham (d. ca. 1010). Bishop Fulbert of Chartres (d. 1028) alluded to it in his sermon for the feast of Mary's Nativity and in one of his prayers. Honorius Augustodunensis

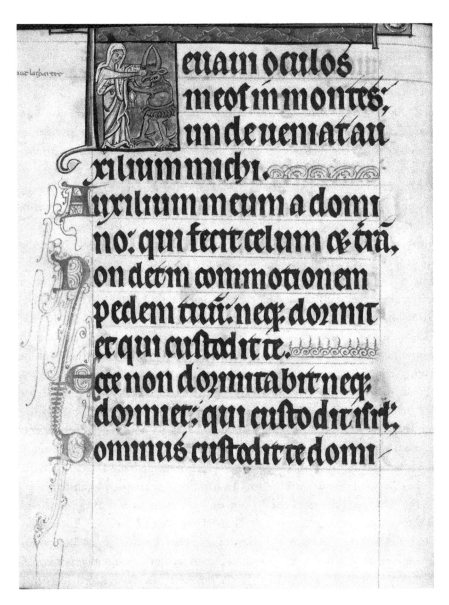

euam oculos
meos in montes;
unde ueniat au
xilium michi.
Auxilium meum a domi
no: qui fecit celum & tram.
on det in commotionem
pedem tuii: neq; dormit
et qui custodit te.
ce non dormitabit neq;
dormier; qui custodit isrl;
ominus custodit te domi

PLATE 21 Mary punches the devil and retrieves the charter for Theophilus. Book of Hours ("The De Brailes Hours"), Oxford, England, ca. 1240. Use of Sarum, with variations. Made by William de Brailes (fl. ca. 1230–1260). London, British Library, Add. 49999, fol. 40v.

Photo courtesy of the British Library, London.

referred to it in his *Sigillum beate Mariae*, a commentary on the liturgical use of the Song of Songs in praise of Mary, and in his sermon for her Assumption. It was included by Dominic of Evesham and William of Malmesbury in their collections of Mary's miracles. Marbod of Rennes (d. 1123), Nigel of Canterbury (ca. 1200), and John of Garland (d. ca. 1272) versified it in Latin. Adgar versified it in Anglo-Norman in the twelfth century; Gonzalo de Berceo put it into verse in Castilian, and King Alfonso sang it in Galician-Portuguese in the thirteenth century. Gautier de Coincy versified it in Old French, and the troubadour Rutebeuf retold it as a play. A Middle English version appears in the *South English Legendary* (composed ca. 1270–1285 in its earliest form). Several Middle German versions survive as plays, and there are also extant versions in Swedish, Italian, Icelandic, and Dutch. The Dominican Vincent of Beauvais (d. 1264?) included it in his *Speculum historiale*, and his confrere Jacobus de Voragine (d. 1298) included it in his *Legenda aurea* in his entry on the Nativity of the Virgin. During the twelfth, thirteenth, and fourteenth centuries, artists crafted it in sculpture at Souillac, Paris, and Ely, and in glass at Laon, Le Mans, Auxerre, Saint-Julien-du-Sault, Troyes, Beauvais, Clermont-Ferrand, Angers, Dreux, Gercy, Lincoln, and York—to name only those cathedrals, chapels, and abbeys whose images survive. William de Brailes retold it in images in the Book of Hours (the earliest extant from England) that he made at Oxford in the 1240s (London, British Library, Add. 49999); the story appears in ten miniatures for the hours of Prime and Terce (fols. 32v–43r). More so than any other of her miracles, the story of Theophilus established Mary's power as an intercessor, particularly her power over the devil. It is the first such story in the West to use the term *mediatrix* in describing her. It is also, not incidentally, the source of the trope of a pact made in writing with the devil, as, for example, by Faust.[136]

But what does the story mean? For many modern readers of the medieval tale, the most arresting character in the narrative is arguably neither Theophilus nor Satan nor even Mary, but the Jewish magician through whom Theophilus makes contact with the devil. To be sure, certain medieval retellings, for example, Gonzalo de Berceo's (for whom the Jew is "the vassal of a very evil lord") and that in Oxford, Bodleian Library, Rawlinson Poetry 225 (a mid–fifteenth century Middle English version of the story in which the Jew tells Theophilus, "I have a lord that hatte Satan") make much of the character of the Jew, as do the manuscript illuminations for the *cantigas* of King Alfonso.[137] But Alfonso himself says only that "on the advice of a Jew he [that is, Theophilus] had signed a letter with the devil in order to gain power and had given the letter into the devil's keeping," while the Jew does not appear at all in William de Brailes's illuminations for the Hour of Terce, only Mary, Theophilus, and the devil—the latter horned, monstrous, and naked but for a fringed red loincloth, whom the Virgin takes out at *"Levavi oculos meos in montes unde veniet auxilium michi"* (Psalm 120:1) with a well-aimed punch.[138] Jacobus de Voragine (who says he took the story from Fulbert of Chartres) relates only that Theophilus "fell into such despair that, in order to regain his honorable post, he sought the advice of a Jewish sorcerer. The sorcerer summoned the devil, who came immediately." Nothing further is said of the Jew.[139] While Vincent of Beauvais, paraphrasing Paul the Deacon, describes the Jew as a "most wicked worker of the diabolic arts, who had already plunged many into the pit of unbelief and perdition," in Herolt's telling, Theophilus is no longer even a cleric, but simply a "certain noble" who, becoming impoverished, "thought of going to the cross-roads and talking with the Devil," apparently without need of any intermediary, Jewish or otherwise.[140] Richard of Saint-Laurent for his part makes no mention whatsoever of the Jew, only that Theophilus was a sinner who denied Mary and her Son.[141] For those like William de Brailes and Richard, concerned above all with the meaning of Mary's Office, the Jewish magician was not essential to the story. From their perspective, what mattered was less how Theophilus entered into his service of the devil, and more how he got out.

Other recent readers have been taken with what appear to be anomalies in the representation of the Virgin, particularly her role in regaining the chirograph or charter with which Theophilus bound himself to Satan's service. According to Boyarin, in the English retellings of the legend, Mary is portrayed primarily as concerned with legal disputes, "both in the literal sense of negotiating contract law and in the more abstract sense of meting out justice," as "Jew, lawyer, trick-ster, mighty, learned, able to penetrate hell and battle or outwit demons."[142] In contrast, for Kate Koppelman what is most striking in the stories, particularly as retold in fourteenth- and fifteenth-century England, is Mary's recourse to verbal and physical aggression, both in her chastisement of Theophilus and in her con-frontation with the devil—a representation purportedly at odds with Mary as a font of mercy and grace and as suppliant of her Son.[143] Arguably, however, neither the presence of the chirograph (the principal marker for Boyarin of Mary's legal activities) nor Mary's "capacity for anger and violence" (as Koppelman puts it) is as anomalous or ambivalent as it might at first seem when we recognize the story as Paul the Deacon of Naples originally translated it—and as Richard alluded to it, using Paul—as a miracle or parable of Wisdom crying out to her children to turn back to her lest they fall into destruction, damnation, and death. Far from being concerned primarily with Mary's recovery of the charter or with her hand-to-hand fight with the devil (which, in Paul's version, is only implied), the story as Paul tells it is above all a lesson in confession, penance, and prayer. It is Theophilus's confession that is at the center of the story, and his sin, not the devil's, that is the focus of Mary's anger (having been exalted above the angels, she is by right the devil's queen; she has no need to be angry at him, he is already damned by his own obstinacy). How later storytellers changed the story is a question for another context. For our purposes, what is significant is the way in which "Theophilus the penitent," as Richard calls him, comes to repent.[144] This is the story as Richard referred to it and which he assumed his readers knew:[145]

It happened that, "before the invasion of the detestable race of the Persians into the Roman republic" (Jacobus adds the date: A.D. 537), there lived in the city of Adana near Tarsus in Cilicia (Jacobus says Sicily) a certain steward of the holy church of God by name Theophilus, "distinguished by his morals and mode of living." Indeed, the people of Adana esteemed and loved him so much that when the bishop of the city died, they petitioned the metropolitan to promote Theophilus to the see. Theophilus, however, flung himself prostrate at the metropolitan's feet "and prayed that no such thing should be done to him, protesting that he was wholly unworthy of the rank of bishop and that he was conscious of his own sins." Seeing Theophilus so loath to consent, the metropolitan promoted another man to the bishopric. Once, however, the new bishop was ordained, certain of the clergy incited him to remove Theophilus and appoint another steward in his place. For a time, Theophilus lived modestly, caring for his own house and doing good deeds, but the "cunning enemy and envious foe of the human race" seeing him thus occupied "made his heart begin to beat with perverse thoughts" and instilled in him such jealousy for the office he had lost and such desire for human glory that Theophilus decided to seek out the help of sorcerers to regain his post.

"Now," as Paul tells it, "there was in that city a certain wicked Hebrew, a practitioner of all sorts of diabolic arts, who had already plunged many into the abyss of the pit of perdition with his faithless arguments." Incited by vainglory and burning with ambition, Theophilus went to the Hebrew's house by night and, throwing himself at his feet, begged him for help against his bishop. The Hebrew "hateful to God" told him to return the next night at the same time and he would take him to his patron who, the "accursed" Hebrew promised, would help Theophilus in what he desired. At midnight the next night (the time, we may note, during which faithful Christians would have been at prayer) the Hebrew led Theophilus to the circus of the city, where he warned him not to make the sign of the cross (that is, the sign of his baptism and anointing as a Christian) whatever he might see or hear. At Theophilus's promise, the Hebrew "showed him suddenly figures clothed in white robes crying out with a multitude of candelabra and, sitting in their midst, the prince." (Paul explains: "It was the devil and his ministers"—the diabolic court here clearly mimicking the heavenly as described in Revelation, with its elders and angels clothed in white and singing amid the seven gold lampstands surrounding the throne.)

The Hebrew, taking his hand, brought Theophilus before the devil and explained that Theophilus wanted his help. To which the devil, having apparently forgotten his role in Theophilus's temptation, responded: "How shall I help him, a man serving his God? But if he desires to be my servant (*meus famulus*) and to be counted among our hosts (*milites*), I will aid him so that he may do more than before and rule over all, even the bishop." Hearing which, Theophilus, clearly given to such gestures, began to kiss the devil's feet and implore him, at which the devil said to the Hebrew: "Let him deny the son of Mary and Mary herself, because they are hateful to me, and let him set down in writing that he denies in everything, and whatever he wants, he shall obtain from me, so long as he denies." "Then Satan entered into the steward, and he replied: 'I deny Christ and his mother.' And, making a chirograph, he sealed the applied wax with his own ring, and both went away with great joy at his perdition." (In the De Brailes Hours [fol. 34r], this scene is elaborated, showing Theophilus, tonsured, kneeling before the devil and clasping the sealed charter [*carta*] between his hands while the devil puts his hands around Theophilus's in the traditional gesture of homage. It is interesting to speculate whether what we see here is not so much the translation of Theophilus into the devil's vassal as such, but rather evidence that such homage itself has its origins less in the military service of secular culture, and more in the devotional tradition of service to Mary and her Son. But let us not digress.) The next day, just as the devil promised, the bishop, "moved, I reckon, by divine providence," restored Theophilus to his former post and gave him authority over the management and possessions of the church and over all the people. The Hebrew, meanwhile, came to him secretly and asked: "Have you seen how fully you have found benefit and speedy aid from me and my patron in that which you prayed for?" And Theophilus said: "I confess it and I give thanks indeed for your mutual action."

But Theophilus was not to enjoy his newfound luxury and power for long. Soon thereafter, God, "the Creator of all things and our redeemer, who desires not the death of sinners, but their conversion and life, mindful of [Theophilus's] former way of living and how he had served God's holy church, and that he had ministered abundantly to the widows, the orphans, and the needy, did not despise his creature, but gave him the conversion of repentance." Accordingly, turning himself away from his arrogance and denial and coming to his senses,

Theophilus began to humble himself and, with fasting, prayers, and vigils, to think on the salvation that he had lost:

> O miserable wretch that I am, what have I done and what have I wrought? . . . Where shall I, unhappy sinner, go, who have denied my Christ and his holy mother and have made myself a servant of the devil through a chirograph of wicked warrant? Who, do you think, will be able to pull it away from the hand of the devil, the destroyer, and help me? Why was it necessary for me to become acquainted with that wicked Hebrew who should be burned? Why indeed? For thus are they honored, who forsaking God and the Lord, run to the devil. . . . Woe to me, wretch, how have I lost the light and gone into the darkness? . . . What help shall I pray for, who am cheated of aid by the devil? I, who am guilty of this thing, I am the author of my soul's perdition, I the betrayer of my salvation. . . . What shall I reply on the day of judgment, when all shall be naked and laid open? . . . Who will pity me? Who will aid me? Who will protect me? Who will be my patron? Verily no one: there no one helps but all render an account for themselves. Woe to my wretched soul! . . . Woe to me, miserable one, who, having stumbled and fallen into the abyss, am unable to rise!

Nevertheless, even as Theophilus was bewailing his state, certain of his misery, God, "who is alone pious and merciful, who despises not his own creature but supports him," encompassed the sinner with another thought:

> Although I know that I have denied the son of God, born of the holy and immaculate always virgin mother Mary, our Lord Jesus Christ, and herself, through that Hebrew whom I came evilly to know, nevertheless I shall go to that same mother of the Lord, holy, glorious, and bright, and her alone I shall entreat with all my heart and soul, and I shall pray and fast in her venerable temple without ceasing, until I obtain mercy through her on the day of judgment.

At once, however, he fell into further doubts:

> But how shall I begin my confession? Trusting in what sort of heart or what state of conscience shall I attempt to move my impious tongue and soiled lips? For what sins shall I first seek remission? And if in rashness I should presume to do this, fire descending from heaven will burn me up, because the world even now will not bear the evils that I, most wretched, have done. Alas, miserable soul [Theophilus, still inspired, told himself], rise up from the darkness that has taken hold of you, and falling down before her, call upon the mother of our

Lord Jesus Christ, because truly she has the power to impose healing penance for such sin.

Much encouraged by such thoughts (prompted, we should note, by God), Theophilus hastened to that "holy and venerable temple of the immaculate and glorious always virgin Mary," where for forty days and forty nights he fasted and prayed that he might be delivered from "that dangerous deceiver and wicked dragon and from the denial which he had made." (Note that Theophilus does not blame the sorcerer for leading him astray, as Adam so famously once blamed Eve. Rather, being truly repentant, he recognizes that he ought to share the Hebrew's punishment, that is, to be burned up for forsaking the Lord and his Mother and serving the devil instead. It was the devil, not the Hebrew magician, who was at the root of his fall. Likewise, it is God who is the author of his redemption.)

"And, verily, after the days [of fasting and prayer] were fulfilled, there appeared manifestly [to him] in the middle of the night that universal aid and ready protection of those who watch for her, the true refuge of Christians who run to her, the way for those who wander, the redemption of captives, the truest light in the darkness, the refuge of the afflicted, the consolation of those in trial, our Lady and truly mother of Christ, saying to him: 'Why, O man, do you persist rashly and disdainfully in asking that I help you, man who has denied my Son, the savior of the world, and me?' " (It is almost as if we hear Wisdom herself, chiding her children from the gates of the city for despising her counsel and hating her instruction, even as she laughs at their destruction and mocks them in their fear [Proverbs 1:20–33]. In the De Brailes Hours [fol. 39v], Mary appears to a kneeling Theophilus at Psalm 119:1: "*Ad Dominum cum tribularer clamavi, et exaudivit me.*") "How," the Lady asked Theophilus, "can I beseech him to forgive you the evils that you have done? With what eyes shall I look on that most merciful face of my Son, whom you have denied, and presume to entreat him for you? . . . For I will not suffer to see my son defamed by insults." (As if to say, with the psalmist: *What shall be given to thee, or what shall be added to thee, to a deceitful tongue* [Psalm 119:3].) I might be able to forgive you, she told him, for the sins you have committed against me, "for so much I love the Christian people, especially those who with right faith and pure conscience run to my temple." (Richard quoted this same passage verbatim more than once.[146]) "But," she cautioned, "I cannot bear to hear or see revilers of my Son, because they need many struggles and labors and pangs of the heart to receive his favor. For he is an exceedingly merciful and very just and pious judge."

But Theophilus persisted: "I know, my Lady, I know that I have sinned greatly against you and am not worthy to ask for mercy; but having an example in those who before sinned against your Son, our Lord, and who merited indulgence for their sins through penitence, therefore I presume to approach you." His examples, taken from both the Old and the New Testaments, run throughout the history of the people of the Lord[147]: the Ninevites, who while not themselves Israelites heeded the word of the Lord and repented at the preaching of Jonah (Jonah 3; Matthew 12:41; Luke 11:32); Rahab, the prostitute of Jericho, who assisted the spies sent by Joshua and so was justified by her works and spared in the destruction of her city (Joshua 2; 6:17–25; Hebrews 11:31; James 2:25); David, who was anointed king and given the gift of prophecy but who fell "into the pit of fornication and homicide" and yet did penance and received yet further gifts (2 Kings [Samuel] 12:1–25); Peter, who denied Christ the Lord not once or twice but three times, and yet through bitter weeping obtained not only indulgence for his sin but even greater honor than before (Matthew 26:69–75; Mark 14:66–72; Luke 22:54–62; John 18:25–27); Zacchaeus, "the prince of the tax-collectors and perverters of the law," who gained salvation when he did penance by giving half his goods to the poor (Luke 19:1–10); Paul, who "was transformed from a persecutor into a vessel of election" by penance (Acts 9:1–30). How else, Theophilus asked, but through penance should the fornicator among the Corinthians be forgiven, "lest Satan get the advantage of him" (1 Corinthians 5:1–5)? How else but through penance did Cyprian, "who had done so many evil things, who cut open pregnant women and was wholly entangled in shameful deeds," receive with the help of Justina not only the remission of sins, but the crown of martyrdom? "Wherefore," Theophilus prayed, "I, too, a sinner, approach you, trusting in the evidence of the penitence of so many and asking for your kind mercy, that you may deign to extend to me the right hand of protection and to grant me indulgence for my sins through your Son, our Lord Jesus Christ, against whom I, a wretch, have sinned."

It is Mary's response to Theophilus's prayer that is the key both to her power and to his salvation, as well as to the meaning of the story.[148] "Confess to me," she said, "O man, that the son whom I bore and you denied, is Christ, the Son of the living God, who will come to judge the living and the dead, and I will entreat him for you and support you." Theophilus, oddly reluctant, demurred: "How shall I presume, my Lady always blessed, I who am unhappy and unworthy, who have a sordid and polluted mouth, who have denied your Son and our Lord, and have been tripped up by the vain desires of this world? And not only that, but I have also defiled the remedy of my soul, I mean the venerable cross and holy baptism which I received, through that written chirograph of most bitter denial." But Mary insisted: "You need only approach and confess him, for he is merciful and will accept the tears of your penitence, just as of all those who come to him purely and sincerely. For on this account, although he is God, he deigned to take flesh from me, with no dishonor to the substance of his Deity, so that he might save the human race." At which, Theophilus bowed his head, confessed, and said:

> *Credo.* I believe, I worship, and I glorify our Lord Jesus Christ, one of the holy Trinity, Son of the living God, who was born ineffably of the Father before the ages, but descended in recent times from heaven and was incarnated true God by the Holy Spirit from you, the holy and immaculate always virgin Mary, and came forth for the salvation of the human race. *Confiteor.* I confess him to be perfect God and perfect man, who on account of us sinners deigned to suffer, to be spat upon and beaten with blows, and to have his hands stretched out upon the life-giving tree, like a good shepherd laying down his life for us sinners. He was buried, rose again, and ascended into heaven in the flesh which he received from you, his most chaste and true mother, and he shall come again in his holy glory to judge the living and the dead and to render to each according to his works. He has no need of an accuser except those works by which our conscience accuses or excuses us and the fire by which each work is examined for what it is. I confess these things with my soul, heart, and body. I worship, adore, and embrace them, and with this my prayerful pledge, made with all the strength of my mind, bring me, holy and immaculate virgin, mother of God, to your Son, our Lord, and do not abhor or despise my prayer, I who have been ravished, tripped up, and deceived, but free me from the iniquities which have seized upon me, and from the blast of the whirlwind which possessed me, who am deprived of the grace of the Holy Spirit.

Satisfied with his confession, Mary, "the holy mother of God, the hope and obstacle of Christians, the redemption of the wandering and the true way of those who flee to her, the font of the wavering, who intercedes for sinners, the refreshment of the poor, the mediator (*mediatrix*) between God and men," said, in effect: Thanks to the baptism you received through my Son and my compassion, I believe you. I shall see what I can do.

This was the miracle. Not that the Virgin returned three days later (days which Theophilus spent in fasting and prayer, fixing his eyes upon the "bright light and ineffable face of the glorious mother of God") with the news that the Lord had accepted his penance if only Theophilus observed in his heart the things that he had confessed until the day of his death; not that, after a further three days, Mary delivered unto him, as if in a vision, the charter of his apostasy with its seal of wax, only for him to awake and find it resting on his breast; not that the next day Theophilus went to the bishop and told him in detail "everything that had been done by the execrable and pernicious Hebrew and sorcerer; of his own arrogance and denial and the chirograph written on account of the vain glory of this world," which chirograph he demanded be read out before everyone there, clergy and laity, women and children alike, so that they would all know what had happened to him and how the charter of denial had been returned to him. Rather, as Theophilus's confession of his sins to the bishop makes clear, it was "his confession to God and our Lord Jesus Christ and his penance" that came about "through miracles" (*per miracula*). Mary's retrieving the chirograph from the devil, while a lively scene for artists and playwrights to portray, was something of an afterthought; it was Theophilus, not Mary, who insisted that he needed it back in order to be sure of his salvation. As Jacobus put it in his retelling, Mary "returned the scroll [Theophilus] had given to the devil [in token of the forgiveness granted him], placing it on his breast as a sign that he need not fear he might still be in the demon's service, and that through her intervention he was a free man."[149]

Far more remarkable, although rarely if ever depicted visually, is Theophilus's transformation after burning the chirograph and hearing mass, for, as Paul the Deacon of Naples put it, "after the completion of the sacred mysteries and the reception of the sacred mysteries, at once the face of the venerable steward shone like the sun, and all who saw the sudden transfiguration of the man glorified God the more, *who alone does great miracles* (Psalm 135:4)." Theophilus, in other words, came out of the Holy of Holies with his face shining like Moses when he came down from the mountain after speaking with the Lord (cf. Exodus 34:29 LXX).[150] As the bishop put it in his sermon to the people following Theophilus's public confession: "For Moses, the lawgiver, fasting for forty days, received graven tablets from God, and this our brother, abiding for forty days in the venerable temple of the immaculate and glorious ever virgin Mary, has received from God by fasting and prayer the former grace that he lost through his denial." More to the point, Theophilus had spent forty days in contemplation of "the bright light and ineffable face of the glorious mother of God," herself, as we have seen, as Wisdom, the *unspotted mirror of God's majesty and the image of his goodness* (Wisdom 7:26). Theophilus, in gazing upon the face of the Mother of the Lord became like her, angelic or rather godlike, transformed through love by grace into the likeness of her Son, regaining that likeness which he lost through sin, and shining with the light of the divine. As Paul put it to the Corinthians (2 Corinthians 3:18 RSV): *And we all, with unveiled face, beholding the glory of the Lord, are being changed into his likeness from one degree of glory to another; for this comes from the Lord who is the Spirit.* Again, as we have already seen, in Richard's words, Mary is called the Mother of beautiful love

> because she makes her lovers and friends to resemble Christ her Son, who is
> most beautiful, reshaping (*refigurans*) the likeness of the Son in them through
> grace, which they lost through sin. This happened with Theophilus: for after he
> was reconciled to the Son through the mother's mediation and had taken holy
> communion, his face shone like the sun.[151]

Theophilus, in other words, was transfigured, like Jesus on Mount Tabor, whom Peter, James, and John beheld with his face shining like the sun and his garments dazzling white, whiter than any fuller on earth could bleach them (Matthew 17:2; Mark 9:3; Luke 9:29): white, that is, like baptismal robes or the linens worn by the high priest as he ministered before the Lord in the Holy of Holies bearing the Name (Exodus 28:36–43; Leviticus 16:1–34); white, that is, like the robes of the angels and elders ministering before the heavenly throne (Revelation 4:4).

With the story of Theophilus, we encounter once again the mystery of the temple tradition into which early and medieval Christians believed themselves to have been baptized so as to sing before the throne of the Lord. Theophilus the Penitent (as Richard styled him) was the model of what Mary's medieval devotees hoped to become as they sang her Hours in her praise. This is the reason that Theophilus's face shone. Confessing the Trinity and partaking of the sacrament of the bread and wine, Theophilus, like every Christian, became once again a servant of the Lord, an angel priest robed in the glory of his Creator and sealed with his Name—that is, with the sign of the cross made on his forehead at baptism (Revelation 19:10, 22:3–4).[152] This, likewise, is why the Hebrew sorcerer told him not to make this same sign as they prepared to meet the devil: the sign of the cross was the sign of the Name before which all creation ought to bow (Isaiah 45:23; Philippians 2:9–11). The devil, of course, had refused to bend his knee to the Name and so had been cast out of heaven (Isaiah 14:12–15; Luke 10:18; Revelation 12:7–9). The Name of the Lord was Theophilus's proper seal, marked in ancient Hebrew as an "X" and transformed by those who bore the Name as Christians into the sign of the cross.[153] We may see the devil and his court as a mockery of the court of heaven; we may also, as Herman Van Nuffel has suggested, read the scene in the circus as a mockery of the sacrament of baptism, in which the baptized assumed the white robes of their angelic status and were given candles as a sign of the light into which they had been reborn.[154] The sacrament is also most likely the source of the "confession" that Theophilus makes to the devil. Before receiving baptism, the catechumens would be questioned: "Do you renounce Satan and all his works?"[155] Instead, in mockery of the baptismal formula, the devil questions Theophilus through the Hebrew sorcerer, his antibaptismal sponsor, saying: "Let him deny the son of Mary and Mary herself, because they are hateful to me." Accordingly, Theophilus renounces the Lord and his mother and writes out with his own hand his anticonfession, which he seals with his ring in mockery of his baptismal seal.

Even so, however, Theophilus is not yet eternally damned, for God "desires not the death of sinners, but their conversion and life." God, as Paul the Deacon of Naples tells the story, brings sinners like Theophilus to repentance and penance, even sinners who have gone so far as to renounce the Lord and serve rather the devil. And how does God bring them to repentance? As the story of Theophilus makes clear, through his Mother: that is, through belief in the Incarnation of the Son who died so that sinners might live. This is why the Hebrew sorcerer is so "wicked," "accursed," and "hateful to God": like Satan, he denies Mary and her Son the worship they are owed as the Lady and Lord bearing the Name. In this denial, he makes a covenant not with life, but, as Isaiah put it, with death (Isaiah 28:15), thinking thereby to enjoy earthly rewards. But in this denial, the sorcerer is deceived, because Satan is *a liar and the father of lies* (John 8:44); his majesty is false, as are his promises. God, however, speaks only the truth, as the Lord said: *I am the way, and the truth, and the life. . . . If you shall ask me anything in my name, that I will do* (John 14:6, 14). The examples of other penitents that Theophilus invokes are examples of God's mercy, his patience and willingness to forgive sinners who come to him and ask. It is not Mary who forgives Theophilus, but God. She is simply, good angel that she is, the Lord's handmaiden (his minister, if you will) and his messenger, carrying the petitions of his servants to him. She is the one who makes the Lord visible, the support for Christians against heresy and the foolishness of denying God, but it is the Lord, as the Apostle Paul put it, who blotted out the chirograph against sinners by nailing it to the cross, thus *despoiling the principalities and powers . . .* [and] *triumphing over them in himself* (Colossians 2:14–15). Mary cannot, from this perspective, as Eileen Power put it in her reading of Mary's miracles, "cheat the Devil of his due," any more than as a good angel she might will to go against the will of God.[156] The devil has no due, he only thinks he does. Everything—adoration, worship, praise, thanksgiving—is due to the Lord, not Satan. Accordingly, the chirograph that Theophilus signed could never be binding on him in the way that he feared; rather—and this arguably is why Mary retrieved it for him—it was valuable only as a witness to his sin and, once read out before the people, could therefore with impunity be burned.

"Come," the bishop cried out to the people after they had heard Theophilus's confession and the chirograph of his denial had been read:

Come, all ye faithful, let us glorify our true Lord Jesus Christ! Come all and behold these wondrous miracles! Come, all ye beloved of Christ and behold him, who does not desire the death of the sinner but instead conversion and eternal life! Come, see, my fathers, the efficacy of penance. Come, see the tears that wash away sins. . . . Come, all ye Christians, and consider the tears which take away the wrath of God. Come and witness of how much avail are the sighs of the soul and a contrite heart. . . . Who is not amazed at the ineffable compassion and charity of God toward us sinners? . . . Let us therefore glorify our God, who has so mercifully given ear to the penitence of him who sought refuge in him through the intervention of the immaculate ever virgin Mary, the mother of God, who is a most true bridge between God and men. . . . She bears our petitions to the one whom she bore, our Lord, and receives indulgence for our sins. Therefore [the bishop prayed], holy mother of God . . . forsake not your humble sheep-fold, but pray for it to the merciful Lord and intercede for it. . . . For in you all us Christians place our hope and to you we flee. . . . For we greet and glorify you and him who was born of you and took flesh from you, our Lord Jesus Christ. And what shall I now speak or say or what manner of praise or glory shall we offer to our Lord God, Jesus Christ the omnipotent, who was born of you? Truly *great are your works, O Lord* (Psalm 103:24), and tongue cannot tell the glory of your miracles.

Theophilus's confession was the miracle, a miracle of intercession and tears, to be sure, but ultimately, as are all miracles, a miracle of God. As his story shows, if Mary has power, it is only because God has power: the power to forgive and to save the creatures that he made. So great is this mystery that some, like the devil, think it is possible to cheat by binding God with a contract, but it is the Lord who made the heavens and the earth, who engraved their bounds and wrote his commandments on the hearts of his creatures. There is nothing the devil can do that can break this bond; only the will of the creatures themselves can do this, made free to accept or reject the covenant of God. No contract that the devil made could be binding against such a covenant, as Theophilus, instructed by Wisdom, at long last realized and confessed. Three days later, worn out with fasting and having distributed all his possessions to the poor, Theophilus died "and departed to the Lord, to whom," Paul the Deacon of Naples reminded his readers, "is the glory, now and forever, throughout all the ages of ages. Amen."[157]

PLATE 22 The woman clothed with the sun, holding the child. Book of Hours, The Netherlands, ca. 1475. Use of Geert Grote. Chicago, The University of Chicago Library, Special Collections 347, fols. 119v-120r.

Photo courtesy of Special Collections Research Center, The University of Chicago Library.

Mary as Bride

A certain sacristan was so devoted to the service of the Virgin that, in Gautier de Coincy's words, "every night, by courtly habit (*par fin usage*), he knelt before the image of our Lady Saint Mary. He never neglected her; upon bare knees and elbows he cried many hot tears. In vain suffering he wearied his flesh, his bones, his ligaments, his veins" (ll. 19–16). "You," the sacristan prayed to her, "are the carbuncle and the jewel which is so brilliant and pure and fine, that it illuminates all of Paradise. Lady, all those in Paradise behold themselves in your shining face" (ll. 40–44, my translation). (We may recall how Theophilus's face shone when he had been in the presence of the Lord.) Burning with desire, the sacristan longed to be able to hold her face in his memory, and so indeed, mindful of his desire, she came to him one night while he was sleeping. It seemed, he dreamed, as if the whole monastery were full of fire:

For before him came a lady, brighter than the midday sun when it is at its highest. She was dressed in a robe, all made of beaten gold, full of precious gems, so bright and glorious [that] the entire monastery shone with the light that they gave off. Her hair was more golden blond and shimmering than fine gold; her eyes so bright they seemed like two stars. Her face [was] more resplendent than emerald or topaz. She had a roseate color so pure and fine, so delightful, so very beautiful—more so than any budding rose. Her face was so pleasing, so clear, so sweet, so lovable, whomseover might behold himself there enough would leave all his troubles behind. She is so beautiful that in this world there is none, whatever skill he might have, who would know how to describe her at all. (ll. 82–107, with changes)

The sacristan, struck mute in wonder at the beauty of the Lady's face, gazed on, at which he noticed that she held in her hands a book, which he then desired to read. She opened it for him, and he beheld that it was beautifully written in letters of red and gold, every letter so well formed that it seemed to have been written by the hand of God. And what did the book say? "Here begins the prophecy of the prophet Isaiah," a book which, as we may recall, itself begins with a vision of the heavenly throne.[158] Overcome with devotion and desire at this revelation, the sacristan began to weep and sigh:

Glorious high queen, great lady, pious and sweet! If your sweetness would not be offended, I ask, I beg that you deign, in your mercy, to ease my fatigue with my mouth by once kissing your very feet. (ll. 153–60)

To which request, she demurred:

I do not wish, my dear sweet friend, that your sainted mouth, which has so often hailed me, ever touch my feet. Rather, dear sweet friend, it would please and suit me if you kissed me with your beautiful mouth on my radiant face. (ll. 161–68)

Overjoyed at the consummation of his desire, the sacristan, leaping to his feet, awoke. That night at Matins, Mary's lover was so overwhelmed at the memory of her face that he could neither sing nor read, for which disobedience he was disciplined the next morning in chapter, but so great was his love, even then he did not make excuse for his silence nor waver in his service to Mary.[159]

Over and over again in the miracle stories, Mary's devotees are described as inflamed with love and overwhelmed by her beauty, beauty likewise reflected in the images sculpted of her, before which her lovers knelt and prayed.[160] According to Caesarius of Heisterbach, the Cistercian convert Walter of Biberach, while still a knight, had been so devoted to the Virgin that even on the way to a tournament, he would stop to hear her Mass, just as a knightly lover might stop to do some service for his earthly lady. One day, as it happened, Walter stayed so long at his prayers that he missed the beginning of the games. At the end of the day, however, a number of knights came to him and declared themselves his prisoners, and he realized that the Blessed Virgin herself had caused him to be honored in this way and "had filled his place during his absence with marvellous might." Eventually, Walter,

> considering how he had hitherto been a layman, and how many benefits he had received from the Blessed Mother of God, was so inflamed with love towards her that he went to a certain poor church dedicated in her honour, and in the presence of the priest, having placed a rope about his neck, he offered himself at her altar as a slave of the soil (*servum glebae*), paying every year a ransom for his life, in the same way as those born slaves were accustomed to do.

Hearing that the Cistercian order was dedicated to the one whose slave (alt. servant or serf) he had become, Walter forsook all his worldly riches and honors and friends so as to spend his days praising her, diligently repeating the psalms, hymns, canticles, and prayers of her Office, which he had learned as a novice. Further, while traveling on the business of his monastery, Walter always carried with him an ivory image of the holy Mother of God, before which he was accustomed to prostrate himself and pray.[161]

Even those not yet devoted to her could be enflamed with love by serving her. Caesarius tells the story of yet another young knight, whom the devil tempted to lust after the wife of his lord. After laboring under this temptation incessantly for a whole year, he at last told his lady how he suffered. Being an honorable matron and faithful to her husband, she rebuffed him, so the knight, now suffering even more, went to a certain hermit and, with many tears, confessed his passion to him. The hermit replied:

> O! if that is all that troubles you, I will give you such advice that your desire may be accomplished. For the coming year, go every day when possible to the church and salute 100 times with the angelic salutation and as many prayers for pardon, Our Lady the Virgin Mary, Mother of God, and through her you will obtain all you wish.

One day, while sitting at the table of his lord, the knight remembered that it was the last day of the year, during which he had paid daily reverence to the Virgin Mary. Immediately, he got up, mounted his horse, and went to the church to say his customary prayers. When he came out of the church, he saw a most beautiful matron, "surpassing the loveliness of all human beauty," holding his horse by the bridle, who (the lady, not the horse) said to him: "Does my appearance please you?" When he replied: "I have never seen anyone half so beautiful as you," she asked him: "Would you be satisfied to have me for a bride?" And he said: "Your beauty might satisfy any king in the world, and he would be judged a happy man as your consort." And she said: "I will be your wife. Come and give me a kiss." And she compelled him to kiss her, saying: "Now are our nuptials begun, and on such and such a day they shall be completed in the presence of my Son." At once, her knightly lover recognized her as the Mother of the Lord "whose chastity delights in human purity," and mounting his horse at her command, he was so completely free of his former temptation that even the wife of his lord was astonished. Soon thereafter, with the hermit at his bedside, he died, and his nuptials were complete.[162]

King Alfonso tells a variant of the same story, in which the knight enters many tournaments and does many great deeds of battle in order to win his lady's love, but she refuses him. After a year of saying two hundred Aves a day in order, as he hoped, to win the first lady's love, the Virgin appears to him, "so beautiful and radiant that he could not gaze upon Her," and says: "Take your hands from your face and look straight at me, for I wear no veil. Between me and the other lady, choose the one who pleases you most, according to your preference." The knight replies: "My Lady, Mother of God, you are the most beautiful thing which these eyes of mine ever gazed upon. Therefore, let me be one of your beloved servants, and I will renounce the other lady." The Virgin tells him that, to win her, he must pray for her for another year in the same way that he prayed for the other, at the end of which, "as I learned, She took him to be with Her."[163]

In Gautier's version of this same story, having said one hundred fifty Aves every day for a year, the knight was so wracked with love for his proud lady that he declared he would die if he could not have her, "so beautiful [was] she that it [seemed to him] that never was there formed by Nature a creature so fair in body, and arm, and hand, and face." One day, as the year was drawing to its close, he happened upon an old chapel, where he found an old image of Our Lady, before which he knelt to pray. Hearing his sighs, the Virgin, in her great courtesy, suddenly appeared to him, and he beheld her "crowned with a crown full of precious stones, so sparkling and so glorious, that for a while his eyes were dazzled by them." Moreover, her garments "glistened and shimmered like unto the rays which shine on a summer's morn," and her face was so beautiful and bright that "happy did that one seem to himself to be who could look long whiles upon it." "Fair friend," the Virgin asked, "is she who is the cause of your sighs, and has so disquieted you, fairer than I?" The knight, however, was "so sore afraid at the brightness that he knew not what to do," so that he covered his face with his hands and fell to the ground in awe and fear. But the bright Lady said to him:

> Friend, be not afraid . . . if I find you a loyal lover, there above, in Paradise, will you find me a loyal friend. . . . Never for my sake strive in any tourney or deeds of chivalry, but if that you would be lord of my love, repeat an hundred and fifty Aves for a year without missing a day. Then will you win me without doubt, and thus will you hold and possess my whole love for ever and ever.

The knight, at once, resolved to become a monk, so as to spend the year remembering her, and at the end, she "took him to eternal life on high, there where all her friends have endless joy and solace of her love."[164]

Sometimes simply seeing a statue of the Virgin was enough to capture a young man's heart and service.[165] One such statue, according to Gautier, had been set up in front of an old church that was being repaired so that the people might leave offerings at its feet. In front of the church, there was a square where the young men were accustomed to play ball. One day, as Gautier tells it, a group of young clerks was playing before the statue, one of them wearing a ring that his beloved had given him. Much fearing to lose or break the ring, the clerk went toward the church to put the ring down somewhere safe, but when he saw the statue and how beautiful it was, he knelt down before it with tears in his eyes, "and in a little while, the desire of his heart was changed." "Lady," he said to the statue,

> henceforth will I serve you all my life long, for never shall I look upon any lady, or damsel, or maiden, so pleasing and so fair. A hundred thousand times fairer and more pleasing are you than she who has given me this ring. To her had I surrendered my every wish, and my whole heart, but for the sake of you I would fain cast her aside, and her love and her jewel. This ring, the which is very beautiful, would I give you out of true love, in token that never will I have lover or wife, save you alone, fair sweet Lady.

With this vow, the clerk placed the ring on the statue's finger, only to his dismay and fear to see the finger bend closed in such a way that he could not remove the ring without breaking it. The people in the square, seeing the ring on the statue, crossed themselves and marveled and counseled the clerk to become a monk, but "he had not enough discretion to keep [the] covenant" he had made with Mary through her image. Rather, he forsook the Lady and took his beloved to wife. But on his wedding night, the Mother of God, now furious, appeared to him in a dream, and showing him the ring still on her finger, she rebuked him, saying:

> In nowise have you done aright or loyally by me . . . Behold the ring of your mistress, the which you gave me in true love . . . A loyal friend would you have had in me if that you had not forsaken me. You give up the rose for the nettle, and the sweet-briar for the elder-bush. So deceived are you by love, that you give up the fruit for the leaf, the sea-lamprey for the river-lamprey, and the honeycomb and the sweet honey for poison and for gall.

"And the clerk sprang up all trembling, for well might it be that he was lost and ruined, since he had angered Our Lady." As Gautier exhorted his audience in conclusion: "Monks and clerics who marry our Lady Saint Mary are married well indeed . . . By God, let us not mismarry! Let us leave *Maros et Marions*, and let us marry Mary, who marries her lovers to heaven."[166]

Who was this Lady to whom so many young knights and monks vowed their service and love? Let us recall what the Lady looked like: her face and her figure shone like the sun; she wore a robe of beaten gold, covered with precious stones, and a sparkling and brilliant crown; she was more beautiful than any other woman, a fitting bride for a king; she compared herself to a rosebush and declared herself sweeter than honeycomb; all Paradise was reflected in her face. Surely we have beheld this Lady before. As the psalmist sang to the Lord and his bride on the day of their espousals:

> *The queen stood on thy right hand in gilded clothing, surrounded with variety.*
> *Hearken, O daughter, and see, and incline thy ear, and forget thy people and thy*
> *father's house, and the king shall greatly desire thy beauty, for he is the Lord, thy*
> *God, and him they shall adore.* (Psalm 44:10–11)

This same Lady was figured in Judith, who was *exceedingly beautiful* (Judith 8:7), and in Esther, whom the king loved more than all the other women brought to his chamber, *for she was exceeding fair, and her incredible beauty made her appear agreeable and amiable in the eyes of all* (Esther 2:15). To those, like Solomon, who loved her and sought her, she was *radiant (clara) and unfading* (Wisdom 6:12), *the brightness of eternal light and the unspotted mirror of God's majesty and the image of his goodness . . . more beautiful than the sun and above all the order of the stars* (Wisdom 7:26, 29). Solomon became a lover of her beauty and wanted to take her for his bride (Wisdom 8:2) because *he that loveth her loveth life, and they that watch for her shall embrace her sweetness* (Ecclesiasticus 4:13). She was exalted *as a rose plant in Jericho* and gave forth *a sweet smell like cinnamon and aromatical balm* (Ecclesiasticus 24:18, 20), and her spirit was *sweet above honey, and* [her] *inheritance above honey and the honeycomb* (Ecclesiasticus 24:27). John saw her come forth from the temple *clothed with the sun, with the moon under her feet, and on her head a crown of twelve stars* (Revelation 12:1). Isaiah promised her: *Thou shalt be a crown of glory in the hand of the Lord, and a royal diadem in the hand of thy God* (Isaiah 62:3), and John saw her coming down out of heaven, *having the glory of God,* [her] *radiance like a most rare jewel, like a jasper, clear as crystal* (Revelation 21:11).

As the bridegroom says of his bride in the "Song of Songs, which is Solomon's" (Song of Songs 4:1, 3–5, 7, 9, 10–11; 6:3, 8–9; 7:1–7, 9):

> *How beautiful art thou, my love; how beautiful art thou!*
> *Thy eyes are doves' eyes, besides what is hid within.*
> *Thy hair is as flocks of goats which come up from Mount Gilead....*
>
> *Thy lips are as a scarlet lace and thy speech sweet.*
> *Thy cheeks are as a piece of pomegranate, besides that which lieth hid within.*
> *Thy neck is as the tower of David, which is built with bulwarks....*
>
> *Thy two breasts like two young roes that are twins which feed among*
> *   the lilies....*
>
> *Thou are all beautiful, O my love, and there is not a spot in thee....*
>
> *Thou hast wounded my heart, my sister, my bride! Thou hast wounded*
> *   my heart with one of thy eyes and with one hair of thy neck.*
> *How beautiful are thy breasts, my sister, my bride!*
> *Thy breasts are more beautiful than wine, and the sweet smell of thy*
> *   ointments above all aromatical spices.*
>
> *Thy lips, my bride, are as a dropping honeycomb; honey and milk are under*
> *   thy tongue, and the smell of thy garments as the smell of frankincense....*
>
> *Thou art beautiful, O my love, sweet and comely as Jerusalem, terrible as an*
> *   army set in array....*
>
> *One is my dove; my perfect one is but one; she is the only one of her mother,*
> *   the chosen of her that bore her.*

The daughters saw her and declared her most blessed, the queens and
    concubines, and they praised her.
Who is she that cometh forth as the morning rising, beautiful as the moon,
    bright as the sun, terrible as an army set in array? . . . .

How beautiful are thy steps in shoes, O prince's daughter!
The joints of thy thighs are like jewels that are made by the hand of a skillful
    workman.
Thy navel is like a round bowl never wanting cups.
Thy belly is like a heap of wheat set about with lilies.
Thy two breasts are like two young roes that are twins.
Thy neck as a tower of ivory.
Thy eyes like the fish pools in Heshbon which are in the gate of the daughter
    of the multitude.
Thy nose is as the tower of Lebanon that looketh toward Damascus.
Thy head is like Carmel, and the hairs of thy head as the purple of the king
    bound in the channels.
How beautiful art thou and how comely, my dearest, in delights!
Thy stature is like to a palm tree, and thy breasts to clusters of grapes. . . .

Thy throat like the best wine, worthy for my beloved to drink and for his lips
    and teeth to ruminate.

Although her poets delighted to praise her in what read now like courtly terms, medieval Christianity did not invent devotion to the Lady; she was there already in the temple tradition, likewise the tradition of her marriage to the Lord. Medieval monks, clerics, and knights may have imagined themselves as her lovers and bridegrooms, but they were hardly the first, as the scriptures made clear. *I came out of the Most High*, Wisdom declares, *the firstborn before all creatures* (Ecclesiasticus 24:5).

> *The Lord possessed me in the beginning of his ways before he made any thing from the beginning. . . . I was with him forming all things and was delighted every day, playing before him at all times.* (Proverbs 8:22, 30)

Solomon, who prayed to the Lord for wisdom (3 Kings 4:29–30), became rich in gold, silver, ivory, garments, and spices (3 Kings 10:23–25), having prized Wisdom above every precious stone and loving her above beauty and health as the light that cannot be extinguished (Wisdom 7:7–11). *Her have I loved*, the king declared, *and have sought her out from my youth and have desired to take her for my bride, and I became a lover of her beauty* (Wisdom 8:2).

What would it be like to take Wisdom for one's bride? King Solomon the Wise knew:

> *Now all good things came to me together with her and innumerable riches through her hands, and I rejoiced in all these, for this wisdom went before me. . . . For she is an infinite treasure to men which they that use become the friends of God, being commended for the gift of discipline.* (Wisdom 7:11–12, 14)

King Alfonso the Wise seems to have known also. As he sang:

> *Holy Mary, Star of Day, show us the way to God and be our guide. . . .*
> You must show us the way in all our deeds to win the true and matchless light which only you can give us, for God would grant it to you, and most willingly bestow it for your sake.
> Your wisdom can guide us far better than any other thing to Paradise, where God has always delight and joy for whoever would believe in Him.[167]

And, again:

> *We should all praise the Virgin with all our hearts, singing in joyous harmony. . . .*
> Because of Adam and Eve, we all fell into the devil's power, but He Who made us had pity on us and became a new Adam who crushed the dragon's head. God bestowed great mercy on the world through this Lady, and the one who serves Her whom God, man and Savior, brought to us acts very wisely, for She fulfilled all that David and Solomon foretold.[168]

For, indeed:

> *Holy Mary restores the good which Eve lost . . .*
> The good which Eve lost when she lost Paradise, Holy Mary recovered through her great wisdom.
> The good which Eve lost when she lost fear of God, Holy Mary regained by believing in Him without question.
> The good which Eve lost by breaking the commandment, Holy Mary regained through good understanding.[169]

This, arguably, is the reason for the some forty-page *du haut en bas* (to put it in courtly terms) meditation in Richard of Saint-Laurent's *De laudibus beatae*

Mariae virginis on the physical beauty of Mary that, as we have seen, so exercised Graef. Richard, like the authors of the Marian liturgy before him, read the description of Solomon's bride in the Song of Songs as a description of Mary, that is, of Wisdom.[170] To meditate on the beauty of Mary was, from this perspective, to meditate on the beauty of Wisdom. And to meditate on Wisdom was, like Solomon, to be transformed, for *she glorifieth her nobility by being conversant with God, yea and the Lord of all things loved her, for it is she that teacheth the knowledge of God (doctrix est enim disciplinae Dei) and is the chooser of his works (electrix operum illius)* (Wisdom 8:3–4). *Take hold on her*, the wise man counseled his children, *and she shall exalt thee; thou shalt be glorified by her when thou shalt embrace her. She shall give to thy head increase of graces and protect thee with a noble crown* (Proverbs 4:8–9). Wisdom, as the firstborn of God and the one with him at the creation, was the seal of resemblance in whose likeness humanity had been made (Ezekiel 28:12). To love her was to be restored, like Adam and Eve, to the image and likeness of God, that is, to become fully human, *little less than the angels . . . crowned with glory and honor . . . and set over the work of* [God's] *hands* (Psalm 8:6–7). It was also, according to the argument of the temple tradition, to restore creation itself to what it was before the fall.[171]

BEAUTIFUL FROM HEAD TO TOE

Thou art all beautiful, O my love, Solomon sang to the Lady in the Song of Songs. As her medieval devotees saw her, Mary, like Wisdom, was all beautiful, the mirror of God's beauty and the image of his goodness. In her was reflected the whole of creation, itself a reflection of the beauty and goodness of God. One might as well ask why God made the heavens and earth beautiful as ask why he made Mary beautiful. To remember her beauty, as the sacristan prayed he might be able to do, was to remember the beauty and goodness of God, the glory for which Adam and Eve had been created, and the image and likeness in which they were made. Like Wisdom, Mary was more beautiful than the sun, moon, and all the stars because she was filled with the light of God, her unveiled face shining with the glory of her creator and Lord. More than just a beautiful woman, as her medieval devotees saw her, she was the image of what every human being was created to be, her physical body transformed by the indwelling of God into a body of light. Those still under the sway of Satan might be tempted to see her as an object of lust, like the daughters of Zion in all their false finery or like Babylon, the mother of harlots, *clothed round about with purple and scarlet, and gilt with gold, and precious stones and pearls* (Revelation 17:4),[172] but those who served Mary knew better, because by serving her they learned who she really was. She was like a gemstone irradiated with the light of God, her exterior beauty signifying her spiritual beauty within. To desire her, as the king desired her (Psalm 44:12), was to desire to become like her, for, as the miracle stories showed, she could wound the heart with but one glance of her eye or one hair of her neck (Song of Songs 4:9)—even, it would seem, when those features were but images themselves rendered by human artists in glass, stone, ivory, or paint.

Every one of her members, or so one of Richard's fellow servants of Mary would have it, was a sign of the wisdom and graces beautifying her soul, "for the same Spirit which enkindled her soul with the vehemence of its heat, also fixed the offices of her members in the same condition. Whence nothing resounded in her movements except the nectar of divine and human wisdom, which the essence or harmony of the divine majesty shares in the Trinity of the Father, Son, and Holy Spirit."[173] She was most beautiful not only among the daughters of men, but also among the ranks of the angels, for it was she who clothed the only begotten Son of God with the substance of her flesh; she was so beautiful, indeed, as the apocryphon *de infantia Salvatoris* says, that no one was able to gaze in full upon her face, so perfectly did she reflect the splendor and glory of God. For if the sons of Israel could not look upon the face of Moses when he came down from Mount Sinai after being in company with the word of the Lord (*sermonis Domini*) (Exodus 34:29; 2 Corinthians 3:13), how much more beautiful, Richard asks, do you think that the face of the Mother of the Word (*Verbi*) must have been?[174] Her beauty is figured in the beauty of all of the women whose corporeal beauty is praised in the scriptures: Sarah, Rebecca, Rachel, the three daughters of Job, Naomi, Abishag, Abigail, Bathsheba, Susanna, Judith, Esther, and others. For, indeed, she whose beauty the king desired is a lesson in virtue and in the knowledge of God from the top of her head to the very bottom of her feet, as Richard of Saint-Laurent, with his usual thoroughness, sought to make clear. As above, all citations from scripture are his.

Head

Thy head is like Carmel, Solomon tells her, *and the hairs of thy head as the purple of the king bound in the channels* (Song of Songs 7:5). *Carmel*, Richard explains, may be interpreted "knowledge of the circumcision," and *the purple of the king bound in the channels* signifies recent events. Mary's head, that is, her mind, was prudently circumcised, and her hairs, that is, her thoughts, were dyed with the memory of the blood poured out by her Son at his Passion. Again, her mind is compared with Carmel on account of the eminence of her contemplation and her knowledge of the divine, as well as on account of the fat of the graces from which come the multiple fruits of her good works, for Carmel is a mountain both fat and high.[175]

Hair

That which is said of the hairs of the Son may also be said of the hairs of the Mother: *His locks as branches of palm trees, black as a raven* (Song of Songs 5:11). Her locks, that is, her holy thoughts, stuck to her head, that is, Christ, through love, rising up like the branches of palm trees from earthly to heavenly things in thinking on the salvation of humankind. They were black on account of her humility and the pains suffered by her Son, and like a raven because she seizes the corpses of sinners away from the devil and incorporates them into the Church. Her thoughts are like hair because they are slender with humility, flexible with obedience and compassion, and subtle with the contemplation of the ineffable divinity. They are yellow like gold through her charity; white like silver through her chastity; and black like a raven through her penance or grief. They grew white through wisdom, especially when, after the Ascension of her Son, she conferred with the apostles on the truth and the whole matter of the Gospels; and they glowed redly through compassion in thinking on the Passion of her Son. "We believe," Richard says, "however, that her hairs were actually blond, like saffron [cf. Song of Songs 4:14], as we see in her relics kept at Rouen." Likewise, her thoughts were golden because they had their origin in the golden head of the divinity, thus they are like flocks of goats that come up from Mount Gilead, that is, from contemplation of the secrets of the highest divinity.[176]

Forehead

The smoothness, whiteness, and ruddiness of her forehead signify the modesty of the Virgin: the smoothness her simplicity, the whiteness her cleanliness, and the redness her love.[177]

Eyes

In their beauty and brightness, Mary's eyes are her understanding and affection (*intellectus et affectus*), or the identity of her thoughts and works, or the simplicity and uniformity of her countenance. Whence the bridegroom says to her: *Behold, thou art beautiful, O my love! behold, thou art beautiful! Thy eyes are as those of doves* (Song of Songs 1:14). He twice says she is beautiful because she is beautiful both outwardly and inwardly, in what ought to be seen with the physical eye and in what ought to be loved by the eye of the mind. She is beautiful in her double love for God and neighbor; in the beauty of her understanding (*intellectus*), which is truth, and in her affection (*affectus*), which is goodness; and in her love for everything good and her hatred for everything evil. The bridegroom continues: *Thou hast wounded my heart, my sister, my bride; thou hast wounded my heart with one of thy eyes and with one hair of thy neck* (Song of Songs 4:9). That is, you have wounded my heart with the wound of love in the unity of your understanding and affection and in the unity of your thoughts through the humility of your voice and mind. Again, what is said of his eyes may be said of hers: *His eyes as doves upon brooks of waters which are washed with milk and sit beside the plentiful streams* (Song of Songs 5:12). The Virgin's eyes are like doves in their simplicity and innocence, gazing upon the past, present, and future in the mirror of the Trinity and wary of the shadow of the hawk, that is, the devil. They live beside the streams of scripture in which the Virgin diligently reads, unlike those equestrian monks who do not stay in their cloisters with their books. *Thy eyes*, the bridegroom tells her yet again, *like the fish pools in Heshbon which are in the gate of the daughter of the multitude* (Song of Songs 7:4), that is, restrained by the grief of penitence, just as a fillet binds a wound and restricts the flow of blood. Her eyes, that is, her intellect and affect, are like fish pools because they contain the waters of doctrine and mercy with which she nourishes the little ones by the gate of the city, which no one can enter except through the waters of baptism. Moreover, her eyes, like her Son's, are like a flame of fire (Revelation 1:14) because they illuminate the elect with the light of wisdom, warm them with the love of justice, terrify the reprobate and demons with the fierceness of her threats, and burn up the unpunished with the fire of damnation, as happened with Julian the Apostate.[178]

Cheeks

Her cheeks are beautiful as the turtledove's (Song of Songs 1:9) because she chews the food of the Gospels, that is, keeps their truth, words, and order of events in her heart (Luke 2:51), for the sake of the apostles, evangelists, and all those who came after them. They are like pieces of pomegranate (Song of Songs 4:3) because they are red on account of her natural beauty, virginal modesty, exceptional love, and singular patience, and white on account of her innocence, virginity, immortality, and immunity from sin. What lies within them is known only to God, for only he who gave her such beauty knows its extent. Like her Son's, her cheeks are as beds of aromatical spices planted by the perfumers (Song of Songs 5:13), that is, the seven spirits which are before the throne (Revelation 1:4) and which are planted in the soul, namely, the spirits of wisdom, understanding, counsel, might, knowledge, piety, and fear of the Lord (Isaiah 11:2).[179]

Face

Mary's face shines with the brightness of the eternal light (Wisdom 7:26) because through her is seen the eternal light, that is, the Father and the Son, so that what the psalmist says applies to her: *In thy light we shall see light* (Psalm 35:10), that is, her servants shall see light in the Son who illuminates her, the true light to whom she gave birth. She is white like the lily (Song of Songs 2:2) and the glory of Lebanon (Isaiah 35:2) in her sanctification from original sin, but red like the burning bush (Exodus 3:2), the reddening star (Numbers 24:17), the planted rosebush (Ecclesiasticus 24:18), and the purple ascent of the litter of Solomon (Song of Songs 3:9–10), for like heated iron she was wholly on fire with love because Christ, who is a consuming fire (Deuteronomy 4:24), dwelled within her and colored her. And note, Richard observes, that Christ twice colored his mother, twice discolored her, and twice recolored her. He colored her in her sanctification, turning her from the black of original sin to the white of immunity, and at his conception through the infusion of an even fuller grace, conserving the whiteness of her virginity and making her red with modesty and love. He discolored her in human opinion, for when she was seen to be with child, she was thought to have been corrupted by adultery, whence she says: *I am black, but beautiful* (Song of Songs 1:4). He discolored her again at his Passion with the blackness of grief, whence she says: *I am dark because the sun has discolored me* (Song of Songs 1:5), that is, my Son suffering eclipse and death. He recolored her at his Resurrection, when the sun rose again, because rising it returns everything to its proper color, even as she rejoiced at her Son's rising again. He recolored her again through the preaching of the apostles, for through their preaching the whole world learned that Christ had been born of the Virgin Mary, for indeed, "*their sound hath gone forth into all the earth*, saying of Christ, *he hath set his tabernacle in the sun*, that is, in her flesh, which he assumed from her" (Psalm 18:5–6). She was also recolored in her Assumption, when she was crowned with glory and honor and colored with the glory of immortality, whence it is sung: *Who is she who comes forth as the rising dawn?* (Song of Songs 6:9).[180]

Ears

Like her eyes, Mary's ears are two, namely her intellect and affect, for truly he has ears to hear who has the sense for retaining and understanding and the affect for loving and deserving those things which are promised him, just as Mary did. He who lacks ears, however, has no care for the heavenly goods promised to him. Therefore, it is written: *He that hath an ear, let him hear what the Spirit saith to the churches* (Revelation 2:7), the Spirit here designating not the person of the Holy Spirit, but the holy and undivided Trinity, which is believed to be one deity and worshipped as one God.[181]

Nose

Mary's nose is like a tower of Lebanon looking toward Damascus (Song of Songs 7:4) because her discretion is always set against the snares of the devil. It is like a tower of Lebanon because in the whiteness of her virginity she treads on the head of the serpent, that is, lust, and because she is founded on the rock, that is, Christ, upon whom she leans (Song of Songs 8:5). The nose is the path of the breath; so, likewise, Mary is the way by which the Holy Spirit comes to her servants for their justification and consolation. Just as the nose serves for the respiration of the soul, that is, the life of the flesh, so Mary serves for the respiration of her servants' life with spiritual hope, whence she says: *In me is all hope of life and virtue* (Ecclesiasticus 24:25). And this is clear with Theophilus and many others, who unless they had hope in her mercy, would have despaired of the mercy of God.[182]

Lips

Again, her lips are her intellect and affect, from which proceed her interior discourse, that is, her thought and desire. They are like a scarlet band (*vitta coccinea*) (Song of Songs 4:3) because they are red with the memory of the Lord's Passion and never allowed to stray far from Christ. Literally, the lips with which she formed her sweet words are called "scarlet" because she was inflamed with love of God and neighbor; these are the same lips with which she makes sweet prayers for her servants in the presence of her Son. Another translation reads: *Your lips are like a scarlet cord* (*funis coccineus*) because in her sweet speech, the preaching of the Trinity is commingled like a triple cord with the scarlet of the Passion.[183]

Mouth

Thy lips, the Son says to his Mother, *are as a dropping honeycomb; milk and honey are under thy tongue* (Song of Songs 4:11). Her servants may well believe, Richard asserts, that the Virgin Mother often kissed her beloved Son and that he returned her kisses, just as she asked: *Let him kiss me with the kiss of his mouth* (Song of

Songs 1:1), especially when he was little and seated on her lap. Therefore, the Son commends his mother for the sweetness of her lips both literally and mystically. Honey and milk, that is, sweetness of every kind is under her tongue, the honey of the wisdom which is given through her to those who are greater, the milk of simple doctrine for those who are little. Likewise, the Son says to his Mother: *The odor of thy mouth like apples* (Song of Songs 7:8), because her prayers (*orationes et preces*) are wholly aromatic, like balsam and cinnamon (Ecclesiasticus 24:20) or like the bowls of incense that are the prayers of the saints (Revelation 5:8). The Son commends the Mother for the fragrance of her prayers because they attract human beings to the worship of the Son, just as the fragrance of apples attracts the hungry to eat.[184]

Throat

Mary's throat, that is, the prayers that proceed from her throat, is like the best wine (Song of Songs 7:9), because those prayers comfort and ease the sorrows of the afflicted. Her prayers are spiced with devotion and stimulate even the lazy to run, love, and pray. For if the words of the wise are goads (Ecclesiastes 12:11), what might her servants think of the words of the Mother of Wisdom? Her prayers pierce even the heart of her Son, whence he says: *Thou hast wounded my heart, my sister, my bride* (Song of Songs 4:9). Her words inebriate the Son and make him forgetful of her servants' sins. Likewise, her words are full of instruction (*doctrina*), delighting the devout and taking them away from the cares of the world. They are like the best wine, however, in that they contain no dregs, nothing evil or foul, but only those things that are worthy for her Son to drink and for his lips and teeth to ruminate.[185]

Neck

Mary is called the neck of the Church because in her womb the human race was joined to Christ, its head, so that in their human nature Christians might be one with God. Just as human words are formed through the mediation of the neck, so Mary is her servants' advocate before her Son, as Bernard prays to her: "Our Lady, our *mediatrix*, our advocate, reconcile us to your Son, commend us to your Son, represent us to your Son." Likewise, just as whatever is necessary to the life of the body—food, drink, medicines, and the like—descends through the neck, so through her mediation Christ, the medicine of Christian souls, whose body and blood is truly food and drink, comes to them. Her neck is beautiful as jewels (Song of Songs 1:9) because her words are fortified with discretion. Likewise, her neck is like a tower of David (Song of Songs 4:4) because she is humble like David, and like a tower of ivory (Song of Songs 7:4) in defense of her innocence and continence.[186]

Shoulders

(Here, as with the other body parts, Richard explains how to read the shoulders *moraliter* with reference to the faithful soul: the right shoulder is piety, the left compassion. He does not, however, give a specific interpretation of Mary's shoulders, perhaps because there is no description of the bride's shoulders in the Song of Songs.)[187]

Arms

(Again, as with the shoulders, Richard seems to have felt the need to describe the arms, but he gives only an indirect account of Mary's arms, suggesting simply that it was either she or the faithful soul who says in the Song of Songs: "*When I had a little passed by them*, here speaking of the watchmen, that is, the angels, *I passed by them*, namely, through contemplating higher things, *I found him whom my soul loveth.* . . . *I held him*, as if by the two arms of twin charity [love of God and love of neighbor] . . . and with the two hands of good works for the honor of God and as an example to neighbor" [Song of Songs 3:4].)[188]

Hands

My hands dropped with myrrh, Mary says, *and my fingers were full of the choicest myrrh* (Song of Songs 5:5). Her hands, that is, her works, and her fingers, that is, the discernment of her works, dripped with myrrh because she was wholly absorbed in spiritual grace so that nothing in her remained of carnal concupiscence. Moreover, what the bride says of the bridegroom may be said of her: *His hands are turned and as of gold, full of hyacinths* (Song of Songs 5:14), that is, her works, like Christ's, were and are wholly circumcised, never deviating from the rule of justice; they were and are golden on account of being worked in wisdom and love, and full of hyacinths because whatever they did or do proceeded wholly and always proceeds from the font of wisdom, shining with heavenly intention. Just as the Father does every work, so every work refers to him and in him through the action of grace, whence the Son says: *The Father who abideth in me, he doth the works* (John 14:10). Like her Son who extended his hands on the cross, Mary opens her hands and extends them to the poor, unlike Eve, who closed her hand over the forbidden fruit.[189]

Breasts

How beautiful are thy breasts, my sister, my bride! Thy breasts (ubera), the Son says, *are more beautiful than wine* (Song of Songs 4:10). He says *ubera* rather than *mammae* or *mammillae* because, while his mother, she is yet virgin; her breasts are full of piety and mercy, better than the wine of the punishing law. Again, the Son says: *I said: "I will go up into the palm tree and will take hold of the fruit thereof, and thy breasts shall be as the clusters of the vine"* (Song of Songs 7:8), as if to say: "I said to my mother that *I will go up into the palm tree*, that is, I will be exalted on the cross, *and will take hold of its fruit*, that is, the benefits arising from my crucifixion . . . for its fruit is for the salvation of all, of which the last part will be the Jews, of whom a remainder shall be saved." Further, concerning the breasts of the Virgin, the companions of Christ, that is, the prophets, say: *Our sister is little and hath no breasts* (Song of Songs 8:8), that is, little in her humility and pure like a tender young heifer, who does not yet have udders (*ubera*). *What shall we do*, Christ asks, *to our sister in the day when she is to be spoken to?* (Song of Songs 8:8), that is, when the archangel Gabriel shall speak to her. The Trinity replies: *If she be a wall, let us build upon it bulwarks of silver; if she be a door, let us join it together with boards or cedar* (Song of Songs 8:9), for she is a wall for Christians' defense and on her the whole Trinity built bulwarks of silver for the defense of the Church, that she might repel enemies with her prayers. She is a door for the Church blocking the way against evil spirits lest they enter into the devout and approach just as they will.[190]

Back

(The backs of Christ, Mary, and the saints are their patience, upright, without any swellings or humps. Sinners, namely, Jews, pagans, heretics, blasphemers, and persecutors of the saints continually put things on their backs and prolong their iniquities, but those who suffer patiently have straight backs. As with the arms and shoulders, there is no description of the bride's or bridegroom's back in the Song of Songs.)[191]

Belly

Mary's belly is *as a heap of wheat, surrounded with lilies* (Song of Songs 7:2), fertile in her virginity, filled with the Son of God who called himself a grain of wheat (John 12:24), and walled round with virtues. Just as she says of the Son, so he says of her: *His belly as of ivory set with sapphires* (Song of Songs 5:14), for their bellies are not like other bellies, like that on which the devil creeps (Genesis 3:14), but just as with ivory is born its whiteness, so with the flesh of Christ and Mary is born the whiteness of virginity, from which greenery is born. Their bellies are picked out with sapphires, that is, conformed to the nature of the angels, for virginity is the sister of the angels, as Thomas the apostle says. Another translation reads: *His belly like an ivory pyx on a sapphire stone*, for in this pyx the Father transmitted to humanity that medicinal ointment, namely the body of Christ, whose odor fills the Church of the faithful and by which the human race is healed.[192]

Navel

The bridegroom says to her: *Thy navel is like a round bowl never wanting cups* (Song of Songs 7:2). The navel, Richard explains, signifies the weakness of carnal concupiscence, whence in Job, the force of Behemoth is said to be in his navel (Job 40:11). But Mary's navel was dried and hardened like seasoned wood, so that like a turned bowl she was free from all temptation both inside and out. This bowl never lacked cups, whether of milk or wine, for when her Son said: *I thirst* (John 19:28), he was given to drink the milk of virginal whiteness mixed with the wine of the mortification of his own flesh.[193]

Legs

The joints of her thighs are *like jewels (monilia) that are made by the hand of a skillful workman* (Song of Songs 7:1) because she is not only chaste and modest, but also a guardian and guide (*monitoria*) for others' chastity, for the Holy Spirit who crafted her extinguished in her the tinder of carnal concupiscence with the dew of celestial grace. Again, what is said of the bridegroom may be said of her: *His legs as pillars of marble that are set upon bases of gold* (Song of Songs 5:15), that is, as temperance in prosperity and patience in adversity, which two columns support and sustain the whole edifice of her virtues.[194]

Feet

The feet signify the affections (*affectus*) because it is with the affections that the mind moves toward itself and toward God and away from itself and from God. The right foot is the desire to please God, the left is the eagerness to be useful to one's brothers, and these two feet carry the soul to heaven. The Mother's feet, that is, her affections, are like fine brass (*aurichalco*) (Revelation 1:15), just like the Son's. For Christ was golden in his patience, never crying out at his flagellation, just as gold makes no sound when it is struck, but he was like bronze in the clear sound of his preaching, as in a burning furnace, because all that he did, he did in the heat of love.[195]

Stature

Thy stature is like to a palm tree, the Son says to his Mother (Song of Songs 7:7), that is, the uprightness of your good intention and the discretion of your holy activity is like to the palm tree, that is, the triumphal tree of the cross, terrible to the evil spirits just as by merit of your uprightness you terrify and drive away evil spirits, too. For indeed, when all the apostles wavered in their faith at the time of the Lord's Passion, his mother stood beside his cross (John 19:25), immovable in her faith. Moreover, just as the sign of the cross is a special armor against the devil, so likewise is the invocation of the name of the blessed Virgin, Mary. *How beautiful*, the Son continues, *are thy steps in shoes, O prince's daughter!* (Song of Songs 7:1), for, he says, *I shod thee with violet coloured shoes* (Ezekiel 16:10), so that her feet, that is, all her thoughts and works would be resplendent with the beauty of spiritual devotion and intention.[196]

Mary as Temple

In the temple tradition, as we have seen, the great desire of the people was to gaze upon the face of the Lord: *My heart hath said to thee, "My face hath sought thee." Thy face, O Lord, will I still seek* (Psalm 26:8).[197] But, the prophets warned, this vision might be lost. *Go*, the voice of the Lord said to the prophet Isaiah, *and thou shalt say to this people: "Hearing, hear, and understand not: and see the vision, and know it not"* (Isaiah 6:9). For the early Christians, the desire—and the anxiety—was the same. *"Dost thou believe in the Son of God?"* Jesus asked the blind man whom he had healed. *"Who is he, Lord, that I may believe in him?,"* the man asked. Jesus said to him: *"Thou hast both seen him; and it is he that talketh with thee."* The man said: *"I believe, Lord,"* and worshipped him. And Jesus said: *"For judgment I am come into this world; that they who see not, may see; and they who see, may become blind"* (John 9:35–39). *No man,* the evangelist John insisted, *hath seen God at any time.* But, he averred, *the Word was made flesh, and dwelt among us, (and we saw his glory, the glory as it were of the only begotten of the Father,) full of grace and truth* (John 1:18, 14).[198] Mary, as the ancient and medieval Christians believed, was the one through whom the Word became flesh, the one through whom Jesus, the Son of the Most High, the Wisdom of God made himself *seen.*

PLATE 23 Mary holds the Lord in her bosom. On the base, she reclines after having given birth, with the Child in the manger and Joseph at her feet. Opening Madonna triptych, France, possibly Sens, ca. 1180–1220. Closed. Baltimore, The Walters Art Museum, Accession number 71.152.

As King Alfonso put it: "[Holy Mary] made us see God, for in no other way could we have seen Him." She "*has the power to bring light to those without it. For She who bore within Her the One who is light has great power to bestow it.*"[199] Again, the king sang:

Glorious Virgin Mother, Daughter and Bride of God, holy, noble, precious, who could know how or be able to praise you?

For God is Light and Day, but because of our base nature we could not see His face except through you, who were the Dawn. . . .

You are the Dawn of the guilty who were blinded by their sins, but they are illumined by you, Holy Mary. . . .

You are the Dawn through which the Sun, Who is Christ, was revealed. . . . God from on high chose to be born of you, His creation, and made you the Dawn. You are Dawn of those who believe and Light of those who do not see God and hold the good as evil because of their benighted heresy which is insane affront, and God cares not for these fools. But through your wisdom, you give them a light like dawn.[200]

Accordingly, the king explained in yet another song, when the angel Gabriel came to her and said, "full of grace," "he caused us to know God, Whom we could not see before. However, later we saw Him clearly."[201] In Caesarius of Heisterbach's words:

Nor ought it to be a matter of wonder . . . that sinners are enlightened by her, for *according to His name, so is His praise unto the world's end* (cf. Psalm 47:11). For the name "Mary" is interpreted "star of the sea" or "light-giver" (*illuminatrix*).[202]

As William of Malmesbury, paraphrasing Anselm of Canterbury, explained in the prologue to his miracle collection, Mary, the Mother of the Lord,

built a temple to the Lord God in her own body. . . . No one had more *understanding* than her, for so clear was her mind, and so aware was she of God, that she fully understood all the good for the present that was involved in the birth, Passion, and Resurrection of the Lord, and the incomparable fruit that would follow in the future. . . . Into this young woman, decked like this with a diadem of virtues, the Son of God poured all of Himself. . . . Finding a young woman possessed of wisdom, the wisdom of God preserved her in that state, that is, kept her safe and pure in heart and body. For it is written: *Wisdom will not enter into a malicious soul, nor dwell in a body subject to sin* (Wisdom 1:40). . . . So, just as God is the Father and Creator of everything, so this virgin is mother and re-creator of everything, because just as nothing exists except what God made, so nothing is re-created except what the son of Holy Mary redeems. Let therefore the faithful soul ascend to the lookout place of the mind, and see, so far as it can, how lofty is Lady Mary's position. All nature was made by God, and God was made from Mary. God, maker of everything, made Himself from Mary, and so re-made everything. . . . God begat (*genuit*) Him through whom everything was made, and Mary bore (*genuit*) Him through whom everything was re-made and saved.[203]

As Anselm himself put it in the greatest of his three prayers to Mary:

O Lady . . . you showed to the world its Lord and its God whom it had not known. You showed to the sight of all the world its Creator whom it had not seen. . . . The world was wrapped in darkness, surrounded and oppressed by demons under which it lay, but from you alone light was born into it, which broke its bonds and trampled underfoot their power.[204]

It was for this reason, according to William, that he had compiled his collection for her. It was through her, "the temple of the Holy Spirit," that he hoped to see God. As he prayed at the conclusion to his collection,

Mary, temple of the Holy Spirit, shade me from the seething heat of vice. Mary, perpetual virgin, cleanse me from the stain and corruption of sin . . . Mary, ladder of God, make me ascend from virtue to virtue, so that as by degrees I grow towards the good I may deserve to come to the highest peak of perfection. . . . Mary, queen of the angels, make me lie hidden at least in the furthest corner of the kingdom of heaven, so that I may see *the God of gods in Sion* (cf. Psalm 83:8).[205]

Mary, as her medieval devotees put it, was the one who had made the Lord visible to the world; it was she who, by giving birth to the Son, made it possible for artists to make images of him as a baby and man. This, arguably, is the reason that French, Flemish, and English Books of Hours contained the cycles of images for which they are famous: not, as has so often been suggested, because the psalms and other texts of the Marian Office were meant somehow to recall episodes in Jesus's or Mary's earthly lives, as if the Office were a retelling of the Gospels like the Franciscan *Meditationes vitae Christi*; but rather because the images, like Mary herself, made the Lord visible in his human form, while the texts praised him as the invisible God known only through his works. Visibly, the Lord lived and died in time in the historical person of Jesus of Nazareth, but invisibly, he reigned in eternity, as the angels and elders sang before his throne. To pray the psalms according to the Hours of the Virgin was to participate bodily and spiritually in this mystery, much as Christ himself had entered into time in order to open eternity to those who worshipped him as Lord. Just as the Marian antiphons framed the psalms, so the illuminations framed the texts, making the Lord praised in the psalms visible to the eye and the mind, without, however, being illustrations of the texts as such. To put it in terms of the temple tradition, the visual images were of time and the earth while the texts were of eternity and heaven. Just as Mary made the Lord visible to the world at his Incarnation, so the images made the story of his earthly life visible to the reader, while the texts that he or she sang and prayed lifted his or her mind and heart to the Lord's eternal presence in heaven. The homelier and more "realistic" or human the visual images (as has often been noted of those typical of many fourteenth- and fifteenth-century Books of Hours), the greater the mystery of how the heavenly Lord praised in the psalms became man, that is, visible on earth.

Who was this Lord whom Mary made it possible to see? According to the psalms that medieval Christians sang nightly in her praise, the Lord her Son was *a great God and a great king above all gods* in whose hands were *all the ends of the earth . . . for the sea is his, and he made it, and his hands formed the dry land* (Psalm 94:3–5). His name was admirable over the whole earth, and his greatness was exalted above the heavens, for he made man and set him over all the works of his hands (Psalm 8:2, 5–7). He made a tabernacle for himself in the sun and as a bridegroom came forth from it like a giant, making a circuit of the heavens in his heat; his judgments were true, more desirable than gold and many precious stones, and there was great reward for his servant in keeping his commandments (Psalm 18:6, 10–12). All the earth belonged to him, for he founded it upon the seas and prepared it upon the rivers, and his holy place was upon the mountain, whose eternal gates he entered as the King of glory, strong and mighty, the Lord of hosts, mighty in battle (Psalm 23:1–3, 8–10). He was beautiful above all the sons of men, and grace poured from his lips; he had a sword girded upon his thigh, and his arrows were sharp. He was beautiful and comely, reigning in truth, mercy, and justice. His throne was eternal and his scepter upright, for he loved justice and hated iniquity; therefore, God had anointed him with the oil of gladness and his garments were perfumed with myrrh, stacte, and cassia from the ivory houses of the daughters of the king. His Mother, the Queen, stood at his right hand to welcome his bride on his wedding day (Psalm 44:3–10). He was a refuge and strength against earthquakes and floods, and he dwelled in the midst of the city in the tabernacle that he had sanctified; when he spoke, the earth trembled, for he was the Lord of armies, *making wars to cease even to the end of the earth* (Psalm 45:2–10). He spoke in his writings of the peoples and princes who lived in the city that he founded, where all who dwelled rejoiced (Psalm 86:6–7). He was to be feared above all gods, for all the gods of the peoples (*gentium*) were devils (*daemonia*), but he made the heavens. He has corrected the earth *which shall not be moved*, and he will come to *judge the world with justice and the people with his truth* (Psalm 95:4–5, 10, 13). Clouds and darkness were round about him as he sat upon his throne; fire went before him to burn his enemies, and the earth trembled at the lightning that went out from his throne. Mountains melted at his presence, and all peoples beheld his glory as the angels adored him (Psalm 96:1–7). His arm was holy, and his right hand wrought salvation, and he revealed his justice to all the earth. At his coming, all the rivers will clap their hands and the mountains rejoice, for *he shall judge the world with justice and the people with equity* (Psalm 97:1–3, 8–9).

"Oh, oh, oh," the visionary beguine Mechthild of Magdeburg (d. ca. 1282/1294) exclaimed as she beheld the Lady (*göttinne*, or "goddess") in her power:

> Three Persons have one name undivided in one God. Gracefully they flow full force toward Mary's countenance, inseparable in one light beam, rightly bestowing the bright light of heavenly honors. With an indescribable greeting it touches her heart, which shines and glows in such a way that the sublime reflection of the Holy Trinity lingers on her countenance. . . . How our Lady feels bliss in the Holy Trinity and how God unites himself to her beyond how he does with all pure persons cannot be expressed in words. But to the degree they were united here on earth, our Lady feels bliss in heaven, and, in like measure, our Lord pours into her, beyond what he does with all the other saints. Our Lady has power over all the devils to keep them away from people. And this is why we like to proclaim our *Ave Maria* in her splendorous presence: so that she might remember us here.[206]

Mary taught medieval Christians to understand Jesus as Lord and God as Trinity, moving them to compose songs and hymns in her praise as the Mother of God. As King Alfonso put it in yet another song (his collection includes more than four hundred), a certain archdeacon of Paris (perhaps the great twelfth-century composer Adam of Saint Victor himself) had been working on a hymn in praise of Mary "which was very well done except for a single rhyme which he still lacked." Stymied, the archdeacon despaired of finding any earthly help, and so went to an altar of the Virgin to beg her to come to his aid and finish the hymn. As King Alfonso explains: "[The hymn] was well composed and praised Her and God and told how disbelievers might understand the Trinity," but the archdeacon could not complete the rhyme. Happily, however,

> while he was praying, he felt in his heart the rhyme he lacked, which was in Latin and said: "Nobile triclinium." There was no phrase which would fit better than this rhyme I quote, which means: noble dwelling, there are three chambers in you: God the Father and His Son and the Holy Spirit came to dwell therein to show us love.

When he had thus finished the hymn, the archdeacon began weeping for joy, at which the statue of the Virgin on the altar leaned down to him, and said: "Many thanks, my lord."[207]

Just as the Lady made the Lord visible on his throne in the temple, so Mary made her Son—and, therefore, his relationship to the Father and Spirit—visible when she bore him in her womb. If, as her medieval poets so often complained, Mary was beyond description, it was not because as a woman, even a virgin woman, she had given birth to a man, even a perfect man, but because as a creature she had given birth to her Creator and Lord. Moreover, she herself was not just any creature, but the most perfect creature the Lord had made, with him from the beginning of his work (Proverbs 8:22–23), herself the most perfect image of him as Creator, reflecting in her beauty his majesty and goodness (Wisdom 7:26), with him forming all things and delighting him every day (Proverbs 8:30–31). How else could she, a mere creature, have contained him who made heaven and earth without herself being a heaven, the Holy of Holies where God set his tabernacle in which to dwell?

THE LORD ENTERS INTO HIS CREATION

Fully to recover the medieval Christian tradition of devotion and prayer that we have been studying would require not only a fuller study of the variants and texts of the Marian Office, but also, if even more dauntingly, a fuller study of the Divine Office, particularly its use of the psalms, as well as a fuller study of the exegetical and devotional tradition dependent upon and supporting the liturgy. In short, it would require us to rethink the whole of the medieval devotion to Mary and Christ, not to mention its basis in scripture.[208] Once again, however, Richard of Saint-Laurent's *De laudibus beatae Mariae virginis* provides us with at least a preliminary way in. If, as we have seen, for Richard, everything in scripture could be read as pointing to Mary, it was only because everything in scripture pointed to God, whose most perfect reflection and revelation she was. Mary was

PLATE 24 In her head or mind, Mary contemplates the Lord enthroned in heaven; in her body, she holds the history of the Incarnation. Reading top to bottom, left to right: trial before Herod, carrying the cross, scourging, Crucifixion surmounted by the Lamb, anointing of the body, Resurrection, women at the empty tomb, the resurrected Lord in the garden with Mary Magdalene. The four evangelists appear in the quarter circles below, left to right: Mark, Matthew, John, Luke. Opening Madonna triptych, France, possibly Sens, ca. 1180–1220. Open, showing scenes of the Passion. Baltimore, The Walters Art Museum, Accession number 71.152.

heaven, sun, moon, dawn, cloud, earth, mountain, fountain, river, ark, throne, tabernacle, bedchamber, house, temple, city of God, tower, ship, garden, flower, and tree because God made her all of these things in order to dwell in her. If, for Richard, as Sarah Jane Boss has put it speaking of this tradition more generally, Mary "is present in all physical things as their foundation," it is because Mary is the one in whom God is present and he is the one whom she shows to the world as Creator of all physical things.[209] From this perspective, to speak of Mary is to speak of God; to describe Mary is to describe God. Indeed, to describe her is the only way to describe God at all, for it is she who, by making him visible, made him possible to describe in human terms. Moreover, she is the one through whom he pours out his love on the world, taking from her body the flesh that he offered as priest on the altar of the cross, "for the flesh of Christ and the flesh of Mary is one as the flesh of mother and son."[210] Through Mary, as Richard puts it, Christians eat the "bread of angels" in the sacrament of the altar because it is from her body that the Son of God took the true food and drink with which he heals humankind.[211]

One with him in the flesh, Mary served the Son of God in all her parts, supporting him with her feet, sustaining him with her legs, carrying him in her belly, nursing him with her breasts, caring for him with her hands, embracing him with her arms, smiling upon him with her lips, kissing him with her mouth, speaking to him with her tongue, smelling him with her nose, listening to him with her ears, seeing him with her eyes, and adoring him with her head[212]—in every way, in other words, revealing him in his humanity even as she worshipped him as God. Above all, however, she served him with her heart, suffering with him through her compassion as he suffered on the cross, so that, as the second Adam, he would not be alone (Genesis 2:18) in saving the human race and condemning the devil.[213] Accordingly, although she gave birth to him at his Nativity without pain, she suffered all the pains of childbirth in her heart when she saw him hanging on the cross, even as she suffered at his Nativity when the devil stood before her wishing through Herod to kill her Son.[214]

Mary suffered as much as she did because she loved God with all her heart, all her soul, and all her mind, delighting in nothing in the world more than God, believing firmly in him, particularly at his Passion, occupying all her senses with God, serving God in her understanding, turning to him in her wisdom, thinking on him in her thoughts, and recalling him in her memory, as the Apostle Paul said (1 Corinthians 14:15): *I will sing with the spirit, I will sing also with the mind*.[215] Mary loved wisely because she was full with the anointing by which she had been taught everything (1 John 2:27); she loved sweetly in her recollection of the mercy by which God sanctified her of original sin, the grace by which he filled her with all virtues and every good work, and the glory which she hoped to receive *supra meritum*; she loved strongly, with all her strength loving him who made her and fearing nothing but him (Ecclesiasticus 7:32); and she loved mindfully, keeping him always in her memory (Ecclesiasticus 37:6), like a bundle of myrrh between her breasts (Song of Songs 1:12).[216] Thus she provides a model of love for other faithful souls, for she was inseparable from God in her love, like a bride for her bridegroom, like a lover for her beloved, like a mother for her only Son. *I held him*, she says in the Song of Songs (3:4), *and I will not let him go*. Her love was insatiable like a fire (Proverbs 30:16), singular, swift, unceasing, fervent, sharp, upright, eager, intimate, ample, affectionate, and tender, for she was the habitation not only of her Son, but of the whole Trinity, and so all three rejoiced in her (Psalm 86:7).[217]

Just as she loved God perfectly as Trinity, so Mary loved her Son perfectly as both God and man. She loved him naturally as his Mother, more, indeed, than any other mother loved her son, because while other sons take their matter from both parents, Christ took all the matter of his flesh from her. She loved him carnally "in the good sense" with all her heart, cherishing and nourishing him out of love for her own flesh. She loved him spiritually with her whole soul because *God is spirit* (John 4:24) and she was one spirit with him (1 Corinthians 6:17). She loved him manfully (*viriliter*) with all her strength, for which reason she is signified by Eve, the *virago* taken out of a man (*vir*), because a man was taken out of her. And she loved bountifully, serving the Son so that he might become a servant to all (Wisdom 9:5), bearing him in her womb, wrapping him in swaddling clothes and laying him in a manger, presenting him in the temple, and standing beside his cross, for, like the Father (John 3:16), Mary so loved the world, that is, sinners, that she gave her only begotten Son for the salvation of the world: "Therefore also it is said in Isaiah 9:6: *A son is given to us*, namely, by the Father, by the mother, by himself, and by the Holy Spirit."[218] Serving her Son, Mary fulfilled all seven works of corporal mercy (Matthew 25:35–36): he was hungry, and she fed him with her milk; he was thirsty, and she gave him her milk to drink; he was a stranger, and she took him into the tabernacle of her virginal womb, and not only the Son, but indeed the whole Trinity, for whom she was a *nobile triclinium*; he was naked, and she covered him with a tunic of her virginal flesh, wrapped him in swaddling clothes as a covering, and laid him in a manger; he was sick, taking on the weaknesses of human nature, and she cared for him as a baby even as she stood beside him as he was wounded for the salvation of his people on the cross; he was imprisoned in the prison of human mortality, being born true man from a true virgin, and she came to him when he was lying in the manger and again when he lay in his tomb.[219]

Over and over again in the Song of Songs Mary is called "bride" (*sponsa*), "beloved" (*dilecta*), and "friend" (*amica*), for Christ was desirous of her as for Jerusalem and Zion (Zechariah 1:14), even as Ahasuerus loved Esther above all other women (Esther 2:17) and the Lord of all things loved Wisdom (Wisdom 8:3). Mary, for her part, served the Lord not out of fear, but love, wishing no other benefit from her loving than the beloved himself. Whence she says in the Song of Songs (2:16): "*My beloved is mine*, as if to say: He alone suffices for me, I seek no other." She is his friend because she was privy to his secrets, especially the mystery of the Incarnation and redemption; because she conformed her will to his in everything, especially when he wished to assume flesh from her; because she fulfilled all his commandments, as he said his friends would (John 15:14); because she was his most faithful helper in the redemption of the world, covering him with the tunic of her virginal flesh which he offered on the cross as a sacrifice to God the Father for the salvation of all; because she never deserted him nor was deserted by him in good times or bad, and because she was proved in distress (Proverbs 17:17); and because she honored him, attributing to him every good thing that she received (Luke 1:49), and he honored her, exalting her above all the choirs of the angels and seating her in glory at his right hand.[220] And she is his bride, for whom he sent from on high (Psalm 17:17), calling to her: *Come from Lebanon, my bride* (Song of Songs 4:8). As the Church sings, she "alone without example" was pleasing to the Lord, that is Christ, who "elected and pre-elected her" to be his bride, adorned her with the gifts of the Holy Spirit, and purified her of original sin. She was joined in marriage to Christ (*conjuncta Christo per verba de praesenti*) at his conception, when she answered the angel: *Be it done to me according to thy word* (Luke 1:38). And she was introduced into the bedchamber of her bridegroom at her Assumption. Just as she gave him from her flesh the flesh in which he suffered, so he gave her as a dowry the twofold gift of grace and glory (Psalm 83:12), cleaving to her as Adam cleaved to Eve (Genesis 2:24), so that they might be *two in one flesh*, Mother and Son, Virgin and Christ. Whence, once again, she says in the Song of Songs (6:2): "*I am my beloved's*, without a [human] father singular and alone, *and my beloved is mine*, singularly and alone [my] son."[221]

But, we might still ask, who was this God of whom the Virgin Mary was beloved, mother, and bride? As Richard and his contemporaries would have it, the question was a tautology. Simply to ask it was to answer it as fully as it could be answered or understood: God was the one of whom the Virgin Mary was lover, mother, and bride. She, as Wisdom, was the one who made him visible to the world as Creator and Lord; she was the one without whom he could not be known, for it was she who had been with him at the beginning of his work

(Proverbs 8:22–23) and who stood by him as it was finished (John 19:26–30). Everything known about God had been made known to the world through her; she was the one who revealed to the world who God is. Insofar as he showed himself to the world through her, God was the one who dwelled in her, his ark, temple, and city; he was the Lord seated above the cherubim on her as his throne. Nevertheless, as her Son, he had further characteristics that Richard averred might be seen through his relationship with her, some of which, to put it mildly, were perhaps more unexpected than others, but all of which, according to Richard, might be discovered in scripture. As above, so below, all citations from scripture are Richard's.

Merchant

As we have already seen in chapter 4, Christ, the Wisdom of the Father, was the captain (*gnavus rector*) and pilot (*gubernator*) of Mary as ship.[222] He was also, somewhat surprisingly, given the purported animosity of medieval theology to commerce, the merchant or entrepreneur (*institor*) for whom that ship was made, "who came through her from heaven into the world to do business, sell, and buy." "Behold," Richard exclaims, "the coin with which he does business (*Ecce moneta de qua negotiatus est*)." Christ is the merchant because he travels hastily day and night to market, just like the merchant (*mercator*) of whom the poet Horace speaks:

> The ready merchant runs to the utmost Indies with speed
> By sea, by rocks, by fire, to shun outrageous need.

He carries his money (*pecuniam*) and the wares (*merces*) of his fatherland with him, and he returns with wares from foreign parts. He offers the wares of his fatherland for sale and persuades men to buy them, whence he says to the angel (*episcopo*) of the church of Laodicea: *I counsel thee to buy of me gold fire tried, that thou mayest be made rich; and mayest be clothed in white garments, and that the shame of thy nakedness may not appear; and anoint thy eyes with eyesalve, that thou mayest see* (Revelation 3:18). "Behold," Richard invites his readers, "the three things sold by Christ: gold against poverty, white clothing against nakedness, and salve for the eyes against blindness."[223]

As merchant, Christ also buys wares from foreign parts, for he buys human souls with the price of his blood (1 Corinthians 6:20) and buys back with that same price those wares foolishly pawned (1 Peter 1:18–19). He is a true merchant, who fashions his own creature, and with his own blood buys and buys back that creature so that that creature may be blessed and free. Therefore, a man ought to say to the devil who tempts him: "I am already purchased, I am not for sale to another." Many, however, have withdrawn themselves from the possession of the Lord and given themselves to the devil, for which they must pay the sevenfold penalty of their sin (Ecclesiasticus 7:3). Christ loves the wares which he buys more than the price that he pays for them and would rather be defrauded in the price that he pays than in the wares which has purchased. He does business as long as the market is open, at whose closing he settles his accounts, for in the present he offers to human beings the price of his Passion and the example of his life to imitate, so that he might make their bodies and souls his own, which transaction he will complete at the judgment. He also exchanges wares for wares, for he took on human nature when the Word was made flesh, and he bestowed upon human beings his divinity; likewise, he was lifted up to heaven in human flesh so that he might make all human beings sharers in his divinity, whence the Church sings, "O marvelous exchange!"[224]

In the meantime, he has under him other merchants (*mercatores*) to whom he entrusts his money to do his business until he comes (Luke 19:13), most notably, the apostles and preachers, and with whom he reckons his accounts (Matthew 25:19). He rejoices when they make money for him (Matthew 25:21, 23), but grieves when they do not and punishes them severely (Matthew 25:30). He is called an entrepreneur (*institor*) because he made everything that exists (Ecclesiasticus 18:1) and because he is earnest in acquiring valuable wares; thus he spent his whole life praying, preaching, casting out demons, and healing the sick so as to acquire these precious wares, that is, souls. He is not only a merchant (*mercator*), but an admirable entrepreneur (*admirabilis institor*) because he gave his creatures his wares, that is, his divinity, and accepted theirs, that is, their humanity, in return. And he is admirable because he sold to those who could not pay (Isaiah 55:1), so that they might acquire wisdom and grace through faith and works.[225]

Flower

Again, as we have already seen in chapter 4, Christ is the flower of the garden, the lily of the valleys and the flower of the field (Song of Songs 2:1).[226] As flower he is *pure* because he is immune from sin (Psalm 25:11); *fragrant* with the odor of good and holy repute (Luke 4:14–15; Song of Songs 1:3); *slight* in his substance, spirit, and soul in his humility (Philippians 2:7) and in his flesh in which he did penance for humanity on the cross (Psalm 21:18); *tender* when he was wounded for sinners' iniquities (Isaiah 53:5) and on account of his love, his jealousy (Exodus 20:5), his pity and compassion (Luke 19:41); *beautiful* in the integrity of his holy way of life on which the angels desire to look (1 Peter 1:12), in his immunity from sin, in the form of his body, particularly as he showed himself to his three friends at his transfiguration, in the whiteness of his virginity and innocence and in the redness of his Passion (Song of Songs 5:10), white in the brightness of the eternal light of his divinity (Wisdom 7:26) and red in the love of the Son for the Father, God for God (1 John 4:16); *concave* through the virtue of humility and in his humanity filled with the honey of divinity; and *multicolored*, purple insofar as he is king and martyr, bronze on account of the virtue of his contemplation, hyacinth and sapphire because he descended from heaven, livid like the violet as he lay in the tomb, white like the lily in his innocence, red like the rose in his love, modesty, and suffering, and yellow like the crocus in his wisdom.[227]

Further, he is *vernal* because he was announced and conceived in the time of flowers, that is, spring (Song of Songs 2:10–14), the time of renewal when all things become young again, birds and beasts bring forth their young, and trees and bushes flower; *pleasant to the touch* in his justification and forgiveness of sinners, sweetly calling them to return to him (Isaiah 30:21); *watery*, that is, succulent, in his compassion and tears (Luke 19:41); *fruit-bearing*, for in the flower there is the hope of fruit just as in Christ there is hope of present and future good (Ecclesiasticus 24:25); *inclined*, because he humbled himself unto death on the cross (Philippians 2:8) and inclining his head, gave up his spirit (John 19:30); *light*, without the weight of sin that presses the soul into hell, so that his flesh is called a "light cloud" (Isaiah 19:1); *common* or open to all to enjoy, a flower of the field, not of the garden; *medicinal*, for in him is found the medicine of the human race; and *delicate*, for as David described his son Solomon (1 Chronicles 22:5), so the Father says of Christ.[228]

Like a flower, he has a mother, that is, the earth, tree, or grass from which he is born without copulation as a male or seed, for according to his humanity Christ has a mother without a father, while according to his divinity he has a father without a mother. He feeds the bees, that is, contemplatives, and provides them with honey and wax (we may recall that Richard described himself as a bee), that is, with the food and drink of eternal safety and satiety, the medicine of eternal incorruptibility, and the splendor of eternal light. He receives the Holy Spirit, as Isaiah (11:1–2) says: *And there shall come forth a rod out of the root of Jesse, and a flower shall rise up out of his root. And the spirit of the Lord shall rest upon him*, because in him alone the plenitude of divinity dwelt corporeally (Colossians 2:9). He gives forth his odor even when he cannot be seen, like Jacob receiving the blessing of his father Isaac (Genesis 27:27), for he is the true wrestler, the son of Isaac from whose lineage Mary descended. He does not harm his mother at his birth, but distinguishes, ennobles, and adorns her, that is, the earth or grass or tree from which he arises. He adorns the head, for he is the crown of the elect that they will not wear if they do not compete (2 Timothy 2:5). And he beautifies the temple, whence roses and lilies are placed around the altars, and it is sung of the blessed Virgin who is the special temple of Christ: "Like a day of spring the flowers of the roses and the lilies of the valleys surround her."[229]

He descends into his garden

Mary, as we saw in chapter 4, is the enclosed garden, into which nothing earthly enters from below, for she was that garden into which no pure man entered, the earth on which no man walked (Jeremiah 2:6), her gate closed to every other creature, whether man, reptile, or beast. Only things from above descended into her at the Incarnation of the Son.[230]

First and foremost, descending into his garden, Christ is the *sun*, for the sun is the eye of the visible world, the light of creatures, and the mirror of the Creator, than which no creature is more beautiful or more useful, shining so brightly that no other lights may be seen. As sun, Christ excels all other lights in magnitude, that is, in his humility; in heat, that is, in his love; in brightness, that is, in his purity; in power, ruling over the year and the day (Psalm 135:8); and in usefulness, that is, in his mercy. Again, the sun is often interpreted as the Father, and its rays or brightness as the Son, who is the brightness of the glory and the figure of the Father (Hebrews 1:3), while its heat is the Holy Spirit, or the love of the Father and the Son. Or, again, the sun that encircles the machine of the world is the power of the Father, its brightness the wisdom of the Son, and its heat the benevolence of the Holy Spirit. At the Incarnation, he hid hides himself under a cloud of flesh in the Virgin's womb (Isaiah 45:15), rising in his Nativity, being eclipsed at his Passion, and rising again at his Resurrection (Ecclesiastes 1:5–6). Now every day he stands at the door, knocking to be let in (Revelation 3:20) by those who confess truthfully, ask forgiveness, praise the Creator, comfort the poor, and instruct the ignorant, thus closing themselves to sin so that the light of the sun, that is, the grace of God might enter their souls and illuminate their minds.[231] Moreover, just as the sun passes through glass, illuminating it and making it bright with its brightness without breaking it by its entry or exit, so the Son of God illuminated the blessed Virgin with the fullness of grace and purified her with his purity without breaking the seal of her modesty at his entry or exit. As a certain poet put it:

> Just as the ray of the sun
> enters without harm
> the window of glass,
> so the Son of God
> even more subtly
> entered the virginal court.

The Virgin is that city of God of which it is said (Revelation 21:18): *The city itself pure gold like to clear glass.*[232]

Again, Christ is called the *Word of the Father* (John 1:1), for six reasons. First, because just as the word makes visible the mind, which is in itself invisible, so the Son shows to the world the Father who is in himself invisible (John 17:6). Second, because just as the word proceeds visibly from the heart or the mind, so the Son proceeds in an incomprehensible manner from the Father, whence the Father says (Psalm 44:2): *My heart hath uttereth a good word.* Third, because just as the word puts on the voice to show the mind, so the Son of God puts on flesh to show the Father. Fourth, because just as the word puts on the voice with the mediation of the tongue, so the Son puts on flesh with the mediation of the Holy Spirit, saying (Psalm 44:2): *My tongue is the pen of the scrivener.* Fifth, because just as the word putting on the voice proceeds from the mouth without harming it, so the Son of God assuming flesh proceeds without corruption or pain from the Virgin at his Nativity, like a bridegroom coming forth from his chamber (Psalm 18:6). And sixth, just as there are three things required for the formation of the voice, namely the palate, the tongue, and the teeth, so all three persons are involved in the Incarnation of the Son, the Father as the palate, the Holy Spirit as the tongue, and the Son as the teeth. In turn, there are seven reasons that the Word descended into the Virgin and became flesh: first, as Ambrose says, "so that flesh might become God"; second, because man is made to the image and likeness of God according to the soul, the Son joined himself to our flesh so that man might be like his creator in both flesh and soul; third, so that the image deformed and effaced through the sin of Adam might be re-imprinted with the seal of the Father, that is, the Son (Haggai 2:24); fourth, because human beings are fleshly and love the flesh, so as to make them love him; fifth, to make himself, who was the food of angels, food for men (Psalm 77:25); sixth, so that the Virgin as nurse might chew him and make him edible for her servants; and seventh, he covered himself with a cloud of flesh so that he might be seen and known by his human creatures and so that his flesh might shield them from the anger of the Father.[233]

Christ is the *splendor* of the Father (Hebrews 1:3) because just as the splendor of the sun is born from the sun and coeval with it, so the Son is born from the Father and coeternal with him; likewise, he is the figure of the substance of the Father because he is the mirror and image of him, for the Father is known in him just as the thing is said to be seen in its image and in a mirror.[234] Christ is the *wind* because he is invisible in his majesty, light without the weight of sin in his humanity, cooling and extinguishing the burning of sin at his first coming, but blowing fiercely at his second.[235] He is the *air* because just as air is the life of the body, so Christ is the life of the soul, and just as a body cannot live without air, so the soul cannot live without the grace of Christ.[236] He is the *snow* because just as the snow and rain come down from heaven to soak the earth and make it grow, so the Word comes forth from the Father to prosper in the things for which it is sent (Isaiah 55:10–11). As snow, Christ covers the impurities of the earth, that is, earthly sins, on the cross, lest they appear before the Father for punishment, while as *rain* he cools the heat of the earth burning with sin, pouring forth water and blood from the font of his body.[237] He descends like a *shower* onto the fleece of the Virgin's womb (Psalm 71:6), humbling himself so as to confound the pride of the devil and making himself an example for human beings. As a shower, he washes the mind of the Virgin with the water of saving wisdom and makes her fruitful in the flesh, cleansing her mind of ignorance and her body of lust and filling her flesh with offspring and her mind with virtue.[238]

He is a *vapor*, that is, the heat of the power of God (Wisdom 7:25), that is, of the Father, for as heat comes from fire, so the Son comes from the Father, expelling the cold of humanity's unfaithfulness and warming his creatures with the love of God.[239] He is a consuming *fire* (Deuteronomy 4:24), inflaming his mother's heart with love and illuminating her mind.[240] He is the *manna* that descended upon the camp (Numbers 11:9), that is, upon the Virgin terrible to the demons (Song of Songs 6:9), with the dew, that is, the Holy Spirit, because he is the bread of angels given to men (Psalm 77:25).[241] And, like the Holy Spirit, he is the *dew* because the works of the Trinity are inseparable from each other. He is the dew of Hermon that descends upon Mount Zion (Psalm 132:3), that is, the blessed Virgin; he is the dew moistening the lily of Israel, again, the Virgin (Hosea 14:6); and he is the dew for whom the holy fathers longed, that it might come down from heaven that the earth might bud forth a Savior (Isaiah 45:8). He is the dew by reason of his origin, because he came from heaven; by reason of his properties, for like the dew he descended secretly and sweetly; and by reason of his operation, for he waters the earth, that is, Mary, and makes it fertile, even as like the dew (Isaiah 26:19) he gives light to Mary, the Church, and the faithful soul.[242]

He is the *angel* of great counsel who entered into Mary, of whom Job (33:23) and Isaiah (63:9) spoke, and of whom more can be found in Revelation.[243] He is a *bird* called from the East (Isaiah 46:11) by the Father at his Ascension, for Christ was always in the East of full knowledge and perfect love. He had the womb of the Virgin for his nest, where he was formed in his humanity, the cross for the perch on which he rested, and the tomb for his mews, where he put off his mortality and passibility like old feathers and assumed the new plumage of immortality and impassibility with which he ascended above the cherubim on the wings of the winds (Psalm 17:11).[244] And he is a *bee*, having both sweetness and a sting. Like a bee, he fed upon the lilies (Song of Songs 2:16) in the country of the angels until, drawn by the sweetness of Mary's virginity, he flew to her to be conceived in Nazareth. He is sweet in his mercy, but stinging in his judgment (John 5:22). He is small among flying things, that is humble, but his fruit, that is the redemption of the world and the liberation of captives, is exceedingly sweet (Ecclesiasticus 11:3). He is like a bee because he carries honey in his mouth through the sweetness of his words (Psalm 118:103), and because just as he dwelt for nine months in the cell of the virginal womb, so he lies hidden in the cells of scripture.[245]

Tree

Like Mary (and Wisdom), Christ is a tree. He is the true *vine* of which the Father is the vinedresser (John 15:1). He was planted at the Incarnation from a shoot of the most pure flesh of the Virgin Mary, cut by the hand of celestial Wisdom through the ineffable operation of the Holy Spirit and formed into his flesh. He grew with his advance in virtue as a child, put forth leaves in his preaching, gave forth his fragrance in his fame, made serpents flee in casting out demons, was fertilized with dung when he was accused of blasphemy, was pruned in his humiliation unto death, was staked out at his Crucifixion, was ditched at his fixing with the nails, was irrigated by his effusion of blood, gave forth his odor at the Passion, flowered in his Resurrection, and fruited in the redemption of the human race.[246] He is the oil and fruit of the *olive* (Job 29:6), inebriating the angels, satiating the saints, giving life to the dead, justifying sinners, making the sad happy, destroying hell, redeeming the world, and opening heaven.[247]

He is chosen like the *cedar* (Song of Songs 5:15), predestined as the Son of God in power (Romans 1:4), that is, in the nature and power of the Godhead, and in the incorruptibility of his flesh.[248] He is the *palm tree* because he is rough, contemptible, and wrinkled below, that is, in the present life (Psalm 21:7), but beautiful above, in his Resurrection and Ascension. His leaves have the appearance of a human hand because he took the form of a man (Philippians 2:7), and they do not fall off (Psalm 1:3) because they treat always of heavenly, not earthly things.[249] He is like the *frankincense* of Lebanon (Song of Songs 5:15), white in his divinity and medicinal in his humility, for everything that flowed from him at his Passion, namely sweat, tears, blood, and water, is as medicine for the human race and gives honor to God.[250] He is the *plane tree* because he has wide leaves, which he stretched out on the cross to make shade for sinners.[251] He is *cinnamon* because he has the color of ash, having no beauty at his Passion (Isaiah 53:2), but concealing a living fragrance underneath.[252] He is a drop of *myrrh* because he by whose price humanity is redeemed is precious (Job 28:13); he is even more precious because he dropped willingly from the tree; he is inwardly bright because he burned with the light of his divinity under the covering of mortality; and he protects the body from stench, worms, and decay, that is, luxuriousness, pride, and greed.[253] He is *balsam* because he protects against the decay of vice and is more precious than all temporal things.[254] And he is the *terebinth* (Ecclesiasticus 24:22), extending his branches on the cross, bearing fruit for sinners in his Passion, dripping with the resin of blood and water, sweat and tears, and driving serpents, that is, vices and demons, away with his odor.[255]

Like Wisdom, the blessed Virgin, the cross, and holy scripture, he is the *Tree of Life* (*lignum vitae*) because his gives life to the world as his fruit.[256] As a *rod* (*virga*), he is a goad for the devil as an ox, a fishing rod for the devil as Leviathan, and birdlime spread on a twig for the devil as a bird (Job 40:10, 20, 24), who moved the Roman princes like his wings to persecute Christ in his members until Christ made their feet, that is, the people, stick fast to him in faith.[257] He is likewise a rod because he is flexible in his humble obedience (Philippians 2:8), slight in his poverty, trembling with natural fear at the prospect of his death (*propassione, sed non passione*), becoming more humble the more he grew, at twelve years old humbling himself before his mother and Joseph, at thirty humbling himself before John the Baptist, and at the end of his life humbling himself even unto death on the cross.[258]

And the spirit of the Lord shall rest upon him, that is, upon the flower that shall arise out of the rod from the root of Jesse (Isaiah 11:1–2). There is here a great mystery. Transitively, the Spirit is of the Lord (*Spiritus Domini*) (2 Corinthians 3:17), but intransitively, it is the Spirit who is the Lord (*spiritus qui est Dominus*) (John 4:24).²⁵⁹ As Richard says earlier, in his description of Christ as flower, this Spirit rested upon Christ most fully because descending upon him at his baptism, it remained on him and never went away (John 1:33).²⁶⁰ According to the Gospel of the Nazarenes (*in Evangelio Nazaraeorum*), "which was written in Hebrew" (quoted, as we saw in chapter 3, by Jerome in his commentary on Isaiah, here quoted by Richard without reference to Jerome):

> It happened that, when the Lord came up out of the water, the whole fount of the Spirit descended and rested upon him, and said to him: "Son, in all the prophets I was waiting for you that you should come and I might rest in you. For you are my rest, you are my first begotten Son, who reigns forever."

As Richard explains: "These Nazarenes were the first faithful, for whose work the Apostles made collections in Jerusalem, for whom there was *one heart and one soul* (Acts 4:32)." They were called "Nazarenes" after Jesus of Nazareth because the name of Christian had not yet been invented.²⁶¹

Eagle

Christ is an eagle, for just as when someone wants to seize her young, the eagle spreads her wings over them and entices them to fly (Deuteronomy 32:11), so when the devil sought to seize the human race, Christ spread his arms like wings upon the cross and ascended where the devil did not dare to touch him "because there is hidden the strength of the Lord by which he vanquishes in the air the powers of the air." Christ is an eagle because the eagle is the king of the birds, that is, of contemplatives, who ascend up to heaven by their way of life. He is called an eagle for the sharpness of his eyes and the keenness of his vision because while a man he always enjoyed the vision of the Father, even while in his mother's womb and hanging upon the cross. There was nothing hidden in the hearts of men, all their thoughts, desires, wishes, and works, that was not revealed to him (Ecclesiasticus 23:28). Looking down from the bosom of the paternal majesty in heaven, he saw the sons of men astray in the sea, that is, the world, and he descended like the eagle from on high to seize them from the grasp of the devil and carry them to the shore of eternal life. He flies higher than all other birds because *none is as holy as the Lord* (1 Kings [Samuel] 2:2), for at his Ascension *he ascended upon the cherubim, and he flew upon the wings of the winds* (Psalm 17:11), that is, over all the powers of the Angels up to the right hand of the Father, albeit in his humanity not, however, above the Seraphim, above which there is nothing except the *gyrochesia*, that is, the holy order of the Trinity.[262]

Like the eagle, he builds his nest in high places, that is, in the hearts of those who scale the heights through the excellence of their life, and abides in the rocks, that is, in those who are firm in their faith, insensible to tribulation, never pierced by the arrows of temptation, dried out by their penitential exercises, and cold in their continence and abstinence (Job 39:27–28). He places an amethyst in his nest as a sign of his royal power (its purple color) and his humility (its violet color) and so as to expel serpents, that is, vices, and the intoxications of carnal delights. Just as the eagle feeds her young with the best partridges, rabbits, and the like, so Christ feeds his people with his own flesh and blood, with the blood which he poured out on the cross, and with his flesh which is true meat (John 6:56) in the sacrament. And just as the eagle places each of her young in the ray of the sun, and those who look upon it keenly and with open eyes, she loves, cherishes, and feeds, while she casts from the nest onto the earth those who close their eyes as if blinded, so Christ, who is the true sun of justice, keeps, embraces, and protects those who look upon his justice and mercy unceasingly with the eye of fear and love, while those who avert their eyes, that is, their intellect and affect from the brightness of the sun, he allows to fall to earth, that is, into earthly desires, where they are blinded spiritually and live in darkness and shadows.[263]

In his turn, the just man, also like an eagle, illuminated by the rays of scripture and the works of Christ, gazes always with the eyes of his intellect and affect, namely by believing and loving, at the sun in its wheel, that is, Christ in his divinity, who has no beginning and end. In the words of the psalmist: *I set the Lord always in my sight* (Psalm 15:8); and: *To thee have I lifted up my eyes who dwellest in heaven* (Psalm 122:1).[264]

Prayer, as medieval theologians from John of Damascus to Dionysius the Carthusian put it, is "a lifting up (*ascensus*) of the mind and soul to God."[265] Trained by Wisdom in the understanding of the scriptures, medieval Christians lifted their minds and souls to God through the psalms and other texts of the Office of the Virgin Mary that they sang in their Lady's praise, longing for the Lord with their intellect and affect even as they visualized him as a baby in his mother's arms. Mary, they believed, was the one who had given birth to God in the flesh so that he might become visible to the world. She was the one who, as his ark, temple, and throne, showed to the world the Creator whom it had not seen, and she was the garden into whom he entered so as to give new life to his creatures. To serve her was to serve God. For those who were able, the most perfect service was to sing with the angels the psalms that they sang before the throne of God, but even those, like the tumbler, who did not know the psalms could serve her with their bodies and hearts, and all could join with the angel Gabriel in his salutation (Luke 1:28):

> Ave, gratia plena, Dominus tecum.
> Benedicta tu in mulieribus.
>
> *Hail, full of grace, the Lord is with you.*
> *Blessed are you among women.*

"Ave, maris stella," Mary's servants sang at Vespers in one of the most popular hymns for her Office:

> Ave, maris stella,
> Dei mater alma
> atque semper virgo,
> felix coeli porta.
>
> *Hail, star of the sea,*
> *nurturing Mother of God,*
> *and ever virgin,*
> *happy gate of heaven.*

> Sumens illud Ave
> Gabrielis ore,
> funda nos in pace,
> mutans Evae nomen.
>
> *Receiving that "Ave"*
> *from the mouth of Gabriel,*
> *establish us in peace,*
> *transforming the name of "Eva."*

> Solve vincla reis,
> profer lumen caecis,
> mala nostra pelle,
> bona cuncta posce.

Loosen the chains of the guilty,
give light to the blind,
drive away our evils,
ask every good thing.

Monstra te esse matrem,
sumat per te precem,
qui pro nobis natus
tulit esse tuus.

Show yourself to be a mother,
through you, let him receive prayer,
who, born for us,
undertook to be your own.

Virgo singularis,
inter omnes mitis,
nos culpis solutos
mites fac et castos.

O singular virgin,
gentle above all others,
make us chaste and gentle,
released from our sins.

Vitam praesta puram,
iter para tutum,
ut videntes Jesum
semper conlaetemur.

Bestow pure life,
prepare a safe way,
that seeing Jesus
we may forever rejoice.

Sit laus Deo patri,
summum Christo decus,
Spiritui sancto
honor, tribus unus.

Praise be to God the Father,
glory to the most high Christ,
to the Holy Spirit,
honor, one to the three.[266]

Mary as medieval European Christians saw her was the Lady of the temple and the Mother of the Lord, Wisdom anointing the eyes of her servants so that they might see her bridegroom coming forth from the bridal chamber of her womb. She was the one who guided Christians to the vision of God as Creator and Lord, the one through whom the Trinity showed itself to the world. She was likewise the most perfect mirror of God, her face shining with the light of the Lord and reflecting him in his glory. Restored to the temple, she was herself the city of God in which the Lamb dwelled, who, passing through the veil into the world, sacrificed himself so as to open a way through the veil into heaven. As her medieval servants imagined her in their devotion, now in heaven as the Tree of Life giving forth its fruit for the healing of nations, she stands beside her Son like a queen, bearing the petitions of her servants to the king and begging that he might stretch out his scepter to her so that they might be saved. In turn, her medieval servants strove to model themselves upon her in her virtues, so that they might serve her as perfectly as she served the Lord, confident that although they would inevitably fall short, she would be there to protect them from the devil and lead them to her Son.

"Blessed are you, Mary, Mother of God," the visionary saint Birgitta of Sweden (d. 1373) apostrophized the Lady:

You are Solomon's temple whose walls were of gold, whose roof shone brightly, whose floor was paved with precious gems, whose whole array was shining, whose whole interior was fragrant and delightful to behold. In every way you are like the temple of Solomon where the true Solomon walked and sat and where he placed the ark of glory and the bright lamp. You, Blessed Virgin, are the temple of that Solomon who made peace between God and man, who reconciled sinners, who gave life to the dead and freed the poor from their oppressor. Your body and soul became the temple of the Godhead. They were a roof for God's love, beneath which the Son of God lived with you in joy after having proceeded from the Father. The floor of the temple was your life arrayed in the careful practice of the virtues. No privilege was lacking to you, but everything you had was stable, humble, devout, and perfect. The walls of the temple were foursquare, for you were not troubled by any shame, you were not proud about any of your privileges, no impatience disturbed you, you aimed at nothing but the glory and love of God. The paintings of your temple were the constant inspirations of the Holy

Spirit that raised your soul so high that there is no virtue in any other creature that is not more fully and perfectly in you. God walked in this temple when he poured his sweet presence into your limbs. He rested in you when the divine and human natures became joined.[267]

In the words of the angels as recorded by King Solomon in the Song of Songs: *Who is she that cometh forth as the morning rising, fair as the moon, chosen as the sun, terrible as an army set in array?* Mary, as her medieval devotees encountered her in her Hours, was the beautiful temple crafted by the true Solomon through which, as her servants, Christians offered their prayers, serving her in the hope that one day they might behold unveiled the face of the Lord, the Maker of heaven and earth whom she had enclosed in her womb.

What would you give to find yourself inside such a tale? One Ave? One hundred fifty Aves? The service of your heart, mind, body, and soul? Mary knew. "Behold," she told the angel. "I am the handmaid of the Lord; let it be to me according to your word" (Luke 1:38 RSV).

PLATE 25 Triptych with Madonna and Child with Crucifixion, Annunciation, Coronation of the Virgin, and Presentation in the temple. Catalonia, Spain, ca. 1340–1348. Circle of Ferrer Bassa (ca. 1290–1348), circle of Arnau Bassa (active ca. 1345–1348). Baltimore, The Walters Art Museum, Accession number 37.468.

Photo courtesy of The Walters Art Museum, Baltimore.

Compline: Sor María de Jesús de Ágreda and the Mystical City of God

In 1637, the abbess of the newly founded convent of the Franciscan order of the Immaculate Conception in the village of Ágreda in northern Spain disclosed to her confessor a remarkable command that the Lord had given her. For ten long years, she confessed, the Lord had been preparing her with many afflictions and illuminations to write the life of his most holy Mother, the Queen and Lady of heaven. The abbess, also named Mary, protested that she was but a "weak woman, wanting in all virtue," who would never have conceived such a work without "the influence and power of the Most High," and begged to be released from this charge, but the Queen of heaven herself pressed her to accept it and promised to help her write down the things that the Lord had shown her. Even the angels weighed in to encourage and instruct her, reassuring her that the Lord had commanded one of them to speed her pen "with lightest breath ... and while gazing on his Majesty, to direct and assist thee by illuminating thy intellect." Hearing of these encouragements, her confessor, Padre Andrés de la Torre, who had known her since she had become abbess ten years before at the age of twenty-five, counseled her to obey, and so trusting in the "great virtue of obedience," she resolved "in the name of the Lord and of my Queen and mistress" to lay aside her reluctance and begin.[1] For eight years she labored to finish the great work, only to be thrown into doubt upon its completion and—abetted by an old confessor (not de la Torre) who believed that women should not write in the Church—burn everything that she had written. Happily, ten years later, in 1655, at the insistence of yet another confessor, Padre Andrés de Fuenmayor, and at the continued urgings of the Lord, the abbess, now aged fifty-three, once again took up her pen to write the history of the Queen.

Abbess Mary, or Sor María as the abbess is generally known, thought it proper at the outset to explain how she came to learn the mysteries recorded in her book. In answer to her prayers and petitions that she might be "guided and led upon the secure paths hidden from the eyes of men," the Lord answered: "Do not fear, soul, nor afflict thyself; for I will give thee a state of mind and show thee a path of light and security, which only its Author himself could know of or even conceive.... I will direct thee toward a hidden path, unobstructed, unfailing and pure; walk thou in it." "And presently," she confessed,

> I felt a change within me and a highly spiritualized state of mind. To my understanding was given a new light, which illuminated it and infused into it a knowledge of all things in God, and of his operations as they are in themselves and as they are known and seen by God, according to the measure of his communication. It is a knowledge of light, holy, sweet and pure, subtle, penetrating, sure and agile, causing love of good and hatred of evil [cf. Wisdom 7:22–23]. It is a breath of the power of God and an emanation of a most subtle light, which acts as a mirror for my understanding [cf. Wisdom 7:25–26]. Thus the higher faculties and the interior perception of my soul began to expand in their activity.

And how they expanded! As Sor María described her experience:

> For the Object, by means of the light which flashed from It, showed Itself to be infinite, though the perception of It remained limited and the understanding finite. It is a vision as it were of the Lord seated on a throne of great majesty, where, always within mortal limitation, I perceive his attributes distinctly. A veil, which seems like purest crystal, intervenes, through which the wonderful attributes and perfections of God appear distinctly and clearly perceptible; yet this vision is not entire, immediate or intuitive, or entirely free from obstruction, but always comes through a medium, which is nothing else than this crystalline covering above mentioned.[2]

Sometimes, the abbess averred, the Lord seated on his throne behind the crystalline veil would manifest himself more clearly than others, depending on the disposition of her soul:

> However, the conviction of the real presence of God in the vision always precedes and impresses itself upon the mind, before one understands fully that which his Majesty speaks. And this knowledge produces a pleasing constraint, powerfully and efficaciously urging the soul onward to love, serve, and obey the Most High. In this vision great truths are made clear; how estimable virtue is, and what a valuable treasure is its exercise and preservation.[3]

So powerfully did this vision work, in fact, that even the body might be affected, becoming "agile and spiritualized during such times, freeing itself from its gross-ness and weight" (that is, levitating).[4] But for the most part, the effects were more affective—and intellectual:

> One feels the uninterrupted activity of love which [the spirit of Christ] causes, and of intimate conversation with God, living and continuous, which rivets the attention of the mind to the things of God and withdraws it from earthly things. Christ manifests Himself as living within the soul, exerting his power and dispersing the darkness by his light. This may be properly desig-nated as standing in the entrance of the house of the Lord; for there the soul beholds the splendor emanating from the beaconlight of the Lamb of God (Revelation 21:23).[5]

And what, irradiated by the splendor of the Lamb, did Sor María see and learn? In a word, everything (cf. Wisdom 7:17–21):

> The ordering of all things, the power of the elements, the beginning, the mid-dle and the end of time, its changes and variations, the onward course of the years, the harmony of all creatures and their innate qualities; all the secrets of men, their acts and their thoughts; how far they stray from the Lord; the dangers in which they live and the errors of their ways; the states and govern-ments, their curtailed existence and their great instability, their beginning and end, the true and the false principles which guide them. All this is learnt and seen distinctly in God through this light, even as far as pertains to the separate individuals and circumstances.[6]

The abbess was, in other words, infused with Wisdom or, as she tended to put it, knowledge (*ciencia infusa*).[7] While in this state of enlightenment, Sor María found herself able to see and recognize both the Queen of heaven and the holy angels, sometimes in the Lord as through a mirror, sometimes in themselves, much, she understood, in the way in which the angels themselves "enlighten, communicate, and speak with each other, when the superior orders enlighten the inferior." "The Lord," she insisted, "is the first cause of this light, but the Queen who has received it in its highest plenitude, communicates it as through a channel to the superior part of my soul, so that I begin to know her excellence, her prerogatives and mysteries in the same manner as an inferior angel perceives that which is communicated to him by the superior spirits." It was in this way, or so she averred, that the abbess learned to know "all the mysteries of the life of the Queen of heaven" that she related in her book.[8] And what mysteries they were—there were hardly words to express them!

For example, Sor María learned that, from the moment of her conception, the Virgin was always accompanied by a host of a thousand angels usually visible only to her in the form of beautiful young men with bodies "like animated crystals bathed in glory,"[9] and that she had dark eyes tending toward green.[10] She learned that the Virgin was the first to take vows of poverty, obedience, chastity, and enclosure,[11] and that she followed a daily rule of study, work, and prayer while living in the temple.[12] She learned that, at the Incarnation, God "could not proceed without the co-operation of most Holy Mary and without her free consent" and that the body of her Son was formed from three drops of blood squeezed from her heart.[13] She learned that when the time came for the Virgin's Son to be born, "her countenance emitted rays of light, like a sun incarnadined, and shone in indescribable earnestness and majesty, all inflamed with fervent love," and that her Son came forth without damage to her virginal integrity, "for He did not divide, but penetrated the virginal chamber as the rays of the sun penetrate the crystal shrine, lighting it up in prismatic beauty."[14] She learned that, at his Passion, the Mother of the Lord prayed to share bodily all the pains and wounds that he suffered "in exact duplication,"[15] and that, accordingly, the Virgin Mary suffered more than the martyrs at the death of her Son, thus fulfilling the first words that he spoke to her as an infant: "Become like unto Me, my Beloved."[16] Likewise, Sor María learned that, three days later, the Virgin overflowed with joy at the very moment when the soul of Christ "entered and gave life to his body," and that when, arisen and glorious, he appeared to her and embraced her, "the glorious body of the Son so closely united itself to that of his purest Mother, that He penetrated into it or She into his, as when, for instance, a crystal globe takes up within itself the light of the sun and is saturated with the splendor and beauty of its light."[17] She learned that, at his Ascension, the Lady was raised up with him and placed at his right hand in fulfillment of what David said in the psalm (Psalm 44:10),[18] and that she then returned to earth just as John says:

"And I John saw the holy city, the new Jerusalem" [Revelation 21:2] ... [that is] the Mother of the Incarnate Word, the true mystical city of Jerusalem, the vision of peace, descending from the throne of God himself to the earth ... clothed as it were with the Divinity and adorned with a new participation in God's attributes, his wisdom, power, holiness, immutability, and amiability, and resembling his Son in her actions and behavior.[19]

Further, Sor María learned that, at the descent of the Holy Spirit at Pentecost, "Mary was transformed and exalted in God . . . and for a short time enjoyed the beatific vision of the Divinity,"[20] and that thereafter she spent all her time praying to her divine Son and "exhorting, instructing, counseling, . . . and distributing graces in diverse manners among the children of the Gospel," catechizing them in the holy faith so that not one of those whom she instructed was lost.[21] She learned, as John saw in Revelation 12, that the Queen of heaven gained a great victory over the demons[22] and that she kept all the feasts of the Church.[23] She learned that the Lady did not age at all after she was thirty-three, although she lived until she was seventy.[24] And she learned that, at the Lady's death, the angels who accompanied her Son to her deathbed "began to sing in celestial harmony some of the verses of the Canticles of Solomon and other new ones" and that she died at three o'clock on a Friday, just like her Son.[25]

Above all, however, Sor María learned that the Queen of heaven, like herself, had been subject to divine illuminations, albeit much more excellent ones than Sor María had ever enjoyed, the first of which occurred at the very moment of the Virgin's conception, when her soul was infused into her body possessed of all the gifts and fruits of the Holy Spirit "so that She knew and was conversant with the whole natural and supernatural order of things . . . from her first instant in the womb of her mother."[26] Even more wonderfully, at the Virgin's birth, the Most High sent a guard of angels to bear her body and soul to the empyrean heaven with songs of joy so that "for a short time [the true ark of the covenant] might rest, not in the house of Obededon, but in the temple of the King of kings and of the Lord of lords, where later it was to be placed for all eternity."[27] There, the child Mary prostrated herself before the royal throne in the presence of the Most High, just as Bathsheba had entered into the presence of her son Solomon, who rose to receive his Mother and seat her beside him as his Queen (3 Kings 2:19). At this point, "[the Virgin's] powers of mind, besides being illumined and prepared by new grace and light, were raised and proportioned to the divine manifestation, and the Divinity displayed Itself in the new light vouchsafed, revealing Itself to Her intuitively and clearly in a most exalted manner. This was the first time," Sor María explained, "in which the most holy soul of Mary saw the blessed Trinity in unveiled beatific vision."[28] It was not to be the last.

As Sor María learned through her own illuminations, the Virgin's most extended vision of the Divinity occurred over the course of the nine days immediately preceding the Incarnation of the Son in her womb, during which God "allowed the river of his Divinity to rush impetuously forth to inundate this City of God with its floods" (Psalm 45:5). On the first day, as Sor María learned, the Princess Mary got up from her couch at midnight "according to the example of her father David" (Psalm 118:62) and prostrated herself "in the presence of the Most High" so as to begin her usual prayers. The angels who attended upon her told her, however, to raise herself up, for the Lord and King was calling her. Turning herself toward the face of the Lord, she replied: "Most high and powerful Master, what wishest Thou to do with me?" And at these words, "her most holy soul was raised in spirit to a new and higher habitation, closer to the same Lord and more remote from all earthly and passing things." In this first vision, in which the Divinity manifested itself "not by an intuitive, but by an abstractive vision," the Virgin "learned most high secrets of the Divinity and its perfections, and especially of God's communications *ad extra* in the work of creation," for the Lord "sought first to prepare the tabernacle or temple, whither He was to descend from the bosom of the eternal Father" by furnishing his chosen Mother with "a clear knowledge of all his works *ad extra*, just as his Omnipotence had made them."[29] (As, we may remember, Pseudo-Albert had likewise claimed.)

Accordingly, on this *first day*, the Lord manifested to his Lady everything that he had made on the first day of the creation of the world, just as it is written in Genesis 1:1–5. She perceived and understood how he created heaven and earth, how the spirit of the Lord hovered over the waters, and how light was made. She knew the size of the earth, its longitude, latitude, and depth, all its countries and climes, hell, limbo, and purgatory, and all the inhabitants therein. She knew all the spheres of heaven, and how the angels were made; she saw the rebellion and fall of the bad angels, and how they were punished.[30]

Likewise, on the *second day*, again in an abstractive manner, the Lady was shown the works performed on the second day of creation (Genesis 1:6–8), when God divided the waters and established the firmament separating the crystal or watery heaven above from the waters of the earth below. On the same day, she saw and perceived the number of the heavens, their latitude and depth, their order, motions, qualities, matter, and form, and the elements with all their changes and accidents in such a way "as to master them and at the same time reserve capacity for knowing many [other creatures of God], if there had existed more to be known."[31]

On the *third day*, the right arm of the Most High "continued to enrich and adorn at the expense of his infinite attributes this most pure spirit and virginal body which He had chosen as his tabernacle, as his temple, and as the holy city of his habitation," now revealing to her the works of the third day of creation (Genesis 1:9–13): how he gathered together the waters to disclose the dry land,

and all the flowers, trees, roots, fruits, and seeds that the earth brought forth, so that the Virgin became more learned in medicine than even those with thorough studies and much experience. "All this," Sor María learned, "our Queen understood and penetrated with the keenest insight more clearly, distinctly and comprehensibly than Adam or Solomon. . . . The most holy Mary knew all that was hidden from sight, as Wisdom says (Wisdom 7:21). . . . Whatever Solomon says there in the book of Wisdom was realized in Her with incomparable and eminent perfection."[32]

On the *fourth day*, in conjunction with a vision of the law of grace which the Redeemer of the world was to establish, the Lord showed the Lady the works of the fourth day of creation (Genesis 1:14–19): the lights of the firmament of heaven, the sun to rule over the day and the moon to rule over the night, along with the stars of the eighth heaven. She understood the material substance of these lights, their form, size, properties, movements, and numbers, as well as the influences that they exerted on the earth. "And," Sor María observed,

> so great was the wisdom, which the most holy Mary drew from these visions, wherein She was taught by the highest Teacher and the Corrector of the wise (Wisdom 7:15), that, if by any means man or angel could describe it, more books would have to be written of this science of our Lady than all those which have been composed in this world concerning all the arts and sciences, and all the inventions of men. And no wonder her science was greater than that of all other men: for into the heart and mind of our Princess was emptied and exhausted the ocean of the Divinity, which the sins and the evil dispositions of the creatures had confined, repressed and circumscribed.[33]

On the *fifth day*, the preparations and enlightenments the Virgin experienced "emitted ever stronger rays of light and divine graces, which flashed into her most holy soul and emptied the treasures of infinity into her faculties, assimilating and transforming the heavenly Lady more and more to a likeness of her God (*assimilando más al ser de Dios, y transformandose más*) in order to make Her worthy of being his Mother." When, at this point, she perceived in the Lord "all the creatures of the past, present, and future," their position in creation, their actions and final ending, she prayed to him to be merciful, saying: "My father David said of Thee and of the eternal Word: 'The Lord hath sworn, and He will not repent: Thou art a priest forever according to the order of Melchisedech' (Psalm 109:4). Let then that Priest come, who is at the same time to be the sacrifice for our rescue; let Him come, since Thou canst not repent of thy promise," at which the Trinity assured her that the eternal Word was soon to be made man.

On this same day, she also knew all the reptiles that creep upon the earth, the birds that inhabit the air, and the fishes that swim in the rivers and seas, and all the forms, conditions, qualities, peculiarities, uses, and connections with which they were created (Genesis 1:20–23).[34]

On the *sixth day*, the Virgin "witnessed, as if She Herself had been present" the creation of the more perfect animals of the earth in all their kinds and species (Genesis 1:24–26), and she knew all their qualities, distinctions, and singularities, and the useful purposes that they serve. She then became aware "how the most blessed Trinity, in order to complete and perfect the world, said: 'Let us make man to our image and likeness' (Genesis 1:26), and how by virtue of this divine decree the first man was formed of the earth as the parent of all the rest." With this awareness, she had insight into the composition of the human soul and its faculties, as well as all the structures and parts of the human body: the bones, veins, arteries, nerves and ligatures, the concourse of humors in their composition of the temperaments, and the faculties of nutrition, growth, and locomotion, all of which she understood "without the least error, better than all the wise men of the world and better than even the angels." She understood the original condition, beauty, and perfection of innocence and grace in which the Lord placed Adam and Eve, and she "perceived how they were tempted and overcome by the astuteness of the serpent (Genesis 2:51), and what were the consequences of their sin." Knowing herself the daughter of these first parents, she humiliated herself before her Creator and took it upon herself to weep as if she had been guilty of all the sins that followed upon their first. So acceptable was this subjection to the Lord that his Majesty decreed "in the presence of his heavenly courtiers" the immediate fulfillment of that which had been prefigured in the history of King Ahasuerus, who repudiated Vashti for her disobedience and raised up Esther in her place.[35]

On the *seventh day*, now filled with the knowledge of all the works of God *ad extra*, the heavenly Lady was once again "called and elevated in spirit, but with this difference, that She was bodily raised by her holy angels to the empyrean heaven, while in her stead one of them remained to represent Her in corporeal appearance." There she beheld the Divinity by abstract vision as on the first six days, but she also heard a voice proceeding from the royal throne and calling her to become "our Bride." When she abased herself before the presence and declared herself its instrument and slave, two seraphim presented themselves in visible form before the throne to attend upon her and, at the divine command, "clothed and adorned [her] with mysterious vestments and jewels" to symbolize her interior graces and privileges as heavenly Queen and Bride. As a complement to the beauty of her tunic, girdle, hair clasp, sandals, bracelets, rings, necklace, earrings, and the embroidered borders on her garment (the meaning of which was still concealed from her), the angels furnished her

> as if with lotions for her face, by illuminating Her with the light drawn from the proximity and participation of the inexhaustible Being and perfection of God himself. For as She was destined actually and truly to shelter within Her virginal womb the infinite perfection of God, it was befitting, that She should have received it beforehand by grace in the highest measure possible to a mere creature.

Thus arrayed, she stood before the Lord "so beautiful and charming, that even the supreme King could desire Her as Bride (Psalm 44:12)."[36]

On the *eighth day*, as the Virgin was praying, wondering who would be the *mediatrix* who would "draw from the celestial altar, as with tongs of gold (Isaiah 6:6), that ember of the Divinity, for the purification of the world," she heard the voice of his Majesty calling to her:

> My Spouse and my Dove, come, my Chosen one (Song of Songs 2:10), for the common law does not apply to thee (Esther 15:13). Thou are exempt from sin and thou art free from its effects since the moment of thy Conception. . . . Come to Me, and be not dismayed in the consciousness of thy human nature; I am He, that raises the humble, and fills with riches those who are poor.

As on the seventh day, she once again felt herself raised bodily to heaven, at which the angels broke out in praise of the Almighty, saying: "Who is this, that ascends from the desert, overflowing with delights? (Song of Songs 8:5). Who is She, that so attracts and compels her Beloved as to bear Him with Her to the earthly habitation?" The Most High received her into his presence and declared her his Queen, at which the holy angels and all the celestial spirits "sung sweet hymns of glory in her honor and in praise of her Author." Giving her leave to ask of him whatever she desired, even to half of his kingdom (Esther 5:3), the Lord answered her petition for the Redeemer of the world to come with the promise that very shortly it should be done. With this assurance and divine promise, the Queen Princess felt herself enlightened and secure, and so closely and intensely was she enveloped by the rays of the sun of justice who was to arise from her, that, still unknowing his purpose for her, "She became Herself the most beautiful aurora, inflamed and refulgent as it were with the fiery clouds of the Divinity, which transformed all things within Her," and she spent the rest of the day, after the angels had returned her to earth, giving praise to the Lord "both in her own name and in that of all the mortals" who would soon be saved.[37]

On the *ninth and last day* of the novena "of immediate preparation of the tabernacle" (cf. Psalm 45:5), the Most High "resolved to renew his wonders and multiply his tokens of love" so as fully to prepare Princess Mary as a woman to be raised to the dignity of being Mother of God. For although God, in descending to become incarnate, "neither could, nor needed to change his essence" in order to unite his person to human nature, "an earthly woman, in ascending to such an excellence that God should unite with Her and become man of her substance, apparently must traverse an infinite space and be raised so far above other creatures, as to approach God's infinite being itself." Accordingly, on this night, as she prepared herself for prayer, the Virgin was again borne body and soul by the angels to the highest heaven and placed in the presence of the throne, at which the divine Majesty raised her up and seated at his side. Again, she saw the Divinity by an abstractive vision and in the Divinity "all things created and many other possible and future ones," but now the fabric of the universe, which she had seen before only in parts, "appeared to Her in its entirety, distinctly pictured as upon canvas, with all the creatures contained therein." As she gazed thus upon the harmony, order, and beauty of creation, the Almighty named her his chosen one and spouse and declared her mistress over all these goods, to possess and dispose of as she wished, so long as she was faithful to him. "Therewith the most blessed Trinity placed a crown upon the head of our Princess Mary, consecrating Her as the sovereign Queen of all creation," at which the heavenly spirits revered her as their legitimate Queen. Finally,

[in] order to put the last touch to this prodigious work of preparing the most holy Mary, the Lord extended his powerful arm and expressly renewed the spirit and the faculties of the great Lady, giving Her new inclinations, habits and qualities, the greatness and excellence of which are inexpressible in terrestrial terms. It was the finishing act and the final retouching of the living image of God, in order to form, in it and of it, the very shape, into which the eternal Word, the essential image of the eternal Father (2 Corinthians 4:4) and the figure of his substance (Hebrews 1:3) was to be cast. Thus the whole temple of most holy Mary, more so than that of Solomon, was covered with the purest gold of the Divinity inside and out (3 Kings 6:30), so that nowhere could be seen in Her any grossness of an earthly daughter of Adam. Her entire being was made to shine forth the Divinity (*Toda quedó deificada con divisas de Divinidad*); for since the divine Word was to issue from the bosom of

the eternal Father to descend to that of Mary, He provided for the greatest possible similarity between the Mother and the Father (*que allasse en ella la similitud possible entre Madre, y Padre*).[38]

Godlike, the Queen, filled with the knowledge of creation, was now ready to become the Mother of God; the living temple was ready to manifest the presence of the Lord, the maker of heaven and earth.

The parallels between Mary's preparation to become the Mother of the Lord and Sor María's account of her own Sapiential infusions are unmistakable: "Become like unto Me," the Son told his Mother. "Contemplate and study thyself in this mirror," the Queen of heaven told her daughter Mary as she taught her about her life and that of her Son.[39] How we read this mirroring—and, thus, Sor María's purpose in (re-)writing her book—is a good litmus test of how far we have come from the ancient and medieval theological tradition in which Richard of Saint-Laurent, Conrad of Saxony, and Pseudo-Albert were writing, likewise from the tradition of prayer in which their readings of scripture were grounded. It is also, therefore, a good litmus test of how well we understand the purpose of Marian devotion and prayer as devotees like Sor María, her contemporaries, and their medieval forebears understood it. If Sor María's work seems strange to us, is it because she was somehow at odds with her tradition? Or is it that we have lost sight of the very tradition in which she was writing?

In her lifetime, Sor María was much revered as a teacher and counselor, not only by her sisters in the convent, but also by Felipe (Philip) IV, the King of Spain, with whom (famously) she carried on a regular correspondence for over twenty years, from 1643 until both their deaths in 1665. Her longtime family friend, Padre José Ximénez de Samaniego, later bishop of Plasencia, began writing her biography (perhaps in anticipation of her consideration for saint-hood) soon after she became even more famous for the hundreds of visions that she had had in her late teens and early twenties of preaching to an unknown people in "Tixtlas." The Franciscan Alonso de Benavides who interviewed her in 1631 identified these people as the Jumanos of northwest Texas, where (at least by the faithful) she is still remembered (and revered) as "the Lady in Blue."[40] Reinforcing the parallelism between Sor María and her model even further, Ximénez de Samaniego's biography would be included in the first edition of (to give it its full title) *Mystica Ciudad de Dios. Milagro de su omnipotencia y abismo de la Gracia. Historia divina y vida de la Virgen Madre de Dios, Reyna y*

Señora nuestra María Santíssima, Restauradora de la culpa de Eva y Medianera de la Gracia. Manifestada en esto ultimos siglos por la misma Señora a su esclava sor María de Iesus, Abadesa de el Convento de la Inmaculada Concepción de la villa de Ágreda, de la Provincia de Burgos, de la Regular Observancia de N. S. P. San Francisco, para nueva luz de el mundo, alegría de la Iglesia Católica y confiança de los mortales, published in Madrid in 1670. In addition to Ximénez de Samaniego's biography of Sor María, this edition would likewise include lengthy endorsements of the *Mystica Ciudad* by Don Diego de Silva, bishop of Guardia, and the Jesuit padre Andrés Mendo of the College of Salamanca, whom King Carlos II had asked to review the book.[41] To put it mildly, the bishop and Jesuit padre could hardly have been more impressed.

According to de Silva: "All this book contains is divine. It manifests the treasures of divinity and eternal incarnate Wisdom in the wonderful life of the great Mother of God . . . I began the examination of this work solely in virtue of obedience, but before I completed it I marveled at its excellence; I began as a critic, but I finished as an admirer."[42] Padre Mendo concurred:

> This work aroused my admiration at every line. I have learned more from it than from all the books to which I have assiduously applied myself for many years. It is unparalleled for clearness, depth and sagacity. . . . It is evident that this doctrine is from heaven, and that the pen which wrote it was guided by a supernatural hand. This work enlightens the mind with a knowledge of the most sublime truths, and inflames the heart with divine love. Whosoever shall read this book with attention will become learned, and whosoever shall meditate on it will be desirous of becoming a saint, for the truths which it contains dispel ignorance and excite one to heroic actions. . . . The Seraphic Order of the great Patriarch St. Francis can well be proud of such a daughter, and although many other members of this order have amassed treasures of spiritual wealth, yet, I think it can be truly said that venerable Sr. Mary of Jesus De Agreda surpasses them all.[43]

The publication of the *Mystica Ciudad* was likewise supported by Bishop Miguel Escartín of Tarazona, who, writing to her confessors just before Sor María's death, had praised the book as written in a "style so sublime, powerful and effective that it penetrates the heart with love for God and his most pure Mother" and pronounced it "in perfect conformity to the evangelical law." "In these writings," Bishop Escartín averred, "we find the real seal of the majesty of God. . . . Hence I see nothing which could give rise to the suspicion that this production is not the work of God."[44] As the Jesuit father Francis de Almada, writing in 1681, put it: "This heavenly authoress explains the most difficult terms in theology with elegance of style, glorious, yet modest and grave words, clearness of expression, deep insight into sacred scripture, and finally, she unites discretion with the most affectionate devotion. . . . It seems evident that her pen was guided by the impulse of the Mother of wisdom."[45]

With such endorsements, it is perhaps unsurprising that Sor María's *Mystica Ciudad de Dios* was an instant—and enduring—success. It was published in Lisbon in 1680 and again in 1681 and 1684; in Perpignan in 1681–1684, 1684, 1685, and 1690; in Barcelona in 1684, 1685, 1689, 1692, and 1694–1696; in Valencia in 1695; in Antwerp in 1692 and 1696; in Seville in 1698; and again in Madrid in 1688 and 1701. It appeared from presses both in Antwerp and Madrid more or less continuously through 1775 (although, notably, not for some years thereafter), and it was printed at least four times in the nineteenth century: Pamplona, 1807; Barcelona, 1860 and 1888; and Valencia, 1872.[46] By 1912, when the first English translation was published in Chicago, it had appeared in eighty-seven editions and had been translated from the original Spanish into Portuguese (1684), French (1695), Italian (1701–1702), Flemish (1713), Latin (1714), German (1715–1718), Polish (1730), Arabic (1736), and Greek (1736).[47] By 1965, the count of complete editions had risen to ninety-two.[48] The most recent critical edition, based on Sor María's autograph manuscript, was published in 1970 in Madrid (like the first, exactly three hundred years earlier), and Sor María's work is still regularly studied in courses on baroque Spanish literature for the beauty of its prose, if not necessarily for its doctrine.[49] This, we should note, is a book nearly 800,000 words long, running to some 2,674 pages in its English translation—at the very least a masterpiece of imagination, not to mention of scribal and editorial endurance, never mind its significance as a work of exegesis and Christian devotion.

Others, however, have been somewhat less impressed. Almost immediately upon its publication, the *Mystica Ciudad* came under suspicion for its (wholly predictable, given Sor María's order) support for the doctrine of the Immaculate Conception (at the time, a matter of intense debate), and on June 26, 1681, it was placed on the Index of Forbidden Books. The decree was lifted only five months later, on November 6, after the whole of Spain was roused to refute it and Bishop Ximénez de Samaniego and the Queen Mother of Spain appealed directly to the pope, but the suspicion about the book raised by the opponents of the doctrine proved more difficult to efface.[50] The case was taken up again in 1696, when 152 masters of theology met at the college of the Sorbonne in thirty-two sessions from July 2 to 14 to review the *Mystica Ciudad*, newly translated into French and published the same year at Marseilles. The Paris masters condemned the work for claiming to have access to mysteries that had not been revealed to the primitive Church (which, in fact, it does, but not without scriptural support[51] and for claiming to record not simply opinions or private visions, but constant and infallible truths (which, again, Sor María does, if in the person of Wisdom).[52] These (arguable) misreadings of the work were found to have been based on faulty translations from the Spanish into French,[53] but again, the taint of censure remained. Over and over again, throughout the early eighteenth century, the work was reexamined and approved by papal commissions (1713, 1730–1734, 1745–1748) and university faculties (four alone in 1729: Salamanca, Alcalá de Hernares, Toulouse, and Louvain), only for the approbations themselves to raise further suspicions (and, arguably, sales).[54] In 1773, in a somewhat desperate effort to quell the criticisms of her life and work, Pope Clement XIV decreed a silence on Sor María's cause for sainthood, effectively leaving both her and her book in an interpretive limbo, despite the formal affirmation of the dogma of the Immaculate Conception by Pope Pius IX in 1854.[55]

Nevertheless, arguably even more devastating to the reputation of Sor María and her Marian masterpiece has been the response from outside the Church. Perhaps most famously, in his *Ancient and Modern History* published in London in 1761, the great French *philosophe* Voltaire described the abbess as "[pretending] to more visions and revelations than all the rest of the mystical tribe put together." As Voltaire's English translators explained in a note: "This enthusiast, who was abbess of a convent at Agreda, pretended to have received divine orders to write the life of the Virgin Mary, which was accordingly published, under the title of the Mystic City of God, and appears to be a strange medley of madness and fanaticism."[56] Some years later, writing in 1787, the Italian adventurer Giacomo Casanova recalled having been given the *Mystica Ciudad* to read while he was imprisoned in Venice in 1755 (for, we may recall, attempting to seduce the nuns in the convent of Saint Justine among other things). Casanova's verdict—after choosing Sor María's book over another by a Jesuit on the devotion to the Sacred Heart, which he thought ridiculous "since the heart seemed no more respectable an organ to me than a lung"—was, if anything, even more damning than his friend Voltaire's.

As Casanova told readers of his autobiography (as translated by Arthur Machen in 1894), in the pages of the *Mystica Ciudad*, he read

the wild conceptions of a Spanish nun, devout to superstition, melancholy, shut in by convent walls, and swayed by the ignorance and bigotry of her confessors. All these grotesque, monstrous, and fantastic visions of hers were dignified with the name of revelations. The lover and bosom-friend of the Holy Virgin, she had received instructions from God Himself to write the life of His divine mother; the necessary information was furnished her by the Holy Ghost.

Noting how Sor María began her account of the Virgin's life not with her birth, but with her Immaculate Conception, and how she described the nine hundred angels helping the Virgin sweep the house at the age of three, Casanova remarked, with a certain ironic degree of sympathy:

> What strikes the judicious reader of the book is the evident belief of the more than fanatical writer that nothing is due to her invention; everything is told in good faith and with full belief. The work contains the dreams of a visionary, who, without vanity but inebriated with the idea of God, thinks to reveal only the inspirations of the Divine Spirit.

Nevertheless, the work failed to inspire him. Quite the reverse:

> The book was published with the permission of the very holy and very horrible Inquisition. I could not recover from my astonishment! Far from its stirring up in my breast a holy and simple zeal of religion, it inclined me to treat all the mystical dogmas of the Faith as fabulous.

Moreover, he predicted:

> Such works may have dangerous results; for example, a more susceptible reader than myself, or one more inclined to believe in the marvellous, runs the risk of becoming as great a visionary as the poor nun herself.

Indeed, under the conditions in which he read it, or so Casanova philosophized, it nearly drove him mad:

> The need of doing something made me spend a week over this masterpiece of madness, the product of a hyper-exalted brain. I took care to say nothing to the gaoler about this fine work, but I began to feel the effects of reading it. As soon as I went off to sleep I experienced the disease which Sister Mary of Agrada [*sic*] had communicated to my mind weakened by melancholy, want of proper nourishment and exercise, bad air, and the horrible uncertainty of my fate. The wildness of my dreams made me laugh when I recalled them in my waking moments. If I had possessed the necessary materials I would have written my visions down, and I might possibly have produced in my cell a still madder work than the one

chosen with such insight by [Dominic] Cavalli [the secretary of the Inquisitors, who had imprisoned him]. This set me thinking how mistaken is the opinion which makes human intellect an absolute force; it is merely relative, and he who studies himself carefully will find only weakness. I perceived that though men rarely become mad, still such an event is well within the bounds of possibility, for our reasoning faculties are like powder, which, though it catches fire easily, will never catch fire at all without a spark. The book of the Spanish nun has all the properties necessary to make a man crack-brained; but for the poison to take effect he must be isolated, put under the Leads [of the Venetian prison], and deprived of all other employments.[57]

It is a verdict that has yet to be properly challenged.

Following in the footsteps of the *philosophes*, Hilda Graef had only scorn for the work, describing it as "damaging" and dismissing it as "a hodgepodge of apocryphal stories and [Sor María's] own fertile imagination . . . [rightly condemned in 1696 for] containing many rash statements and hallucinations apt to expose the Catholic religion to ridicule."[58] Even among Sor María's more recent admirers, at least in English-language scholarship, there is evident uncertainty about how to assess the *Mystica Ciudad* as a theological work. T. D. Kendrick, writing in 1967, while describing the *Mystica Ciudad* as "an original, lively, and powerful book," nevertheless faults Sor María for not being able "to bring herself to accept in full the brutal implications of the perfect humanity of Jesus."[59] (It would be interesting to know what Kendrick would make of the story that filmmaker Mel Gibson drew upon the *Mystica Ciudad*, among other sources, as the basis for his famously brutal representation of the Passion in his 2004 blockbuster, *The Passion of the Christ*.[60]) Clark Colahan, who has worked more closely than almost anyone else with Sor María's writings, editing and translating several of her shorter works and even examining some of the books still at the convent in Ágreda that she may have used in writing the *Mystica Ciudad*, still finds it difficult to explain Sor María's "[daring] to assert that it was a woman who had become equal to God the father," albeit "fully in harmony with the Marian worship of her century," other than in terms of Sor María's own family life, as a projection of her own mother as head of her family household and as a way to escape from the "patriarchal views of women that undermined her childhood."[61] (One wonders, then, what Richard of Saint Laurent's or Pseudo-Albert's motivation in imagining Mary as so filled with Wisdom as to become like God could have been.) Likewise, Nathan Mitchell, in his wide-ranging study of the role of Marian devotion in the Catholic Reformation, describes the *Mystica Ciudad* above all as a historical novel. Like Colahan, Mitchell notes that in imagining herself in conversation with the Virgin, Sor María was drawing on a long, particularly Franciscan tradition of meditations on the life of Christ, but he nevertheless reads her imaginings more as an exercise in Renaissance "self-fashioning" than as a primarily theological or devotional endeavor with specifically scriptural roots.[62] Most recently, Marilyn Fedewa has suggested that Sor María may best be read not as a peculiarly Catholic or even Christian thinker, but rather as expressing "timeless truths offered by highly evolved seers of many religious and wisdom traditions," thus, arguably, effacing the very Wisdom Sor María sought to describe. Now, it seems, the only way to explain Sor María is as an empowered woman, somehow going against tradition (in Fedewa's words, "the paternalistic church-state of Inquisition-era Spain") in order to imagine Mary as "spiritual mother of all creation."[63] (Perhaps Sor María had been reading Anselm.)

Part of the problem, of course, is that unlike Richard of Saint Laurent, Conrad of Saxony, or Pseudo-Albert, Sor María did not reveal her (written) sources other than scripture, whether because she was a woman or because she was a more imaginative writer, it is difficult to say. (While one of her confessors believed that women should not write, two of them actively encouraged her to do so, and we have seen how many men, even men of the "paternalistic church-state of Inquisition-era Spain," supported her in her life and work, sometimes, as with Benavides, perhaps more enthusiastically than even Sor María might have wished.) Nor, arguably, has it helped that her supporters have so often insisted that "in this book there is something more than human"—a sort of reverse criticism by way of praise, suggesting that because the book is so good, it cannot possibly have been written by someone relying on mere human resources of imagination and reading. As doctors of theology Hermann Damen and Anton Parmentier of the university of Louvain put it in 1715: "There are contained in this work such noble, such devout circumstantial and pertinent discourses, as cannot be the result of mere discursive thought. . . . Therefore, just as 'Ciudad' must without a doubt be attributed to the venerable Mother of Agreda . . . so she cannot have composed it without particular help from on high."[64]

Help from on high Sor María may have had (and why not?), but it is also likely that she had help from on earth. According to Ximénez de Samaniego, she could read Latin, although she could not speak it, and she was able to distinguish good translations from bad. She understood the significance of the scriptures, particularly the psalms and lessons of the Office, and she was able to interpret them with admirable clarity and accuracy in both letter and spirit.[65] We should not, therefore, be surprised that the *Mystica Ciudad* contains multiple extended exegeses of the principal Marian texts with which we have been concerned: Proverbs 8:22–31[66]; Proverbs 31[67]; Revelation 12:1–18[68]; and Revelation 21[69]; while references to the Psalms, the Song of Songs, and Ecclesiasticus are abundant throughout. Nor is it an accident that so much of Sor María's work is supported by scripture, any more than Richard's or Conrad's or Pseudo-Albert's had been. For Sor María, as for Richard, Conrad, and Pseudo-Albert, to understand Mary was to be able to read scripture as it should be read, as a record of the Lord's promise to become incarnate as the Christ, the high priest anointed by Wisdom. Accordingly, throughout Sor María's work, Mary is read as the city, temple, and ark of the Lord, which he prepared from the beginning of his work as his habitation and dwelling on earth—images that, as we have seen, had been at the heart of the temple tradition of devotion to the Lady since the beginning.

Most modern scholars have remarked how Sor María depends upon the apocryphal stories of Mary's childhood and death, well-known to all medieval Christians from sermons, liturgy, drama, and art.[70] Arguably far more remarkable is Sor María's knowledge of what Mary knew, particularly what the Virgin learned about the works of creation during the first six days of her mystical novena. As abbess, Sor María was responsible for building up the new convent's library,[71] and her own writings evidence extensive reading not only in scripture, but also in all of the arts and sciences, including in particular the highly topical realms of geography and cosmography. In her youth, she composed a two-part work in which she described herself as being given a vision of "all the face of the earth, the sea, some of the big rivers, the animals, the inhabitants, the cities and kingdoms, and the diversity of creatures," and of "the heavenly and elemental spheres from the empyrean heaven to the center of the earth."[72] Her sources, according to Colahan, included such standard textbooks as the 1524 *Cosmographia* of Peter Bienewitz (known as Apianus), widely used throughout Europe and available from 1575 in a Castilian translation.[73] According to her confessor, Padre Andrés de Fuenmayor, Sor María could speak knowledgeably about all the sciences: in philosophy, about the beginnings, composition, and nature of elemental bodies and their properties; in astronomy about the magnitude of the heavens, stars, and planets, their locations, distances, sizes, movements, and *fluxios*; in cosmography, about the division and description of the earth, the differences between the nations, all their properties, customs, and laws; in mathematics, about dimensions and figures; and in arithmetic, about its beginnings and rules—better even than a man with formal training (*mas consumado*) in such studies.[74]

For all her experiences of mystical illumination, Sor María was also therefore clearly a voracious reader. Judging from the volumes now still in the convent library, her favorite authors seem to have been her compatriots Teresa of Ávila (d. 1582) and the Dominican friar Luis of Granada (d. 1588).[75] Teresa is, of course, still famous as one of Spain's great sixteenth-century mystics, but Luis is somewhat less well-known, although, as Colahan notes, "histories of Spanish literature [will] tell you that he was much read by all of the great Spanish mystics"[76]—including, it would seem, Sor María. Most notably, Sor María seems to have depended upon Friar Luis for her account of what Mary learned from God about creation, although Friar Luis himself would insist that Mary had no opportunity to acquire such knowledge.[77] According to Friar Luis, just as now all creatures are mirrors in which the saints behold the beauty of God, so God becomes for the saints in heaven a mirror (*espejo*) in which they behold all creatures.[78] Further, Friar Luis provided an account of the works of creation, including the world and its parts, the sun, the planets, the moon, the stars, the four elements and their regions, the plants and fruits of the earth, the properties of all the animals, the faculties of the soul, and all the members of the body with all their functions and parts.[79] Likewise, Friar Luis wrote "memorials" of the life of Jesus and Mary in which he called upon the reader to imagine the thoughts and emotions of God and his Mother,[80] asking Mary in particular what she—the Queen of heaven, gate of paradise, Lady of the world, sanctuary of the Holy Spirit, throne of Wisdom, temple of the Living God, *secretaria* of Christ, and witness of all his works—felt in her heart as she held in her arms the one who holds up the heavens.[81]

Sor María's other most likely sources have yet to be clearly identified.[82] If, in fact, as her biographer asserts, she was able to read Latin, it would be interesting to know whether she or perhaps one of her confessors had access to Richard of Saint Laurent's *De laudibus beatae Mariae virginis*, newly published in Antwerp (at that time, controlled by Spain) in 1625. Or perhaps she had read or heard about Conrad of Saxony's *Speculum beatae Mariae*, circulating since the later Middle Ages as the work of his (and her) fellow Franciscan Bonaventure, and also available in print.[83] Pseudo-Albert's *Mariale* may likewise have been accessible to her, having been published among the works of Albert the Great at Lyons in 1651. Certainly, her potential sources (other than the Lord and his Mother) were manifold. Colahan suggests that she may have drawn upon traditions of Christianized kabbalah that she discovered in Luis de Granada's works (although, as Margaret Barker has shown for temple mysticism more generally, what similarities there are in such early modern works may depend as much upon Christianity's own roots in the temple tradition as upon more recent interactions between Christian and Jewish mystics—thus, arguably, the underlying sympathy between Marian devotion and kabbalah, both highly focused on angels and angelic wisdom).[84] Nathan Mitchell points to the works of Franciscans, including the Capuchin Lawrence of Brindisi (d. 1619), the preacher Bernadino of Siena (d. 1444), and the Subtle Doctor John Duns Scotus (d. 1308)—the latter most famous in Marian circles for his defense of the doctrine of the Immaculate Conception—as potential sources for some of Sor María's teaching on the Virgin.[85] As Padre Mendo recognized, Sor María was clearly familiar with Bonaventure's description of the triple way of purgation, illumination, and union,[86] nor was she likely to have been unaware that the great Franciscan teacher had been declared a doctor of the church by Pope Sixtus V in 1588. As Mitchell points out, several of the Seraphic Doctor's works had been printed or reprinted at Venice between 1593 and 1609, making them, like those of Richard and Pseudo-Albert, newly available for purchase for the convent's collection.[87] Other potential models that have been suggested include the works of such late medieval visionaries as the Dominican tertiary Catherine of Siena (d. 1380) and Birgitta of Sweden, likewise given to having conversations with the Virgin. Or perhaps Sor María had read such late medieval Franciscan classics as the *Meditationes vitae Christi*, in which the reader is encouraged to imagine herself in the presence of the Virgin and her Son at each of the canonical hours as Christ suffered and died, or the *Arbor vitae crucifixae Jesu Christi* of Ubertino of Casale (d. 1329), in which the Virgin is described as so filled at the Annunciation with the plenitude of divinity "compared with which every other form of cognition [of God] can justly be called a shadow"—albeit, Ubertino would caution, Mary's contemplation in this life was "still short of the beatific vision."[88]

More than her particular sources, however, what matters most for our purposes is that Sor María was clearly steeped in the exegetical and liturgical tradition we have been studying: she imagined herself within it as Mary's devotees had done for centuries, just as we have done. By definition, hers was an exercise in both intellect and affect, knowledge and devotion, science and mysticism, precisely because it was an exercise grounded in Wisdom and in love for her Son, through whom the world was created and who entered through her into his creation in order to create it anew. If, with Voltaire and Casanova, we are only able to read Sor María's work as evidence of madness, then we condemn not only the whole of the theological and devotional tradition in which she was working, including the use of the imagination, but also the very foundations of modern science, grounded as it was in the belief that human beings might achieve understanding of creation through the exercise of the intellect with which they were made in the image and likeness of God. Like Solomon the Wise, Sor María was filled with the knowledge of creation, of the trees and the beasts, of birds, reptiles, and fish, and the kings of the earth—or, at the very least, the king of Spain—came to learn from her (3 Kings 4:33–34). She became, in other words, the very image of the Lady who had been exalted above the angels to share in their wisdom. As we have seen, according to her medieval devotees like Richard, Conrad, and Pseudo-Albert, Mary as Queen of angels participated in and bestowed upon her devotees an angelic understanding of God as Creator of heaven and earth. It was through her that they received the light with which to see God.

"From what papers or books," the inquisitor Antonio del Moral asked the forty-eight-year-old abbess when, in 1650, she came under suspicion of being involved in a plot against the king, and del Moral was sent to interrogate her about her life and works, including a litany which she had written when she was nineteen, "did you get the praises for Our Lady? Or, in what part of the scriptures or in which authors have you read any of them? Or, did any other person tell these praises to you so that you could write them down?" Sor María answered:

Certainly, I was inspired by the Sacred Scriptures, particularly by Proverbs and the Song [of Songs]. But no one helped me to write them, and the real "book" where I found them was in the light of the Lord and his divine intelligence. It was as though, at the instant that I thought of writing them, that I saw them all written out in a divine handwriting.

"What is the meaning," del Moral continued, "of the verse [in the litany] which says: 'Immaculate and most perfect mirror of the divinity'? How is this possible?" Sor María replied:

Sometimes when we look into a mirror, we may observe something new. When we look at Mary—as into a mirror—we know the Most Holy Mother participated in our redemption by taking the flesh of the Son of God into her womb. We also know that God is said to have created man in his image and likeness. In partaking of man's redemption, it seemed to me that the Most Holy Mary helped to restore man's resemblance to God, and in doing so by virtue of her own immaculate purity, she acts as a mirror in producing the most genuine likeness of God.[89]

Even if, with Voltaire and Casanova, we no longer share Sor María's vision of Mary and God, perhaps now thanks to our study of the longer tradition in which she was writing and praying, we can understand why, when she looked at herself in the reflection of the Virgin Mary, Sor María says that she beheld the Wisdom with which she, as all human creatures, had been made, the mirror of God's majesty and the image of his goodness (Wisdom 7:26). As her ancient, medieval, and early modern devotees like Sor María beheld themselves in her, Mary was the mirror of the Divinity; she was the model of mystical illumination and the vision of God, the Queen of the angels and the Mother of God, as like to her Son as it is possible for a creature to be, enthroned beside him in heaven and absorbed in the contemplation of the Divine. For his part, del Moral concluded his examination:

> I recognize in [Sor María] much virtue deeply rooted In charity, and a great intel ligence of the Sacred Scriptures. . . . In my estimation, those who initiated this line of inquiry embellished and made unwarranted suppositions, because they did not have reasonable cause to begin with . . . Regarding what she signed under [Benavides's] order [about her bilocation], we consider it an "indiscreet obedi- ence," and attribute it to the inexperience of youth and gender. As for the subject now, I say that she is a catholic and faithful Christian, well-founded in our holy faith. She embroidered no fiction into her accounts, nor was she deluded by the devil. This is my best judgment, which I humbly yield.[90]

APPENDIX

Handlist of Manuscripts and Printed Editions of Richard of Saint-Laurent's *De laudibus beatae Mariae virginis libri XII*

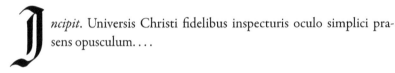*ncipit.* Universis Christi fidelibus inspecturis oculo simplici præsens opusculum. . . .

- Prologus secundus: Dictum est Joanni sancto theologo . . .
- I Ave Maria gratia plena . . . Tres salutationes celebriores ceteris in Evangelio reperimus . . .

MANUSCRIPTS[1]

*Arras, Bibliothèque municipale, 109, fols. 1–207
- Fifteenth century, from the Benedictine monastery of Saint Vaast in Arras

Auch, Bibliothèque municipale, 3, fols. 1–282
- 1302, from the Cistercian monastery of Gimont

Basel, Universitätsbibliothek, A.VI.10, fols. 1–328
- Fifteenth century, on paper, possibly from the Franciscan Barfüsserkloster, Basel

Cesena, Biblioteca Comunale Malatestiana, Piana 3.183, fols. 153v–178r
- First half of fifteenth century
- Third item in a miscellany including Bernardus de Parentinis, Thomas Aquinas, and Aldobrandinus de Tuscanella

*Douai, Bibliothèque municipale, 387, fols. 1–[479]
- Third quarter of thirteenth century, from the Benedictine monastery of Anchin

Florence, Museo Horne, Manoscritti, N 5/27, fol. 1r–341v
- First half of fourteenth century

Frankfurt-am-Main, Stadt.-u. Universitätsbibliothek, Cod. Barth. 77, fols. 1–394
- 1462, copied by Martin Hugonis and Johannes Streler in Straßburg, for the Dominican cloister at Frankfurt

Graz, Universitätsbibliothek, Cod. 446, 2 vols.
- Fifteenth century, on paper, from the Benedictine monastery of Saint Lambrecht, Styria

Krakow, Biblioteka Jagiellonska, 1240, fol. 100r: "Tres salutationes celebriores..."
- 1456, 1467, miscellany copied by Iohannes de Slupcza of Krakow

Krakow, Biblioteka Jagiellonska, 1289, fols. 1r–251v
- ca. 1420

Krakow, Biblioteka Jagiellonska, 1433, fols. 2r–v, 4v (excerpts)
- ca. 1452–1460, miscellany copied by Iohannes de Slupcza of Krakow

Krakow, Biblioteka Jagiellonska, 1441, fols. 10v–49r, 53r–309r
- Middle of the fifteenth century, Prussia
- Incomplete, with Albert of Brixen, *Liber de doctrina dicendi et tacendi*, fols. 49r–52v

Leipzig, Universitätsbibliothek, 275, fols. 146v–415r
- Fifteenth century, on paper
- Fifth item in a miscellany including Ildefonsus of Toledo (as Augustine), Johannes Anglicus, Gilbert of Hoyland, and an anonymous treatise on Mary written in Venice in 1371.

Milan, Biblioteca Nazionale Braidense, AG IX 30, fols. 99r–209v
- 1455–1456, made at the command of Dominico de Dominici, bishop of Torcello and Brescia, at the monastery of Saint Cyprian in Murano
- Copied with Servasanctus of Faenza, *Mariale*, fols. 2v–98v

Munich, Bayerische Staatsbibliothek, Clm 3790, fols. 1r–331r
- 1434/1466, Southern Germany, on paper

Pamplona, Biblioteca Capitular de la Catedral, 63, fols. 1–131: lib. 1–lib. 6, cap. 1
- Fifteenth century, on paper

*Paris, Bibliothèque nationale, nat. lat. 3173, fols. 1–358
- Sent by Richard from Picardy to Hugh of Saint Cher, cardinal of Santa Sabina (1244–1263): "Hoc volumen est conventus fratrum predicatorum Lugdunensis, quod fuit domini Hugonis, Tit. S. Sabine presbiteri cardinalis, cui missum fuerat de Picardia ab auctore ejus mediantibus aliquibus."
- Includes Richard's four sermons on the feasts of the Virgin

Paris, Bibliothèque nationale, nat. lat. 3697, fols. 1–94: lib. 1
- Beginning of the fourteenth century
- First item in a miscellany, including Innocent III, Hugh of Saint Cher, and Paul of Hungary, among others

*Paris, Bibliothèque nationale, nat. lat. 16498, fols. [46–143]
- Thirteenth century; one in a set of four volumes of sermons and other materials collected by Jean d'Essonnes

*Paris, Bibliothèque nationale, nat. lat. 17492, fols. 1–237
- 1240–1260; given by Galéran de Penderef, cantor and canon of Notre Dame, to the library of the cathedral along with the *Postilla* of Nicholas of Lyra in the early fifteenth century

Sélestat, Bibliothèque municipale, 62
- 1509, on paper; purchased by Lord Johanne Schetzil Argentorat for preaching in the parish church of Sletzstat

Stuttgart, Wurtemburgischen Landesbibliothek, HB I.25, fols. 8–252
- 1465–1470, on paper, parchment endpapers from Konstanz

Trier, Stadtbibliothek und Stadtarchiv, 730/282a quart, fols. 1–273
- Fifteenth century, from the Augustinian house of Eberhardsklausen

Trier, Stadtbibliothek und Stadtarchiv 734/285 quart, fols. 1r–312v
- Fifteenth century, willed in 1466 to the Collegiatstift Pfalzel by Magister Johannes von Amelburg

*Troyes, Bibliothèque municipale, 828, 2 vols., fols. 1–315, 1–279
- Thirteenth to fourteenth century, from the Cistercian monastery of Clairvaux

*Troyes, Bibliothèque municipale, 1743, fols. 1–417
- Fourteenth century, from the Cistercian monastery of Clairvaux, with concordance

Uppsala, Universitetsbibliotek, C 404, fols. 153r–159v: lib. 4, cap. 1–14; lib. 12, cap. 6.4
- Thirteenth and fourteenth century, miscellany, including sermons and other spiritual tractates

Vitry-le-François, Bibliothèque municipale, 49, fols. 1–353
- Thirteenth century, from the Cistercian monastery of Trois-Fontaines

Wellesley, Wellesley College, 19, fols. 1–503
- Second half of the thirteenth century, Paris or French Flanders, most likely Dominican, with thirteen historiated initials

Fragment: Italian, ca. 1300, lib. 12, cap. 6, §24.
- Image posted by Dianne Tillotson http://medievalwriting.50megs.com /scripts/examples/smallgothic2.htm

PRINTED EDITIONS

Strasbourg: Johann Mentelin, not after 1473
- Bound with pseudo-Albert, *Mariale, sive CCXXX quaestiones*

*Strasbourg: Martin Flach, 1493
Cologne: Heinrich Quentell, 1500
*Cologne, 1509[2]
*Ed. Jean Bogard, as Richard's. Douai and Antwerp: Martin Nutium, 1625
*Ed. Petrus Jammy, in Albert the Great, *Opera omnia*, 20. Lyon: C. Prost, 1651
Ed. Augustus and Aemilius Borgnet, in Albert the Great, *Opera omnia*, 36. Paris: L. Vivès, 1898
- Attributed to Richard in the introduction to the set 1 (1890):XLVIII–XLIX

Notes

NOTES TO THE READER

1.   On this method of inquiry in medieval grammatical instruction, see Minnis and Scott, *Medieval Literary Theory*, 12–15. For the *accessus* as used in introducing commentary on scripture, particularly the Psalms, see Gross-Diaz, *Psalms Commentary*, 66–96. For a more extended use of this method in introducing medieval techniques of prayer, see Fulton Brown, "My Psalter, My Self."

INVITATORY

1.   Scarry, *Body in Pain*, 162–63.
2.   James, *Varieties of Religious Experience*, 464, citing Sabatier, *Esquisse d'une philosophie*, 24–26.
3.   On the medieval understanding of prayer as described here, see Fulton Brown, "Prayer," "What's in a Psalm?," "Oratio," "My Psalter, My Self," "Praying by Numbers," and "Praying with Anselm." On the history of ancient and medieval prayer, see also Boynton, "Prayer as Liturgical Performance"; Jaye, *Artes Orandi*; Hammerling, *History of Prayer*; and Cottier, *La Prière en latin*. On Christian prayer generally, see Zaleski and Zaleski, *Prayer*; Chase, *Tree of Life*; *Catechism of the Catholic Church*, part 4, chap. 3, art. 1–4, §2558–2865, 711–56; von Speyr, *World of Prayer*, trans. Harrison; von Balthasar, *Prayer*, trans. Harrison; and Heiler, *Prayer*.
4.   Weil, "Reflections on the Right Use of School Studies," 57.
5.   Benedict of Nursia, *Regula* 19.7, ed. Fry et al., *RB 1980*, 216: "et sic stemus ad psallendum ut mens nostra concordet voci nostrae."
6.   For the now classic definition of "flow" oft invoked in studies of attention and absorption, see Csikszentmihalyi, *Flow*. On the experience of absorption in prayer, see Luhrmann, *When God Talks Back*, 189–226.
7.   Hildegard of Bingen, *Scivias*, pars 2, visio 2, cap. 2, ed. Führkötter and Carlevaris, 126; trans. Hart and Bishop, 162. On Hildegard's understanding of the Incarnation as a revelation of the Trinity, see Fulton Brown, "Hildegard of Bingen's Theology."
8.   Lewis, "Meditation in a Toolshed," 607–10. Subsequent quotations in this section are to these pages.
9.   So, for example, Luhrmann, *When God Talks Back*, feels compelled to ask about the evangelical Christians whose prayer practices she studies, "But are they crazy?" (chap. 8). She says, no, not necessarily, but the question lingers.
10. This is the principal argument in Cary, *Good News for Anxious Christians*.
11. See Feuerbach, *Essence of Christianity*, trans. Eliot, for his critique of God as an artifact of human species consciousness.

12. Anselm of Canterbury, *Proslogion*, cap. 1, ed. Schmitt, *Opera omnia* 1:100; trans. Ward, 244 (with changes). On Anselm's understanding of prayer, see Fulton Brown, "Anselm and Praying with the Saints"; and Edsall, "Learning from the Exemplar."

13. Cited by James, *Varieties of Religious Experience*, 464. The parliamentarian John Milton (d. 1674) was even more critical of the use of set prayers, or in his words, the "servile yoke liturgy" as found in the Anglican Book of Common Prayer, which he considered not just worthless, but tyrannical: "to imprison and confine by force, into a pinfold of set words, those two most unimprisonable things, our prayers, and that divine spirit of utterance that moves them, is a tyranny that would have longer hands than those giants who threatened bondage to heaven" (*Eikonoklastes* [1649], cited by Jacobs, *The Book of Common Prayer*, 68).

14. On this metaphor of mental "machines," see Carruthers, *Craft of Thought*, 23.

15. Gadamer, *Truth and Method*, 122, 451–52.

16. Rubin, *Mother of God*, xxii, explicitly took this assumption as the inspiration for her book on Mary: "The question that animated my interest from the start was this: how did Mary, about whom so little is said in the gospels, become this familiar global figure?" For similar apologies on the value of Mary's cult, albeit from radically different perspectives, see Warner, *Alone of All Her Sex*, 3–4; and Pelikan, *Mary Through the Centuries*, 8.

17. As, for example, in Bartlett, *Why Can the Dead Do Such Great Things?*, 157: "It has been pointed out that the New Testament gives such a bare and colourless picture of Mary that subsequent generations of worshippers could fill her out with almost any of the qualities they required."

18. For recent ecumenical arguments in favor of the older tradition of seeing Mary, see Boss, *Mary*; Carlson, *Why Mary Matters*; and Nichols, *There Is No Rose*. For a more explicitly devotional version of the argument I make in this book, see Hahn, *Hail, Holy Queen*.

19. The impressions given here of the prevailing arguments in the scholarship are general ones, based on my reading over the past decade or so, as well as on conversations with fellow scholars in the field. For an in-depth introduction to this scholarship, focusing on the development of the Book of Hours as a type of book, see the essays collected in Hindman and Marrow, *Books of Hours Reconsidered*. Compared with the attention given to the Books as books, discussions of the ways in which medieval Christians read and understood the Marian Office are for the most part nonexistent. For the only efforts to explain the texts of the Office of which I am aware, see Baltzer, "Little Office," 471–74 (who suggests a reading of the Office as it was said in the cathedral of Paris); Reinburg, "Popular Prayers," 70–75 (who offers a sketch of the main texts in the Use of Paris); Donovan, *The De Brailes Hours*, 42–104 (who concentrates on the relationship between the psalms texts and the images in a particular manuscript); and Wieck, *Painted Prayers*, 52–54, and "The Book of Hours," 492–94 (who suggests in outline a way of reading the relationship between the psalms and their antiphonal frames). Taunton, *Little Office of Our Lady*, offers an extended reading of the whole Office based on a more modern understanding of the devotion.

20. For influential expressions of this conviction, see Epilogue, "Compline."

21. Tellingly, even modern exegetes broadly sympathetic to a more "traditional" approach to reading scripture have qualms about medieval exegetical practice. See, for example, Waltke and Houston, *Psalms as Christian Worship*, 490: "Medieval exegetes went much further with the text than modern students, since allegorical and anagogical approaches suggest an innate hiddenness, which was exaggerated by clericalism, suggesting it was a special kind of text that needed to be interpreted as a sort of theological riddle."

22. De Lubac, *Exégèse médiévale* (1959–1964), the first three volumes of which have been published in translation as *Medieval Exegesis* (1998–2009) in the Eerdmans series Ressourcement: Retrieval & Renewal in Catholic Thought. My impression of Catholic reticence at embracing the medieval modes comes from Joseph Ratzinger, Pope Benedict XVI's introduction to his *Jesus of Nazareth: From the Baptism in the Jordan to the Transfiguration* (2007), where he reflects on the gap between

the "historical Jesus" and the "Christ of faith" in Catholic exegesis since the 1950s. Pope Benedict calls explicitly for a recognition of the limits of the historical-critical method on which modern studies of the "historical Jesus" have depended and for a re-incorporation of the "living tradition of the whole Church" into contemporary interpretation of the scriptures, but this re-incorporation does not include, at least in Pope Benedict's own account of the Jesus of the Gospels, the medieval traditions that de Lubac described.

23. For the still classic description of the medieval practice of *lectio divina*, see Leclercq, *Love of Learning*. For modern invitations to the practice, see Pennington, *Lectio Divina*; and Casey, *Sacred Reading*.

24. In large part, this reticence is arguably a function of the way in which, as scholars mindful of our better angels, we have tended to divide up our fields of study, with medievalists in one camp and Old and New Testament scholars in two others. As the poet says, "For fools rush in . . ." For the story of the tumbler who made himself a fool for Mary, see chap. 5, "How to Serve Mary."

25. See chap. 4, *Lectio prima. Ars grammatica*.

26. On the ongoing complexities of this relationship, see Nirenberg, *Anti-Judaism*.

27. The earliest known examples of these Trinitarian "shrine Madonnas" date to the last decades of the thirteenth century. The iconography remained popular through the end of the fifteenth. Gertsman, *Worlds Within*, provides stunning reproductions of some dozen of these Madonnas, nine of which open to show the Trinity, along with a complete list of the known examples (thirty-eight extant, four in photographs).

1. THE HOURS OF THE VIRGIN

1. For *Marking the Hours*, Duffy consulted some eight hundred Books of Hours from England. Leroquais catalogued more than three hundred in the Bibliothèque nationale in Paris. As de Hamel, "Books of Hours and the Art Market," shows, many (perhaps most) Books of Hours are still in private collections. Delaissé, "Importance," 203, coined the phrase "the late medieval best-seller" for the books, which Hamburger, "Another Perspective," 139, would now challenge, at least for Germany. On manuscript numbers, see also de Hamel, "Books of Hours: 'Imaging' the Word." On the production of and markets for manuscript Books of Hours, see Hindman and Marrow, ed., *Books of Hours Reconsidered*, parts II and IV; de Hamel, *History*, 184–98; Harthan, *Books of Hours*; Rogers, "Patrons"; and van Bergen, "Production." On the current state of research on Books of Hours, see Hindman, "Introduction."

2. On printed Books of Hours, see Hoskins, *Horae*; Lacombe, *Livres d'heures*; Labarre, "Heures (Livres d'Heures)"; Hindman and Marrow, ed., *Books of Hours Reconsidered*, part VI; Reinburg, *French Books*, 15–83; Reinburg, "Books of Hours"; Erler, "Devotional Literature"; Dondi, "Books of Hours"; Bowen, *Christopher Plantin's Books of Hours*; and Winn, *Anthoine Vérard*, 219–36, 495–500; Winn, "Printing"; Winn, "Illustrations"; and Winn, "Vérard's Hours."

3. For introductions to the contents of the Books of Hours, see Drigsdahl, *Introduction and Tutorial*; Leroquais, *Les livres d'heures*, 1: xiv–xxxii; Harthan, *Books of Hours*, 14–19; Wieck, *Time Sanctified*; Wieck, *Painted Prayers*; and Wieck, "Book of Hours."

4. See Duffy, *Marking the Hours*, for the way in which medieval English readers adapted their books. Reinburg, *French Books*, calls the books "archives of prayer" that readers would personalize and draw on for the creation of their own practices of prayer.

5. For variations in the title of the Office, see Leroquais, *Les livres d'heures manuscrits*, 1: xvii–xviii.

6. On the development of the primer, see Clanchy, "ABC Primer." On its contents, see Bishop, "On the Origin of the Prymer." On the laity's access to the texts in the Books of Hours, see Kennedy, "Reintroducing the English Books of Hours." For the Psalter and the Office of the Virgin as the basic texts with which medieval Christians learned to read, see Black, "Curriculum," 140–41, and below, n. 125.

7. Waterton, *Pietas Mariana Britannica*, 1:31.

8. Bowen, *Christopher Plantin's Books of Hours*, 4n7, and 63. For the Tridentine Decree on the revision of the catechism (promulgated 1566), breviary (promulgated 1568), and missal (promulgated 1570), see Waterworth, ed. and trans., *Canons and Decrees*, 25th Session, December 1563, 279. As Bowen notes, the decree does not, however, explicitly mention the reform of the Book of Hours. According to Witcombe, "Christopher Plantin's Papal Privileges," 139, all older versions of the Hours were officially prohibited by a papal bull dated March 11, 1571. Antwerp printer Christopher Plantin received his privilege to print the new version in March 1572.

9. That is, the selection of hymns, chants, psalms, lessons, prayers, and other texts specific to the liturgy of a particular church or diocese.

10. Drigsdahl, *Hore Beate Marie Virginis*, gives incipits for eighty-five different Uses, but notes in *New Tests for the Localization of the Hore Beate Marie Virginis* that he has identified some six hundred different variants. Drigsdahl's lists of identifying incipits are more extensive than those published by Madan, "Hours of the Virgin Mary (Tests for Localization)," and Plummer, " 'Use' and 'Beyond Use,' " but he acknowledges that even his lists are incomplete. For a fuller account of the difficulties in establishing the variety of Uses, see Hindman, "Introduction," 8–9; and Cavet, "Les Heures de la Vierge." On the Uses of the Low Countries, including Grote's, see Marrow, "Notes on the Liturgical 'Use,' " and Korteweg, "Books of Hours." See Hamburger, "Another Perspective," on the complexity of the Uses in Germany. For incipits of the Office according to the Use of Rome, see Wieck, *Time Sanctified*, 159–61. *The Little Office of the Blessed Virgin Mary in Latin and English* (2007) follows the Use of Rome.

11. For the variety of chants, see Hesbert, *Corpus Antiphonalium Officii* [hereafter CAO], for each of the different feasts (Purification, Annunciation, Assumption, Nativity), both secular and monastic cursus. On the complexities of the liturgy of the Virgin at just one cathedral, see Fassler, *Virgin of Chartres*.

12. Fulton [Brown], "The Virgin Mary and the Song of Songs," chap. 2; Fulton [Brown], " 'Quae est ista' "; Barré, "Antiennes et répons."

13. For the weekly and festal cycles of psalms on which the Marian Office was modeled, see Harper, *Forms*, 258–63; Tolhurst, *Monastic Breviary*, 6:125–27; and Roper, *Medieval English*, 75–81. For introduction to the music of the Divine Office, see Fassler, *Music in the Medieval West*.

14. Pantin, "Instructions for a Devout and Literate Layman," 399. For evidence that "every devout Christian man or woman" said the Marian Office, in addition to the evidence of the Books of Hours themselves, see de Hamel, *History*, 168, for Eustache Deschamps' (1346–1406) description of the bourgeois wife who feels she is "not properly fitted out unless she owns a Book of Hours"; Roper, *Medieval English*, 71–89, 209–10, 219–38, 260–66, on the Office as said in the Benedictine convents; *Book of the Knight*, ed. Wright, 7–8, for Geoffroy's advice to his daughters on how to say their Matins; Van Engen, *Sisters and Brothers*, 101, 125, 140, 271, 308, on the Hours said by the sisters and brothers of the Common Life; Cullum and Goldberg, "How Margaret Blackburn Taught Her Daughters," and Rudy, "An Illustrated Mid-Fifteenth-Century Primer," on the use of the primer for teaching children; and Duffy, *Marking the Hours*, and Reinburg, *French Books*, on the owners and users of Books of Hours generally. As Duffy, "Elite and Popular Religion," 142, observes: "At every level … the Book of Hours is a bridging text, holding together rather than polarizing the conventions of lay and clerical piety, the belief systems and devotional practices of educated and ignorant, rich and poor, orthodox and marginal."

15. See Duffy, *Marking the Hours*, 4, on the mistaken cataloguing of many Books of Hours in the eighteenth and nineteenth centuries as "Missals." As de Hamel, "Books of Hours and the Art Market," 47, somewhat wryly observes: "In Europe there was, and perhaps to some extent still is, a lingering sense that Books of Hours are not serious manuscripts, and that they are somehow frivolous, pretty but tinselly bits of bijouterie for the pleasure of millionaires and private collectors but not really

for the puritan shelves of scholarly libraries, beside uncials and classical texts." Leroquais, *Les livres d'heures*, I: i–ii, made a similar complaint almost ninety years ago. More recent studies of particular Books of Hours, including Donovan, *The De Brailes Hours*, Higgitt, *Murthly Hours*, Smith, *Art, Identity and Devotion*, and Smith, *Taymouth Hours*, have sought to put the texts into conversation with the images, but for the most part even these excellent studies tend to take the Hours of the Virgin for granted so as to concentrate on the more idiosyncratic visual elements in each book.

16. Tellingly, German Books of Hours from before the second half of the fifteenth century are for the most part without illustration. See Hamburger, "Another Perspective."

17. Radulph of Rivo (d. 1403), *De canonum observantia*, ed. Hittorp, cols. 1145–47; Bishop, "On the Origin of the Prymer," 234. As Reinburg, *French Books*, 18, notes, while the contents of Books of Hours, including the Office of the Virgin, were "largely liturgical . . . they were not 'official,' if that term implies supervision by church authorities. Until the late sixteenth century, the book of hours was largely free of official control."

18. Bishop, "On the Origin of the Prymer," 226–35.

19. Battifol, *History of the Roman Breviary*, trans. Baylay, 147–49.

20. On these early Offices generally, see Baltzer, "Little Office," who also edits the Office as it was kept at the cathedral in Paris in the thirteenth century; Roper, *Medieval English*, 209; and Tolhurst, *Monastic Breviary*, 6:121–22. Editions in Dewick, *Facsimiles* (see next note); Leclercq, "Formes anciennes" (Monte Cassino, 434, fols. 2–3, tenth-century psalter with eleventh-century additions; Vatican, Bibliotheca Apostolica Vaticana, Chigi C.VI.173, fols. 4–5v, late eleventh- to early twelfth-century prayer book; Paris, Bibliothèque nationale, lat. 5371, fols. 237v–240, eleventh-century legendary from the Benedictine abbey of Mouzon with twelfth-century additions); Leclercq, "Formes anciennes" (Vatican, Bibliotheca Apostolica Vaticana, Ottoboni latin 453, fol. 85r, eleventh-century copy of Gregory's homilies on Ezekiel bound with thirteenth-century copy of Gregory's homilies on the Gospels; Vatican, Bibliotheca Apostolica Vaticana, Barberini latin 523, fols. 122–123v, and Fribourg, Universitätsbibliothek, L 18, fols. 154v–156v, late twelfth-century Cistercian breviaries); Canal, "Oficio parvo de la Virgen" (Paris, Bibliothèque nationale, lat. 3719, fols. 93–100v, late twelfth-century liturgical book from the Benedictine abbey of Saint Martial of Limoges; Paris, Bibliothèque nationale, lat. 10433, fols. 226–249v, late twelfth-century psalter from Westminster); and *Officium beatae Mariae virginis secundum consuetudinum monachorum monasterii Sanctae Crucis Fontis Avellanae*, PL 151, cols. 970–74 (twelfth-century breviary from Peter Damian's community at Fonte Avellana). I have also transcribed the office of the Virgin in London, British Library, Add. 21927, fols. 101v–115v, a late twelfth-century psalter for a Benedictine abbey in the diocese of York, but which Tolhurst (6:122) claims was in use at Muchelney, Somerset. According to Hamburger ("Another Perspective," 103), Oxford, Bodleian Library, Canon. liturg. 277, "a late eleventh-century book of monastic hours and offices for use in a Benedictine nunnery . . . written in a variant of Beneventan script in Dadar (Dalmatia)," is "perhaps the earliest, extant Book of Hours," but as the script is unfamiliar to me, I have not yet been able to determine whether it contains a Marian Office. Many images of the manuscript are available digitally on ARTstor (www.artstor.org).

21. London, British Library, Cotton Tiberius A. iii, fols. 107v–115v, miscellany from Christ Church, Canterbury; and London, British Library, Royal 2 B. V, fols. 1–7, psalter from Saint Mary's, Winchester, the Nunnaminster; both ed. Dewick, *Facsimiles*. Comparative chart of incipits in Roper, *Medieval English*, 220–26; discussion in Roper, 71–75; Clayton, *Cult*, 70–77; Tolhurst, *Monastic Breviary*, 6:121–24. Both Offices depend to a certain extent on the repertoire of hymns, antiphons, responsories, and versicles for the Marian feasts, but even those few texts they do share do not typically appear at the same place in each Office. Moreover, the two Offices differ completely in their selection of readings: the one (Royal 2 B. V), most likely composed for the community of Saint Mary's, Winchester, takes all of its lessons from the Song of Songs; the other (Cotton Tiberius A. iii), copied at Canterbury, takes its lessons from various nonscriptural sources, including an

eighth-century sermon by Ambrosius Autpertus once attributed to Augustine and a ninth-century retelling of the legend of Theophilus (Clayton, *Cult*, 71, citing Dewick, *Facsimiles*, xviii, and Barré, *Prières*, 132). Neither of these sets of lessons reappears in any later known Use, whether of the twelfth or subsequent centuries.

22. Interestingly, Henry Adams deals very little with prayer in his *Mont Saint Michel and Chartres* (privately published 1904), despite his insistence that even in Shakespeare's day, "the Virgin still remained and remains the most intensely and the most widely and the most personally felt, of all characters, divine or human or imaginary, that ever existed among men. Nothing has even remotely taken her place" (242). On Adams's image of the Virgin, see below, chaps. 4 and 5.

23. Millett, "*Ancrene Wisse* and the Book of Hours"; Duffy, *Marking the Hours*, 6–7.

24. Donovan, *The De Brailes Hours*. Duffy, *Marking the Hours*, 58–59, notes that the De Brailes Hours was rather "clumsily altered" by the addition of the Vespers of the Virgin as observed by the Dominicans in England: "This clumsy and very noticeable change, made before the whole book was bound for the first time, was most likely made so that the owner could recite Vespers along with the Dominican friars who were her spiritual advisers."

25. For the history of devotion to Mary in this period generally, see Boss, ed., *Mary: The Complete Resource*; Ellington, *From Sacred Body to Angelic Soul*; Fulton [Brown], *From Judgment to Passion*; Gambero, *Mary in the Middle Ages*; Iogna-Prat, Palazzo, and Russo, eds., *Marie*; Pelikan, *Mary Through the Centuries*; Reynolds, *Gateway to Heaven*; Rubin, *Mother of God*; and Morgan's three essays on "Texts and Images in Marian Devotion."

26. De Hamel, *A History of Illuminated Manuscripts*, 170: "Monks and nuns, of course, were obliged to read their Breviary the same number of times a day, and the central text of a Book of Hours [i.e., the Hours of the Virgin] is basically only a shorter and lay version of the same round of monastic prayers." Duffy, *Marking the Hours*, 60, notes that Books of Hours contained the full text of the Office for the Dead as it was said in public prayers, but still insists that the Office of the Virgin was "simplified" and "abbreviated." Cf. Wieck, *Time Sanctified*, 27.

27. Norris's best-selling *The Cloister Walk* gives a personalized introduction to the Benedictine practice of saying the Divine Office, while Tickle, *Divine Hours*, provides short daily offices of "fixed-hour prayer" to be said morning, midday, and evening throughout the year.

28. Which, as we shall see in chap. 3, may have some basis in fact, in the sense that the psalms used in the Marian Office first appear in the Carolingian liturgies for Mary's feasts, but it seems doubtful that at this early stage there was a daily Office of the Virgin independent of the observation of her feasts.

29. Bishop, "On the Origin of the Prymer," 226–27, citing Martène, *De antiquis monachorum ritibus*, lib. I, c. 2, para. 17 (my translation).

30. On Alcuin's votive Mass, see Roper, *Medieval English*, 42–43; Clayton, *Cult*, 62–63; and Gougaud, *Dévotions*, 65–73. Alcuin composed a votive Mass to Mary, but it was only a few decades after his death that its observance was fixed to Saturdays. See Barré and Deshusses, "A la recherché du Missel d'Alcuin," 28. For the text of the Mass, see Alcuin, *Liber sacramentorum*, cap. 7, PL 101, col. 455. On the Saturday office of the Virgin kept at Einsiedeln in the late tenth century, see Bishop, "On the Origin of the Prymer," 225–26. This was an observance of three lessons said from the octave of Easter to Advent, apparently in addition to the ordinary ferial office for the day. According to Roper, *Medieval English*, 91 and 239–41, the Saturday commemorative Office is documented for English Benedictine monasteries only from the mid-twelfth century onward.

31. Hugh of Flavigny, *Chronicon*, ed. Pertz, MGH Scriptores 8, lib.I, 365. See also Bertarius Virdunensis, *Continuatio*, PL 132, col. 517; Bishop, "On the Origin of the Prymer," 225. On the setting at Verdun, see Healy, *Chronicle*.

32. Gerhard, *Vita Sancti Udalrici*, ed. Berschin and Häse, 112–14, also PL 135, col. 1016; Bishop, "On the Origin of the Prymer," 225. On the significance of Ulric's canonization, see Vauchez, *Sainthood*, trans. Birrell, 22.

33. Wulfstan, *Life of St. Aethelwold*, ed. and trans. Lapidge and Winterbottom, lxviii–lxix; *De horis peculiaribus*, PL 137, col. 107–8; trans. Clayton, *Cult*, 67n58 (with changes). See also Barré, *Prières anciennes*, 133.

34. Roper, *Medieval English*, 66–67; Clayton, *Cult*, 67–68.

35. *Aelfwine's Prayerbook*, ed. Günzel, 53–55, 128–36.

36. Roper, *Medieval English*, 67–68; Clayton, *Cult*, 68–70; Tolhurst, *Monastic Breviary*, 6:120–21. For the secular and monastic cycles of psalms, see Harper, *Forms*, 258–59.

37. *Regularis concordia*, ed. and trans. Symons, 14. On the antiphons as suffrages, see Clayton, *Cult*, 62–65.

38. Binns, *Dedications*, 90.

39. Bertarius Virdunensis, *Continuatio excerpti*, PL 132, col. 517; cited by Bishop, "On the Origin of the Prymer," 225, from MGH Scriptores iv 46.

40. Hugh of Flavigny, *Chronicon*, ed. Pertz, MGH Scriptores 8, lib. I, 365.

41. Fulton [Brown], *From Judgment to Passion*, 60–141.

42. For the pope's institution of the Office, see Dominic of Evesham, *De miraculis Sanctae Mariae*, cap. 8, ed. Canal, 31–33; and Jennings, "Origins of the 'Elements Series,' " 92. See *Miracula Sanctae Virginis Mariae*, ed. Dexter, 15, where Mary teaches a "uir religiosus" the Office of Compline. On the miracles associated with Mary's Office, see Ihnat, "Marian Miracles," 78–84. On these Marian miracle collections more generally, see Ward, *Miracles*, 132–65, and below chap. 5.

43. See above, n. 21.

44. Ker, *Catalogue*, no. 186, 240–48.

45. Dewick, *Facsimiles*, xiii.

46. Lanfranc of Bec, *Decreti Lanfranci*, ed. and trans. Knowles; Bishop, "On the Origin of the Prymer," 227; Roper, *Medieval English*, 51–52, 69.

47. Ker, *Catalogue*, no. 249, 318–20.

48. Dewick, ed., *Facsimiles*, cols. 1–2; trans. Clayton, *Cult*, 74n76.

49. Roper, *Medieval English*, 72, citing Ker, *Catalogue*, nos. 186 and 249.

50. On Edburga and her cult at Winchester, see Braswell, "Saint Edburga," and Ridyard, *Royal Saints*, 96–139.

51. Dewick, *Facsimiles*, xi–xii.

52. Clayton, *Cult*, 76, suggests probably not.

53. To complicate matters further, Cotton Tiberius A.iii contains liturgical details, including the invocation of saints (Swithun and Birinus) more closely associated with Winchester than Canterbury, leading some to suggest that the manuscript itself depends upon a Winchester exemplar (Roper, *Medieval English*, 71). And yet, as noted above, n. 21, there is very little possibility of the two Marian offices being at all directly dependent upon each other.

54. Peter Damian, Letter 142, ed. Reindel, *Epistolae*, 3:518–20; trans. Blum and Resnick, *Letters* 5:141–42; Battifol, *History*, trans. Baylay, 147–48; Bishop, "On the Origin of the Prymer," 226. On Peter's devotion to Mary generally, see Blum, *St. Peter Damian*, 157–64; and Gambero, *Mary*, 95–101.

55. John of Lodi, *Vita b. Petri Damiani*, c. 15, ed. Freund, 242; PL 144, col. 132; Battifol, *History*, trans. Baylay, 149.

56. Peter Damian, Letter 17, ed. Reindel, *Epistolae*, 1:156, 164–66; trans. Blum, *Letters*, 1:145–46, 155–57.

57. Peter Damian, Letter 17, ed. Reindel, *Epistolae*, 1:166–67; trans. Blum, *Letters*, 1:157–58.

58. Peter Damian, Letter 166, ed. Reindel, *Epistolae*, 4:231–32; trans. Blum and Resnick, *Letters* 6:228–29. "Milk" was to become one of the most widely circulated of the Marian miracle stories. See *Miracula Sanctae Virginis Mariae*, ed. Dexter, 54–57; Southern, "English Origins," 184; Ihnat, "Marian Miracles," 78.

59. On the examples that follow, see also Leclercq, "Fragmenta mariana," 294–95; Canal, "El oficio parvo," 463–65; and Bishop, "On the Origin of the Prymer," 228–31.

60.   [Turgot of Durham and Saint Andrew's], *Vita S. Margaritae Reginae Scotiae*, 333; Donizo of Canossa, *Vita Mathildis*, lib. 2, cap. 21, ed. Simeoni, 106, and PL 148, col. 1035.

61.   Fulton [Brown], *From Judgment to Passion*, 286–88.

62.   Honorius, *Gemma animae*, lib. 2, cap. 63, PL 172, cols. 637–38.

63.   *Vita Gundulfi*, ed. Thomson, 67; PL 159, col. 834.

64.   Canal, "El oficio parvo," 464n4; citing Thurston and Slater, eds., *Eadmeri monachi cantuariensis tractatus*, 104, citing London, British Library, Harley 1005, fols. 217v–18, from Bury St. Edmunds.

65.   Southern, "English Origins," 199–200; Southern, *Making*, 251–54. On the Feast of the Conception as promoted through the collections of miracle stories made in England, see Ihnat, "Marian Miracles," 84–95.

66.   Gregory, *Epistola* I, 47 (February 16, 1074), PL 148, cols. 327–28; trans. Emerton, 23–24: "prostrata coram illa ex corde contritio et humiliato lacrymas effunde." On Gregory's advice to Matilda about how to pray to Mary, see Fulton [Brown], *From Judgment to Passion*, 225.

67.   Gerhoh of Reichersberg (d. 1169), *Commentarius aureus in Psalmos, In psalmus 39*, PL 193, col. 1436: "Nam et in coenobiis canticum novum celebratur, cum a tempore praedicti papae septimi Gregorii cursus beatae Mariae frequentatur."

68.   William, *Constitutiones Hirsaugiensis*, lib. 2, cap. 54, PL 150, col. 1121; cf. ed. Elvert and Englebert, 1:114.

69.   Ulrich, *Antiquiores consuetudines*, lib. 3, cap. 13, PL 149, col. 758.

70.   Bernard, *Ordo Cluniacensis*, lib. 1, cap. 23, ed. Herrgott, *Vetus disciplina monastica*, 189. On Ulrich and Bernard as sources for the Cluniac liturgy, see Boynton, "Customaries."

71.   Leclercq, "Fragmenta Mariana," 295, citing Mansi, *Sacrorum conciliorum*, vol. 20, col. 821. According to Leclercq, Mansi was citing from the late twelfth-century chronicle of Geoffrey de Vigeois. Thierry Ruinart (1657–1709) cites the same chronicle in his *Vita Urbani II*, cap. 226, PL 151, col. 183. Gougaud, *Dévotions et pratiques ascétiques*, 73n18, cites the passage from Labbé, *Nova bibliotheca manuscripta*, 2:292: "statutum est ut horae B. Virginis quotidie dicantur officiumque ejus diebus Sabbati fiat. Ex quo mos in quibusdam Ecclesiis inolevit facere novem lectiones cum novem responsoriis et aliis necessariis, nisi in quadragesima vel nisi adsit festum duplex." Canal, "El oficio parvo," 466n14, notes that the story was likewise picked up by Radulph of Rivo (*De canonum observantia*, ed. Hittorp, col. 1145).

72.   Peter, *Statuta congregationis cluniacensis*, cap. 60, ed. Avagliano and Constable, 90–91; PL 189, col. 1041–42. For the Virgin's instructions on how to say Compline, *Miracula Sanctae Virginis Mariae*, ed. Dexter, 15; Dominic of Evesham, *De miraculis*, cap. 9, ed. Canal, 33–34; and Heidelberg, Universitätsbibliothek Cod. Sal. IX 42a, fol. 33v-34v (with thanks to Alison Beach for bringing this manuscript to my attention).

73.   Gerardus Itherius, *Vita S. Stephani*, cap. 20, PL 204, cols. 1017–18.

74.   Peter de Honestis, *Regula clericorum*, lib. 3, cap. 17, PL 163, col. 738–39; Bishop, "On the Origin," 230, citing Amort, *Vetus disciplina canonicorum*, 1:373.

75.   Manegold, *Constitutiones Marbacenses*, cc. 5–12, 24, and 52, ed. Siegwart, 106–19, 127–31, 155; Bishop, "On the Origin," 230–31, citing Amort, *Vetus disciplina canonicorum*, 1:386–89, 391–92, and 400–401.

76.   Peter's customary was approved by Pope Paschal in 1117 (Amort, *Vetus disciplina canonicorum*, 1:338–39). On Marbach as a center of Augustinian reform, see Constable, *Reformation*, 109–10.

77.   Bishop, "On the Origin," 228–29, citing *Institutiones rerum praemonstratensium*, dist. 1, cap. 1–2, in Martène, *De antiquis ecclesiae ritibus*, 3:325. On the Premonstratensian devotion to Mary, see Petit, *La spiriutalité*, 223, 253–59; *Spirituality*, trans. Szczurek, 301–9.

78.   Leclercq, "Fragmenta Mariana," 295n21, citing Canivez, "Le rite cistercien," 300, notes that the choral recitation of the Marian Office among the Cistercians is attested with certitude only from 1374, although there are hints that it may have been in place by 1237. A form of the Office seems, however, to have been available for private use from the late twelfth century, as attested in at least

two manuscripts: Vatican, Bibliotheca Apostolica Vaticana, Barberini lat. 523, fols. 122–123v, and Fribourg, Universitätsbibliothek, L 18, fols. 154v–156v. See above, n. 20.

79. Canivez, ed., *Statuta capitulorum*, 1:60 (A.D. 1157).

80. Canal, "El oficio parvo," 467, citing Lisiard, *Ordinarium ecclesiae Laudunensis*, ed. Chevalier, 3–18, 34, 58–59, 63, 74, 108, and 150.

81. **Cambrai:** Canal, "El oficio parvo," 466n13, citing Cambrai, Bibliothèque municipale 193, fols. 80v–83v; **Chartres:** Canal, "El oficio parvo," 468–69, citing Delaporte, *L'Ordinaire chartrain*, 75, 90, 98, 134, 145; Canal, "En torno a S. Fulberto de Chartres," 219–20, citing Chartres, Bibliothèque municipale 162, fols. 247v–248, and Chartres, Bibliothèque municipale, nouv. acq. 4, fols. 139v–140; Fassler, *Virgin*, 109, 425–26; **Paris:** Baltzer, "Little Office of the Virgin," 463–65; **Reims:** Bishop, "On the Origin of the Prymer," 232n2, citing London, British Library, Royal 11 B.xiii, ed. Chevalier, "Ordo legendi et cantandi Remensis ecclesiae," in *Sacramentaire et martyrologe*, 261–305, at 271 (although this may be referring to the Saturday Office).

82. Baltzer, "Little Office," 465.

83. *Antiphonaire monastique*, 7–8, 59, 272–73, and 310; Roper, *Medieval English*, 260–66 (Table 4:10). The antiphoner was copied ca. 1230.

84. Bishop, "On the Origin of the Prymer," 233, citing *De officiis ecclesiasticis tractatus*, c. 52, ed. Jones, *Vetus registrum Sarisberiense*, 1:90, on the vespers of Saint Mary at Sarum. See Donovan, *The De Brailes Hours*, 176–80, on the Sarum Use in the Book of Hours. For the full text of the Sarum Use in Middle English, see Maskell, *Monumenta ritualia*, 3: 3–81. On the Marian liturgy at the cathedral, including the daily Marian Mass (introduced in the 1220s), the Saturday commemorative Mass and Office, the Masses on Mary's feast days (Conception, Purification, Annunciation, Assumption, Nativity, and, from the mid-fifteenth century, the Visitation, Presentation of the Virgin in the Temple, and Compassion), and the Marian Hours, see Morgan, "Marian Liturgy." The Little Hours of the Marian Office were recited daily in the Lady Chapel before the Marian Mass, while Matins, Lauds, and Vespers were sung in choir following the same offices for the day.

85. Canal, "Oficio parvo," 498–99, and Canal, "El oficio parvo," 470, citing Van Dijk and Walker, *Origins*, 129–30, 191, and *passim*; and Righetti, *Manuale*, 2:523–25. Canal notes that the two oldest known copies of the breviary adopted by Saint Francis both contain the *Officium B. M. Virginis secundum consuetudinum romanae ecclesiae* (Assisi, Convent of Saint Damiano, fols. CCLIX–CCLXv; Munich, Convent of Saint Ana, fols. 226–28; MS cited by Van Dijk). For the Roman Marian Office as described in the *Ordo Breviarii* of 1243–1244 by the Franciscan Haymo of Faversham, see Van Dijk, ed., *Sources*, 2:185–91.

86. Thomas of Cantimpré, "Defense of the Mendicants," trans. Tugwell, *Early Dominicans*, 135–36. Cf. Robert Kilwardby, "Letter to Dominican Novices," trans. Tugwell, *Early Dominicans*, 149: "First of all, you should know that, before our Order arose, certain holy people were vouchsafed revelations from God, which we now have in writing, showing that the prayer of the glorious Virgin obtained this Order from her Son, when he was angry at the sins of the world, for the reconciliation of sinners. And it is not unreasonable to believe that it is from her too that the Order's progress and advancement and its guidance and preservation come." Early versions of the Dominican Office appear in Rome, Santa Sabina XIV L 1 (Humbert's Codex), and London, British Library, Add. 23935, both of which were made in Paris in the mid-thirteenth century (Baltzer, "Little Office," 482n20). On Humbert's Codex, see Boyle and Gy, *Aux origins de la liturgie dominicaine*.

87. Humbert, *De eruditione praedicatorum (On the Formation of Preachers)*, Sermons for Saints and Feast Days no. VII, trans. Tugwell, *Early Dominicans*, 355. On Humbert's reforms of the Dominican Office, see Brett, *Humbert of Romans*; and Bonniwell, *History*, 130–47.

88. Dominican Constitutions of 1228, dist. 1, cap. 1, ed. Thomas, *De oudste constituties*, 312–13; trans. Tugwell, *Early Dominicans*, 457. On the Dominican devotion to Mary, see Fassler, "Music and the Miraculous."

89. Humbert, *De eruditione praedicatorum*, lib. 2, sermo 97, in Casagrande, ed., *Prediche alle donne*, 49; cited by Millett, "*Ancrene Wisse*," 38n63.

90. See above, n. 20.

91. For contents of some early Books of Hours, see Wieck, *Time Sanctified*, 171–72, 207, 221–22; and Morgan, "English Books of Hours," 75–87.

92. Donovan, *The De Brailes Hours*, 125–27, 130–1; Duffy, *Marking the Hours*, 8–10.

93. Donovan, *The De Brailes Hours*, 88–95, 130; Duffy, *Marking the Hours*, 58–59. The alteration involved adding three psalms, according to Donovan's chart on 180: Psalm 109 (*Dixit Dominus*), 112 (*Laudate pueri*), and 147 (*Lauda Jerusalem*; although the chart says "*Lauda verbum*"). This still leaves out Psalm 126 (*Nisi Dominus*). Psalm 121 (*Laetatus sum*) appears as the first psalm in the Sarum Use for Vespers.

94. *Ancrene Wisse: A Corrected Edition*, part 1, ed. Millett, 1:9: "Euchan segge hire Ures as ha haued iwriten ham" (Cambridge, Corpus Christi College 402, fol. 6r); trans. Millett, 9: "Each of you should say her Hours as she has them written down." According to Millett ("*Ancrene Wisse*," 26), the word order makes it clear that the anchoresses did their own copying, rather than having the text copied for them. Cf. Aelred, *De institutione inclusarum*, chap. 9, ed. Talbot, "The 'De institutis inclusarum,' " 184.

95. *Ancrene Wisse: A Corrected Edition*, part 1, ed. Millett, 1:7–19, trans. Millett, 7–19, trans. White, 9–26. For the Virgin's ascent of the steps, see Jacobus de Voragine, *Legenda aurea*, cap. 131 (Nativity of the Virgin), trans. Ryan, 2:152. On the Gradual Psalms as read in the Marian Office, see below, chap. 3, "The Seven Hours of the Day: Terce, Sext, and None."

96. *Ancrene Riwle: Introduction and Part I*, ed. and trans. Ackerman and Dahood, 36.

97. Millett, "*Ancrene Wisse*," 32–34, citing Thomas, ed., *De oudste constituties*, dist. 1, cap. 1, 314–15. See also Millett, "Origins of *Ancrene Wisse*."

98. Millett, "*Ancrene Wisse*," 27; *Ancrene Wisse: A Corrected Edition*, part 1, ed. Millett, 1:9–10, 19, trans. Millett, 9–10, 19, trans. White, 13, 26.

99. Simons, *Cities of Ladies*, 113–17.

100. Jacques de Vitry, *Vitae Mariae Oigniacensis*, lib. 1, cap. 29, trans. King, 59; Thomas of Cantimpré, "Life of Margaret of Ypres," cap. 21, trans. King and Newman, 183; *Vita Beatricis*, lib. 1, cap. 4, trans. De Ganck, 30–31. Beatrice's biographer records that the Cistercian nuns at Florival discouraged her in this "burdensome practice" (*oneroso labore*). Perhaps it was one that she had developed herself, having memorized the Psalter by age five. Perhaps it was one that she learned while living with the beguines at Zoutleeuw before she joined the convent at the age of eight.

101. Oliver, "Devotional Psalters." On the daily recitation of the Hours of the Virgin at the Wijngaard in Bruges, see Hoornaert, "La plus ancienne règle," 8, 53. For the Dominicans' role in encouraging these devotions, see Simons, "Beguine Movement," 87–89; and Meersseman, "Frères Prêcheurs."

102. See Simons, *Cities of Ladies*, 80–85, on the beguines' role as teachers.

103. Millett, "*Ancrene Wisse*," 37n48: "The term *clerici* is not always used in the same sense in these regulations: it seems to mean sometimes 'cleric' as opposed to 'lay', sometimes 'in minor orders' as opposed to 'priest', and sometimes simply *litteratus* (i.e. fully literate in Latin, as opposed to literate in the vernacular or illiterate)."

104. Millett, "*Ancrene Wisse*," 29–30; Meersseman, ed., *Dossier*, 99–100, 105 (*Memoriale* of 1221–28); 133 (*Regula* of Caro, 1284); 139 (*Regula* of the bishop Guidaloste for the *Vestitae* of Saint Francis at Prato, 1284); 146–47 (*Regula* of Munio of Zamora for the brothers and sisters of the Penitence of Saint Dominic, 1285); 283 (*Propositum* of the Poor Catholics, 1208); 287 (*Propositum* of the Poor Catholics, 1212); and 294 (*Regula militie Jesu Christi* of Barthélemy de Vicence O.P., 1235). On the role of the confraternities in educating the laity in devotion to Mary, see Clark, "Cult of the Virgin Mary."

105. Meersseman, ed., *Dossier*, 300: "Clerici divina officia studeant celebrare, alii vero fratres, qui non sunt clerici et sciunt legere, dicant, si voluerint, officium beate Marie virginis." Cf. the statutes for the twelfth-century knights of Santiago: Leclercq, "La vie et la prière," 353, 355.

106. On the presence of married laity among the hospital workers, see Farmer, "Leper in the Master Bedroom."

107. Le Grand, *Statuts*, 37–38. Cf. the similar provisions for the hospital at Lille (ca. 1250) (Le Grand, *Statuts*, 64–65).

108. For example, Swanson, *Religion*, 62–63, 97, 100, 117, 221, 305–6; and Swanson, "Prayer," 130–38.

109. Le Grand, *Statuts*, 202: "Et qui horas beate Marie scierit et dicere maluerit ad hoc [the above-mentioned *Paters* and *Aves*] non tenetur." Cf. the statutes for Troyes (1263) (Le Grand, *Statuts*, 108): "Quicumque sciet horas Beate Marie, tam soror quam frater laycus et clericus non in sanctis ordinibus, regulariter teneatur quotidie dicere integer, et a numero Pater noster absolvatur." Also, those for the hospital at Vernon (end of the reign of Saint Louis) (Le Grand, *Statuts*, 165): "Les sereurs et li frère qui sauront les hores Nostre Dame ne sunt pas tenu à dire tant *Pater noster* ne *Ave Maria*."

110. Duffy, *Marking the Hours*, 10, 179n2 and 180n22, citing a database compiled by Nigel Morgan: thirteenth century, 30 manuscripts; fourteenth century, 104 manuscripts; fifteenth century, 610 manuscripts; sixteenth century, 28 manuscripts. Morgan, "English Books of Hours," 94–95, includes a partial list of these manuscripts.

111. Leroquais, *Livres d'heures*, lists 313 manuscripts in the main catalogue, plus 24 in the Supplement.

112. Hamburger, "Another Perspective," 107–108, with many thanks for sharing an early version of this article with me while I was working on this chapter.

113. Hamburger, "Another Perspective," 99–104. See Harrsen, *Cursus Sanctae Mariae*, 32–35, for the liturgical Use; and Suckale-Redlefsen, "Buchkunst," 248, for the association with Hedwig. Harrsen argues that the book was most likely commissioned for Agnes of Bohemia (d. 1282) by her aunt Kunegunde, wife of the Markgraf Henry of Mähren. Agnes spent three years at Trebnitz when she was a child, before returning to court life at Prague at the age of six. Images of the manuscript are available on the Morgan Library website (http://ica.themorgan.org/manuscript/143915).

114. Hamburger, "Another Perspective," 104. On these prayer books, see also Hamburger, "*Liber precum*"; Cermann, *Gebetbücher* (with thanks to Jeffrey Hamburger for drawing Cermann's research to my attention); Klemm, "Das sogenannte Gebetbuch der Hildegard"; *Hildegard-Gebetbuch*; and Ochsenbein, "Deutschprachige Privatgebetbücher." For Books of Hours with texts in French, see Brayer, "Section d'ancien français."

115. Hamburger, "Another Perspective," 108, citing Vienna, Österreichische Nationalbibliothek, Cod. 2745, and Giessen, Universitätsbibliothek, Hs. 878, as examples of manuscripts from Austria, Bavaria and/or Bohemia; and Freiburg, Universitätsbibliothek, Hs. 476, from a house of Dominican nuns on the Upper Rhine.

116. Van Engen, *Sisters and Brothers*, 98 and 271, citing Van Dijk, *Prolegomena*, 615, for the number of manuscripts. But on 583, Van Dijk says there are "mehr als 800." On the sources for Grote's Use, see Korteweg, "Books of Hours," 246–54. Korteweg's study draws on an extensive database of manuscripts produced in the Northern Netherlands (Byvanck), part of which may be accessed online at http://manuscripts.kb.nl.

117. Geert Grote, *Getijdenboek*, ed. Van Wijk; Van Engen, *Sisters and Brothers*, 271; Newman, *God and the Goddesses*, 222. For the Hours of Holy Wisdom, see Geert Grote, *Getijden van de Eeuwige Wijsheid*, ed. Weiler; and Henry Suso, *Horologium Sapientiae*, ed. Künzle, 606–18.

118. Van Engen, *Sisters and Brothers*, 271. See de Hamel, "Books of Hours: 'Imaging' the Word," 137–43, on books of Hours as a source of Scripture.

119. Van Engen, *Sisters and Brothers*, 48–55, for the regions and cities with houses of Modern Devout.

120. Van Engen, *Sisters and Brothers*, 191, on the brothers' book production. Sisters tended to work in textiles.

121. Van Engen, *Sisters and Brothers*, 100–101, 271–76, citing Hyma, "The 'De libris teutonicalibus,'" 61–70; and idem, "Het traktaat 'Super modo Vivendi,'" 56–71.

122.   Zerbolt, "De libris teutonicalibus," ed. Hyma, 69 (see note 21).

123.   The literature on known owners of Books of Hours is almost as extensive as book ownership itself. For an introduction to the range of ownership, see Duffy, *Marking the Hours*; Reinburg, *French Books*; Wieck, *Time Sanctified*; Wieck, *Painted Prayers*; Harthan, *Books of Hours*; Higgit, *Murthly Hours*; Smith, *Art, Identity, and Devotion*; Smith, *Taymouth Hours*; Hindman and Marrow, *Books of Hours Reconsidered*; Hughes, *Religious Life of Richard III*, 104–52; Rogers, "Patrons and Purchasers"; Bennett, "Transformation of the Gothic Psalter"; Bennett, "A Thirteenth-Century French Book of Hours for Marie"; Bennett, "Devotional Literacy"; Morgan, "English Books of Hours"; Korteweg, "Books of Hours"; Hamburger, "Another Perspective"; Cullum and Goldberg, "How Margaret Blackburn Taught Her Daughters"; Booton, "Breton Book of Hours"; Holladay, "Education of Jeanne d'Evreux"; Kamerick, "Patronage and Devotion"; and Waterton, *Pietas Mariana Britannica*, 1:122–25.

124.   Digital version available online through the university website in Digital Special Collections (www.leiden.edu). See Bennett, "Transformation," 212n9, on the psalters owned by Blanche of Castile (d. 1252).

125.   Jean de Joinville, *Vie de Saint Louis*, trans. Shaw, part 2, cap. 1, 182, on Louis's instruction by his mother; part 2, cap. 18, 336–37, on how he made his children learn their Hours of Our Lady and "repeat to him the Hours each day, so as to accustom them to hear these regularly when they came to rule over their own lands." There is an extensive discussion in the scholarly literature on the ways in which medieval people learned to read and to what degree of fluency. For an introduction, see Clanchy, "Images of Ladies," Clanchy, "Did Mothers Teach Their Children to Read?," and Clanchy, "ABC Primer." See Reinburg, *French Books*, 89, on how important it was for late medieval book owners to be able to say their prayers in Latin, according to the ancient tradition: "To pray meant repeating the words of others. . . . Knowing Latin grammar was beside the point." Arguably, even lay Christians like Margery understood something of the Latin, if only indirectly, by virtue of their priests' and other spiritual advisors' oral translations. As Zieman, *Singing the New Song*, 131, notes: "Layfolk were probably far more motivated to learn to read the single book or prayer roll they had acquired than to possess a generalized skill. . . . Learning to read a Book of Hours (among other books) in the terms of a repertory-based literacy was a social practice, whereby texts were transmitted from person to person as much as they were transmitted from page to person." Mary's mother Saint Anne is often depicted teaching the Virgin herself to read, typically from a psalter or Book of Hours. See Sheingorn, " 'Wise Mother' "; Scase, "St. Anne and the Education of the Virgin"; Eastmond, "Reading Art, Looking at Books"; and Orr, "Fitzherbert Hours."

126.   *Vita Beatricis*, lib. 1, cap. 20, 38; lib. 3, cap. 230, ed. and trans. De Ganck, 24–25, 44–45, 268–69.

127.   Bell, "Medieval Woman Book Owners," 161–62, citing Panofsky, *Early Netherlandish Painting*, 1:68.

128.   De Hamel, *History*, 184–85.

129.   Rogers, "Patrons," 1165–81; Van Bergen, "Production," 271–83.

130.   Rogers, "Books of Hours," 48; cf. Duffy, *Marking the Hours*, 25.

131.   On Browne's book (Philadelphia, Free Library, Widener 3), see Duffy, *Marking the Hours*, 21 and plates 16–17. Digital images at http://libwww.freelibrary.org/medievalman.

132.   *Book of Margery Kempe*, lib. 1, cap. 9, ed. Windeatt, 82–83. Duffy, *Marking the Hours*, 58, says that Margery was saying Matins, but her book says she was in the church of Saint Margaret at N., hearing Mass (*heryng hir messe*).

133.   *Book of Margery Kempe*, lib. 1, cap. 58, ed. Windeatt, 278–80.

134.   For the price of books in the fourteenth century, see Bell, "Medieval Woman Book Owners," 154. For the spread of book ownership down the social scale, see Reinburg, "Books of Hours," 70–71.

135.   Duffy, *Marking the Hours*, 58, makes much the same point. Paradoxically, in this age of digital books, texts have typographically become once again markedly more fluid.

136.   On early editions and print runs, see Reinburg, "Books of Hours," 73–74; Reinburg, *French Books*, 37–43; Winn, *Anthoine Vérard*, 219–36; Dondi, "Books of Hours," 53–70, 212–23; Bowen, *Christopher Plantin's Books of Hours*, 22–54, 263–66; Hoskins, *Horae*; and Bohatta, *Bibliographie*.

137. Hoskins, *Horae*, 1. Both editions are now known only from fragments, neither of which includes the Office of the Virgin, making their Use impossible to determine.

138. Winn, "Anthoine Vérard, Publisher and Bookseller"; Winn, "Hore beate virginis."

139. Hoskins, *Horae*, 1–9.

140. Bowen, *Christopher Plantin's Books of Hours*, 25, citing Moreau, *Inventaire chronologique*.

141. Duffy, *Marking the Hours*, 36, 121, for the number of English-market editions. Duffy gives 760 as the number of printed editions, but this is likely from Bohatta, *Bibliographie*, with whose figures Reinburg, "Books of Hours," 73, takes issue. According to Reinburg, Bohatta lists 740 Paris editions, but the more recent inventory made by the Bibliothèque nationale lists only 595. For further discussion, see Reinburg, *French Books*, 37–40. It is not clear where Duffy gets his number of 114 editions for England. Hoskins, *Horae*, lists 115 for before 1535, but only 94 before 1530 for the Sarum Use. Another three were produced for the York Use.

142. Duffy, *Marking the Hours*, 58.

143. See Duffy, *Marking the Hours*, 58–60, who argues against the contention that Books of Hours may be best seen as a "symptom or a cause of rising individualism and isolation."

144. *A Relation, or Rather a True Account of the Island of England*, trans. Sneyd, 23.

145. Pius V, *Quod a nobis* (1568), in *Magnum Bullarium Romanum*, vol. IV, part 3, no. 87, para. 9, 23.

146. On this model of prayer, see Giardini, "Unceasing Prayer."

147. Clement, *Stromateis* 7.35, trans. Oulton, 114–15; Tertullian, *De oratione*, cap. 25, ed. and trans. Evans, 34–35; Hippolytus, *Traditio apostolica*, cap. 36, trans. Dix, 62–65; Origen, *De oratione*, 12.2, trans. Greer, 104–5; Cyprian, *De dominica oratione*, cap. 35, trans. Stewart-Sykes, 91–92. See Phillips, "Prayer in the First Four Centuries A.D.," 37–45; and Stewart, "Prayer."

148. Cited by Taft, *Liturgy*, 33.

149. On the history of prayer according to the schedule of the Divine Office on which the Marian Hours were modeled, see Taft, *Liturgy*; Woolfenden, *Daily Liturgical Prayer*, 201–28; McKinnon, "Origins of the Western Office"; Black, "Divine Office"; Mitchell, "Liturgical Code"; Battifol, *History*, trans. Baylay; Stewart, *Cassian*, 100–113; Stewart, "Prayer"; de Vogüé, "Prayer"; and de Vogüé *Rule*, 127–72, 251–57. On the history and definition of Christian prayer more generally, see above, "Invitatory", n. 3.

150. Tertullian, *De oratione*, cap. 25, ed. and trans. Evans, 34–35.

151. Hippolytus, *Traditio apostolica*, cap. 36, ed. Hamman, *Early Christian Prayers*, trans. Mitchell, 254–55; cf. trans. Dix, 62–68.

152. Hippolytus, *Traditio apostolica*, cap. 36, trans. Taft, *Liturgy of the Hours*, 24.

153. Basil, *Great Asketikon [Long Rules]* 37:2–5, trans. Taft, *Liturgy*, 85–86; cf. trans. Wagner, 309–10. Cassian, *De institutis coenobiorum*, lib. 3, cap. 3, trans. Ramsey, 59–62.

154. Basil, *Great Asketikon [Long Rules]* 37:2–5, trans. Taft, *Liturgy*, 85–86; cf. trans. Wagner, 309–11.

155. Cassian, *De institutis coenobiorum*, lib. 3, cap. 4, trans. Ramsey, 62–63.

156. McKinnon, "Origins," 71; Taft, *Liturgy*, 206–9.

157. Cassian, *De institutis coenobiorum*, lib. 3, cap. 4, trans. Ramsey, 63.

158. Benedict, *Regula*, cap. 16, ed. Fry et al., *RB 1980*, 210–11; cf. de Vogüé, *Rule*, 127–39.

159. Smaragdus, *Commentaria in regulam*, lib. 3, cap. 16, trans. Barry, 326–37. For the interpretation of the Hours in the *Regula Cassiani*, see Ledoyen, "La *Regula Cassiani*," 177.

160. Hrabanus, *De institutione clericorum*, lib. 2, caps. 1–9, ed. Zimpel, 344–51; also PL 107, cols. 325–29. On the terminology for Matins and Lauds, see Taft, *Liturgy*, 77n2. For the manuscripts of Hrabanus's work, see Zimpel, 160–230.

161. Tickle, *Divine Hours*, 1/2/3: viii–xii, emphasizes the fact of the schedule rather than its typological significance.

162. Peter Damian, Letter 17, ed. Reindel, *Epistolae*, 1:156; trans. Blum, 1:146. According to Peter, the vices are pride, avarice, vainglory, anger, envy, lust, and spiritual torpor.

163. Honorius, *Gemma animae*, lib. 2, cap. 54, PL 172, col. 633; Johannes Beleth, *Summa de ecclesiasticis officiis*, cap. 28, ed. Douteil, 2:55; Sicardus, *Mitrale*, lib. 4, cap. 3, PL 213, col. 160; Durandus, *Rationale*

divinorum officiorum, lib. 5, cap. 1.4, ed. Davril and Thibodeau, 2:10–11. On this symbolism, see also Ohly, "Cathedral as Temporal Space," 217–19.

164.   Honorius, *Gemma anima*, lib. 2, cap. 53, PL 172, cols. 632–33; cf. trans. Ohly, "Cathedral as Temporal Space," 215–16; and Sicardus, *Mitrale*, lib. 4, cap. 3, PL 213, col. 160.

165.   Beleth, *Summa de ecclesiasticis officiis*, cap. 27, ed. Douteil, 2:54. Cf. Sicardus, *Mitrale*, lib. 4, cap. 3, PL 213, col. 160; and Durandus, *Rationale divinorum officiorum*, lib. 5, cap. 1.3, ed. Davril and Thibodeau, 2:10.

166.   Goscelin, *Liber confortatorius* lib. 3, cap. 7, ed. Talbot, 83; cited by McNamer, "Reading," 79n35. Cf. trans. Otter, as *Book of Encouragement and Consolation*, 99–100. On Goscelin's advice to Eva about how to say the Psalms, see below, chap. 3, "The Seven Hours of the Day: Terce, Sext, and None."

167.   Peter Damian, Letter 17, ed. Reindel, *Epistolae*, 1:159–60; trans. Blum, 1:149–50.

168.   Rupert, *Liber de divinis officiis*, lib. 1, caps. 1–8, ed. Haacke, 7–10. Cf. Honorius, *Gemma animae*, lib. 2, cap. 55, PL 172, cols. 633–34; Beleth, *Summa de ecclesiasticis officiis*, cap. 29, ed. Douteil, 2:57; Sicardus, *Mitrale*, lib. 4, cap. 3, PL 213, col. 161; Adam of Dryburgh, *Liber de ordine, habitu et professione*, sermo 9.8, PL 198, cols. 526–27; Durandus, *Rationale divinorum officiorum*, lib. 5, cap. 1.6, ed. Davril and Thibodeau, 2:12.

169.   See Fulton [Brown], *From Judgment to Passion*, on the interdependence between devotion to Christ and Mary more generally in medieval exegesis and prayer.

170.   Anselm of Lucca, *Oratio 3*, ed. Wilmart, "Cinq texts," 63–64; trans. Fulton [Brown], *From Judgment to Passion*, 225–26.

171.   Pseudo-Bonaventure, *Meditationes Vitae Christi*, caps. 74–80, trans. Taney et al., 236–68. On the authorship of the *Meditationes*, see McNamer, "Origins of the *Meditationes*," who complicates the attribution to John. On the importance of the *Meditationes* for the development of late medieval devotion to Christ and Mary, particularly the invitation to share with Mary in Christ's suffering at the Passion, see McNamer, *Affective Meditation*, 86–115; Bestul, *Texts*, 111–44; and Karnes, *Imagination*, 141–78.

172.   *Meditationes Vitae Christi*, caps. 74–75, trans. Taney et al., 238–39, 243.

173.   *Meditationes Vitae Christi*, cap. 75, trans. Taney et al., 245.

174.   *Meditationes Vitae Christi*, cap. 78, trans. Taney et al., 256.

175.   *Meditationes Vitae Christi*, cap. 79, trans. Taney et al., 258.

176.   Gertrude, *Legatus divinae pietatis*, lib. 3, cap. 46, ed. Doyère, *Oeuvres spirituelles*, 3:206–13; trans. Sister Mary Frances Clare, 227–30; trans. Winkworth, 214–16; trans. Barratt, 148–50. See below, chap. 2, "Saying the Ave," for Gertrude's experience of saying the Ave Maria.

177.   For the context at Syon Abbey, see Yardley, *Performing Piety*, 203–27. For the effect on the nuns of reading the *Myroure*, see Bryan, *Looking Inward*, 75–104.

178.   *Myroure of oure Ladye*, part 1, caps. 1 and 3, ed. Blunt, 11–12, 15.

179.   *Myroure of oure Ladye*, first prologue, ed. Blunt, 4–5.

180.   *Myroure of oure Ladye*, part 1, caps. 2–3, ed. Blunt, 13–15. The author of the *Myroure* would seem to be drawing on Durandus, *Rationale divinorum officiorum*, lib. 5, cap. 1.8, ed. Davril and Thibodeau, 2:13, for his Marian exegesis of the Hours, but with changes. For Christ's appearances after the Resurrection as recapitulated in the Hours, see Honorius, *Gemma animae*, lib. 2, cap. 56–57, PL 172, col. 634; Sicardus, *Mitrale*, lib. 4, cap. 3, PL 213, col. 161; and Durandus, *Rationale divinorum officiorum*, lib. 5, cap. 1.6, ed. Davril and Thibodeau, 2:12.

181.   On the implications of this liturgical way of thinking for the medieval understanding of time more generally, see Fassler, "Liturgical Framework." For the laity's knowledge of the christological significance of the hours, see Fulton Brown, "Exegesis, Mimesis, and the Voice of Christ."

182.   Williams, "English Reformers," 239–43.

183.   The quotation is from Reinburg, "Popular Prayers," 70: "The 'hours' of the Little Office recall significant episodes in Mary's life: the Annunciation, Visitation, Nativity, Annunciation to the Shepherds, Epiphany, Purification, the Flight into Egypt, and the Coronation." Cf. Reinburg, *French Books*, 17:

"Divided into eight canonical hours, the hours of the Virgin celebrated Mary by marking the significant events of her life." Also de Hamel, "Books of Hours: 'Imaging' the Word," 140: "The Hours of the Virgin, as its name implies, honours events in the life of the Virgin Mary." Note, however, that de Hamel is here speaking specifically of the images in Books of Hours, not the text of the Office itself.

184. Donovan, *The De Brailes Hours*, Appendix 1, 171–75; pl. 4, 8, and 10; and figs. 37, 42, and 52. This manuscript is fully digitized online at www.bl.uk/manuscripts/FullDisplay.aspx?ref=Add _MS_49999. On the Infancy cycle as found in later Books of Hours, see Wieck, *Time Sanctified*, 60–72; and Vanwijnsberghe, "Le cycle de l'Enfance." The story of the Wandering Jew who accosted Jesus at the Crucifixion, converted, and spent the rest of his life as a wandering preacher of Christ appears in Roger of Wendover's (d. 1236) *Flores historiarum* (ca. 1228) and was reiterated in his *Chronica majora* by Matthew Paris (d. 1259), Roger's successor as chronicler of Saint Albans. For the later history of this legend, see Cohen, "The 'Wandering Jew.' "

185. Illuminated folios digitized online at www.bl.uk/catalogues/illuminatedmanuscripts/record .asp?MSID=8851&CollID=28&NStart=1151.

186. Donovan, *The De Brailes Hours*, Appendix 3, 188–89, and figs. 88 and 93; Backhouse, *Illuminated Page*, fig. 71; Princeton Index of Christian Art, online at http://ica.princeton.edu.

187. Leroquais, *Les livres d'heures*, 1: xvii: "A leur suite, relégué depuis longtemps parmi les supplements du bréviaire, se trouve un office abrégé, notablement plus court que les precedents et intitulé: *Officium parvum beatae Mariae virginis.*" Leroquais himself notes that this title was not that found in most manuscripts; its "littleness" seems to have been emphasized only much later in its use.

188. *Antiphonaire monastique*, 7; Roper, *Medieval English*, 260. At Paris in the thirteenth century, the canons seem to have said all three nocturns with all nine lessons each night (Baltzer, "Little Office," 465–66). Other early Offices of three nocturns: Vatican, Biblioteca Apostolica Vaticana, Chigi, C.VI.173 (eleventh to twelfth century); Paris, Bibliothèque nationale, lat. 3719 (late twelfth century: Saint Martial of Limoges); Paris, Bibliothèque nationale, lat. 10433 (late twelfth century: Westminster). On these early Offices, see above, n. 20.

189. On the Saturday commemorative Office of the Virgin, see Roper, *Medieval English*, 91–137. For the alternation of the nocturns over the course of the week, see Baltzer, "Little Office," 465–66. For the structure of the Divine Office generally, see Harper, *Forms*, 86–108.

190. As with all things having to do with the Hours of the Virgin, there were exceptions. The Uses of Sarum (ed. Maskell) and York (ed. Wordsworth) have only one nocturn, but both Rome (*Little Office*) and Paris (ed. Baltzer) have three.

191. Dewick, ed., *Facsimiles*, Cotton Tiberius A.iii, fol. 108: "Spiritus sanctus in te descendit, Maria, ne timeas habens in utero filium dei." Cf. CAO #5006: "Spiritus sanctus in te descendet Maria ne timeas habebis in utero filium dei alleluia."

192. Dewick, ed., *Facsimiles*, Royal 2 B. V, fol. 1v: "Exaltata es, sancta Dei genitrix, super choros angelorum ad celestia regna." Cf. CAO #2762.

193. Facchini, *San Pier Damiani*, 387: "Benedicta tu in mulieribus et benedictus fructus ventris tui." Cf. CAO #1709.

194. Paris, Bibliothèque nationale, lat. 5371, fol. 237v, ed. Leclercq, "Formes anciennes," 98 ("<IN> NOCTURNO"): "Precibus et meritis beatissimae Dei genitricis Mariae et omnium sanctorum, misereatur nostri et saluet nos omnipotens Dominus." No CAO parallel found.

195. London, British Library, Add. 21927, fol. 102: "Sicut letantium omnium nostrum habitatio est in te, sancta Dei genitrix." Cf. CAO #4936.

196. Paris, Bibliothèque nationale, lat. 10433, fol. 227v, ed. Canal, "Oficio parvo," 511: "Celi reginam Mariam te iure fatemur, ex cuius thalamo processit iustitie sol." Cf. CAO #1838.

197. CAO #8375. For the text of the hymn, see Raby, *Medieval Latin Verse*, no. 59, 79–80; AH 2, nr. 27, 38–39; and AH 50, nr. 72, 86–88. On the late medieval English translations of this hymn, see Pezzini, "Translations," 253–54. For the hymn as recited in the Marian Office, see chap. 3 in this volume.

198. CAO #8362. Paris, Bibliothèque nationale, lat. 10482, fol. 306, ed. Baltzer, "Little Office," 474.

199. Madan, "Hours of the Virgin Mary (Tests for Localization)"; updated in "The Localization of Manuscripts." Plummer, " 'Use' and 'Beyond Use,' " proposes checking the following in addition to the Madan items: the first lesson and its responsory at Matins; the first psalm antiphon, the chapter and the antiphon for the canticle at Lauds; the antiphons and chapters from Terce and Sext; the first psalm antiphon, chapter, and antiphon for the canticle at Vespers; and the same for Compline.

200. Drigsdahl, *New Tests for the Localization of the Hore Beate Marie Virginis*.

201. For full comparisons of the two Offices, see Dewick, ed., *Facsimiles*, xiv–xix; and Roper, *Medieval English*, 71–75, 220–26. For complete descriptions of the manuscripts, see Ker, *Catalogue*, 240–48 (no. 186), 318–20 (no. 249). "The Nunnaminster" is so called because it was "the nuns' minster" (OE: *mynster*, from L: *monasterium*). It was known as Saint Mary's Abbey after the Conquest.

202. Baltzer, "Little Office," 480.

203. *Antiphonaire monastique*, 7–8, 59, 162, 272–73, and 310; Roper, *Medieval English*, 260–66.

204. Tolhurst, ed., *Monastic Breviary of Hyde Abbey*, 2: fols. 442–447v.

205. For example: Chicago, The University of Chicago, Regenstein Library, Special Collections 344 (Use of Rome); 345 (Use of Rome); 346 (Use of Rome).

206. On these additional items, see Leroquais, *Les livres d'heures*, 1: xxi–xxii, xxiv–xxxii; Wieck, *Time Sanctified*, 89–96, 103–23; Wieck, "Book of Hours," 496–98, 502–8; and Duffy, *Stripping of the Altars*, 233–65. See Drigsdahl, *Introduction and Tutorial*, for fuller descriptions.

207. De Hamel, *History*, 184–85; Rogers, "Patrons."

208. Zerbolt, "De libris teutonicalibus," ed. Hyma, 66–70.

209. Saenger, "Books of Hours." For a rich discussion of the aural dimension of such reading practices, see Dillon, *Sense of Sound*, 175–286. On the concern for understanding and the place of private prayer in the liturgy, see Boynton, "Prayer," Constable, "Concern for Sincerity," and Leclercq, "Culte liturgique." On the importance given to training the attention for saying the psalms, see Fulton Brown, "My Psalter, My Self." On the laity's ability to understand what they were reading, see above, n. 125.

210. Winn, *Anthoine Vérard*, 217–32, 495–500; and Winn, "Hore beate virginis Marie ad usum Sarum."

211. Bowen, *Christopher Plantin's Books of Hours*, 36–37.

212. Witcombe, "Christopher Plantin's Papal Privileges," 139–42. For the number of editions after 1571, see Bowen, *Christopher Plantin's Books of Hours*, 274–76. Plantin had already published some twenty-six editions of *Horae* before the 1571 revision.

213. In essence, Book of Hours were the personalized smartphones of their day, with arguably much the same democratizing effects on portraiture and self-expression, not to mention the passion for decorative covers. For the multitude of ways in which medieval owners personalized their Books, see Reinburg, *French Books*; Duffy, *Marking the Hours*; Kamerick, *Popular Piety*, 155–90; Sand, *Vision, Devotion, and Self-Representation*, 149–210; Smith, *Art, Identity and Devotion*; Ashley, "Creating Family Identity"; Bennett, "Making Literate Lay Women Visible"; Gelfand and Gibson, "Surrogate Selves"; Rudy, "A Pilgrim's Book of Hours"; and Sandler, "Wilton Diptych."

214. See above, "Invitatory," n. 19, for the almost complete lack of discussion on the meaning of the Marian Office in the scholarship. Reinburg, *French Books*, 209, acknowledges that there is "a grain of truth" to the argument that Books of Hours were "an artifact of Marian piety," but she does not offer an analysis of the Marian Hours in her discussion of Marian prayer as it appears in the Books, other than through the illuminations of the Annunciation that typically accompany Matins (212–18). Duffy, *Marking the Hours*, mentions the Hours of the Virgin only in passing (5–6). Hindman and Marrow, ed., *Books of Hours Reconsidered*, include sections on the prehistory, production, Uses, workshops, illustrations, and printing history of the Books of Hours, but no discussion of the contents of the Hours themselves.

2. AVE MARIA

1. For the opening of the night Office or Matins of the Virgin as described here, see *Ordinal and Customary of the Abbey of Saint Mary, York*, ed. [McLachlan] and Tolhurst, 1:46; *Horae Eboracenses*, ed. Wordsworth, 37–38; and Roper, *Medieval English*, 85–87, 297–98. According to Roper, this is the fullest account that we have of how the daily Marian Office was kept in an English Benedictine house; it is the fullest of which I am aware for any monastic community, whose customaries tend to be our most detailed sources for such practices generally. Cf. Van Dijk, ed., *Sources*, 2:187; Lisiard de Laon, *Ordinarium*, ed. Chevalier, 8; and Baltzer, "Little Office," 466, 474. For the general structure of the Divine Office on which the Marian Office was modeled, see Harper, *Forms*, 73–108. For the musical setting of the Divine Office in which the Marian Office was said, see Fassler, *Music*, 59–66; and Hiley, *Western Plainchant*, 25–30, 88–108. For Psalm 94 as cited and translated here, see *Little Office of the Blessed Virgin Mary in Latin and English*, 2–3; *Vulgate Bible, Douay-Rheims*, ed. Edgar, 3:407–8; and Taunton, *Little Office*, 94–104, with changes. For interpretation, see *Myroure*, part 2, ed. Blunt, 84–89; and Cassiodorus, *Expositio*, Psalm 94, trans. Walsh, 2:408–15.

2. "Gloria Patri et Filio et Spiritui Sancto. Sicut erat in principio et nunc et semper et in saecula saeculorum. Amen. [*Glory be to the Father, and to the Son, and to the Holy Spirit. As it was in the beginning, is now, and ever shall be: world without end. Amen.*]" This doxology (hymn of praise) was also sung at the end of each psalm in the Divine Office as well as after the last responsory in Matins. On the history of this doxology, see Thurston, *Familiar Prayers*, 178–92.

3. For the beads and ring bequeathed by Isabella in 1401 to hang before the image of the Virgin at Saint Mary's, York, see Waterton, *Pietas*, 2:264. For the probable location of the image of the Virgin in the church, see Morgan, "Marian Liturgy," 100–2 (on the image in the cathedral at Salisbury); and Waterton, *Pietas*, 2:259–63 (on the images in the cathedral at York). For the structure of the abbey, see Norton, "Buildings of St. Mary's Abbey." For the use of Marian images in the liturgy more generally, see Palazzo, "Marie," 317–22. The image would most likely have been a seated Virgin holding the Child or "Throne of Wisdom" (*Sedes Sapientiae*), although if it were newer it might have been a standing figure. On the difficulty of knowing what kind of image there might have been at York, see Morgan, "Text and Images . . . in Fourteenth-Century England," 37–38. On the most likely types for such an altar image, see Forsyth, *Throne*. On the complexity of the response to such images, see Jung, "Tactile"; and below, n. 116. On the role of such images in Marian miracle stories, see below, chap. 5.

4. For the invitation to imagine yourself present at the Annunciation, see Pseudo-Bonaventure, *Meditationes vitae Christi*, cap. 4, trans. Taney et al., 13; and Nicholas Love, *Mirror*, ed. Sargent, 23. On this late medieval style of meditation generally, see McNamer, *Affective Meditation*. On Mary at the Annunciation as a model for prayer, see Miles, "Origins"; Otter, "Entrances"; Purtle, "Iconography"; Reinburg, *French Books*, 212–18; and Schreiner, "Marienverehrung."

5. For the sweet taste in the mouth on saying the Ave Maria, see Caesarius, *Dialogus miraculorum*, dist. 7, cap. 49, ed. Strange, 2:69–70; Herolt, *Promptuarium Discipuli*, cap. 71, trans. Swinton-Bland, 99–100; and below, n. 54.

6. For Mary's admonition to slow down at the recitation of the Ave Maria, see *Liber de miraculis sanctae Dei genitricis Mariae*, cap. 32, ed. Pez, reprinted and ed. Crane, 40–41; London, British Library, Cotton Cleopatra C. X, trans. Thurston, "Our Popular Devotions II: The Rosary," 411–12; Alfonso, *Cantigas*, no. 71, trans. Kulp-Hill, 93–94; and below, n. 67.

7. Richard of Saint-Laurent, *De laudibus beatae Mariae virginis*, lib. 1, cap. 3, n. 2, ed. Borgnet, 19. On the invitation to share in Mary's compassion more generally, see Fulton [Brown], *From Judgment to Passion*.

8. CAO #8375: *Quem terra, pontus, aethera*. For the full text of the hymn, see below, opening page of chap. 3.

9. Bernard, *Sermones super Cantica canticorum*, Sermon 3.1, ed. Leclercq et al., 1:14, PL 183, col. 794, trans. Walsh and Edmonds, 1:16 (with changes); cf. Stock, *Implications of Literacy*, 419. On the kinds of experience that Bernard encouraged his brothers to extract from their reading of the Song of Songs, see Engh, *Gendered Identities*.

10. Adams, *Education*, chap. 25, 309.

11. For these prevailing psychological explanations for the appeal of Mary's cult, see Carroll, *Cult*; Ruether, *Mary*; Waller, *Virgin Mary*; and Warner, *Alone of All Her Sex*.

12. For the reformers' critiques, see Kreitzer, *Reforming Mary*; Williams, "English Reformers"; Williams, "Virgin Mary in Anglican Tradition"; MacCullough, "Mary and Sixteenth-Century Protestants"; Freeman, "Offending God"; and Waller, "The Virgin's 'pryvytes.'" For the image of Mary as goddess, see Ashe, *The Virgin*; Baring and Cashford, *Myth of the Goddess*, 547–608; Benko, *Virgin Goddess*; Borgeaud, *Mother of the Gods*, 120–132; and Galland, *Longing for Darkness*. A Google search on "Virgin Mary goddess" reveals that this is a lively and ongoing conversation. On the problem with this argument *ad deam* as an explanation for the early development of Marian devotion, see Shoemaker, *Mary*, 9–14, and below, chap. 3, n. 106.

13. On the image of Mary in the Catholic Church following Vatican II, see Spretnak, *Missing Mary*; and Thompson, "Vatican II and Beyond," in Graef, *Mary* (2009).

14. For further introduction to this understanding of Mary as it is newly emerging from the medieval sources, see Boss, *Empress and Handmaid*; Donavin, *Scribit Mater*; Fassler, *Virgin of Chartres*; Fulton [Brown], *From Judgment to Passion*; Fulton [Brown], "Mary"; Fulton Brown, "Mary in the Scriptures"; Miles, "Mary's Book"; Mossman, *Marquard von Lindau*, 243–334; Newman, *Frauenlob's Song of Songs*; Newman, *God and the Goddesses*, 245–90; and Robinson, *Imagining the Passion* (with the caveats expressed in Fulton Brown, *Speculum* 89.3 [2014]: 817–19). For the contrast of the medieval image of Mary with that developed in the nineteenth and twentieth centuries, see Pope, "Immaculate and Powerful," and below, chap. 5.

15. For this emphasis on Mary as a type of the Church, see Barré, "Marie et l'Église"; Coathalem, *Le parallelisme*; de Lubac, *Splendour of the Church*, 268–87; *Lumen Gentium*, chap. 8; *Catechism of the Catholic Church*, part 1, chap. 3, art. 9, para. 6, §963–72, 273–76; and Llamas, "Mary, Mother and Model." For medieval images of Mary read as images of the Church, see Thérel, *Le triomphe*; Gold, *The Lady and the Virgin*, 56–61; and Katzenellenbogen, *Sculptural Programs*, 60–65. For additional citations from post–Vatican II magisterial documents, see "Mary and the Church: Figure and Model of the Church," compiled by M. Jean Frisk for The Marian Library/International Marian Research Institute, Dayton, http://campus.udayton.edu/mary/resources/documents/docs4-2. html. Nevertheless, as O'Carroll, *Theotokos*, s.v. "Type of the Church," 346–48, notes: "The modern Popes had frequently spoken of Mary's relationship with the Church; but never before Vatican II, of Mary as type or figure of the Church. . . . With the exception of St. Albert the Great, the great Scholastic Doctors did not develop the theme. Nor is it found in subsequent literature until the 'return to the sources,' and the ecumenical approach of the present age." For further discussion on the tensions that developed between the *ressourcement* supporters of the newer "ecclesio-typical" Mariology and those who would argue for a more "christo-typical" approach, see Nichols, *There is No Rose*, 131–50. As Nichols notes, it is one thing to say that the ancient and medieval sources to which the *ressourcement* writers sought to return make use of the Mary-Church motif; it is wholly another to insist that it is the *dominant* theme of the Mariology of the premodern period.

16. CAO #2762: "Exaltata es sancta Dei genitrix super choros angelorum ad caelestia regna."

17. Jacobus, *Mariale*, lib. 5, cap. 2, 127–28. For the image of Mary as a leader in actual battles, see Remensnyder, *La Conquistadora*; Pentcheva, *Icons*; and Fassler, *Virgin*, 12–23.

18. Anselm, *Oratio 5*, ed. Schmitt, 3:13, trans. Ward, *Prayers*, 107.

19. Dionysius, *De oratione*, section 1, trans. Ní Riain, 202; John of Damascus, *De fide orthodoxa* 3.24, cited by Thomas Aquinas, *Summa theologiae* 2a 2ae q. 83 a. 1, 3:1841b: "Oratio est ascensus mentis in Deum." On this medieval definition of prayer, see above, "Invitatory," n. 4.

20. Anselm, *Oratio 7*, ed. Schmitt, 3:22, trans. Ward, *Prayers*, 121: "mater rerum recreatarum."

21. Dante, *Paradiso* canto 32.85–87, ed. Petrocchi, trans. Mandelbaum: "la faccia che a Cristo / più si somiglia."

22. Hildegard, *Symphonia*, no. 20, stanza 4a, ed. and trans. Newman, 130–31: "O quam magnum est / in viribus suis latus viri, / de quo Deus formam mulieris produxit, / quam fecit speculum / omnis ornamenti sui / et amplexionem / omnis creature sue."

23. For examples, see Salzer, *Die Sinnbilder*.

24. Bruno of Segni (d. 1123), *Sententiae*, lib. 5, cap. 1, PL 165, col. 1022: "virgo Maria portabit in utero Christum, quem totus mundus capere non potest."

25. Gautier, *Les Miracles de Nostre Dame*, trans. Belduc, "Poetics of Authorship," 133–34, cited by Rubin, "Mary and the Middle Ages," 228. On the manuscripts and composition of Gautier's collection of miracles, see Krause and Stones, ed., *Gautier de Coinci*.

26. On the this development of the Ave Maria, see Savonarola, *Esposizione sopra l'Ave Maria*, trans. Ferrigno; *Lexikon der Marienkunde*, s.v. "Ave Maria"; LeClercq, "Marie (Je vous salue)"; Thurston, "Our Popular Devotions V: The Angelus"; and Anderson, "Enhancing the *Ave Maria*." The concluding clause is typically rendered: "Holy Mary, Mother of God, pray for us sinners, now and at the hour of our death."

27. Kreitzer, *Reforming Mary*, 30–36; Ellington, *From Sacred Body*, 213–26.

28. Letter X: Latimer to Morice, *Works*, 2:360, cited by Williams, "English Reformers," 241.

29. Letter X: Latimer to Morice, *Works*, 2:360, cited by Williams, "English Reformers," 241.

30. Grindal, *Remains*, 163; cited by Williams, "English Reformers," 242.

31. Sabatier, *Esquisse*, 24–26, cited by James, *Varieties*, 464, my emphasis. Cf. Heiler, *Prayer*, xix: "Whenever a suppliant writes down in words his most fervent prayers, he feels only too deeply that the written words are but a faint reflection of the burning prayer of his heart."

32. For sympathetic accounts of the rosary as a practice, see Wilkins, *Rose-Garden Game*; Miller, *Beads*; and Wills, *The Rosary*. For the history of the medieval practice, see Winston-Allen, *Stories of the Rose*. For further discussion of the significance and experience of such numbered prayers, see Fulton [Brown], "Praying by Numbers."

33. So, for example, Gass, *Chanting*, recommends the Ave Maria alongside chants from various Hindu, African, Buddhist, Islamic, Jewish, shamanic, and Native American traditions, as all being grounded in a "core of shared truth that lies at the heart of all spiritual paths: the knowledge of a divine, creative force that permeates all of reality, and the belief that something of that divine nature lives within each of us" (65). In Gass's words (203): "Chanting . . . is a powerful means of aligning our bodies, hearts, and minds to the wavelength of Spirit. Our restless minds find peace in the repeating, rhythmic vibrations of chant. Our wandering hearts find a home in devotion to the Source of all love. And the anxiety of our grasping ego is channeled into praise and gratitude to the Creator. As our being begins to resonate with the frequency of Spirit, we will sometimes have the experience of oneness with God." On the mechanism and efficacy of such attentional practices as currently understood, see Csikszentmihalyi, *Flow*; and Luhrmann, *When God Talks Back*, 189–226.

34. *Myroure of oure Ladye*, part 1, cap. 12, ed. Blunt, 32–35.

35. Thurston, "Our Popular Devotions II: The Rosary," 407: "The earlier ascetics do not seem to have picked out this psalm or that, because it appealed to them, or because it chimed in with the particular mood in which they happened to find themselves. They looked upon prayer not subjectively but objectively. They chanted the psalms not because they liked to say them, but because they thought that God liked to hear them, and had put them there to be said."

36. Augustine, *In Psalmum CXLIV enarratio*, PL 36, col. 1869, CSEL 95.5:101, my translation: "ut bene ab homine laudetur Deus, laudavit se ipse Deus; et quia dignatus est laudare se, ideo invenit homo quemadmodum laudet eum."

37. Jacobus, *Mariale*, lib. 1, cap. 16, 42: "Ista salutatio in secretario Trinitatis Dei facta est." This phrase does not appear in the works of Bernard or indeed anywhere in the texts included in the Patrologia Latina, the Brepols Library of Latin Texts, or the Analecta Hymnica.

38. Richard, *De laudibus*, lib. 1, cap. 1, n. 2, ed. Borgnet, 8: "O beata Virgo, congaudeo et congratulor saluti et gloriae tuae."

39. Jacobus, *Mariale*, lib. 17, cap. 1, 358–61.

40. Richard, *De laudibus*, lib. 1, cap. 3, n. 2, ed. Borgnet, 19.

41. Richard, *De laudibus*, lib. 1, cap. 7, n. 10, ed. Borgnet, 55; trans. Thurston, "Our Popular Devotions V: The Angelus," 491, with changes.

42. Richard, *De laudibus*, lib. 2, cap. 2 4, ed. Borgnet, 82–106. For Richard's instructions on how to serve Mary more fully, see below, chap. 5.

43. Thurston, "Our Popular Devotions V: The Angelus," 483–88; Thurston, *Familiar Prayers*, 90–108; d'Achery and Mabillon, eds., *Acta sanctorum ordinis S. Benedicti*, 7: lviii–lx. See also Laurenceau, "Les debuts," 238–42; and Anderson, "Enhancing the *Ave Maria*," 37–41. For the Ave Maria as invitatory in the earliest Offices of the Virgin, see Dewick, ed. *Facsimiles*: Cotton Tiberius A.iii, fol. 107v, and Royal 2.B.V, fol. 1v.

44. Peter Damian, Letter 106, ed. Reindel 3:174; trans. Blum, *Letters*, 4:179–80.

45. Thurston, *Familiar Prayers*, 98–106; Bridgett, *Our Lady's Dowry*, 175–99.

46. Franco, *De gratia Dei*, lib. 6, PL 166, col. 745, trans. Thurston, *Familiar Prayers*, 101.

47. Baldwin, *Tractatus septimus: De salutatione angelica*, ed. Bell, 193–94, PL 204, cols. 467, 469, trans. Bell, *Spiritual Tractates*, 191–92.

48. Elisabeth, *Libri visionum*, lib. 1, §VI, ed. Roth, 6, trans. Clark, *Complete Works*, 47.

49. *Vita [Hermanni Iosephi] auctore canonico Steinfeldensi synchrono*, c. 3, AASS, April vol. 1, dies 7, 693, trans. Thurston, *Familiar Prayers*, 97–98.

50. Jacques de Vitry, *Vita Mariae Oigniacensis*, lib. 1, cap. 9.29, ed. Huygens, 73; AASS June iv, die 23, col. 643; Thurston, "Genuflexions and Aves II," 550–51.

51. Thomas of Cantimpré, "Life of Margaret of Ypres," cap. 21, trans. King and Newman, 183. On Margaret's recitation of the Mary-psalters, see Meersseman, "Les frères prêcheurs," 75–76.

52. *Vita Beatricis*, lib. 1, cap. 4, trans. De Ganck, 30–31.

53. For introduction to these collections of miracle stories, see Ward, *Miracles*, 132–65; Boyarin, *Miracles of the Virgin in Medieval England*; Wilson, *Stella Maris*; Timmons and Boenig, *Gonzalo de Berceo*; Cooke et al., "Miracles of the Virgin" (including cross-references to variants on almost two hundred miracles told in Middle English); Southern, "English Origins"; and Jennings, "Origins." For their importance for our understanding of the devotion to the Virgin, see below, chap. 5.

54. Caesarius, *Dialogus Miraculorum*, dist. 7, cap. 49, ed. Strange, 2:69–70. Cf. Herolt, *Promptuarium Discipuli*, cap. 71, trans. Swinton-Bland, 99–100. On this metaphor of sweetness in the encounter with God, see Fulton [Brown], " 'Taste and See.' " On sweetness understood as a property of beautiful speech, see Carruthers, *Experience*, 80–107; and Carruthers, "Sweetness."

55. William of Malmesbury, *De laudibus et miraculis*, lib. 2, cap. 10, ed. and trans. Thomson and Winterbottom, 39–40; Herolt, *Promptuarium Discipuli*, cap. 32, trans. Swinton-Bland, 53–54.

56. William of Malmesbury, *De laudibus et miraculis*, lib. 2, cap. 16, ed. and trans. Thomson and Winterbottom, 55–56. Cf. Gonzalo de Berceo, *Milagros*, no. 2, trans. Mount and Cash, 32–35; John of Garland, *Stella maris*, no. 36, ed. Wilson, 126–27.

57. Dominic of Evesham, *De miraculis sanctae Mariae*, cap. 10, ed. Canal, 34. Cf. *Miracula*, ed. Dexter, no. iv, 18–19.

58. Jacobus, *Legenda aurea*, cap. 51 (Annunciation), trans. Ryan, 1:201. Cf. *The South English Legendary*, in *Miracles of the Virgin in Middle English*, trans. Boyarin, 46–49.

59. Southern, *Making*, 248: "Like the rain, this protective power of the Virgin falls on the just and the unjust alike—provided only that they have entered the circle of her allegiance." For further examples of this insistence, see below, chap. 5.

60. Clark, "Cult," 234.

61. Guibert, *De laude sanctae Mariae*, cap. 12, PL 156, col. 573–74.

62. Crane, "Miracles," 246–47; Gautier, *Les Miracles de Nostre Dame*, ed. Koenig, 3:35–41, trans. Blumenfeld-Kosinski, 640–42; Alfonso, *Cantigas*, no. 68, trans. Kulp-Hill, 90; Jean Gobi, *Scala coeli*, ed. Polo de Beaulieu, no. 645, 438–39; Herolt, *Promptuarium Discipuli*, caps. 46–47, trans. Swinton-Bland, 73–75.

63. Guibert, *De laude sanctae Mariae*, cap. 12, PL 156, col. 573.

64. Crane, "Miracles," 247.

65. Alfonso, *Cantigas*, no. 68, trans. Kulp-Hill, 90.

66. Cf. Mary's delight at the Aves offered by Countess Ada of Avesnes as recounted by Herman of Tournai (d. 1147), *Liber de restauratione S. Martini Tornacensis*, cap. 57, ed. Huygens, 99–102; MGH Scriptores 14, 298–99, trans. Nelson, 79; trans. Thurston, *Familiar Prayers*, 103. For the story of the knight saved from a demon by his Aves, see Jacobus, *Legenda aurea*, cap. 51 (Annunciation), trans. Ryan, 1:201–2; Crane, "Miracles," 270–72; and Herolt, *Promptuarium Discipuli*, cap. 68, trans. Swinton-Bland, 96.

67. Alfonso, *Cantigas*, no. 71, trans. Kulp-Hill, 93. Cf. Crane, "Miracles," 256 (where the nun is from Saxony); *Liber de miraculis*, cap. 32, ed. Pez, reprinted Crane, 40–41 (where the nun and her convent are named); London, British Library, Cotton Cleopatra C.X, ed. and trans. Thurston, "Our Popular Devotions II: The Rosary," 411–12 (where, again, she is called Eulalia); Gautier, *Les Miracles de Nostre Dame*, I Mir 29, ed. Koenig, 2:273–84, trans. Poquet, cols. 482–88 (where she says one hundred fifty Aves before an image of the Virgin); and Savonarola, *Esposizione*, trans. Ferrigno, 164–65. Crane, "Miracles," 256; Thurston, "Our Popular Devotions II: The Rosary," 4122; and Cooke, "Miracles," 3523, list further examples.

68. *Liber de miraculis*, ed. Pez, cap. 32, 40; Thurston, "Our Popular Devotions II: The Rosary," 4121.

69. Ludolph of Saxony, *Vita Jesu Christi*, pars 1, cap. 5.27, ed. Rigollot, 1:52, trans. Clark, "Cult," 236: "Est tibi, Virgo Maria, quasi osculum, audire hunc versum Angelicum *Ave*. Toties enim beatissima oscularis, quoties per *Ave* devote salutaris. Ergo, fratres carissimi, ad imaginem ejus accedite, genua flectite, oscula ei imprimite, *Ave, Maria* dicite." This passage does not appear in the works of Bernard.

70. Gertrude, *Legatus*, lib. 4, cap. 12, ed. Clément, *Oeuvres spirituelles* 4:132; trans. Sister Mary Frances Clare, 368, with changes.

71. On the composite authorship of Gertrude's *Legatus*, see Finnegan, *Women*, 76–78; Harrison, " 'Oh! What Treasure Is in This Book?' "; and Harrison and Bynum, "Gertrude." On the complexities of Gertrude's devotion to Mary, see Clark, "An Uneasy Triangle," and Elkins, "Gertrude the Great." For the importance of the liturgy in Gertrude's devotions, see Harrison, " 'I Am Wholly Your Own,' " and Vagaggini, *Theological Dimensions*, trans. Doyle and Jurgens, 741–803.

72. Gertrude, *Legatus*, lib. 4, cap. 12, ed. Clément, *Oeuvres spirituelles* 4:136; cf. trans. Sister Mary Frances Clare, 370; and trans. Vagaggini, *Theological Dimensions*, trans. Doyle and Jurgens, 767.

73. Clark, "An Uneasy Triangle," 46, citing Clément, *Oeuvres spirituelles*, 4:142–431. Gertrude offered a similar devotion on the feast of Mary's Nativity, "having said as many *Ave Marias* as she had remained days in her mother's womb" (*Legatus*, lib. 4, cap. 51, ed. Clément, *Oeuvres spirituelles*, 4:418; trans. Sister Mary Frances Clare, 453).

74. Gertrude, *Legatus*, lib. 4, cap. 12, ed. Clément, *Oeuvres spirituelles*, 4:142–44; cf. trans. Sister Mary Frances Clare, 373.

75. Gertrude, *Legatus*, lib. 4, cap. 51, ed. Clément, *Oeuvres spirituelles*, 4:430; cf. trans. Sister Mary Frances Clare, 458.

76. Gertrude, *Legatus*, lib. 5, cap. 3.2, ed. Clément, *Oeuvres spirituelles*, 5:68–71.

77. Mansi et al., eds., *Sacrorum conciliorum*, vol. 23, col. 432: "Item praecipimus, quod quilibet Christianus, et quaelibet Christiana, omni die dicat septies suum *Pater noster*: quia septies in die debet laudare Dominum, juxta Prophetam: *Septies in die laudem dixi tibi*. Similiter septies, *Ave Maria*, et bis suum *Credo*; et ad hoc faciendum moneatur frequenter, et ad sciendum cogatur." For further references, see Clark, "Cult," 232–33, citing Paris (1198), Salisbury (1217), Béziers (1246), Le Mans (1247), Albi

(1254), Norwich (1257), Liège (1287), Bergen (1320), Drontheim (1351), and Skalholt (1354); and Morgan, "Texts and Images . . . in Thirteenth-Century England," 74–75n4, citing Salisbury (1219), Coventry (1224), Exeter (1225), Lincoln (1239?), Norwich (1243), Winchester (1247?), Durham (1249), Chichester (1245), Ely (1256), London (1259), Winchester (1265), and Exeter (1287). On this conciliar legislation, see also Beissel, *Geschichte der Verehrung Marias*, 229–30.

78. *Ancrene Wisse: A Corrected Edition*, part 1, ed. Millett, 8–10, 19, trans. Millett, 8–10, 19; trans. White, 11–13, 26.

79. See above, chap. 1, "A Little History of the Office."

80. Le Grand, *Statuts*, 65.

81. Meersseman, "Les Congrégations," 38–46.

82. Meersseman, "Les Congrégations," XLI (1312), cap. 4, 127–28. The *lauda* translates: "Blessed be the name of Our Lord Jesus Christ and his sweet mother Virgin Mary."

83. *Regula Fratrum et Sororum Ordinis de Penitentia Beati Dominici*, cap. 6, ed. Meersseman, *Dossier*, 147–48.

84. This is a chant from the Office for the Dead. CAO #4617: "Requiem aeternam dona eis domine et lux perpetua luceat eis. [*Lord, grant them eternal rest and let perpetual light shine upon them.*]"

85. Meersseman, "Les Congrégations," XLI (1312), cap. 4 and 6, 127–29. The *lauda* translates: "Blessed be that Lord, who created, appeared to, and nourished us, and by the mercy of God may every faithful departed soul rest in holy peace. Amen." With thanks to Robert Fulton for help with the translation.

86. *Regula Fratrum et Sororum Ordinis de Penitentia Beati Dominici*, cap. 6, ed. Meersseman, *Dossier*, 147–48.

87. Thurston, *Familiar Prayers*, 112; Clark, "Cult," 233; Clanchy, "ABC Primer," 24–28; Rudy, "An Illustrated Mid-Fifteenth-Century Primer," 67, 70. For the Ave as part of the Office in the vernacular, see *The Prymer or Lay Folks' Prayer Book* [Cambridge, University Library, Dd. 11. 82; ca. 1420–1430], ed. Littlehales, part 1, 1; Haimerl, *Mittelalterliche Frömmigkeit*, 150–51 (Cgm 136 [1475], fol. 146v; and Cgm 87 [1420], fol. 1r); and above, chap. 1, nn. 114–22. For the Ave Maria translated, paraphrased, and glossed, see John Mirk, *Instructions for Parish Priests*, ed. Peacock, 13, ll. 422–25; Wells, *Manual*, 530; Bridgett, *Our Lady's Dowry*, 186–89; Gros, *Ave Vierge Marie*, 109–50; Scott-Stokes, ed., *Women's Books*, 76–87; Revell, *Fifteenth-Century English Prayers*, 50 (London, British Library, Royal 17 C. XVII, fol. 91) and 97 (London, British Library, Add. 10036, fols. 92r–v); Saupe, ed., *Middle English Marian Lyrics*, 55–58 (Oxford, Bodleian Library, Bodleian 21700 [Douce 126], fol. 92r–v); and Rothenberg, *Flower*, 162–72.

88. Meersseman, "Les Congrégations," 27–32, 61–68; Meersseman, "La predication dominicaine," 131–61; and Nicola da Milano, *Collationes de beata virgine*, ed. Mulchahey. On the friars' audiences for their sermons, see d'Avray, *Preaching*, 29–43; Corbari, *Vernacular Theology*; Lesnick, *Preaching*; and Muessig, ed., *Preacher*. On the friars' training as preachers, see Roest, *History*, 272–324.

89. See, for example, Jacobus de Voragine, O.P., *Sermones de sanctis*, sermones xcviii–ciiii; Bartolomeo da Breganze, O.P., *I "Sermones de beata virgine,"* ed. Gaffuri, sermones 38–103; Bonaventure, O.F.M., *Sermones de b. Virgine Maria*, 657–87 (Sermones I–VI De Annunciatione); and Matthew of Aquasparta, O.F.M., *Sermones de beata Maria virgine*, ed. Piana, 48–94. On these late medieval Marian sermons generally, see Ellington, *From Sacred Body*. On the Franciscan preaching collections, see Roest, *Franciscan Literature*, 1–119. For further examples, see van der Heijden and Roest, *Franciscan Authors*.

90. *Speculum seu salutatio beatae Mariae virginis*, ed. Martinez, trans. Sister Mary Emmanuel. For additional commentaries on the Ave Maria, see *Speculum*, ed. Martinez, 71–73n42.

91. Richard, *De laudibus beatae Mariae virginis*, ed. Borgnet, vol. 36; Pseudo-Albertus Magnus, *Mariale, sive CCXXX quaestiones super Evangelium "Missus est Angelus Gabriel"*, ed. Borgnet, vol. 37.

92. Servasanctus, *Mariale, sive De laudibus Virginis Mariae*; Jacobus, *Mariale, seu Sermones aurei de beata Maria virgine*. On Servasanctus as a preacher, see d'Avray, "Philosophy"; and Oliger, "Servasanto

da Faenza." In addition to the sermons that he preached on the Marian feasts (see above, n. 89), Jacobus also touched on Marian themes in the sermons he preached during Lent. See *Sermones Quadrigesimales*, ed. Maggioni, nos. 203, 217, 230, 244, 258, 272, 277, 278, 286, and 287. These Lenten sermons survive in some 309 known manuscripts.

93. Conrad, *Speculum*, ed. Martínez, 113–33. On the contents, structure, and themes of Conrad's *Speculum*, see Girotto, *Corrado di Sassonia*, 132–47; and Prinzivalli, "Il 'Commento all'Ave Maria.' "

94. On Richard's popularity as an author and the manuscripts and editions of his work, see Chatillon, "L'héritage littéraire"; Colasanti, "Il 'De Laudibus B.M.V.' "; Glorieux, *Répertoire*, 1:330–31; Roten, "Richard v. St. Laurentius"; Solignac, "Richard de Saint-Victor"; www.mirabile.it, s.v. "Richardus de Sancto Laurentio"; and www.manuscripta-mediaevalia.de, s.v. "ricardus de laudibus." On the *Mariale* of Pseudo-Albert, see Fries, "Die unter dem Namen" (including its sources and influence); Kolping, "Zur Frage" (with descriptions of the manuscripts); Korosak, *Mariologia*, 3–18; and Pelster, "Zwei Untersuchungen." See appendix for a handlist of Richard's manuscripts.

95. On the manuscripts of Servasanctus's *Mariale*, see Bandini, *Catalogus*, 4:309–10 (on Florence, Laurenziana Cod. Plut.35.sin.4, which belonged to Servasanctus's convent at Santa Croce; manuscript digitized online at TECA digitale as "Anonymi De laudibus beatae Mariae"); Hermann, *Die italienischen Handschriften*, 152–53 (on Vienna, Österreichische Nationalbibliothek 1389, acquired by Archbishop Ernestus of Prague [d. 1364] from Bologna and given to the Augustinian house at Glatz); James, *On the Abbey of S. Edmund*, 65–66 (on Ipswich Museum No. 4); Koehler, "Onze manuscrits"; Koehler, "Une liste d'*Ave*"; and Robinson, *Imagining the Passion*, 184–93 (on Madrid, Biblioteca Nacionale de España 8952, mistakenly identified as the work of anonymous compilers at the cathedral of Ávila).

96. Jacobus, *Mariale*: Hamburg: Johann and Thomas Borchard, 1491 (digitized at http://diglib.hab.de /inkunabeln/510-theol-2f-2/start.htm); Venice: Simon de Luere for Lazarus de Suardis, de Saviliano, 1497 (digitized at https://books.google.com/books?id=t1wCQxpTtE8C&dq=mariale&source =gbs_navlinks_s); and Paris: per Philippe Pigouchet expensis Jean Petit, 1503 (digitized at www .mdz-nbn-resolving.de/urn/resolver.pl?urn=urn:nbn:de:bvb:12-bsb10165719-2). Rudolph Clutius, O.P., edited a new edition published in Mainz (Sumptibus Petri Cholini, 1616), which was reprinted in Lyon (Apud Joann. Mattaeum Mart., 1688), and Antwerp (Apud Henricum & Cornelium Verdussen, 1712). For manuscripts, see Kaeppelli, *Scriptores Ordinis Praedicatorum Medii Aevi*, 2:367–68. Publication information given here and in nn. 97-99 and 101 taken from entries in WorldCat, the Incunabula Short Title Catalogue (www.bl.uk/catalogues/istc), the Universal Short Title Catalogue (http://ustc.ac.uk), and Pettegree and Walsby, *French Books III & IV*.

97. Conrad, *Speculum beatae Mariae virginis*: Augsburg: Anton Sorg, 1476 and 1477; Antwerp: Gheraert Leeu, 1487; Basel: Michael Furter, 1506; and s.l.: 1521 (digitized at www.mdz-nbn-resolving.de/urn /resolver.pl?urn=urn:nbn:de:bvb:12-bsb10188904-7).

98. Richard, *De laudibus beatae Mariae virginis*: Strasbourg: Johann Mentelin, not after 1473, bound with the *Mariale, sive CCXXX quaestiones super Evangelium* (digitized at http://daten .digitale-sammlungen.de/~db/0007/bsb00078847/images/); Strasbourg [Argentine]: Martin Flach [Simus], 1493 (digitized at http://diglib.hab.de/inkunabeln/448-1-theol-2f-4/start.htm); and Cologne: Heinrich Quentell, 1502 and 1509. *Mariale, sive CCXXX quaestiones super Evangelium "Missus est Angelus Gabriel"*: Cologne: Ulrich Zell, 1473; Strasbourg: Johann Mentelin, not after 1473, bound with Richard's *De laudibus beatae Mariae virginis*; Basel: Michael Wenssler, not after 1474; Strasbourg: Martin Schott, not after 1486; Milan: Ulrich Scinzenzeler, per Alvise Serrazzoni, 1488 (digitized at http://gateway.proquest.com/openurl?url_ver=Z39.88-2004&res_dat=xri:eurobo :&rft_dat=xri:eurobo:rec:ita-bnc-in2-00001211-001); Lyon: Johannis Cleyn, 1503 (digitized at https://books.google.com/books?id=xGo2ahYxw4cC&dq=mariale&source=gbs_navlinks_s); and Venice: per Lazzaro Soard, 1504 (digitized at www.mdz-nbn-resolving.de/urn/resolver .pl?urn=urn:nbn:de:bvb:12-bsb10188002-4).

99. Ed. Jean Bogard, as *Domini Richardi a Sancto Laurentio qui ante quadrigentos annos floruit de laudibus b. Mariae Virginis libri XII. Mira pietate, ac eruditiones referti, accesserunt similis argumenti S. Anselmi Cantuariensis Archiepiscopi oratio ad B. Virginem, sive meditatio de laude meritorum eiusdem. Omnia ex m.s. nunc primum edita: una cum B. Hildephonsis Archiepis. Toletani libris duobus de perpetua Virginitate, & Parturitione B. Mariae, & Sermonibus de eadem: item D. Amedei Episcopi Lausanie de Maria Virginea Matre Homiliis octo recognitii. Adjecti multiplices indices* (Douai: Typis Ioannis Bogardi; Antwerp: Apud Martinum Nutium, 1625; digitized at https://books.google.com /books?id=YuJdYy-yRHMC&dq=de+laudibus+b.+mariae+virginis&source=gbs_navlinks_s); ed. Pierre Jammy, in Albertus Magnus, *Opera quae hactenus haberi potuerunt* (Lyon: Claudius Prost et al., 1651), vol. 20 (along with the *Mariale, sive CCXXX quaestiones super Evangelium*).

100. On the history of these attributions, see Graef, *Mary*, 1:266–73.

101. Vienna, Österreichische Nationalbibliothek 1389, ed. Bohuslao Balbino, as *Mariale, sive liber de praecellentibus et eximiis SS. Dei genitricis Mariae supra reliquas creaturas praerogativis, ex arcanis S. Scripturae, SS. Patrum, theologiae et philosophiae naturalis mysteriis concinnatus ab Ernesto Primo Archiepiscopo Pragensi ante annos CCLXXXIX. conscriptus atque hoc demum anno piissimis Ferdinandi Tertii, Romanorum Imperatoris erga SS. Dei Virginem auspiciis lucem editus. Opus omnibus sacrarum litterarum studiosis sed praecipue concionatoribus apprime utile* (Prague: Typis Caesareo-Academicis, 1651; digitized at https://books.google.com/books?id=l_BVAAAAcAAJ &dq=mariale+1651&source=gbs_navlinks_s). For Servasanctus as the author of the *Mariale*, see Bartos, "Mariale Servasancti et Mariale Arnesti."

102. On the evening recitation of the Ave Maria as promoted especially by the Franciscans from 1269, see Graef, *Mary*, 1:308; Waterton, *Pietas*, 1:143–47; Thurston, "Angelus"; and Henry, "Angelus." On the development, proliferation, and significance of images of the Annunciation, see Blum, *New Art*, 163–90; Miles, "Origins"; Purtle, "Iconography"; Reinburg, *French Books*, 212–18; Robb, "Iconography"; Van Dijk, "Angelic Salutation" (with special emphasis on images inscribed with the Ave Maria); and Wenzel, "Die Verkündigung." On responses to such images, see Schneider, "Site and Insight"; and Williamson, "Altarpieces." On the Annunciation in the liturgy, see Robertson, "Remembering the Annunciation." On the development of the rosary, see Fracheboud, "Cistercian Antecedents"; Fulton [Brown], "Praying by Numbers"; Miller, *Beads*; Mitchell, *Mystery*; Thurston, "Our Popular Devotions: II. The Rosary"; Wilkins, *Rose-Garden Game*; Winston-Allen, *Stories*; and Winston-Allen, "Tracing the Origins." On Mary-psalters, see below, "Aves in the Psalms."

103. *Le ménagier de Paris*, cited by Alexandre-Bidon, "Des femmes de bonne foi," 122.

104. Honorius Augustodunensis, *Sigillum beatae Mariae*, PL 172, col. 499–500; trans. Carr, *Seal*, 53, with changes. On these Marian commentaries on the Song of Songs more fully, see Fulton [Brown], *From Judgment to Passion*, 244–464; Fulton [Brown], "Mimetic Devotion"; Matter, *Voice of My Beloved*, 151–77; and Astell, *Song of Songs*, 42–72.

105. Rupert, *Commentaria in Cantica Canticorum*, lib. 1, ed. Haacke, 10, ed. Deutz, 1:120–21; trans. Fulton [Brown], *From Judgment to Passion*, 324.

106. Alan, *Compendiosa in Cantica Canticorum*, cap. 1, PL 210, cols. 53–54.

107. Philip, *Commentaria in Cantica Canticorum*, lib. 1, cap. 3, PL 203, col. 194.

108. Amadeus, *De Maria virginea matre*, homilia 3, PL 188, cols. 1318–19, trans. Perigo, 26, with changes.

109. Cf. Aelred, *De institutis inclusarum*, cap. 29, ed. Talbot, 200, trans. Macpherson, 80: "O sweet Lady, with what sweetness you were inebriated, with what a fire of love you were inflamed, when you felt in your mind and in your womb the presence of majesty, when he took flesh to himself from your flesh and fashioned for himself from your members in which all the fullness of the Godhead might dwell in bodily form."

110. Ludolph, *Vita Jesu Christi*, pars 1, cap. 5.27, ed. Rigollot, 1:52.

111. Aelred, *De institutis inclusarum*, cap. 29, ed. Talbot, 200; trans. Macpherson, 80 with slight changes; cited by Ludolph, *Vita Jesu Christi*, pars 1, cap. 5.26, ed. Rigollot, 1:52.

112. Walter, *Marie Carmina*, stanzas 1–8 (including stanzas 5a and 5b), ed. Rigg, *Poems*, 188–89; stanza 4, trans. Rigg, *History*, 220; remaining stanzas, my translation, with apologies to Walter for making merry with his meter. On Walter as a poet, see also Rigg, "Walter." On Walter's Marian poetry, see Donavin, *Scribit Mater*, 127–41; and Dzon, "Conflicting Notions." For a somewhat playful reading of his interest in Mary, see Sutherland, "Amplification." On this inexpressibility topos, see Linn, "If All the Sky."

113. Kreitzer, *Reforming Mary*, 31.

114. On the Ebstorf map, see Kupfer, "Reflections"; Miller, *Die Ebstorfkarte*; Kugler, *Die Ebstorfer Weltkarte*; and Areford, "The Passion Measured," 233. On the Hereford map, see Harvey, *Mappa Mundi*; and Kline, *Maps*. On the Marian imagery of the Hereford map, see Kupfer, *Art and Optics*, 44–49, 129–33, and *passim* (with thanks for sharing her work in manuscript). On the Annunciation frame, see Bailey, "Discovery." On the larger symbolism of these *mappa mundi*, see Kupfer, "Medieval World Maps."

115. Oxford, Bodleian Library, Bodleian 270b, fol. 1v, reproduced by Kline, *Maps*, fig. 8.7; Vienna, Österreichische Nationalbibliothek 1179, fol. 1v, reproduced by Zahlten, *Creatio mundi*, fig. 269; and Toledo, Archivio capitular, *Bible moralisée* of Louis IX, fol. 1v. Images digitized on The Warburg Institute Iconographic Database (http://warburg.sas.ac.uk/vpc/VPC_search/main_page.php), s.v. "Religious Iconography: Biblical Cycles: Manuscripts: Bible moralisée:[version]:Genesis."

116. For extant examples of the many statues of Mary as *Sedes sapientiae* ("seat of Wisdom") from Belgium, Germany, and France, see Forsyth, *Throne*. For such images in Spain as represented in the Escorial and Florence manuscripts of King Alfonso's *Cantigas*, see Keller and Cash, *Daily Life*, plates 1, 3, 7, 8, 10–14, 19, 30, 32, 38, 39, 41, 44, 47, 49, 50, 60, 67, 69, and 70. On the images of Mary in England, most destroyed at the Reformation, see Waterton, *Pietas*, 1:221–56, and 2: *passim*. For the image of the seated Virgin holding the Child in Italy, including in apse mosaics and panel paintings, see Belting, *Likeness and Presence*, 377–408; Lloyd, "Mary, Queen of Angels"; Norman, *Siena*; and Williamson, *Madonna*. On such images in the Latin East, see Folda, "Icon to Altarpiece." On the importance, significance, and complexity of response to these images, see Bynum, "Avoiding the Tyranny"; Bynum, "Crowned"; Camille, *Gothic Idol*, 220–41; Fassler, *Virgin*, 205–41; Forsyth, "Magi"; Gertsman, *Worlds Within*, 101–48; Gold, *The Lady and the Virgin*; Kamerick, *Popular Piety*; Smith, "Bodies"; Webb, "Image"; Webb, "Queen"; and Ziegler, "Medieval Virgin." For more recent examples of such images' cultic use, see Orsi, *Madonna*; and Remensnyder, *La Conquistadora*, 362–69, on the image in Santa Fe, New Mexico.

117. Tolkien, "Athrabeth Finrod ah Andreth," in *Morgoth's Ring*, ed. Christopher Tolkien, 322. On the importance of Catholicism for Tolkien's fiction, see Tolkien, *Letters*, ed. Carpenter, no. 142 (To Robert Murray, SJ), 213 (To Deborah Webster), and 320 (To Mrs. Ruth Austin); Birzer, *Tolkien's Sanctifying Myth*; Caldecott, *Power*; Milbank, *Chesterton*; and Philip and Carol Zaleski, *Fellowship*.

118. On Mary's purported passivity at the Incarnation, see Daly, *Gyn/Ecology*, 85 (who describes the Annunciation as a rape of Mary's "mind/will/spirit"); de Beauvoir, *Second Sex*, 189 (who hears Mary's response to the angel as "the rehabilitation of woman by the achievement of her defeat"); and Ruether, *Sexism*, 139 (who says that within "patriarchal theology" Mary represents the "good feminine" or "spiritual principle of passive receptivity to the regenerating powers of God"). More recently, Hazelton, *Mary*, 136, has graphically imagined Mary being overwhelmed at the moment of Jesus's conception by a mysterious force she cannot resist or name: "She knows what is happening, but it takes place so fast that she has no time to react. Not even to protest, let alone struggle. The weight is the worst of it. It bears down on her. It pins her to the ground and smothers her like a huge dark cloud until she can't speak, can't cry out, has no voice at all. A giant hand seems to cover her face—her eyes, her nose, her mouth. She is suffocating. No sight, no voice, no breath in her for so long that she is sure she will never see, speak, breathe again. And then, as quickly as it began it is over." It is still a rape, but one to which Mary responds courageously.

119. Anselm, *Oratio 7*, ed. Schmitt, 3:20–22, trans. Ward, *Prayers*, 117–21. On Anselm's prayers to Mary, see Fulton [Brown], *From Judgment to Passion*, 232–43; Fulton [Brown], "Praying with Anselm"; and Fulton Brown, "Anselm and Praying with the Saints." For further discussion of Anselm's understanding of Mary's role in redemption, see Larson, "Passive Instrument"; and Gambero, *Mary*, 109–116. For the circulation and influence of Anselm's prayers in the later Middle Ages, see Cottier, *Anima mea*. On the bodily grounding for the twinned metaphors of container and way, see Johnson, *Body*.

120. Hildegard, *Scivias* I.4.8, ed. Führkötter and Carlevaris, 72, trans. Hart and Bishop, 116. For Hildegard's understanding of Mary, see Newman, *Sister*, 156–95; Garber, "Where Is the Body?"; and Holsinger, *Music*, 87–136. On Hildegard's understanding of the Incarnation as revelation, see Fulton Brown, "Hildegard of Bingen's Theology."

121. Hildegard, *Scivias*, III.13.1, ed. Führkötter and Carlevaris, 615; trans. Hart and Bishop, 525; cf. *Symphonia*, trans. Newman, 115.

122. For examples, see Lechner, *Maria Gravida*, figs. 26, 135, 155/XXI, 155/XXVIII, 162 (most missing their crystals). One of the most famous of these images is that of the Visitation from the Dominican convent of Katharinenthal in Switzerland, now in the Metropolitan Museum in New York, where both Mary and Elizabeth were originally shown with babies shining from their bodies. See Jung, "Crystalline Wombs"; Hamburger and Marti, *Crown*, 48–52; digital image at www.metmuseum. org/collection/the-collection-online/search/464596. Significantly, it was not only Mary through whom God's light was believed to have shone into the world, although it was of course historically only she through whom God had become incarnate. In the Middle Ages, the bodily relics of the saints were often displayed in reliquaries set with lenticular crystals backed with gold or silver foil so as to suggest that the crystals (or relics) themselves were emitting (heavenly) light. See Hahn, "Reliquaries."

123. Adam, "Splendor Patris et figura," AH 54, nr. 100, 154; trans. Newman, *Symphonia*, 272. On Adam's sequences as they were performed at Notre Dame in Paris, see Fassler, *Gothic Song*. On this imagery of Mary as a sun-filled crystal, see Gros, "La *Semblance*"; and Fassler, *Virgin*, 141–42, where it is used by Ivo of Chartres. For this stanza as quoted by Richard of Saint-Laurent, see below, chap. 4, "Lectio prima. . . . Temple."

124. *In antiphonam Salve Regina*, sermo 3.2, PL 184, col. 1069. The most comprehensive introduction to these catalogues of names remains Meersseman, *Hymnos Akathistos*. See also Meersseman, " 'Virgo a doctoribus praetitulata,' " where Meersseman argues for an "erneuerten Mariologie" based on this tradition of titles. Sinués Ruíz, "Advocaciones de la Virgen," edits another anonymous catalogue of titles from the twelfth century found in Arxiu de la Corona d'Arago, Ripoll 193, suggesting that these lists of names were current throughout Europe, including the Iberian peninsula. On this catalogue, see also Stewart, "*Domina Misericordiae*," 126–35.

125. Frauenlob, *Marienleich*, strophes 11–13, trans. Newman, *Frauenlob's Song of Songs*, 23–27.

126. Phillips, " 'Almighty and al merciable queene,' " 86–87: "The result may be a deeply mysterious, powerfully attractive, and reverent splendour, but the verbal artifice, semantic alienations and dichotomies that play a part in creating the particular type of jewelled and mentally dazzling hyperbole to which writers of late medieval marian praise are so often drawn could be seen also as expressions of unresolved contradictions in the elevation to so high a place in theology and devotion of a woman, in a society that gives women and female qualities in general little power or respect." For the reformers' critique, see Kreitzer, *Reforming Mary*.

127. Richard, *De laudibus*, lib. 10, cap. 11, ed. Borgnet, 491.

128. Richard, *De laudibus*, lib. 6–12, ed. Borgnet, 320–841. As Franklin-Brown, *Reading the World*, has shown, such encyclopedism was a feature of thirteenth-century thinking generally. Franklin-Brown does not, however, include these Marian encyclopedias in her discussion.

129. Frauenlob, *Marienleich*, strophes 9, 11, and 12, trans. Newman, *Frauenlob's Song of Songs*, 19–25.

130. Jacobus, *Mariale*, lib. 1, cap. 16, 43.

131.   *Rosarius*, ed. Sandqvist. On this work, see also Gros, "Du sommaire encyclopédique"; and Kunstmann, "Vertus et propriétés."

132.   Walter of Wimborne, *Ave Virgo Mater Christi*, stanzas 4–5, 7, 9–10, 14–15, 20, ed. Rigg, *Poems*, 146–50. For Walter's use of Richard, see Rigg, *Poems*, 21. For a fuller citation of Walter's *Ave*, see below, "Aves in the Psalms."

133.   *Pace* Phillips, " 'Almighty and al merciable queene,' " 99, who would see in such exuberant verbal play little more than an effort on the part of their clerical authors to "move the vision of female power [elicited by the various titles of Mary] towards the safely abstract and the linguistic" and thus "[recoup any] potential awe for a female cosmic power back securely into the authority of clerkes." Rubin, *Mother*, 268–82, while less critical of the clerics' efforts, nevertheless attributes them more to the clerics' desire to display their cleverness and inventiveness than to any theological urgency.

134.   Jacobus, *Mariale*, lib. 10, cap. 2, 203–4.

135.   Dante, *Paradiso*, canto 31.136–38, ed. Petrocchi, trans. Mandelbaum: "e s'io avessi in dir tanta divizia / quanta ad imaginar, non ardirei / lo minimo tentar di sua delizia." On the centrality of Mary in Dante's vision, see McInerney, *Dante*.

136.   *Den lof van Maria ghemaect op drie stauen*, ed. Brinkman and Schenkel, *Het handschrift-Van Hulthem* 1: 264–71; Warner, "Men of Letters," 221–22.

137.   Bonaventure, "De annuntiatione b. virginis Mariae," sermo I, *Opera omnia*, 9:657. On Bonaventure's understanding of Mary, see Gambero, *Mary*, 206–15; and Kirwin, "Sermons."

138.   Bonaventure, "De Purificatione B. Virginis Mariae," sermo IV, *Opera omnia*, 9:651.

139.   Bonaventure, "De Annuntiatione b. Virginis Mariae," sermo VI, *Opera omnia*, 9:683.

140.   Bonaventure, "De Nativitate b. Virginis Mariae," sermo V, *Opera omnia*, 9:717.

141.   Bonaventure, "De Nativitate b. Virginis Mariae," sermo II, *Opera omnia*, 9:709.

142.   Bonaventure, "De Purificatione b. Virginis Mariae," sermo IV, *Opera omnia*, 9:651.

143.   Bonaventure, "De Annuntiatione b. Virginis Mariae," sermo IV, *Opera omnia*, 9:671–72.

144.   This discussion was, of course, encouraged by the definition of the dogma of the Immaculate Conception in 1854. For introduction to the history of the debate over the dogma, including its medieval formulations and liturgical observance, see John Duns Scotus, "Was the Blessed Virgin Conceived in Original Sin?," in *Four Questions*, trans. Wolter, 34–75; Adams, "Immaculate Conception"; Bishop, "On the Origins of the Feast of the Conception"; Boss, "Development"; Clayton, *Cult*, 25–51; Fehlner, "Predestination"; Graef, *Mary*, 1:298–306, 310–11; Izbicki, "Immaculate Conception"; Jugie, *L'Immaculée conception*; Mayberry, "Controversy"; Mildner, "Immaculate Conception"; Nichols, *There is No Rose*, 45–65; O'Connor, *Dogma*; Reynolds, *Gateway*, 330–69; and Twomey, *Serpent*.

145.   Pseudo-Albert, *Mariale*, quaestiones 96–110, ed. Borgnet, 157–66.

146.   Graef, *Mary*, 1:272–73. According to Graef, here Pseudo-Albert most decidedly went *too far*: "All of this is deduced from the words of the angel—which, incidentally, as we saw in the first chapter, did not mean 'full of grace' at all, but 'highly favoured one.' " In her view, such "extravagant deductions from [the] principle of the fullness of grace, despite [the author's] statement in the preface that he does not wish to praise the blessed Virgin with lies" more than "justify Laurentin's remark that the work 'manifests the first symptoms of decadence,' though Richard of St.-Laurent's earlier work certainly shows them, too." For my answer to Graef's critiques of Pseudo-Albert and Richard, see below, chap. 4.

147.   Pseudo-Albert, *Mariale*, quaestio 111, ed. Borgnet, 167–68. As Donavin, *Scribit Mater*, beautifully shows, this image of Mary as *magistra* of the arts was somewhat more mainstream than Graef realized. See also Fassler, *Virgin*, 223–41, on the images of the liberal arts as they appear in the sculptural and liturgical program at Chartres, particularly the tympanum of the southern portal of the west façade where Mary is depicted as *Sedes Sapientiae*; Courtenay, "Magisterial Authority," on the representation of Mary as the patron of the arts on seals of the masters of theology and of the university of Paris; Fanger, *Rewriting Magic*, for the Benedictine monk John of Morigny's (magical) efforts to attain learning through prayer to Mary; Miles, "Mary's Book," for Mary's association with learning

and books; Mossman, *Marquard*, 243–334, on the image of Mary as prayerful contemplative and model seeker of Wisdom; and Stotz, "Les artes liberales," on the sequence *Si fuerit in triuio* celebrating Mary as beyond all human knowledge. See above, chap. 1, n. 125, on Mary as a model for learning to read. See below, chap. 4, for Mary as a teacher of the three arts of the Word.

148. Volfing, *Heinrich von Mügeln*, 122, 133, 185–86; Newman, *Frauenlob's Song of Songs*, 150–51.

149. Pseudo-Albert, *Mariale*, quaestiones 44–94, ed. Borgnet, 87–153.

150. Pseudo-Albert, *Mariale*, quaestiones 112–122, ed. Borgnet, 168–175.

151. Pseudo-Albert, *Mariale*, quaestiones 17–20, ed. Borgnet, 40–47. On Pseudo-Albert's sources for this physiognomy, see Resnick, "Ps.-Albert the Great."

152. Pseudo-Albert, *Mariale*, quaestiones 151–161, 167–193, ed. Borgnet, 220–34, 252–80. Cf. CAO #2762: "Exaltata es sancta Dei genitrix super choros angelorum ad caelestia regna."

153. Thomas Aquinas, "The Hail Mary, or the 'Angelic Salutation,' " trans. Shapcote, *Three Greatest Prayers*, 165–68. On Thomas's understanding of Mary more generally, see Gambero, *Mary*, 234–42.

154. CAO #7569: "Sancta et immaculata virginitas quibus te laudibus referam nescio. R: Quia quem caeli capere non poterant tuo gremio contulisti." Responsory for the feast of the Nativity (Christmas), widely used in the Office of the Virgin as the first responsory for Matins.

155. AH 11, nr. 83, 54: "Virgo dei genitrix, quem totus non capit orbis / in tua se clausit viscera factus homo." Hymn for the Assumption, used in the Office of the Virgin at Paris at Lauds and Compline (Baltzer, "Little Office," 476, 480).

156. Conrad, *Speculum*, V.2, ed. Martínez, 224–25; trans. Sr. Mary Emmanuel, 39–41, with changes. On Conrad's understanding of Mary more generally, see Gambero, *Mary*, 216–21.

157. Conrad, *Speculum*, V–VII, ed. Martínez, 220–88; trans. Sr. Mary Emmanuel, 37–76.

158. Conrad, *Speculum*, VI.III.5, ed. Martínez, 250–51; trans. Sr. Mary Emmanuel, 55–56, citing CAO #3877: "Nesciens mater virgo virum peperit sine dolore salvatorem saeculorum, ipsum regem angelorum sola virgo lactabat ubere de caelo pleno." Antiphon for the Nativity (Christmas), used at Hyde Abbey as the first antiphon for Matins and Vespers in the Office of the Virgin from Christmas to the Purification (*Monastic Breviary*, ed. Tolhurst, 3: fol.444–444v).

159. Conrad, *Speculum*, VII.1, ed. Martínez, 270; trans. Sr. Mary Emmanuel, 65.

160. Conrad, *Speculum*, VII.5, ed. Martínez, 278–79; trans. Sr. Mary Emmanuel, 70–71.

161. Conrad, *Speculum*, VIII.I, ed. Martínez, 291; trans. Sr. Mary Emmanuel, 78. Here Conrad goes on to quote Anselm, *Oratio 7*, ed. Schmitt, 3:18: "Regina caeli et domina mundi . . ."

162. Conrad, *Speculum*, VIII.II, ed. Martínez, 299–309; trans. Sr. Mary Emmanuel, 83–89.

163. Conrad, *Speculum*, VIII.II, ed. Martínez, 309–24; trans. Sr. Mary Emmanuel, 90–97.

164. Conrad, *Speculum*, IX–XI, ed. Martínez, 325–87; trans. Sr. Mary Emmanuel, 98–132.

165. Meersseman, *Hymnos Akathistos*, 2:53–62, 222–29.

166. On the circumstances of this conciliar acclamation, see below, chap. 3, "Miriam, the Mother of the Son of the Most High."

167. On the performance, origins, and dating of the "Akathistos," see Peltomaa, *Image*, 21–22, 49–114; and below, chap. 3. At present, the hymn is sung in the Orthodox church every year on Friday evenings in Lent, in parts over the first four weeks and in full on the evening of the fifth.

168. Meersseman, *Hymnos Akathistos*, 1:49–57 (discussion), and 1:100–27 (edition). See also Huglo, "L'ancienne version latine," who argues (Meersseman demurs) that the Latin translation was made around 825 at the monastery of Saint-Denis.

169. Meersseman, *Hymnos Akathistos*, 1:67–86 (discussion), and 1:148 (edition of *Ave maris stella*); CAO #8272; many versions in AH. On the "Ave maris stella," see Lausberg, *Hymnus "Ave maris stella"*; Fassler, *Music*, 3–10; Krass, " 'Ave Maris Stella' "; Pezzini, "Late Medieval Translations"; Reynolds, *Gateway*, 194; Szövérffy, *Marianische Motivik*, 14–15; and Weber, "Ambrose Autpert" (who rejects Lausberg's thesis that Ambrosius was the author). For the text of the hymn, see below, the concluding section of chap. 5.

170. Meersseman, *Hymnos Akathistos*, 1:165–66; AH 19, nr. 22, 24–25, Brussels, Bibliothèque royale, 8860–67, tenth century: "Dawn . . . Blessed house . . . Dove . . . Bringing forth a son to lofty David . . . Rod come forth from the root of Jesse."

171. Meersseman, *Hymnos Akathistos*, 2:12–21 (discussion), and 2:79–159 (editions). AH 35 and 36 contain many examples of such psalters.

172. Meersseman, *Hymnos Akathistos*, 2: 22–28; Winston-Allen, *Stories*, 13–30. These Ave-psalters should be distinguished from that more famous *Psalterium B. Mariae Virginis* attributed to Bonaventure, in which every psalm is rewritten in honor of the Virgin.

173. Meersseman, *Hymnos Akathistos*, 2:13, 79–96; AH 35, nr. 13000, 189–99. Dreves lists sixteen manuscripts, Meersseman another two, but neither notes Arundel 157. According to the online catalogue description, this manuscript was copied in the early thirteenth century in Oxford, and was possibly associated with the Augustinian priory of Saint Frideswide. Fols. 19–131 contain a psalter; fols. 132–185 contain the Office of the Dead and the Hours of the Virgin (fols. 159v–85), along with other devotional pieces. *Ave porta paradisi* appears on fols. 146–59. The manuscript is particularly remarkable for containing one of the earliest Western images of the Veronica (fol. 2), the image of Christ impressed on the cloth which Veronica offered him to wipe his face on the way to the Cross. On the images and devotions found in English psalters, including a list of those containing Mary psalters and the Hours of the Virgin, see Morgan, "Patrons." For the history of the Veronica, see Hamburger, "Vision."

174. Meersseman, *Hymnus Akathistos*, 2:79, puts the prayer at the beginning of the psalter, but in Arundel 157, the prayer (as cited here) appears at Psalm 26 (fol. 148).

175. Psalm and psalter verses given as they appear in Arundel 157, fol. 146–146v. In the manuscript, the psalm verses are written in red with blue initial capitals, while the Aves are written in gold. With thanks to Ann W. Astell for inspiring this method of analysis through her own work on the Marian psalters.

176. Conrad, *Speculum*, XVI.3, ed. Martínez, 486; trans. Sr. Mary Emmanuel, 188.

177. Richard, *De laudibus*, lib. 12, cap. 6, §18, ed. Borgnet, 776.

178. Conrad, *Speculum*, XII.3, ed. Martínez, 393–94; trans. Sr. Mary Emmanuel, 136.

179. Conrad, *Speculum*, VII.5, ed. Martínez, 278; trans. Sr. Mary Emmanuel, 70.

180. Conrad, *Speculum*, VII.1, ed. Martínez, 270–71; trans. Sr. Mary Emmanuel, 66, citing Bernard, *Sermo 52: De domo divinae Sapientiae, id est Virgine Maria*, 4, ed. Leclercq et al. 6.1:276; PL 183, cols. 675–76.

181. Richard, *De laudibus*, lib. 1, cap. 5, n. 3, ed. Borgnet, 37–38.

182. Richard, *De laudibus*, lib. 1, cap. 3, n. 1, ed. Borgnet, 17–18.

183. Conrad, *Speculum*, IX.II.4, ed. Martínez, 350; trans. Sr. Mary Emmanuel, 113.

184. Bonaventure, "De Purificatione b. Virginis Mariae," sermo IV, *Opera Omnia*, 9:651.

185. Jacobus, *Mariale*, lib. 18, cap. 2, 392–94.

186. Richard, *De laudibus*, lib. 11, cap. 31, n. 1, ed. Borgnet, 523.

187. On the law of sanctuary, see Shoemaker, *Sanctuary*. On the story of Theophilus, see Reynolds, *Gateway*, 197–99; O'Carroll, *Theotokos*, 341–42; Graef, *Mary*, 1:170–71, 204–5; and below, chap. 5, "The Miracle of Theophilus."

188. Jacobus, *Mariale*, lib. 4, cap. 6, 120.

189. Richard, *De laudibus*, lib. 10, cap. 11, ed. Borgnet, 491.

190. AH 35, nr. 11000, 153: "Ave, cuius viscera natum ediderunt, cuius ad interitum, *gentes fremuerunt*. Audi voces supplicum, qui te pie quaerunt, mali causas removens, quae nos invenerunt."

191. AH 35, nr. 10000, 137: "Ave, nostri *salus* morbi, per quam vita datur orbi nato Dei filio, per quam hostis ars confusa et in plebem est effusa Dei *benedictio*."

192. Meersseman, *Hymnos Akathistos*, 2:133–34; AH 35, nr. 9000, 123–24, stanzas 1.1, 1.5, 1.9, 1.14, and 1.21. On Engelbert and his works, see Fowler, "Chronology"; and Tomaschek, ed., *Abt Engelbert*. In addition to his Mary-psalter, Engelbert was also the author of a lengthy work *De gratiis et virtutibus beatae et gloriosae semper virginis Mariae*, which Mossman calls "the last great Latin *summa*

Mariana of our period [i.e., that of Marquard's predecessors and contemporaries up to the end of the fourteenth century]" and "the apogee of the Latin tradition presenting Mary as a mystical contemplative" (*Marquard*, 314). In composing this *summa*, Engelbert drew on the Pseudo-Albertine *Mariale, sive CCXXX quaestiones super Evangelium*, his personal copy of which, heavily annotated, is still in the library at Admont (Stiftsbibliothek, Cod. 272). On the parallels between the two works, see Fries, "Die unter dem Namen," 53–66 (who assumed that the author of the *Mariale* used Engelbert, rather than the reverse). According to Fowler, *Intellectual Interests*, 193–94, the *De gratiis* is extant in some dozen or so manuscripts, mainly from the southeastern Germanic region near Admont.

193. Walter, *Ave Virgo Mater Christi*, stanzas 1–10, ed. Rigg, *Poems*, 146–48. On Walter as poet, see above, n. 112

194. For example, perhaps one of the most ingenious, stanza 61, trans. Rigg, *History*, 219: "Removing death you're ablative, / Since of a son you're genitive, / Conceived immaculate. / You wash away our tears and pain; / As dative you give back again / Our long-lost free estate." See Donavin, *Scribit Mater*, 127–41, for Walter's emphasis on Mary as teacher of grammar and rhetoric. On the Victorine models for Walter's poetry, see Fassler, *Gothic Song*, 290–320.

195. See above, n. 112.

196. Walter, *Marie Carmina*, stanza 207, ed. Rigg, *Poems*, 220.

197. In Hebrew, Mary's name was *Miryam* (מִרְיָם), the name of the sister of Moses. In Aramaic it would have been *Maryam* (מִרְיָם), which was rendered in the Greek New Testament as *Mariam* (Μαριάμ). See Wikipedia, s.v. "Miriam (given name)"; Maas, "Name"; and Bardenhewer, *Der Name Maria*.

198. Richard, *De laudibus*, lib. 1, cap. 2, n. 3, ed. Borgnet, 13.

199. Bernardino, *Mariale*: Milan: Uldericus Scinzenzeler, 1492; Milan: Leonardus Pachel, 1493; Strasburg: Martin Flach,1496, 1498, 1502; Lyon: Johannis Cleyn, 1502, 1511, 1515; Nuremberg: A. Koberger, 1503; Hagenau: Johannes Rynmann, Henricus Gran, 1506, 1508, 1513, 1519; and Lyon: Antonius du Ry, Jacobus and Franciscus de Giuta, 1525; Brescia: Pietro Maria Marchetti, 1588; Cologne: Anton Hierat, 1607. Citations taken from the Newberry Library copy of the 1511 edition of Johannis Cleyn, digitized at www.mdz-nbn-resolving.de/urn/resolver.pl?urn=urn:nbn:de:bvb:12-bsb10165291-7. The 1588 edition is digitized at https://books.google.com/books?id=rrf-UE6oIdUC&dq=mariale +busti+1588&source=gbs_navlinks_s. The twelve parts deal with Mary's Immaculate Conception, Nativity, name, way of life, Annunciation, blessings, childbearing, Purification, figures, compassion, Assumption, and coronation. As popular as this work was in its own day, it is now (as Hilda Graef put it) "quite forgotten"—rightly, as far Graef was concerned (*Mary*, 1:320–22): "The wildest legends and the most exaggerated claims are mixed up with sound Mariological statements in a hodgepodge of a book whose style is as impossible as its contents." She notes in particular that Bernardino follows Pseudo-Albert in attributing to Mary "the knowledge of rhetoric, logic, physics, metaphysics and all other possible departments of knowledge to perfection; for if anyone else had this knowledge, God must have given it in a much higher degree to his Spouse." In René Laurentin's words as cited by Graef: "One realizes the decadence of the period which has established the reputation of this compilation whose sometimes excellent ideas are only too often drowned in a mass of extreme or inconsistent opinions. . . . A purification was necessary." Gambero, *Mary*, 321–22, reiterates Laurentin's critique: "We have already mentioned that many exaggerations, trifles, and banalities are mixed in with more valuable material [in Bernardino's *Mariale*]. This may be considered telling evidence of the decadence that infected the historical period in question."

200. Bernardino, *Mariale*, pars 3: "De nominatione Marie," sermo 3, fol. 107v: "Immensitas quippe glorie eius omnis humani sermonis excedit inopiam."

201. Bernardino, *Mariale*, pars 3: "De nominatione Marie," sermo 5, fol. 113r–v.

202. Bernardino, *Mariale*, pars 3: "De nominatione Marie," sermo 3, fol. 108: "Nec mirum si thesaurum immensum sapientie habuit cum in ea Christus requieuerit in quo sunt omnes thesauri sapientie et scientie dei secundum apostolum ad Colossians."

203. Bernardino, *Mariale*, pars 3: "De nominatione Marie," sermo 1, fol. 100. Although he gives the citations from scripture in full, here Bernardino simply lists his other authorities with short title references: "Hieronymus *super Mattheum* [probably not Jerome, possibly Paschasius Radbertus, ed. Paulus, 1:20–112, PL 120, cols. 43–102, who talks at length about Christ's genealogy] et Ambrosius *in sermone de nativitate virginis* [definitely not Ambrose, but difficult to identify, most likely Fulbert of Chartres, a great eleventh-century promoter of the feast of Mary's Nativity; see Fulbert, *Sermo IV: De nativitate beatissimae Mariae virginis: Approbate consuetudines*, trans. Fassler, *Virgin of Chartres*, 426–29, where Fulbert describes Mary's name as "received by divine dispensation"] et Bernardus *super missus est* [alias *In laudibus virginis matris*, ed. Leclercq et al., 4:13–58] et Anselmus *in liber de conceptu virginali* c. ii [ed. Schmitt, 2:141–42] et Bartholomeus de Pisis *in liber beate virginis fructu. viii.*" Bartholomew of Pisa is also known as Bartholomew Rinonico (d. 1401). According to Van der Heijden and Roest, *Franciscan Authors*, Bartholomew's *De vita et laudibus beatae Mariae virginis libri sex* (composed 1382; printed Venice: Dusinelli, 1596) depicts Mary as "a tree bearing the fruit of many virtues." Bartholomew is better known for his work on Saint Francis's conformity to Christ (*De conformitate vitae beati Francisci ad vitam Domini Nostri Jesu Christi*, composed between ca. 1385 and 1390; printed Milan: Gottardo da Ponte, 1510; alias "*Alcoranus Franciscanorum*").

204. Bernardino, *Mariale*, pars 3: "De nominatione Marie," sermo 1, pars 1, fols. 100–101, citing Paschasius, *Cogitis me*, c. 15, ed. Ripberger, no. 92, 151; PL 30, col. 138: "Quam si diligentius aspicias, nihil virtutis est, nihil speciositatis, nihil candoris gloriaeque, quod ex ea non resplendeat." On the importance of this sermon for the liturgy of the feast of the Assumption, see Fulton [Brown], " 'Quae est ista.' "

205. Bernardino, *Mariale*, pars 3: "De nominatione Marie," sermo 1, pars 2, fol. 101.

206. Bernardino, *Mariale*, pars 3: "De nominatione Marie," sermo 1, pars 3, fols. 102–105.

207. Bernardino, *Mariale*, pars 3: "De nominatione Marie," sermo 3, fols. 107v–110v.

208. Bernardino, *Mariale*, pars 3: "De nominatione Marie," sermo 4, fols. 110v–113.

209. Bernardino, *Mariale*, pars 3: "De nominatione Marie," sermo 5, fols. 113v–118.

210. Bernardino, *Mariale*, pars 3: "De nominatione Marie," sermo 6, fols. 118–122v.

211. Bernardino, *Mariale*, pars 3: "De nominatione Marie," sermo 6, fol. 120, cf. Jerome, *Liber interpretationis Hebraicorum nominum*, ed. de Lagarde, 137; PL 23, col. 841: "Mariam plerique aestimant interpretari, illuminant me isti, vel illuminatrix, vel smyrna maris, sed mihi nequaquam videtur. Melius autem est, ut dicamus sonare eam stellam maris, sive amarum mare: sciendumque quod Maria, sermone Syro domina nuncupetur." On the history of this etymology attributed by the mid-ninth century to Jerome (who more likely explained the name as *stilla maris* or "drop of the sea"), see Maas, "Name"; and Bardenhewer, *Der Name Maria*, 51–75. On the hymn, see above, n. 169

212. Conrad, *Speculum*, III, ed. Martínez, 175; trans. Sr. Mary Emmanuel, 15 (with changes).

213. Conrad, *Speculum*, III.II, ed. Martínez, 184–85; trans. Sr. Mary Emmanuel, 18–19.

214. Jacobus, *Mariale*, lib. 11, cap. 4, 235–39.

215. Richard, *De laudibus*, lib. 1, cap. 3, nn. 1–3, ed. Borgnet, 17–21.

216. Bernard of Clairvaux, *In laudibus virginis matris [Super "Missus est"]*, homilia 2.17, ed. Leclercq et al., 4:34–35, trans. Saïd, 30–31; cited by Richard, *De laudibus*, lib. 1, cap. 3, n. 3, ed. Borgnet, 24; Jacobus, *Mariale*, lib. 11, cap. 4, 238; Conrad, *Speculum*, III.II, ed. Martínez, 188–89; and Bernardino, *Mariale*, pars 3: "De nominatione Marie," sermo 6, fol. 120. For Dante's description of Bernard as Mary's "faithful" one, see *Paradiso*, canto 31, ed. Petrocchi, trans. Mandelbaum.

217. On this iconography, see above, n. 102.

218. Servasanctus, *Mariale*, praefatio, citing Bede, *Homilia XLVII*, ed. Giles, *Complete Works*, 5:360–68; *Homilia prima. In festo annuntiationis beatae Mariae*, PL 94, cols. 9–14; CCSL 122:14–20. According to Fassler, *Virgin*, 117, this sermon "circulated widely as part of the homiliary of Paul the Deacon," making it one of the best-known texts on the Annunciation. It is known to have been used for this feast from the eleventh century at Chartres.

219. Technically, what Servasanctus is doing here would have been quite literally elementary for his audience, schooled as even the youngest readers would have been in the practice of identifying the various parts of speech and declining or parsing a text beginning from its letters and moving through syllables and words to phrases and sense. Exactly what he is counting is another matter: he seems to be declining Luke 1:28: "Et ingressus angelus ad eam dixit: Ave gratia plena: Dominus tecum: benedicta tu in mulieribus," but only the number of words (fifteen) is correct. He counts six extra letters and two extra syllables. Bede gives the verse as "Et ingressus *autem* angelus ad eam dixit: Ave gratia plena: Dominus tecum: benedicta tu in mulieribus," which brings the syllable count to Servasanctus's thirty-seven, but does not add enough letters and makes the word count wrong. The thousands of boys and girls the chronicler Giovanni Villani tells us were attending school in Florence in 1283 (Thorndike, "Elementary and Secondary Education," 402) would doubtless have noticed the discrepancy. On the textbooks and exercises they would have been using to learn to decline the parts of speech before moving on to syntax, see Black, "Curriculum," 140–45; Black, "Vernacular," 703–5; Copeland and Sluiter, *Medieval Grammar*, 87–90 (Donatus, *Ars Minor*); and Reynolds, "Two Documents."

220. Here Servasanctus is more likely citing the Franciscan Alexander of Hales (d. 1245), *Summa theologica*, liber 3, pars 2, inquisitio 3, tractatus 2, sectio 1, quaestio 2, tit. 4, cap. 3, art. 2, num. 344, ed. Collegii S. Bonaventurae, vol. 4, part 1, 512, who cites "the Philosopher."

3. ANTIPHON AND PSALM

1. For the night Office as it continues here, see *The Ordinal and Customary of Saint Mary, York*, ed. [McLachlan] and Tolhurst, 1:46; *Horae Eboracenses*, ed. Wordsworth, 39; and Roper, *Medieval English*, 86–87. On the structure and musical performance of the Marian Office, see above, chap. 2, n. 1.

2. CAO #8375: *Quem terra, pontus, aethera*, stanzas cited as they appear with the concluding *Gloria tibi, Domine*, in *Horae Eboracenses*, ed. Wordsworth, 38–39, my translation. The full hymn consists of eight stanzas. Typically, in the Marian Office, stanzas 1, 2, 4, and 5 would be sung at Matins, stanzas 6–8 at Lauds.

3. CAO #1709: "Benedicta tu in mulieribus, et benedictus fructus ventris tui." The psalm would be introduced with the antiphon's incipit. The antiphon would be sung in full at the end of the psalm.

4. For Psalm 8 as cited and translated here, see *Little Office of the Blessed Virgin Mary in Latin and English*, 5–6; *Vulgate Bible, Douay-Rheims*, ed. Edgar, 3:166–67; and Taunton, *Little Office*, 109–114, with changes.

5. On this doxology, sung at the end of each psalm, see above, chap. 2, n. 2.

6. For the reading you have been doing, see Cassiodorus, *Expositio Psalmorum*, Psalm 8, trans. Walsh, 1:109–116. See below, n. 199, for why you would have been reading Cassiodorus as well as Augustine on the Psalms.

7. For this desire to extract the sweetness of spiritual understanding from the letter of the psalms, see Stephen of Sawley, *De informatione mentis*, ed. Mikkers, 259, trans. O'Sullivan, *Treatises*, 125. On the method of exegesis you are using, see below, n. 16.

8. Cassiodorus, *Expositio Psalmorum*, Psalm 8:2, trans. Walsh, 1:110.

9. You have also been reading Peter Lombard (d. 1160), *Commentarius in Psalmos Davidicos*, PL 191, col. 123–24, who cites Augustine, Cassiodorus, and the Carolingian Remigius of Auxerre (d. 908) on this verse. Peter's commentary was read throughout the later Middle Ages as the basis for the study of the Psalms in the schools. See Colish, *Peter Lombard*, 1:155–225; and Colish, "*Psalterium Scholasticorum*."

10. Here you have been reading Augustine, *Enarrationes in Psalmos*, Psalm 8:3, trans. Boulding, 1:132.

11. Augustine, *Enarrationes*, Psalm 8:4, trans. Boulding, 1:133.

12. Cassiodorus, *Expositio*, Psalm 8:2, trans. Walsh, 1:110; Augustine, *Enarrationes*, Psalm 8:6–7, trans. Boulding, 1:135.

13. Cassiodorus, *Expositio*, Psalm 8:6, trans. Walsh, 1:113. Italics in original.

14. Cassiodorus, *Expositio*, Psalm 8:10, trans. Walsh, 1:115.

15. On the appearance and placement of this image, see above, chap. 2, n. 3. On the significance of the Child's smile, see Binski, "Angel Choir"; Jung, "Tactile," 232–40; and Svanberg, "Gothic Smile."

16. On these traditional metaphors for exegesis, see Ohly, "Problems," 69–70; and de Lubac (trans. Sebanc and Macierowski), *Medieval Exegesis*, 1:1–3.

17. In this meditation, you would seem to have been reading Stephen of Sawley, *De informatione mentis*, ed. Mikkers, 259, trans. O'Sullivan, *Treatises*, 126–27.

18. For the medieval tradition of reading Mary herself as the model contemplative, see Mossman, *Marquard*, 243–334. For Mary as a model reader, see Miles, "Mary's Book." For Mary as a reader of the Psalms, see also Otter, "Entrances."

19. There is arguably much to be learned about this experience from the Psalms commentaries themselves, but there is as yet no comprehensive study of this tradition. There has been some scholarly work done on the Psalms as they were prayed, but relatively little attention has been given to what we can learn about this practice from the commentaries. As with the Books of Hours, much more work has been done on the psalters as books than on medieval commentary on and use of the Psalms as such. For introduction, see Van Deusen, ed., *Place*; Holladay, *Psalms*; Waltke and Houston, *Psalms*; Bennett, "Transformation"; Black, "Psalm Uses"; Boynton, "Prayer"; Büttner, ed., *Illuminated Psalter*; Cochelin, "When Monks Were the Book"; Daley and Kolbet, eds., *Harp*; Driscoll, "Seven Penitential Psalms"; Fassler, "Psalms"; Gross-Diaz, *Psalms Commentary*; Kuczynski, *Prophetic Song*; Mayr-Harting, "Praying the Psalter"; Morrison, "Church"; Panayotova, "Illustrated Psalter"; Sutherland, "Performing the Penitential Psalms"; Toswell, *Anglo-Saxon Psalter*; and Zinn, "Psalms."

20. Stephen, *De informatione mentis*, ed. Mikkers, 259–61, trans. O'Sullivan, *Treatises*, 125–27: "We are aware that different methods of psalmody affect people in different ways . . . So you see, my friend, it is very difficult for me to lay down a formula in these matters."

21. Honorius, *Gemma animae*, lib. 2, PL 172, cols. 615–42; Rupert, *De divinis officiis*, lib. 1, cap. 1–15, ed. Haacke, 7–13. On the symbolism each attributes to the Hours, see above, chap. 1, "Seven times a day I have praised you." On the Marian Office, Honorius, *Gemma animae*, lib. 2, c. 63, says only: "We sing the hours of the Virgin (*cursum de sancte Marie*) and all the saints not constrained by any law, but on account of devotion, so that, because as useless servants (*servi inutiles*) we negligently pay the debt of service, we may offer our gifts to the friends of the Lord, so that through them we make our service (*obsequium*) acceptable and obtain the grace of our Lord." On this understanding of the Marian Office as service, see below, chap. 5.

22. Leclercq, *Love of Learning*, trans. Misrahi, 237. Later medieval commentators like the Augustinian canon Jan Mombaer (d. c. 1501) were less reticent. For Mombaer's instructions on how to say the Divine Office, see his "Directorium Solvendarum Horarum," in *Rosetum*, 124–99; and Fulton Brown, "My Psalter, My Self."

23. Adams, *Mont Saint Michel*, 88; *Education*, chap. 25, 306. On Adams's response to Chartres, see also below, chap. 4.

24. See above, chap. 2, nn. 126 and 133.

25. Stephen, *De informatione mentis*, ed. Mikkers, 261; trans. O'Sullivan, *Treatises*, 130, with changes.

26. The list is from Servasanctus's *Mariale*.

27. At least, roughly: Servasanctus typically gives more than one citation as reference; this count includes only the primary citations for each name. Titles taken from the New Testament include fig tree (Luke 21:29), castle (Luke 10:38), fishnet (Matthew 13:47), treasure chest (Matthew 12:35), handmaiden (Luke 1:38), and *Magnificata* (Romans 16:6).

28. See above, chap. 2, "Naming Mary."

29. *Speculum virginum*, part 5, trans. Newman, 284–85.

30. On the problem with explaining these references as dependent on a parallel between Mary and the (likewise feminine) Church, see above, chap. 2, n. 15.

31. Cf. Maunder, "Origins," 23: "To discover anything approaching devotion to Mary in the New Testament period is next to impossible, of course." Likewise, Shoemaker, *Mary*, would date the cult to the latter half of the second century, when the earliest extracanonical sources appear.

32. *Speculum virginum*, part 5, trans. Newman, 285–86.

33. On the significance of the Psalms generally in the New Testament, including for Matthew, see Moyise and Menken, eds., *Psalms*.

34. On the way in which this disagreement was portrayed in the New Testament and its long-term effects on Jewish-Christian relations, see Nirenberg, *Anti-Judaism*, 48–86.

35. Barker, *Temple Themes*, 24 (her emphasis).

36. Calvin, *Institutes*, bk. 1, chap. 13, section 10, trans. Beveridge, 1:158–59.

37. *Speculum virginum*, part 5, trans. Newman, 285.

38. Truth be told, even the modern Catholic tradition of Marian exegesis is now largely reticent in comparison with the medieval. For modern discussions of Mary that include the Old Testament images, without, however, giving them any more robust exegetical justification than "the Sacred Tradition," see Scheeben, *Mariology* 1:17–41; Masini, *Il lezionario mariano*; and Manelli, "Mystery." In contrast, see Hahn, *Hail, Holy Queen*, 49–67, who reads the Woman of the Apocalypse unambiguously as Mary revealed as the ark of the new covenant. On the iconography of the Immaculate Conception associated with this image, see Vetter, "Mulier Amicta Sole"; Vloberg, "Iconography"; and Stratton, *Immaculate Conception*.

39. On this ambiguity in the Old Saxon *Heliand*, see Fulton [Brown], *From Judgment to Passion*, 37. On the difficulty in reconciling Protestant and Catholic scholarship on the origins of Mary's cult, see Shoemaker, *Mary*, 7–8.

40. Kort, *"Take, Read,"* offers a succinct description of this disruption generally.

41. Barker's recovery of what she calls "the Temple tradition" began with a study of the Old Testament pseudepigraphal Book of 1 Enoch, cited by the New Testament epistle of Jude (1:14–15) and considered canonical in the Ethiopian tradition (*Older Testament* [1987]; *Lost Prophet* [1988]). She has developed her larger argument over the course of seventeen books "which form a sequence, later volumes building on her earlier conclusions" (www.margaretbarker.com). *Temple Theology* (2004) gives a concise overview of the major themes of this tradition. *Mother of the Lord* (2012) gives the fullest account of the place of the Lady in the tradition; "Wisdom Imagery" (2011) gives the best summary of this aspect of the tradition.

42. For these additional scriptures, see Barnstone, *Other Bible* (with bibliography); Charles, *Apocrypha*; Charlesworth, *Old Testament Pseudepigrapha*; Schneemelcher, *New Testament Apocrypha*; and Elliott, *Apocryphal New Testament*. The Old Testament Apocrypha (1–2 Esdras, Tobit, Judith, Wisdom, Ecclesiasticus or Sirach, Baruch, and 1–4 Maccabees) were included in the third-century B.C.E. Alexandrian translation of the Hebrew scriptures known as the Septuagint and were quoted by the early Christians as scripture. On the importance of the Septuagint for the Christian tradition, including its Apocrypha, see Law, *When God Spoke Greek*. As Law notes (74): "None of these apocryphal works achieved canonical status in the Hebrew Bible, and this decision internal to early Judaism exercised a profound impact on Christian thinking for centuries to come." The Vulgate includes the Septuagint Apocrypha among the texts of the Old Testament, but the Anglican Bible excerpts them as "deuterocanonical." They do not appear at all in the Revised Standard Version based on the Masoretic text, the Hebrew Bible as revised by Jewish scholars (the "Masoretes") between the sixth and ninth centuries C.E. On the process by which early Christianity separated itself from Judaism generally, see Dacy, *Separation*. On the complexity of distinguishing between Christians and Jews in this early period, see Murray, "Jews," who, like Barker, suggests describing those who dissented against the scribal establishment of the first-century Jerusalem temple as "Hebrews."

43. Dever, *Did God Have a Wife?*, 212–19, describes these reforms as an attempt to eradicate the "folk" religion of ancient Israel.

44. I am assured by my readers for the press that most mainstream biblical scholars would insist that it is not. On the other hand, John W. Rogerson, professor emeritus of Biblical Studies at the University of Sheffield, for one, seems to have a fairly high estimation of Barker's scholarship, as he asked her to contribute the section on Isaiah for the *Eerdmans Commentary on the Bible*, which he coedited with James D. G. Dunn, Lightfoot Professor Emeritus of Divinity at the University of Durham. Barker herself has served as president of the Society for Old Testament Study (1998).

45. Mowinckel, *Psalms in Israel's Worship*, trans. Ap-Thomas. On Mowinckel's "cult-functional" approach in the larger history of modern Psalms exegesis, see Waltke and Houston, *Psalms*, 98–100, who dismiss Mowinckel's description of the fall Enthronement festival, for which he argues many of the royal psalms were originally written, as "pagan."

46. Psalm 148:7, depending, of course, on which translation you use. In the Septuagint, they are δράκοντες; in the Vulgate, they are *dracones*; in the RSV, they are sea monsters. Biblical scholarship is no less perilous territory than medieval studies, witness what Moore and Sherwood, *Invention*, call the "Great Testamentary Divide" that opened in the nineteenth century between those who self-identify as "Old Testament scholars" vs. "New Testament scholars" rather than risk the interpretational rift. It is time to brave the interdisciplinary deeps! See below, nn. 66, 134, 147, 199, and 253, for some of the more formidable dragons.

47. Barker, "Wisdom Imagery," 92–93. On this symbolism of the temple more fully, see Barker, *Gate of Heaven*; and *Great High Priest*, 146–228. On this symbolism as it appears in the New Testament, see Barker, *On Earth*. On the temple in early and medieval Christian interpretation, see O'Brien, *Bede's Temple*; and Whitehead, *Castles*, 7–27.

48. Barker, "Wisdom Imagery," 97, citing *Exodus Rabbah* XLVIII.4, trans. S. M. Lehrman (1939).

49. Barker, "Wisdom Imagery," 106. On the Lady more fully, see Barker, *Great High Priest*, 228–61; and *Mother of the Lord*.

50. Barker, *Temple Theology*, 7. On these Old Testament names of God, see Barker, *Older Testament*, 104–24, 246–60; Biale, "God with Breasts"; Eissfeldt, "El and Yahweh"; and Miller, *Religion*, 1–29. See above, n. 36, on Calvin's identification of the Angel of Israel with Christ. On the importance of such angel christologies for the development of devotion to Mary, particularly in stories about her Dormition, see Shoemaker, *Ancient Traditions*, 212–32; and Shoemaker, *Mary*, 100–29.

51. Barker, *Temple Themes*, 80. On the different versions of Deuteronomy and their importance for early Christianity, see also Law, *When God Spoke Greek*, 24–25, 47–48, 75–76, 91–94, 109, 170, and *passim*.

52. Barker, *Temple Themes*, 121. On Yahweh as the Angel more fully, see Barker, *Great Angel*. On the unity in plurality, see Barker, *Temple Mysticism*. On the importance of angels in this tradition, see Barker, *Angels*.

53. Barker, *Temple Themes*, 121–22. On the temple priesthood more fully, see Barker, *Great High Priest*, 103–45; and *Hidden Tradition*, 54–76.

54. Barker, *Temple Themes*, 91.

55. Barker, *Temple Themes*, 74.

56. Barker, *Temple Themes*, 221–38; and *Temple Mysticism*, 81–95.

57. Barker, *Temple Themes*, 135–65. On this emphasis on seeing the Lord and the tensions between the Deuteronomic and temple traditions more fully, see Barker, *King of the Jews*.

58. Barker, *Temple Themes*, 142, her emphasis.

59. On the importance of the throne in the temple tradition, see Barker, *Temple Mysticism*, 97–132; and *Gate of Heaven*, 133–77. On the cultic function of these enthronement psalms, see Mowinckel, *Psalms*, 1:106–92; and Morgenstern, "Cultic Setting." On the importance in Christianity of the desire to see the Lord, see Kirk, *Vision of God*.

60. Lombard, *Commentarius in Psalmos Davidicos*, PL 191, cols. 57–59, trans. Minnis, *Medieval Literary Theory*, 108–10.

61.   Barker, *Temple Themes*, 75. On the identification of Jesus with the Lord of the psalms, see Menken, "Psalms in Matthew's Gospel," 69: "In the ancient Greek translations of the Old Testament, the divine name יהוה is usually translated as κύριος, 'Lord'. Because early Christians considered Jesus as κύριος, they easily applied Old Testament statements about God as 'Lord' to him (see, e.g., Isa. 40:3 in Matt. 3:3 and parallels)."

62.   Barker, *Revelation*, 125–26. On Revelation as a description of Christian worship, see also Taunton, *Little Office*, 6–11.

63.   Barker, *Revelation*, 259–60, citing 1 Enoch 14:9–12, and Josephus, *Jewish Antiquities* 8.74, trans. Marcus.

64.   Barker, *Revelation*, 328–33; and *Mother*, passim. On the long Judeo-Christian tradition associating the Lady with Wisdom, see Schäfer, *Mirror of His Beauty*. On the significance of such feminine images of the divine for medieval Christianity, see Newman, *God and the Goddesses*.

65.   On this identification of the Lady, see Barker, *Temple Theology*, 88–91; *Great High Priest*, 229–61; "Wisdom Imagery"; and *Mother of the Lord*.

66.   As with the arguments in favor of seeing Mary as a goddess (see above, chap. 2, n. 12), there is a lively and ongoing debate in Old Testament scholarship whether Yahweh had a consort, usually identified with the Asherah. For discussion, see Ackerman, "Queen Mother"; Albright, "Evolution"; Dahood, "Ancient Semitic Deities"; Day, "Asherah"; Dever, "Asherah, Consort"; Dever, *Did God Have a Wife?* (who says yes); Dijkstra, "El"; Emerton, "New Light"; Hadley, *Cult*; Meshel, "Did Yahweh Have a Consort?"; Miller, *Religion*, 29–45; Smith, *Early History*, 108–47; Wiggins, "Myth"; and Wiggins, "Of Asherahs and Trees" (who questions the association with trees). The debate is an old one. G. K. Chesterton's *The Ball and the Cross* (1909) involves a duel between a Roman Catholic and an atheist who would insist that Our Lady was a Mesopotamian goddess.

67.   Barker, *Temple Themes*, 57, citing Numbers Rabbah XV.10, trans. J. J. Slotki (1939).

68.   Barker, "Wisdom Imagery," 98.

69.   Barker, *Great High Priest*, 230.

70.   Barker, *Great High Priest*, 247. On the baking of cakes for the Queen of Heaven, see also Dever, *Did God Have a Wife?*, 234, who also identifies the disks held by the female figures as cakes made in molds.

71.   Barker, *Great High Priest*, 248, citing Leviticus Rabbah XI.9, trans. J. J. Slotki (1939).

72.   Barker, *Temple Themes*, 126–27.

73.   Barker, *Temple Theology*, 77, citing Babylonian Talmud *Horayoth* 12a, trans. I. Epstein (1961).

74.   Barker, *Great High Priest*, 240–41, citing 1Q Isaa. Barker reiterates this reading of Isaiah 7:11 in her entry on Isaiah in the *Eerdmans Commentary*, ed. Dunn and Rogerson, 506 (see above, n. 44).

75.   Barker, *Mother*, 180. On the role of the queen mother in ancient Israelite religion, see Ackerman, "Queen Mother." On the divine identity of the king in these royal psalms, see Mowinckel, *Psalms*, 1:42–80.

76.   Barker, *Mother*, 125; and *Temple Themes*, 97.

77.   Barker, *Temple Themes*, 236.

78.   Barker, *Temple Themes*, 237–38; and *Temple Theology*, 81–82.

79.   Barker, *Temple Theology*, 87–88; *Temple Themes*, 160; and *Mother*, 231–55.

80.   Like Barker, Dever associates the devotion to the Asherah with the piety of the common people of ancient Israel, particularly that of the women, as against the public cult of the Jerusalem Establishment with its "orthodox priests; . . . prophetic guild (often close to the crown); . . . literati; [and] politically correct theology" represented by the Deuteronomists and Jeremiah (*Did God Have a Wife?*, 190).

81.   *Jewish Antiquities* 11.5.7, trans. Marcus. On this nomenclature, see Murray, "Jews," 198–99.

82.   On these communities, see Barker, *Mother*, 20–25. Here, it should be noted, is where Barker's argument becomes historically speaking most speculative: How, exactly, were memories of the older tradition preserved? As noted above (n. 42), Barker's evidence includes not only the texts

subsequently considered as part of the revealed canon of scripture in the Christian and rabbinic traditions, but also those texts that were later deemed apocryphal, pseudepigraphal, or in some other way not authoritative or orthodox. As John McDade, S.J., puts it in his foreword to her *Temple Theology*: "The great puzzle is how early Christian reflection on Jesus emerged so clearly, so rapidly and with such a high degree of definition. What patterns of interpretation, already in Jewish religion, crystallized around the person of Jesus Christ and his work [and his Mother]?" Barker's project is to discern these theological patterns in the texts that were available to Jesus, his followers, and their near contemporaries, not to provide a social history of their authors. Law, *When God Spoke Greek*, demonstrates how important the Septuagint and its apocrypha were for the development of Christianity, including the variants on the translation of the (subsequently) canonical texts of the Old Testament that Barker points to. It is beyond the scope of the present book (and my expertise) to test the claims that Barker has made about texts like 1–3 Enoch, *Jubilees*, 2 Baruch, *Testament of the Levi*, *Apocalypse of Abraham*, *Apocalypse of Moses*, *Assumption of Moses*, *Ascension of Isaiah*, the Ugaritic texts, the commentaries of Philo of Alexandria, the Qumran texts, *Letter of Barnabas*, *Clementine Recognitions*, the Gnostic Gospels, the Mishnah, the Tosefta, the Jerusalem and Babylonian Talmuds, the Targumim, the Midrashim, and the Merkavah texts. In the above account of Barker's reconstruction of the temple theology on which the early Christians drew, I have concentrated on highlighting primarily those texts and images that play a significant role in the later medieval devotion to the Virgin, particularly through the psalms and other texts used in her Office. To properly test Barker's conclusions would require another book. For an alternative reading of many of these same sources, see Hurtado, *One God*; and *Lord Jesus Christ*.

83.   On the composition of these texts, see *Eerdmans Commentary*, ed. Dunn and Rogerson, 763–98. On their place in the tradition of Wisdom literature more generally, see Kampen, *Wisdom Literature*, and Schroer, *Wisdom*.

84.   1 Enoch 42:1–3, trans. Charles, *Apocrypha* 2:213.

85.   Cf. Dever, *Did God Have a Wife?*, 301–3, who points to the importance of the Shekinah in thirteenth-century C.E. Jewish Kabbala as evidence that the Asherah did not go away, but was rather driven underground "where she was almost forgotten for centuries, until popular piety *and* archeology rediscovered and revived her." Deustsch, *Lady Wisdom*, argues that the evangelist Matthew brings Wisdom back in Jesus. Schroer, *Wisdom*, 132–63, sees Sophia in the dove that hovered over Jesus at his baptism. Barker's argument is that the Asherah has been hiding in plain sight in the way in which early Christian exegetes read the scriptures about Mary. In her postscript to *Mother*, 375, Barker says she plans a second volume to "trace the story of the Lady through her years of exile from Jerusalem, and then how she returned with the Christian proclamation that the Virgin had conceived [again] and borne a child." The next section of our argument here must be therefore somewhat provisional, pending Barker's fuller account.

86.   Barker, *Mother*, 43. Dever, *Did God Have a Wife?*, 213–14, suggests that the *battîm* (lit. "houses" or "temples") that the women were weaving might have been " 'tent-shrines' (as the earlier Tabernacle?). That cannot be proven, but it would make sense. Around both ancient and modern shrines in the Middle East one finds pavilions made of hanging fabrics."

87.   For the analysis that follows, see Barker, *Christmas*, 128–50.

88.   Tischendorf, ed., *Evangelia Apocrypha*, 1–50; de Strycker, *La forme*, 64–191; trans. Elliott, *Apocryphal New Testament*, 57–67; and Barker, *Christmas*, 151–61. For context, see Elliott, "Mary." This text was extremely popular and survives in at least 140 manuscripts in Greek; it was translated into Coptic, Syriac, Armenian, Georgian, Ethiopian, Slavonic (169 manuscripts extant), Arabic, and Latin. In the Eastern Church, its narrative provided the basis for the development of the Marian feasts of the Virgin's Nativity (September 8), and Conception (December 9) and was regularly cited by preachers from the eighth century on (Cunningham, "Use"). Although the *Protevangelium* itself was listed among the works to be rejected by the faithful in the so-called Gelasian Decree of ca. 500, its account

of Mary's infancy and childhood was popularized in the West by the *Gospel of Pseudo-Matthew* (ed. Tischendorf, *Evangelia*, 51–112; Gijsel, *Pseudo-Matthaei Evangelium*; Clayton, *Apocryphal Gospels*, 323–27) and the *Libellus de nativitate sanctae Mariae* (ca. 1000, ed. Tischendorf, *Evangelia*, 113–21; and Beyers), the former extant in upward of 200 manuscripts from the ninth through the fifteenth centuries, the latter in more than 140. The *Gospel of Pseudo-Matthew* was known in Mercia in the ninth century and translated into Old English before the twelfth (ed. and trans. Clayton, *Apocryphal Gospels*, 164–209). In the eleventh century, Fulbert of Chartres drew on the *De nativitate Mariae* in composing his sermon *Approbate consuetudinis* (PL 141, cols. 320–24, trans. Fassler, *Virgin*, 426–29); Fulbert's sermon was to become the standard reading for the Feast of Mary's Nativity throughout the later Middle Ages (Fassler, *Virgin*, 81–89). Sometime around 1130, the Norman poet Wace used the *De nativitate Mariae* as a source for his versified life of the Virgin in Old French (ed. and trans. Blacker et al., *Hagiographical Works*, 57–146). In the thirteenth century, Jacobus de Voragine drew extensively on this tradition for his entry on the Nativity of Mary in his *Legenda aurea* (cap. 131). As Shoemaker notes (*Mary*, 48–49), given its importance in both the Eastern and Western traditions, it is somewhat anomalous to describe the *Protevangelium* as an apocryphon: "It is true, of course, that the *Protevangelium* is an extracanonical text that treats events and characters from the biblical tradition … But at the same time the influence of this particular narrative on the subsequent Christian tradition is so vast that it must also be regarded in a certain sense as 'quasi-canonical.' " As Elliott puts it (*Apocryphal New Testament*, 48): "The influence of PJ was immense, and it may be said with some confidence that the developed doctrines of Mariology can be traced to this book." On the *Protevangelium* in the early apocryphal tradition, see also Shoemaker, "Between Scripture," who notes that "the overwhelming majority of the manuscripts [of the *Protevangelium*] are liturgical in nature, meaning that the *Protevangelium*'s traditions formed a regular part of Christian worship" (499).

89. Elliott, *Apocryphal New Testament*, 50. In contrast, Shoemaker, *Mary*, 59, notes how the *Protevangelium* "envisions Mary as a physical embodiment of holiness much in the same way that the Temple served as an unmatched locus of divine sanctity on earth."

90. Barker, *Great High Priest,* 257–58; and *Christmas*, 142–43. Constas, "Weaving," 181, cites Smid, *Protevangelium*, 75–80, as noting "that the Mishnah called for the preparation of two curtains every year to be woven by 82 young girls." Smid elaborates, citing Samuel Krause, *Synagogale Altertümer* (Berlin: B. Harz, 1922), 378: "These women, a Jewish kind of hierodules, presumably had their place of work within the area of the temple, as indeed they were paid out of the Temple monies."

91. Barker, *Temple Theology*, 29–30.

92. Barker, *Temple Theology*, 83.

93. Barker, "Wisdom Imagery," 97, her emphasis, citing *Exodus Rabbah* XLVIII.4, trans. S. M. Lehrman (1939); cf. Barker, *Mother*, 66–67.

94. Barker, *Christmas*, 141–42.

95. For these early debates, see Shoemaker, *Mary*, 64–129, who discusses the existing evidence from the second, third, and fourth centuries, including the writings of Justin Martyr (d. 165), Irenaeus of Lyons (d. 202), Tertullian (d. ca. 225), Clement of Alexandria (d. ca. 215), Origen of Alexandria (d. 253/254), the *Gospel of Mary*, Tatian's *Diatesseron* (composed between 150 and 180), the *Gospel of Thomas*, the *Gospel of Philip*, the *Pistis Sophia*, the *Gospel (Questions) of Bartholomew*, and the *Book of Mary's Repose* (which represents Mary as a teacher of wisdom and the mother of the Great Cherub of Light).

96. Epiphanius, *Panarion* 79.1.7, trans. Shoemaker, "Cult," 76–77, citing Holl and Dummer, ed., 3:473–74.

97. Epiphanius, *Panarion*, 79.2.3, trans. Williams, 2:621, although Abel, Cain, Enoch, Abraham, Melchizedek, Isaac, and Jacob had sacrificed to God, along with a long list of other patriarchs. NB: the inclusion of Enoch and Melchizedek.

98. Epiphanius, *Panarion*, 79.8.1–2, trans. Williams, 2:627–28.
99. Shoemaker, "Cult," 77. On Epiphanius's description of the Kollyridians, see also Shoemaker, "Epiphanius"; and *Mary*, 145–65.
100. Epiphanius, *Panarion*, 79.4.6, trans. Williams, 2:624.
101. Epiphanius, *Panarion*, 79.5.2–3, trans. Williams, 2:624–25.
102. Epiphanius, *Panarion*, 79.3.1, trans. Williams, 2:622.
103. Epiphanius, *Panarion*, 79.5.4, 7.1, trans. Williams, 2:625, 626.
104. Ed. and trans. Wright, "Departure." Shoemaker has studied this work extensively and is preparing a critical edition for the Corpus Christianorum Series Apocryphorum. See his *Mary*, 130–65; "Epiphanius"; "Apocrypha and Liturgy"; and "Cult," 78–79. Although Shoemaker does not highlight it, this account is full of the kind of imagery Barker would point to as an appeal to the temple tradition, particularly the welcome that Mary receives from the sun and the moon, the rain and the dew, the fire and flame, the lightnings and thunders, and all the angels as she enters the twelve gates of the heavenly Jerusalem and the vision that she enjoys of the Trinity in the place "where Enoch dwells . . . and in which he prays" (Wright, "Departure," 2:157–58). According to the *Book of Jubilees* (2:2–3), the creatures worshipping Mary are the powers created on Day One, the first day of Creation, the great secret of the Holy of Holies (Barker, *Temple Tradition*, 19–21). See below, nn. 318–19.
105. Wright, "Departure," 2:153.
106. Here Shoemaker, *Mary*, which appeared in print just as I was revising this section, is essential. Like Barker, Shoemaker would insist that there is no need to look to some external cause, whether "ancient goddess traditions, psychoanalysis, the 'eternal feminine,' or the anthropology of sacrifice," in order to explain the origins of Marian piety in early Christianity. In his words: "In my opinion, much current scholarship on the origins of Marian devotion suffers from a crisis of both overexplanation and insufficient information. Numerous studies have been published that would purport to explain devotion to the Virgin Mary as a result of some foreign impulse that has intruded upon the Christian faith or as something fully comprehensible only in light of some modern intellectual discourse that reveals the peculiar logic underlying such reverence for Mary. Indeed, works that take such an approach are often among the studies most cited by non-specialists, particularly because they appear to operate outside of the confessional interests that govern other more theologically oriented works. Nevertheless, it is hard not to see such approaches as a kind of extension of the more avowedly Protestant view of Marian cult as something grafted onto the Christian tradition only at a rather late stage. As a result, Marian piety is effectively made out to be something so exotic, so discordant with the fabric of the Christian faith that external influences must be identified in order to understand its very existence. . . . So much emphasis on discovering the skeleton key that unlocks the mystery of Christian devotion to Mary has left us without an account of Marian piety that describes how the basic principles undergirding these influential beliefs and practices actually arose from a logic that was native to the early Christian tradition itself. Instead, devotion to the Virgin is presented as something largely anomalous to the Christian tradition, a historical oddity that requires some sort of dramatic explanation for its genesis. . . . Protestant writers have often emphasized the influence of ancient goddess traditions in order to make devotion to Mary appear as something alien to the Christian tradition, framing the rise of Marian cult in terms of her gradual 'deification' rather than as a rather ordinary element of late ancient piety. So while parallels between ancient goddess traditions and early Marian piety of course remain significant for the historian of religion, they simply do not explain the emergence of Christian devotion to Mary and likewise should not be allowed to control its interpretation in the way that one finds in much previous scholarship" (11–14). Unlike Barker, however, Shoemaker would argue that the rise of devotion to Mary is best understood as a relatively ordinary outgrowth of the late antique cult of the saints, with an emphasis on Mary as a "saint among saints who was revered for her exceptional purity and holiness as well as her intimacy with her son, a more modest status that she retains, more or less, in much of the Christian East up until the present"

(16). He would specifically caution us here not to use the later medieval developments in Marian devotion as a way of understanding the earlier cult. We have been warned!

107. Alan, *Liber parabolarum*, cap. 5, PL 210, col. 591: "Mille viae ducunt homines per saecula Romam."

108. Schaff, *Creeds*, 2:57–61.

109. Shoemaker, *Mary*, 68–73, on the *Sub tuum praesidium*, generally regarded as the oldest known Marian prayer. In the Middle Ages, it was used regularly in the Office of the Virgin as an antiphon (CAO #5041), as we shall see below. For the text of the prayer as it appears in Greek in the earliest extant papyrus, see Stegmüller, "Sub tuum praesidium."

110. On these early feasts, see Shoemaker, *Mary*, 178–86; Shoemaker, *Ancient Traditions*, 78–141; Shoemaker, "Cult," 74–76; Shoemaker, "Marian Liturgies"; and Shoemaker, "(Re?)Discovery"; and Fassler, "First Marian Feast." On the hymnography for these early feasts and its importance for the Nestorian controversy, see also Carlton, " 'Temple.' "

111. Constas, *Proclus*, 58. There is considerable debate on the significance of this moment in the history of Christianity. On Proclus, Nestorius, Cyril of Alexandria, and the Council of Ephesus, see Shoemaker, *Mary*, 205–28 (who concludes that it was "Marian piety in the form of the devotional title Theotokos that gave rise to the Third Council, rather than vice-versa" [228]); Limberis, *Divine Heiress* (who argues that the Constantinopolitan image of Mary depends heavily on "imperial panegyric and indigenous Byzantine goddess traditions" [146]); Price, "*Theotokos*" (who argues that the council made no formal proclamation of the title *Theotokos* and that to focus on the council as giving the "decisive spur to the cult of the Virgin" overstates the importance of Mary in the Nestorian controversy [100]); and Atanassova, "Did Cyril of Alexandria Invent Mariology?" (who says, yes, in the context of his christology).

112. This was the second church built on the same site, completed in 415 under Emperor Theodosius II. According to Cyril Mango, s.v. "Hagia Sophia in Constantinople," *Oxford Dictionary of Byzantium*, ed. Alexander Kazhdan (Oxford: Oxford University Press, 1991), the dedication to *Hagia Sophia* is attested only from "ca. 430."

113. Proclus, *Homily 1.1*, trans. Constas, 137.

114. Socrates, *Historia ecclesiastica* 7.29.7, cited by Constas, *Proclus*, 47.

115. On the current debate over Pulcheria's importance in this controversy, see Shoemaker, *Mary*, 205–22, who argues against the tendency to underplay her role.

116. Constas, *Proclus*, 50. On the portrait and the robe, see Shoemaker, *Mary*, 212–13, who follows Richard Price in observing that it seems unlikely Nestorius actually defaced an imperial portrait, but insists that there is more likely something to the story other than fabrications by Nestorius's supporters.

117. Socrates, *Historia ecclesiastica* 7.32.1–2, cited by Constas, *Proclus*, 52.

118. Constas, *Proclus*, 51.

119. Constas, *Proclus*, 51.

120. *Vaticanus Graecus* 1431, in *Acta conciliorum oecumenicorum* I.I.I, ed. Schwartz, 103, cited by Constas, *Proclus*, 60.

121. Proclus, *Homily 1.9*, trans. Constas, 147.

122. Proclus, *Homily 1.1*, trans. Constas, 137.

123. Cf. Barker, *Mother*, 60–61.

124. Proclus, *Homily 1.1*, trans. Constas, 137.

125. Constas, *Proclus*, 134–35, 348–49. On the importance of weaving in Proclus's imagery of the Virgin, see also Constas, "Weaving."

126. Cf. Constas, "Weaving," 177: "Although by now well-worn to the point of a perhaps tedious familiarity, these typological images were, in the fifth century stunningly innovative and provoked euphoric reactions from late-antique audiences. In fact, the nearly exhaustive profusion of Old Testament Marian typologies in the writings of Proclus is without precedent in the whole of early Christian literature, and would later determine the basic features of all subsequent Byzantine

Mariology." Our question, of course, is whether Proclus invented these typologies or was drawing on an older tradition to which we no longer have full access.

127. Proclus, *Homily 1.2*, trans. Constas, 139.

128. Proclus, *Homily 5.3*, trans. Constas, 263.

129. Proclus, *Homily 2.9–10*, trans. Constas, 173, citing Zechariah 4:2.

130. Proclus, *Homily 1.3*, trans. Constas, 139.

131. Proclus, *Homily 4.2*, trans. Constas, 231, 233.

132. Barker, *Mother*, 148. On Wisdom as with God at creation, see Deutsch, *Lady Wisdom*, 15–16.

133. Barker, *Mother*, 371–72. Hahn, *Hail, Holy Queen*, 31–45, has an illuminating meditation on Mary as the New Eve in the writings of the early Fathers which supports this interpretation.

134. As with the role of the Asherah in ancient Israelite religion (see above n. 66), so there is a lively and ongoing debate about whether and how Jesus himself was identified as Wisdom in early Christianity. For discussion, see Ashton, "Transformation"; Deutsch, *Lady Wisdom*; Douglas, *Early Church Understandings*; Dunn, "Jesus"; Lee, *Jesus*, 123–44; Osmer, *Pratical Theology*, 86–100; and Schroer, *Wisdom*, 113–63.

135. Philo, *On Fugitives* XX, trans. Yonge, 2:216–17. On the elemental symbolism of the veil, see Philo, *On the Life of Moses* VI, trans. Yonge, 3:93: "Moreover, [Moses] chose the materials of this embroidery, selecting with great care what was most excellent out of an infinite quantity, choosing materials equal in number to the elements of which the world was made, and having a direct relation to them; the elements being the earth and the water, and the air and the fire. For the fine flax is produced from the earth, and the purple from the water, and the hyancinth colour is compared to the air (for, by nature, it is black), and the scarlet is likened to fire, because each is of a red colour; for it followed of necessity that those who were preparing a temple made by hands for the Father and Ruler of the universe must take essences similar to those of which he made the universe itself."

136. Proclus, *Homily 1.8–9*, trans. Constas, 145, 147.

137. *Acta conciliorum oecumenicorum* I.5.I, ed. Schwartz, 37, cited by Constas, *Proclus*, 66; also PL 48, cols. 782–85. Nestorius's impromptu sermon is extant only in Latin.

138. *Sermo IV: De incarnatione, qui primus atque extemporalis adversus Procli orationem panegyricam in Virginem* Θεοτοκον, PL 48, col. 782.

139. *Acta conciliorum oecumenicorum* I.5.I, ed. Schwartz, 38, cited by Constas, *Proclus*, 67.

140. Nestorius, *Homily 1*, trans. Norris, 124–25.

141. *Acta conciliorum oecumenicorum* I.1.2, ed. Schwartz, 102, cited by Shoemaker, *Mary*, 225. On the setting for the council, see Shoemaker, *Mary*, 224–25.

142. Tanner, *Decrees*, 59.

143. Atanassova, "Did Cyril of Alexandria Invent Mariology?," 115.

144. Tanner, *Decrees*, 50–52.

145. As Fassler, "First Marian Feast," 38, notes, Nestorius's and Cyril's christological differences had deep exegetical roots: while the Alexandrian school of exegesis is known for its focus on allegory, the Antiochene teachers whom Nestorius followed preferred a more "literal and historical hermeneutic". In Fassler's words (n. 60): "Some scholars believe that the Antiochene emphasis on literal interpretation of scripture was, in part, a result of Jewish influence."

146. Bouriant, *Actes*, 50.

147. As with the role of the Asherah in the ancient temple (see above n. 66) and the place of Wisdom in the new (see above n. 134), so with the development of the cult of the Virgin in late antiquity, there is a lively and ongoing debate of which readers should be aware. While Shoemaker, *Mary*, places the origins of devotion to the Virgin "as a figure in her own right" possibly as early as the third century with the appearance of the intercessory prayer *Sub tuum praesidium*, certainly by the late fourth century with the appearance of feasts in her honor, Price, "*Theotokos*," would insist that there is no evidence for her cult until well after the council of Ephesus. Cameron, "Theotokos," argued

that devotion to the Virgin was well established in Constantinople during the sixth century with the adoption of most of her major feasts and the dedication of the city to her protection (see below n. 149), but Pentcheva, *Icons,* sees no active cult in the imperial city, at least with respect to the use of processional icons, until after the defeat of iconoclasm in the ninth century. Writing in 2011, Brubaker and Cunningham, *Cult,* xxi, signaled a general consensus among Byzantinists pointing to "the ninth or tenth century" for the development of the Virgin's actual "cult," acknowledging, however, "that there are numerous pre-iconoclast monuments to and portraits of the Virgin [whose] character is uncertain." Much depends on how we define "cult."

148. *Akathistos,* ed. and trans. Peltomaa, *Image,* 1–19.

149. On the tradition associating the "Akathistos" with the lifting of the siege, see Peltomaa, *Image,* 21–22, 27; and Cameron, "Theotokos." On Pulcheria as the foundress of the church at Blachernai, see Shoemaker, *Mary,* 220–21 (who here revises his earlier account in "Cult of Fashion," in which he follows Bissera Pentcheva in questioning the attribution to Pulcheria). On the relic of the Virgin's veil, see Cameron, "Virgin's Robe"; Carr, "Threads of Authority"; and Maguire, "Body."

150. On the Virgin's defense of the city, see Pentcheva, *Icons,* 38–43. On the siege, see Kaegi, *Heraclius,* 133–41.

151. Peltomaa, *Image,* 49–114.

152. Barker, "Wisdom Imagery." See also the detailed structural analysis in Peltomaa, *Image,* 115–218; and Peltomaa, "Epithets."

153. Cf. Barker, *Mother,* 97–98, on the tower as the Holy of Holies; and "Wisdom Imagery," 106–7, on the Lady as the genius of the city of Jerusalem.

154. On the bronze sea, see Barker, *Gate of Heaven,* 65–67.

155. Peltomaa, *Image,* 22; Pentcheva, *Icons,* 66–67.

156. Limberis, *Divine Heiress,* 89–97, 121–42; Pentcheva, *Icons,* 12–21. Cf. Angelova, *Sacred Founders,* 234–59, who points to the associations between the pagan goddesses and the empresses to argue that "[had] Christianity not become an imperial religion, the idea of the Virgin Mary as queen might not have come into existence" (240).

157. Andrew, *On the Nativity IV,* 2, trans. Cunningham, 127–28.

158. As Barker, *Mother,* 268, notes, remarking on the consistency of this imagery, surely the burden at this point is on those who would look outside the tradition for explanations. In her words: "Either the Christian writers of the sixth century CE engaged in a complex research exercise to recover images of the Lady in the temple, before composing their hymns and homilies, or else they were heirs to an unbroken tradition that knew more about the signs and symbols of the Lady than is apparent to the methods of modern critical biblical scholarship."

159. Modestus, *On the Dormition,* 10, trans. Daley, 94–97.

160. John of Damascus, *On the Dormition III,* 5, trans. Daley, 237.

161. Germanus, *On the Entrance I,* 14–17, trans. Cunningham, 159–60.

162. See Barker, *Mother,* 156–57, on the significance of the calf and its association with Asherah.

163. See Barker, *Mother,* 182–206, on the Lady and her holy mountains.

164. Germanus, *On the Annunciation,* 3, trans. Cunningham, 224–26.

165. Germanus, *On the Annunciation,* 4, trans. Cunningham, 233.

166. Andrew, *On the Nativity IV,* 2, trans. Cunningham, 128–32.

167. Andrew, *On the Dormition III,* 6, trans. Daley, 141.

168. John of Damascus, *On the Dormition II,* 2, trans. Daley, 206. As Louth, "John," 158–59, observes of John's imagery in these homilies (his emphasis): "What is striking about the examples that John chooses (or rather the tradition which John is following has chosen) is that they are all *places* where God is to be found, and most of these examples are *cultic*: the Virgin is the place where God is encountered and *worshipped* . . . Mary is, if you like, *theotopos*—'place of God'!"

169. Andrew, *On the Annunciation,* 6, trans. Cunningham, 207.

170. Andrew, *On the Nativity IV*, 7, trans. Cunningham, 138.

171. Andrew, *On the Dormition II*, 15, trans. Daley, 133.

172. Andrew, *On the Nativity IV*, 1, trans. Cunningham, 125.

173. Andrew, *On the Nativity IV*, 6, trans. Cunningham, 137–38.

174. Andrew, *On the Dormition III*, 13, trans. Daley, 147–48.

175. Germanus, *On the Dormition I*, 8, trans. Daley, 160.

176. Germanus, *On the Dormition I*, 11, trans. Daley, 164.

177. Germanus, *On the Dormition I*, 5, trans. Daley, 157.

178. John of Damascus, *On the Nativity*, 6, trans. Cunningham, 62.

179. John of Damascus, *On the Dormition I*, 1, trans. Daley, 183; *On the Dormition II*, 12, 14, trans. Daley, 215–16, 217–18.

180. John of Damascus, *On the Dormition II*, 15–16, trans. Daley, 220–21.

181. Shoemaker, *Ancient Traditions*, 38–46, 146–68, 232–56; "Death and the Maiden"; "Virgin Mary's Hidden Past"; and *Mary*, 100–29.

182. John of Thessalonica, *Dormition*, 13, trans. Daley, 64–67. For this scene in the narrative, see also Germanus, *On the Dormition II*, 9, trans. Daley, 176–77; and John of Damascus, *On the Dormition II*, 13, trans. Daley, 216–17. For the scene in the Ethiopic and Syriac versions of what Shoemaker argues is the oldest complete narrative, the *Book of Mary's Repose*, see Shoemaker, *Ancient Traditions*, 327–32. For the scene as it was retold in the West, see Pseudo-Melito, *Transitus*, cc. 11–14, ed. Haibach-Reinisch, in Clayton, *Apocryphal Gospels*, 340–41; cf. trans. Elliott, *Apocryphal New Testament*, 712–13. For the reservations about these stories in the West, see Fulton [Brown], " 'Quae est ista.' "

183. John of Thessalonica, *Dormition*, 3, trans. Daley, 50.

184. Shoemaker, " 'Let Us Go,' " argues for reading the story in its immediate sixth-century context, pointing to the continuing tensions in the empire between Christians, Judaizing Christians, and proselytizing Jews.

185. John of Euboea, *On the Conception*, 4, 11, trans. Cunningham, 175, 183.

186. John of Euboea, *On the Conception*, 11, 17, trans. Cunningham, 185, 188.

187. John of Euboea, *On the Conception*, 14, trans. Cunningham, 185.

188. John of Euboea, *On the Conception*, 16–17, trans. Cunningham, 187–88.

189. Roughly; it's complicated. For our purposes, the oldest useful sources are those which indicate the chants and psalms to be used for Mary's feasts. These date from around the eighth century. See Fassler, "First Marian Feast," 68–78, for the psalms and chants used in Constantinople; see Fulton [Brown], " 'Quae est ista,' " 101–16, and Fulton [Brown], "Virgin Mary," 86–149, for those used in the West. There are lectionaries in Armenian and Georgian for the Marian feasts as they were observed in Jerusalem that are even older, but these do not include the texts for the Office, only the Mass, albeit with very important references to the psalm verses that were sung for these liturgies.

190. On the introduction of the Marian feasts to the Orthodox liturgical calendar, see Cameron, "Theotokos," 95–96; Cunningham, *Wider Than Heaven*, 19–28; and Ekonomou, *Byzantine Rome*, 260 (with bibliography). See Ledit, *Marie*, on the image of the Virgin in these liturgies.

191. On the introduction of these feasts to the Roman calendar and the West more generally, see Botte, "La première fête"; Capelle, "La liturgie mariale"; Clayton, *Cult*, 25–29; Ekonomou, *Byzantine Rome*, 257–64; *Liber pontificalis*, ed. Duchesne, 1:376; Frénaud, "Le culte"; Fulton [Brown], "Virgin Mary," 27–51; MacGregor, "Candlemas"; Palazzo and Johansson, "Jalons liturgiques"; and Reynolds, *Gateway*, 186–90. On the Anglo-Saxon observances, see Clayton, *Cult*, 30–47; and Clayton, "Feasts."

192. See above, chap. 2, n. 168, on the knowledge of the "Akathistos" in the West.

193. In the late eleventh century, Honorius Augustodunensis's students asked just this question about the Marian use of the Song of Songs: "To the excellent master," they wrote him, "from the assembly of students; may you see in Zion the God of Gods [NB: the emphasis on seeing God]. The convent of all the brothers thanks you because the Spirit of Wisdom working through you in the *Elucidarius*

lifted so many veils for them. We all beg you, therefore, to undertake a new work and show us, in the spirit of Charity, why the Gospel text *Jesus entered into a certain town* [Luke 10:38] and the Canticle of Canticles are read on the feast of Mary, although they do not seem to pertain to her at all" (*Sigillum*, PL 172, col. 495; trans. Carr, 47). As I show in " 'Quae est ista,' " the Song of Songs had been used in the West as a source for antiphons for the Feast of the Assumption since as early as the ninth century as a way of celebrating the *historia* of the Virgin's Assumption without having to use the apocryphal accounts of her death; it was only in the late eleventh century, however, that commentators like Honorius attempted to explain in full this choice of texts. See Fulton [Brown], *From Judgment to Passion*, for the way in which Honorius and his twelfth-century successors read the Song as a dialogue between Christ and his Mother.

194. *Catechism of the Catholic Church*, part 2, chap. 1, article 2, para. 3, §1124, 318: "The law of prayer is the law of faith: the Church believes as she prays."

195. As Arnold of Bonneval (d. ca. 1157) put it in his *De laudibus beatae Marie virginis*, alluding to Hebrews 9:1–5 (PL 189, cols. 1729–30, trans. Fassler, *Virgin*, 231): "Behold the tabernacle of God, having within it the Holy of Holies, the rod of the signs, the tablets of the testament, the altar of incense, the twin cherubim gazing at each other, the manna, and the Mercy Seat fully exposed without the cloud. The shrine that is the Virgin contained these things in itself, not in figure, but in very truth (*Haec non in figuris, sed in ipsa veritate sacrarium Virginis in se continebat reposita*), revealing law and discipline to the world, the sweet smell of zeal, the fragrance of chastity, the concord of the testaments, the bread of life, a food not completely consumable, sanctity, humility, and the sacrifice of obedience, the safe port of repentance for all the shipwrecked."

196. Wieck, *Painted Prayers*, 53.

197. Baltzer, "Little Office," 471.

198. Taunton, *Little Office*, 25–26.

199. Another dragon (see above, n. 46): as with the observance of the feasts of the Virgin, so with devotion to Mary more generally, the West seems to have lagged behind the East. Nevertheless, given how thoroughly our reading of Barker has challenged the prevailing narrative of how Mary's cult developed in the East, to my mind it would at this point in our scholarship be perilous to suggest why the West followed a different route—if, in fact, it did. We may note that the church of Santa Maria Maggiore was built under Pope Sixtus III (r. 432–440), immediately following the Council of Ephesus (Rubery, "Pope John's Devotion," 160–65), while Ambrose of Milan (d. 397) described Mary as an *aula pudoris*, a royal hall "rendered perpetually sacred by the presence of the Emperor" (Brown, *Body*, 353–56). Likewise dragonish is the history of commentary on the Psalms. See above, n. 19, for introductory bibliography. On the reception and importance of Augustine's and Cassiodorus's commentaries in the West, see Pollmann and Otten, *Oxford Guide*, s.v. "Enarrationes in Psalmos" (Hildegund Müller) and "Cassiodorus" (Maria Becker); Gross-Diaz, *Psalms Commentary*; and Waltke and Houston, *Psalms*, 48–53. Müller (1:413) notes of Augustine's commentary "almost every monastery owned a full copy of the work."

200. On this method, see de Lubac, *Exégèse medievale*. As the famous late medieval distich put it (as cited by de Lubac): "The letter teaches events, allegory what you should believe, morality teaches what you should do, anagogy what mark you should be aiming for."

201. Cassian, *Collationes*, 14.8, trans. Gibson, 438.

202. For a similar exercise to the one I propose here, see Fassler, "Hildegard," who offers a reading of the antiphons composed by the Benedictine abbess for her sisters to sing at Lauds as frames for their psalmody. This is a methodology that I have been working to develop for some time. I attempted a more modest version of this exercise in Fulton [Brown], " 'Quae est ista,' " where I suggested a reading of the antiphons for the Feast of the Assumption as an *historia* of Mary's death. I lay out the argument in favor of this kind of exercise more fully in Fulton [Brown], "Praying with Anselm." In "Exegesis, Mimesis, and the Voice of Christ," I suggest a reading of Francis's Office of the Passion as

framed by his knowledge of the *tituli* for the psalms identifying the psalms as spoken by Christ. In "My Psalter, My Self," I show how the late fifteenth-century Augustinian canon Jan Mombaer used a similar technique of imagining himself as the author of the psalms for helping his brothers pay attention while singing the Office.

203. Clayton, *Cult*, 44, 269–70. On the knowledge of Greek in the Latin West in the early Middle Ages, see Herren, ed., *Sacred Nectar*.

204. Reynolds, *Gateway*, 204n83, and 269n63, specifically takes me to task for not giving sufficient attention in *From Judgment to Passion* to these connections between the Eastern and Western traditions of Marian devotion. In my defense, I acknowledged there (216–17) that there was more work to be done, but at the time I had no idea how much; my guess now, after learning what I have about the Western tradition so as to make sense of Mary's Office, is that the roots go even deeper than I have the space to articulate here. See McCormick, *Origins*, on the regular interactions between Frankish Europe and the Eastern Mediterranean prior to the tenth century.

205. Fassler, *Music*, 49, describing the development of early tonaries, notes: "In this period, Frankish cantors were studying theoretical principles learned from and about Byzantine liturgical music and adapting them to their own use. Theoretical ideas that first developed in Jerusalem, and spread from there all over the Byzantine Empire, were transmitted to the Roman world through the Franks in the late eighth century and received in a variety of ways throughout the ninth century." According to Ekonomou, *Byzantine Rome*, 250–53, chanting in Greek was standard practice in the churches of Rome during the late seventh and early eighth centuries, "with Greek consistently taking precedence over Latin." On the imagery from the Psalms and other texts of the Old Testament in the Eastern liturgies of the Virgin, see Ledit, *Marie*, 64–97.

206. Ekonomou, *Byzantine Rome*, 260–64. In " 'Quae est ista,' " I examine the evidence for the Carolingian's knowledge of the Eastern stories of the Dormition, including the sermons for the Feast of the Assumption by Ambrosius Autpertus (d. 784) and Paschasius Radbertus (d. 865). Ambrosius was a native of Provence who became abbot of San Vincenzo al Volturno, near Monte Cassino. There were significant communities of Greek-speaking monks in southern Italy and Sicily in Ambrosius's day, including refugees from iconoclasm who almost certainly brought with them the sermons of such prominent iconodules as Germanus, Andrew, and John of Damascus (Graef, *Mary*, 1:165–70). I discuss Ambrosius's sermon for the Assumption in more detail in "Virgin Mary," 158–60. As Fassler, *Virgin*, 119–20, shows, Ambrosius's sermon for the Purification (PL 89, cols. 1291–1304) became an important source for the Marian liturgy at Chartres. On Paschasius's sermon for the Assumption, see below, "Psalm 23 *Domini est terra*."

207. On the translation of the "Akathistos," see above, chap. 2, n. 168. Dyer, "Celebration," shows in detail how the observance of *Hypapante* or Candlemas was adopted in Rome in the seventh century, possibly thanks to the presence there of communities of Greek and Syrian monks, possibly during the pontificate of Theodore I (r. 642–649), the son of a bishop of Jerusalem. On the Jerusalem liturgy for the feast, see Denysenko, "*Hypapante*." In addition, Wenger, *L'assomption*, 140–84, would point to a tenth-century manuscript from the monastery of Reichenau (Karlsruhe, Badische Landesbibliothek, Cod. Augiensis LXXX, fols. 107–122v) containing a ninth-century sermon in Latin for the Assumption comprising excerpts from the Dormition sermons of Andrew, Germanus, John of Damascus, and Cosmas Vestitor (late eighth–early ninth century). As Wenger (341–62) shows, this sermon was an important source for Jacobus de Voragine's sermon for the Assumption in his *Legenda aurea*. On this sermon and its transmission, see also Philippart, "Jean Évêque d'Arezzo," and Mayr-Harting, *Ottonian Book Illumination*, 1:139–55.

208. CAO, siglum C; PL 78, cols. 641–850. On this manuscript, see Jacobsson, "Antiphoner"; and Haggh, "From Auxerre," 173–74n26. On its antiphons for the Feast of the Assumption, see Fulton [Brown], " 'Quae est ista,' " 101–16. On the antiphons for the Marian Offices more generally, see Barré, "Antiennes."

209. McCormick, *Origins*, 401, 647, 668, 720.

210. As edited by Hesbert, CAO, vol. 1: C: Paris, Bibliothèque nationale, MS lat. 17436 (ninth century); G: Durham, Chapter Library, B.III.11 (eleventh century); B: Bamberg, Staatliche Bibliothek, Cod. lit. 23 (late twelfth century); E: Ivrea, Biblioteca capitolare, Cod. 106 (eleventh century); M: Monza, Biblioteca capitolare, Cod. C-12/75 (eleventh century); and V: Verona, Biblioteca capitolare, Cod. XCVIII (eleventh century). The psalmody for the Marian feasts in the *cursus monasticus* includes twelve psalms in two nocturns: I: 8, 18, 23, 44, 45, 47; II: 84, 86, 95, 96, 97, 98. The oldest witness for this psalmody is the Hartker antiphoner (Saint Gall, Stiftsbibliothek, Cod. 390–91, ca. 980–1000). Hesbert edits this *cursus* in vol. 2. For details on the Marian psalmody as it appears in the CAO, see Fulton [Brown], "Virgin Mary," 94–104.

211. Hesbert, ed., *Antiphonale Missarum Sextuplex*, no. 140; *Liber antiphonarius*, PL 78, cols. 649, 655, 702, 704.

212. As both Frénaud, "Le culte," and Maître, "Du culte mariale," note, this same psalmody is used in the *cursus Romanus* for the Common of Virgins. Given, however, that our earliest witness to this common use is the same ninth-century antiphoner as that which gives us the psalmody for the feasts of the Virgin (see above, n. 208), it is difficult to know whether the Marian psalmody was taken from that for the Common of Virgins or vice versa. Frénaud argues for the latter (the Marian psalmody as the source) on the basis of the psalmody for the Feasts of the Circumcision and Octave of the Nativity of the Lord (a.k.a. Christmas), while Maître points out that the two uses share only a handful of antiphons; I made a similar argument in "Virgin Mary," 102–130, on the basis of the antiphons taken from the Song of Songs. Much depends on the way in which we tell the history of the cult of Mary. While Cameron, "Cult of the Virgin," 17, argues that the development of devotion to the Virgin lagged behind that of virgin saints like Thecla, Shoemaker, *Mary*, 235–36, concludes the reverse, particularly for the Virgin's liturgies.

213. *Liber responsalis*, PL 78, cols. 745–46, 798–99. Effectively, the psalmody and antiphons of the first two nocturns are taken from the Purification; that of the third from the Assumption. Cf. Hesbert, CAO, for parallels with the other early antiphoners. On the complicated links between the Frankish and Roman liturgies, see Fassler, *Music*, 36–40. See Barré, "Antiennes," for what we can know about the sources of the antiphons. In his sermon for the Nativity of the Virgin (PL 101, col. 1301), Ambrosius Autpertus quotes the antiphon for Vespers that was sung with the Magnificat (CAO #3852; PL 78, col. 802): "O quam beata Dei genitrix virgo! cujus nativitas gaudium annuntiavit in universo mundo, ex qua sol justitiae Christus Dominus Deus noster exortus est, qui exsolvens culpae veteris maledictionem dedit nobis benedictionem, et confundens mortem donavit nobis vitam sempiternam." This antiphon, as Baumstark, *Comparative Liturgy*, 99, notes, was translated from the Greek *apolytikion* for the same feast. The antiphoner of Compiègne also contains two processional antiphons for the Purification in both Latin and Greek: Χαιρε κεχαριτωμένη (*Ave, gratia plena*) and Κατακόσμησον τον νυμφωνά σου Σιων (*Adorna thalamum tuum Zion*) (*Liber antiphonarius*, PL 78, col. 653). On the use of these processional antiphons in Rome, see below, n. 234.

214. CAO #1709: "Benedicta tu in mulieribus, et benedictus fructus ventris tui." See also above, n. 3.

215. Taunton, *Little Office*, 108.

216. Barker, *Mother*, 336–37.

217. Barker, *Mother*, 339; see also 168, 292–93.

218. Augustine, *Enarrationes*, Psalm 18(2):1, trans. Boulding, 1:204.

219. Augustine, *Enarrationes*, Psalm 18(1):6, trans. Boulding, 1:200, with changes.

220. Cassiodorus, *Expositio*, Psalm 18:5–6, trans. Walsh, 1:197.

221. Augustine, *Enarrationes*, Psalm 18(2), trans. Boulding, 1:204.

222. Cassiodorus, *Expositio*, Psalm 18: Division, trans. Walsh, 1:195.

223. CAO #4942: "Sicut myrrha electa, odorem dedisti suavitatis, sancta Dei genitrix."

224. Taunton, *Little Office*, 116.

225. Wyatt, "Liturgical Context." See also Barker, *Mother*, 369–71.

226. Cassiodorus, *Expositio*, Psalm 23:1, trans. Walsh, 1:241.

227. Augustine, *Enarrationes*, Psalm 23:3–4, trans. Boulding, 1:246; Cassiodorus, *Expositio*, Psalm 23:4, trans. Walsh, 1:243.

228. Cassiodorus, *Expositio*, Psalm 23:6, trans. Walsh, 1:244.

229. Cassiodorus, *Expositio*, Psalm 23:8, trans. Walsh, 1:245.

230. Augustine, *Enarrationes*, Psalm 23:8, trans. Boulding, 1:247.

231. Cassiodorus, *Expositio*, Psalm 23: Conclusion, trans. Walsh, 1:246.

232. CAO #1438: "Ante thorum hujus Virginis frequentate nobis dulcia cantica dramatis."

233. Taunton, *Little Office*, 127.

234. Fulton [Brown], " 'Quae est ista,' " 109, citing Barré, "Antiennes," 214, on the source for the antiphon. See Dyer, "Celebration," 51–56, on the processional antiphon *Adorna thalamum tuum* translated from the Greek Κατακόσμησον τον νυμφῶνά σου Σιων (Adorn thy bridal chamber, O Zion), sung at Vespers for the feast of *Hypapante*. *Adorna thalamum tuum* was sung in Rome for the feast of the Purification, introduced by the Greek popes sometime in the seventh century. Dyer argues that the chant was introduced to the Roman liturgy most likely in the eighth century. The antiphon greets Mary as "heavenly gate" (*celestis porta*) who carries in her arms the King of glory (*regem gloriae*) and light of light (*lumen luminis*). In the Greek version, she is also called "throne of the cherubim" bearing the "cloud of light."

235. Paschasius, *Cogitis me*, ed. Ripberger; also PL 30, cols. 122–42.

236. Dahood, *Psalms*, 1:150–53 (Psalm 24); Taunton, *Little Office*, 129.

237. Barker, *Temple Themes*, 147; *Mother*, 98.

238. Barker, *Temple Themes*, 160–61.

239. CAO #4987: "Specie tua et pulchritudine tua intende, prospere procede, et regna."

240. Cassiodorus, *Expositio*, Psalm 44: Division, trans. Walsh, 1:440.

241. Fulton [Brown], "Virgin Mary," 101, 105, 110. See also the uses listed for the antiphon in CANTUS.

242. Taunton, *Little Office*, 139.

243. Augustine, *Enarrationes*, Psalm 44:1, trans. Boulding, 2:280.

244. Cassiodorus, *Expositio*, Psalm 44:5, trans. Walsh, 1:443.

245. Augustine, *Enarrationes*, Psalm 44:1, trans. Boulding, 2:282.

246. Cassiodorus, *Expositio*, Psalm 44:8, trans. Walsh, 1:445.

247. Augustine, *Enarrationes*, Psalm 44:8, trans. Boulding, 2:297.

248. Mowinckel, *Psalms*, 1:74–75, describes Psalm 44 [45] as "the only example in the whole of Israelite psalm poetry of a true hymn to the king. . . . [Both] in Babylonia and in Egypt the direct 'hymn to the king', who is more or less clearly described and praised as a god, is quite common, but of this type of poem we have only one actual example in the book of Psalms—the wedding psalm, Ps. 45."

249. Cassiodorus, *Expositio*, Psalm 44:10, trans. Walsh, 1:447.

250. Wyatt, " 'Araunah.' "

251. Barker, *Mother*, 79–80. On role of the queen mother in the ancient temple cult, see also Ackerman, "Queen Mother"; and Dever, *Did God Have a Wife?*, 214, citing Ackerman.

252. Barker, *Mother*, 179–80.

253. Again, a dragon (see above n. 46): Why was this tradition of interpretation apparently unknown in the Latin West until after the seventh century? Our concern at the moment is to construct a reading of the Psalms as the compilers of her Office may have read them. In the West, if they were reading commentaries on the Psalms, they would be reading Augustine and Cassiodorus. And yet, the antiphons associated with the psalms for the Marian feasts suggest that the composers of the liturgy must have known the Eastern traditions, otherwise they would not have been observing her feasts in the first place. Perhaps here we have the real origins of the tensions that persist to this day between those who would see Mary's role as Queen of heaven as essential to Christianity and those who worry about elevating her "too much"?

254. Chrysippus, *Oratio in Sanctam Mariam*, 2, ed. Jugie, 339; trans. Fassler, "First Marian Feast," 56.

255. Shoemaker, "Virgin Mary's Hidden Past"; and "Mother's Passion."

256. Maximus, *Life*, cap. 7, trans. Shoemaker, 41.

257. Maximus, *Life*, cap. 103, trans. Shoemaker, 130.

258. Germanus, *On the Entrance I*, 6, trans. Cunningham, 151–52.

259. Andrew, *On the Dormition III*, 6, 8, trans. Daley, 141, 143–44. On the importance of Andrew's homilies for the development of the cult of the Virgin in the West, see Ekonomou, *Byzantine Rome*, 259–60, 264.

260. Cassiodorus, *Expositio*, Psalms 44 and 45, trans. Walsh, 1:415, 452.

261. Cassiodorus, *Expositio*, Psalm 45: Division, trans. Walsh, 1:452–53.

262. Augustine, *Enarrationes*, Psalm 45:1, trans. Boulding, 2:310–11.

263. CAO #1282: "Adjuvabit eam Deus vultu suo: Deus in medio ejus, non commovebitur."

264. Augustine, *Enarrationes*, Psalm 45:5, trans. Boulding, 2:316–17.

265. Cassiodorus, *Expositio*, Psalm 45:5–6, trans. Walsh, 1:455.

266. Taunton, *Little Office*, 159.

267. Modestus, *On the Dormition*, 10, trans. Daley, 95.

268. John of Damascus, *On the Nativity*, 9, trans. Cunningham, 67.

269. John of Damascus, *On the Dormition I*, 12, trans. Daley, 197.

270. John of Euboea, *On the Conception*, 17, trans. Cunningham, 188.

271. John of Damascus, *On the Dormition I*, 1, trans. Daley, 183.

272. It is something of a mystery why the Western Fathers do not seem to have had access to the Eastern traditions before the sixth or seventh century, likewise why when they did learn of them (as, for example, with the Marian apocrypha condemned by the so-called Gelasian Decree), they were largely suspicious (on which suspicions, see Fulton [Brown], " 'Quae est ista,' " 82–91). Nor is it easy to explain why, after the seventh century, the West became so much more receptive to the Marian devotions of the East, even if they still had their suspicions about some of the stories that they heard. My guess at the moment is that it has something to do with the Lady's relationship to cities.

273. Cassiodorus, *Expositio*, Psalm 86:1, trans. Walsh, 2:336.

274. Augustine, *Enarrationes*, Psalm 86:1, trans. Boulding, 4:246.

275. Augustine, *Enarrationes*, Psalm 86:2–3, trans. Boulding, 4:247.

276. Cassiodorus, *Expositio*, Psalm 86: Division, trans. Walsh, 2:337.

277. Taunton, *Little Office*, 168.

278. CAO #4936: "Sicut laetantium omnium nostrum habitatio est in te, sancta Dei genitrix."

279. Barker, *Mother*, 94; *Great High Priest*, 232, 236–37; "Wisdom Imagery," 106; and *Revelation*, 319–23.

280. Augustine, *Enarrationes*, Psalm 86:4–5, trans. Boulding, 4:253–54. Cf. Psalm 142:1, trans. Boulding, 6:345–46, where the woman-city is clearly the mother of Jesus in the flesh. For this passage, see below, text at n. 453.

281. Barker, *Mother*, 25, 191–93.

282. Germanus, *On the Consecration*, 1–2, trans. Cunningham, 247.

283. Cassiodorus, *Expositio*, Psalm 95:1, trans. Walsh, 2:415, citing 1 Esdras 2.

284. Cassiodorus, *Expositio*, Psalm 95:1, trans. Walsh, 2:415; Augustine, *Enarrationes*, Psalm 95:1, trans. Boulding, 4:423–25.

285. Cassiodorus, *Expositio*, Psalm 95: Division, trans. Walsh, 2:415.

286. Cassiodorus, *Expositio*, Psalm 95:2–3, trans. Walsh, 2:416–17.

287. Augustine, *Enarrationes*, Psalm 95:5, trans. Boulding, 4:428–29.

288. Cassiodorus, *Expositio*, Psalm 95:5, trans. Walsh, 2:418.

289. CAO #2924: "Gaude, Maria Virgo, cunctas haereses sola interemisti in universo mundo." This, thanks to its use by Gautier de Coinci in one of his most famous miracle stories (book 2, miracle 13), is perhaps the antiphon that modern scholars are most familiar with in association with the

Virgin Mary. In Gautier's story, the chant as sung by a boy excites a Jew to murder him, but the murder is discovered when the dead boy continues to sing. In his *Canterbury Tales*, Chaucer gave the same story to the Prioress, although in her telling, the "litel clergeon" sings *Alma redemptoris mater*. Haggh, "From Auxerre to Soissons," traces the composition of the chant in its various forms back to the ninth century, when a rather different miracle was associated with it. According to a story recounted by the Carolingian music scholar Aurelian of Réôme, the responsory's composer "was a certain Roman, Victor by name, who was blind from birth," who had learned the melodies of the chants of the singers by memory. One day "as he sat before the altar of St. Mary in the House which is called the Rotunda [actually, as Haggh shows, a crypt near the abbey of Saint-Germain in Auxerre], the divine will being favorable, he composed this response and immediately merited to be illumined with sight, of which he had already been long deprived, and to receive genuine brightness" (trans. Haggh, 175). According to Aurelian, the responsory was controversial because it was not taken from the *historiae*, that is, Haggh explains (176–78), "from one of several books of the Bible that usually furnished responsory texts as did the Psalms and, for the period after Pentecost, the books of Kings, Wisdom, Job, Tobias, Judith, Esther, Maccabees, and Ezechial." For our purposes, it is surely significant that the miracle Aurelian invoked to justify the use of the responsory "to venerate St. Mary, the Mother of God, and to refute the insanity of the Jews and the impudent superstitions of heretics" involved curing its composer of blindness. We may recall that one of Wisdom's attributes in the temple tradition was to give sight to those who served her.

290. Taunton, *Little Office*, 174–75.
291. Müller, "*Enarrationes*," 1:414, notes: "[Augustine's] explanations [of the Psalms] are based solely on the Latin versions of the Septuagint, with occasional recurrences to the Greek original; the Hebrew text, or its translation by Jerome, is of no interest to him."
292. Augustine, *Enarrationes*, Psalm 95:1, trans. Boulding, 4:425.
293. Cassiodorus, *Expositio*, Psalm 95:10, trans. Walsh, 2:421.
294. Justin Martyr, *Dialogue with Trypho*, cap. 73, trans. Dods and Reith, 235 (NB: this is still a live debate; cf. n. 2: "These words were not taken away by the Jews, but added by some Christian—Otto. [A statement not proved].") On the work of the correcting scribes, see Levin, *Father*, 70–107.
295. Barker, *Mother*, 162.
296. Levin, *Father*, 95–96, highlights this passage as one that gave particular difficulty to the correcting scribes thanks to its "traces of polytheism": "The non-Massoretic text makes excellent sense philologically, given the theology which prevailed in that region: each nation has its patron god, as a result of an original, mythical division of the earth."
297. Barker, *Temple Themes*, 230.
298. Augustine, *Enarrationes*, Psalm 96:1, trans. Boulding, 4:439; Cassiodorus, *Expositio*, Psalm 96:1, trans. Walsh, 2:424.
299. Augustine, *Enarrationes*, Psalm 96:1, trans. Boulding, 4:441.
300. Cassiodorus, *Expositio*, Psalm 96:2, trans. Walsh, 2:425.
301. Augustine, *Enarrationes*, Psalm 96:2, trans. Boulding, 4:442.
302. CAO #2217: "Dignare me laudare te, Virgo sacrata: da mihi virtutem contra hostes tuos."
303. Taunton, *Little Office*, 185.
304. *Akathistos*, ed. and trans. Peltomaa, *Image*, 1–19.
305. Proclus, *Homily 1.1*, trans. Constas, 137.
306. Andrew, *On the Nativity IV*, 2, trans. Cunningham, 130. Jacob of Serug (d. 521) likewise saw Mary on Ezekiel's throne (see Golitzin, "Image").
307. Barker, *Mother*, 201–4, 255–70, 336–37.
308. Barker, *Mother*, 202.
309. Barker, *Mother*, 205.
310. Barker, *Mother*, 50.

534 ~@ 3. ANTIPHON AND PSALM

311. Barker, *Mother*, 35, 73–75, 145, 174, 259–65.

312. Cassiodorus, *Expositio*, Psalm 97:1, trans. Walsh, 2:430–31.

313. Augustine, *Enarrationes*, Psalm 97:2–3, trans. Boulding, 4:460–61.

314. Cassiodorus, *Expositio*, Psalm 97:3, trans. Walsh, 2:432. Italics in original.

315. Cassiodorus, *Expositio*, Psalm 97: 4–9, trans. Walsh, 2:433–35.

316. CAO #4332: "Post partum virgo inviolata permansisti: Dei genitrix, intercede pro nobis."

317. Barker, *Temple Themes*, 142.

318. Fragments of *Jubilees* appear in the Dead Sea Scrolls, including the description of creation (see Martínez, *Dead Sea Scrolls*, 238–40). It is considered canonical in both the Jewish and Christian Ethiopian traditions. For discussion of the text, its composition, and provenance, see Charlesworth, *Old Testament Pseudepigrapha*, 2:35–50.

319. *Jubilees* 2:2–3, trans. Charles, *Apocrypha*, 2:13–14.

320. Barker, *Temple Themes*, 226. Readers of Tolkien will doubtless here recall the creation of Arda through the singing of the Ainur as told in the *Ainulindalë*.

321. 1 Enoch 39:12, trans. Charles, *Apocrypha*, 2:211.

322. Barker, *Temple Themes*, 227.

323. Barker, *Temple Themes*, 227.

324. Barker, *Temple Themes*, 230.

325. Barker, *Mother*, 99.

326. Barker, *Mother*, 209.

327. Barker, *Mother*, 373.

328. Barker, *Mother*, 336–37, rereading Genesis 1:28.

329. 1 Enoch 40, trans. Charles, *Apocrypha*, 2:211–12.

330. Taunton, *Little Office*, 195.

331. John of Damascus, *On the Nativity*, 6, trans. Cunningham, 61.

332. Germanus, *On the Dormition I*, 10, trans. Daley, 163.

333. John of Euboea, *On the Conception*, 17, trans. Cunningham, 188.

334. For the psalmody of the Divine Office generally, see Harper, *Forms*, 67–72, 242–59; for the psalmody of the Marian feasts generally, see Harper, *Forms*, 260–63. For the psalms in the Marian Office according to the various Uses cited here, see *Officium beatae Mariae virginis*, PL 151, cols. 970–74 (Fonte Avellana); Leclercq, "Formes anciennes," 92–94 (Monte Cassino); London, British Library, MS Add. 21927, fols. 101v–115v (twelfth-century England, possibly Muchelney); Roper, *Medieval English*, 227–37 (England, ca. 1050–1521); Baltzer, "Little Office," 474–81 (Paris); Donovan, *The De Brailes Hours*, 171–74 (Oxford, Dominican); Tolhurst, ed., *Monastic Breviary*, fols. 442–447v (Hyde Abbey); Geert Grote, *Getijdenboek*, ed. Van Wijk; Maskell, ed., *Monumenta*, 3:3–81 (Sarum); Wordsworth, ed., *Horae Eboracenses*, 37–58 (York); Wieck, *Time Sanctified*, 159–61 (Rome). My analysis here also draws on the tables of Uses compiled by Drigsdahl, *Index to a Selection of Uses*.

335. CAO #2450: "Dum esset rex in accubitu suo, nardus mea dedit odorem suavitatis." See below, for the use of this antiphon at Vespers.

336. On the *Protevangelium* and its reception in the West, see above, n. 88.

337. *Gospel of Pseudo-Matthew*, cap. 6, ed. and trans. Clayton, *Apocryphal Gospels*, 176–77 (Old English); ed. Tischendorf, *Evangelia*, 62–64 (Latin). For the manuscripts, see Gijsel, *Pseudo-Matthaei Evangelium*, 503.

338. Hrotsvitha, *Maria*, ed. and trans. Wiegand, 32–33.

339. Otfrid, *Evangelienbuch*, ed. Wolff, 20–21, trans. Miles, "Origins," 645.

340. *Liber responsalis*, PL 78, col. 799; Barré, "Antiennes," 222–23. See above, n. 208.

341. Augustine, *Enarrationes*, Psalm 92:1, trans. Boulding, 4:360–61.

342. Augustine, *Enarrationes*, Psalm 92:2, trans. Boulding, 4:367.

343. Augustine, *Enarrationes*, Psalm 92:3–4, trans. Boulding, 4:369.

344. Barker, *Mother*, 345; cf. Genesis 1:6–8. Mowinckel, *Psalms*, 163–64, reads the psalm as celebrating Yahweh's "victory over the powers of chaos, over primeval ocean and demons."

345. CAO #1503: "Assumpta est Maria in caelum, gaudent angeli, laudantes benedicunt Dominum."

346. John of Damascus, *On the Dormition I*, 9, 11, trans. Daley, 194, 196.

347. Taunton, *Little Office*, 233.

348. Augustine, *Enarrationes*, Psalm 94:2, trans. Boulding, 4:412.

349. Cassiodorus, *Expositio*, Psalm 26:6, trans. Walsh, 1:266.

350. Augustine, *Enarrationes*, Psalm 32(2):3, trans. Boulding, 1:401.

351. Augustine, *Enarrationes*, Psalm 96:3–4, trans. Boulding, 4:349.

352. Augustine, *Enarrationes*, Psalm 94:1, trans. Boulding, 4:409.

353. Augustine, *Enarrationes*, Psalm 83:5, trans. Boulding, 4:194, with changes.

354. Augustine, *Enarrationes*, Psalm 99:2, trans. Boulding, 5:15.

355. Cassiodorus, *Expositio*, Psalm 99:3, trans. Walsh, 2:444.

356. Augustine, *Enarrationes*, Psalm 99:4–5, trans. Boulding, 5:27–28.

357. CAO #3707: "Maria Virgo assumpta est ad aethereum thalamum, in quo Rex regum stellato sedet solio."

358. Cassiodorus, *Expositio*, Psalm 62: Division, trans. Walsh, 2:83.

359. CAO #3261: "In odorem unguentorum tuorum currimus: adolescentulae dilexerunt te nimis."

360. See above, n. 193.

361. Theodore the Studite, *On the Dormition*, 1, trans. Daley, 250.

362. Augustine, *Enarrationes*, Psalm 62:2, trans. Boulding, 3:234.

363. John of Damascus, *On the Dormition II*, 10, trans. Daley, 214.

364. John of Damascus, *On the Dormition I*, 11, trans. Daley, 196.

365. Theoteknos, *On the Dormition*, 7, trans. Daley, 77; Germanus, *On the Dormition II*, 4, trans. Daley, 173.

366. Pseudo-Melito, *Transitus B2*, cap. 7, ed. Tischendorf, 129; John of Thessalonica, *On the Dormition*, 4, trans. Daley, 51.

367. See above, "The Lord and the Lady of the Temple."

368. On this theme in the temple tradition, see Barker, *Mother*, 250–51, 285–86, 298. On this song and the other Septuagint additions to Daniel, see *Eerdmans Commentary*, ed. Dunn and Rogerson, 803–6.

369. Augustine, *De civitate Dei*, lib. 11, cap. 9, trans. Bettenson, 438–40.

370. See above, "Psalm 97 *Cantate Domino*."

371. Barker, *Temple Themes*, 226.

372. CAO #1705: "Benedicta, filia, tu a Domino; quia per te fructum vitae communicavimus."

373. Augustine, *Enarrationes*, Psalm 68(1):3, trans. Boulding, 3:371.

374. Augustine, *Enarrationes*, Psalm 128:1–3, trans. Boulding, 6:120.

375. *Akathistos*, strophes 9 and 13, ed. and trans. Peltomaa, 8–13.

376. John of Damascus, *Canon*, Odes 7–8, trans. Daley, 244–45.

377. Augustine, *Enarrationes*, Psalm 149:2, trans. Boulding, 6:497.

378. On these psalms as hymns of praise in the temple, see Mowinckel, *Psalms*, 1:81–105.

379. Barker, *Temple Themes*, 142–43.

380. CAO #4418: "Pulchra es et decora, filia Jerusalem: terribilis ut castrorum acies ordinata."

381. Barker, *Mother*, 134–35.

382. *Akathistos*, prooemium II, ed. and trans. Peltomaa, 2–3.

383. Andrew of Crete, *On the Dormition III*, 11–12, trans. Daley, 146–47.

384. On the Virgin as defender of Constantinople, see above, "Mary, the Theotokos, the Living Temple of God." For her similar reputation in the West, see Carr, "Threads"; Fassler, *Virgin*, 12–23; and Remensnyder, *La Conquistadora*.

385. See above, n. 334, for references to these Uses.

386. On the rainbow, see Barker, *Mother*, 203, 219–22, 244, 250, 273–74.

387. On all of these antiphons, their use for the Feast of the Assumption, and their relationship to the Office for the Common of Virgins, see Fulton [Brown], "Virgin Mary," 94–130. On the antiphons *in evangelio* in the antiphoner of Compiègne used as the *historia* for the feast of the Assumption, see Fulton [Brown], " 'Quae est ista,' " 101–16. On the antiphoner of Albi, see http://cantusdatabase.org/source/374102/f-ai-44.

388. CAO #1503: "Assumpta est Maria in caelum, gaudent angeli, laudantes benedicunt Dominum."

389. Augustine, *Enarrationes*, Psalm 53:1–2, trans. Boulding, 3:41–44.

390. Maximus, *Life*, cap. 125, trans. Shoemaker, 149.

391. Maximus, *Life*, cap. 128, trans. Shoemaker, 154.

392. Augustine, *Enarrationes*, Psalm 53:8, trans. Boulding, 3:51–52.

393. Maximus, *Life*, cap. 130, trans. Shoemaker, 156.

394. Barker, *Mother*, 262–63.

395. Theoteknos, *On the Dormition*, 9–10, trans. Daley, 78–79.

396. Andrew, *On the Nativity IV*, 2, trans. Cunningham, 128; *On the Annunciation*, 4, trans. Cunningham, 201–2.

397. Augustine, *Enarrationes*, Psalm 84:12, trans. Boulding, 4:216.

398. Cassiodorus, *Expositio*, Psalm 84:11–12, trans. Walsh, 2:325–26.

399. CAO #3707: "Maria Virgo assumpta est ad aethereum thalamum, in quo Rex regum stellato sedet solio."

400. CAO #3261: "In odorem unguentorum tuorum currimus: adolescentulae dilexerunt te nimis."

401. CAO #4418: "Pulchra es et decora, filia Jerusalem: terribilis ut castrorum acies ordinata."

402. Dahood, *Psalms*, 3:195 (Psalm 120); McKinnon, "Fifteen Temple Steps," 39–42.

403. Dahood, *Psalms*, 3:194 (Psalm 120).

404. Augustine, *Enarrationes*, Psalm 89:7–10, trans. Boulding, 4:308 (on the number of the psalms); Psalm 83:6–7, trans. Boulding 4:196 (on the meaning of the steps).

405. Augustine, *Enarrationes*, Psalm 83:6–7, trans. Boulding, 4:196; Psalm 119, trans. Boulding, 5:497–98.

406. Cassiodorus, *Expositio*, Psalm 119, trans. Walsh, 3:260.

407. Augustine, *Enarrationes*, Psalm 38:1, trans. Boulding, 2:168–69; Cassiodorus, *Expositio*, Psalm 119, trans. Walsh, 3:267.

408. Jacobus de Voragine, *Legenda aurea*, cap. 131 (Nativity of the Virgin), trans. Ryan, 2:152.

409. Granger, "Reading Her Psalter," 308–9.

410. See above, "The Seven Hours of the Day."

411. Goscelin, *Liber confortatorius*, ed. Talbot, 83; trans. Otter, 100–101.

412. Otter, "Entrances," 285–86. On the monastic use of the Gradual Psalms, see Knowles, "Monastic Horarium."

413. For Mary's exegesis of the Gradual Psalms as we follow her up the temple steps at Terce, Sext, and None, see N-Town, *Mary Play*, 175–76.

414. Augustine, *Enarrationes*, Psalm 119:1–2, trans. Boulding, 5:501.

415. Cassiodorus, *Expositio*, Psalm 119:1–2, trans. Walsh, 3:261–62.

416. CAO #3707: "Maria Virgo assumpta est ad aethereum thalamum, in quo Rex regum stellato sedet solio."

417. Andrew, *On the Dormition III*, 11, trans. Daley, 146.

418. Pseudo-Melito, *Transitus B2*, cap. 2, ed. Tischendorf, 125–26.

419. Barker, *Mother*, 313, listing the psalms according to the Hebrew numbering: Psalm 115:15, 121:2, 124:8, 134:3, and 146:5–6 RSV.

420. Cassiodorus, *Expositio*, Psalm 120:1, trans. Walsh, 3:266.

421. Modestus, *On the Dormition*, 9, trans. Daley, 94.

422. Germanus, *On the Dormition I*, 11, trans. Daley, 165.

423. CAO #3261: "In odorem unguentorum tuorum currimus: adolescentulae dilexerunt te nimis." (The italic *m* in the title of the antiphon is present because the title is given two different ways

in the sources: "In odore" and "In odorem." It is the same CAO number (#3261) but with two different spellings.)

424. Dahood, *Psalms*, 3:208–9 (Psalm 123).

425. Cassiodorus, *Expositio*, Psalm 122, trans. Walsh, 3:277.

426. Augustine, *Enarrationes*, Psalm 122:1, trans. Boulding, 6:31.

427. Cassiodorus, *Expositio*, Psalm 123: Division, trans. Walsh, 3:282.

428. Augustine, *Enarrationes*, Psalm 123:1–2, trans. Boulding, 6:43–45.

429. John of Damascus, *On the Nativity*, 6, trans. Cunningham, 61–62.

430. John of Euboea, *On the Conception*, 16, trans. Cunningham, 187.

431. Augustine, *Enarrationes*, Psalm 124:1, trans. Boulding, 6:56.

432. Germanus, *On the Entrance I*, 10, trans. Cunninghamn, 157.

433. CAO #4418: "Pulchra es et decora, filia Jerusalem: terribilis ut castrorum acies ordinata."

434. Augustine, *Enarrationes*, Psalm 125:1, trans. Boulding, 6:68–72.

435. Andrew, *On the Dormition II*, 4, trans. Daley, 121.

436. Andrew, *On the Dormition III*, 4, trans. Daley, 139.

437. Andrew, *On the Dormition III*, 9, trans. Daley, 144–45.

438. Augustine, *Enarrationes*, Psalm 126:1, trans. Boulding, 6:83–86.

439. Augustine, *Enarrationes*, Psalm 126:2, trans. Boulding, 6:88–91.

440. Cassiodorus, *Expositio*, Psalm 126:3, trans. Walsh, 3:299.

441. Augustine, *Enarrationes*, Psalm 127:1–4, trans. Boulding, 6:103–6.

442. Barker, *Temple Themes*, 137–43.

443. Cassiodorus, *Expositio*, Psalm 109:1, trans. Walsh, 3:116.

444. Augustine, *Enarrationes*, Psalm 109, trans. Boulding, 5:263.

445. Dahood, *Psalms*, 3:112 (Psalm 110).

446. Barker, *Temple Themes*, 92, 97, 196. Mowinckel, *Psalms*, 1:63–64, likewise associates this psalm with the anointment ritual: "Ps. 110 . . . evidently belongs to the moment when the king is led forth to ascend his throne. The king's throne was in the East looked upon as a symbol of the throne of the deity. It is on a throne flanked by winged lions (cherubs), like that of Solomon, that the deity himself sits in Syro-Canaanite pictures. Such a winged lion throne (empty!) stood in the Temple in Jerusalem also, and it was supposed that 'Yahweh who sits upon the cherubim' was seated on it invisibly. When the king as the 'son of Yahweh' seats himself on his throne, this is a symbolic expressions of the fact that he, as Yahweh's appointed governor, sits on the Lord's own throne."

447. Throckmorton, ed., *Gospel Parallels*, 11 (at Matthew 3:16–17).

448. Throckmorton, ed., *Gospel Parallels*, 13 (at Matthew 4:8).

449. Jerome, *Commentaria in Isaiam*, PL 24, col. 405: "Sed et in Evangelio quod juxta Hebraeos scriptum, Nazaraei lectitant, Dominus loquitur: *modo me tulit mater mea, Spiritus sanctus*. Nemo autem in hac parte scandalizari debet, quod dicatur apud Hebraeos spiritus genere feminino, cum nostra lingua appelletur genere masculino, et Graeco sermone neutro. In divinitate enim nullus est sexus."

450. On this association of the dove at Jesus's baptism with Wisdom, see also Schroer, *Wisdom*, 132–63.

451. CAO #2450: "Dum esset rex in accubitu suo, nardus mea dedit odorem suavitatis." On the manuscript transmission of this antiphon, see above, n. 387.

452. Barker, *Mother*, 125; *Temple Themes*, 97.

453. Augustine, *Enarrationes*, Psalm 142:1, trans. Boulding, 6:345–46.

454. On the exegesis of Mary as the Woman of Revelation 12, see Manelli, "Virgin Mary," 115–18; Lobrichon, "La Femme," and Bergamini, "From Narrative to Ikon."

455. Modestus, *On the Dormition*, 10, trans. Daley, 96–97.

456. Germanus, *On the Dormition I*, 3, trans. Daley, 154–55.

457. Augustine, *Enarrationes*, Psalm 109:4, trans. Boulding, 5:280.

458. See above, n. 379.

459. Augustine, *Enarrationes*, Psalm 112:1–3, trans. Boulding, 5:297.

460. CAO #3574: "Laeva ejus sub capite meo, et dextera illius amplexabitur me."
461. Augustine, *Enarrationes*, Psalm 112:7–9, trans. Boulding, 5:303.
462. Eusebius, *Preparatio*, lib. IX, cap. 29, trans. Gifford, cited by Barker, *Mother*, 204.
463. Barker, *Mother*, 205.
464. It is this antiphon that is inscribed on the scroll that Mary holds in the famous twelfth-century apse mosaic in Santa Maria in Trastevere, Rome, where Mary is depicted crowned and enthroned at her Son's right hand. Christ holds a book that is inscribed with the opening of the great respond for the feast of the Assumption (CAO #7826): "Veni, electa mea et ponam in te thronum meum: *Come, my chosen one, and I will place my throne in you.*" On this mosaic, see Fulton [Brown], *From Judgment to Passion*, 398–404.
465. See above, "Psalms 119 *Ad Dominum . . .*"
466. CAO #3878: "Nigra sum sed formosa, filiae Jerusalem: ideo dilexit me rex, et introduxit me in cubiculum suum."
467. Taunton, *Little Office*, 387.
468. Boss, "Black Madonnas," discusses the various theories put forward to explain these images; Begg, *Cult*, provides a gazetteer. The most famous of these images is arguably Our Lady of Le Puy, in southern France, although the current statue is a copy of the medieval one, which was burnt in 1794. The majority of the medieval Black Madonnas were sculpted in the twelfth or thirteenth centuries, although their legends often claim that they are older.
469. Leithart, "Like the Tents."
470. See Barker, *Christmas*, 120–21, citing Justin, *Dialogue with Trypho*, cap. 78, on the possibility that the Magi came from Arabia.
471. CAO #3470: "Jam hiems transiit, imber abiit et recessit: surge, amica mea, et veni."
472. See above, "Psalms 125 *In convertendo . . .*"
473. John of Damascus, *On the Dormition II*, 10, trans. Daley, 214.
474. John of Damascus, *On the Dormition III*, 2, trans. Daley, 232.
475. Dahood, *Psalms*, 3:241 (Psalm 132).
476. CAO #4988: "Speciosa facta es et suavis in deliciis tuis, sancta Dei genitrix." On the source for this antiphon, see de Bruyne, "Anciennes versions latines," 103.
477. Taunton, *Little Office*, 391.
478. On Jerusalem as the "vision of peace," see Cassiodorus, *Expositio*, Psalm 147:12, trans. Walsh, 3:445.
479. Germanus, *On the Entrance I*, 10, trans. Cunningham, 156–57.
480. Cassiodorus, *Expositio*, Psalm 128: Division, trans. Walsh, 3:307.
481. Cassiodorus, *Expositio*, Psalm 128:1–4, trans. Walsh, 3:307–9.
482. Cassiodorus, *Expositio*, Psalm 128: Division, trans. Walsh, 3:307.
483. Cassiodorus, *Expositio*, Psalm 129, trans. Walsh, 3:311.
484. On these psalms in the medieval tradition, see Driscoll, "Seven Penitential Psalms." The designation comes from Cassiodorus, *Expositio*, Psalm 50: Conclusion, trans. Walsh, 1:511–12.
485. Augustine, *Enarrationes*, Psalm 130, trans. Boulding, 6:138–39.
486. Augustine, *Enarrationes*, Psalm 130, trans. Boulding, 6:137, 141.
487. On the churches honoring the Virgin in Rome built between the fifth and eighth centuries, see Rubery, "Pope John VII's Devotion."
488. Barker, "Life-Bearing Spring"; Cunningham, *Wider Than Heaven*, 24–25.
489. MacGregor, "Candlemas," 137. On Sergius's introduction of the processions, see *Liber pontificalis*, ed. Duchesne, 1:376; and Ekonomou, *Byzantine Rome*, 260–64. On the route and chants for the procession, see also Dyer, "Celebration."
490. Barker, *Christmas*, 88–89.
491. CAO #5041: "Sub tuum praesidium confugimus, sancta Dei genitrix: nostras deprecationes ne despicias in necessitatibus; sed a periculis cunctis libera nos semper, Virgo gloriosa et benedicta." On the origins of this antiphon as a prayer, see above, n. 109.

4. LESSON AND RESPONSE

1. See above, chap. 2, n. 3.

2. On what Gabriel found Mary reading, see Miles, "Origins"; Miles, "Mary's Book"; and Frey, "Maria Legens."

3. Your reflections on the lessons and responses follow the Use of Rome. For the place of these readings and chants in the Divine Office, see Hiley, *Western Plainchant*, 47–76. For their performance in the Office of the Virgin, see Roper, *Medieval English*, 86–87. Our meditation here is somewhat freeform, moving with the inspiration of the Spirit from hour to hour, rather than reproducing the practice of a single hour. For a more precise description of the way in which the responsories for Mary's feasts would have been performed, see Fassler, "Mary's Nativity," 416–22. On the use of the Song of Songs in the Marian liturgy, see Fulton [Brown], "Virgin Mary," 70–149; " 'Quae est ista' "; and *From Judgment to Passion*, 248–54, 265–75. On the use of Ecclesiasticus, Wisdom, and Proverbs for the lessons for the Marian liturgy, see Newman, *God*, 194–206; Catta, "Sedes Sapientiae"; Seethaler, "Die Weisheitstexte"; Capelle, "La liturgie," 236–37; Frénaud, "Le culte," 188–90. These readings are attested for Mary's feasts as early as ca. 700 in the West.

4. CAO #7569. The singing of the responsories for the Divine Office was especially elaborate. Typically, the cantor would begin the respond (R.) and the choir would then join in. The cantor would then sing the verse (V.), after which the choir would repeat the ending of the respond (from *). The verse for this responsory in the Roman Use for the Marian Office is the same as the antiphon for the first psalm at Matins: "Benedicta tu in mulieribus, et benedictus fructus ventris tui."

5. Cf. CAO #6163: "Beata es Maria quae omnium portasti creatorem saeculorum; genuisti qui te fecit et in aeternum permanes virgo." The verse for this responsory is "Ave, Maria, gratia plena, dominus tecum."

6. CAO #6725. There are two verses for this responsory: "Ora pro populo, interveni pro clero, intercede pro devoto femineo sexu. Sentiant omnes tuum juvamen, quicumque celebrant tuam sanctam commemorationem"; and the Gloria Patri.

7. Peter Lombard, *Sententiae*, lib. 3, dist. 3, cap. 1–2, trans. Silano, 3:9–11.

8. Peter Lombard, *Sententiae*, lib. 1, dist. 2, cap. 4.8, trans. Silano, 1:16–17.

9. On the tensions within the medieval tradition as to the identity of Wisdom, see Newman, *God*, 190–244.

10. Latimer, Letter 31, ed. Corrie, 1:393–95. On the burning of the Virgin's statues in the late summer of 1538, see Waller, *Virgin Mary*, 1. Waterton, *Pietas*, includes a catalogue of the many statues of the Virgin that were destroyed at this time.

11. On these debates, see above, chap. 2, n. 15.

12. On Adams's importance for American medieval studies, see Morrison, "Henry Adams."

13. Adams, *Education*, 308–10.

14. Adams, *Mont Saint Michel*, 5.

15. Adams, *Mont Saint Michel*, 87–102.

16. Adams, *Mont Saint Michel*, 94, Adams's somewhat free translation of the Latin.

17. Adams, *Mont Saint Michel*, 141, 186.

18. Adams, *Mont Saint Michel*, 98–100.

19. Fassler, *Virgin*, 217–19, her emphasis on *seen*. The full text of the Advent antiphon (CAO #4156) is: "Omnis vallis implebitur et omnis mons et collis humiliabitur et videbit omnis caro salutare dei."

20. Fassler, *Virgin*, 220–21. For the full text of the sequence, *Salve Mater Salvatoris, Vas electum*, sung for the Nativity of the Virgin, see AH 54, nr. 245, 383–86.

21. Yet another dragon (see above, chap. 3, nn. 46, 66, 134, 147, 199, and 253). As one of my angels for the press remarked at this point in my argument: "It is true that Mary is not mentioned much in the *Sentences* and other theological texts of the twelfth and thirteenth centuries, and this is because the subject matter of theology during this period was God and spiritual substances. However, the

academic study of theology was not the place where one found salvation (*salus*). This was found in liturgy and devotion, to which theology was, in effect, subordinate. The cult of the Virgin is thus part of the work of salvation."

22. Conrad, *Speculum*, IX.4, ed. Martínez, 338; trans. Sr. Mary Emmanuel, 105, with changes.

23. Gambero, *Mary*, 216–21, judges Conrad as "faithful to the tradition of the Church," but he does not explore the way in which Conrad reads scripture in any depth, nor does he account for the images of Mary with which, as we shall see, Conrad's commentary is full.

24. Graef, *Mary*, 1: vii–viii.

25. For their publication history, see above, chap. 2, nn. 91, 94, and 98-99.

26. See above, chap. 2, n. 146.

27. Graef, *Mary*, 1:270.

28. Graef, *Mary*, 1:266–69.

29. Richard, *De laudibus*, lib. 4, cap. 1, n. 2, ed. Borgnet, 167.

30. See above, chap. 3, n. 195. The abbey of Bonneval was in the diocese of Chartres.

31. Etymologically, the "lessons" (*lectiones*) of the Divine Office are "readings": thus the pun in this chapter's title. Although it would have been helpful to have been able to include a reading of Servasanctus's *Mariale*, given that we are following the structure of the Office, it makes sense to have only three lessons. I hope to offer a reading of Servasanctus in a future study.

32. Richard, *De laudibus*, prolog. 1 and 2, ed. Borgnet, 1–4.

33. Mossman, *Marquard*, 279, notes simply, following Beumer, "Mariologie," 27, that Richard's work is "predominantly exegetical," while "its Mariology is not underpinned by any one guiding principle" other than "an assimilation of Mary to Christ" [*eine Angleichung Mariens an Christus*]. While much more sympathetic than Graef, Mossman is more concerned with the way in which Richard describes Mary as a contemplative reader of scripture than with the way in which Richard discovered her in the scriptures. Beumer argues, in contrast, that Richard's work may be taken as evidence for the burgeoning popular devotion (*Volksfrömmigkeit*) of his day. Both, as we shall see, are accurate, if incomplete assessments of Richard's depiction of Mary.

34. Richard, *De laudibus*, prolog. 1, ed. Borgnet, 1–2.

35. Richard, *De laudibus*, prolog. 2, ed. Borgnet, 3.

36. On Paschasius's sermon for the Assumption, see above, chap. 3, "Psalm 23 *Domini est terra*." On Richard's sources more generally, see Beumer, "Mariologie," 20–21; Colasanti, "Il 'De laudibus,'" 15–22 (who gives the citation counts); and the index to Jean Bogard's 1625 edition (see above, chap. 2, n. 99). These identifications depend for the most part on Richard's own citations, which are legion.

37. This manuscript is now Paris, Bibliothèque nationale, nat. lat. 3173, with the inscription (fol. 2): "Hoc volumen est conventus Fratrum Praedicatorum lugdunensium, quod fuit D. Hugonis tit. S. Sabine presbyteri cardinalis, cui missum fuerat de Picardia ab auctore eius mediantibus aliquibus." See Fries, "Die unter dem Namen," 22; and Chatillon, "L'héritage," 162n37.

38. Richard, *De laudibus*, lib. 1, cap. 7, n. 3, ed. Borgnet, 51; lib. 4, cap. 19, ed. Borgnet, 226; lib. 12, cap. 5, n. 3, ed. Borgnet, 709.

39. *Transitus*: Richard, *De laudibus*, lib. 4, cap. 6, n. 2, ed. Borgnet, 186 (as "Miletus"); lib. 6, cap. 13, n. 4, ed. Borgnet, 357 (as "Hieronymus").

40. Richard, *De laudibus*, lib. 5, cap. 2, n. 5, ed. Borgnet, 283.

41. Richard, *De laudibus*, lib. 10, cap. 25, ed. Borgnet, 501–2, citing the last three stanzas of the conductus *Veri floris sub figura* (AH 20, nr. 19, 50–51). See Herrad, *Hortus*, fol. 90r, ed. Green, 1:142.

42. On Herrad's bee imagery, see Griffiths, *Garden*, 82–107.

43. Richard, *De laudibus*, lib. 3, cap. 9, ed. Borgnet, 153; lib. 4, cap. 34, n. 1, ed. Borgnet, 269; lib. 6, cap. 5, n. 2, ed. Borgnet, 333; lib. 10, cap. 10–11, ed. Borgnet, 490–91; lib. 10, cap. 21, ed. Borgnet, 499; lib. 10, cap. 30, n. 10, ed. Borgnet, 519, and n. 19, 523.

44. Richard, *De laudibus*, lib. 12, cap. 7, §4, nn. 1–6, ed. Borgnet, 830–31.

45. Richard, *De laudibus*, lib. 12, cap. 7, §4, n. 7, ed. Borgnet, 832.
46. Richard, *De laudibus*, lib. 12, cap. 7, §4, n. 18, ed. Borgnet, 834.
47. Richard, *De laudibus*, prolog. 1, ed. Borgnet, 3; cf. lib. 9, cap. 2, n. 1, ed. Borgnet, 427.
48. Richard, *De laudibus,* lib. 4 cap. 31, n. 3, ed. Borgnet, 257.
49. Richard, *De laudibus*, lib. 4, cap. 31, nn. 3–5, ed. Borgnet, 258.
50. Richard, *De laudibus*, lib. 4, cap. 31, n. 7, ed. Borgnet, 259, citing Ralph of Escures (as Anselm), *Homilia IX. In Evangelium secundum Lucam*, PL 158, col. 648. On this twelfth-century homily, see Fulton [Brown], *From Judgment to Passion*, 261.
51. Richard, *De laudibus*, lib. 4, cap. 31, nn. 10–11, ed. Borgnet, 260.
52. Graef, *Mary*, 1:266.
53. Richard, *De laudibus*, lib. 4, cap. 34, n. 1, ed. Borgnet, 269.
54. Richard, *De laudibus*, lib. 4, cap. 17, n. 6, ed. Borgnet, 219.
55. Richard, *De laudibus*, lib. 10, cap. 21, ed. Borgnet, 498–99.
56. Richard, *De laudibus*, lib. 10, cap. 31, n. 27, ed. Borgnet, 535.
57. Richard, *De laudibus*, lib. 2, cap. 3, n. 1, ed. Borgnet, 89; lib. 12, cap. 6, §18, n. 4, ed. Borgnet, 777.
58. Richard, *De laudibus,* lib. 7, cap. 1, n. 1, ed. Borgnet, 362.
59. Richard, *De laudibus*, lib. 10, cap. 31, n. 1, ed. Borgnet, 523; cf. lib. 10, cap. 30, n. 1, ed. Borgnet, 512.
60. Richard, *De laudibus*, lib. 10, cap. 8, n. 1, ed. Borgnet, 487.
61. Richard, *De laudibus*, lib. 2, cap. 1, n. 4, ed. Borgnet, 60, citing "Alcuin."
62. Graef, *Mary*, 1:267.
63. Richard, *De laudibus*, lib. 1, cap. 4, n. 3, ed. Borgnet, 30.
64. Richard, *De laudibus*, lib. 3, cap. 1, ed. Borgnet, 143.
65. Richard, *De laudibus*, lib. 5, cap. 1, n. 1, ed. Borgnet, 275. You can tell how important Richard thinks it is to understand this mystery by how many analogies he gives.
66. Richard, *De laudibus*, lib. 5, cap. 1, n. 1, ed. Borgnet, 275.
67. Richard, *De laudibus*, lib. 5, cap. 1, n. 1, ed. Borgnet, 276.
68. Richard, *De laudibus,* lib. 10, cap. 2, n. 2, ed. Borgnet, 457.
69. Richard, *De laudibus*, lib. 10, cap. 2, n. 8, ed. Borgnet, 462.
70. Richard, *De laudibus*, lib. 10, cap. 2, n. 14, ed. Borgnet, 466.
71. Richard, *De laudibus*, lib. 10, cap. 2, n. 15, ed. Borgnet, 467.
72. Richard, *De laudibus*, lib. 2, c. 1, n. 29, ed. Borgnet, 77.
73. Richard, *De laudibus*, lib. 12, cap. 5, §9, ed. Borgnet, 701.
74. Richard, *De laudibus*, lib. 9, cap. 1, n. 8, ed. Borgnet, 425. On Mary as a seal, see Fulton [Brown], *From Judgment to Passion*, 254–65.
75. Richard, *De laudibus*, lib. 9, cap. 1, n. 8, ed. Borgnet, 425.
76. Richard, *De laudibus*, lib. 5, cap. 2, n. 19, ed. Borgnet, 290.
77. Richard, *De laudibus*, lib. 7, cap. 10, n. 1, ed. Borgnet, 395.
78. Richard, *De laudibus*, lib. 1, cap. 5, n. 3, ed. Borgnet, 38; cf. lib. 2, cap. 1, n. 38, ed. Borgnet, 81; lib. 2, cap. 3, n. 4, ed. Borgnet, 90, and n. 5, 94; lib. 4, cap. 5, ed. Borgnet, 183; lib. 7, cap. 10, n. 1, ed. Borgnet, 394; and lib. 10, cap. 2, n. 12, ed. Borgnet, 464.
79. On this method of reading things through their properties, see Thorndike, "Properties."
80. Richard, *De laudibus*, lib. 2, cap. 3, n. 5, ed. Borgnet, 94.
81. Barker, *Lost Prophet*, 71. For those schooled in medieval significs: what Barker calls "parables," Auerbach might rather call *figurae*, while Ohly would describe them as signs (*signa*) or traces of God (*vestigia Dei*). See Auerbach, *Mimesis*, 73–76, 156–62, 194–202; Ohly, "Problems," 68–82; and Ohly, "On the Spiritual Sense."
82. Richard, *De laudibus*, lib. 7, cap. 10, n. 1, ed. Borgnet, 395.
83. Richard, *De laudibus*, lib. 4, cap. 20, n. 2, ed. Borgnet, p 228. We may recall that "Angel of Great Counsel" was the Septuagint translation of the titles listed in Isaiah 9:6. See above, chap. 3, text at n. 327.

84. Richard, *De laudibus*, lib. 1, cap. 3, n. 1, ed. Borgnet, 17–18.
85. Richard, *De laudibus*, lib. 1, cap. 3, n. 2, ed. Borgnet, 18–19.
86. Richard, *De laudibus*, lib. 6, cap. 1, n. 1, ed. Borgnet, 320–21.
87. Richard, *De laudibus*, lib. 6, cap. 1, n. 2, ed. Borgnet, 321–23.
88. Richard, *De laudibus*, lib. 6, cap. 1, nn. 3–4, ed. Borgnet, 323–24. See below, chap. 5, "The Miracle of Theophilus," for why Theophilus's face shone.
89. Richard, *De laudibus*, lib. 6, cap. 1, n. 9, ed. Borgnet, 325–26.
90. Richard, *De laudibus*, lib. 6, cap. 9, nn. 1–5, ed. Borgnet, 343–45.
91. Richard, *De laudibus*, lib. 6, cap. 9, nn. 6–8, ed. Borgnet, 345–47, citing CAO #3985: "O admirabile commercium! Creator generis humani animatum corpus sumens de virgine nasci dignatus est et procedens homo sine semine largitus est nobis suam deitatem." Typically, in citing from the songs of the liturgy, Richard cites only the incipit, suggesting that he expected his readers to be able to fill in the rest.
92. Richard, *De laudibus*, lib. 6, cap. 13, n. 1, ed. Borgnet, 353.
93. Richard, *De laudibus*, lib. 6, cap. 13, n. 2, ed. Borgnet, 353–54.
94. Richard, *De laudibus*, lib. 6, cap. 13, n. 3, ed. Borgnet, 354–55.
95. Richard, *De laudibus*, lib. 6, cap. 13, n. 4, ed. Borgnet, 356.
96. Cf. CAO #3707: " Maria Virgo assumpta est ad aethereum thalamum, in quo Rex regum stellato sedet solio." See above, chap. 3, "Psalm *99 Jubilate Deo*." for this antiphon at Lauds.
97. Richard, *De laudibus*, lib. 6, cap. 13, n. 4, ed. Borgnet, 356–57. "Jerome" here is, of course, Paschasius Radbertus, *Cogitis me*, cap. 4, PL 30, col. 126, ed. Ripberger, no. 24, 119. On this sermon, see above, chap. 3, "Psalm 23 *Domini est terra*."
98. Richard, *De laudibus*, lib. 6, cap. 13, n. 4, ed. Borgnet, 358–59.
99. Richard, *De laudibus*, lib. 7, cap. 1, n. 1, ed. Borgnet, 361–64.
100. Richard, *De laudibus*, lib. 7, cap. 1, n. 1, ed. Borgnet, 364–65.
101. Richard, *De laudibus*, lib. 7, cap. 3, n. 1, ed. Borgnet, 371–72.
102. Richard, *De laudibus*, lib. 7, cap. 3, n. 1, ed. Borgnet, 372, citing *Salve Mater Salvatoris, Vas electum*, AH 54, nr. 245, strophe 17, 384: "Sol luna lucidior, / Et luna sideribus, / Sic Maria dignior / Creaturis omnibus." Another strophe of the same "childish jingle" cited by Adams.
103. Richard, *De laudibus*, lib. 7, cap. 3, n. 1, ed. Borgnet, 372–73.
104. Richard, *De laudibus*, lib. 7, cap. 3, nn. 2–5, ed. Borgnet, 373–74.
105. Richard, *De laudibus*, lib. 7, cap. 3, nn. 6–9, ed. Borgnet, 374–75, citing CAO #2924: "Gaude, Maria Virgo, cunctas haereses sola interemisti in universo mundo." See above, chap. 3, "Psalm 95 *Cantate Domino*." for this antiphon at Matins. Again, Richard cites only the incipit.
106. Oddly, since this is not the model of the universe with which Richard's contemporaries would have been familiar. The usual order of the planets was that followed by Dante in his *Paradiso*: Earth, Moon, Mercury, Venus, Sun, Mars, Jupiter, Saturn, Fixed Stars, Primum Mobile, Empyreum.
107. Richard, *De laudibus*, lib. 7, cap. 4, nn. 1–3, ed. Borgnet, 377–78.
108. Richard, *De laudibus*, lib. 7, cap. 4, nn. 4–7, ed. Borgnet, 379–80.
109. Richard, *De laudibus*, lib. 7, cap. 7, n. 1, ed. Borgnet, 384, citing CAO #7756: "Te laudant angeli, sancta Dei genetrix, quae virum non cognovisti et dominum in tuo utero bajulasti. V. Concepisti per aurem dominum nostrum ut benedicta dicaris inter omnes mulieres." Also citing Theodulus, *Ecloga*, l. 38, ed. Osternacher, 32: "Aurea per cunctas disponens saecula terras."
110. Richard, *De laudibus*, lib. 7, cap. 7, n. 2, ed. Borgnet, 384–85.
111. Richard, *De laudibus*, lib. 7, cap. 7, n. 3, ed. Borgnet, 385–86.
112. Richard, *De laudibus*, lib. 7, cap. 7, n. 4, ed. Borgnet, 386–87.
113. Richard, *De laudibus*, lib. 7, cap. 7, n. 6, ed. Borgnet, 389–90, citing CAO #7878: "Vidi speciosam sicut columbam ascendentem desuper rivos aquarum, cujus inaestimabilis odor erat nimis in vestimentis ejus; et sicut dies verni circumdabant eam flores rosarum et lilia convallium."
114. Richard, *De laudibus*, lib. 7, cap. 12, nn. 1–2, ed. Borgnet, 397–99.

115. Richard, *De laudibus*, lib. 8, cap. 1, nn. 1–3, ed. Borgnet, 400–402.

116. Richard, *De laudibus*, lib. 8, cap. 1, nn. 4–11, ed. Borgnet, 402–408.

117. Richard, *De laudibus*, lib. 8, cap. 1, n. 12, ed. Borgnet, 408–10.

118. Richard, *De laudibus*, lib. 8, cap. 5, ed. Borgnet, 415–17.

119. Richard, *De laudibus*, lib. 9, cap. 1, nn. 1–7, ed. Borgnet, 422–24.

120. Richard, *De laudibus*, lib. 9, cap. 3, nn. 1–7, ed. Borgnet, 429–32.

121. Richard, *De laudibus*, lib. 10, cap. 1, n. 1, ed. Borgnet, 447–48.

122. Richard, *De laudibus*, lib. 10, cap. 1, nn. 4–8, ed. Borgnet, 450–51. This is one of the passages that Graef (*Mary*, 1:266) singled out for particular censure as going *too far* in identifying Mary with her Son.

123. Richard, *De laudibus*, lib. 10, cap. 1, nn. 9–12, ed. Borgnet, 451–53. This is the one place where Richard explicitly cites a text from the Marian Office. As usual, he gives only the incipit of the verse ("Memento salutis auctor, etc."), but he is most likely citing the hymn sung at the Little Hours in the Use of Rouen: "Veni, creator spiritus, / mentes tuorum visita: / imple superna gratia, / quae tu creasti pectora. // Memento, salutis auctor, / quod nostri quondam corporis, / ex illibata virgine / nascendo formam sumpseris. // Maria, mater gratiae, / mater misericordiae, / tu nos ab hoste protege / in hora mortis suscipe. // Gloria tibi, domine, / qui natus es de virgine / cum patre et sancto spiritu / in sempiterna saecula. Amen." See Drigsdahl, *Index to a Selection of Uses*, on this Use. For the hymn as it was sung in the Marian Office, see *Horae Eboracenses*, ed. Wordsworth, 47–54 *passim*.

124. Richard, *De laudibus*, lib. 10, cap. 1, nn. 13–15, citing Edmund of Canterbury, *Psalterium beatae Mariae*, AH 35, nr. 10000, prima quinquagena, strophe 38, 139: "Ave, dives arca Christi, / Quae thesaurum effudisti, / Quo ditantur omnia." On these rhymed psalters, see above, chap. 2, "Aves in the Psalms."

125. Richard, *De laudibus*, lib. 10, cap. 1, nn. 16–18, ed. Borgnet, 454–56.

126. Richard, *De laudibus*, lib. 10, cap. 2, nn. 1–2, ed. Borgnet, 456–57.

127. Richard, *De laudibus*, lib. 10, cap. 2, n. 4, ed. Borgnet, 458–59. Here Richard betrays his familiarity with the bestiaries. On the elephant and its tower, see Druce, "Elephant."

128. Richard, *De laudibus*, lib. 10, cap. 2, nn. 5–12, ed. Borgnet, 459–64.

129. Richard, *De laudibus*, lib. 10, cap. 2, nn. 16–23, ed. Borgnet, 467–71. Again, Richard gives only the incipit, so it is difficult to know which form of the penitential *Confiteor* he had in mind. For one version of the *Confiteor* in use at Rouen in the thirteenth century, see *Lay-Folks Mass Book*, ed. Simmons, 186–87.

130. Richard, *De laudibus*, lib. 10, cap. 28, nn. 1–6, ed. Borgnet, 503–507.

131. Richard, *De laudibus*, lib. 10, cap. 29, n. 1, ed. Borgnet, 508–509.

132. Richard, *De laudibus*, lib. 10, cap. 29, n. 2, ed. Borgnet, 509–12.

133. Richard, *De laudibus*, lib. 10, cap. 30, n. 1, ed. Borgnet, 512–13.

134. Richard, *De laudibus*, lib. 10, cap. 30, nn. 2–8, ed. Borgnet, 513–18.

135. Richard, *De laudibus*, lib. 10, cap. 30, n. 10, ed. Borgnet, 519–20, citing Master Peter Comestor, *Historia scholastica*, III Regum, cap. 22, PL 198, cols. 1367–68.

136. On this prayer, sung in Rouen as a hymn in the Office of the Virgin, see above, n. 123.

137. Richard, *De laudibus*, lib. 10, cap. 31, nn. 1–2, ed. Borgnet, 523–25.

138. Richard, *De laudibus*, lib. 10, cap. 31, nn. 3–13, ed. Borgnet, 525–29, citing Edmund of Canterbury, *Psalterium beatae Mariae*, AH 35, nr. 10000, tertia quinquagena, strophe 47, 149: "Ave, lucis janua / Portarum praecipua, / Patens regi gloriae." See above, n. 124.

139. Richard, *De laudibus*, lib. 10, cap. 31, n. 16, ed. Borgnet, 529–30, citing Adam of Saint Victor, *Splendor Patris et figura*, AH 54, nr. 100, 154: "Si crystallus sit humecta, / Atque soli sit subjecta, / Scintilla igniculum: / Nec crystallus rumpitur, / Nec in partu solvitur / Pudoris signaculum." On this imagery, see above, chap. 2, nn. 122–23.

140. Richard, *De laudibus*, lib. 10, cap. 31, nn. 17–20, ed. Borgnet, 530–31.

141. Richard, *De laudibus*, lib. 10, cap. 31, nn. 21–45, ed. Borgnet, 532–38.

142. Richard, *De laudibus*, lib. 11, cap. 1, n. 1, ed. Borgnet, 539, citing Isidore, *Etymologies*, XV.ii.1, trans. Barney et al., 305.

143. Richard, *De laudibus*, lib. 11, cap. 1, nn. 2–7, ed. Borgnet, 540–42.

144. Richard, *De laudibus*, lib. 11, cap. 1, nn. 8–12, ed. Borgnet, 542–44, citing CAO #4936: "Sicut laetantium omnium nostrum habitatio est in te, sancta Dei genitrix"; and CAO #5041: "Sub tuum praesidium..." On these antiphons, see above, chap. 3, "Psalm 86 *Fundamenta eius*" and "Compline, sung at bedtime."

145. Richard, *De laudibus*, lib. 11, c. 1, nn. 14–41, ed. Borgnet, 545–59.

146. Richard, *De laudibus*, lib. 11, cap. 1, nn. 42–49, ed. Borgnet, 559–65. Given the specificity of his description of Mary as city, Richard would seem to have a rather particular city in mind, perhaps even his own city of Rouen, which was still in his day a major trading center and riverine port. Elsewhere, speaking of Mary's love for God, Richard notes that it was "generous and wide: because she both loved and loves everything which is of God, Saracens, Jews, and Christians, albeit in different ways" (*De laudibus*, lib. 4, cap. 17, n. 7, ed. Borgnet, 222). It is perhaps not insignificant that Rouen in Richard's day had both a Jewish quarter located close to the cathedral and at least one family called "Salehadin." On Richard's fellow citizens, see Six, "Burgesses"; and Brenner and Hicks, "Jews." With thanks to Christopher Loveluck for advice about medieval Rouen.

147. Richard, *De laudibus*, lib. 11, cap. 5, nn. 1–3, ed. Borgnet, 573–76.

148. Richard, *De laudibus*, lib. 11, cap. 8, n. 1, ed. Borgnet, 578–79.

149. Richard, *De laudibus*, lib. 11, cap. 8, nn. 2–4, ed. Borgnet, 579–82.

150. Richard, *De laudibus*, lib. 11, cap. 8, nn. 5–10, ed. Borgnet, 582–85. For Richard's description of Christ as merchant more fully, see below, chap. 5, "The Lord enters into his Creation: Merchant."

151. Richard, *De laudibus*, lib. 11, cap. 8, n. 12, ed. Borgnet, 589.

152. Richard, *De laudibus*, lib. 12, cap. 1, nn. 1–4, ed. Borgnet, 600–602, citing Ekbert of Schönau, *Ad beatam virginem Deiparam*, PL 184, col. 1012.

153. Richard, *De laudibus*, lib. 12, cap. 1, §1, nn. 1–7, ed. Borgnet, 605–608.

154. Richard, *De laudibus*, lib. 12, cap. 1, §2, nn. 1–3, ed. Borgnet, 608–609.

155. Richard, *De laudibus*, lib. 12, cap. 1, §3, nn. 1–4, ed. Borgnet, 609–11.

156. Richard, *De laudibus*, lib. 12, cap. 1, §4, nn. 1–4, ed. Borgnet, 611–12.

157. Richard, *De laudibus*, lib. 12, cap. 1, §5, nn. 1–5, ed. Borgnet, 612–13, citing Anselm, *Oratio 7*, ed. Schmitt, 3:21, trans. Ward, *Prayers*, 120; see above, chap. 2, n. 119.

158. Richard, *De laudibus*, lib. 12, cap. 1, §6, nn. 1–5, ed. Borgnet, 613–15.

159. Richard, *De laudibus*, lib. 12, cap. 1, §7, nn. 1–2, 4–5, ed. Borgnet, 615–17.

160. Richard, *De laudibus*, lib. 12, cap. 1, §8, nn. 1–3, 10, ed. Borgnet, 617–18, 621–22.

161. Richard, *De laudibus*, lib. 12, cap. 1, §9, nn. 1, 4–6, ed. Borgnet, 622–24.

162. Richard, *De laudibus*, lib. 12, cap. 1, §10, nn. 1–6, ed. Borgnet, 625–27.

163. Richard, *De laudibus*, lib. 12, cap. 1, §11, nn. 1–4, ed. Borgnet, 627–29.

164. Richard, *De laudibus*, lib. 12, cap. 1, §12, nn. 1–8, 10, ed. Borgnet, 629–33, 637, citing Hugh of Saint Victor, *De Verbo incarnato*, collatio 3, PL 177, col. 322. On the tumbler who leapt and danced before Mary's image at the monastery of Clairvaux, see below, chap. 5, "How to Serve Mary."

165. Richard, *De laudibus*, lib. 12, cap. 4, nn. 2–25, 28, ed. Borgnet, 653–60, 662–64.

166. Richard, *De laudibus*, lib. 12, cap. 4, n. 30, ed. Borgnet, 664–67.

167. Richard, *De laudibus*, lib. 12, cap. 4, n. 33, ed. Borgnet, 669–70.

168. Richard, *De laudibus*, lib. 12, cap. 4, n. 29, ed. Borgnet, 664.

169. Richard, *De laudibus*, lib. 12, cap. 4, n. 40, ed. Borgnet, 674–75.

170. Richard, *De laudibus*, lib. 12, cap. 6, §1, nn. 1–2, ed. Borgnet, 715.

171. Richard, *De laudibus*, lib. 12, cap. 6, §2, nn. 1–2, ed. Borgnet, 734–35.

172. Richard, *De laudibus*, lib. 12, cap. 6, §3, n. 1, ed. Borgnet, 739–40.

173. Richard, *De laudibus*, lib. 12, cap. 6, §4, nn. 1–4, ed. Borgnet, 741–44.

174.   Richard, *De laudibus*, lib. 12, cap. 6, §5, nn. 1–2, ed. Borgnet, 745–46.

175.   Richard, *De laudibus*, lib. 12, cap. 6, §6, n. 1, ed. Borgnet, 751.

176.   Richard, *De laudibus*, lib. 12, cap. 6, §7, nn. 1–3, ed. Borgnet, 753–54.

177.   Richard, *De laudibus*, lib. 12, cap. 6, §8, n. 2, ed. Borgnet, 756.

178.   Barker would be pleased to hear it. See above, chap. 3, n. 82.

179.   Richard, *De laudibus*, lib. 12, cap. 6, §9, nn. 1–3, ed. Borgnet, 758–60. On similar miracles attested to Mary's servants, see above, chap. 2, "Saying the Ave."

180.   Richard, *De laudibus*, lib. 12, cap. 6, §10, nn. 1–4, ed. Borgnet, 761–64.

181.   Richard, *De laudibus*, lib. 12, cap. 6, §11–15, ed. Borgnet, 764–69.

182.   Richard, *De laudibus*, lib. 12, §16, n. 5, ed. Borgnet, 771–73.

183.   Richard, *De laudibus*, lib. 12, cap. 6, §17, nn. 1–2, ed. Borgnet, 774–75.

184.   Richard seems to be thinking here of the seated images of the Virgin holding the Son in her lap, while at the same time of the images of her standing under the cross. Perhaps he means the images of her as seat of Wisdom placed on the altar next to the crucifix.

185.   Richard, *De laudibus*, lib. 12, cap. 6, §18, nn. 4, 9, ed. Borgnet, 778, 780.

186.   Richard, *De laudibus*, lib. 12, cap. 6, §20, nn. 1–5, ed. Borgnet, 786–92.

187.   Richard, *De laudibus*, lib. 12, cap. 6, §20, nn. 15–23, ed. Borgnet, 795–99, citing the ending to the antiphon *Salve, Regina, mater misericordiae* (CANTUS #204367): "O clemens, O pia, O dulcis, Virgo Maria!" Fassler, *Music*, 170–71, notes that the Dominicans made this antiphon "one of the most beloved pieces of music in Europe" by instituting a daily procession at Compline, during which they would sing Salve Regina with the people while walking from their own church to the church of the laity. For the full text of the antiphon, see below chap. 5, at n. 11.

188.   Richard, *De laudibus*, lib. 12, cap. 6, §21–33, ed. Borgnet, 810–18. One is almost tempted to start looking for Ents, with Asherah not far behind. Servasanctus gives a similarly impressive catalogue of trees.

189.   Amadeus, *De Maria virginea matre*, homilia 1, PL 188, cols. 1303–8, trans. Perigo, 1–7; ed. Bogard (1625), with Richard, *De laudibus*, cols. 1144–48. Perhaps sensing this camaraderie between Richard and Amadeus, Cistercian Publications used an image from a manuscript of one of Richard's other works on their paperback cover of Perigo's translation of Amadeus (1979). See plate 18.

190.   Conrad, *Speculum*, prologus, ed. Martínez, 141–48, trans. Sr. Mary Emmanuel, vii–xi, with changes. Martínez indicates Conrad's sources in his critical edition. Here "Jerome" is Paschasius, *Cogitis me*, cap. 4, PL 30, col. 126, ed. Ripberger, no. 24, 119.

191.   Girotto, *Corrado*, 142–46, gives a list.

192.   Conrad, *Speculum*, VIII.II.4, ed. Martínez, 309–14, citing the antiphon for Christmas (CAO #2938): "Genuit puerpera regem cui nomen aeternum et gaudium matris habens cum virginitate pudoris, nec primam similem visa est nec habere sequentem, alleluia."

193.   Conrad, *Speculum*, VIII.II.4.1–4, ed. Martínez, 314–24.

194.   Conrad, *Speculum*, VIII, ed. Martínez, 324.

195.   Conrad, *Speculum*, I, ed. Martínez, 149–50.

196.   Conrad, *Speculum*, prologus, ed. Martínez, 145–46: "Haec omnia diligenter pensata, pium lectorem piumque auditorem movere debent merito."

197.   Conrad, *Speculum*, I, ed. Martínez, 150.

198.   On the mnemonic techniques used by the friars, see Rivers, *Preaching*. On their training as preachers, see Roest, *History*, 272–324.

199.   Conrad, *Speculum*, VII.5, ed. Martínez, 280.

200.   Conrad, *Speculum*, III.I, ed. Martínez, 175–83.

201.   Conrad, *Speculum*, III.II, ed. Martínez, 183–89.

202.   Conrad, *Speculum*, III.III, ed. Martínez, 189–90, trans. Sr. Mary Emmanuel, 21–22.

203.   Conrad, *Speculum*, III.III.3, ed. Martínez, 194.

204. Conrad, *Speculum*, III.IV, ed. Martínez, 195–97, citing Ambrosius Autpertus, *De assumptione*, cap. 5, PL 39, col. 2131.

205. Conrad, *Speculum*, VI.I, ed. Martínez, 238; cf. Martínez, 177n6, on Conrad's text: *In me omnis gratia vitae et veritatis*; not as it appears in the Sixto-Clementina edition: *viae et veritatis*. Richard's reading of the text shows similar variation. See above, "Mother."

206. Conrad, *Speculum*, VI.I, ed. Martínez, 238–42.

207. Conrad, *Speculum*, VI.II, ed. Martínez, 242–47.

208. Conrad, *Speculum*, VI.III, ed. Martínez, 248–56.

209. Conrad, *Speculum*, VI.IV.1–2, ed. Martínez, 256–59, citing the "modern" Bonaventure, *Breviloquium*, pars 7, cap. 7, ed. *Opera omnia* 5:288.

210. Conrad, *Speculum*, VI.IV.2, ed. Martínez, 259–63, citing Bernard, *De dominica infra octavam Assumptionis*, cap. 3, ed. Leclercq et al., 5:264, PL 183, col. 431; Ambrosius Autpertus, *De assumptione*, cap. 11, PL 39, col. 2134; and Pseudo-Augustine, *De assumptione*, cap. 6, PL 40, col. 1146. On the importance of this latter sermon for the doctrine of Mary's bodily assumption, see Fulton [Brown], *From Judgment to Passion*, 391–93.

211. Conrad, *Speculum*, VII.1, ed. Martínez, 267–71, trans. Sr. Mary Emmanuel, 65.

212. Conrad, *Speculum* VII.2, ed. Martínez, 271–73, trans. Sr. Mary Emmanuel, 67.

213. Conrad, *Speculum*, VII.3, ed. Martínez, 273–75.

214. Conrad, *Speculum*, VII.4, ed. Martínez, 276–78, trans. Sr. Mary Emmanuel, 70, citing Bernard, *De dominica infra octavam Assumptionis*, cap. 2, ed. Leclercq et al., 5:263, PL 183, col. 430.

215. Conrad, *Speculum*, VII.5, ed. Martínez, 278–80, trans. Sr. Mary Emmanuel, 70–71, with changes.

216. Conrad, *Speculum*, VII.6, ed. Martínez, 280–82.

217. Conrad, *Speculum*, VII.7, ed. Martínez, 282–84.

218. Conrad, *Speculum*, VII.8, ed. Martínez, 284–86. Antonomasia is the substitution of an epithet for a proper name.

219. Conrad, *Speculum*, VII.9, ed. Martínez, 286–87, citing Paschasius, *Cogitis me*, cap. 15, PL 30, col. 139, ed. Ripberger, no. 95, 153; and Anselm, *Oratio 7*, ed. Schmitt, 3:21.

220. Conrad, *Speculum*, VIII.I, ed. Martínez, 289–91.

221. Conrad, *Speculum*, VIII.I, ed. Martínez, 290–99.

222. Conrad, *Speculum*, VIII.II, ed. Martínez, 299–309.

223. See above, "*Lectio ii. Ars rhetorica.*"

224. Conrad, *Speculum*, IX, ed. Martínez, 325–26, citing Anselm, *Oratio 7*, ed. Schmitt, 3:22.

225. Conrad, *Speculum*, IX, ed. Martínez, 327–33.

226. Conrad, *Speculum*, IX.I.4, ed. Martínez, 337–38, citing Paschasius, *Cogitis me*, cap. 13, PL 30, col. 136, ed. Ripberger, no. 82, 146.

227. Conrad, *Speculum*, IX.I.4, ed. Martínez, 339–40, citing Bernard, *In assumptione beatae Mariae. Sermo I*, cap. 3, ed. Leclercq et al., 5:230, PL 183, col. 416.

228. Conrad, *Speculum*, X.I, ed. Martínez, 352–59, citing "Innocent": "Ave, Dei mater alma, quae ex dignitate, qua Dei mater es, imperare potest angelis et daemonibus! Compesce daemones, ne nobis noceant; praecipe angelis, ut nos custodiant." Martínez was not able to identify this quotation; a Google search returns only Conrad's *Speculum*.

229. Conrad, *Speculum*, X.II, ed. Martínez, 359–71, quotation at 368–69.

230. Conrad, *Speculum*, XI, ed. Martínez, 372–73.

231. Conrad, *De assumptione sanctae Mariae, sermo I*, ed. Martínez, 525–33.

232. Conrad, *De eodem, sermo II*, ed. Martínez, 533–41.

233. Conrad, *Speculum*, XII.I–III, ed. Martínez, 388–411.

234. Conrad, *Speculum*, XII.IV, ed. Martínez, 411–12.

235. Conrad, *Speculum*, XIII, ed. Martínez, 419–37.

236. Conrad, *Speculum*, XIII.7, ed. Martínez, 434–36, citing *Sermo "Adest nobis,"* cap. 3: Pseudo-Augustine, *Sermo 194: De annuntiatione Dominca II*, PL 39, col. 2106; Pseudo-Fulbert, *Sermo 9: De annuntiatione*

Dominica, PL 141, col. 338. This sermon was read at Chartres from the eleventh century for the Feast of Mary's Nativity. See Fassler, *Virgin*, 421, for its location in the liturgy.

237. Conrad, *Speculum*, XIV, ed. Martínez, 438–39, citing Bede, *Homilia II: In festo visitationis beatae Mariae . . . "Lectio quam audivimus,"* PL 94, col. 16; CCSL 122:23.

238. Conrad, *Speculum*, XIV, ed. Martínez, 438–60.

239. Conrad, *Speculum*, XV, ed. Martínez, 461–80.

240. Conrad, *Speculum*, XV.4, ed. Martínez, 474, trans. Sr. Mary Emmanuel, 180, with changes; paraphrasing Bede, *In evangelium s. Lucae*, lib. 1, cap. 1, PL 92, col. 321; CCSL 120:37.

241. Conrad, *Speculum*, XV.5, ed. Martínez, 475–76, citing John of Damascus, *De fide orthodoxa*, 4.14, PG 94, col. 1159; versio Burgundio cap. 87, n. 6, ed. Buytaert, 321.

242. Conrad, *Speculum*, XV.4, ed. Martínez, 473–74.

243. Conrad, *Speculum*, XVI.1–6, ed. Martínez, 481–92.

244. Conrad, *Speculum*, XVI.7–12, ed. Martínez, 492–504.

245. See above, n. 36.

246. On the rhetorical significance of this focus on place, see Carruthers, *Craft of Thought*. See above, chap. 3, n. 168, for the Orthodox emphasis on Mary as place.

247. On this methodology, see Novikoff, *Medieval Culture of Disputation*.

248. Graef, *Mary*, 1:271–72.

249. Graef, *Mary*, 1:273, referring to her earlier discussion at 1:8.

250. Graef, *Mary*, 1:273, citing Laurentin, *Court Traité*, 67.

251. Kolping, "Zur Frage"; and Mossman, *Marquard*, 295.

252. Fries, "Die unter dem Namen," 18–22.

253. Barker, *Mother*, 333–42. On Pseudo-Albert's sources, see Fries, "Die unter dem Namen."

254. Pseudo-Albert, *Mariale*, quaestio 27, §2, ed. Borgnet, 59.

255. Pseudo-Albert, *Mariale*, solutio ad praedicta, a quaestione XXXVI ad XLIII, §2, ed. Borgnet, 85; quaestio 120, ed. Borgnet, 174.

256. Pseudo-Albert, *Mariale*, solutio ad praedicta, a quaestione XXXVI ad XLIII, §2, ed. Borgnet, 86–87.

257. Pseudo-Albert, *Mariale*, quaestio 44, ed. Borgnet, 89.

258. Pseudo-Albert, *Mariale*, quaestio 44, ed. Borgnet, 89, citing Bernard, *In laudibus virginis matris [Super "Missus est"]*, homilia 4.4, ed. Leclercq et al., 4:50, trans. Saïd, 49.

259. Pseudo-Albert, *Mariale*, proemium, ed. Borgnet, 1–3, citing Augustine, *Confessiones* 12.31, trans. Pine-Coffin, 308; and John of Damascus, *De fide orthodoxa*, 4.14, PG 94, col. 1157; versio Burgundio cap. 87, n. 6, ed. Buytaert, 321, identified by Graef, *Mary*, 1:272. Conrad cites from this same passage (see above, n. 241).

260. Pseudo-Albert, *Mariale*, quaestiones 3–6, 14–20, ed. Borgnet, 15–20, 34–47.

261. Pseudo-Albert, *Mariale*, quaestio 12, ed. Borgnet, 29–31.

262. Pseudo-Albert, *Mariale*, quaestio 29, ed. Borgnet, 60–63.

263. Pseudo-Albert, *Mariale*, quaestio 30, ed. Borgnet, 63–65, citing Bernard, *In laudibus virginis matris*, homilia 3.1, ed. Leclercq et al., 4:36, trans. Saïd, 33–34.

264. Pseudo-Albert, *Mariale*, quaestio 31, ed. Borgnet, 65–68.

265. Pseudo-Albert, *Mariale*, quaestio 32, ed. Borgnet, 68–69.

266. Pseudo-Albert, *Mariale*, quaestio 35, ed. Borgnet, 74.

267. Pseudo-Albert, *Mariale*, solutio ad praedicta, a quaestione XXXVI ad XLIII, ed. Borgnet, 82.

268. Pseudo-Albert, *Mariale*, quaestio 44, ed. Borgnet, 87–89. See above, at n. 257.

269. Pseudo-Albert, *Mariale*, quaestio 45, ed. Borgnet, 90.

270. Pseudo-Albert, *Mariale*, quaestiones 46–61, ed. Borgnet, 90–104.

271. Pseudo-Albert, *Mariale*, quaestio 51, ed. Borgnet, 97.

272. Pseudo-Albert, *Mariale*, praemittenda ad solutionem praecedentium quaestionum, ed. Borgnet, 104–18.

273. Pseudo-Albert, *Mariale*, responsio ad quaestiones XLV–XLIX, ed. Borgnet, 112; discussion in Mossman, *Marquard*, 300.

274. Pseudo-Albert, *Mariale*, responsio ad quaestiones XLV–XLIX, ed. Borgnet, 110–12. As Mossman, *Marquard*, 300, comments: "This [argument] implies, logically, the total deification of the mind." Barker might argue that it also implies, sapientially, the total identification of Mary with Wisdom, the cloud surrounding the Lord as he appeared in his glory, his face shining like the sun and his garments white as snow.

275. Pseudo-Albert, *Mariale*, quaestio 62, ed. Borgnet, 118–19.

276. Pseudo-Albert, *Mariale*, quaestio 63, ed. Borgnet, 119–20. The Philosopher is Aristotle, but Pseudo-Albert is paraphrasing.

277. Pseudo-Albert, *Mariale*, quaestio 64, ed. Borgnet, 120–21.

278. Pseudo-Albert, *Mariale*, quaestio 65, ed. Borgnet, 121–22.

279. Pseudo-Albert, *Mariale*, quaestiones 66–69, ed. Borgnet, 122–25.

280. Pseudo-Albert, *Mariale*, responsio ad quaestiones LXII, LXIII, etc., de donis, ed. Borgnet, 125–26.

281. Pseudo-Albert, *Mariale,* quaestiones 112–18, ed. Borgnet, 168–73.

282. Pseudo-Albert, *Mariale,* quaestio 95, ed. Borgnet, 153–57. On Pseudo-Albert's use of Pseudo-Dionysius, see below, "Q. 152 *Whether if, as Dionysius says...*"

283. Pseudo-Albert, *Mariale*, quaestio 97, ed. Borgnet, 158.

284. Pseudo-Albert, *Mariale*, quaestiones 98–102, ed. Borgnet, 159–61.

285. Pseudo-Albert, *Mariale*, quaestiones 103–110, ed. Borgnet, 161–66.

286. Pseudo-Albert, *Mariale*, quaestio 111, ed. Borgnet, 166–68.

287. Pseudo-Albert, *Mariale*, quaestio 152, ed. Borgnet, 223–24, citing Pseudo-Dionysius, *De coelesti hierarchia*, cap. 11, as translated from the Greek by John Scotus Eriugena, *Expositiones*, PL 122, col. 230; *De coelesti hierachia*, trans. Parker, 38, with changes. On the Dionysian angelic hierarchies and their importance in thirteenth-century scholastic thought, see Keck, *Angels*, parts I–II.

288. Pseudo-Albert, *Mariale*, quaestio 152, ed. Borgnet, 224, citing Ralph of Escures (as Augustine), *Homilia IX. In Evangelium secundum Lucam*, PL 158, col. 648, with Pseudo-Albert's changes. See above, n. 50, where Richard cites the same sermon as Anselm's.

289. Pseudo-Albert, *Mariale*, quaestio 152, ed. Borgnet, 224, citing Pseudo-Dionysius, *De coelesti hierarchia*, cap. 3, as trans. by John Scotus Eriugena, *Expositiones*, PL 122, col. 174, reading *actio deiformi* rather than *operatio* (Pseudo-Albert).

290. Pseudo-Albert, *Mariale*, quaestiones 153–58, ed. Borgnet, 225–30.

291. Pseudo-Albert, *Mariale*, quaestiones 159–61, ed. Borgnet, 231–34, citing CAO #7878: "Vidi speciosam sicut columbam ascendentem desuper rivos aquarum, cujus inaestimabilis odor erat nimis in vestimentis ejus; et sicut dies verni circumdabant eam flores rosarum et lilia convallium." Accident and essence (or substance) are Aristotelian terms. Here Pseudo-Albert cites Hugh of Saint Victor as "the Commentator," on the properties of the Cherubim and Seraphim (*Super ierarchiam Dionisii*, lib. 6, cap. 7, ed. Poirel, 553–68; PL 175, cols. 1034–44).

292. Pseudo-Albert, *Mariale*, quaestio 162, ed. Borgnet, 234–25, citing Pseudo-Dionysius, *De coelesti hierarchia*, cap. 12, as trans. by John Scotus Eriugena, *Expositiones* (PL 122, col. 233), with changes; cf. *De coelesti hierarchia*, trans. Parker, 38. It is not clear which translation Pseudo-Albert was using; it does not seem to be Hugh's version either. There may be an error in the edition.

293. Pseudo-Albert, *Mariale*, quaestio 162, ed. Borgnet, 235–37.

294. Pseudo-Albert, *Mariale*, quaestio, 164, ed. Borgnet, 240–41, citing CAO #5448: "Virgo dei genetrix quem totus non capit orbis in tua se clausit viscera factus homo: vera fides geniti purgavit crimina mundi et tibi virginitas inviolata manet."

295. Cf. Peter Comestor, *Historia scholastica*, III Regum, cap. 22, PL 198, cols. 1367–68. See above, "House," for Richard's correct use of the same passage.

296. Pseudo-Albert, *Mariale*, quaestio 164, ed. Borgnet, 241–45.

297. Antiphon for the Assumption (CAO #4425): "Quae est ista quae ascendit sicut aurora consurgens, pulchra ut luna, electa ut sol, terribilis ut castrorum acies ordinata?"

298. The list of palaces is Adams's (*Mont Saint Michel*, 88).

299. On this hymn, see above, n. 123.

5. PRAYER

1. Your prayers (*orationes*) follow the Use of Rome. See Reinburg, *French Books*, for a fuller discussion of the prayers of the Marian Office as acts of speech modeled both on audiences before a secular lord and on the exchange of contracts or oaths. See above, "Invitatory," for the understanding of prayer we are drawing on here.

2. This is one of the most ancient prayers of the Marian Office. It appears as the collect for Matins in the eleventh-century Office for the Virgin used at Saint Mary's, Winchester (London, British Library, Royal 2 B.V, ed. Dewick, *Facsimiles*, col. 6). It also appears in the Gregorian *Liber sacramentorum* (PL 78, col. 52; ed. Deshusses, 1:128), as a prayer for the Feast of the Annunciation.

3. This prayer appears in the Gregorian *Liber sacramentorum* (PL 78, col. 132; ed. Deshusses, 1:262), as a prayer for the Vigil of the Assumption. At Fonte Avellana in the eleventh century, it was said in the Marian Office at None (PL 151, col. 972).

4. As per Richard of Saint-Laurent's instructions. See above, chap. 2, at n. 41.

5. Another ancient prayer: it appears as the collect for Terce in the Office of the Virgin said in the eleventh century at Canterbury (London, British Library, Cotton Tiberius A. iii, ed. Dewick, *Facsimiles*, cols. 29–30); and at Vespers in the Office said at Winchester (Royal 2 B.V, ed. Dewick, *Facsimiles*, col. 16). In the Gregorian *Liber sacramentorum* (PL 78, col. 37; ed. Deshusses, 1:112), it is the prayer for the Octave of the Nativity (January 1).

6. Because if you do, the devils will be sure to collect them, like coin clippings stolen from the money of God's service, to use them against you in the judgment (*Myroure*, part 1, 20, ed. Blunt, 53–54).

7. This prayer was used in the eleventh century at Canterbury as a collect for the Marian Office at Lauds (Cotton Tiberius A. iii, ed. Dewick, *Facsimiles*, col. 24). It appears in the Gregorian *Liber sacramentorum* (PL 78, col. 133; ed. Deshusses, 1:262) at the Vigil for the Assumption.

8. In the Gregorian *Liber sacramentorum* (PL 78, col. 133; ed. Deshusses, 1:263), the prayer for the Mass on the Feast of the Assumption. It was used at Canterbury at Matins (Cotton Tiberius A.iii, ed. Dewick, *Facsimiles*, col. 22) and at Winchester at Terce (Royal 2 B.V, ed. Dewick, *Facsimiles*, col. 11).

9. You have been reading Cassian, *Collationes*, conferences 9–10; and Hugh of Saint Victor, *De virtute orandi*. This prayer was used in the eleventh century at Winchester at Lauds (Royal 2 B.V., ed. Dewick, *Facsimiles*, cols. 7–8). It appears in Alcuin's *Liber sacramentorum* as the collect for the Saturday Mass of the Virgin (PL 101, col. 455).

10. This prayer was used as early as the twelfth century in England for the Marian Office at Terce (London, British Library, Add. 21927, fol. 103v).

11. CANTUS #204367. For the history and miracle stories associated with this antiphon, see Thurston, "Notes on Familiar Prayers VIII: The *Salve Regina*"; and Canal, *Salve Regina*. According to Thurston, it is first mentioned definitively around 1135 as being sung as an antiphon for the procession for the Feast of the Assumption at the monastery of Cluny.

12. You are not alone in this vision, others have described it, too. See Caesarius, *Dialogus Miraculorum*, dist. 7, cap. 20, 24, 37, ed. Strange, 2:25–28, 33–35, 45–49, trans. Scott and Swinton Bland, 1:481–85, 490–92, 506–10; and Underhill, *Miracles*, 167–77, 233–44.

13. Mechthild of Magdeburg saw her face shining in this way (*Das fliessende Licht*, lib. 6, cap. 39, trans. Tobin, 265).

14. Perhaps you have been reading Gautier's account of her miracles, so as to learn from her. On these miracle stories as forms of instruction, see Waters, *Translating Clergie*, 164–208; and Ihnat, *Mother*, 100–37.

15. The Cistercian monk Bertram of Karixtus heard this song (Caesarius, *Dialogus Miraculorum*, dist. 7, cap. 37, ed. Strange, 2:46, trans. Scott and Swinton Bland, 1:507), as did a penitent who wandered all the way to Alexandria to discover someone who might teach him how to be relieved of his sin (Alfonso, *Cantigas*, no. 65, trans. Kulp-Hill, 83–86, who notes that the angels do not need books to sing the Virgin's Hours).

16. Here you seem to have been reading one of the earlier collections of Latin miracles (*Latin Miracles*, trans. Timmons and Boenig, 43) as well as Caesarius (*Dialogus Miraculorum*, dist. 7, cap. 2, ed. Strange, 2:3, trans. Scott and Swinton Bland, 1:455).

17. All popular stories: *Latin Miracles*, trans. Timmons and Boenig, 33 (Ebbo); 48–51 (pregnant abbess); 40–41 (Virgin as bride).

18. See above, chap. 4, n. 146.

19. Barker, *Temple Themes*, 73–78; *Revelation*, 123–26, 333–37; and *Great High Priest*, 103–45.

20. On the importance of this verse for the early Christians and the absence of the passage from the modern Hebrew, see Law, *When God Spoke Greek*, 48, 109. As Law comments (94): "Whether the New Testament authors intentionally chose the Septuagint over the Hebrew, whether they were aware of the different textual options, is another question altogether, but often their Septuagint readings had, even if only coincidentally, a more suitable message for their purposes than the Hebrew." Barker would say there was no coincidence. On the corrections made to the Hebrew text by the ancient and medieval rabbinic scribes, including the passage from Deuteronomy 32, see Levin, *Father of Joshua*, 70–107.

21. Jordan, *Liber vitasfratrum*, cap. 15, trans. Deighan, 197. On this understanding of prayer as a service of praise offered with the angels, see Fulton Brown, "Prayer"; and Ratzinger, "Address to the Collège": "For Benedict, the words of the Psalm: *coram angelis psallam Tibi, Domine*—in the presence of the angels, I will sing your praise (cf. [137:1])—are the decisive rule governing the prayer and chant of the monks. What this expresses is the awareness that in communal prayer one is singing in the presence of the entire heavenly court, and is thereby measured according to the very highest standards: that one is praying and singing in such a way as to harmonize with the music of the noble spirits who were considered the originators of the harmony of the cosmos, the music of the spheres." For Tolkien's reflection on this service, see Tolkien, *Letters*, ed. Carpenter, no. 310 (To Camilla Unwin): "So it may be said that the chief purpose of life, for any one of us, is to increase according to our capacity our knowledge of God by all the means we have, and to be moved by it to praise and thanks. . . . And in moments of exaltation we may call on all created things to join in our chorus, speaking on their behalf, as is done in Psalm 148, and in The Song of the Three Children in Daniel II [the *Benedicite*]. PRAISE THE LORD . . . all mountains and hills, all orchards and forests, all things that creep and birds on the wing."

22. Dionysius, *De oratione*, section 30, trans. Ní Riain, 259.

23. On the Sanctus as sung for the Mass, see Fassler, *Medieval Music*, 70–71. In the Jewish liturgy, the "Holy, holy, holy" of the seraphim "[forms] part of the Amidah, a central prayer of blessing said while standing and facing the Ark that houses the Torah scrolls." The Mass Sanctus adds the Benedictus, which the people sang as Jesus entered into Jerusalem on Palm Sunday (Matthew 21:9, Mark 11:9–10).

24. On this understanding of the Mass, see Keck, *Angels*, 174–79. For the Mass preface as cited here, see *Liber sacramentorum*, PL 78, col. 30. For the meditations that the laity were encouraged to make at this time, see Kumler, *Translating Truth*, 103–59.

25. Philip and Carol Zaleski, *Prayer*, part IV, survey these concerns.

26. Adams, *Mont Saint-Michel*, 238, 246–47, 249.

27. Adams, *Mont Saint-Michel*, 260–61.

28. Graef, *Mary*, 1:268–69, citing Richard, *De laudibus*, lib. 6, cap. 9, nn. 3–5, ed. Borgnet, 344–45.

29. Saint-Omer, Bibliothèque municipale, 174; digitized at http://bvmm.irht.cnrs.fr/resultRecherche /resultRecherche.php?COMPOSITION_ID=18774. On the contents and influence of this treatise, see Chatillon, "L'héritage," 149–54.

30. Graef, *Mary*, 1: viii, citing Newman, *Certain Difficulties Felt by Anglicans*, new ed. (1892), vol. 2, 115.

31. Luther, *Large Catechism*, trans. Fischer, 65.

32. Priestley, *General History*, 1:385, emphasis his.

33. Sabatier, *Esquisse*, 24–26, cited by James, *Varieties*, 464.

34. Heiler, *Prayer*, 104.

35. Heiler, *Prayer*, xix.

36. Like, in fact, the Office of the Virgin. See above, chap. 1.

37. Underhill, *Miracles*, xiv.

38. Power, "Introduction," xviii–xix, citing Coulton, *Five Centuries of Religion* (1923), I:155.

39. Southern, *Making*, 248–50. For his fuller proof of the origins of the collections, see Southern, "English Origins." On the importance of Southern's argument for the subsequent historiography of these collections, see Boyarin, *Miracles of the Virgin in Medieval England*, 4–6; and Ihnat, "Marian Miracles," 65–70.

40. Flory, *Marian Representations*, 108–9.

41. William, *De laudibus et miraculis*, prologus 40, ed. and trans. Thomson and Winterbottom, 13–14, translators' emphasis.

42. Dominic, *De miraculis*, ed. Canal, 258.

43. Ward, *Miracles*, 164: "When the stories were read in a court or hall, the religious purpose soon merged with the magical elements in romance; the later forms of such stories are of knights devoted to great ladies, rather than to the Queen of Heaven, but the seeds of romance lay in the Mary stories of the earlier period."

44. Carter, "Historical Content," 139, who suggests that the story of Ebbo may lie behind the later Robin Hood legends. The reference to the story of Julian is from William's commentary on Jeremiah. For Ebbo, see William, *De laudibus et miraculis*, lib. 2, cap. 37, ed. Thomson and Winterbottom, 102–103.

45. Boyarin, *Miracles of the Virgin in Medieval England*, 7, citing Boyd, ed., *Middle English*, 10; Rubin, *Gentile Tales*, 7; and Ward, *Miracles*, 133.

46. See above, chap. 4, at nn. 34, 190, and 259.

47. Barker, *Creation*, 215, 247.

48. Barker, *Lost Prophet*, 65–76.

49. Barker, *Creation*, 239, citing *Exodus Rabbah* XLVIII.4, trans. S. M. Lehrman (1939).

50. Barker, *Creation*, 31, her translation of the psalm.

51. Dominic, *De miraculis*, prologus, ed. Canal, 256, citing CAO #4081: "O sapientia quae ex ore altissimi prodisti attingens a fine usque ad finem fortiter suaviter disponensque omnia veni ad docendum nos viam prudentiae." This is the first of the great O antiphons sung at Vespers in the last seven days of Advent, the season before Christmas.

52. Dominic, *De miraculis*, prologus, ed. Canal, 256–58.

53. Dominic, *De miraculis*, cap. 1–4, ed. Canal, 259–71. The title for the series is Adolfo Mussafia's. See Jennings, "Origins," 84n2.The remaining ten stories do not follow such an explicit organizing schema, although Dominic offers similar justifications for including each one.

54. Dominic, *De miraculis*, incipit, ed. Canal, 258.

55. As Donatus explained in his *Ars Maior*, the great medieval textbook of grammar on which Dominic and his brothers would have been regularly drilled (III.2, trans. Copeland and Sluiter, *Medieval Grammar*, 95): "A solecism contains words which are in conflict or incongruent among themselves, while barbarisms occur in individual written or spoken words."

56. Augustine, *De catechizandis rudibus*, cap. 10.15, trans. Salmond.

57. Augustine, *De doctrina christiana*, lib. 4, trans. Shaw.

58. Augustine, *De doctrina christiana*, lib. 1, cap. 14, trans. Shaw. Here Augustine is talking about the foolishness of the Incarnation when the Word took on human flesh, but his words apply to his understanding of the scriptures as well. He discusses the obscurities in scripture in lib. 2, cap. 6; on their grammatical crudeness, see lib. 4, cap. 20.

59. Auerbach, "*Sermo Humilis*," 50–51. For the effects of their training in the liberal arts on the Fathers' reading of the scriptures and its importance for the Christian tradition, see Morrison, "Incentives."

60. Waters, *Translating Clergie*, 165. Flory, *Marian Representations*, 18, likewise comments on the character of the miracle stories as Wisdom literature. In his view, however, the stories, like Mary, serve to confound "reformist Church policies" rather than to instruct in doctrine.

61. For examples of miracles in which devotion to Mary gives sight to the blind, see Bull, *Miracles*, part I, nos. 16, 21, 23; and part II, nos. 18, 19, 36. For cures of the deaf, see part I, nos. 33, 39; and part II, no. 48. As an example of her taking sight away as a punishment, see part II, no. 9.

62. For examples of her rebukes, see Bull, *Miracles*, part I, nos. 3, 6, 24, 45, 47; part II, nos. 6, 8, 11, 26, 27, 30, 35; and part III, nos. 4, 7, 8, 11, 14.

63. This story was first edited by Wilhelm Foerster in "Del tumbeor Nostre-Dame," and since has become one of the best-known miracles of the Virgin. Adams, *Mont Saint-Michel*, 265–68, reads it at once as an example of abbatial patience and as somehow more modern than medieval in its "quiet sense of humor that pleases modern French taste as much as it pleased the Virgin." Perhaps most beautifully, Tomie dePaolo retold and illustrated it as *The Clown of God* (1978). It has been frequently translated. Here I use Wicksteed (1904); see also Kemp-Welch, *Of the Tumbler*, 3–33. For the story's reception in the late nineteenth and twentieth centuries, see Ziolkowski, "Juggling." Ziolkowski is preparing a fuller study entitled *The Juggler of Notre Dame: Medieval Meets Medievalism*.

64. On these variations in the complexity of service that Mary's devotees might offer her, see above, chap. 2, "Saluting Mary: Ave."

65. Trans. Bull, *Miracles*, part I, no. 34, 122–23; cf. Alfonso, *Cantigas*, no. 8, trans. Kulp-Hill, 13–14, where the musician is a fiddler and the drop of wax a whole candle; and Gautier, *Les Miracles*, II Mir 21, ed. Koenig, 4:175–89, trans. Pouquet, cols. 309–22, where the minstrel requests the candle in payment. On the jongleurs' devotion to the Virgin, see Symes, "Lordship"; and "Confraternity."

66. Alfonso, *Cantigas*, no. 267, trans. Kulp-Hill, 324–25.

67. Alfonso, *Cantigas*, no. 121, trans. Kulp-Hill, 149; cf. Herolt, *Promptuarium Discipuli*, cap. 70, trans. Swinton-Bland, 98–99, where Mary's servant is a certain clerk.

68. Caesarius, *Dialogus Miraculorum*, dist. 7, cap. 24, ed. Strange, 2:33–35; trans. Scott and Swinton-Bland, 1:490–92.

69. Caesarius, *Dialogus Miraculorum*, dist. 7, cap. 50, ed. Strange, 2:70–71; trans. Scott and Swinton-Bland, 1:535–36; cf. Herolt, *Promptuarium Discipuli*, cap. 60, trans. Swinton-Bland, 84–85, where the monk says simply, "Mary, Mother of Grace, Mary, Mother of Mercy."

70. *Latin Miracles*, trans. Timmons and Boenig, 32; cf. Gonzalo, *Milagros*, no. 5, trans. Mount and Cash, 41–42; and William of Malmesbury, *De laudibus et miraculis*, lib. 2, cap. 36, trans. Thomson and Winterbottom, 101.

71. Caesarius, *Dialogus Miraculorum*, dist. 7, cap. 19, ed. Strange, 2:25; trans. Scott and Swinton-Bland, 1:481.

72. Herolt, *Promptuarium Discipuli*, cap. 72, trans. Swinton-Bland, 100.

73. Alfonso, *Cantigas*, no. 55, trans. Kulp-Hill, 71–72; Caesarius, *Dialogus Miraculorum*, dist. 7, cap. 34, ed. Strange, 2:42–43; trans. Scott and Swinton-Bland, 1:502–3.

74. Caesarius, *Dialogus Miraculorum*, dist. 7, cap. 45, ed. Strange, 2:63–64; trans. Scott and Swinton-Bland, 1:526–28; Herolt, *Promptuarium Discipuli*, cap. 15, trans. Swinton-Bland, 32–33. Cf. Jacobus, *Legenda aurea*, cap. 131, trans. Ryan, 2:155, where the woman holds the Virgin's son hostage for the release of her son from captivity.

75. Herolt, *Promptuarium Discipuli*, cap. 19, trans. Swinton-Bland, 35–36, cited by Herolt from Vincent of Beauvais, *Speculum historiale*, lib. 7, cap. 99. Cf. Alfonso, *Cantigas*, no. 89, trans. Kulp-Hill, 114.

76. Alfonso, *Cantigas*, no. 167, trans. Kulp-Hill, 202, translator's italics. These latter two examples may be contrasted with those more famous stories like Chaucer's "Prioress's Tale," in which unbelieving Jews and Saracens appear as foils for faithful Christians, although, as we have noted, there are many stories in which Mary likewise punishes Christians for their unbelief. On Mary's relationship

with the Jews as portrayed in her miracles, see Frank, "Miracles" (who contextualizes Chaucer's story); Rubin, *Gentile Tales*, 7–28 (who focuses on the story of the Jewish boy); and Ihnat, *Mother of Mercy*, who discusses the importance of these stories in the monastic culture of twelfth-century Anglo-Norman England. Elsewhere, Ihnat, "Getting the Punchline," 415, points to William of Malmesbury's strong anti-Jewish invective as an example of his own discomfort with the presence of Jews in twelfth-century England, including a story that he relates in his *Gesta regum Anglorum* about an attempt under William Rufus by certain Jews of Rouen "to recall to the Jewish faith some who had abandoned their mistaken ways." As we have noted (above, n. 18), Richard of Saint-Laurent, as canon of Rouen, seems to have had a rather different perspective on Mary's relationship with both Saracens and Jews. On Mary imagined as protectress of the Jews, see Fulton [Brown], *From Judgment to Passion*, 280–85, 441–43. On the significance of the Jew in the story of Theophilus, see below, "The Miracle of Theophilus." For Mary's role in the *Cantigas* as defender of Christians against the Saracens of Spain, see Remensnyder, *La Conquistadora*. On the stories as expressing the threats Christian poets felt about Judaism, see Nirenberg, *Aesthetic Theology*, 79–127.

77. Wilson, *Stella Maris*, v–ix, gives a list of known collections extant in Latin, Anglo-Norman, Old French, Provençal, Castilian, Galician-Portuguese, Italian, Middle English, German, Icelandic, and Old Norse. Thomson and Winterbottom include a handlist of manuscripts containing stories in Latin as an appendix to their edition of William of Malmesbury's *De laudibus et miraculis*. See Cooke, "Miracles," for a catalogue of the 171 stories extant in Middle English. Cooke, 3178, gives an estimate of more than two thousand stories extant in Latin and the vernaculars. Like Books of Hours, such stories are difficult to count.

78. William of Malmesbury, *De laudibus et miraculis*, lib. 1, cap. 2, ed. Thomson and Winterbottom, 21: "I shall compose my unfolding narrative in such a way as to show that the blessed Virgin has poured out the bowels of her compassion on every rank, every condition of men, and on both sexes." Cf. Wilson, *Stella Maris*, 20, who notes a similar promise made by a compiler working in the thirteenth century at St. German-des-Prés.

79. Gonzalo, *Milagros*, no. 1, trans. Mount and Cash, 28–31.

80. Gonzalo, *Milagros*, no. 12, trans. Mount and Cash, 64–67.

81. Gonzalo, *Milagros*, no. 16, trans. Mount and Cash, 77–80. On the angel in the furnace, see Barker, *Great Angel*, 7. On the *Benedicite* as sung in Mary's Office, see above, chap. 3, "Lauds . . . Daniel 3:57–88, 56."

82. Gautier, *Les Miracles*, I Mir 21, ed. Koenig, 2:197–204, trans. Flory, *Marian Representations*, 63–67.

83. Jacques de Vitry, *Exempla*, no. CCXCVI, ed. Crane, 124–25, trans. Flory, *Marian Representations*, 90. The role of the Jew needs to be read not only in the context of contemporary social relations (here, the Jew as moneylender promising to make the Christian rich), but also in the context of the Wisdom tradition. Here, Mary, not earthly commerce, is the source of riches, much as Solomon said (Proverbs 3:13–15).

84. Alfonso, *Cantigas*, no. 290, trans. Kulp-Hill, 350, translator's italics.

85. Richard, *De laudibus*, lib. 2, cap. 4, n. 13, ed. Borgnet, 106; lib. 1, cap. 2, n. 3, ed. Borgnet, 13; lib. 4, cap. 6, n. 2, ed. Borgnet, 187.

86. On these images, see above, chap. 2, n. 116.

87. On the throne in the temple, see above, chap. 3, "The Lord and the Lady of the Temple."

88. To the examples cited above, nn. 65–76, may be added Caesarius, *Dialogus Miraculorum*, dist. 7, cap. 29, ed. Strange, 2:38–39, trans. Scott and Swinton-Bland, 1:497–98; Alfonso, *Cantigas*, no. 288, trans. Kulp-Hill, 348–39.

89. Alfonso, *Cantigas*, no. 202, trans. Kulp-Hill, 243. For Adam's sequence, see above, chap. 4, n. 20.

90. Ziolkowski, "Juggling," 160.

91. Richard, *De laudibus*, lib. 12, cap. 1, §12, n. 10, ed. Borgnet, 637.

92. The tumbler at Clairvaux may not have been alone in his athletic psaltery: see Bayless, "Humour," 27, on the jugglers accompanying King David in London, British Library, Cotton Tiberius C.VI,

a Gallican psalter with an interlinear Old English gloss produced ca. 1060 at Winchester; and Cambridge, Trinity College, B.5.26, a copy of Augustine's commentary on the psalms made at Christ Church, Canterbury, between 1070 and 1100—both places where the Hours of the Virgin were already being said. See Fulton Brown, "Delight," on the significance of this comic tumbling.

93. Alfonso, *Cantigas*, no. 296, trans. Kulp-Hill, 359.

94. Alfonso, *Cantigas*, no. 311, trans. Kulp-Hill, 376, translator's italics.

95. Richard, *De laudibus*, lib. 1, cap. 7, n. 10, ed. Borgnet, 55.

96. See appendix for a handlist of manuscripts and editions. See below, "Compline," on the gaps in our knowledge about how the medieval devotion to Mary was preserved into the seventeenth and eighteenth centuries. Graef, *Mary*, 2:1–77, surveys a number of works that might fall into this category, but typically dismisses them much as she had Richard's. Perhaps the most intriguing is a series of one hundred devotions published by the Jesuit Père Paul de Barry (d. 1661), as *Le Paradis ouvert à Philagie par cent dévotions à la Mère de Dieu, aisées à pratiquer*. According to Graef (47), Barry's recommendations were roundly criticized by Blaise Pascal (d. 1662) as "a superstitious and purely external cult of the blessed Virgin."

97. Richard, *De laudibus*, lib. 2, cap. 3, n. 1, ed. Borgnet, 90.

98. Richard, *De laudibus*, lib. 2, cap. 3, nn. 2–4, ed. Borgnet, 90–92.

99. Richard, *De laudibus*, lib. 2, cap. 3, nn. 5–8, ed. Borgnet, 94–97.

100. Richard, *De laudibus*, lib. 2, cap. 3, nn. 9–10, ed. Borgnet, 97–99.

101. Richard, *De laudibus*, lib. 2, cap. 3, nn. 11–18, ed. Borgnet, 99–102. For the calamities that Peter Damian described, see above, chap. 1, "A Little History of the Office."

102. Richard, *De laudibus*, lib. 2, cap. 4, nn. 1–6, ed. Borgnet, 102–104. The story of Barlaam and Josaphat is a Christianized telling of the conversion of Siddhartha Gautama, a.k.a. Josaphat. The doctrine of images on which Barlaam relies (as Richard paraphrases it) comes from John of Damascus. For the Greek version of this passage, see *Barlaam and Ioasaph*, cap. 19, ed. and trans. Woodward and Mattingly, 280–81.

103. Richard, *De laudibus*, lib. 2, cap. 4, nn. 7–14, ed. Borgnet, 104–106. For the stories of Ildefonsus and Bonus, see William of Malmesbury, *De laudibus et miraculis*, lib. 1, cap. 2 and 6, ed. Thomson and Winterbottom, 23–25, 30–32. For the story of Theophilus, here cited by Richard *verbatim*, see below, "The Miracle of Theophilus."

104. Richard, *De laudibus*, lib. 2, cap. 5, nn. 1–3, ed. Borgnet, 107–109, citing Anselm, *Oratio 7*, ed. Schmitt 3:22, trans. Ward, *Prayers*, 121. For the litanies, see Meersseman, *Der Hymnos Akathistos*, 2:222–31.

105. Richard, *De laudibus*, lib. 2, cap. 5, nn. 4–5, ed. Borgnet, 110–12.

106. Richard, *De laudibus*, lib. 2, cap. 5, nn. 6–9, ed. Borgnet, 113–16.

107. Richard, *De laudibus*, lib. 2, cap. 5, n. 10, ed. Borgnet, 116–18.

108. Richard, *De laudibus*, lib. 2, cap. 5, n. 12, ed. Borgnet, 120–24.

109. Richard, *De laudibus*, lib. 2, cap. 7, nn. 1–22, ed. Borgnet, 126–33, citing Paschasius, *Cogitis me*, cap. 16, PL 30, col. 139, ed. Ripberger, no. 99, 154–55.

110. Richard, *De laudibus*, lib. 2, cap. 1, n. 3, ed. Borgnet, 60.

111. Alfonso, *Cantigas*, no. 130, trans. Kulp-Hill, 161, translator's italics.

112. Alfonso, *Cantigas*, no. 50, trans. Kulp-Hill, 66, translator's italics.

113. Richard, *De laudibus*, lib. 4, cap. 30, n. 2, ed. Borgnet, 255.

114. Power, "Introduction," xxix.

115. Ward, *Miracles*, 162.

116. Flory, *Marian Representations*, 20–21. My point here is the durability of this interpretation in the scholarship, not, as one of my readers for the press suggested, to shame my colleagues. We moderns have all misread the medieval devotion to Mary for some time now, having lost the exegetical key. On how we lost it, see below, "Compline: Sor María de Jesús de Ágreda."

117. Richard, *De laudibus*, lib. 2, cap. 1, nn. 1–42, ed. Borgnet, 59–82.

118. Adams, *Education*, 310. For a powerful reflection on the way in which Adams reflects modern scholarship's continuing anxiety over the reality of such forces, see Hollywood, *Acute Melancholia*, 2–43.

119. Boss, *Mary*, argues that devotion to Mary is critical to a proper relationship to the created world. Barker, *Creation*, puts it, if anything, even more strongly: without Wisdom, all of creation is at risk.

120. Herolt, *Promptuarium Discipuli*, cap. 50, trans. Swinton-Bland, 76–77.

121. Richard, *De laudibus*, lib. 6, cap. 9, n. 3, ed. Borgnet, 344.

122. Graef, *Mary*, 1:268.

123. Richard, *De laudibus*, lib. 2, cap. 1, n. 23, ed. Borgnet, 70.

124. Richard, *De laudibus*, lib. 1, cap. 7, n. 10, ed. Borgnet, 55.

125. Richard, *De laudibus*, lib. 4, cap. 30, n. 1, ed. Borgnet, 254.

126. John of Italy, *Vita s. Odonis*, cap. 20, PL 133, cols. 71–72.

127. *Miracula*, ed. Dexter, no. xxvii, 42–43.

128. Pseudo-Albert, *Mariale*, quaestio 162, ed. Borgnet, 236.

129. Richard, *De laudibus*, lib. 2, cap. 1, n. 19, ed. Borgnet, 68–69.

130. Richard, *De laudibus*, lib. 2, cap. 2, n. 14, ed. Borgnet, 87.

131. Richard, *De laudibus*, lib. 4, cap. 21, n. 2, ed. Borgnet, 228–29.

132. Richard, *De laudibus*, lib. 4, cap. 23, n. 1, ed. Borgnet, 237–38.

133. Richard, *De laudibus*, lib. 4, cap. 23, n. 5, ed. Borgnet, 240.

134. Richard, *De laudibus*, lib. 4, cap. 6, nn. 1–2, ed. Borgnet, 185–87.

135. Boyarin, *Miracles of the Virgin in Medieval England*, 43.

136. On Theophilus in the miracle collections and in Aelfric's homilies, see Boyarin, *Miracles of the Virgin in Medieval England*, 42–103. On Theophilus in Hrotsvitha, Rutebeuf, and the plays, see Lazar, "Theophilus." On Theophilus in Fulbert, see Fassler, *Virgin*, 88, 426–29. On Theophilus in Honorius, see Fulton [Brown], *From Judgment to Passion*, 219–20, 281–82. On the images of Theophilus in stone, glass, and manuscript, see Cothren, "Iconography"; Davis, "Canonical Views"; and Fryer, "Theophilus." On Theophilus in the De Brailes Book of Hours, see Donovan, *De Brailes Hours*, 69–81. On the title *mediatrix*, see Gripkey, *Blessed Virgin Mary*, 11. On Theophilus as the origin of the Faust legend, see Palmer and More, *Sources*.

137. Gonzalo, *Milagros*, no. 25, trans. Mount and Cash, 129–47; Boyd, ed., *Middle English Miracles*, 68–87; Patton, "Constructing the Inimical Jew."

138. Alfonso, *Cantigas*, no. 3, trans. Kulp-Hill, 5–6; Donovan, *The De Brailes Hours*, 75; London, British Library, Add. 49999, fol. 40v.

139. Jacobus, *Legenda aurea*, cap. 131, trans. Ryan, 2:157.

140. Vincent, *Speculum historiale*, lib. 21, cap. 69; Herolt, *Promptuarium Discipuli*, cap. 42, trans. Swinton-Bland, 68–69.

141. Richard, *De laudibus*, lib. 4, cap. 6, n. 2, ed. Borgnet, 187, and *passim*.

142. Boyarin, *Miracles of the Virgin in Medieval England*, 88, 103.

143. Koppelman, "Devotional Ambivalence."

144. Richard, *De laudibus*, lib. 11, cap. 1, n. 49, ed. Borgnet, 565.

145. Our telling follows Paul the Deacon of Naples, *Miraculum S. Mariae: De Theophilo penitente*, ed. Petsch, 1–10; trans. Palmer and More, 60–75.

146. Richard, *De laudibus*, lib. 2, cap. 4, n. 14, ed. Borgnet, 106; lib. 4, cap. 17, n. 7, ed. Borgnet, 222: "qui recta fide et pura conscientia currunt ad templum suum."

147. Boyarin, *Miracles of the Virgin in Medieval England*, 60, identifies the citations.

148. For Theophilus's prayer as it circulated as an independent devotion, see Barré, *Prières anciennes*, 185–93.

149. Jacobus, *Legenda aurea*, cap. 131, trans. Ryan, 2:157.

150. Barker, *Temple Mysticism*, 53–62; *Temple Themes*, 154–65.

151. Richard, *De laudibus*, lib. 6, cap. 1, n. 4, ed. Borgnet, 324.

152. Barker, *Temple Themes*, 10, 74, 76, 100, 113.

153. Barker, *Temple Themes*, 122.

154. Van Nuffel, "Le pacte"; cf. Barker, *Temple Themes*, 99–134.

155. For these baptismal confessions or "scrutinies," see Keefe, *Water*, 2:127–30 (list); and Cramer, *Baptism*, 142–44, 195–96.

156. Power, "Introduction," xxx.

157. Waters, *Translating Clergie*, 206, comes to a similar conclusion in her reading of Gautier's miracles: "Just as the devils' claim that Mary scandalously overturns Jesus' righteous judgment is carefully answered in the miracles, the suggestion that she saves the undeserving is shown to be incorrect, and both claims fail because they undervalue, or misunderstand, the love that binds both devotee and Christ to Mary, their mediatrix. Worthless though they may appear in the eyes of the devils (and of many of those on earth . . .), Mary's sinful devotees have in fact done the one thing that can save them; their continual practice both manifests and constitutes their love and faith, demonstrating that they have learned what is most important": how to pray.

158. See Lapostelle, "Images," 61–65, on the iconography associated with this miracle in the manuscripts.

159. Gautier, *Les Miracles*, I Mir 31, ed. Koenig, 3:11–22, trans. Pouquet, cols. 333–40, selections trans. Flory, *Marian Representations*, 60–62, with changes. With thanks to Daisy Delogu for help with the translation.

160. On this response to Mary's images, see Smith, "Bodies."

161. Caesarius, *Dialogus Miraculorum*, dist. 7, cap. 38, ed. Strange, 2:49–54, trans. Scott and Swinton-Bland, 1:510–15.

162. Caesarius, *Dialogus Miraculorum*, dist. 7, cap. 32, ed. Strange, 2:40–41, trans. Scott and Swinton-Bland, 1:499–501. Cf. Herolt, *Promptuarium Discipuli*, cap. 27, trans. Swinton-Bland, 45–47.

163. Alfonso, *Cantigas*, no. 16, trans. Kulp-Hill, 24–25.

164. Gautier, *Les Miracles*, I Mir 41, ed. Koenig, 3:150–64, trans. Pouquet, cols. 531–42, trans. Kemp-Welch, 37–47.

165. See Baum, "Young Man," on this tradition.

166. Gautier, *Les Miracles*, I Mir 21, ed. Koenig, 2:197–204, trans. Pouquet, cols. 355–60, trans. Kemp-Welch, 61–67. Cf. Alfonso, *Cantigas*, no. 42, trans. Kulp-Hill, 55–56; Vincent of Beauvais, *Speculum historiale*, lib. 7, cap. 87.

167. Alfonso, *Cantigas*, no. 100, trans. Kulp-Hill, 125, translator's italics.

168. Alfonso, *Cantigas*, no. 270, trans. Kulp-Hill, 328, translator's italics.

169. Alfonso, *Cantigas*, no. 320, trans. Kulp-Hill, 388, translator's italics.

170. On the twelfth-century commentaries on the Song of Songs in which this description is elaborated, see Fulton [Brown], *From Judgment to Passion*.

171. Barker, *Mother*, 333–74; and *Creation*, 237–38.

172. See Barker, *Revelation*, 279–84, on the identity of the Harlot City opposed to the Heavenly Bride.

173. Richard, *De laudibus*, lib. 5, cap. 2, n. 1, ed. Borgnet, 280, citing *quidam*.

174. Richard, *De laudibus*, lib. 5, cap. 2, n. 1, ed. Borgnet, 279–80, citing *Liber de infantia Salvatoris*, Hereford version, cap. 24, ed. James, 25. On the relationship of this text to the *Protevangelium of James*, see Elliott, *Apocryphal New Testament*, 108–9.

175. Richard, *De laudibus*, lib. 5, cap. 2, n. 2, ed. Borgnet, 280–81.

176. Richard, *De laudibus*, lib. 5, cap. 2, nn. 3–6, ed. Borgnet, 281–83. On the relics of Mary's hair, including the one kept at Rouen, see Durand, "Holy Hair."

177. Richard, *De laudibus*, lib. 5, cap. 2, n. 7, ed. Borgnet, 283.

178. Richard, *De laudibus*, lib. 5, cap. 2, nn. 8–10, ed. Borgnet, 283–85. For the miracle of Julian, see William of Malmesbury, *De laudibus et miraculis*, cap. 2, ed. and trans. Thomson and Winterbottom, 21–22; and Dominic of Evesham, *De miraculis*, cap. 4, ed. Canal, 269–71.

179. Richard, *De laudibus*, lib. 5, cap. 2, nn. 13–15, ed. Borgnet, 286–88.

180. Richard, *De laudibus*, lib. 5, cap. 2, nn. 19–23, ed. Borgnet, 290–93.

181. Richard, *De laudibus*, lib. 5, cap. 2, n. 25, ed. Borgnet, 293.

182. Richard, *De laudibus*, lib. 5, cap. 2, n. 26, ed. Borgnet, 295.

183. Richard, *De laudibus*, lib. 5, cap. 2, n. 29, ed. Borgnet, 297–98.

184. Richard, *De laudibus*, lib. 5, cap. 2, nn. 31–33, ed. Borgnet, 299–300.

185. Richard, *De laudibus*, lib. 5, cap. 2, nn. 36–37, ed. Borgnet, 301–2.

186. Richard, *De laudibus*, lib. 5, cap. 2, nn. 38–41, ed. Borgnet, 302–4, citing Bernard, *In Adventu*, homilia 2.5, ed. Leclercq, 4:174, PL 183, col. 43.

187. Richard, *De laudibus*, lib. 5, cap. 2, nn. 44–45, ed. Borgnet, 305–6.

188. Richard, *De laudibus*, lib. 5, cap. 2, n. 46, ed. Borgnet, 306.

189. Richard, *De laudibus*, lib. 5, cap. 2, nn. 47–50, ed. Borgnet, 306–8.

190. Richard, *De laudibus*, lib. 5, cap. 2, nn. 55–59, ed. Borgnet, 310–13.

191. Richard, *De laudibus*, lib. 5, cap. 2, n. 62, ed. Borgnet, 314.

192. Richard, *De laudibus*, lib. 4, c. 12, nn. 1–2, ed. Borgnet, 198–99; lib. 5, c. 2, n. 63, ed. Borgnet, 314–15, citing Aldhelm of Malmesbury (d. 709), *De laudibus virginitatis*, cap. 23, PL 89, col. 121, on the Apostle Thomas.

193. Richard, *De laudibus*, lib. 5, cap. 2, n. 66, ed. Borgnet, 316.

194. Richard, *De laudibus*, lib. 5, cap. 2, n. 70, ed. Borgnet, 317.

195. Richard, *De laudibus*, lib. 5, cap. 2, n. 71, ed. Borgnet, 317–18.

196. Richard, *De laudibus*, lib. 5, cap. 2, n. 74, ed. Borgnet, 319.

197. On this desire, see Barker, *Temple Mysticism*; *Revelation*; *Temple Themes*; and *Great High Priest*.

198. See Barker, *King of the Jews*, 159–87, 288–99, on the significance of what John is saying here.

199. Alfonso, *Cantigas*, no. 92, trans. Kulp-Hill, 117, translator's italics.

200. Alfonso, *Cantigas*, no. 340, trans. Kulp-Hill, 413, translator's italics.

201. Alfonso, *Cantigas*, no. 415, trans. Kulp-Hill, 500.

202. Caesarius, *Dialogus Miraculorum*, dist. 7, cap. 8, ed. Strange, 2:12, trans. Scott and Swinton-Bland, 1:465.

203. William, *De laudibus et miraculis*, prologus 10–11, 16–17, 29–30, ed. and trans. Thomson and Winterbottom, 3, 5–6, 9, paraphrasing Anselm, *Oratio 7*, ed. Schmitt, 3:22–24.

204. Anselm, *Oratio 7*, ed. Schmitt, 3:20, trans. Ward, 118. On Anselm's prayers to Mary, see Fulton [Brown], *From Judgment to Passion*, 232–43; "Anselm"; and "Praying with Anselm."

205. William, *De laudibus et miraculis*, epilogus 9, ed. and trans. Thomson and Winterbottom, 134.

206. Mechthild, *Das fliessende Licht*, lib. 6, cap. 39, trans. Tobin, 265. On Mechthild's use of the title *göttine*, see Newman, *God and the Goddesses*, 274–76. For Pseudo-Albert's use of the title *dea*, see above, chap. 4, "*Q. 162 Whether the Name . . . ?*"

207. Alfonso, *Cantigas*, no. 202, trans. Kulp-Hill, 243. For Adam's sequence, see above, chap. 4, n. 20.

208. Obviously, an enormous project. See the scholarship cited above, chap. 2, n. 14, for the recent work that medievalists have done rethinking the devotion to the Virgin. See above, chap. 3, n. 19, for recent work on rethinking the place of the Psalms. See Fassler and Baltzer, *Divine Office*, on the importance of the Office for our understanding of medieval Christianity. See Ohly, *Sensus Spiritualis*, on rethinking our understanding of medieval exegesis as a way of seeing. See Mossman, *Marquard*, 243–334, who offers a valuable survey of Mary as a model contemplative touching on many of the texts we have been reading here, including Richard, Conrad of Saxony, and Pseudo-Albert. See Kirk, *Vision of God*, on this desire to see God as fundamental to the Christian tradition. See Hamburger, *Rothschild Canticles*, for the realization of this desire in one exquisite fourteenth-century devotional manuscript. See Newman, *God and the Goddesses*, for a rethinking of the place of monotheism in medieval images of the divine. See Bynum, *Christian Materiality*, and Ritchey, *Holy Matter*, on the importance of the material, created world in this tradition. See Carruthers, *Experience,* and Astell, *Eating Beauty*, on the aesthetic appreciation of this beautiful world. See Fulton Brown, "Hildegard of Bingen's Theology of Revelation," for a rereading of Hildegard's theological understanding of her visions; Fulton Brown, "Exegesis," on the way in which an

understanding of the exegesis of the Psalms affects our reading of even such figures as Saint Francis, famous for his devotion to the humanity of Christ; and Fulton Brown, "Three-in-One," for the place of the Trinity in this devotion.

209.   Boss, *Mary*, 5.

210.   Richard, *De laudibus,* lib. 2, cap. 2, n. 3, ed. Borgnet, 83. On this understanding of the unity of Christ and Mary's flesh, see Fulton [Brown], *From Judgment to Passion,* 383–97.

211.   Richard, *De laudibus,* lib. 2, cap. 2, n. 12, ed. Borgnet, 86. On the Eucharistic bread as the "bread of angels," see Barker, *Temple Themes,* 201–19; *Great High Priest,* 87–95; and above, n. 23.

212.   Richard, *De laudibus,* lib. 3, cap. 1, ed. Borgnet, 143; cf. lib. 2, cap. 2, nn. 3–22, ed. Borgnet, 83–89.

213.   Richard, *De laudibus,* lib. 2, cap. 2, n. 2, ed. Borgnet, 83.

214.   Richard, *De laudibus,* lib. 4, cap. 14, n. 1, ed. Borgnet, 209. On the tradition of Mary's compassion at the suffering of her Son, see Fulton [Brown], *From Judgment to Passion.*

215.   Richard, *De laudibus,* lib. 4, cap. 17, n. 2, ed. Borgnet, 214.

216.   Richard, *De laudibus,* lib. 4, cap. 17, nn. 2–6, ed. Borgnet, 216–19.

217.   Richard, *De laudibus,* lib. 4, cap. 17, n. 7, ed. Borgnet, 219–22.

218.   Richard, *De laudibus,* lib. 4, cap. 18, nn. 1–6, ed. Borgnet, 222–25.

219.   Richard, *De laudibus,* lib. 4, cap. 34, nn. 1–6, ed. Borgnet, 268–71.

220.   Richard, *De laudibus,* lib. 6, cap. 2, ed. Borgnet, 328–30.

221.   Richard, *De laudibus,* lib. 6, cap. 6, nn. 1–2, ed. Borgnet, 337–38, citing CAO #1563: "Beata Dei genetrix, Maria virgo perpetua, templum domini, sacrarium spiritus sancti, sola sine exemplo placuisti Domino Jesu Christo; ora pro populo, interveni pro clero, intercede pro devoto femineo sexu."

222.   See above, chap. 4, n. 146. According to Six, "Burgesses," Rouen in Richard's day had a thriving merchant class, including many Jews and at least one Muslim convert to Christianity—a circumstance not, perhaps, incidental to Richard's positive portrayal of Christ as merchant as well as his insistence that Mary loves all God's children, "albeit in different ways."

223.   Richard, *De laudibus,* lib. 11, cap. 8, nn. 10–11, ed. Borgnet, 585–86, citing Horace, *Epistolae,* 1.1, trans. John Weever, *Antient Funeral Monuments of Great Britain, Ireland and the Islands* (London: W. Tooke, 1767), 134, with changes.

224.   Richard, *De laudibus,* lib. 11, cap. 8, n. 11, ed. Borgnet, 586–87, citing CAO #3985: "O admirabile commercium . . ." For the antiphon in full, see above, chap. 4, n. 91.

225.   Richard, *De laudibus,* lib. 11, cap. 8, n. 11, ed. Borgnet, 588.

226.   See above, chap. 4, "Flower."

227.   Richard, *De laudibus,* lib. 12, cap. 4, nn. 2–9, ed. Borgnet, 653–57.

228.   Richard, *De laudibus,* lib. 12, cap. 4, nn. 10–18, ed. Borgnet, 657–59.

229.   Richard, *De laudibus,* lib. 12, cap. 4, nn. 19–25, ed. Borgnet, 659–60, citing CAO #7455b: "Sicut dies verni circumdabant eam flores rosarum et lilia convallium."

230.   Richard, *De laudibus,* lib. 12, cap. 5, ed. Borgnet, 676.

231.   Richard, *De laudibus,* lib. 12, cap. 5, §1, nn. 1–4, ed. Borgnet, 676–79.

232.   Richard, *De laudibus,* lib. 12, cap. 5, §1, n. 5, ed. Borgnet, 683, citing AH 20, nr. 33, 60: "Ut solis radius / Intrat innoxius / Fenestram vitream, / Sic Dei Filius / Imo subtilius / Aulam virgineam."

233.   Richard, *De laudibus,* lib. 12, cap. 5, §2, nn. 1–2, ed. Borgnet, 684–86, citing Ambrose, *De virginibus,* lib. 1, cap. 3, PL 16, col. 192.

234.   Richard, *De laudibus,* lib. 12, cap. 5, §3, n. 1, ed. Borgnet, 689.

235.   Richard, *De laudibus,* lib. 12, cap. 5, §4, n. 2, ed. Borgnet, 691.

236.   Richard, *De laudibus,* lib. 12, cap. 5, §5, n. 2, ed. Borgnet, 691.

237.   Richard, *De laudibus,* lib. 12, cap. 5, §6–7, ed. Borgnet, 692–93.

238.   Richard, *De laudibus,* lib. 12, cap. 5, §8, nn. 1–2, ed. Borgnet, 693–95.

239.   Richard, *De laudibus,* lib. 12, cap. 5, §9, ed. Borgnet, 700.

240.   Richard, *De laudibus,* lib. 12, cap. 5, §10, ed. Borgnet, 701–2.

241. Richard, *De laudibus*, lib. 12, cap. 5, §11, nn. 1, 4, ed. Borgnet, 702, 705.

242. Richard, *De laudibus*, lib. 12, cap. 5, §12, nn. 1–3, ed. Borgnet, 707–9.

243. Richard, *De laudibus*, lib. 12, cap. 5, §13, ed. Borgnet, 711.

244. Richard, *De laudibus*, lib. 12, cap. 5, §14, n. 1, ed. Borgnet, 711–12.

245. Richard, *De laudibus*, lib. 12, cap. 5, §15, nn. 1–2, ed. Borgnet, 712–14.

246. Richard, *De laudibus*, lib. 12, cap. 6, §1, nn. 10, 13, ed. Borgnet, 724–26.

247. Richard, *De laudibus*, lib. 12, cap. 6, §2, nn. 3–4, ed. Borgnet, 737.

248. Richard, *De laudibus*, lib. 12, cap. 6, §4, n. 5, ed. Borgnet, 744.

249. Richard, *De laudibus*, lib. 12, cap. 6, §5, n. 4, ed. Borgnet, 749.

250. Richard, *De laudibus*, lib. 12, cap. 6, §7, n. 5, ed. Borgnet, 755.

251. Richard, *De laudibus*, lib. 12, cap. 6, §8, n. 1, ed. Borgnet, 756.

252. Richard, *De laudibus*, lib. 12, cap. 6, §9, ed. Borgnet, 761.

253. Richard, *De laudibus,* lib. 12, cap. 6, §10, n. 3, ed. Borgnet, 762.

254. Richard, *De laudibus*, lib. 12, cap. 6, §15, n. 4, ed. Borgnet, 768.

255. Richard, *De laudibus*, lib. 12, cap. 6, §16, n. 4, ed. Borgnet, 770–71.

256. Richard, *De laudibus*, lib. 12, cap. 6, §18, n. 15, ed. Borgnet, 781.

257. Richard, *De laudibus*, lib. 12, cap. 6, §20, nn. 39–40, ed. Borgnet, 802–803.

258. Richard, *De laudibus*, lib. 12, cap. 6, §20, n. 55, ed. Borgnet, 808–809.

259. Richard, *De laudibus*, lib. 12, cap. 6, §20, n. 56, ed. Borgnet, 809.

260. Richard, *De laudibus*, lib. 12, cap. 4, n. 21, ed. Borgnet, 659.

261. Richard, *De laudibus*, lib. 12, cap. 6, §20, n. 56, ed. Borgnet, 809; see above, chap. 3, n 449. On the significance of this passage for the identity of the Spirit at Jesus's baptism, see Barker, *Christmas*, 40–41; *Creation*, 256; and *Temple Themes*, 111, 127, who argues that here the Spirit is described as Jesus's mother, a.k.a. Wisdom.

262. Richard, *De laudibus*, lib. 12, cap. 7, §2, nn. 1–2, ed. Borgnet, 819–20. Here Richard is drawing on a very long tradition. On the symbolism of Christ as eagle in its ancient and medieval contexts, see Wittkower, "Eagle."

263. Richard, *De laudibus*, lib. 12, cap. 7, §2, n. 3, ed. Borgnet, 820–21. For the eagle's amethyst, see Anthony of Padua's (d. 1231) sermon on the saints compared with eagles (trans. Neale, *Mediaeval Preachers*, 235–36).

264. Richard, *De laudibus*, lib. 12, cap. 7, §2, n. 6, ed. Borgnet, 824–25.

265. See above, "Invitatory."

266. Meersseman, *Hymnos Akathistos*, 1:148; trans. *Liber Hymnarius* (Solesmes, 1983), with changes. On the composition and authorship of the hymn, see above, chap. 2, n. 167.

267. Birgitta, *Liber caelestis*, lib. 3, cap. 29, trans. Searby, ed. Morris, 1:316–17. On this imagery as realized by Birgitta in the liturgy and architecture at the monastery she founded at Vadstena, see Urberg, "Music." For the Virgin as temple in the motet Guillaume Dufay composed for the dedication of the cathedral of at Florence in 1436, see Wright, "Dufay's 'Nuper rosarum flores.' "

COMPLINE: SOR MARÍA DE JESÚS DE ÁGREDA AND THE MYSTICAL CITY OF GOD

1. María, *Mystica Ciudad*, Introduction §1–13, trans. Blatter, 1:1–13.

2. María, *Mystica Ciudad*, lib. 1, cap. 2, §14, trans. Blatter, 1:36.

3. María, *Mystica Ciudad*, lib. 1, cap. 2, §15, trans. Blatter, 1:37.

4. As, indeed, Sor María was seen by her sisters to do. See Fedewa, *María*, 34–40.

5. María, *Mystica Ciudad*, lib. 1, cap. 2, §15–17, trans. Blatter, 1:38.

6. María, *Mystica Ciudad*, lib. 1, cap. 2, §19, trans. Blatter, 1:40.

7. Fedewa, *María*, 211–12; Ximénez de Samaniego, *Vida*, cap. 21, ed. Seco Serrano, 322–23.

8. María, *Mystica Ciudad*, lib. 1, cap. 2, §124–25, trans. Blatter, 1:43–45.

9. María, *Mystica Ciudad*, lib. 1, cap. 14, §202, trans. Blatter, 1:168; cap. 23, §363, trans. Blatter, 1:292–93.

10. María, *Mystica Ciudad*, lib. 3, cap. 10, §115, trans. Blatter, 2:95.

11. María, *Mystica Ciudad*, lib. 2, cap. 2, §440, trans. Blatter, 1:345.

12. María, *Mystica Ciudad*, lib. 2, cap. 4, §470, trans. Blatter, 1:364.

13. María, *Mystica Ciudad*, lib. 3, cap. 11, §136–37, trans. Blatter, 2:109–110.

14. María, *Mystica Ciudad*, lib. 4, cap. 10, §475–77, trans. Blatter, 2:398–99.

15. María, *Mystica Ciudad*, lib. 6, cap. 12, §508, trans. Blatter, 3:486–87.

16. María, *Mystica Ciudad*, lib. 6, cap. 22, §670, 687, trans. Blatter, 3:647, 663; cf. lib. 2, cap. 18, §577, trans. Blatter, 489.

17. María, *Mystica Ciudad*, lib. 6, cap. 26, §758–60, trans. Blatter, 3:731–32.

18. María, *Mystica Ciudad*, lib. 6, cap. 29, §802, trans. Blatter, 3:773.

19. María, *Mystica Ciudad*, lib. 7, cap. 2, §18, trans. Blatter, 4:46.

20. María, *Mystica Ciudad*, lib. 7, cap. 5, §62, trans. Blatter, 4:86.

21. María, *Mystica Ciudad*, lib. 7, cap. 6, §87, 91, trans. Blatter, 4:107, 110.

22. María, *Mystica Ciudad*, lib. 8, cap. 7, §505–28, trans. Blatter, 4:444–60.

23. María, *Mystica Ciudad*, lib. 8, cap. 12–16, §611–96, trans. Blatter, 4:522–602.

24. María, *Mystica Ciudad*, lib. 8, cap. 19, §736, trans. Blatter, 4:622.

25. María, *Mystica Ciudad*, lib. 8, cap. 19, §740–42, trans. Blatter, 4:626–27.

26. María, *Mystica Ciudad*, lib. 1, cap. 16, §227, trans. Blatter, 1:185.

27. María, *Mystica Ciudad*, lib. 1, cap. 21, §331, trans. Blatter, 1:266–67.

28. María, *Mystica Ciudad*, lib. 1, cap. 21, §333, trans. Blatter, 1:267–68.

29. María, *Mystica Ciudad*, lib. 3, cap. 1, §4–8, trans. Blatter, 2:25–27.

30. María, *Mystica Ciudad*, lib. 3, cap. 1, §9, trans. Blatter, 2:28.

31. María, *Mystica Ciudad*, lib. 3, cap. 2, §17, 23, trans. Blatter, 2:34, 37.

32. María, *Mystica Ciudad*, lib. 3, cap. 3, §27, 29, trans. Blatter, 2:40, 41–42.

33. María, *Mystica Ciudad*, lib. 3, cap. 4, §39, 41, trans. Blatter, 2:48–49.

34. María, *Mystica Ciudad*, lib. 3, cap. 5, §47, 52, 54–56, trans. Blatter, 2:53, 56–59.

35. María, *Mystica Ciudad*, lib. 3, cap. 6, §60, 62–64, trans. Blatter, 2:62–64.

36. María, *Mystica Ciudad*, lib. 3, cap. 7, §70–83, trans. Blatter, 2:68–74, with changes.

37. María, *Mystica Ciudad*, lib. 3, cap. 8, §88–95, trans. Blatter, 2:77–82.

38. María, *Mystica Ciudad*, lib. 3, cap. 9, §99–105, trans. Blatter, 2:85–89.

39. María, *Mystica Ciudad*, lib. 5, cap. 12, §142, trans. Blatter, 3:129.

40. How and whether she actually appeared to the Jumanos remains a mystery. Later in life, Sor María suggested that perhaps "an angel, taking on my looks, appeared there and preached and taught them the catechism, while here the Lord showed me what was going on there as an answer to my prayers [to preach to the people of the New World]" (Colahan, *Visions*, 122). Modern scholars have tended to be somewhat more skeptical about the possibility of her bilocation than even Sor María's seventeenth-century inquisitors. See Colahan, *Visions*, 93–127, for Benavides's and Sor María's reports on her visions; and Pichardo, "Miraculous Journeys," for additional sources, including excerpts from Ximénez de Samaniego's biography. On the importance of this tradition for the history of the conversion of the peoples of the American Southwest, particularly the region around Amarillo, Texas (where, by the by, I grew up), see Donahue, "Mary of Agreda"; Fedewa, *María*, 43–68; Hickerson, "Visits"; Kessell, "Miracles or Mystery"; and MacLean, "María."

41. Fedewa, *María*, 251–52.

42. *Life*, trans. Pandolfi, 141.

43. *Life*, trans. Pandolfi, 142–43.

44. *Life*, trans. Pandolfi, 140–41.

45. *Life*, trans. Pandolfi, 144–45.

46. Varas García, "Ágreda," 31–34; Solaguren, Martínez Moñux, and Villasante, "Introducción," cii–ciii.

47. Blatter, *Mystical City*, 1: Special Notice to the Reader; *Life*, trans. Pandolfi, 191–93; Solaguren, Martínez Moñux, and Villasante, "Introducción," cii–civ.

48. Kendrick, *Mary*, 163; Solaguren, Martínez Moñux, and Villasante, "Introducción," ci–ciii. Pérez-Rioja (1965), "Proyeccion," counts 89 complete editions and 68 summaries and anthologies; Colahan (1988), "Mary," 53, says that it has been "published some 250 times."

49. Fedewa, *María*, xiii.

50. Fedewa, *María*, 252–57.

51. María, *Mystica Ciudad*, lib. 1, cap. 1, §10, trans. Blatter, 1:33–34.

52. Artola Arbiza and Mendía, *La venerable*, 107.

53. Artola Arbiza and Mendía, *La venerable*, 110.

54. Artola Arbiza and Mendía, *La venerable*, 98, 123–28, 133–52.

55. Fedewa, *María*, 257; Artola Arbiza and Mendía, *La venerable*, 208–13.

56. Voltaire, *Ancient and Modern History*, trans. Smollett et al., 9:125–26.

57. Casanova, *Memoirs*, trans. Machen, vol. 2, episode 10 "Under the Leads," chap. 26 www.gutenberg .org/files/39302/39302.txt.

58. Graef, *Mary*, 2:53–55.

59. Kendrick, *Mary*, 86.

60. Fedewa, *María*, 5, 104, 267.

61. Colahan, *Visions*, 149, 159–60.

62. Mitchell, *Mystery*, 130–45.

63. Fedewa, *María*, 6.

64. Blatter, *Mystical City*, 2: Testimonies.

65. Ximénez de Samaniego, *Vida*, cap. 21, ed. Seco Serrano, 322; María, *Autenticidad*, A77-4, 429 (trans. Fedewa, *María*, 185–86).

66. María, *Mystica Ciudad*, lib. 1, cap. 5, §52–74, trans. Blatter, 1:62–74.

67. María, *Mystica Ciudad*, lib. 2, cap. 22–23, §772–802, trans. Blatter, 1:587–610.

68. María, *Mystica Ciudad*, lib. 1, cap. 8–10, §94–133, trans. Blatter, 1:93–124.

69. María, *Mystica Ciudad*, lib. 1, cap. 17–19, §244–309, trans. Blatter, 1:198–249; lib. 7, cap. 2–3, §10–36, trans. Blatter, 4:39–63.

70. Fedewa, *María*, 101; Mitchell, *Mystery*, 134; Colahan, *Visions*, 152–54; Kendrick, *Mary*, 82, who insists, however, that "it is wrong to imagine her [depending on a library and the prompting of learned friars or] searching for material in obscure apocryphal sources, or borrowing without acknowledgment as [was suggested by Cardinal Gotti in the eighteenth century]." On these stories, see above, chap. 3, n. 88.

71. Fedewa, *María*, 251.

72. Trans. Colahan, *Visions*, 47–91. For lists of Sor María's works, see Serrano y Sanz, *Apuntes*, 1:571–601; Uribe, "Fondo Agredano," 261–73; and Varas García, "Ágreda."

73. Colahan, *Visions*, 21–23.

74. Serrano y Sanz, *Apuntes*, 1:578.

75. Colahan, *Visions*, 151–53.

76. Colahan, "Mary," 55.

77. Granada, *Obras*, 8:41. According to Friar Luis, the Virgin Mary spent her days celebrating the Office.

78. Granada, *Obras*, 1:125.

79. Granada, *Obras*, vol. 9.

80. Granada, *Obras*, vols. 6 and 8.

81. Granada, *Obras*, 8:89–90; Colahan, *Visions*, 152–53.

82. Solaguren, Martínez Moñux, and Villasante, "Introducción," li–liii, suggest Jacobus, *Legenda aurea*, and Vincent of Beauvais, *Speculum historiale*, along with the works they found in the convent library,

but argue that much of Sor María's information must have been acquired in conversation with her confessors as well as through the texts of the liturgy. For other popular works of the period that Sor María might have been reading, most particularly the Discalced Carmelite José de Jesús de María's *Historia de la Vida y Excelencias de la Virgen Maria Nuestra Señora* (1652), see Johnson, "Mary."

83. Vázquez Janiero, "Libros," 175. With thanks to Daniel Gullo for advice on Spain's early modern libraries.
84. Colahan, *Visions*, 154–55; Barker, *Temple Mysticism*.
85. Mitchell, *Mystery*, 132–33.
86. *Life*, trans. Pandolfi, 143.
87. Mitchell, *Mystery*, 142.
88. Ubertino, *Arbor*, lib. 1, cap. 7–8, trans. Mossman, *Marquard*, 304–6.
89. María, *Autenticidad*, Q78–A78, 430–31, trans. Fedewa, *Maria*, 186–87.
90. María, *Autenticidad*, 436–37, trans. Fedewa, *Maria*, 192–93.

APPENDIX: HANDLIST OF MANUSCRIPTS AND PRINTED EDITIONS OF RICHARD OF SAINT-LAURENT'S *DE LAUDIBUS BEATAE MARIAE VIRGINIS LIBRI XII*

1. Starred items listed by Glorieux, *Répertoire*, 1:330–31. Additional items based on the digitized manuscripts and catalogue descriptions currently available online as well as through the *In Principio* database at Brepolis. The list is almost certainly incomplete; every time I have made searches to double-check the descriptions, I have found additional copies of Richard's work. I have consulted only the Wellesley manuscript in person, thus far the only example that I have found with illuminations. Corrections and additions welcome!
2. I have not been able to verify this edition cited by Glorieux. It may be a misidentification of Sélestat, Bibliothèque municipale, 62.

Bibliography

ABBREVIATIONS

AASS — *Acta sanctorum quotquot toto orbe coluntur*. Ed. J. Bollandus and G. Henschenius. Antwerp and Brussels, 1643–present.

AH — *Analecta hymnica medii aevi*. Ed. Guido Maria Dreves and Clemens Blume, with Henry M. Bannister. 55 vols. Leipzig: Fues, etc., 1886–1922.

CANTUS — CANTUS A Database for Latin Ecclesiastical Chant http://cantus.uwaterloo.ca

CAO — *Corpus Antiphonalium Officii*. Ed. René-Jean Hesbert. 6 vols. Rerum Ecclesiasticarum Documenta, Series Maior. Fontes 7–12. Rome: Casa Editrice Herder, 1963–1979.

CCCM — Corpus christianorum, continuatio medievalis

CCSL — Corpus christianorum, series latina

CCM — Corpus consuetudinum monasticarum

CF — Cistercian Fathers Series

Cgm — Codices germanici monacenses, Bayerische Staatsbibliothek, Munich

CSEL — Corpus scriptorum ecclesiasticorum latinorum

DACL — *Dictionnaire d'archéologie chretienne et de liturgie*. Ed. F. Cabrol and H. Leclercq. 15 vols. Paris: Letouzey et Ané, 1924–1953.

DSAM — *Dictionnaire de spiritualité, ascétique et mystique, doctrine et histoire*. Ed. M. Viller et al. Paris: Beauchesne, 1932–1994.

EETS — Early English Text Society: e.s. Extra Series; o.s. Original Series

HBS — Henry Bradshaw Society

LXX — Septuagint

MGH — Monumenta Germaniae historica

PG — *Patrologia cursus completus: series graeca*. Ed. J.-P. Migne. 162 vols. Paris: Migne, 1857–1866.

PL — *Patrologia cursus completus: series latina*. Ed. J.-P. Migne. 221 vols. Paris: Migne, etc., 1841–1864.

RSV — Revised Standard Version

SF — Spicilegium Friburgense

HOURS OF THE VIRGIN: PRINTED EDITIONS

Baltzer, Rebecca A. "The Little Office of the Virgin and Mary's Role at Paris." In *The Divine Office in the Latin Middle Ages*, ed. Fassler and Baltzer, 463–84.

Canal, José M. "Oficio parvo de la Virgen: Formas viejas y formas nuevas." *Ephemerides Mariologicae* 11 (1961): 497–525.

Dewick, E. S., ed. *Facsimiles of Horae de Beata Maria Virgine, from English MSS. of the Eleventh Century.* HBS 21. London: Harrison and Sons, 1902.

Geert Grote. *Het Getijdenboek van Geert Grote, naar het Haagse handschrift 133 E 21 uitgegeven.* Ed. Nicolaas Van Wijk. Leidsche drukken en herdrukken. Kleine reeks 3. Leiden: Brill, 1940.

Horae Eboracenses: The Prymer or Hours of the Blessed Virgin Mary according to the use of the illustrious church of York, with other devotions as they were used by the lay-folk in the Northern province in the XVth and XVIth centuries. Ed. Christopher Wordsworth. Publications of the Surtees Society 132. Durham, U.K.: Andrews/London: Bernard Quaritch, 1920.

Leclercq, Jean. "Formes anciennes de l'Office marial." *Ephemerides liturgicae* 74 (1960): 89–102.

———. "Fragmenta mariana." *Ephemerides liturgicae* 72 (1958): 292–305.

The Little Office of the Blessed Virgin Mary in Latin and English. In conformity with the 1961 Editio Typica of the Roman Breviary being that permitted by Summorum Pontificum. *Including the Gregorian Chant appointed to be used in the Office.* London: Baronius, 2007.

Maskell, William, ed. *Monumenta ritualia ecclesiae Anglicanae, or, Occasional offices of the church of England according to the ancient use of Salisbury, the Prymer in English, and other prayers and forms.* 2d ed. 3 vols. Oxford, U.K.: Clarendon, 1882.

Officium beatae Mariae virginis secundum consuetudinum monachorum monasterii Sanctae Crucis Fontis Avellanae. PL 151, cols. 970–74.

The Prymer, or Lay Folks' Prayer Book, edited from the ms. Dd 11.82, ab. 1420–30 A.D., in the library of the University of Cambridge. Ed. Henry Littlehales. 2 vols. EETS o.s. 105, 109. London: Kegan Paul, Trench, Trübner, 1895–1897.

Tolhurst, J. B. L., ed. *The Monastic Breviary of Hyde Abbey, Winchester: MSS Rawlinson liturg. e. 1*, and Gough liturg. 8, in the Bodleian Library, Oxford.* 6 vols. HBS 69–71, 76, 78, 80. London: Harrison, 1932–1942.

PRINTED SOURCES AND TRANSLATIONS

Adam of Dryburgh [Adamus Scotus]. *Liber de ordine, habitu et professione canonicorum ordinis Praemonstratensis.* PL 198, cols. 439–610.

Aelfwine's Prayerbook (London, British Library, Cotton Titus D. xxvi + xxvii). Ed. Beate Günzel. HBS 108. London: Boydell, 1993.

Aelred of Rievaulx. *De institutis inclusarum.* Ed. C. H. Talbot, "The 'De institutis inclusarum' of Ailred of Rievaulx." *Analecta sacri ordinis cisterciensis* 7.3–4 (1951): 167–217. Trans. Mary Paul Macpherson, as "A Rule of Life for a Recluse," in *The Works of Aelred of Rievaulx: Treatises and Pastoral Prayer*, 43–102. CF 2. Kalamazoo, Mich.: Cistercian Publications, 1971.

Alan of Lille. *Compendiosa in Cantica Canticorum ad laudem deiparae virginis Mariae.* PL 210, cols. 51–110.

Alcuin of York. *Liber sacramentorum.* PL 101, cols. 445–66.

Alexander of Hales. *Summa theologica.* Ed. Collegii S. Bonaventurae. 4 vols. in 5. Quaracchi: Ex Typographia Collegii S. Bonaventurae, 1924–1948.

Alfonso X, King of Castile and Leon. *Cantigas de Santa María.* Trans. Kathleen Kulp-Hill, as *Songs of Holy Mary of Alfonso X, the Wise.* Medieval and Renaissance Text and Studies 173. Tempe, AZ: Arizona Center for Medieval and Renaissance Studies, 2000.

Amadeus of Lausanne. *De Maria virginea matre. Homiliae octo.* PL 188, cols. 1303–46. Trans. Grace Perigo, as *Eight Homilies on the Praises of Blessed Mary.* CF 18B. Kalamazoo, Mich.: Cistercian Publications, 1979.

Ambrosius Autpertus. *Opera*. Ed. Robert Weber. 3 vols. CCCM 27, 27A–B. Turnhout, Belgium: Brepols, 1975–1979.

——. *Sermo de assumptione*. Ed. Weber, *Opera*, 3:1027–36. As Augustine, *Sermo CCVIII. In festo Assumptionis B. Mariae*, PL 39, cols. 2130–34.

——. *Sermo de lectione evangelica . . .in purificatione s. Mariae*. PL 89, cols. 1291–1304.

——. *Sermo de nativitate perpetuae virginis Mariae*, as Alcuin, PL 101, cols. 1300–1308.

Amort, Eusebius, ed. *Vetus disciplina canonicorum regularium et saecularium*. 2 vols. Venice: Apud Joannem Baptistam Recurti, 1747.

Ancrene Riwle: Introduction and Part I. Ed. and trans. Robert W. Ackerman and Roger Dahood. Medieval & Renaissance Texts & Studies 31. Binghamton, N.Y.: Medieval & Renaissance Texts & Studies, State University of New York, 1984.

Ancrene Wisse: A Corrected Edition of the Text in Cambridge, Corpus Christi College, MS 402, with variants from other manuscripts. Ed. Bella Millett, drawing on the uncompleted edition by E. J. Dobson, with glossary and additional notes by Richard Dance. 2 vols. EETS 325–326. Oxford: Oxford University Press, 2005–2006. Trans. Bella Millett, as *Guide for Anchoresses: A Translation Based on Cambridge, Corpus Christi College MS 402*. Exeter Medieval Texts and Studies. Exeter: Exeter University Press, 2009. Also trans. Hugh White. Harmondsworth: Penguin, 1993.

Andrew of Crete. *On the Dormition of Our Most Holy Lady, the Mother of God I–III*. PG 97, cols. 1045–1109. Trans. Daley, *On the Dormition*, 103–52.

——. *On the Nativity of the Supremely Holy Theotokos I–IV*. PG 97, cols. 805–81. Trans. Cunningham, *Wider Than Heaven*, 71–138.

——. *Oration on the Annunciation of the Supremely Holy Lady, Our Theotokos*. PG 97, cols. 881–913. Trans. Cunningham, *Wider Than Heaven*, 197–219.

Anselm of Canterbury. *S. Anselmi Cantuariensis archiepiscopi opera omnia*. Ed. F. S. Schmitt. 6 vols. Edinburgh: Nelson, 1946–1961.

——. *De conceptu virginali et de originali peccato*. Ed. Schmitt, *Opera omnia*, 2:137–73.

——. *Orationes sive meditationes*. Ed. Schmitt, *Opera omnia*, 3:3–91. Trans. Benedicta Ward, in *The Prayers and Meditations of Saint Anselm, with the Proslogion*. Harmondsworth: Penguin, 1973.

——. *Proslogion*. Ed. Schmitt, *Opera omnia*, 1:93–122. Trans. Ward, in *Prayers and Meditations*, 238–67.

Anselm of Lucca. *Orationes*. Ed. André Wilmart, "Cinq textes de prière composés par Anselme de Lucques pour la comtesse Mathilde." *Revue d'ascétique et de mystique* 19 (1938): 23–72.

Antiphonaire monastique XIII siècle. Le Codex F. 160 de la Bibliothèque de la Cathédrale de Worcester. Paléographie musicale 12. Tournai: Desclée, 1922. Reprint, Berne: Herbert Lang, 1971.

Arnold of Bonneval. *De laudibus beatae Mariae virginis*. PL 189, cols. 1725–34.

Augustine of Hippo. *Confessiones*. Trans. R. S. Pine-Coffin, as *Confessions*. Harmondsworth, U.K.: Penguin, 1961.

——. *De catechizandis rudibus*. Trans. S. D. F. Salmond, as *On the Catechising of the Uninstructed*. Nicene and Post-Nicene Fathers, First Series 3. Buffalo, N.Y.: Christian Literature Publishing, 1887. Revised and edited for *New Advent* by Kevin Knight. www.newadvent.org/fathers/1303.htm.

——. *De civitate Dei*. Trans. Henry Bettenson, as *City of God*. Harmondsworth: Penguin, 1984.

——. *De doctrina christiana*. Trans. J. F. Shaw, as *On Christian Doctrine*. Nicene and Post-Nicene Fathers, First Series 2. Buffalo, N.Y.: Christian Literature Publishing, 1887. www.ccel.org/ccel/augustine/doctrine.html.

——. *Enarrationes in Psalmos*. Ed. Clemens Weidmann, Hildegund Müller, and Franco Gori. 3 vols. CSEL 93–95. Vienna: Verlag der Österreichischen Akademie der Wissenschaften, 2001–2005. Also PL 36, cols. 67–1027. Trans. Maria Boulding, as *Expositions of the Psalms*. 6 vols. New York: New City, 2000–2004.

Baldwin of Canterbury. *Tractatus diversi*. Ed. David N. Bell, in *Balduini de Forda Opera: Sermones. De commendatione fidei*, 1–339. CCCM 99. Turnhout, Belgium: Brepols, 1991. Also PL 204, cols. 403–572. Trans. David N. Bell, as *Spiritual Tractates*. 2 vols. CF 38, 41. Kalamazoo, Mich.: Cistercian Publications, 1986.

Barlaam and Ioasaph. Ed. and trans. G. R. Woodward and Harold Mattingly. Loeb Classical Library 34. Cambridge, Mass.: Harvard University Press, 1914.

Barnstone, Willis, ed. *The Other Bible: Jewish Pseudepigrapha, Christian Apocrypha, Gnostic Scriptures, Kabbalah, Dead Sea Scrolls.* New York: HarperCollins, 2005.

Bartholomew of Pisa. *De conformitate vitae beati Francisci ad vitam Domini Nostri Jesu Christi.* Analecta Franciscana 4–5. Quaracchi: Collegii S. Bonaventurae, 1906–1912.

———. *De vita et laudibus beatae Mariae virginis libri sex.* Venice: P. Dusinelli, 1596.

Bartolomeo da Breganze. *I "Sermones de beata virgine" (1266).* Ed. Laura Gaffuri. Fonti per la Storia della Terraferma Veneta 7. Padua. Editrice Antenore, 1993.

Basil of Caesarea. *Great Asketikon.* Trans. Sister M. Monica Wagner, as "The Long Rules." In *Saint Basil: Ascetical Works,* 223–337. The Fathers of the Church 9. Washington, D.C.: Catholic University of America Press, 1950.

Bede the Venerable. *The Complete Works of Venerable Bede, in the original Latin, collated with the manuscripts and various printed editions, accompanied by a new English translation of the historical works, and a life of the author.* Ed. J. A. Giles. 12 vols. London: Whittaker, 1843–1844. Also *Bedae Venerabilis Opera.* Ed. D. Hurst. CCSL 118A, 119, 119A-B, 120, 121, 121A, 122, 123A-C. Turnhout, Belgium: Brepols, 1955–2001. Also PL 90–95.

Benedict of Nursia. *Regula.* Ed. and trans. Timothy Fry et al., in *RB 1980: The Rule of St. Benedict in Latin and English with Notes,* 156–297. Collegeville, Minn.: Liturgical, 1981.

Bernard of Clairvaux. *S. Bernardi opera omnia.* Ed. Jean Leclercq, C. H. Talbot, and H. M. Rochais. 8 vols. Rome: Editiones cistercienses, 1957–1977. Also PL 182–83.

———. *De dominica infra octavam Assumptionis b.v. Mariae sermo. De verbis Apocalypsis.* Ed. Leclercq et al., *Opera omnia,* 5:262–74. Also PL 183, cols. 429–38.

———. *In assumptione beatae Mariae. Sermo I. De gemina assumptione.* Ed. Leclercq et al., *Opera omnia,* 5:228–31. Also PL 183, cols. 415–17.

———. *In laudibus virginis matris.* [*Super "Missus est"*]. Ed. Leclercq et al., *Opera omnia,* 4:13–58. Trans. Marie-Bernard Saïd, as *Homilies in Praise of the Blessed Virgin Mary.* CF 18A. Kalamazoo, Mich.: Cistercian Publications, 1993.

———. *Sermones super Cantica canticorum.* Ed. Leclercq et al., *Opera omnia* 1–2. Trans. Kilian J. Walsh and Irene M. Edmonds, as *On the Song of Songs I–IV.* CF 4, 7, 31, and 40. Kalamazoo, Mich.: Cistercian Publications, 1981, 1983, 1979, and 1980.

Bernard of Cluny. *Ordo Cluniacensis.* Ed. Marquard Herrgott, in *Vetus disciplina monastica,* 134–364. Paris: C. Osmont, 1726.

Bernardino de Busti. *Mariale eximii viri Bernardini de Busti ordinis seraphici Francisci de singulis festivitatibus Beate Virginis per modum sermonum tractans. Omni theologia copiosum denique utriusque iuris autoritatibus applicatis et arte humanitatis refertum in omnibus allegationibus promptissimum.* Lyon: Johannis Cleyn, 1511.

Bertarius Virdunensis. *Continuatio.* PL 132, cols. 517–28.

Birgitta of Sweden. *Liber caelestis.* Trans. Denis Searby, ed. Bridget Morris, as *The Revelations of St. Birgitta of Sweden.* 4 vols. Oxford: Oxford University Press, 2006–2015.

Bonaventure of Bagnoreggio. *Opera Omnia.* Edita studio et cura PP. Collegii a S. Bonaventura. 11 vols. Ad Claras Aquas-Quaracchi: Ex typographia Collegii S. Bonaventurae, 1882–1902.

———. *Sermones de Beata Virgine Maria.* In *Opera Omnia* 9: 633–721.

Bouriant, Urbain, ed. *Actes du concile d'Éphèse: Texte copte publié et traduit.* Mémoires publiès par les membres de la Mission archéologique française au Caire 8.1. Paris: Ernest Leroux, 1892.

Boyd, Beverly, ed. *The Middle English Miracles of the Virgin.* San Marino: Huntingdon Library, 1964.

Brinkman, Herman, and Janny Schenkel, eds. *Het handschrift-Van Hulthem: Hs. Brussel, Koninklijke Bibliotheek van België,* 15.589–623. 2 vols. Hilversum: Verloren, 1999.

Bruno of Segni. *Sententiae.* PL 165, cols. 875–1078.

Bull, Marcus. *The Miracles of Our Lady of Rocamadour: Analysis and Translation.* Woodbridge, U.K.: Boydell, 1999.

Caesarius of Heisterbach. *Dialogus Miraculorum. Textum ad quatour codicum manuscriptorum editionisque prinicipis fidem accurate recognovit Josephus Strange*. Ed. Joseph Strange. 2 vols. Cologne: J. M. Heberle, 1851. Trans. H. von E. Scott and C. C. Swinton Bland, as *The Dialogue on Miracles*. 2 vols. London: Routledge, 1929.

Calvin, John. *Institutes of the Christian Religion*. Trans. Henry Beveridge. 3 vols. Edinburgh: Calvin Translation Society, 1845–1846.

Canivez, Joseph-Marie, ed. *Statuta capitulorum generalium ordinis Cisterciensis ab anno 1116 ad annum 1786*. 8 vols. Louvain: Bureaux de la Revue, 1933–1941.

Casagrande, C., ed., *Prediche alle donne del secolo xiii: Testi di Umberto da Romans, Gilberto da Tournai, Stefano di Borbone*. Nuovo Corona 9. Milan: Bompiani, 1978.

Casanova, Giacomo. *Memoirs of Jacques Casanova de Seingalt*. Trans. Arthur Machen. 6 vols. New York: G. P. Putnam, 1894. www.gutenberg.org/files/39302/39302.txt

Cassian, John. *Collationes patrum XXIV*. Trans. Edgar C. S. Gibson. Nicene and Post-Nicene Fathers, Second Series 11. New York: Christian Literature Company, 1894.

——. *De institutis coenobiorum*. Trans. Boniface Ramsey, as *The Institutes*. Ancient Christian Writers 58. New York: Newman, 2000.

Cassiodorus. *Expositio Psalmorum*. Ed. M. Adriaen, CCSL 97–98. Turnhout, Belgium: Brepols, 1958. Trans. P. G. Walsh, as *Explanation of the Psalms*. 3 vols. Ancient Christian Writers 51–53. New York: Paulist Press, 1990–1991.

Catechism of the Catholic Church. 2d ed. New York: Doubleday, 1995.

Charles, R. H. *The Apocrypha and Pseudepigrapha of the Old Testament in English*. 2 vols. Oxford, U.K.: Clarendon, 1913.

Charlesworth, James H. *The Old Testament Pseudepigrapha*. 2 vols. New Haven: Yale University Press, 2009–2010.

Chevalier, Ulysse, ed. *Sacramentaire et martyrologe de l'Abbaye de Saint Remy. Martyrologe, calendrier, ordinaires, et prosaire de la Métropole de Reims (VIIIe–XIIIe siécles)*. Bibliothèque liturgique 7. Paris: Picard, 1900.

Chrysippus of Jerusalem. *Oratio in Sanctam Mariam Deiparam*. Ed. Martin Jugie, *Homélies mariales byzantine II, Patrologia Orientalis* 19.3 (1925): 336–43.

Clement of Alexandria. *Stromateis*. Trans. J. E. L. Oulton, in *Alexandrian Christianity: Selected Translations of Clement and Origen*, 93–165. Library of Christian Classics 2. London: SCM, 1954.

Conrad of Saxony. *Speculum seu salutatio beatae Mariae virginis ac sermones mariani*. Ed. Pedro de Alcántara Martínez, Bibliotheca Franciscana Ascetica Medii Aevi 11. Rome: Collegium S. Bonaventurae ad Claras Aquas, 1975. Trans. Sr. Mary Emmanuel as Saint Bonaventure, *The Mirror of the Blessed Virgin Mary*. St. Louis, MO: Herder, 1932.

Copeland, Rita, and Ineke Sluiter, eds. *Medieval Grammar and Rhetoric: Language Arts and Literary Theory, AD 300–1475*. Oxford: Oxford University Press, 2009.

Crane, T. F. "Miracles of the Virgin." *Romanic Review* 2.3 (July–September 1911): 235–79.

Cunningham, Mary. *Wider Than Heaven: Eighth-Century Homilies on the Mother of God*. Crestwood, N.Y.: St. Vladimir's Seminary Press, 2008.

Cyprian of Carthage. *De dominica oratione*. Trans. Alistair Stewart-Sykes, in *On the Lord's Prayer: Tertullian, Cyprian and Origen*, 65–93. Crestwood, N.Y.: St. Vladimir's Seminary Press, 2004.

d'Achery, Luc, and Jean Mabillon, eds. *Acta sanctorum ordinis S. Benedicti in saeculorum classes distributa*. 6 vols. in 9. Venice: S. Coleti & J. Bettinelli, 1733–1738.

Daley, Brian E., trans. *On the Dormition of Mary: Early Patristic Homilies*. Crestwood, N.Y.: St. Vladimir's Seminary Press, 1998.

Dante Alighieri. *Divina commedia: Inferno, Purgatorio, Paradiso*. Ed. Giorgio Petrocchi. Milan: Mondadori, 1966–1967; 2d ed. Florence: Le Lettere, 1994. Trans. Allen Mandelbaum. 3 vols. New York: Random House, 1980–1984; online with Italian at www.worldofdante.org. Also trans. Mark Musa, as *The Divine Comedy*. 3 vols. Harmondsworth: Penguin, 1984–1986.

De Barry, Paul. *Le Paradis ouvert à Philagie par cent dévotions à la Mère de Dieu, aisées à pratiquer*. Lyon: Pierre and Claude Rigaud, 1644.

Delaporte, Yves, ed. *L'Ordinaire chartrain du XIII siècle*. Société archéologique d'Eure-et-Loir Mémoires 19. Chartres: Société archéologique d'Eure-et-Loir, 1953.

Deshusses, Jean. *Le sacramentaire grégorien. Ses principales formes d'après les plus anciens manuscrits*. 3 vols. SF 16, 24, 28. Fribourg: Universitätsverlag, 1971–1982.

De Strycker, Émile. *La forme la plus ancienne du Protévangile de Jacques: Recherches sur le papyrus Bodmer 5 avec une édition critique*. Subsidia hagiographica 33. Brussels: Société des Bollandistes, 1961.

Dionysius the Carthusian. *De oratione*. Trans. Íde M. Ní Riain, as "Prayer." In *The Spiritual Writings of Denis the Carthusian*, 199–272. Dublin: Four Courts, 2005.

Dominic of Evesham. *De miraculis sanctae Mariae*. Ed. José M. Canal, in *El libro "De miraculis sanctae Mariae" de Domingo de Evesham (m.c. 1140)*. Studium Legionense 39. Leon: Studium Legionense, 1998.

Donizo of Canossa. *Vita Mathildis carmine scripta a Donizo presbytero*. Ed. Luigi Simeoni. Rerum Italicarum Scriptores 5.2. Bologna: N. Zachinelli, 1930–1934. Also PL 148, cols. 939–1036.

Durandus, William. *Guillelmi Duranti rationale divinorum officiorum*. Ed. A. Davril and T. M. Thibodeau. 3 vols. CCCM 140, 140A, 140B. Turnhout, Belgium: Brepols, 1995–2000.

Elisabeth of Schönau. *Libri visionum et epistolae*. Ed. F. W. E. Roth, *Die Visionen und Briefe der hl. Elisabeth sowie dei Schriften der Äbte Ekbert und Emecho von Schönau*. 2d ed. Brünn: Verlag der "Studien aus dem Benedictiner-und-Cistercienser-Orden," 1886. Trans. Anne L. Clark, as *Elisabeth of Schönau: Complete Works*. New York: Paulist Press, 2000.

Ekbert of Schönau. *Ad beatam virginem Deiparam. Sermo panegyricus*. PL 184, cols. 1009–14.

Elliott, J. K. *The Apocryphal New Testament: A Collection of Apocryphal Christian Literature in an English Translation*. Oxford, U.K.: Clarendon, 1993.

Engelbert of Admont. *De gratiis et virtutibus beatae et gloriosae semper virginis Mariae tractatus*. In Bernard Pez, *Thesaurus anecdotorum novissimus, seu Veterum Monumentorum, praecipue Ecclesiasticorum, ex Germanicis potissimum Bibiothecis adornata Collectio recentissima*, vol. 1, cols. 503–762. Augsburg: Sumptibus Philippi, Martini, & Johanni Veith Fratrum, 1721.

Epiphanius of Salamis. *Panarion*. Ed. Karl Holl and Jürgen Dummer. In *Epiphanius*. 2d ed. Die griechischen christlichen Schriftsteller der ersten drei Jahrhunderte 25, 31, 37. Leipzig: Hinrichs/Berlin: Akademie-Verlag, 1915, 1980, 1985. Trans. Frank Williams, as *The Panarion of Epiphanius of Salamis*. 2 vols. Nag Hammadi Studies 35–36. Leiden: Brill, 1987, 1994.

Eusebius of Caesarea. *Preparatio evangelica*. Trans. E. H. Gifford, as *Preparation of the Gospel*. Oxford: Oxford University Press, 1903.

Foerster, Wilhelm. "Del tumbeor Nostre-Dame." *Romania* 2 (1873): 315–25. Trans. Philip H. Wicksteed, as *Our Lady's Tumbler: A Twelfth Century Legend done out of Old French into English*. Portland, Maine: Thomas B. Mosher, 1904.

Franco of Afflighem. *De gratia Dei libri XII*. PL 166, cols. 717–808.

Gautier de Coinci. *Les Miracles de Nostre Dame*. Ed. V. Frederic Koenig. 4 vols. Geneva: Droz, 1955–1970. Trans. l'abbé Poquet, as *Les miracles de la Sainte Vierge*. Paris: Parmantier: Didron, 1857. Selections trans. Renate Blumenfeld-Kosinski, in *Medieval Hagiography: An Anthology*, ed. Thomas Head, 627–54. New York: Routledge, 2001. Also selections trans. Kemp-Welch, *Of the Tumbler*.

Geert Grote. *Getijden van de Eeuwige Wijsheid naar de Vertaling van Geert Grote*. Ed. Anton Weiler. Baarn, The Netherlands: Ambo, 1984.

Geoffroy de La Tour Landry. *The Book of the Knight of La Tour Landry: Compiled for the Instruction of His Daughters*. Ed. Thomas Wright. EETS o.s. 33. London: N. Trübner, 1868.

Gerardus Itherius. *Vita S. Stephani*. PL 204, cols. 1005–46.

Gerhard of Augsburg. *Vita Sancti Uodalrici: Die älteste Lebensbeschreibung des heiligen Ulrich: lateinisch-deutsch, mit der Kanonisatiosurkunde von 993*, ed. Walter Bershin and Angelika Häse. Editiones Heidelbergenses 24. Heidelberg: Universitätsverlag C. Winter, 1993. Also *Vita S. Udalrici Augustani Episcopi*. PL 135, cols. 1009–58.

Gerhoh of Reichersberg. *Commentarius aureus in Psalmos et cantica ferialia.* PL 193, cols. 619–1814; PL 194, cols. 9–998.

Germanus of Constantinople. *On the Entrance into the Temple I–II.* PG 98, cols. 292–320. Trans. Cunningham, *Wider Than Heaven,* 145–72.

——. *On the Most Venerable Dormition of the Holy Mother of God.* PG 98, cols. 340–72. Trans. Daley, *On the Dormition,* 153–81.

——. *Oration on the Annunciation of the Supremely Holy Theotokos.* Ed. D. Fecioru, "Un nou gen de predica in omiletica ortodoxa," *Biserica Ortodoxa Romana* 64 (1946): 65–91, 180–92, 386–96. Also PG 98, cols. 320–40. Trans. Cunningham, *Wider Than Heaven,* 221–46.

——. *Oration on the Consecration of the Venerable Church of Our Supremely Holy Lady, the Theotokos, and on the Holy Swaddling Clothes of Our Lord Jesus Christ.* PG 98, cols. 372–84. Trans. Cunningham, *Wider Than Heaven,* 247–55.

Gertrude the Great. *Legatus divinae pietatis.* Ed. and trans. Pierre Doyère, Jean-Marie Clément et al., *Oeuvres spirituelles,* vols. 2–5. Trans. Sister Mary Frances Clare, as *The Life and Revelations of Saint Gertrude, Virgin and Abbess, of the Order of St. Benedict.* 2d ed. London: Burns & Oates; New York: Benziger, 1870. Trans. Alexandra Barratt, as *The Herald of God's Loving Kindness.* 2 vols. CF 35, 63. Kalamazoo, Mich.: Cistercian Publications, 1991. Trans. Margaret Winkworth, as *The Herald of Divine Love.* New York: Paulist Press, 1993.

——. *Oeuvres spirituelles.* Ed. and trans. Jacques Houlier, Pierre Doyère, and Jean-Marie Clément. 5 vols. Sources chrétiennes 127, 139, 143, 255, and 331. Paris: Éditions du Cerf, 1967–1986.

Gonzalo de Berceo. *Milagros de Nuestra Señora.* Trans. Richard Terry Mount and Annette Grant Cash, as *Miracles of Our Lady.* Studies in Romance Languages 41. Lexington: University Press of Kentucky, 1997.

Goscelin of Saint Bertin. *Liber confortatorius.* Ed. C. H. Talbot, "The Liber Confortatorius of Goscelin of Saint Bertin." *Studia Anselmiana* 37. Analecta monastica series 3 (1955): 1–117. Trans. Monika Otter, as *The Book of Encouragement and Consolation: The Letter of Goscelin to the Recluse Eva.* Cambridge, U.K.: Brewer, 2004.

Granada, Fray Luis de. *Obras.* 18 vols. Madrid: Antonio de Sancha, 1786–1789.

Gregory VII. *Registrum.* PL 148, cols. 285–644. Selections trans. Ephraim Emerton, *The Correspondence of Pope Gregory VII: Selected Letters from the Registrum.* Records of Western Civilization. New York: Columbia University Press, 1990.

Grindal, Edmund. *The Remains of Edmund Grindal, D.D.: Successively Bishop of London and Archbishop of York and Canterbury.* Ed. William Nicholson. Parker Society 19. Cambridge: Cambridge University Press, 1843.

Guibert of Nogent. *De laude sanctae Mariae.* PL 156, cols. 537–77.

Henry Suso. *Horologium Sapientiae.* Ed. Pius Künzle. SF 23. Freiburg: Universitätsverlag, 1977.

Herman of Tournai. *Liber de restauratione ecclesie Sancti Martini Tornacensis.* Ed. R. B. C. Huygens. CCCM 236. Turnhout, Belgium: Brepols, 2010. Also MGH Scriptores 14, 274–317. Trans. Lynn Harry Nelson, as *The Restoration of the Monastery of Saint Martin's of Tournai.* Washington, D.C.: Catholic University of America Press, 1996.

Herolt, Johannes. *Promptuarium Discipuli de miraculis Beate Marie Virginis.* Trans. C. C. Swinton-Bland, as *Miracles of the Blessed Virgin Mary.* London: Routledge, 1928.

Herrad of Hohenbourg. *Hortus deliciarum.* Ed. Rosalie Green. 2 vols. Studies of the Warburg Institute 36. London: Warburg Institute, 1979.

Herrgott, Marquard, ed. *Vetus disciplina monastica.* Paris: C. Osmont, 1726.

Hesbert, René-Jean, ed. *Antiphonale Missarum Sextuplex.* Brussels: Vromant, 1935.

Hildegard-Gebetbuch: Faksimile-Ausgabe des Codex-Latinus Monacensis 935 der Bayerischen Staatsbibliothek. Wiesbaden: Reichert, 1982.

Hildegard of Bingen. *Scivias.* Ed. Adelgundis Führkötter and Angela Carlevaris. CCCM 43–43A. Turnhout, Belgium: Brepols, 1978. Trans. Columba Hart and Jane Bishop. New York: Paulist Press, 1990.

——. *Symphonia: A Critical Edition of the Symphonia armonie celestium revelationum: Symphony of the Harmony of Celestial Revelations.* Ed. and trans. Barbara Newman. Ithaca, N.Y.: Cornell University Press, 1988.

Hippolytus of Rome. *Traditio apostolica [Apostolikē paradosis].* Trans. Gregory Dix, as *The Treatise on the Apostolic Tradition of St. Hippolytus of Rome, Bishop and Martyr.* 2d rev. ed with corrections by Henry Chadwick. London: Alban, 1991. Also in A. G. Hamman, *Early Christian Prayers.* Trans. Walter Mitchell. Chicago: Regnery, 1961.

Honorius Augustodunensis. *Gemma animae.* PL 172, cols. 541–738.

———. *Sigillum beatae Mariae.* PL 172, cols. 495–518. Trans. Amelia Carr, as *The Seal of Blessed Mary.* Peregrina Translation Series 18. Toronto: Peregrina, 1991.

Hrabanus Maurus. *De institutione clericorum libri tres.* Ed. Detlev Zimpel. Freiburger Beiträge zur mittelalterlichen Geschichte. Studien und Texte 7. Frankfurt am Main: Lang, 1996. Also PL 107, cols. 293–420.

Hrotsvitha of Gandersheim. *Maria.* Ed. and trans. Sister M. Gonsalva Wiegand, in *The Non-Dramatic Works of Hrosvitha,* 14–73. Ph.D. dissertation, Saint Louis University, 1936.

Hugh of Flavigny. *Chronicon.* Ed. Georg Heinrich Pertz. MGH Scriptores 8:288–502.

Hugh of Saint Victor. *De Verbo incarnato collationes seu disputationes tres.* PL 177, cols. 315–24.

———. *De virtute orandi.* PL 176, cols. 977–88. Trans. Hugh Feiss, as "On the Power of Prayer." In *Writings on the Spiritual Life: A Selection of Works of Hugh, Adam, Achard, Richard, Walter, and Godfrey of St. Victor,* ed. Christopher Evans, 315–47. Victorine Texts in Translation 4. Turnhout, Belgium: Brepols, 2013.

———. *Super ierarchiam Dionisii.* Ed. Dominic Poirel. CCCM 178. Turnhout, Belgium: Brepols, 2015. Also PL 175, cols. 923–1154.

In antiphonam Salve Regina, Sermones IV. PL 184, cols. 1059–1078.

Isidore of Seville. *Etymologies.* Trans. Stephen A. Barney, W. J. Lewis, J. A. Beach, and Oliver Berghof. Cambridge: Cambridge University Press, 2006.

Jacobus de Voragine. *Legenda aurea.* Trans. William Granger Ryan, as *The Golden Legend: Readings on the Saints.* 2 vols. Princeton, N.J.: Princeton University Press, 1993.

———. *Mariale, seu Sermones aurei de beata Maria virgine.* Paris: Hippolytus Walzer, 1888.

———. *Sermones Quadrigesimales.* Ed. Giovanni Paolo Maggioni. Edizioni nazionale dei testi mediolatini 13. Florence: Sismel edizioni dei Galluzzo, 2005.

———. *Sermones de sanctis per anni totius circulum concurrentibus.* Lyon: Jacques Giunta, 1546.

Jacques de Vitry. *The Exempla, or Illustrative Stories from the Sermones Vulgares.* Ed. T. H. Crane. London: David Nutt, for the Folk-lore Society, 1890.

———. *Vitae Mariae Oigniacensis.* Ed. R. B. C. Huygens. CCCM 252. Turnhout, Belgium: Brepols, 2012. Also AASS June 4, dies 23, cols. 636–66.

Jean de Joinville. *Vie de Saint Louis.* Trans. Margaret R. B. Shaw, as *Life of Saint Louis.* In *Chronicles of the Crusades,* 161–353. Harmondsworth: Penguin, 1963.

Jean Gobi. *Scala coeli.* Ed. Marie Anne Polo de Beaulieu, as *La scala coeli de Jean Gobi.* Sources d'histoire médiévale. Paris: Edition du Centre national de la recherche scientifique, 1991.

Jerome. *Commentaria in Isaiam.* PL 24, cols. 17–678.

———. *Liber interpretationis Hebraicorum nominum.* Ed. Paul de Lagarde. CCSL 72. Turnhout, Belgium: Brepols, 1959. Also PL 23, cols. 771–858.

Johannes Beleth. *Summa de ecclesiasticis officiis.* Ed. Herbert Douteil. 2 vols. CCCM 41–41A. Turnhout, Belgium: Brepols, 1976.

John Duns Scotus. *Four Questions on Mary.* Trans. Allan B. Wolter. Text Series 22. St. Bonaventure, N.Y.: Franciscan Institute Publications, 2000.

John Mirk. *Instructions for Parish Priests: Edited from Cotton ms. Claudius A.II.* Ed. Edward Peacock. EETS o.s. 31. London: Trübner, 1868.

John of Damascus. *Canon for the Dormition of the Mother of God.* Ed. Wilhelm von Christ and Matthaiso K. Paranikas, *Anthologia Graeca Carminum Christianorum,* 229–32. Leipzig: Teubner, 1871. Trans. Daley, *On the Dormition,* 241–46.

———. *De fide orthodoxa. Versions of Burgundio and Cerbanus.* Ed. Eligius M. Buytaert. Franciscan Institute Publications 8. St. Bonaventure, N.Y.: Franciscan Institute, 1955. In Greek: PG 94, cols. 790–1228.

———. *On the Dormition of the Holy Mother of God I–III*. Ed. Bonifatius Kotter, *Die Schriften des Johannes von Damaskos*, 5:461–555. Berlin: Walter de Gruyter, 1988. Also PG 96, cols. 700–61. Trans. Daley, *On the Dormition*, 183–239.

———. *An Oration on the Nativity of the Holy Theotokos Mary*. Ed. Kotter, *Die Schriften*, 5:169–82. Trans. Cunningham, *Wider Than Heaven*, 53–70.

John of Euboea. *Homily on the Conception of the Holy Theotokos*. PG 96, cols. 1460–1500. Trans. Cunningham, *Wider Than Heaven*, 173–95.

John of Garland. *Stella maris*. Ed. Wilson, *The Stella Maris of John of Garland*, 87–154.

John of Italy. *Vita s. Odonis abbatis Cluniacensis secundi*. PL 133, cols. 43–86.

John of Lodi. *Vita b. Petri Damiani*. Ed. Stephan Freund, *Studien zur literarischen Wirksamkeit des Petrus Damiani*, 203–65. MGH Studien und Texte 13. Hannover: Hahnsche Buchhandlung, 1995. Also PL 144, cols. 113–46.

John of Thessalonica. *The Dormition of Our Lady, the Mother of God and Ever-Virgin Mary*. Ed. Martin Jugie, *Homélies mariales byzantine II, Patrologia Orientalis* 19.3 (1925): 375–436. Trans. Daley, *On the Dormition*, 47–70.

John Scotus Eriugena. *Expositiones super Ierarchiam caelestem S. Dionysii*. PL 122, cols. 125–266.

Jordan of Saxony. *Liber vitasfratrum*. Trans. Gerard Deighan, as *The Life of the Brethren*. Villanova, Penn.: Augustinian, 1993.

José de Jesús de María. *Historia de la Vida y Excelencias de la Virgen Maria Nuestra Señora*. Amberes: Canisio, 1652.

Josephus. *Jewish Antiquities*. Trans. H. St. J. Thackeray, Ralph Marcus, Allen Wikgren, and Louis H. Feldman. 9 vols. Loeb Classical Library. Cambridge, Mass.: Harvard University Press, 1930–1965.

Justin Martyr. *Dialogue with Trypho*. Trans. Marcus Dods and George Reith. Ante-Nicene Fathers 1. Buffalo, N.Y.: Christian Literature Publishing, 1885.

Kemp-Welch, Alice. *Of the Tumbler of Our Lady and Other Miracles*. New York: Oxford University Press, 1908.

Labbé, Philippe, ed. *Nova bibliotheca manuscriptorum librorum*. 2 vols. Paris: Apud Sebastianum Cramoisy et Gabrielem Cramoisy, 1657.

Lanfranc of Bec. *Decreta Lanfranci monachis Cantuariensibus transmissa*. Ed. David Knowles. CCM 3. Siegburg: F. Schmitt, 1967. Trans. David Knowles, as *The Monastic Constitutions of Lanfranc*. London: Nelson, 1951.

Latin Miracles of the Virgin. Trans. Patricia Timmons and Robert Boenig, in *Gonzalo de Berceo and the* Latin Miracles of the Virgin, 29–65. Farnham, U.K.: Ashgate, 2012.

Latimer, Hugh. *The Works of Hugh Latimer, sometime Bishop of Worcester, martyr, 1555*. Ed. George Elwes Corrie. 2 vols. Parker Society 27–28. Cambridge: Cambridge University Press, 1844.

The Lay-Folks Mass Book; or the Manner of Hearing Mass. Ed. Thomas Frederick Simmons. EETS 71. London: EETS, 1879.

Le Grand, Léon. *Statuts d'hotels-Dieu et de léproseries. Recueil de textes du XIIᵉ au XIVᵉ siècle*. Paris: Picard, 1901.

Libellus de nativitate sanctae Mariae. Ed. Rita Beyers. Corpus Christianorum Series Apocryphorum 10. Turnhout, Belgium: Brepols, 1997.

Liber antiphonarius. PL 78, cols. 641–724.

Liber de infantia Salvatoris. Ed. M. R. James. *Latin Infancy Gospels: A New Text with a Parallel Version from Irish*. Cambridge: Cambridge University Press, 1927.

Liber de miraculis sanctae Dei genitricis Mariae. Published at Vienna, in 1731 by Bernard Pez. Reprinted and ed. T. F. Crane. Cornell University Studies in Romance Languages and Literatures 1. Ithaca, N.Y.: Cornell University Press, 1925.

Liber pontificalis. Ed. Louis Duchesne. 2 vols. Bibliothèque des écoles françaises d'Athènes et de Rome. Paris: Ernest Thorin, 1886–1892.

Liber responsalis sive antiphonarius. PL 78, cols. 725–850.

Liber sacramentorum. PL 78, cols. 25–240.

Lisiard de Laon. *Ordinarium ecclesiae Laudunensis*. Ed. Ulysse Chevalier, in *Ordinaires de l'Eglise cathedral de Laon (XII–XIII siècles)*, 1–188. Bibliothèque liturgique 6. Paris: Alphonse Picard, 1897.

Ludolph of Saxony. *Vita Jesu Christi*. Ed. L. M. Rigollot. 4 vols. Paris: Victor Palmé, 1870.

Lumen Gentium. Dogmatic Constitution on the Church, solemnly promulgated by His Holiness Pope Paul VI on November 21, 1964. www.vatican.va/archive/hist_councils/ii_vatican_council/documents /vat-ii_const_19641121_lumen-gentium_en.html.

Luther, Martin. *The Large Catechism of Martin Luther*. Trans. Robert H. Fischer. Philadelphia: Fortress, 1959.

Magnum Bullarium Romanum: Bullarum, privilegiorum ac diplomatum Romanorum Pontificum amplissima collectio. 15 vols. in 13. Graz: Akademische Druck-u. Verlagsanstalt, 1964–1966.

Manegold of Lautenbach. *Constitutiones Marbacenses*. Ed. Josef Siegwart, as *Die Consuetudines des Augustiner-Chorherren-Stiftes Marbach im Elsass (12. Jh.)*. SF10. Freiburg: Universitätsverlag, 1965. Also ed. Eusebius Amort, in *Vetus disciplina canonicorum*, 1:383–431.

Mansi, Giovanni Domenico et al., eds. *Sacrorum conciliorum, nova et amplissima collectio: cujus Johannes Dominicus Mansi et post ipsius mortem Florentius et Venetianus editores ab anno 1758 ad annum 1798 priores triginta unum tomos ediderunt, nunc autem continuat et absoluta*. 54 vols. Paris: H. Welter, 1901–1927.

Marbode of Rennes. *Historia Theophili metrica*. PL 171, cols. 1593–1604.

Margery Kempe. *The Book of Margery Kempe*. Ed. Barry Windeatt. Harlow: Longman, 2000.

María de Jesús de Ágreda. *Autenticidad de la* Mística Ciudad de Dios *y biografía de su autora*. Barcelona: Heredos de Juan Gili, Editores, 1914.

——. *Mystica Ciudad de Dios. Milagro de su omnipotencia y abismo de la Gracia. Historia divina y vida de la Virgen Madre de Dio. . . .* 8 books in 3 vols. Madrid: Bernardo de Villa-Diego, 1670; Lisbon: Miguel Manescal, 1684. Trans. George J. Blatter as Fiscar Marison, as *Mystical City of God. The Miracle of His Omnipotence and the Abyss of His Grace. The Divine History and Life of the Virgin Mother of God . . .* 8 books in 4 vols. Chicago: Theopolitan, 1914.

Martène, Edmond, ed. *De antiquis ecclesiae ritibus libri tres*. Editio novissima. 4 vols. Antwerp and Venice: J. B. Novelli, 1763–1764.

——. *De antiquis monachorum ritibus*. 5 vols. Lyon: Anisson, Posuel et Rigaud, 1690.

Matthew of Aquasparta. *Sermones de beata Maria virgine*. Ed. Caelestinus Piana. Bibliotheca Franciscana Ascetica Medii Aevi 9. Quaracchi, Florence: Collegii S. Bonaventurae, 1962.

Maximus the Confessor. *The Life of the Virgin*. Trans. Stephen J. Shoemaker. New Haven: Yale University Press, 2012.

Mechthild of Magdeburg. *Das fliessende Licht der Gottheit*. Trans. Frank Tobin, as *The Flowing Light of the Godhead*. New York: Paulist Press, 1998.

Le ménagier de Paris. Ed. Georgine E. Brereton and Janet M. Ferrier. Oxford, U.K.: Clarendon, 1981. Trans. Gina L. Greco and Christine M. Rose, as *The Good Wife's Guide*. Ithaca, N.Y.: Cornell University Press, 2009.

Miracles of the Virgin in Middle English. Ed. and trans. Adrienne Williams Boyarin. Peterborough, Ont.: Broadview, 2015.

Miracula Sanctae Virginis Mariae. Ed. Elise Forsythe Dexter. University of Wisconsin Studies in the Social Sciences and History 12. Madison: [University of Wisconsin Press], 1927.

Modestus of Jerusalem. *An Encomium on the Dormition of Our Most Holy Lady, Mary, Mother of God and Ever-Virgin*. PG 86, cols. 3277–3312. Trans. Daley, *On the Dormition*, 83–102.

Mombaer, Jan. *Rosetum exercitiorum spiritualium et sacrarum meditationum*. Milan: Apud Hieronymum Bordonum & Petrum Martyrem Locarnum, 1603.

The Myroure of Oure Ladye, containing a devotional treatise on divine service, with a translation of the offices used by the sisters of the Birgittine Monastery of Sion, at Isleworth, during the fifteenth and sixteenth centuries. Ed. from the original black-letter text of 1530 A.D. Ed. John Henry Blunt. EETS, e.s. 19. London: N. Trübner, 1873.

Neale, J. M. *Mediaeval Preachers and Mediaeval Preaching: A Series of Extracts, translated from the Sermons of the Middle Ages, Chronologically Arranged*. London: J. C. Mozley, 1856.

Nestorius. *Homily 1*. Trans. Richard A. Norris Jr., *The Christological Controversy*, 123–31. Philadelphia: Fortress, 1980.

Nicholas Love. *The Mirror of the Blessed Life of Jesus Christ: A Reading Text*. Ed. Michael G. Sargent. Rev. ed. Exeter: University of Exeter Press, 2004.

Nicola da Milano. *Collationes de beata virgine: A Cycle of Preaching in the Dominican Congregation of the Blessed Virgin Mary at Imola, 1286–1287. Edited from Firenze, Biblioteca nazionale centrale, MS Conv. Soppr. G.7.1464*. Ed. M. Michèle Mulchahey. Toronto Medieval Latin Texts 24. Toronto: Pontifical Institute of Mediaeval Studies, 1997.

Nigel of Canterbury. *Miracula Sanctae Dei Genitricis Virginis Marie, Versifice*. Ed. Jan Ziolkowski. Toronto Medieval Latin Texts 17. Toronto: Centre for Medieval Studies, 1986.

N-Town. *The Mary Play*. In *Medieval Drama: An Anthology*, ed. Greg Walker, 167–95. Oxford: Blackwell, 2000.

The Ordinal and Customary of the Abbey of Saint Mary, York (St. John's College, Cambridge, ms. D. 27). Ed. the Abbess of Stanbrook [Laurentia McLachlan] and J. B. L. Tolhurst. 3 vols. HBS 73, 75, 84. London: Henry Bradshaw Society, 1936, 1937, 1951.

Origen of Alexandria. *De oratione*. Trans. Rowan A. Greer, in *Origen*, 81–170. New York: Paulist Press, 1979.

Otfrid von Weissenburg. *Evangelienbuch*. Ed. Oskar Erdmann. 6th ed., ed. Ludwig Wolff. Altdeutsche Textbibliothek 49. Tübingen: Niemeyer, 1962.

Pandolfi, Ubaldus de, trans. *Life of Venerable Sister Mary of Jesus—D. Agreda*. Evansville, Ind.: Keller-Crescent, 1910.

Paschasius Radbertus. *De assumptione sanctae Mariae virginis [Cogitis me, o Paula et Eustochium]*. Ed. Albert Ripberger, *Der Pseudo-Hieronymous-Brief IX "Cogitis me": Ein erster marianischer Traktat des Mittelalters von Paschasius Radbert*. SF 9. Fribourg: Universitätsverlag, 1962. Reprint CCCM 56C, 99–172. Turnhout, Belgium: Brepols, 1985. Also *Epistola 9: Ad Paulam et Eustochium*, PL 30, cols. 122–42.

——. *Expositio in Matheo libri XII*. Ed. Beda Paulus. 3 vols. CCCM 56, 56A, 56B. Turnhout, Belgium: Brepols, 1984. Also PL 120, cols. 31–994.

Paul the Deacon of Naples. *Miraculum S. Mariae: De Theophilo penitente*. Ed. Robert Petsch, in *Theophilus: Mittelniederdeutsches Drama in Drei Fassungen Herausgegeben*, 1–10. Heidelberg: Carl Winter's Universitätsbuchhandlung, 1908. Also AASS, February 1, dies 4, cols. 483–87. Trans. Palmer and More, *Sources*, 60–75.

Peter Comestor. *Historia scholastica*. PL 198, cols. 1053–1722.

Peter Damian. *Epistolae*. Ed. Kurt Reindel, *Die Briefe des Petrus Damiani*. 4 vols. MGH Die Briefe der deutschen Kaiserzeit 4. Munich: MGH, 1983. Also PL 144 and 145. Trans. Owen J. Blum and Irven Michael Resnick. 6 vols. The Fathers of the Church, Medieval Continuation 1–3, 5–7. Washington, D.C.: Catholic University of America Press, 1989–2005.

Peter de Honestis. *Regula clericorum*. Ed. Eusebius Amort, in *Vetus disciplina canonicorum*, 1:338–82. Also PL 163, cols. 703–48.

Peter Lombard. *Commentarius in Psalmos Davidicos*. PL 191, cols. 61–1296.

——. *Sententiae*. Trans. Giulio Silano, as *The Sentences*. 4 vols. Toronto: Pontifical Institute of Mediaeval Studies, 2007–2010.

Peter the Venerable of Cluny. *Statuta congregationis cluniacensis*. Ed. Faustino Avagliano and Giles Constable. CCM 6: Consuetudines Benedictinae variae, saec. XI–saec.XIV. Siegburg: F. Schmitt, 1975. Also PL 189, cols. 1025–48.

Philip of Harvengt. *Commentaria in Cantica canticorum*. PL 203, cols. 181–490.

Philo of Alexandria. *The Works of Philo Judaeus, the Contemporary of Josephus*. Trans. C. D. Yonge. 4 vols. London: Henry G. Bohn, 1854–1855.

Proclus of Constantinople. *Homilies 1–5*. Ed. and trans. Constas, in *Proclus of Constantinople*, 125–272.

Pseudo-Albertus Magnus. *Mariale, sive CCXXX quaestiones super Evangelium "Missus est Angelus Gabriel."* Ed. Augustus and Aemilius Borgnet, in *B. Alberti Magni Ratisbonensis Episcopi, Ordinis Praedicatorum, Opera omnia* 37, 5–341. Paris: L. Vivès, 1898.

Pseudo-Augustine. *De assumptione beatae Mariae virginis*. PL 40, cols. 1141–48.

Pseudo-Bonaventure. *Meditationes vitae Christi*. Trans. Francis X. Taney, Anne Miller, and C. Mary Stalling-Taney, as John of Caulibus, *Meditations on the Life of Christ*. Asheville, N.C.: Pegasus, 2000.

——. *Psalterium B. Mariae Virginis*. In Bonaventure, *Opera omnia*, 14:199–226. Paris: L. Vivès, 1864–1871.

Pseudo-Dionysius. *De coelesti hierarchia*. Trans. John Parker, in *The Celestial and Ecclesiastical Hierarchy of Dionysius the Areopagite*, 15–49. London: Skeffington and Son, 1894.

Pseudo-Matthaei Evangelium. Ed. Jan Gijsel. Corpus Christianorum Series Apocryphorum 9. Turnhout, Belgium: Brepols, 1997.

Pseudo-Melito. *Transitus B2*. Ed. Monika Haibach-Reinisch, *Ein neuer "Transitus Mariae" des Pseudo-Melito: Textkritische Ausgabe und Darlegung der Bedeutung dieser Urspruenglicheren Fassung fuer Apokryphenforschung und lateinische und deutsche Dichtung des Mittelalters*. Bibliotheca Assumptionis B. Virginis Mariae 5. Rome: Pontificia Academia Mariana Internationalis, 1962. Also Tischendorf, *Apocalypses apocryphae*, 125–36; Clayton, *Apocryphal Gospels*, 334–43. Trans. Elliott, *Apocryphal New Testament*, 708–14.

Raby, F. J. E., ed. *The Oxford Book of Medieval Latin Verse*. Oxford, U.K.: Clarendon, 1959.

Radulph of Rivo. *De canonum observantia*. Ed. Melchior Hittorp, in *De divinis catholicae ecclesiae officiis et mysteriis*, cols. 1103–78. Paris: 1610.

Regularis Concordia. Ed. and trans. Thomas Symons, as *The Monastic Agreement of the Monks and Nuns of the English Nation*. London: Nelson, 1953.

A Relation, or Rather a True Account of the Island of England with sundry particulars of the customs of these people, and of the royal revenues under King Henry the Seventh about the year 1500. Trans. Charlotte Augusta Sneyd. Works of the Camden Society 37. London: Camden Society, 1847.

Richard of Saint-Laurent. *De laudibus beatae Mariae virginis libri XII*. Ed. Augustus and Aemilius Borgnet, in *B. Alberti Magni Ratisbonensis Episcopi, Ordinis Praedicatorum, Opera omnia* 36. Paris: L. Vivès, 1898.

Rosarius. Ed. Sven Sandqvist, as *Le bestiaire et le lapidaire du Rosarius (B.N. f. fr. 12483)*. Études romanes de Lund 55. Lund: Lund University Press, 1996.

Rupert of Deutz. *Commentaria in Canticum Canticorum de Incarnatione Domini*. Ed. Rhabanus Haacke. CCCM 26. Turnhout, Belgium: Brepols, 1974.

——. *Liber de divinis officiis*. Ed. Rhabanus Haacke. CCCM 7. Turnhout, Belgium: Brepols, 1967.

Saupe, Karen, ed. *Middle English Marian Lyrics*. Middle English Texts. Kalamazoo, Mich.: Published for TEAMS by Medieval Institute Publications, Western Michigan University, 1998.

Savonarola. *Esposizione sopra l'Ave Maria*. Florence: Bartolommeo di Libri, 1496. Trans. James Ferrigno, as "Exposition . . . Concerning the Prayer to the Glorious Virgin." In Ayo, *Hail Mary*, 152–65.

Schneemelcher, Wilhelm, ed. *New Testament Apocrypha*. Trans. R. McL. Wilson. 2 vols. Louisville, Ky.: Westminster John Knox, 2003.

Schwartz, Eduard, ed. *Acta conciliorum oecumenicorum*. 4 tomes, 15 volumes. Berlin: Walter de Gruyter, 1914–1984.

Scott-Stokes, Charity, ed. *Women's Books of Hours in Medieval England*. Woodbridge, U.K.: Brewer, 2006.

Servasanctus of Faenza. *Mariale, sive De laudibus Virginis Mariae*. Ed. Bohuslao Balbino, as Ernestus of Prague, *Mariale sive Liber de praecellentibus et eximiis SS. Dei genitricis Mariae supra reliquas creaturas praerogativis, ex arcanis S. Scripturae, SS. Patrum, theologiae et philosophiae naturalis mysteriis concinnatus*. Prague: Typis Caesareo-Academicis, 1651.

Sicardus of Cremona. *Mitrale, seu De officiis ecclesiasticis summa*. PL 213, cols. 13–436.

Sinués Ruíz, Atanasio, ed. "Advocaciones de la Virgen en un códice del siglo XII." *Annalecta Sacra Tarraconensia* 21 (1948): 1–34.

Six Books Dormition Apocryphon. Ed. William Wright, "The Departure of My Lady Mary from This World." *Journal of Sacred Literature and Biblical Record* 6–7 (1865): 417–48, 129–60.

Smaragdus of Saint-Mihiel. *Commentaria in regulam Sancti Benedicti*. Trans. David Barry, as *Commentary on the Rule of Saint Benedict*. Cistercian Studies Series 212. Kalamazoo, Mich.: Cistercian Publications, 2007.

Speculum virginum. Selected excerpts, trans. Barbara Newman. In *Listen Daughter*, ed. Mews, 269–96.

Stephen of Sawley. *De informatione mentis circa psalmodiam diei et noctis.* Ed. Edm. Mikkers, "Un traité inédit d'Étienne de Salley sur la psalmodie." *Cîteaux: Commentarii Cistercienses* 23 (1972): 245–88. Trans. Jeremiah F. O'Sullivan, as "On the Recitation of the Divine Office," in *Treatises,* 125–85. CF 36. Kalamazoo, Mich.: Cistercian Publications, 1984.

Tanner, Norman P., ed. *Decrees of the Ecumenical Councils.* Vol. 1, *Nicaea I to Lateran V.* London: Sheed and Ward; Washington, D.C.: Georgetown University Press, 1990.

Tertullian. *De oratione.* Ed. and trans. Ernest Evans, *Q. Septimii Florentis Tertulliani De oratione liber/Tertullian's Tract on the Prayer.* London: SPCK, 1953.

Theodore the Studite. *Encomium on the Dormition of Our Holy Lady, the Mother of God.* PG 99, cols. 720–30. Trans. Daley, *On the Dormition,* 249–57.

Theodulus. *Ecloga.* Ed. Joannes Osternacher. Urfahr: Verlag des bischöflichen Privatgymnasiums am Kollegium Petrinum, 1902.

Theoteknos of Livias. *An Encomium on the Assumption of the Holy Mother of God.* Ed. Wenger, *L'assomption,* 272–91. Trans. Daley, *On the Dormition,* 71–81.

Thomas, A. H., ed. *De oudste constituties van de Dominicanen: Voorgeschiedenis, Tekst, Bronnen, Onstaan en Ontwikkelung (1215–1237).* Bibliothèque de la Revue d'Histoire Ecclésiastique 42. Leuven: 1965.

Thomas Aquinas. *Summa theologiae.* Cura et studio Instituti Studiorum Medievalium Ottaviensis. 5 vols. Ottawa: Studii Generalis O. Pr., 1941–1945.

Thomas Aquinas. *The Three Greatest Prayers: Commentaries on the Lord's Prayer, the Hail Mary, and the Apostles' Creed.* Trans. Laurence Shapcote. Manchester, N.H.: Sophia Institute, 1990.

Thomas of Cantimpré. "Life of Margaret of Ypres." Trans. Margot H. King and Barbara Newman, in *The Collected Saints' Lives: Abbot John of Cantimpré, Christina the Astonishing, Margaret of Ypres, and Lutgard of Aywières,* ed. Barbara Newman, 163–206. Medieval Women Texts and Contexts 19. Turnhout, Belgium: Brepols, 2008.

Throckmorton, Burton H., Jr., ed. *Gospel Parallels: A Synopsis of the first three Gospels with alternative readings from the manuscripts and noncanonical parallels.* 4th ed. rev. Nashville: Nelson, 1979.

Thurston, Herbert, and Thomas Slater, eds. *Eadmeri monachi cantuariensis tractatus de conceptione sanctae Mariae.* Freiburg im Breisau: Herder, 1904.

Tischendorf, Constantine, ed. *Apocalypses apocryphae Mosis, Esdrae, Pauli, Johannis, item Mariae dormitio: additis evangeliorum et actuum apocryphorum supplementis.* Leipzig: H. Mendelssohn, 1866.

——. *Evangelia Apocrypha.* 2d ed. Leipzig: H. Mendelssohn, 1876.

Tugwell, Simon, ed. and trans. *Early Dominicans: Selected Writings.* Mahwah, N.J.: Paulist Press, 1982.

[Turgot of Durham and Saint Andrew's]. *Vita S. Margaritae Reginae Scotiae.* AASS, June 2, dies 10, cols. 328–35.

Ulrich of Zell. *Antiquiores consuetudines cluniacensis monasterii.* Ed. Kassius Hallinger. CCM 7: Consuetudines Cluniacensium antiquiores cum redactionibus derivatis. Siegburg, Germany: Schmitt, 1983. Also PL 149, cols. 635–778.

Underhill, Evelyn, ed. and trans. *The Miracles of Our Lady Saint Mary Brought Out of Divers Tongues and Newly Set Forth in English.* New York: Dutton, 1906.

Van Dijk, S. J. P., ed. *Sources of the Modern Roman Liturgy: The Ordinals by Haymo of Faversham and Related Documents 1243–1307.* 2 vols. Leiden: Brill, 1963.

Vetus registrum Sarisberiense, alius dictum Registrum S. Osmundi episcopi: The Register of S. Osmund. Ed. and trans. W. H. Rich Jones. 2 vols. Rerum Britannicarum medii aevi scriptores 78. London: Longman, 1883–1884.

Vincent of Beauvais. *Speculum historiale.* Venice: Apud Dominicum Nicolinum, 1591.

Vita Beatricis. Trans. Roger De Ganck, assisted by John Baptist Hasbrouck, as *The Life of Beatrice of Nazareth.* CF 50. Kalamazoo, Mich.: Cistercian Publications, 1991.

Vita Gundulfi. Ed. Rodney Thomson, as *The Life of Gundulf, Bishop of Rochester.* Toronto: Published for the Center for Medieval Studies by the Pontifical Institute of Mediaeval Studies, 1977. Also PL 159, cols. 813–36.

Vita [Hermanni Iosephi] auctore canonico Steinfeldensi synchrono. AASS, April 1, dies 7, cols. 686–710.

Voltaire. *Ancient and Modern History.* 9 vols. Trans. T. Smollett et al. London: J. Newbery, 1761.

Wace. *The Hagiographical Works: The Conception Nostre Dame and the Lives of St. Margaret and St. Nicholas.* Trans. Jean Blacker, Glyn S. Burgess, and Amy V. Ogden. Studies in Medieval and Reformation Traditions 169: Texts and Sources 3. Leiden: Brill, 2013.

Walter of Wimborne [Gauterus de Wymburnia]. *The Poems of Walter of Wimborne.* Ed. A. G. Rigg. Studies and Texts 42. Toronto: Pontifical Institute of Mediaeval Studies, 1978.

Waterworth, J., ed. and trans. *The Canons and Decrees of the Sacred and Oecumenical Council of Trent.* London: Dolman, 1848.

William of Hirsau. *Constitutiones Hirsaugienses.* Ed. Candida Elvert and Pius Engelbert. 2 vols. CCM 15. Siegburg, Germany: Schmitt, 2010. Also PL 150, cols. 927–1146.

William of Malmesbury. *De laudibus et miraculis sanctae Mariae.* Ed. and trans. R. M. Thomson and M. Winterbottom, as *The Miracles of the Blessed Virgin Mary.* Woodbridge, U.K.: Boydell, 2015.

Wulfstan of Winchester. *Life of St. Aethelwold.* Ed. and trans. Michael Lapidge and Michael Winterbottom. Oxford: Oxford University Press, 1991.

Ximénez de Samaniego, José. *Prologo galeato. Relación de la vida de la venerable madre sor María de Jésus . . .* Madrid: Imprenta de la Causa de la V. Madre, 1721. Ed. D. Carlos Seco Serrano, in *Cartas de Sor María de Jesús de Ágreda y de Felipe IV.* Biblioteca de Autores Españoles 109: Epistolario Español 5, 269–385. Madrid: Ediciones Atlas, 1958.

SCHOLARLY STUDIES

Ackerman, Susan. "The Queen Mother and the Cult in Ancient Israel." *Journal of Biblical Literature* 112.3 (1993): 385–401.

Adams, Henry. *The Education of Henry Adams: An Autobiography.* Cambridge: Printed at the Riverside Press for the Massachusetts Historical Society, 1918; reprint, New York: Barnes & Noble, 2009.

——. *Mont Saint Michel and Chartres.* Harmondsworth: Penguin, 1986.

Adams, Marilyn McCord. "The Immaculate Conception of the Blessed Virgin Mary: A Thought-Experiment in Medieval Philosophical Theology." *Harvard Theological Review* 103.2 (2010): 133–59.

Albright, W. F. "The Evolution of the West-Semitic Divinity 'An-'Anat-'Attâ." *American Journal of Semitic Languages and Literatures* 41.2 (1925): 73–101.

Alexandre-Bidon, Danièle. "Des femmes de bonne foi: La religion des mères au moyen âge." In *La Religion de ma Mère: Le rôle des femmes dans la transmission de la foi,* ed. Jean Delumeau, 91–122. Paris: Les Éditions du Cerf, 1992.

Anderson, Michael Alan. "Enhancing the *Ave Maria* in the Ars Antiqua." *Plainsong and Medieval Music* 19.1 (2010): 35–65.

Angelova, Diliana N. *Sacred Founders: Women, Men, and Gods in the Discourse of Imperial Founding, Rome Through Early Byzantium.* Berkeley and Los Angeles: University of California Press, 2015.

Areford, David. "The Passion Measured: A Late-Medieval Diagram of the Body of Christ." In *The Broken Body: Passion Devotion in Late-Medieval Culture,* eds. A. A. MacDonald, H. N. B. Ridderbos, and R. M. Schlusemann, 211–38. Mediaevalia Groningana 21. Groningen: Egbert Forsten, 1998.

Artola Arbiza, Antonio M., and Benito Mendía. *La venerable M. María de Jesús de Ágreda y la Inmaculada Concepción: El proceso eclesiástico a la Mística Ciudad de Dios.* Soria: Las Heras, 2004.

Ashe, Geoffrey. *The Virgin: Mary's Cult and the Re-emergence of the Goddess.* London: Routledge, 1976.

Ashley, Kathleen. "Creating Family Identity in Books of Hours." *Journal of Medieval and Early Modern Studies* 32.1 (2002): 145–65.

Ashton, John. "The Transformation of Wisdom: A Study of the Prologue of John's Gospel." *New Testament Studies* 32 (1986): 161–86.

Astell, Ann W. *Eating Beauty: The Eucharist and the Spiritual Arts of the Middle Ages.* Ithaca, N.Y.: Cornell University Press, 2006.

——. *The Song of Songs in the Middle Ages*. Ithaca, N.Y.: Cornell University Press, 1990.

Atanassova, Antonia. "Did Cyril of Alexandria Invent Mariology?" In *Origins*, ed. Maunder, 105–25.

Auerbach, Erich. *Mimesis: The Representation of Reality in Western Literature*. Trans. Willard R. Trask. Princeton, N.J.: Princeton University Press, 1953.

——. "*Sermo Humilis*." In *Literary Language and Its Public in Late Latin Anquity and in the Middle Ages*, trans. Ralph Manheim, 25–81. Bollingen Series 74. Princeton, N.J.: Princeton University Press, 1993.

Ayo, Nicholas. *The Hail Mary: A Verbal Icon of Mary*. Notre Dame: University of Notre Dame Press, 1994.

Backhouse, Janet. *The Illuminated Page: Ten Centuries of Manuscript Painting in the British Library*. Toronto: University of Toronto Press, 1998.

Bailey, Martin. "The Discovery of the Lost Mappamundi Panel: Hereford's Map in a Medieval Altarpiece?" In *The Hereford World Map: Medieval World Maps and Their Context*, ed. P. D. A. Harvey, 79–93. London: British Library, 2006.

Bandini, Angelo Maria. *Catalogus codicum bibliothecae Mediceae Laurentianae*. 4 vols. Florence: [Typis Caesareis], 1774–1777.

Bardenhewer, Otto. *Der Name Maria: Geschichte der Deutung desselben*. Biblische Studien 1.1. Freiburg im Breisgau: Herder, 1895.

Baring, Anne, and Jules Cashford. *The Myth of the Goddess: Evolution of an Image*. London: Arkana, 1991.

Barker, Margaret. *Christmas: The Original Story*. London: SPCK, 2008.

——. *Creation: A Biblical Vision for the Environment*. London: Clark, 2010.

——. *An Extraordinary Gathering of Angels*. London: Spruce, 2004.

——. *The Gate of Heaven: The History and Symbolism of the Temple in Jerusalem*. London: SPCK, 1991.

——. *The Great Angel: A Study of Israel's Second God*. Louisville, Ky.: Westminster John Knox, 1992.

——. *The Great High Priest: The Temple Roots of Christian Liturgy*. London: Clark, 2003.

——. *The Hidden Tradition of the Kingdom of God*. London: SPCK, 2007.

——. "Justinian's 'New Church' and the Entry of the Mother of God Into the Temple." *Sourozh* 103 (2006): 15–33.

——. *King of the Jews: Temple Theology in John's Gospel*. London: SPCK, 2014.

——. "The Life-Bearing Spring." In *Origins*, ed. Maunder, 127–35.

——. *The Lost Prophet: The Book of Enoch and Its Influence on Christianity*. London: SPCK, 1988.

——. *The Mother of the Lord*. Vol. 1, *The Lady in the Temple*. London: Bloomsbury, 2012.

——. *The Older Testament: The Survival of Themes from the Ancient Royal Cult in Sectarian Judaism and Early Christianity*. London: SPCK, 1987.

——. *On Earth as It Is in Heaven: Temple Symbolism in the New Testament*. London: Clark, 1995.

——. *The Revelation of Jesus Christ Which God Gave to Him to Show to His Servants What Must Soon Take Place (Revelation 1.1)*. Edinburgh: Clark, 2000.

——. *Temple Mysticism: An Introduction*. London: SPCK, 2011.

——. *Temple Themes in Christian Worship*. London: Clark, 2007.

——. *Temple Theology: An Introduction*. London: SPCK, 2004.

——. "Wisdom Imagery and the Mother of God." In *Cult of the Mother of God*, ed. Brubaker and Cunningham, 91–108.

Barré, Henri. "Antiennes et répons de la Vierge." *Marianum* 29 (1967): 153–254.

——. "Marie et l'Église du Vénérable Bède à Saint Albert le Grand." In *Marie et l'Église. Bulletin de la Société Française d'Études Mariales* 9–11, vol. 1, 59–143. Paris: Lethielleux, 1952–1954.

——. *Prières anciennes de l'occident à la Mère du Sauveur: Des origines à saint Anselme*. Paris: Lethielleux, 1963.

Barré, Henri, and J. Deshusses. "A la recherché du Missel d'Alcuin." *Ephemerides Liturgicae* 82 (1968): 1–44.

Bartlett, Robert. *Why Can the Dead Do Such Great Things?: Saints and Worshippers from the Martyrs to the Reformation*. Princeton, N.J.: Princeton University Press, 2013.

Bartos, F. M. "Mariale Servasancti et Mariale Arnesti de Pardubic." *Antonianum* 18 (1943): 175–77.

Battifol, Pierre. *History of the Roman Breviary*. Trans. Atwell M. Y. Baylay, from the third French edition. London: Longmans, Green, 1912.

Baum, Paul Franklin. "The Young Man Betrothed to a Statue." *PMLA* 34 (1909): 523–79.

Bäumer, Remigius, and Leo Scheffczyk, eds. *Marienlexikon*. 6 vols. St. Ottilien: EOS, 1988–1994.

Baumstark, Anton. *Comparative Liturgy*. Rev. Bernard Botte. Trans. F. L. Cross. London: A. R. Mowbray, 1958.

Bayless, Martha. "Humour and the Comic in Anglo-Saxon England." In *Medieval English Comedy*, ed. Sandra M. Hordis and Paul Hardwick, 13–30. Turnhout, Belgium: Brepols, 2007.

Begg, Ean. *The Cult of the Black Virgin*. London: Penguin, 1985.

Beissel, Stephen. *Geschichte der Verehrung Marias in Deutschland während des Mittelalters: Ein Beitrag zur Religionswissenschaft und Kunstgeschichte*. Freiburg im Breisgau: Herdersche Verlagshandlung, 1909.

Belduc, Michelle. "The Poetics of Authorship and Vernacular Religious Devotion." In *Varieties of Devotion in the Middle Ages and the Renaissance*, ed. Susan Karrant Nunn, 125–43. Arizona Studies in the Middle Ages and the Renaissance 7. Turnhout, Belgium: Brepols, 2003.

Bell, Susan Groag. "Medieval Woman Book Owners: Arbiters of Lay Piety and Ambassadors of Culture." In *Women and Power in the Middle Ages*, ed. Mary C. Erler and Maryanne Kowaleski, 149–87. Athens: University of Georgia Press, 1988.

Belting, Hans. *Likeness and Presence: A History of the Image Before the Age of Art*. Trans. Edmund Jephcott. Chicago: University of Chicago Press, 1994.

Benko, Stephen. *The Virgin Goddess: Studies in the Pagan and Christian Roots of Mariology*. Studies in the History of Religions (*Numen* Book Series) 59. Leiden: Brill, 1993.

Bennett, Adelaide. "Devotional Literacy of a Noblewoman in a Book of Hours of ca. 1300 in Cambrai." In *Manuscripts in Transition: Recycling Manuscripts, Texts and Images*, ed. Brigitte Dekeyzer and Jan Van der Stock, 149–57. Paris: Uitgeverij Peeters, 2005.

——. "Making Literate Lay Women Visible: Text and Image in French and Flemish Books of Hours, 1220–1320." In *Thresholds of Medieval Visual Culture: Liminal Spaces*, ed. Elina Gertsman and Jill Stevenson, 125–58. Woodbridge, U.K.: Boydell, 2012.

——. "A Thirteenth-Century French Book of Hours for Marie." *Journal of the Walters Art Gallery* 54 (1996): 21–50.

——. "The Transformation of the Gothic Psalter in Thirteenth-Century France." In *The Illuminated Psalter*, ed. Büttner, 211–21.

Bergamini, Laurie Jones. "From Narrative to Ikon: The Virgin Mary and the Woman of the Apocalypse in Thirteenth Century English Art and Literature." Ph.D. dissertation, University of Connecticut, 1985.

Bestul, Thomas. *Texts of the Passion: Latin Devotional Literature and Medieval Society*. Philadelphia: University of Pennsylvania Press, 1996.

Beumer, Johannes. "Die Mariologie Richards von Saint-Laurent." *Franziskanische Studien* 41 (1959): 19–40.

Biale, David. "The God with Breasts: El Shaddai in the Bible." *History of Religions* 21.3 (1982): 240–56.

Binns, Alison. *Dedications of Monastic Houses in England and Wales, 1066–1216*. Studies in the History of Medieval Religion 1. Woodbridge, U.K.: Boydell, 1989.

Binski, Paul. "The Angel Choir at Lincoln and the Poetics of the Gothic Smile." *Art History* 20.3 (1997): 350–74.

Birzer, Bradley J. *J.R.R. Tolkien's Sanctifying Myth: Understanding Middle-Earth*. Wilmington, Del.: ISI, 2002.

Bishop, Edmund. "On the Origin of the Prymer." In *Liturgica Historica: Papers on the Liturgy and Religious Life of the Western Church*, 211–37. Oxford, U.K.: Clarendon, 1918.

——. "On the Origins of the Feast of the Conception of the Blessed Virgin Mary." In *Liturgica Historica*, 238–59.

Black, Jonathan. "The Divine Office and Private Devotion in the Latin West." In *The Liturgy of the Medieval Church*, ed. Heffernan and Matter, 45–71.

——. "Psalm Uses in Carolingian Prayer Books: Alcuin and the Preface to *De psalmorum usu*." *Mediaeval Studies* 64 (2002): 1–60.

Black, Robert. "The Curriculum of Italian Elementary and Grammar Schools, 1350–1500." In *The Shapes of Knowledge from the Renaissance to the Enlightenment*, ed. Donald R. Kelley and Richard H. Popkin, 137–63. Archives Internationles d'Histoire des Idées/International Archives of the History of Ideas 124. Dordrecht, Netherlands: Kluwer, 1991.

——. "The Vernacular and the Teaching of Latin in Thirteenth and Fourteenth-Century Italy." *Studi Medievali*, 3d ser. 37 (1996): 703–51.

Blum, Owen J. *St. Peter Damian: His Teaching on the Spiritual Life*. Washington, D.C.: Catholic University of America Press, 1947.

Blum, Shirley Nielsen. *The New Art of the Fifteenth Century: Faith and Art in Florence and the Netherlands*. New York: Abbeville, 2015.

Bohatta, Hanns. *Bibliographie der Livres d'Heures (Horae B.M.V.), Officia, Hortuli Animae, Coronae B.M.V., Rosaria und Cursus B.M.V. des XV und XVI Jahrhunderts*. 2d ed. Vienna: Gilhofer and Ranschburg, 1924.

Bonniwell, William R. *A History of the Dominican Liturgy 1215–1945*. 2d ed. New York: Wagner, 1945.

Booton, Diane E. "A Breton Book of Hours for M. de Fontenay, Lady of Chasné." *Scriptorium* 58.2 (2004): 174–201.

Borgeaud, Philippe. *Mother of the Gods: From Cybele to the Virgin Mary*. Trans. Lysa Hochroth. Baltimore, Md.: Johns Hopkins University Press, 2004.

Boss, Sarah Jane. "Black Madonnas." In *Mary: The Complete Resource*, ed. Boss, 458–75.

——. "The Development of the Doctrine of Mary's Immaculate Conception." In *Mary: The Complete Resource*, ed. Boss, 207–35.

——. *Empress and Handmaid: On Nature and Gender in the Cult of the Virgin Mary*. London: Cassell, 2000.

——. *Mary*. New Century Theology. London: Continuum, 2004.

Boss, Sarah Jane, ed. *Mary: The Complete Resource*. London: Continuum, 2007.

Botte, Bernard. "La première fête mariale de la liturgie romaine." *Ephemerides liturgicae* 47 (1933): 425–30.

Bowen, Karen Lee. *Christopher Plantin's Books of Hours: Illustration and Production*. Bibliotheca Bibliographica Neerlandica 32. Nieuwkoop, Netherlands: De Graaf, 1997.

Boyarin, Adrienne Williams. *Miracles of the Virgin in Medieval England: Law and Jewishness in Marian Legends*. Cambridge, U.K.: Brewer, 2010.

Boyle, Leonard, and Pierre-Marie Gy, eds. *Aux origines de la liturgie dominicaine: le manuscrit Santa Sabina XIV L 1*. Documents, études et répertoires 67. Rome: Ecole française de Rome/Paris: CNRS, 2004.

Boynton, Susan. "The Customaries of Bernard and Ulrich as Liturgical Sources." In *From Dead of Night to End of Day: The Medieval Customs of Cluny: Du coeur de la nuit à la fin du jour: les coutumes clunisiennes au Moyen Age*, ed. Susan Boynton and Isabelle Cochelin, 109–30. Disciplina monastica 3. Turnhout, Belgium: Brepols, 2005.

——. "Prayer as a Liturgical Performance in Eleventh- and Twelfth-Century Monastic Psalters." *Speculum* 82 (2007): 896–931.

Boynton, Susan, and Diane J. Reilly, eds. *The Practice of the Bible in the Middle Ages: Production, Reception, and Performance in Western Christianity*. New York: Columbia University Press, 2011.

Braswell, Laura. "Saint Edburga of Winchester: A Study of Her Cult, A.D. 950–1500, with an Edition of the Fourteenth-Century Middle English and Latin Lives." *Mediaeval Studies* 33 (1971): 292–333.

Brayer, Édith. "Section d'ancien français: Livres d'heures contenant des textes en français." *Bulletin d'information de l'institut de recherché et d'histoire des texts* 12 (1963): 31–102.

Brenner, Elma, and Leonie V. Hicks. "The Jews of Rouen in the Eleventh to the Thirteenth Centuries." In *Society and Culture*, ed. Hicks and Brenner, 369–82.

Brett, Edward Tracy. *Humbert of Romans: His Life and Views of Thirteenth Century Society*. Studies and Texts 67. Toronto: Pontifical Institute of Mediaeval Studies, 1984.

Bridgett, T. E. *Our Lady's Dowry; or How England Gained and Lost That Title: A Compilation*. 2d ed. London: Burns and Oates, 1875.

Brown, Peter. *The Body and Society: Men, Women, and Sexual Renunciation in Early Christianity*. New York: Columbia University Press, 1988.

Brubaker, Leslie, and Mary B. Cunningham, eds. *The Cult of the Mother of God in Byzantium: Texts and Images*. Farnham, U.K.: Ashgate, 2011.

Bryan, Jennifer. *Looking Inward: Devotional Reading and the Private Self in Late Medieval England.* Philadelphia: University of Pennsylvania Press, 2008.

Büttner, F. O., ed. *The Illuminated Psalter: Studies in the Content, Purpose and Placement of Its Images.* Turnhout, Belgium: Brepols, 2004.

Bynum, Caroline Walker. "Avoiding the Tyranny of Morphology; or, Why Compare?" *History of Religions* 53 (2014): 341–68.

——. *Christian Materiality: An Essay on Religion in Late Medieval Europe.* New York: Zone, 2011.

——. " 'Crowned with Many Crowns': Nuns and Their Statues in Late-Medieval Wienhausen." *Catholic Historical Review* 101.1 (2015): 18–40.

Caldecott, Stratford. *The Power of the Ring: The Spiritual Vision Behind* The Hobbit *and* The Lord of the Rings. New York: Crossroad, 2012.

Cameron, Averil. "The Cult of the Virgin in Late Antiquity: Religious Development and Myth-Making." In *The Church and Mary*, ed. Swanson, 1–21.

——. "The Theotokos in Sixth-Century Constantinople: A City Finds Its Symbol." *Journal of Theological Studies* n.s. 29.1 (1978): 79–108.

——. "The Virgin's Robe: An Episode in the History of Early Seventh-Century Constantinople." *Byzantion* 49 (1979): 42–56.

Camille, Michael. *The Gothic Idol: Ideology and Image-Making in Medieval Art.* New York: Cambridge University Press, 1989.

Canal, José M. "El oficio parvo de la Virgen de 1000 a 1250." *Ephemerides Mariologicae* 15 (1965): 463–75.

——. "En torno a S. Fulberto de Chartres (†1028): El clamor liturgico 'In spiritu humilitatis.' El oficio parvo mariano." *Ephemerides liturgicae* 80 (1966): 211–25.

——. *Salve Regina misericordiae: Historia y leyendas en torno a esta antífona.* Temi e testi 9. Rome: Edizioni di storia e letteratura, 1963.

Canivez, J. J. "Le rite cistercien." *Ephemerides liturgicae* 63 (1949): 276–311.

Capelle, B. "La fête de la Vierge à Jérusalem au Ve siècle." *Le Muséon* 56 (1943): 1–33.

——. "La liturgie mariale en occident." In *Maria*, ed. du Manoir, I:217–45.

Carlson, Kristofer. *Why Mary Matters: Protestants and the Virgin Mary.* 4th ed. Norfolk, Va.: Dormition, 2014.

Carlton, C. Clark. " 'The Temple That Held God': Byzantine Marian Hymnography and the Christ of Nestorius." *St. Vladimir's Theological Quarterly* 50.1–2 (2006): 99–125.

Carr, Annemarie Weyl. "Threads of Authority: The Virgin Mary's Veil in the Middle Ages." In *Robes and Honor: The Medieval World of Investiture*, ed. Stewart Gordon, 59–93. New York: Palgrave, 2001.

Carroll, Michael P. *The Cult of the Virgin Mary: Psychological Origins.* Princeton, N.J.: Princeton University Press, 1986.

Carruthers, Mary. *The Craft of Thought: Meditation, Rhetoric, and the Making of Images, 400–1200.* Cambridge Studies in Medieval Literature 34. Cambridge: Cambridge University Press, 1998.

——. *The Experience of Beauty in the Middle Ages.* Oxford-Warburg Studies. Oxford: Oxford University Press, 2013.

——. "Sweetness." *Speculum* 81.4 (2006): 999–1013.

Carter, Peter. "The Historical Content of William of Malmesbury's Miracles of the Virgin Mary." In *The Writing of History in the Middle Ages: Essays Presented to Richard William Southern*, ed. R. H. C. Davis and J. M. Wallace-Hadrill, 127–65. Oxford, U.K.: Clarendon, 1981.

Cary, Phillip. *Good News for Anxious Christians: 10 Practical Things You Don't Have to Do.* Grand Rapids, Mich.: Brazos, 2010.

Casey, Michael. *Sacred Reading: The Ancient Art of Lectio Divina.* Ligouri, Mo.: Ligouri/Triumph, 1996.

Catta, Étienne. "Sedes Sapientiae." In *Maria*, ed. du Manoir, VI:689–866.

Cavet, Laurent. "Les Heures de la Vierge: identification liturgique et origine du manuscrit." In *Les manuscrits liturgiques*, ed. Olivier Legendre and Jean-Baptiste Lebigue. *Ædilis, Actes. Séminaires et tables rondes* 9. Paris-Orléans: IRHT, 2005. http://aedilis.irht.cnrs.fr/liturgie/06_2.htm.

Cermann, Regina. *Gebetbücher A-F.* In *Katalog der deutschsprachigen illustrierten Handschriften des Mittelalters*, ed. Hella Frühmorgen-Voss and Norbert H. Ott. Stoffgruppe 43. Bd. 5.1. Munich: In Kommission beim Verlag C. H. Beck, 2014.

Chase, Steven. *The Tree of Life: Models of Christian Prayer.* Grand Rapids, Mich.: Baker Academic, 2005.

Chatillon, Jean. "L'héritage littéraire de Richard de Saint-Laurent." *Revue du moyen age latin* 2.1 (1946): 149–66.

Clanchy, Michael. "The ABC Primer: Was It in Latin or English?" In *Vernacularity in England and Wales, c. 1300–1550*, ed. Elizabeth Salter and Helen Wicker, 17–39. Utrecht Studies in Medieval Literacy 17. Turnhout, Belgium: Brepols, 2011.

——. "Did Mothers Teach Their Children to Read?" In *Motherhood, Religion, and Society in Medieval Europe, 400–1400: Essays Presented to Henrietta Leyser*, ed. Conrad Leyser and Lesley Smith, 129–53. Farnham, U.K.: Ashgate, 2011.

——. "Images of Ladies with Prayer Books: What Do They Signify?" In *The Church and the Book*, ed. R. N. Swanson, 106–22. Studies in Church History 38. Woodbridge, U.K.: Boydell, 2004.

Clark, Anne L. "The Cult of the Virgin Mary and Technologies of Christian Formation in the Later Middle Ages." In *Educating People of Faith: Exploring the History of Jewish and Christian Communities*, ed. John Van Engen, 223–50. Grand Rapids, Mich.: Eerdmans, 2004.

——. "An Uneasy Triangle: Jesus, Mary and Gertrude of Helfta." *Maria: A Journal of Marian Studies* 1 (2000): 37–56.

Clayton, Mary. *The Apocryphal Gospels of Mary in Anglo-Saxon England.* Cambridge Studies in Anglo-Saxon England 26. Cambridge: Cambridge University Press, 1998.

——. *The Cult of the Virgin Mary in Anglo-Saxon England.* Cambridge Studies in Anglo-Saxon England 2. Cambridge: Cambridge University Press, 1990.

——. "Feasts of the Virgin in the Liturgy of the Anglo-Saxon Church." *Anglo-Saxon England* 13 (1984): 209–33.

Coathalem, H. *Le parallelisme entre la Sainte Vierge et l'Eglise dans la tradition latine jusqu'à la fin du XIIe siècle.* Analecta Gregoriana 74, Series Facultatis Theologicae, sectio B, no. 27. Rome: Apud Aedes Universitatis Gregorianae, 1954.

Cochelin, Isabelle. "When Monks Were the Book: The Bible and Monasticism (6th to 11th Centuries)." In *The Practice of the Bible*, ed. Boynton and Reilly, 61–83.

Cohen, Richard I. "The 'Wandering Jew' from Medieval Legend to Modern Metaphor." In *The Art of Being Jewish in Modern Times*, ed. Barbara Kirshenblatt-Gimblett and Jonathan Karp, 147–75. Philadelphia: University of Pennsylvania Press, 2008.

Colahan, Clark. "Mary of Agreda, the Virgin Mary, and Mystical Knowing." *Studia mystica* 3 (1988): 53–65.

——. *The Visions of Sor María de Ágreda: Writing Knowledge and Power.* Tucson: University of Arizona Press, 1994.

Colasanti, Giovanni M. "Il 'De laudibus B.M.V.' di Riccardo da San Lorenzo († c. 1260): Breve studio introduttivo e sintesi dottrinale." *Marianum* 23 (1961): 1–49.

Colish, Marcia L. *Peter Lombard.* 2 vols. Leiden: Brill, 1994.

——. "*Psalterium Scholasticorum*: Peter Lombard and the Emergence of Scholastic Psalms Exegesis." *Speculum* 67.3 (1992): 531–48.

Constable, Giles. "The Concern for Sincerity and Understanding in Liturgical Prayer, Especially in the Twelfth Century." In *Classica et Mediaevalia: Studies in Honor of Joseph Szövérffy*, ed. Irene Vaslef and Helmut Buschhausen, 17–30. Washington, D.C.: Classical Folia Editions, 1986.

——. *The Reformation of the Twelfth Century.* Cambridge: Cambridge University Press, 1998.

Constas, Nicholas. *Proclus of Constantinople and the Cult of the Virgin in Late Antiquity: Homilies 1–5, Texts and Translations.* Supplements to Vigiliae Christianae 66. Leiden: Brill, 2003.

——. "Weaving the Body of God: Proclus of Constantinople, the Theotokos, and the Loom of the Flesh." *Journal of Early Christian Studies* 3.2 (1995): 169–94.

Cooke, Thomas D., with Peter Whiteford and Nancy Mohr McKinley. "Miracles of the Virgin" [under section heading XXIV: "Tales: Pious Tales"]. In *A Manual of Writings in Middle English, 1050–1500*, ed. Albert E. Hartung, 9:3177–258 and 3501–51. New Haven: Connecticut Academy of Arts and Sciences, 1993.

Corbari, Eliana. *Vernacular Theology: Dominican Sermons and Audience in Late Medieval Italy.* Trends in Medieval Philology 22. Berlin: De Gruyter, 2013.

Cothren, Michael W. "The Iconography of Theophilus Windows in the First Half of the Thirteenth Century." *Speculum* 59.2 (1984): 308–41.

Cottier, Jean-François. *Anima mea: Prières privées et textes de dévotion du moyen âge latin. Autour des "Prières ou Méditations" attribuées à Saint Anselme de Cantorbéry (XIe–XIIe siècle).* Recherches sur les Rhétoriques Religieuses 3. Turnhout, Belgium: Brepols, 2001.

Cottier, Jean-François, ed. *La Prière en latin, de l'antiquité au XVIe siècle: Formes, évolutions, significations.* Turnhout, Belgium: Brepols, 2006.

Courtenay, William J. "Magisterial Authority, Philosophical Identity, and the Growth of Marian Devotion: The Seals of the Parisian Masters, 1190–1308." *Speculum* 91.1 (2016): 63–114.

Cramer, Peter. *Baptism and Change in the Early Middle Ages, c. 200–c. 1150.* Cambridge Studies in Medieval Life and Thought, 4th ser. 20. Cambridge: Cambridge University Press, 1993.

Csikszentmihalyi, Mihaly. *Flow: The Psychology of Optimal Experience.* New York: Harper and Row, 1990.

Cullum, Patricia, and Jeremy Goldberg. "How Margaret Blackburn Taught Her Daughters: Reading Devotional Instruction in a Book of Hours." In *Medieval Women: Texts and Contexts in Late Medieval Britain: Essays for Felicity Riddy*, ed. Jocelyn Wogan-Browne, Rosalynn Voaden, Arlyn Diamond, Ann Hutchison, Carol M. Meale, and Lesley Johnson, 217–36. Medieval Women: Texts and Contexts 3. Turnhout, Belgium: Brepols, 2000.

Cunningham, Mary B. "The Use of the *Protevangelium of James* in Eighth-Century Homilies on the Mother of God." In *Cult*, ed. Brubaker and Cunningham, 163–78.

Dacy, Marianne. *The Separation of Early Christianity from Judaism.* Amherst, N.Y.: Cambria, 2010.

Dahood, Mitchell J. "Ancient Semitic Deities in Syria and Palestine." In *Le antiche divinità semitiche*, ed. J. Bottéro, M. J. Dahood, and W. Caskel, 65–94. Studi Semitici 1. Rome: Centro di Studi Semitici, 1958.

——. *Psalms I–III.* 3 vols. Anchor Yale Bible 16, 17, 17A. New Haven: Yale University Press, 1965–1970.

Daley, Brian E., and Paul R. Kolbet, eds. *The Harp of Prophecy: Early Christian Interpretation of the Psalms.* Christianity and Judaism in Antiquity 20. Notre Dame: University of Notre Dame Press, 2015.

Daly, Mary. *Gyn/Ecology: The Metaethics of Radical Feminism.* Boston: Beacon, 1978.

Davis, Michael T. "Canonical Views: The Theophilus Story and the Choir Reliefs at Notre-Dame, Paris." In *Reading Medieval Images: The Art Historian and the Object*, ed. Elizabeth Sears and Thelma K. Thomas, 102–16. Ann Arbor: University of Michigan Press, 2002.

d'Avray, D. L. "Philosophy in Preaching: The Case of a Franciscan Based in Thirteenth-Century Florence (Servasanto da Faenza)." In *Literature and Religion in the Later Middle Ages: Philological Studies in Honor of Siegfried Wenzel*, ed. Richard G. Newhauser and John A. Alford, 263–73. Medieval & Renaissance Texts & Studies 118. Binghamton: Center for Medieval and Early Renaissance Studies, State University of New York at Binghamton, 1995.

——. *The Preaching of the Friars: Sermons Diffused from Paris Before 1300.* Oxford, U.K.: Clarendon, 1985.

Day, John. "Asherah in the Hebrew Bible and Northwest Semitic Literature." *Journal of Biblical Literature* 105.3 (1986): 385–408.

De Beauvoir, Simone. *The Second Sex.* Trans. Constance Borde and Sheila Malovany-Chevallier. New York: Vintage, 2011.

De Bruyne, D. "Les anciennes versions latines du Cantique des Cantiques." *Revue bénédictine* 38 (1926): 97–122.

De Hamel, Christopher. *A History of Illuminated Manuscripts.* 2d ed. London: Phaidon, 1994.

——. "Books of Hours and the Art Market." In *Books of Hours Reconsidered*, ed. Hindman and Marrow, 41–50.

——. "Books of Hours: 'Imaging' the Word." In *The Bible as Book: The Manuscript Tradition*, ed. John L. Sharpe III and Kimberly Van Kampen, 137–43. London: British Library & Oak Knoll Press, in association with The Scriptorium: Center for Christian Antiquities, 1998.

Delaissé, L. M. J. "The Importance of Books of Hours for the History of the Medieval Book." In *Gatherings in Honor of Dorothy E. Miner*, ed. Ursula McCracken, Lilian M. C. Randall, and Richard Randall, 203–25. Baltimore, Md.: Walters Art Gallery, 1974.

De Lubac, Henri. *Exégèse médiévale: Les quatre sens de l'Écriture*. 2 vols. in 4. Théologie: Études publiées sous la direction de la Faculté de Théologie S. J. de Lyon-Fourvière 41.1–2, 42, and 59. Paris: Aubier, 1959–1964. Trans. by Marc Sebanc and E. M. Macierowoski as *Medieval Exegesis: The Four Senses of Scripture*. 3 vols. Ressourcement: Retrieval & Renewal in Catholic Thought. Grand Rapids, Mich.: Eerdmans, 1998–2009.

——. *The Splendour of the Church*. Trans. Michael Mason. London: Sheed and Ward, 1956; reprint, 1979.

Denysenko, Nicholas. "The *Hypapante* Feast in Fourth to Eighth Century Jerusalem." *Studia Liturgica* 37 (2007): 73–97.

Deutsch, Celia M. *Lady Wisdom, Jesus, and the Sages: Metaphor and Social Context in Matthew's Gospel*. Valley Forge, Penn.: Trinity, 1996.

Dever, William G. "Asherah, Consort of Yahweh? New Evidence from Kuntillet 'Ajrûd." *Bulletin of the American Schools of Oriental Research* 255 (1984): 21–37.

——. *Did God Have a Wife? Archeology and Folk Religion in Ancient Israel*. Grand Rapids, Mich.: Eerdmans, 2005.

De Vogüé, Adalbert. "Prayer in the Rule of Saint Benedict." *Monastic Studies* 7 (1969): 113–40.

——. *The Rule of Saint Benedict: A Doctrinal and Spiritual Commentary*. Trans. John Baptist Hasbrouck. Cistercian Studies Series 54. Kalamazoo, Mich.: Cistercian Publications, 1983.

Dillon, Emma. *The Sense of Sound: Musical Meaning in France, 1260–1330*. New Cultural History of Music. New York: Oxford University Press, 2012.

Dijkstra, Meindert. "El, YHWH and Their Asherah: On Continuity and Discontinuity in Canaanite and Ancient Israelite Religion." In *Ugarit: Ein ostmediterranes Kulturzentrum im Alten Orient. Ergebnisse und Perspektiven der Forschung. Band I: Ugarit und seine altorientalische Umwelt*, ed. Manfried Dietrich and Oswald Loretz, 43–73. Münster: Ugarit, 1995.

Donahue, William H. "Mary of Agreda and the Southwest United States." *The Americas* 9.3 (1953): 291–314.

Donavin, Georgiana. *Scribit Mater: Mary and the Language Arts in the Literature of Medieval England*. Washington, D.C.: Catholic University of America Press, 2012.

Dondi, Cristina. "Books of Hours: The Development of the Texts in Printed Form." In *Incunabula and Their Readers: Printing, Selling, and Using Books in the Fifteenth Century*, ed. Kristian Jensen, 53–70. London: British Library, 2003.

Donovan, Claire. *The De Brailes Hours: Shaping the Book of Hours in Thirteenth-Century Oxford*. London: British Library/Toronto: University of Toronto Press, 1991.

Douglas, Sally. *Early Church Understandings of Jesus as the Female Divine: The Scandal of the Scandal of Particularity*. London: Bloomsbury, 2016.

Drigsdahl, Erik. *Hore Beate Marie Virginis—Index to a Selection of Uses*. Copenhagen: Center for Handskriftstudier i Danmark. http://manuscripts.org.uk/ www.chd.dk/use/index.html.

——. *Introduction and Tutorial: Books of Hours*. Copenhagen: Center for Handskriftstudier i Danmark. http://manuscripts.org.uk/ www.chd.dk/tutor/index.html.

——. *New Tests for the Localization of the Hore Beate Marie Virginis*. Copenhagen: Center for Handskriftstudier i Danmark. http://manuscripts.org.uk/ www.chd.dk/use/hv_chdtest.html.

Driscoll, Michael. "The Seven Penitential Psalms: Their Designation and Usages from the Middle Ages Onwards." *Ecclesia Orans* 17 (2000): 153–201.

Druce, G. C. "The Elephant in Medieval Legend and Art." *Archeological Journal* 76 (1919):1–73.

Duffy, Eamon. "Elite and Popular Religion: The Book of Hours and Lay Piety in the Later Middle Ages." In *Elite and Popular Religion: Papers Read at the 2004 Summer Meeting and the 2005 Winter Meeting of the Ecclesiastical History Society*, ed. Kate Cooper and Jeremy Gregory, 140–61. Woodbridge, U.K.: Published for the Ecclesiastical History Society by the Boydell Press, 2006.

——. *Marking the Hours: English People and Their Prayers, 1240–1570*. New Haven: Yale University Press, 2006.

——. *The Stripping of the Altars: Traditional Religion in England, c. 1400–c.1580.* New Haven: Yale University Press, 1992.

Du Manoir, Hubert, ed. *Maria: Études sur la sainte Vierge.* 8 vols. Paris: Beauchesne, 1949–1971.

Dunn, James D. G. "Jesus: Teacher of Wisdom or Wisdom Incarnate?" In *Where Shall Wisdom Be Found? Wisdom in the Bible, the Church, and the Contemporary World,* ed. Stephen C. Barton, 75–92. Edinburgh: Clark, 1999.

Dunn, James D. G., and John W. Rogerson. *Eerdmans Commentary on the Bible.* Grand Rapids, Mich.: Eerdmans, 2003.

Durand, A. "The Holy Hair of Our Lady." *Donahoe's Magazine* 5.1 (1881): 301–10.

Dyer, Joseph. "The Celebration of Candlemas in Medieval Rome." In *Music, Dance and Society: Medieval and Renaissance Studies in Memory of Ingrid G. Brainard,* ed. Ann Buckley and Cynthia J. Cyrus, 37–70. Kalamazoo, Mich.: Medieval Institute Publications, 2011.

Dzon, Mary. "Conflicting Notions of *Pietas* in Walter of Wimborne's *Marie Carmina.*" *Journal of Medieval Latin* 15 (2005): 67–91.

Eastmond, Elizabeth. "Reading Art, Looking at Books, Watching Screens: Learning to Read in a 15th-Century Prayer Book, Learning to Read Today." In *A Book in the Hand: Essays on the History of the Book in New Zealand,* ed. Penny Griffith, Peter Hughes, and Alan Loney, 202–23. Auckland: Auckland University Press, 2000.

Edsall, Mary Agnes. "Learning from the Exemplar: Anselm's *Prayers and Meditations* and the Charismatic Text." *Mediaeval Studies* 72 (2010): 161–96.

Eissfeldt, Otto. "El and Yahweh." *Journal of Semitic Studies* 1.1 (1956): 25–37.

Elkins, Sharon. "Gertrude the Great and the Virgin Mary." *Church History* 66.4 (1997): 720–34.

Ellington, Donna Spivey. *From Sacred Body to Angelic Soul: Understanding Mary in Late Medieval and Early Modern Europe.* Washington, D.C.: Catholic University of America Press, 2001.

Elliott, J. K. "Mary in the Apocryphal New Testament." In *Origins,* ed. Maunder, 57–70.

Ekonomou, Andrew. *Byzantine Rome and the Greek Popes: Eastern Influences on Rome and the Papacy from Gregory the Great to Zacharias, A.D. 590–752.* Lanham, Md..: Lexington, 2007.

Emerton, J. A. "New Light on Israelite Religion: The Implications of the Inscriptions from Kuntillet 'Ajrud." *Zeitschrift für die alttestamentliche Wissenschaft* 94 (1982): 2–20.

Engh, Line Cecilie. *Gendered Identities in Bernard of Clairvaux's "Sermons on the Song of Songs": Performing the Bride.* Europa Sacra 15. Turnhout, Belgium: Brepols, 2014.

Erler, Mary C. "Devotional Literature." In *The Cambridge History of the Book in Britain.* Vol. 3, *1400–1557,* ed. Lotte Hellinga and J. B. Trapp, 495–525. Cambridge: Cambridge University Press, 2008.

Facchini, Ugo. *San Pier Damiani: L'eucologia e le preghiere. Contributo alla storia dell'eucologia medievale. Studio critico e liturgico-teologico.* Bibliotheca "Ephemerides Liturgicae" Subsidia 109. Rome: CLV-Edizioni Liturgiche, 2000.

Fanger, Claire. *Rewriting Magic: An Exegesis of the Visionary Biography of a Fourteenth-Century French Monk.* Magic in History. University Park: Pennsylvania State University Press, 2015.

Farmer, Sharon. "The Leper in the Master Bedroom: Thinking Through a Thirteenth-Century Exemplum." In *Framing the Family: Narrative and Representation in the Medieval and Early Modern Periods,* ed. Rosalynn Voaden and Diane Wolfthal, 79–100. Tempe, Ariz.: Arizona Center for Medieval and Renaissance Studies, 2005.

Fassler, Margot E. "The First Marian Feast in Constantinople and Jerusalem: Chant Texts, Readings, and Homiletic Literature." In *The Study of Medieval Chant: Paths and Bridges, East and West,* ed. Peter Jeffrey, 25–87. Woodbridge, U.K.: Boydell, 2001.

——. *Gothic Song: Victorine Sequences and Augustinian Reform in Twelfth-century Paris.* Cambridge: Cambridge University Press, 1993.

——. "Hildegard and the Dawn Song of Lauds: An Introduction to Benedictine Psalmody." In *Psalms in Community: Jewish and Christian Textual, Liturgical, and Artistic Traditions,* ed. Harold W. Attridge and Margot E. Fassler, 215–39. Symposium Series 25. Atlanta: Society of Biblical Literature, 2003.

——. "The Liturgical Framework of Time and the Representation of History." In *Representing History, 900–1300: Art, Music, History*, ed. Robert A. Maxwell, 149–72. University Park: Pennsylvania State University Press, 2010.

——. "Mary's Nativity, Fulbert of Chartres, and the *Stirps Jesse*: Liturgical Innovation circa 1000 and Its Afterlife." *Speculum* 75.2 (2000): 389–434.

——. "Music and the Miraculous: Mary in the Mid-Thirteenth-Century Dominican Sequence Repertory." In *Aux origines de la liturgie dominicaine*, ed. Boyle and Gy, 229–78.

——. *Music in the Medieval West*. Western Music in Context. New York: Norton, 2014.

——. "Psalms and Prayers in Daily Devotion: A Fifteenth-Century Devotional Anthology from the Diocese of Rheims: Beinecke 757." In *Worship in Medieval and Early Modern Europe: Change and Continuity in Religious Practice*, ed. Karin Maag and John D. Witvliet, 15–40. Notre Dame: University of Notre Dame Press, 2004.

——. *The Virgin of Chartres: Making History Through Liturgy and the Arts*. New Haven: Yale University Press, 2010.

Fassler, Margot E., and Rebecca Baltzer, eds. *The Divine Office in the Latin Middle Ages: Methodology and Source Studies, Regional Developments, Hagiography*. Oxford: Oxford University Press, 2000.

Fedewa, Marilyn H. *María of Ágreda: Mystical Lady in Blue*. Albuquerque: University of New Mexico Press, 2009.

Fehlner, Peter M. "The Predestination of the Virgin Mother and Her Immaculate Conception." In *Mariology*, ed. Miravalle, 213–76.

Feuerbach, Ludwig. *The Essence of Christianity*. Trans. George Eliot. New York: Harper, 1957.

Finnegan, Mary Jeremy. *The Women of Helfta: Scholars and Mystics*. Athens: University of Georgia Press, 1991.

Flory, David. *Marian Representations in the Miracle Tales of Thirteenth-Century Spain and France*. Washington, D.C.: Catholic University of America Press, 2000.

Folda, Jaroslav. "Icon to Altarpiece in the Frankish East: Images of the Virgin and Child Enthroned." In *Italian Panel Painting of the Duecento and Trecento*, ed. Victor M. Schmidt, 123–45. Studies in the History of Art (Washington, D.C.), Symposium Papers 38. Washington, D.C.: National Gallery of Art/New Haven: Yale University Press, 2002.

Forsyth, Ilene H. "Magi and Majesty: A Study of Romanesque Sculpture and Liturgical Drama." *Art Bulletin* 50.3 (1968): 215–22.

——. *The Throne of Wisdom: Wood Sculptures of the Madonna in Romanesque France*. Princeton, N.J.: Princeton University Press, 1972.

Fowler, George B. "The Chronology of the Writings of Engelbert of Admont O.S.B. (ca. 1250–1331)." In *Paradosis: Studies in Memory of Edwin A. Quain*, 121–34. New York: Fordham University Press, 1976.

——. *Intellectual Interests of Engelbert of Admont*. Studies in History, Economics and Public Law 530. New York: Columbia University Press, 1947.

Fracheboud, André. "Cistercian Antecedents of the Rosary." *Cistercian Studies Quarterly* 33.2 (1998): 165–84.

Frank, Robert Worth, Jr. "Miracles of the Virgin, Medieval Anti-Semitism, and the 'Prioress's Tale.'" In *The Wisdom of Poetry: Essays in Early English Literature in Honor of Morton W. Bloomfield*, ed. Larry D. Benson and Siegfried Wenzel, 177–88. Kalamazoo, Mich.: Medieval Institute Publications, 1982.

Franklin-Brown, Mary. *Reading the World: Encyclopedic Writing in the Scholastic Age*. Chicago: University of Chicago Press, 2012.

Freeman, Thomas S. "Offending God: John Foxe and English Protestant Reactions to the Cult of the Virgin." In *The Church and Mary*, ed. Swanson, 228–38.

Frénaud, G. "Le culte de Notre Dame dans l'ancienne liturgie latine." In *Maria*, ed. du Manoir, 6:157–211.

Frey, Winfried. "Maria Legens—Mariam Legere: St. Mary as an Ideal Reader and St. Mary as a Textbook." In *The Book and the Magic of Reading in the Middle Ages*, ed. Albrecht Classen, 277–93. New York: Garland, 1998.

Fries, Albert. "Die unter dem Namen des Albertus Magnus überlieferten mariologischen Schriften." *Beiträge zur Geschichte der Philosophie und Theologie des Mittelalters* 37.4 (1954): 5–80.

Fryer, Alfred C. "Theophilus, the Penitent, as Represented in Art." *Archaeological Journal* 92 (1935): 287–333.

Fulton Brown, Rachel. "Anselm and Praying with the Saints." In *Experiments in Empathy: The Middle Ages*, ed. Karl F. Morrison and Rudolph M. Bell, 92–112. Turnhout, Belgium: Brepols, 2013.

——. "Delight." In *High Medieval: Literary Cultures in England*, ed. Elizabeth M. Tyler and Jocelyn Wogan-Browne. Oxford Twenty-First Century Approaches. Oxford: Oxford University Press, forthcoming.

——. "Exegesis, Mimesis, and the Voice of Christ in Francis of Assisi's *Office of the Passion.*" *Medieval Journal* 4.2 (2014) 39–62.

——. *From Judgment to Passion: Devotion to Christ and the Virgin Mary, 800–1200*. New York: Columbia University Press, 2002.

——. "Hildegard of Bingen's Theology of Revelation." In *From Knowledge to Beatitude: St. Victor, Twelfth-Century Scholars and Beyond. Essays in Honor of Grover A. Zinn*, ed. E. Ann Matter and Lesley Smith, 300–27. Notre Dame: University of Notre Dame Press, 2013.

——. "Mary." In *Christianity in Western Europe c. 1000–c.1500*, ed. Miri Rubin and Walter Simons, 283–96. Cambridge History of Christianity 4. Cambridge: Cambridge University Press, 2009.

——. "Mary in the Scriptures: The Unexpurgated Tradition." The Theotokos Lectures in Theology 7. Milwaukee: Marquette University Press, 2014.

——. "Mimetic Devotion, Marian Exegesis and the Historical Sense of the Song of Songs." *Viator* 27 (1996): 85–116.

——. "My Psalter, My Self; or How to Get a Grip on the Office According to Jan Mombaer: An Exercise in Training the Attention for Prayer," *Spiritus* 12 (2012): 75–105.

——. "Oratio." In *The Cambridge Companion to Christian Mysticism*, ed. Patricia Z. Beckman and Amy Hollywood, 167–77. Cambridge: Cambridge University Press, 2012.

——. "Prayer." In *The Oxford Handbook of Christian Monasticism*, ed. Bernice M. Kaczynski. Oxford: Oxford University Press, forthcoming.

——. "Praying by Numbers." *Studies in Medieval and Renaissance History*, 3rd ser. 4 (2007): 195–250.

——. "Praying with Anselm at Admont: A Meditation on Practice." *Speculum* 81.3 (2006): 700–33.

——. Review of Cynthia Robinson, *Imagining the Passion in a Multiconfessional Castile: The Virgin, Christ, Devotions, and Images in the Fourteenth and Fifteenth Centuries. Speculum* 89.3 (2014): 817–19.

——. " 'Quae est ista quae ascendit sicut aurora consurgens?': The Song of Songs as the *Historia* for the Office of the Assumption." *Mediaeval Studies* 60 (1998): 55–122.

——. " 'Taste and See That the Lord Is Sweet' (Ps. 33:9): The Flavor of God in the Monastic West." *Journal of Religion* 86.2 (2006): 169–204.

——. "Three-in-One: Making God in Twelfth-Century Liturgy, Theology, and Devotion." In *European Transformations: The Long Twelfth Century*, ed. Thomas F. X. Noble and John Van Engen, 468–97. Notre Dame: University of Notre Dame Press, 2012.

——. "The Virgin Mary and the Song of Songs in the High Middle Ages." Ph.D. dissertation, Columbia University, 1994.

——. "What's in a Psalm? British Library, MS Arundel 60 and the Stuff of Prayer." In *Rome and Religion in the Medieval World: Studies in Honor of Thomas F. X. Noble*, ed. Valerie L. Garver and Owen M. Phelan, 235–52. Farnham, U.K.: Ashgate, 2014.

Gadamer, Hans-Georg. *Truth and Method*. 2d rev. ed. Trans. Joel Weinsheimer and Donald G. Marshall. New York: Continuum, 1994.

Galland, China. *Longing for Darkness: Tara and the Black Madonna. A Ten-Year Journey*. New York: Viking Penguin, 1990.

Gambero, Luigi. *Mary in the Middle Ages: The Blessed Virgin Mary in the Thought of Medieval Latin Theologians*. Trans. Thomas Buffer. San Francisco: Ignatius, 2005.

Garber, Rebecca L. R. "Where Is the Body?: Images of Eve and Mary in the *Scivias.*" In *Hildegard of Bingen: A Book of Essays*, ed. Maud Burnett McInerney, 103–32. New York: Garland, 1998.

Gass, Robert, with Kathleen Brehony. *Chanting: Discovering Spirit in Sound*. New York: Broadway, 1999.

Gelfand, Laura D., and Walter S. Gibson. "Surrogate Selves: The *Rolin Madonna* and the Late-Medieval Devotional Portrait." *Simiolus: Netherlands Quarterly for the History of Art* 29.3/4 (2002): 119–38.

Gertsman, Elina. *Worlds Within: Opening the Medieval Shrine Madonna*. University Park: Pennsylvania State University Press, 2015.

Giardini, Fabio. "Unceasing Prayer." *Angelicum* 72.2 (1995): 281–312.

Girotto, Samuele. *Corrado di Sassonia: Predicatore e Mariologico del sec. XIII*. Biblioteca di Studi Francescani 3. Florence: Edizioni "Studi francescani," 1952.

Glorieux, P. *Répertoire des maitres en théologie de Paris au XIIIe siécle*. 2 vols. Paris: J. Vrin, 1933–1934.

Gold, Penny Schine. *The Lady and the Virgin: Image, Attitude, and Experience in Twelfth-Century France*. Women in Culture and Society Series. Chicago: University of Chicago Press, 1985.

Golitzin, Alexander. "The Image and Glory of God in Jacob of Serug's Homily, 'On That Chariot That Ezekiel the Prophet Saw.'" *St. Vladimir's Theological Quarterly* 47:3–4 (2003): 323–64.

Gougaud, Louis. *Dévotions et pratiques ascétiques du Moyen Âge*. Paris: Desclée de Brouwer, 1925.

Graef, Hilda. *Mary: A History of Doctrine and Devotion*. 2 vols. London: Sheed and Ward, 1963, 1965; reprint in one vol., 1985. Reprinted with a new chapter by Thomas A. Thompson on Vatican II and beyond, 401–55. Notre Dame: Ave Maria Press, 2009.

Granger, Penny. "Reading Her Psalter: The Virgin Mary in the N-Town Play." In *Psalms in the Early Modern World*, ed. Linda Phyllis Austern, Kari Boyd McBride, and David L. Orvis, 299–314. Farnham, U.K.: Ashgate, 2011.

Griffiths, Fiona. *The Garden of Delights: Reform and Renaissance for Women in the Twelfth Century*. Philadelphia: University of Pennsylvania Press, 2007.

Gripkey, Mary Vincentine. *The Blessed Virgin Mary as Mediatrix in the Latin and Old French Legend Prior to the Fourteenth Century*. Washington, D.C.: Catholic University of America Press, 1938.

Gros, Gérard. *Ave vierge Marie: Étude sur les prières mariales en vers français, XIIe–XVe siècles*. Lyon: Presses universitaires de Lyon, 2004.

——. "Du sommaire encyclopédique à la compilation mariale: Étude su la moralisation des choses dans le *Rosarius* (Paris, Bibl. nat., fr. 12483)." In *Le divin, discours encyclopédiques: Actes du Colloque de Mortagne-au-Perche, 3–4 avril 1993*, ed. Denis Hüe, 181–200. Cahiers Diderot 6. Caen: Paradigme, 1994.

——. "La *Semblance* de la *verrine*: Description et interprétation d'une image mariale." *Le Moyen Âge* 97 (1991): 217–57.

Gross-Diaz, Theresa. *The Psalms Commentary of Gilbert of Poitiers: From* Lectio Divina *to the Lecture Room*. Leiden: Brill, 1996.

Hadley, Judith M. *The Cult of Asherah in Ancient Israel and Judah: Evidence for a Hebrew Goddess*. Cambridge: Cambridge University Press, 2000.

Haggh, Barbara. "From Auxerre to Soissons: The Earliest History of the Responsory *Gaude, Maria Virgo* in Gautier de Coinci's *Miracles de Nostre Dame*." In *Gautier de Coinci*, ed. Krause and Stones, 167–93.

Hahn, Cynthia. "Reliquaries: Boundaries of Vision." In *Papers from the Symposium Semantics of Vision: Art Production and Visual Cultures in the Middle Ages*, ed. Raphaelè Preisinger. Forthcoming.

Hahn, Scott. *Hail, Holy Queen: The Mother of God in the Word of God*. New York: Doubleday, 2001.

Haimerl, Franz Xavier. *Mittelalterliche Frömmigkeit im Spiegel der Gebetbuchliteratur Süddeutschlands*. Münchener Theologische Studien I: Historische Abteilung 4. Munich: Zink, 1952.

Hamburger, Jeffrey F. "Another Perspective: The Book of Hours in Germany." In *Books of Hours Reconsidered*, ed. Hindman and Marrow, 97–152.

——. "A *Liber precum* in Sélestat and the Development of the Illustrated Prayer Book in Germany." *Art Bulletin* 73 (1991): 206–36.

——. *The Rothschild Canticles: Art and Mysticism in Flanders and the Rhineland Circa 1300*. New Haven: Yale University Press, 1990.

——. "Vision and the Veronica." In *The Visual and the Visionary: Art and Female Spirituality in Late Medieval Germany*, 317–82. New York: Zone, 1998.

Hamburger, Jeffrey F., and Susan Marti, eds. *Crown and Veil: Female Monasticism from the Fifth to the Fifteenth Centuries*. New York: Columbia University Press, 2008.

Hammerling, Roy, ed. *A History of Prayer: The First to the Fifteenth Century*. Brill's Companions to the Christian Tradition. Leiden: Brill, 2008.

Harper, John. *The Forms and Orders of Western Liturgy from the Tenth to the Eighteenth Century: A Historical Introduction and Guide for Students and Musicians*. Oxford, U.K.: Clarendon, 1991.

Harrison, Anna. " 'I Am Wholly Your Own': Liturgical Piety and Community Among the Nuns of Helfta." *Church History* 78.3 (2009): 549–83.

——. " 'Oh! What Treasure Is in This Book?' Writing, Reading, and Community at the Monastery of Helfta." *Viator* 39.1 (2008): 75–106.

Harrison, Anna, and Caroline Walker Bynum. "Gertrude, Gender and the Composition of the *Herald of Divine Love*." In *Freiheit des Herzens: Mystik bei Gertrud von Helfta*, ed. Michael Bangert, *Mystik und Mediävistik*, 2:57–76. Münster: Lit, 2004.

Harrsen, Meta. *Cursus Sanctae Mariae: A Thirteenth-century manuscript, now M. 739 in the Pierpont Morgan Library, probably executed in the Premonstratensian monastery of Louka in Moravia, at the instance of the Margravine Kunegund, for presentation to her niece, Saint Agnes*. New York: Pierpont Morgan Library, 1937.

Harthan, John. *Books of Hours and Their Owners*. London: Thames and Hudson, 1977.

Harvey, P. D. A. *Mappa Mundi: The Hereford World Map*. 2d ed. Hereford: Hereford Cathedral, 2002.

Hazelton, Lesley. *Mary: A Flesh-and-Blood Biography of the Virgin Mother*. New York: Bloomsbury, 2004.

Healy, Patrick. *The Chronicle of Hugh of Flavigny: Reform and the Investiture Contest in the Late Eleventh Century*. Aldershot, U.K.: Ashgate, 2006.

Heffernan, Thomas J., and E. Ann Matter, eds. *The Liturgy of the Medieval Church*. 2d ed. Kalamazoo, Mich.: Medieval Institute Publications, Western Michigan University, 2005.

Heiler, Friedrich. *Prayer: A Study in the History and Psychology of Religion*. Oxford: Oxford University Press, 1932.

Henry, W. "Angelus." *Dictionnaire d'archéologie chrétienne et de liturgie* 1.2 (1907): 2068–78.

Hermann, H. J. *Die italienischen Handschriften des Dugento und Trecento. Teil 2: Oberitalienische Handschriften der zweiten Hälfte des 14. Jahrhunderts*. Leipzig: Hiersemann, 1929.

Herren, Michael W., with Shirley Ann Brown, eds. *The Sacred Nectar of the Greeks: The Study of Greek in the West in the Early Middle Ages*. King's College London Medieval Studies 2. London: King's College, 1988.

Hickerson, Nancy P. "The Visits of the 'Lady in Blue': An Episode in the History of the South Plains, 1629." *Journal of Anthropological Research* 46.1 (1990): 67–90.

Hicks, Leonie V., and Elma Brenner, eds. *Society and Culture in Medieval Rouen, 911–1300*. Studies in the Early Middle Ages 39. Turnhout, Belgium: Brepols, 2013.

Higgit, John. *The Murthly Hours: Devotion, Literacy and Luxury in Paris, England and the Gaelic West*. London, British Library; Toronto: University of Toronto Press, 2000.

Hiley, David. *Western Plainchant: A Handbook*. Oxford: Oxford University Press, 1993.

Hindman, Sandra. "Introduction: Books of Hours—State of the Research. In Memory of L. M. J. Delaissé." In *Books of Hours Reconsidered*, ed. Hindman and Marrow, 5–16.

Hindman, Sandra, and James H. Marrow, eds. *Books of Hours Reconsidered*. Studies in Medieval and Early Renaissance Art History. Turnhout, Belgium: Brepols/Harvey Miller, 2013.

Holladay, Joan A. "The Education of Jeanne d'Evreux: Personal Piety and Dynastic Salvation in Her Book of Hours at the Cloisters." *Art History* 17.4 (1994): 585–611.

Holladay, William L. *The Psalms Through Three Thousand Years: Prayerbook of a Cloud of Witnesses*. Minneapolis, Minn.: Fortress, 1993.

Hollywood, Amy. *Acute Melancholia and Other Essays: Mysticism, History, and the Study of Religion*. New York: Columbia University Press, 2016.

Holsinger, Bruce. *Music, Body, and Desire in Medieval Culture: Hildegard of Bingen to Chaucer*. Stanford: Stanford University Press, 2001.

Hoornert, Rodolphe. "La plus ancienne règle du Béguinage de Bruges." *Annales de la Société d'Émulation de Bruges* 72 (1930): 1–79.

Hoskins, Edgar. *Horae Beatae Mariae Virginis, or, Sarum and York Primers with Kindred Books, and Primers of the Reformed Use, Together with an Introduction.* London: Longmans Green, 1901.

Hughes, Jonathan. *The Religious Life of Richard III: Piety and Prayer in the North of England.* Thrupp, Stroud: Sutton, 1997.

Huglo, Michel. "L'ancienne version latine de l'hymne acathiste." *Le Muséon* 64 (1951): 27–61.

Hurtado, Larry W. *Lord Jesus Christ: Devotion to Jesus in Earliest Christianity.* Grand Rapids, Mich.: Eerdmans, 2003.

——. *One God, One Lord: Early Christian Devotion and Ancient Jewish Monotheism.* 2d ed. London: Continuum, 1998.

Hyma, Albert. "The 'De libris teutonicalibus' by Gerard Zerbolt of Zutphen." *Nederlandsch Archief voor Kerkegeschiednis* n.s. 17 (1924): 42–70.

——. "Het traktaat 'Super modo Vivendi devotorum hominum simul commorantium' door Gerard Zerbolt van Zutphen." *Archief voor de geschiedenis van het Aartsbisdom Utrecht* 52 (1926): 1–100.

Ihnat, Kati. "Getting the Punchline: Deciphering Anti-Jewish Humour in Anglo-Norman England." *Journal of Medieval History* 38.4 (2012): 408–23.

——. "Marian Miracles and Marian Liturgies in the Benedictine Tradition of Post-Conquest England." In *Contextualizing Miracles in the Christian West: New Historical Approaches*, ed. Matthew M. Mesley and Louise E. Wilson, 63–97. Medium Aevum Monographs n.s. 32. Oxford: Society for the Study of Medieval Languages and Literatures, 2014.

——. *Mother of Mercy, Bane of the Jews: Devotion to the Virgin Mary in Anglo-Norman England.* Princeton, N.J.: Princeton University Press, 2016.

Iogna-Prat, Dominique, Éric Palazzo, and Daniel Russo, eds. *Marie: Le culte de la Vierge dans la société médiévale.* Paris: Beauchesne, 1996.

Izbicki, Thomas M. "The Immaculate Conception and Ecclesiastical Politics from the Council of Basel to the Council of Trent: The Dominicans and Their Foes." In *Reform, Ecclesiology, and the Christian Life in the Late Middle Ages*, 4:145–70. Aldershot, U.K.: Ashgate, 2008.

Jacobs, Alan. *The Book of Common Prayer: A Biography.* Lives of Great Religious Books. Princeton, N.J.: Princeton University Press, 2013.

Jacobsson, Ritva. "The Antiphoner of Compiègne: Paris, BNF lat. 17436." In *The Divine Office*, ed. Fassler and Baltzer, 147–78.

James, Montague Rhodes. *On the Abbey of S. Edmund at Bury. I, The Library. II, The Church.* Cambridge: Cambridge Antiquarian Society, 1895.

James, William. *The Varieties of Religious Experience: A Study in Human Nature.* Ed. with introduction by Martin E. Marty. Harmondsworth: Penguin, 1982.

Jaye, Barbara. *Artes Orandi.* Typologie des sources du moyen âge occidental 61.2. Turnhout, Belgium: Brepols, 1992.

Jennings, J. C. "The Origins of the 'Elements Series' of the Miracles of the Virgin." *Mediaeval and Renaissance Studies* 6 (1968): 84–93.

Johnson, Mark. *The Body in the Mind: The Bodily Basis of Meaning, Imagination, and Reason.* Chicago: University of Chicago Press, 1987.

Johnson, Trevor. "Mary in Early Modern Europe." In *Mary: The Complete Resource*, ed. Boss, 363–84.

Jugie, Martin. *L'Immaculée conception dans l'écriture sainte et dans la tradition orientale.* Bibliotheca Immaculatae Conceptionis, Textes et Disquisitiones. Collectio edita cura Academiae Marianae Internationalis 3. Rome: Academia Mariana and Officium Libri Catholici, 1952.

Jung, Jacqueline E. "Crystalline Wombs and Pregnant Hearts: The Exuberant Bodies of the Katharinenthal Visitation Group." In *History in the Comic Mode: Medieval Communities and the Matter of Person*, ed. Rachel Fulton [Brown] and Bruce W. Holsinger, 223–37. New York: Columbia University Press, 2007.

——. "The Tactile and the Visionary: Notes on the Place of Sculpture in Medieval Religious Imagination." In *Looking Beyond: Visions, Dreams, and Insights in Medieval Art and History*, ed. Colum Hourihane, 203–40. Princeton, N.J.: Index of Christian Art, 2010.

Kaegi, Walter E. *Heraclius, Emperor of Byzantium*. Cambridge: Cambridge University Press, 2003.

Kaeppeli, Thomas. *Scriptores Ordinis Praedicatorum Medii Aevi*. 4 vols. Rome: Instituto storico Dominicano, 1970–1993.

Kamerick, Kathleen. "Patronage and Devotion in the Prayer Book of Anne of Brittany, Newberry Library MS 83." *Manuscripta* 39.1 (1995): 40–50.

——. *Popular Piety and Art in the Late Middle Ages: Image Worship and Idolatry in England, 1350–1500*. New York: Palgrave, 2002.

Kampen, John. *Wisdom Literature*. Grand Rapids, Mich.: Eerdmans, 2011.

Karnes, Michelle. *Imagination, Meditation and Cognition in the Middle Ages*. Chicago: University of Chicago Press, 2011.

Katzenellenbogen, Adolf. *The Sculptural Programs of Chartres Cathedral: Christ-Mary-Ecclesia*. Baltimore, Md.: Johns Hopkins University Press, 1959.

Keck, David. *Angels and Angelology in the Middle Ages*. Oxford: Oxford University Press, 1998.

Keefe, Susan A. *Water and the Word: Baptism and the Education of the Clergy in the Carolingian Empire*. 2 vols. Notre Dame: University of Notre Dame Press, 2002.

Keller, John Esten, and Annette Grant Cash. *Daily Life Depicted in the "Cantigas de Santa Maria."* Lexington: University Press of Kentucky, 1998 [2015].

Kendrick, T. D. *Mary of Ágreda: The Life and Legend of a Spanish Nun*. London: Routledge and Kegan Paul, 1967.

Kennedy, Kathleen E. "Reintroducing the English Books of Hours, or 'English Primers.' " *Speculum* 89.3 (2014): 693–723.

Ker, N. R. *Catalogue of Manuscripts Containing Anglo-Saxon*. Oxford, U.K.: Clarendon, 1957.

Kessell, John L. "Miracles or Mystery: María de Ágreda's Ministry to the Jumanos Indians of the Southwest in the 1620s." In *Great Mysteries of the West*, ed. Ferenc Morton Szasz, 121–44. Golden, CO: Fulcrum, 1993.

Kirk, Kenneth E. *The Vision of God: The Christian Doctrine of the Summum Bonum*. Bampton Lectures 1928. 2d ed. London: Longmans Green, 1932.

Kirwin, P. George F. "The Sermons of Saint Bonaventure on Mary and Their Relationship to the Cult of Mary." In *De cultu mariano saeculis XII–XV: Acta Congressus Marianologici-Mariani Internationalis Romae anno 1975 celebrati*. Vol. 4, *De cultu mariano apud scriptores ecclesiasticos saec. XII–XIII*, 447–65. Rome: Pontificia academia Mariana internationalis, 1979.

Klemm, Elisabeth. "Das sogenannte Gebetbuch der Hildegard von Bingen." *Jahrbuch der Kunsthistorischen Sammlungen in Wien* 74 (1978): 29–78.

Kline, Naomi Reed. *Maps of Medieval Thought: The Hereford Paradigm*. Woodbridge, U.K.: Boydell, 2001.

Knowles, David. "The Monastic Horarium 970–1120." *Downside Review* 51 (1933): 706–25.

Koehler, Théodore. "Onze manuscrits du 'Mariale' de Servasanctus de Faenza, OFM (d. ca. 1300)." *Archivum Franciscanum Historicum* 83:1–2 (1990): 96–117.

——. "Une liste d'*Ave* en l'honneur de la Vierge Marie: 24 titres empruntés à l'éloge de la Sagesse." *Revue française d'histoire du livre* 61:74–75 (1992): 5–22.

Kolping, Adolf. "Zur Frage der Textgeschichte, Herkunft und Entstehungszeit der anonymen 'Laus Virginis' (bisher *Mariale* Alberts des Grossen)." *Recherches de Théologie ancienne et médiévale* 25 (1958): 285–328.

Koppelman, Kate. "Devotional Ambivalence: The Virgin Mary as 'Empresse of Helle.' " *Essays in Medieval Studies* 18 (2001): 67–82.

Korosak, Bruno. *Mariologia S. Alberti Magni eiusque coaequalium*. Bibliotheca Mariana Medii Aevi: Textus et Disquisitiones 8. Rome: Academia Mariana Internationalis, 1954.

Kort, Wesley. *"Take, Read": Scripture, Textuality, and Cultural Practice*. University Park, PA: Pennsylvania State University Press, 1996.

Korteweg, Anne S. "Books of Hours from the Northern Netherlands Reconsidered: The Uses of Utrecht and Windesheim and Geert Grote's Role as a Translator." In *Books of Hours Reconsidered*, ed. Hindman and Marrow, 235–61.

Krass, Andreas. " 'Ave Maris Stella' und 'Ave Praeclara Maris Stella' in einem deutschen Mariengebetbuch." *Zeitschrift für deutsches Altertum und deutsche Literatur* 140 (2011): 190–99.

Krause, Kathy M., and Alison Stones, eds. *Gautier de Coinci: Miracles, Music and Manuscripts*. Medieval Texts and Cultures of Northern Europe 13. Turnhout, Belgium: Brepols, 2006.

Kreitzer, Beth. *Reforming Mary: Changing Images of the Virgin Mary in Lutheran Sermons of the Sixteenth Century*. Oxford Studies in Historical Theology. Oxford: Oxford University Press, 2004.

Kuczynski, Michael P. *Prophetic Song: The Psalms as Moral Discourse in Late Medieval England*. Philadelphia: University of Pennsylvania Press, 1995.

Kugler, Hartmut. *Die Ebstorfer Weltkarte*. 2 vols. Berlin: Akademie, 2007.

Kumler, Aden. *Translating Truth: Ambitious Images and Religious Knowledge in Late Medieval England and France*. New Haven: Yale University Press, 2011.

Kunstmann, Pierre. "Vertus et propriétés de la Vierge dans le Bestiaire, le Lapidaire et le Plantaire du *Rosarius* (BNF fr. 12483, ms. du xiv s.)." *Le moyen français* 55–56 (2004): 205–217.

Kupfer, Marcia. *Art and Optics in the Hereford Map: An English Mappa Mundi, c 1300*. New Have: Published for the Paul Mellon Centre for Studies in British Art, by Yale University Press, 2016.

——. "Medieval World Maps: Embedded Images, Interpretive Frames." *Word & Image* 10.3 (1994): 262–88.

——. "Reflections in the Ebstorf Map: Cartography, Theology and *dilectio speculationes*." In *Medieval Geographies: Cartography and Geographical Thought in the Latin West and Beyond: 300–1600*, ed. Keith D. Lilley, 100–26. Cambridge: Cambridge University Press, 2013.

Labarre, Albert. "Heures (Livres d'Heures)." DSAM 7.1 (1969): 410–31.

Lacombe, Paul. *Livres d'heures imprimés au XVe et au XVIe siècle conservés dans les bibliothèques publiques de Paris*. Paris: Imprimerie nationale, 1907.

Lapostelle, Christine. "Images et apparitions: Illustrations des 'Miracles de Nostre Dame.' " *Médiévales* 2 (1982): 47–66.

Larson, Atria A. "Passive Instrument and Active Intercessor: Anselm's View of Mary's Role in Redemption." *Cistercian Studies Quarterly* 41.1 (2006): 31–50.

Laurenceau, Jean. "Les debuts de la recitation privee de l'antienne 'Ave Maria' en occident avant la fin du XIe siècle." In *De cultu mariano saeculis VI–XI: Acta Congressus Mariologici Mariani Internationalis in Croatia anno 1971 celebrati*, 2:231–46. 5 vols. Rome: Pontificia Academia Mariana Internationalis, 1972.

Laurentin, René. *Court Traité de théologie Mariale*. 4th ed. Paris: Lethielleux, 1959.

Lausberg, Heinrich. *Der Hymnus "Ave maris stella."* Abhandlungen der Rheinisch-Westfälischen Akademie der Wissenschaften 61. Opladen: Westdeutscher, 1976.

Law, Timothy Michael. *When God Spoke Greek: The Septuagint and the Making of the Christian Bible*. Oxford: Oxford University Press, 2013.

Lazar, Moshe. "Theophilus: Servant of Two Masters. The Pre-Faustian Theme of Despair and Revolt." *Modern Language Notes* 87.6 (1972): 31–50.

Lechner, Gregor Martin. *Maria Gravida: Zum Schwangerschaftsmotiv in der bildenden Kunst*. Münchner kunsthistorische Abhandlungen 9. Munich: Schnell und Steiner, 1981.

Leclercq, Henri. "Marie (Je vous salue)." DACL 10:2043–62.

Leclercq, Jean. "Culte liturgique et prière intime dans le monachisme au moyen âge." *La Maison-Dieu* 69 (1962): 39–55.

——. *The Love of Learning and the Desire for God: A Study of Monastic Culture*. Trans. Catherine Misrahi. 3rd ed. New York: Fordham University Press, 1982.

——. "La vie et la prière des chevaliers de Santiago d'après leur règle primitive." *Liturgia II: Scripta et documenta* 10 (Montserrat, 1958): 347–57.

Ledit, Joseph. *Marie dans la Liturgie de Byzance*. Théologie historique 39. Paris: Beauchesne, 1976.

Ledoyen, Henri. "La *Regula Cassiani* du CLM 28118 et La Règle Anonyme de L'Escorial A.I.13." *Revue Bénédictine* 94 (1984): 154–94.

Lee, Bernard J. *Jesus and the Metaphors of God: The Christs of the New Testament*. Conversation on the Road Not Taken 2. New York: Paulist Press, 1993.

Leithart, Peter J. "Like the Tents of Kedar." *First Things* 1.7.12. www.firstthings.com/blogs/leithart/2012/01 /like-the-tents-of-kedar.

Leroquais, Victor. *Les livres d'heures manuscrits de la Bibilothèque nationale*. 3 vols. and supplement. Paris and Macon: Protat Frères, 1927–1933.

Leonick, Daniel R.. *Preaching in Medieval Florence: The Social World of Franciscan and Dominican Spirituality*. Athens: University of Georgia Press, 1989.

Levin, Saul. *The Father of Joshua/Jesus*. Binghamton, N.Y.: State University of New York, 1978.

Lewis, C. S. "Meditation in a Toolshed." Originally published in *The Coventry Evening Telegraph* (17 July 17 1945); reprinted in *Essay Collection and Other Short Pieces*, ed. Lesley Walmsley, 607–10. London: HarperCollins, 2000.

Lexikon der Marienkunde. Ed. Konrad Algermissen, Ludwig Böer, Georg Englhardt, Carl Feckes, Michael Schmaus, and Julius Tyciak. 8 parts in 1 vol. Regensburg: Pustet, 1957–1967.

Limberis, Vasiliki. *Divine Heiress: The Virgin Mary and the Creation of Constantinople*. London: Routledge, 1994.

Linn, Irving. "If All the Sky Were Parchment." *Publications of the Modern Language Association (PMLA)* 53 (1938): 951–70.

Llamas, Enrique. "Mary, Mother and Model of the Church." In *Mariology*, ed. Miravalle, 551–604.

Lloyd, Joan Barclay. "Mary, Queen of the Angels: Byzantine and Roman Images of the *Virgin and Child Enthroned with Attendant Angels*." *Melbourne Art Journal* 5 (2001): 5–24.

Lobrichon, Guy. "La Femme d'Apocalypse 12 dans l'exégèse du haut Moyen Age latin (760–1200)." In *Marie*, ed. Iogna-Prat et al., 407–39.

Louth, Andrew. "John of Damascus on the Mother of God as a Link Between Humanity and God." In *Cult of the Mother of God*, ed. Brubaker and Cunningham, 153–61.

Luhrmann, T. M. *When God Talks Back: Understanding the American Evangelical Relationship to God*. New York: Vintage, 2012.

Maas, Anthony. "The Name of Mary." *The Catholic Encyclopedia*. Vol. 15. New York: Appleton, 1912. www .newadvent.org/cathen/15464a.htm.

MacLean, Katie. "María de Ágreda, Spanish Mysticism, and the Work of Spiritual Conquest." *Colonial Latin American Review* 17:1 (2008): 29–48.

MacCullough, Diarmaid. "Mary and Sixteenth-Century Protestants." In *The Church and Mary*, ed. Swanson, 191–217.

MacGregor, Alistair. "Candlemas: A Festival of Roman Origin." In *Origins*, ed. Maunder, 137–53.

Madan, Falconer. "Hours of the Virgin Mary (Tests for Localization)." *Bodleian Quarterly Record* 3 (1920): 40–44. Updated in "The Localization of Manuscripts," in *Essays in History Presented to Reginald Poole*, ed. H. W. C. Davis, 5–29. Oxford, U.K.: Clarendon, 1927.

Maguire, Henry. "Body, Clothing, Metaphor: The Virgin in Early Byzantine Art." In *Cult of the Mother of God*, ed. Brubaker and Cunningham, 39–51.

Maître, Claire. "Du culte marial à la célébration des vierges: À propos de la psalmodie de matins." In *Marie: Le culte de la Vierge*, ed. Iogna-Prat et al., 45–63.

Manelli, Settimio M. "The Virgin Mary in the New Testament." In *Mariology*, ed. Miravalle, 47–119.

Manelli, Stefano. "The Mystery of the Blessed Virgin Mary in the Old Testament." In *Mariology*, ed. Miravalle, 1–46.

Marrow, James H. "Notes on the Liturgical 'Use' of the Hours of the Virgin in the Low Countries." In *Manuscript en miniature: Studies aangeboden an Anne S. Korteweg*, ed. Jos Biemans, Klass van der Hoek, Kathryn M. Rudy, and Ed van der Vlist, 279–94. Zuphen: Walburg, 2007.

Martínez, Florentino García. *The Dead Sea Scrolls Translated: The Qumram Texts in English*. 2d ed. Trans. Wilfred G. E. Watson. Grand Rapids, Mich.: Eerdmans, 1996.

Masini, Mario. *Il lezionario mariano: Commento esegetico e pastorale del lezionario liturgico*. Brescia: Queriniana, 1975.

Matter, E. Ann. *The Voice of My Beloved: The Song of Songs in Western Medieval Christianity*. Philadelphia: University of Pennsylvania Press, 1990.

Maunder, Chris, ed. *The Origins of the Cult of the Virgin Mary*. London: Burns and Oates, 2008.

Maunder, Chris. "Origins of the Cult of the Virgin Mary in the New Testament." In *Origins*, ed. Maunder, 23–39.

Mayberry, Nancy. "The Controversy Over the Immaculate Conception in Medieval and Renaissance Art, Literature, and Society." *Journal of Medieval and Renaissance Studies* 21.1 (1991): 207–24.

Mayr-Harting, Henry. *Ottonian Book Illumination: An Historical Study*. 2d ed. 2 vols. in 1. London: Harvey Miller, 1999.

——. "Praying the Psalter in Carolingian Times: What Was Supposed to Be Going on in the Minds of Monks." In *Prayer and Thought in Monastic Tradition: Essays in Honour of Benedicta Ward SLG*, ed. Santha Bhattacharji, Rowan Williams, and Dominic Mattos, 77–100. London: Bloomsbury, 2014.

McCormick, Michael. *Origins of the European Economy: Communications and Commerce, A.D. 300–900*. New York: Cambridge University Press, 2001.

McInerney, Ralph. *Dante and the Blessed Virgin*. Notre Dame: University of Notre Dame Press, 2010.

McKinnon, James W. "The Fifteen Temple Steps and the Gradual Psalms." In *The Temple, Church Fathers, and Early Western Chant*, Essay 16:29–59. Aldershot, U.K.: Ashgate, 1998.

——. "The Origins of the Western Office." In *The Divine Office in the Latin Middle Ages*, ed. Fassler and Baltzer, 63–73.

McNamer, Sarah. *Affective Meditation and the Invention of Medieval Compassion*. Philadelphia: University of Pennsylvania Press, 2009.

——. "The Origins of the *Meditationes Vitae Christi*." *Speculum* 84 (2009): 905–55.

——. "Reading the Literature of Compassion: A Study in the History of Feeling." Ph.D. dissertation, Harvard University, 1998.

Meersseman, G[illes] G[érard], ed. *Dossier de l'ordre de la Pénitence au xiiie siècle*. SF 7. Freiburg: Universitätsverlag, 1961.

——. "Les Congrégations de la Vierge (Études sur les anciennes confréries dominicaines III)." *Archivum Fratrum Praedicatorum* 22 (1952): 5–176.

——. "Les frères prêcheurs et le mouvement dèvot en Flandre au XIIIe s." *Archivum Fratrum Praedicatorum* 18 (1948): 69–130.

——. *Der Hymnos Akathistos im Abendland*. 2 vols. SF 2–3. Freiburg: Universitätsverlag, 1958–1960.

——. "La predication dominicaine dans les congrégations mariales en Italie au XIIIe siècle." *Archivum Fratrum Praedicatorum* 18 (1948): 131–61.

——. " 'Virgo a doctoribus praetitulata': Die marianischen Litaneien als dogmengeschichtliche Quellen." *Freiburger Zeitschrift für Philosophie und Theologie* 1 (1954): 129–78.

Menken, Maarten J. J. "The Psalms in Matthew's Gospel." In *Psalms*, ed. Moyise and Menken, 61–82.

Meshel, Ze'ev. "Did Yahweh Have a Consort? The New Religious Inscriptions from the Sinai." *Biblical Archeological Review* 5 (1979): 24–35.

Mews, Constant, ed. *Listen Daughter: The Speculum Virginum and the Formation of Religious Women in the Middle Ages*. New York: Palgrave, 2001.

Milbank, Alison. *Chesterton and Tolkien as Theologians: The Fantasy of the Real*. London: Clark, 2007.

Mildner, F. M. "The Immaculate Conception in England up to the Time of John Duns Scotus." *Marianum* 1 (1939): 86–99, 200–221; and 3 (1940): 284–306.

Miles, Laura Saetveit. "Mary's Book: The Annunciation in Medieval England." Ph.D. dissertation, Yale University, 2012.

——. "The Origins and Development of the Virgin Mary's Book at the Annunciation." *Speculum* 89.3 (2014): 632–69.

Miller, John D. *Beads and Prayers: The Rosary in History and Devotion.* London: Burns & Oates, 2001.

Miller, Konrad. *Die Ebstorfkarte: Eine Weltkarte aus dem 13. Jahrhundert.* Stuttgart: J. Roth, 1900.

Miller, Patrick D. *The Religion of Ancient Israel.* London: SPCK, 2000.

Millett, Bella. "*Ancrene Wisse* and the Book of Hours." In *Writing Religious Women: Female Spiritual and Textual Practices in Late Medieval England,* ed. Denis Renevey and Christiana Whitehead, 21–40. Toronto: University of Toronto Press, 2000.

——. "The Origins of *Ancrene Wisse:* New Answers, New Questions." *Medium Aevum* 61.2 (1992): 206–28.

Minnis, A. J., and A. B. Scott, with David Wallace. *Medieval Literary Theory and Criticism c. 1100–c. 1375: The Commentary Tradition.* Rev. ed. Oxford, U.K.: Clarendon, 1988.

Miravalle, Mark, ed. *Mariology: A Guide for Priests, Deacons, Seminarians, and Consecrated Persons.* Goleta, Calif.: Seat of Wisdom Books, Queenship, 2007.

Mitchell, Nathan D. "The Liturgical Code in the Rule of St. Benedict," in *RB 1980,* ed. Fry, 379–414.

——. *The Mystery of the Rosary: Marian Devotion and the Reinvention of Catholicism.* New York: New York University Press, 2009.

Moore, Stephen D., and Yvonne Sherwood. *The Invention of the Biblical Scholar: A Critical Manifesto.* Minneapolis, Minn.: Fortress, 2011.

Moreau, Brigitte. *Inventaire chronologique des editions Parisiennes du XVIe siècle . . . d'après les manuscrits de Philippe Renouard.* 4 vols. (for the years 1501–1535). Paris: Service des travaux historiques de la ville de Paris, 1972–.

Morgan, Nigel. "English Books of Hours, c. 1240–c.1480." In *Books of Hours Reconsidered,* ed. Hindman and Marrow, 65–95.

——. "Marian Liturgy in Salisbury Cathedral." In *The Medieval English Cathedral: Papers in Honour of Pamela Tudor-Craig. Proceedings of the 1998 Harlaxton Symposium,* ed. Janet Backhouse, 89–111. Donington, U.K.: Shaun Tyas, 2003.

——. "Patrons and Their Devotions in the Historiated Initials and Full-Page Miniatures of 13th-Century English Psalters." In *The Illuminated Psalter,* ed. Büttner, 309–22.

——. "Texts and Images of Marian Devotion in English Twelfth-Century Monasticism, and Their Influence on the Secular Church." In *Monasteries and Society in Medieval Britain: Proceedings of the 1994 Harlaxton Symposium,* ed. Benjamin Thompson, 117–36. Stamford, U.K.: Paul Watkins, 1999.

——. "Texts and Images of Marian Devotion in Fourteenth-Century England." In *England in the Fourteenth Century: Proceedings of the 1991 Harlaxton Symposium,* ed. Nicholas Rogers, 30–53. Stamford, U.K.: Paul Watkins, 1993.

——. "Texts and Images of Marian Devotion in Thirteenth-Century England." In *England in the Thirteenth Century: Proceedings of the 1989 Harlaxton Symposium,* ed. W. M. Ormrod, 69–104. Stamford, U.K.: Paul Watkins, 1991.

Morgenstern, Julian. "The Cultic Setting of the 'Enthronement Psalms.'" *Hebrew Union College Annual* 35 (1964): 1–42.

Morrison, Karl F. "The Church as Play: Gerhoch of Reichersberg's Call for Reform." In *Popes, Teachers, and Canon Law in the Middle Ages,* ed. James Ross Sweeney and Stanley Chodorow, 114–44. Ithaca, N.Y.: Cornell University Press, 1989.

——. "Henry Adams (1838–1918)." In *Medieval Scholarship: Biographical Studies on the Formation of a Discipline,* ed. Helen Damico and Joseph B. Zavadil, 1:115–30. New York: Garland, 1995.

——. "Incentives for Studying the Liberal Arts." In *The Seven Liberal Arts in the Middle Ages,* ed. David L. Wagner, 32–57. Bloomington: Indiana University Press, 1983.

Mossman, Stephen. *Marquard von Lindau and the Challenges of Religious Life in Late Medieval Germany: The Passion, the Eucharist, the Virgin Mary.* Oxford: Oxford University Press, 2010.

Mowinckel, Sigmund. *The Psalms in Israel's Worship.* Trans. D. R. Ap-Thomas. 2 vols. in 1. Grand Rapids, Mich.: Eerdmans, 2004.

Moyise, Steve, and Maarten J. J. Menken, eds. *The Psalms in the New Testament.* London: Clark, 2004.

Muessig, Carolyn, ed. *Preacher, Sermon, and Audience in the Middle Ages*. New History of the Sermon 3. Leiden: Brill, 2002.

Müller, Hildegund. "*Enarrationes in Psalmos*." In *Oxford Guide*, ed. Pollman and Otten, 1:412–17.

Murray, Robert. "Jew, Hebrews and Christians: Some Needed Distinctions." *Novum Testamentum* 24.3 (1982): 194–208.

Newman, Barbara. *Frauenlob's Song of Songs: A Medieval German Poet and His Masterpiece*. University Park: Pennsylvania State University Press, 2006.

——. *God and the Goddesses: Vision, Poetry, and Belief in the Middle Ages*. Philadelphia: University of Pennsylvania Press, 2003.

——. *Sister of Wisdom: Hildegard of Bingen's Theology of the Feminine*. Berkeley and Los Angeles: University of California Press, 1987.

Nichols, Aidan. *There Is No Rose: The Mariology of the Catholic Church*. Minneapolis, Minn.: Fortress, 2015.

Nirenberg, David. *Aesthetic Theology and Its Enemies: Judaism in Christian Painting, Poetry, and Politics*. Lebanon, N.H.: Brandeis University Press, 2015.

——. *Anti-Judaism: The Western Tradition*. New York: Norton, 2013.

Norman, Diana. *Siena and the Virgin: Art and Politics in a Late Medieval City State*. New Haven: Yale University Press, 1999.

Norris, Kathleen. *The Cloister Walk*. New York: Riverhead, 1996.

Norton, Christopher. "The Buildings of St Mary's Abbey, York and Their Destruction." *The Antiquaries Journal* 74 (1994): 256–88.

Novikoff, Alex. *The Medieval Culture of Disputation: Pedagogy, Practice, and Performance*. Philadelphia: University of Pennsylvania Press, 2013.

O'Brien, Conor. *Bede's Temple: An Image and Its Interpretation*. Oxford: Oxford University Press, 2015.

O'Carroll, Michael. *Theotokos: A Theological Encyclopedia of the Blessed Virgin Mary*. Rev. ed. Wilmington, Delaware: Glazier, 1983.

Ochsenbein, Peter. "Deutschprachige Privatgebetbücher vor 1400." In *Deutsche Handschriften 1100–1400: Oxforder Kolloquium, 1985*, ed. Volker Honemann and Nigel F. Palmer, 379–98. Tübingen: Niemeyer, 1988.

O'Connor, Edward Dennis. *The Dogma of the Immaculate Conception: History and Significance*. Notre Dame: University of Notre Dame Press, 1958.

Ohly, Friedrich. "The Cathedral as Temporal Space: On the Duomo of Siena." In *Sensus Spiritualis*, trans. Northcott, 136–233.

——. "On the Spiritual Sense of the Word in the Middle Ages." In *Sensus Spiritualis*, trans. Northcott, 1–30.

——. "Problems of Medieval Significs and Hugh of Folieto's 'Dove Miniature.' " In *Sensus Spiritualis*, trans. Northcott, 68–135.

——. *Sensus Spiritualis: Studies in Medieval Significs and the Philology of Culture*. Trans. Kenneth J. Northcott. Chicago: University of Chicago Press, 2005.

——. "Typology as a Form of Historical Thought." In *Sensus Spiritualis*, trans. Northcott, 31–67.

Oliger, L. "Servasanto da Faenza O.F.M. e il suo 'Liber de Virtutibus et Vitiis.' " In *Miscellanea Francesco Ehrle. Scritti di storia e paleografia I: Per la storia della teologia e della filosofia*, 148–89. Studi e testi 37. Rome: Biblioteca Apostolica Vaticana, 1924.

Oliver, Judith. "Devotional Psalters and the Study of Beguine Spirituality." *Vox Benedictina* 9 (1992): 199–225.

Orsi, Robert A. *The Madonna of 115th Street: Faith and Community in Italian Harlem, 1880–1950*. New Haven: Yale University Press, 1985.

Orr, Michael. "The Fitzherbert Hours (Dunedin Public Libraries, Reed MS 5) and the Iconography of St. Anne Teaching the Virgin to Read in Early Fifteenth-Century England." In *Migrations: Medieval Manuscripts in New Zealand*, ed. Stephanie Hollis and Alexandra Barratt, 216–31. Newcastle, U.K.: Cambridge Scholars, 2007.

Osmer, Richard Robert. *Practical Theology: An Introduction*. Grand Rapids, Mich.: Eerdmans, 2008.

Otter, Monika. "Entrances and Exits: Performing the Psalms in Goscelin's *Liber confortatorius*." *Speculum* 83.2 (2008): 283–302.

Palazzo, Éric. "Marie et l'élaboration d'un espace ecclésial au haut Moyen Age." In *Marie: Le culte de la Vierge*, ed. Iogna-Prat et al., 313–25.

Palazzo, Éric, and Ann-Katrin Johansson. "Jalons liturgiques pour une histoire du culte de la Vierge dans l'Occident latin (Ve–XIe siècles)." In *Marie: Le culte de la Vierge*, ed. Iogna-Prat et al., 15–43.

Palmer, Philip Mason, and Robert Pattison More. *The Sources of the Faust Tradition: From Simon Magus to Lessing*. New York: Oxford University Press, 1936.

Panayatova, Stella. "The Illustrated Psalter: Luxury and Practical Use." In *The Practice of the Bible*, ed. Boynton and Reilly, 247–71.

Panofksy, Erwin. *Early Netherlandish Painting: Its Origins and Character*. 2 vols. Cambridge, Mass.: Harvard University Press, 1953.

Pantin, W. A. "Instructions for a Devout and Literate Layman." In *Medieval Learning and Literature: Essays Presented to Richard William Hunt*, ed. J. J. G. Alexander and M. T. Gibson, 398–422. New York: Oxford University Press, 1976.

Patton, Pamela A. "Constructing the Inimical Jew in the *Cantigas de Santa Maria*: Theophilus's Magician in Text and Image." In *Beyond the Yellow Badge: Anti-Judaism and Antisemitism in Medieval and Early Modern Visual Culture*, ed. Mitchell B. Merback, 233–56. Leiden: Brill, 2011.

Pelikan, Jaroslav. *Mary Through the Centuries: Her Place in the History of Culture*. New Haven: Yale University Press, 1996.

Pelster, Franz. "Zwei Untersuchungen über die literarischen Grundlagen für die Darstellung einer Mariologie des hl. Albert des Grossen." *Scholastik* 30 (1956): 388–402.

Peltomaa, Leena Mari. "Epithets of the Theotokos in the *Akathistos Hymn*." In *Cult of the Mother of God*, ed. Brubaker and Cunningham, 109–116.

——. *The Image of the Virgin Mary in the Akathistos Hymn*. The Medieval Mediterranean: Peoples, Economies and Cultures, 400–1453, 35. Leiden: Brill, 2001.

Pennington, M. Basil. *Lectio Divina: Renewing the Ancient Practice of Praying the Scriptures*. New York: Crossroad, 1998.

Pentcheva, Bissera V. *Icons and Power: The Mother of God in Byzantium*. University Park, Penn.: Pennsylvania State University Press, 2006.

Pérez-Rioja, Jose Antonio. "Proyeccion de la Venerable María de Ágreda: Ensayo para un bibliografia de fuentes impresas." *Celtiberia* 29 (1965): 77–122.

Petit, François. *La spiritualité des Prémontrés au XIIe et XIIIe siècles*. Études de théologie et d'histoire de la spiritualité 10. Paris: Vrin, 1947. Trans. Victor Szczurek, ed. Carol Neel, as *Spirituality of the Premonstratensians: The Twelfth and Thirteenth Centuries*. Cistercian Studies Series 242. Trappist, Ky.: Cistercian Publications/Collegeville, Minn.: Liturgical, 2011.

Pettegree, Andrew, and Malcolm Walsby, eds. *French Books III & IV: Books Published in France Before 1601 in Latin and Languages Other Than French*. 2 vols. in 1 online. Leiden: Brill, 2012.

Pezzini, Domenico. "Late Medieval Translations of Marian Hymns and Antiphons." In *The Medieval Translator/Traduire au Moyen Age 5*, ed. Roger Ellis and René Tixier, 236–63. Turnhout, Belgium: Brepols, 1996.

Philippart, Guy. "Jean Évêque d'Arezzo (IXè s.), Auteur du 'De assumptione' de Reichenau." *Analecta bollandiana* 92 (1974):345–46.

Phillips, Helen. " 'Almighty and al mercible queene': Marian Titles and Marian Lyrics." In *Medieval Women: Texts and Contexts in Late Medieval Britain: Essays for Felicity Riddy*, ed. Jocelyn Wogan-Browne et al., 83–99. Turnhout, Belgium: Brepols, 2000.

Phillips, L. Edward. "Prayer in the First Four Centuries A.D." In *A History of Prayer*, ed. Hammerling, 31–58.

Pichardo, José Antonio. "The Miraculous Journeys of Mother María de Jesús de Ágreda to La Quivira." In *Pichardo's Treatise on the Limits of Louisiana and Texas*, 2:465–509. Trans. Charles Wilson Hackett. Austin: University of Texas Press, 1934.

Plummer, John. " 'Use' and 'Beyond Use.' " In Wieck, *Time Sanctified*, 149–67.

Pollmann, Karla, and Willemien Otten, eds. *The Oxford Guide to the Historical Reception of Augustine*. 3 vols. Oxford: Oxford University Press, 2013.

Pope, Barbara Corrado. "Immaculate and Powerful: The Marian Revival in the Nineteenth Century." In *Immaculate and Powerful: The Female in Sacred Image and Social Reality*, ed. C. W. Atkinson, C. H. Buchanan, and M. R. Miles, 173–200. Boston: Beacon, 1985.

Power, Eileen. "Introduction." In Johannes Herolt, *Miracles of the Blessed Virgin Mary*, trans. Swinton Bland, ix–[xxxv].

Price, Richard M. "The *Theotokos* and the Council of Ephesus." In *Origins*, ed. Maunder, 89–103.

Priestley, Joseph. *A General History of the Christian Church to the Fall of the Western Empire*. 2 vols. Birmingham, U.K.: Thomas Pearson, 1790.

Prinzivalli, Emanuela. "Il 'Commento all'Ave Maria' di Corrado di Sassonia: A proposito di un libro recente." *Ricerche Teologiche* 10 (1999): 169–78.

Purtle, Carol J. "The Iconography of Prayer, Jean de Berry, and the Origin of the Annunciation in a Church." *Simiolus* 20.4 (1991): 227–39.

Ratzinger, Joseph, Pope Benedict XVI. "Address to the Collège des Bernardins, Paris, 12 September 2008." https://w2.vatican.va/content/benedict-xvi/en/speeches/2008/september/documents/hf_ben-xvi _spe_20080912_parigi-cultura.html.

——. *Jesus of Nazareth: From the Baptism in the Jordan to the Transfiguration*. Trans. Adrian J. Walker. New York: Doubleday, 2007.

Reinburg, Virginia. "Books of Hours." In *The Sixteenth-Century French Religious Book*, ed. Andrew Pettegree, Paul Nelles, Philip Conner, 68–82. Aldershot, U.K.: Ashgate, 2001.

——. *French Books of Hours: Making an Archive of Prayer, c. 1400–1600*. Cambridge: Cambridge University Press, 2012.

——. "Hearing Lay People's Prayer." In *Culture and Identity in Early Modern Europe, 1500–1800: Essays in Honor of Natalie Zemon Davis*, ed. Barbara Diefendorf and Carla Hesse, 19–39. Ann Arbor: University of Michigan Press, 1993.

——. "Popular Prayers in Late Medieval and Reformation France." Ph.D. dissertation, Princeton University, 1985.

Remensnyder, Amy G. *La Conquistadora: The Virgin Mary at War and Peace in the Old and New Worlds*. Oxford: Oxford University Press, 2014.

Resnick, Irven. "Ps.-Albert the Great on the Physiognomy of Jesus and Mary." *Mediaeval Studies* 64 (2002): 217–40.

Revell, Peter. *Fifteenth-Century English Prayers and Meditations: A Descriptive List of Manuscripts in the British Library*. Garland Reference Library of the Humanities 19. New York: Garland, 1975.

Reynolds, Brian. *Gateway to Heaven: Marian Doctrine and Devotion, Image and Typology in the Patristic and Medieval Periods*. Vol. 1, *Doctrine and Devotion*. Hyde Park, N.Y.: New City, 2012.

Reynolds, Robert L. "Two Documents Concerning Elementary Education in Thirteenth-Century Genoa." *Speculum* 12.2 (1937): 255–56.

Ridyard, Susan. *The Royal Saints of Anglo-Saxon England: A Study of West Saxon and East Anglian Cults*. Cambridge Studies in Medieval Life and Thought 4. Cambridge: Cambridge University Press, 1988.

Righetti, Mario. *Manuale di storia liturgica*. 3 vols. Milan: Àncora, 1950–1956.

Rigg, A. G. *A History of Anglo-Latin Literature, 1066–1422*. Cambridge: Cambridge University Press, 1992.

——. "Walter of Wimborne, O.F.M.: An Anglo-Latin Poet of the Thirteenth Century." *Mediaeval Studies* 33 (1971): 371–78.

Ritchey, Sara. *Holy Matter: Changing Perceptions of the Material World in Late Medieval Christianity*. Ithaca, N.Y.: Cornell University Press, 2014.

Rivers, Kimberly A. *Preaching the Memory of Virtue and Vice: Memory, Images, and Preaching in the Late Middle Ages*. SERMO 4. Turnhout, Belgium: Brepols, 2010.

Robb, David M. "The Iconography of the Annunciation in the Fourteenth and Fifteenth Centuries." *Art Bulletin* 18.4 (1936): 480–526.

Robertson, Anne Walters. "Remembering the Annunciation in Medieval Polyphony." *Speculum* 70.2 (1995): 275–304.

Robinson, Cynthia. *Imagining the Passion in a Multiconfessional Castile: The Virgin, Christ, Devotions, and Images in the Fourteenth and Fifteenth Centuries.* University Park: Pennsylvania State University Press, 2013.

Roest, Bert. *Franciscan Literature of Religious Instruction Before the Council of Trent.* Studies in the History of Christian Traditions 117. Leiden: Brill, 2004.

——. *A History of Franciscan Education (c. 1210–1517).* Education and Society in the Middle Ages and Renaissance 11. Leiden: Brill, 2000.

Rogers, Nicholas. "Books of Hours Produced in the Low Countries for the English Market." M.Litt. Dissertation, University of Cambridge, 1984.

——. "Patrons and Purchasers: Evidence for the Original Owners of Books of Hours Produced in the Low Countries for the English Market." In *"Als Ich Can": Liber Amicorum in Memory of Professor Dr. Maurits Smeyers,* ed. Bert Cardon, Jan Van der Stock, Dominique Vanwijnsberghe, with the collaboration of Katharina Smeyers, Karen Decoene, Marjan Sterckx, and Bart Stroobants, 1165–81. Paris: Uitgeverij Peeters, 2002.

Roper, Sally. *Medieval English Benedictine Liturgy: Studies in the Formation, Structure, and Content of the Monastic Votive Office, c. 950–1540.* New York: Garland, 1993.

Roten, J. "Richard v. St. Laurentius." In *Marienlexikon,* ed. Bäumer and Scheffczyk, 5:486–88.

Rothenberg, David J. *The Flower of Paradise: Marian Devotion and Secular Song in Medieval and Renaissance Music.* Oxford: Oxford University Press, 2011.

Rubery, Eileen. "Pope John VII's Devotion to Mary: Papal Images of Mary from the Fifth to the Early Eighth Centuries." In *Origins,* ed. Maunder, 155–99.

Rubin, Miri. *Gentile Tales: The Narrative Assault on Late Medieval Jews.* New Haven: Yale University Press, 1999.

——. "Mary and the Middle Ages: From Diversity to Discipline." *Studies in Church History* 43 (2007): 212–29.

——. *Mother of God: A History of the Virgin Mary.* New Haven: Yale University Press, 2009.

Rudy, Kathryn M. "An Illustrated Mid-Fifteenth-Century Primer for a Flemish Girl: British Library, Harley MS 3928." *Journal of the Warburg and Courtauld Institutes* 69 (2006): 51–94.

——. "A Pilgrim's Book of Hours: Stockholm Royal Library A233." *Studies in Iconography* 21 (2000): 237–79.

Ruether, Rosemary Radford. *Mary: The Feminine Face of the Church.* London: SCM, 1979.

——. *Sexism and God-Talk: Toward a Feminist Theology.* Boston: Beacon, 1983.

Sabatier, Auguste. *Esquisse d'une philosophie de la religion d'après la psychologie et l'histoire.* 2d ed. Paris: Fischbacher, 1897.

Saenger, Paul. "Books of Hours and the Reading Habits of the Later Middle Ages." *Scrittura e civiltà* 9 (1985): 239–69.

Salzer, Anselm. *Die Sinnbilder und Beiworte Mariens in der deutschen Literatur und lateinischen Hymnenpoesie des Mittelalters. Mit berücksichtigung der patristischen literatur. Eine literar-historische studie.* Programm des k.k. Ober-Gymnasiums der Benedictiner 20–28. Linz, 1886–1894.

Sand, Alexa Kristen. *Vision, Devotion, and Self-Representation in Late Medieval Art.* Cambridge: Cambridge University Press, 2014.

Sandler, Lucy Freeman. "The Wilton Diptych and Images of Devotion in Illuminated Manuscripts." In *The Regal Image of Richard II and the Wilton Diptych,* ed. Dillian Gordon, Lisa Monnas, and Caroline Elam, 137–55. Coventry, U.K.: Miller, 1997.

Scarry, Elaine. *The Body in Pain: The Making and Unmaking of the World.* Oxford: Oxford University Press, 1985.

Scase, Wendy. "St. Anne and the Education of the Virgin: Literary and Artistic Traditions and Their Implications." In *England in the Fourteenth Century: Proceedings of the 1991 Harlaxton Symposium*, ed. Nicholas Rogers, 81–96. Stamford, U.K.: Watkins, 1993.

Schäfer, Peter. *Mirror of His Beauty: Feminine Images of God from the Bible to the Early Kabbalah*. Princeton, N.J.: Princeton University Press, 2002.

Schaff, Philip. *The Creeds of Christendom with a History and Critical Notes*. 3 vols. New York: Harper & Brothers, 1890.

Scheeben, M. J. *Mariology*. Trans. T. L. M. J. Geukers. 2 vols. in 1. St. Louis, Mo.: Herder, 1946–1948.

Schneider, Leah Buturain. "Site and Insight: Picturing the Annunciation as a Means of *Imitatio Mariae* in Medieval Devotional Praxis." *Magistra* 22.1 (2016): 41–72.

Schreiner, Klaus. "Marienverehrung, Lesekultur, Schriftlichkeit: Bildungs-und frömmigkeitsgeschichtliche Studien zur Auslegung und Darstellung von 'Mariä Verkündigung." *Frühmittelalterliche Studien* 24 (1990): 314–68.

Schroer, Silvia. *Wisdom Has Built Her House: Studies on the Figure of Sophia in the Bible*. Trans. Linda M. Maloney and William McDonough. Collegeville: Liturgical, 2000.

Seethaler, Paula. "Die Weisheitstexte in der Marienliturgie." *Benediktinischer Monatschrift zur Plege religiösen und geistigen Lebens* 34 (1958):111–20.

Serrano y Sanz, Manuel. *Apuntes para una biblioteca de escritoras españolas desde el año 1401 al 1833*. 2 vols. Madrid: 1903–1905.

Sheingorn, Pamela. " 'The Wise Mother': The Image of St. Anne Teaching the Virgin Mary." *Gesta* 32.1 (1993): 69–80.

Shoemaker, Karl. *Sanctuary and Crime in the Middle Ages, 400–1500*. New York: Fordham University Press, 2011.

Shoemaker, Stephen J. *Ancient Traditions of the Virgin Mary's Dormition and Assumption*. Oxford: Oxford University Press, 2002.

——. "Apocrypha and Liturgy in the Fourth Century: The Case of the 'Six Books' Dormition Apocryphon." In *Jewish and Christian Scriptures: The Function of "Canonical" and "Non-Canonical" Religious Texts*, ed. James H. Charlesworth and Lee Martin McDonald, 153–63. London: Clark, 2010.

——. "Between Scripture and Tradition: The Marian Apocrypha of Early Christianity." In *The Reception and Interpretation of the Bible in Late Antiquity*, ed. Lorenzo DiTommaso and Lucian Turcescu, 491–510. Bible in Ancient Christianity 6. Leiden: Brill, 2008.

——. "The Cult of Fashion: The Earliest *Life of the Virgin* and Constantinople's Marian Relics." *Dumbarton Oaks Papers* 62 (2008): 53–74.

——. "The Cult of the Virgin in the Fourth Century: A Fresh Look at Some Old and New Sources." In *Origins*, ed. Maunder, 71–87.

——. "Death and the Maiden: The Early History of the Dormition and Assumption Apocrypha." *St. Vladimir's Theological Quarterly* 50:1–2 (2006): 59–97.

——. "Epiphanius of Salamis, the Kollyridians, and the Early Dormition Narratives: The Cult of the Virgin in the Fourth Century." *Journal of Early Christian Studies* 16.3 (2008): 371–401.

——. " 'Let Us Go and Burn Her Body': The Image of the Jews in the Early Dormition Traditions." *Church History* 68.4 (1999): 775–823.

——. "Marian Liturgies and Devotion in Early Christianity." In *Mary: The Complete Resource*, ed. Boss, 130–45.

——. *Mary in Early Christian Faith and Devotion*. New Haven: Yale University Press, 2016.

——. "A Mother's Passion: Mary at the Crucifixion and Resurrection in the Earliest *Life of the Virgin* and Its Influence on George of Nikomedia's Passion Homilies." In *Cult of the Mother of God*, ed. Brubaker and Cunningham, 53–67.

——. "The (Re?)Discovery of the Kathisma Church and the Cult of the Virgin in Late Antique Palestine." *Maria: A Journal of Marian Studies* 2 (2001): 21–72.

——. "The Virgin Mary's Hidden Past: From Ancient Marian Apocrypha to the Medieval *Vitae Virginis.*" *Marian Studies* 60 (2009): 1–30.

Simons, Walter. *Cities of Ladies: Beguine Communities in the Medieval Low Countries, 1200–1565.* Philadelphia: University of Pennsylvania Press, 2001.

——. "The Beguine Movement in the Southern Low Countries: A Reassessment." *Bulletin de l'institut historique belge de Rome* 59 (1989): 63–105.

Six, Manon. "The Burgesses of Rouen in the Late Twelfth and Early Thirteenth Centuries." In *Society and Culture,* ed. Hicks and Brenner, 247–76.

Smid, Harm R. *Protevangelium Jacobi: A Commentary.* Trans. G. E. van Baaren-Pape. Assen: Van Gorcum, 1965.

Smith, Katherine Allen. "Bodies of Unsurpassed Beauty: 'Living' Images of the Virgin in the High Middle Ages." *Viator* 37 (2006): 167–87.

Smith, Kathryn A. *Art, Identity and Devotion in Fourteenth-Century England: Three Women and Their Books of Hours.* Toronto: University of Toronto Press, 2003.

——. *The Taymouth Hours: Stories and the Construction of Self in Late Medieval England.* London, British Library/Toronto: University of Toronto Press, 2012.

Smith, Mark S. *The Early History of God: Yahweh and the Other Deities in Ancient Israel.* 2d ed. Grand Rapids, Mich.: Eerdmans, 2002.

Solaguren, Celestino, Angel Martínez Moñux, and Luis Villasante. "Introducción." In Sor María de Jesús de Ágreda, *Mistica Ciudad de Dios: Vida de Maria,* xi–cv. Madrid: Fareso, 1970.

Solignac, Aimé. "Richard de Saint-Laurent." DSAM 13 (1988): 590–93.

Southern, R. W. "The English Origins of the 'Miracles of the Virgin.'" *Mediaeval and Renaissance Studies* 4 (1958): 176–216.

——. *The Making of the Middle Ages.* New Haven: Yale University Press, 1953.

Spretnak, Charlene. *Missing Mary: The Queen of Heaven and Her Re-emergence in the Modern Church.* New York: Palgrave Macmillan, 2004.

Stegmüller, Otto. "Sub tuum praesidium: Bemerkungen zur ältesten Überlieferung." *Zeitschrift für katholische Theologie* 74.1 (1952): 76–82.

Stewart, Kathleen Anne. "*Domina Misericordiae*: Miracle Narratives and the Virgin Mary, 1130–1230." Ph.D. dissertation, University of California, Berkeley, 2006.

Stewart, Columba. *Cassian the Monk.* Oxford Studies in Historical Theology. Oxford: Oxford University Press, 1998.

——. "Prayer." In *The Oxford Handbook of Early Christian Studies,* ed. Susan Ashbrook Harvey and David G. Hunter. Oxford Handbooks Online. Oxford: Oxford University Press, 2009.

Stock, Brian. *The Implications of Literacy: Written Language and Models of Interpretation in the Eleventh and Twelfth Centuries.* Princeton, N.J.: Princeton University Press, 1983.

Stotz, Peter. "Les artes liberales et la louange de la Vierge: La séquence mariale *Si fuerit in trivio.*" In *Hortus troporum: Florilegium in honorem Gunillae Iversen. A Festschrift in Honour of Professor Gunilla Iversen on the Occasion of Her Retirement as Chair of Latin at Stockholm University,* ed. Alexander Andrée and Erika Kihlmann, 124–37. Acta Universitatis Stockholmiensis: Studia Latina Stockholmiensia 54. Stockholm: Stockholms Universitet, 2008.

Stratton, Suzanne L. *The Immaculate Conception in Spanish Art.* Cambridge: Cambridge University Press, 1994.

Suckale-Redlefsen, Gude. "Buchkunst zur Zeit der Andechs-Meranier in Bamberg." In *Die Andechs-Meranier in Franken: Europäisches Fürstentum im Hochmittelalter. Katalog der Ausstellung Bamberg 1998,* ed. Lothar Hennig, 239–61. Mainz: Zabern, 1998.

Sutherland, Annie. "Performing the Penitential Psalms in the Middle Ages." In *Aspects of the Performative in Medieval Culture,* ed. Almut Suerbaum and Manuele Gragnolati, 15–37. Berlin: De Gruyter, 2010.

Sutherland, Jennifer. "Amplification of the Virgin: Play and Empowerment in Walter of Wimborne's *Marie Carmina.*" In *Virginity Revealed: Configurations of the Unposssessed Body,* ed. Judith Fletcher and Bonnie MacLachlan, 128–48. Toronto: University of Toronto Press, 2007.

Svanberg, Jan. "The Gothic Smile." In *Künstlerischer Austausch/Artistic Exchange: Akten des XXVIII. Internationalen Kongressus für Kunstgeschichte Berlin, 15–20 Juli 1992,* ed. Thomas W. Gaehtgens, 2:357–70. Berlin: Akademie, 1993.

Swanson, R. N., ed. *The Church and Mary: Papers Read at the 2001 Summer Meeting and the 2002 Winter Meeting of the Ecclesiastical History Society.* Studies in Church History 39. Woodbridge, U.K.: Boydell, 2004.

——. "Prayer and Participation in Late Medieval England." *Studies in Church History* 42 (2006): 130–39.

——. *Religion and Devotion in Europe, c. 1215–c. 1515.* Cambridge: Cambridge University Press, 1995.

Symes, Carol. "The Confraternity of Jongleurs and the Cult of the Virgin: Vernacular Devotion and Documentation in Medieval Arras." In *The Church and Vernacular Literature in Medieval France,* ed. Dorothea Kullmann, 176–97. Toronto: Pontifical Institute of Mediaeval Studies, 2009.

——. "The Lordship of Jongleurs." In *The Experience of Power in Medieval Europe, 950–1350,* ed. Robert F. Berkhofer III, Alan Cooper, and Adam J. Kosto, 237–52. Aldershot, U.K.: Ashgate, 2005.

Szövérffy, Joseph. *Marianische Motivik der Hymnen: Ein Beitrag zur Geschichte der marianischen Lyrik im Mittelalter.* Medieval Classics: Texts and Studies 18. Leyden: Classical Folia Editions, 1985.

Taft, Robert. *The Liturgy of the Hours in East and West: The Origins of the Divine Office and Its Meaning for Today.* Collegeville, Minn.: Liturgical, 1986.

Taunton, Ethelred L. *The Little Office of Our Lady: A Treatise Theoretical, Practical, and Exegetical.* London: John Bale, Sons & Danielsson, 1903.

Thérel, Marie-Louise. *Le triomphe de la Vierge-Église: À l'origine du décor du portail occidental de Notre-Dame de Senlis: Source historiques, littéraires et iconographiques.* Paris: Editions du Centre National de la Recherche Scientifique, 1984.

Thorndike, Lynn. "Elementary and Secondary Education in the Middle Ages." *Speculum* 15.4 (1940): 400–408.

——. "The Properties of Things of Nature Adapted to Sermons." *Medievalia et humanistica* 12 (1958): 78–83.

Thurston, Herbert. "Angelus." *The Catholic Encyclopedia.* New York: Appleton, 1907. www.newadvent.org/cathen/01486b.htm.

——. *Familiar Prayers: Their Origin and History.* Westminster, Md.: Newman, 1953.

——. "Genuflexions and Aves: A Study in Rosary Origins." *The Month* 127 (1916): 441–51; 127 (1916): 546–59.

——. "Our Popular Devotions V: The Angelus." *The Month* 98 (1901): 483–99.

——. "Our Popular Devotions II: The Rosary." *The Month* 96 (1900): 403–18, 513–27, 620–37; 97 (1901): 67–79, 172–88, 286–305, 383–404.

——. "Notes on Familiar Prayers VIII: The *Salve Regina.*" *The Month* 127 (1916): 248–60, 300–14.

Tickle, Phyllis. *The Divine Hours: Prayers for Summertime, Prayers for Autumn and Wintertime, Prayers for Springtime. A Manual for Prayer.* 3 vols. New York: Image/Doubleday, 2006.

Timmons, Patricia, and Robert Boenig. *Gonzalo de Berceo and the Latin Miracles of the Virgin: A Translation and a Study.* Farnham, U.K.: Ashgate, 2012.

Tolkien, J. R. R. *Letters.* Ed. Humphrey Carpenter with Christopher Tolkien. Boston: Houghton Mifflin, 1981.

——. *Morgoth's Ring: The Later Silmarillion.* Part 1, *The Legends of Aman.* Ed. Christopher Tolkien. The History of Middle Earth 10. Boston: Houghton Mifflin, 1993.

——. "On Fairy Stories." In *The Tolkien Reader,* 33–99. New York: Del Rey, 1966.

Tomaschek, Johann, ed. *Abt Engelbert von Admont (reg. 1297–1327).* Admont: Benediktinerstift Admont, 1998.

Toswell, T. J. *The Anglo-Saxon Psalter.* Medieval Church Studies 10. Turnholt: Brepols, 2014.

Twomey, Lesley K. *The Serpent and the Rose: The Immaculate Conception and Hispanic Poetry in the Late Medieval Period.* Studies in Medieval and Renaissance Traditions 132. Leiden: Brill, 2008.

Urberg, Michelle Ann. "Music in the Devotional Lives of the Birgittine Brothers and Sisters at Vadstena Abbey (c. 1373–1545)." Ph.D. dissertation, University of Chicago, 2016.

Uribe, Ángel. "Fondo Agredano de la Biblioteca de Aránzazu." *Archivo Ibero-Americano* 27 (1967): 249–304.

Vagaggini, Cyprian. *Theological Dimensions of the Liturgy: A General Treatise on the Theology of the Liturgy.* Trans. Leonard J. Doyle and W. A. Jurgens from the fourth Italian edition, revised and augmented by the author. Collegeville: Liturgical, 1976.

Van Bergen, Saskia. "The Production of Flemish Books of Hours for the English Market: Standardization and Workshop Practices." In *Manuscripts in Transition: Recycling Manuscripts, Texts and Images. Proceedings of the International Congress held in Brussels (5–9 November 2002)*, ed. Brigitte Dekeyzer and Jan Van der Stock, 271–83. Paris: Uitgeverij Peeters, 2005.

Van der Heijden, Maarten, and Bert Roest. *Franciscan Authors, 13th–18th Century: A Catalogue in Progress.* http://users.bart.nl/~roestb/franciscan.

Van Deusen, Nancy, ed. *The Place of the Psalms in the Intellectual Culture of the Middle Ages.* Albany, N.Y.: State University of New York, 1999.

Van Dijk, Ann. "The Angelic Salutation in Early Byzantine and Medieval Annunciation Imagery." *Art Bulletin* 80.3 (1999): 420–36.

Van Dijk, Rudolf Th. M. *Prolegomena ad Gerardi Magni Opera Omnia.* Corpus Christianorum Continuatio Mediaevalis 192. Turnhout: Brepols, 2003.

Van Dijk, S. J. P, and J. Hazelden Walker, *The Origins of the Modern Roman Liturgy: The Liturgy of the Papal Court and the Franciscan Order in the Thirteenth Century.* Westminster, Md.: Newman, 1960.

Van Engen, John. *Sisters and Brothers of the Common Life: The Devotio Moderna and the World of the Later Middle Ages.* Philadelphia: University of Pennsylvania Press, 2008.

Van Nuffel, Herman. "Le pacte avec le diable dans la littérature médiévale." *Anciens pays et assemblées d'états/ Standen en Landen* 39 (1966): 27–43.

Vanwijnsberghe, Dominique. "Le cycle de l'Enfance des petites heures de la Vierge dans les livres d'heures des Pays-Bas méridionaux: Un bilan intermédiaire." In *Manuscripten en miniaturen: Studies aangeboden aan Anne S. Korteweg bij haar afscheid van de Koninklijke Bibliotheek*, ed. Jos Biemans, Klass van der Hoek, Kathryn M. Rudy, and Ed van der Vlist, 355–65. Zutphen: Walburg, 2007.

Varas García, Julio C. "Ágreda, María de Jesús de, O.I.C. (Ágreda, Soria, 1602–1665)." In *Diccionario filológico de literatura española. Siglo XVII*, ed. Pablo Jauralde Pou, Delia Gavela, and Pedro C Rojo Alique, 1:3–58. Madrid: Castalia, 2010.

Vauchez, André. *Sainthood in the Later Middle Ages.* Trans. Jean Birrell. Cambridge: Cambridge University Press, 1997.

Vázquez Janiero, Isaac. "Libros y lectores de S. Buenaventura en España y Portugal durante la edad media y el renacimiento." In *Bonaventuriana. Miscellanea in onore di Jacques Guy-Bougerol*, ed. Francisco de Asís Chavero Blanco, 2:135–75. Rome: Edizioni Antonianum, 1988.

Vetter, Ewald M. "Mulier Amicta Sole und Mater Salvatoris." *Münchner Jahrbuch der Bildenden Kunst*, 3rd ser. 9–10 (1958–1959): 32–71.

Vloberg, Maurice. "The Iconography of the Immaculate Conception." In *The Dogma of the Immaculate Conception: History and Significance*, ed. Edward Dennis O'Connor, 463–512. Notre Dame: University of Notre Dame Press, 1958.

Volfing, Annette. *Heinrich von Mügeln. 'Der meide kranz': A Commentary.* Münchener Texte und Untersuchungen zur deutschen Literatur des Mittelalters 111. Tübingen: Niemeyer, 1997.

Von Balthasar, Hans Urs. *Prayer.* Trans. Graham Harrison. San Francisco: Ignatius, 1986.

Von Speyr, Adrienne. *The World of Prayer.* Trans. Graham Harrison. San Francisco: Ignatius, 1985.

Waller, Gary. *The Virgin Mary in Late Medieval and Early Modern English Literature and Popular Culture.* Cambridge: Cambridge University Press, 2011.

——. "The Virgin's 'pryvytes': Walsingham and the Late Medieval Sexualization of the Virgin." In *Walsingham in Literature and Culture from the Middle Ages to Modernity*, ed. Dominic James and Gary Waller, 113–30. Farnham, U.K.: Ashgate, 2010.

Waltke, Bruce K., and James M. Houston, with Erika Moore. *The Psalms as Christian Worship: A Historical Commentary*. Grand Rapids, Mich.: Eerdmans, 2010.

Ward, Benedicta. *Miracles and the Medieval Mind: Theory, Record and Event, 1000–1215*. Rev. ed. Philadelphia: University of Pennsylvania Press, 1987.

Warner, Geert. "Men of Letters: Medieval Dutch Literature and Learning." In *University, Council, City: Intellectual Culture on the Rhine (1300–1500)*, ed. Laurent Cesalli, Nadja Germann, and Maarten J. F. M. Hoenen, 221–46. Turnhout, Belgium: Brepols, 2007.

Warner, Marina. *Alone of All Her Sex: The Myth and the Cult of the Virgin Mary*. New York: Knopf, 1976.

Waters, Claire M. *Translating Clergie: Status, Education, and Salvation in Thirteenth-Century Vernacular Texts*. Philadelphia: University of Pennsylvania Press, 2016.

Waterton, Edmund. *Pietas Mariana Britannica: A History of English Devotion to the Most Blessed Virgin Marye Mother of God, With a catalogue of shrines, sanctuaries, offerings, bequests, and other memorials of the piety of our forefathers*. 2 vols. in 1. London: St. Joseph's Catholic Library, 1879.

Webb, Diana. "Image and Pilgrimage: The Virgin Mary in the Later Middle Ages." In *Mary for Time and Eternity: Papers on Mary and Ecumenism Given at International Congresses of the Ecumenical Society of the Blessed Virgin Mary at Chester (2002) and Bath (2004), a Conference at Woldingham (2003), and Other Meetings in 2005*, ed. William M. McLoughlin and Jill Pinnock, 349–66. Leominster: Gracewing, 2007.

——. "Queen and Patron." In *Queens and Queenship in Medieval Europe: Proceedings of a Conference Held at King's College London, April 1995*, ed. Anne J. Duggan, 205–221. Woodbridge, U.K.: Boydell & Brewer, 1997.

Weber, Robert. "Ambrose Autpert serait-il l'auteur de l'hymne 'Ave maris stella'?" *Revue bénédictine* 88.1–2 (1978): 159–66.

Weil, Simone. "Reflections on the Right Use of School Studies with a View to the Love of God." In *Waiting for God*, trans. Emma Craufurd, 57–65. New York: Putnam, 1951; reprint edition, New York: Perennial Classics, 2001.

Wells, John Edwin. *A Manual of the Writings in Middle English, 1050–1400*. New Haven: Yale University Press, 1916.

Wenger, Antoine. *L'assomption de la T.S. Vierge dans la tradition byzantine du VIe au Xe siècle*. Archives de l'Orient chrétien 5. Paris: Institut français d'études byzantines, 1955.

Wenzel, Horst. "Die Verkündigung an Maria: Zur Visualisierung des Wortes in der Szene oder: Schriftgeschichte im Bild." In *Maria in der Welt: Marienverehrung im Kontext der Sozialgeschichte 10.–18. Jahrhundert*, ed. Claudia Opitz et al., 23–52. Zürich: Chronos, 1993.

Whitehead, Christiana. *Castles of the Mind: A Study of Medieval Architectural Allegory*. Cardiff: University of Wales Press, 2003.

Wieck, Roger S. "The Book of Hours." In *The Liturgy of the Medieval Church*, ed. Heffernan and Matter, 473–513.

——. *Painted Prayers: The Book of Hours in Medieval and Renaissance Art*. New York: Braziller, 1998.

——. *Time Sanctified: The Book of Hours in Medieval Art and Life*. New York: Braziller, 1988.

Wiggins, Steve A. "Of Asherahs and Trees: Some Methodological Questions." *Journal of Ancient Near Eastern Religions* 1.1 (2001): 158–87.

——. "The Myth of Asherah: Lion Lady and Serpent Goddess." *Ugarit-Forschungen* 23 (1991): 383–94.

Wilkins, Eithne. *The Rose-Garden Game: The Symbolic Background to the European Prayer-Beads*. London: Gollancz, 1969.

Williams, Paul. "The English Reformers and the Blessed Virgin Mary." In *Mary: The Complete Resource*, ed. Boss, 238–55.

——. "The Virgin Mary in Anglican Tradition." In *Mary: The Complete Resource*, ed. Boss, 314–39.

Williamson, Beth. "Altarpieces, Liturgy, and Devotion." *Speculum* 79.2 (2004): 341–406.

——. *The Madonna of Humility: Development, Dissemination and Reception, c. 1340–1400*. Bristol Studies in Medieval Cultures. Woodbridge, U.K.: Boydell, 2009.

Wills, Gary. *The Rosary: Prayer Comes Round*. New York: Viking, 2005.

Wilson, Evelyn. *The Stella Maris of John of Garland, edited together with a study of certain collections of Mary legends made in northern France in the twelfth and thirteenth centuries.* Cambridge, Mass.: Published jointly with Wellesley College by the Medieval Academy of America, 1946.

Winn, Mary Beth. *Anthoine Vérard, Parisian Publisher 1485–1512: Prologues, Poems, and Presentations.* Geneva: Librairie Droz, 1997.

——. "Anthoine Vérard, Publisher and Bookseller." 2003. www2.kb.dk/elib/mss/verard/Av-dk.htm. Accessed 3 August 2015.

——. "Hore beate virginis Marie ad usum Sarum." 2003. www2.kb.dk/elib/mss/verard/index-en.htm. Accessed 3 August 2015.

——. "Illustrations in Parisian Books of Hours: Borders and Repertoires." In *Incunabula and Their Readers: Printing, Selling and Using Books in the Fifteenth Century,* ed. Kristian Jensen, 31–52, 209–11. London: British Library, 2003.

——. "Printing and Reading the Book of Hours: Lessons from the Borders." *Bulletin of the John Rylands University Library of Manchester* 81.3 (1999): 177–204.

——. "Vérard's Hours of February 20, 1489/90 and Their Biblical Borders." *Bulletin du bibliophile* 2 (1991): 299–330.

Winston-Allen, Anne. *Stories of the Rose: The Making of the Rosary in the Middle Ages.* University Park: Pennsylvania State University Press, 1997.

——. "Tracing the Origins of the Rosary: German Vernacular Texts." *Speculum* 68:3 (1993) 619–636.

Witcombe, Christopher L. C. E. "Christopher Plantin's Papal Privileges: Documents in the Vatican Archives." *De Gulden Passer* 69 (1991): 133–43.

Wittkower, Rudolf. "The Eagle and the Serpent." *Journal of the Warburg and Courtauld Institutes* 2.4 (1939): 293–325.

Woolfenden, Gregory W. *Daily Liturgical Prayer: Origins and Theology.* Liturgy, Worship, and Society. Aldershot, U.K.: Ashgate, 2004.

Wright, Craig. "Dufay's 'Nuper rosarum flores,' King Solomon's Temple, and the Veneration of the Virgin." *Journal of the American Musicological Society* 47 (1994): 395–427, 429–41.

Wyatt, N[icolas]. " 'Araunah the Jebusite' and the Throne of David." *Studia Theologica* 39 (1985): 39–53.

——. "The Liturgical Context of Psalm 19 and Its Mythic and Ritual Origins." *Ugarit Forschungen* 27 (1995): 559–96.

Yardley, Anne Bagnall. *Performing Piety: Musical Culture in Medieval English Nunneries.* New York: Palgrave Macmillan, 2006.

Zahlten, Johannes. *Creatio mundi: Darstellungen der sechs Schöpfungstage und naturwissenschaftliches Weltbild im Mittelalter.* Stuttgart: Klett-Cotta, 1979.

Zaleski, Philip, and Carol Zaleski. *The Fellowship: The Literary Lives of the Inklings: J.R.R. Tolkien, C.S. Lewis, Owen Barfield, Charles Williams.* New York: Farrar, Straus and Giroux, 2015.

——. *Prayer: A History.* Boston: Houghton Mifflin, 2005.

Ziegler, J. E. "The Medieval Virgin as Object: Art or Anthropology?" *Historical Reflections/Réflexions Historiques* 16.2–3 (1989): 251–64.

Zieman, Katherine. *Singing the New Song: Literacy and Liturgy in Late Medieval England.* Philadelphia: University of Pennsylvania Press, 2008.

Zinn, Grover. "The Psalms at the Abbey of St. Victor: From the Novice's *schola* to the Heights of *contemplatio*." In *Transforming Relations: Essays on Jews and Christians Throughout History in Honor of Michael A. Signer,* ed. Franklin T. Harkins, 75–100. Notre Dame: University of Notre Dame Press, 2010.

Ziolkowski, Jan. "Juggling the Middle Ages: The Reception of *Our Lady's Tumbler* and *Le Jongleur de Notre-Dame.*" *Studies in Medievalism* 15 (2006): 157–97.

Index of Scriptural Citations

Genesis
1:1, 257
1:1–3, 274
1:1–5, 464
1:6, 270
1:6–8, 464, 535n344
1:9, 277
1:9–13, 464
1:10, 314
1:14, 270
1:14–19, 465
1:16, 271, 272
1:20–23, 466
1:24–26, 466
1:26, 466
1:26–27, 325
1:26–27 RSV, 132
2:5–6, 275
2:6, 279, 300
2:7, 361
2:8, 299
2:8–9, 298
2:9, 87, 305
2:10, 298, 318
2:10–14, 149, 279
2:11–12, 275
2:12, 273
2:15, 285, 298, 299
2:18, 397, 441
2:24, 443
2:51, 466
3, 193
3:14, 431
3:15, 265, 288, 325
3:24, 298
6:14, 297

7:16, 120
8:4, 278
8:6–11, 317
12:4–7, 127
14:18, 294
14:18–20, 120
15:1, 341
16:14, 295
16:15, 227
21:8–21, 227
21:33, 295
22:14, 278
24:18–19, 399
25:13, 227
26:12, 275
27:27, 315, 342, 447
28:12–13, 290
28:17, 257, 290
28:17 LXX, 155
30, 96
30:37–39, 306
31:21, 278
32:30, 116
47:25, 393

Exodus
3, 127
3:2, 140, 367, 427
3:2–3, 303
3:3 LXX, 154
3:5, 240
3:5 LXX, 154
3:14, 239
6:3, 120
12:5, 301
13:21, 288

13:21–22, 188
14:24, 188
15:18, 316
15:20 LXX, 158
15:20–21, 386
16:33, 291
17:6, 306
20:5, 446
20:12, 390
23:14–17, 212
24:15–18, 189
25:3–4, 113
25:4, 253
25:10, 187
25:23–30, 128, 148
25:31–37, 127
25:40, 121
26:1, 134, 391
26:1–13, 227
26:3, 383
26:14, 244
26:31–33, 245
28:9–12, 289
28:33–34, 134
28:36–38, 120
28:36–43, 411
30:22–33, 129
30:34–38, 150
31:18, 58
33:9, 189
34:29, 424
34:29 LXX, 410
34:29–35, 244
35:25–26, 295
35:31, 367
35:31 RSV, 361

36:8–17, 227
37:1, 319
37:1–2, 280, 319
37:6, 289

Leviticus
1, 387
15:19, 134
16:1–34, 120, 411
16:1–34 LXX, 157
16:4, 135
23:40, 320
24:5–9, 128
26:2, 382
26:11, 286
26:13, 388

Numbers
4:25, 227
6:14 LXX, 153
10:11–12, 286
11:9, 449
12, 136
14:8, 275
16:31–32, 278
17:1–11, 134
17:8, 84, 306, 317, 318
17:10, 325
20:1–2 RSV, 136
20:8, 340
20:11, 306
24:5–6, 286, 295
24:17, 98, 293, 305, 312, 325,
  380, 427

Deuteronomy
4:6, 189
4:11–12 RSV, 122
4:24, 268, 427, 449
6:4 RSV, 120
8:7–9, 275
8:7–10, 295
8:9, 295
11:11–12, 277
16:16, 212
31:26, 255
32:2, 96–97
32:8–9, 120, 127, 186
32:11, 452
32:39, 392
32:43, 349

Joshua
2, 408

Judges
6:36–38, 140
18:7, 294

Ruth
1:20, 312
3:10, 310
4:11, 317

1 Kings (1 Samuel RSV)
1:22–28 RSV, 196
2:1–10 RSV, 201
2:2, 452
2:8, 225
2:30, 367, 393
14:26, 295
14:27, 306
16:13 RSV, 129
23:19 RSV, 209
25, 96, 398
25:3, 316
25:32–33, 320
25:41, 310, 400

2 Kings (2 Samuel RSV)
3, 96
5:9, 294
6:1–7, 159
6:12, 268
6:12–15 RSV, 174
6:14, 301
6:14–16, 379
6:16–19 RSV, 122
7:2 RSV, 227
7:29, 80
12:1–25, 408
14, 398, 400
20:14–22, 398
23:4, 274, 317
23:8, 257
23:15, 340

3 Kings (1 Kings RSV)
1 RSV, 177
1:1–4, 96
1:1–13 RSV, 227
1:17–21, 367, 384
2:19, 58, 266, 319, 463

2:19–20, 398
4:22–28, 295
4:29–30, 421
4:32, 361
4:33–34, 478
5:17–18, 293
6:3, 290
6:7, 278
6:8, 291
6:29, 287
6:30, 468
6:30 RSV, 125
7:2, 288, 341
7:15, 288
7:46–50, 277
7:47, 291
8:1–6, 157
8:1–11 RSV, 122
8:6, 318
8:10–11 RSV, 189
8:11, 84
8:11–12, 315
8:12, 300
8:12 RSV, 189
8:13, 315
8:27, 83, 119
9:3, 288
10:1–2, 84, 319
10:2–3, 267
10:13, 267
10:18, 319
10:18–19, 259
10:18–20, 283
10:20, 316
10:23–25, 421
12:28 RSV, 212
15:1–13 RSV, 132
15:2 RSV, 177
15:9–13 RSV, 177
15:10 RSV, 177
22:42 RSV, 177

4 Kings (2 Kings RSV)
2:20, 291
4:4, 315
8:26 RSV, 177
12:1 RSV, 177
14:2 RSV, 177
15:2 RSV, 177
15:33 RSV, 177
18:1–8 RSV, 122

18:2 RSV, 177
18:32, 321
21:1 RSV, 177
21:19 RSV, 177
22:1 RSV, 177
23 RSV, xxxiii, 117
23:6 RSV, 127
23:6–7 RSV, 119
23:7, 367
23:7 RSV, LXX, 133
23:31 RSV, 177
23:36 RSV, 177
24:8 RSV, 177
24:18 RSV, 177

1 Chronicles
4:21, 295
15:16, 121
15:25–28, 174
15:27, 379
15:28 RSV, 122
16:4 RSV, 190
16:4–6 RSV, 121
16:7–11, 349
16:7–11 RSV, 121
16:23–34, 186
17:1, 227
22:5, 446
25:1 RSV, 122
25:7 RSV, 122
28:11–19, 367
28:18–19, 361
29:20–23, 121

2 Chronicles
1:15, 295
3–5, 118, 123
3:6, 288
4:2, 149
4:18, 291
5:8, 80
5:12–13 RSV, 122, 125
5:13–14, 190, 245
5:13–14 RSV, 122, 123
7:15–16, 367, 384
7:16, 257
15:16 RSV, 177
29:25–28 RSV, 122

1 Esdras
2, 184

Nehemiah
8:6, 382

Tobit
4:16, 295
12:15, 382
13:13, 294

Judith
1:1–3, 294
6:7, 294
8:7, 419
8:8, 317
8:29, 385
11:19, 313
13, 96
13:22, 320

Esther
2:7, 397
2:15, 419
2:17, 319, 443
4:11, 305, 306, 318
5, 209
5:3, 467
6:7–8, 341
7, 209
7:2, 267
7:2–3, 398
8:5, 400
10:6, 340
15, 209
15:3, 367, 385
15:4, 399
15:13, 467
15:15, 84

Job
4:16, 273
9:10, 361
10:11, 265
14:2, 318
25:5, 271
26:7, 277
28:12–19, 172
28:13, 451
29:4–6, 257
29:6, 450
30:30, 340
33:23, 450
33:26, 393

37:18, 270
38:4 RSV, 191
38:7, 203, 252, 273
38:7 RSV, 191
38:12, 318
38:33, 268
39:27–28, 453
40:10, 451
40:11, 432

Psalms (Vulgate numbering,
    unless RSV)
1, 86, 194
1:1, 340
1:3, 87, 451
1:3–4, 322
2, 194, 222
2:1, 91
2:7, 222, 350
2:9, 84, 224, 318
2:12, 87, 91
3:3, 91
3:5, 88
3:9, 91
4, 195
4:6 LXX, 151
4:7, 89
4:8, 320
5, 86, 194
5:3, 383
5:6, 270
5:8, 89
5:13, 341
6, 18, 232
7:12, 285
8, 3, 40, 105–106, 168, 170,
    246
8:2, 95, 437
8:5–6, 348
8:5–7, 437
8:5–9, 193
8:6–7, 423
9:5, 284
9:8–9, 284
10, 86
10:5, 289
10:8, 316
11:4 RSV, 123
12, 4, 195
12:1, 260
14:1, 285

15:8, 453
16:3, 340
17:11, 450, 452
17:17, 443
18, 3, 168, 171–72, 174, 176, 220, 246
18:1–5, 351
18:2, 270
18:2 LXX, 152
18:3 LXX, 155
18:5–6, 427
18:5–6 LXX, 155
18:6, 144, 176, 268, 285, 286, 437, 448
18:7, 266
18:10, 220
18:10–12, 437
18:11, 183
21:7, 451
21:18, 340, 446
22:3 RSV, 123
22:1, 294, 296
22:5, 299
23, 3, 168, 172–75, 187, 229, 246
23:1, 277, 314, 316
23:1–3, 437
23:8, 177
23:8–10, 437
23:10, 319
24:7–10 RSV, 123
24:5, 296
25, 86
25:8, 393
25:11, 445
26:8, 433
27:7–9 RSV, 123
27:7, 302, 318
27:29, 314
28:3, 270
28:9, 289
30, 4, 195
30:17, 246
31:16 RSV, 123
31, 18, 232
32:13 LXX, 155
33:4, 386, 388
34:1–2, 296
35, 86
35:10, 260, 427
36:31, 295

37, 18, 232
37:10, 382
41:1, 202
41:3, 300
41:8, 83
42, 4, 195
44, 3, 168, 169, 175–79, 246, 531n248
44:2, 255, 448
44:3, 264, 313, 319
44:3–10, 437
44:8, 267
44:8 LXX, 179
44:10, xxxii, 208, 237, 266, 318, 319, 462
44:10 LXX, 154
44:10–11, 419
44:11, 311
44:11–12 LXX, 155, 161
44:12, 424, 467
44:13 LXX, 179
44:14, 310, 399
44:14 LXX, 178, 179
44:15–16, 201
44:15 LXX, 161, 178
45 RSV, 130
45:9 RSV, 130
45:10 RSV, 130
45, 3, 168, 179–81, 246
45:1 LXX, 181
45:2–10, 438
45:4 LXX, 181
45:5, 198, 277, 279, 464, 468
45:5 LXX, 155, 180, 181
45:5–6, xxi
45:6 LXX, 155, 161
46:8, 383
47:2, 294, 391
47:3–4 LXX, 152
47:11, 435
47:12, 218
49:10, 295
49:11, 295
49:23, 384
50, 18, 20, 66, 232, 368
50:19, 289, 387
51:10 LXX, 154
53, 9, 168, 194, 195, 209–10
54, 86
54:23, 392
55:3, 277

56:8, 386
57:12, 321
58:18, 397
60:4, 296, 367, 392
62, 3, 168, 194, 201–203
62:2, 29
62:7–8, 29
64:4–5 LXX, 181
64:5, 257, 288
64:5–6, 289
64:9, 27
64:10, 277, 279
64:11, 300
66, 3, 86, 168, 194, 203
66:6–7, 321
66:7, 83
67:5 LXX, 155
67:14–18, 206
67:16–17, 278
67:16–18, 217
67:16 LXX, 154
67:17, 278
67:17 LXX, 154
67:33–34 LXX, 155
69:17 RSV, 123
70:6, 386
71:6, 449
71:6 LXX, 155
71:8, 267
72:24, 399
73:12, 277
74, 86
75:3, 257, 270, 284, 293, 317
77:25, 351, 448, 449
77:43, 294
79:2–8, 221
80:1 RSV, 123
80, 86
83:8, 436
83:12, 443
84, 168, 195, 210–11
84:2, 277, 320
84:3, 277
84:9, 391
84:11–12 LXX, 210
84:12, 320
84:12 LXX, 154
84:13, 80, 277, 320
84:13 LXX, 211
85, 86
85:5, 316

86, 3, 4, 168, 181–84, 246
86:1, 293
86:2, 293
86:2 LXX, 184
86:3, 223, 291, 293, 341, 391, 399
86:3 LXX, 155, 181
86:4, 293, 295
86:4 LXX, 183
86:5, 224, 293
86:5 LXX, 154, 183
86:6, 293
86:6–7, 438
86:7, 257, 294, 341, 442
87:3, 398
88:12, 316
88:38, 113, 270, 284, 285, 316, 319, 385
90, 195
90:1 LXX, 144
90:6, 28
90:9, 268
90:10, 270
90:11, 267, 298, 299
92, 3, 168, 194, 197–99
92:5, 310
94, xxxvii, 3, 48–51
94:1, xxiii
94:1–5, 349
94:3–5, 437
95, 3, 168, 169, 184–87, 229, 246
95:1–2, 352
95:1–2 LXX, 161
95:4–5, 438
95:10, 187, 438
95:11, 314
95:13, 438
96:10 RSV, 185
96, 3, 86, 168, 169, 187–89, 246
96:1–2, 352
96:1–7, 438
97, 3, 168, 189–94, 246
97:1–3, 438
97:4 LXX, 161, 194
97:8–9, 438
97:9 LXX, 194
98:5, 390
99:1 RSV, 118, 123
99, 3, 86, 168, 194, 199–201

101, 18, 232
101:13, 316
103:2, 270
103:5, 294
103:13, 320
103:18, 300
103:24, 361, 413
103:19, 270
103:27, 282
104:2, 386
104:39, 275, 319
105:24 LXX, 154
109, 4, 86, 115, 169, 195, 221–24, 229, 537n446
109:2, 280, 305
109:2–3, 172
109:3, 130, 148, 198, 266, 320, 367
109:4, 350, 465
109:4 LXX, 151
109:6, 287
110 RSV, 115, 130
110:2–3 RSV, 130
110:4 RSV, 119
112, 4, 169, 195, 224–26
112:2–3, 316
113:23, 215
113:24 LXX, 155
116, 4, 168, 195, 211
117, 9, 195
117:23, 297
118, 3, 9, 195, 213
118:1–16, 194
118:17–32, 194
118:37, 316
118:62, 26, 28, 30, 464
118:91, 271
118:103, 450
118:104, 334
118:105, 334
118:164, 13, 26, 28, 386
119, 3, 195, 214–15
119–127, 168
119–133, 18, 207
119:1, 407
119:2–5, 227
119:3, 407
119:5 LXX, 207
120, 3, 195, 215–16
120:1, 403
120:8, 213

121, 3, 4, 169, 195, 215–16, 221, 226–28, 229
121:1, 213
121:2, 384
122, 3, 4, 195, 216
122:1, 453
123, 3, 4, 195, 216–17
123:8, 215
124, 3, 4, 195, 217–18
125, 3, 4, 195, 218–19
126, 3, 4, 169, 195, 219–20, 228–29, 229
126:3, 341
127, 3, 220–21
128, 3, 4, 169, 195, 214, 231–32
129, 3, 4, 18, 169, 214, 232
130, 3, 4, 169, 195, 214, 233–35
131, 4, 195, 229
131:3–5, 30
131:4–5 LXX, 155
131:8, 228, 282
131:8 LXX, 154, 179, 201, 228–29
131:11, 320
131:13 LXX, 154
131:14, 256, 265
132, 4
132:3, 449
133, 4, 195
133:3, 215
134:6, 316
135:4, 410
135:8, 447
136:1, 382
136:4, 386
136:6, 382
137:1, 351, 550n21
137:2, 383
140:2, 29, 30, 350
140:3–4, 388
142, 18, 232
142:6, 340
143:2, 399
144, 57
144:2, 385
144:13, 316
144:17, 316
144:21, 384
145:5–6, 215
146:5, 316
147, 4, 169, 195, 229–30

147:1, 166
147:2, 299
147:3, 294
148, 3, 66, 352, 550n21
148–150, 41, 168, 194,
    205–207, 224
148:7, 519n46
148:11–12, 316
149, 3
150, 3, 66, 86
150:4, 371

Proverbs
1:5, 296
1:20, 353
1:20–33, 367, 407
1:20–33 LXX, 159
1:22–26, 353
1:22 RSV, 133
1:23 RSV, 129
3:8, 272
3:13, 225
3:13 RSV, 127
3:13–14 RSV, 172
3:13–15, 553n83
3:15 RSV, 127
3:16, 225
3:18, 119, 225, 367, 392
3:18 RSV, 127
3:19–20, 225
4:8–9, 382, 423
4:16, 303
7:17, 383
7:20, 340
7:21–22, 367
8:17, 381, 391
8:19, 322, 393
8:20–21, 392
8:22, 119, 257, 421
8:22–23, 439, 444
8:22–31, xxv, 192, 246, 367,
    475
8:22–31 RSV, 131, 170
8:23, 198
8:30, 135, 142, 148, 211, 421
8:30–31, 379, 439
8:35, 391
9:1, 90, 257, 283, 286, 287, 295,
    297, 313, 333, 341
9:4–5, 353
9:5, 340, 367
9:5–6 RSV, 128

9:11, 393
11:2, 331
11:30, 320, 322
12:14, 322
12:23 LXX, 187
14:1, 391
17:17, 443
20:8, 267
29:25, 264
30:16, 442
31, 475
31:10, 265, 266, 284, 340
31:16, 322
31:14, 296, 340
31:17, 384
31:21–22, 391
31:26, 295
31:29, 101, 316, 319
31:29 LXX, 155

Ecclesiastes
1:4, 277
1:5–6, 447
1:7, 312, 314
2:4–5, 303
8:3, 382
12:11, 429

Song of Songs (Song of
    Solomon), 2, 51, 53, 78,
    173–74, 175, 209, 332, 402,
    423, 443, 489n21, 527n193,
    530n212, 539n3
1:1, 69, 177, 272, 428–29
1:2, 94
1:2–3, 201, 202
1:3, 33, 202, 227, 388, 445
1:4, 202, 227, 427
1:4–5, 227
1:5, 427
1:9, 426, 429
1:11, 223
1:12, 442
1:14, 425
1:15, 318
1:16, 288
2:1, 302, 445
2:1–2, 202
2:2, 302, 427
2:4, 301
2:6, 202, 225, 286
2:10, 467

2:10–12, 201, 228
2:10–13, 203
2:10–14, 302, 446
2:11, 228
2:12, 318
2:13, 228
2:14, 386
2:15, 202
2:16, 443, 450
2:17, 202
3:1, 202
3:2, 202, 294
3:3, 202
3:4, 202, 430, 442
3:6, 84, 174, 202, 318, 325
3:6 LXX, 179
3:7, 298
3:7 LXX, 154, 179
3:9, 337
3:9 LXX, 154
3:9–10, 427
3:10, 288
3:10 LXX, 179
3:11, 177, 203, 284, 299, 341
3:11 LXX, 179
3:11 RSV, 130
4:1, 252, 420
4:3, 426, 428
4:3–5, 420
4:4, 174, 295, 333, 430
4:7, 176, 202, 258, 306, 420
4:7 LXX, 154
4:8, 267, 443
4:8 LXX, 154
4:9, 420, 424, 426, 429
4:10, 431
4:10 LXX, 154, 179
4:10–11, 420
4:11, 313, 428
4:11 LXX, 154, 179
4:12, 51, 113, 299, 339
4:12 LXX, 155
4:13–14, 300, 301
4:14, 425
4:15, 278, 295
4:16, 297, 300
5:1, 301
5:2, 215
5:4, 273
5:5, 430
5:7, 202
5:10, 271, 320, 446

5:11, 425
5:12, 426
5:13, 426
5:14, 398, 430, 431
5:15, 288, 432, 451
5:16, 273
6:1, 299
6:2, 443
6:3, 53, 206, 392, 420
6:3 LXX, 179
6:8, 168, 223, 237, 271, 293
6:8 LXX, 179
6:8–9, 420
6:9, 53, 84, 168, 174, 199, 223,
    237, 261, 270, 272, 274, 312,
    314, 317, 319, 367, 427, 449,
    457
7:1, 432, 433
7:1–7, 420
7:2, 291, 431, 432
7:4, 295, 426, 428, 430
7:5, 424
7:6 Vetus Latina, 229
7:7, 433
7:8, 429, 431
7:9, 420, 429
8:3, 225
8:5, 199, 301, 428, 467
8:6, 279, 289
8:8, 431
8:9, 294, 431
8:11, 322

Wisdom of Solomon, 53, 133, 332
1:3, 387
1:40, 435
3:11, 321
6:12, 419
6:13–17, 327
6:16, 382
6:17, 393
6:20, 326, 336
7:7–11, 421
7:8–9, 381
7:9, 183
7:10–11, 381
7:11, 336, 339
7:11–12, 326, 422
7:14, 392, 422
7:15, 465
7:17–21, 461
7:21, 287, 297, 465

7:22–23, 460
7:25, 150, 182, 183, 230, 361, 449
7:25–26, 144, 337, 460
7:26 xxv, 77, 112, 251, 259, 275,
    320, 323, 410, 419, 427, 439,
    446, 479
7:27, 392
7:28, 183
7:29, 183, 312, 419
8:1, 183, 230, 340
8:2, 119, 182, 381, 419, 422
8:3, 316, 443
8:3–4, 423
8:4, 256
9:4, 230
9:5, 442
9:7–8, 230
9:9, 230
9:17, 129, 149
10:1–2, 183
10:1–21, 367
10:10, 230
10:12, 393
10:15–19 LXX, 188
10:21, 362
11:21, 361
14:5, 296
16:20, 113, 280
18:15, 320

Ecclesiasticus Iesu, Filii Sirach,
    53, 132–33
1:9, 385
1:17–18, 264
1:22, 320
4:15, 389, 390
4:16, 382
7:3, 445
7:32, 442
7:33–36, 383
11:3, 450
15:1, 388
15:9, 386
16:30, 314
18:1, 445
18:3–4, 384
18:30, 387
23:28, 452
24:2, 361
24:5, 240, 257, 367, 421
24:5–14, 142–43
24:6, 263, 392

24:6–7, 188
24:7, 288, 319, 336, 337
24:8, 284
24:11, 256, 298
24:11–12, 222
24:12, 285
24:11–13, 168, 238
24:12, 73, 80, 81, 112, 119, 172,
    186
24:14, 96, 169, 229, 237, 257,
    267, 301, 387
24:14–16, xxi
24:15, 222, 283, 316, 399
24:15–16, 168, 186, 238
24:16, 223, 315
24:17, 303
24:17–19, 126, 186
24:17–20, 168, 239
24:17–23, 300
24:18, 302, 303, 420, 427
24:19, 303, 304, 321
24:19–20, 223
24:20, 295, 304, 315, 420, 429
24:20–21, 129, 171
24:21, 295, 304
24:22, 304, 451
24:22–23, 126
24:23, 148, 303, 318, 320
24:24, 101, 169, 231, 239, 263,
    310, 319
24:24–25, 380
24:25, 101, 264, 265, 313, 314,
    329, 428, 446
24:25–31, 240
24:26, 264, 301, 340, 388
24:27, 172, 420
24:29, 367, 392
24:29–31, 327
24:30, 381
24:30–31, 255
24:31, 101, 252, 308, 359, 383, 385
24:32, 253
24:35–36, 256
24:35–37, 279
24:39, 382
24:40, 280
24:40–41, 126
24:40–43, 136
24:41, 96, 339, 341
24:42, 279, 300
24:46, 259
26:19, 313

26:21, 270
26:23, 288
29:15, 398
32:7, 291
35:11, 388
37:6, 442
38:4, 295, 300, 333, 341
38:28, 287
39:1–3, 256
39:17–20, 388
39:20, 385
40:17, 319
42:16, 287, 312, 316
43:2, 80, 283, 291, 296, 339, 316
43:6–7, 273
43:10, 268
43:15, 274
43:24, 315, 341
43:33, 384
50:6, 311, 315
50:10, 291

Isaiah
1:16, 387
2:2, 278
4:2, 320
6:1, 84, 315, 349
6:1 LXX, 154, 179, 188
6:1–2, 148
6:1–3, 123
6:1–3 RSV, 123
6:1–4, 125
6:3, 80, 316
6:3 RSV, 191
6:4 RSV, 123
6:5–7 RSV, 191–92
6:6, 467
6:6–7 LXX, 154
6:7, 239
6:9, 433
6:10, 140
7:10–11 RSV, 129
7:11, 520n74
7:14, 129, 137, 140, 192, 246,
    293, 325, 367
7:14 LXX, 154
8:1, 255
8:1 LXX, 154
8:3–4 LXX, 154
8:6, 279
9:6, 229, 263, 367, 442

9:6 LXX, 193, 541n83
9:6 RSV, 130
11:1, xlii, 80, 84, 293, 302, 305,
    306, 318
11:1 LXX, 154
11:1–2, 302, 446, 451
11:1–3, 313
11:1–3 RSV, 129
11:2, 222, 265, 427
11:2–3, 82, 326, 331
11:3–4 RSV, 192
11:6 RSV, 183
11:9 RSV, 183
11:10 LXX, 154
13:2–6, 206
14:12–15, 411
16:5, 316, 339
19:1, 140, 244, 275, 337, 446
19:1 LXX, 155, 188
19:9, 295
19:24–25, 320
22:22, 299
24:16, 283, 299
26:1, 294
26:9, 30
26:19, 450
27:9, 321
28:5, 302
28:15, 412
29:11, 255
29:11 LXX, 154
29:14, 353
30:21, 446
30:26, 272
31:9, 388
33:20, 273, 286
33:21 RSV, 198
33:22, 316
35:1, 318
35:2, 295, 399, 427
38:20, 386
40:5, 234
40:9, 194
40:12, 277
40:20, 297
40:22, 270
41:13, 299
41:17, 340
42:6, 299
42:8, 399
42:11 RSV, 227

44:23 RSV, 192
45:8, 270, 314, 449
45:15, 275, 280, 300, 447
45:23, 121, 378, 384, 411
45:24, 58
46:11, 450
46:13, 294
48:2, 294
49:13–18 RSV, 192
49:15, 382
52:1, 295, 300
52:10, 234
52:11, 326
53:2, 272, 277, 451
53:5, 446
54:11–12, 183
55:1, 445
55:10–11, 449
57:19, 321
58:7, 341
58:11, 300
58:12, 294
59:20 LXX, 154
60:1 RSV, 228
60:2–3 RSV, 228
60:6–7 RSV, 227–28
60:9, 295
60:14, 294
60:17, 295
60:18, 294
60:19, 294
60:21, 295
61:10, 183
62:2, 329
62:3, 420
62:3–5 RSV, 182
62:5, 131
62:6, 294
62:12, 294
63:9, 450
65:18, 294
66:1, 270
66:8, 333
66:23, 383

Jeremiah
1:11, 306
1:18, 288
2:6, 277, 447
2:13, 279
5:21, 140

10:6, 316
14:21, 285
17:8, 300, 305
17:12, 257
23:24, 168, 287
29:11, 283, 382
31:12, 295
31:21–22, 393
31:22, 73, 277, 285, 333
31:22 LXX, 155
31:23, 116, 320
31:33, 282
31:38, 293, 294
31:39–40, 294
44:15–19, 119, 128, 132, 188
44:15–23, 137
44:18, 367
49:28–29, 227

Lamentations
4:4, 282, 341

Baruch
3:38, 275

Ezekiel
1:4–14, 124
1:4–28, 123, 148, 244
1:20–21, 132
1:24 RSV, 125
1:26, 140, 237, 319, 337, 367
1:26–27, 378
1:26–28, 132
1:27 LXX, 155
1:27–28, 188
1:28 LXX, 155
2:9–3:1 LXX, 154
3:12, 320, 399
3:12 LXX, 155
5:5, 294
10, 132
10:4, 399
10:15, 367
16:8, 277
16:10, 433
17:23, 322
20:15, 275
27:17, 295
27:21 RSV, 227
28:12, 423
36:35, 299

44:1, 113
44:1–2, 140, 144, 148,
44:1–2 LXX 153, 155
44:1–3, 290
44:2, 315, 339
44:2 LXX, 154
44:2–3, 325
44:3, 283
46:1, 288
47:7, 300
47:10, 295
47:12, 300, 321

Daniel
2:34, 278
2:45, 88,
2:45 LXX, 154
3, 203
3:39, 289
3:56, 3, 168, 194, 203–205,
  550n21
3:57, 384
3:57–88, 3, 168, 194, 203–205,
  550n21
4:7–9, 304
4:9, 321
7:9–10, 378
7:10, 336
9:21, 193
12:1, 398

Hosea
2:16 RSV, 192
2:18 RSV, 192
2:19–20, 310
2:20, 267
2:20 RSV, 192
11:9, 293
14:6, 273, 449
14:9, 320

Joel
2:22, 321
2:31, 272
3:18, 279

Jonah
3, 408

Micah
4:2, 256

4:13 RSV, 206
5:2–4 RSV, 170, 192

Nahum
1:4, 302

Habakkuk
1:13, 382
2:2–3, 255
3:3, 278
3:3 LXX, 154

Haggai
2:24, 448

Zechariah
1:3, 393
1:14, 443
4:2, 141, 148
11:7, 306
12:10 LXX, 194
13:1, 279, 340
14:10, 294

Malachi
1:11, 95
2:7, 280
3:1, 80, 116
4:2, 127

1 Maccabees
6:37, 284

Matthew
1:1, 255
1:18–2:23, xxxi
1:21, 155
1:23, 140
2:2, 284
2:9–11, 228
3:16–17 RSV, 222
5:3–11, 82
5:3–12, 326
5:18, 99
6:5–6, 26
6:7, 26
6:11, 282
6:21, 337
6:33, 264
8:24, 297
9:15, 175

11:9, 325
11:15, 140, 311
11:27, 255
11:28, 301
12:35, 517n27
12:41, 408
12:46–50, xxxi
13:33, 340–41
13:46, 381
13:47, 517n27
15:8, 383
16:16 RSV, 115
16:18, 293
17:1–8, 331
17:2, 411
17:26, 279
18:4, 271
19:14, 367
20:28, 267
21:9, 550n23
22:41–46 RSV, 115, 221
23:37, 364
24:30 RSV, 192, 246
25:19, 445
25:21, 445
25:23, 445
25:30, 445
25:31, 246
25:31–33 RSV, 193
25:35–36, 442
26:64, 246
26:69–75, 408
27:45, 27
27:46–50, 27
27:51, 135
28:9–10, 35

Mark
1:10–11 RSV, 222
2:19, 175
3:31–35, xxxi
4:11, 361
6:3, xxxi
9:1–7, 331
9:3, 411
9:22, 271
10:14, 367
11:9–10, 550n23
12:1, 299
12:30, 353
12:35–37 RSV, 115, 221

14:66–72, 408
15:25, 27
15:33, 27
15:34–37, 27
15:38, 135
16:9, 35
16:14–20, 36

Luke
1:26–27, 155
1:26–29, xxi
1:26–33, 194
1:26–38, 99
1:26–2:52, xxxi
1:27, 93–94
1:28, xxiv, 48, 67, 99, 134, 299, 454, 516n219
1:30, 155
1:31, 155, 325
1:32, xxiv, 136
1:32 RSV, 115
1:32–35, 155
1:34, 313
1:35, xxiv, xxvi, 263, 277, 333, 399
1:35 RSV, 115
1:38, 54, 73, 88, 310, 313, 443, 517n27
1:40, 313
1:41, 58
1:42, 53, 104, 134, 135, 155
1:43, 310
1:44, 301
1:45, 155
1:46, 155, 313
1:46–47, 155, 200
1:46–55, 4, 42, 198, 368
1:48, 135
1:49, 443
1:49–50, 200
1:52, 201
1:52–53, 225
1:54, 225
1:55, 225
1:56, 267
1:68–79, 3, 41
1:74–75, 387
2:14 RSV, 192
2:19, 108, 326
2:29–32, 4, 42, 234
2:35, 33, 312

2:41, 212
2:51, 333, 426
3:5, 244
3:21–22 RSV, 222
3:38, 194
4:14–15, 445
5:34–35, 175
7:26, 325
8:11, 299
9:28–36, 331
9:29, 411
10:18, 411
10:22, 255
10:38, 517n27, 528n193
10:38–42, 336
10:42, 264
11:27, 155, 385
11:32, 408
13:20, 341
18:16, 367
18:19, 391
19:1–10, 408
19:13, 445
19:41, 446
20:41–44 RSV, 115, 221
21:29, 517n27
22:54–62, 408
23:25, 399
23:43, 399
23:44, 27
23:44–46, 27
23:45, 135
24:13–35, 36
24:45, 256

John
1:1, 448
1:1–5 RSV, 143
1:9, 263
1:14, xxxiii, 141, 229, 359, 385, 433
1:14 RSV, 122
1:18, xxxiii, 433
1:33, 452
2:1–11, 367
2:1–12, xxxi
2:3, 313, 384, 398, 399, 400
2:4, 265
2:5, 313
2:12, 222
3:16, 442

4:14, 340
4:20–21, 278
4:24, 442, 452
5:22, 450
5:27, 285
6:35, 239
6:51, 340
6:56, 453
8:12, 239
8:36, 399
8:44, 399, 412
9:6, 263
9:7, 279
9:35–39, 433
10:30, 143
11:25, 239
12:24, 431
12:26, 196
12:41 RSV, 123
13:13, 257
14:6, 239, 412
14:10, 430
14:14, 412
14:16, 397
14:21, 391
15:1, 299, 450
15:5, 239
15:14, 443
16:13, 332, 334
16:15, 266
17:6, 448
18:25–27, 408
19:2, 136
19:17–30, xxxi
19:23, 142
19:25, 136, 433
19:25–27, 367
19:26, 265
19:26–30, 444
19:28, 432
19:30, 446
19:34, 27
20:1–18, 35
20:19, 36
21:4–14, 35

Acts of the Apostles
1:14, 26, 273
2:1–4, 27, 29
2:14–15, 27
2:34–35, 115

3:1–10, 27, 29
4:12, 94
4:32, 452
7:49, 270
9:1–30, 408
10:9–16, 27, 29
16:25, 28, 30

Romans
1:4, 451
1:20, 80
5:1, 229
5:4, 264
8:21, 287
8:26, 26, 397
8:38–39, 264, 332
12:1, 388
12:1–2, 350
12:15, 388
13:1, 397
16:6, 517n27

1 Corinthians
1:18–19, 353
1:24, 240
1:24 RSV, 143, 149
1:30, 257
2:8, 300
2:15, 333
3:9, 299
3:11, 197
5:1–5, 408
6:17, 265, 442
6:19, 350
6:20, 266, 444
9:22, 364
10:4, 116, 294
12:8–10, 326, 332
12:9–10, 82
13:1, 252
13:9, 326
13:12, 260
13:13, 100
14:15, xxvi, 386, 441
15:47, 349
15:49, 349

2 Corinthians
3:13, 424
3:17, 452
3:18 RSV, 410

4:4, 468
5:13–14, 364
8:9, 388
9:15, 273
12:3, 331

Galatians
3:27–28, 350
4:4, 155
4:26, 181
5:22–23, 82, 270, 386

Ephesians
4:11, 82
6:11, 297

Philippians
2:7, 445, 451
2:7–8, 364
2:8, 446, 451
2:9–10, 248, 367
2:9–11, 351, 411
2:9–11 RSV, 121
2:10, 399
2:10–11, 94
4:5, 388

Colossians
1:15, 228, 251, 378
1:15–16, 351
1:15–17 RSV, 143
1:19, 251
1:19–20, 351
2:3, 95, 240, 258, 283, 298, 340
2:9, 116, 447
2:14, 400
2:14–15, 412

1 Thessalonians
5:17, 26, 384

1 Timothy
2:1, xxv
2:8, 383
6:15, 338

2 Timothy
2:5, 393, 447

Hebrews
1:2–3 RSV, 143

1:3, 264, 447, 449, 468
1:6, 349
1:8, 284
1:14, 297, 336
2:16, 303, 393
4:14, 156
4:14–5:10, 367
5:5–6, 115, 350
5:5–6 RSV, 222
5:6, 119, 151
5:8–10 RSV, 121
5:10, 141
6:7, 300
7:25, 397
8, 175
8:5 RSV, 121
8–9, 244
9, 127, 245
9:1–5, 528n195
9:4, 156, 280, 319, 325
9:11, 157
9:24, 157
9:24 RSV, 121
9:28, 396
10:19–20, 367, 396
10:19–20 RSV, 135
11:10, 278, 294, 296
11:31, 408
12:22, 228
12:23, 229
12:29, 268, 303

James
1:17, 263, 299
2:2, 116
2:25, 408
3:17, 288

1 Peter
1:12, 446
1:13, 286
1:18–19, 444
2:5, 295
2:9, 350
2:21, 363

1 John
2:2, 282
2:20, 332, 350

2:27, 334, 350, 441
4:7–12, xxiii
4:8, 342
4:16, 446

Jude
1:14–15, 133

Revelation (Apocalypse)
1:1, 124
1:4, 426
1:8, 107, 305
1:11, 256
1:13, 135
1:14, 426
1:15, 432
2:7, 428
2:17, 51
3:7, 283, 299
3:12, 125
3:18, 273, 444
3:20, 447
4, 127
4–5, 225
4:2 RSV, 124
4:2–11, 378
4:4, 411
4:5 RSV, 124
4:6, 198
4:8, 350
4:8 RSV, 124, 191
4:10, 238
4:11, 204, 350
4:11 RSV, 124, 191
5:1, 255
5:4, 101
5:8, 429
5:9 RSV, 124, 192
5:13 RSV, 226
7:13–14, 350
10:8–11, 255
10:9, 255
11:19, 127, 283
12, 225, 463
12:1, 97, 117, 246, 284,
    319, 341, 420
12:1–2, 119, 183
12:1–6, 131, 192
12:1–6 RSV, 128

12:1–18, 475
12:5, 224
12:7–9, 411
12:16, 277
12:17, 367
14:1–3, 163, 186
14:1–3 RSV, 125
14:3, 289
14:4, 204
14:14, 275
15:2, 198
15:2–4 RSV, 125
17:4, 423
18:1, 312
19:8, 119
19:10, 411
19:16, 338
21, 192, 367, 475
21:2, 182, 246, 462
21:3, 286
21:5, 287
21:9–21, 119
21:10–11, 294
21:10–21, 183
21:11, 294, 420
21:12, 294
21:16, 126, 183, 294
21:18, 273, 294, 448
21:21, 294
21:22, 182, 295
21:22 RSV, 126
21:23, 461
21:24, 294
21:25, 294
21:27, 183, 287, 294, 300
22:1–2, 127, 199
22:1–2 RSV, 126
22:2, 87, 193, 246, 300,
    321, 367
22:3–4, 350, 393, 411
22:5, 199
22:14 RSV, 229
22:16, 183, 367
22:16 RSV, 128
22:17, 383
22:18–19, 329

Index of Manuscripts Cited

Admont, Stiftsbibliothek
  Cod. 272, 514n192
Albi, Bibliothèque municipale Rochegude
  44, 209
Arxiu de la Corona d'Arago
  Ripoll 193, 510n124
Assisi, Convent of Saint Damiano
  Breviary, 493n85

Bamberg, Staatliche Bibliothek
  Cod. lit. 23, 530n210
Brussels, Bibliothèque royale
  8860–67, 513n170

Cambrai, Bibliothèque municipale
  193, 493n81
Cambridge, Corpus Christi College
  402, 494n94
Cambridge, Trinity College
  B.5.26, 554n92
Cambridge, University Library
  Dd.11.82, 506n87
Chartres, Bibliothèque municipale
  162, 493n81
  nouv. acq. 4, 493n81
Chicago, The University of Chicago Library
  Special Collections 26, plate 6
  Special Collections 184, plate 7
  Special Collections 344, 500n205
  Special Collections 345, 500n205
  Special Collections 346, 500n205
  Special Collections 347, plates 19
    and 22
  Special Collections 348, plate 3

Durham, Chapter Library
  B.III.11, 530n210

Florence, Laurenziana
  Cod. Plut. 35.sin.4, 507n95
Freiburg, Universitätsbibliothek
  476, 495n115
Fribourg, Universitätsbibliothek
  L 18, 489n20, 493n78

Giessen, Universitätsbibliothek
  878, 495n115

Heidelberg, Universitätsbibliothek
  Cod. Sal. IX 42a, 492n72

Ipswich, Ipswich Museum
  4, 507n95
Ivrea, Biblioteca capitolare
  Cod. 106, 530n210

Karlsruhe, Badische Landesbibliothek
  Cod. Augiensis LXXX, 529n207

Leiden, Universiteitsbibliotheek
  BPL 76 A, 23
London, British Library
  Add. 10036, 506n87
  Add. 21927, 40, 489n20, 499n195, 534n334,
    549n10
  Add. 23935, 493n86
  Add. 48985, 39
  Add. 49999, xxxix, 5, 16, 18, 38, 402, 405, 407,
    490n24, 555n138, plate 21

Arundel 157, 86–91, 513nn173–175
Cotton Cleopatra C.X, 501n6, 505n67
Cotton Nero A.xiv, 19
Cotton Tiberius A.iii, 10–11, 41–42, 59, 489n21,
    491n53, 499n191, 504n43, 549nn5, 7, and 8
Cotton Tiberius C.VI, 553n92
Cotton Titus D.xxvi+xxvii, 9
Egerton 1139, plate 9
Egerton 1151, 38–39, plate 4
Harley 1005, 492n64
Lansdowne 383, plate 10
Royal 2 B.V, 11–12, 42, 59, 489n21, 499n192,
    504n43, 549nn2, 5, 8, and 9
Royal 11 B.XIII, 493n81
Royal 17 C.XVII, 506n87

Madrid, Biblioteca Nacionale de España
  8952, 507n95
Monte Cassino
  434, 489n20
Monza, Biblioteca capitolare
  Cod. C-12/75, 530n210
Munich, Bayerische Staatsbibliothek
  Cgm 87, 506n87
  Cgm 136, 506n87
Munich, Convent of Saint Ana
  Breviary, 493n85

New York, Pierpont Morgan Library
  M. 739, 21–22, 495n113

Oxford, Bodleian Library
  Bodleian 270b, 509n115
  Bodleian 21700 [Douce 126], 506n87
  Canon. liturg. 277, 489n20
  Rawlinson Poetry 225, 402

Paris, Bibliothèque nationale
  lat. 3173, 540n37

lat. 3719, 489n20, 499n188
lat. 5371, 489n20, 499n194
lat. 10433, 489n20, 499nn188 and196
lat. 17436, 167, 169–70, 173–74, 197, 208–209,
    530nn 210 and 213, 536n387
lat. 10482, 500n198
Philadelphia, Free Library
  Widener 3, 496n131

Rome, Santa Sabina
  XIV L 1, 493n86

Saint Gall, Stiftsbibliothek
  Cod. 390–91, 530n210
Saint Omer, Bibliothèque municipale
  174, 550n29, plate 18
's-Heerenberg, Huis Bergh
  52, inv.-no. 239, 21

Toledo, Archivio capitular
  Bible moralisée of Louis IX, 509n115

Vatican, Bibliotheca Apostolica Vaticana
  Barberini latin 523, 489n20, 493n78
  Chigi C.VI.173, 489n20, 499n188
  Ottoboni latin 453, 489n20
Verona, Biblioteca capitolare
  Cod. XCVIII, 530n210
Vienna, Österreichische Nationalbibliothek
  Cod. 1179, 509n115
  Cod. 1389, 507n95, 508n101
  Cod. 1857, plate 8
  Cod. 2745, 495n115

Wellesley, Wellesley College
  19, plates 12–17, 20

General Index

Aaron, high priest, 121, 128, 134, 136, 306, 361

Abigail, wife of David, 96, 398, 400, 424

Abishag, the Sunamite, 96, 398, 424

accessus, xvii, 255

Adam, as high priest, 118, 170; as image of the
Creator, 170, 193, 325, 349–50, 423; created by
Wisdom, 142, 361

Adam of Saint-Victor, 75, 242, 379, 438, 543n139

Adams, Henry, on Chartres, 241–45, 249–51, 255;
on Mary's appeal, 5, 52, 109, 342, 490n22; on
miracle stories, 354–58, 378, 390, 394, 552n63

Adgar, Anglo-Norman poet, 402

Aelfric of Eynsham, 400

Aelfwine of Winchester, 9–10

Aelred of Rievaulx, 18, 71, 508n109

Aethelwold of Winchester, 8–10

Ahasuerus, king of Persia, 267, 305–306, 398, 443,
466

"Akathistos," 148–51, 175, 188, 204; performance
of, 85, 207, 512n167; translated into Latin 85,
162, 164, 167

Alan of Lille, 69, 138, 253

Albertus Magnus, 79

Alcuin of York, 8, 253

Alfonso X, the Wise (el Sabio), king of Castile and
Leon, *cantigas* of, 62–63, 374–80, 389, 402,
417, 422, 435, 438

Alleluia, meaning of, 206, 224

Amadeus of Lausanne, 70–71, 307

Ambrose of Milan, 95, 253, 448, 528n199

Ambrosius Autpertus, 309, 312, 314, 490n21,
529n206, 530n213

anchoresses, 18–20, 65, 494n94

Ancrene Wisse, 18–19, 65, 494n94

Andrew of Crete, on Mary in scripture, 150,
154–56, 174, 178–19, 188, 207, 211, 214; on
Mary's Dormition, 218–19; relationship with
popes, 167

angels: and kabbalah, 477; around heavenly throne,
xxiv, 124–26, 163, 206, 245, 347–52, 405, 411,
437–38, 454, 467; as guards, 298–99, 319,
328–29, 371, 398, 462–64, 473; baptized as,
258, 297, 350, 411–12; cherubim, 118–19, 123,
127, 140, 142, 148, 151, 155, 156, 161, 188–89,
205, 216, 244, 286, 307–308, 323, 337, 444,
450, 452, 522n95, 528n195, 531n234, 537n446;
hierarchies of, 83–84, 100, 108, 112, 314, 326,
335–38, 443, 452–53; names of, 120; seraphim,
123, 148, 156, 191–92, 205, 337, 453, 466,
550n23; singing at Assumption, 198–99, 200,
202, 205, 237, 268, 273–74, 463; singing at
creation, 131–32, 190–91, 203–204, 394–95;
see also Gabriel

Anna, mother of Mary, 134, 137, 161, 178, 196, 279

Anselm of Bec, archbishop of Canterbury, 14, 253;
Proslogion, xxx, 260; prayer to Mary, 53–54,
74–75, 94, 112, 253, 300, 309, 316–17, 384,
435–36

Anselm of Bury St. Edmunds, 14, 360

Anselm of Lucca, 32

Antiphoner of Compiègne, *see* Paris, Bibliothèque
nationale, lat. 17436

antiphons, oldest Marian, 167, 169–70, 197,
208–209; by incipit (CAO #):
    Adjuvabit eam (1282), 532n263
    Ante thorum (1438), 531n232
    Assumpta est (1503), 535n345, 536n388
    Ave Maria (1041, 1539), 48 and *passim*

Beata Dei genetrix (1563), 558n221

Benedicta, filia (1705), 535n372

Benedicta tu (1709), 499n193, 516n3, 530n214

Celi reginam (1838), 499n196

Dignare me (2217), 533n302

Dum esset rex (2450), 209, 534n335, 537n451

Exaltata es (2762), 499n192, 502n16, 512n152

Gaude, Maria Virgo (2924), 532n289, 542n105

Genuit puerpera (2938), 545n192

In odorem unguentorum (3261), 535n359, 536nn400 and 423

Jam hiems (3470), 538n471

Laeva ejus (3574), 538n460

Maria Virgo assumpta est (3707), 535n357, 536nn399 and 416, 542n96

Nesciens mater (3877), 512n158

Nigra sum (3878), 538n466

O quam beata (3852), 530n213

O admirabile commercium (3985), 542n91, 558n224

O sapientia (4081), 551n51

Omnis vallis (4156), 539n19

Post partum (4332), 534n316

Precibus et meritis (not found), 499n194

Pulchra es (4418), 535n380, 536n401, 537n433

Quae est ista (4425), 548n297

Requiem aeternam (4617), 506n84

Salve regina (CANTUS 204367), 76, 347–38, 355, 374, 382, 398, 545n187

Sicut laetantium (4936), 499n195, 532n278, 544n144

Sicut myrrha (4942), 530n223

Specie tua (4987), 531n239

Speciosa facta (4988), 538n476

Spiritus sanctus in te (5006), 499n191

Sub tuum praesidium (5041), 524n109, 538n491, 544n144

Virgo dei genetrix (5448), 548n294

Aristotle, 101, 254, 294, 297, 331, 334

Arnold of Bonneval, 249, 307, 399, 528n195

Asherah, consort of Yahweh, 119, 127–28, 132–33, 177, 187, 241, 520n66, 521n85

Astarte, goddess, 127

Athanasius of Alexandria, 253

Athena, goddess, 150

Athirat, goddess, 127–30, 134

Auerbach, Erich, 365–66, 541n81

Augustine of Hippo, as authority, 240, 260, 282, 309, 328, 333, 383, 531n253; *De doctrina*

christiana, 363–66, 380; *Enarrationes in psalmos*, 57–58, 106, 164–66, 171–233 *passim*

Ave psalters, xxxviii, 61, 69, 85–93; see also Edmund of Abingdon, Walter of Wimborne

Baldwin of Ford, archbishop of Canterbury, 60

Baltzer, Rebecca, 16, 164–65

Barker, Margaret, as Old Testament scholar, 117–18, 518nn41 and 42, 519n44, 520n82; on creation, 190–93, 226, 523n104, 555n119; on Mary, 133–36, 233, 521n85, 526n158, 548n274; on the origins of Christianity, xxxii-xxxiii, 115–16, 550n20; on parables, 261, 360–61, 365; on the psalms, 170–233 *passim*; on the temple tradition, 118–33, 349, 477

Barlaam and Ioasaph, 383, 554n102

Bartlett, Robert, 486n17

Basil of Caesarea, 27–28, 253

Bathsheba, mother of Solomon, 177, 266, 384, 398, 424, 463

Beatrice of Nazareth, 19, 23, 61, 494n100

beguines, 19–20, 23, 60–61, 438, 494n100

Bede, the Venerable, 99, 253, 320–21, 384, 516n219

Benavides, Alonso de, 469, 475, 480

Benedict of Nursia, Rule of, xxvi, 8, 11–12, 18, 27–29, 34, 37, 211, 352

Benedict XVI, pope, alias Joseph Ratzinger, 486n22, 550n21

Benedictines, 11–12, 33, 42–43, 54–55, 60, 62, 68, 69, 91, 108–109, 249, 324, 481–82, 489n20, 501n1, 511n147, 528n202, plate 10

Benedictus, *see* Luke 1:68–79

Berengerius of Verdun, 8

Bernard of Clairvaux, as authority, 253, 309; on angels, 328–29; on Mary, 89, 314–15, 318, 326–27, 429; on the name of Mary, 98–99; on the Song of Songs, 51–52

Bernard of Cluny, 15

Bernardino de Busti, 94–97, 100, 514n199, 515n203

Bernerius, provost of Verdun, 8, 10

Beseleel (Bezaleel), builder of the tabernacle, 153, 280, 297, 319, 361

Birgitta (Bridget) of Sweden, 456–57, 478

Birgittines, 34–36, 57

Boethius, 253, 391

Bonaventure of Bagnoreggio, 478; attribution of works to, xxxvi, 33, 68, 477, 513n172; on Mary, 80–81, 90, 119

Books of Hours: as smartphones, 500n213;
    illuminations in, xxxi, xxxix, 1–2, 4–5, 38–39,
    68–69, 163, 402, 405, 407, 436–37, 500n214;
    manuscript lists of, 487n1, 488n15; origins of,
    1, 5, 16, 18–19, 21–26, 43–44, 384, 486n19;
    see also plates 3, 4, 6, 7, 8, 19, 21, 22
Boss, Sarah Jane, 441, 555n119
Boyarin, Adrienne Williams, 360, 400, 403

Caesarius of Heisterbach, 61, 373–74, 415–17, 435
Calvin, John, 116
Casanova, Giacomo, 472–74, 478–79
Cassian, John, 27–29, 166
Cassiodorus, as authority, 253, 531n253;
    Expositio Psalmorum, 106–107, 164–66,
    171–233 *passim*
Catherine of Siena, 478
Catholics: as critics of Marian devotion, xxxii, 52,
    109, 117, 241, 247–48, 474–75, 502n15, 518n38,
    520n66, 523n106
Caxton, William, printer, 25
Chartres, cathedral of, 16, 52, 241–45, 342, 394,
    511n147
Chaucer, Geoffrey, 533n289, 552n76
Christ, Jesus:
    as Angel of Great Counsel, 130, 136, 193, 229, 263,
        312, 323, 450, see also Isaiah 9:6
    as bridegroom, 69–70, 171–72, 175–79, 220–21,
        225, 252, 258, 286–87, 302, 437, 442–43, 448,
        see also Psalm 18:6
    as eagle, 452–53
    as flower, 153, 302–303, 318, 445–47
    as fruit, 83, 87, 150, 277, 301, 304–305, 307,
        320–22, 393, see also Luke 1:42
    as high priest, 121, 130, 136, 142, 144, 156–57,
        170, 175, 179, 192, 195–97, 198, 221–24, 287,
        303, 349–50, 367, 476, see also Psalm 109:3,
        Hebrews 4:14
    as king of glory, 123–24, 172–75, 318–19, 338–39,
        437–38, 531n234
    as Logos, 143–45; as Lord (*Adonai*), xv, 120
    as merchant, 266, 296–98, 444–45
    as Morning Star, 128, 130, 141, 148, 149, 172,
        182–83, 198, 246, 311, 315, 367
    as second Adam, 140, 193–94, 275, 284–85, 299,
        422, 441
    as sun, 447–48, of justice 97, 263, 268, 272, 275,
        290, 300, 304, 447–48, 453
    as tree, 87, 298, 450–52

as Word of the Father, 448–49
as Yahweh, 121, 124, 132, 136, 172, 222, see also
    God, as Yahweh
titles of, 437–38, 443–53
see also Wisdom
Christophorus I, bishop of Venice, 85, 167
Chrysippus of Jerusalem, 177–78
Chrysostom, John, 253
Cicero, Marcus Tullius, 254, 272, 362–64
Cistercians, 15–16, 21, 23, 51, 61, 70–71, 86, 108, 111,
    251, 253, 303, 307, 324, 368–71, 373, 381, 386,
    415–16, 481, 484, 489n20, 492n78, 494n100,
    545n189, 549n15
Clark, Anne, 62
Clayton, Mary, 167
Clement of Alexandria, 26
Clement XIV, pope, 472
Colahan, Clark, 474, 476–77
confraternities, 19–20, 66–67
Conrad of Saxony, as preacher, 309, 360: *Speculum
    beatae Mariae*, xxxii, xxxvi–xxxviii, 54, 83–85,
    87–89, 97, 119, 165–66, 249, 309–23, 342–43;
    manuscripts of, 67–68; modern reception of,
    246–47, 477
Constas, Nicholas, 139, 524n126
Coulton, G. G., 358, 390
Cromwell, Thomas, 241
Cyprian of Carthage, 26, 253
Cyril of Alexandria, 145–46, 240, 253, 286, 524n111,
    525n145

Dahood, Mitchell, 174, 212, 222
Damian, Peter, see Peter Damian
Dante Alighieri, 54, 79, 98
David, king of Israel, 115, 129, 177, 187, 209, 268,
    398, 400, 408; appointing temple singers,
    121–23, 174, 190, 349; dancing before the ark,
    301, 379–80; see also Psalms
De Brailes Hours, see London, British Library,
    Add. 49999
De Hamel, Christopher, 488n15, 490n26,
    499n183
De Lubac, Henri, xxxii
Deogratias of Carthage, 363–64, 380
Deschamps, Eustache, 24, 44
Deuteronomists, 117, 122, 130, 132, 188–89, 215,
    520n80
Dever, William G., 520n80, 521nn85 and 86
Dionysius the Carthusian, 53, 351, 453

Divine Office, xxxi, 6–8, 15–16, 18, 20, 66–67, 107–109, 162, 166, 169, 195, 209, 439; as service, 57–58, 350–51; symbolism of, 26–32

Dominic of Evesham, 10, 360–63, 365–66, 402

Dominicans, xxxii, 2, 17–19, 22, 43, 53, 67–68, 78, 83, 111, 195, 207–208, 214, 254, 324, 351, 402, 476, 478, 482, 484, 490n24, 493n86, 510n122, 545n187, plates 12, 15, and 16

dragon(s), 284, 287, 407, 422; in psalms, 118, 206, 352; in Revelation, 128; in scholarship, 395, 519n46, 520n66, 525nn134 and 147, 528n199, 531n253, 539n21, 557n208

Drigsdahl, Erik, 41, 488n10

Duffy, Eamon, 25, 487n1, 488n14, 490nn24 and 26, 497n141, 500n214

Durandus, William, 31

Edberga of Winchester, 11

Edmund of Abingdon, archbishop of Canterbury, 91, 543nn124 and 138

Ekbert of Schönau, 253, 298, 309

Ekonomou, Andrew, 167

Elisabeth of Schönau, 60

Elliott, J. K., 135, 522n88

Elijah, prophet, 137, 298

Elizabeth, cousin of Mary, 53, 56–57, 108, 251, 264, 267–68, 274, 320, 322

Engelbert of Admont, 91, 112

Enoch, 31, 191, 193, 298, 522n97, 523n104; book of, 125, 133, 518n41

Ephesus, council of, 85, 138, 145–47, 158, 185, 233, 524n111, 525n147

Epiphanius of Salamis, 136–38

Ernestus of Prague, archbishop, 68

Escartín, Miguel, on Sor María, 470

Esther, queen, 209, 267, 385, 397–400, 419, 424, 443, 466

Eusebius of Caesarea, 27, 226

Eustochium, daughter of Paula, 17, 387

Eva of Wilton, recluse, 31–32, 213

Eve, 75, 142, 284, 294, 325, 393, 407, 422–23, 430, 443, 466

face, shining, xxxii, 123, 260, 265, 347, 410–11, 423, 427, 456, 548n274

Fassler, Margot, 244–45, 528n202, 529n205

Fedewa, Marilyn, 475

Felipe IV, king of Spain, 469

Feuerbach, Ludwig, xxix

Flory, David, 359, 390

Franciscans, xxxii, xxxvi, 16–17, 20, 32, 67–68, 72, 78, 80, 83, 94, 99, 163, 246, 309, 436, 459, 469, 475, 477–78, 481

Franco of Afflighem, 59

Fuenmayor, Andrés de, 459, 476

Fulbert of Chartres, 253, 400, 403, 522n88

Fulgentius of Ruspe, 253

Gabriel, angel, xxiii–xxiv, 33, 48–49, 53–54, 56–58, 72–73, 108, 115, 197, 213, 215, 263, 267, 274, 285, 299, 309, 311, 328–29, 431, 435, 454; as intercessor, 193; at the Dormition, 178; in *Protevangelium of James*, 134–36; see also Luke 1:26–38

Gallus, Thomas, 253

Gambero, Luigi, 247

Gass, Robert, 503n33

Gautier de Coinci, 55, 354, 376–77, 402, 414–15, 417–19

Geert Grote, 2, 22–23, 43; see also Hours of the Virgin, Uses of

genuflections, 19, 59–61, 65, 68, 248, 330, 372, 385; see also Mary, Virgin: images of, devotions before

Geoffroy de la Tour Landry, 2

Gerhard of Augsburg, 8

Germanus I of Constantinople, on Mary as temple, 157, as city, 182–84; on Mary's entry into the temple, 178, 218, 231, 233; on the Spirit, 224; on titles of Mary, 152–54, 194, 215

Gertrude the Great of Helfta, 33–34, 37–38, 63–65

Gibson, Mel, 474

God: as *artifex*, 74, 103, 120, 252, 257, 286; as Creator, 53, 73–75, 80–81, 101, 104–107, 111, 120, 131–32, 144–45, 170, 342–43, 405, 435–36, 441, 503n33, see also Ecclesiasticus 24:11–13; as El, 120, 127, 172, 215; as El Shaddai, 120, 127, 206, 208; as Trinity, xxvi, xxxiii, 64, 69, 75, 90, 171, 244–45, 257, 260, 282, 296–97, 310–11, 342–43, 354–55, 359, 409, 424, 428, 438–39, 442, 463, 466, plate 2, see also Mary, Virgin, as triclinium; as Yahweh, 119–21, 191, 215, 535n344, 537n446, see also Christ, Jesus, as Yahweh

Gonzalo de Berceo, 376, 402

Goscelin of Saint Bertin, 31–32, 213–15

Gospel of Pseudo-Matthew, 196, 201, 522n88

Gospel of the Hebrews (Nazarenes), 222–24, 452

Graef, Hilda, on Bernardino de Busti, 514n199; on Mary, 342; on Paul de Berry, 554n96; on Pseudo-Albert, 81, 324, 328, 511n146; on Richard of Saint-Laurent, 247–48, 256, 258, 355, 381, 390, 394, 396, 423, 543n122; on Sor María, 474

Granada, Luis de, 476–77

Grandmontines, 15

Gregory I, pope, 253, 489n20; prayer of, 43

Gregory III, pope, 167

Gregory VII, pope, 14, 17

Grindal, Edmund, archbishop of Canterbury, 56

Guibert of Nogent, 62

Gundulf of Bec, 6, 14

Haggh, Barbara, 533n289

Hahn, Scott, 486n18, 518n38, 525n133

Hazelton, Lesley, 509n118

Hedwig of Silesia, 21–22

Heiler, Friedrich, 357, 503n31

Heinrich von Meissen/Frauenlob, 77–78, 112

Heinrich von Mügeln, 82

Henry of Ghent, 79–80

Henry Suso, 22

Heraclius, emperor, 147

Hermann Joseph, 60

Herolt, Johannes, 378, 403

Herrad of Hohenbourg, 254

Hilary of Poitiers, 253

Hildegard of Bingen, xxvi, 54–55, 75, 112–13, 528n202

Hippolytus of Rome, 26–27

Holbein, Hans, 25

Holy Spirit: as advocate, 397; as mother, 222–24, 452; as weaver, 141; as Wisdom, 129, 257, 297, see also God, as Trinity; seven gifts of, 29, 31, 35, 82, 84, 181, 257, 288, 289, 312–13, 326, 331–32, 443, 463, see also Isaiah 11:1–3

Honorius Augustodunensis, 14, 31, 108–109, 400, 517n21, 527n193

Horace, poet, 254, 444

hospitals, 20, 65–66, 294

Hours of the Virgin: origins of, xxxi–xxxiii, 7–26, 233–34; psalmody of, 164–70, 194–97, 207–209; structure of, 3–4, 37–44; Uses of, 2, 6–7, 24–26, 40–44, 194–95, 207–209, defined, 488n9; earliest, 489nn20–21; method for identifying, 41, 488n10, 500n199:
    Arras, 46

Canterbury, Christ Church, 10–11, 40–42, 195, see also London, British Library, Cotton Tiberius A.iii

Châlons-sur-Marne, plate 6

Dominican, 17–18, 43, 195, 207, 214

Fonte Avellana, 40, 194–95, 207

Geert Grote, 2, 22–23, 40, 43, 195, 207, 214, plates 19 and 22

Ghent, plate 7

Hyde Abbey, 42–43, 195

Monte Cassino, 194–95, 207

Mouzon, 40

Muchelney, 40, 194, 207, see also London, British Library, Add. 21927

Nevers, plate 3

Oxford, 195, 207, 214

Paris, 16, 40–41, 43–44, 194–95, 207, 214

Premonstratensian, 21–22

Rome, xvii, 2, 16–17, 40, 44, 167–70, 195, 197, 207–209, 211, 214, 222–23, 230, 539n3, 549n1, plates 8 and 11

Rouen, 43–44, 343, 543n123

Saint Alban's, 207

Sarum, 2, 16, 24–25, 40, 43–44, 195, 207, 214, plate 21

Westminster, 40

Winchester, Nunnaminster, 11–12, 40–42, 195, 207, see also London, British Library, Royal 2 B. V

Worcester, 42

York, 2, 40, 43, 195, 501n1, 516n1

Hrabanus Maurus, 29–30, 253

Hrotsvitha of Gandersheim, 196–97, 400

Hugh of Cluny, 15

Hugh of Flavigny, 8–10

Hugh of Saint Cher, 254, 483

Hugh of Saint Victor, 253, 301, 548n291

Humbert of Romans, 17

hymns, by incipit:
    Ave, maris stella, 4, 42, 85, 97, 454–56
    Memento, salutis auctor, 343, 543n123
    O quam glorifica luce coruscas, 41
    Salve, mater salvatoris, 242, 245, 270
    Splendor Patris et figura, 75, 290
    Quem terra, pontus, aethera, 3, 41, 51, 103–104
    Veni, creator spiritus, 543n123
    Veri floris sub figura, 540n41
    Virgo dei genitrix, 512n155

Ignatius of Antioch, 253
Ildefonsus of Toledo, 253, 376, 383, 482
Innocent III, pope, 16, 253, 483
Isabella, wife of William Belgrafe, 48
Isidore of Seville, 254, 272–73, 291
Isis, goddess, 150

Jacobus de Voragine: *Legenda aurea*, 212–13,
    402–404, 410, 522n88, 529n207, 561n82;
    Mariale, 53, 58, 67–68, 78–79, 90, 97, 166
Jacques de Vitry, 60, 359, 376–77
James, William, xxv, 356
Jean Gobi, 62
Jeanne of Lille, countess, 65
Jerome, 56, 212, 253, 260; on Mary's name, 97, 175;
    on the Spirit, 222, 452; *see also* Paschasius
    Radbertus
Jerusalem: allegory of, 166; as bride, 131, 182, 246;
    as "vision of peace," 230, 267, 294, 462; church
    of Mary in, 233; feast of Mary in, 138, 164,
    177–78, 527n189
Jesus of Nazareth, *see* Christ, Jesus
Jews, as enemies of Mary, 158–59, 532n289, 552n76;
    as interpreters of scripture, xxxiii, 114–16,
    141, 143, 185–86, 533n294; Mary's prayers for,
    348, 375, 544n146, 553n76, 558n222; origin of
    name, 132, 186, 518n42
Joachim, father of Mary, 134, 137, 151
Johannes Beleth, 31
John Duns Scotus, 477–78, 511n144
John Halgrin of Abbeville, 253
John of Caulibus, 33
John of Damascus, 253, 321, 328, 333, 554n102; on
    Mary's Nativity, 181, 194, 217–18; on prayer,
    53, 453; on the Dormition, 151–52, 157–58, 181,
    198–99, 201–202, 205, 228–29, 526n168
John of Euboea, 159, 181, 194, 218
John of Garland, 402
John of Thessalonica, 158
John the Baptist, 58, 267, 285, 301, 325, 451
John the Evangelist, 27, 30, 33, 38, 99, 137, 285, 299,
    331, 411; *see also* Index of Scriptural Citations:
    John, 1 John, Revelation
Jordan of Saxony, 351
Joseph, husband of Mary, 134–35, 451, plate 434
Josephus, historian, 125, 132
Josiah, king of Israel, xxxiii, 117, 119, 122, 127, 129,
    132–33, 183, 187
Jubilees, book of, 190–91, 203, 523n104, 534n318

Judith, widow, 96, 313, 317, 385, 419, 424, 518n42
Justin Martyr, 186
Justinian I, emperor, 233

Kendrick, T. D., 474, 561n70
Kerver, Thielman, printer, 25, 236
Kollyridians, 136–37
Koppelman, Kate, 403

Lanfranc of Bec, archbishop of Canterbury, 11
Langton, Stephen, archbishop of Canterbury, 91
Latimer, Hugh, bishop of Worcester, 56, 241
Laurentin, René, 324, 511n146, 514n199
Law, Timothy, 518n42, 521n82, 550n20
Leclercq, Jean, 109
lectio divina, xxxii, 240
Leithart, Peter, 227
Leroquais, Victor, 21, 499n187
Levites, temple priests, 121–22
Lewis, C. S., xxvi-xxx, 44
Liber de infantia salvatoris, 254, 424
liberal arts, xvii, 254; education in, 360–66,
    496n125, 516n219, 551n55; Mary's knowledge
    of, 81–82, 324, 333–34, 511n147, 514n199
Limberis, Vasiliki, 150
Lisiard of Laon, 16
literacy: of clergy, 494n103; of laity, 19–26, 488n14,
    496n125, 516n219; of women, 17–26, 459,
    475–80, 496n125
Lombard, Peter, *see* Peter Lombard
Louis IX, king of France, 23, 496n125
Louth, Andrew, 118, 526n168
Lucan, poet, 254
Ludolph of Saxony, 63, 70–71
Luther, Martin, 56, 356

Madan, Falconer, 41, 500n199
Maerlant, Jacob von, 79
Magnificat, *see* Luke 1:46–55
Manegold of Lautenbach, 6, 15
mappa mundi, 73
Marbod of Rennes, 402
Margaret of Scotland, 14
Margaret of Ypres, 19, 60–61
Margery Kempe, 6, 24
María de Jésus de Ágreda, Sor, bilocation, 560n40;
    life of Virgin Mary, 462–69; reception of
    work, 469–75; sources of work, 475–80,
    561n82; visions of, 459–62

Marie d'Oignies, 19, 60

Mary of Burgundy, book of Hours of, plate 8

Mary, Virgin:

 as advocate, 13, 96, 210, 255, 265–66, 333, 347, 392, 397–98, 429

 as ark, 80, 174–75, 186–87, 228–29, 280–83

 beauty of, 116, 177–79, 182, 248, 254, 318, 414–33, 466–69

 in battle, 53, 147, 174, 206–207, 284–85, 297, 348, 403

 as bedchamber, 176, 286–87

 as blessed among women, 53, 83, 104, 134, 170, 273, 319–20, 325

 as book, 101, 255–56

 bread of, 35, 119, 128, 137, 211, 229, 280–82, 294, 296–98, 304–305, 307, 340–41, 353, 441, 528n195

 as bride, 69–71, 85, 119, 146–50, 175–79, 182–84, 201–203, 225, 227–28, 310–11, 414–32, 443, 466–69

 childhood of, in temple, 133–35, 196–97, 201, 462

 as city of God, 180–84, 198–99, 228–30, 291–95, 462

 as cloud, 142, 187–90, 244–45, 275, 315, 337

 compassion of, for Son, 441–42

 contemplation of, 81–82, 218, 219, 246, 268, 295–96, 301, 317–19, 330–31, 335, 337, 424–25, 441–43, 478

 as crystal, 75, 82, 290, 448, 462

 as dawn, 273–74, 317, 435

 dormition of, 137, 158–59, see also Mary, Virgin: feasts of

 as earth, 275–78

 as elephant, 53, 283–84

 as exalted above the angels, 83, 335–38, 404, 478–79

 faith of, 34, 52, 95, 100, 268, 270, 271, 277, 297, 326, 330–31, 333, 341, 463

 as filled with Wisdom, 81–83, 257–60, 314, 326–27, 333–35, 463–69

 as flower, 302–303

 as fountain, 278–79, 339–40

 as full of grace, 83–84, 312–16, 325–26, 329, 331–35, 339–42

 as garden, 298–301, 447–50

 as goddess, xxxiii, 52–53, 137, 150, 157, 241, 338–39, 438, 502n12, 523n106, 524n111

 as godlike, 258–60, 308, 330–31, 337, 339, 410, 468–69

 as good woman, 265–66

 as heaven, 83, 141, 154, 156, 238, 268–70

 as house, 80, 287–88, 341

 as magistra, 256, 282, 511n147

 as mater misericordiae, 96, 347, 397, 399

 as mediatrix, 96, 255, 317, 336, 359, 390, 396, 402, 409, 429, 467, 556n157

 as mirror, 54–55, 89, 101, 156, 259–60, 332, 423, 461, 469, 479, see also Wisdom 7:26

 as moon, 84, 176, 272–73, 314, 319, 385

 as mother, 52, 54, 74–75, 80, 119, 133–46, 176–79, 182–84, 186, 222–24, 263–65, 355, 396–97, 441–42, 463–69

 as mountain, 88, 154, 206, 217–18, 278, 283–84

 name of, 93–99, 263, 311–12, 328–29, 435

 physical appearance of, 82–83, 324, 328, 414–33

 prayer life of, 196–97, 462

 as priest, 325–26, see also Mary, Virgin: bread of

 as prophetess, 82, 150, 154, 155, 158, 325

 as queen, 112, 135–37, 161, 163, 177–79, 188, 209, 231, 241–45, 266–68, 318–19, 338–39, 347, 371, 378, 396–97, 404, 419–20, 463–69, 526n156

 reasons to serve, 390–93

 relics of: hair, 254, 425; veil, 147, 245

 as river, 149–50, 175, 180–81, 198, 279–80

 Saturday Mass and Office of, 8, 40, 297, 373, 378, 383–84, 387, 490n30, 493n84

 as ship, 296–98, 340, 444–45

 as star of the sea, 85, 97–99, 112, 198, 263, 311–12, 328, 337, 435, 454

 as sun, 171–72, 223–24, 270–71, 285, 312, 361–62

 as tabernacle, 73, 80–81, 113, 157–58, 171–72, 180–81, 184, 189, 219, 222–23, 227, 244–45, 285–86, 341, 437–38, 464, 468, 528n195

 as temple, 80, 89–90, 135, 141, 145, 146–157, 233, 244–45, 289–91, 433–39, 456–57, 464, 468–69

 as Theotokos, 85, 138–46, 149–50, 154, 162, 178, 184, 185, 207, 209, 233, 524n111, 525n147

 as throne, 77, 141–42, 161, 181, 187–89, 194, 197–99, 231, 241, 258–59, 283–85, 315, 319, 337

 titles of, xxxii, 54–55, 76–81, 84–86, 91–93, 99, 111–14, 119–20, 146–55, 236, 306–307, 367–68, 399–400

 as tower, 174, 263, 295–96, 392, 428, 430

 as tree, 87, 112, 148, 186–87, 193, 239, 303–306, 307, 321–22, 392 as triclinium, 77, 90, 119, 255, 257, 342, 379, 439, 442

as type of the Church, 52, 165, 241, 502n15; as virgin, 134, 161, 177–78, 196, 201, 289, 326, 333, 336, 384, *see also* Isaiah 7:14

visions of, 57, 60, 62, 64, 438, 456–57, 461–69

weaving of, 81, 141–42, 196–97, 333; temple veil, 133–35

womb of, crystalline, 510n122

see also Wisdom

Mary, Virgin, cathedrals of, 16, 241–42, 342, 394; Santa Maria Maggiore, 233–34, 528n199; *see also* Chartres

Mary, Virgin, feasts of, 2, 37–38, 40, 67, 150, 383–84, 387, 463; Annunciation, 63–64, 67, 80, 152, 515n218; Conception, 14, 159, 167, 194, 218, 521n88; Dormition (Assumption), 53, 151–52, 156–57, 173–74, 197, 198–99, 205, 207, 208–209, 227, 228, 253–54, 337, 387, 400, 527n193, 538n464; Entry into the Temple, 152; introduction into Latin West, 162, 167, 233–34, 529n206, 531n253; oldest, 137–38, 177–78, 233; psalmody for, 169–70, 194–97, 207–209, 530n212; Nativity of the Virgin, 150, 181, 194, 400, 515n203, 521n88, 522n88; Purification, 529n207, 530n213, 531n234

Mary, Virgin, images of, 17, 75, 97, 99, 277, 304–305, 378, 393, 424, 436, 439, 501n3, 510n122, 538n468, 545n184; Black Madonnas, 227–28, 538n468; burned, 241; devotions before, 56, 58–60, 65, 73, 290, 301, 372, 374, 377–79, 382–84, 415, 418; Notre Dame de la Belle Verrière, 243–45; Opening Madonnas, xxxiii, plates 1–2, 23–24; *Sedes sapientiae*, 241, 378, 501n3, 509n116, 511n147, plate 5; Santa Maria in Trastevere, 538n464; with Theophilus, 402; *see also* Books of Hours, illuminations in

Masoretic Hebrew Bible, xvi, 518n42

Matilda of England, queen, 14,

Matilda of Tuscany, countess, 6, 14, 32–33

Maximus the Confessor, 178, 209–10, 253

Mechthild of Magdeburg, 438

Meersseman, G. G., 85, 167

Melchizedek, king and priest, 119–21, 130, 141, 151, 196, 222–24, 294–95, 303, 307, 349–50, 465, 522n97

Melisende of Jerusalem, psalter of, plate 9

Mendo, Andrés, on Sor María, 470

Merchant(s), 24, 167, 266, 295, 296–98, 371, 558n222; Christ as, 444–45

Millett, Bella, 18–19, 494nn 94 and 103

Milton, John, 486n13

miracles of the Virgin, xxxvi, xxxviii–xxxix, 254, 333, 368–80, 389, 414–19; collections of, 14, 360–63, 375–76, 435–36; modern criticisms of, 354, 357–59, 366–67, 390, 504n59, 556n157; stories: Adam of Locheim, 372; almsman, 373; betrothed to statue, 377, 418–19; Ebbo the thief, 360; Eulalia, 63; gambler, 377; "Gaude Maria Virgo," 532n289; Jewish boy, 376; Jewish woman in childbirth, 375; Jostius of Saint Bertin, 304; Julian the Apostate, 360; knight of Provence, 371; laybrother, 373; Mary as bride, 416–18; Mary as *mater misericordiae*, 397; merchant of Portugal, 371–72; minstrel of Rocamadour, 371; Moorish woman, 375; mother holds Child hostage, 374; pregnant nun, 374; "Prioress's Tale," 552n76; sacristan, 414–15; saying Aves and Hours of the Virgin, 10, 12–14, 61–63, 395–96; sweetness in mouth, 61; tumbler of Clairvaux, 368–71, 379, 381, 552n63; Walter of Biberach, 415–16; woman who said Aves, 373; *see also* Alfonso the Wise, Anselm of Bury St. Edmunds, Caesarius of Heisterbach, Dominic of Evesham, Gonzalo de Berceo, Guibert of Nogent, Ildefonsus of Toledo, Jacques de Vitry, Paul the Deacon, Theophilus, William of Malmesbury

Miriam, sister of Moses and Aaron, 119, 136, 158, 361, 386, 514n197

Mitchell, Nathan, 474, 477–78

Modern Devout, 23

Modestus of Jerusalem, 151, 181, 215, 224

Moses, brought forth water, 306, 340; built tabernacle, 113, 121, 286, 525n135; face shone, 410, 424; lawgiver, 122, 132, 136, 158, 171–72; saw burning bush, 127, 154, 156, 239–40, 303; vision on Mount Sinai, 189, 191, 226

Mossman, Stephen, 330, 513n192, 540n33

Mowinckel, Sigmund, 118, 537n446

Munio de Zamora, 66

music: at creation, 190–91; in Office, 163, 190–92, 199–200, 347–52; in Revelation, 124–26; in temple, 121–23, 197

Myroure of oure Ladye, 34–36, 57, 549n6

Nebuchadnezzar, king of the Chaldeans, 203–204, 227, 376

Nestorius of Antioch, 139–40, 145–46, 185, 240, 525n145

Nichols, Aidan, 502n15

Nigel of Canterbury, 402

Noah, builder of the ark, 31, 273, 290, 317

Norbert of Xanten, 15

Norris, Kathleen, 7

N-Town *Mary Play*, 213, 214–231 *passim*

Nuffel, Herman von, 411

Nunc Dimittis, *see* Luke 2:29–32

Odilia of Liège, 19

Odo of Cluny, 397

oil, anointing, 128–30, 172, 176, 178–79, 195–96, 222, 230, 267, 315–16, 349–50, 353, 404, 456

Oliver, Judith, 19

Ordericus Vitalis, 8

Origen of Alexandria, 26, 222, 253

Otfrid von Weissenburg, 197

Otter, Monika, 213

Ovid, poet, 254

parables, 256, 261, 360–61, 365–66, 541n81

Paschasius Radbertus, as Bernard, 95; as Jerome, 253–54, 309, 316–17, 322, 387, 515n203; on the Song of Songs, 174

Paul, apostle, 8, 26, 28, 30, 121, 408; in ecstasy 330–31, 333; *see also* Index of Scriptural Citations: Romans, 1 and 2 Corinthians, Galatians, Ephesians, Philippians, 1 Thessalonians, and 1 and 2 Timothy

Paul the Deacon of Naples, 400–13

Paula, mother of Eustochium, 17, 387

Peltomaa, Leena Mari, 147, 150

Pentcheva, Bissera, 150, 526n147

Peregrinus, master, 113–14, 116

Persephone, goddess, 137

Peter, apostle, 8, 10, 36, 115; at Mary's death, 158–59; at prayer, 27–28, 30; at transfiguration, 331, 411; denied Christ, 32, 38, 39, 408

Peter Comestor, 253, 288, 341

Peter Damian, 253; promotes Hours of the Virgin, 5–6, 10, 12–15, 19, 26, 30–32, 39–40, 59, 253, 382–83; *see also* Hours of the Virgin, Uses of, Fonte Avellana

Peter de Honestis, 15

Peter Lombard, 81, 123, 240, 245, 516n9

Peter the Deacon, 7–9

Peter the Venerable of Cluny, 15

Philip of Harvengt, 69–70

Phillips, Helen, 510n126, 511n133

Philo of Alexandria, 144, 525n135

phoenix, 78, 92, 271

Pius V, pope, 26, 44

Pius IX, pope, 472

Plantin, Christopher, printer, 44, 488n8

Power, Eileen, 358, 390, 412

prayer: as advocate, 398; as service, 7, 37, 57–58, 347–54, 380–89, 454; defined, xxv–xxvi, xxix–xxx, 53–54, 356–57, 453; numbered, 56–57, 60–61; of Theophilus, 406–409; oldest Marian, 138, 235; precedes doctrine, 164; regular, 26–32, 196–97, 213–14

prayers, by incipit:
Beatae et gloriosae, 347
Concede, misericors Deus, 346
Concede nos famulos tuos, 346
Deus, qui de beatae Mariae, 345
Deus, qui salutis aeternae, 346
Deus, qui virginalem aulam, 345
Famulorum tuorum, 346
Sancta Maria, succurre miseris, plate 9
Sub tuum praesidium, 138, 524n109, 525n147

Premonstratensian canons, 15–16, 21, 60, 69–70, 386

Priestley, Joseph, 356

Proclus of Constantinople, 138–42, 144–45, 188, 233

Protestants: as critics of Marian devotion, 52, 56–57, 109, 117, 132, 241, 247, 523n106

Protevangelium of James, 133–38, 196, 201, 521n88

Psalms: and King David, 121–23; commentaries on, 108–109, 123, 164–65; Gradual, 1, 15, 18, 26, 195, 207–208, 211–21, 230–33; in Marian liturgies, 165–67, 169–70, 208–209, 233–34; Penitential, 1, 15, 18, 20, 22, 26, 66, 232; in temple, 121–24, 130–31; *see also* Index of Scriptural Citations: Psalms

psalters: manuscripts, 5, 11, 17, 19, 21–23, 197, 489nn20–21; *see also* plates 9, 10

Pseudo-Albert, as scholastic, 324, 360, 366–67: *Mariale*, xxxii, xxxvi–xxxviii, 165–66, 324–42, 397; manuscripts of, 68; modern reception of, 246–49, 324, 474–79, 484; on Mary's knowledge, 81–83, 331–35

Pseudo-Dionysius, 333, 335–38

Pulcheria, empress, 139, 141, 145–47

Rachel, wife of Jacob, 96, 424

Ralph of Escures, 336

Raphael, angel, 193, 382

Rebecca, wife of Isaac, 399, 424

regular canons (Augustinians), 15, 68, 75, 386, 483

Regularis concordia, 9, 11

Reinburg, Virignia, 486n19, 487n4, 489n17,
    496n125, 497n141, 498n183, 500n214, 549n1

Remigius of Auxerre, 253

responsories, recitation of, 539n4; by incipit
    (CAO #):

    Beata es (6163), 238, 539n6

    Felix namque (6725), 239, 539n6

    Sancta et immaculata (7569), 238, 512n154, 539n4

    Sicut dies verni (7455b), 558n229

    Te laudant angeli (7756), 542n109

    Veni, electa mea (7826), 538n464

    Vidi speciosam (7878), 542n113, 548n291

Rhea, goddess, 150

Richard of Saint-Laurent, 53, 67, 265, 355, 390; *De
    laudibus beatae Mariae virginis*, xxxii-xxxiii,
    xxxvi-xxxviii, 76–78, 87, 89–90, 165–66,
    251–308; manuscripts of, 67–68, 481–84,
    plates 12–17, 20; method of, 251–55, 360, 363,
    366–67; modern reception of, 246–49, 474–
    79; on Christ, 439–53; on Mary as intercessor,
    395–400, 403–404, 407; on Mary's beauty,
    422–33; on Mary's name, 94, 97–98, 199, 263;
    on serving Mary, 58, 342–43, 348, 378–94

Richard of Saint Victor, 253

Robert Kilwardby, 493n86

Rogers, Nicholas, 24

rosary, 7, 56–57, 69, 86; *see also* Ave psalters

Rouen, city of, 43, 295, 342, 394, 544n146, 553n76,
    558n222; relic of Mary's hair at, 254, 425;
    Richard of Saint-Laurent in, 53, 67, 265, 355,
    390

Rubin, Miri, 486n16

Rufo de Gurgone, 20

Rupert of Deutz, 32, 69, 109

Rutebeuf, 359, 376, 402

Sabatier, Auguste, xxv, xxx, 350, 356–57, 381

Saenger, Paul, 43

Saracens, 348, 544n146, 552n76

Satan, 158, 402–12, 423

Scarry, Elaine, xxiii, xxviii-xxix

schools, 23, 240, 253, 255, 261, 334, 372, 516n219,
    516n9

scriptures: allegory in, xxxii, 261, 525n145,
    528n200; apocrypha, 135, 174, 254, 474, 476,
    518n42, 520n82, 521n88, 523n104, 527n182,
    528n193, 532n272; exegesis of, xxxii, 106–111,
    164–66, 439, 486nn22-21, 541n81, 557n208;
    metaphors in, 76, 80, 94, 99, 305, 307; read
    through Mary, 107–118, 249, 252–61, 307–308,
    475–76, 518n38, 521n85, 554n116

Sedulius, poet, 253

Seneca, philosopher, 254

Septuagint, xv-xvii, 120, 130–31, 150, 186, 199,
    203, 212, 254, 349, 518n42, 519n46, 521n82,
    533n291, 550n20

Sergius I, patriarch, 147

Sergius I, pope, 162, 167, 234

sermo humilis, 364–66

Servasanctus of Faenza: *Mariale*, 111–12, 165–66,
    540n31, 545n188; manuscripts of, 67–68,
    482, 507n95, 508n101; method of, 99–101,
    394–95, 516n219, 517n27; modern reception
    of, 246–47

Servetus, Michael, 116

Sheba, queen of, 227, 267

Shoemaker, Stephen, 158, 178, 522nn88 and 95,
    523nn104 and 106, 525n147

Sicardus of Cremona, 31, 38

Silva, Diego de, bishop of Guardia, on Sor María,
    470

Sirach, Jesus Ben, 132–33; *see also* Index of
    Scriptural Citations: Ecclesiasticus

Six Books Dormition Apocryphon, 137–38, 523n104

Sixtus III, pope, 528n199

Sixtus V, pope, 85, 478

Smaragdus of Saint-Mihiel, 29–30

Socrates, historian, 139

Solomon, king of Israel, 122, 157, 177, 189, 219,
    266–67, 283, 288, 361, 384, 398, 446; *see also*
    Index of Scriptural Citations: Proverbs,
    Ecclesiastes, Song of Songs, Wisdom

Southern, R. W., 14, 358–360, 504n59

Speculum virginum, 113–14

Stephen, cardinal priest, 59

Stephen of Muret, 15

Stephen of Sawley, 108–109, 111

Taunton, Ethelred, 109, 164, 166, 170–230 *passim*
temple: as place of prayer, 90, 233, 257, 289, 394, 457; symbolism of, 118–19; worship in, 120–26; *see also* Mary, Virgin, as temple; veil, temple, symbolism of
Teresa of Ávila, 476
Tertullian, 26–27
Theodora, virgin, 113–114, 116
Theodosius I, emperor, 139
Theodulus, poet, 253
Theophilus, miracle of, xxxviii–xxxix, 90, 348, 362, 400–14, 490n21, 553n76; in Conrad of Saxony, 317, 319; in Richard of Saint-Laurent, 254, 265, 267, 271, 290, 296, 304, 384, 391–92, 400, 428
Theoteknos of Livias, 210
Thermutis, goddess, 137
Thomas, apostle, 432
Thomas Aquinas, 53, 83, 481
Thomas Gallus, 253
Thomas of Cantimpré, 61
Thurston, Herbert, 59, 503n35
Tickle, Phyllis, 7, 30
Tolkien, J. R. R., xix, 74, 534n320, 550n21
Torre, Andrés de la, 459
transfiguration, 331, 410–11, 446
Transitus Mariae, 354
Trent, council of, xxxvi, 2, 16, 208
troubadour(s), 242, 376
Tyche, goddess, 150

Ubertino of Casale, 478
Ulric of Augsburg, 8–10
Ulrich of Zell, 15
Underhill, Evelyn, 357–58, 360
unicorn, 91
Urban II, pope, 15

Vatican, second council of, 52, 241, 247, 502n15
Venantius Fortunatus, 41, 120
Venus, goddess, 241, 283
Veronica, image of the, 513n173
Vérard, Antoine, printer, 25, 44
veil, temple, symbolism of, 118–19, 144, 198, 244, 391, 525n135; woven by Mary, 134–36, 142, 155, 367–68

Victoria, goddess, 150
Vincent of Beauvais, 402–403
Virgil, poet, 254, 272, 362–63
Voltaire, *philosophe*, 472, 478–79
Vostre, Simon, printer, 25, 44

Wace, Norman poet, 522n88
Walter of Biberach, 415–16
Walter of Wimborne, 72, 78, 91–94, 112
Ward, Benedicta, 360, 390
Waters, Claire, 366, 556n157
Weil, Simone, xxv
Wieck, Roger, 164, 486n19
William de Brailes, 5, 18, 38–39, 401–403; *see also* London, British Library, Add. 49999
William of Auvergne, 253
William of Hirsau, 14–15
William of Malmesbury, 360, 366, 376, 402, 435–36, 553n76
Williams, Rowan, 118
Wisdom, xxxiii, 84, 89, 139, 140–44, 149, 170, 210–11, 222–23, 230, 353–54, 359–66, 379–80, 461; as bride, 182–83, 422–23, 443–44; Asherah as, 126–33, 177, 521n85; Christ as, 143–45, 151, 240, 256–60, 263, 284, 286–88, 296–97, 307, 337–38, 392, 470–71, 525n134; Mary as, 101, 117, 119, 135–36, 146, 195–96, 237–40, 246, 252–61, 280, 308, 326–27, 332, 336, 366–67, 381–82, 394, 435–36, 456; rejected by Jews, 159, 185–86, 188–89, 226, 378; speaking in parables, 256, 261, 360–62, 365–66; *see also* Mary, Virgin, bread of; oil, anointing; Index of Scriptural Citations: Proverbs, Wisdom of Solomon, Ecclesiasticus
Wulfstan of Winchester, 8, 16
Wyatt, Nicolas, 172, 177

Ximénez de Samiego, José, 469–71, 475

Zacharias, high priest, 231
Zachary, pope, 7
Zerbolt, Gerhart, 23, 43
Ziolkowski, Jan, 379

9 780231 181693